MARK

Volume 27

THE ANCHOR BIBLE is a fresh approach to the world's greatest classic. Its object is to make the Bible accessible to the modern reader; its method is to arrive at the meaning of biblical literature through exact translation and extended exposition, and to reconstruct the ancient setting of the biblical story, as well as the circumstances of its transcription and the characteristics of its transcribers.

THE ANCHOR BIBLE is a project of international and interfaith scope: Protestant, Catholic, and Jewish scholars from many countries contribute individual volumes. The project is not sponsored by any ecclesiastical organization and is not intended to reflect any particular theological doctrine. Prepared under our joint supervision, THE ANCHOR BIBLE is an effort to make available all the significant historical and linguistic knowledge which bears on the interpretation of the biblical record.

THE ANCHOR BIBLE is aimed at the general reader with no special formal training in biblical studies; yet, it is written with most exacting standards of scholarship, reflecting the highest technical accomplishment.

This project marks the beginning of a new era of cooperation among scholars in biblical research, thus forming a common body of knowledge to be shared by all.

William Foxwell Albright
David Noel Freedman
GENERAL EDITORS

THE ANCHOR BIBLE

MARK

A NEW TRANSLATION
WITH INTRODUCTION
AND COMMENTARY
BY

C. S. Mann

DOUBLEDAY & COMPANY, INC.
GARDEN CITY, NEW YORK
1986

Library of Congress Cataloging in Publication Data
Bible. N.T. Mark. English. Mann. 1986.
Mark: a new translation with introduction and
commentary.
(The Anchor Bible; v. 27)
Includes bibliographies and index.
1. Bible. N.T. Mark—Commentaries. I. Mann, C. S.
(Christopher Stephen), 1917– . II. Title.
III. Series: Bible. English. Anchor Bible. 1964;
v. 27.
BS192.2.A1 1964.G3   vol. 27 220.7′7 s
[BS2583]   [226′.3077]
ISBN 0-385-03253-6
Library of Congress Catalog Card Number: 85-4433

Dedicated to
Addison G. Wright, S.S., S.T.D.,
the kindest of critics and a valued friend
and to
Timothy Baker
William Betteridge
Richard Vaughan Case
Timothy Curtis
Sean Thomas Flynn
Pauline Hayward
Kevin Tatum
in thanksgiving for their entrance into
the community of faith.

PREFACE

"For in a commentary you have to say something on everything, whether you have anything to say or not. This is why most commentaries in my experience are duller than books written by the same persons, even on the same subject." The words are those of the late J. A. T. Robinson *(Wrestling with Romans,* Westminster Press, 1979). In the same preface he went on to plead for work which offered "a sort of conducted tour in biblical literature for the student and the educated layman" rather than commentaries by "academics writing with one eye on their colleagues and their research reputation." Whether he would have approved of this work on Mark's gospel is now matter purely for speculation. But in embarking on this task I tried to keep in mind the student in a theological school, the minister teaching adult education classes, and the enquiring layman searching for information. Academic scholars are generally well aware of the opinions of their colleagues, and there are innumerable periodicals in which research projects are described and theses proposed for attention and appraisal. Furthermore, the professional academic has no difficulty in tracing whence this or that particular idea arose or how it was developed. Yet even in writing for a broader field than that of academic scholarship there is a duty on the part of the author to declare how conclusions were reached and to cite the material which helped reach them. To that end, bibliographies are appended at the end of various sections, containing books and articles which in the view of the author are important and often formative.

New Testament scholarship and scholarly interests appear to pursue a path of cycles. Twenty years ago we were immersed in Luke-Acts and related studies. Shortly thereafter interest moved to the Johannine literature, and then for a short time there was renewed interest in Matthew. The past ten years have seen a proliferation of books and articles on Mark, though most of these (thanks to a new concern about the sociology of early Christianity) reflect a search for the community which produced Mark's work. The suggested solutions have been many and varied, and we are now far removed from the comparatively simple thesis of a "Roman" gospel written around the reminiscences of Peter.

If there is renewed interest in Mark, the fascination of the problem of synoptic relationships is still with us and is destined to continue into the foreseeable future. This work embraces the theory which has come to be known as "the Griesbach hypothesis," after its principal proponent more

than a century ago. What was once a very insignificant minority view has in
the past few years achieved more than a little respectability—a state of affairs
which could hardly have been predicted in the era of B. H. Streeter's monu-
mental study of gospel origins. It had not occurred to this writer to question
the assumption of Markan priority until in conversation R. V. G. Tasker
remarked that "the priority of Mark is assuredly not one of the assured
results of New Testament scholarship." Shortly thereafter the pioneering
work of W. R. Farmer compelled me to reexamine the presuppositions upon
which the familiar two-document hypothesis had been built. My debt to
W. R. Farmer is incalculable, not only for valuable advice and for support in
writing this work, but also for personal friendship and hospitality. My debt to
him will be sufficiently obvious to the student of New Testament origins all
through this commentary. It was through Farmer that I was privileged to
meet Dom Bernard Orchard, whose charts of synoptic relationships have
proved highly illuminating.

If the assumed priority of Mark is being questioned, it ought surely not to
be forgotten that the two-document hypothesis and the positing of a "sayings
source" in "Q" precisely underpinned some of the cherished theological opinions of "liberal" nineteenth- and twentieth-century scholarship. The advantage of the two-document hypothesis, with Mark as the prior and "simple"
gospel, is that it allows us to postulate some "fact" behind the belief in the
risen Jesus as Messiah and Lord (whether of the Church, the Age to Come, or
the world), and that "fact" can be anything from the preacher of the Fatherhood of God and the brotherhood of man to the existential decision-demand-
ing Jesus of Bultmann. Thus there is fascination with the progression from
Judaism to Hellenism in early Christianity, and the supposed simplicity of
Mark allows us to see Jesus as a man of unique God-consciousness or as the
man who calls to freedom, or to authentic existence (whatever that may
mean), or to the liberation of the oppressed. This can effectively evade the
central issue in all New Testament study—that from our earliest sources
(Paul's letters) Jesus is known as risen, and as Lord. But that central confession can be muted, blurred, and eroded altogether and dismissed as a "Hellenizing" of an original message.

The two-document hypothesis aids this process, even though many of its
proponents would reject it. If one of the earliest sources we have is "Q" or
some such series of sayings of Jesus, then we may conclude that the earliest
followers saw Jesus as a Wisdom teacher; but certainly no statement of a
"christological" nature can be found there. In the same way, if the gospels
were constructed by various communities, unidentified and perhaps unidentifiable, then it may be permissible to see their christological statements, or
the implications of what they say of Jesus, as pure constructs of the community, reflecting their own needs rather than the fact of who Jesus was. It is
possible to fasten onto Jesus whatever portrait one wishes, and then demon-

strate through community handling of the material that the original Jesus was wholly misunderstood by overlaid christological confessions. The process ends, as in many books on christology, with Paul and John being seen as the last elements in a progression from "lower" to "higher" christology.

In all of this Mark seems more than qualified to be the "simple gospel" of the liberal, humanitarian nineteenth-century quest. It has no embarrassing material such as the virginal conception, it lacks controversial items like the Petrine promise, and has no highly colored resurrection appearances. To be sure, it has the apocalyptic drama of Chapter 13, but that is manifestly not a Markan composition and might therefore be ignored. But the pace of Markan studies at the present time, and their scope, suggest that "simple" is hardly the adjective to use. The individual pericopae are tightly organized, with an economy of words which can be deceiving. No time is lost in explanation, save where some readers might be puzzled by unfamiliar customs. This commentary urges the view that the author of Mark was writing for urgent, immediate use, and was prepared to discard any material which did not meet the needs of the situation. This commentary also urges that Mark is—as the Griesbach hypothesis holds it to be—a digest, or conflation, of Matthew and Luke with a strong bias in favor of Matthew's order and Matthew's material. Now, while a coincidence of order as between Matthew and Mark is perfectly explicable on the two-document hypothesis, what is significant—and generally not noticed—is the *internal* coincidence of order in Mark's pericopae as compared with those of Matthew. Although it is entirely appropriate for an author or editor conflating or making a digest of one or more documents to follow fairly closely the internal order of each section of his major document, it is wholly otherwise with an author with far more material of his own than the minor source which he is embodying. In other words, it is understandable that Mark would preserve in each section of his work the internal order of the two major documents he was using. But there seems no very good reason why Matthew or Luke, faced with a relatively short document and having considerable documentary resources of their own, should have reproduced the internal order of the individual units of Mark.

Much work remains to be done on the manner in which Mark edited his material, and there are several paths which might usefully be followed. In the past it was often suggested that Mark's work was, if not ill-organized, at least haphazard. It is with gratitude therefore that I include in this commentary some work done by my friend and former colleague, the Reverend Laurence F. X. Brett (editor of *Share the Word*), in an examination of Markan literary devices. Equally, much has yet to be done in the area of Markan language. The Latinisms in Mark have been remarked on for many years, but how much can be detected of Semitic influence in the gospel? Professional opinion is still very divided, and a recent publication can speak of Markan syntax in a title which is its own spokesman: *Semitic Interference in Markan Syntax* (by

Elliott C. Maloney, SBL Dissertation Series, Missoula, Mont.: Scholars Press, 1981). We are a long way yet from determining to what extent ordinary people in the Middle East in the first century were bilingual (or even, in the case of the much-traveled, trilingual), but every minor inscription, every scrap of papyrus helps us to piece together the background against which Jesus and his first followers lived. It was an age which, for all the security that the Roman imperial system apparently provided, had disturbing shadows of disaster to come. For Jesus, the dazzling splendor of a yet-unfinished temple held promise only of future ruin. Jesus came, if nothing else, as the eschatological prophet of the "last days." Mark's gospel allows little time for the exploration of theological niceties and nuances—the times were far too perilous and the days too short.

Our own age ought at least to appreciate the urgency of Mark. We are in far too serious a predicament to emasculate eschatology into the existential decision of the individual, fascinating though that may be. To quote the late W. F. Albright, we need to pay heed to "the contemporary fulfillment of eschatological prophecy in part, at least, by the realization of man's age-old dream of discovering how to destroy himself and the entire world as we know it."

The expression of thanks is always an unenviable task, for so many people have in innumerable ways helped in the completion of this work that a risk is run of overlooking significant help. But I here pay tribute to those without whom the task of preparing this work would have been even more formidable than it has proved to be. First, there is my continued indebtedness to W. F. Albright, whose zeal and dedication in biblical studies provided inspiration to so many men and women. It is right to pay tribute to Bishop John Robinson of gracious memory—pastor, mentor, and personal friend—for the many hours spent by me in his company. He shared few of my ideas about synoptic relationships, but was unfailingly encouraging. To the patience of librarians at the University of London, the Bodleian Library in Oxford, and the Library of Congress I owe much for their help in tracing obscure references. Successive librarians of St. Mary's Seminary and University in Baltimore (Messrs. Robert Matthews, Norman Desmaris, and David Siemsen) and students at St. Mary's helped considerably by putting bibliographical material in order. Of particular help to me were Ms. Mary Becker, Ms. Winnie Hart, and Ms. Mary Jinno. Two editors of the Anchor Bible series (Ms. Sally Waterman, and Ms. Eve Roshevsky) have been unfailingly helpful and supportive. To Dr. David Noel Freedman, the General Editor, I owe far more than I can express for his patience and wisdom. Dr. Astrid Beck, Dr. Marsha Dutton, and Ms. Susan Wyman, of the University of Michigan, performed miracles by deciphering what I fondly call my handwriting.

The dedication pays a different kind of tribute. First, to my friend and former colleague Father Addison G. Wright, for the many hours I spent with him in the pursuit of biblical studies, and especially in the field of New Testament origins. We disagree in many of our views of synoptic relationships, but he has always been most helpful. Secondly, the dedication to my godchildren bears witness to the happiness they have always given me in that capacity.

C. S. Mann
Baltimore, 1985

CONTENTS

TRANSLATION AND COMMENTARY

PRINCIPAL ABBREVIATIONS

AB	Anchor Bible
AnBib	Analecta Biblica
ASTI	Annual of the Swedish Theological Institute
ATR	Anglican Theological Review
BEvT	Beiträge zur evangelischen Theologie
Bib	Biblica
BJRL	Bulletin of the John Rylands Library
BTB	Biblical Theology Bulletin
BZ	Biblische Zeitschrift
CBQ	The Catholic Biblical Quarterly
CQR	Church Quarterly Review
DCG	Dictionary of Christ and the Gospels
DSS	Dead Sea Scrolls
EphTheolLov	Ephemerides Theologicae Lovanienses
EspVie	Esprit et Vie
EvTh	Evangelische Theologie
ExpT	Expository Times
FRLANT	Forschungen zur Religion und Literatur des Alten und Neuen Testaments
HeyJour	Heythrop Journal
HTR	Harvard Theological Review
HUCA	Hebrew Union College Annual
Int	Interpretation
JAAR	Journal of the American Academy of Religion
JBC	Jerome Biblical Commentary
JBL	Journal of Biblical Literature
JJS	Journal of Jewish Studies
JournEvThSoc	Journal of the Evangelical Theological Society
JR	Journal of Religion
JSNT	Journal for the Study of the New Testament
JTC	Journal of the Interdenominational Theological Center
JTS	Journal of Theological Studies
KJV	King James Version
LXX	The Septuagint
M	Mishna
MT	The Massoretic Text
NKZ	Neue kirkliche Zeitschrift
NovTest	Novum Testamentum
NRTh	Nouvelle Revue Théologique

NTAbh	Neutestamentliche Abhandlungen
NTS	New Testament Studies
NZTR	Neue Zeitschrift für Systematische Theologie und Religionsphilosophie
RevBib	Revue Biblique
RevExpos	Review and Expositor
RevTheolLouv	Revue Théologique de Louvain
RevTheolPhil	Revue de théologie et de philosophie
RevThom	Revue Thomiste
RGG	Die Religion in Geschichte und Gegenwart
RHPR	Revue d'histoire et de philosophie religieuses
RSR	Recherches de Science Religieuse
RSV	Revised Standard Version
RV	Revised Version, 1881
SBL	Society of Biblical Literature
SBT	Studies in Biblical Theology
SEA	Svensk Exegetisk Årsbok
SJT	Scottish Journal of Theology
SNTS	Society for New Testament Studies
ST	Studia Theologica
StEv	Studia Evangelica
Supp	Supplement
TB	Babylonian Talmud
TDNT	Theological Dictionary of the New Testament (English translation of *TWNT)*
ThL	Theologische Literaturzeitung
TheolBeit	Theologische Beiträge
TheolPrakQuart	Theologisch-Praktische Quartalschrift
TheolZeit	Theologische Zeitschrift
ThS	Theological Studies
ThViat	Theologia Viatorum
TNTS	Twelve New Testament Studies (J. A. T. Robinson)
TSK	Theologische Studien und Kritiken
TTZ	Trierer theologische Zeitschrift
TU	Texte und Untersuchungen
TWNT	Theologisches Wörterbuch zum Neuen Testament (ed. G. Kittel)
TY	Jerusalem Talmud
USQR	Union Seminary Quarterly Review
VT	Vetus Testamentum
ZAW	Zeitschrift für die Alttestamentliche Wissenschaft
ZDPV	Zeitschrift des Deutschen Palatina-Vereins
ZNW	Zeitschrift für die Neutestamentliche Wissenschaft
ZTK	Zeitschrift für Theologie und Kirche

GENERAL BIBLIOGRAPHY

Unless indicated otherwise, all references to works by Lagrange, Lane, Lohmeyer, Rawlinson, Taylor, Turner, and Swete are to the commentaries on the Gospel of Mark compiled by those authors. References to Bultmann, unless otherwise noted, are to his *History of the Synoptic Tradition*. References to rabbinic material, whether to Mishnah, Midrash, or Talmud, are to the English edition by the Soncino Press (London).

Commentaries

The following commentaries on Mark have been consistently used by the writer:

Lagrange, M.-J. *Évangile selon Saint Marc.* Paris: Gabalda, 1920 and following.

Lane, W. L. *Commentary on the Gospel of Mark.* Grand Rapids, Mich.: Eerdmans, 1974.

Lohmeyer, E. *Das Evangeliums des Markus.* Göttingen: Vandenhoeck and Ruprecht, 1959.

Rawlinson, A. E. J. *The Gospel According to St. Mark.* Westminster Commentaries. London: Methuen, 1925.

Swete, H. B. *The Gospel According to St. Mark.* 3rd ed. London: Macmillan, 1909 (reprinted 1920).

Taylor, V. *The Gospel According to St. Mark.* 2nd ed. London: Macmillan, 1966; New York: St. Martin's Press, 1966.

Turner, C. H. *The Gospel According to St. Mark.* London: SPCK, 1929. Reprinted from *A New Commentary on Holy Scripture*, edited by C. Gore, H. L. Goudge, A. Guillaume, London: SPCK, 1928, pp. 42-124.

Synopses

A suitable synopsis of the three gospels is essential, and the following are recommended:

Farmer, W. R. *Synopticon.* Cambridge University Press, 1969. This is in Greek with a color arrangement to show agreements between the gospels.

Huck, A. *Synopse der drei ersten Evangelien mit Beigabe der johannischen Parallelstellen.* Tübingen: J. C. B. Mohr, 9th ed., 1935. Translation by

F. L. Cross as *Synopsis of the First Three Gospels with the Addition of the Johannine Parallels.* Oxford: Basil Blackwell, 1951.

Orchard, J. B. *A Synopsis of the Four Gospels.* Macon, Ga.: Mercer University Press, 1982. This, along with the charts in the same author's *Matthew, Luke and Mark,* is arranged according to the Griesbach hypothesis.

Swanson, R. J. *Horizontal Line Synopsis of the Gospels.* Dillsboro, N.C.: Western North Carolina Press, 1975. A Greek version is also available.

Throckmorton, B. H. *Gospel Parallels.* 4th ed. Nashville: Thomas Nelson, 1979. This follows the arrangement of the Huck synopsis.

Other Books

Abrahams, I. *Studies in Pharisaism and the Gospels.* Cambridge: KTAV. 1st series, 1917; 2nd series, 1924.

Albright, W. F. *History, Archaeology, and Christian Humanism.* New York: McGraw-Hill, 1964.

Albright, W. F. and Mann, C. S. *Matthew.* AB Vol. 26. Garden City, N.Y.: Doubleday, 1971.

Aulén, Gustav. *Jesus in Contemporary Historical Research.* Philadelphia: Fortress Press, 1976. Translation by I. H. Hjelm of *Jesus i nutida historisk forskning.* Stockholm, 1973.

Bacon, B. W. *Is Mark a Roman Gospel?* Cambridge: Klaus Reprints, 1919.

———. *Studies in Matthew.* London: Constable, 1930; New York: Henry Holt, 1930.

Barbour, R. S. *Traditio-Historical Criticism of the Gospels: Some Comments on Current Methods.* London: SPCK, 1947.

Barrett, C. K. *The Holy Spirit and the Gospel Tradition.* London: SPCK, 1947.

Black, M. *An Aramaic Approach to the Gospels and Acts.* Oxford University Press, 1946.

Blass, F. *A Grammar of New Testament Greek.* Translation by H. St. John (London, 1905). Revised (with A. Debrunner) as *Grammatik des neutestamentlichen Griechisch.* 6th ed. Göttingen: Vandenhoeck and Ruprecht, 1931, with additions in 1943; reprinted 1976. Translation by R. W. Funk as *Greek Grammar of the New Testament.* University of Chicago Press, 1961.

Blunt, A. F. W. *The Gospel According to St. Mark.* Oxford: Clarendon Press, 1929.

Bultmann, R. *The History of the Synoptic Tradition.* New York: Harper and Row, 1963. Translation by J. Marsh of *Die Geschichte der synoptischen Tradition.* 3rd ed. Göttingen: Vandenhoeck and Ruprecht, 1957.

———. *The Theology of the New Testament.* London: SCM Press, 1952; New

York: Scribner, 1952. Translation by K. Grobel of *Theologie des Neuen Testaments.* Tübingen: J. C. B. Mohr, 1948.

Burkitt, F. C. *The Gospel History and Its Transmission.* 3rd ed. Edinburgh: T. & T. Clark, 1911.

Bussmann, W. *Synoptische Studien.* 3 parts. Halle: Waisenhaus, 1925-31.

Butler, B. C. *The Originality of St. Matthew: A Critique of the Two-Document Hypothesis.* Cambridge University Press, 1951.

Cadoux, A. T. *The Historic Mission of Jesus.* London: T. & T. Clark, 1937.

――――. *The Sources of the Second Gospel.* London: Macmillan, 1935.

Carrington, P. *The Primitive Christian Calendar.* Cambridge University Press, 1952.

Charles, R. H. *The Apocrypha and Pseudepigrapha of the Old Testament.* 2 vols. Oxford: Clarendon Press, 1913; reprinted 1976.

Charlesworth, J., ed. *The Old Testament Pseudepigrapha.* Vol. 1: *Apocalyptic Literature and Testaments.* Garden City, N.Y.: Doubleday, 1983.

Corley, B., ed. *Colloquy on New Testament Studies.* Macon, Ga.: Mercer University Press, 1983.

Crum, J. M. *St. Mark's Gospel: Two Stages of Its Making.* Cambridge: W. Heffer, 1936.

Cullmann, O. *Christ and Time.* Philadelphia: Westminster Press, 1950 and following. Translation by F. Filson of *Christus und Zeit.*

――――. *The Christology of the New Testament.* London: SCM Press, 1959; Philadelphia: Westminster Press, 1959. Translation by S. C. Guthrie and C. A. M. Hall of *Die Christologie des Neuen Testaments.*

Dalman, G. *Jesus-Jeschua.* Leipzig, 1922 (Supp 1929); Darmstadt, 1967. Translation by P. Levertoff. London: Collins, 1929.

――――. *The Words of Jesus.* Edinburgh: T. & T. Clark, 1902. Translation by D. M. Kay of *Die Worte Jesu.* Leipzig: J. C. Heinrich, 1898, 1930.

Davies, W. D. *Christian Origins and Judaism.* London: Arno Press, 1962.

Davies, W. D. and Daube, D. *The Background of the New Testament and Its Eschatology.* Studies in Honour of C. H. Dodd. Cambridge University Press, 1956.

Dodd, C. H. *The Bible and the Greeks.* London: Hodder and Stoughton, 1935.

――――. *History and the Gospel.* London: Nesbit, 1938.

Easton, B. S. *The Gospel Before the Gospels.* London: George Allen and Unwin, 1928; New York: Scribner, 1928.

Farmer, W. R. *The Synoptic Problem.* London and New York: Macmillan, 1964.

Farrer, Austin. *A Study in Mark.* London: Dacre Press, 1951.

Filson, Floyd. *A New Testament History.* London: SCM Press, 1964.

Finegan, Jack. *Handbook of Biblical Chronology.* Princeton University Press, 1964.

Finkel, Asher. *The Pharisees and the Teacher of Nazareth.* Leiden: E. J. Brill, 1964.

Gaston, Lloyd. *Horae Synopticae Electronicae.* Missoula, Mont.: SBL, 1973.

Glasson, T. F. *The Second Advent.* London: Epworth Press, 1945.

Gowan, Donald E. *Bridge Between the Testaments.* Pittsburgh: Pickwick Press, 1976.

————. *The Greek New Testament.* Edited by K. Aland, M. Black, B. M. Metzger, and A. Wikgren. The United Bible Societies, 1975.

————. *The Greek New Testament: Being the Text Translated in the New English Bible.* Edited by R. V. G. Tasker. Oxford and Cambridge: The University Presses, 1961.

————. *The New Testament in the Original Greek.* Edited by F. J. A. Hort and B. F. Westcott. Cambridge University Press, first published 1882.

————. *Novum Testamentum Graece.* Edited by A. Souter. Oxford: Clarendon Press, 1953.

Harvey, A. E. *Jesus and the Constraints of History.* Philadelphia: Westminster Press, 1982.

Hatch, E. and Redpath, H. A. *A Concordance to the Septuagint.* 2 vols. Oxford University Press, 1897 and following.

Hawkins, J. C. *Horae Synopticae.* Oxford University Press, 1909.

Hengel, M. *Judaism and Hellenism.* Philadelphia: Fortress Press, 1974. Translation by J. Bowden of *Judentum und Hellenismus Studien zur ihrer Begegnung unter besonderer Berücksichtigung Palästinas bis zur Mitte 2 Jhr.s v.Chr.* Tübingen: J. C. B. Mohr, 1973.

Hennecke, E. and Schneemelcher, W. *New Testament Apocrypha.* 2nd ed. London: Lutterworth Press, 1965.

Hoskyns, E. and Davey, N. *The Riddle of the New Testament.* 3rd ed. London: Faber and Faber, 1937; Naperville, Ill.: Allenson, 1947.

James, M. R. *The Apocryphal New Testament.* Oxford University Press, 1924.

Jeremias, J. *New Testament Theology I: The Proclamation of Jesus.* Translation by J. Bowden of *Neutestamentliche Theologie I: Die Verkündigung Jesu.* Gütersloh: Mohn, 1971.

Kähler, M. *The So-Called Historical Jesus and the Historic, Biblical Christ.* Philadelphia: Fortress Press, 1964. Translation by E. Braaten of *Der sogennante historische Jesu und der geschichtliche, biblische Christus.* New ed. edited by E. Wolff. Munich: Kaiser, 1953.

Kealey, S. P. *Mark's Gospel: A History of Its Interpretation.* Philadelphia: Fortress Press, 1982.

Kittel, G., ed. *Theological Dictionary of the New Testament.* 10 vols. Grand Rapids, Mich.: Eerdmans, 1964-76. Translation by G. W. Bromiley of *Theologisches Wörterbuch.* Stuttgart: W. Kohlhammer, 1933 and following.

Klausner, J. *Jesus of Nazareth.* London: Menorah, 1929.

Klostermann, E. *Das Markusevangeliums.* 4th ed. Tübingen: J. C. B. Mohr, 1950; reprinted 1976.

Knox, W. L. M. *The Sources of the Synoptic Gospels.* 2 vols. Cambridge University Press, 1951.

Kümmel, W. G. *Introduction to the New Testament.* London: SCM Press, 1966; Nashville: Abingdon Press, 1966. Translation by A. J. Mantill of *Einleitung in das Neue Testament.* Heidelberg: Quelle and Meyer, 1965.

Lagrange, M.-J. *L'Évangile de Jésus-Christ.* Paris: Lecoffre, 1929.

Lampe, G. W. H. *Patristic Greek Lexicon.* Oxford: Clarendon Press, 1961 and following.

Liddell, H. G. and Scott, R. *A Greek-English Lexicon.* Oxford: Clarendon Press, 1869 and following.

Lightfoot, R. H. *The Gospel Message of St. Mark.* Oxford: Clarendon Press, 1950.

———. *History and Interpretation in the Gospels.* London: Hodder and Stoughton, 1935.

Lindars, B. *New Testament Apologetics.* London: SCM Press, 1961.

Longenecker, R. N., and Tenney, M. C. *New Dimensions in New Testament Study.* Grand Rapids, Mich.: Zondervan, 1974.

Manson, T. W. *Jesus the Messiah.* London: Hodder and Stoughton, 1943.

———. *The Teaching of Jesus.* Cambridge University Press, 1935.

Marxsen, W. *Der Evangelist Markus.* 2nd ed. Göttingen: Vandenhoeck & Ruprecht, 1959.

Meyer, A. *Die Entstehung des Markusevangeliums.* Festgabe F. A. Julicher. Tübingen: J. C. B. Mohr, 1927.

Mitton, C. L. *The Gospel According to St. Mark.* London: Macmillan, 1957.

Moore, G. F. *Judaism in the First Centuries of the Christian Era.* Cambridge, Mass.: Harvard University Press, 1927.

Moule, C. F. D. *An Idiom Book of New Testament Greek.* Cambridge University Press, 1953.

Moulton, J. H. and Howard, W. F. *A Grammar Book of New Testament Greek (Prolegomena).* 3rd ed. Edinburgh: Darby Books, 1908; Vol. 2, 1929.

Moulton, J. H. and Milligan, G. *The Vocabulary of the Greek New Testament.* London: Gordon Press, 1914-29.

Neusner, J., ed. *Christianity, Judaism and Other Greco-Roman Cults.* Studies for Morton Smith at Sixty. 4 parts. Leiden: E. J. Brill, 1975.

Nineham, D. E. *Saint Mark.* Harmondsworth, Middlesex: Penguin Books, 1963.

Nineham, D. E., ed. *Studies in the Gospels: Essays in Memory of R. H. Lightfoot.* Oxford: Basil Blackwell, 1955.

Oesterley, W. O. E. *The Gospel Parables in the Light of Their Jewish Background.* London: Macmillan, 1936.

Radermakers, J. *La Bonne Nouvelle de Jésu selon Saint Marc.* 2 vols. Brussels: Institut d'Études Théologiques, 1974.

Ramsey, A. M. *The Glory of God and the Transfiguration of Christ.* London: Longman, Green, 1949.

Richardson, A. *The Miracle Stories of the Gospels.* London: SCM Press, 1941.

Robinson, J. A. T. *Jesus and His Coming.* London: SCM Press, 1957.

————. *Twelve New Testament Studies.* London: SCM Press, 1962.

Robinson, J. M. *The Problem of History in Mark.* Naperville, Ill.: Allenson, 1957.

Robinson, J. M. and Koester, H. *Trajectories Through Early Christianity.* Philadelphia: Fortress Press, 1971.

Sanders, E. P. *The Tendencies of the Synoptic Tradition.* SNTS Monographs No. 9. Cambridge University Press, 1969.

Schweitzer, A. *The Quest of the Historical Jesus.* 3rd ed. London: A. & C. Black, 1954. Translation by W. Montgomery of *Von Reimarus zu Wrede,* 1906; and of the later German ed., *Die Geschichte der Leben-Jesus-Forschung,* 1910.

Seyffert, O. *Dictionary of Classical Antiquities.* 3rd ed. Revised by H. Nettleship and J. E. Sandys. London: Swan Sonnenschein, 1900.

Stanton, V. H. *The Gospels as Historical Documents.* Vols. 1-3. Cambridge University Press, 1903-20.

Stauffer, E. *New Testament Theology.* London: SCM Press, 1955. Translation by J. Marsh of *Die Theologie des Neuen Testaments.* Stuttgart: Kohlhammer, 1955.

Strack, H. L. and Billerbeck, P. *Kommentar zum Neuen Testament aus Talmud und Midrasch.* Munich: Beck, 1922-61.

Streeter, B. H. *The Four Gospels: A Study of Origins.* London: Macmillan, 1924 and later editions.

Sykes, S. W. and Clayton, J. P., eds. *Christ, Faith and History.* Cambridge and New York: Cambridge University Press, 1978.

Taylor, V. *Jesus and His Sacrifice.* London: Macmillan, 1937 and 1948.

————. *The Person of Christ in New Testament Teaching.* 2nd ed. London: Macmillan, 1963.

Tuckett, C. *The Revival of the Griesbach Hypothesis.* London and New York: Cambridge University Press, 1983.

Wellhausen, J. *Einleitung in die drei ersten Evangelien.* 2nd ed. Berlin: Georg Reimer, 1911.

Williams, C. S. C. *Alterations to the Test of the Synoptic Gospels and Acts.* Oxford University Press, 1951.

Wrede, W. *Das Messiasgeheimnis.* 3rd ed. Göttingen: Vandenhoeck and Ruprecht, 1963.

Zimmerli, W. and Jeremias, J. *The Servant of God.* London: SCM Press, 1957.

Introduction

1. THE GOSPEL—PROCLAMATION AND DOCUMENTATION

A. The Gospel

The Gospel—or, as the word has been rendered wherever possible in this commentary, the Proclamation—is the message that God's righteous purposes for Israel have reached both goal and climax in and through the ministry and person of Jesus; the Gospel is the assertion that in and through that ministry and person of Jesus, viewed as messiah and harbinger of a New Age, the Reign of God is declared to all people willing to submit to its demands. As the earliest written interpretation of this Proclamation in our NT writings, Paul's letters speak of a salvation offered without distinction to all people—an interpretation based on the universality of sin, which knows no distinction between Jew and non-Jew, between those within the Sinai Covenant and those yet outside it. If Paul's understanding of the matter brought him bitter criticism and even persecution from Jews, Christians, and non-Christians alike, as seeming to undermine the privilege inherent in being the People of the Covenant; and if, too, the fall of Jerusalem in A.D. 70 rendered many of Paul's controversies academic (notably that surrounding the admission of Gentiles to the Church), nevertheless an important point emerged—the total dependence of the Proclamation made by Jesus on the OT understanding of God's dealings with Israel. Without the OT, there is no understanding of the Proclamation enshrined in the NT.

For all the Greek dress in which the message and ministry of Jesus come to us, for all the use which Paul makes of the stock-in-trade of current Stoic vocabulary, it is inescapable that the Gospel—as recorded in our documents —asserts a Reign of God which presuppose a covenant-making and covenant-demanding God, in the terms of the OT. The pivotal point of Jesus' teaching ministry is viewed by the first three of the evangelists as the acknowledgment by Peter, as spokesman for the rest, that Jesus was the expected Messiah. The fourth evangelist has a similar declaration of Jesus' messiahship built around John the Baptist's denial of any role for himself save that of "voice." While it is true that our four existing documents were compiled—so far as we can judge—for diverse audiences, and that these audiences to some extent dic-

tated the varying emphases and preoccupations of the four evangelists, nevertheless all four works assume a ministry of Jesus within the confines of the
Covenant people of Israel. All four equally assume a demand by Jesus to be
heard—and obeyed—both as authentic messenger of the Sinai Covenant, fulfilling its demands, and as Messiah inaugurating a New Age.

Although our four gospels are the primary and principal source material
for the life and ministry of Jesus, it would be wholly misleading to speak of
them as being in any sense "lives of Jesus." Certainly the gospels are not
biographical in any sense in which our own age would understand the term,
nor were they intended to be. But an entirely understandable preoccupation,
in the three centuries after the fall of Jerusalem, with what has come to be
called "christology" effectively set a pattern, persisting into our own times,
whereby the gospels were regarded as "christocentric." In other words, attention shifted from *God's* act *in Jesus,* which is the focus of the gospels, to a
concern with the person and ministry of Jesus exclusively. Given the momentous nature of Jesus' claim to be agent and instrument of God in the inauguration of his reign, it is not surprising to find throughout the NT writings
wholly different ways of understanding, and responding to, the person and
ministry of Jesus. (One author, for example, has persuasively argued for two
contrasting understandings of Jesus' role and ministry, reported from the lips
of Peter, in Acts. See J. A. T. Robinson, "The Most Primitive Christology of
All?" TNTS, 1962.) When therefore we come to deal with Mark's contribution to the understanding of Jesus—insofar as such a contribution is open to
our inspection—it will be of paramount importance to see it in NT perspective. To approach the person and ministry of Jesus as though both existed in a
kind of vacuum does violence to the framework, and to the milieu, in which
Jesus lived and taught.

B. What Is a Gospel?

A recent study (John Drury, "What Are the Gospels?" *ExpT* 87.1975-76, pp.
324-28) has demonstrated how difficult it is to arrive at an adequate definition
of what we mean when we describe the four first books of the NT as "gospels." The title as such is a mere convention, and has no foundation in primitive Christian practice (Justin Martyr describes our documents as "memoirs"
of the apostles—*Apologia* 1.67—or "memoirs which we call gospels"—ibid.,
1.66, cf. 1.33). Our present documents are hardly interested at all in the
human aspects of the man Jesus; we know nothing of his appearance or
habits, save by inference, and no appeal is made or implied in the gospels to

admire the man Jesus as someone who dramatically influenced his own times. The call of Jesus to the disciples, to the crowds, and to those who would share with him in the messianic blessings, is to "follow" him, not merely to imitate an example.

The literary form known to us as "gospels" sprang from the life, witness, and experience of the early Christian community, the Church. It is precisely here that our difficulties lie. For not only did the writers of our gospels live by the faith that in Jesus the God of Israel had sent to the chosen people the long-expected Messiah; they also believed that in Jesus God had given Israel his definitive "Word" for all generations. Furthermore, these evangelists were part and parcel of a community which proclaimed that this promised Messiah, this Jesus, was not only the "Son of Man" in the terms of Daniel and Enoch, but also "Son" in relation to God in a fashion which far transcended Israel's relationship of "Sonship" to God. Most of all, the later NT writers proclaimed—and the community taught—that God's act in Jesus had been one of universal redemption, manifested in and accomplished by the sacrificial death of the Messiah—a sacrificial death accepted by God and sealed in his raising of the Messiah from the tomb. *The* witness of the apostles, and of the NT, was that these same apostles had been eyewitnesses to this risen Messiah. From all of this witness and preaching issued a single call to all people—to the Jew first, and then to the Gentile—that people should repent and believe in this proclamation of God's redemptive act in Jesus.

No commentator, no NT scholar, can be wholly dispassionate about his material. He will bring to his work a whole mass of presuppositions—historical, sociological, cultural—which belong to the tradition in which he was raised. Above all, he cannot long pretend to remain neutral with regard to the central belief proclaimed by the message of the NT. But when that has been said, it is the business of the commentator to deal as faithfully as he can with the material before him, and endeavor to convey to his readers the message of the text itself.

All this is simply to state this commentator's view that the central theme of the Proclamation is God's deliverance of people from the dominion of sin and death in and through the sacrificial self-giving of The Man, Jesus-Messiah. The NT writers view this sacrificial self-giving as reaching its climax in the Passion, and its acceptance by God in the Resurrection. But if one demands further contemporary particularity in the phrase "deliverance of man," the best answer is found in a paraphrase of the words of Jesus—that people need now, as then and always, to be delivered from "the self" in order to find the *true* self—or rather to be found by God. What is therefore under discussion is the whole person: in solitude, in society, in quest of meaning, in life, and in history. And it is plain that the interpretative emphasis on the various facets of "deliverance" will shift from one age to another and from one dominant culture to another.

All that a commentary of this character can hope to accomplish is to take the tradition as one evangelist received it and apprehended it, and attempt to relate both the tradition and the evangelist's understanding of it to the wider background of Judaism and the Hellenistic world in which the tradition was articulated. It is the responsibility of the student and the reader, in every generation, to remember the claim of the NT writers that the tradition is "Word of God," and so of universal applicability. To say precisely how that tradition ought to be applied in greatly dissimilar cultures and circumstances is not the responsibility of the commentary, but it is important to see what interpretations have been offered in the past.

To seek answers to the question "Is there one particular kind of judgment which one can apply to every variety of material calling itself a gospel?" is in the end to bring up a whole variety of possible answers to questions of canonicity, inspiration, and the historical circumstances which prompted the Church at various times to declare what is, or is not, NT scripture. For example, the *Gospel of Thomas,* recently discovered at Nag Hammadi, poses its own unique questions in this respect: there are no immutable and unchangeable sets of criteria. But varying interpretations of this Proclamation all assume that there *is* a residual, unchangeable core, even if the interpretation currently being commended is presented—in contrast to all others—as *the* valid interpretation.

There is always a tendency to erect a present interpretation as valid for all time. Here one may contrast the cultural assumptions of the Middle Ages in the West, and their implication that there really was a "Christendom," with the underlying assertions of Paul van Buren *(The Secular Meaning of the Gospel,* London: SCM, 1963). The limitations of our own cultural horizons can stultify and even suffocate the liberation preached by Paul as the essence of the Proclamation.

Even the term "the Gospel of Jesus Christ" is not free of ambiguity, and some writers on NT subjects have made the most of this very ambiguity. The phrase may mean either the Gospel proclaimed by Jesus, understood as having to do with an imminent Reign of God, or the Gospel centered in the acts performed by God in and through Jesus.

What has customarily been called "liberal" theology concentrated almost entirely on the first of these alternatives, sometimes asserting, but nearly always implying, that the proclamation of the Kingdom by Jesus had an interior, ethical emphasis. Sometimes allied with this understanding was an interpretation of the Reign of God as concerned almost wholly with the sphere of life lived in society, with all its multifarious activities. From such a background of interpretation came the "social Gospel."

For some—if not all—liberal commentators on the gospels the shift of emphasis to christology was unhappy, if not downright mistaken. To be sure, such a shift of emphasis was to be found in Paul's letters, but that could be—

and was by some—explained as being due to the corrupting Hellenistic influence to which the apostle was considered subject.

To assert in reply to the liberal unhappiness with christocentrism that it was certainly to be found in the apostolic preaching, especially in the early speeches in Acts, was to invite complete skepticism as to the veracity of Luke's reporting of the preaching, and an equal skepticism concerning the historicity of Acts in general.

One result of the Renaissance was an interpretation of the Gospel in terms of an individual and interior pietism. The Puritan understanding of the Gospel has often been assumed to be concerned exclusively with this pietist individualism, but it should not be forgotten that medieval religion could be, and often was, highly individualist and pietist.

Whatever the emphases and varying interpretations of previous ages and of our own time, there is an element of truth in each of them. This makes the task of defining the term "gospel," as applied to a written document, at once simple and complex. It is simple to the extent that we intuitively grasp the broad outlines of the content of the Proclamation of the Reign of God by Jesus, simple in that we can grasp the transition from the proclaimed righteousness of the Reign of God to the Pauline Jesus who *is* the righteousness of God. Even the titles which are used of Jesus in our four gospels—Messiah, Shepherd, Lord, Son of Man, Son of David, Word, Lamb of God—bear witness to the manner in which the declaration of the righteousness of God inevitably became the theological concepts of Paul. They also bear witness to the possibilities of changes of emphasis from one cultural climate to another.

In whatever way we understand the term "gospel" as applied to the four NT documents, we shall seriously misunderstand their import if we regard them as being simply lives of Jesus. Since the nearest literary form which we have to the four gospels is biography, there is a natural tendency to seek biographical detail—which is for the most part lacking—and in so doing to miss the characteristics which mark them off from all biography. The gospels are primarily theological documents, and all else is subordinated to the conditions which each evangelist received and which he transmitted to his hearers and readers.

Nor is this all. Behind each evangelist's tradition, or series of traditions, there lies a history of transmission both oral and written. In some cases we can see the process of transmission at work. Yet another factor to be considered is one without which there is no understanding of the gospels, and certainly no understanding of the NT as a whole. This factor, which gave rise to the whole tradition enshrined in our gospels, is the picture of Jesus held by the early Christian community. Whatever may have been the history of individual elements of narratives, units of teaching material, or the framework of the history of Jesus' early ministry, the traditions in our four gospels unanimously present Jesus to us as one who did not merely proclaim the dawning

Reign of God, but demanded people's allegiance to himself as the divinely ordained instrument through which that Reign would be inaugurated.

The early Church in the Pauline letters and in Acts comes to our notice as a community which based its claim to acceptance by Jew and Gentile alike, and its demand for repentance, not only on an assertion that Jesus was the promised Deliverer but also on the conviction that the community experienced and witnessed certain historical events in its life which validated its beliefs about Jesus. It is this assertion, this proclamation, which dominates and gives unity to the four gospels, whatever their varying traditions or individual preoccupations.

The great services rendered by the discipline known as *Formgeschichte* (in English, usually "form criticism") have been many and impressive. The discipline may be said to have begun with Hermann Gunkel in his important and pioneering work *Genesis* (Göttingen: Vandenhoeck & Ruprecht, 1901. English translation by W. H. Carruth, *The Legends of Genesis: The Biblical Saga and History.* New York: Schocken Books, 1901). It is fair to say that this tool of biblical studies has had its most extensive application (in recent years) in the field of NT studies. While the past few years have seen an increasingly severe criticism of some of the more confident statements made by protagonists of the "form-critical" school, nevertheless in some sense most writers on NT subjects, and especially on the gospels, are by implication "form critics."

Valuable as the discipline has been in calling attention to the various strata in the gospel tradition—short "pronouncement stories," "miracle stories," "parables," and so forth—form criticism has undoubtedly been more a child of its time than some of its disciples have so far admitted. It is far too readily assumed that a current interest in "structuralism" in literature can be carried into the gospel traditions, with a consequent analysis of the forces motivating the evangelists or the compilers of the tradition. Nor is this all. It is not a long step from such an analysis to a consideration of the gospels from a purely psychological viewpoint, regarding them purely as vehicles for producing some desired effect in the reader. Significantly, some of the more prominent writers of the form-critical school have concentrated heavily on written gospels as comprehended under the broad heading of "preaching." Wholly divorced from considerations of history, it would be perfectly possible to compile a narrative about, say, Napoleon, with precisely the same end in view—that is, to produce a dramatic effect on the reader.

It cannot be denied that for the worshiping Christian congregation the events of the ministry of Jesus can be, and ought to be, renewed and revivified by effective preaching. But it is precisely because such preaching can be readily adapted by a process known to psychologists as "conditioning" that all preaching needs to be examined in the light of, and certainly always followed by, the discipline of teaching. Our NT sources speak regularly of both *kerugma* (preaching) and *didachē* (teaching) and although the lines of demarcation are sometimes not clear in those sources, nevertheless the distinction is there. Each sustains the other.

Whatever the desire on the part of the early Christian community to persuade by preaching, and inform by teaching, it is impossible to imagine a situation in Judaism in which isolated collections of sayings, or groups of sayings, could have generated their own motive power. The message of a messiah who called people into a New Age through the gateway of repentance could only have been nullified by the scandalous pivot of that message —a redemptive death accomplished by one condemned by law—if lacking the solid support provided by an account of the life and ministry of that messiah, as witnessed by those who had known him. At the very foundation of the Proclamation lies the history of Jesus of Nazareth. According to some writers on NT subjects, the reason for the tradition's being committed to writing must be found in the concept of *parousia*—a response to the promise (whether real or misunderstood) of a renewed manifestation of Jesus to his followers, differentiated from his first appearance by its glory. For these followers, the disappointment of this expectation aroused fears for the preservation of the traditions concerning the ministry and passion of Jesus, and so prompted the compilation of our present gospels.

Now, it is true that a diminishing interest in and concern for this *parousia* in the writings of Paul tends to support the view that in the earliest period after the ministry of Jesus there was an intense expectation of a second appearing of Jesus in glory. Assuming, however, that Paul was responsible for the letter to Ephesus either in whole or in part, it is crucial to note that this letter makes no mention of a *parousia* expectation at all. Further, one may seriously doubt whether this explanation for the writing down of the tradition will satisfy. Indeed, the argument can be turned around to suggest that the primitive community hastened to make accurate records of the ministry and mission of Jesus precisely *because* of its expectation of an early return of Jesus in glory. There is ample OT precedent for the compilation of written records, even when national fortunes were at a very low ebb, as in Isaiah's time, or even at full ebb tide, as in Jeremiah's.

It was fashionable and even academically acceptable up to quite recent times to maintain a high degree of skepticism with regard to the possibility of knowing anything at all of the "Jesus of History," and also—and even more pronouncedly—with regard to the recorded utterances of Jesus. While the old skepticism with regard to the historicity of the gospel records of Jesus has given way to the "new quest for the historical Jesus," one may wonder whether this "new quest" has as yet taken sufficient cognizance of the increasingly known contemporary background of Jesus' life. What is certain is that attempts to see in the gospel accounts yet another Hellenistic *theios anēr*, "divine man"—however superior in some respects to other examples of the genre—must be dismissed. There is no known example of legends of a *theios anēr* until some time after the NT books were circulating and being read.

If the gospels, as individual books containing traditions about the ministry of Jesus as it proclaims the Reign of God, enshrine *the* Gospel, and this Gospel is accepted as universally applicable, then some further consideration of the response to that Gospel in succeeding ages is surely in order. If the Gospel is to be regarded as universally applicable, then it is applicable to the whole person, and not simply to his internal intellectual or emotional responses. Equally, if universally applicable, then the word of God enshrined in the Gospel cannot be simply directed to one society, whether contemporary with the ministry of Jesus or our own. If the "salvation" offered in our NT documents is universal, then we must expect that its manifestation will change its emphasis from one period to another, from one culture to another, and language will in all kinds of subtle ways influence the manner in which the Gospel is apprehended.

Deliverance—from fear, death, astral domination—in the days of the Roman Empire was the quest of many of the mystery religions. There is enough evidence in the letters of Paul to suggest that the promise of "deliverance" brought into the early Christian community many pagans whose mistaken apprehensions of this deliverance and redemption had frequently to be corrected. Even in the compass of the NT books, a shift in emphasis can be easily discovered. For while Jesus appears often to have conceived his mission in terms of Representative Israel, Paul's emphasis on universality of redemption sprang ultimately from a premise of the universality of sin. The operative factor in Paul's theology of Jesus' sacrificial ministry and death was the role of Jesus as Second Adam, the Representative Man, who wrought the reconciliation of mankind with the Father in his identification with us.

When we pass beyond the boundaries of the NT writings and wish to speak of a final, irreducible, and unchanging deposit of faith in the interpretation of the ministry and work of Jesus, then it is proper to ask by what standards we measure that deposit. It is perfectly true that we can, and do, appeal to the Bible. In so doing, we frequently forget that what we have before us in English has come to us through Greek, in part Latin, Anglo-Saxon, and Middle English. Our claims for a "contemporary" understanding of the Gospel cannot possibly be confined to a quest for contemporaneity in language. In whatever language the gospels are presented to us, an obligation is laid on us to understand the processes of conciliar definition and condemnation of heresy by which previous generations came to understand the nature of the tradition. Even beyond the processes by which the tradition has come to us, there is the whole world of history, culture, and archeology whose lights must be brought to bear upon the written traditions enshrined in the four gospels.

The tradition, as it is preserved for us in the four gospels and proclaimed and explained by Paul and later writers, in the end drives us back to the question frequently posed by the late Canon Sir Edwyn Hoskyns: "Who are the Jews?" All our quests for new situations in a new age, and our desire to give the Gospel a "contemporary" interpretation, in the end prove to be far too confining. We are never aware of our own limitations, though we are often painfully aware of the limitations of past interpretations of the Gospel. The merely "situational" is frequently an enslavement even when it is not purely ephemeral.

C. The Marks of a Gospel

Granted that in the course of Christian history some documents came to be molded in patterns already existing in Hellenistic literature—"revelations," "words of the wise," "deeds of the mighty," etc.—how can we determine with any precision what constitutes a "gospel" so as to mark it off from all other literary productions? If we hold that a gospel is in the main kerygmatic, what determining characteristics exist which can set a gospel apart from later imitations? (This question is wholly apart from the very vexed and confusing debates as to canonicity and inspiration. Cf., e.g., James C. Turro and Raymond E. Brown, "Canonicity," in *JBC* 67, Englewood Cliffs, N.J.: Prentice Hall, 1968, pp. 515-34; Richard F. Smith, "Inspiration and Inerrancy," in *JBC* 66, pp. 499-514.) By what criteria do we judge, say, Elizabethan drama? What is there in common between Ben Jonson's quest for a true balance of the "unities" and Shakespeare's free use of every technique open to him? Yet both are subsumed in the same "Elizabethan drama" genre.

James M. Robinson *("Logos sophōn.* Zur Gattung der Spruchquelle Q," in *Zeit und Geschichte: Dankesgabe an R. Bultmann,* edited by R. Dinkler, Tübingen: Mohr, 1964, pp. 77ff.) has pleaded that the same principles applied to identify smaller units in form-critical analysis should now be applied to whole documents. He suggests that we may discern from the intention of the evangelists in the smaller units the total theological preoccupation in the whole resulting work. But this method of arriving at a definition of the genre "gospel" is seriously flawed unless we can identify—as some others seek to do —the post-Easter theological and social concerns of the community which produced the gospel.

If it is possible to infer from the state of the material which we now have that Matthew's work was intended to be a kind of "guide to the perplexed"; if we can determine that Matthew was composed to establish the rules by which the Christian community must live through the earthly Kingdom of the Son in order to be found acceptable to the (final) Kingdom of the Father—then not only are valid comparisons possible between Matthew and the Essene *Rule of the Community* or the *Didachē,* but we may also determine the fashion in which the tradition of Jesus' ministry was seen by the evangelist. If so, which of these elements are shared with Mark in such a way that the term "gospel" can apply to his work, too? Luke, for all his concern for a continuing community in Luke-Acts (cf. the use of the word "disciple" for *all* believers), succeeds in presenting the tradition as a series of "confrontation stories" between the Spirit-endowed messengers of God on the one hand and the inimical members of the established order on the other. How then does Mark compare with this work, or Matthew with either? It would seem that the use by the early Christian Church of the term "gospel" for all three of these (not to mention John) makes the problem of identifying the genre almost insoluble. Perhaps we have to fall back on the confused field of canonicity, and conclude that what we have in our present four documents is a division of a far wider *genus* "canon." Yet if the earliest attestation of the use of the word "gospel" to describe the documents is given by Irenaeus and Clement of Alexandria (the first writers known to use the plural), then we must assume that in the early community there was *a* gospel, known in a plurality of forms, whether in oral form or committed to writing. Perhaps the best we can do is to suggest that what partly determined the inclusion of our present documents in the existing canon was that each embodied in its own fashion an apprehension of "gospel" as "proclamation," as distinct from other writings—whether "orthodox" or "heretical"—which contained simply sayings, signs, or manifestations of deity.

It is in this sense that Mark appears most closely to approximate Paul's use of the term "gospel" (cf. Rom 1:1ff., 1 Cor 15:1ff., and Mark 1:15; 8:35; 10:29; 13:10; 14:9). M. Dibelius (1934) found it possible to reject Mark as a gospel, using a criterion of "message of salvation," and on the same grounds found it possible to accept Matthew as precisely fulfilling that criterion. It is difficult to see where this might lead. For if Matthew, considered *purely as instruction,* be accepted and Mark rejected, then we must expect the *Gospel of Thomas* (and just possibly John) to qualify, and two synoptic documents to be rejected.

These considerations are offered as examples of the very fluid state of the current debate on "genre criticism" which is engaging the attention of New Testament scholars. If we have tentatively agreed on the norm "proclamation" as being the characteristic which distinguished our four documents as "gospels," we may now turn our attention to Mark as example.

Much has turned in the past upon the supposed Markan "secrecy" motif. Bultmann maintained that the so-called "messianic secret" was not merely an editorial device, but a necessary declaration of faith in a Messiah for whom semi-anonymity was characteristic. To this, Hans Conzelmann responded with a denial ("Gegenwart und Zukunft in der synoptischen Tradition," *ZTK*

54.1957, pp. 277-96; English translation by J. Wilson, "Present and Future in the Synoptic Tradition," in H. Braun, *God and Christ, JTC* 5.1968, pp. 26-44), asserting that Mark's traditions were already heavily loaded with messianism and that the "messianic secret," already present in the traditions Mark used, was therefore an underpinning device in his work. (It is incidentally worth noting that any adherent of the Griesbach hypothesis of synoptic origins, on which see below, would not be surprised by this—cf. Matt 16:20.) But there is more than this: for Conzelmann the "secrecy" motif is of the very essence of the literary type we call "gospel" (cf. English edition, ibid., p. 41). This point was not fully developed by Conzelmann until the publication of his work on the passion narratives *(Zur Bedeutung des Todes Jesu,* edited by F. Viering, Gütersloh: Gütersloher Verlagshaus Gerd Mohn, 1967; English translation by C. Consar, "History and Understanding in the Passion Narratives of the Synoptic Gospels," *Int* 24.1970, pp. 178-97). Here Conzelmann rejects the old contention that the gospels are merely passion narratives with an extended introduction, and goes on to demand why the introduction was necessary and why the form we have come to call "gospel" was invented. It is not enough, he maintained, to reply that the introduction material was merely "there"—given the theology of the tradition and the theological preoccupations of Mark. Since the passion of Jesus is for Conzelmann *the* key to understanding the work and ministry of Jesus, he regards the messianic secret as the *means* by which all this work and ministry was accomplished, and *the* secret is the application of the theology of the cross to the whole work of Jesus. The Passion was the necessary condition of entrance into glory, and was also the determinative of faith after the Easter experience.

When we go on to inquire of Conzelmann *why* Mark imposed a theology of the cross on the material he found—if indeed that is what he did—then the answers are less satisfactory. For Conzelmann, all the titles are blanketed under a single understanding of the theology of the cross, and the titles themselves (as understood in some sections of Judaism) are irrelevant. It is quite imperative then to ask why the evangelist did not seek wholly different titles. Assuming Conzelmann's thesis is correct, we might reasonably expect that the evangelist would impose upon his material wholly different categories —perhaps with major emphasis on the "servant" motifs of Second Isaiah. Further, if Mark was writing for a predominantly Gentile community— which the present commentator does not accept—then we are entitled to ask what meaning, if any, would have been given the word "Christos" by a Hellenistic Greek audience.

Conzelmann's original suggestion has given rise to suggestions which may be thought to be implied in it. Most cogently argued has been the proposition that if Mark imposed a theology of the cross upon his traditions, then the audience to which the work was addressed must have had (or been in danger of taking up) an understanding of Jesus as *theios anēr,* and of discipleship as a sharing in the same endowment of miraculous powers. It is suggested that Mark controverts this incipient error by the juxtaposition of the passion narrative and the introductory material.

While all this is of considerable interest as speculation, two immediate questions spring to mind. First, in what area and at what stage in the community's history did this incipient heresy begin to manifest itself in serious dimensions? To this question, there has so far been no satisfactory reply. Secondly, the motif of a suffering "Son of Man" is so deeply embedded in the tradition that we may ask at what stage the evangelist imposed upon the introductory material the theological orientations of his passion narrative.

The suggestion that what we have in the gospels is a Christian aretalogy— an account of a "divine man," or hero, moving through manifold trials to the inevitable triumph of virtue at the end—has at first sight something to commend it. But some qualifications are necessary, and they are such as to call in question the validity of the whole concept. The movement in the gospels is not from hazard to victory; rather, the passion-resurrection narratives qualify and inform all that has gone before, and without those narratives much of the preceding material is void of meaning. If the superficial form of the gospel narratives is that of aretalogy, then it must be said that in order to include the gospels in that category such a drastic redefinition of aretalogy would have to be offered as virtually to exclude all other contenders. Rather than engage in such a self-defeating procedure, we almost inevitably reach the conclusion that our gospels are what the opening words of Mark assert them to be— proclamation.

2. THE COMPOSITION OF THE GOSPELS

A. The Background of the Tradition

Any attempt to explain the form and order of Mark's gospel must, if it is to be intelligible, give some account of factors which have led the commentator to his conclusions. Account must be rendered of how, and why, he has rejected other explanations; why he has chosen to question some tentative conclusions of NT scholarship and accept others; why he feels that this process of sifting leads to more convincing explanations than some commonly offered. This introduction will therefore attempt to indicate the author's presuppositions before offering his own—admittedly tentative—hypothesis for consideration.

In the first place, the author sees no good reason to suppose that any single writer of our four canonical gospels was any other than a Jewish Christian. Admittedly, the phrase "Jewish Christian" needs careful documentation in the light of what is now known of the extent of sectarianism in the Jewish world of the first century. It is necessary, for example, to draw some distinction between the carefully garnered traditions of Jesus' attitude to the Law preserved in Matthew and the lesser attention paid to such material in Luke. While it is possible to presuppose a more "orthodox" Jewish background for Matthew, it would nevertheless be decidedly ill-advised to base major conclusions on the comparative lack of legal material in Luke. I think that either the third evangelist had been nurtured in circles which sat loosely under the Mosaic Law or he was not concerned for its place in the new era which grew out of the ministry of Jesus. We may speculate, then (assuming that Luke's gospel originally began at Chapter 3), as to the sources from which his narratives were added, and with what motives, and ask from what "sectarian" sources did the well-known canticles of the first two chapters come to the author (or authors). Even if we take the gospel of Mark as the literary source of Matthew and Luke, it will be of more than passing moment to inquire why Mark has been preserved at all, in view of its apparently "formless" character and episodic nature, especially in light of the fact that the other evangelists had access to other Palestinian traditions.

Other considerations must be taken into account when we come to the fourth gospel. Granted that the author (like the synoptists) was a Jew, we find ourselves wondering precisely what kind of audience John had in mind when he used vocabulary which—while familiar to Greek-speaking Jews—carried meanings valid for, and understood by, an educated Greek. A similar ambivalence may be found in some passages of Paul's letters. For example, it is legitimate to speculate what degree of explanation was necessary for the word *Christos* when the writings passed beyond the confines of Greek-speaking Jews—a transition which was certainly early. It has been suggested from time to time that the familiar gospel title "Son of Man" fell into disuse in the period represented by Acts precisely because the term was not understood in the Hellenistic world—a suggestion which, even if not accepted as a sufficient explanation, nevertheless draws attention to the inherent difficulties posed in the passage of the gospel into a wider world.

If, then, in addition to seeing the ministry of Jesus amidst its Jewish environment and background—viewed almost entirely in the terms of the OT— we posit a Jewish background for the evangelists, it is imperative to ask what accommodation the writers made to a nascent Hellenistic Christianity. We are therefore faced with the necessity of determining (a) how the transmission of the gospel fared during the period covered by the remainder of the NT, which in its turn depends upon (b) the possible dates of the gospel material. It is hoped that the other sections of this part of the Introduction will sufficiently indicate the present writer's presuppositions in both respects. This section will show how, and in what respects, the writer sees the Jewish heritage of this one evangelist in particular, and his approach to collecting reminiscences of Jesus' ministry and message.

B. Oral Tradition

NT scholars are agreed that there was a period, long or short, before the sources of our present gospels were committed to written form. But by no means all NT scholars are agreed on the importance of this oral tradition, or on the validity of that tradition in the period in question. To that must be added a similar lack of unanimity as to what part—if any—was played by the believing and worshiping community in committing oral sources to writing. To what extent, for example, was the anxiety of a Jewish Christian community about the continuing validity of the Law responsible for the legal material in Matthew? And, to pursue this matter a little further, was such a community *itself responsible* for the inclusion in Matthew of the injunction in 23:2? In view of the continuing debate on the extent to which we may, or may not, be able to recall the *ipsissima verba* of Jesus from our gospel sources, the writer on the NT gospel tradition will find himself choosing between a denial of oral tradition and an affirmation of it which may often appear to be too confining. (Cf. H. Riesenfeld, 1970, and Howard Teeple, "The Oral Tradition That Never Existed," *JBL* 89.1970, pp. 56-68.)

Enough is now known of rabbinic oral tradition to suggest that the process of oral transmission of the early gospel sources must be taken very seriously indeed. To be sure, it is possible to treat oral transmission with altogether too much rigidity (cf. B. Gerhardsson, 1961 and 1964). In general, Scandinavian scholars have been far more alive to the part played by oral tradition in the gospels than has been the case elsewhere. Although it is fair to point out that the existence of the Icelandic saga has contributed largely to this awareness, it is possible to be somewhat surprised at the less than enthusiastic fashion in which the known facts about oral tradition were embraced elsewhere. Great numbers of oral traditions are found in the United States today, many of them only discovered by scholars in the past thirty years. (Cf. in this connection the work of Cecil Sharpe and Maud Karpeles in the Appalachian oral tradition during the early decades of the twentieth century.) We have no particular reason today to be as skeptical of the oral tradition as was Samuel Johnson (cf. John Wain, *Samuel Johnson,* New York: Viking Press, 1974, pp. 328-29).

Even at our great remove from the first century we can learn much about the methods of the leading influence in Jewish learning in that period—Rabbinic Pharisaism. That Jesus himself was aware of the immense influence exercised by "oral Torah," or rabbinic and legal commentary on the written Law, is evidenced by his excoriation of Pharisee lawyers as overscrupulous and pettifogging in Matt 23 (cf. Albright-Mann, AB *Matthew,* Introduction, pp. cvi-cxxiii). Words from the Torah with commentary by a notable teacher were treasured by pupils and reflected upon, and they soon hardened into positive precept. The words of notable rabbis were committed to memory, fixed through recital, and enshrined almost as sacred words—a process to which the Mishnah bears ample testimony. Some of the great teachers of the time have given us an insight into part of the method by which their teaching was safeguarded: repeating and memorizing the important texts, even before apprehending their real meaning, with unbroken dependence on the teacher, who would safeguard the tradition by handing it on only to qualified pupils.

This whole process was perpetuated in various ways, in homes, in synagogues, in gatherings of learned men, and in the courts, by men who made it their business to take note of and to record such traditions—the scribes. Familiar as we are with the extraordinary care taken by Isaiah or Jeremiah to preserve teaching accurately through circles of pupils (and Jeremiah had little confidence that much would survive a national disaster), we often find ourselves unwilling to accord the same desire for preservation to Jesus and his disciples. Yet enough is known on two counts to give us some leads in the matter: first, Jesus was evidently regarded and addressed as "Rabbi," with all that this entailed; secondly, the information on the relations between student and teacher in the learning process leads us to assume that Jesus' teaching methods were those of his own time. It should be noted that our information on these matters derives from Judea; how far such methods were employed in Galilee we have few means of knowing.

A further note must be added to this discussion of the oral tradition. The discoveries at Qumran have demonstrated the care taken to preserve the texts of biblical and other writings, and incidentally give us some insights into the methods employed, including the use of a scriptorium. If, indeed, the so-called "Temple Scroll" was an attempt deliberately to write scripture (cf. the use of the first person singular for God, as in Deuteronomy), then we are that much closer to being able partially to explain the compilation of what we call the gospels. (Incidentally, the present writer believes that the sealed manuscripts of Qumran were neither being cast into a *genizah* of unwanted or damaged books nor yet being hidden against a time of distress, but were being deliberately stored to provide master copies for reference purposes.)

One final consideration must be added before we pass to other modes of interpretation of the tradition within Judaism. Although the spoken word was in some ways regarded as more potent than the written—a usage which persists in English to this day in sayings such as "Don't say that!"—yet the written word provided the framework for other modes of expression; it was in fact vital to all the exercise of *midrash* (homily) as fount for oral traditions of law and custom. It cannot be too strongly emphasized that in the rabbinic tradition no word of scripture could be regarded as superfluous. So much was this the case that identical words, or even words vaguely similar or from similar contexts, could be and often were used to interpret each other. The development of the synagogue after the Exile guaranteed that by NT times the reasonably educated Jew knew most of his Scriptures by heart.

C. Written Tradition and Interpretation

Various methods of interpreting the written tradition in Judaism were known and regarded as wholly legitimate. First of all, there was *halakah,* concerned particularly with the written Law and the analysis of varying opinions as to how the Torah had come to be interpreted. It was in this sense that Rabbi Akiba held that tradition "is a fence around the Law" (M *Aboth* 3:18). In general, *halakah* was characterized by a very precise attention to words and phrases. Some interesting examples of this occur in Paul's letters; cf. Gal

3:15-18. The much more free and wide-ranging method known as *midrash* can best be described as homily or exposition and, with one important qualification, this is the way in which the gospel of Matthew is written. In Matthew, the use of the OT by the evangelist is a very striking example of the method now so well known from Qumran—that of *pesher* (cf. Albright-Mann, AB *Matthew*, pp. lviii-lxxiii). In effect, *the whole context* of Matthew's OT quotations is to provide background for his narrative of events and teaching in the ministry of Jesus.

Matthew includes other indications of the adoption of common Jewish learning methods—for example, the well-known memory aid of "inclusion" (cf. J. C. Fenton, *Saint Matthew,* London and Baltimore: Penguin Books, 1963, pp. 53ff.). There are equally striking examples in Matthew of the "refrain" device, in the framing of autonomous sections by repeated phrases or formulas. Mark, too, has characteristic words and phrases (see below), but in his case the task of memorization appears to be dependent on the episodic character of his compilation—cf. the "typical day" in the ministry of Jesus (1:21-34).

In the transition from oral to written tradition, certain changes inevitably occur. Some fairly well-defined characteristics are thought to mark the change, but for material such as the gospels there are factors at work which are alien to other transmitted traditions. We may, for example, examine the interpretation of the tradition in the Pauline corpus and watch the emergence, in the later letters like Colossians and Ephesians, of a "cosmic" approach to the ministry and person of Jesus. While passages like Eph 1:10,20, 22-23 are consonant with some manifestations of messianic hope in contemporary Judaism, a gap is already forming between the tradition of the early Pauline letters—which clearly express the role of Jesus as God's *agent* in redemption—and a later tradition which is concerned rather with Jesus-in-himself.

Considerable caution is called for in assessing the part played by felt community needs in shaping the original oral tradition into written form. The attempt to confine the genesis of certain forms in the written tradition to homilies in the early Church, or to real or supposed life situations in missionary enterprise, requires some assumptions that may be unwarranted. It is surely illegitimate to imagine, or to infer from the very meager evidence open to our inspection, that any one facet of community experience was the exclusive point of departure for some particular body of material. We may reasonably infer—in the absence of parallel texts elsewhere—that the so-called "Matthean exception" in the teaching on divorce (Matt 5:32) may be a piece of community legislation; but its provenance, and still less the date of the legislation in question, cannot be inferred from the text.

D. The Context of Composition

We may be reasonably certain, at all events from the crisis which Paul confronted in 1 and 2 Thessalonians, that the death of individual believers posed considerable problems for those who understood—or misunderstood—the New Age to have been inaugurated by the mission and ministry of Jesus. Equally, we may compare and contrast present/realized and future/end-of-time eschatology in the gospels, and try to determine on that basis whether Jesus regarded himself as the eschatological prophet of the last days, or as a present, suffering Son of Man in humility, or as a coming Son of Man yet to be revealed. Any such analysis must finally return to a community which consisted of those who proclaimed they had experienced God's act of salvation in Jesus. We cannot, that is to say, contemplate the ministry of Jesus untrammeled by the mediation of a believing community. Yet in saying this we are making the same judgment that must be made about the books of the OT, whether historical or prophetic, and about the later speculative pseudepigraphical books. And if Israel was a believing community, she was also a worshiping community.

Form criticism has provided us with a series of categories through which we may hope to penetrate, through the present written forms of the texts, to original oral sources behind them. But the reasons given for writing down the texts are as diverse as the vocabularies in which the hypothetical reasons are commended: expectation of an imminent *parousia,* to demonstrate the community's preparedness; bewilderment at a delay of the expected *parousia,* to sustain faith; a felt need to guard the tradition from false teaching by restating a supposedly primitive tradition; a concern on the part of an evangelist to propound his own theological interpretation of the salvation event. The situation is not made easier when to this catena of often contradictory hypotheses is added the interposition of more than one redactor.

To one context, however, remarkably little attention has been paid—that of worship. There seems to be no good reason to be skeptical of the assertion in Acts 2:42 and 46-47 that assiduity in customary and common worship characterized the early Jerusalem community. Nor is there any good reason to think that the earliest missionary enterprises (cf. Acts 8:1-4) were content simply with proclamation *(kerugma)* and teaching *(didachē)* and left the neophytes with no instruction in prayer, public or private. But the proclamation that in Jesus God had decisively and once for all acted to rescue and redeem Israel (universalism was a later refinement, so far as we can judge) opened the way for a new understanding of man's approach to God. In no area of worship can this have been more dramatically true than in the context of the Passover *Haggadah*. It is regrettable that the seminal suggestions of David Daube in this regard—references to which will be found in the bibliography appended to this section—should have met with minimal subsequent study. It is a commonplace to give attention to the liturgical recitation of some parts of the text (e.g., Chronicles), but the possibility that our gospels were similarly used (particularly the passion narrative) has received little examination.

Space does not permit any examination in detail of this matter. But we may too long have been mesmerized by paying close attention to a single aspect of form criticism—the distinguishing marks of certain classes of material in the synoptic gospels—while at the same time neglecting to pursue further enquiry and ask in what context(s) the identified units were used.

The matter of the *Sitz im Leben* of the gospel pericopae has been raised in recent years with some urgency in two publications: M. D. Goulder's *Midrash and Lexicon in Matthew* (London: SPCK, 1974) and—far nearer to this commentary—John Bowman's *The Gospel of Mark: The New Christian Jewish Passover Haggadah* (1965). It may reasonably be contended that Bowman attempted to prove too much, but the author performed a signal service by calling attention once again to the matrix of worship as formative of collective traditions. In the view of this writer, it is of some interest to note that Goulder, in an appendix to the work already mentioned, maintains that there is a "lectionary" origin for Mark's gospel. Despite the fact that our best and most reliable information on synagogue lectionaries long postdates the NT books, and despite the plethora of suggestions that *all* the gospel material was arranged in orderly fashion for planned reading of some kind, certain puzzling features remain about some gospel manuscripts. We have as yet no wholly satisfactory explanation for the "chapter divisions" *(kephalaia)* in some manuscripts of the gospels, unless such headings indicated a division of the material for reading in an assembly. Codex Sinaiticus is certainly the best known of such examples for all four gospels, though the papyrus p[75] has the *kephalaia* for Luke. Very strong reservations may properly be expressed here on some of the specific suggestions in Goulder's work. It is, however, encouraging to find that new questions of gospel formation may still be raised.

A phenomenon associated with Qumran's cave 7 may have some bearing on our subject. There was found on the cave floor, in inked letters—evidently impressed from a long-vanished papyrus or parchment—the Greek phrase *en tais graphais.* So far as is known, the phrase is confined to NT scripture (Matt 21:42; Luke 24:27; Acts 17:2,18,24,28; Rom 1:2; 1 Cor 15:3,4). This unexplained discovery does inevitably pose a question for which we have no answer at the present time: were members of the Qumran community, or later refugees associated with the site, self-consciously engaged in writing "scripture"? So far as the Essenes are concerned, the answer (at all events from the evidence of the so-called Temple Scroll and the *War Scroll)* would appear to be affirmative. This so far isolated example of a Greek NT phrase may be some indication that our gospels were quite simply and directly intended to be "scriptures of fulfillment." It must be emphasized, however, that any such suggestion is plainly speculative.

Other suggestions have from time to time been made urging a typological foundation for the formation of the gospel tradition. Such works are included in the bibliography following this section; but it should be noted that such essays into typology have not normally been greeted with much enthusiasm and certainly have not been pursued within recent years.

Bibliography

THE COMPOSITION OF THE GOSPELS

Aalen, S. "St. Luke's Gospel and the Last Chapters of I Enoch." *NTS* 13.1967, pp. 1-13.

Bowman, John. *The Gospel of Mark: The New Christian Jewish Passover Haggadah.* Leiden: E. J. Brill, 1965.

Burkitt, F. C. *The Gospel History and Its Transmission.* Edinburgh: T. & T. Clark, 1906.

Daube, David. "The Earliest Structure of the Gospels." *NTS* 5.1.1959, pp. 174-87.

———. "He That Cometh." 1966 Lecture of the London Diocesan Council for Christian-Jewish Understanding. London: St. Paul's Cathedral, 1966.

———. *The New Testament and Rabbinic Judaism* (esp. Part 2, Chaps. 8 and 9, Section 5, and Part 3, Chap. 10). London: Athlone Press, University of London, 1956.

Dodd, C. H. *The Apostolic Preaching and Its Development.* London: Hodder & Stoughton, 1936.

———. *History and the Gospel.* London: Nisbet, 1938.

———. "The Primitive Catechism and the Sayings of Jesus." In *New Testament Essays: Studies in Memory of Thomas Walter Manson,* edited by A. J. B. Higgins. Manchester University Press, 1939, pp. 106-19.

Dungan, D. L., and Cartlidge, D. R. *Sourcebook of Texts for the Comparative Study of the Gospels: Literature of the Hellenistic and Roman Period Illuminating the Milieu and Character of the Gospels.* 3rd ed. Missoula, Mont.: Scholars Press, 1973.

Enz, J. J. "Exodus as a Literary Type of John," *JBL* 76.3.1957, pp. 208-15.

Fitzmyer, J. A. "Memory and Manuscript: The Origins and Transmission of the Gospel Tradition," *ThS* 23.1962, pp. 442-57.

Gerhardsson, Birger. *Memory and Manuscript: Oral Tradition and Written Transmission in Rabbinic Judaism and Early Christianity.* Acta Seminarii Neotestamentici Upsaliensis 22. Lund: Gleerup; Copenhagen: Munksgaard, 1961.

————. *Tradition and Transmission in Early Christianity.* Coniectanea Neotestamentica 20. Lund: Gleerup; Copenhagen: Munksgaard, 1964.

Grant, F. C. *The Gospels: Their Origin and Growth.* London: Faber & Faber, 1957.

Kee, Howard Clark. *Jesus in History.* 2nd ed. New York: Harcourt Brace Jovanovich, 1977.

Lapide, P. "Hebräisch im Evangelium." *Judaica* 33.1.1977, pp. 7-29.

Manek, J. "Exodus in Luke." *NovTest* 2.1.1957, pp. 8-23.

Moule, C. F. D. *The Birth of the New Testament.* New York: Harper & Row, 1962.

————. "The Intention of the Evangelists." In *New Testament Essays: Studies in Memory of Thomas Walter Manson,* edited by A. J. B. Higgins. Manchester University Press, 1959, pp. 165-80.

Riesenfeld, Harald. *The Gospel Tradition.* Philadelphia: Fortress Press, 1970.

Simon, Ulrich E. "The Problem of Biblical Narrative." *Theology* 42.1969, pp. 243-53.

————. *Story and Faith.* London: SPCK, 1975.

Vajta, Vilmos. *The Gospel as History.* Philadelphia: Fortress Press, 1975.

FORM CRITICISM

Baur, Ferdinand Christian. *Kritische Untersuchungen über die kanonischen Evangelien.* Tübingen: L. F. Fues, 1847.

Bornkamm, Günther. *Jesus of Nazareth.* Translation by Irene and Fraser McLuskey with James M. Robinson. London: Hodder & Stoughton, 1960, pp. 9, 22.

Bultmann, Rudolf. *History of the Synoptic Tradition.* Translation by John Marsh. New York: Harper, 1963.

————. *Jesus and the Word.* Translation by Louise Pettibone Smith and Erminie Huntress Lantero. New York: Scribner's, 1958, p. 8.

————. "The Primitive Christian Kerygma and the Historical Jesus." In *The Historical Jesus and the Kerygmatic Christ,* edited and translated by Carl E. Braaten and Roy A. Harrisville. New York: Abingdon, 1964, pp. 15-42.

————. "The Study of the Synoptic Gospels." In *Form Criticism,* edited and translated by Frederick C. Grant. New York: Harper, 1962, p. 55.

Carlston, Charles Edwin. "A Positive Criterion of Authenticity?" *Biblical Research* 7.1962, pp. 33-44.

Conzelmann, Hans. "Jesus Christus." In *Religion in Geschichte und Gegenwart III.* Tübingen: J. C. B. Mohr, 1959, pp. 619-53.

————. "Zur Methode der Leben-Jesu-Forschung." *ZTK* 56.1959, pp. 2-13. English translation by Carl E. Braaten and Roy A. Harrisville, "The Method of the Life of Jesus Research," in *The Historical Jesus and the Kerygmatic Christ: Essays on the New Quest of the Historical Jesus.* New York: Abingdon Press, 1964, pp. 54-68.

Davies, W. D. *Invitation to the New Testament.* Garden City, N.Y.: Doubleday, 1966.

Lachmann, Karl. "De ordine narrationum in evangeliis synopticis." *TSK* 8.1835, pp. 570ff.

Ladd, George Eldon. *The New Testament and Criticism.* Grand Rapids, Mich.: Eerdmans, 1967.

Lightfoot, Robert Henry. *The Gospel Message of St. Mark.* Oxford: Clarendon Press, 1950.

———. *History and Interpretation in the Gospels.* London: Hodder & Stoughton, 1935.

———. *Locality and Doctrine in the Gospels.* London: Hodder & Stoughton, 1938.

McArthur, Harvey K. "A Survey of Recent Gospel Research." *Int* 18.1964, pp. 39-55.

McKnight, Edgar V. *What Is Form Criticism?* Philadelphia: Fortress Press, 1970.

Manson, T. W. *Studies in the Gospels and Epistles.* Philadelphia: Westminster Press, 1962, p. 6.

———. *The Teaching of Jesus: Studies of Its Form and Content.* 2nd ed. Cambridge University Press, 1935.

Newman, S. A. Review of *Rediscovering the Teaching of Jesus* by Norman Perrin. *The Quarterly Review* 28.1968.

Perrin, Norman. *Rediscovering the Teaching of Jesus.* New York: Harper & Row, 1967.

Reimarus, Hermann Samuel. *Von dem Zwecke Jesu und seiner Jünger: Noch ein Fragment des Wolfenbüttelschen Ungenannten,* edited by Gotthold Ephraim Lessing. Brunswick: G. E. Lessing, 1778.

Reimer, G. *Einleitung in die drei ersten Evangelien.* Berlin, 1905.

Riesenfeld, Harald. *The Gospel Tradition and Its Beginnings: A Study in the Limits of "Formgeschichte."* London: A. R. Mowbray, 1957.

Robinson, James M. *A New Quest of the Historical Jesus.* SBT 25. London: SCM Press, 1959.

Schmidt, Karl Ludwig. *Der Rahmen der Geschichte Jesu.* Berlin: Trowitsch, 1919; reissued by *Wissenschaftliche Buchgesellschaft,* 1964.

Schweitzer, Albert. *The Mystery of the Kingdom of God: The Secret of Jesus' Messiahship and Passion.* Translation by Walter Lowrie. New York: Dodd, Mead, 1914.

———. *The Quest of the Historical Jesus: A Critical Study of Its Progress from Reimarus to Wrede.* Translation by W. Montgomery. 2nd English ed. London: Black, 1910.

Strauss, David Friedrich. *Das Leben Jesu, kritisch bearbeitet.* 2 vols. Tübingen: C. F. Osiander, 1835, 1836. English translation by George Eliot, *The Life of Jesus Critically Examined.* 4th ed. 3 vols. London: Chapman Brothers, 1840.

Streeter, Burnett Hillman. *The Four Gospels: A Study of Origins.* Rev. ed. London: Macmillan, 1930.

Taylor, Vincent. *The Formation of the Gospel Tradition.* London: Macmillan, 1933; 2nd ed., 1935.

Weiss, Johannes. *Das Älteste Evangelium.* Göttingen: Vandenhoeck & Ruprecht, 1903.

Weisse, Christian Hermann. *Die evangelisch kritisch und philosophisch bearbeitet.* 2 vols. Leipzig: Breitkopf & Hartel, 1838.

Wrede, William. *Das Messiasgeheimnis in den Evangelien.* Göttingen: Vandenhoeck & Ruprecht, 1901; reissued, Vandenhoeck & Ruprecht, 1963, p. 130.

REDACTION CRITICISM

Bultmann, R. *Die Geschichte der synoptischen Tradition.* Göttingen: Vandenhoeck & Ruprecht, 1921. English translation by J. Marsh, *The History of the Synoptic Tradition.* New York: Harper & Row, 1963.

Conzelmann, H. *Theology of St. Luke.* Translation by G. Buswell. New York: Harper & Row, 1960.

Davies, W. D., and Daube, D., eds. *The Background of the New Testament and Its Eschatology.* Studies in Honour of C. H. Dodd. Cambridge University Press, 1954, 1964.

Dibelius, M. *Die alttestamentlichen Motive in der Leidensgeschichte des Petrus- und Johannes-Evangeliums.* ZAW Supp. 33. Giessen: Alfred Toppelmann, 1918.

————. *Die Formgeschichte des Evangeliums.* Tübingen: J. C. B. Mohr (Paul Siebeck), 1919; English translation by B. L. Woolf, *From Tradition to Gospel.* New York: Scribner's, 1935.

Dungan, D. L. "Reactionary Trends in the Gospel Producing Activity of the Early Church: Marcion, Tatian, Mark." In *L'évangile selon Marc: Tradition et rédaction,* edited by M. Sabbe. Bibliotheca ephemeridum theologicarum lovaniensium 34. Gembloux: Duculot; Louvain: Leuven University Press, 1974.

Farmer, W. R. "Redaction Criticism and the Synoptic Problem." *One Hundred Seventh Annual Meeting Seminar Papers.* Vol. 1. SBL, 1971.

Feine, P., Behm, J., and Kümmel, W. G. *Introduction to the New Testament.* Translation by A. J. Mattil, Jr. New York and Nashville: Abingdon, 1966.

Fuller, R. H. *A Critical Introduction to the New Testament.* Naperville, Ill.: Allenson, 1966.

Grant, F. C. Preface to *Form Criticism, Two Essays on New Testament Research* by R. Bultmann and K. Kundsin. Translation by F. C. Grant. New York: Harper Torchbooks, 1966 (1934).

Haenchen, E. *Der Weg Jesu.* Berlin: Alfred Topelmann, 1966.

Kähler, Martin. *Der sogenannte historische Jesus und der geschichtliche, biblische Christus.* Leipzig: A. Deichertsche Verlagsbuchhandlung, 1892. New edition by E. Wolf, *Theologische Bücherei.* Munich: Kaiser, 1953. English translation by Carl E. Braaten, *The So-called Historical Jesus and the Historic Biblical Christ.* Philadelphia: Fortress Press, 1964.

Lightfoot, R. H. *History and Interpretation in the Gospels.* The Bampton Lectures. New York: Harper & Bros., 1934.

————. *Locality and Doctrine in the Gospels.* New York and London: Harper & Bros., 1938.

Lindars, B. *New Testament Apologetic.* Philadelphia: Westminster Press, 1962.

Lohse, E. *The New Testament Environment,* English translation by J. E. Steely. London: SCM; Nashville: Abingdon, 1976.

Marxsen, W. *Der Evangelist Markus. Studien zur Redaktionsgeschichte des Evangeliums.* Göttingen: Vandenhoeck & Ruprecht, 1956, 1959. English translation by

R. A. Harrisville, *Mark the Evangelist.* New York and Nashville: Abingdon, 1969.

Marxsen, W. *Introduction to the New Testament.* Translation by G. Buswell. Philadelphia: Fortress Press, 1968.

Nineham, D. E., ed. *Studies in the Gospels: Essays in Memory of R. H. Lightfoot.* Oxford: Basil Blackwell, 1955.

Perrin, N. "The Creative Use of the Son of Man Traditions by Mark." *USQR* 23. 1967-68.

————. *The Kingdom of God in the Teaching of Jesus.* Philadelphia: Westminster, 1963.

————. *Rediscovering the Teaching of Jesus.* New York: Harper & Row, 1967.

————. "The Son of Man in the Synoptic Tradition." *Biblical Research* 13.1968, pp. 3-25.

————. "The Wredestrasse Becomes the Hauptstrasse: Reflections on the Reprinting of the Dodd Festschrift." *JR* 46.2.1966, pp. 296-300.

Rhode, J. *Rediscovering the Teaching of the Evangelists.* Translation by D. M. Barton. Philadelphia: Westminster Press, 1969.

Sabbe, M., ed. *"L'évangile selon Marc: Tradition et rédaction.* Bibliotheca ephemeridum theologicarum lovaniensium 34. Gembloux: Duculot; Louvain: Leuven University Press, 1974.

Schmidt, K. L. *Der Rahmen der Geschichte Jesu.* Berlin: Trowitsch & Sohn, 1919.

Schweitzer, A. *The Quest of the Historical Jesus.* New York: Macmillan, 1961 (1910).

Stein, R. H. "What is Redaktionsgeschichte?" *JBL* 88.1.1969, pp. 45-56.

Todt, H. E. *The Son of Man in the Synoptic Tradition.* Translation by Dorothea M. Barton. Philadelphia: Westminster Press, 1965.

Wellhausen, J. *Das Evangelium Matthaei* (1904); *Das Evangelium Marci* (1903); *Das Evangelium Lucae* (1904); *Einleitung in die drei ersten Evangelien* (1905). Berlin: Georg Reimer, 1903-5.

Westcott, B. F. *Introduction to the Study of the Gospels.* New York: Macmillan, 1882 (1851).

Worden, Ronald D. "Redaction Criticism of Q: A Survey." *JBL* 94.4.1975, pp. 532-46.

SOME CRITICAL APPROACHES TO MARK

Baltensweiler, H. *Die Verklärung Jesu.* Zürich: Zwingli, 1959.

Brun, Lyder. *Die Auferstehung Christi in der urchristlichen Ueberlieferung.* Oslo: H. Aschehoug (W. Nygaard), 1925.

Burch, Ernest W. "Tragic Action in the Second Gospel: A Study in the Narrative of Mark." *JR* 11.1931, pp. 346-58.

Burkill, T. A. *Mysterious Revelation.* Ithaca, N.Y.: Cornell University Press, 1963.

Busch, Friedrich. *Zum Verständnis der synoptischen Eschatologie, Markus 13 neu untersucht.* Gütersloh: Bertelsmann, 1938.

Conzelmann, Hans. "Geschichte und Eschaton nach Mark 13." *ZNW* 50.1959, pp. 210-21.

──────. *The Theology of St. Luke.* Translation by Geoffrey Buswell. New York: Harper & Row, 1961.

Ebeling, H. J. *Das Messiasgeheimnis und die Botschaft des Marcus-Evangelisten.* Berlin: Alfred Topelmann, 1939.

Grundmann, W. *Das Evangelium nach Markus.* Berlin: Evangelische Verlagsanstalt, 1959.

Keck, Leander. "The Introduction to Mark's Gospel." *NTS* 12.1966, pp. 352-70.

──────. "Mark 3:7-12 and Mark's Christology." *JBL* 84.1965, pp. 341-58.

Kee, Howard Clark. "Mark as Redactor and Theologian: A Survey of Some Recent Markan Studies." *JBL* 90.3.1941, pp. 333-36.

Kelber, Werner H. *The Kingdom in Mark: A New Place and a New Time.* Philadelphia: Fortress Press, 1974.

Kline, M. G. "The Old Testament Origins of the Gospel Genre." *Westminster Theological Journal* 38.1.1975, pp. 1-27.

Koester, Helmut. "Häretiker im Urchristentum." *RGG* 3.1959, pp. 17-21.

──────. "One Jesus and Four Primitive Gospels." *HTR* 61.1968, pp. 203-47.

Kuby, Alfred. "Zur Konzeption des Markus-Evangeliums." *ZNW* 49.1958, pp. 52-64.

Lightfoot, R. H. *The Gospel Message of Mark.* Oxford: Clarendon Press, 1950.

──────. *Locality and Doctrine in the Gospels.* London: Hodder & Stoughton, 1968.

Lohmeyer, Ernst. "Die Verklärung Jesu nach Markus-Evangelium." *ZNW* 21.1922, pp. 185-215.

Luz, Ulrich. "Das Geheimnismotiv und die Markanische Christologie." *ZNW* 56.1965, pp. 9-30.

Marxsen, Willi. *Mark the Evangelist.* Translation by R. A. Harrisville et al. Nashville: Abingdon, 1969.

Matera, F. J. "Interpreting Mark—Some Recent Theories of Redaction Criticism." *Louvain Studies* II.1968, pp. 113-31.

Meagher, J. C. "Die Form- und Redaktionsungeschichtliche Methoden: The Principle of Clumsiness and the Gospel of Mark." *JAAR* 43.3.1975, pp. 459-72.

Meye, Robert P. *Jesus and the Twelve.* Grand Rapids, Mich.: Eerdmans, 1968.

Nierynck, Franz. *Duality in Mark: Contributions to the Study of Markan Redaction.* Bibliotheca ephemeridum theologicarum lovaniensium 31. Gembloux: Duculot, 1972.

Perrin, Norman. "The Christology of Mark: A Study in Methodology." Paper presented at the Seminar on Christology of the New Testament, Annual Meeting of the Studiorum Novi Testamenti Societas, Newcastle upon Tyne, England, August 1970.

Parker, Pierson. *The Gospel Before Mark.* University of Chicago Press, 1953.

──────. "A Second Look at *The Gospel Before Mark.*" *JBL* 100.3.1981, pp. 389-413.

Quesnell, Quentin. *The Mind of Mark.* Analecta Biblica 30. Rome: Pontifical Biblical Institute, 1969.

Robinson, James M. *The Problem of History in Mark.* Naperville, Ill.: Allenson, 1957.

──────. "The Problem of History in Mark Reconsidered." *USQR* 30.1965, pp. 131-47.

Schniewind, J. *Das Evangelium nach Markus.* Göttingen: Vandenhoeck & Ruprecht, 1949.

Schreiber, Johannes. "Die Christologie des Markusevangelium." *ZTK* 58.1961, pp. 154-83.

Schweizer, Eduard. *The Good News According to Mark.* Translation by D. H. Madbig. Richmond, Va.: John Knox Press, 1970.

———. "Mark's Contribution to the Quest of the Historical Jesus." *NTS* 10.1964, pp. 421-32.

———. "Die theologische Leistung des Markus." *EvTh* 24.1964, pp. 337-55.

Trocmé, Etienne. *La formation de l'Évangile selon Marc.* Paris: Presses Universitaires de France, 1963.

Tyson, Joseph. "The Blindness of the Disciples in Mark." *JBL* 80.1961, pp. 261-68.

Waetjen, Herman. "The Ending of Mark and the Gospel's Shift in Eschatology." *ASTI,* Vol. 6. Leiden: E. J. Brill, 1965, pp. 114-31.

Weeden, T. J. *Mark—Traditions in Conflict.* Philadelphia: Fortress Press, 1971.

Worden, R. D. "Redaction Criticism of Q: A Survey." *JBL* 94.4.1975, pp. 532-46.

3. PROPOSED DISCIPLINES
IN GOSPEL STUDIES

A. The New Quest for the Historical Jesus

One of the results of the identification of layers of material in the written gospels has been a rapidly expanding series of proposed methods to elucidate the primary gospel message. While these various modern methods have called attention to ways in which we may proceed in evaluating an individual evangelist's handling of his sources or in tentatively identifying his dominant concerns, it would be rash to conclude that any one of the proposed methods has been uniformly successful. Indeed, one or two of the methods appear to exclude all the others, and proponents of them are occasionally somewhat too enthusiastic over what can at best be tentative conclusions.

The attempt to uncover the varied forms of the oral tradition underlying the gospels—an attempt characterized by the term "form criticism"—gave impetus to renewed attempts to answer the question: "How much can we know of the historical figure of Jesus, and to what extent has the life of Jesus of Nazareth been overlaid by imaginative and adulatory material from a later period?" The attempt by Albert Schweitzer to depict Jesus as a thoroughgoing eschatological prophet, convinced that his own role was central in an impending divine intervention and who yet died disillusioned, was altogether too simple, adequate only as an explanation of one aspect of Pauline interpretation. Yet in a period preoccupied with Jesus as a humanitarian preacher of the "fatherhood of God and the brotherhood of man" Schweitzer rendered a singular service in recalling to scholarly attention the unquestionably eschatological, "otherworldly" emphasis in the teaching of Jesus, an element undoubtedly present in Paul's writings.

There is always the danger, in an enterprise such as the "new quest" for the historical Jesus, that any work proclaimed to be "determined only by the evidence" or "free from doctrinal bias" will nevertheless carry with it the presuppositions and preoccupations of the writer. There can be as little real expectation of freedom from doctrinal bias on the part of a writer committed by confession to the definitions of Nicaea and Chalcedon as on the part of a writer committed in advance to the view that Jesus was a simple, itinerant preacher of no particular learning. Unhappily for both cases, the gospels supply us with remarkably little biographical detail, and the theological statements of Paul about Jesus give no ground for the kind of examination of the human psyche of Jesus so assiduously courted today. But the insistent demand for some clarification of the relationship between Jesus of Nazareth and the divine messiah proclaimed by the Church must be met.

If the possibility of making statements of a historical character about the life of Jesus becomes merely peripheral, it must be insisted that Christianity, as it has been interpreted by confessing Christians since apostolic times, is on its deathbed. For the claim of historical Christianity has always been that God spoke definitively in Jesus, whose place in history can be verified historically ("suffered under Pontius Pilate") and interpreted theologically ("sits at the right hand of God the Father"); this claim admits of either affirmation or denial, but hardly of doubt. For all that, the man of faith must also affirm that the very accounts of the history of Jesus are the work of men of like faith, whose lives were molded by and who lived in the context of a confessional community. The skeptic must concede some historical core in the oral tradition behind the gospels, however much he may insist that the NT as the "Church's book" is hardly an impartial witness.

The matter was put in focus sharply by a statement of Leander E. Keck in a recent work (A Future for the Historical Jesus: The Place of Jesus in Preaching and Theology, Nashville and New York: Abingdon Press, 1971, p. 125): "to the extent that [a Christian's] faith is shaped by his perception of what the text says, and what is going on in it, his faith is contingent on scholarly probabilities." This does, however, raise in acutest form the question whether one's trust in God would be shattered, or severely eroded at least, by any possible discovery that deliberately fraudulent material was incorporated in the gospel narrative, since the Christian's access to God is said to be through Jesus.

If, however, Martin Kähler (see bibliography at the end of this section) could state in unmistakable terms that the Christ of faith in the gospels does present us with a living portrait of a man, the preoccupation of the early decades of this century with the "proclaimed" Christ led to a total skepticism as to the possibility of knowing anything substantial about Jesus of Nazareth. Though nothing was produced by Jesus of a literary character, yet the earliest years of the Christian tradition had left a very extensive body of written material. No matter that this material had obviously been shaped by the presuppositions of the authors—so went the theory—at least there was a whole series of data upon which to work. But of the man Jesus we could know nothing. We could only know the apprehensions of those who contributed to the consolidation of the Church's faith; we can see Mark's interest in a "messianic secret" or Matthew's possible preoccupation with a new lawgiver, but we can see Jesus himself only after his ministry has become "my-thologized."

From this, yet another critical assumption followed. This assumption soon ceased to be a hypothesis (at least in the minds of its proponents). Though it was impossible to deny the existence of Jesus, yet (it was said) his person was comparatively insignificant in the formation of faith. While it might be true that Jesus was totally demanding in his call for man's obedience to God, all this was also true of the prophets under the old Covenant. Perhaps it is to Rudolf Bultmann most of all that we owe what has come to be—in some critical circles at any rate—an almost total divorce between the faith of the NT and the person and proclamation of Jesus. If indeed Bultmann's words are to be taken in the literal sense (though in some ways this can be a remark-ably frustrating exercise), then his assertion that the message of Jesus is "not part of the theology" of the NT but is simply one of its "presuppositions" *(voraussetzungen)* comes perilously close to relegating Jesus to comparative insignificance (cf. R. Bultmann, *The Theology of the New Testament,* 1952, p. 3). To be sure, there are other presuppositions, with some of which Jesus could be identified, such as messianic expectation and the eschatological de-mand of the Day of God. But the boundaries of such presuppositions were extended to encompass other elements, real or imaginary, of which a full-grown gnosticism and Hellenistic mythology were but two.

Of course, extending the presuppositional boundaries ultimately depends on the dates one ascribes to the gospels. The presumption of a mythic motif of the *theios anēr,* or "divine man," must deal with the fact that the motif in question does not really become discernible until the second century of the Christian era. Similarly, it is not without considerable hazard that we attempt to identify a full-grown "gnosticism" in our sources when we consider that the philosophical-religious speculation in question did not achieve anything approaching maturity until the early years of the same century. And it is at least open to question whether it would ever have become a widespread phe-nomenon at all, had there not been already a proclamation about the presence of God's act in Jesus. (Cf. W. F. Albright, "Simon Magus as the 'Great Power of God,' " Appendix 7, in Johannes Munck, *The Acts of the Apostles,* A.B., Garden City, N.Y.: Doubleday, 1967.)

In short, a skeptical response in this century to the possibility of recon-structing a biography of Jesus of Nazareth has gone well beyond an agnosti-cism with regard to the possibility, and has developed on the part of some into an outright assertion that the person of Jesus and anything we can know of him is a chimera. The proper task of NT scholarship on this view is to examine the apostolic proclamation and the message of God's reconciling activity preached par excellence by Paul. If any summary was needed of the present confused and confusing state of NT studies, then the article by

J. Schreiber listed in the bibliography following this section would be a good starting point. Little has changed in the more than ten years since the publication of that article.

B. Proclamation and History

It is of the highest importance that we make a clear distinction between two different elements in the critical inquiry. There is, first, the attempt to write the biography of Jesus; this must be abandoned until or unless we are in possession of indubitably authentic material contemporary with the gospels. But this is by no means the same thing as an attempt to discover to what extent—if at all—the documents we possess show a radical shift away from the person of Jesus and his own proclamation of the Kingdom. In other words, biography or no, we are driven back to ascertain the character of Jesus' mission and message. It is the theme of the apostolic preaching that God's proffered salvation was made through Jesus. The sources—and the writings of Paul anterior to the gospels—demand an explanation of the situation antecedent to a proclamation of a Risen Savior in the aftermath of an "Easter faith." There is no such thing as an idea ready-born, without a history, and for all the concern of the NT material outside the gospels with theological ideas, we are driven back to asking what gave the ideas impetus. The only reply from the NT itself is that it was Jesus and his ministry and message. The suggestion that much, if not most, of what we have in the gospels is heavily overlaid retrojectively by the theologizings of the early community is one which defies all the rules of historical criticism, and—if made in other contexts—would be treated with less than seriousness. Certainly the NT writings sprang from a community, and a community living in the faith that God had intervened in the person of Jesus, acknowledged as his Anointed Servant; but it is a remarkably naïve view which looks at the gospels as primarily intended for external consumption. At the same time the letters of Paul, theological as they are, and concerned again and again to appeal to the events of the cross and resurrection, were manifestly not propaganda documents by a community to outsiders.

The apostolic preaching and the letters of Paul are concerned with interpretation—history is, after all, event plus interpretation. But the interpretations offered by Paul—that in raising Jesus from the dead God had declared him to be Son (Rom 1:4), that the death of Jesus was for our sins (1 Cor 15:3) —raises in the most acute form two inseparable questions. First, did the events described take place, and secondly, assuming them to be historical events, how far has interpretation been imposed on the events without justifying evidence? We are inexorably driven to inquire how Jesus himself viewed his ministry, and whether the interpretation of that event is demonstrably a prophecy after the event invented by the early Christian community. Whatever may have been the relationship between Paul and the Jerusalem community from time to time, the appeal of both Paul and the first chapters of Acts (assuming those chapters to be even partly accurate) is the same. It is an appeal back to a known history of a known man. But all of this argues that the early Christian community's proclamation of Jesus as Savior must have been capable of being sustained in disciplined historical inquiry by the interpretation of Jesus' ministry and message on the part of those who were closest to the events. Faith in God's act of salvation in Jesus is one thing, but it is quite another to assert or imply that whether or not the historical Jesus had real existence is immaterial to faith.

To be sure, there is no such thing as a disembodied historian, or—in the present instance—a commentator who can divest himself of a committed ground of faith. We shall not be as rash as were those in the last century who saw a biography of Jesus in the modern sense as a real possibility. We have become increasingly aware in the past forty years of the limits imposed on such a possibility, and some of the tools of modern critical scholarship have materially assisted in the process of penetrating beyond our written sources. It is to some of those modern critical disciplines that we now turn our attention.

C. Form Criticism

Beginning with the important work of Hermann Gunkel in the first quarter of this century, NT scholars were not slow to see the implications of form criticism as a primary tool in distinguishing strands of tradition behind the written sources. Certainly, so far as the gospels are concerned, there has been, and continues to be, widespread skepticism about the historical accuracy of much of the reporting, whether of the narrative of events or of the words of Jesus. Part of the difficulty obviously arises from the fact that the gospels are sui generis: not biography; they purport to encapsulate a once-for-all decisive act of God in Jesus, within the framework of a Judaism which was at home with the idea of divine intervention.

Even granted that layers of interpretative material have been added to an original oral tradition, the problem was not that of identifying strata in the material, but of coming to terms with the dating of the material when identified. How long was the period of oral transmission? How quickly did the oral tradition harden into fixed forms? How much oral material was there? How long was the process of committing the oral tradition to written form and was that done in Hebrew/Aramaic or in Greek?

The answer to the second question has largely determined the response of redaction criticism (of which we shall treat later), and the very existence of redaction criticism as a NT discipline has been dependent upon the answer. Much NT scholarship has opted for the years A.D. 80 to 100 as the period in which Matthew, Luke, and John were disseminated. Several important consequences flow from positing this period in the first century for the final form of three of the gospels. First, we know almost nothing of this temporal limbo in Church history, and it is therefore comparatively easy to *assume* the accuracy of a hypothesis (of this more will be said in the section on dating and chronology). Second, on the basis of an assumed accuracy the period of oral transmission is regarded as fairly substantial in length, with a consequent freedom to assume a considerable number of editors. Third, the length of time assumed for the organization of oral tradition into written form allows for a considerable and even decisive part to be played by unidentified (and unidentifiable) "communities" with one or another special interest. Fourth, the hypothesizing of late dates for written form and dissemination has carried with it the assumption that the Mediterranean world was dotted with a very considerable number of stable Christian communities, each apparently with its own theological concerns, whether orthodox or "heretical." Perhaps more serious than these considerations is the assumption—or the assumed truth of a hypothesis—that the Hellenistic world witnessed in the period under discussion a proliferation of refined ideas of some sophistication, such as the quest for *gnosis* or speculations about *theios anēr,* all of which can be found reflected in the NT writings.

Form criticism—which properly includes identification of the genre of literary forms in the text, the composition of forms and their present place and function in the text, the history (if recoverable) of those forms, and the intention of the writers in using them—has been employed by scholars with considerable success. No one would deny that various oral traditions have been molded together in our present narratives of the resurrection of Jesus, some of them almost impossible to reconcile with the others, some with a frankly apologetic motif, and yet others couched in the familiar terms of the apocalyptic. The hard core of the apostolic proclamation remains: that Jesus was raised from the dead. An empty tomb which had terrified some members of the community and perhaps caused others to flee from Jerusalem was later seen to be the sacramental sign of an eschatological act of God in the endtime. The identification of the role of any interest group in shaping this material is always in the final analysis the individual judgment of the individual scholar, and in the absence of firm evidence should be treated as such. It is, for example, hard to discover precisely why the Johannine account of the trial of Jesus should have perpetrated the error of inserting part of the sentence of crucifixion (the flogging) into the narrative before the passing of the sentence itself. We may identify this as an insertion by some later editor, but that is a far cry from identifying either the editor or his motivation.

Perhaps the least defensible judgment on the part of some proponents of form criticism has been the assertion that we cannot recover anything genuinely from the ministry and teaching of Jesus, and—this being the case—must content ourselves with an existential encounter with a message of salvation proclaimed by enthusiastic followers. There is something here of romanticism, akin to the ideals of chivalry centered on the legendary representation of King Arthur, rather than a quiet determination to arrive at the truth of the matter. To be sure, a man's life might be radically changed could he but be persuaded that redemption from sin was a present possibility, held out in a once-for-all act of God for all people in the person of Jesus. But one may question whether this confidence of faith could long survive the discovery that those who proclaimed it felt its historical basis to be irrecoverable and indeed irrelevant.

Form criticism, along with the need to recover the basic oral tradition of the ministry and words of Jesus, has been responsible for a steady growth in the methods of academic study; out of it grew the next discipline we must discuss.

D. Redaction Criticism

Redactional study, to recover strata of tradition, must begin with the documents we possess and endeavor to discover therein the concerns and interests of the authors themselves and the imprint which those authors may have left on the tradition. At present the method, insofar as it relates to the synoptic gospels, relies almost wholly on the assumption that Matthew and Luke can be identified with certainty as resting on Mark. In consequence, attempts to identify Markan contributions to the tradition present some difficulties. For example, attempts to isolate Mark's use of three-fold units have necessarily ended up in a cul-de-sac, for Matthew uses the same familiar rabbinic mnemonic device, though with far greater sophistication. We should not be overly optimistic about what Mark may have done with the original tradition by his device of the "messianic secret," assuming such a device to be a reality. A plethora of messianic hopes and expectations immediately preceded the ministry of Jesus, and Jesus himself may well have viewed them in his ministry in different ways in different periods. To urge silence upon an enthusiastic protagonist of any one view would have been prudent, if the ministry was not to come to a premature end. Mark may well have preserved more carefully than either Matthew or Luke a clear tradition which was no longer a matter of concern when the ministry was ended. Furthermore, there is good rabbinic evidence for the belief that the identity of the Messiah would be unknown until openly declared by God—a belief which finds partial expression outside the gospels (e.g., Acts 2:36 and 3:20; Rom 1:4).

It may be doubted whether Markan sources are recoverable at all, on the generally accepted theory of synoptic origins. If, as the present writer believes, Mark is a digest and a conflation of Matthew and Luke, then it is permissible to attempt to demonstrate the use which Mark made of what he found. If Mark is indeed prior in time, it may well be that all we can undertake is a painstaking analysis of Markan vocabulary and linguistic style, since his sources are irrecoverable. It is worth pointing out that even an analysis of Markan vocabulary is not likely to lead to unanimity among those undertaking this task.

At first glance it might be thought that redaction criticism is on safer ground in assessing traditions found in more than one source. First given prominence by B. H. Streeter (1924: especially pp. 223-70), this approach seeks to validate as authentic those sayings that are found in more than one tradition; obviously sayings found in all four are given high marks for authenticity. But there are some severe drawbacks. Once again almost all depends on one's viewpoint as to the solution of the synoptic problem. Mark's recording of Jesus' sharing of table fellowship with nonobservant Jews (2:15-17) is not known to us in any other gospel tradition, even though Jesus' concern for such folk is plain enough. On the usual "two-source" theory (Mark and Q, together with special-Matthew and special-Luke) it is hard to know why Matthew and Luke omitted significant material such as Mark 2:15-17; but this kind of consideration fades into insignificance in dealing with the narratives of the Resurrection. Manifestly, the ending of Mark at 16:8 leaves us with no agreed attestation dependent on an original source, while the narratives themselves display a remarkable independence of each other. Perhaps C. H. Dodd has given us the best treatment possible in the circumstances ("The Appearances of the Risen Christ: An Essay in Form Criticism of the Gospels," in D. E. Nineham, 1955, pp. 9ff.). For all the difficulties which the theory must encounter if Markan priority is denied, redaction criticism continues to rely on attestation in more than one source as an important criterion for determining a genuine tradition.

This criterion of confirmation and agreement from multiple sources can be further refined when applied to a tradition appearing in more than one literary form—parables, sayings, pronouncements, and the like. C. H. Dodd (1938) declared that the method was used by E. Hoskyns and N. Davey

(1931). Though at first sight this method of determining elements of the oral tradition behind the written sources seems attractive, it has two obvious if not fatal limitations. First, in order to have determinative value, far more literary forms are necessary than we possess at present, for the limited character of the source material we possess may indicate (on the usual two-source theory) merely a dependence on the principal source. If all the "forms" presently found in the synoptic tradition owe their first shaping to one evangelist, then we are far from authenticating any oral tradition. Secondly, even if we tentatively identify a short saying as a "pronouncement" belonging to the oral tradition behind our present sources, this is far from a positive assertion that any saying is of unquestioned authenticity.

Redaction criticism of the gospel of Mark operates at two levels. First, it is applied to the synoptic problem: any determination of editorial influence in comparing any two documents must plainly be based on a previous determination as to which of the documents was written or compiled first. The prevailing critical opinion of Markan priority obviously dominates the redaction criticism field at the present time; examples of the results will be mentioned from time to time in this commentary and may be found in the books listed in the various bibliographies. At another level, the method can be applied to the gospel of Mark itself, with attention directed to the theological motifs thought to underlie the editorial methods of the evangelist.

It is not inappropriate to note some examples of recent work in this field. Perhaps one of the most penetrating discussions has come from Franz Nierynck (1972), whose painstaking analysis serves to cast serious doubts on an overenthusiastic embracing of redaction criticism to achieve certitude in determining original sources as against editorial revision. A study of doublets and dualities in Mark leads Nierynck to ask whether the theological stamp of a final redactor was not so dominating as to render the original sources beyond adequate recovery. In addition, we are indebted to the same work for calling attention to a phenomenon which appears characteristic of spoken style—that of making a broad statement in one sentence and then proceeding to refine it by words or phrases in succeeding sentences. What emerges from this work is certainly an important tool for identifying Markan style, while at the same time cautioning against a too easy assumption of "assured results" in redaction criticism.

Alongside Nierynck's book we may usefully set two other recent studies of Mark which work from the principles of redaction criticism. The first is by W. H. Kelber (1974). Some prominent features of the book must be summarized in order to identify the method under discussion. Mark is said to have been composed in response to a critical situation arising after A.D. 70, before which certain Christians had been persuaded that the final manifestation of the Kingdom would take place in or around Jerusalem. The whole gospel is seen as a polemic against such a false premise and the promises attendant thereupon, in the interests of an assertion that the "new place and the new time" would be a *parousia* in Galilee. This thesis not only informs the whole book—so much so that the author does not even suggest that the supposed polarization between Jerusalem and Galilee might reflect states in Jesus' ministry—but also demands an audience possessing various hidden reference marks by which alone the gospel can be understood. In fact, a whole series of presuppositions are required for this thesis. It is surely straining credulity almost to the breaking point to assert that the disciples—certainly represented by Mark as possessing an adequate share of human frailty—so failed Jesus that the pattern persisted beyond the Resurrection, of which they did not hear. Again, as with so many other essays in this discipline, almost all depends on the twin factors of date and synoptic relationships. Kelber further posits that in the seventies there existed no other traditions which might have produced some emphatic protests against what on any showing must have been a radical reworking of accepted tradition. Equally, if Matthew and Luke differ from Mark, especially in the so-called "minor agreements,"[1] can we assume as readily as Kelber does that the differences are a theological revision of Mark? In fact Kelber's thesis would have been far more convincing had the author based it on Griesbach's premises.

It is difficult to escape the conclusion that the first readers or hearers of our present gospels must have been remarkably sophisticated in intellect to have laid bare the theological nuances offered to us by some redaction critics. A second study (T. J. Weeden, 1971) works on the hypothesis that Mark contains two contrasting if not mutually exclusive christologies. In light of the many-faceted messianic expectations current in the time of Jesus, and considering the felt impossibility of using any one of them exclusively of Jesus, this is a vastly overstated thesis. The hypothesis could easily give way to another: that the evangelist found conflicting christologies in his sources and willy-nilly incorporated them all. In other words, Mark's final manuscript can be explained on Weeden's thesis as that of an author-compiler rather than that of redactor. To the foregoing cautions, one final note may be added. Neither the identification of classes of material by form criticism nor the discussion of theological motifs, real or supposed, by redaction criticism can in any way

[1] Mark	2:12	=	Matt	9:7	=	Luke	5:25
	3:1	=		12:9-10	=		6:6
	4:10	=		13:10	=		8:9
	4:36	=		8:23	=		8:22
	8:29	=		16:16	=		9:20
	13:19	=		24:21	=		21:23
	14:47	=		26:51	=		22:49-50
	15:43	=		27:57	=		23:50
	16:8	=		28:8	=		24:9

determine for us whether the editorial process was completed before the individual pericopae were incorporated into the first written forms, and this is at least a possibility to be taken into account.

E. Tendency Criticism

Other methods of approach, or criteria of judgment, have developed from redaction criticism, and at first glance there seems to be positive gain in exploring what happens to strands of the tradition as they pass from one written form to another. The various assumptions behind this method must be kept in mind: first, Markan priority is assumed, and the progression of material from that source, from Q through Matthew and Luke, can be traced with more or less accuracy. There is in this method a further presupposition —that the same factors of adjustment and assimilation were also at work in the oral tradition and that by a right discernment of "tendencies" it should be possible to arrive at the purely primitive and original oral tradition.

Various tendencies thought to be operative in the period of oral transmission and in the assumed transmission from Mark and Q to other sources have been identified by writers in the NT field. It is generally thought, for example, that sayings of Jesus changed comparatively little, while at the same time crudities of grammar were refined, Hebraisms and Aramaisms disappeared, and the central core of narrative sections exhibited more stability than the beginnings and endings. There is considerable merit in this approach, but here again almost all depends on the view taken of the problem of synoptic relationships. Granted that Mark preserves Aramaic expressions where Matthew and Luke do not, even to the unpracticed eye Matthew is a more "Jewish" document than Mark. That there will always be an element of the subjective in this approach seems inevitable, since much will depend on the literary presuppositions of the scholar who uses the method. If the final word on this subject has not been said, the most trenchant criticism of it so far belongs to E. P. Sanders (1969), and caution in the use of the method certainly seems in order.

F. The Test of Discontinuity

Attempts have been made in the past, and continue to be made, to establish authenticity for sayings of Jesus on the basis of a supposed radical difference between Jesus and the Judaism from which he sprang. On the basis of this discontinuity or dissimilarity, anything which could have derived from contemporary Judaism has often been excluded from the teachings of Jesus. The process has been applied to the teaching of the early community, which is similarly denied to Jesus. So far was the process carried by Bultmann some ten years ago that he appeared willing to characterize the teaching of Jesus as distinctively eschatological. It must be said with considerable emphasis that to apply the principle of discontinuity in seeking to separate Jesus or the NT writings from "Judaism" is altogether too naïve. If there is one thing which the discoveries of the past thirty years have taught us, it is the sheer impossibility of comprehending under any single banner of "Judaism" the manifold varieties of traditions, sectarian and otherwise, which could with more or less reality claim to be Jewish.

The attempt to establish some principles of discontinuity between Jesus and the early Christian community may be thought to have some merit, especially when the incipient breach between church and synagogue is thrown into relief. But for this kind of hypothesis to have any validity for continuing research, the following conditions would have to be met: (1) it should be determined to what extent the Christian community in one area may have preserved the teaching of Jesus with more or less fidelity compared with Christian communities in some other area; and (2) far more access to other teachings of Jesus than we presently possess would be needed to say what *was* distinctive about the teaching of Jesus in contradistinction to the Judaism of his own day. Further confident assertions about what was the teaching of the early Christian community—even accepting for the moment that there was a homogeneous whole which could be so described—are only too likely to be disproved by the next turn of the spade.

There is certainly some attractiveness in this approach; judging, however, by the extraordinary variety presented by Judaism in the time of Jesus, those who propound it must be prepared for the disappearance of "distinctiveness" as a proper description of any single element in the teaching of Jesus. Short of a credal statement of unquestioned authenticity from the earliest days of the community, there is no way we can establish an "orthodoxy" by which to measure some purely local and apparently aberrant feature.

Similarly, the attempt to secure principles of authentication by identifying "modified" traditions from "primitive" or unmodified traditions seems a completely reasonable procedure. Paul, for example, is careful to tell the Corinthians that he is offering his own commentary rather than a dominical command in 1 Cor 7:12, even though his own charge arises from the command previously asserted in that verse. So, too, we may identify the "Matthean exception" of Matthew as "community modification." But in order to prove modification beyond doubt we would need to know whether the modification was indeed such or a wholly independent tradition.

Reservations similar to those expressed above must also be entered in considering the tool of gospel criticism sometimes referred to as a principle of "coherence." The authenticity of units of the tradition dealing with Jesus' teaching and ministry can—so the hypothesis holds—be determined with some degree of accuracy by assessing whether such units cohere with various other controls, such as the sociopolitical or religious circumstances in which any event or saying is reported, and above all by assessing their coherence with other elements determined to be characteristic of Jesus. The latter point has already to some extent been examined. But the claim of this effort to be partly determinative of authenticity must be doubted. At the very most, the verdict which can be rendered is "This could have happened," but certainly not "This did happen." It is said, for example, by those best qualified to judge that the "Hornblower" novels of the late C. S. Forester showed a very remarkable degree of accuracy and grasp of historical detail, and this at a distance of over a century from the events. As a cautionary tale, the treatment at first accorded by at least one reviewer to the book *Flashman: From the Flashman Papers* by George M. Fraser (London: Jenkins, 1969) would suggest some hesitation in applying criteria of authenticity. One critic of impeccable credentials hailed the fictional work as adding immeasurably to our knowledge of the Victorian scene, only to have the ground cut from under his feet some months later by the confession of the "editor" of the papers that the whole work was fiction from beginning to end.

Proceeding from these considerations, we may call attention next to matters of style and language. The present writer sees no reason substantially to change anything he wrote in his 1967 summary of the languages current among Jews in first-century Palestine. (See "The Customary Languages of the Jews," Appendix 9 in Johannes Munck, *The Acts of the Apostles,* AB, Garden City, N.Y.: Doubleday, 1967, pp. 313ff.) Compare in this connection J. A. Fitzmyer, "The Language of Palestine in the First Century A.D." *(CBQ* 32.4.1970, pp. 501ff.)

What emerges from recent debates about the language spoken by Jesus is that the question is far from settled. Attempts to determine the authenticity of some saying of Jesus by translating the Greek into Aramaic without at the same time taking into account a possible Hebrew original can be regarded as assuming far too much. Perhaps we can say with some confidence that Jesus' ordinary speech was Aramaic, but it is at least possible that in expounding material for rote learning Jesus may have used Hebrew. Even if we maintain that a pre-Hellenic form is closer to the original tradition, we must bear in mind the possibility of a Semitic author or editor using Greek directly and not in translation.

Similarly, attempts to establish authenticity by examining what can only be described as Jesus' literary style, whether poetic or rhythmic, run the risk of being subject to the presuppositions and even the prejudices of the exegete. Attention was called to some distinctively rabbinic pedagogic features in the formation of Matthew (cf. Albright-Mann, 1971, pp. lvii ff.) as throwing some light on the operation of the oral tradition, but there is no way we can be certain that the device belonged to Jesus and not the evangelist. Again, the manner of speech attributed to Jesus in the synoptics does not run into the very real difficulty encountered in the fourth gospel—that of determining where the words of Jesus end and those of the evangelist begin. Here, one of the tools commended to us by some scholars—that of confirmation in more than one source—is notoriously lacking; and the degree of John's dependence on the synoptic gospels is still a debatable question which may be impossible to solve. Moreover, some degree of peril attaches to any assumption of a uniform style in the speech of Jesus on all occasions. Such an assumption runs contrary to all the experience of other public figures known to us, and contradicts the fashion in which all of us employ variegated literary styles for the various circumstances in which we are called upon to speak or write.

G. Historical Circumstances

It is nowadays customary to lay the burden of proof on those who accept at face value the recorded sayings of Jesus. One of the results of gospel criticism in the past fifty years has been an increasing reluctance to accept the recorded sayings without qualification, and at the same time an increased readiness to ascribe many such utterances to the early Christian community. Presumably there is some *via media* between a fundamentalist position, which treats the recorded utterances of Jesus in the gospels as *ipsissima verba,* and the skepticism which attributes all genius of insight to the early Church. But a *via media* is not easily arrived at, even if all NT scholars agreed on the dating or the sequence of the gospels. The role assigned to the creativity of the early Christian community will plainly be considerably enlarged by a date of A.D. 80 to 90 as against a date preceding the fall of Jerusalem in A.D. 70.

In practice we tend to assume the accuracy of reported occurrences or recorded statements in the contemporary scene unless we have the strongest possible grounds for assuming a fatal bias or prejudice on the part of the reporter. Even then, some correctives can be brought to bear on the contemporary scene from other reports or reporters. It is well, however, to avoid too sanguine an attitude. No one who has carefully compared the accounts of "special reporters" at one and the same event can fail to be impressed and even astonished by the divergent accounts of different "eyewitnesses" to that event.

In general, in the total absence of participation on our part in human events, we accept as a principle of action and belief the reliability of those who report and describe those events to us. We have every initial right to accept this principle of reliability of reporting in the case of the recorded words of Jesus and the events which evoked and surrounded those words. We may have cause on more than one occasion—or even on many occasions—to revise our original assumption of reliability, but the *fundamental* assumption from which all historical investigation proceeds is the reliability of those reporting incidents and utterances. We may therefore *initially* assume the reliability of the recorded words of Jesus, and of the events of the ministry and its outcome; but—and this has been an increasingly urgent call from scholars in recent years—how certain can we be that any pericope under investigation is *intended* as recorded history, and not as a theological reflection of the author or editor? Again, in reverse, what grounds do we have in any given instance to deny to the reported speaker some recorded utterance? For example, an assurance that the Matthean exception of Matt 5:32 belongs to the legislative concerns of the early community must take into account the variety of opinions offered by teachers contemporary with Jesus on matters arising from the Mosaic Law. Similarly, the confidence expressed in years past in *denying* to Jesus certain utterances on the grounds of theological content must be drastically reduced in the light of proliferating material associated with the Dead Sea sect.

Our gospels do claim to be recording history—Luke's claim to Theophilus is explicit enough—and must be judged on that claim. Even when we are certain that we are face to face with interpretation or even (in the case of the fourth gospel) when it appears impossible to separate comment from the words of Jesus, we must still presume that the evangelist was intending to convey history (that is, event plus interpretation). But we are right to demand to know whether a particular incident is indeed historical narrative and not disguised theological lesson (Matt 2 is of some interest here). At the same time, caution is required in denying words to a purported speaker, and far weightier reasons must be adduced for denying sayings to Jesus than are very often produced. The present writer, for example, sees no valid reason for denying to Jesus the pictorial accounts in which the temptation narratives are enshrined, in spite of the well-grounded suggestion that the narratives in fact belong to a later stage of the ministry and represent a somewhat enigmatic summary of possible responses to three distinct periods of ministry.

Relatively new on the scene of gospel criticism is the attention currently paid to what are described as "trajectories" in early Christian thought, constituting a new and valuable discipline. The classic statement of this new school of criticism belongs to James M. Robinson and Helmut Koester (1971). As stated in various essays, the authors' views present a refreshing contrast to the presuppositions which have governed NT studies all through this century. The authors are surely right in wishing to abandon what they describe as the "traditional static" approach to NT studies (p. 9). Particularly interesting in this field of inquiry is the dubious value which Robinson and Koester see as attaching to the contemporary labels of NT research, generally known as "backgrounds": Semitic, Palestinian, Hellenistic, and the like. Rightly they have refused to be mesmerized by an undemonstrable "correspondence between geographical and cultural boundaries" (p. 8). What is proposed in place of the common attempt to identify backgrounds is an investigation of the "trajectories" traced by various Christian phenomena as they are modified by factors such as environment and local historical situations.

Some may perhaps feel less confidence in another position of the authors—namely, their belief that primitive Christianity produced a series of confrontations between differing facets of development, which resulted in a sharpening antithesis between "orthodoxy" and "heresy" leading ultimately to "early Catholicism." The difficulty with this thesis, which in one way or another has been propounded before, lies in identifying as "orthodox" the process by which one development triumphed over another. The Donatist controversy with Augustine, for example, may be seen as nationalist strife rather than as serious theological debate. While we may admit with Robinson and Koester that primitive Christianity can only be described as a somewhat inchoate and amorphous mass of religious responses to faith in Jesus and his proclaimed resurrection glory, there are hazards in some of the steps taken by these authors. For example, to trace the situation in which "Son of God" came to be understood in terms of preexistence as Christianity became less identified with Judaism does indeed involve us in the process which Robinson and Koester would wish us to avoid—i.e., a discussion of the influence of a vaguely defined "Hellenism" on the gospels.

One essay in the book under discussion inevitably raises the whole matter of synoptic relationships once more. "One Jesus and Four Primitive Gospels" (pp. 158ff.) rightly calls attention to the fact that each gospel has its own particular theological concern or concerns. But short of a final and irrefutable proof that one particular gospel was written before the others and that the others had access to it as a prior source, we are in no position to say that any particular theological concern represented a reaction for or against a previously written and accessible account. Moreover, while we may speculate as to why the Semitic term "Son of Man" finds no expression in the Pauline letters, it is not safe to assume that the majority of Paul's converts were Gentiles. When we find an archaic term, "the Righteous One," on the lips of Stephen (Acts 7:52) and again on the lips of Paul in the same source (Acts 22:14), and elsewhere in the NT, some baffling questions inevitably surface as to date, provenance, and "Semitic background." Not the least of our difficulties lies in knowing precisely where pockets of Semitic-speaking Christians may have existed in the second half of the first century.

There is no doubt that in the current state of NT studies Robinson and Koester have presented us with a viable discipline, in strong contrast to a current antihistoricism on the one hand and the imposition of impossible historical criteria on the other. Yet it is well to remember that we are able to "judge the value of a movement, or of a method, only by inadequate criteria, and to set up such criteria as absolute guides is the most dangerous possible procedure. . . ." (W. F. Albright, *History,* 1965, p. 140). To be sure, Robinson and Koester do not claim any finality for their method, and to express doubts about a tentative proposal must seem unfair. But the present writer must be allowed to ask if it is possible, in the final analysis, to trace the path of a particular phenomenon through the NT writings without taking some fundamental data or fixed points from which the "trajectory" began. The character of any datum or fixed point at its beginning is of capital importance if we are to trace the development of the datum and assess at the same time the phenomena which reacted upon that datum. As was to be expected in view of the authors' tentative approach to their task, no firm guidance is offered by Robinson and Koester in dealing with this problem. Yet the question of gospel material remains fundamental, and a trajectory through the synoptics and John must inevitably begin with some hypothesis about priority. It must equally posit some hypothesis as to the origin of the tradition which Paul declared himself to have "received."

Robinson and Koester are at times insistent that for the purposes of their proposed task the distinction between "canonical" and "uncanonical" in Christian writings can be dismissed. This is defensible from the viewpoint of a historian interested in early Christian origins and the development of ideas. But on the premises of the authors of this important work, "trajectories" have recognizable starting points, and one of them, which emerged in the early Christian community, was a conviction of the necessity of presumed apostolic authorship for attestation as genuine. Now that form criticism has called attention to the development of local interests in the formation of the gospel tradition, on the very grounds proposed by Robinson and Koester, it is imperative not only that the earliest datum be open to inspection—if that is possible—but that the grounds on which material was accepted or rejected also be open to inspection. Unfortunately for any purely historical approach to the question, the earliest datum discoverable to us is the faith that Jesus was God's messiah, and that God had raised him from the dead. We are here in the realm of the parahistorical and the theological, beyond history. Almost every element of gospel criticism proposed for inspection and acceptance finally depends on the ever-present and allied questions of synoptic priority in the dating of the NT gospel material. The present writer's approach to synoptic relationships will be examined later in this Introduction.

4. SYNOPTIC RELATIONSHIPS AND THE SUPPOSED PRIORITY OF MARK

The early centuries of the Christian era, which saw the first allusions to, and commentaries on, the four gospels, and also witnessed the first lectionary cycles, gave scant attention to the gospel of Mark. The fourth century witnessed the verdict of Augustine of Hippo that Mark was an abbreviated version of Matthew *(De consensu evangelistarum* 1.2.4). Commentaries on Mark were written, both during the Middle Ages and at the time of the Reformation and subsequent to it, but the prevalent view was usually that of Augustine, and Mark's gospel was to a large extent neglected.

The early years of the nineteenth century saw the first tentative approaches to a radical reexamination of the assumptions of the preceding centuries. It is unnecessary in a commentary of this character to detail all the steps of this reexamination, but some stages in the process must be mentioned.

At the beginning, the existence of an oral tradition of a more or less fixed character, derived from the apostles and by them transmitted to early Christian teachers and preachers, seemed to answer satisfactorily the question, "How did the written gospels come into being?" It was not until 1835 that the first major step toward modern critical scholarship was taken. In that year Karl Lachmann first called attention to the fact that the great diversity of the synoptic gospels was more apparent than real—that if Matthew and Luke were examined and compared to Mark, the picture was relatively simple. The hypothesis of the dependence of Matthew and Luke on Mark, once accepted —as in general it was by the end of the first quarter of this century—was further refined by Holtzmann's suggestion of a tradition of sayings called the Q ("Quelle") source. Thus was produced the "two-source" hypothesis: the priority of Mark as the foundation of Matthew and Luke, and along with it an explanation of material common to both but not found in Mark. The present century began with an increasing acceptance of the theory, and to this day, for all the attempts made from time to time to call the hypothesis in question, it is almost axiomatic in NT critical circles that to question the priority of Mark is an exercise in futility.

From the beginning of this century up to the present, the acceptance of Markan priority in synoptic relationships has led to a torrent of critical work on Mark. It is not too much to say that it has been emphasis on the *theological* concerns of the evangelists which has led to skepticism in many quarters as to the possibility of knowing anything at all of the life of Jesus. With these theological concerns, as they affect Mark, we shall be concerned elsewhere in this Introduction. Here it is sufficient to indicate that in some circles the specific theological contributions of Matthew and Luke are seen as reactions against, or modifications and developments of, theological concerns thought to exist in Mark.

The scope of the Anchor Bible series, and the audience of general readers envisaged by the editors of this series, would seem to rule out in this commentary any extended treatment of what is called "the synoptic problem." Nonetheless it must be noted that for more than fifty years Mark has been commonly assumed to be the prime source and foundation for Matthew and Luke. So much is this the case that Vincent Taylor can say, "Mark is our earliest gospel used as a source by Matt and Luke," and indeed "in a modern commentary it is no longer necessary to prove the priority of Mark" (The Gospel According to St. Mark, 1966, p. 11). A commentator on Mark, especially in a work designed for the general public, is under serious obligation to explain his position if he finds himself unable to accept what is unquestionably a majority view. A commentator may express reservations about the assumed priority of Mark in dealing with Matthew's gospel, but it is quite another matter to embark on a commentary on Mark and at the same time remain content with expressing reservations. Any reservations as to a view accepted by the vast majority of one's academic contemporaries must be stated with a reasonable fullness, consonant with the audience envisaged for the series.

No attempt will be made in this introduction to sketch the history of academic attention to the synoptic problem. Possibly the fullest historical survey at present available in English is W. R. Farmer's The Synoptic Problem, which has the advantage of being eminently readable and in essentials not beyond the competence of the interested layman. Farmer's own solution to the relationship among the first three gospels has not met with general acceptance, and the present writer must say at once that he finds Farmer's thesis (largely a reformulation of the Griesbach hypothesis) far more acceptable than the present majority view.

The Griesbach hypothesis, to which reference will be made frequently, can be very simply stated. Griesbach held that Mark was written later than Luke, and was dependent on both Matthew and Luke. Moreover, the hypothesis holds, Mark almost never diverged from Matthew in order, and very seldom in content, unless for some purpose he was following for a time the order and content of Luke.

The commonly accepted solution to the relationships among the synoptic gospels can be easily represented as follows:

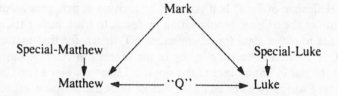

The diagrammatic simplicity of the solution is attractive. Ostensibly, it not only provides the simplest solutions to problems of possible literary dependence—after all, one of the three synoptic gospels must have been written first—but also provides a *terminus a quo* for religious and theological development. It ought not to be forgotten, as Farmer rightly points out (p. 19), that the modern search for solutions has been theologically motivated. Granted that the earliest oral Christian traditions must sooner or later have been committed to writing, how far is it possible to go behind our present written sources to an original source or sources? As far as this quest was concerned, John could be left safely where Schleiermacher had put it, a "spiritual" gospel theologically important and even normative for later Christianity, but of little value as testimony to the events in the life and ministry of Jesus (Farmer, p. 15n.).

We should neither underestimate nor misunderstand the theological motivations of those who first proposed solutions to the synoptic problem in the last century. Faced with what for convenience may be called the "developing" or "emerging" christology of (for example) Ephesians, scholars asked to what extent the theological message and concerns of the gospel writers were founded in the ministry and the message of Jesus himself. Such a question carried with it a need to find the earliest ascertainable written traditions of that ministry and message. In light of the manifest differences among the first three NT documents—not to mention the contrast between those three and the fourth NT document—it was imperative that the whole question of priority be discussed, and if possible firm conclusions reached, before matters of early Christian belief could be rightly discussed. With this desire to reach behind the canon in an attempt to establish the priority of its parts in time, there can be no quarrel.

Built into the inquiry, however, were some other considerations, often not overtly expressed, together with some presuppositions inherited from the eighteenth century and often unconsciously assumed. What, for example, was the role of the apostle Paul in the development of primitive Christian theology? There was no cause to dispute *in broad outline* the account of his ministry in Acts, and his letters were certainly earlier than the written gospel tradition. But for all his Pharisaic upbringing, there appeared to be an element of Greek cosmopolitanism in his background. How far then was a simple Palestinian proclamation transformed, if not distorted, by the presumed Hellenism of Paul? Is it possible, by arriving at firm conclusions as to the nature of the original proclamation by Jesus, to trace such a transformation at the hands of Paul (or of any other NT writer, for that matter)?

Another eighteenth-century legacy in the nineteenth-century feast of reason was the rise in importance of the empirical sciences. Not a few Christians had become seriously alarmed at the almost nonexistent space left for miracles and the paranormal by the "closed system" scientific view of the universe with which the nineteenth century had opened. Yet the gospel accounts were full of miracle stories, and the climax of the ministry of Jesus in the narratives as they stood was the raising of Jesus from the dead. The use of the miracle narratives as evidential proof of the uniqueness of Jesus sprang in the end from the same set of assumptions as those of the eighteenth-century naturalist about the nature of the universe. Even if the assumed closed system of the universe here and there admitted of some puzzling variations, there was widespread discomfort and embarrassment among many Christians with respect to miracles. No matter what comparisons might be made between miracles in the OT and those in the NT, to the eventual dismissal of testimony from both, neither the Pauline letters nor the speeches in Acts could be construed as suggesting in any way that Christian faith rested ultimately on anything other than the proclaimed resurrection of Jesus. Did this proclamation rest on the earliest ascertainable traditions? What of the passion and resurrection predictions on the lips of Jesus in the gospels, and especially the synoptic gospels?

From the foregoing it will be seen that apart from any questions of literary relationships among the first three gospels, there were other factors at work which rendered the pursuit of documentary priority a matter of the highest importance. Reduced to the simplest terms, this was a "quest for the historical Jesus"—a quest which has noticeably attracted renewed attention in the second half of this century and which is discussed elsewhere in this introduction. Every age conducts its theological and historical investigations against a background of its own cultural concerns and presuppositions; our own age is no exception to this. If therefore the age that witnessed the quest for the historical Jesus was fascinated by the supposed predictabilities in the natural order, it must also be said that it was an age when virtually nothing was known of the period in Judaism between the testaments. (The pioneering work of R. H. Charles was a brilliant exception to this generalization.) Other areas were equally unknown, or at best ill-explored. Roman provincial legal practice in the NT period is an example.

Our own times have witnessed a proliferation of factual information documenting NT times which can only be described as an explosion. At the same time there has been a similar explosion of factual data, and of inquiry growing therefrom, in the realm of the natural sciences. The field of NT studies has seen no diminution of effort focusing on the theological concerns of the NT writers, and a future historian of NT studies may find it somewhat daunting to undertake a listing of discernible trends in NT academic writing in the period from 1950 onward. But it must be said that for the most part the supposed validity of the two-document hypothesis has not been seriously questioned.

Literary relationships can sometimes be the least rewarding of all studies, and often frustrating in the seemingly impossible task of choosing between various hypotheses. Some fascinating hypotheses can be and have been adduced to account for the relationship between (for example) the Rule of St. Benedict and the *Regula Magistri*. But the advent on the critical scene of the Qumran *Manual of Discipline* (1QS) has injected into even that possible relationship complicated considerations of the part which Nilus of Ancyra and even the community discipline of the *Therapeutae* of Philo may have played.

The author of this commentary wishes to state his own position about the present state of affairs in synoptic studies, and give his reasons for hesitating to accept the traditional two-document hypothesis as in any sense an established tool of NT criticism.

1. The majority view that Mark was written first and that Matthew and Luke are substantially dependent upon Mark cannot be adequately proved; indeed, the premise of Markan priority allows for far too many obstinate surds in the calculation of relations for the view to be sustained.

2. The argument "from simplicity to artifice" generally employed in some studies of the synoptic problem to support Markan priority has three serious flaws. First, as noted in countless other studies of literary dependence or interdependence, an ostensibly simple document is often simply a précis of another, more elaborate one. Second, the argument fails to account for the high degree of artifice and detail exhibited in the individual and self-contained pericopae in Mark. Finally, and most serious of all, it fails to explain why Matthew and Luke—granted the theological ideas said to be elaborated by each—should have felt themselves bound by the historical framework of Mark.

3. An examination of the order of Matthew and Luke as against Mark produces far more additional questions than answers. The agreements of Luke and Matthew against Mark are by no means the "minor agreements" commonly so described in some works on the synoptic problem. The assumption of Markan priority is totally unable to explain why Mark follows Matthew quite closely when Luke's order is different from that of Matthew.

4. The advocates of Markan priority must somehow find a satisfactory explanation for the fact that Matthew and Luke almost never agree against Mark. But when they do, the occasions are notable. Matthew and Luke, for example, put the cleansing of the temple on the same day as Jesus' entry into Jerusalem, where Mark has it on the day following. If Mark was the prior document, known to both Matthew and Luke and used by both, then why did the other two writers feel compelled to change his record? Assuming that

neither knew the account of the other, as the argument usually does, this would be remarkable, to say the least.

5. The only hypothesis which adequately explains the difference in order between Mark and the other two synoptists is the assumption that when Mark found his two sources at variance he made a choice between them, following one or the other. Certainly he does not depart from *both* in order.

6. An examination of the content of Mark reveals that few sayings or incidents in Mark are not similarly represented in Matthew and Luke. The only substantial exceptions to this are two miracles (7:32-35, 8:22-26) and a parable (4:26-29). On any theory of Matthean and Lucan dependence, we are compelled to ask why these were omitted. A theory which posits Markan dependence on the others allows for Mark's incorporating material known to him but absent from the sources before him. But there is more to be said than that. Streeter's statement (1930, p. 151)—"The relative order of incidents and sections in Mark is in general supported by Matt and Luke; where either of them deserts Mark the other is usually found supporting him"—is far less convincing than is supposed by those who have followed him. The real question, on the hypothesis of Markan priority, is why Matthew and Luke do not differ from their exemplar more frequently than they do, particularly when one recalls that each has material peculiar to himself. In fact it is possible to be even more critical of Markan priority by asking a further question: since it is assumed on this hypothesis that both Matthew and Luke depended on Mark but were unknown to each other, why then does Matthew usually follow Mark when Luke goes his own way, and why does Luke similarly follow Mark when Matthew departs from Mark's order?

7. If we assume that there was a recognizable body of material which could for convenience be called a "foundation source or sources," we are then left bewildered by this curious alternation of rejection of the Markan order by Matthew and Luke. Why does their rejection of this order not coincide more frequently than it does, if in fact Mark is the nearest to the foundation sources? The picture is made more rather than less confused if Luke was written with full knowledge of both Matthew and Mark.

8. Streeter familiarized the whole English-speaking world with the "minor agreements" of Matthew and Luke as against Mark (1930, p. 153). The phenomenon can be simply stated: when all the synoptic gospels are in parallel, the agreements between Matthew and Luke against Mark are minor and erratic, as compared with the occasions of agreement of Matthew and Mark against Luke and of Luke and Mark against Matthew. Several points should be considered here. To begin with, this "minor agreements" material is far less—almost insignificant—when compared with agreements of Mark and Luke against Matthew or agreements of Matthew and Mark against Luke. It is necessary to explain this phenomenon far more convincingly than is commonly done by the upholders of Markan priority. For if either Matthew or

Luke is placed third in the order of appearance of the gospels, with the third writer being aware of both Mark as primary source and the second writer as secondary source, then both the agreements and the divergences are somewhat more than surprising, and even—on the basis of redaction history— quite unreasonable. Moreover, on the usual premises, some convincing explanation must be found for the closer relationship of Luke 9:51-18:14 with Matthew than with Mark.

By far the simplest literary explanation of this phenomenon of "minor agreements" against Mark by Matthew and Luke lies in assuming that Mark had Matthew and Luke in front of him and—where they agreed with one another—went his own way when this did not affect the general purpose of the texts in front of him. The present writer believes that this is the most reasonable explanation of the vast majority of the concurrences of Matthew and Luke against Mark. Finally, on the hypothesis that Mark was third, we can far more satisfactorily account for Mark's agreements with Matthew against Luke and with Luke against Matthew. By assuming that Mark, with both sources in front of him, followed first one and then the other where they differed from one another, even on occasion putting both aside, we can account for obstinate literary problems in a way which the Markan priority hypothesis does not. What is manifestly not solved, however, is the problem of priority as between Matthew and Luke.

9. We are so accustomed to the attempted demonstrations of the redaction of Markan material in Matthew and Luke that it is fatally easy to overlook the real difficulties in the theory. This is especially true of the consideration briefly examined in the preceding paragraph, and in particular when applying this to order as distinct from content. As we have already seen, when the three synoptists do not agree in order, Matthew and Mark will agree against Luke or Luke and Mark against Matthew. Now, if Mark's wording corresponds very closely to that of either Matthew or Luke when his order is common to one of them but different from the other, then it is remarkably difficult on the hypothesis of Markan priority to explain why—for example— Matthew knew when to begin his copying of Mark at the point where Luke's order departs from that of Mark. By the same token, the same considerations apply to Luke's copying of Mark where Matthew deserts the Markan order. For if both Matthew and Luke were using Mark as a prime source, unknown to each other, then we must further inquire how either Matthew or Luke knew when to return to a common order with each other and with Mark.

Once we assume that Mark was the third gospel to be committed to writing, the whole redactional process becomes at once far simpler and more convincing, not to say more manageable. For if Mark elected to follow Matthew's order rather than Luke's, it would have been wholly natural for him to pay closer attention to the text of Matthew. Similarly, a choice to follow Luke's order would find Mark paying closer attention to Luke's text. It is certainly true that there is no absolute rule of thumb in the method outlined above, but there is enough consistency in Mark's method to make this hypothesis a more viable one than making Mark the first source of Matthew and Luke.

10. The whole process of redaction in the synoptic gospels is far more clearly seen if we work on the hitherto unpopular view that Mark was the third in order to be written. One important matter is undecided, as we noted above: that of the order of the appearance of Matthew and Luke. There is very extensive parallel material in Matthew and Luke, and two solutions are possible: (1) Matthew made use of Luke or Luke made use of Matthew, or (2) each is independent of the other and both are using common sources. The adoption of (2) obviously brings with it the question, "What common source or sources?"

As already indicated, the present writer is unconvinced that posited Markan priority answers any questions adequately, and is at the same time convinced that the hypothesis of Markan priority raises far more difficult questions than its proponents admit. Some of these questions have been examined above. The view taken here is that in assessing the relationship between Matthew and Luke we should keep two factors in mind: (a) similarity of material, without strong and convincing agreement suggesting direct dependence of one evangelist on the other, *may* argue a common source or sources; but (b) convincing argument in favor of direct dependence of one on the other *does* argue that one author directly copied the other.

11. The arguments proposed above are supported by the "Gnostic" text known as *The Gospel of Truth*. Whatever the precise period of *The Gospel of Truth* may eventually prove to be, and whatever its provenance, its importance lies in the new dimension it gives to the word "gospel." There is virtually no narrative here, no attempt to provide even a recognizable outline of anything which might be called a "life of Jesus." Short of the dramatic discovery of new documents closely resembling our present four gospels, therefore, we have two gospels (Matthew and Luke) which very closely parallel each other, together with a third (Mark) which this commentator believes was compiled with the aid of the other two. The fourth gospel, for all its greater concentration on the reflective and theological, is recognizably set in the same mold as the other three—namely, a theology of the life and ministry of Jesus. For all the revived interest in any parallel, real or supposed, between the gospels and contemporary biographical literature in the Hellenistic world, no convincing evidence has yet been produced to make our own four canonical gospels anything other than sui generis. But in this collection we have two gospels of great similarity in content and in form, and though any biographical account must proceed from birth to death, yet the parallels in form and content between Matthew and Luke are striking and the similarity is unmatched (so far as we know) in any contemporary or near-contemporary

Hellenistic literature. One comment needs to be added here. It is in the highest degree unlikely that two writers, each working quite independently of the other, should have produced such strikingly similar work.

12. The similarity between Matthew and Luke is demonstrable. The view taken above is that Mark was derived from both. But there remains the further question: which is prior in time? It is impossible to account for the close relationship of Matthew and Luke in both shape and content by supposing both to be dependent on Mark, unless we allow for the possibility of a plethora of sources to account for the body of material common to Matthew and Luke but absent from both Mark and John. The problem of priority between Matthew and Luke is thus not an easy one, and requires that the following considerations be kept in mind.

First, if the early tradition that Mark was Roman is correct, then it must be asked, and asked insistently, why any Palestinian gospel tradition was compelled to await the arrival from Rome of some documentary basis before such Palestinian tradition could be committed to writing. Secondly, enough is known from archaeology and contemporary sources to indicate that conditions in Palestine were far too chaotic after A.D. 60 to allow for anything like the academic calm envisaged by most proponents of Markan priority. It is hard to imagine any circumstances in which a group of Jewish sectarians (whose loyalty was in question on both sides) would be compelled to await patiently the arrival of a Roman gospel before committing Palestinian traditions to writing. Luke's preface to his gospel begins with a statement that "many" have taken in hand the task of editing or arranging a coherent account *(diēgēsis)* of the "events which have happened among us." Luke presumably includes himself among the "many." But we lack information as to the number of attempts made or the number of persons so engaged. Here it is appropriate to mention an important work published in 1954, *The School of St. Matthew* (Krister Stendahl, *Acta Seminarii Neotestamentici Upsaliensis* XX, Uppsala: Almquist & Wiksells, 1954). Apart from the conclusions in that work (p. 34) about the order of appearance of our present gospels, which this writer is unable to accept, Stendahl rightly called attention to the extent to which Matthew's use of texts from the Hebrew Bible resembled the *pesher* (commentary) methods of the Essene sectarians. (Cf. also in this connection Albright-Mann, 1971, Introduction, pp. xliv ff.) Considerably more is now known of Jewish literary methods than was the case when Stendahl's work was first published, but the supreme importance of that work was that it provided an important clue to an understanding of the background of Matthew's gospel. "The Matthaean school must be understood as a school for teachers and church leaders, and for this reason the literary work of that school assumes the form of a manual for teaching and administration within the church. As we shall see, the Matthaean type of midrashic interpretation is not principally the halakic or the haggadic one favored by the rabbinic schools, but it closely approaches what has been called the *midrash pesher* of the Qumran sect, in which the OT texts were not primarily the source of rules, but the prophecy which was shown to be fulfilled" (op. cit., p. 35). Perhaps the term "school" is unfortunate, conveying more of the German *Schule* in the formal academic sense than may have been intended, rather than an informal "circle," but the meaning is plain. For Stendahl, Matthew's gospel represented the end product of a sifting and ordering of tradition along lines familiar to us from the Dead Sea sectarians. But was Luke referring to such a process in his preface? Did he mean us to understand that he was familiar with the work of the Matthean "circle"? It is Farmer's consistent position that the relationships between the synoptic gospels are explicable only on the supposition that Luke made painstaking and lengthy examination of Matthew and in the light of what he found determined to write his own carefully ordered narrative. Farmer suggests that the present gospel of Matthew is itself a single *diēgēsis*—the end product of a reflection upon traditions which go back to the period of those who were intimate witnesses of the nativity of Jesus.

13. Admittedly, there is much in Farmer's hypothesis that is attractive to the present writer. But some serious questions remain unanswered—notably, why did Luke not make substantial use of the nativity narratives in Matthew? Perhaps because Matthew is far more Palestinian-Jewish in orientation than Luke. Farmer does use this consideration in arguing that Luke was written after the emergence of the Church into the wider Hellenistic world. The retention of some Aramaic expressions in Mark could equally well be used, and has been used, to urge the priority of Mark, a conclusion which Farmer would reject.

It is the view of the present writer that Mark is dependent on both Matthew and Luke, but that no absolutely certain grounds exist for determining priority between Matthew and Luke. At first sight it would seem much more likely that Matthew and Luke represent independent attempts to sift the traditions known to both, and at the same time include the traditions peculiar to each. If Matthew represents a specifically Palestinian tradition, with very strong emphasis on the Jewish background of Jesus' ministry and teaching, while Luke represents an Antiochian (Syrian) understanding of that tradition, then both may well have been working with the same basic source material independently. Unfortunately, this does not answer the question: what sources? To that extent, therefore, the reader may well feel that the whole argument has come full circle, and that we are now back again to the point where the two-document hypothesis begins—with the thesis that the earliest source which both Matthew and Luke used was Mark. Enough has been said, however, to make the writer's position clear—namely, that Markan priority, as an explanation for the form and content of Matthew and Luke, is at best debatable and at worst indefensible. On the views here expressed, no sound hypothesis at present exists for any identification of the sources of material held in common by Matthew and Luke.

It is true that Griesbach—to whose work this writer is a fairly recent convert—was fascinated in 1783 by the notion that there was a primary gospel source used by both Matthew and Luke, and Eichorn and others pleaded for a single Aramaic source. But too much has been accomplished in the field of form criticism for such a thesis to stand. Form criticism has served to demonstrate that our present documents contain different strata of the tradition. For example, material belonging to a "sayings of Jesus" source can hypothetically be divided into (a) sayings going back to Jesus himself and (b) others which have been subject to editorial change (for the latter, compare Matt 19:9 and 5:32). Whatever the vagaries of form criticism in the hands of some of its more ardent disciples, it has freed us from the necessity of postulating some "Q" or "primal source"—instead, anyone who works in gospel studies must accustom himself or herself to think of a whole range of possible sources.

It may well be objected that once a series of "sayings-sources" has been admitted to the discussion, the very simplicity of the Griesbach theory of synoptic relationships is severely eroded, if not destroyed. What purports to be a simple solution to the problem of synoptic relationships in diminishing the number of hypotheses is destroyed—it may be said—once collections of material are allowed. But this judgment misses the point. What the Griesbach theory does is to challenge an unnecessary proliferation of hypothetical sources, whether the sources are in "collections" or not. It may often be true that the simplest solutions are the right ones, though this is not always *necessarily* true. Griesbach avoids an unrestrained multiplication of hypothetical sources.

Any hypothesis of synoptic relationships must be founded on the presupposed existence of traditions about the words and ministry of Jesus. But it is surely sound procedure to attempt some explanation of the obvious verbal agreements between the gospels without an appeal to sources which in the nature of the case are hypothetical. This done, we are then free to seek some theory to explain the existence of (for example) parables in Luke not found in Matthew. There is urgent need for the NT scholar to submit to one of the accepted canons of literary criticism: if evidence requires an otherwise unknown source, then such may be posited to explain phenomena otherwise impossible to explain, even if no direct evidence for such a source can be found. In terms of synoptic study, this implies that the parable material common to Matthew and Luke ought first to be examined on the hypothesis that one copied from the other.

It is here that the Griesbach theory has the twin merits of (1) comparative simplicity and (2) conformity to the accepted canons of literary criticism. The Griesbach theory requires that we examine all the parables in Luke which are paralleled in Matthew and take seriously the possibility that they were copied from Matthew before coming to the conclusion that Luke's version has come from some source or sources independent of Matthew. There is no adequate reason to resort to a sayings collection to account for the material common to Matthew and Luke (cf. Albert Fuchs, *Sprächliche Untersuchungen zu Mathäus und Lukas: Ein Beitrag zur Quellenkritik,* AnBib 49.1971). Such resort can only succeed in maintaining Markan priority and explaining the agreements of Matthew and Luke against Mark by positing a "Deutero-Mark" among the sources. It is however essential, on the Griesbach theory, to presuppose a body of parable material used by Luke—material, moreover, which is independent of Matthew. In short, what the Griesbach theory demands is that we examine the phenomena of the relationships among the synoptic gospels without resorting to Q. In other words, if the relationships among the synoptic gospels can be explained by a hypothesis in which Matthew is first, Luke second, and Mark dependent on both, then sound literary analysis would suggest that this arrangement be examined *before* resorting to one which necessitates positing another collection of material. If it is possible, for example, to explain the text of Luke by recognizing that in most of his material he has modified Matthew, then the accepted canons of literary analysis compel us to take this possibility seriously. At all events, that possibility delivers us from a special "John the Baptist" tradition, and possibly from a "miracles source." NT scholarship ought rightly to be concerned with answering the question, "How far are we dependent upon purely hypothetical sources to explain the evidence before us?" It is certainly possible to suppose that a considerable body of material was known to Matthew and Luke without in the least being committed to the status which Q has commonly been accorded. If, however, we can begin to look afresh at Q as a loose collection of sayings known to Matthew and Luke and for which Luke exercised a fairly frequent preference in his adaptation of Matthew, then there is a real possibility of renewed discussion of the synoptic problem. The contest between a rigidly held two-document hypothesis and an equally rigidly held Griesbach hypothesis must ultimately end in stalemate.

It will be plain from the foregoing that the present writer is far from sanguine about the possibilities of any reasonable treatment of synoptic relationships on the two-document hypothesis. We are pleading here for a realistic form-critical and redaction-critical assessment of the material *on the supposition that Luke worked with Matthew.* What emerges, on the Griesbach theory of relationships, is that we do not find Luke's manner of dealing with his material in any way foreign to the author who produced Luke-Acts. Essentially, then, we have in Luke—apart from Chapters 9-18—a work which proceeds through Matthew's outline, not once but many times freely incorporating material from other traditions known to him, or even substituting material for the Matthean (for example, the nativity accounts, the genealogy, and the resurrection narratives). For Chapters 12-18, Luke plainly uses the outline of another body of material, often using material from Matthew but not in the Matthean order. At 18:15 Luke returns to Matthew's order and uses it freely to the end of his narrative.

All of this procedure on the part of Luke is understandable in the light of accepted canons of secular literary criticism. But when the gospel of Mark is made the central pivot of a treatment of synoptic relationships, and the supposed dependence of Matthew and Luke on Mark is treated as a matter separate from their hypothetical dependence on Q, then the result is difficult to chart. What ensues is a literary jungle, in which differences in the order of Q material as between Matthew and Luke are used as a demonstration that Luke did not know Matthew (and so render Q a necessary intrusion). Such was the position of Streeter; it was quite effectively and just as logically reversed by Taylor with the assertion that *similarity* of order in the use of Q material led to the conclusion that both Matthew and Luke knew of the existence of Q.

In light of the above, the parallelism of Matthew and Luke is startling. It is all the more arresting if early dates are posited for our present written sources (as proposed by C. F. D. Moule, the late W. F. Albright, and most recently J. A. T. Robinson). The position adopted by Albright and the present writer in the Anchor Bible *Matthew*—a modified Augustinian view of the independence of Matthew and Luke of each other—cannot, I am persuaded, any longer stand. (It is appropriate here to remark that, when that work had gone to press, Albright was already seriously considering the viability of the Griesbach hypothesis.)

Anyone attempting to place the gospels of Matthew and Luke in a time other than the civil and religious limbo of the two decades between A.D. 80 and 100—where the consensus of a majority places the composition of the gospels—must face the problem of the relationship between Matthew and Luke. On every possible count, Matthew must be regarded as the most fundamentally "Jewish" of the synoptic gospels, and on this premise alone we are entitled to ask what manner of Jewish Christian community, circle, or individual would find it possible or even desirable to produce our present Matthew at any time after the horrors of A.D. 66-70. We are compelled to reexamine, on the very grounds of its "Jewishness," the whole question of the priority of Matthew raised in acute form by Griesbach. "First the Jew, and then the Greek" would not only do justice to the realities of the missionary situation of the primitive Christian community, but would also do justice to the manifest differences in orientation between Matthew and Luke, for all their similarities in literary respects.

Considerable time has been spent on this matter—admittedly at a very general level—because, in the writer's view, the options formerly believed to have been closed by the two-document hypothesis are in fact wide open. The

task of the NT scholar at the end of the twentieth century must be to bring
together the lessons of all related disciplines—historical, archaeological, sociological, and cultural—and then ally these disciplines with those commonly
associated with biblical studies. It is, for example, no service to NT studies to
"compass sea and land" to find one *theios anēr* as an explanation of gospel
treatments of Jesus when there is an abundant diversity of "messianic" speculation already at hand in sectarian Judaism of the NT period. Equally, we are
not entitled to channel the gospels into a period of which we know very little,
either in social and political history or indeed in literary history, until we
have produced convincing arguments against the thesis of the tradition's urgent committal to written form in the worsening atmosphere of A.D. 60-65.
By the same token, NT scholarship must guard against the recent tendency to
proliferate early Christian communities of varying theological hues to explain
every facet of theological speculation unless there is solid historical evidence
to support such a wide spectrum of communities. Similarly, much firmer
evidence than is commonly adduced must be demanded for the current vogue
of invoking an editor or editors in every discernible unit or block of units in
the gospels: experience of an academic seminar, or of a "school" (in the sense
employed by Stendahl), serves to qualify severely the hypothesis of independent editorial hands.

    14. If it be conceded—at any rate for the sake of argument—that Mark is a
conflation and a digest (although highly competent and theologically well
honed) of both Matthew and Luke, then what becomes of the testimony of
Papias that Mark was largely the reminiscences of Peter and furthermore
compiled in Rome? The witness of Papias must be taken seriously, as indeed
must all ancient traditions. But if it should prove correct that Mark is a
conflation and a digest of Matthew and Luke, then we are at all events
delivered from the absurdity of supposing that no Palestinian tradition could
be committed to writing before the discovery of a Roman manuscript, and
that on the verge of the first Jewish war!

    We are entitled, however, before proceeding further, to examine the exter-
nal early evidence about synoptic composition. Papias gives us no indication
of the order in which the gospels appeared. The statement of Clement of
Alexandria may be significant because of his apparent lack of concern with
questions of literary relationship: he asserts that he received from the elders
the tradition that the gospels with genealogies were written before those without them. Here we have a second-century statement implying that Mark
postdates Matthew and Luke. Whether or not Justin Martyr actually quotes
Mark—and this is disputed—in the *Dialogue with Trypho* (Sections I and VI),
this seems to be reminiscent of Mark's gospel. It would be rash to assume
that, while we have definite quotations from Matthew and Luke in Justin and
earlier writers but nothing definitely identifiable from Mark, there is no certain external evidence of Mark before the second century. If Mark was a local

production, compiled from the traditions embodied in Matthew and Luke and serving a comparatively limited purpose (of which more will be said later), then the fact that his work is not quoted more widely is explicable. Furthermore, early Christian writers who had access to all three synoptic gospels would probably, in the present writer's view, have taken the stance later expressed by Augustine that Mark was a plodding imitator of Matthew. What does seem to emerge from the non-use of Mark is an implication that Matthew and Luke were earlier documents, and so used more frequently, while Mark is a purely local document and a digest which later came to be circulated.

15. The whole vexed question of synoptic relationships has been under review recently from a wholly different angle. Robert Lindsey and David Flusser of Hebrew University in Jerusalem have suggested that priority ought to be given to Luke. Briefly, the thesis as presented by Lindsey (in *A Hebrew Translation of the Gospel of Mark,* Jerusalem: Dagith Publishers, 1971) goes as follows: a modern attempt to translate Mark into Hebrew for Jewish Christians in Israel resulted in a twofold discovery: (a) the Greek word order and idioms were more like Hebrew than like literary Greek, and (b) there were many non-Hebraisms—to use Lindsey's phrase—in Mark. This forced Lindsey to "suspect that the writer had used a Greek text which had itself been translated quite literally from a Semitic original, but that he had also thoroughly edited this text by inserting frequent expressions and phrases which were more Greek than Semitic and, in any case, were not part of his source." Lindsey reports his growing accumulation of evidence that Luke contained none of the "non-Hebraisms" found in Mark, while Matthew appeared to reject about half of them, accepting others and using them in "Markan" contexts. Further, according to Lindsey, "where Matthew was not parallel to Mark . . . his text showed the same ease of translation as that of Luke." Two results came from this study: first, the reluctant abandonment by Lindsey of any notion of Markan priority; and second, the emerging necessity in Lindsey's view of positing an Ur-gospel, or principal source, in Semitic form to explain the comparative purity of the Hebraic form and vocabulary of Luke. Lindsey's "inescapable" conclusion is that the priority of Luke is the only hypothesis which adequately deals with the whole vexed matter of synoptic relationships, above all with respect to "translation Greek."

16. Lindsey is perfectly correct to call attention to the embarrassment caused to the proponents of Markan priority by the so-called minor agreements between Matthew and Luke against Mark. The agreements are by no means "minor," if only because the simplicity of the two-document hypothesis will not accommodate the agreements. To assert that the sources of Matthew and Luke were Mark and Q material, a known source and an unknown, inevitably leads to the suggestion that there was in fact an Ur-Markus or a source gospel of some kind to explain the agreements of Matthew and Luke

against Mark. Otherwise we are left to the suppositious mercies of an unnumbered and anonymous collection of editors and redactors or copyists, all of them apparently highly sophisticated scholars. Yet another factor can be added to this confused and often confusing discussion from a much neglected work by the late Vincent Taylor, published in 1927 *(Behind the Third Gospel: A Study of the Proto-Luke Hypothesis,* Oxford: Clarendon Press, 1927; cf. also *The First Draft of Luke's Gospel,* London: SPCK, 1927), suggesting that the removal of all Markan material from our present Luke leaves a consistent and continuous narrative. This sequence of Taylor's never met with anything approaching an enthusiastic response; but it is fair to suggest that this lack of enthusiasm was due to the potential damage by Taylor's thesis to the strongly entrenched presupposition of the majority of NT scholars that Mark was the primary source of both Matthew and Luke. Moreover, Taylor's view carries with it the implication of a source (document?) already in existence by the time Mark came to the author's notice, or—to quote Taylor—"a first-class authority comparable to Mark." *(Behind the Third Gospel,* p. 254). Both Taylor's thesis of a "proto-Luke" and Lindsey's thesis of Lucan priority as an Ur-gospel imply their rejection of all notions of a Markan source of primitive theological simplicity, later worked upon and elaborated by two evangelists and by unidentified and unidentifiable editors and redactors. Perhaps there never was after all much substance to a supposed theological simplicity or an undeveloped primitive theology in Mark. Enough information is now at hand from studies of sectarian literature to assert quite positively that the single term "kingdom of God" was a theological idea of quite extraordinary complexity by the time the ministry of Jesus began. At the same time, the proclamation by Jesus recorded in Mark that his kingdom was dawning in his own person not only produces questions about the circumstances and scope of Jesus' education and his sense of vocation; it must also pose serious questions for those who maintain Markan priority coupled with assertions of a message of primitive simplicity supposedly to be found in Mark.

Any attempt at a short summary of the past and present state of synoptic studies is difficult in a commentary of this scale. It must be said that all the old apparent certainties are in question if not in the process of dissolution. There has been of late an increasing movement away from the priority of Mark, which was a hypothesis widely touted in the past as an assured result of NT studies. Largely abandoned, too, is the once widely held view of Mark as a "primitive" theological understanding of the ministry and the message of Jesus. But though both positions may have existed in a state of mutual partnership in some circles, in the interests of a "developed" or even transformed theology in Matthew and Luke—assuming them to be dependent on Mark— they were not in fact necessarily dependent on each other. It is significant, however, that each idea served to support the other, and the assumption of Markan priority made it possible to speak with confidence about the redactions made by others in the interests of one or more theological emphases. Equally, the search for the primitive data in the records of the life and ministry of Jesus made it possible to speak and write confidently of the introduction of Hellenistic or other elements into the stark simplicity of the Markan account.

Within recent years all this confidence has been increasingly called in question by a growing number of NT scholars unable to accept the assumptions of previous synoptic criticism. But nothing approaching the unanimity found among upholders of the two-document hypothesis is to be discovered among its current critics. We have seen that the Matthean priority espoused by W. R. Farmer does not commend itself to Lindsey, while a fairly lengthy oral tradition posited by Riesenfeld *(The Gospel Tradition,* 1970) would appear unacceptable to Lindsey. There may well be hitherto undiscovered historical facts or even other documentary fragments and inscriptions which will serve to illumine, or even decide, the relationships undoubtedly existing between the synoptic gospels. We argue that Mark was a conflation and an adaptation of Matthew and Luke composed and edited for a particular purpose. We are still left with the undecided question of priority between Matthew and Luke. The material common to Matthew and Luke, and used by Mark, the so-called minor agreements of Matthew and Luke against Mark, and the source material commonly known as "Q," together with the material peculiar to Matthew and material peculiar to Luke, all seem to lead to the insistent question, "Was Luke dependent on Matthew, or Matthew on Luke?" Perhaps we are asking the wrong question; perhaps we ought to ask, "What were the characteristics of the original (oral and/or written?) source or sources used and edited by Matthew and Luke with results later to be conflated by Mark?"

It must be admitted at once that the divergent hypotheses of Farmer and Lindsey are both persuasive. But attractive though it may be to suppose that behind Matthew and Luke there was an Ur-gospel from which both drew independently, and that Mark then drew from both, clearly such a supposition flies in the face of the accepted canons of literary criticism. The literary relationships between Matthew and Luke are so close, especially when they agree against Mark, that it is far more acceptable to posit the dependence of one on the other than to suppose that our present Matthew and Luke are completely independent of each other. For the present writer the hypotheses of both Lindsey and Farmer appear to be inconclusive, and both are attended with considerable difficulty. If, as Albright maintained, Luke was a Jew, and compiled his gospel for the benefit of the Antiochene community, and if furthermore Matthew's gospel is an orderly presentation of Palestinian traditions collected by him, then it is at least possible that what we have are two independent works. Yet, as will at once be obvious, the similarities between Matthew and Luke, particularly in regard to the so-called Q material, compel the hypothesis that behind both gospels was a Palestinian tradition, or series of traditions, of the life, ministry, and message of Jesus which had very early hardened in oral form or had even to a large extent been committed in fixed form in writing before Matthew and Luke began work. But the form in which we have our present Matthew and Luke renders it equally impossible to claim that either could be considered an Ur-gospel or primitive source material. The present writer believes that although the relationships between Matthew and Luke are firmly established, there is no adequate evidence at the present moment to indicate which of the two, Matthew or Luke, first committed the traditions he knew to fixed form in writing. On balance, the advantage seems to lie with Matthew with its strongly Jewish and Palestinian emphasis.

It is often forgotten that the two-document hypothesis, as first enunciated, arose from the view that Matthew and Luke were independent of each other, and that behind all the synoptic gospels there was a single source from which all the evangelists copied. This thesis has carried with it some corollaries which even now are hardly appreciated. If Matthew and Luke were independent of each other and (as Holtzmann maintained in 1863) drew upon a gospel he identified as Ur-Markus and upon a "sayings-source" (first identified with the *logia* of Papias and later by the appellation "Q"), then some sources must have existed from which both copied. But once we abandon the idea of independence, a very feeble case is left for earlier sources, and particularly for Q. It is hardly conceivable that Matthew and Luke would independently have copied a "gospel" anything like our present Mark unless they also copied Q.

Holtzmann's later belief that Matthew had known and used Luke was one he succeeded in holding alongside his continued belief that Matthew (and so Luke) had used the source akin to Mark, and had also used Q. It was left to B. H. Streeter so to shape and refine the two-document hypothesis that to all intents and purposes it has held sway ever since. In the face of the canons of literary criticism in other fields he rejected the simplest solution—that the Q material shared by Matthew and Luke was copied by Luke from Matthew— and maintained the independence of Matthew and Luke. But this solution of the problem succeeded only because Streeter made the whole matter of the so-called minor agreements of Matthew and Luke against Mark a far more fragmentary phenomenon than in fact it is. The more than two hundred agreements of Matthew and Luke against Mark were divided by Streeter into numerous categories, each category being examined in isolation from the rest. Until fairly recent times, Streeter's fragmented treatment was almost universally accepted. It carried with it an inability to examine individual pericopae for possible evidence of literary dependence as between Matthew and Luke. But it is becoming increasingly clear to some NT scholars that the "minor" agreements of Matthew and Luke are by no means minor and are not to be dismissed so easily. They remain an obstinate item in the calculations of the traditional two-document hypothesis, and at the very least they seriously suggest a literary dependence between Matthew and Luke. E. P. Sanders ("The Argument from Order and the Relationships between Matthew and Luke," *NTS* 15.1968-69, pp. 249-61) cogently drew attention to agreements between Matthew and Luke in sentence order, word order, and order of pericopae. More recently, Robert Morgenthaler *(Statische Synopse,* Zürich and Stuttgart: Gotthelf, 1971) has developed Sanders' argument further, though still holding to Markan priority. W. R. Farmer ("The Two-Document Hypothesis as a Methodological Criterion in Synoptic Research," *ATR* 488.1966, pp. 380-96; and "A Response to Robert Morgenthaler's *Statische Synopse,"* Bib 54.3.1973, pp. 429ff.) was correct in pointing out that form criticism has been largely independent of the two-document hypothesis and that indeed much of the work of form criticism has militated against the theory.

The two-document hypothesis is currently under attack, and with it the whole notion of Markan priority, but it is well to include here two observations (one of which has already been made) which properly belong in any conclusion to this discussion. First, the assertion of Markan priority, along with the implied dependence of Matthew and Luke, served very well the theological "liberalism" of an era which espoused it so enthusiastically. For Markan priority does shelve the awkwardness of having to reckon with embarrassing matters such as the virginal conception and the bodily resurrection of Jesus in a primary source. Markan priority also made it unnecessary to deal with the possibility that the "church" belonged to a stage in the formation of the tradition prior to Mark. Secondly, it is hard to escape the conclusion that—in spite of all claims to the contrary—there is nowhere any solid and incontrovertible evidence for either the two-document hypothesis or the existence of Q. What was always at best one possibility among several other proposed solutions to the synoptic problem during the last century gained acceptance over its rivals not because of any compelling force inherent to it, but because of the simplicity which Mark was thought to represent and which accorded well with contemporary theological thought. "A study of the history of the Two-Document hypothesis will verify the fact that there is no article, or series of articles, nor any monograph or any book in which the priority of Mark or the existence of Q has ever been conclusively proven" (W. R. Farmer in his work just cited above).

Recent unpublished work by Joseph B. Tyson of Southern Methodist University has served to cast further doubt on the viability of the two-document hypothesis. In spite of painstaking analyses such as that of Dennis Norlin ("Once More—Statistics and Q," *HTR* 64.1.1971, pp. 59-78), Tyson's work has shown that a study of sequential parallelism in the synoptic gospels does not demand any one solution to the problem, but does suggest that hypotheses which lean toward the solution posed by Griesbach are more likely to prove correct.

The publication of Bernard Orchard's *Matthew, Luke and Mark* (Manchester, U.K.: Koinonia Press, 1976) introduces into the discussion a new element: the author provides a chart of all the pericopae of the synoptic gospels with which his thesis may be tested. (A somewhat similar tool, in English and Greek, has been published recently: Reuben J. Swanson, *The Horizontal Line Synopsis of the Gospels,* Dillsboro, N.C.: Western North Carolina Press, 1975; Greek text 1978.) Orchard's chart demonstrates the difficulties attendant on the assumption of the two-document hypothesis that Matthew and Luke are essentially expansions of Markan material. The subject will not be pursued further in this section, and both works are commended to the student.

Markan priority was too easily assumed to be an almost unassailable bastion in NT studies—particularly after its popularization by Streeter—and has remained a majority opinion up to the present time. In recent years a particular minority view appears to have gained something more than mere respectability. Perhaps nowhere is this better exemplified than in the acceptance by a major theological institution in this country of Longstaff's thesis on Mark as a possible conflation. Longstaff's plea, that Mark exhibits all the classical signs commonly accepted as evidence of conflation, should not in any future discussion be ignored.

It is fair to say that many of the older presuppositions no longer appear as impressive as once they did, and the reappraisal of synoptic relationships in recent years has demonstrated (at least to this writer) the vulnerability of positions formerly thought to be fundamental. One may hope that the Griesbach hypothesis will be given its proper place in any new attempt to examine the synoptic gospels, and not be treated, as so often in the past, as a skeleton at the feast.

Bibliography

Abbott, E. A. "Gospels." In Encyclopaedia Britannica. 9th ed. New York and Chicago: Britannica Publishing Co., 1892.

————. *The Corrections of Mark.* London: A. & C. Black, 1901.

————, and Rushbrooke, W. G. *The Common Tradition of the Synoptic Gospels.* London: Macmillan, 1894.

Augustine. *De consensu evangelistarum* 1.2-3.

Badham, F. P. *Mark's Indebtedness to S. Matthew.* New York: E. R. Herrick, 1897.

Barr, Allan. *A Diagram of Synoptic Relationships.* Edinburgh: T. & T. Clark, 1938.

Baur, F. C. *Das Marcusevangelium.* Tübingen: J. B. C. Mohr, 1851.

————. *Kritische Untersuchungen über die kanonischen Evangelien.* Tübingen: L. F. Fues, 1847.

Beare, Francis W. "On the Synoptic Problem: A New Documentary Theory." In

Gospel Studies in Honor of Sherman Elbridge Johnson, edited by Massey H. Shepherd, Jr., and Edward C. Hobbs. *ATR* Supp Series 3, 1974, pp. 15-28.

Benoit, André. "The Transmission of the Gospel in the First Centuries." In *The Gospel As History,* edited by Vilmos Vatja. The Gospel Encounters History 4. Philadelphia: Fortress Press, 1975.

Benoit, P., and Boismard, M.-E. *Synopse des quatre évangiles en français avec parallèles des apocryphes et des pères.* Vol. 1, 2nd ed., edited by P. Sandevoir. Vol. 2, *Commentaire,* by M.-E. Boismard, A. Lamouille, and P. Sandevoir. Paris: Éditions du Cerf, 1967.

Bleek, F. *Introduction to the New Testament.* Translation by William Urwick of *Einleitung in das Neuen Testament.* Edinburgh: T. & T. Clark, 1869; rev. 3rd ed., 1875; 4th ed., 1886.

Boismard, M.-E. "Influences matthéennes sur l'ultime rédaction de l'évangile de Marc." In *L'évangile selon Marc: Tradition et rédaction,* edited by M. Sabbe. Bibliotheca ephemeridum theologicarum lovaniensium 34. Gembloux: Duculot; Louvain: Leuven University, 1974, pp. 93-101.

———. "The Two-Source Theory at an Impasse." *NTS* 26.1.1979, pp. 1-17.

Brown, J. P. "An Early Revision of the Gospel of Mark." *JBL* 78.3.1959, pp. 215-27.

Buchanan, George W. "Has the Griesbach Hypothesis Been Falsified?" *JBL* 93.4.1974, pp. 550-72.

Bultmann, Rudolf. *Primitive Christianity in Its Contemporary Setting.* London and New York: Thames & Hudson, 1956.

———. *The Theology of the New Testament.* 2 vols. New York: Scribner's, 1951, 1955.

Bundy, W. E. *Jesus and the First Three Gospels.* Cambridge: Harvard University Press, 1955.

Burkitt, F. C. *The Gospel History and Its Transmission.* 2nd ed. Edinburgh: T. & T. Clark, 1907.

———. *Two Lectures on the Gospels.* London and New York: Macmillan, 1901.

Butler, B. C. *The Originality of St. Matthew: A Critique of the Two-Document Hypothesis.* Cambridge University Press, 1951.

Chapman, John. *Matthew, Mark and Luke: A Study in the Order and Interrelation of the Synoptic Gospels.* London: Longman, Green, 1937.

Conzelmann, Hans. *Theologie als Schriftauslegung: Aufsätze zum Neuen Testament.* BEvT 65. Munich: Kaiser, 1974.

Credner, C. A. *Einleitung in das Neuen Testament.* Halle, 1836.

Davidson, Samuel. *An Introduction to the Study of the New Testament: Critical, Exegetical, and Theological.* London: Longman, 1868.

Devish, M. "La relation entre l'évangile de Marc et le document Q." In *L'évangile selon Marc: Tradition et rédaction,* edited by M. Sabbe. Bibliotheca ephemeridum theologicarum lovaniensium 34. Gembloux: Duculot; Louvain: Leuven University, 1974, pp. 59-91.

De Wette, W. M. L. *Lehrbuch der historischen-kritischen Einleitung in die kanonischen Bücher des Neuen Testaments.* 5th ed. Berlin, 1858.

Dibelius, Martin. *Botschaft und Geschichte.* 2 vols. Tübingen: J. C. B. Mohr, 1953, 1956.

————. *A Fresh Approach to the New Testament and Early Christian Literature.* Hertford: Ivor Nicholson & Watson, 1936.

Dungan, D. L. "Mark—the Abridgement of Matthew and Luke." *Perspective* 11.2-3.1970, pp. 51-97.

Eichhorn, Johann G. "Über die drei ersten Evangelien." *Allgemeine Bibliothek der biblischen Literatur* 5.1974, pp. 759-996.

Elliott, J. K. "The Synoptic Problem and the Laws of Tradition—A Cautionary Note," *ExpT* 82.5.1971, pp. 148-52.

Ewald, Heinrich. *Jahrbücher der biblischen Wissenschaft.* Göttingen, 1848.

Farmer, W. R. "A Fresh Approach to Q." In *Christianity, Judaism and Other Greco-Roman Cults,* edited by Jacob Neusner. Section 12, vol. 1, Studies in Judaism in Late Antiquity. Leiden: E. J. Brill, 1975, pp. 39-50.

————. "Modern Developments of Griesbach's Hypothesis." *NTS* 23.3.1977, pp. 275-95.

————. *Occasional Notes on Some Points of Interest in New Testament Studies.* Dallas: Perkins School of Theology, 1980.

————. *The Synoptic Problem.* New York: Macmillan, 1964.

————. "The Synoptic Problem: The Inadequacies of the Generally Accepted Solution." *Perkins Journal* 23.4.1980, pp. 20-28.

————. "The Two-Document Hypothesis as a Methodological Criterion in Synoptic Research." *ATR* 48.1966, pp. 380-96.

Fee, G. D. "A Text-Critical Look at the Synoptic Problem." *NovTest* 22.1.1980, pp. 12-28.

Filson, Floyd V. *Origins of the Gospels.* New York: Abingdon, 1938.

Fitzmyer, J. A. "The Priority of Mark and the 'Q' Source in Luke." *Perspective* 11.1-2.1970, pp. 131-70.

Fuchs, Albert. *Sprachliche Untersuchungen zu Mathäus und Lukas: Ein Beitrag zur Quellenkritik.* AnBib 49. Rome: Pontifical Biblical Institute, 1971.

Fuller, R. H. "Baur versus Hilgenfeld: A Forgotten Chapter in the Debate on the Synoptic Problem." *NTS* 24.3.1978, pp. 355-71.

————, Sanders, E. P., and Longstaff, T. R. W. "The Synoptic Problem: After Ten Years." *Perkins Journal* 28.1975, pp. 63-74.

Gieseler, J. C. *Historisch-kritischer Versuch über die Entstehung und die frühesten Schicksale der schriftlichen Evangelien.* Leipzig, 1818.

Goodspeed, E. J. *Introduction to the New Testament.* University of Chicago Press, 1937.

Goulder, M. D. "On Putting 'Q' to the Test." *NTS* 24.2.1978, pp. 218-34.

Grant, F. C. *The Gospels: Their Origin and Growth.* London: Faber & Faber, 1941.

Griesbach, J. J. *Inquisitio in Fontes, unde Evangelistae Suas de Resurrectione Domini Narrationes Hauserint.* Jena, 1783. Later in *Commentatio qua Marci Evangelium totum e Matthaei et Lucae Commentariis Decerptum Esse Monstratur.* Jena, 1789-90. Revised in *Commentationes Theologicae,* edited by J. C. Velthausen, C. Th. Kuinoel, and G. A. Ruperti. Vol. 1. Leipzig, 1794, pp. 360ff.

Hawkins, J. C. *Horae Synopticae.* 2nd ed. Oxford: Clarendon, 1909.

Herder, Johann G. *Christliche Schriften.* Vol. 3. Riga, 1797. Republished in *Sämliche Werke, zur Religion und Theologie.* Stuttgart and Tübingen, 1830.

Honoré, A. M. "A Statistical Study of the Synoptic Problem." *NovTest* 10.2-3.1968, pp. 95-147.

Howard, George. "Stylistic Inversion and the Synoptic Tradition." *JBL* 97.3.1978, pp. 375-89.

Jameson, H. G. *The Origin of the Synoptic Gospels.* Oxford: Blackwell, 1922.

Jepsen, A. "Anmerkungen eines Aussenseiters zum Synoptikerproblem." *NovTest* 14.2.1972, pp. 106-14.

Knox, W. L. *The Sources of the Synoptic Gospels.* 2 vols. Cambridge University Press, 1953, 1957.

Lachmann, Karl. "De ordine narrationum in evangeliis synopticis." *TSK,* 1835, pp. 570ff.

Lessing, G. E. *New Hypothesis Concerning the Evangelists Regarded as Merely Human Historians.* Translation of "Neue Hypothese über die Evangelisten als bloss menschliche Geschichtschreiber betrachtet," in *Theologische Nachlass,* Berlin, 1784. In *Lessing's Theological Writings,* edited and translated by Henry Chadwick. Stanford University Press, 1957.

Léon-Dufour, X. "Interprétation des évangiles et problème synoptique." *EphTheolLov* 43.1.1967, pp. 5-16.

Lindsey, Robert. *A Hebrew Translation of the Gospel of Mark.* Jerusalem: Dagith Publishers, 1971.

Linton, Olaf. "The Q-Problem Reconsidered." In *Studies in New Testament and Early Christian Literature,* edited by David E. Aune. Leiden: E. J. Brill, 1972, pp. 43-60.

Longstaff, T. R. W. "A Critical Note in Response to J. C. O'Neill." *NTS* 23.1.1976, pp. 116-17.

―――. *Evidence of Conflation in Mark? A Study in the Synoptic Problem.* Thesis, Union Theological Seminary, New York, 1972.

―――. "The Minor Agreements: An Examination of the Basic Argument." *CBQ* 37.2.1975, pp. 184-92.

Lummis, E. W. *How Luke Was Written.* Cambridge University Press, 1915.

Metzger, Bruce. *Index to Periodical Literature on Christ and the Gospels.* Vol. 6. New Testament Tools and Studies. Grand Rapids, Mich.: Eerdmans, 1970.

Michaelis, J. D. *Einleitung in die göttlichen Schriften des neuen Bundes.* Göttingen: 1788. Translated by Herbert Marsh as *Introduction to the New Testament.* 4th ed., 1801.

Morgenthaler, Robert. *Statische Synopse.* Zürich and Stuttgart: W. Gotthelf, 1971.

Moule, C. F. D. *The Birth of the New Testament.* 2nd ed. London: A. & C. Black, 1965.

―――. *The Phenomenon of the New Testament.* London: SCM Press, 1967.

―――. "Urmarcus redivivus? Examen critique de l'hypothèse des insertions matthéennes dans Marc." In *L'évangile selon Marc: Tradition et rédaction,* edited by M. Sabbe. Bibliotheca ephemeridum theologicarum lovaniensium 34. Gembloux: Duculot; Louvain: Leuven University, 1974, pp. 103-45.

Neirynck, Franz, ed., with Hansen, Theo., and van Sebgroeck, Franz. *The Minor Agreements of Matthew and Luke Against Mark with a Cumulative List.* Gembloux: Duculot, 1974.

Neusner, Jacob. *Early Rabbinic Judaism* (especially "The Rabbinic Traditions About the Pharisees: The Problem of Oral Transmission," pp. 73ff., and "The Written Tradition in Pharisaism before 70," pp. 90ff.). Studies in Judaism in Late Antiquity 13. Leiden: E. J. Brill, 1975.

Norlin, Dennis. "Once More—Statistics and Q." *HTR* 64.1.1971, pp. 59-78.

O'Neill, J. C. "The Synoptic Problem." *NTS* 21.1974-75, pp. 273-85.

Orchard, Bernard. *Matthew, Luke and Mark.* Manchester, U.K.: Koinonia Press, 1975.

———, and Longstaff, T. R. W., eds. *J. J. Griesbach: Synoptic and Text-critical Studies, 1776-1976.* Society for New Testament Studies Monograph Series 34. New York and London: Cambridge University Press, 1978.

O'Rourke, J. J. "Some Observations on the Synoptic Problem and the Use of Statistical Procedures." *NovTest* 16.1974, pp. 272-77.

Parker, Pierson. *The Gospel Before Mark.* University of Chicago Press, 1953.

Peabody, David. "A Pre-Markan Prophetic Sayings Tradition and the Synoptic Problem." *JBL* 97.3.1978, pp. 391-409.

Reicke, B. "Griesbach und die synoptische Frage." *TheolZeit* 32.6.1976, pp. 341-59.

Riddle, D. W. *The Gospels: Their Origin and Growth.* University of Chicago Press, 1939.

Riesenfeld, Harald. *The Gospel Tradition.* Philadelphia: Fortress Press, 1970.

Riesner, R. "Wie sicher ist die Zwei-Quellen Theorie?" *TheolBeit* 8.2.1977, pp. 49-73.

Rist, J. M. *On the Independence of Matthew and Mark.* Cambridge University Press, 1977.

Ritschl, A. B. "Über den gegenwärtigen Stand der Kritik der synoptischen Evangelien." In *Theologische Jahrbücher,* 1851.

Roloff, Jurgen. "The Historicity of the Scriptures and the Witness to the One Gospel." In *The Gospel as History,* edited by Vilmos Vatja. The Gospel Encounters History 4. Philadelphia: Fortress Press, 1975, pp. 11-142.

Ropes, J. H. *The Synoptic Gospels.* Cambridge, Mass.: Harvard University Press, 1934. Reissued 1960 with preface by D. E. Nineham.

Rushbrooke, W. G. *Synopticon, An Exposition of the Common Matter of the Synoptic Gospels.* London, 1880.

Sanday, William. *The Authorship and Historical Character of the Fourth Gospel, Considered in Reference to the Contents of the Gospel Itself.* London, 1872.

———. "A Plea for the Logia," *ExpT* 9.1901, pp. 471-73.

———. "A Survey of the Synoptic Question." *Expositor,* 4th series, 3.3.1891, pp. 307ff.

———, ed. *Studies in the Synoptic Problem.* Oxford: Clarendon Press, 1911.

Sanders, E. P. "The Argument from Order and the Relationship Between Mark and Luke." *NTS* 15.1968-69, pp. 249-61.

———. *The Tendencies of the Synoptic Tradition.* Cambridge University Press, 1969.

Schleiermacher, Friedrich. "Über die Zeugnisse des Papias von unsern beiden ersten Evangelien." *TSK,* 1832, pp. 735-68.

Sieffert, F. L. *Über den Ursprung des ersten kanonischen Evangeliums, eine kritische Abhandlung.* Königsberg, 1832.

Simpson, R. T. "The Major Agreements of Matthew and Luke against Mark." *NTS* 12.3.1966, pp. 273-84.

Solages, Bruno de. *La composition des évangiles.* Leiden: E. J. Brill, 1974.

———. *A Greek Synopsis of the Gospels.* English translation by J. Baissus. Leiden: E. J. Brill, 1959.

Stanton, Vincent H. *The Gospels as Historical Documents.* 3 vols. Cambridge University Press, 1903.

Stendahl, Krister. *The School of St. Matthew.* Acta Seminarii Neotestamentici Upsaliensis XX. Lund: Gleerup, 1954.

Stonehouse, N. B. *Origins of the Synoptic Gospels.* Grand Rapids, Mich.: Eerdmans, 1963.

Storr, G. Ch. *Über den Zweck der evangelischen Geschichte und der Briefe Johannis.* Tübingen, 1786.

Streeter, B. H. *The Four Gospels.* London: Macmillan, 1924; rev. ed., 1930.

Swanson, Reuben. *The Horizontal Line Synopsis of the Gospels.* Western North Carolina Press, 1975.

Talbert, Charles H., and McKnight, Edgar V. "Can the Griesbach Hypothesis Be Falsified?" *JBL* 91.3.1972, pp. 338-68.

Taylor, Vincent. *Behind the Third Gospel: A Study of the Proto-Luke Hypothesis.* Oxford: Clarendon Press, 1927.

———. *The First Draft of Luke's Gospel.* London: SPCK, 1927.

———. *The Formation of the Gospel Tradition.* London: Macmillan, 1933.

———. *The Gospels: A Short Introduction.* London: Macmillan, 1930.

Thomas, R. L. "An Investigation of the Agreements Between Matthew and Luke Against Mark." *JournEvThSoc* 19.2.1976, pp. 103-12.

Tigay, Jeffrey. "An Empirical Basis for the Documentary Hypothesis." *JBL* 94.3.1975, pp. 329-42.

Turner, C. H. "Marcan Usage: Notes Critical and Exegetical on the Second Gospel." *JTS,* 1924, pp. 377ff.

———. *The Study of the New Testament, 1883-1920.* Oxford University Press, 1920.

Von Simons, E. *Hat der dritte Evangelist den kanonischen Matthäus benutzt?* Bonn, 1880.

5. THE PURPOSE OF MARK

A. The Date of Mark's Gospel

Almost all NT disciplines of interpretation depend overtly or covertly on the dating proposed for the various books. The method known as form criticism would appear to be exempt from this general judgment, save that it has moved away from the identification of layers of material toward far wider judgments as to date and provenance of the material identified. Tendency criticism can only rightly be used if there is a *terminus a quo* dating of some of the material, allowing for a later "tendency" or development in other parallel or near-parallel material. Long or short, oral transmission of gospel material came to an end with written records, resulting in parallel and independent or primary traditions and dependent, written traditions; the length of the period of oral transmission is related to the handling of the material transmitted, involving revision, manipulation, and even distortion. It is therefore important to determine, if possible, which gospel was first committed to writing, since there are reasonable grounds for believing that such a gospel preserves the oral tradition in something near to primitive purity.

Two conditions appear to be necessary for this belief. First, it would be necessary to demonstrate (or to assume, in the absence of firm proof) that the evangelist was simply concerned with recording the tradition, and that his account, whatever editorial methods he might employ, represented a faithful record. Yet the gospels grew out of the needs of a worshiping and confessing community, and any view of an evangelist as a disinterested reporter is suspect, if not to be rejected outright. Faith in Jesus as Messiah, and in Jesus as raised from the dead, would for most commentators rule out a view of the account as nothing more than faithful chronicle. Second, and perhaps even more important, we would need some assurance that even the *first* written gospel was not written as a polemic against some growing misunderstanding of the tradition. (Such an interpretation of Mark has prompted Theodore J. Weeden's study *Traditions in Conflict,* Philadelphia: Fortress Press, 1971.)

The two conditions outlined above would seem, on some theories at least, to preclude Mark's identification as a "primitive" gospel from which the other synoptists were in part derived. In spite of the fact that Mark contains no obstinate items such as a miraculous conception and birth, no uncompromising assertion of the bodily resurrection of Jesus, it yet possesses a high degree of theological sophistication in its picture of Jesus at war with evil. Moreover, the deceptively abrupt pericopae in Mark often hide from us the considerable artifice in their internal construction. In addition, the designation of Mark as a "gospel of conflict," while it reflects an undoubted truth about the Markan account, finds commentators in substantial disagreement as to what the central conflict or conflicts may be. Matthew and Luke, while they have their own manner of presentation, appear not to highlight the theme of conflict to the extent Mark does. It is easier, if we insist on emphasizing the theme of "conflict" in Mark, to suppose that Mark responded to what he considered serious omissions in Matthew and Luke. This would be even more impressive as a hypothesis if (as on some redaction-history theories) Mark's own community had a turbulent history not found in the Matthean and Lucan communities.

But is this after all convincing?

Behind much that has been written about the synoptics in the past eighty years there have been two almost wholly unspoken assumptions. The first is that the period of oral transmission was relatively long; we now know, from Qumran preeminently, of quite extensive literary activity in the period. The second assumption is that in the course of some thirty to forty years there was a steady proliferation of Christian communities, mainly Gentile in origin, with sufficient sophistication to appreciate the letters of Paul, but equally subject to philanderings with all manner of specious aberrations from the primitive faith. One may question whether the Christian communities were quite so numerous as many writers assume. Tertullian's famous jibe *(Apologia* 27) about Christians having infiltrated all levels of society was made, after all, in the second century. It is obviously important to say whether one supposes, for example, that Matthew's gospel was written in Antioch in A.D. 65 or 95. In favorable circumstances, thirty years may well have given the local Christian community a chance for speedy growth. Many solutions to NT problems propounded by students of redaction history assume a long period of relative calm in which there was apparently considerable comparison of manuscripts, and considerable editing and reissuing of revised "editions," of what eventually coalesced into the present three synoptic gospels.

Whether such a period of comparative calm ever really existed is open to doubt. Conditions in Syria-Palestine in the decade preceding the outbreak of the first Jewish War in A.D. 66 were emphatically not such as to encourage the quiet academic pursuit of editing or a proliferation of manuscripts of recollected tradition. In addition, the more we discover distinctively Semitic or Jewish characteristics in the gospels, the less likely it seems that the tradition was edited for the needs of, or transformed by the pressures of, a Hellenistic community interest. Nor is it any longer possible to argue convincingly for an emergent "high christology" in John versus a simple portrait of an itinerant preacher in Mark, unless we are prepared to dismiss the evidence of the Pauline letters by the way and contend that Mark's exorcism stories are transferred from some unknown wonder-working source.

Perhaps the time has come to look once more at what the various available traditions say about Mark's gospel. A good starting point is C. F. D. Moule's provocative statement in *The Birth of the New Testament* (New York: Harper & Row, 1962) that there may be "extremely little in the New Testament later than A.D. 70" (see pp. 121-23). The same point was made in various places, and in similar terms, by the late W. F. Albright (e.g., in *History*, 1964, p. 295; and see also *From the Stone Age to Christianity*, Garden City, N.Y.: Doubleday, 1941, p. 387; and "Recent Discoveries in Palestine and the Gospel of St. John," in *The Background of the New Testament and its Eschatology: Studies in Honor of C. H. Dodd*, Cambridge University Press, 1965, pp. 160ff.). J. A. T. Robinson has again called attention to the inescapable fact that one traumatic event after the resurrection of Jesus which shaped the destiny of the Christian community is never mentioned in the NT—namely, the fall of Jerusalem in A.D. 70 *(Redating the New Testament*, Philadelphia: Fortress Press, 1976). The fall of the city and of the temple is predicted in quite unequivocal terms, even though these terms are drawn from the language of apocalyptic. The silence of the NT writings on the destruction of the city, if it had happened when the books were first shaped, is astonishing. An event so momentous, if prior to the first writing down of the oral traditions, would certainly have produced something along the general lines of "We told you so."

As it is, however, even Luke's second volume (if such Acts is) comes to an end with Paul's house imprisonment; the author is apparently unaware of anything subsequent thereto. Far more impressive is the total silence of Hebrews on the fall of Jerusalem. It is not merely that the author of that book consistently uses the present tense about the sacrificial system—that could conceivably be a kind of "Platonic" historical present. Far more important, there could hardly have been a single crisis subsequent to the ministry of Jesus which more emphatically underlined the author's main arguments (cf. Heb 8:13; 9:8 and 9) than the fall of Jerusalem and the end of temple sacrifices.

In questions of dating, it is worth paying attention to Hebrews, for not only does it fail to call attention to an event which—if it had already occurred—would be critical to the author's argument; it also embodies almost incidentally a considerably developed theological stance in regard to both the humanity and the divinity of Jesus (cf. 5:7-8; 10:32). A reference to the Apocalypse is also in order. Only two possible catastrophes can be envisaged there —either the fall of Rome at some date in the future, or the fall of Jerusalem as imminent. In the latter case, the assertion of the absence of a temple would be highly significant, and would emphasize even more strongly the silence of Hebrews.

Now, whether Mark was the first tradition committed to writing or, as this author believes, a digest of already existing documents, we are dealing with a book which preserves traditions of Jesus' predictions of the fall of Jerusalem and contains strong statements about Jesus' relationship with God along with an emphasis on his humanity. The total silence of the NT on the fall of Jerusalem was made the *terminus a quo* for his part by the late S. G. F. Brandon (see bibliography), who began with a special reference to Mark as a prior source. The thesis was, broadly, that from Mark onward the entire history of the period before A.D. 70 had been rewritten to hide the fact that Jesus and the members of the early Christian community had in their several ways been identified with the revolt which collapsed. If Brandon's contentions have been severely criticized, and even hardly accepted, he did NT scholarship a service by pointing to a significant silence in the NT writings. The simplest explanation of all—that the event had not in fact happened before the writing down—may in the end prove to be the most convincing. Even if we accept as reasonable only the hypothesis that Hebrews antedates the fall of Jerusalem, one major criterion by which judgment is brought to bear on Mark—that of Christology—assumes far less impressive proportions.

The commonly accepted dating of Mark (65-70) depends in part, if not wholly, on the assumption that the work was committed to writing after the death of Peter, or even on account of Peter's death. This by no means agrees with the assertion of Clement of Alexandria that Mark was written as an account of the Lord's doings for the benefit of those who were being taught during Peter's time in Rome (Clement of Alexandria, cited by Eusebius, *Ecclesiastical History* 6.14.6b). The sense of the quotation in Eusebius does not compel us to assume that Mark's work was done at the same time as Peter's preaching, for the same passage goes on to declare that "when Peter knew of it, he neither actively prevented nor encouraged the work." This does not sound as though Peter was in Rome at all at the time, and another quotation from Clement (in Eusebius, *Ecclesiastical History* 2.15.2) seems to preclude Peter's presence in the city: "when the apostle knew what had been done [it having been revealed to him by the spirit] he was pleased by the eagerness of the men, and ratified the writing for reading [or study, Greek *enteuxis*] in the congregations." The *Anti-Marcionite Prologue* (second century A.D.) speaks of Mark having compiled his work *post excessionem Petri,* and this is generally assumed to indicate Peter's death. Indeed, Irenaeus *(Adv Haer* 3.1.2) asserts that Mark, the "disciple and interpreter of Peter," committed to writing the things taught by Peter after the departure (Greek *exodos)* of Peter and Paul.

Even though Luke uses the word *exodos* (9:31) as "departure" in reference to Jesus' death, his use of the word is deliberately ambiguous, and quite certainly the translation "decease" of KJV is incorrect. Luke's primary reference is to *exodos* in the terms of the redemptive history of the Hebrew Bible; the identification of the word with Jesus' death as "departure" is secondary.

T. W. Manson (1962, p. 40) suggested that Peter made a visit to Rome between A.D. 55 and 60, and that Mark, who had been his interpreter on this occasion, was urged on Peter's *leaving the city* to put in order the material communicated by the apostle. This suggestion of Manson has not generally met with wide acceptance, but it is possible to link it with historical sources already at our disposal, and even to refine the dating.

Justin Martyr *(Apologia* 1.26) dates the arrival of Simon Magus in Rome in the reign of Claudius (died A.D. 54), while Eusebius *(Ecclesiastical History* 2.14.6) declares that Peter followed close upon him. In addition to this, Hippolytus *(Refutations* 6.15) maintains that Peter met Simon Magus when they were both in the city. Now Eusebius' second quotation from Clement, implying some kind of recognition by Peter of Mark's work, sounds clearly secondary to the first quotation, and does not have about it the ring of authenticity possessed by the first. But if we accept the first Clementine tradition as genuine, and put it alongside the testimony of Justin, Hippolytus, and Eusebius, then we are left with the date of A.D. 55 for the first draft of Mark's composition, assuming that Mark was persuaded to begin his editorial work when Peter left Rome.

Several things follow from this. First of all, we are free to think that Peter was not the sole, or even primary, source of the tradition treasured by the community in Rome, and that Mark and the community may have known that tradition before Peter's visit. Indeed, taken at face value, the first quotation from Clement would almost appear to imply that it was Peter's teaching in Rome which prompted demands that Mark commit the tradition to writing. Eusebius *(Ecclesiastical History* 2.15.1) makes, or appears to make, a clear distinction between the unwritten tradition and Peter's teaching. Secondly, if Mark was used by Luke and Matthew in their works, an early date of A.D. 55 would give enough time both for such use and for community-interest processes to be at work. If, as the writer of this commentary believes, Mark was derivative of Matthew and Luke, the evidence of Clement and Irenaeus is far more cogent. Mark, not himself an eyewitness of the ministry of Jesus, must have relied for information on oral tradition, just as did his first teachers and erstwhile companions Paul and Luke. Acting as Peter's interpreter provided an opportunity to hear an eyewitness at first hand; afterward, in the light of that experience and in comparison with sources already known, he could commit the tradition to writing. Thirdly, this dating prompts us to inquire why Mark is cast in the form in which we have it—brief and self-contained pericopae during the ministry, preparatory to a lengthy treatment of the passion and death of Jesus.

Admittedly Mark, as a composition derived and conflated in part from

Matthew and Luke, is not at first glance impressive. True, there are arresting examples of detail which appear to owe everything to an eyewitness account; and, significantly, nearly all of them are in the fifty or so verses which are peculiar to Mark. Assuming the traditional account of the composition of Mark to be accurate, we are entitled to ask why such a bald narrative— particularly if the author had had access to the reminiscences of Peter— should have been produced at all. It is therefore appropriate here to state the author's reasons for writing Section B of this chapter.

1. If we assume that Mark brought with him to Palestine his own composition, however much of it may have been garnered from Peter, then we suggest the situation which he found was of such urgency as to compel him to abandon any idea of publishing his own material in full.

2. We may well agree with T. A. Burkill (1972) that some Markan choice of material was dictated by a controversy over the status of Gentiles, but given the wholly changed circumstances after A.D. 70, a date and a *Sitz im Leben* for Mark prior to A.D. 70 seems to be demanded; the controversy became a dead issue thereafter.

3. The fact that Matthew and Luke were already in hand made Mark's urgent task of conflation substantially easier; his choice of materials was dictated by a rapidly worsening crisis situation.

4. Luke's adaptation of the Matthean tradition for a largely Gentile audience (compare his extension of the title "Disciple" beyond the confines of the Twelve) was too prolix for use and at the same time had largely fragmented the apocalyptic material of Matthew into other contexts.

5. Mark's Chapter 13 must be regarded as crucial to his whole enterprise.

B. The Occasion of Mark's Gospel

Assuming Mark to be a conflated digest of Matthew and Luke, it is important to inquire why the work was written at all. This question is open to discussion, initially without reference to dates.

Various suggestions have been made from time to time on the composition of the gospels in general; for example, the late Philip Carrington espoused for many years the cause of linking the composition of the gospels to a primitive Christian calendar. More recently, Daube pleaded for a closer examination of the relationship between the composition of the gospels and Jewish liturgical material. John Bowman has linked the whole of Mark to a revised Christian Jewish Passover Haggadah. Although Bowman has succeeded partially in explaining the compact and self-contained style of the pericopae in Mark, the crucial Chapter 13 is largely left out of his account—as is the swift movement of the whole gospel to the Passion narrative, which is a complete unit, can be detached from the remainder, and is *almost* a second division of the gospel.

The present writer has come to the conclusion that some recent viewpoints can accommodate both the Griesbach hypothesis on synoptic origins and an explanation of (a) the compact organization of the individual pericopae in Mark, (b) the strong note of urgency throughout the gospel, and (c) the apocalyptic material in Mark 13 as against the eschatological material in Matthew and Luke.

Theodore Weeden (1971) argues that Mark's opponents are being castigated in Chapter 13, and that 13:5-6 are meant to describe them. According to Weeden, these opponents who claimed messiahship and claimed to be the returned Jesus sustain his thesis by suggesting that for Mark the *parousia* was an extrahistorical event, cosmic, Danielic; none of the contending messiahs could qualify. Mark was compelled to provide some relationship between the *parousia* and current events, which he calls "sorrows," only the "beginning" and not "the end" mentioned in 13:3 as the goal of those who persevere and are granted salvation. Even the flight and the setting up of the abomination that makes desolate are not the end, since the *parousia* of the Son of Man can only come at the end of tribulation (v. 24). The opponents, according to Weeden, occur again in vv. 21 and 22; in v. 21 they point to others as messiah. V. 22 calls all the opponents "impostors," despite the fact that they can do wonders. They are not described as Christians, who are called "the elect." If we seek to identify these opponents of Mark, it is easy to describe them as non-Christian Jews, but it is necessary to be more precise than this. Weeden calls attention to the fact that v. 21 has "if anyone says to you . . . ," one of eight such phrases in this chapter. Weeden suggests that what is being corrected by the Passion narrative of Mark is a Hellenistic *theios anēr* Christology in the first part of the gospel. Therefore, concludes Weeden, the heretics described in Chapter 13 are *theioi andres* becoming messiahs. For Weeden, the assertion of the messianic "I am" (13:6) is of considerable importance for estimating this chapter.

Hans Conzelmann provides answers to the puzzles of Chapter 13 from a theological angle. For Conzelmann the question is how to relate the *parousia* to an imminent expectation. Therefore, for him, 13:24 represents a distinction between a historical time of final evil and the supernatural incursion of the *parousia*. In strong contrast to Willi Marxsen, Conzelmann believes that although Mark 13:1-23 is historicized, Mark did not intend the chapter as a description of contemporary events. Conzelmann does not deal specifically with vv. 5,6,22, and 23, but he notes that Mark has to deal with a current belief that the fall of the temple and of Jerusalem marked the end of the age. Conzelmann does not see vv. 1-23 as a historical outline of the experiences of Mark's community.

For Marxsen, Chapter 13 is emphatically bound up with the experiences of the community. As Jesus had passed through the cross to the triumph of resurrection, so the community would go through tribulation to the *parousia*. Marxsen seeks to identify the crisis through which the community was passing. He believes that vv. 5-6 refer to various "messiahs"—for example, John of Gischala, or Josephus, who came to prominence in the war of A.D. 66-70 (it is important for Marxsen that such messianic pretenders must be Galileans —Galilee being a center of revolutionary activity). In contrast to Conzelmann, Marxsen finds the separation of present and future at v. 14, and not at v. 24. The impostors of vv. 23 and 24 had then not appeared when the chapter was written. They would appear after the defilement of the temple (v. 14), which would heighten expectation of the end and prompt the appearance of pseudo-prophets and pseudo-messiahs. The context, then, is one in which moderates and zealots are both confronting Christian Jews about their loyalty, and in such a situation some Christian Jews might easily defect to revolutionary parties of one kind or another.

In summary, Weeden begins with problems in Hellenistic religious curiosity, and Conzelmann begins with problems posed in theology by a delayed *parousia*, while Marxsen's starting point is the problem of suffering in the community. Left out of account in this discussion is the question of dating. If one can believe with C. F. D. Moule and J. A. T. Robinson that any date after A.D. 70 is improbable, it is worth bearing in mind that nothing would have pleased sectarian Judaism better than an opportunity to say "I told you so." It is precisely this kind of talk which we find lacking in the NT material, unless we believe with J. Massyngberde Ford (AB *Revelation,* Garden City, N.Y.: Doubleday, 1975) that the last book of the NT celebrates the triumph of Rome over Jerusalem. Often neglected is the nature of the crisis posed for any Christian in the period immediately before the first Jewish War by a messianic confession linked to the proclamation of an impending Reign of God. Roman authority would find it difficult to believe protestations of a peaceful kingdom, while Jews who saw no reason to throw in their lot with the new messianic movement would wish to know how the confession of Jesus as messiah affected the loyalties of Christian Jews. From either side, the Christian Jews would find themselves under constant attack, or at least under enduring suspicion.

The first Jewish War of 66-70 had long been in the making, and it is clear from contemporary sources that by A.D. 60 many were aware that a confrontation between Rome and the Jewish desire for deliverance was inevitable.

Let us consider the interplay of three commonly held views about the making of the present Markan gospel: the tradition of Roman authorship; the tradition of Petrine reminiscences; and the common view that Chapter 13 is an important clue about the final composition of the gospel. By denying implicitly the tradition of Roman authorship, Weeden, Conzelmann, and

Marxsen can maintain Markan priority and at the same time salvage something of the old synoptic theory. It is worth asking whether some credence can be given to the old tradition of Roman authorship alongside the questions and solutions posed by the Griesbach hypothesis.

The present writer believes that Mark's *original* composition drew largely on the reminiscences of Peter, along with an already formalized passion narrative. The self-contained and highly structured pericopae of this gospel have often been commented on, but it is important to try to discover in what context these pericopae took shape. Both Carrington and Bowman produced arresting suggestions as to how this came about, but it seems that at least in the case of Carrington the hand was overplayed (cf. W. D. Davies in the Dodd *Festschrift*). The pericopae in Mark, if nowhere else, bear signs of being used as easily remembered short sections, and whatever their origin the paragraph arrangements in Codex Vaticanus need to be explained.

The suggestion here made is that Mark brought back to Palestine with him a narrative like the one in Mark 1-14. Chapter 13 is crucial. If Mark is the prior source of the synoptic written tradition and Matthew and Luke followed, it is not obvious why they managed as they did some elements of Mark 13. For example, why should Matthew transfer Mark 13:10 to Matt 24:14? The Matthean context is one whole piece, but in the Markan context this verse is oddly out of place. In our view, Mark brought with him 12:41-44, which Luke abbreviated and used, as Mark did, to open the eschatological discourse.

Again, the omission by Luke of the major thesis of Mark 13:21-23 (= Matt 24:23-25) is astonishing if he had Mark before him. If we suppose rather that Matthew and Mark, with substantially the same material, worked against a background of Palestinian ferment, then the sense of urgency for Luke, probably in Antioch, was not so marked and the material could be foreshortened to Luke 17:23. But much more than that, Luke has his own arrangement of this material in 17:22-37, removed from the passion context, and specifically concerned with the signs of the dawning Reign of God in response to the Pharisees. The sense of apocalyptic urgency is missing.

Perhaps the most illuminating example is the abbreviation in Mark of Matt 24:29-31: the "standard of The Man" (Matt 24:30) is missing, and the mourning of the tribes of the earth finds no mention. Immediately following upon the lesson of the fig tree (Matt 24:32-33 = Mark 13:28-29) comes the description of the *parousia*. Now the parable of the fig tree and the succeeding section are concerned, the first by illustration, the second by direct warning, with Israel and her response to the call of God. (N.B. the 1973 article by Derrett on fig trees, noted in the bibliography at the end of this section.) But significantly, what we have in Mark is a self-contained pericope made up of Matt 25:14-15b,24-42 (expanded), and 25:13. Whether the warnings contained here refer to a manifestation of The Man, considered as a return in glory to the scene of former ministry; to an impending catastrophic event; or in some sense to a combination of both at some distant date, it is clear that the Markan section is far more urgent in immediate warning than the Matthean version, not to mention the truncated Lucan parallel.

There seems to be no good reason for Mark to have survived at all, save on the supposition that our present gospel at least partially embodies some reminiscences of Peter. The attitude of the early Church to Mark's gospel was one of almost complete neglect. Aside from considerations of Petrine memories enshrined, what would prompt an evangelist to issue a gospel version in an environment which already had both a strong written tradition (on the Griesbach hypothesis, Matthew) and yet other traditions still circulating in oral or written form?

The material we have just examined may serve in part to answer the question. *If* the evangelist left Rome before Peter's final days there, and if too (cf. Weeden) he was in Palestine to witness the first threatening clouds of impending struggle, then it is reasonable to suppose that he found the comparative prolixity of Matthew, with its lengthy teaching sections in measured tread, lacking in urgency for a rapidly deteriorating situation. For Christians whose loyalty was soon to be put to the severest tests from both Roman and Jewish sides, what was imperative was a far shorter compendium, with narrative and teaching drastically reduced in volume, and with a note of warning decisively emphasized wherever possible. What resulted was the present gospel of Mark, with a clamorous note of urgency underlined even by grammatical usage: note the constant intrusion of *euthus,* "immediately," in the narratives of the ministry.

How far can this hypothesis be proved? At the present state of our knowledge, not at all, although there are scattered indications which tend to support it. In what follows, the author assumes the validity of the Griesbach hypothesis—the dependence of Mark on Matthew and Luke.

1. The principal parable section in Mark 4 consists of material dealing with the Reign of God directly; the "case law" parables reflecting Matthew's concern with the relationship of Jew and Gentile in the community are missing. (Mark contents himself on that issue with the healing of the pagan in 7:24-30.)

2. The miracles are all demonstrations of the irruption of God's sovereignty through Jesus, and like Matthew the evangelist repeats the "messianic banquet" motif of Chapter 6 in Chapter 8.

3. Questions about the authority of Jesus are crucial, given the abbreviated compass of Chapters 1-10, but the sum total of the teaching of Jesus is alluded to, rather than expounded at length.

4. The circumstances of composition outlined above support the view that Mark's gospel did indeed end at 16:8 and was deliberately so ordered, and that the abruptness was in line with Mark's purpose in compiling his mate-

rial. The gospel begins with no genealogy but with an abrupt introduction to
John and his mission. The reader is plunged immediately into a narrative of
conflict: the conflict between Jesus and evil, criticism, misunderstanding, misapprehension of his mission (even on the part of his followers), and finally the
crucial test, the passion. If the readers of Mark were startled by the omission
of any resurrection narrative, then they were—on the view of this commentator—meant to be startled. Were they not "terrified" like the women in 16:8?
If they knew the true "ending" of Mark's narrative, then they also knew the
true "ending" of the present distress.

In the light of all this, what of the suggestions of Weeden and Conzelmann
with which we began? They share an important insight: that this gospel was
written as a response to a situation. The view of the present writer is that the
solution of Marxsen to the problems posed by Chapter 13 is far and away the
most convincing, although it is not necessary to make Mark 13 a free composition owing almost nothing to the teaching of Jesus, nor to assume that it
was a direct response to a war already in progress. Quite to the contrary, the
political ferment in Palestine in the decade preceding the first Jewish War
(A.D. 66-70) made the condition of Christians, as sectarian Jews, increasingly
open to hostile question from patriot groups, pacifists, and Romans alike; it is
not in the least necessary to assume that Mark 13 was written against the
background of a rebellion already in being.

At the same time, Conzelmann's thesis of problems raised by a delayed
parousia appears to read far too much into the language of apocalyptic. Although Conzelmann insists that 13:1-23 was not intended to be used as an
account of contemporary events, yet he holds that the evangelist was attempting to deal with the equation between destruction of the temple and the end of
the world. Assuming the Thessalonian letters of Paul to be among the first
written by the apostle, we find (far removed from Jerusalem) considerable
doubts and hesitations being expressed by Paul's converts. Equally, assuming
Ephesians to be Pauline (though this is less clear), it is possible to trace a
steady decline in Paul's interest in *parousia*. From the questions and doubts of
2 Pet 3:3-12 to the millenarianism of the second century and beyond, the
expectation of a visible and dramatic manifestation of Jesus and his kingdom
has fascinated orthodox and heretic alike.

The difficulty posed by Weeden's attempt to penetrate behind Mark 13 lies
in a too ready assumption that the concept of *theios anēr* as an articulate facet
of religious thought was already in full flower in the first century A.D., and
further that it exercised a close-to-catastrophic influence on Christian Jews in
the second half of the first century. Not only is it impossible to speak with any
confidence of *theios anēr* as a recognizable single concept in Hellenism much
before the second century; there was also enough speculative material already
to hand in the pseudepigrapha to provide Jewish models for any number of
messianic or semimessianic figures.

In sum, the present commentator finds himself agreeing with Weeden, Conzelmann, and Marxsen that Mark was compiled in response to a conflict and crisis situation. This writer does not believe that the crisis had to do with either Hellenistic religiosity or theological investigations about the *parousia*. He does believe that Mark is an edited and conflated version of Matthew-Luke, composed in response to a situation already fraught with danger for Christian Jews—and for Gentile Christians also—before the Jewish War broke out in A.D. 66. Moreover, the sense of impending doom raised questions about the relationship of sufferings, the "birth pangs" of the Messiah, to the End; the atmosphere elicited the question: Do all these signs portend a messianic intervention? But it is not easy to believe that either Matthew or Mark composed an apocalypse in response. It is altogether likely that the ordinarily perceptive Jew, which we may take Jesus to have been, *could* have and with other models before him *would have* expressed hopes and fears for the future as early as A.D. 30, and that Matthew's tradition recorded those hopes and fears, and Mark's editing heightened them.

In his "Towards an Interpretation of the Gospel of Mark" (1971), Norman Perrin (p. 5) lists five "endings" of Mark (conclusions of sections 1:16-3:6; 3:13-6:6a; 6:7-8:22; 8:27-10:45; 11:11-12:44)—each ending, with the exception of the last, with a typical Markan summary or story. The final section ends with a twofold climax—the apocalyptic discourse and the Passion narrative—while the fourth section contains the three passion predictions (8:31; 9:31; 10:33-34) made in Caesarea Philippi, Galilee, and Capernaum on the road to Jerusalem. Perrin holds, in our view rightly, that Mark cannot be understood apart from his proleptically oriented purpose of looking to the central events in Jerusalem. "Son of God" in 1:1 is immediately reinterpreted in terms of "Son of Man," and the terms "Messiah" (8:29; 13:21) and "Son of David" (11:10; 12:35) are in context sharply contracted in meaning. With all of this we can be in substantial agreement, and agree with the author that Mark wishes his readers and/or hearers to understand Jesus in the light of the passion. We are compelled to disagree with Perrin's view that Mark's purpose is polemically directed against a false "Divine Man" miracle-working christology. If what has been argued above is correct, then the evangelist was confronting not a false christology but a gnawing and growing doubt in a steadily deteriorating situation, as to the legitimacy of the new faith and the ability of Jesus to save. If what was being hoped for was a resurgence of national existence and political future, then Mark's task was to present messiahship in the terms drastically reinterpreted by Jesus, and to present resurrection as that which came only at the end of persecution and terror.

C. Method

Granted that Mark's gospel responds to a situation for which neither Matthew nor Luke was suited, in what way did it accomplish its purpose? On the hypothesis we have adopted there ought to be firm indications that the evangelist was deliberately choosing and framing material with the following questions in mind.

1. In a worsening and darkening political situation, and with so many messianic claimants being heard, what certainty was there that Jesus was the messiah?

2. If the community was under continual pressure from both Jew and Gentile, how could people believe in the promises of the messianic age?

3. Had Jesus really ushered in the age of messianic blessings, or was there to be some infinitely prolonged time of suffering not spoken of by Jesus, or even deliberately hidden from his followers?

4. In the face of what was happening to the community, what was to be its shape in the future, i.e., was the messianic community to be Jewish or Gentile?

It can tentatively be demonstrated, though certainly not proved, that the method Mark employed was wholly adequate for his purpose, and served the embattled Palestinian community he sought to assist. We may usefully begin with two common assertions about Mark: first, that it is a gospel built around the theme of conflict, and secondly, that the whole gospel up to the Passion narrative beginning in Chapter 14 is a prologue to it. With some qualifications, we may accept the first assertion. The second, however, is dependent on the view that Mark's framework for the ministry of Jesus is in reality no framework at all, and that the individual elements of narrative and teaching in Chapters 1-13 were chosen by the evangelist as typical examples from existing material. Our contention is that the "ministry" section of Mark is highly selective and tightly organized to indicate the evangelist's concern with the four topics noted above, and that though the Passion narrative is lengthy and important it grows out of the previous section and is in no way independent of it.

Since the present writer is convinced of the persuasive character of Griesbach's hypothesis, he must indicate the manner in which the evangelist ordered his material. Nothing is more important than to discover *why* Mark chose his material in the fashion he did. First and foremost, in striking contrast to Matthew and Luke, the evangelist focuses his attention and ours on the *events* of the ministry of Jesus; the element of teaching is almost at a minimum. The emphasis on proclamation of a dying, risen messiah so characteristic of Paul and the speeches in Acts is absent. If the evangelist is deliberately concentrating on events, then it seems reasonable to suppose that his arrangement of the narrative will be an indication of his purpose. Moreover, such a supposition demands the corollary that the writer had command of material from which to make careful selection. There was always something odd about the suggestion that Mark's narrative up to Chapter 14 was simply prologue. It is true that Mark's editorial additions serve very well as an answer to the second question posed above; it is equally true that his Passion narrative, apart from such answers to questions, makes no radical departure from what he found in Matthew and Luke. We must assume that Mark's method of composition in the material preceding the passion amply demonstrates his theological concerns. This chapter will seek to prove that assumption.

Strangely, the Markan passion account lacks any direct suggestion that the death of Jesus was regarded by the evangelist as being an atoning sacrifice. If it is pleaded that 10:45 and 14:24 do carry such an implication, one should recall that 10:42-45 is found in Luke 22:25-27 in a eucharistic context, and further that Mark is less concerned with "ransom" than with the one who came to serve. Only special pleading can attach any fundamentally sacrificial meaning to the death of Jesus in Mark. The evangelist's concerns lie elsewhere. To say that for Mark the Passion narrative enshrines the account of the Servant obedient to death is not to minimize the narrative—sheer length would militate against such a judgment—but rather to assert that the narrative answers the concerns of his audience in a vital and direct fashion. It is also a judgment which carries with it the implication that the main theological thrust of the gospel must be found in Chapters 1-13.

Conflict Is Introduced: 1:1-15

Whatever interpretation we offer of the term "Son of God" in apposition to "Jesus-Messiah," the evangelist certainly understood the term to apply to Jesus. Such an assurance to his readers, preoccupied with the four questions we outlined, was vital. The assurance is followed by the introduction of John and Jesus as heralds of the eschatological age. Sealed with God's favor, and imbued with the enabling Spirit, Jesus is represented as being driven into the desert to do battle with Satan. Mark's foreshortening of the accounts he inherited allows him to see the temptation tradition simply as conflict, with a tacit assumption that Jesus emerges as victor—an assumption which is demanded in the first major section of the gospel and certainly in the exorcism stories. The victory of Jesus, actual and proleptic, ushers in a summary of

Jesus' mission. Significantly, the Community words "preach," "proclamation," "repent," and "believe" have as their object the phrase "the Kingdom of God," which is not the proclamation of the Community—it proclaimed "Jesus and the resurrection." It is of paramount importance therefore to attempt some identification of the term's meaning for Mark.

No extended treatment of the phrase "Kingdom of God" will be given in this introduction. Instead, the following notes indicate the position of this commentary on the phrase, using the instance of 1:15 as sufficient evidence.

1. There is in Mark no sharp division between "Kingdom of God" and "Kingdom of Heaven" as in Matthew, where the contrast emphasizes the distinction between the *time of the Church* and the *end-time*. For Mark, the "Kingdom of God" is all of a piece with the Kingdom of Heaven, and the evangelist refuses to follow his principal source in this area.

2. There is no way of proving that Mark intended the phrase "Kingdom of God" as an equivalent for "the Church," but this seems the most obvious sense on the basis of the connection in Mark between the Kingdom of God and the Community.

3. Unlike Matthew, Mark is not concerned with the "last things" and with the final end-time of judgment. His concern is with the Community, already under severe pressure and a sense of impending crisis. Significantly, the apocalyptic material in Mark 13 has no mention of the Kingdom of God. This Kingdom throughout the gospel is "received" and "entered"; the believer is said to be "close to" that Kingdom (9:47; 10:14 and 23; 12:34). In Chapter 4, the phrase is used three times (vv. 11,26,30), notably at a point where the evangelist is beginning to speak of the Community.

4. If we are surprised that Mark has little apparent interest in apocalyptic, then our surprise, in view of the four issues posed in the first paragraph of this section, may be due to our lack of appreciation of Mark's principal concern, the continuity of the Community. Mark's readers are not being summoned to some apocalyptic moment, but challenged to see, in the continuity of the Community, the fruits of a battle already joined in Jesus and won.

First Results of Victory: Jesus Acts: 1:16-3:35

Two pieces of tradition selected by Mark are at first sight merely "typical" incidents: the series of events at Capernaum and the introduction of the conflict-theme. This is simply first sight, and nothing more. Had Mark wished to emphasize conflict between Jesus and his critics he would surely have made more of the conflict. So too with Capernaum: Mark's interests do not lie in any specific events there. The evangelist declares his intentions in 1:34,39, for though he alludes to Jesus' teaching activity he uses no examples, and emphasizes instead the activity of Jesus in power. The whole section begins and ends with this emphasis, and the summary in 3:7-12 plainly indicates that the evangelist's concern is with the healing activity of Jesus but particularly his activity as exorcist. Moreover, between the two blocks of material Mark has inserted yet another healing story (1:40-45).

The call of the disciples in this first section finds commentators puzzled by the pericope, but we wish to maintain that the inclusion of the call was demanded by Mark's own arrangement of material. First, the Community material begins in Chapter 4, leading to the mission-charge in 6:7-12. But secondly, and far more important, the evangelist is concerned with emphasizing that the mighty power of Jesus had been handed on to the Community, and it is within that Community (and not elsewhere) that his harried audience must find confidence and strength. All of this has been accomplished by Mark's drastic editing of Matthew and Luke, his elimination of material extraneous to his purpose. (The Markan parallels to Matt 4:23-25 are instructive in this respect. The reader is invited to refer to Orchard's Chart III and to pp. 13 and 14 in Swanson's *Horizontal Line Synopsis of the Gospels* for illustrations of the point.)

So, then, Jesus performs works of power. But wherein was the source of that power? The answer lies in what appears to be another "conflict with enemies" theme; but it is hard to identify the enemies. The assumption on the part of Jesus' family that he was mad is matched by the accusation of the scribes that Jesus has an alliance with evil. But these two examples are not simple confrontations: on the contrary, the reader is now, and only now, informed of the real issue of the conflict in the desert temptations. Far from the Matthean emphasis on Jesus as the "recapitulation of Israel" in the desert, Mark gives his explanation only here. That explanation is to point to Jesus as Victor, exploiting in his own works an eschatological victory which looks to its consummation.

The Church: 4:1-8:21

Mark's purpose cannot accommodate the Matthean scheme of the body of Community teaching: the times are perilous, and already the infant Community is terrified by the onslaught of evil. The closing of the section at 3:35 points the way to the next part, where the believer who fulfills God's will is already part of the eschatological family of Jesus.

Nevertheless, this "church" section of Mark is not easy to handle: there is teaching introduced for the first time; the death of John is in this section; and there are narratives without any reference to the works of Jesus. The familiar pattern of severe curtailment of the Matthean model is evident, as again will be plain from Chart III in Orchard. But is there a single thread which binds the diverse elements together? Can we discern a central Markan motif in this disparate selection of material? We wish to maintain that there are two Markan motifs in this section of his gospel: one concerns the Church and its ambivalent position toward Judaism and the Gentiles; the other—which dominates the first—is christological. These two motifs can be summarized as follows:

1. Mark's understanding of the Church is set in the interpretation of the parable of the sower in 4:14-20—that of apparent failure and promise of a better future; however, this might differ from meanings in the Matthean context. The Church *is* the Kingdom of God. The collection of sayings in vv. 26-32 carries the same message of apparent failure as against real but hardly perceived success.

2. Mark's next transposition, from Luke, of the Matthean material brings him naturally to the mission of the disciples, and the short notes in 5:7,12ff. underline the ongoing and victorious warfare against Satan.

3. The mission of the disciples leads naturally into the first account of the feeding—allowing, that is, for a very considerable omission on the part of the evangelist of the material before him. The mission, followed by the account of the execution of John by Herod, serves, like the parable of the sower, to raise questions and provide an answer. The apparent success of the mission is followed by the disaster of John's murder. Was not this total failure of an apparently God-given message? Mark, following Matthew's order, returns immediately to the works of Jesus in the first account of the feeding. It is important here to notice that it is in this narrative that Mark inserts the "shepherd" notes from Matt 9:36, establishing the messianic shepherd theme where Matthew does not. The precise symbolism of the number "twelve" implied by Mark in this narrative is far from clear, though that number is in constant use in early Christian catacomb iconography. So far, we have a purely Jewish shepherd-messiah motif in the first feeding pericope.

4. The second feeding narrative is of a different character, however. Once again, Matthew's order provides the evangelist with his point of departure. Between the first and the second feedings there are further assertions of Jesus' ongoing victory, first over natural forces and then in healings. These are followed immediately by two crucially important pericopae: the discourse on the tradition of the elders (7:1-23) and the account of the Canaanite woman. In dealing with oral tradition as against the Torah, the evangelist can claim that the Law of Moses is inescapable because it is the Word of God, and the oral tradition (and commentary on that Law) may be set aside as necessity demands. But in that case, what was to become of the conflict between Jew and Gentile in the crisis situation already confronting the Palestinian community? (Mark's added notes at 7:3-4 are clear evidence of an increasing tension, and also evidence of a need to provide explanations for Jewish sensitivities.) Here Mark must be charged with manipulating the evidence: if the Torah was valid as an expression of God's will, then no amount of denigration of oral

METHOD 89

tradition will alter the case. Yet Mark follows the judgment of Jesus on the Pharisaic and scribal traditions with a very strained explanation in v. 19, which may be what Jesus meant. Mark has already laid the groundwork for this very difficult interpretation in vv. 8 and 13, and in this fashion can proceed with the journey of Jesus into predominantly Gentile Galilee in 7:24, here following the lead of Matthew—a lead which suits his purpose admirably. Matthew is content with "Canaanite" as a description of the woman with the possessed daughter, but it is Mark who identifies her further. Similarly, the grammatically difficult v. 31 serves only to emphasize that Jesus is ministering in Gentile territory. All in all, it is hard to escape the conclusion that Mark is deliberately heightening Matthew's account so as to put the second feeding within a Gentile context. Whether or not there ever was a second feeding, or whether Matthew originally incorporated two different traditions out of caution, we cannot know. Mark has his own purpose here, and it is straightforward enough: Gentiles will not be excluded from the messianic banquet.

5. It is from the above interpretation of the second feeding as Gentile-oriented that we can discern the meaning of Mark's condensation of the sign-seeking delegation in 8:11-13. The Matthean version does not depend on the context as heavily as does Mark's version. The only interpretation which adequately explains the incident is that the Pharisees are seeking some authoritative sign that embracing Gentiles within the compass of the messianic ministries is in accordance with the will of God.

Thus far, the discussion has been about the Community. In Mark's own time, under suspicion or attack from both Jew and Gentile, the evangelist was compelled to answer the question, "Is this Community in its present form what Jesus intended it to be?" But intertwined with that question was the other question of christology. Christology was vital for the answer to the question Christians posed about their own Community.

Mark's christology question is found in 4:41, at the end of the first miracle narrative in this part of his gospel. If the first part of the gospel introduces, and the second part affirms, an answer to the question in 4:41, it is nevertheless true that a full declaration is not undertaken until the next part. The reader, in a series of juxtaposed pericopae, is being asked to weigh the evidence fully. No facile answers will suffice. If in essence the christological answer is given at the very beginning of the work (1:21-28), Mark is aware that this is not the complete answer. Healing stories were common currency, whether credible or not. What is true of the miracle narratives in the next part is their heightened character. All the "nature" miracles are in this section: Jesus is seen expelling demons; raising a child; healing a woman merely by the touch of his clothes. "Who is this?" (4:41) is the question the reader is urged to consider. But the negative element is also strongly present in this part. Jesus is a mere craftsman, Herod has taken his measure (and can dispose of him as he has of John), and not even those closest to Jesus are able to penetrate beneath the surface of things (6:52). If the crowd can be held responsible for incomprehension at 4:12, the disciples can be equally faulted. What is startling is the linking of the failure of the disciples with their failure to grasp the true meaning of the feeding. If they cannot understand that, then *all* is failure. It is hard not to conclude that the reader, a member of a terrified community, is being asked to consider how far *he* understands the twin polarity of the section: "Who is this?" and "Can he provide for his people?" (It is well to call attention here to the healing of the demoniac in 5:1-20. Mark is faithful to the outline, for all the theological thrust of his condensations and omissions and occasional rearrangement of Matthean material. The demoniac narrative was in his sources in its present place, and it served well enough to pose again the question in 4:41, the more so in that the healed man's response was to engage in evangelization. It may even be said to provide a Gentile introduction to the second feeding narrative.)

Jesus as Example for the Church: 8:22-10:52

The vital concern of the evangelist in the whole of his work is that the members of the Community for which he is writing shall see, and see clearly, two things: who Jesus is; and what the Community must be in discipleship to its Lord. Significantly, then, this part of the gospel opens and closes with healings of the blind. Nor is the second healing without another significance: "Son of David, have pity on me." Son of David merely? Son of David, in anticipation of the entry into Jerusalem? The material in between has long been known as "discipleship" material and does not call for extended examination. The structure is interesting, and again depends on Matthean order, but the scheme is such that faithfulness to the Matthean order produces something approaching chaos in one part of the pattern.

A table of this section can be constructed as on the following page.

The first subsidiary section is certainly an inserted section, but the connections between the various parts is at first sight not obvious, and this difficulty is compounded by the severely confused and conflated state of 9:14-29. Elijah, and the identification of him with John, can be explained on the score that Elijah in his own time was persecuted and was finally vindicated. The link between the boy who was apparently dead and the material preceding—Elijah, the passion prediction—must lie in the fact that the demoniac was only apparently dead, and was raised. Mark's scheme is clear enough: the way of Jesus must be the way of the Church. Mark's use of the Matthean order has meant that so far as this first subsidiary section is concerned, the connections are not as clear as perhaps they might have been.

The intent of the scheme outlined below is simple: each passion pre-

PASSION PREDICTION SECTIONS WITH SUBSIDIARY SECTIONS

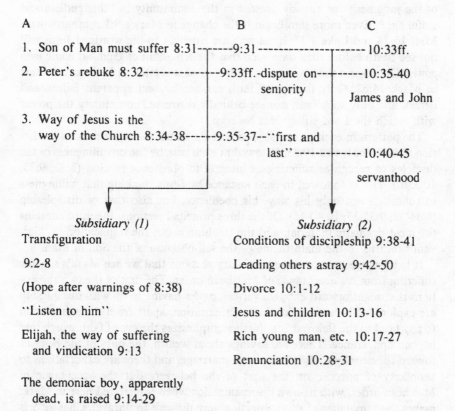

A   B   C

1. Son of Man must suffer 8:31------9:31-------------------- 10:33ff.

2. Peter's rebuke 8:32--------------9:33ff.-dispute on--------10:35-40
                                     seniority
                                                         James and John

3. Way of Jesus is the
   way of the Church 8:34-38------9:35-37--"first and
                                     last"-------------- 10:40-45

                                                         servanthood

Subsidiary (1)   *Subsidiary (2)*

Transfiguration   Conditions of discipleship 9:38-41

9:2-8   Leading others astray 9:42-50

(Hope after warnings of 8:38)   Divorce 10:1-12

"Listen to him"   Jesus and children 10:13-16

Elijah, the way of suffering   Rich young man, etc. 10:17-27
and vindication 9:13
                                     Renunciation 10:28-31
The demoniac boy, apparently
dead, is raised 9:14-29

(Conflated and confused section)

diction is followed by the inability of the disciples to understand, or even by their outright refusal to accept what they hear. Each failure of the disciples is followed by teaching on the way of the Son of Man as providing an example for the Church. The subsidiary sections appear to be designed as commentary on the preceding material.

Matthew's order has been followed, but there are significant changes in the main material. Mark 8:34 has the crowds as well as the disciples. The Community is now wider than the one for whom the discipleship sayings were first enunciated. Similarly, in 8:35 "the Proclamation" is added to Jesus as adequate motivation for the denial of self—the physical presence of Jesus has been removed, and the suffering Community must be prepared to suffer for the Proclamation which Jesus announced, and in obedience to which he too was done to death. Mark emphasizes his own immediacy here: he omits the "for what he has done" (Matt 16:27, cf. Mark 8:38) because the dividing lines of the judgment are already present in the community in "this godless and sinful age." Even more significant is the change in Mark's 9:1 compared with Matt 16:28 and Luke 9:27: some who are listening to the words of Jesus will not see death before they have seen that the Kingdom of God *has come with power.* Once again the emphasis is on *seeing,* as it is later on in the crucial text in Mark 14:62. Only the eye of faith can see beyond apparent failure and defeat, and only such faith can see behind a distressed community the power with which the Lord still guides his own.

The pattern in each principal section is the same: there is a passion prediction at 8:31, 9:31, and 10:33, followed in each case by the unwillingness of the disciples to recognize suffering as integral to obedience to God (8:32; 9:33; 10:35ff.). This is followed in each instance by Jesus teaching that willingness to submit is not only his way, his obedience, but also that of discipleship (8:34-38; 9:35-37; 10:40-45). Of the three principal sections, the third contains the most dramatic material, and the teaching about the implication of "Servant" returns to the main theme of the self-oblation of the Son of Man.

It is when we turn to these subsidiary sections that we see Mark's scheme suffering from his acceptance of Matthean order. The first of the two subsections is straightforward enough: various topics having to do with discipleship are explored. The account of the transfiguration, apart from the exhortation to pay heed to the Beloved Son, further emphasizes the eye of faith which sees beyond appearance. There are sayings about wealth, the duty of the believer toward the neophyte, and divorce and marriage, and there are exhortations to simplicity of purpose on the part of the believer. But the acceptance of Matthean order, with its own disorganization when transferred here in Mark, makes the remainder of this subsection very difficult to unravel. Chapter 9 is confused in vv. 9-13, though the meaning is clear enough, and Mark's readers would remember the account of John's death and make the necessary connections. The healing of the epileptic in vv. 14-29 is very difficult to accommodate in the present Markan scheme of "principal section followed by subsidiary section," for it is a confused narrative. (Why was the crowd amazed? And what is the point of Jesus' question at 9:16?) Mark's principal sections are self-explanatory in following Matthew's order, but by following the Matthean order in the subsidiary section the point of the main section is almost lost. Perhaps Mark made the best of the material he found—one may suspect that vv. 14-29 are a conflation of two, if not three stories—and allowed the material two implied motifs: (a) bewildered lack of faith on the part of the disciples and (b) the "rising" theme in the healing of the epileptic which underscores the "will be raised" in the passion prediction. Only one who can himself look forward to his own vindication—his "rising"—can raise others.

It is of paramount importance that we rightly evaluate the material in this section of the scheme. In any commonly accepted sense, no christology is being espoused or expounded. The sole aim of the evangelist was to emphasize the true character of discipleship, *and in so doing* to raise the question in acute form: "What kind of person can demand a suffering, obedient discipleship, and what is the outcome promised?" If the second part of the scheme raised the question only in terms of calling the inner circle, this question is now posed in its most acute form for all believers.

Judgment on Israel: 11:1-13:2

This part of Mark's scheme is concerned with Jesus' judgment on the old order, beginning with the entry into Jerusalem but focused on and in the temple. Although it has a legitimate use and has been canonized by long usage, the phrase "the cleansing of the temple" can obscure the account Mark inherited. The vivid Markan addition in 11:11 in fact served to concentrate attention on the temple rather than on the entry into Jerusalem, and the use of a quotation, so rare in Mark, even to the extent of significantly correcting Matthew—by amplification of the text—lends added emphasis. Mark's concentration on the temple is further heightened by a detail found only in his gospel at 11:16. If most commentators see in the incident a messianic assertion, for Mark the principal concern is Jesus' judgment on the temple and all it stood for, once again driving home, purely by implication, the question, "Who is this?" This is underlined by the Markan detail in 11:18—it was the judgment on the old order which caused members of the priestly party to seek Jesus' death.

The emphasis on the end of the old order is carried into the deliberate sundering of the fig tree incident (whether originally a parable or not) and the insertion of the temple incident in vv. 15-19. By this rearrangement of the Matthean order, Mark has succeeded in driving home the theme of judgment on the old order. Whether or not 11:27-33 originally belonged to the episode in the temple, Mark has left the order he found unchanged, and in so doing has underscored the dominant theme of this part: Jesus invoked divine judgment on a recalcitrant Israel. If anything more was wanted, Mark omits (if he then had access to it) Matthew's parable of the two sons (Matt 21:28-32) and proceeds immediately to the parable of the wicked tenants. The point of this parable in its present Markan context is not in danger of being lost by the intervening Matthean material, and for all Mark's determination to abbreviate, the psalm quotation is left standing in 12:10, as is also "they tried to arrest him" as an audience identification, looking back to 11:27.

If this part be considered as concluding with the judgment pronounced against the temple in 13:1-2, it must be admitted that on any documentary hypothesis which argues for the priority of Mark and attempts to discover an overall unity of purpose and method in Mark, there is no obvious purpose in the three narratives in 12:13-27. On a theory of dependence, however, it is comparatively simple to conceive of Mark leaving the order as he found it and relying on the fact that the word "scribe" in all three provided an underlying unity among the forces hostile to Jesus. The messianic question about David, together with the pericopae about the widow, simply do not fit; they have been inherited from his predecessors.

With the conclusion of this part, Mark has ended his summary-conflation of the challenge posed by the acts of Jesus, and the scene shifts from the earthly ministry of Jesus to the exalted mission of The Man. One final note is demanded here. Did Jesus intend, in the parable of the vineyard and the wicked tenants, to be understood as referring to his own impending death or to the future destruction of the temple by the Romans? The link with the death of Jesus is at best tenuous, depending on the tearing of the veil and the accusation by the Jews (deliberately branded as false) that he would destroy the temple and build another. Given the circumstances we have posed for the publication of his gospel, it is inherently probable that Mark intended to refer, like his predecessors, but with more urgency, to the imminent fall of both city and temple. As more than once urged by Albright, by the end of the fifth decade of the first century the lines were already drawn, and no particular prescience was required to see the inevitable end of Jerusalem-based Judaism.

The Community and the Future

Chapter 13 will be examined in detail in the commentary, but a short summary is provided for the sake of rounding off this part of the introduction. Mark's organization of conflated and severely condensed material has emphasized the following: in the ministry and works of Jesus, Satan has been overthrown and his empire imperiled; the chosen few have been gathered, and the conditions of discipleship laid down; official Judaism has been placed under the judgment of dissolution, and the new Community of Jew and Gentile will replace it. Jesus must now go the way of all people, to death, looking to his vindication, his "being raised." Attention must now move from the "has been" to the "will be."

Little comfort is to be found in the expectations of Mark 13, and it has already been suggested that the evangelist did indeed end his account at 16:8: "they were terrified." There are no promises, as in Matthew and Luke, of a continuing presence, aid, and sustaining power, no promise of the Spirit, no apparent relationship between the vindicated coming Man and the suffering Community. We believe that this was deliberate on Mark's part. We have seen that Mark's christology is by no means of a primitive character, and it is on this that the whole gospel depends, by implication. The bewildered and suffering Community, about to face even more severe trials, must first come to terms with the question, "Who is this?" Then, and only then, would its members be in a position to ask why, in the providence of God, such a person endured suffering, looking only to final vindication, and not expecting any dramatic intervention until his full mission was accomplished. What was true of him will be true of the messianic Community.

Bibliography

Aalen, S. "St. Luke's Gospel and the Last Chapters of 1 Enoch." *New Testament Scholar* 13.1967, pp. 1-13.

Albright, W. F. *From the Stone Age to Christianity.* Garden City, N.Y.: Doubleday, 1941.

————. *New Horizons in Biblical Research.* Oxford University Press, 1966.

————. "Recent Discoveries in Palestine and the Gospel of St. John." In *The Background of the New Testament and Its Eschatology: Essays in Honour of C. H. Dodd,* edited by W. D. Davies and D. Daube. Cambridge University Press, 1965.

Baltensweiler, H. *Die Verklärung Jesu.* Zürich: Zwingli, 1959.

Beare, Francis W. *The Earliest Records of Jesus.* Nashville: Abingdon Press, 1962.

Best, Ernest. "Mark's Preservation of the Tradition." In *L'évangile selon Marc: Tradition et rédaction,* edited by M. Sabbe. Bibliotheca ephemeridum theologicarum lovaniensium 34 (Gembloux: Duculot; Louvain: Leuven University, 1974.

————. *The Temptation and the Passion: The Marcan Soteriology.* Society for New Testament Studies Monograph Series, No. 2. New York: Cambridge University Press, 1965.

Bowman, John. *The Gospel of Mark: The New Christian Jewish Passover Haggadah.* Leiden: E. J. Brill, 1965.

Brandon, S. F. G. *The Fall of Jerusalem and the Christian Church.* London: SPCK, 1951.

Branscomb, B. H. *The Gospel of Mark.* London: Hodder & Stoughton, 1937.

Brun, Lyder. *Die Auferstehung Christi in der urchristlichen Überlieferung.* Oslo: H. Aschehoug & Co. (W. Hygaard), 1965.

Burch, Ernest W. "Tragic Action in the Second Gospel: A Study in the Narrative of Mark." *JR* 11.1931, pp. 346-58.

Burkill, T. A. "Blasphemy: St. Mark's Gospel as Damnation-History." Vol. 1 in *Christianity, Judaism and other Greco-Roman Cults: Studies for Morton Smith at Sixty,* edited by Jacob Neusner. Studies in Judaism in Late Antiquity 12. Leiden: E. J. Brill, 1975.

————. *Mysterious Revelation: An Examination of the Philosophy of St. Mark's Gospel.* Ithaca: Cornell University Press, 1963.

————. *New Light on the Earliest Gospel: Seven Markan Studies.* Ithaca and London: Cornell University Press, 1972.

Burkitt, F. C. *The Gospel History and Its Transmission.* Edinburgh: T. & T. Clark, 1906.

Busch, Friedrich. *Zum Verständnis der synoptischen Eschatologie, Markus 13 neu untersucht.* Gütersloh: Bertelsmann, 1938.

Butterworth, R. "The Composition of Mark 1-12." *HeyJour* 13.1.1972, pp. 5-26.

Carrington, Philip. *According to Mark.* Cambridge University Press, 1960.

—. *A Running Commentary on the Oldest Gospel.* New York: Cambridge University Press, 1960.

—. *The Primitive Christian Calendar: A Study in the Making of the Markan Gospel.* New York: Cambridge University Press, 1952.

Conzelmann, Hans. "Geschichte und Eschaton nach Mk. 13." *ZNW* 50.1959, pp. 212ff.

—. *The Theology of St. Luke.* Translation by Geoffrey Buswell. New York: Harper & Row, 1961.

Crossan, J. D. "A Form for Absence: The Markan Creation of Gospel." *Semeia* 12.78.1966, pp. 41-55.

Cullmann, Oscar, and Y. Menoud, P. H., eds. *Aux Sources de la tradition Chrétienne* (M. Maurice Goguel à l'occasion de son soixante-dixième anniversaire). Delachaux & Niestlé, 1950.

Daube, David. "He That Cometh" (1966 Lecture of the London Diocesan Council for Christian-Jewish Understanding). London: St. Paul's Cathedral, 1966.

—. "The Earliest Structure of the Gospels." *NTS* 5.1.1958-59, pp. 174-87.

—. *The New Testament and Rabbinic Judaism* (especially Part 2, Chaps. 8 and 9, Section 5, and Part 3, Chap. 10). University of London, Athlone Press, 1956.

Dautzenberg, A. "Zur Stellung des Markusevangeliums in der Geschichte der urchristlichen Theologie." *Kairos* 18.4.1976, pp. 282-91.

Davies, W. D. "Reflections on Archbishop Carrington's *The Primitive Christian Calendar.*" In *The Background of the New Testament and Its Eschatology: Studies in Honor of C. H. Dodd,* edited by W. D. Davies and D. Daube. Cambridge University Press, 1956, pp. 124-53.

Derrett, J. D. M. "Fig Trees in the New Testament." *HeyJour* 14.3.1973, pp. 249-65.

Dodd, C. H. *The Apostolic Preaching and Its Development.* London: Hodder & Stoughton, 1936.

—. *History and the Gospel.* London: Nisbet, 1938.

—. "The Primitive Catechism and the Sayings of Jesus." In *New Testament Essays: Studies in Memory of Thomas Walter Manson,* edited by A. J. B. Higgins, Manchester University Press, 1959, pp. 106-19.

Dungan, David L., and Cartlidge, David R. *Sourcebook of Texts for the Comparative Study of the Gospels: Literature of the Hellenistic and Roman Period Illuminating the Milieu and Character of the Gospels.* 3rd ed. Missoula, Mont.: Scholars Press, 1973.

Ebeling, H. J. *Das Messiasgeheimnis und die Botschaft des Markus-Evangelisten.* Berlin: Alfred Töpelmann, 1939.

Enz, J. J. "Exodus as a Literary Type of John." *JBL* 76.3.1957, pp. 208-15.

Fitzmyer, J. A. "Memory and Manuscript: The Origins and Transmission of the Gospel Tradition." *ThS* 23.1962, pp. 442-57.

Fuller, R. H. *The New Testament in Current Study.* New York: Scribner's, 1962.

Gerhardsson, Birger. *Memory and Manuscript: Oral Tradition and Written Transmission in Rabbinic Judaism and Early Christianity.* Acta Seminarii Neotestamentici Upsaliensis 22. Lund: Gleerup; Copenhagen: Munksgaard, 1961.

————. *Tradition and Transmission in Early Christianity.* Coniectanea Neotestamentica 20. Lund: Gleerup; Copenhagen: Munksgaard, 1964.

Goulder, M. D., and Sanderson, M. L. "Genesis in Luke." *JTS* 8.1.1957, pp. 12-30.

Grant, F. C. *The Gospels: Their Origin and Growth.* London: Faber & Faber, 1957.

Grundmann, W. *Das Evangelium nach Markus.* Berlin: Evangelische Verlagsanstalt, 1959.

Haenchen, Ernst. *Der Weg Jesu.* Berlin: Walter de Gruyter, 1968.

Hegermann, H. "Bethsaida und Gennesar. Eine traditions-und-redaktions-geschichtliche Studie zu Mc 4-8." *Judentum, Urchristum, Kirche* 1960, pp. 130-40.

Hendriks, W. M. A. "Zur Kollectionsgeschichte der Markusevangeliums." In *L'évangile selon Marc: Tradition et rédaction,* edited by M. Sabbe. Bibliotheca ephemeridum theologicarum lovaniensium 34. Gembloux: Duculot; Louvain: Leuven University, 1974, pp. 35-37.

Hoskyns, Edwyn, and Davey, F. N. *The Riddle of the New Testament.* 3rd ed. London: Faber & Faber, 1937.

Karnetzki, M. "Die Gegenwart des Freudenboten. Zur letzten Redaktion des Markus-Evangeliums." *NTS* 23.1.1976, pp. 101-8.

Keck, Leander. "The Introduction to Mark's Gospel." *NTS* 12.1965-66, pp. 352-70.

————. "Mark 3.7-12 and Mark's Christology." *JBL* 84.4.1965, pp. 341-58.

Kee. H. C. *The Community of the New Age: Studies in Mark's Gospel.* Philadelphia: Westminster Press, 1977.

————. "Mark's Gospel in Recent Research." *Int.* 32.4.1978, pp. 353-68.

Kelber, Werner H. *The Kingdom in Mark.* Philadelphia: Fortress Press, 1973.

Kiddle, M. "The Death of Jesus and the Admission of the Gentiles in St. Mark." *JTS* 35.1934, pp. 45-50.

Knigge, Heinz-Dieter. "The Meaning of Mark." *Int* 22.1968, pp. 64-66.

Knox, W. L. *The Sources of the Synoptic Gospels.* Cambridge University Press, 1953.

Koester, Helmut. "Häretiker im Urchristentum." *RGG* 3.1959, pp. 17-21.

————. "One Jesus and Four Primitive Gospels." *HTR* 61.1968, pp. 203-47.

Kuby, A. "Zur Konception des Markus-Evangeliums." *ZNW* 49.1958, pp. 52-65.

Lane, W. L. "From Historian to Theologian: Milestones in Markan Scholarship." *RevExpos* 75.4.1978, pp. 601-17.

————. "The Gospel of Mark in Current Study." *Southwestern Journal of Theology* 21.1.1978, pp. 7-21.

Lang, F. G. "Kompositionsanalyse des Markusevangeliums." *ZTK* 74.1.1977, pp. 1-24.

Lightfoot, R. H. *The Gospel Message of St. Mark.* Oxford University Press: 1962.

————. *Locality and Doctrine in the Gospels.* London: Hodder & Stoughton, 1938.

Lohmeyer, Ernst, "Die Verklärung Jesu nach dem Markus-Evangelium." *ZNW* 21.1922, pp. 185-215.

Longstaff, T. R. W. *Evidence of Conflation in Mark: A Study in the Synoptic Problem.* Dissertation. Union Theological Seminary, 1973.

Luz, Ulrich. "Das Geheimnismotiv und die Markanische Christologie." *ZNW* 56.1965, pp. 9-30.

Manek, J. "Exodus in Luke." *NovTest* 2.1.1957, pp. 8-23.

Mann, Jacob. *The Bible as Read and Preached in the Old Synagogue.* 2 vols. New York: KTAV, 1966.

Manson, T. W. *Studies in the Gospels and Epistles.* Manchester University Press, 1962.

Martin, R. P. "The Theology of Mark's Gospel." *Southwestern Journal of Theology* 21.1.1978, pp. 23-36.

Matera, F. J. "Interpreting Mark: Some Recent Theories of Redaction Criticism." *Louvain Studies* 2.1968, pp. 113-31.

Marxsen, Willi. "Mark the Evangelist: Studies on the Redaction History of the Gospel." Translation by James Boyce et al. of *Der Evangelist Markus,* 2nd ed. Göttingen: Vandenhoeck & Ruprecht, 1959.

Meye, Robert P. *Jesus and the Twelve.* Grand Rapids, Mich.: Eerdmans, 1968.

Moule, C. F. D. *The Birth of the New Testament.* New York: Harper & Row, 1962.

———. "The Intention of the Evangelists." In *New Testament Essays: Studies in Memory of Thomas Walter Manson,* edited by A. J. B. Higgins. Manchester University Press, 1959, pp. 165-80.

Nierynck, Franz. *Duality in Mark: Contributions to the Study of Markan Redaction.* Bibliotheca ephemeridum theologicarum lovaniensium 31. Gembloux: Duculot, 1972.

Perrin, Norman. "The Christology of Mark: A Study in Methodology." *JR* 51, July 1971.

———. "The Interpretation of the Gospel of Mark." *Int* 30.2.1976, pp. 115-24.

———. "Towards an Interpretation of the Gospel of Mark." In *Christology and a Modern Pilgrimage,* edited by Hans D. Betz. Claremont, Calif.: The New Testament Colloquium, 1971.

Petersen, N. R. " 'Point of View' in Mark's Narrative." *Semeia* 12.1978, pp. 97-121.

Pryke, E. J. *The Redactional Style in the Markan Gospel.* New York: Cambridge University Press, 1977.

Quesnell, Quentin. *The Mind of Mark.* Analecta Biblica No. 38. Rome: Pontifical Biblical Institute, 1969.

Radermakers, J. "L'évangile selon Marc: Structure et théologie." In *L'évangile selon Marc: Tradition et rédaction,* edited by M. Sabbe. Bibliotheca ephemeridum theologicarum lovaniensium 34. Gembloux: Duculot; Louvain: Leuven University, 1974.

Räiänen, Heikki. *Das "Messiasgeheimnis" im Markus-evangelium: Ein redaktionskritischer Versuch.* Helsinki: Finnish Exegetical Society, 1976.

Riesenfeld, Harald. *The Gospel Tradition.* Philadelphia: Fortress Press, 1970.

Rigg, H. A., Jr. "Papias on Mark." *NovTest* 1.1956, pp. 161-83.

Robinson, J. M. "The Literary Composition of Mark." In *L'évangile selon Marc: Tradition et rédaction,* edited by M. Sabbe. Bibliotheca ephemeridum theologicarum lovaniensium 34. Gembloux: Duculot; Louvain, Leuven University, 1974.

———. *The Problem of History in Mark.* SBT No. 21. Naperville, Ill.: Allenson, 1957.

Sabbe, M., ed. *L'évangile selon Marc: Tradition et rédaction.* Bibliotheca ephemeridum theologicarum lovaniensium 34. Gembloux: Duculot; Louvain: Leuven University, 1974.

Schniewind, J. *Das Evangelium nach Markus.* Göttingen: Vandenhoeck & Ruprecht, 1949.

Schweizer, Eduard. "Das Evangelium nach Markus." In *Das Neue Testament Deutsch.* Göttingen: Vandenhoeck & Ruprecht, 1968.

————. "Mark's Contribution to the Quest of the Historical Jesus." *NTS* 10.1964, pp. 421-32.

————. "Die theologische Leistung des Markus." *EvTh* 24.1964, pp. 337-55.

Schreiber, Johannes. "Die Christologie des Markusevangelium." *ZTK* 58.1961, pp. 154-83.

Simon, Ulrich. "The Problem of Biblical Narrative." *Theology* 72.1969, pp. 243-53.

————. *Story and Faith.* London: SPCK, 1975.

Taylor, V. *The Gospel According to St. Mark.* London: Macmillan; New York: St. Martin's Press, 1952, pp. 90-113.

Trocmé, Étienne. *La formation de l'évangile selon Marc.* Paris: Presses Universitaires de France, 1963.

Turner, Nigel. "Modern Issues in Biblical Studies: The Tradition of Mark's Dependence upon Peter." *ExpT* 71.9.1960, pp. 104-7.

Vajta, Vilmos. *The Gospel as History.* Philadelphia: Fortress Press, 1975.

Vassiliadis, P. "Behind Mark: Towards a Written Source." *NTS* 20.2.1974, pp. 155-60.

Vielhauer, Philip. "Erwägungen zur Christologie das Markusevangeliums." In *Zeit und Geschichte* (Bultmann Festschrift), edited by Erich Kinkler. Tübingen: J. C. B. Mohr, 1964.

Weeden, T. J. *Mark—Traditions in Conflict.* Philadelphia: Fortress Press, 1971.

Wendland, Paul. *Die hellenistisch-römische Kultur in ihren Beziehungen zu Judentum und Christentum. Die urchristlichen Literaturformen* (Handbuch zum N.T. I. 2-3), 2nd and 3rd ed. Tübingen: J. C. B. Mohr.

6. JESUS IN MARK'S GOSPEL

A. Chronology

The years since the publication of *The Problem of History in Mark* (James Robinson, 1957) have not witnessed any diminution of interest in the attempts to evaluate the element of the historical in Mark. Nowhere is this more evident than in the realm of attempted reconstructions of the life of Jesus. Such reconstructions are made more difficult, if not impossible, if based on the understanding that Mark's work was dictated by theological considerations, alongside which strictly historical or chronological elements were almost secondary. If Mark is a conflation of Matthew and Luke, as the present writer believes, and moreover a conflation prepared under the pressure of particular circumstances, then we are very unlikely to find any consistent attempt by Mark to provide a historical framework for the ministry. It does seem possible from Matthew and Luke, and with full attention to Mark, to delineate key areas of Jesus' ministry together with the response Jesus made to his ministry in the light of developing circumstances.

Jesus' ministry in all the synoptic gospels is represented as inheriting the preaching of John—involving a call to repentance in the face of the imminent Reign of God (Matt 3:1-6; Luke 3:1-6; Mark 1:1-6). Following John's testimony to Jesus (Matt 3:11-12; Luke 3:15-18; Mark 1:7-8) and Jesus' baptism by John (Matt 3:13-17; Luke 3:21-22; Mark 1:9-11), Mark drastically curtails the temptation narrative and represents Jesus as taking up John's proclamation (Matt 4:17; Mark 1:15) in the same call to repentance as John, but with the important qualification that the time had come (Mark 1:15). There is a significant new note in the account from Mark: "After John had been arrested" (1:14), Jesus went to Galilee. It is a commonplace of NT scholarship that the author of the fourth gospel knew a tradition of a ministry of Jesus in Judea and Samaria, though, like the synoptists, that evangelist concentrated his attention on the Galilean ministry. But what characterized this Judean ministry? Luke provides no help at this juncture, since we are told of Jesus' putative age when he "began his ministry" (with John?) and after the temptation narrative Jesus is said to have "returned to Galilee" (Luke 4:16), specifically to Nazareth.

The severe curtailment of the Matthean and Lucan material by Mark introduces the Markan characteristic of conflict almost at once, following the call of the first disciples: first a conflict with evil (Mark 1:21-28) and then a conflict with the interpreters of the Law (Mark 2:2-12)—both, significantly, in the context of healing. It is perhaps useful to consider whether or not, or how much of, the teaching preserved in Chapters 5-7 of Matthew belongs to a *Judean* ministry, in spite of the geographical notes about Galilee, rather than to the Galilean ministry. Obviously germane to the discussion at this point is John 4:1-3 (cf. John 4:43 and 2:12). Unfortunately we are in doubt as to how much teaching and preaching went on in Judea. Plainly, the call of the disciples in Galilee could hardly have been Jesus' first meeting with these men (cf. John 1:35-50). But was this formal call a response to a time of probation in a Judean ministry? The answer must be that we simply do not know. In the light of Matt 4-12 (= Mark 1-4), this writer has come to the conclusion that the first period of Jesus' ministry, of unknown duration and concluding with John's imprisonment, was characterized by Jesus' (and some disciples'?) carrying on of John's proclamation of repentance. Perhaps Jesus assumed that the proclamation of the Reign of God was its own authentication; however, he may have seen himself at this stage as the instrument of that reign as well as its proclaimer.

The arrest of John in Matthew and Mark clearly marked the end of a period of ministry of which we know little. Matthew speaks of Jesus having "withdrawn" into Galilee. While that part of the country, along with Judah, was subject to the jurisdiction of Herod Antipas, the Greek verb *anachōreō* often carried the meaning of "take refuge in." Jesus may have concluded that however his ministry was to be conducted in the future, the period just ended was either characterized by failure or was not the way God would usher in his reign. Matt 14:13 speaks of another "withdrawal" upon hearing news of John, though Mark 6:32 gives another reason for the retreat.

The Galilean ministry is presented to us in the synoptic gospels as a period of miracles of healing and exorcism, coupled with occasions of public preaching (mainly through parable) and of instruction provided exclusively for the inner circle of disciples. Apart from occasional geographical notes, we are unable to say whether all the incidents recorded in Mark 1-9 took place in the order in which they are presented to us, though if we assume that Matthew had the rudiments of a historical outline of events, then the evangelist follows Matthew's order. There is a further difficulty here. Whereas Mark plunges us immediately into a whole series of conflicts and mounting crises in Jesus' ministry, Luke's gospel defers the element of conflict and Matthew represents the ministry as a gradually escalating series of crises, both internal and external. Though for Matthew and Luke the final crisis is reached when Jesus puts Galilee behind him and goes to Jerusalem, Mark from the beginning compels us to regard the events in Jerusalem as but the final inevitable outcome of a crisis present at the outset of the preaching ministry. The reason for this treatment of the material has been explored already.

The third stage in the ministry (Judea and Jerusalem) is introduced by both Mark and Matthew at the transfiguration. It is here that Mark's genius as an editor is seen at its purest. Concerned only with the immediate and desperate needs of a community in trial, he omits the promise to Peter (as concerned with a continuing community) and then, with Matthew, passes from a saying about the meaning of discipleship to the transfiguration and the first prediction of the passion. The identification of the figure of The Man with suffering begins at this point in the narrative, even though the Markan material has long accustomed us to conflict in the ministry.

It is difficult to evade the conclusion that the three distinct periods of ministry as outlined for us in the synoptic gospels represent three distinct apprehensions on the part of Jesus of his vocation; they range from his identification with John's preaching of an imminent Reign of God, through Jesus' identification of the inauguration of the Reign in his own works of healing and exorcism, to the final realization by Jesus that the role of Representative Israel inevitably involved suffering and death. It is tempting to see in this three-stage ministry some connection with the threefold temptation narrative of Matthew and Luke. If indeed Jesus saw himself at the outset of his ministry as in some sense Representative Israel, then, using the Matthean narrative, the "public appeal" of John's ministry is answered by Jesus (or the response is forced upon him by circumstance) to the effect that the will of God does not lie in that direction. This identification is admittedly not very convincing, though the second temptation, and its rejection, does answer somewhat better to the second temptation in Matthew (4:5-7). Reliance on works of power, healings, and exorcisms was not the way in which God would finally declare himself. The third test is the culmination in the series in Matthew (though not in Luke) and concerns the way in which radical evil must be met. No matter how Jesus came to revise his own earlier apprehensions of his ministry, by the time he knew that he "must" go to Jerusalem (Matt 16:21, omitted by Mark, but cf. Luke 18:31) the whole character of his ministry had changed. There would still be questions to be confronted (some of which Matthew exemplified in parables: 20:1-16,21,28-32, and 33-46; 22:1-14; 24:1-30), and conflict would be heightened, but the Reign of God could only be inaugurated in a final confrontation with evil. The days of proclamation, of healing and exorcism, were over. There was no room for compromise here, and the declaration of God's overlordship of humanity carried with it humanity's oblation of itself.

Any sacrificial interpretation of the third stage of Jesus' ministry which purports to be supplied by the words and understanding of Jesus himself must necessarily depend on the view that present to the mind of Jesus, especially in the final Judean and Jerusalem period, was the vocation of the Suffering

Servant of Isaiah (42:1-4; 49:1-6; 50:4-9; 52:13-15; and particularly Chapter 53).

If Mark provides no satisfactory chronological framework in his gospel, he does offer two interpretations of the ministry of Jesus. One interpretation, that of providing for the immediate needs of a suffering community plagued with doubt, has been discussed in the previous section. The second is distinct from, but allied with, the first. The community for which the gospel was compiled had to be assured not only of a divinely promised outcome of good (because guaranteed in Jesus) but also of the cosmic significance of God's victory in Jesus. This aspect of Mark's gospel will not be examined in detail here but will be explored in the "Miracles" section in Chapter 7.

The following tabulation indicates the way in which Mark preserves the chronological development of Jesus' ministry and of the crises by which that ministry was attended.

A. *Internal Conflict*	B. *External Conflict*
1. The disciples are concerned about visible success. Jesus replies with a parable (Mark 4:1-9; cf. Matt 13:3-9): the mission must go on, regardless of results.	1. The apparent success at Capernaum (Mark 1:21-28) and the events following seem canceled by the opposition of the lawyers (Mark 2:1-12).
2. The disciples are doubtful as to how or when the kingdom will come. A parable emphasizes (a) the miraculous character of God's working and (b) the fact that the issues and results belong to God (Mark 4:30-34; cf. Matt 13:31-32; Luke 13:18-19). The immediate juxtaposition of the stilling of the storm (without Matthew's intervening material) underlines the necessity of faith. It asserts that God is in control of events, not human beings.	2. The call of a disciple (Mark 2:13) raises questions about Jesus' table fellowship with nonobservant Jews (Mark 2:15-17), his attitude toward oral law (Mark 2:23-28) and toward religious observance (Mark 2:18-22; 3:1-6). Opposition hardens.
3. Mounting opposition raises doubts among the disciples as to Jesus' consorting with nonobservant Jews. Mark includes a section on "clean" and "unclean" and the healing of the Syrophoenician's daughter.	3. The opposition spreads to Jesus' own family circles (Mark 3:20-27). Jesus demands allegiance to himself as an outward token of obedience to God's will (Mark 3:31-35).

A. *Internal Conflict*	B. *External Conflict*
	4. At the end of the ministry the breach between Jesus and the interpreters of the Law is final (Mark 12:38-40).

It is hard to determine precisely what place in this chronicle of official opposition and the disciples' doubts is occupied by the public enthusiasm of the crowds following upon the feeding narrative (6:53-56). Clearly in the fourth gospel (John 6:15) this represents a high point in the enthusiastic response of the uncommitted. It may also in its present position in Mark represent a climactic eschatological demonstration of the true nature of the ministry, before the transfiguration and the first prophecy of the passion. Here Mark is faithful to the Matthean tradition.

B. Christology in Mark

Granted the reasons proposed above for the compiling of Mark, it would seem urgent for the evangelist to substantiate his promise of ultimate deliverance by heightened claims for the person of Jesus in his gospel. For the proponent of Markan priority, there is the alleged advantage of seeing "developed" christology in Matthew over and against a more primitive strand of tradition in Mark from which both Matthew and Luke were derived. It is doubtful how far this position can be sustained. Some account must be given of the "developed" christology of the Pauline letters (for the most part, on any present showing, anterior in time to Mark). Are we to assume that Mark represents a "downgrading" of Pauline christology, a conservative reaction against it, or the preservation of the primitive tradition otherwise in danger of being overwhelmed by an enthusiastic and growing adulation of Jesus? The task of interpretation is not made easier by those who would find in Mark the conscious revolt against *theios anēr* speculation, for it is necessary to demonstrate *where* this speculation arose, and at what date. Nor does the Jewish cast of Matthew's christology support the hypothesis of Markan priority with its assumption of a "primitive" character in Mark. It was rightly pointed out by Robinson that Mark casts the ministry and message of Jesus in "cosmic" terms, and Matthew can hardly be regarded as heightening that process.

"Son" Titles Other than "The Man"

1. The only passage in the gospels where Jesus is described as son of Mary is Mark 6:3, but here the text is uncertain and even suspect. Though Jesus is not described in this gospel as "the son of Joseph" (cf. Luke 3:23, 4:23; John 1:45, 6:42), there is no statement by Mark, as there is in Matthew and Luke, of the virginal conception of Jesus.

2. On any showing, the evangelist's emphatic designation of Jesus as "Son of God" in 1:1 performs a similar service as do Matthew's and Luke's genealogies and their accounts of God's miraculous intervention in the conception of Jesus. Essentially, the evangelist is doing what John does in the prologue of his gospel, demonstrating that Jesus was Word of God in human flesh. Whether the text of Mark 1:1 is original—in whatever sense—in its present form (some manuscripts omit *Son of God),* it undergirds the whole gospel. Whether Mark understood Son of God in any Nicean and Chalcedonian sense of "divinity" is a matter of considerable doubt, aside altogether from the fact that the evangelist would hardly have recognized the terms in which those conciliar definitions were expressed. While the Davidic king is spoken of as God's "Son" in the OT, this is always in an "adoptive sense" familiar throughout the history of Near Eastern monarchies. What is not open to our inspection is how this phrase would have been understood in Hellenistic circles. Neither is it possible to determine the reason for the omission of the title in some admittedly secondary texts, unless it be by *homoioteleuton.*

3. The "sonship" of Jesus' baptism (1:11) is of crucial importance, and translations of the adjective *agapētos* (usually "beloved") may vary considerably. The tenor of the declaration is clear enough. Jesus is declared to be Messiah, however messiahship is understood. There was in the century immediately preceding the ministry of Jesus very considerable messianic speculation, and the term *"agapētos"* can bear the translation "Chosen One" or "Elect" (cf. here Isa 42:1; 45:4; 65:9 and 22). Difficulties attend any comparative use of the *Mesalē Hanoch,* the "parables" or "sayings" of Enoch, for there is no consensus among scholars as to the date or provenance of the work: it may well be either a Jewish work with Christian interpolations or a Christian work drawing on Jewish sources.[2] The work does refer to an "elect one" associated with "the elect" (cf. *1 Enoch* 37-71) but it would be idle to pretend that *Enoch* can be used unreservedly. There is a short "Elect of God" text from Qumran (4QMess ar). It is tantalizingly short, has so far failed to

---

[2] Both estimates, representing two facets of critical scholarship, must be revised in the light of the discovery of parts of *Enoch* at Qumran—though admittedly not containing the "Son of Man" sections of 37-71.

convince all scholars that the text has any messianic reference at all, and may even be considered an astrological text. J. A. Fitzmyer treats the fragment (see bibliography, p. 122) with exemplary caution, and he rightly points out that the appellation "elect" is used in the OT of David (Ps 89:3), of the Servant (Isa 42:1), and of Moses (Ps 106:23). He doubts whether the phrase in this Aramaic fragment can be regarded as in any sense messianic. He refers to the use of the title at John 1:34, where Jesus is undoubtedly Messiah. With Fitzmyer's verdict that "this represents the usual NT piling up of titles with which we are all familiar," no scholar will disagree. But whether this NT practice was solely a response of the community to the pressure of interpreting the event of Jesus in OT terms, or whether it was a development of an interpretation initiated by Jesus, is a consideration we must defer until later.

The Man/The Son of Man

The term rendered "Son of Man" in most translations has alone produced whole libraries of commentary, and all that can be attempted here is a summary of the ideas which appear to have informed the title, together with some comments on how the term is used in Mark.

Messianic expectation in the period prior to, and coincidental with, the ministry of Jesus presents a confused picture, with no easily identifiable lines of development in any one area. This being so, we ought not to be particularly surprised if the term "Son of Man" defies encapsulation. Designating a figure of prophetic authority, bearing the Word of God, the term is prominent in Ezekiel; as a surrogate term for the final vindication of God's people, it refers to the central figure in Dan 7. It is in *Enoch* that the term finds its widest variety of expression. Attention was called earlier to the widespread disagreement among scholars as to the viability of any use of *Enoch* in NT study. Insofar as we can draw conclusions from the shift in emphasis between Ezekiel and Daniel, and further in *Enoch,* we may infer that the groups which used the term in Daniel, and subsequently, looked for a more dramatic act of intervention on God's part than was represented by any future anointed king. This intervention seems to have been conceived in terms of a transcendent, semihuman, semidivine being who in *some* sense preexisted with God and to whom the term "Son of Man" was applied. (On the whole complicated concept of preexistence see R. G. Hamerton-Kelly, *Preexistence, Wisdom, and the Son of Man,* SNTS Monograph Series 21, London and New York: Cambridge University Press, 1973.)

The background of the designation "Son of Man" is historically complex (cf. S. Mowinckel, *He That Cometh,* Oxford: Blackwell, 1956) and will not be pursued here. The translation of the Aramaic *bar naša* by the Greek *huios tou anthropou* is literal, and would not have been easily understood in purely

Hellenistic circles; our own term "Son of Man" is equally an overtranslation. J. A. Fitzmyer, in his examination of the Qumran material, persuasively argued for the translation "The Man" (in *The Genesis Apocryphon of Qumran Cave 1*, Rome: Pontifical Biblical Institute, 1966) and that is our translation here.

"The Man" can be, and is, an expression which embodies whole realms of ideas—from that of an authoritative representative and spokesman to a figure encapsulating a whole people. In Mark the term is used almost wholly in a context of suffering. The notes of triumph which so characterize Matthew's use of the term and the role of judgment assigned to "The Man" in John are less strongly emphasized in Mark. Furthermore, apart from the instance in 2:10, Mark's narrative begins to use the term only after the question posed in 8:29. There are certainly good grounds for supposing that Mark's text in 2:1-12 is a composite text (cf. Taylor, pp. 191ff.). If Mark is dependent on Matthew, then there is a possible explanation for the intrusion of "The Man" in this early chapter of Mark, before the Petrine confession. Matthew does use the term before the Petrine confession, and does not give the same central place to the term. If therefore Mark is following Matthew in 2:1-12, then he has abandoned his scheme on this occasion in favor of preserving a conflict story intact.

To a large extent, the view taken by any commentator on Jesus' identification of "The Man" with suffering and death must depend on another set of considerations: namely, on what may be inferred of Jesus' education, and also on how the commentator regards that elusive quality "religious genius" as exhibited in Jesus. Of the first we have no direct information, and the tradition in Luke 2:40-52 speaks only of a growing devotion and awareness. But unless we are to dismiss the extraordinarily rich variety of quotations of, and allusions to, the Hebrew scriptures and the intertestamental literature in our sources as the work of the early community, we are bound to inquire (along with some of Jesus' listeners) whence he derived all this learning. The suggestion has been made from time to time that a period of residence among the Essenes may well have provided Jesus with both the broad scope of his eschatological language and his expectation of an imminent Reign of God. Short of some contact with sectarian Judaism, it is difficult to envisage any other source for the deep imprint in our gospels (and not least the fourth gospel) of vocabulary which appears to have been inspired by groups such as the Essenes. Any attempt to deal with the religious consciousness of Jesus must run the risk of falling into the trap of mere psychological speculation. But (with a special reference to Jesus' vital link between The Man and suffering) it is singularly difficult to accord to (for example) Joseph Smith the designation of "religious genius," in his case wholly deserved, without at the same time according the same appellation to Jesus as he is depicted in our sources.

It is important here to emphasize that there are several distinct yet related steps in the identification of The Man and suffering: the links forged between the Servant of Isa 42-53 in 4 Esdras and *1 Enoch* (the Ethiopic text) are not to be dismissed lightly, as the following tabulation should make clear.

Light to the peoples	Isa 42:6; 49:6	*Enoch* 48:4
the "elect" or "Chosen One"	42:1	39:6; 40:5, et al.
The Righteous One	53:11	38:2; 53:6
named before creation	49:1	48:3
hidden, known to God	49:2	48:6; 62:7
kings will serve him	49:7; 52:13-15	46:4ff.; 62:1
The Man is "my servant" and is "being preserved"	49:2	4 Esdras 13:32,37,52; 14:9

The fact that the term "The Righteous One" is preserved in several important contexts in the NT (Acts 7:52, 22:14; 1 John 2:1, obscured in most English versions; 1 Pet 3:18), along with an important reference in Matt 10:41, suggests that the connection between the roles of "The Man" and "the Servant" in *Enoch* was an important factor in forming the vocabulary attributed to Jesus in the Passion sayings. (Heb 10:37,38 joins "The Righteous One" and "The Elect One" in a pastiche of quotations including Hab 2:4.) "The Righteous One" as a technical term is also found in the Qumran *Hôdāyôt (Thanksgiving Psalms,* 1QH), and lines 14-17 in an unpublished translation prepared by the late W. F. Albright and the present commentator can be rendered as follows:

> Thou alone didst create the Righteous One
> and from the womb thou hast prepared him (or made him ready)
> for the time of favor
> to be kept in thy covenant
> and walk in all (thy ways)
> and to forgive him with thy many mercies
> and to relieve all the distress of his soul
> for eternal salvation and for everlasting salvation
> without lack of anything
> and thou hast singled out a herald to bring in
> glad news of his glory.

(The "herald" occurs again in 18, line 13.) What is of moment here is the non-Essene character of the *Thanksgiving Psalms,* and the predestinarian character of much of the material would have been equally at home among the Sadducees. Despite the fact that the Wisdom of Solomon is known to us only in Greek, some writers have hazarded the guess that Aramaic or Syriac sources underlie the use of *Dikaios* in (at least) Chapter 2. It is interesting that The Righteous One is described, and his actions spelled out, in the same fashion as the descriptions of the Right Guide in the Qumran literature.

A recognition of the links between Daniel, *Enoch,* and the *Thanksgiving Psalms,* together with the persistent occurrence of The Righteous One as a figure from 2 Isaiah through Wisdom and Qumran is enough to suggest that a knowledge of speculative Jewish literature would have provided Jesus with ample material with which to make the connection between the apocalyptic Son of Man and the inevitability of suffering. The same speculative questions are at work in the Servant Songs of 2 Isaiah, in Daniel, *Enoch,* the *Thanksgiving Psalms,* and 4 Esdras, to name the principal sources, and all the questions concern either the identity of God's intervening agent or the means by which such intervention will accomplish salvation for Israel.

It is well to attempt to disarm one possible criticism at this juncture. Although it is true that the fragments of *Enoch* discovered so far at Qumran do not contain any of the vital "Son of Man" material in *Enoch* 37-71, the fragments do indicate that *Enoch* was acceptable material there. Furthermore, the absence of any specifically Christian overtones, e.g., references to redemptive suffering, in the section in question—overtones which cloud all debate on the *Testaments of the Twelve Patriarchs*—gives good reason to think it legitimate to use the *Enoch* materials.

The passion predictions will be dealt with in their proper place in the commentary; here it must suffice to make one observation. Aside from a first-century social and political climate in which any proclamation of an imminent Reign of God would involve the proclaimer in a violent conflict with one group or another, there are more than enough references to suffering *apart from* passion predictions to suggest that Jesus should have seen his ministry ending in violence and bloodshed. *In themselves,* predictions of suffering and even of violent death were in the circumstances not remarkable. What is noteworthy and arresting is the interpretation given to the specific passion predictions. It is the contention of this commentary that such interpretation was the result of meditation on the roles of Son of Man, Elect One, and Servant in the "canonical" and deuterocanonical sources. Present and future in the role of Son of Man are interwoven in our sources, and Mark is no exception.

The Son of Man sayings in the third person have caused much difficulty to commentators; the suggestion is often made that such third-person usage casts serious doubt upon Jesus' identification of himself with the apocalyptic future Son of Man. It is doubtful whether such skepticism is soundly based. Although the Aramaic phrase does not mean "I," this is not to say that in some instances it could not have been substituted for "I" in the gospel tradition; wherever this might have been done, the association of Son of Man both with the end-time and with suffering is so deeply rooted in our sources that community editing is highly unlikely. The term in our gospels is never found on anyone's lips apart from Jesus (except John 12:34, where the term is being thrown back to Jesus as a challenge). At no time is the term used in any statement made *about* Jesus, whether in the confessional sense or not. The early Christian community, apart from the saying attributed to Stephen in Acts 7:56, did not use the term, although the Pauline contrasts of Adam-Jesus, First Man-Last Man, certainly imply a knowledge of the term. Yet the term was eschewed by the early Christians as open to misunderstanding (no Greek could have been faulted for understanding the term as "somebody's son"), and its retention in the gospels can only be explained adequately on the ground that "The Man" was embedded in the sayings tradition from the beginning and in some sense goes back to Jesus himself. The usage attributed to Jesus in our gospels can be tabulated as follows:

1. Nowhere is there any indication that Jesus saw himself as forerunner to another "Coming One" (cf. Matt 11:5ff.), and the claim to be fulfiller, deeply embedded in the Pauline letters, would appear to rule out the possibility of another Coming One.

2. Apart from any links with sectarian and deuterocanonical literature, the term ultimately rests in biblical sources in Dan 7, and there are other instances of sayings dependent on Dan 7: for example, Luke 12:32 (cf. the use of *basileia,* "kingdom," in Dan 7:18-27); Matt 19:28 (cf. Luke 22:28,30)—compare the use of *thronoi,* "thrones," in Dan 7:9 and *kritērion* in Dan 7:10. This does not exhaust Dan 7 as a source; the plural *ouranoi,* "heavens," occurs again only at Luke 22:69 and in the so-called speech of Stephen at Acts 7:56 (cf. Dan 7:13).

3. As will be indicated in the commentary, Daniel plays an important part in the apocalyptic Mark 13, and hence the influence of Daniel is by no means confined to Son of Man sayings.

4. It has been claimed that at no point in the gospels is any connection made between the Reign of God and The Man, that the two concepts stand side by side, and that links between them were made only in the course of compilation and redaction. By way of demonstration, the following passages are adduced: Matt 10:7-23 (Mark 8:38-9:1; Luke 17:21-22); Matt 13:37, 13:43; Luke 21:27, 21:31; and Matt 25:31-34. This claim is far too sweeping. To assert that the preaching of Jesus was that of the Eschatological Prophet proclaiming the Reign of God, and that the association of the proclamation with The Man sayings is the work of the community, is to ignore two considerations: first, the literature of Judaism immediately prior to Jesus, especially in sectarian speculation, was characterized by a similar dissociation between Son of Man speculation on the one hand and an eschatological dream of a Reign of God on the other; secondly, the sayings of Jesus concerned with the suffering Son of Man are, on the most critical analysis, so integral a part of

the primitive tradition that we are bound to associate them also with the person who proclaimed an imminent Reign of God.

5. If the proclamation of the Reign of God is to be understood as a rallying point of hope for the future, and therefore as appealing to an expectation known and understood in a variety of ways to Judaism in the time of Jesus, then it must be noted that "The Man" was a far more esoteric term than was "Reign of God," no matter how much eschatological and apocalyptic hope it might have shared with the concept of Reign of God. A further note should be added. Jesus is consistently represented in our sources as addressing his public preaching and teaching to the *crowds* under the term "Reign of God," while the use of "Son of Man" is reserved for private teaching to the disciples. (Attention was called to this distinction between audiences in the AB *Matthew*, pp. cxxxviiff.) Unless this distinction is kept in mind, the proximity of the two terms in Luke 17:20,24 will lead to the confusion inherent in the critical claim discussed in paragraph 4 above. So far as Mark is concerned, the covert character of the Son of Man sayings is only made overt in Jesus' examination before the Council (14:62). One apparent exception (8:38) is discussed in the commentary.

6. As already noted, Jesus' sayings may be legitimately seen as inferring that he saw himself as forerunner to a future Son of Man. But now we are in a position to carry the examination further. The juxtaposed "I" and "The Man" in Luke 12:8 have been cited by some as an example of the complete distinction between Jesus and the Son of Man. But the parallel Matt 10:32 has "I" in place of Luke's "Son of Man," and on almost every grammatical score the Matthean version is earlier. Some other parallels are instructive here: Matt 10:32 = Luke 12:8; Mark 14:62 = Luke 22:69; Matt 19:28 = Luke 22:28-30. It is possible that the early written tradition changed some sayings from "I" to "The Man" and vice versa, but any such attempted exercise inevitably brings us back to the hidden agenda of synoptic relationships.

7. Whatever else has been manifested during the course of the past thirty years, it has been established beyond question that "messianic expectation" (a term covering also anticipated salvific intervention by God) in the century anterior to the ministry of Jesus cannot be confined in any single easily identifiable pattern. Some of the facets of this kind of expectation have already been briefly examined. Once admit the "religious genius" of Jesus in seeing connections between the Elect One, the Righteous One, the Servant, and The Man, and the way is open to yet another interpretation which Jesus gave to the last of these. Jesus in private teaching makes a firm distinction between Son-of-Man-Present and Son-of-Man-Future. He is not yet The Man, but he will be in the glory of vindication. He therefore speaks of himself proleptically in The Man sayings which have to do with anticipated passion and death. This facet of interpretation ought not to occasion any surprise. Paul refers to, and by

implication gives assent to, one commonly accepted current of opinion about messiahship: that the identity of the messiah would not be known until his assumption to God (Rom 1:3-4).

8. One final question remains to be examined, i.e., the manner in which Jesus is represented as speaking of the "coming" of the Son of Man. It has for some years been fashionable in certain critical circles to dismiss the realized eschatology of C. H. Dodd and to ignore the impressive accumulation of data and interpretation in J. A. T. Robinson's *Jesus and His Coming*. The crucial phenomena are the usage of two Greek words: *parousia,* literally "presence, manifestation," and *erchesthai,* "to come." This very complicated question was examined to some extent in *Matthew* (Anchor Bible, Introduction, pp. xcviiff., with particular reference to Dan 7:13), to which the reader is referred. The feature peculiar to Matthew is the word *parousia* (Matt 24:3,27,37,39). It would be hazardous to conclude that the word necessarily carries an implication in Matthew of the "return" of Jesus in glory to the Christian community or to the world at large. The usage of *parousia* in Matt 24:3 may be editorial, but its use in vv. 37 and 39 seems best understood in terms of the end-time, when the continuing kingdom of The Man is summoned to judgment, and given up by him to the Father. Mark 14:62 will be examined in the commentary proper, particularly as it compares with the other synoptic texts. However, it is important to recognize at this juncture the faithfulness of our sources to the traditions of Judaism as we presently know them.

Whether the term "The Man" is to be understood in terms of "corporate identity" (cf. T. W. Manson, 1935, pp. 211ff.; ibid., "The Son of Man in Daniel, Enoch, and the Gospels," *BJRL* 32.1949, pp. 171ff.) or as an ideal figure, it is clear that there was no tradition in Judaism (sectarian or otherwise) of a *descent* of The Man in glory from the heavens. It is in this light that Mark's use of *erchesthai* must be evaluated. So far as our present knowledge goes, Dan 7:13 is the seminal passage from which all speculative writing concerning the Son of Man grew, and which Albright and the present writer render (AB *Matthew,* p. xcvii and n. 17) as "And behold on the clouds how The Man was coming!" The one who is truly The Man comes *to* the Lord of Time; this is the only "coming" known to Jewish tradition before and during the time of Jesus. If we must speak in terms of "movement" in considering the texts concerning The Man in glory, then the text in Daniel, together with the *Enoch* material, speaks of a movement *upward,* to God. Whence, then, came the element of a "downward" movement, particularly associated with *parousia* in the Pauline letters (see especially 1 Thess 4:16)? Perhaps some understanding of this Pauline emphasis on *parousia* as "return" can be found in the nature of sayings about The Man in such passages as Matt 24:27 (cf. Luke 17:24), 37, and 39 (cf. Luke 17:26); Luke 17:30; Mark 13:26 (cf. John 1:51) and 13:27, to mention a few eschatological sayings. The assumption underlying all the sayings is that the prophecy of Dan 7:13 will be fulfilled *when the sufferings of the community have reached a point of crisis.* The association of a suffering people with The Man in Dan 7 is of critical importance here. If therefore the persecution which follows the death of Stephen, together with the hardening of opposition to the community in Jerusalem, persuaded Paul that the "coming" of The Man was *not* coincidental with his resurrection-exaltation, then it is possible that here we have some explanation for the strong emphasis on *parousia* as "return." One should add, however, that in the Pauline letters subsequent to 1 and 2 Thessalonians—if one accepts Ephesians as even in part genuinely Pauline—the emphasis on *parousia* diminishes to the vanishing point.

It was left to the early Church to coin the phrase "Second Coming." With the legitimacy or otherwise of that expression, and with its virtual canonization in the credal statements of the Council of Nicea in A.D. 325, we are not here concerned. Suffice it to say that this commentator finds no adequate grounds for a "descent" of The Man from exaltation glory in our earliest gospel traditions.

It will be plain in the course of the commentary how deeply indebted is the writer to the work of M. D. Hooker *(The Son of Man in Mark,* London: SPCK, 1957), but nothing would excuse the writer's failure to advise his readers of his own interpretation of the material. In summary, therefore, the present writer finds:

1. The difficulty of making any firm distinction between the individual and the corporate in Dan 7—on any showing the *terminus a quo* of all such material in later writing—must also make for hesitation in assuming too easily that the term "Son of Man" in our gospels is always exclusively individual.

2. This hesitation is reinforced when considered alongside the variations in usage between the "Righteous One" and "righteous ones" in Wis 2 and 3, and the use of the singular in Qumran 1QH, the *Thanksgiving Psalms.* The same singular/plural interchange with regard to the righteous is also found in *Enoch,* and though the "Elect One" of 4QMess from Qumran is a single figure, in all instances so far known to us the salvific figure of The Man, the Righteous One, or the Elect One always involves in some fashion or other the fortunes of a community of adherents or disciples.

3. The present writer remains unimpressed by arguments that Jesus could not have used, or did not use, the term "The Man" either of himself alone or in association with his followers. Aside from the use of the term for an "authority" figure in Ezekiel, the only convincing interpretation of the temptation narratives in Matthew and Luke requires the belief that Jesus envisaged his ministry as reliving the whole spiritual experience of Israel (cf. AB *Matthew,* pp. 35 and 36). If Jesus so understood his ministry and regarded himself as at least the herald and prophet of the eschatological age, there

would be nothing improbable (in the light of the intertestamental literature) in his appropriating to himself and the infant community a title which referred to both suffering and vindication.

4. The tendency on the part of some commentators to find in the early Christian community the source of The Man sayings must inevitably face questions as to the theological and religious sophistication of the early community, not to mention the date of the original sources, and must also deny to Jesus any new religious insights. Apart from the raising of Jesus from the dead, this last consideration leads the present writer to some skepticism as to how the early community could possibly have survived. If the title was a retrojection to the original sources, we are entitled to ask why some care was not taken to perpetuate the title elsewhere, notably in Acts. We may reasonably ask further why Paul, who could be counted upon to know the term well enough, sedulously avoided it and used *Christos* instead, certainly as obscure in meaning to Greeks as "The Man."

5. The present writer, in common with many of his British colleagues, holds in the main to a "realized eschatology" and finds the attempted "proleptic Son of Man" in R. H. Fuller *(The Mission and Achievement,* London: SCM, 1954, pp. 95-108) untenable. To be sure, Fuller has recently refined substantially his own earlier approach (cf. *The Foundations of New Testament Christology,* New York: Scribner's, 1965, p. 112). It is difficult to see how the former position can be sustained, though admittedly it solved some of the questions raised by an apparent *parousia* interpretation for The Man sayings. But in no place in the gospels does The Man appear as one "yet-to-be-designated." To the contrary, all the sayings which speak of vindication speak of the vindication of one who is now The Man. Moreover, the "coming" of The Man is bound up in our sources with the inauguration of the Reign of God, and no room is left for any interim period between that proclamation and the coming of the Son of Man. Apart from the puzzling exception of Acts 7:52, the NT writers outside the gospels used terms other than "The Man," apparently as being more appropriate to the Son-of-Man-now-exalted.

6. The text in Dan 7:13 provides us with a figure of The Man who is vindicated, representative of his persecuted but now victorious followers, and leaves no room for a figure who is hidden-though-designated and who will in some future manifestation come *from* the Father.

The Messiah

The comparative rarity of the term "Messiah/*Christos*" in the synoptic gospels is noticeable, especially since the word is used so often in the Pauline letters. It is a commonplace among scholars to suggest that its absence in the synoptic gospels, or the paucity of references to the use of the term by Jesus, was dictated by the political and even revolutionary overtones which the word carried in his own time. Questions may be raised as to how persuasive this argument is. Essene literature and beliefs were known to considerable numbers of people, and for all the revolutionary character of some of the literature in terms of messianic expectation, the Essenes were not the objects of political hostility before A.D. 66, nor were they the leaders of any popular, enthusiastic political movement.

In the synoptic gospels (Matt 22:42, Mark 12:35, Luke 20:41), Jesus either dismisses the Davidic messiahship as peripheral to interpretation of his own ministry, or casts doubt on it as too confining. While the injunction to silence about messiahship in Mark 8:30 (cf. Matt 16:20, Luke 9:21) may be regarded as safeguarding the ministry from premature disclosure and misunderstood interpretation, our gospel sources seem to reflect an attitude on the part of Jesus which sought the interpretation of his vocation and ministry rather in terms of the Servant-Chosen One-The Man as far more embracing than any other figure.

The wide use of *Christos* in Paul, in the light of the synoptic usage, demands more questioning than it commonly receives. The term must have been as unintelligible to pagan Greeks as the phrase *huios tou anthrōpou,* "Son of Man," and though Paul certainly knew the latter term, we may reasonably inquire about the background of the majority of his congregations if he could use the term *Christos* so freely. The Pauline letters demand an understanding of Judaism and of scripture which militates against any suggestion that his congregations were overwhelmingly Gentile. We may reasonably infer that in the beginning of Paul's ministry the majority of Paul's converts were either Jews or Gentile God-fearers, for whom the speculative literature of Palestinian Judaism was either alien or unknown but by whom the Septuagintal *Christos* was well understood.

Supposed Contributions from the World of Hellenism

Confident assertions about what Mark did with his sources are meaningless unless the common assumption of Markan priority is abandoned. On that assumption, we have no evidence whatsoever as to sources. On the face of it, Mark's gospel presents us with a man who performed great and notable acts of power, though usually in response to faith and trust on the part of those for whom the acts were done. To construct from this apparent slender framework a deceptively imposing edifice of speculation as to the manner in which Mark transformed, or gave new theological dimensions to, the tradition is an exercise of questionable value.

One of the ideas often presented for inspection is that of the Markan transformation of the *theios anēr* motif, alluded to above. Here it must suffice to say that, even allowing a certain range of distribution of the term *theios anēr* in the first century of the Christian era, the proponents of this understanding of the Markan handling of the tradition must inform us more precisely of the extent to which such a category was immediately recognizable as a single identifiable phenomenon. The steps by which the wonder-worker *(thaumaturge)*, a type supposedly instantly recognizable in the Hellenistic world, was transformed by Mark into the humble Servant cannot, for all the special pleading, be identified unless (on the usual Markan priority theory) we are in possession of anterior sources. But the picture is far more complex than this. Even granted this transformation at the hands of Mark, enough of the tradition has been left with us to give us the phenomenon of a wonder-worker who commanded the beneficiaries of his works to be silent and who, so far from advertising his claims, shrank from public acclamation. Above all, in Mark (who is so often cast in the role of the transforming theologian) the humility of the *thaumaturge* is complicated by the linking of his works with the imminent Reign of God. We may suspect that any instant recognition of Jesus as a *thaumaturge* by the Hellenistic world would have been highly problematic. A recent and balanced study of the famous wonder-worker Apollonius of Tyana does nothing to revise this estimate. (Cf. G. Petzke, *Die Traditionem über Apollonius von Tyana und Das Neue Testament: Studia ad Corpus Hellenisticum Nov. Test. I.* Leiden: E. J. Brill, 1970.) We must conclude that the person and ministry of Jesus would have frustrated any easy categorization by anyone expecting to find yet another "divine man" with miraculous powers. Certainly the evidence in our synoptic gospels suggests that Jerusalem-centered Judaism found Jesus a constant and irritating enigma.

Lord

We are on no easier ground in dealing with the Greek *kurios,* "Lord." Bousset was originally responsible for the view that while Jesus may have been addressed in Syria-Palestine as *mar,* "Master" (cf. 1 Cor 16:22), it was only within the wider framework of Hellenism that the invocation *kurios,* "Lord," was possible—an invocation which had its roots in Hellenistic salvation religions. This view, in which Bousset was followed by Hahn, can no longer stand. Not only does the Qumran material (particularly IQapGen, the *Genesis Apocryphon)* show that *mar* could be used as a form of address for God himself; it could also be used of pagan gods as well as of human masters and teachers. The Greek *kurios* was familiar enough to Greek-speaking Jews as an appellation for deity, as attested by Josephus and Philo (Josephus, *Antiquities* 5.121; Philo Judaeus, *De Mutatione Nom.* 3.11ff.).

The Septuagint quotations in the NT are evidence of the use of *kurios* for Yahweh, the name of God. It has been objected by Conzelmann that Septuagint quotations in the NT are not wholly reliable evidence, since all early complete editions of the Septuagint are of Christian origin, and other methods of representing the divine name are known to us from Jewish sources. (See Conzelmann, *Grundriss der Theologie*, pp. 102ff.; English Translation, pp. 83ff.) Such an objection depends in the end on a dating which would allow quite substantial rewriting of the Septuagint for specifically Christian ends, and it may be doubted whether the physical circumstances existed for such an enterprise between A.D. 64 and 130. (See also K. Berger, "Die königlichen Messiastraditionem des Neuen Testaments," *NTS* 20.1.1973-74, pp. 1-44.)

The problem is to relate these phenomena to the NT writings, and especially to the gospel traditions, without in some fashion invoking later christological definitions like those of Nicea and Chalcedon. If *mar* was a human title, so too was *kurios,* and the vocative *kurie* was the equivalent of our "sir." The Aramaic liturgical formula in 1 Cor 16:22 cannot be anything save an invocation of Jesus, however construed (cf. W. F. Albright and C. S. Mann, "Two Texts in I Corinthians," *NTS* 16.1969-70, pp. 271-76)—an invocation, moreover, such as might be addressed to a divinity. When we urge that the use of *kurios* carries with it a suggestion of divinity, especially in phrases such as *Kurios Iēsous,* we must avoid the temptation to read conciliar definitions into the NT writings. For the phrase "Jesus-Messiah is Lord, to the glory of God the Father" (Phil 2:11) may mean simply that Jesus is Lord of the community he founded. The hymn in any case is an ascription of praise to the Father, not to Jesus.

In Mark's gospel, *kurios* is applied to Jesus far less frequently than it is in Matthew and Luke. In Mark 2:28, it probably means "Master" of the Sabbath, though this is certainly a substantial claim, while in 5:19 almost certainly the term is applied to the Father. Instances of *kurios* at 7:28 and 11:3 do not appear to mean more than "sir" or "master," though 11:3 could be read as referring to a demand of God upon a lender's property. Mark 11:9, a partial quotation from Ps 118:26, certainly refers to God, as do the quotations in 12:11,29,30,36, while 13:20 quite certainly refers to the Father and not to Jesus. Two instances in the concluding part of Mark 16 do apply to Jesus, but they appear to be out of character with what we have so far seen of Mark's usage, and the passage is of doubtful authenticity.

Conclusions

What can be said with anything approaching certainty about the way in which Jesus regarded his own person and ministry? The majority view holds that any attempt at retrieval of the human consciousness of Jesus results only in minimal success. Yet some impressive inferences from the synoptic mate-

rial are possible, making the transition from the oral tradition of Jesus' sayings to the christological statements of Paul somewhat less startling. To begin
with, any dating of the synoptic material earlier than, say, A.D. 80 leaves a
very short time-span for a whole "school" of interpreters to bring together
diverse literature of a sectarian and nonsectarian messianic character and
weave its many elements into a convincing pattern in and around the sayings
of Jesus. As an achievement, this would be impressive at any time, but our
knowledge of social and political conditions in Syria-Palestine at any time
after A.D. 62 makes such a process inconceivable. Furthermore, one must ask
precisely what kind of audience was intended to be the recipient of material
so heavily saturated with allusion and half-allusion to specifically Jewish literature, some of which has only been clarified for us since 1947. Again, what is
so impressive and so startling is to find so many titles and matching strands of
expectations, drawn together in the synoptic material and reinterpreted, all
treated as substantiating a short public ministry.

Surpassing all the expectations gathered around the person and ministry of
Jesus must be the way in which Jesus identified himself and his mission with
the totality of Israel and its mission. This is nowhere more demonstrable than
in the temptation narratives in Matthew and Luke (cf. AB *Matthew*, pp. 30-
37, and J. A. T. Robinson, "The Temptations," in *TNTS*). That Mark was
aware of a far more detailed written tradition than his own brief account
encompasses (1:12-13) is clear from the vocabulary he uses. We would be
missing the point if we did not take notice that Matthew's highly selective
vocabulary in his first two temptation narratives uses the word "desert"—and
for Israel the desert experience was the formative period of the espousals with
Yahweh, the Covenant, and above all the test of faithfulness to the demand of
God. In the temptation stories of Matthew and Luke, the quotations from
Deuteronomy are crucial: Israel as the child of God failed to respond to
God's demand; Jesus as the Chosen One responds perfectly at every point
where Israel did not. Unless we are to suppose that the temptation narrative
is an invention of the early community, we must also find significance in the
emphasis placed upon the obedience of Jesus in the Pauline writings, in 1
Peter, and above all in Hebrews. Linked with that obedience, both in Paul
and in Hebrews, is the sinlessness of Jesus, which in OT terms meant embracing the will of God without reservation. Here again we have an emphasis on
the role of Jesus as the representative of Israel. This could be expanded—as,
even more, could the comment—by examining at length the concept of the
Servant-Righteous One of Isa 53:11 as the dominant redemptive theme underlying Jesus' ministry, which would have to be balanced against the representative character of The Man in Dan 7:13 insofar as this illuminates the
theme. Here again, the triumph of the representative of Israel in Daniel glides
easily into the world-dominating figure depicted in *Enoch* and characteristic
of the passages about The Man-in-Judgment in Matthew.

What is so signally distinctive in this combination of notes of expectation is not so much that they concentrate on the single person of Jesus, but that their significance is seen to extend beyond the confines of Israel. It is a truism of Pauline studies that the apostle arrived at his theme of the universality of God's redemptive act in Jesus through his conviction of the universality of sin. But is this the best statement of the matter? Paul's concern for what he "received" from the tradition persuades us to look again at the ministry of Jesus, and the way in which the biblical tradition finds expression there. "Messianism" is almost insignificant when set alongside the way in which the ministry of Jesus encompasses the whole vocation of the Israel of God and responds to that vocation in total submission. It is important, then, to take into account the special nature of Israel's vocation, epitomized by Ps 8, its classical expression in the OT: Israel is intended to stand for and encapsulate the human race in quasi-priestly fashion. It makes no difference that the vocation expressed in the Servant Songs of Second Isaiah gave way to the nationalism of Third Isaiah (Isa 60) or to the fierce pride of Nehemiah—the tradition of that vocation is of the essence of biblical faith. This being so, the role of Jesus as the representative of Israel assumes dimensions far beyond the confines of Israel. It is small wonder that Paul transforms the concept of The Man through the universalism of Ps 8 and links it to Jesus, finding ultimately that he can only express the tradition in terms of the first and last Adams.

This "encapsulation" of various expectations in the person of Jesus within the gospel tradition is impressive, but pales in significance when compared with the notion of Jesus as identifying all humanity with himself. Once again, we would be bound to inquire how long this process took *if* we deny that the identification was in *some* measure made by Jesus himself, even if by allusion and implication rather than direct assertion. For all the pivotal place occupied by the Right Guide in the Qumran writings, there is no suggestion that he was regarded as being in any sense the focus and fulfillment of the various forms of expectation expressed by the Essenes. There is nothing remotely resembling the claim that in the Right Guide was to be found Representative Man.

A final point remains to be made in this section. It has been many times suggested that Jesus envisaged himself as the Prophet of the End-Time (Cullmann, 1959, Part I, Section 2). The role of the Eschatological Prophet in Judaism fails to explain why Jesus came to be seen as the agent of creation as well as its consummation. Further, the suggestion has been made that there was a cultus devoted to Wisdom in the years immediately before the ministry of Jesus which influenced the early Church. We can see the personification of Wisdom at work in the Wisdom literature of the intertestamental period, in which Wisdom is praised and given a place at the creation. It is another thing to find evidence for the existence of congregations worshiping Wisdom before the Christian era. Even could it be proved that such worship existed, the identification of Wisdom with a recently executed Man must be explained, and evidence must also be found to demonstrate that Wisdom already in some sense occupied a mediating role in worship. So far, no such evidence exists. The language of mediation was certainly widespread, as was also the language associated with Wisdom: the combination of the two in NT usage must be explained by something more convincing than references to an ephemeral "Hellenism." How long a period of development are we to allow for the unquestionably early incidence of such language in Paul? Paul was certainly in the best position to know how revolutionary his thinking was in terms of Judaism, and yet it is from the focal point of Judaism-fulfilled that he consistently argues. We are at least entitled to infer that the tradition he had "received" allowed for such development and indeed gave it birth.

Bibliography

"SON OF MAN"

Abbott, E. A. *The Message of the Son of Man.* London: Macmillan, 1909.

———. "The Son of Man." *Diatessarica* VIII. Cambridge University Press, 1910.

Andel, van, C. P. *De Structur van de Henoch-traditie en het Nieuwe Testament.* Utrecht: 1955 (Summary in English, pp. 114-27).

Ashby, E. "The Coming of the Son of Man." *ExpT* 72.1961, pp. 360-63.

Barrett, C. K. "The Background of Mark 10.45." In *New Testament Essays,* edited by A. J. B. Higgins. Manchester University Press, 1959, pp. 1-18.

———. "New Testament Eschatology." *SJT* 6.1953, pp. 136-55, 225-43: I—"Jewish and Pauline Eschatology"; II—"The Gospels."

———. "Stephen and the Son of Man." *Apophoreta* (Festschrift für Ernst Haenchen), edited by W. Eltester. Berlin: 1964, pp. 32-38.

Baumgartner, W. M. "Ein vierteljahrhundert Danielforschung." In *Theologische Rundschau,* Neue Folge, 11te Jahrgang. Tübingen: J. C. B. Mohr, 1939, pp. 59-83, 125-44, 201-28.

Beasley-Murray, G. R. *A Commentary on Mark Thirteen.* London: Macmillan, 1957.

———. *Jesus and the Future.* London: Macmillan, 1954.

Bentzen, A. *King and Messiah.* London: SCM Press, 1955. Translation of *Messias-Moses Redivivus-Menschensohn.* Zurich: 1948.

Black, M. "The Eschatology of the Similitudes of Enoch." *JTS,* new series, 3.1952, pp. 1-10.

———. "Servant of the Lord and Son of Man." *SJT* 6.1953, pp. 1-11.

———. "The Son of Man Problem in Recent Research and Debate." *BJRL* 45.1963, pp. 305-18.

————. "Unsolved New Testament Problems: The 'Son of Man' in the Teaching of Jesus." *ExpT* 60.1949, pp. 32-36.

Boobyer, G. H. *St. Mark and the Transfiguration Story.* Edinburgh: T. & T. Clark, 1942.

Bornkamm, G. *Jesus of Nazareth.* Translation by Irene and Fraser McLuskey with James M. Robinson of *Jesus von Nazareth.* New York: Harper Brothers, 1960.

Borsch, Frederick H. *The Christian and Gnostic Son of Man.* Naperville, Ill.: Allenson, 1970.

————. *The Son of Man in Myth and History.* London: SCM Press; Philadelphia: Westminster Press, 1967.

Bowman, J. W. *The Intention of Jesus.* Philadelphia: Westminster Press, 1943.

Brown, Raymond E. *Jesus: God and Man.* New York: Macmillan; London: Collier-Macmillan, 1967.

Bultmann, R. *Jesus and the Word.* Translation by Louise Pettibone Smith and Erminie Huntress Lanterno of *Jesus.* New ed. London and New York: Scribner's, 1958.

Burkitt, F. C. "Four Notes on the Book of Enoch." *JTS* 8.1907, pp. 444-47.

Campbell, J. Y. "The Origin and Meaning of the Term 'Son of Man.'" *JTS* 42.1947, pp. 145-55.

Casey, Maurice. *Son of Man: The Interpretation and Influence of Daniel.* London: SPCK, 1979.

Conzelmann, H. "Gegenwart und Zukunft in der synoptischen Tradition." *ZTK* 54. 1957, pp. 277-96.

————. *An Outline of the Theology of the New Testament.* London: SCM Press; New York: Harper & Row, 1969. Translation of *Grundriss der Theologie des Neuen Testaments.* Munich: Kaiser Verlag, 1967.

Coppens, J. "Le chapitre VII de Daniel." *EphTheolLov* 39.1963, pp. 87-94.

————. Article in *L'évangile selon Marc: Tradition et rédaction,* edited by M. Sabbe. Bibliotheca ephemeridum theologicarum lovaniensium 34. Gembloux: Duculot; Louvain: Leuven University, 1974.

————. "Le fils d'homme danielique, vizir céleste?" *EphTheolLov* 40.1964, pp. 72-80.

————. "L'origine du symbole 'Fils d'homme,'" *EphTheolLov* 39.1963, pp. 100-4.

————. "Les Saints dans le Psautier." *EphTheolLov* 39.1963, pp. 485-500.

————. "Les Saints du Très-Haut sont-ils à identifier avec les Milices Célestes?" *EphTheolLov* 39.1963, pp. 94-100.

————. "Le Serviteur de Yahvé et le fils d'homme danielique: sont-ils les figures messianiques?" *EphTheolLov* 39.1963, pp. 104-13.

————, and Dequeker, L. *Le fils de l'homme et les Saints du Très-Haut en Daniel VII, dans les Apocryphes et dans le Nouveau Testament.* Louvain: Leuven, 1961.

Creed, J. M. "The Heavenly Man." *JTS* 26.1925, pp. 113-36.

Cross, F. M., and Freedman, D. N. "The Blessing of Moses." *JBL* 67.1948, pp. 191-210.

Davies, W. D. "Unsolved New Testament Problems: The Jewish Background of the Teaching of Jesus: Apocalyptic and Pharisaism." *ExpT* 59.1948, pp. 233-37.

Descamps, A. L. "Pour une histoire du titre 'Fils de Dieu': Les antécédents par rapport à Marc." In *L'évangile selon Marc: Tradition et rédaction.* Bibliotheca ephemeridum theologicarum lovaniensium 34. Gembloux: Duculot; Louvain: Leuven University, 1974, pp. 529-71.

Dodd, C. H. "The Fall of Jerusalem and the 'Abomination of Desolation.'" *The Journal of Roman Studies* 37.1947, pp. 47-64.

———. *The Parables of the Kingdom.* 3rd ed. London: Nisbet, 1936.

Drummond, J. "The Use and Meaning of the Phrase 'The Son of Man' in the Synoptic Gospels." *JTS* 2.1901, pp. 350-58, 539-71.

Emerton, J. A. "The Origin of the Son of Man Imagery." *JTS,* new series, 9.1958, pp. 225-42.

Engnell, I. "The 'Ebed Yahweh' Songs and the Suffering Messiah in 'Deutero-Isaiah.'" *BJRL* 31.1948, pp. 54ff.

———. *Studies in Divine Kingship in the Ancient Near East.* 2nd ed. Oxford: Blackwell, 1967.

Fascher, E. "Theologische Beobachtungen zu *dei." Neutestamentliche Studien für Rudolf Bultmann.* Beihefte zur A.N.T.W. 21.1954, pp. 228-54.

Fitzmyer, J. A. "The Aramaic 'Elect of God' Text from Qumran Cave IV." *CBQ* 27.4.1965, pp. 348-72.

Glasson, T. F. "The Son of Man Imagery: Enoch xiv and Daniel vii." *NTS* 23.1.1976, pp. 82-90.

Grant, Michael. *Jesus: An Historian's View of the Gospels.* London and New York: Scribner's, 1977.

Grasser, Erich. "Jesus in Nazareth." *NTS* 16.1969-70, pp. 1-24.

Higgins, A. J. B. *The Son of Man in the Teaching of Jesus.* New York: Cambridge University Press, 1981.

Hooker, Morna D. *The Son of Man in Mark.* London: SPCK, 1967.

Horstmann, M. *Studien zur markinischen Christologie: Mk 8:27-9:13 als Zugang zum Christusbild des zweiten Evangeliums.* Münster: Aschendorff, 1969.

Hoskyns, E. C. "Jesus the Messiah." In *Mysterium Christi,* edited by G. K. A. Bell and A. Deissmann. London, New York, and Toronto: 1930, pp. 67-89.

Hunter, A. M. *The Gospel According to Saint Mark.* London: Harper, 1948.

Jeremias, J. "Die aramaische Vorgeschichte unserer Evangelien." *ThL* 74.1949, pp. 527-32.

———. *The Parables of Jesus.* Translation by S. H. Hooke. London and New York: Scribner's, 1963.

Käsemann, E. *Essays on New Testament Themes.* Translation by W. J. Montague of *Exegetische Versuche und Besinnungen,* vol. I. 2nd ed. London: SCM Press, 1960.

Kümmel, W. G. *Promise and Fulfillment.* Translation by Dorothea M. Barton of *Verheissung und Erfüllung,* 3rd ed. London: 1957; Naperville, Ill.: Allenson, 1957.

Klausner, J. *Jesus of Nazareth.* London and New York: Macmillan, 1926.

Kraeling, C. H. *Anthropos and Son of Man.* New York: Columbia University Press, 1927.

Lietzmann, H. *Der Menschensohn.* Freiburg and Leipzig: Herder, 1896.

Morgenstern, J. "The 'Son of Man' of Daniel 7-13f." *JBL* 80.1961, pp. 65-77.

Otto, R. *The Kingdom of God and the Son of Man.* London: Lutterworth Press, 1938.

Translation by Floyd F. Filson and Bertram Lee Woolf of *Reichgottes und Menschensohn* (rev. ed.). Munich: Beck, 1934.

Perkins, Pheme. "Gnostic Christologies and the New Testament." *CBQ* 43.4.1981, pp. 590-606.

Pesch, R., and Schnackenburg, R., eds. *Jesus und der Menschensohn.* Freiburg: Herder, 1975.

Preiss, T. *Le fils de l'homme.* Montpellier: Faculté de théologie Protestante, 1955.

——. "The Mystery of the Son of Man." In *Life in Christ,* edited by H. Knight. London: SCM Press, 1957, pp. 43-60.

Sidebottom, E. M. "The Son of Man in the Fourth Gospel." *ExpT* 68.1957, pp. 231-35, 280-83.

Stauffer, E. "Messias oder Menschensohn." *NovTest* I. Leiden: 1956, pp. 81-102.

Taylor, V. "The 'Son of Man' Sayings Relating to the Parousia." *ExpT* 58.1947, pp. 12-15.

——. "Unsolved New Testament Problems: The Messianic Secret in Mark." *ExpT* 59.1948, pp. 145-51.

Teeple, Howard M. *The Mosaic Eschatological Prophet.* Philadelphia: SBL, 1957.

Thompson, G. H. P. "The Son of Man: The Evidence of the Dead Sea Scrolls." *ExpT* 72.1961, p. 125.

Vielhauer, P. "Jesus und der Menschensohn." *ZTK* 60.1963, pp. 133-77.

Volz, P. *Die Eschatologie der judischen Gemeinde im neutestamentlichen Zeitalter.* Tübingen: J. C. B. Mohr, 1934.

Wifall, Walter. "Son of Man: A Pre-Davidic Social Class?" *CBQ* 37.3.1975, pp. 341-42.

THE BEGINNINGS OF CHRISTOLOGY

Aulén, Gustaf. *Jesus in Contemporary Historical Research.* Translation by I. H. Hjelm. Philadelphia: Fortress Press, 1976.

Benoit, P. "Jésus et le serviteur de Dieu." In *Jésus aux origines de la christologie,* edited by J. Dupont. Bibliotheca ephemeridum theologicarum lovaniensium 40. Gembloux: Duculot; Louvain: Leuven University, 1975.

Betz, H. Dieter. "Jesus as Divine Man." In *Jesus and the Historian,* edited by F. Thomas Trotter (Festschrift for E. C. Colwell). Philadelphia: Westminster Press, 1965.

——, ed. *Christology: A Modern Pilgrimage.* Missoula, Mont.: SBL, 1971.

Betz, Otto. "The Concept of the So-Called 'Divine Man' in Mark's Gospel." In *Studies in the New Testament and Early Christian Literature: Essays in Honour of Allen P. Wikgren,* edited by David A. Aune. Leiden: E. J. Brill, 1972, pp. 229-41.

Descamps, A. L. "Porte christologique de la recherche historique sur Jésus." In *Jésus aux origines de la christologie,* edited by J. Dupont. Bibliotheca ephemeridum theologicarum lovaniensium 40. Gembloux: Duculot; Louvain: Leuven University, 1975.

Dupont, J., ed. *Jésus aux origines de la christologie.* Bibliotheca ephemeridum theologicarum lovaniensium 40. Gembloux: Duculot; Louvain: Leuven University, 1975.

Fitzmyer, J. A. "Methodology in the Study of the Aramaic Substratum of Jesus' Sayings in the New Testament." In *Jésus aux origines de la christologie,* edited by J. Dupont. Bibliotheca ephemeridum theologicarum lovaniensium 40. Gembloux: Duculot; Louvain: Leuven University, 1975.

Fuller, Reginald H. *The Foundations of New Testament Christology.* New York: Scribner's, 1965.

Harvey, A. E. *Jesus and the Constraints of History* (Bampton Lectures, 1980). London: Duckworth, 1982.

Holladay, Carl. *"Theios anēr" in Hellenistic Judaism.* Missoula, Mont.: Scholars Press, 1974.

Horstmann, Maria. *Studien zur markinischen Christologie.* NTAbh, Neue Folge, Vol. 6. Münster: Verlag Aschendorf, 1969.

Hoskyns, Sir Edwyn C. "The Christ of the Synoptic Gospels." In *Essays Catholic and Critical,* edited by E. G. Selwyn. 3rd ed. London: SPCK, 1950.

Jeremias, Joachim, and Zimmerli, Walther. *The Servant of God.* SBT, Vol. 20 (rev. ed.). London: SCM Press, 1965.

Lane, W. L. *"Theios anēr* Christology and the Gospel of Mark." In *New Dimensions in New Testament Study,* edited by Richard H. Longenecker and Merrill C. Tenney. Grand Rapids, Mich.: Zondervan, 1974.

Levey, Samson H. *The Messiah: An Aramaic Interpretation: The Messianic Exegesis of the Targum.* Cincinnati, New York, Los Angeles, and Jerusalem: Hebrew Union College, 1974.

Lindars, Barnabas. "Jesus as Advocate: A Contribution to the Christology Debate." *BJRL* 62.2.1980, pp. 476-97.

Linnemann, E. "Hat Jesus Nahewartung gehabt?" In *Jésus aux origines de la christologie,* edited by J. Dupont. Bibliotheca ephemeridum theologicarum lovaniensium. Gembloux: Duculot; Louvain: Leuven University, 1975.

Lohse, Eduard. "Apokalyptik und Christologie." *ZNW* 62.1971, pp. 48-67.

Mauer, Christian. "Das Messiasgeheimnis des Markusevangeliums." *NTS* 14.1967-68, pp. 515-28.

McKelvey, R. J. "Christ the Cornerstone." *NTS* 8.1961-62, pp. 352-59.

Perrin, Norman. "The Christology of Mark: A Study in Methodology." *JR* 51.1971, pp. 173-87.

Robinson, J. A. T. *The Human Face of God.* Philadelphia: Westminster Press, 1973.

Rosa, Peter de. *Jesus Who Became Christ.* London: Collins, 1974.

Sahlin, H. "Zum Verständnis der christologischen Anschauung des Markusevangeliums." *ST* 31.1.1977, pp. 1-19.

Schneider, Franz. *Jesus der Prophet.* Orbis biblicus et orientalis 2. Fribourg: Universitätsverlag; Göttingen: Vanderhoeck & Ruprecht, 1973.

C. The Jesus of History and the Christ of Faith

This section will discuss some of the views held by modern scholars on the problem of the historical Jesus as against the proclaimed Risen Lord of the Church. The full bibliography for this section should be consulted for varying opinions. What has come to be known as "the quest for the historical Jesus" began in the eighteenth century, and Jeremias singles out 1778 as the year in which H. S. Reimarus first seriously recognized that the Jesus of history and the Messiah proclaimed in the gospels and by the Church were not the same. Reimarus also believed that a biography of Jesus "as he really was" could be reconstructed. Although Reimarus' portrayal of the historical Jesus is, as Jeremias notes, "clearly absurd and amateurish," he nevertheless raised a question which could not be evaded: "Who really was Jesus of Nazareth?" Thus the age of the "old quest" was inaugurated and the result was a library of books and essays in which the life of Jesus was described and modernized according to each author's own personal viewpoint. Although Jeremias remarks that "dogma was replaced by psychology and fantasy," scholars of the old quest did possess some positive characteristics: (1) a firm knowledge of the historical documents, (2) a sincere concern for the historical Jesus, and (3) source criticism, the acknowledged nineteenth-century tools and contributions to present-day studies.

Between 1900 and 1940 the pendulum swung again, this time in reverse, as optimism was replaced by pessimism. It was concluded on scientific and theological grounds that the true biography of Jesus could never be written. The future of the nineteenth-century quest for the historical Jesus was exposed by Albert Schweitzer's famous book *Von Reimarus zu Wrede* (1906). He proposed that the key to the historical Jesus was an element previously overlooked, that of eschatology. Scholars generally reject Schweitzer's view that Jesus was a noble but mistaken and disappointed thoroughgoing eschatologist. However wrong Schweitzer may have been, he did nevertheless restore eschatology to a place of respectability in theological debate.

Form criticism was developed during this period by three German scholars —Bultmann, Dibelius, and Schmidt. Proponents of this discipline tend to stress heavily the role of the early Church in transmitting, shaping, and even creating material about Jesus. As a result of debates among form-critical scholars it was concluded that any attempt to get behind the postresurrection community to the historical Jesus was doubtful at best, and at worst impossible. Preoccupation with the historical Jesus was determined to be a fruitless undertaking and the emphasis was shifted instead to the *kerugma.* The view that developed during this phase, which lasted until the mid-1930s, rejected the possibility or even the desirability of a life of Jesus, and proponents saw in this a defense of what faith really must mean. Bultmann seems to have relished this "historical unreliability"; for him, "all the old life of Jesus fantasies could burn, as they have no value for faith."

There has been since then another swing of the pendulum, this time back to renewed interest in the Jesus of history. The extremes of the "old quest" have been avoided: it was Käsemann, one of Bultmann's own pupils, who helped bring the pendulum back toward the center in 1953 with a paper proposing a new quest which would avoid the errors of the nineteenth century. It was suggested that a quest back through the proclamation would find behind it a Jesus consistent with the Church's proclamation. It was this "new quest" that provided the immediate background for Jeremias' essay, *The Problem of the Historical Jesus,* which is concerned with the problem of separation of the gospel of Jesus from the preaching of the early Church.

For Jeremias it is evident that an attempt must be made to uncover the historical Jesus and his message for two compelling reasons. The first is the sources: every verse of the gospels tells us that the origin of Christianity lies not in the proclamation, not in the resurrection experience of the disciples, not in a "Christ idea," but in the appearance of Jesus of Nazareth in the history of humanity. The second is the proclamation itself: the Church's preaching refers to a historical event—God revealing himself in an event in history. For these two reasons we need to know who the Jesus of history was and what was the content of his teaching.

Jeremias states that while the dangers do exist of ending up once again with results similar to those of the nineteenth century, the present position is markedly different since scholars are better equipped to avoid the mistakes of the "old quest" for the historical Jesus. If the attempt is made with rigid discipline and critical resources are applied conscientiously to the study of the historical Jesus, the final result (according to Jeremias) is always the same: "We find ourselves confronted with God himself." Through the words and acts of Jesus at every turn the challenge to faith is presented; hence study of the historical Jesus and his message is the prime task of NT scholarship.

Jeremias concludes that the gospel message of Jesus and the proclamation are inseparable, for the gospel of Jesus remains dead history without the witness of the faith by which the Church continually reiterates, affirms, and attests its gospel. Apart from Jesus and his gospel the proclamation is merely the proclamation of an idea or a theory. It is the historical Jesus and his message which is the sole preoccupation of the *kerugma.* The Church's response presupposes an act of God in history, and the witness to the revelation presupposes the revelation itself.

More recent scholars have not been slow to take up Jeremias's challenge.

The core of Schweitzer's argument was that the quest for the historical Jesus was not historical enough. Instead of following through with historical research wherever it might lead, liberal scholarship always stopped at the point at which a Jesus was presented who was almost an image of the scholar himself. Schweitzer contended that if the research was carried through to the end, Jesus would be discovered to be an apocalyptic fantasist. Disappointed in his expectations, this Jesus was deluded enough to attempt to force the hand of God by his own sufferings—sufferings that would prove to be the beginning of the End.

Schweitzer's work was important, as Perrin has noted. Liberal scholarship had indeed tended to bias the picture of the historical Jesus with its own ideals, and the omission of eschatology had been spectacular. Thus, subsequent attempts to carry on the quest for a historical Jesus who is the concern of faith had to take Schweitzer's work seriously. This, again according to Perrin, was precisely what Jeremias encountered during the writing of *The Problem of the Historical Jesus.*

Christology, the Church's response to the history of Jesus, was regarded (prior to the rise of gospel criticism) as the essential core of the actual historical teaching of Jesus. This traditional view rested in the main on the fourth gospel, since it is only in this account that Jesus' proclamation is almost entirely "christological." Once the historicity of John was in large measure abandoned (cf. R. H. Fuller, *The Foundations of New Testament Christology),* scholars were thrown back on the synoptic gospels as the main evidence for the historical Jesus.

Although the synoptic tradition contains christological material, the bulk of this material (for example, the infancy narratives, the baptism, the miracle stories, the temptation narrative, Peter's confession, the transfiguration, the passion narratives, and the resurrection stories) took shape after the resurrection and reflects the messianic belief of the postresurrection Church. It is in the light of this that Fuller assigns these narratives to the theology of the community. What is left, according to Fuller, is only a small body of christological material in the synoptic sayings of Jesus. Fuller then goes on to analyze that body of material and attempts to discover an authentic minimum "compatible with the implicit self-understanding already extracted from his more characteristic teaching."

Jesus' proclamation of the Kingdom was not an abstract idea but the historic proclamation of an event. Jesus' words and deeds are accordingly "present actualizations of the future Kingdom of God." God is present in Jesus, acting eschatologically through Jesus. Jesus' ethical teaching points in the same direction as he confronts human beings with the direct demand of God. According to Fuller, the majority of Jesus' sayings about his death contain either explicit christology or an explicit soteriology, and therefore must be assigned to the primitive Church rather than to Jesus himself. However,

Fuller calls attention to two passages which pass his specific test of critical method: (1) Luke 13:32—here Jesus' death at Jerusalem is stated in terms free of any church theology; Jesus accepts the inevitability of his death as part of his eschatological ministry; (2) Mark 14:25—here Jesus makes a distinction between himself and his disciples; the meal is his last on earth, and between Jesus at the Supper and the consummation of the Kingdom lies the decisive event of his own death, part of God's eschatological action in him. Fuller concludes that Jesus' death, like his words and deeds, implies a christology. He is also concerned with finding a point of contact in Jesus' history for the subsequent proclamation of the Church. The implicit christology found in the words and works of Jesus is enough to rescue a historical basis for the proclamation. Fuller proceeds to reexamine the seven titles used or implied in the sayings of Jesus—Messiah, Son of David, Son of God, Servant, Lord, Son of Man, Prophet. He concludes that it is the implicit, unexpressed figure of the eschatological prophet which gives a unity to all of Jesus' historical activity. If the implied self-understanding of his role in terms of eschatological prophet is taken away, the whole ministry falls into a series of unrelated if not meaningless fragments. "The basic datum of New Testament christology is not the concept of Jesus as eschatological prophet, but his proclamation and activity which confront men and women with the saving act of God breaking into history and his utter commitment and entire obedience to the will of God which made him the channel of that saving activity. To interpret this datum in terms of explicit christology was the task of the post-Easter church in whose *kerugma* the Proclaimer became the Proclaimed." Fuller is therefore concerned with the separation of the implicit historical christology and the post-Easter church. For him, this is entirely possible using scientifically based methods of traditional-historical criticism.

Fuller's thesis rests in large part on the abandonment of the historicity of John; primary consideration is given to the synoptic gospels. Although Fuller readily admits that some Johannine sayings may well go back to Jesus himself, Jesus' christological utterances in the fourth gospel are beyond doubt church formulation. Therefore the whole discussion of the historical Jesus seems for Fuller to hinge on this opening qualification.

Few have done more in this generation to reassess the historicity of the fourth gospel than R. E. Brown. In his *New Testament Essays* (Milwaukee: Bruce Publishing Co., 1965) and in his massive commentary on the *Gospel According to John* (AB, Garden City, N.Y.: Doubleday, 1966, 1970), Brown stresses that the historicity is a problem with two sides, positive and negative. The positive side must include the historical characteristics of the Johannine tradition which are too often neglected; Brown further calls attention to the historical limits inherent in John which forbid its interpretation *merely* as history. Brown begins his essay in *New Testament Essays* as follows: "It is well known that the categorical rejection of the historicity of John, so familiar in earlier critical exegesis, can no longer be maintained. We may still find writers stating that the Fourth Gospel cannot be seriously considered as a witness to the historical Jesus, but these represent a type of uncritical traditionalism which arises with age, even in heterodoxy." There are, at any rate, fewer supporters of the view that John is a late second century document which lies closer to Gnosticism and the Hellenistic world than to the Palestinian era of Jesus. Brown summarizes the reasons for the shift in opinion he has led: (1) The Rylands and Bodmer papyri make it virtually impossible to date the final writing of the gospel much later than A.D. 100. (2) Gnostic writings indicate that Gnosticism (particularly in the *Gospel of Truth)* is quite different from the thought pattern of John; though the Gnostics certainly favor John, there is evidence too for the orthodox use of John in the second century. (3) The Palestinian aspects of the Johannine tradition have been better verified in recent years. No other gospel gives us such a wealth of place names, exact locations, lists of persons, which can no longer be rejected as artificial since we now have a much improved knowledge of Palestinian geography. (4) The discoveries at Qumran indicate that many features of vocabulary, mentality, and theological outlook of John were current at Qumran during the lifetime of Jesus. Qumran provides the real Palestinian background against which the Jesus of John's gospel can be plausibly identified. (5) The basic assumption of the past concerning the relation of John to the synoptic gospels has been fallacious: if the synoptic gospels are histories and John claims to be historical, then it should agree with them. The fallacy is the use of categories like history and biography in the modern sense. Rather, the tradition behind the synoptic gospels is that of the preaching and teaching of the early community which comes from eyewitnesses and may therefore be presumed to be historical. Three stages of development can be identified: what Jesus said and did; what the apostles preached; and what the evangelists wrote.

The differences between John and the synoptic gospels (at least as they relate to historicity) are not as acute as might seem at first sight. Brown maintains that what the synoptic gospels portray is not a detailed history but a simplified outline of the ministry as presented in the early proclamations; it is therefore possible that John's more detailed outline is historical. The chronological differences on the date of the Last Supper have not been solved.

The Johannine tradition is in essence not dependent on the synoptic gospels, and indeed is viewed by most scholars as an independent proclamation and teaching document. While it was fashionable in the past to view the Johannine discourses as the theological reflections of John himself, since they do not resemble Jesus' way of speaking in the synoptics, the new and increased emphasis on the originality of the Johannine tradition ought to cause a rethinking of this position. The vocabulary of the Johannine Jesus, measured against the discoveries at Qumran, is not as strange as might appear at first sight. Although the synoptic gospels preserve materials that reflect the life of the community and even of Jesus himself before that community, the old contrast between the synoptic gospels as history and the fourth gospel as interpretation no longer makes adequate sense. There is no reason why John could not contain primitive independent tradition; it is hazardous to assume that all tradition was channeled through the synoptic gospels. John's use of sources creates difficulty, since under his hand they lose their identity and become his own. John is a gospel, and gospels deal with the words and deeds of Jesus within a historical framework. The appearance of the written gospels, it has been suggested, was a reaction in first-century Christianity against tendencies already present in Paul but going to extremes in apocalypticism and gnosticism. The fact remains, however, that no matter how largely the faith of the Church is written into the gospels, that faith is referred to the historical Jesus in a recognizable historical setting.

The problem with finding the historical Jesus began with the early Church, since the primitive Christian community saw the resurrection as the real starting point of christology. The early Church did not attribute a christological function to the Jesus of the pre-Easter experience—that function was dependent on the resurrection; this seems to have been the view of Paul himself.

The major event in the history of Christian thought was the writing of the gospels. Mark therefore (if Mark was indeed the prior document), begins a revolutionary era when the gospel is placed against the futurist stance taken by the primitive Church and by Paul. The writing of the gospels, in whatever order they may have come, presents a relationship between the proclamation of the community and the pre-Easter Jesus. The shift to the historical Jesus provides a corresponding change in the beginning point of christology—that is to say, from the resurrection to the baptism of John. The proclamation is not in the parahistorical field, but begins with the appearance of Jesus on the stage of history. It is not without significance that the conflict between Jesus and Satan in Mark is presented in cosmic language.

In his quest for the total picture of NT christology, Oscar Cullmann proceeded in a purely analytical fashion. Investigation of all the titles which the first Christians conferred upon Jesus is in his view the best approach, and he therefore examines the precise meaning of each title as it appears throughout the NT books. His method is to differentiate by analysis the given titles in order to identify the characteristics of each title—the significance in Judaism and in the general history of each title; the sense in which Jesus applied this or that christological definition to himself, if indeed he did so; and how the title was understood by the different NT writers.

Cullmann leans toward agreement with Käsemann, T. W. Manson, and Fuchs in his conclusion that the results of form criticism demand an answer to the question of the historical Jesus. It seems to him improper to abandon the quest even when there are false consequences of past mistakes. For

Cullmann a thoroughgoing skepticism in using the gospels as historical sources is unjustified. On the contrary, we ought to be encouraged to use the Church's faith in Jesus to discover the historical truths behind that faith.

Cullmann attempted to arrive at the self-consciousness of Jesus by use of form-critical examination of the gospel tradition, in order to distinguish between places where the evangelists plainly express their own views and places where they report the words of Jesus. He makes the claim that the christology of the NT is not a myth externally imposed on an essentially nonhistorical proclamation. For Cullmann, all christology is ultimately founded upon the life of Jesus. Cullmann's methodology is to dissect every christological title into its diverse components and then to reconnect them with an insight which enables one to see the patterns implied. In his work there is a connection between (1) examination of christological titles, (2) gospel historicity, and (3) the place of faith in the fact of redemptive history.

For Fuchs, as expressed in his *Studies of the Historical Jesus,* there is nothing significant about the raising of Jesus from death apart from faith in the Jesus of history. It is essentially the words of Jesus, and not the titles ascribed to him, that provide a historical record of Jesus' life and ministry. Since Jesus' life and ministry was itself the real framework of his proclamation, it follows that the framework of the historical record is the words of Jesus himself: it is his words which give rise to his deeds.

Fuchs attempts to interrelate faith, conduct, and Jesus' words and actions. His method is to confront the problem of the historical Jesus by utilizing the synoptic gospels to supplement a discussion on faith in Paul. As Jesus was representative of faith, so faith became representative of Jesus. It follows that if faith is representative of Jesus, then preaching or proclamation is seen as the new representation of God. Thus faith knows that in the proclamation of the resurrection, the historical Jesus has come to us. Fuchs concludes that the test for the historical Jesus leads to theology rather than away from it. His attempt to show subsequent cause-and-effect relationships in his quest for the historical Jesus leads to the conclusion that faith is the essential key to the problem. It must be said, however, that the argument based on "faith" would be familiar to the reader of Richard Whately's *Historic Doubts Relative to Napoleon Bonaparte,* and might suggest that it would be as easy to write an existentialist "Life of Napoleon" as an existentialist "Life of Jesus."

Perrin gives the verdict that "Fuchs places upon faith an extreme emphasis arriving at a point at which faith is practically personified." Indeed, the intricate cause-and-effect relationship in Fuchs, which seems to hinge sometimes on cause and sometimes on effect in order to arrive at the end product, is an extremely difficult relationship to follow in his argumentation.

Perrin's book *Rediscovering the Teaching of Jesus* is perhaps one of the best and most critical essays in the new quest for the historical Jesus. Perrin demands that the problem—in order for its true nature to be understood—be set in its historical perspective; in one respect the question of the historical Jesus is as old as Christian faith itself. Faith, by definition, is both faith in a historical figure, Jesus, a man from Nazareth, and faith in the Messiah, a para-historical title. The question is how these two are related to one another in the same person. Perrin discusses the work of his predecessors in delineating the background of the modern quest for the historical Jesus. He then describes three different kinds of knowledge involved in any discussion of the historical Jesus: (1) descriptive historical knowledge of Jesus of Nazareth; (2) aspects of this historical knowledge which can become significant to us in our own times; and (3) knowledge of Jesus which is only significant in the context of Christian faith. Perrin asserts that descriptive historical knowledge can be achieved through use of appropriate methods in interpretation. Some of this knowledge will be found directly significant to us today only if a point of contact is established between the past and the present. It therefore follows that faith-knowledge becomes significant to us at the level of religious faith, belief, and commitment, and has a value beyond that ascribed to any historical knowledge. In short, historical knowledge of Jesus of Nazareth has become historic knowledge (i.e., has assumed a direct significance for the present) as the events from the pre-Easter ministry assume a direct significance for a future time. Faith-knowledge depends upon a special work that is attributed to the person concerned, and knowledge of that person may then assume a significance beyond the historic. One can attribute historic significance to almost any number of people from the past, but faith-knowledge can only be attributed to Jesus the Messiah.

For Perrin, historical knowledge is significant in that it can help provide faith with its necessary content and it can contribute to formation of the faith image. In addition, historical knowledge of Jesus can be directly relevant to faith, apart from aiding in the formation of the faith image.

Perrin summarizes his position on the significance of knowledge of the historical Jesus for faith as follows: (1) historical knowledge only plays a part in the content of the proclamation of the Church, which helps to provide content for a faith which gives its allegiance to Jesus; (2) due to the varieties of Christian proclamations and the nature of the synoptic gospel material (earthly Jesus = risen Lord), the historical knowledge of Jesus must be used to test the validity of the claim of any given form of the Church's proclamation to be *Christian* proclamation; (3) historical knowledge of the teaching of Jesus can be directly applied to the situation of the believer in any age. If Perrin's book can be described as "minimalist," it is nevertheless one of the best presentations of the "historical Jesus" perspective found up to the present time. It is clear that Perrin, unlike Fuchs, is concerned with relating the historical fact of the pre-Easter Jesus to the Christian faith in a risen Lord.

Each of the authors we have considered approached the problem with his own particular style and method, each attempting to contribute specific knowledge and fresh insight to an old problem. Jeremias asserts that the Church is dead historically without the witness of faith by the Church, and that apart from Jesus the *kerugma* is merely proclamation of an idea or theory. Schweitzer claimed that the historical quest was not historically rigorous enough—it always stopped short, and thus all historical research resulted in an image of the scholar himself. Fuller approached the problem through the synoptic gospels, working from the denial of the historicity of John. Fuchs laid heavy emphasis on faith in his search for the historical Jesus. E. L. Titus *(The Message of the Fourth Gospel,* New York: Abingdon Press, 1957) believed that the gospels were a return to the historical Jesus, a reaction in first-century Christianity against a tendency already present to dehistoricize Jesus. Cullmann elaborated a precise, analytical christological method in his quest for the historical Jesus and his subsequent reflections on acceptance of faith in Jesus as the center of redemptive history. Brown defends the historical authenticity of John and the assertion that the historical tradition behind the synoptic gospels is that of the preaching and teaching Church. Perrin presents a clear, concise association between historical knowledge of Jesus and faith. All of these works play their part in explicating the problem, if not in providing any definitive answers.

Although it is apparent that the gospels were intended to be read as testimony of faith and not as detailed, historical, factual accounts, it is also true that each of the gospels portrays Jesus as a historical figure. The proclamation that God entered history at a specific time and place in the person of Jesus is accepted as fact. No historian would deny that something happened in the pre-gospel era or that some change did take place in the followers of Jesus from the time of the raising of Jesus to the time of Pentecost. The disciples would not preserve records of cowardice if not true; the gospel was boldly preached to the world with no concern for physical danger; the historicity of the dramatic growth of the proclaimed faith is undeniable. The facts are that the disciples spoke of the resurrection as a historical occurrence, that inconsistencies in the gospel accounts tend to verify their honesty rather than their contrivance, that the primary tradition rested on the witness of two or three women which no Jew would have invented. These are a few factual points which are incapable of refutation. The subsequent problem of separating Jesus' actual words and deeds from what the apostles preached and what the evangelists wrote is a never-ending task which will be constantly revised and altered as NT scholarship increases in knowledge and refinement.

134 INTRODUCTION

Bibliography

Althaus, Paul. "Das sogenannte Kerygma und der historische Jesus: Zur Kritik der heutigen Kerygma-theologie." In *Beiträge zur Förderung christlicher Theologie* 48. Gütersloh: Bertelsmann, 1958. Translation by David Cairns, *The So-called Kerygma and the Historical Jesus.* Edinburgh: Oliver & Boyd, 1959. U.S. ed., *Fact and Faith in the Kerygma of Today.* Philadelphia: Muhlenberg, 1960.

Anderson, Hugh. *Jesus and Christian Origins: A Commentary on Modern Viewpoints.* New York: Oxford University Press, 1964.

Baird, J. Arthur. *Audience Criticism and the Historical Jesus.* Philadelphia: Westminster Press, 1969.

Bornkamm, Günther. *Jesus of Nazareth.* Translation by Irene and Fraser McLuskey with James M. Robinson. New York: Harper, 1960.

Braaten, Carl E., and Harrisville, Roy A., eds. *The Historical Jesus and the Kerygmatic Christ: Essays on the New Quest of Historical Jesus.* New York: Abingdon, 1964.

————, eds. *Kerygma and History: A Symposium on the Theology of Rudolf Bultmann.* New York: Abingdon, 1962.

Brown, Raymond E., S.S. "After Bultmann, What?—An Introduction to the Post-Bultmannians." *CBQ* 26.1964, pp. 1-30.

Bultmann, Rudolf. *Theologie des Neuen Testaments.* Tübingen: J. C. B. Mohr, 1948-53, 1965. Translation by Kendrick Grobel, *Theology of the New Testament.* 2 vols. New York: Scribner's, 1951-55.

————. "Die Unsterblichen." In *Jesus.* Berlin: Deutsche Bibliothek, 1926, Vol. 1, p. 143. Translation by Louise Pettibone Smith and Erminie Huntress, *Jesus and the Word.* New York: Scribner's, 1934, p. 155.

————. *Das Urchristentum im Rahmen der antiken Religionen.* Zürich: Artemis-Verlag, 1949, 1954. Translation by R. H. Fuller, *Primitive Christianity in Its Contemporary Setting.* New York: Meridian, Living Age Books, 1956.

Cahill, P. Joseph, S.J. "Rudolf Bultmann and Post-Bultmannian Tendencies." *CBQ* 26.1964, pp. 153-78. Reprinted in *New Theology No. 2,* edited by M. E. Marty and D. G. Peerman. New York: Macmillan, 1965, pp. 224-54.

Case, Shirley Jackson. "The Life of Jesus During the Last Quarter Century." *JR* 5.1925, pp. 561-75 (covering 1900-25).

————. *Jesus Through the Centuries.* University of Chicago Press, 1932.

Crossan, John D. *In Parables: The Challenge of the Historical Jesus.* New York: Harper & Row, 1973.

Dahl, Nils A. "Der historische Jesus als geschichtswissenschaftliches und theologisches Problem." *Kerygma und Dogma* 1.1955, pp. 104-32. Translation, "The Problem of the Historical Jesus." In *Kerygma and History: A Symposium on the Theology of Rudolf Bultmann,* edited by Carl E. Braaten and Roy A. Harrisville. New York: Abingdon, 1962, pp. 138-71.

Dalman, Gustav. *Die Worte Jesu mit Berücksichtigung des nachkanonischen jüdischen Schrifttums und der aramäischen Sprache erörtert.* Leipzig: J. C. Hinrichs, 1898,

1930. Translation by D. M. Kay, *The Words of Jesus Considered in the Light of Post-Biblical Jewish Writings and the Aramaic Language.* Edinburgh: T. & T. Clark, 1902.

Dupont, J. "Conclusion des journées bibliques: les énigmes de l'histoire de Jésus." In *Jésus aux origines de la christologie,* edited by J. Dupont. Bibliotheca ephemeridum theologicarum lovaniensium 40. Gembloux: Duculot; Louvain: Leuven University, 1975, pp. 351-56.

Ebeling, Gerhard. *Die Geschichtlichkeit der Kirche und ihre Verkündigung als theologisches Problem.* Tübingen: J. C. B. Mohr, 1954. Translation by Grover Foley, *The Problem of Historicity in the Church and Its Proclamation.* Philadelphia: Fortress Press, 1967.

Enslin, Morton S. *The Prophet from Nazareth.* New York: McGraw-Hill, 1961.

Fuchs, Ernst. "Die Frage nach dem historischen Jesus." *ZTK* 53.1956, pp. 210-29; Translation by A. Scobie, "The Quest of the Historical Jesus." In *Studies of the Historical Jesus.* SBT 42. London: SCM, 1964, pp. 11-31.

Fuller, Reginald H. *Kerygma and Myth.* Edited by H. W. Bartsch. London: SPCK; Greenwich, Conn.: Seabury, 1953, Vol. 1, pp. 11-21.

————. *The New Testament in Current Study* (esp. pp. 25-53). New York: Scribner's, 1962.

————. *The Foundations of New Testament Christology.* New York: Scribner's, 1965.

Gloege, Gerhard. *The Day of His Coming: The Man in the Gospels.* Translation by Stanley Rudman. Philadelphia: Fortress Press, 1963.

Goguel, Maurice. *Jesus and the Origins of Christianity.* Translation by Olive Wyon. New York: Macmillan, 1933. Paperback, New York: Harper & Row, 1960.

Grant, Robert M. *The Earliest Lives of Jesus.* London: SPCK; New York: Harper, 1961.

Guillet, Jacques. *The Consciousness of Jesus.* New York: Newman Press, 1971.

Heitsch, Ernst. "Die Aporie des historischen Jesus als Problem theologischer Hermeneutik." *ZTK* 53.1956, pp. 192-210.

Hunter, A. M. "The Life of Christ in the Twentieth Century." *ExpT.* 61.1950, pp. 131-35. Reprinted in *Interpreting the New Testament, 1900-1950.* Philadelphia: Westminster Press, 1951, pp. 49-60.

Jeremias, Joachim. *The Central Message of the New Testament.* London: SCM; New York: Scribner's, 1965.

————. "Characteristics of the *ipsissima vox Jesu.*" In *The Prayers of Jesus.* SBT, 2nd series, 6. London: SCM, 1967.

————. *Jerusalem in the Time of Jesus.* Philadelphia: Fortress Press, 1969.

————. *Jesus' Promise to the Nations.* SBT 24. London: SCM; Naperville, Ill.: Allenson, 1958.

————. *New Testament Theology I: The Proclamation of Jesus.* New York: Scribner's, 1971.

————. *The Origins of Infant Baptism: A Further Study in Reply to Kurt Aland* (Studies in Historical Theology 1). London: SCM; Naperville, Ill.: Allenson, 1963.

————. *The Prayers of Jesus.* SBT, 2nd series. London: SCM; Naperville, Ill.: Allenson, 1967. A selection from the author's collected essays, *Abba: Studien zur neutestamentliche Theologie und Zeitgeschichte.* Göttingen: Vandenhoeck & Ruprecht, 1966.

―――. *The Problem of the Historical Jesus.* Translation by Norman Perrin. Philadelphia: Fortress Press, 1964.

―――. *The Sermon on the Mount.* Translation by Norman Perrin. Facet Books, Biblical Series 2. Philadelphia: Fortress Press, 1963, pp. 19-21.

―――. *Unknown Sayings of Jesus.* London: SPCK; Greenwich, Conn.: Seabury, 1957. Rev. ed., 1964.

―――, with Walter Zimmerli. *The Servant of God.* SBT 20. London: SCM; Naperville, Ill.: Allenson, 1957. Rev. ed., 1965.

Kähler, Martin. *Der sogenannte historische Jesus und der geschichtliche, biblische Christus.* Leipzig: A. Deichertsche Verlagsbuchhandlung, 1892, 1896.

Käsemann, Ernst. "Blind Alleys in the 'Jesus of History' Controversy." In *New Testament Questions of Today.* Translation by W. J. Montague. Philadelphia: Fortress Press, 1969, pp. 23-65.

―――. "Das Problem des historischen Jesus." *ZTK* 51.1954, pp. 125-53. Translation by W. J. Montague, "Essays on New Testament Themes." SBT 41. London: SCM, 1964, pp. 15-47.

―――. "Die neue Jesus-Frage." In *Jésus aux origines de la christologie,* edited by J. Dupont. Bibliotheca ephemeridum theologicarum lovaniensium 40. Gembloux: Duculot; Louvain: Leuven University, 1975, pp. 47-57.

Keck, Leander. *A Future for the Historical Jesus.* Nashville and New York: Abingdon Press, 1971.

Kümmel, W. G. "Jesusforschung seit 1950." *Theologische Rundschau,* Neue Folge 31.1966, pp. 15-46, 289-315.

Leipoldt, J. *Vom Jesusbilde der Gegenwart.* Leipzig: Dörffling & Franke, 1913, 1925.

Lohse, Eduard. "Die Frage nach dem historischen Jesus in der gegenwarten neutestamentlichen Forschung." In *Die Einheit des Neuen Testaments: exegetische Studien zur Theologie des Neuen Testaments* (collected essays). Göttingen: Vandenhoeck & Ruprecht, 1973.

Longenecker, Richard N. "Literary Criteria in Life of Jesus Research: An Evaluation and Proposal." In *Current Issues in Biblical and Patristic Interpretation: Studies in Honor of Merrill C. Tenney Presented by His Former Students,* edited by Gerald F. Hawthorne. Grand Rapids, Mich.: Eerdmans, 1975.

Manson, T. W. "The Life of Jesus: Some Tendencies in Present-day Research." In *The Background of the New Testament and Its Eschatology* (in honor of Charles Harold Dodd), edited by W. D. Davies and D. Daube. Cambridge University Press, 1956, pp. 211-21.

―――. "The Quest of the Historical Jesus (continued)." In *Studies in the Gospels and Epistles,* edited by Matthew Black. Philadelphia: Westminster Press, 1962, pp. 3-12.

McArthur, Harvey K. *The Quest Through the Centuries: The Search for the Historical Jesus.* Philadelphia: Fortress Press, 1966.

McCasland, S. Vernon. *The Pioneer of Our Faith: A New Life of Jesus.* New York: McGraw-Hill, 1964.

Mitchell, E. K. "History of the Life of Christ." In *Recent Christian Progress.* New York: Macmillan, 1909, pp. 118-26.

Mitton, C. Leslie. *Jesus: The Fact Behind the Faith.* Grand Rapids, Mich.: Eerdmans, 1974.

Mounce, R. H. *The Essential Nature of New Testament Preaching.* Grand Rapids, Mich.: Eerdmans, 1960, pp. 40-43, 133.

Nineham, D. E. "Some Reflections on the Present Position with Regard to the Jesus of History." In *Historicity and Chronology in the New Testament.* London: SPCK, 1965.

Perrin, Norman. *Rediscovering the Teaching of Jesus.* New York: Harper, 1967.

Potterie, I. de la, ed. *De Jésus aux évangiles: tradition et rédaction dans les évangiles synoptiques.* Bibliotheca ephemeridum theologicarum lovaniensium 25. Gembloux: Duculot; Louvain: Leuven University, 1967.

Prenter, Regin. "Works and Words of Jesus Christ." In *The Gospel as History,* edited by Vilmos Vatja. The Gospel Encounters History 4. Philadelphia: Fortress Press, 1975, pp. 3-42.

Reumann, John. *Jesus in the Church's Gospels.* Philadelphia: Fortress Press, 1968.

Rigaux, Béda. "Jésus-Christ devant l'histoire et la dialectique." *Revue générale belge* 94.1958-59, pp. 1-16.

Ristow, Helmut, and Matthiae, Karl, eds. *Der historische Jesus und der kerygmatische Christus: Beiträge zum Christus-verständnis in Forschung und Verkündigung.* Berlin: Evangelische Verlagsanstalt, 1962.

Robinson, James M. "Kerygma and History in the New Testament." In *The Bible and Modern Scholarship,* edited by J. P. Hyatt. New York: Abingdon, 1965.

————. "A New Quest of the Historical Jesus." SBT 25. London: SCM; Naperville, Ill.: Allenson, 1959. German translation, *Kerygma und historischer Jesus.* Zürich: Zwingli-Verlag, 1960.

————. "The Recent Debate on the New Quest." *Journal of Bible and Religion* 30.1962, p. 207.

Rowlingson, D. T. "The Continuing Quest of the Historical Jesus." In *New Testament Studies: Critical Essays in New Testament Interpretation with Special Reference to the Meaning and Worth of Jesus,* edited by E. P. Booth. New York: Abingdon-Cokesbury, 1942, pp. 42-69 (covers 1918-1942).

Schlier, H. "amēn." In *Theologisches Wörterbuch zum Neuen Testament.* Vol. 1. Edited by G. Kittel. Stuttgart: W. Kohlhammer, 1933, pp. 339-42, esp. 341-42. Translation by G. W. Bromiley, *Theological Dictionary of the New Testament.* Vol. 1. Grand Rapids, Mich.: Eerdmans, 1964, pp. 335-38.

Schnackenburg, Rudolf. "Jesusforschung und Christusglaube." *Catholica* 13.1959, pp. 1-17.

Schubert, Kurt, ed. *Der historische Jesus und der Christus unseres Glaubens: eine katholische Auseinandersetzung mit der Folgen der Entmythologisierungtheorie.* Vienna and Freiburg: Herder, 1962.

Schweitzer, Albert. *Geschichte der Leben-Jesu-Forschung.* Tübingen: J. C. B. Mohr, 1906, 1913, 1951. Translation by W. Montgomery, *The Quest of the Historical Jesus: A Critical Study of its Progress from Reimarus to Wrede.* London: A. & C. Black, 1910, 1911.

Stanton, G. N. *Jesus of Nazareth in New Testament Preaching.* New York: Cambridge University Press, 1975.

Stauffer, Ethelbert. *Jesus and His Story.* Translation by Richard and Clara Winston. New York: Knopf, 1959.

Vermes, Geza. *Jesus the Jew.* New York: Macmillan, 1973.

Whately, Richard. *Historic Doubts Relative to Napoleon Bonaparte.* 4th British ed. Cambridge: Brown, Shattuck, 1832; Philadelphia: J. M. Campbell, 1946.

Zahrnt, Heinz. *The Historical Jesus.* Translation by J. S. Bowden. New York: Harper, 1963.

7. THE KINGDOM IN MARK

A. Miracles

Just as facts come to us in the reports of an interpreting mind, so too with phenomena outside received empirical knowledge: the events known to us in the gospels as miracles are mediated through the interpreting minds of the community and the evangelists. Any attempt to get behind the record to ascertain the "fact" of what happened in each and every instance must reckon with the mediating interpretation of a believing and religious mind.

This must not be taken to imply that what in the gospels and in common speech are called "miracles" do not happen. Only a mind confined by the mechanistic and determinist mold of one kind of nineteenth-century understanding of the physical sciences can maintain the posture that the physical universe is a completely predictable machine. Doubtless if all the evidence were in—or rather if all the evidence were open to our inspection—some apparently aberrant phenomena in nature could after all be fitted into a framework of the laws of nature where they cannot now be accommodated. The commentator on the gospels, whether a believer or not, must come to terms not only with the believing minds which recorded the tradition of the miracles, but also with the belief in supernatural causation in the time of the ministry of Jesus. In such a context, *immediate* causes were not considered as important as the remote, divine causes. The commentator must also deal with the texts and the records he has from the hands of the people who asserted that events of a supernatural character had taken place; he must also deal with the assertion that Jesus considered such events to be an integral part of his ministry.

Some general comments are therefore in order at this point. The early community certainly shared the belief that miracles were bound up with the preaching of Jesus (cf. Acts 2:22, 10:36-38). To suggest that the miracles were understood *by Jesus* as having evidentiary significance attaching to his person is to misunderstand the records. It is *partly* on this misunderstanding that some of the recent concern with Jesus as *theios anēr* (not to mention *thaumatourgos)* is based. If indeed *(pace* Bultmann) the miracles were added by the evangelists to reinforce the image of Jesus as wonder-worker, it is surely pertinent to ask why those same evangelists left standing the record that publicity about his works of healing compelled Jesus to seek privacy (Mark 7:36, 8:10, 9:30). In the face of the gospel tradition, we may well hesitate to give unqualified acceptance to the view that miracles can be used to demonstrate the validity of the Christian faith. Jesus asserted that even false prophets could work wonders capable of deceiving holy men (Mark 13:22,23). Moreover, the acceptance of supranatural phenomena as establishing, or tending to establish, the truth of Christian faith inevitably raises legitimate questions about similar phenomena in other religious systems. It is one thing to say that we would expect a definitive act of God to be accompanied by supranormal signs; it is a completely different thing to suggest that the presence of such signs is a guarantee of such a definitive act. Jesus apparently refused to accede to the request that he perform signs to authenticate his mission from God (Matt 4:6, 12:38-42; Luke 4:23; Mark 6:1-6, 8:11-13, 15:31-32).

It is important to remember that the vocabulary of the NT preserves subtleties in language which are not reflected by the English "miracle" (Latin *miraculum*). The NT *teras,* "portent" (used in the Septuagint as translation for Hebrew *môpet,* "portent, wonder"), is never used alone, perhaps because *teras* is the preferred word in Hellenistic wonder tales for supranormal occurrences; it is always used alongside *sēmeion,* "sign," to designate the words of Jesus. In so doing, the NT not only preserves one strand of Hebrew usage, since *môpet* is used with *ôt,* "sign," but also does justice to the use of *môpet* to describe any symbolic act, not necessarily miraculous.

The signs of Jesus are in our gospels inextricably linked with the proclamation of the Reign of God. This is not to say that the signs are merely authenticating tokens. Quite to the contrary, miracle as the power of God was seen by Jesus as one means of the Reign of God's entry into an area long dominated by powers of evil. God's entrance into a world dominated by evil, personified in the person of Satan, links the miracles of healing and the exorcisms. Dramatic though the latter may be in our records, they share the same characteristic as the healings from sickness. Both healings and exorcisms are seen as a restoration of order to a creation characterized by disorder, and so under the dominion of Satan. While it is true that the popular orthodoxy of the OT was that disease and sickness were a result of or a punishment for sin, it would be far too simplistic to take this as Jesus' sole motivation for his work of healing and exorcism. Despite the fact that Augustine of Hippo was only too ready to attribute all human ills to his poorly defined concept of original sin, and the fact that many human ills are indeed a direct result of sin, Jesus is reported on two important occasions to have rejected the widespread orthodoxy of his own time (Luke 13:1-5; John 9:3). Nevertheless, the healing ministry of Jesus does emphasize the fundamental unity of human existence in classical Hebrew thought: being delivered from the bondage of the evil of sickness and disease meant also being delivered from one form of bondage to Satan. This mode of thought in the ministry of Jesus is demonstrated clearly in the language employed, for example, in Luke 4:39—in which the "rebuke" administered to the fever is in Mark (1:25, 3:12, 9:25) used of confrontation with a demon; see the commentary on Mark 1:25.

All of this suggests an approach to works of healing which in our frame of reference we find alien and even unacceptable. Yet our ability to recognize epilepsy (Mark 9:14-29) or psychosomatic illnesses in the gospel narratives may well lead us to forget that element in the works of Jesus which sees the ministry as concerned with reestablishing the unity of the Reign of God in a creation characterized by disorder, sin, and the reign of Satan. The healing works of Jesus are, to use a more familiar terminology, an outward and sacramental sign of a dawning but invisible Reign of God.

The first work of healing recorded by Mark (1:21-28) is not only an exorcism, in which the dominion of Satan is challenged by Jesus and defeated; it is also a healing which occurs on a Sabbath. To see in this incident a confrontation with the then current understanding of Sabbath rest, or to see Jesus as a "new Moses" superseding the old legislation, is to miss the point. It has been observed more than once in the past thirty years that God's rest from the activity of creation on the seventh day is reaffirmed in Jesus' action. The emphasis on the use of the Sabbath for healing and exorcism springs from the fact that there is in the ministry of Jesus a *new* creation-activity. Like the first creation, it is concerned with order and unity, but this time it is not creation from nothing; it is *restoration* to life and salvation.

It is from this point of view that we must approach the miracles in the gospels. Attention has already been called to the comparative absence in Hebrew thought of any prolonged examination of the varieties of causation, apart from God as the cause of everything. One prophet found it possible to attribute evil to God in specific human situations (Amos 3:6). By the time of the ministry of Jesus, this view had undergone considerable erosion, if not total obliteration. The transformation of the figure of Satan from a "prosecuting attorney" in Job to the embodiment of malevolence meant that manifestations of evil could be explained through satanic dominion. The healing ministry of Jesus is the challenge of a dawning Reign of God to the entrenched power of evil, in exorcism, in healings, and in the accounts of the raising of the dead. A note of caution is in order at this point. There is no suggestion in the gospels of a metaphysical dualism in the universe; such dualism as we find is ethical and moral. At no point do the evangelists suggests that the ultimate power of God is in question; that disorder and chaos, sin and rebellion, have made serious inroads in the creation is nowhere denied, but everywhere the triumph of God is asserted.

It is appropriate to consider first the nature miracles, especially the "rebuking" of the wind during the storm on the lake (Mark 4:37-41). The natural order is never neutral in the Bible, and Jesus' injunction to the sea, "Be silent" (Mark 4:39), uses the same vocabulary as the command to a demon in Mark 1:25. Whatever may be our own explanation in terms of secondary causality, the NT lesson is clear enough—God's order has triumphed over chaos. A similar looking forward to such restoration finds notable expression in Rom 8:22.

We may wish to inject a sober note of later medical knowledge into the accounts of Jesus raising the dead, and conclude that perhaps we are confronted with the resuscitation of persons in a diabetic coma. Equally, we may wish to call attention to meteorological phenomena associated with large bodies of land-locked water in the narrative in Mark 4:37-41. But in both cases we shall not only be bringing considerations to bear of which the first century was ignorant; we shall also be missing the point which the evangelists were making about the ministry of Jesus. We may be in agreement with J. F. Stenning (in *A New Commentary on Holy Scripture,* edited by Charles Gore, Henry Leighton Goudge, and Alfred Guillaume, London: SPCK, 1928, p. 239, col. 2) on the unfortunate Uzza (2 Sam 6:1-7), but we shall overlook the unity of mind, body, and soul in biblical thought. We shall certainly not be attending to the evangelist's assertion that "salvation" is a declaration of the sovereignty of God by whatever means this is brought about. In the biblical view, the "natural" realm and the "spiritual" realm are one entity, and salvation is the restoration of unity to a fragmented creation: the wholeness of humanity and of creation was outwardly manifested in what we call health, whether of mind or of body. Similarly, the wholeness of creation was a wholeness where things inimical to people would be conquered by the assertion of God's rule.

Still to be considered is the element of faith, or trusting belief, in the gospel works. We have become accustomed in our discussion of "faith healing" to ask questions which the gospels do not ask: we demand to know the object of faith, whether it is the healer as agent or God as author. Significantly, our NT sources are content to record the demand for faith, or the commendation of a faith already active. The gospels would appear to suggest that our modern concerns are, in their terms, misplaced and that the faith which alone can embrace the acts of God is simply an openness to God's activity as the necessary prerequisite through which that activity can operate.

Bibliography

Ambrozic, Aloysius M. *The Hidden Kingdom.* CBQ Monograph Series 2. Washington, D.C.: Catholic Biblical Association of America, 1972.

Bacon, Benjamin W. "The Markan Theory of Demonic Recognition of the Christ." *ZNW* 6.1905, pp. 153-58.

Bartsch, Hans-Werner. "Parusieerwartung und Osterbotschaft." *EvTh* 7.1947-48, pp. 115-26.

————. "Zum Problem der Parusieverzögerung bei den Synoptischen," *EvTh* 19.1959, pp. 117-30.

Bickermann, E. "Das leere Grab." *ZNW* 23.1924, pp. 281-92.

————. "Das Messiasgeheimnis und die Komposition des Markus-evangeliums." *ZNW* 22.1923, pp. 122-40.

Black, Matthew. "The Kingdom of God Has Come." *ExpT* 63.1952, pp. 289-90.

Boobyer, G. H. "The Redaction of Mark IV.1-34." *NTS* 6.1921, pp. 225-35.

Bornkamm, Barth G., and Held, H. J. *Tradition and Interpretation in Matthew* (esp. pp. 15-38). Translation by Percy Scott. London: SCM Press, 1963.

Bousset, W. *Kyrios Christos.* Translation by John E. Steely. 6th ed. Nashville: Abingdon Press, 1970.

Burkill, T. Alec. "The Hidden Son of Man in St. Mark's Gospel." *ZNW* 52.1961, pp. 189-213.

Busse, Ulrich. *Die Wünder der Propheten Jesus: Die Rezeption, Komposition und Interpretation der Wünder-Tradition im Evangelium des Lukas.* Stuttgart: Katholischer Bibelwerk, 1977.

Campbell, J. Y. "The Kingdom of God Has Come." *ExpT* 48.1936, pp. 91-94.

Carlston, C. E. *The Parables of the Triple Tradition.* Philadelphia: Fortress Press, 1975.

Colani, T. *Jésus-Christ et les croyances messianiques de son temps.* Strasbourg: Treuttel & Wurtz, 1864.

Dodd, C. H. "The Kingdom of God Has Come." *ExpT* 48.1936, pp. 138-42.

Ebeling, Hans Jurgen. *Das Messiasgeheimnis und die Botschaft des Markus-Evangelisten.* Berlin: Alfred Topelmann, 1939.

Feuillet, A. "Le règne de Dieu et les miracles de Jésus après les Évangiles synoptiques." *EspVie* 87.49.1977, pp. 655-69.

Fuller, R. H. *The Mission and Achievement of Jesus.* London: SCM Press; Chicago: Allenson, 1954.

Grant, Robert M. "The Coming of the Kingdom of God." *JBL* 67.1948, pp. 297-303.

Harder, Gunther. "Das eschatologische Geschichtsbild der sogenannten kleinen Apokalypse Markus 13." *ThViat* 4.1952, pp. 71-107.

————, "Das Gleichnis von der selbstwachsenden Saat. Mark. 4.26-29." *ThViat* 1.1948-49, pp. 51-70.

Hiers, Richard. *The Kingdom of God in the Synoptic Tradition.* Gainesville, Fla.: University of Florida Press, 1970.

————. "Purification of the Temple: Preparation for the Kingdom of God." *JBL* 90.1.1971, pp. 82-90.

Hutton, W. R. "The Kingdom of God Has Come." *ExpT* 64.1952, pp. 89-91.

Kee, Howard C. *Community of the New Age.* Philadelphia: Westminster Press, 1977.

————. "The Terminology of Mark's Exorcism Stories." *NTS* 14.1968, pp. 232-46.

Kelber, Werner H. *The Kingdom in Mark.* Philadelphia: Fortress Press, 1974.

Knigge, Heinz-Dieter. "The Meaning of Mark." *Int* 22.1968, pp. 53-70.

Kümmel, Werner G. *Promise and Fulfillment.* Translation by Dorothea Barton. London: SCM Press, 1966.

Lambrecht, Jan. "Die Redaktion der Markus-Apokalypse." Analecta Biblica 28. Rome: Pontifical Biblical Institute, 1967.

Luz, Ulrich. "Das Geheimsmotiv und die Markinische Christologie." ZNW 56.1965, pp. 9-30.

Manson, T. W. "The EGO EIMI of the Messianic Presence in the New Testament." JTS 48.1947, pp. 59-61.

Mussner, Franz. "Die Bedeutung von Mk 1.14f. für die Reichgottesverkündigung Jesu." TTZ 66.1957, pp. 257-75.

————. "Gottesherrschaft und Sendung Jesu nach Mk 1.14f. zugleich ein Beitrag über die innere Struktur des Markusevangeliums." In Praesentia Salutis. Düsseldorf: Patmos-Verlag, 1967.

Nineham, Dennis E. "The Order of Events in St. Mark's Gospel." In Studies in the Gospels, edited by D. E. Nineham. Oxford: Blackwell, 1955.

Perrin, Norman. "The Creative Use of the Son of Man Traditions by Mark." USQR 23.1968, pp. 357-65.

————. Jesus and the Language of the Kingdom. Philadelphia: Fortress Press, 1976.

————. The Kingdom of God in the Teaching of Jesus. Philadelphia: Fortress Press, 1963.

————. A Modern Pilgrimage in New Testament Christology. Philadelphia: Fortress Press, 1974.

————. "Towards an Interpretation of the Gospel of Mark." In Christology and a Modern Pilgrimage, edited by Hans D. Betz. Claremont, Calif.: New Testament Colloquium, 1971.

Riesenfeld, Haarald. Jésus transfiguré: L'arrière-plan du recit évangelique de la transfiguration de notre Seigneur. Acta Seminarii Neotestamentici Upsaliensis 16. Copenhagen: Ejnar Munksgaard, 1947.

Schnackenburg, Rudolf. God's Rule and Kingdom. Translation by John Murray. New York: Herder & Herder, 1963.

Schulz, Siegfried. "Die Bedeutung des Markus für die Theologie-geschichte des Urchristentums." Studia Exegetica ii, TU 87. Berlin: Akademie-Verlag, 1964.

Smith, Charles W. F. "No Time for Figs." JBL 79.1960, pp. 315-27.

Turner, C. H. "Marcan Usage: Notes Critical and Exegetical on the Second Gospel." JTS 1923-28.

Weihnacht, Harald. Die Menschwerdung des Sonnes Gottes im Markusevangelium. Tübingen: J. C. B. Mohr, 1972.

Weiss, Johannes. Jesus' Proclamation of the Kingdom of God. Translation with introduction by R. Hiers and D. Larrimore Holland. Philadelphia: Fortress Press, 1971.

Werner, Eric. " 'Hosanna' in the Gospels." JBL 65.1946, pp. 97-122.

Zerwick, M. Untersuchungen zum Markus-Stil: Ein Beitrag zur stilistisch Durcharbeitung des Neuen Testaments. Rome: Pontifical Biblical Institute, 1937.

Ziesler, J. A. "The Transfiguration Story and the Markan Soteriology." ExpT 81.1970, pp. 263-68.

B. Parables

The general problems of parables are treated in the Anchor Bible *Matthew*. Parable material in Matthew's gospel was almost always cast in "case law" form and demanded an answer to a hypothetical case. *In general,* the Matthean parable tradition calls for a decision on the "case" of the vocation of Israel as the chosen people of God at a time when, in Jesus, the Reign of God is proclaimed as imminent and people are called to respond to its proclamation. If, as we contend, the most convincing solution to the synoptic problem is the Griesbach hypothesis, we must consider in what terms, if any, parable material in Mark was modified from the models in Matthew and Luke.

What must immediately strike the reader of the synoptic gospels is their agreement that Jesus accomplished the bulk of his general teaching by means of parable/allegory. In connection with this it is instructive to notice the way in which Mark amplifies and explains the sayings of Jesus which concern his teaching methods. The point not only exemplifies the way Mark deals with his sources, but also sheds additional light on his reasons for writing his gospel. John's gospel also emphasizes that Jesus taught in figurative speech, *paroimia* (John 16:25).

We are confronted with several separate but related questions. Does the gospel tradition (Matt 13:34-35; Mark 4:11,33,34; Luke 10:21,23; John 16:25) accurately describe the pedagogical method of Jesus? For example, did Jesus use the kind of figure found in Mark 4:13ff.? How faithfully have our gospels conveyed the earliest tradition? Historically, there is no good reason to deny to Jesus a method of teaching deeply entrenched in the Hebrew Scriptures (cf., e.g., 2 Sam 12:1-4 and Isa 5:1-7, both illustrative of the "Covenant lawsuit" theme in the prophetic tradition). Moreover, in spite of the fact that the NT outside the gospels does not develop or even continue the teaching method of Jesus, rabbinic examples of parables can be found well into the fourth century A.D. It is at least possible that the *absence* of parables in the non-gospel NT tradition is mute witness to the claim made by the synoptic writers that Jesus employed the method only for "those outside"; the NT books are works compiled within the boundaries of a believing community and not primarily for evangelism. If there is no good reason to except Jesus from the exercise of a known and ancient teaching method, there is at the same time good reason to suppose that unless Jesus had employed the method, there would have been little point in introducing the material in books written for believers.

We must now turn to the vital passage, Mark 4:33-34. The distinction in Matthew between teaching imparted privately to the inner circle on the one hand, and the parable method employed with the crowds on the other, is examined in the Anchor Bible *Matthew*. What is instructive in Mark 4:33-34 is the expansion of the Matthean comment. It has been pleaded by some that despite Mark's desire to produce a gospel which served an immediate purpose, it was necessary for him to reassure his readers that they had indeed heard the gospel in its fullness, that there were no "secret teachings" as yet undisclosed, and that in spite of the brevity imposed on the material, nothing of moment had been omitted. But the validity of this view must obviously depend on our ability to determine the kind of questioning in the early community to which Mark 4:33-34 would be at best an insignificant answer. Moreover, the approach fails to account for the patchwork quality of Mark 4, to which attention will be called later.

Mark 4:33-34 is preceded by a section paralleled in Matthew and Luke: the parable of the sower, an explanation for such methods in teaching, the interpretation of the parable, the saying about the lamp, and related lessons from that saying (Mark 4:10-22). Then Mark combines a series of sayings from Matthew and Luke, emphasizing that nothing has been deliberately concealed in the proclamation of the gospel, and that only obduracy on the part of the hearers can obscure the message (Mark 4:21-25 is a digest of Matt 5:15, 10:26, 7:2, and 25:29 with Luke 12:2, 8:16-18, 6:38, 19:26). From whatever source it was derived, the Markan parable of the seed growing secretly (4:26-29) is vital assurance to his readers that the purposes of God cannot be negated: the Kingdom will come to fruition even though its growth is for the time being hidden from view. The parable of the mustard seed in Mark (4:30-32) is far more polished and emphatic than in either Matthew (13:31-32) or Luke (13:18-19) and serves the same end as the preceding parable of the seed. In the light of all this, it is imperative to consider the following verses in Mark, vv. 33 and 34, as against v. 11 in the same chapter. Jeremias *(The Parables of Jesus,* English translation by S. H. Hooke, London, 1963, p. 16) proposes a translation of v. 11b: ". . . those outside are confronted by riddles"—in contrast with the secret knowledge possessed by the inner circle. Jeremias further contends that his translation can be justified by the parallel between *mustērion* in v. 11a and *parabolē* in v. 11b, with the additional comment that the sayings concern the obscurity of Jesus' teaching and have no bearing on the interpretation of parables. This, in common with other proposals, is too simple. But it must be said that much of the continuing debate on the material in Mark 4 is due to the character of the chapter itself, where (in at least one instance) Mark is apparently drawing on material which was not part of his original source or sources.

The contribution of Wrede (1963) to the debate, issuing in his famous enunciation of the "messianic secret" as the key to Mark's work, has been seminal, though perhaps few would accept the thesis now without severe qualification. In recent years that thesis has been succinctly stated again by D. E. Nineham (1963, p. 126): "Mark thought that the parables were intended to wrap up our Lord's teaching and make it obscure, and so prevent it from having its full impact on those who were not meant to be enlightened and saved by it." From this view the present writer emphatically dissents, as will be clear from preceding material in this section; nor is it easier to give assent to Nineham's further judgment that believers have access to the meaning of parables because they see them from the far side of the salvation events of crucifixion and exaltation. The difficulty with this view, as with its predecessor in Wrede, is that Mark does not invariably think of parables as instruments of obfuscation. On the contrary, the parable of the tenant winegrowers (12:1-12), described as such in 12:1, was certainly understood, and Mark implies that Jesus meant it to be understood. Again, Mark 7:14 speaks of the parable which Jesus explicitly expected to be understood. It is difficult to know what to make of the assertion that the obscurity of Jesus' teaching and the faithlessness of the disciples (cf. 4:13, 7:18, 8:17ff.) were all dramatically changed by the events of Easter. It must be said that if so much was changed, then Mark has been remarkably careless in handling his tradition, since Jesus is represented as expressing astonishment at the obduracy of the disciples (8:17), while 4:34 certainly does not suggest any kind of post-Easter faith. No more impressive is the theory, propounded in the last decade, that Mark's gospel reflects a period in the early community when Christians needed to be reassured that the tradition accurately reflected the authentic teaching of Jesus, and for this reason Mark invests the teaching of Jesus with an "esoteric quality" which needed interpretation to the inner group of disciples. This sounds oddly anticipatory of Morton Smith's *Secret Gospel* (cf. appended notes to Chapter 10 in the commentary). But apart from such an odd connection, it is only in Mark 4 that there is even the faintest hint of an esoteric dimension in the teaching. The teaching of Jesus in Mark—apart from instances where there is a note indicating that it was addressed to "the disciples"—is mainly public. But most important of all, Evans' proposition is singularly ill-served by the evangelist, for it is Mark who is constantly reminding us of the inadequacy of the disciples to whom supposedly hidden interpretations were given.

C. F. D. Moule has introduced an element of textual interpretation all too frequently absent in these debates. Moule believes that Mark does not employ Isa 6:9-10 literally. The evangelist simply provides a contrast between two diverse groups: for one group (the outsiders) the parable remains a mere story, while for the other (those already beginning to respond to Jesus) further explanations are sought. This is emphatically less tortuous, and does far more justice to the text, than the two views already mentioned. Yet even here we must express reservations. The overall picture of the disciples in Mark is not wholly that of a trusted inner circle of those beginning to understand and so seeking enlightenment. The failure to understand, along with Jesus' astonishment at such failure, is a prominent element in Mark (cf. 7:13,14, and 18).

Perhaps one element in the continuing debate as to the place of parables in the Markan scheme is our own failure to see them as part of a whole pattern of teaching. Not only are the parables set in the context of Jesus' whole ministry of proclamation, but that proclamation in Mark is characterized from the beginning as beset by opposition, obstinate refusal to understand, and even total rejection. If parables and sayings produced hostility and misunderstanding, then this was all of a piece with the way in which Mark understood the whole ministry. The disciples, so far from being eager recipients of esoteric teaching, emerge in almost as bad a light as Jesus' opponents and critics. In short, the Markan theme of conflict, humiliation, opposition, and final rejection is basic to the whole tenor of his work. The difficulty with the Markan parable material is that it is almost inextricably interwoven with "sayings" material, as a glance at the table in Taylor's commentary will demonstrate (Introduction, VIII.5, pp. 85-88). But on any showing it is Mark 4 which, as most commentators agree, most clearly indicates how the evangelist viewed his tradition.

There are, however, verses in Mark 4 which do not fit the Markan theme just described. For example, 4:11ff. certainly is an intrusion into the flow from 4:10 to the explanation of 4:14. Jeremias *(Parables,* pp. 13ff.) offers the suggestion that v. 11 originally was not confined to parable teaching, but was a saying (similar to Matt 11:25-27) concerned with the whole ministry and identity of Jesus. But if this is so, then under what influence did Mark adapt the saying to parable teaching? The simplest explanation is that whatever tradition Mark inherited was adapted by him in the light of Matt 13:10-15, and that Matthew's "case law" sense of *parabolē* (Hebrew *māšāl)* has been somewhat awkwardly fitted into a Markan scheme concerned with humiliation and rejection in the ministry. Certainly 4:33,34 accords well with the careful distinctions in Matthew between the crowd and the inner circle. (That Mark had access to sources other than Matthew and Luke and his own tradition seems confirmed by the very odd and non-Markan phrase in v. 34— *tois idiois mathētais*—"to his own disciples," a *hapax legomenon* in Mark, who otherwise uses *hoi methētai autou*—"his disciples.")

The editorial hand of Mark can be seen in the series of sayings in 4:21-32. They are joined by the phrase "he said to them" (vv. 21,24,26,30) and it is certainly the case that the sayings are of a different character from vv. 11ff. and v. 34. Moreover, vv. 33-34 would have come conveniently after the parable of the sower, or in the position occupied by the parallel in Matthew. If the parable of the sower is challenge and "case law" in the Matthean sense, then the sayings of 4:23-25 are an exhortation to watchfulness for those who already discern the meaning. How far can we identify Mark's use of sources in his Chapter 4? Verse 13 appears to be Markan—it effectively nullifies the sense of vv. 31 and 34. In v. 10, *erōtan* is not the usual Markan word for "to ask" (it is used again only at 7:26), for *eperōtan* is his preferred verb, which he uses more than twenty times. Again, the phrase "the Twelve and others who were around him" stands alone: comparable verses at 7:17 and 9:28 all have quite common Markan characteristics of vocabulary. It is possible that 4:10 was added from one of his sources as preparatory to v. 11. Mark's 4:9 seems clearly to have been taken from the Matthean context (Matt 13:1-9), where it is entirely in place, and added by Mark to the account to assist his own tradition of 4:21-32 (cf. 7:14 and 8:18).

If Mark then, out of respect for a tradition which he found, inserted its wording into what seemed to him an appropriate place, yet did not change it to fit his own overall theological concerns, we can easily find ourselves accusing him of inconsistency. But Mark's respect for traditions which he found is impressive: he uses the two Matthean accounts of the feeding of the crowds for no apparent reason other than respect for the tradition. But consistency in an evangelist may well be the hobgoblin of critics: Mark allows the tradition to stand in 9:9ff. and 9:31ff., where the disciples are represented as being totally unable to comprehend the passion predictions, while 8:31ff. does imply *some* understanding at least.

We now need to examine the parable audience in our gospels. A series of parallels in 4:11a and 4:11b should be noticed:

4:11a	4:11b
the mystery of the Reign of God	everything
is given	comes (literally "is")
to you	to those outside
(with exposition)	in parables

The parenthetical clause in 11a is demanded by the parallel. Although Jeremias allows that *en parabolais* refers directly to the manner in which the teaching was given, he does not see that *mustērion* refers to content. He therefore fails to find a parallel for *parables.* The word *everything* plainly parallels *mystery;* cf. v. 34, which refers to all things being expounded to disciples.

The contrast (as in Matt 13:11 and Luke 8:10) in 4:34 is between "cases" to outsiders and "all things" to insiders. But can this be substantiated? Does Mark 4:11 and 33,34 (cf. Luke 10:21,23 and John 16:25) describe the actual practice of Jesus? If so, to what extent have the evangelists, or the primitive communities, faithfully mirrored this tradition? T. W. Manson *(The Teaching of Jesus,* Cambridge University Press, 1935, pp. 57ff.) classifies parables under various headings, with further refinement among individual sayings and parables (as we commonly understand them) between those explained and those left unexplained. Some single sayings hardly demand explanation, and stand on their own. One vital consideration must be borne in mind, and that is the audience to which, as the evangelists inform us, the parables were addressed. The "disciples" must be divided into the Twelve and the general body of followers. In addition, there are the "crowds" (mainly not marked by any further distinction) and Jesus' critics (variously, Pharisees, Sadducees, priests, and scribes).

We shall be concerned solely with Mark here, though the reader is assured that schemes such as that presented here validate for the other synoptics the tentative conclusions drawn from Mark. For our purposes, we must separate the "case" parables and the sayings into four separate groups, as follows: (1) The allegorical group includes sayings where some elements, if not every single item, have some kind of explanation. The explanations *tend* to be separated from the main body of the material, sometimes at the end, sometimes relegated to a different occasion (cf. Matt 13:24-30; Mark 4:13-20 and 7:15-24). (2) A closely allied category includes the kind of material which explains the parable, and its application, usually at the end. If this is removed, the parable remains without explanation. (3) Self-explanatory material is derived from its *Sitz im Leben,* often dialogue, which serves as adequate exposition. (4) Some material, self-explanatory like that in (3), calls for no explanation because the parables are either complete in themselves or have the explanation interwoven with the material. With these divisions, the Markan material can be classified as follows:

	The Twelve	Followers	Crowds	Critics
(1) Allegory	7:17-23	4:13-20		3:26
(2) Explained		4:22		
(3) *Sitz im Leben*	9:49-50			
	13:34			
(4) Unexplained			4:30-32	2:19-20
				2:21
				2:22
				3:27
				12:1-2

"Explained" material—to Twelve and followers = 6

—to crowds and critics   = 1

"Unexplained"   —to Twelve and followers = 0

—to crowds and critics   = 6

The tabulation bears out the sayings in Mark 4:11 and 34. All except one item of the explained material is addressed to the groups composed of the Twelve and the followers; six items in the table, directed at the crowds and the critics, are left without explanation. Some caution is perhaps called for in connection with 9:49-50 and 13:34: here we have examples of explanation in context, but the chart effectively demonstrates that the bulk of unexplained material is addressed to crowds and critics; there is only one example of explained material, 3:26, directed at Jesus' opponents. Comparison of the Markan data with Matthew and Luke throws some light on the way Mark used his material. In Matthew, seven parables and/or sayings are explained to the Twelve and the general body of followers, and two are explained to Jesus' critics. Matthew has three instances of unexplained material directed to the Twelve and the followers, with two "unexplained" examples directed at the opposition. In Luke, there are fourteen examples explained to the Twelve and the followers, two explained to the crowds, and a surprising eight explained to the opposition. In the "unexplained" category there are three addressed to the Twelve and the followers, with three addressed to the crowds and four to the opposition.

In general, then, Jesus appears not to have dealt with the inner meaning of the Kingdom with the crowds or his critics, contenting himself with stating "cases" or even riddles, while reserving explanatory matter for the inner circle and/or the general body of the disciples. The Markan scheme outlined in the chart is remarkably consistent, and those of the other evangelists only slightly less so. But the impressive fact is that the exceptions in all the synoptics to the general rule derived from Mark 4:11,33-34 are so few. It is safe to say that the *Sitz im Leben* of the parables and sayings, with the distinction made between the followers on the one hand and the crowds and critics on the other, was carefully preserved. It is possible that this scheme was imposed by the early Christian community, but for the results to have been achieved with such unanimity would be little less than astounding. It is difficult to escape the conclusion that the "secret" of the interpretation of the parables and sayings is so consistently a part of the tradition that it was indeed, as Mark in 4:11,33, and 34 asserts, Jesus' own purpose. Reference will be made in the commentary to the problems of 4:11, widely regarded as redactional but defended by Räisänen (1973) as certainly Markan. Some answer is demanded of the question posed by the redaction critics and by Räisänen: *"Cui bono?"* The bewilderment of the Jewish Christian community hypothesized above in 5A ("The Date of Mark's Gospel") would appear to this writer to demand some such editorial insertion by the evangelist. Why was the Kingdom not openly proclaimed to all? If the secrets of the Kingdom were the possession of the inner circle, then why did they desert Jesus at the moment of crisis? The answer of the evangelist is that they too had failed to grasp the implications of Jesus' teaching. If the community to which this gospel is addressed fails likewise to appropriate the full meaning of the parables, then that community, already panic-stricken, will go down to ignominy and defeat; its members must look beyond the passion, as they were told to do in the message delivered to them by those who first preached the word.

Bibliography

Biser, Burgen. *Die Gleichnisse Jesu*. Munich: Kösel-Verlag, 1965.

Burkill, T. Alec. "The Cryptology of the Parables in St. Mark's Gospel." *NovTest* 1.1956, pp. 246-62.

Carlston, E. *The Parables of the Triple Tradition*. Philadelphia: Fortress Press, 1975.

Crossan, J. D. *In Parables*. New York: Harper & Row, 1976.

Dodd, C. H. *The Parables of the Kingdom*. London: Nisbet, 1935.

Dupont, Jacques. *Pourquoi des Paraboles? La méthode parabolique de Jésus*. Paris: Éditions du Cerf, 1977.

Edlund, Conny. *Das Auge der Einfalt: Eine Untersuchung zu Math. 6.22-23 und Luk. 11.34-35*. Copenhagen: Ejnar Munksgaard, 1952.

Eichholz, George. *Einführung in die Gleichnisse*. Neukirchen-Vluyn: Neukirchener Verlag des Erziehungsvereins GmbH., 1963.

Feldman, Asher. *The Parables and Similes of the Rabbis*. London: Cambridge University Press, 1924.

Glen, John S. *The Parables of Conflict in Luke*. Philadelphia: Westminster Press, 1962.

Glover, Carl. *Messages from the Parables*. London: Independent Press, 1956.

Gutzmiller, Richard. *Die Gleichnisse der Herrn*. Einsiedeln: Benzinger, 1960. Translation by Arlene Swidler, *The Parables of the Lord*. New York: Herder & Herder, 1964.

Huffmon, Norman A. "Atypical Features in the Parables of Jesus." *JBL* 97.2.1978, pp. 207-20.

Jeremias, J. *Die Gleichnisse Jesu*. Zürich: Zwingli-Verlag, 1947; Göttingen: Vandenhoeck & Ruprecht, 1965. Translation by S. H. Hooke, *The Parables of Jesus*. London: SCM; New York: Scribner's, 1954. Rev. ed., 1963.

Kahlefeld, Heinrich. *Gleichnisse und Lehrstücke im Evangelium*. Frankfurt: J. Knecht, 1963.

Kirkland, J. R. "The Earliest Understanding of Jesus' Use of Parables: Mark IV.10-12 in Context." *NovTest* 19.1.1977, pp. 1-21.

Lohse, Eduard. *Die Einheit des Neuen Testaments: Exegetische Studien zur Theologie des Neuen Testaments*. Göttingen: Vandenhoeck & Ruprecht, 1973, pp. 49ff.

Masson, Charles. *Les Paraboles de Marc IV*. Paris: Delachaux & Niestlé, 1945.

Michaelis, Wilhelm. *Die Gleichnisse Jesu*. Hamburg: Furche, 1956.

Patte, Daniel, ed. *Semiology and Parables: Exploration of the Possibilities Offered by Structuralism for Exegesis*. Pittsburgh Theological Monographs Series 9. Pittsburgh: Pickwick Press, 1976.

Räisänen, Heikki. *Die Parabeltheorie im Markusevangelium*. Schriften der finnischen exegetischen Gesellschaft 26. Helsinki: Finnish Exegetical Society; Leiden: E. J. Brill, 1973.

Trocmé, E. "Why Parables? A Study of Mark IV." *BJRL* 59.2.1977, pp. 458-71.

Via, Dan Otto, Jr. *The Parables: Their Literary and Existential Dimension.* Philadelphia: Fortress Press, 1967.

C. The Reign/Kingdom

At the heart of the proclamation of Jesus was the imminent dawning of the Reign of God. (The Greek *basileia,* normally translated "kingdom," is far better understood as being a sovereignty constituted of those responding to a demand of God which calls people to allegiance. "Kingdom" has a spatiotemporal connotation which is foreign to the teaching of Jesus.) The frequency in the gospels of the phrase "Reign of God" and "heavenly Reign" is in strong contrast to the paucity of such phrases in Jewish literature contemporary with Jesus—not to mention the comparatively infrequent use of the phrase in the remainder of the NT.

The terminology used in the synoptic gospels is by no means free of debate. The term *basileia tou theou,* "the Reign of God," is found alongside *he basileia tōn ouranōn,* "the heavenly Kingdom." Although the terms ostensibly have the same meaning ("the heavens" being a reverential expression, used to avoid the name of God), a strong case can be made for a differentiation in usage in Matthew's gospel (cf. Albright-Mann, AB *Matthew,* Introduction, pp. c-cv). It is maintained there that the term "Kingdom of Heaven" had specific reference to the continuing community of the Gospel, in contradistinction to the final Reign of God, the Father, after judgment had been passed on the community of the Gospel. This view has been disputed (cf. William O. Walker, Jr., "The Kingdom of the Son of Man and the Kingdom of the Father in Matthew," *CBQ* 30.1968, pp. 573-79), but it still seems to the present writer that Günther Bornkamm (1956) has the best of the argument to date.

One problem with the terminology of the Reign of God in the gospels is the absence of comparative evidence in other Jewish sources. Expectations of a manifold and bewildering complexity and variety existed, but the term "the heavenly Reign" is not attested where on most grounds we might have expected it, in the intertestamental literature. The earliest instance of its use outside the gospels is an occurrence in R. Johanan ben Zakkai (c. A.D. 75). But the fact that the expression occurs at that time should give us pause. It demonstrates very clearly that however Jesus' critics and even his followers may have understood the Reign of God, it could not easily in R. Johanan's time have had overtones of conquest and military adventure.

The bibliography at the end of this section will serve to indicate the interest aroused by the theme of the Kingdom among NT writers in recent years. Much of that discussion has involved imposing on the evangelists whole systems of finely honed theological motifs which speak much of the concerns—social, theological, and other—of the latter part of the twentieth century. Too often it appears that the metaphorical and poetic character of the language employed in the gospels is forgotten, and precise delineations are demanded of material which cannot, and was not intended to, bear the weight placed upon the language. (Cf. in this connection the highly instructive correspondence item "Preparing Scientific Papers" in *Nature*, Vol. 268, July 1977, for a "treatment" of P. B. Shelley's "Ozymandias.") It is far too often forgotten that Jesus never described the Kingdom, and the sayings are introduced by phrases such as "The Reign of God is like . . ."

The most detailed and convincing recent treatment of the theme of the Reign of God in Mark is that of Ambrozic (1975). His thesis is that there are three aspects under which Mark collects the "Kingdom" sayings: (a) the arrival of the Reign in the person of Jesus, especially in his ministry; (b) the hidden character of that Reign in the life of the community; and (c) the promise of further revelation. Ambrozic rightly, in our view, asserts that the tension among these three aspects is "the very flesh and blood of the Second Gospel" (p. 24).

All that is proposed in this section of the Introduction is briefly to discuss the characteristics of the Reign in Mark. Extended treatment of individual sayings will be found in the commentary. In Mark the Reign of God "has come" in the person of Jesus; the decisive intervention of God has begun to take place. The past ages are over, as is also the time of expectation, and in the ministry and teaching of Jesus the sovereign rule of God is now being inaugurated. This Reign breaks in during the ministry by means of the words and actions of Jesus. This irruption of divine activity is especially seen in the healings and exorcisms, as signs of the reassertion of God's order in a world characterized by disorder and sin. The state of affairs inaugurated by Jesus is a wholly new event, an occasion of joy (cf. Mark 2:19-20), and while Jesus will only be with his disciples continually when the Reign has fully come (9:1), even times of distress have a new character, for the end is assured.

The nature of the Reign is misunderstood (and so, *pari passu,* the power of God is misunderstood) even by those closest to Jesus, who think him mad. But the cardinal outward manifestation of the Reign is the gathering together in fellowship with Jesus, now in the ministry and hereafter in the community, of those committed to doing the will of God (cf. 3:31-35). To find in Jesus' proclamation of the new divine activity some new principle of ethics (cf. T. A. Burkill, *Mysterious Revelation,* Ithaca, N.Y.: Cornell University Press, 1963,

p. 2n.) is to fall into the same error that causes Mark to excoriate Jesus' critics—a failure to understand that the fundamental questions revolved around the identity of Jesus as the inaugurator, and the eschatological nature of his mission. The questioners in 2:18-22, for example, cannot distinguish between Jesus and John. The Reign of God commands love and loyalty from those committed to it in childlike trust (cf. 10:15): it is hidden from the untrusting and the unloving, who in their ignorance only ask for a sign, in spite of the signs already given (cf. 8:11-13).

Jesus deliberately confides the secrets of the eschatological age to those committed to God and to him, in faith and love. But the growth of the Kingdom, for all the manifestations of its presence in healing and exorcism, and in the words of Jesus, is hidden. Significantly, the one parable peculiar to Mark (4:26-29) emphasizes the faith in the sovereign power of God demanded of the disciple (= the community), stressing the attitude of the farmer, confident of the outcome, while knowing that he himself can contribute nothing to growth. Aims and methods are the only activities permitted to human endeavor: the results belong to God. It is of more than passing moment that this Markan parable should be found in the section of the gospel which concentrates on the Church. In the study of this parable, homiletic enthusiasm which concentrates on silent, gradual growth is sadly misplaced. There is certainly silent and concealed growth, but the thrust of the parable is directed to the miracle of a munificent harvest from such insignificant beginnings. As in all the other nature parables, there are two emphases: the power of God, and the person of Jesus as the agent of that power. It is more than likely that those to whom the parable was addressed were dissatisfied with the lack of dramatic or even apocalyptic manifestations in the ministry of word and healing.

The Reign of God, now only breaking through in the ministry of Jesus, had long been known in the heavenly council *(mustērion,* 4:11). Only in the final days was it being manifested, presented to people for their doom or destiny. Because it is from God, the opportunity will not recur. In the final denouement of the ministry even the enemies of Jesus will be challenged to "see" the Reign of God come with power (9:1). Further discussion will be provided in the commentary ad loc., but a short summary is required here. Most commentators are hesitant about Dodd's translation of 9:1: ". . . the bystanders . . . shall come to see that the Kingdom of God has already come at some point before they became aware of it" *(The Parables of the Kingdom,* p. 53n. 1). The debate about "realized eschatology" shows no sign of ending soon, and this passage is crucial to Dodd's wholehearted espousal of that view of eschatology. Although his translation of the passage, coupled with the equally important 14:62, certainly does justice to the understanding of the passion in John's gospel, it does not by itself convey the theological understanding of Jesus' ministry in Mark. Indeed, left in isolation 9:1 would undoubtedly have given rise to a general diffusion of the difficulties outlined in the Thessalonian letters. But linked with 14:62 the verse under discussion demands that we pay adequate attention to the focal character of the passion as it is understood in John and Matthew.

The change in Acts from Jesus' emphasis on the Reign to a preaching focused on Jesus and the resurrection is most noticeable. While the change cannot be linked *definitely* with a shift from eschatological expectation to the organizational concerns of a continuing community (Thessalonians for example, succeeds in combining both concerns), it is plain to any reader of the NT that the Reign of God was understood as having in some sense "arrived" during the ministry of Jesus and through his person. The anxieties and doubts of an early Christian community (such as the one for which Mark wrote) could hardly be quieted by references to the past, even references to the victories of Jesus in healing and exorcism. However fundamental to our understanding of the gospels is the basic theme of the dawning of the Reign of God in the ministry of Jesus, it is equally fundamental to the gospels to recognize the Reign-yet-to-be which cannot be identified with the continuing community. This is as true of John's gospel as it is of the three synoptic documents.

This section must end, as it began, with a warning against overweening confidence in any attempt to invest the language of eschatology with precise meanings which such language cannot carry. The immense number of books dedicated to the theme of the Kingdom, from the seminal *Kingdom of Christ* of F. D. Maurice to James Cone's *Theology of Liberation,* ought to give pause to any who would provide an easy encapsulation of the wealth of ideas subsumed under the injunction: "Repent! The Reign of God is upon you!"

Bibliography

Few topics in gospel studies have generated as much discussion in this century as the phrase variously translated as "Kingdom of God" or "Reign of God" in our gospels. Proposed meanings have ranged from an inner possession of the meaning of God's rule in the hearts and minds of men and women on the one hand, to an interpretation of Jesus as some near-identification with the Zealots on the other. The bewildering array of opinion on this phrase will continue to engage academic scholars in spirited debate, and there appears to be no hope at present of a consensus in the matter.

The difficulty of interpreting the phrase is enhanced when Jesus is regarded as having sometimes acted as a predictive prophet in his use of it. Alongside this is the often unspoken stance of some more conservative scholars that Jesus cannot have been mistaken in his prophecies of "the End," whether seen in terms of Israel or the world. Nowhere is this more clearly seen than in commentaries on Mark 9:1 (and par.). Did

Jesus anticipate that the end of his ministry would usher in the Reign of God coming in power? Or did he look to a time beyond that ministry, however soon that time might be, when his band of followers would be clothed in power—i.e., was Jesus looking to the time of the first post-Easter Pentecost? It has long been characteristic of some British scholars to espouse what has come to be called "realized eschatology" as being the theology which informs not only much of the fourth gospel, but also—rightly understood—much of the Synoptics. To a large extent this view was that of the present writer and the late W. F. Albright in *Matthew* (1971). In the intervening period, and as the research into the historical and cultural background of the person and ministry of Jesus has progressed, it has become increasingly clear as this commentary took shape that this view must still be taken seriously as an explanation of the ministry of Jesus.

For a careful historical survey of the debate, the reader is commended to Norman Perrin's *The Kingdom of God in the Teaching of Jesus* (1963). The bibliography that follows does not pretend in any way to be exhaustive, but is intended simply to indicate where the main materials are to be found. It must be emphasized that the debate continues, and that every commentary on the gospels will inevitably reflect that ongoing concern.

Ambrozic, Aloysius M. *The Hidden Kingdom: A Redactional-Critical Study of the References to the Kingdom of God in Mark's Gospel. CBQ* Monograph Series 2, 1975.

Beasley-Murray, G. R. *Jesus and the Future.* London: Macmillan; New York: St. Martin's Press, 1954.

Black, Matthew. "Servant of the Lord and Son of Man." *SJT* 6.1.1953-54, pp. 1-11.

Bornkamm, Günther. *Jesus von Nazareth.* Stuttgart: W. Kolhammer Verlag, 1956. English translation, *Jesus of Nazareth.* New York: Harper & Bros., 1960.

Burkitt, F. C. "The Eschatological Idea in the Gospels." In *Essays on Some Biblical Questions of the Day,* edited by H. B. Swete. London: Macmillan, 1909.

———. "The Parable of the Wicked Husbandmen." In *Transactions of the Third International Congress for the History of Religions,* edited by P. S. Allen and J. de M. Johnson. Oxford University Press, 1908.

Chilton, Bruce David. *God in Strength: Jesus' Announcement of the Kingdom.* Studien zum Neuen Testament und seiner Umwelt B/1. Freistadt: F. Plocht, 1979.

Cullmann, Oscar. *Christ and Time.* Philadelphia: Westminster Press, 1950. Translation by Floyd V. Filson of *Christus und Zeit.*

———. "The Return of Christ." In *The Early Church,* edited by A. J. B. Higgins. London: SCM Press, 1956.

Dalman, G. *Jesu-Jeschua.* New York: Macmillan, 1929.

———. *Die Worte Jesu.* Leipzig: J. C. Heinrich, 1898, 1930. Translation by D. M. Kay, *The Words of Jesus.* Edinburgh: T. & T. Clark, 1902.

Dodd, C. H. *The Coming of Christ.* Cambridge University Press, 1951.

———. *The Kingdom of God and History.* London: Nisbet, 1938.

———. *The Parables of the Kingdom.* London: Nisbet, 1935, 1948.

Easton, B. S. *Christ in the Gospels.* New York: Scribner's, 1930.

Fuller, R. H. *The Mission and Achievement of Jesus.* London: SCM Press, 1954.

Glasson, T. F. *The Second Advent.* London: Epworth Press, 1945.

Grant, F. C. *The Gospel of the Kingdom.* New York: Macmillan, 1940.

Hunter, A. M. *The Words and Works of Jesus.* Philadelphia: Westminster Press, 1950.

Jeremias, J. *New Testament Theology I: The Proclamation of Jesus.* New York: Scribner's, 1971. Translation by John Bowden of *Neutestamentliche Theologie I: Die Verkündigung Jesu.* Gütersloh: Gerd Mohn, 1971.

————. *The Parables of Jesus.* Translation by S. H. Hooke. Rev. ed. New York: Scribner's, 1963.

Knox, John. *The Death of Christ.* London: Collins, 1967.

————. *Jesus Lord and Christ.* New York: Harper & Row, 1958.

Kümmel, W. G. *Verheissung und Erfüllung.* Translation by D. M. Barton, *Promise and Fulfillment.* Naperville, Ill.: Allenson, 1957.

Manson, T. W. "The Life of Jesus: Some Tendencies in Present-Day Research." In *The Background of the New Testament and Its Eschatology,* edited by W. E. Davies and D. Daube. Cambridge University Press, 1956.

————. "Realized Eschatology and the Messianic Secret." In *Studies in the Gospels,* edited by D. E. Nineham. Oxford: Basil Blackwell, 1955.

————. *The Sayings of Jesus.* Cambridge University Press, 1937.

————. *The Servant Messiah.* New York and Cambridge: Cambridge University Press, 1966.

Manson, William. *Christ's View of the Kingdom of God.* (Cambridge University Press), 1918; New York: Moran, 1918.

————. *Jesus the Messiah.* London: Hodder & Stoughton, 1943.

Otto, Rudolf. *Reichgottes und Menschensohn.* 1934. Translation by Floyd Filson and Bertram Lee Woolf, *The Kingdom of God and the Son of Man.* London: Lutterworth Press, 1938.

Perrin, Norman. *The Kingdom of God in the Teaching of Jesus.* Philadelphia: Westminster Press, 1963.

————. *Rediscovering the Teaching of Jesus.* New York: Harper & Row, 1967.

Rauschenbusch, W. *A Theology for the Social Gospel.* Nashville: Abingdon Press, 1957.

Robinson, J. A. T. *Jesus and His Coming.* London: SCM Press, 1957.

Robinson, J. M. *A New Quest for the Historical Jesus.* London: SCM Press, 1959.

Schleiermacher, F. *Der Christliche Glaube.* Translation by H. R. Mackintosh and J. S. Stewart, *The Christian Faith.* New York: Harper & Row, 1963.

Schlosser, J. *Le Règne de Dieu dans les dits de Jésus.* Études Bibliques. Paris: Gabalda, 1980.

Schnackenburg, R. *God's Rule and Kingdom.* New York: Herder & Herder, 1963.

Schweitzer, Albert. *The Mystery of the Kingdom of God.* New York: Dodd, Mead, 1914. Translation by W. Lowrie of *Das Messianitäts- und Leidensgeheimnis Jesu.*

————. *The Quest of the Historical Jesus.* London: A. & C. Black, 1910, 1911, 1954.

Taylor, Vincent. *The Name of Jesus.* New York: St. Martin's Press, 1953.

————. *The Life and Ministry of Jesus.* London: Macmillan, 1954.

Wilder, Amos N. *Eschatology and Ethics in the Teaching of Jesus.* New York and London: Harper & Row, 1939.

8. PRINCIPAL TEXTS OF MARK

GREEK MANUSCRIPTS (UNCIALS)

		Contents	*Century*
ℵ	Sinaiticus	whole gospel	4th
A	Alexandrinus	whole gospel	5th
B	Vaticanus	whole gospel	4th
C	Ephraemi	1:17-6:31; 8:5-12:29; 13:18-16:20	5th
D	Bezae	whole gospel	5th
L	Regius	omits 10:16-30; 15:2-20	8th
M	Campianus	whole gospel	9th
N	Purpureus Petropolitanus	5:20-7:4; 7:20-8:32; 9:1-10:43; 11:7-12:19; 14:25-15:23; 15:33-42	6th
U	Nanianus	whole gospel	9th or 10th
W	Washington	omits 15:13-38	5th
Δ	Sangallensis	whole gospel	9th or 10th
Θ	Koridethi	whole gospel	7th-9th
Π	Petropolitanus	omits 16:18-20	9th
Σ	Rossanensis	omits 16:14-20	6th
Φ	Beratinus	omits 14:62-16:20	6th
Ψ	Laurensis	has 9:5-16:20	8th or 9th

PAPYRUS

P45	Chester Beatty	4:36-40; 5:15-26, 38-6:3; 6:16-25, 36-50; 7:3-15, 25-8:1; 8:10-26, 34-9:8; 9:18-31; 11:27-33; 12:1, 5-8, 13-19, 24-28	3rd

	Contents	*Century*
MINUSCULES		
Family 1	including: 1 Basle, 118 Oxford, 131 Rome, 209 Venice, 22 Paris, 1582 Athos Batopedi	10th-15th
Family 13	including: (a) 13 Paris, 346 Milan, 543 Michigan, 836 and 828 Grotta Ferrata; (b) 69 Leicester, 124 Vienna, 788 Athens; (c) 983 Athos, 1689 Serres	12th-15th
28	Paris	11th-12th
33	Paris	9th-10th
157	Rome	12th
565	Leningrad	9th
579	Paris	13th
700	London	11th-12th
892	London	9th-10th
1071	Athos	12th
1342	Jerusalem	11th
1424	Drama	9th

LATIN VERSIONS

The Old Latin

a	Vercellensis	omits 1:22-34; 4:17-24, 26-5:19; 15:15-16:20	4th
b	Veronensis	whole gospel	5th
c	Colbertinus	whole gospel	12th
d	Latin side of D	whole gospel	5th
e	Palatinus	1:20-4:8; 4:19-6:9; 12:37-40;	5th
	(in text, like k)	13:2-8, 24-27, 33-36	
f	Brixianus	omits 12:5-13:32; 14:70-16:20	6th
ff²	Corbeiensis II	whole gospel	5th-6th
g¹	Sangermanensis I	whole gospel	9th
g²	Sangermanensis II	whole gospel	10th
i	Vindobonensis	2:17-3:29; 4:4-10:1; 10:32-14:36; 15:33-40	5th-6th

		Contents	*Century*
k	Bobiensis	8:8-11, 14-16, 19-16:8, and shorter ending	4th-5th
l	Rehdigeranus	whole gospel	8th
m	(Speculum) Attributed wrongly to Augustine	11:25ff.	8th
n	Fragmenta Sangallensia (Text like a)	7:13-31; 8:32-9:10; 13:2-20; 15:22-16:13	4th-5th
o	Fragmentum Sangallense	16:14-20	7th
q	Monacensis	omits 1:7-22; 15:5-36	7th
r¹	Usserianus I	omits 14:58-15:4	7th
r²	Usserianus II	omits 3:24-4:19; 5:31-6:13; 15:17-41	7th
δ	(Latin side of Δ)	whole gospel	9th-10th
aur	Aureus	whole gospel	9th

The Vulgate

VG	The edition of J. Wordsworth and H. J. White (Oxford: Clarendon Press)		1911

THE SYRIAC VERSIONS

sys	Sinaiticus	1:12-44; 2:21-4:17; 4:41-5:26; 6:5-16:8	4th
syc	Curetonianus	has only 16:17-20	5th
sype	Peshitta	the whole gospel in many manuscripts	5th
syhl	Harclean	whole gospel	7th
syhier	Jerusalem	contained in gospel lectionaries	6th

THE EGYPTIAN VERSIONS

sa	Sahidic	mainly fragments and some manuscripts	3rd-4th
bo	Bohairic	fragments and some manuscripts	6th

Contents

Century

The Georgian Version

geo¹	Adysh,	omits 16:9-20	9th
geo²	A: Athos	omits 16:9-20	10th
	B: Leningrad		

The Armenian Version

arm	some Armenian manuscripts omit 16:9-20, but one which contains it refers to "the elder Ariston"—see section on the Anonymous Ending	5th

The Ethiopic Version

aeth	the oldest manuscript is possibly 13th c, deriving from a 5th c. (?)	5th

The Church Fathers

These writers quote either extensively or partially from Mark:

Writer	Century	Writer	Century
Ambrose	4th	Eusebius of Caesarea	4th
Aphraat	4th	Gregory Naziensis	4th
Athanasius	4th	Gregory of Nyssa	4th
Augustine	4th-5th	Hilary	4th
Basil of Caesarea	4th	Hippolytus	3rd
Chrysostom	4th-5th	Irenaeus	2nd
Clement of Alexandria	2nd-3rd	Jerome	4th-5th
Cyprian	3rd	Justin Martyr	2nd
Cyril of Alexandria	4th-5th	Origen	3rd
Cyril of Jerusalem	4th	Tatian	2nd
Ephraem Syrus	4th	Tertullian	2nd-3rd
Epiphanius	4th	Victor of Antioch	5th

Note: Textual analysis, and textual criticism, as the process by which we determine which is the preferable reading in the Greek of any given New Testament text, together comprise a technical discipline full of pitfalls for the unwary. It does not follow, for example, that the oldest text is necessarily the best, for it might be that in some particular case an early writer with purposes of his own to serve might have changed the Greek which he had before him in order to give expression to those purposes. Tatian, for example, in the second century began disseminating his views that the scriptures of the Old Testament reflected a view of God which Christians ought not to hold—his *Diatessaron* therefore expunges all quotations from the Old Testament. Therefore, even though he is an early writer, it is necessary to look at Tatian's writings with caution.

Similarly, lectionary texts (thanks to an increasing interest in early New Testament manuscripts as possibly divided for lectionary purposes) have again been seen as a fruitful source of Greek readings, though lectionary texts are all relatively late.

Two names will always be associated with the work of establishing the best Greek text of the New Testament, and their work is still a highly important reference tool: F. J. A. Hort, and B. F. Westcott, *The New Testament in the Original Greek,* first published by the Cambridge University Press in 1882. Their work has been subject to revision and suggestion ever since, but one of their contributions for which they will long be remembered is the proposal that various principal manuscripts can be broadly divided into geographical families, as follows:

Alexandria:	B; ℵ, L, sa, bo; C, 33, Δ, Ψ; 579, 892; Origen, Cyril of Alexandria
Antioch:	sy^s; sy^c; sy^{pe}; sy^{hi}; sy^{hier}
Caesarea:	Θ 565; P^{45} fam; 1 Fam 13, 28, 700, W (5:13-16), geo; 1424, N, Σ, Φ; 1071, arm; Origen, Eusebius
Italy and Gaul:	D; b, a; ff^2, i, r; ff, g, l, q; Tatian, Irenaeus
Carthage:	k; W (1-5:30), e; c; m; Cyprian

After a century, Hort and Westcott is still one of the truly great works of textual analysis, but discoveries since the beginning of this century—notably that of the Chester Beatty papyrus (P^{45})—means that reassessment is constantly being made, while papyrus fragments are still capable of shedding light on grammatical usage in the New Testament era.

Two Greek editions of the New Testament have been used in the preparation of this commentary:

The Greek New Testament, edited by Kurt Aland, Matthew Black, Carlo M. Martini, Bruce M. Metzger, and Alan Wikgren. New York, London, Amsterdam, Würtemburg, United Bible Societies, 1966.

The Greek New Testament, edited by R. V. G. Tasker. Oxford and Cambridge
   University Presses, 1964.

Note: For the benefit of a beginning student in Greek, who may be using an
analytical concordance, I have generally left all single-word citations of
Greek in the case or tense in which they are used in the gospel.

9. WORD USAGE IN MARK COMPARED WITH MATTHEW

The publication of Lloyd Gaston's *Horae Synopticae Electronicae* (Missoula, Montana: SBL, 1973), together with a republication of John Hawkins's *Horae Synopticae* (Oxford: Oxford University Press, 1968) has provided us with statistical analysis from two points of view: the strictly "proportional word count" of Hawkins on the one hand, and the more elaborate scheme of Gaston, with its tabulation of relationships between words in the synoptic gospels and in the Q source. What is appended below is a word count comparing Matthew and Mark in instances where (on any showing in NT scholarship) there has been dependence, literary relationship, or simply borrowing. If Gaston's book begins with the unannounced premise that in large measure the two-document hypothesis must stand, it is hoped that the listings here given, going in a descending scale from highest incidence to lowest, may provide the student with some comparative tools.

Matthew	Mark		Matthew	Mark
62	6	*idou* (behold)		
57	4	*oun* (therefore)		
44	4	*patēr* (Father = God)		
30	2	*ereō* (speak)		
26	2	*ponēros* (evil)		
18	1	*apodidōmi* (give, render)		
17	1	*hopōs* (how, that)		
13	1	*hupocritēs* (hypercritical)		
12	1	*plēroō* (fulfill)		
10	1	*anachōreō* (withdraw)		
10	1	*hēgemon* (ruler, governor)		
10	1	*misthos* (reward)		
9	1	*dōron* (gift)		
9	1	*thēsauros* (treasure)		
9	1	*nai* (yes)		
		eisporeuomai (enter)	1	8
		euthus (immediately)	7	42
30	5	*doulos* (slave)		

Matthew	Mark		Matthew	Mark
20	5	*heōs* (until)		
		anistēmi (rise)	3	17
15	3	*prospherō* (offer, bring)		
14	2	*laos* (people)		
12	3	*pente* (five)		
12	2	*ouai* (woe)		
		akathartos (unclean)	2	11
11	2	*probaton* (sheep)		
10	2	*mellō* (shall, to come)		
9	2	*peinaō* (be hungry)		
7	1	*echthros* (enemy)		
7	1	*Saddukaios* (Sadducee)		
6	1	*kerdainō* (gain)		
6	1	*skotos* (darkness)		
6	1	*chara* (joy)		
6	1	*thelēma* (will, purpose)		
		parististēmi (stand by)	1	6
5	1	*anti* (for)		
5	1	*archōn* (ruler)		
5	1	*astēr* (star)		
5	1	*kleptō* (steal)		
5	1	*kruptos* (secret, hidden)		
5	1	*miseō* (hate)		
5	1	*nosos* (disease)		
5	1	*pro* (before)		
5	1	*petra* (rock)		
5	1	*phileō* (love)		
5	1	*phoneuō* (kill, murder)		
5	1	*ochlos* (crowd)		
4	1	*doxadzō* (glorify)		
4	1	*ekastos* (every one)		
4	1	*ergadzomai* (work)		
		mēketi (no more)	1	4
4	1	*moicheuō* (commit adultery)		
4	1	*orkos* (oath)		
4	1	*seismos* (earthquake)		
		existēmi (be astonished)	1	4
20	6	*men* (truly, indeed)		
12	4	*pur* (fire)		
10	3	*prosōpon* (face, presence)		

Matthew	Mark		Matthew	Mark
9	3	*naos* (ship)		
7	2	*baptistēs* (baptizer)		
		theōreō (perceive)	2	7
		ouketi (no more)	2	7
6	2	*Hēsaias* (Isaiah)		
6	2	*lupeō* (be sad)		
3	1	*aitia* (cause)		
3	1	*apodēmeō* (go on a journey)		
3	1	*astheneō* (be weak)		
3	1	*astheneis* (weak, sick)		
3	1	*Beelzeboul* (Beelzebul)		
3	1	*gaster* (be pregnant)		
3	1	*deka* (ten)		
		derō (beat, hit)	1	3
3	1	*diaskorpidzō* (scatter)		
3	1	*eudokeō* (be pleasing)		
3	1	*thrix* (hair)		
3	1	*kēnsos* (tribute, tax)		
3	1	*klēronomeō* (inherit)		
3	1	*koilia* (womb)		
3	1	*koptō* (lament)		
3	1	*kraspedon* (border, hem)		
3	1	*kullos* (maimed)		
		kōluō (forbid)	1	3
3	1	*manthanō* (understand)		
3	1	*hou* (where)		
3	1	*periagō* (go about)		
3	1	*piprasko* (sell)		
		plērōma (fullness)	1	3
3	1	*porneia* (sexual misconduct)		
3	1	*potamos* (river)		
3	1	*sophia* (wisdom)		
		stachus (ear of corn)	1	3
3	1	*stratiōtēs* (soldier)		
		phaneros (openly known)	1	3
3	1	*chōris* (without)		
		pseudomartureō (bear false witness)	1	3
3	1	*pseudoprohētēs* (false prophet)		

Matthew	Mark		Matthew	Mark
3	1	*matigoō* (flog)		
		sindōn (winding sheet)	1	3
		hupokatō (under)	1	3

The proportions of usage as between Matthew and Mark are given in diminishing sequence and diminishing frequency, and the third section represents a proportion of three to one. However, it is not the occurrence of words which is important. Hawkins (pp. 168ff.) provides us with thirty-four varying short sentences or combinations of words which appear to be habitual expressions of Matthew. Of the examples given, fourteen appear also in Mark, but significantly in no place where there is not other evidence of copying between Matthew and Mark. But there are no lists in Hawkins which are a reverse situation—i.e., words and phrases which are habitual to Mark and are also found in Matthew.

The tabulations given above represent a listing of words which occur more than three times in either Matthew or Mark, and moreover in passages where there is evidence of copying activity from one or the other.

It cannot be said that such statistical analysis is more than tentative in assessing the dependence of one document on another. Not only would there be need to examine carefully what words there are for which no satisfactory substitute existed in Koinē Greek—in which case the significance of the words themselves is thus diminished—but it would be necessary to have far more information than of course we have as to the original forms of the tradition in its oral state. It is, however, hoped that this listing may encourage the student to pursue the matter further.

Since the present writer believes that Matthew was Mark's prime source, no attempt has been made to correlate the tables above with Luke. Such correlations are indeed made in Gaston's work, where it must be borne in mind that the two-document hypothesis is assumed as valid.

Grammatical Constructions Peculiar to, or Characteristic of, Mark

Exaggerated use of the third person plural impersonal (active voice) as a substitute for the passive—1:32, 2:3, 7:32, 8:22, 10:13, 12:13, 13:26, 15:27.

Distributive singular (employed for a collective idea or used figuratively)—6:52, 7:21, 8:17.

"To believe *in*" (1:16 is peculiar to NT usage and is not found elsewhere).

Redundant use of the pronoun—1:7, 6:22, 7:23.

erchetai (come) as a substitute for the passive of *pherō* (bring)—4:21.

dia cheiros (through his hand) as a periphrastic formula for *autō*—6:2.

ekporeuomai (to go out) in the genitive absolute introducing a sentence about Jesus "going out"—10:17, 10:46, 13:1. The usage is not found in the rest of the NT.

epi with the accusative in place of *peri* (of, concerning)—5:21, 6:34, 8:2, 9:12,13,22.

ho estin (that is), used to introduce a translation or explanation—3:18; 5:41; 7:11,34; 12:42; 15:16,22,34,42. Cf. Matt 27:33, Acts 1:12, 4:36. The use is not found in Luke.

Duplication used in the distributive form—*duo duo* (6:7), "two by two"; *symposia symposia* (6:39), "by groups"; *prasiai prasiai* (6:40), "group by group." The words of 6:39 and 6:40 are unique in the NT. N.B.: Two Church Fathers (Epiphanius and Origen) read *desmas desmas* in Matt 13:30 (bundle by bundle).

Nominative case with the definite article instead of the vocative—*to karasion* (little girl), 5:41; *to alalon kai kōron* (dumb and deaf spirit), 9:25; *ho theos mou, ho theos mou* (my God, my God), 15:34; *ho patēr* (Father), 14:36. Whereas 5:41 and 15:34 appear to be due to translation, 9:25 (with its use of *alalos*—on which see the *hapax legomena)* may well be an original source. Note that some texts of Matt 27:29 are parallel to Mark 15:19, where Mark has the vocative case. Mark 9:19 uses the vocative case.

Use of *archomai* (begin) with the infinitive: As used by Mark, there are twenty-six occasions of this verb with the infinitive. Five cases mean "begin," while three can be called auxiliary, but the following are clearly redundant: 2:23; 5:17; 6:55; 8:11; 10:28,41; 11:15; 14:65,69. It is worthy of notice that of the twelve uses of *archomai* in Matthew, seven clearly mean "begin," five are doubtful, but no example is redundant. Thirteen uses in Luke clearly demand "begin" as translation, fourteen examples are doubtful, but there is no case of redundancy.

HAPAX LEGOMENA IN MARK

alalos (dumb)—7:37; 9:17; 9:25.

aphrizō (foam, *verb)*—9:18; 9:20.

thambeō, thambeomai (to be amazed)—1:27; 9:15; 10:24; 10:32; 14:33; 16:6.

kenturiōn (centurion)—15:39,44,45.

sunthlibō (press closely)—5:24,32.

thugatrion (young daughter)—5:23, 7:24.

ARAMAIC WORDS IN MARK

talitha koum (rise, young maid)—5:41.
ephatha (be opened)—7:34.
Abba (Father)—14:36.
Ēloi Ēloi lama sabachthani (my God, my God, why have you deserted me?) —15:34.
kopazō (cease)—4:39, 6:51; also Matt 14:32. (These are the only NT uses of the verb.)
enagkalizomai (take in one's arms)—9:36, 10:16. Not attested until after the NT period.

Characteristic Phrases and Usages

In compiling this material, the writer acknowledges with gratitude the original impetus provided by Dr. David Peabody, of Nebraska Weslyan University in Lincoln, who kindly shared with me some preliminary work of his own.

kai elegen autois (and he said to them)—2:27; 3:23; 4:2,11,21,24; 6:4,10; 7:9,14; 8:21; 9:1,31; 11:17. The phrase is used when the other two evangelists agree on the use of *eipen* and can be described as redactional. The phrase never occurs in Matthew, and in Luke it appears in a parallel passage (2:27 = Luke 6:5). *Kai elegen* is found alone at 4:9,26,30,41; 14:36. This phrase too, as a substitute for *eipen* or *legon,* may also be redactional.

blepete (second person imperative of *blepō),* meaning "watch" or "beware" —4:24; 8:15; 12:38; 13:9,23,33.

kairos (season), used absolutely of eschatological time—1:15; 13:33.

diēgeomai (tell, declare), used with a form of *horaō* (see, witness)—5:16; 9:9. The word is not common in the NT (cf. Luke 8:39; 9:10; Acts 8:33, 9:27, 12:17; Heb 11:32).

eperotaō (ask), used twenty-six times in Mark, as against eight in Matthew (seven of which are in parallel), seventeen in Luke (nine of which are in parallel), twice in John, and four times in the rest of the NT.

eisporeuomai (go out). In all of the NT, there are eighteen uses, of which Mark has eight. Mark 1:21; 4:19 (= Luke 8:16); 5:40; 6:56; 7:15,18 (= Matt 15:17); 7:19; 11:2 (= Luke 19:30).

euangelion (proclamation), used absolutely of "the Gospel"—1:15; 8:35; 10:29; 13:10; 14:9; 16:15. The phrase *euangelion Iēsou Christou* (the Gospel of Jesus-Messiah) at 1:1 is unique in the NT.

arrōstos (sick). There are five uses in the NT. Mark has three—6:5,13; 16:18.

ton logon ("the word," accusative case), used absolutely as "the word"—2:3, 4:33, 8:32. Cf. the prologue of John, and Luke 1:3.

ta pneumata ta akatharta (the unclean spirits), used by Mark in place of *daimonia* (demons) or *daimonizomenos* (demon-possessed). There are eleven uses in Mark, two in Matthew, and six in Luke—Mark 1:23 (= Luke 4:34); 1:26,27 (= Luke 4:36); 3:11 (= Luke 6:18); 3:30; 5:2,8 (= Luke 8:29); 5:13; 6:7 (= Matt 10:1); 7:25; 9:25 (= Luke 9:42). Cf. also Matt 12:43 = Luke 11:24.

palin (again). Mark uses the word twenty-six times, of which twenty are instances where there is no relationship of copying with the other synoptics. Luke uses the word only three times, Matthew sixteen—of which five are in Markan parallels.

ptuas (spittle). As a means of healing, found only in Mark 7:33, 8:23; and in John 9:6.

polla (much), used as an adverb to lend emphasis to the predicate in Mark 3:12; 5:10,23,38,43; 6:20; 9:26. Hawkins adds 1:45 and 15:3. See also 6:34, 9:12, 12:27. These last instances are somewhat doubtfully in the same category as those first listed.

prōi (in the morning): Of twelve uses in the NT, six are in Mark—1:35; 11:20 (= Matt 21:18); 13:35; 15:1; 16:2,9.

suzeitein (to question). In ten NT uses, Mark has six—1:27; 8:11; 9:10,14,16; 12:28. The remaining Luke-Acts uses do not parallel Mark.

Satana (Satan): The word is always used by Mark where the other gospels have *diabolos* (devil) or *ho ponēros* (the vile one). Mark 1:13 (= Matt 4:1, Luke 4:2); 3:26 (= Matt 12:26, Luke 11:18); 4:15 (= Matt 13:19, Luke 8:12); 8:33 (= Matt 16:23).

pherō (carry): Mark uses the word sixteen times, as against four for Matthew (three of which are parallel with Mark) and Luke four times (one of which is parallel with Mark). Eight of the Markan uses refer to carrying a sick person.

hēdeōs (gladly): unique to Mark in the gospels. Found also in Paul's 2 Corinthians.

pas ho ochlos (all the crowd)—2:13; 4:1; 9:15; 11:18.

eneken emou kai eneken tou euangeliou (on account of me, on account of the gospel)—8:35; 10:30.

kai daimonia polla exebalen (and he cast out many demons)—1:34; 6:13.

peprōmenē kardia (hard heart)—6:52; 8:19 (cf. 3:5).

ho estin methermēneuomenon (translated, that is)—5:41, 15:22,34. This phrase is not used elsewhere. Cf. Matt 1:23; John 1:41; Acts 4:36 for all other NT uses of *methermēneoumai*.

kai diesteilato antois hina medeni (medeis) (charge strictly)—5:43, 7:36, 9:9. Also *kai diestellato autois legōn*—8:15. There is a textual problem at Matt 16:20 where some texts have *epitimao* (= Mark 8:30).

meta treis hēmeras anastēnai (after three days rise)—8:31. Also *meta treis hemeras anastēsetai* (be raised)—9:31, 10:34. The other evangelists prefer *tē tritē hēmera* (on the third day), and also use the verb *egeirō.* Mark 9:31 = Matt 16:21, Luke 9:22. Matt 17:23 = Mark 9:31, and Mark 10:41 = Matt 20:19, Luke 18:32.

Use of verb *epitithēmi* (lay) with *cheiras* (hands) in healing—5:23 (= Matt 9:18); 6:5; 7:32; 8:23,25; 16:18.

periblepō (look around)—characteristics of Jesus in Mark 3:5,34; 5:32; 9:8; 10:23; 11:11. These examples, with the Lucan parallel 6:10, make up the whole NT use.

kai exerato didaskein (and he began to teach)—4:1; 6:2,34; 8:31.

kai (parakalein) auton hina . . . (and they implored him that)—5:10 (= Luke 8:31); 5:12 (= Luke 8:32); 5:18,23 (= Matt 9:18, Luke 8:42); 6:56 (= Matt 14:36); 7:32; 8:22.

kai proskalesamenos . . . (and calling [crowds or disciples, he said])— 3:13,23; 7:14; 8:1,34; 12:43; 15:44.

kai edidasken kai elegen outois (and he taught them and said)—4:2, 9:31, 11:17. For a slightly different formula with similar verbs, cf. 8:31, 12:35.

In situations where Jesus enters a house, or finds himself in a position in which the crowds make it impossible for him to do something, there is usually a double negative construction in the sentence—2:1,4; 3:20; 6:4; 7:25. (The use of *ou mē* results in constructions like "He was not, not able, to enter the house.") Grammarians have commented on this usage in Mark frequently.

kai elegen . . . en te didachē autou (elegen) (and he said in his teaching)— 4:2, 12:38.

kai erchontai eis . . . (and he went into)—8:22; 10:46; 11:15,27; 14:32. For a similar construction with other verbs, cf. 3:1,20; 5:1; 9:33; 11:11.

10. NOTE ON TRANSLITERATION

The rendering of Greek into English has been done as literally and in as straightforward a manner as possible. In spite of the general use of *psyche,* for example, in all manner of contexts, that Greek word has been reproduced in this work as *psuchē.* There seems to be no good reason to confuse a beginning Greek student by a suggestion that miniscule (lowercase) Greek had any letter like "y."

The transliteration of Hebrew, as a vowel-less language, has its own peculiar problems. The general reader may well be aware of *elohim* from Young's *Analytical Concordance* and elsewhere, but he/she may be pardoned for wondering what has happened to the word when confronted by *'ĕlōhîm* in an academic periodical, while the transformation of *onniyoth* (little ships) into *'oniyyôt* would be baffling. This author has witnessed no less than five attempted conventions for Hebrew transliteration since 1950, and feels nothing but sympathy for the enquiring general reader. Accordingly, renderings of Hebrew words in this book (save where directly quoting from other works) are best described as eclectic. It is nevertheless hoped that they are intelligible. Those of us who write on Biblical subjects for general consumption ought not to be encouraged to pursue a vocation of *obscuritas gratia obscuritatis.*

11. SUGGESTIONS FOR AN ANALYSIS OF MARK'S ARRANGEMENT

Laurence F. X. Brett

Recent biblical scholarship has paid greater attention to the Gospel of Mark, with an increased interest paid to the narrative techniques that the evangelist used in arranging the various traditions he has received. As a result of such studies, undertaken from a variety of disciplines, this gospel emerges as a highly skilled composition, with various patterns of arrangement becoming increasingly obvious. The studies to date, however, have yet to reveal an overall schema to the entire gospel, while each attempt to uncover a unifying pattern has added to our insights.

The process of seeking one particular key to the organization of Mark's material, while answering some questions, has often raised additional questions. For example, are the uncovered patterns original to the evangelist? Do such recurring patterns have a role to play in the interpretation of the traditions presented?

What follows may appear to be yet another attempt to organize the evangelist's material for him. Consequently, the given outline represents mere suggestions for an analysis of the arrangement of Mark's gospel. As such, it is offered as a possible starting point for further studies, while at the same time it builds upon the suggestions advanced by Markan scholars, notably Achtemeier.

The suggestions that follow are based upon recurring patterns within individual units, and upon the distinctive elements of arrangement that have been suggested by others. In many cases they are meant to look at the proposals that have already drawn some degree of acceptance, but with certain refinements that attempt to solve obvious impasses that have arisen from setting individual units into the overall plan of this gospel.

I. Recurring Patterns in Mark

A study of the individual traditions reveals recurring patterns within Mark's arrangement, and in many cases the appearance of rearrangement suggests itself. It is not the purpose of this brief Appendix to state the source for such composition, but merely to indicate that the structures involved do present themselves for our consideration. A brief table of supposed patterns, it is suggested, best prefaces any outline that takes such arrangements into account. From a study of the individual pericopes, as well as larger sections, these patterns (found to recur with sufficient frequency to suggest a model of arrangement) can be seen to emerge:

A. Brackets. It has been pointed out that Mark is fond of enclosing material(s) within similar traditions. Perhaps the most noteworthy example is that portion which presents the three predictions of the Passion within the cures of those who were blind (at 8:22-26 and 10:46-52). Both healings "bracket" the intervening material, and the use of such incidents to interpret that intervening section has been made by many commentators.

B. Developed Frames. Similar to the use of "brackets" is the use of incidents, at the beginning and end of a particular section, that are not entirely parallel, as with the use of brackets. A case in point, suggested below in Part One, are the episodes that take place at the Sea of Galilee. The opening incident presents the call of the first disciples, who leave their boats to follow Jesus (1:16-20). The closing incident also takes place *upon* the Sea of Galilee, where Jesus and his disciples are *in a boat* (8:14-21). In most cases where this is seen to occur, both "frames" are related, but one (usually the closing frame) is larger and more developed. This is certainly the case in the final segment of Part Two, in which the curious episode at 14:51-52 would appear to be developed in 16:1-8.

C. Organizational Clues. There appears to be a use of "organizational clues" that project, or retroject, into complete segments. The appearance of "Elijah and Moses" at 9:4, for example, might offer clues to the arrangement of the intervening materials that separate the prediction sequences (preparing for the blocks of material at 9:9-29 and 10:1-31, respectively). Again, the mention of the "yeast" of Herod or Pharisees (at 8:15) could well look back at those blocks of material in which Herod (6:14-29) and the Pharisees (7:1-23) figure prominently, and their opposition to Jesus is related. The reverse order of the caution made by Jesus (with the Pharisees mentioned before Herod) further enhances this suggestion, since the "yeast" of Herod is described before the encounter with the Pharisees.

D. Reversal. A reversal of order becomes apparent within smaller sections as well. In the description of the multitudes that came to Jesus, in 3:7-12, the geographical references (in which the use of prepositions reveals an interesting arrangement) are preceded and followed by phrases in which the order of words is reversed: *polu plēthos* (v. 7b), and *plēthos polu* (v. 8).

E. Parallelism. The common device of parallelism makes its appearance in Mark in a number of places. One such example is in 3:24-25, in which the fates of "a kingdom" and "a household" are described identically. In that same section, 3:20-30, one may detect something of a parallelism in the arrangement of key words—*hamartēmata* and *blasphēmiai* in v. 28; and *blasphēmēsē* in v. 29. and *hamartēmatos* in v. 29.

F. Chiasmus. Not uncommon in Mark, the chiasmic pattern is exemplified best, perhaps, at 8:10-13, as follows:

embas, ēlthen	10	*Ti . . . smeion; tautē semeion*	12
semeion	11	*embas apēlthen*	13
	10		12
	11		13

It can be noted that Mark's use of chiasmus frequently makes use of a double reference within one of the units, as in v. 12.

G. Play on Words. Within that same pericope, a play on words may also be detected, again a not infrequent occurrence within Mark. Within v. 11, we find: *suzētein autō, zētountes par'autou*

H. Hanging Chain. Of all the devices that may be seen in Mark, the most noteworthy is that arrangement of verses which can best be described as a "hanging chain." The verses are linked together to form a catenary, with the weightiest material at the center. The first and final verses display similarities to one another, and quite often such similarity can be found in the corresponding verses that emanate in either direction from the central verse(s), as follows:

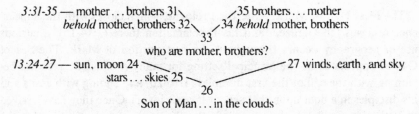

3:31-35 — mother... brothers 31\ /35 brothers... mother
behold mother, brothers 32\ /34 *behold* mother, brothers
33
who are mother, brothers?
13:24-27 — sun, moon 24 ⟍ 27 winds, earth, and sky
stars... skies 25 ⟍
26
Son of Man... in the clouds

I. Insertion. Markan studies have long observed the insertion of one tradition within another, as in the case of the healing of a woman (5:25-34) told within the story of the healing of a young girl (5:21-24, continued in 5:35-43). The common factor here may simply be that both cures involve women, one of whom suffered for "twelve years," while the other was a "child of twelve."

It would seem, however, that the insertion of a story within a story does more than simply conjoin episodes bearing a similarity. The cleansing of the temple, at 11:15-19, is told within the story of the cursing of a fig tree, which is first cursed by Jesus (11:12-14) and afterward seen to have withered (11:20-25). It has been observed that the incident involving the tree serves to interpret the action whereby the temple is cleansed.

J. Sequences: The arrangement of similar pericopes in sequence has been accepted as a Markan device (as with the disputes between Jesus and the Pharisees in 2:18-3:6). But it has also been pointed out that the evangelist favors arranging dissimilar materials in a sequential pattern. The most notable arrangement involves the three predictions of the Passion, each of which is followed by a *misunderstanding* on the part of disciples, a *teaching* that corrects such failure to fathom, and a final *insight* into the role of Jesus, one that has implications for discipleship. (This will be seen in the outline of the opening segment of Part Two in the format that follows.)

II. An Outline of Mark

Many have held that Mark falls into two sections of equal length, with the suggestion that Peter's confession of faith, falling at the center of this gospel, is central to the gospel. To a large degree, the division into fairly equal halves can be maintained, but without singling out a particular incident as pivotal. With some refinement, the Gospel of Mark can be seen as falling into two halves, the first ending with the vital question, "Do you still not understand?" (8:21).

The First Half of Mark: After the Prologue, which closes with the appearance of Jesus "in Galilee," and his Proclamation there (1:14-15), a curious use of geography occurs throughout the first portion of Mark. The Sea of Galilee appears to be the principal setting for many significant episodes, beginning with the call of the first disciples (1:16-20) and ending with Jesus and his disciples in a boat upon that sea, or lake (8:14-21). Once they have arrived at Bethsaida (in 8:22), there is no further mention of Lake Galilee for the remainder of the Gospel.

In the outline that follows, the Sea of Galilee is significant throughout the first segment, involving the call and eventual selection of disciples (1:16-3:19), and provides us with the central incidents for the second and third segments (the storm on the sea, at 4:35-41, and the appearance of Jesus upon the water, at 6:45-52). Marked by countless crossings, Part One can be seen to make use of the Sea of Galilee as its principal reference point, until the closing scene upon that sea, with its series of questions which Part Two it would appear, was designed to answer.

The Second Half: From 8:22 until the ending of this gospel at 16:8, geography can once again be seen to play a role (albeit minor to theological considerations) as the second half of Mark develops. The opening segment presents a movement from Galilee to the gates of Jerusalem; the middle segment concerns itself with the ministry of Jesus in and around Jerusalem itself, and the final portion of the gospel (bracketed with references to "flight") presents the Passion narrative. Whereas Part One can be divided into segments of almost equal length, give or take a verse, Part Two presents its three segments in unequal lengths, the last being the briefest within the entire gospel, and the central section, with the eschatological discourse at its center, as the longest. It is the centricity of the discourse of Chapter 13 that dictates the prominence given to the central section of Part Two, contrary to those divisions of Mark, based upon measurement of verses, which would see the eschatological discourse as extrinsic to the original development of Mark's arrangement.

Accordingly, this outline is proposed as a suggestion for an analysis of Mark's arrangement; the geographical references are maintained for reference points only, so as not to overlay any thematic or theological development upon the format proposed. That such development can be detected within the six segments suggested is not to be denied; but that is not the province of the following proposal. The apparent organization of materials happily coincides (a word used with caution) with the geographical developments, and although the proposed arrangements would appear to be based upon recurrent patterns, the use of such geographical references is meant to avoid the suggested divisions as being either definitive or determined.

THE PROLOGUE—1:1-15

PART ONE—1:16 to 8:21, Episodes At or Near the Sea of Galilee

> Segment One—1:16 to 3:19
> Segment Two—3:20 to 6:6
> Segment Three—6:7 to 8:21

PART TWO—8:22-16:8, From Galilee to Jerusalem, Ministry in Jerusalem, and the Climax At and Near Golgotha

> Segment Four—8:22 to 11:10
> *Transition at 11:11*
> Segment Five—11:12 to 14:50
> *Transition at 14:51-52*
> Segment Six—14:53 to 16:8

III. A Detailed Analysis

Each of the units described above is first presented in diagram form, followed by an explanation of the components of that unit, and a consideration of such components individually. The individual "segments" have been numbered sequentially so as not to disturb the basic unity of the gospel's development.

A. The Prologue—1:1 to 15

Title—1:1-2, Introducing Prologue and Gospel

a	b	a'
John	**Jesus and John**	**Jesus**
1:3-7	1:8-10	1:11-15
3—"a voice"	8—water, Spirit	11—"a voice"
4—Setting	9—Jesus, John	12—Setting
5—Results	10—water, Spirit	13—Results
6, 7a—"proclaims"		14—"proclaims"
7b—Proclamation		15—Proclamation

Explanation: The opening verses form a "title," which may be considered as a single unit. It introduces what follows in the prologue, and serves to introduce the entire gospel as well. The similarity between the beginnings of "blocks" of material relating to John and Jesus respectively would demand a division of the quotation after v. 2.

a, a′: The prologue itself would appear to set the appearances of John and Jesus in parallel arrangement, separated by a unit in which both figures appear together. The parallel descriptions both begin with "a voice," and all that follows would appear to be set in identical order. By the use of such an arrangement, the superior role of Jesus is subtly heightened.

b: To enhance the superiority of Jesus, the central section describes the encounter between both figures in as brief a manner as possible, almost in an abbreviated manner. The comparison between both would thus be brought out by the comparison between "water" and "Spirit," made in vv. 8 and 10, which bracket the actual encounter. It may even be that the mention of Jesus before the mention of John, in v. 9, reverses the order of the actual appearance of both.

B. Part One—1:16 to 8:21

Representing those incidents taking place at the Sea of Galilee, where this half of the gospel begins and ends, after which Lake Galilee is not mentioned again.

Segment One—1:16 to 3:19

a	b	c	b′	a′
1:16-20	1:21-2:12	2:13-17	2:18-3:12	3:13-19
Call of four disciples	Sequence of cures, last involving a conflict	Call of Levi	Sequence of conflicts, last involving a cure	Choice of the twelve

Explanation: Luke's description of Jesus as "a prophet powerful in word and deed in the eyes of God and all the people" (Luke 24:19) could provide the description of the traditions concerning Jesus, set within the context of his choice and final selection of disciples "whom he would send to preach the good news" (3:19).

b, b′: The central figure is Jesus himself, who is revealed as "powerful" in "word" (sequence of conflicts) and in "deed" (sequence of healings) in these blocks of material. Conflict enters into the final cure (2:1-12), just as a cure provides the setting for the final conflict (3:1-6); the second block of material leads into a final consideration of the merciful power of Jesus (6:7-12). The notion of conflict, however, is not entirely absent, as demons refer to Jesus by a title (3:11) that points ahead to the "final conflict" at Golgotha (15:39), where that title again appears.

a, c, a': Incidents concerning the choice of disciples provide a cohesive framework into which the traditions concerning Jesus appear to be anchored. The call of the first four disciples, and the call of Levi, take place by the sea. The final portion takes place on a mountain, but only after Jesus withdrew toward the lake of Galilee "with his disciples" (3:7), so that the summary concerning the merciful cures of Jesus also serves to prepare for the selection of the Twelve. The opening scene (a) will perform double duty, and serve as a "frame" with the closing scene of Part One, at 8:14-21, where those called to leave their boats appear in a boat with the Teacher.

Segment Two—3:20 to 6:6

a	b	c	b'	a'
3:20-35	Teachings	4:35-41	Cures	6:1-6
The true family of Jesus	4:1-20 Teaching within a teaching 4:21-34 Further teaching	Jesus calms the Sea of Galilee	5:1-20 Explusion of demons 5:21-43 Cure within a cure	Supposed family of Jesus

Explanation: Jesus is again seen as "powerful" in "word" (teachings) and in "deed" (cures), a power made obvious in his calming of troubled sea and disturbed disciples, who form his genuine family, in contrast to blood relatives, or his supposed family.

c: In this and the following segment, the power of Jesus is revealed upon the Sea of Galilee. A great calm comes over the sea, and a great awe overtakes the disciples.

b, b': Words and deeds again provide a revelation of Jesus. These blocks of material form something of a chiasmic pattern, excepting the central portion (c). A "teaching within a teaching" (parable of the seed, with its explanation interpreting the parable and the explanation that follows) can be seen to interact with the cure of a woman inserted within a cure. The "further teaching" (4:21-34) interprets the use to which the parable of the seed is to be put, just as the expulsion of demons (5:1-20) interprets the cures that follow.

a, a': These sections serve to bracket this segment. The sections also serve as *developed frames,* for the final section (supposed family of Jesus) relates to the opening section, in which the blasphemy of the scribes is itself bracketed by references to "family" (3:20-21 and 3:31-35). By its length the first section prepares for the rejection that is central to the final section.

A Further Note: The bracketed material in "a" develops a theme found in the prologue, where Jesus is called "more powerful" (1:7).

Segment Three—6:7 to 8:21

a	b	a'
6:7-33	6:45-52	6:53-7:37
"The yeast of Herod"	Jesus walks upon the Sea	"The yeast of Pharisees"
6:34-44	Ending:	8:1-9
Feeding of the five thousand	"minds closed"	Feeding of the four thousand

8:10-13   Transition to close of Part One
8:14-20   Closing scene: warning against
                "years of Pharisees and yeast
                of Herod"

Explanation: Once again, as in Segment Two, a scene upon the Sea of Galilee is the centerpiece, but this time with an emphasis upon the "closed minds" of the disciples who are present. This factor bears heavily upon the closing scene.

a, a': The closing scene itself, with its warnings against the "yeast of the Pharisees and the yeast of Herod," provides a clue to the organization of the entire segment. Set within the mission of apostles and their return is an account of Herod's wickedness (6:14-29); following the walking upon the sea, a second section deals with the perversity of the Pharisees, itself bracketed by a reference to miracles (6:53-56) and two cures (7:24-30 and 31-37). Those latter cures involve Gentile regions, thus setting the conflict with Pharisees over "clean" and "unclean" into a real situation.

Both sections, dealing with Herod and the Pharisees, are followed by multiplications of loaves. The idea of the first as a "Jewish feeding" is reinforced by the mission of the Twelve and mention of Herod; the concept of the second as a "Gentile feeding" is enhanced by the discussion concerning cleanliness and the cures that take place in Gentile areas.

Transition: Mark 8:10-13 serves as a transition to the final scene in Part One. It is carefully constructed, and prepares the reader for the significance of that closing scene.

Closing Scene: Part One ends where it began, at the Sea of Galilee. With a series of questions, the blindness of the disciples is made apparent. With its mention of "yeasts" and references to the two feedings, this scene brings Segment Three to an end; with its very setting, within a boat upon the sea, it brings Part One to its close; the first "half" of Mark's gospel is over.

This scene prepares us for the opening segment of Part Two, a segment that will begin and end with the restoration of sight to people who were blind.

C. Part Two—8:22 to 16:8

As in Part One, the second "half" of Mark's gospel may also be arranged in three segments. All of Part One was seen to have taken place near the Sea of Galilee. In this portion each segment details geographical movements:

Segment Four—from Galilee to Jerusalem;
Segment Five—in and around Jerusalem;
Segment Six—the Final Hour, to and from Golgotha.

Segment Four—8:22 to 11:10

Frame I   8:22-26—a blind person *sees* . . .
             8:27-30—who Jesus is.

I		II		III	
8:31-9:10	9:11-29	9:30-50	10:1-31	10:32-45	
P 8:31	Elijah	P 9:30-32	Moses	P 10:32-34	
M 8:32-33	section	M 9:33-34	section	M 10:35-41	

      T 8:34-9:1   T 9:35-37   T 10:42-44
      I 9:2-10   I 9:38-50   I 10:45

Frame II   10:46-51—a blind person *sees* . . .
                 11:1-10—who Jesus is.

Key: P = Prediction of Passion
        M = Misunderstanding by disciple(s)
        T = Teaching to correct misunderstanding
        I = Insight into role of Messiah

Explanation: The three predictions of the Passion have been received, generally, as the basis for the organization of the traditions within this unit. The entire segment is bracketed by *frames;* the cures of blind persons, *together* with the titles accorded to Jesus, unite two incidents into a single frame. The first frame is the cure of the man at Bethsaida coupled with Peter's "title" of "Messiah"; the second frame is the cure of Bartimaeus coupled with the "title" accorded Jesus by the crowds, the one "who comes in the name of the Lord" (11:10). Both "titles" come toward the end of their respective pericopes. Mark 11:1-10 is a description of events *prior* to the actual entry into Jerusalem, which occurs quietly at 11:11, a verse that may serve as a transition to the next segment.

I, II, III: These sections follow parallel formats. Jesus predicts his sufferings and immediately afterward a misunderstanding by a disciple (or by disciples) takes place. To correct those misunderstandings, Jesus offers a teaching, and finally an insight is given into the true role of Jesus as Messiah. The final insight is but a single verse!

Moses, Elijah Sections: To separate the three sections concerning the predictions, two blocks of material have been arranged from various traditions. There does appear to be some factor that determines their arrangement, and the first "insight" (at 9:2-10) provides a suggested clue. Elijah appears before Moses, an arrangement that has intrigued commentators and readers alike. The two figures appearing in the Transfiguration narrative, it would seem, color the intervening material that separates the "predictions," providing *organizational clues.*

In 9:11-13 the discussion centers around Elijah. In what follows, from v. 14 to v. 29, the work of Elijah may be suggested. His first miracle involved the cure of a young lad who was severely ill, and for whom Elijah prayed three times (1 Kgs 17:7-24); at his cure, the mother professed her belief that Elijah truly spoke "the word of the Lord." The cure of this lad ends with a reference to prayer as the only way to expel the type of demon who had possessed the child. The material in 10:1-31 appears to be related to the figure of Moses, who is explicitly mentioned in 10:3, even as the Law of Moses is quoted in 10:19. The two sections, on divorce (10:1-12) and on riches (10:17-31), bracket a central episode that also involves children.

Further Note: The "insight" of Section III, confined to a single verse, would appear to be separate from the "teaching" found in 10:42-44. That teaching does correct the "misunderstanding" of the disciples (James and John), and v. 45 corroborates that teaching; but it appears to stand apart, since it is not addressed to the disciples in the second person, and would therefore qualify as an "insight" together with 9:2-10 and 9:38-50.

TRANSITION—III

This verse represents the actual entry into Jerusalem. As such, it appears to stand somewhat apart from what precedes and follows. As a transitional statement, it concludes Segment Four, which takes Jesus from Galilee *to* Jerusalem, and it sets the stage for Segment Five, the incidents *in and around* Jerusalem.

Segment Five—11:12 to 14:50

This segment would appear to be more highly organized than any other and is the lengthiest of all. The discourse of Chapter 13 is the centerpiece of this entire portion, and the parables at its conclusion may be seen to provide *organizational clues* to the material that brackets this segment.

	d	c'
12:38-13:2	Eschatological discourse	14:1-11
Bracketed episode of a woman's kind deed (12:41-44)	Setting: 13:3-4	Bracketed episode of a woman's kind deed (14:3-9)
	I—13:5-23	
	II—13:24-27	
	III—13:28-36	
	Parable of a fig tree Parable of servants in charge	
	Conclusion—13:37	

Explanation: The eschatological discourse, itself a highly organized tradition, would seem not only to be central to this central segment of Part Two, but to dominate its entire arrangement. Bracketed episodes frame the discourse and call attention to its significance.

d: The great discourse, apart from its setting (with questions answered within the discourse), and its conclusion (which takes up the opening caution), falls into three units:

I (13:5-23): Like the other units, this opening portion appears to be arranged in the "hanging chain" pattern, with the caution to be "on guard" at start and finish. The central portions each begin with the word *hotan*

$$
\begin{array}{ccc}
-5 & & 23 - \\
\text{false claims refuted} - 6 & & 21\text{-}22 - \text{false claims refuted} \\
\textit{when} \text{ you hear} - 7\text{-}10 & & 14\text{-}20 - \textit{when} \text{ you see} \\
& 11\text{-}13 & \\
& \textit{when} \text{ you are handed over} &
\end{array}
$$

II (13:23-27): The central promise of the entire discourse is bracketed by references to the elements of creation, framing the appearance of the Lord of Creation (v. 26).

III (13:28-36): The parables about the fig tree (vv. 28-29) and the servants given appointed tasks (vv. 34-36) surround central teachings, the final statement (v. 33) preparing for the concluding statement (v. 37) with its caution to be "on guard" (thus bringing the entire discourse to its opening command, as an *inclusio).*

c, c': Bracketing the eschatological discourse are two deeds which are themselves, in turn, bracketed by materials which interpret the deeds, and vice versa. The "widow's mite" and the anointing at Bethany are set within words that denote opposition *by* Jesus (against hypocrisy), and opposition to Jesus (betrayal by Judas).

a	b	b'	a'
11:12-25	11:27-33	14:12-31	14:32-50
Parable of the fig tree, from Chapter 13, is enacted; the temple is cleansed.	Jesus is challenged Jesus replies 5 times: 12:1-12	Passover prepared Betrayal foretold	Parable of the servants, from Chapter 13, is enacted; Jesus is arrested.

12:13-17	Passover
12:18-27	partaken
12:28-34	
12:35-37	Denial foretold

Explanation: The two parables that conclude the eschatological discourse, at the center of this entire segment, shed light on the opening and closing episodes; both appear to take place outside Jerusalem proper.

a, a′: The parable of the fig tree finds its enactment in the cursing of the fig tree, and its subsequent withering, incidents that bracket the cleansing of the temple. The movement here is to and from the Holy City.

The parable of the servants appears to be acted out in the events at Gethsemane (14:32-42), and the arrest announced in the final verse (v. 42) is told next (14:43-50). It is curious to note that Jesus is seen at prayer only twice, although he returns three times. The wording of this episode appears to reflect the parable of 13:34-36, as Jesus returns and catches his disciples "asleep." Whereas the discourse of Chapter 13 announced, at its center, the glorious coming of the "Son of Man," the events at Gethsemane proclaim, at the center of this section, the "handing over" of the "Son of Man."

b, b′: Although both sections are not parallel to each other, both are arranged in sequence. In the first the authority of Jesus is challenged, to which five "replies" are then given. In the second, the preparation of the Passover and the actual meal follow sequentially with episodes announcing both the betrayal of Judas and the denial by Peter.

TRANSITION—14:51-52

This brief passage, like the transition that joined the first two segments of Part Two, serves to join what precedes and follows it. With mention of the young man's flight, the flight of disciples is recalled. The attempt to "seize" him prepares us for what follows, as Jesus is "led away."

As we approach the final segment of Part Two, this scene, however brief, will serve to frame the entire Passion account (which this outline determines to begin at 14:53). The "linen cloth" looks ahead to the burial cloth of Jesus, just as the unusual word *neaniskos* prepares us for the "young man" whom the women will encounter at the tomb (16:5).

Segment Six—14:53 to 16:8

The materials in this final segment form the climax to the entire Gospel of Mark. The first portion represents Questionings; the second describes the Movement to Golgotha; the Crucifixion comes next, followed by the Resurrection narrative, which concludes the gospel.

1. Questionings—14:53 to 15:15

a	b	a'
Jesus before Sanhedrin	Peter before inquisitors	Jesus before Pilate
14:53-59	14:66-72	15:1-5
53, 54—Setting	67—Question	2a—Question
55-59—Death sentence testimony	68—Reply	2b—Reply
	69—Question	4—Question
	70a—No Reply	5—No reply
14:60-65		
	70b—Question	15:6-15
60—Question	71—Reply	
61a—no reply		6-8—Setting
		9-15—Death
61b—Question		sentence
62—Reply		given

Explanation: Jesus is questioned by religious and civil authorities, episodes that bracket a central section in which one of his disciples is questioned regarding his relationship to Jesus. One can only think of the central section to part one of the eschatological discourse that refers to what happens "when" a disciple is "led away, being handed over," at 13:11-13.

b: Peter is questioned by bystanders, and although the second query is met by a denial, the actual reply is not recorded.

a, a': The opening portion of "a' " is set in relationship to the closing scene of the first block of material (a). In that opening block, the figure of Peter is introduced, setting the stage for the central tradition.

2. The Way to Golgotha—15:16-24

This portion would suggest a rearrangement of the traditions received. Its opening verses (15:16-20) trace the pattern described as a "hanging chain," with the weightiest verse containing the title "King of the Jews" (v. 18). The figure of Simon of Cyrene (a model disciple?) appears within the route to Golgotha, and this section ends with a brief summary of the actual Crucifixion. Throughout, however, the emphasis is upon what the soldiers did: the mockery of Jesus, the pressing into service of a passerby, and the incidents involving the wine and the garments of Jesus. John's brief statement could well sum up this portion: "This is what the soldiers did" (John 19:24).

3. The Final Hours—15 to 16:8

I	15:25-32	third hour	25-27: Action	29:32: Reaction
II	15:33-41	sixth to ninth hours	33-34: Action 37-38: Action	35-36: Reaction 39: Reaction 1 40-41: Reaction 2
III	15:42-47	evening	42-46: Action	47: Reaction
IV	16:1-8	early next morning	1-7: Action	8: Reaction

Explanation: The climactic scenes to the Gospel of Mark appear as a sequence of events, each of which is introduced by a reference to that "hour" when the event took place. For every "action" there is a corresponding "reaction," which may be termed a "reaction on the part of bystanders." The first three reactions involve various personages: the jeerers; a few of the bystanders and "someone" from their number; and a centurion, with his declaration of faith. The last three reactions involve the same persons, the "women who had followed Jesus"; their reactions, if that term can be kept, are their observations of the death, burial, and empty tomb, the last leading to a further reaction to the message they receive.

Actions: The Crucifixion is the first in the sequence of events, followed by the only "word" which Mark records, the death of Jesus with its attendant tearing of the sanctuary curtain, the detailed account of burial, and the discovery of the empty tomb, with its message from the "young man" seated there.

Reactions: The reactions on the part of those who did *not* follow Jesus have a marked movement: at first, there is open hostility; next, misunderstanding takes place, tinged by some hostility; finally, a declaration of faith is given.

As for the women who had followed Jesus, the reactions simply record the fact that they "observed" each event; the final reaction, of course, apart from that of witnessing the empty tomb and the appearance of the "young man," is their departure in fear and bewilderment.

Note of the Final Scenes, III and IV: The last three scenes all mention the women, listed at the end of the first two of these scenes, and at the beginning of the last, thus reversing the order. One may see in this arrangement the evangelist's choice of 16:1-8 as the closing scene of the gospel.

Apart from such a reversal of order, one may also detect in the closing two scenes a "developed frame." Scene III mentions *sindona* twice; Scene IV introduces *neaniskos*. This would indicate a reference to the *transitional scene* of 14:51-52, which might be renamed as a "frame" that is developed in the closing scenes of burial and empty tomb. Yet the term "transitional scene" is favored, since it relates to the preceding verse (14:50), the "flight" of disciples, a reference repeated in the final verse of the gospel (16:8).

Note on Arrangement According to "Hours": While it is conceded that a reference to time introduces each of the events, is this, in itself, a key to the arrangement? One may find confirmation in the fact that Scene II, with its double "actions" and "reaction," the last reaction itself twofold (that of the centurion, and the witness of women), is introduced by a reference to *two* "hours," the sixth and the ninth. As to the last scene, with only one activity taking place, the references to time are twofold: we are told that the "Sabbath" is over and that it is "early." However, the reference to the "next day" can be taken to clearly separate the events of burial and empty tomb; the reference to "early" morning becomes the only reference to the "hour" of the day, and the above arrangement can be maintained. (In addition, the references in Scenes III and IV, to the Sabbath, and to the Sabbath as ended, might be seen to form an inclusion with the opening scenes of the ministry— 1:21, and 1:32,35.) The final brief sentence is to some a summary of the very emotion which may have occasioned the Gospel of Mark:

ephobounto gar (they were afraid).

A Final Note: The suggestions presented remain precisely that—suggestions. No mention has been made of the difficulties that this analysis presents, difficulties that may be attributed to the rearrangement of the received traditions. As stated at the outset, these views are offered to advance the cause of Markan studies and not to anticipate a conclusion of them.

TRANSLATION
AND COMMENTARY

PART I
CONFLICT IS JOINED 1:1-1:15

1. The Preaching of John the Baptizer
(1:1-8) = Matt 3:1-12; Luke 3:1-9; John 1:19-28

1 ¹The beginning of the Proclamation of Jesus-Messiah (Son of God): ²Just as it was written in Isaiah the prophet:
"Pay attention: I send my messenger before your face.
He will prepare the way.
³A voice calling, "In the desert make ready the Lord's road! Make for him a straight way to travel."
⁴So John, the one who baptized, appeared in the desert, proclaiming a baptism of repentance for the forgiveness of sins, ⁵and everyone from the region of Judea, and all the people of Jerusalem, were going out to him. Those who confessed their sins he baptized in the Jordan River. ⁶John was dressed in clothes made from camels' hair, with a band of hide round his waist. He ate locusts and wild honey. ⁷In his proclamation, he said, "The one who is coming after me is greater than I am. I am not fit to unfasten his sandals. ⁸I have baptized you with water; he will baptize you with the holy Spirit."

Comment

It has long been customary to regard Mark's prologue as ending at v. 13 (so it was regarded by Taylor and more recently by Lane). But the present writer is convinced of the persuasiveness of Keck's argument that the first section should end at 1:14-15 (cf. L. Keck, "The Introduction to Mark's Gospel," *NTS* 12.1966, pp. 352-70), for it is only when the eschatological conflict between the Tempter and Jesus has been joined and decided that any ministry of proclamation is possible.

The prologue is characterized by its brevity and its condensation of sources: there is no introduction of John the Baptist, no indication of any connection between Jesus and John, and no explanation of the location of the baptisms in the desert. Perhaps if v. 1 is a title (which is Taylor's view but is not reflected in this commentary), the verse is intended as a summary of the whole. If this is so, then as a summary of the intent of Mark's work it could not be bettered. A reference should be made to O. J. F. Seitz, *"Praeparatio evangelica* in the Markan Prologue," *JBL* 82.3.1963, pp. 201-6, for the intriguing suggestion that the prologue is dominated by a series of interrelated themes, some of which are to be found in the Qumran *Manual of Discipline.* The themes in question, according to Seitz, are: (a) preparation in the desert, (b) repentance and turning from evil, (c) confession of sin, (d) baptism, or washing with water, (e) baptism—or cleansing—by the holy Spirit, (f) time of testing, (g) the appointed time. This is not the place to enter upon a lengthy discussion upon the relationship of Jesus and his followers to sectarian Judaism, but the article in question demonstrates the possibility that the links between the Proclamation of John—and later Jesus—and the Essene community were not merely coincidental.

Notes

1:1. *beginning:* The Greek term *archē* implies the beginning of a new reality effected by God through Jesus. But the word also seems to imply a transformation of already existing concepts, especially that of messianism.

Proclamation: Characteristically this is used in the NT of the Proclamation of salvation, but the Greek *euangelion* was rare in classical Greek. It carried with it not only an emphasis on "good news," but also a subsidiary meaning of amnesty on the accession of a sovereign.

Jesus-Messiah: Jesus is the rendering into Greek of the familiar Hebrew *Yešûa'* from a previous *Yōšūa',* and remotely from *Yahōsû'.* The first element, *Yāhū,* means "Yahweh, the Lord," and the second is probably derived from *yāša',* "to aid, save." A fair translation would be "O Lord, save." We have hyphenated *Messiah* with *Jesus,* as this best fits the sense here. It is often asserted, and perhaps too confidently, that the Greek *Christos* speedily became a proper name. But at the time of the compilation of Mark there was no sharp distinction between the definite and the indefinite article in Aramaic, and the suffix *a* came to be affixed to both definite and indefinite nouns. The absence of a definite article in *koinē* Greek *may* therefore represent a translation from Hebrew or Aramaic.

Son of God: There seems no good reason, in view of the manuscript evidence, to omit this designation. Not only is the title found elsewhere in Mark (3:11, 5:7, 15:39), but Jesus is also the "Son, the Beloved" (1:11, 9:7) and "Son of the Blessed" (14:61). The designation may be simply messianic (in the old "royal" sense—cf. Ps 2:7) but in light of the remainder of Mark, it is almost certainly far more than that (cf. P. Lamarche, "Commencement de l'évangile de Jesus Christ, Fils de Dieu (Marc 1:1),"

NRTh 92.10.1970, pp. 1024-36). But the Markan sense seems to fall short of the cosmic role of Jesus as found in Phil 2:6 or in Ephesians 1.

2. *Just as it was written:* The Greek tense is perfect, with the sense of a past event with continuing effects. This common formula for quotations is found only here in Mark.

in Isaiah the prophet: Some lesser manuscripts read *in the prophets,* but this is evidently done in response to the realization that the first quotation is not from Isaiah.

Pay attention: The familiar *kai idou* of Matthew and Luke is omitted in Mark, and we have the simple *idou* (pay attention).

I send my messenger: In Mark the verb *apostellō* (to send) occurs twenty times. In the papyri it is customarily found in expressions of commissioning. The first part of the quotation is an almost exact duplication of the *LXX* of Exod 23:20. The second part depends on the Hebrew of Mal 3:1 rather than on *LXX.* The same arrangement is found in Matt 11:10 and Luke 7:27, except for the addition of *before you* at the end of the quotation. Mark, for all the brevity and compression of his prologue, found it essential to include a composite quotation which was evidently part of a whole series of *testimonia* associated with John the Baptizer. If—with Taylor, Lagrange, Rawlinson, and H. Holtzmann*—the view is taken that v. 2 is an insertion into the text of Mark—breaking the connection between *Isaiah* in v. 1 and *A voice calling* in v. 3— then it is necessary to assume that this is either the responsibility of a copyist, or Mark himself is dependent on prior sources. There are problems with the quotations, especially if they are regarded as originally *testimonia* attached to the person of John (cf. J. A. T. Robinson's essay—"Elijah, John, and Jesus"—in *TNTS).*

3. There is no justification from the Hebrew text of Isa 40:3 for any punctuation of this verse which does not associate *in the desert* with *make ready.*

desert: The wilderness dominates the prologue. Traditionally, the wilderness area was considered the haunt of demons, and a fitting scene for conflict between God and evil.

Lord (Greek *kurios):* Used in Mark fifteen times, the title here means "God," though it is possible that Mark here uses the term in a messianic sense also. *Lord* is used of God at 5:19 and 12:30 and so also in OT citations at 11:9; 12:11,29-30,36-37. The word is used for *master* in 2:28, 11:3, 12:9, 13:35; for *sir* in 7:28; and as *Lord,* applied to Jesus, in 16:19-20 (the dubious ending of the gospel). The change from *kurios* as God in *LXX* to *kurios* as Lord in the NT is commented on by Matthew Black (1946). The usage in Mark is not as simple as the above listing would appear to indicate. *Kurios* is never used of Jesus, except as an address at 7:28 and only with the article at 11:3 (where the sense is ambiguous, it may mean simply "master" or it may equally have a messianic sense, which is the translation we have preferred). In 2:28 the use is predicative, as also in 12:9 and 13:35. Whereas Luke uses *Kurios* with the article sixteen times, Mark's anarthrous use is Matthean.

4. *So John, the one who baptized:* Rather than use a punctuation pausal mark, we have placed a period at the end of v. 3, and carried the sense of the connection of v. 3 with v. 4 by this translation (cf. Taylor, *Saint Mark,* p. 154). John is prominent in Mark (1:6,9,14; 2:18; 6:14-25; 8:28; 11:30,32), though Mark assumes that his readers

---

* H. Holtzmann, *Die Synoptiker (Hand-Commentar zum Neuen Testament,* Tübingen: J. C. B. Mohr, 1901.

are familiar with some details of John's background. The emphasis on *the desert* in this prologue recalls the view much canvassed in the past decade that John was brought up and nurtured by the Essene community at Qumran. There would appear to be nothing to militate against this view, though there is no firm evidence for it. We know that it was a common custom at Qumran for the community to rear boys (especially orphans), and if there is any historical accuracy in Luke's report that John's parents were old, then there may well have been some urgency in sending John to the Essene community.

proclaiming a baptism: There is no present evidence for the existence of any sectarians practicing baptism before John, apart from the lustrations which were part of Essene discipline. Later on there were many such baptistic sects, including some Gnostics and the Mandeans (the latter group claiming John as spiritual progenitor). Compare the following: W. H. Brownlee, "John the Baptist in the Light of Ancient Scrolls," in *The Scrolls and the New Testament,* edited by Krister Stendahl, London: SCM Press, 1958, pp. 33-54; C. H. H. Scobie, *John the Baptist,* London: SCM Press, 1964; John Pryke, "Eschatology in the Dead Sea Scrolls," in *The Scrolls and Christianity,* SPCK Theological Collections 11, London: SPCK, 1969, pp. 45-57; and H. H. Rowley, "Jewish Apocalyptic and the Dead Sea Scrolls, Ethel M. Wood Lecture, London: Athlone Press, University of London, 1957.

of repentance for the forgiveness of sins: An alternative rendering of this Semitism would be. "A baptism which symbolized repentance" (cf. C. F. D. Moule, 1953, p. 70). John's baptism was preparatory and designed for those who were repentant and desired pardon.

forgiveness: The Greek word *aphesis* is a common word in the papyri for the remission of debts.

5. *were going out:* The tense is imperfect, implying a constant procession of people. On the variant Greek spellings of Jerusalem in the gospels and Acts, see now J. K. Elliott, "Jerusalem in Acts and the Gospels," *NTS* 23.4.1977, pp. 462-69.

6. *was dressed:* The connection between John and Elijah—later an important theme —is here implied by a reference to clothing: cf. 2 Kgs 1:8.

locusts: A common item of diet then and now in the Near East, high in vitamin content. There is no justification for the identification of the word with "carob," the pods of the carob tree, sometimes known as "St. John's bread." Epiphanius *(Heresies* 30:13) is authority for the statement that the Ebionites of his own time (c. 315-403) changed the word to "cakes" in deference to their vegetarian view, and Tatian (second century) had from a similar concern changed the word to "milk."

7. The terse summary of John's mission leaves the impression that the evangelist assumed knowledge of Matt 3:2. The announcement that his mission was but a *praeparatio evangelica,* with no further characterization of the nature of the preaching, is odd, if Mark is regarded as the prime source for the other synoptists. But it fits well with Mark's concentration on the person and ministry of Jesus.

is coming: The present tense here sounds a note of urgent immediacy.

after me: The word *me* is omitted by two manuscripts.

greater (or *stronger):* The comparative is of the substantive *ischuros* (used in 3:27 of Satan). The word is found with some frequency in the NT, used to describe Satan, angels, oppressors, and God. Here the term implies that the Coming One (cf. Mal 3:1ff., 4:5ff., 3:23-24) is the deliverer and even the judge of the end-time. John does not make any identification of the Coming One, and only juxtaposition with the baptismal scene which follows allows us to find here a primitive christology. (Cf. also Lohmeyer, p. 18, for the suggestion that *after*—Greek *opisō*—denotes a slave-overlord relationship, producing the paradox that the one following behind his master is at the same time the judge and deliverer. This suggestion, though interesting, does not appear to be demanded by the sense of the saying. See also Lane, p. 52, who follows Lohmeyer here.)

8. *I have baptized:* The aorist tense *ebaptisa* ought not to be presented so as to suggest the Baptizer as saying, "I baptized, but now that the Coming One is to be here. . . ." Rather the tense should be understood as a stative perfect. Matt 3:11 has *I am baptizing.* It is at least a possibility, assuming Markan dependence on Matthew, that Mark consciously altered Matthew's tense in order to emphasize a discontinuity between the ministry of John and that of Jesus.

with water . . . with the holy Spirit: There is a contrast between the baptism of John and that of the Coming One. The gospels represent John as himself distinguishing between his baptismal ministry and that of Jesus. Mark reproduces the Lucan statement (Luke 3:3) that John preached a baptism of repentance, whereas Matt 3:11 has the Baptizer himself declaring the purpose of his ministry.

with the holy Spirit (omitting *in,* with some manuscripts): The phrase in 1:10,12 is *the Spirit* and in 3:29, 12:36, and 13:11 is *the holy Spirit.* Matt 3:11 and Luke 3:16 have *with the holy Spirit and with fire.* The outpouring of the Spirit was a well-known feature of speculation about the end-time (cf. Joel 2:28ff., Isa 44:3, Ezek 36:26ff., *T Levi* 18), though nowhere described as bestowed by the messiah. The phrasing of this passage has in our own time been obscured by the insistence of some Pentecostalist groups that two different "baptisms" are described in the phrase used by Matthew and Luke. The evidence from the Dead Sea Scrolls is, however, clear and certain that their phrase is a hendiadys (cf. J. A. T. Robinson, "The Baptism of John and the Qumran Community" in *TNTS*). Carl-Martin Edsman in *Le Baptême de Feu* (Leipzig: A. Lorenz, 1940, pp. 1ff.) discusses all this against the background of some later Christian notions of a baptism by fire either at the end of life, or the end of the age, with special reference to Origen's *Homily 24* on Luke. Unfortunately this important monograph missed the fact of the hendiadys.

Taylor suggests that the original saying spoke merely of a baptism by fire—i.e., of judgment (cf. Amos 7:4, Isa 31:9, Mal 3:2, 1 Cor 3:13, 2 Thess 1:7) and that *with the holy Spirit* was introduced under the influence of later Christian baptism (J. E. Yates, "The Form of Mark 1:8," *NTS* 4.1958, pp. 334-38).

2. The Baptism of Jesus
(1:9-11) = Matt 3:13-17; Luke 3:21-22

1   9 At this time it happened that Jesus came from Nazareth in Galilee and was baptized by John in the Jordan. 10 At the moment when
Jesus was coming up out of the water, he saw heaven being torn apart,
and the Spirit like a dove descending to him. 11 A voice came from
heaven, "You are my Son, the Beloved. On you my favor rests."

Comment

This pericope, unlike others in the Markan tradition, begins and ends
abruptly. It may have been for the evangelist an inserted item, but as part of
the tradition he was compiling, it was impossible to omit. The pericope, in its
brevity, bears all the marks of an insertion into an already conflated document. The "Spirit" motif of v. 8 is taken up again in v. 12.

Mark is apparently recording, or inserting, an early part of the historical
tradition, and whether the imagery employed suggests a vision, or some spiritual apprehension by Jesus, it is not necessary (cf. Bultmann, *Theology,* 1921,
p. 264) to judge the account to be a faith legend, still less to attribute the
whole account to some typically *theios anēr* mythology. That the baptism is
basic to the tradition is evidenced by the changes in the evangelists' handling
of the material. Luke apparently wished to underline the visibility of the
appearance of the Spirit to all. Mark uses Luke's second person speech in his
account, preferring it to Matthew's third-person speech.

To attempt some kind of investigation of Jesus' consciousness at the time of
his baptism is to engage in speculation. What is open to our investigation is
what the evangelist understood by his handling of the tradition in the narrative. The identification of Jesus as Representative Israel, found in Matt 3:15,
is not to Mark's purpose. But Mark shares with Matthew and Luke the
central understanding of the baptism in the tradition as the beginning of the
messianic age. This theme is emphasized in the scriptural quotations:

a. The opening of the heavens is neither simply a device of apocalyptic, nor
the necessary prelude to a vision, but a precondition of the coming of the
Spirit, and as such is found in ancient accounts of theophanies. In this con-

nection Isa 64:1 provides an interesting parallel, set in a context of desire for the dawn of the eschatological age.

b. The desire expressed in the book of Isaiah is here fulfilled, and the Spirit is given. This is not all. The coming of the Spirit happens as Jesus comes up from the water, and there is a reminiscence of Isa 63:11, all the more impressive in that the Isaianic reference is in a context of anticipation of an expected Second Deliverance (the first being the Exodus from Egypt). The linking of the baptism of Jesus with the beginning of a second Exodus often finds expression in Christian baptismal liturgies.

c. The voice from heaven has often been described in commentaries as not only an assertion of relationship (based on Ps 2:7) but also the first identification of Jesus with the Servant of Isaiah (42:1), the latter effectively providing the framework of Jesus' understanding of his ministry. This was called in question by G. Vermes *(Scripture and Tradition in Judaism,* Leiden: E. J. Brill, 1961, pp. 193-227, especially p. 223), and a recent article (Robert J. Daley, "The Soteriological Significance of the Sacrifice of Isaac," *CBQ* 39.1.1977, pp. 45-75) has called attention once more to the strong possibility that it is Genesis 22 which lies behind the voice in the baptismal accounts. The suggestion of both authors—that the authenticating voice points to a soteriological interpretation of Jesus' ministry—is certainly more persuasive than the weight placed on Psalm 2 and Isaiah 42. It must be noted, however, that such an interpretation would demand that the evangelists were aware of soteriological speculation about Isaac among the Palestinian rabbis. Equally, the weight often placed on the baptism of Jesus as being in some fashion the dawn of his messianic consciousness fails to account for the soteriological significance attaching to baptism in the NT letters, unless this was first grounded in a primary significance attaching to the baptism of Jesus. (The reader is referred to Daley's article, with its invaluable bibliographical references, and see further references in the notes.) On the baptism of Jesus cf. three articles by A. Feuillet: "La Baptême de Jésus d'apres l'Évangile selon Saint Marc 1.9-11," *CBQ* 21.4.1959, pp. 468-90; "La Baptême de Jésus," *RevBib* 71.3.1964, pp. 321-54; and "La personnalité de Jésus entrevue à partir de sa soumission au rite de repentance du précurseur," *RevBib* 77.1.1970, pp. 30-49. Also cf. S. Gero, "The Spirit as a Dove at the Baptism of Jesus," *NovTest* 18.1.1976, pp. 17-35.

Notes

9. *At this time:* A vague note of time, found also in 8:1, 13:17,24. It seems to be a later editorial insertion. The whole phrase *At this time . . . came* is Semitic in character. The use of *it happened* is common in Luke, but rare in Mark.

10. *he saw:* The subject of the verb refers to Jesus, but it is impossible to determine

whether Mark is describing (in our terms) a vision or an objective event. The bystanders are not apparently witnesses to any visible phenomenon. It is equally difficult to determine whether the early tradition, shared by all three synoptic gospels, was a theologizing of the baptism of Jesus, or whether the tradition as we now have it rests upon Jesus' own understanding of the event communicated in private teaching.

being torn apart: The Greek participle describes action taking place. Matthew and Luke use the passive form of the verb *anoigō,* "to open," but Mark's use considerably heightens the dramatic effect. (A similar apocalyptic image is found in 15:38.) There are further examples of the image in the NT: John 1:32ff.; Acts 10:19, 12:12; Rom 8:16,26ff.; and in *T 12 Patr (T Levi* 2:6, 5:1, 18:6; *T Judah* 24:2) and in *Apoc Bar* 22:1.

the Spirit: The more usual Hebrew term would be *Spirit of God* (cf. Matt 3:16) or *the holy Spirit* (cf. Luke 3:22), but Mark's abbreviation here is not a change in idea. The passages in the pseudepigraphical literature cited previously connect the opening of the heavens with revelation, and additional references associate the coming of the Spirit with the Messiah (cf. *1 Enoch* 49:3, 62:2; *Pss Sol* 17:42; *T Levi* 18:6ff.; *T Judah* 24:2). The idea has its foundation in Isa 61:1. We use the term "messiah" to designate no more—though no less—than the Servant-Messenger of God.

to him: Lohmeyer's caution (p. 23) is important here. Mark's account does not speak of any endowment of the Spirit given to Jesus, but simply of the Spirit coming to Jesus. The manuscript evidence, furthermore, is confused. Both Matthew and Luke have *ep' auton* (upon him), but we have preferred Mark's *eis auton* as well attested in the manuscripts and as being the more difficult reading. If our preference is correct, then Mark's change in the texts he had before him was designed to exclude any suggestion that Jesus' subsequent ministry was simply the result of interior compulsion.

like a dove: Luke 3:22 adds emphasis to this part of the tradition by adding "in bodily form," which is partly in accord with Luke's habit of providing additional physical details to narrative. The term itself is obscure, and the dove as a sign of Israel is late, while the identification of the dove with the Spirit is even later (cf. *Tg Cant* 2:12) and rejected by Strack-Billerbeck (Vol. 1, p. 125). The published material on this matter is of formidable dimensions, and much of it has been conveniently summarized in the article by Gero (1976, pp. 17-35) cited at the end of the preceding comment. The explanation provided by Gero is as convincing as anything else current. The "dove" element, missing in the *Gospel of the Hebrews,* is provided by the *Odes of Solomon* 24: "The dove flew upon (the head of our Lord) the Messiah, because he was the head. And she sang over him and her voice was heard. And the inhabitants feared and the strangers were disturbed. The bird let down its wings and the creeping things died in their holes. . . ." The setting of this passage is almost certainly the baptism of Jesus. There is no reason to identify the dove with the Spirit, since what is being presented is an epiphany or "cosmic catastrophe" described in very unclear terms: the dove and the voice have a revelatory function. The descent of a bird—especially a dove—upon a chosen person is a common motif in ancient Near Eastern legend. The ode in question—Christian in its present form—may represent the first linkage of the common dove-election motif with the baptismal setting in a form "as yet unassociated with the parallel but independent motif of the descent of the Spirit" (p. 19). Gero contends that the evangelist had available to him a story which linked two divine messengers in the context of the baptism of Jesus, and rather than present separate descents for each, he amalgamated them. The *Gospel of the Hebrews* had a tradition of the descent of the Spirit, which spoke to, and in, Jesus, while the *Odes of Solomon* preserved a tradition of a dove (not yet identified with the Spirit) which flew down upon Jesus and revealed his status to the world.

Gero's interesting suggestion raises questions once again about the provenance and the dating of the *Testaments of the Twelve Patriarchs* which are beyond the scope of this commentary but certainly demand study.

11. *A voice:* The sentence is abrupt, and our translation—"came"—reflects an *egeneto* which is missing in some manuscripts of Mark. Taylor (p. 161) suggests that the absence of the verb may be explained by an overliteral translation of an Aramaic original. Luke 3:22 supplies the verb *genesthai.* The *voice* (whether this explains the experience of Jesus himself, or is an early theological reflection in the tradition) has its background in the *bāt qôl* often found in the rabbinical literature (cf. Strack-Billerbeck Vol. 1, pp. 125-32 for examples). A story of Rabbi Jose (c. A.D. 150) in TB *Berakot* relates his hearing the divine voice "like the cooing of a dove" in the ruins of Jerusalem.

You are my Son, the Beloved: In the Greek of *LXX,* nearly half of all uses of *agapētos,* "beloved," with "son," mean "only." P. G. Bretscher ("Exodus 4:22-23 and the Voice from Heaven," *JBL* 87.3.1968, pp. 301-11) believes that the strongest emphasis in this authenticating voice is the idea of Israel as God's only son, his beloved, and contends that *prōtotokos* ("first-born, only"—referring to a child) "seems to stand behind" uses of *agapētos, monogenēs* (only-begotten), and *eklēktos* (chosen). In Matthew *Beloved* is a separate title, in apposition, as it is also in the *LXX* of Gen 22:2 and Isa 52:1. The first part of the Proclamation in Matthew, therefore, appears to be a Proclamation of messiahship (by being cast in the third person), though the element of Jesus as Representative Israel (especially in the temptation narrative later) is also prominent. Gero (v. 10, above) places much stronger emphasis on the Isaac parallel than on the Servant of Deutero-Isaiah. The complexity of the declaration in this verse —composed as it is of elements of Genesis 22, Psalm 2, and Isaiah 42 and 44—can hardly be exaggerated, since it combines motifs from the soteriological ideas of Genesis 22, a messianic designation in Psalm 2, and the Servant of Isaiah 42. The combination of motifs is startling, yet all the elements are at home in Palestinian Judaism. If we can agree with Taylor (p. 162), what is given here is an insight into Jesus' awareness of his intimate relationship with God which preceded any consciousness of messianic vocation.

3. The Temptations of Jesus
(1:12-13) = Matt 4:1-11; Luke 4:1-13

1   [12] Immediately the Spirit drove him into the desert. [13] He remained in the desert forty days, where he was tempted by Satan. He was there among the wild beasts, but angels came and helped him.

Comment

The temptation narrative in Mark is brief and differs in style from the preceding material: the historic present makes its first appearance; the verb follows the subject; and Taylor (p. 162) suggests the possibility of a rhythmic structure which he characterizes as b/ab (was in the desert; tempted by Satan; among wild beasts). P. Pokorný ("The Temptation Stories and Their Intention," *NTS* 20.2.1974, pp. 115-27) is certainly correct in considering the brief temptation account in Mark as not derived from Matthew and Luke, though it is perhaps less convincing—in the absence of parallels from the intertestamental literature—to see in this brief account a "Jewish Adam-apocalypse" with Jesus as type and Adam as antitype. The account is linked closely with the baptism (cf. *kai euthus,* "immediately") and as such signals the opening of the eschatological warfare centered in and focused upon Jesus.

Notes

12. *Immediately the Spirit drove him:* Mark uses the verb *ekballō* seventeen times in all, and the association of the verb with exorcism (eleven times) compels a translation such as "drove" or "impelled." Mark here uses the dramatic historic present indicative. A recent article (F. C. Synge, "A Matter of Tenses—Fingerprints of an Annotator in Mark," *ExpT* 88.6.1977, pp. 168-71) suggests that the present indicative tense in this instance, as in v. 21 (cf. 2:18; 3:20; 4:1; 6:1,30; 7:1; 8:22a; 10:1,46; 11:15,27a; 14:53) comes from an editor whose work can be traced as an "*i*-dotter," but who avoided tampering with the text in any major way and so eroding the prestige of the original. See also the use of the present indicative in aorist narratives (5:15; 8:6a; 10:49; 16:2,4). It seems equally possible to suggest that this annotator was engaged in heightening Mark's original work based on Matthean sources. See also below under 5:22-43.

13. *desert:* The wilderness areas were commonly believed to be the habitation of demons (cf. Kittel, article on *erēmos, TWNT* Vol. 2, pp. 657ff.). It is interesting here to see something of the character of Markan conflation. "Into the desert" (Matt 4:1-2) is reproduced in Mark 1:12, while the Lucan 4:1-2 is found in Mark 1:13. This cannot be explained by a Matthean choice of one phrase and a Lucan choice of another. Moreover, as Feuillet pointed out more than a decade ago (1960, pp. 49-73), the links between baptism and temptation, or between the crossing of the Red Sea and the desert sojourn—links carefully preserved in Matthew and Luke—are broken in Mark. It is almost impossible to understand the Markan account without recourse to the other synoptists. Even the apparently primitive detail of the wild beasts in v. 13 may be the Markan equivalent of the defeat of Satan, and Matthew and Luke have primitive traditions (e.g., the hunger of Jesus and the victory over Satan) which find no place in Mark. Feuillet concludes that Mark is an abridgement of a source preserved more fully in Matthew and Luke. The abridgement (or in our view the conflation) of the sources of Matthew and Luke depends on two considerations: the evangelist wishes to avoid any suggestion that Jesus was at any point not master of events—a suggestion which might have been conveyed by a fuller temptation narrative—and he wants to pass immediately from the temptation to the working out of the drama following the arrest of John.

was tempted: The verb *peirazō* ought to be understood in the sense of "to wage war on"—the first engagement in the eschatological conflict.

Satan: Evil and temptation in the biblical material are not easily summarized. The Hebrew figure of the *śāṭān* appears in Job 1-2 as a member of the heavenly assembly and there acts as a kind of prosecuting attorney; similarly, 1 Chr 21:1 embodies a similar tradition about the *śāṭān*. Job certainly antedates Chronicles, and perhaps (in chapters 1-2) by as much as two centuries. Ps 109:6 also has the *śāṭān*. Zech 3:2 shows a slight change in that the prosecutor becomes more obviously an adversary.

The intertestamental literature, under the influence of Iranian dualism, produces numerous examples of a dominion of God and a beneficent providence set in sharp contrast to a malignant dominion of evil (cf. the *mastema* figure of Job). The figure of the *śāṭān* now becomes wholly evil, and is no longer a member of the heavenly assembly. We have no information as to the steps by which *śāṭān* became *diabolos*, the devil, but in the NT literature generally the prince of the dominion of evil is *diabolos*, dedicated to man's destruction through temptation. A *diabolos* is literally an accuser, and the corresponding *diabolē*, though sometimes used in the sense of "enmity," is most often used as "calumny," notably in *LXX. LXX* also uses *diabolos* for Hebrew *śāṭān* even in its earlier sense of adversary or opponent. (Josephus never uses *diabolos*, or any other name, for Satan.) It is important not to confuse *diabolos* with *daimōn* (demon), which can be either good or evil, or even morally neutral.

Essene theology demonstrates a thoroughgoing dualism (probably developed from Zoroastrianism in some form) with the "good Spirit" (i.e., the holy Spirit) in total opposition to the "evil Spirit" (i.e., Satan), though all is finally under divine rule.

among the wild beasts: This Markan addition to the temptation story is characterized by the use of *meta*, a preposition which elsewhere in Mark suggests close and intimate communion (cf. 3:14, 5:18, 14:67). The reference to animals, which may be an allusion to Isa 11:6-8, 65:25, and Hos 2:18, suggests (according to Jeremias) the

restoration of paradise. H.-G. Leder ("Sundenfallerzählung und Versuchungsge-
schichtliche: Zur Interpretation von Mc 1.12f," *ZNW* 54.3-4.1963, pp. 188-216) finds
in this account a christological motif: the eschatological warfare with Satan has been
joined, and Jesus in his ministry is proleptically the triumphant Son of Man. He denies
that there is any Adam-Christ typology, deriving from Genesis 3 here, pleading that
there is no clear example in Jewish literature of angels ministering to Adam; however,
cf. *Ber. Sanh.* 59b. (Cf. also J. Jeremias, 1963, pp. 278-97.)

angels came and helped him: The Greek *angelos* is in both *LXX* and the NT notoriously difficult to interpret in many places. Since in Mark the word is always used of
"heavenly beings," we have allowed the translation *angels.*

4. The Beginnings of Ministry
(1:14-15) = Matt 4:12-17; Luke 4:14-15

1   ¹⁴ After John had been arrested, Jesus went to Galilee, heralding
the Proclamation of God: ¹⁵ "The time has come," he said, "and God's
Reign is upon you. Repent, and believe the Proclamation."

Comment

Attention has already been called in the Introduction to the three distinct
parts of Jesus' ministry and the association of those stages with three distinct
understandings of his ministry. Of the Judean ministry, John alone provides
us with information, though Matthew and Luke imply its existence. The
opening of the Galilean ministry, consequent upon the arrest of John, finds
Mark assuming a knowledge of the arrest of the Baptizer either from Luke or
from some other source. It has been pointed out, however, that there is a gap
between vv. 13 and 14 in which the tradition of a Judean mission could be
accommodated. Matters extraneous to the central thrust of Mark's message
(the crisis provoked by Jesus' words and works) are excluded.

It has been suggested that the whole complex of 1:14-3:6 was intended by
Mark to represent a series of events in the ministry, "typical days," with 1:29-
39 furnishing one such day. We believe this view must be rejected. Each
pericope of Mark is self-contained and tightly organized, and the notes of
time are often simply introductory matter with no particular reference to the
sequence of events. Not only so, but the material in this section is intended to
introduce the theme of eschatological conflict as quickly as possible. Chronology and geography *of themselves* are not important to the evangelist. His

dominant concern is the crisis in the community to which he addresses himself.

Notes

14. *After:* Reading *meta de* rather than *kai meta* found in other manuscripts.

arrested (Greek *to paradothēnai,* literally "the delivering up"): The absence of a qualifying clause such as "to prison" may be a Markan device for making a parallel between the experience of John and that of Jesus, or the expression may link (cf. Taylor, p. 165) the delivering up with the fulfilling of the will of God. The articular infinitive is found fifteen times in Mark.

Galilee: Mark says nothing of any place where Jesus went; the scene is almost immediately set by the lakeside.

heralding: The verb *kērussō* was customarily associated in Hellenistic Greek with a proclamation of importance made by a herald carrying a trumpet. In classical times the person of the herald was legally inviolate.

Proclamation: This translation of *euangēlion* has been used out of a sense of the debasement of the word "gospel," which is attached to any program its proponents feel is important (e.g., "the social gospel"). As "good news" the *euangēlion* was most commonly used in antiquity of news of victory; so much was this the case that good fortune was held to attend the very words of the Proclamation, and the word could be used as a religious term, in that offerings accompanied the reception of news of victory (cf. Philostratus, *Life of Apollonius* Vol. 8). In the imperial cult the accession of a new sovereign is a *euangēlion,* for the king was regarded as a "divine man" whose birth and later accession as protector of the state brought *sotēria* (wholeness, salvation). Similar sentiments are found in Psalm 72. For a very full treatment of the word, cf. Kittel, *TWNT* Vol. 2, pp. 721-27. Cf. also Adolf Deissmann, *Licht vom Osten: Das Neue Testament und die neuemdekten Texte der hellenistisch-romischen Welt* (Tübingen: J. C. B. Mohr, 1909; English translation by R. M. Strachan, *Light from the Ancient East,* New York: G. H. Doran, 1927, from the fourth German edition). Such forms continued into the Middle Ages. Paul in Gal. 5:1 expresses the sense attempted in this translation. Dr. Thomas McAdoo has called my attention to the linking of *euangēlion* with *sotēria* in Aeschylus, *Agamemnon* 6.4.6.

of God: The genitive can mean "from God" or "about God," but the former sense appears preferable. Some manuscripts add the phrase "of the Kingdom" before the genitive *of God,* but this is likely to be a scribal addition.

15. *The time:* The notion of *kairos,* "appointed time," is found also in 13:33. For OT background, cf. Ezek 7:12; Dan 12:4,9; Zeph 1:12; and in the NT cf. also Gal 4:4 and Eph 1:10. The content of the idea is eschatological—the determination of time fulfilled is in the hands of God.

he said: Read *kai legōn hoti.* Kai is widely omitted by the manuscripts, as is *legōn,* but *legōn hoti* is found in Mark thirty-eight times and should stand here. The evangelist generally avoids indirect speech; this construction can be used for something said repeatedly.

God's Reign: The phrase is used fourteen times (1:15; 4:11,26,30; 9:1,47; 10:14-

15,23,25; 12:34; 14:25; 15:43). The phrase refers to the rule of God, his dominion, and sovereignty. There is a full discussion of it in the commentary by Turner, Introduction, pp. 114-16, where it is rightly pointed out that the idea of God's kingly rule also implies a visible community. There is no fine distinction, such as is characteristic of Matthew, between the Reign of God and the Son's mission in this gospel (cf. Albright-Mann, AB *Matthew*, Introduction, VI-VIII, pp. lxxxi-cv).

Hardly anything was more destructive of the Proclamation of Jesus in the Middle Ages, both east and west, than the ready—and total—identification of the Reign of God with ecclesiastical rule and order. In our own time the idea of the Kingdom has been debated in another fashion. Jesus never stated precisely what the Kingdom *is*, but spoke in similitudes—"the Kingdom is like . . ."—and for modern commentators the problem is the possibility of communicating the reality of the Kingdom in nonreligious language, or (put more simply) of speaking of God in a "secular" fashion. The reader is commended to the following: Ian T. Ramsey, *Models and Mystery* (Whidden Lectures for 1963, New York and London: Oxford University Press, 1964); E. L. Mascall, *The Secularization of Christianity* (London: Darton, Longman and Todd, 1965); Norman Perrin, *The Kingdom of God in the Teaching of Jesus* (London: SCM Press, 1963); Perrin, *Jesus and the Language of the Kingdom* (Philadelphia: Fortress Press, 1976); Amos Wilder, *Early Christian Rhetoric: The Language of the Gospel* (Cambridge, Mass.: Harvard University Press, 1971).

is upon you: The note of immediacy in the Greek *ēngiken* is not easily conveyed in English. Jesus spoke of the Kingdom as future (14:25, cf. Luke 11:2) but also proclaimed that the Kingdom was present in his own person and mission. C. H. Dodd popularized the expression "realized eschatology" and contended that most, if not all, of the "futurist" eschatology ought *stricto sensu* to be understood in the sense of a present, irrupting eschatology in the words of Jesus. The present writer, acknowledging his indebtedness both to the late W. F. Albright and to J. A. T. Robinson, would find little reason to change the notes and comments to chapters 24 and 25 in the AB *Matthew* (pp. 285-305). The element of "futurist" eschatology in the gospels has always seemed to this writer to have been exaggerated; scholars have tended to minimize the sense of immediate urgency with which Jesus invested contemporary apocalyptic language. The discussion of this point in Lohmeyer (p. 30) is important, as are also two articles bearing on this question (J. Y. Campbell, "The Kingdom of God Has Come," *ExpT* 48.1936-37, pp. 91-94; and J. M. Creed, "The Kingdom of God Has Come," *ExpT* 48.1936-37, pp. 184-85).

F. Mussner ("Die Bedeutung von Mc 1.4f. für die Reichgottesverkündigung," *TTZ* 66.5.1957, pp. 257-75) does not agree with Dodd's plea that *ēngiken* means "has arrived" but admits that "God's Kingdom is upon you" is parallel to "the time has come": the Reign of God begins with the words and works of Jesus. Taylor (p. 167) agrees that Jesus "believed the *Basileia* to be present in Himself and in His ministry." Cf. also C. H. Dodd, *The Parables of the Kingdom* (London: Nisbet, 1961) and R. H. Lightfoot (1935), especially pp. 65ff. and 107, n. 1.

Repent: The verb *metanoeō* is used in *LXX* to translate Hebrew *niḥam*, "to be sorry," but (following Taylor) the context suggests that the NT usage reflects Hebrew *šûb*, "to return, repent" (cf. William L. Holladay, *The Root Šûbh in the Old Testament*, Leiden: E. J. Brill, 1958).

believe: Or "put your trust in." Here only in the NT does *en* (in) occur with *pisteuō* (to believe). Commentators have paid considerable attention to the presence of *en*. If *euangēlion* is used in the sense of "Proclamation" or "good news," then the sense would seem to demand "put your trust in. . . ." It is not likely that Mark has imposed a theology of his own on the opening message of the ministry of Jesus by a meaning such as "the Christian message." Cf. Wellhausen (1911), p. 7; Klostermann (1950), pp. 4ff; J. Weiss, *Das Urchristentum,* Göttingen: Vandenhoeck and Ruprecht, 1917, p. 137.

PART II
THE ACTS OF JESUS—1:16-3:35

5. First Disciples
(1:16-20) = Matt 4:18-22; Luke 5:1-11

1 [16] As [Jesus] was walking by the Sea of Galilee, he saw Simon and his brother Andrew casting a net in the sea—they were fishermen. [17] "Come with me," Jesus said to them, "and I will make you fishers who catch men." [18] At once they left their nets and followed him. [19] When he had gone a little farther, he saw two other brothers, James and John, Zebedee's sons, who were in their boat preparing their nets. [20] He immediately summoned them, and—leaving their father Zebedee in the boat with the hired hands—they went to follow him.

Comment

Mark follows Matthew's narrative order, even when his own theme of conflict must be postponed and not followed up naturally—as on other grounds we might have expected—from v. 15. The disciples play an important role in vv. 29ff. and so must be introduced. The geographical details provided by Matt 4:13 are omitted, and Mark's account begins abruptly at 1:16. The narrative of the calling of the two sets of brothers implies that they left all behind them and followed Jesus on first acquaintance. This must certainly have been the intention of the evangelist, and in all probability it was derived from early Christian preaching. But it was almost imperative to supply the details of the Judean ministry from John 1:35ff. to account for an earlier acquaintance with Jesus which would have predisposed the first disciples to accompany him when he made his appearance in Galilee.

The judgments made by commentators on this section are widely varied; some are mutually incompatible. Taylor (p. 168) finds the accounts resting on Petrine reminiscences, with their eyewitness details. K. L. Schmidt *(Der Rahmen der Geschichte Jesu,* Berlin: Kaiser Verlag, 1919, p. 44) thinks that the constant repetition of detail is an indication that we are within the circles of the earliest tradition. Bultmann *(History,* pp. 26ff.) puts the narratives under the heading of a biographical apothegm, presenting an idealized scene deriving from a "fishers of men" saying. Lohmeyer (pp. 31-33) finds in it part of a whole cycle of manifestation stories about Jesus as the Son of Man. The present writer believes that the repetitive character of the narrative, in both Matthew and Luke, would be more at home in the simpler historical narratives of the Hebrew Bible than in a cycle of manifestation stories. Bultmann's characterization of the narrative seems to be apt, even if a verdict of idealization seems unduly skeptical.

Notes

16. *As Jesus was walking by:* Mark's verb, *paragō,* is unusual in combination with *para,* as Taylor remarks (p. 168). It is possible that the original tradition simply gave him *paragōn* and he added *para tēn thalassan* from Matthew. Black (1946, p. 96) maintains that the use of Greek *thalassa* to describe a lake reflects Semitic usage—i.e., Hebrew *ym.*

Simon: The word occurs seven times in Mark (1:16,29ff.,36; 3:16; 14:37) and *Peter* nineteen times. The tradition of Papias, that Mark was the interpreter of Peter, would seem to be confirmed by the frequency with which Mark mentions Peter. Simon is used when Jesus addresses the apostle here and in 14:37, otherwise in narrative before the change recorded in 3:16.

Andrew: Apart from the note that Andrew was Simon's brother and that he lived with him in Capernaum, we know nothing of him as a member of the inner circle of disciples.

17. *Come with me* (literally, "Come after me"): Call and discipleship (following) are prominent in Mark (cf. 1:20; 2:14ff.; 8:34,34b). The idiom is Semitic.

fishers who catch men: Literally, "I will make you become fishers. . . ." Mark adds *genesthai,* "to become," to Matthew's phrase. The fishing metaphor is almost certainly derived from Jer 16:16. As a symbol for missionary enterprise, fishing is found also in Matt 13:47 (cf. Luke 5:1ff. and John 21:4-8), and see also Ezek 47:10. For the element of eschatological warning in the fishing metaphor, cf. C. W. F. Smith, "Fishers of Men," *HTR* 52.1959, pp. 187-203).

18. *At once:* The theme of renunciation in the teaching of Jesus is continually emphasized in the gospels, and this theme is here given its first expression. The detail of leaving *their nets* underlines the finality of the response to Jesus. Cf. Lohmeyer, p. 32.

19. The only information we have on James *(Iakōbos)*—in Mark 1:19,29; 3:17; 5:37; 9:2; 10:35,41; 13:3; 14:33—is that he was John's brother and, together with his brother and Peter, was present at the raising of Jairus' daughter, at the Transfiguration, the Mount of Olives, and Gethsemane, and that he craved with his brother some degree of eminence at the coming of the kingdom. The other Jameses are apparently distinct figures; for James the brother of Jesus, see 6:3; James the son of Alphaeus, see

3:18; and James the Less, see 15:40. From early times the question of the identity of James the Less (15:40) with James the son of Alphaeus has been argued, and the conventional view has been that the two are identical, though perhaps a majority of modern scholars holds that they are two different individuals. A convenient summary of the discussion is to be found in John L. McKenzie, S.J., *Dictionary of the Bible*, New York: Macmillan; London: Collier-Macmillan, 1965, p. 411. Zebedee is mentioned only in connection with his sons. The one reference to John not in association with James is 9:38.

The pericope of the first disciples is vital to Mark's scheme. It anticipates—as R. P. Maye correctly observes in *Jesus and the Twelve: Discipleship and Revelation in Mark's Gospel* (Grand Rapids, Mich.: Eerdmans, 1968), pp. 83ff.—the call of the Twelve in 3:13-19 and the mission of the Twelve in 6:7-13, and most important of all it looks to the conclusion of the gospel and the mission of the community.

preparing their nets: The use of the verb *katartizō* (restore, mend, perfect) by Paul (Rom 9:22; 1 Cor 1:10; 2 Cor 13:11; Gal 6:1; 1 Thess 3:10) and by the author of Hebrews (10:5) and of 1 Peter (5:10), together with the emphasis on fishing for men, suggests that the theme of the future mission of the Church was in the forefront of the mind of the evangelist (cf. Matt 4:21).

20. *hired hands:* The word *misthōtos* is peculiar to Mark. Luke 5:10 speaks of some of these disciples as "partners." Certainly in the circumstances of Galilee at that time, it is unlikely that fishermen were necessarily poor.

6. The Man with the Unclean Spirit (1:21-28) = Luke 4:31-37

1 ²¹ They went to Capernaum, and on the Sabbath he went to synagogue and taught. ²² The people were astounded at his teaching, for he taught as an authority in his own right, unlike the scribes. ²³ There was a man in the synagogue with an unclean spirit, and he screamed: ²⁴ "What do you want with us, Jesus of Nazareth? You have come to destroy us! I know who you are—God's Holy One." ²⁵ Jesus commanded him: "Silence! Come out of him!" ²⁶ The unclean spirit threw the man into convulsions, and then with a loud shout left him. ²⁷ They were all astounded, and so began to ask one another, "What is this? A new teaching? He speaks with authority. When he gives orders to unclean spirits they obey him." ²⁸ The report about him spread rapidly everywhere in the district of Galilee.

Comment

The general description of the Galilean ministry in Matt 4:23-25 is expanded by Mark and used as a basis for a series of pericopae. There is certainly either a confusion or a conflation of traditions here. The "they" of v. 21a becomes "he" in v. 21b; the "they" goes back to vv. 16-20, and Mark here depends on his other sources for what may originally have come to him as a healing story about Jesus.

Taylor (pp. 170-71, cf. Introduction, pp. 90-92) argues that the series of pericopae which begins here and continues to 1:39 belonged to "the earliest personal testimony." We may accept this verdict, though taking into account the present writer's view of Markan dependence on Matthew and Luke it must be said that this collection appears to have been made to demonstrate, as typical of the Galilean ministry, the authority of Jesus' teaching and his challenge to the dominion of evil (cf. Matt 4:13; 7:28,29; Luke 4:31-37).

Notes

21. *Capernaum:* One of the few places identified by Mark as associated with Jesus' ministry, it is identified with the site of Tel Ḥûm on the northwestern shore of Lake Galilee. Mark mentions the place again at 2:1 and 9:33, and it is perhaps implied in 5:21ff.

Sabbath: The origin of the seventh day as a compulsory day of rest is obscure: the Old Testament (Gen 2:2ff.) links it with the merciful providence of God. For fuller information on the Sabbath, cf. Kittel, *TWNT* ad loc. The Greek *sabbaton* is Semitic in origin and, though it is a second declension noun, always in the New Testament it takes a dative plural ending, *sabbasin*. The plural is common when feasts are under discussion. T. A. Burkill's suggestion (in *Mysterious Revelation: An Examination of the Philosophy of Mark's Gospel,* Ithaca, N.Y.: Cornell University Press, 1963, p. 34) that the evangelist is attempting by this plural to depict Jesus' ministry in some general, overall fashion is not justified by the usages of NT Greek.

synagogue: The first attestation of synagogues as places of assembly for instruction and prayer is in Egypt toward the end of the third century B.C.; in Palestine they are attested c. 200 B.C. (cf. Sir 51:23). The origins of the synagogue would appear to be far older, however, since the centralization of worship in Jerusalem after 621 B.C., along with the fact that the majority of Jews were thereby denied access to sacrificial worship, must perforce have led to the proliferation of nonsacrificial places of assembly. During the Babylonian exile (597-539 B.C.), we know that exiles gathered for prayer and instruction wherever this was possible (cf. Ezek 8:1; 14:1; 33:30ff., and John Bright, *A History of Israel,* Philadelphia: Westminster Press, 1959, pp. 422ff.).

taught: In spite of the fact that Mark uses the verb *didaskō* seventeen times, no hint is given of the content of such teachings. Either Mark assumes that such omission can be supplied by his readers, or his purpose, to record the actions of the one who proclaims the Reign of God, makes extended treatments of teaching otiose.

22. *astounded* (Greek *ekplēssomai):* Found also at 6:2, 7:37, 10:26, and 11:18, this word expresses profound amazement.

authority: The Greek *exousia,* used eight other times in Mark (cf. 1:27; 2:10; 3:15; 6:7; 11:28,29,33; 13:34), means in general freedom or power to act and in the NT carries the meaning of "authority." The authority here ascribed to Jesus is that of assurance of truth, commonly attributed to authentic prophets.

unlike the scribes: Lane (p. 72) somewhat overstates the case for scribes' being considered theologians of equal competence with the rabbis. Cf. *The Jewish Encyclopedia* (New York and London: Funk and Wagnalls) ad loc. on the subject. Given any body of law, there will naturally and rapidly spring up a body of persons competent in the recording of case-law decisions and reinterpretations. Ability to recall the minutiae of former decisions makes such persons particularly valuable. (In the British legal system, there is immense influence wielded by "managing clerks" in barristers' and solicitors' offices.) David Daube (in *The New Testament and Rabbinic Judaism,* London: University of London, Athlone Press, 1959, pp. 205-33) contrasts the ability to lay down binding decisions *(rešūt),* charateristic of the rabbis, with the inability of the scribes *(soperîm)* to do so. Cf. also Daube, *"Exousia* in Mark 1:22 and 27," *JTS* 39.1938, pp. 45ff. For other views cf. A. W. Argyle ("The Meaning of *exousia* in Mark 1:22,27," *ExpT* 80.11.1969, p. 343) and J. Jeremias in *TWNT,* Vol. 1, pp. 740ff. Cf. also Lohmeyer, p. 35.

23. We omit *euthus,* "immediately," whether this qualified "was" or "unclean spirit," though the word is found in many manuscripts.

with an unclean spirit: Luke has an extended phrase, including *echōn* (having) where Mark's simple *en* (in) is reminiscent of the Hebrew *bĕ* (with). Mark uses *akatharton pneuma* (unclean spirit) eleven times, just as frequently as *daimonion* (demon). *Daimōn,* with the same meaning, is used once. It may be that Mark here indicates a difference in demon possession, but—with Turner, p. 173—it is preferable to see here a religious judgment on the part of the evangelist: possession leaves people at the mercy of a nonritual uncleanness which makes them unfit for communion with God.

24. The cry of the possessed is the language of terror, and a declaration of Jesus' avowed intent: Jesus' presence implies a judgment for all. The "us" in the narrative may well include the audience in this judgment as well as the demonic powers, though this is doubtful. *What do you want with us?* (literally, "What is there common to us and to you?" probably has as background the same kind of expression as is found in the Hebrew of, e.g., Judg 11:12 or 1 Kgs 17:18, in the sense of "Why do you interfere with us?"

Jesus of Nazareth: An article of F. Mussner ("Ein Wortspiel in Mark 1:24?" *BZ* 4.2.1960, pp. 285-86) suggests that a comparison with the dedication of Samson in Judg 13:7 helps us to understand the meaning of "Jesus of Nazareth . . . God's Holy One" as lying in *n'zîr 'ēlōhîm (nazaraoin theou* in *LXX* Codex A, together with *hagion theou* in *LXX* Codex B), so that there is a combination of both *LXX* texts. The author suggests that there is play on words in *Iēsou Nazarēne* (Hebrew *Y'šûa' hannāṣrî).* "Holy One of God" would therefore be an interpretation of Jesus' place name as well as a revelation of his true nature. The suggestion is useful in that it does not require taking *God's Holy One* as a messianic title, for which there is no present evidence. For similar expressions, cf. Ps 116:15; 2 Kgs 4:9 *(LXX); T Levi* 18; *1 Enoch* 69:27. The unclean spirit in this cry recognizes that the presence of God can destroy the dominion of evil. J. Weiss, in the original edition of his *Das Markusevangelium* (Vol. 1 in the series *Die Schriften des Neuen Testaments,* Göttingen: Vandenhoeck and Ruprecht, 1917), speaks of the man's discernment of the consequences to Satan's realm of the proclamation of the Kingdom. See also J. M. Robinson (1957), pp. 29ff.

25. *commanded:* The Greek *epitimaō* is also used in 4:39; 8:32,33; 9:25; 10:13. The translation "to command" has been chosen for several reasons. In the first place, the usual rendering, "to rebuke," fails to do justice to the overwhelming evidence in Greek authors for the sense of "to take the measure of, put a price upon"; in legal terms it is used of a judge reaching a determination in a case. The word is important in exorcism contexts in the NT: there are five instances in Matthew, eleven in Luke. H. C. Kee ("The Terminology of Mark's Exorcism Stories," *NTS* 14.2.1968, pp. 232-46) suggests Hebrew *q'r* (to rebuke) as the source of the word. He adduces in favor of its technical use in Qumran literature and Jewish apocalyptic literature as the commanding word of God, spoken either by God or one of his representatives, whereby evil powers are brought into submission in preparation for God's rule. However, he rightly points out that rabbinic exorcism accounts do not assert the subjugation of evil powers as a prerequisite for the Reign of God.

Here we may try to dismiss the specter of the oft-touted Hellenistic element in the gospel exorcism and miracle stories. This "Hellenistic" hypothesis has been adduced with much frequency in the past forty years and in some quarters has achieved the status of an article of faith. The verb here used, *epitimaō,* is without parallel in the Hellenistic miracle accounts. Moreover, the propagators of the Hellenistic thaumaturge theories do not remind us—as in fairness they ought—that in all such Greek literature the significance of exorcisms and the like had nothing to do with any proclamation, but had everything to do with investing the wonder-worker with mysterious and awe-inspiring power: hearers or readers of such stories would have been puzzled by references to either forgiveness of sin or a Reign of God. Superficially the accounts of healings and exorcisms in the gospels have much in common with Hellenistic miracle stories (description of a person's symptoms and state; description of the cure, with words—if any—uttered by the wonder-worker; admiration of the bystanders; and subsequent behavior of the former sufferer). Ten minutes of exposure to television news programs at the national level in prime time would be enough to convince the most hardened skeptic that the true parallel to Hellenistic wonder stories lies in advertisers' claims for the panaceas being offered on modern commercial television. See Albright-Mann, AB *Matthew,* Introduction X, "Miracles in Matthew," pp. cxxiv ff.

"Silence! . . .": The verb *phimoō* is used in the NT generally in the sense of "to muzzle, bind" (cf. 1 Cor 9:9, 1 Tim 5:18) or "to silence" (Mark 4:39; Matt 22:12,34; Luke 4:35; 1 Pet 2:15). The command underscores Jesus' acceptance of contemporary beliefs about demon possession.

26. *threw . . . into convulsions* (Greek *sparassō,* cf. *susparassō* in Luke 9:42): We may wish to conclude that the man was an epileptic, or that the exorcism produced psychosomatic symptoms of a violently convulsive character. We should remember,

however, that our superior wisdom in the matter is no fit vantage point from which to judge the beliefs of people who lived two millennia ago.

27. *astounded:* The verb *thambeō* is very strong; it is found in the classical authors and sometimes in *LXX* to express deep amazement. This amazement has two roles: (a) a recognition on the part of bystanders that something wholly new is at work in the person and ministry of Jesus, far removed from the practices of professional wonder-workers, and (b) the teaching of Jesus. On *authority* and *teaching,* cf. notes on v. 22.

unclean spirits: Cf. v. 34. Mark makes no distinction between demons and unclean spirits.

28. *report* (Greek *akoē*): Coupled with the genitive to mark the subject of the report, cf. Nah 1:12, Jer 6:24 *(LXX)*.

district of Galilee: Mark's note is vague and is probably intended to refer to the neighborhood of Capernaum.

7. Healings
(1:29-34) = Matt 8:14-17; Luke 4:38-41

1　 29 On leaving the synagogue, they went straight to the house of Simon and Andrew, and James and John went with them. 30 Simon's mother-in-law was in bed with fever, and at once they told him about her. 31 He went to her, took her by the hand, and helped her up. The fever left her, and she waited on them. 32 The same evening, after sunset, they brought to him all who were sick or demon-possessed; 33 and all the town was there, gathered at the door. 34 He healed many who had various diseases, and drove out many demons. He would not allow the demons to speak, because they knew who he was.

Comment

Unlike those miracle stories in the gospels which have often been labeled "Hellenistic wonder stories," this account in vv. 29-31 is characterized by great economy. There are no details of any words of Jesus, no account of the symptoms of the sickness, and no mention of any amazement on the part of the bystanders. The Markan account contains details lacking in Matthew and Luke (the accompanying disciples—Andrew, James, and John—*took her by the hand and lifted her up);* Luke's medical vocabulary is simplified here. The phrase *at once they told him about her* reads very much like a Petrine reminiscence. Lohmeyer (p. 40) finds that this narrative alone in Mark has such features of recollection.

Notes

29. *Simon and Andrew, and James and John:* Bultmann *(History,* 3rd ed., p. 227), faced with the awkward grammatical structure of the sentence, finds the four names a Markan peculiarity, an addition to the text. Turner (p. 16) seems far more convincing in his suggestion that the awkwardness disappears if the sentence is cast back into direct speech from Peter: "We came into our house with James and John."

30. *mother-in-law* (Greek *penthera):* It would seem from 1 Cor 9:5 that Peter's wife was accustomed to going with him on missionary journeys.

with fever: The Greek verb *puressō* is found also in Matthew and the cognate *puretō* is used in Luke; both are rare in classical writers and are not represented in the papyri. Luke refers to a "high fever."

at once: Either informing Jesus of her condition and hoping for healing, or excusing an apparent lack of hospitality.

31. *took her by the hand:* A gesture in healing stories which is characteristic of Mark—cf. 9:27.

on them: Mark and Luke vary from Matthew's *on him* (8:15)—i.e., Jesus, referring instead to the number of those accompanying Jesus.

32. The remainder of the narrative in this section is connected by Mark with the preceding account of Peter's mother-in-law, but the implication that the subsequent events all took place in the evening of the same day can hardly be realistic. Luke 4:40 avoids *the same evening* of Matthew and Mark. Matthew's narrative is formal and stylized, while the Markan narrative, with its vivid detail in v. 33, can with fair assurance be described as reminiscence, preferred by Mark to the accounts he had before him.

The same evening: Mark's double phrasing—*opsias de genomenēs,* "when evening had come," and *hote edusen ho hēlios,* "when the sun had set"—may be either a more precise definition of time or, since Matthew has the first phrase and Luke something like the second, a combination of the two. In Matthew's account, the connection of this narrative with the Sabbath is not made, whereas in Mark these healings and exorcisms occur after sunset when the Sabbath was ended. But it must be noted that the healing of Simon's mother-in-law was a Sabbath event and so a resumption of God's creative activity. Luke's account is, as always, a heightened narrative full of dramatic detail.

brought: Literally, "kept on bringing." This use of the imperfect would appear to underline the "timeless" character of this narrative as an illustration of Jesus' ministry. Cf. *prosenegkan,* "they brought," in Matt 8:16.

34. *healed:* Classically, and in the papryi, Greek *therapeuō* means "to treat medically," but whatever meaning Luke may have given to the verb, it is unlikely to have been understood in any technical sense by Mark.

many (Hebrew *rabbîm):* The word is one of Mark's frequent Semitisms (cf. Lohmeyer, p. 41). The text at this point is a conflated one, drawing together Matthew's 8:16b and the tradition in Matt 12:16, together with Mark's own 3:12.

allow (Greek *ēphien*, from *aphiēmi*, "to permit"): Taylor (p. 181, cf. p. 174) calls attention to the "uncanny knowledge of the possessed." Some Markan manuscripts, instead of the simple statement that the spirits knew him, have the same reading as Luke 4:41: "they knew him to be the Messiah," obviously the work of later assimilation. One text of Mark (D-Codex Bezae) conflates the ordinary reading with a parallel: "and he healed them and he threw out demons from those who had demons."

Beginning with the commands to silence, W. Wrede *(Das Messiasgeheimnis in den Evangelien,* Göttingen: Vandenhoeck and Ruprecht, 1900) constructed his argument that Mark imposed a theology of the "messianic secret" upon the narrative of the ministry. Jesus' requests for silence in Mark are frequent; cf. 1:25,34; 3:2; 5:43; 7:24,36; 8:30; 9:9,30. These *commands* are reinforced by the contrast between private teaching to the inner circle and the enigma of Jesus' teaching to the crowds; even to the inner circle much remains obscure (9:32). It has often been suggested that the command to silence grew out of a desire not to compromise messiahship by permitting public confession to be confused by militarist ambitions. However, it must be said that the narrative contains items which do not easily fit the theory: the crucifixion— whether a Roman judicial sentence or the result of popular demand of a section of the Jews in Jerusalem—is represented as a response to a messianic pretender; messianic tension of some kind is discernible in the examination of Jesus before the Sanhedrin; and the proclamation of a crucified messiah by Paul must have some preresurrection basis.

The "secrecy" motif is too strongly entrenched in the narrative to be dismissed lightly. Some commentators have overreacted to Wrede's suggestion that the messianic secret was theologically imposed by the evangelist. We would suggest that the theme was indeed imposed, but by Jesus himself. The silence had to do with messiahship, but not on the political grounds of possible identification with political militancy. The time of healing and exorcism belonged to the second period of the ministry (cf. Introduction, Chapter 6, Part 1, "Chronology"). It is impossible for us to enter into the human consciousness of Jesus and perilous to speculate beyond what evidence we have. Whatever consciousness Jesus had of messiahship *as such* at this period in his ministry, he appears to have imposed silence in order to preserve his sense of vocation intact. For the time being, his actions and his teaching must be their own authentication, and the whole matter of messiahship must await the seal and vindication of God, however these might come. (Cf. H. H. Graham, "The Gospel According to St. Mark: Mystery and Ambiguity," *ATR* Supp. 7.1976, pp. 43-55; and J. J. Kilgallen, "The Messianic Secret and Mark's Purpose," *BTB* 7.2.1977, pp. 60-65.)

8. Preaching
(1:35-39) = Luke 4:42-44

1 35 The next morning, a long time before sunrise, he rose and went out and went to a lonely place, where he prayed. 36 But Simon and those with him searched for him, found him, and said, 37 "They are all looking for you." 38 He replied, "Let us move on to the next villages in the neighborhood. I have to proclaim the message there, too—that is what I came to do." 39 So he went all through Galilee, preaching in synagogues and casting out demons.

Comment

This short pericope is unlike most Markan narratives in that it depends upon the preceding material. It is not derived from Matthew, and is certainly far more vivid in style than Luke's stereotyped account. Lohmeyer (p. 42) finds it a traditional piece, and the style suggests reminiscence by one of the participants.

Notes

35. *rose and went out:* Mark's gospel has many examples of a verb of motion preceded by unnecessary participles. While Semitic in character, it is not exclusively so.

where he prayed (literally, "continued in prayer"). For other examples of Jesus' prayers in Mark, cf. 6:46; 14:35,39. Luke is the evangelist we most readily associate with Jesus' prayers, and if his work was dependent on Mark, it is strange that he omits this example.

36. *searched* (Greek *katadiōxen*): A vivid word in Greek—almost "hunted down" —the employment of which seems to indicate a tradition of personal reminiscence.

38. *the next:* Greek *ekomenos* is rare in the NT. *Villages* (Greek *kōmopolis*) is not found in *LXX* and is comparatively rare, denoting a small country town.

that is what I came to do: Some commentators have suggested that the word "came" is intended by Mark in a Johannine sense, indicating a mission from the Father. This seems, however, to strain the plain sense of the sentence, and it is best to understand it as meaning "came to Galilee."

39. Cf. 1:34 and 3:7,8. This terse summary of the purpose of the Galilean mission is considerably shorter than the Matthean summary (Matt 4:23) or the Lucan parallel with its inclusion of Judea (Luke 4:44). The Matthean summary "pattern" of Matt 4:23, 9:35, and 8:16 is recognizable, but Mark's parallels are hardly close.

9. The Leper
(1:40-45) = Matt 8:1-4; Luke 5:12-16

1   40 A leper came to Jesus and knelt before him, asking help. "If you are willing," he said, "you can heal me." 41 In compassion [indignation] he stretched out his hand, touched him, and said to him, "I am willing. Be clean." 42 At once the leprosy left him and he was clean. 43 Then Jesus sent him away with the stern warning: 44 "Take care that you say nothing to anyone. Go and show yourself to the priest, and then make the offering Moses ordered for your cleansing, as evidence to them that you are clean." 45 But the man went away and began to make the news public, so much so that he could no longer show himself in any town, but remained outside in the open country. But people kept coming to him from everywhere.

Comment

Mark omits all of Matthew 5-7, as extended notes of Jesus' teaching are no part of his purpose, and he picks up the Matthean account from Matt 8:2 without any note of setting. The evangelist here isolates one of the three-healings group of Matt 8:1-18 to provide an isolated pericope. In the Markan account there are no details of place or time, and the incident is chosen as a "typical" healing. The incident may further serve, by details lacking in Matthew, to illustrate Jesus' attitude to the Law (which Matthew treats far more lengthily in 5-7). To assert, from an assumed Markan priority, that Matthew and Luke omit the healed man's disobedience, as well as the indignation of Jesus, in the interests of an increasingly reverential attitude to Jesus, is to pass over the salient fact that the evangelists saw moral or theological questions involved in narratives of miracles. They felt free to omit or to include details. What Matthew or Luke possessed in their respective traditions, apart from the bare facts of the incident, we do not know, but Mark's version, with its vivid detail, may owe far more to an original oral reminiscence than to the other evangelists.

Notes

40. *leper:* The generic term "leprosy" (Greek *lepra)* included many skin ailments—psoriasis, vitiligo, elephantiasis—and it must not be concluded that Hansen's disease (the causative agent of which was first isolated in 1871) is intended here. The all-embracing Greek term is of no assistance in defining precisely the ailment, but whatever affliction the man had, the severe restrictions of the Mosaic Law would hold (Leviticus 12-14). Talmudic regulations may be found in *The Jewish Encyclopedia,* Vol. 8, ad loc.

In some manuscripts of Mark, *Sir* precedes the sufferer's request. This may be assimilation to Matthew, but since the manuscripts in question are Alexandrian, African, and Caesarean, the address is entitled to the benefit of the doubt, even though not included in our translation.

If you are willing: Cf. 9:22. In the present instance, doubt is not expressed.

heal: The verb *katharizō* is relatively late and was used of a declaration of cleansing and healing, as well as of the act of healing.

41. *indignation:* The reading *orgistheis* has been put in brackets in the translation as an alternative to *splanchnistheis* (felt compassionate). The more difficult reading of "indignation" can easily be understood as being changed to "compassion," but it would be very difficult to imagine a change from "compassion" to "indignation." Suggestions that the indignation followed "If you are willing, you can heal me" are gratuitous. The man was expressing simple trust. The suggestion of the late W. F. Albright, that Jesus was indignant at the man's disregard of legal prescriptions for isolation of such sufferers, is possible. But more likely is an indignation at the Satanic disorder in God's creation.

stretched out his hand: Bultmann *(History,* p. 227) sees in this a stylistic device to be expected in miracle narratives. The feature of Jesus' touching people is, however, common in Mark (7:33, 8:23, 10:13) and is not confined to miracle narratives. In this particular instance it serves to emphasize not only the pity of Jesus for sufferers, but also—in the light of succeeding material—the increasing alienation of Jesus from the conventional wisdom of his own time and his own people.

42. *At once . . . and he was clean:* The whole phrase is an interesting example of Mark's conflation of Matt 8:3 and Luke 5:13.

43. *sent him away:* Literally, "drove him away." The emotion demonstrated here perhaps arises from exhaustion after a period of healing, or perhaps (and more likely in view of Jesus' words) from a desire on Jesus' part to protect himself from a reputation as a wonder-worker.

stern warning: The rare verb *embrimaomai* is a strong word, for which there is no satisfactory English equivalent.

44. Here is another example of what is loosely called the "messianic secret," to which reference has already been made.

Go and show yourself: The injunction to silence is followed by the command to fulfill

the Levitical precept (Lev 13-14 passim), and it is worthy of notice that in this instance Jesus is represented as upholding the Law. The priests would have assured
themselves of the man's renewed health *before* permitting the compulsory offering to
be made.

as evidence to them: Swete (p. 31) suggests that this would be proof to the clergy
that there was a prophet among the people, suspected by some to be the Messiah. This
seems to read too much into the text. The Markan text differs from Matt 8:4 and Luke
5:14. Matthew's version is ". . . make the offering Moses commanded, for a proof to
them," while Luke has "make an offering for your cleansing, as Moses commanded,
for a proof to them." Mark's version has all the indications of a clarification: the proof
in question appears to be that of the healer's allegiance to the Law.

45. *But the man went away:* Allen *(The Gospel According to St. Mark,* London and
New York: Macmillan, 1915, p. 64) and Klostermann (pp. 24ff.) make the suggestion
that the phrase *ho de exelthōn*—literally, "the one who went out," or "the one, going
out"—applies to Jesus and that *tou logou* (translated here by "news") should be
rendered "gospel" or "message of salvation." Recently, J. K. Elliott ("Is *ho exelthōn* a
Title for Jesus in Mark 1:45?" *JTS* 27.2.1976, pp. 402-5) moved the argument a stage
farther by urging that *ho exelthōn* is together a substantive (as in the first literal gloss
above), with *de* as a connective particle. *Ho exelthōn,* he thinks, is not a primitive
Christian *title* for Jesus, but one which stands in the same descriptive category as "the
Coming One" of Mark 11:9 and parallels—Matt 23:39 = Luke 13:35; Matt 11:3 =
Luke 7:19-20; John 1:15, 6:14; Acts 19:4; Heb 10:37. He would connect this with 1:38
("That is what I came to do"). The view of this commentator is that the evidence is
too slender, given (a) the close connection in our text between the sense of vv. 44 and
45, and (b) the use of *logos* in Mark, which, though it generally means "gospel" in
Chapters 1-4, cannot easily be so translated here.

began: The word *erxato* occurs twenty-six times with the infinitive in Mark, as
against six such constructions in Matthew, but Luke has the construction twenty-
three times, five of them in Markan contexts. Taylor (pp. 63ff.) finds that this construction is "probably Semitic."

make . . . public: The word *diaphēmizo* is late in Greek. The account of the man's
disobedience is peculiar to Mark, and the verse has its own inner contradictions, as
K. L. Schmidt *(Der Rahmen der Geschichte Jesu,* Berlin: Kaiser Verlag, 1919, p. 66)
observes, suggesting that *phanerōs* ("openly") was added by Mark. After the stress on
"openly," it is to be expected that a statement will be made that Jesus could only enter
a town in secret. Perhaps the most that can be said is that the verse provides a very
good climax to the story.

10. The Paralytic: Beginnings of Opposition (2:1-12) = Matt 9:1-8; Luke 5:17-26

2 [1] After some days, when he returned to Capernaum, the news spread that he was at home, [2] and so many people gathered together that there was no room left, not even at the door. While he was speaking the message to them, [3] a man was brought to him who was paralyzed. Four men were carrying him, [4] but because of the crowd they could not bring him near. So they opened up the roof over the place where Jesus was, and when they had dug through (the roof), they lowered the paralyzed man down on his stretcher. [5] When Jesus saw their faith, he said to the paralyzed man, "My son, your sins are forgiven." [6] There were some scribes sitting there, questioning in their minds: [7] "How can this man talk like that? He is blaspheming—who except God alone can forgive sins?" [8] Jesus was aware in his own mind of what they were thinking, and so said to them, "Why are you thinking such things? [9] Is it easier to say to this paralyzed man 'Your sins are forgiven' or to say 'Stand up, take your bed, and walk?' [10] But so that you may know that The Man has authority on earth to forgive sins" he turned to the paralyzed man— [11] "I tell you, stand up, take your stretcher, and go home." [12] Then he got up, at once took up his bed, and went out in full view of everybody, so that they were astounded and praised God: "We have never," they said, "seen anything like this."

Comment

Commentators on this section are divided as to its unity. Bultmann (History, 1957, pp. 12-14, 227) finds two distinct elements in coalescence: a "saying" (apothegm) source in 5b-10a, and a miracle narrative in 1-5a, 10b-12, citing several authors in support. Rawlinson (p. 25) rejects the interpolation view of the "saying" section but contends that there was expansion of the incident in the light of controversy between early Christianity and Judaism. Taylor (p. 191) embraces Bultmann's view, but the present writer finds the suggestion of

Weiss (p. 156) more attractive—the episode is derived from what the author calls "the Apostolic Source" represented by Matt 9:1-8 but supplemented by Petrine reminiscences. Certainly the material is such that a twofold origin may be demanded by the material. There are indications of this state of affairs in the following particulars: first the very vivid details in 3-5a (the breaking of the roof, the crowds) all appear to be derived from early tradition. But secondly, the section 5b-10a seems to come from a far different background, and the phrase *he turned to the paralytic man* has all the marks of an editorial and copied interjection. Not only so, but vv. 11ff. carry the account of the cure, but the evangelist's *everybody* leaves open the false(?) impression that the scribes also are included. Perhaps 5b-10a comes from a background of an original pronouncement story (cf. vv. 16ff.,18-20,23-26, and 3:1-6). But far more likely is the suggestion of Taylor (p. 192) that the whole unit is an uneven narrative from which separate elements are ready to be separated.

The most persuasive attempt in fairly recent years to plead for the unity of 2:1-12 came from R. T. Mead ("The Healing of the Paralytic—A Unit?" *JBL* 80.4.1961, pp. 348-54). Mead builds upon the undeservedly neglected work of David Daube *(The New Testament and Rabbinic Judaism,* Jordan Lectures, 1952, London: The University of London, Athlone Press, 1956, especially pp. 170-75) in the area of "tripartite forms." Mead believes that Daube's work on this particular form—the components of which are (a) revolutionary action, either on the part of Jesus or his disciples; (b) protest; and (c) silencing of the critics—amply demonstrates that this form can be found at least seven times in the synoptists. Mead further maintains that this form adequately solves the exegetical problems of our present passage, with the possible exception of the shift of address in v. 10. If—he contends—this shift had not occurred, the unity of the passage could not have been challenged successfully. H. Simonsen ("Zur Frage der grundlegenden Problematik in form- und redaktionsgeschichtlicher Evangelienforschung," *ST* 26.1.1972, pp. 1-23) similarly argues for the unity of the passage under discussion, and believes that the healing is subordinate to the forgiveness of sins. By contrast, T. L. Budesheim ("Jesus and the Disciples in Conflict with Judaism," *ZNW* 62.3-4.1971, pp. 190-201) finds the passage (along with various other conflict and healing narratives) significant mainly as exhibiting a breach between Jesus (as *theios anēr)* and Judaism, with attempts to involve the disciples discernible in the text. Christian heretics also figure prominently on the enemies' list, and—given a presumably late date for Budesheim's community redactor—one is surprised not to find proto-Gnosticism among the contenders. By contrast, Joanna Dewey ("The Literary Structure of the Controversy Stories in Mark 2:1-3:6," *JBL* 92.3.1973, pp. 394-401) is prepared to support Markan authorship of the whole unit, bearing in mind the chiastic structure, which Dewey finds to be deliberate.

Recently it has been suggested by A. B. Kolenkow ("Healing Controversy as a Tie Between Miracle and Passion Material for a Proto-Gospel," *JBL* 95.4.1976, pp. 623-38) that both Mark and John closely tie "conflict" material with the inevitability of the passion, and hence the author finds the material in Mark ending at 3:6 (with the threat to kill Jesus) closely linked in thought with John 5:8. While the whole article is provocative and interesting, it seems too strained to carry the thought of this self-contained pericope into the beginning of the next chapter, unless (with Dewey) we accept the unity of *structure* in the whole unit. The present writer finds this a far more convincing explanation than the fragmented solutions proposed by many commentators. The primary concern of 2:1-12 is that of forgiveness, and Mark's *Sitz im Leben* demanded as much attention to the problem as that of Matthew and Luke. Indeed, the problems of Mark's community may well have been more urgently directed to this theme than those of his predecessors. (Cf. P. Mourton Beernaert, "Jésus controversé: Structure et théologie de Marc 2:1-3:6," *NRTh* 95.2.1973, pp. 129-49.)

Notes

1. *After some days:* There is clearly a clean break in Mark at this point (cf. Nineham, 1963, p. 89), and the interval may well have been weeks.

when he returned (Greek *kai eiselthōn palin):* This broken construction (literally, "coming again") is characteristic of Mark, and some manuscripts attempted to improve matters by adding a finite verb. *Palin,* originally meaning "back," was used in later Greek to mean "again" and is used twenty-eight times in Mark.

at home (Greek *en oikō):* From the evidence of the papyri, this translation is clearly demanded, but whose home (unless it was Peter's) is in doubt.

2. The crowd scene recalls 1:33. *No room left* is the best translation we can offer for a somewhat complicated Greek construction. *Not even at the door*—perhaps meaning "out in the open street"—would indicate that the house was a comparatively modest one, with no courtyard.

3. *was brought:* For Mark's use of *erchetai,* see the Introduction, "Characteristic Words and Phrases."

paralyzed (Greek *paraluticos,* cf. 2:4ff.,9ff.; Matt 4:24; 8:6; 9:2,6): The Greek word is *late,* not being found in the classical literature or in *LXX.* Luke uses *paralelumenos.*

Four men were carrying him is peculiar to Mark, and has signs of being a detail remembered by an eyewitness.

4. *crowd* (Greek *ochlos):* Though the crowd has been implied in the text, this is the first of the thirty-seven times Mark uses the word.

opened up the roof (Greek *apostegazō,* literally "to unroof"): This is a rare word, and the following details underline the fact of a flat roof with an earth covering. Luke's version (5:19) implies a tiled roof, where Mark evidently draws on eyewitness testimony. Matthew has no such details, and one must conclude either that Mark was correcting Luke's record or that Luke was embellishing Mark.

stretcher (Greek *krabbatos*): A poor man's bed roll or mat, this was capable of being let down through a small aperture, unlike the *kline* which Matthew and Luke have in their texts.

5. *faith* (Greek *pistis*) (cf. 4:40, 5:34, 10:52, 11:22) = confident, believing trust: The word is less common in Mark than the verb "to trust, believe in."

My son (Greek *teknon*) is an affectionate form of address, which Luke does not preserve (he uses "man").

forgiven (Greek *aphiemi*, from *aphiemi*): It is important to notice Mark's tense: the present tense is used with the meaning "your sins are at this moment forgiven." The statement is declaratory, a meaning somewhat lost in Luke's use of the perfect tense *(apheontai*, found also in some manuscripts of Mark). There is no present evidence linking the messianic vocation with the remission of sin, and we are therefore compelled to fall back on the view that Jesus' declaration of forgiveness rested upon his own understanding of "Son of Man" as a term for a close and intimate relationship with God and a relationship with men as God's messenger. As noted previously, there is no example in the gospels of Jesus saying "I forgive."

6. *in their minds* (literally, "in their hearts"): The phrase is Hebraic, the heart being the locus of reasoning and decision making. The thoughts of the scribes were visible, presumably, in their expressions.

7. *How can this man. . . :* It must be noted that the charge of blasphemy is not made directly, and is tentative. But forgiveness was reserved to God (cf. Exod 34:6ff.; Isa 43:25, 44:22), and so to claim this right to forgive was tantamount to blasphemy. This interpretation of the attitude of the scribes belongs to the tradition behind the written NT material (cf. with this and the parallel passages of John 5:18, 8:48-59). In this instance we may rightly regard the tradition as being carefully preserved—a subsequent heightening of the narrative by the later community would surely have had the scribes give verbal expression to their attitude.

8. *aware in his own mind* (Greek *dialogizomai*): The word does not carry the meaning of prior knowledge, but rather an awareness arrived at by a concentration of attention—cf. 2:8 and 5:30. There is certainly no question of supernatural knowledge involved here, but rather discernment. *In his own mind:* literally "spirit," cf. 5:30 and 8:12.

9. Jesus' question is addressed to the authentication of the claim to forgive sins by the visible sign of healing. But underlying it all is the larger issue of authority, the sign of healing being a declaration of the validity of his own mission. Unquestionably Jesus would have found it easy to subscribe to the commonly accepted view of his own time that there was a strong and even decisive connection between sin and bodily sickness. There is evidence enough that he did not invariably make this connection (cf. John 9:2 and especially Luke 13:1-5). Yet he appears to have observed how intimately physical, mental, and spiritual conditions interact upon one another, and it is possible that in this instance Jesus intuitively understood that the paralysis was psychosomatic in character and that the declaration of pardon was intended also as a declaration of healing.

10. See the appended note, " 'Son of Man' in 2:10."

12. *astounded* (Greek *existasthai*): This is a very strong word. It is to be noted that the amazement is directed to the immediate cure, and not to the dialogue of Jesus with

his critics. Matthew's version has "who has given such power to men," and this certainly refers to the healing.

Appended Note—"Son of Man" in 2:10

1. The phrase is regarded by most critics as an addition by the primitive Christian community, especially with regard to accommodating this instance into other known uses of the term.

2. In all the synoptic gospels, the appearance of the term before the confession of Peter or the passion predictions is an anomaly, and it is Caesarea Philippi which is accepted by most commentators as the *terminus a quo* of authenticity. The result is near unanimity in dismissing this instance as a primitive Christian creation.

3. If the explanation for this theologizing by the early Church is sought in terms of a claim by the early missionaries to forgive sin, then some explanation is surely demanded as to the authority of that claim, if Jesus himself did not make the claim. The attempt to find here an evangelist's substitution of the terms for a personal pronoun fails when we ask why the evangelist did not introduce the term in far more vital contexts having to do with Jesus' anticipation of suffering and vindication.

4. To find, with a considerable number of critics, that the term is a misunderstanding of "a man" is to leave the charges of Jesus' opponents unanswered and unanswerable. The claim is made by Jesus for himself as Son of Man, and not on his own behalf as *a* man.

5. There is the further matter of the difficult grammatical construction of v. 10 after the *hina* clause, "so that you may know," as a parenthesis. Some writers indeed have suggested that the straightforward progression of the narrative has been broken by "but so . . . forgive sins," which is regarded as an intrusion. In light of both major theories of gospel origins, this is odd. On a basis of Markan priority, we are left wondering why Matthew and Luke—so often credited with improving Mark's grammar and style—left matters as they found them. If, as this commentator holds, Mark was a redactor and synthesizer, then it is odd that he did not attempt to eliminate the ambiguities.

6. The suggestion that the *hina* clause was an imperative, and describes a challenge from Jesus to his opponents, has been made from time to time, and the evidence of *hina* in imperative clauses is documented by C. F. D. Moule, 1953, pp. 144ff. More persuasively, perhaps, we may link the clause with similar grammatical material in Mark 14:49 and John 9:2ff., where in both cases alternatives are offered: in John and in Mark there is a link being made by some between sin and disease. The example in Mark 2:10 provides not a

blatant manipulation of the original oral tradition but an explanation of why Jesus acted as he did: he could after all simply have told the man to go home. (On the grammatical usage, see further below on 14:49.) Form criticism fails us here: the only explanation which fits all the facts is that Jesus acted as he did precisely that men may know that the Son of Man already has authority on earth to pardon.

7. If the story cannot be separated into two, then we are bound to ask why Jesus acted as he did in response to the faith of the man's friends. If Jesus used these words, then the assumption must be that they answered the paramount concern of the sufferer—and this aside from all speculation about whether Jesus accepted the common view of sickness as linked with sin.

8. The reaction of the critics was predictable. Jesus had made a claim for which there was no supporting evidence. But to omit vv. 6-10 (which is current majority wisdom) as an insertion or an invention of the Palestinian community (cf. Lewis S. Hay, "The Son of Man in Mark 2:10 and 2:28," *JBL* 89.1.1970, pp. 69ff.) is hardly satisfactory. Even supposing that the verses belong to a later occasion and were inserted here, they belong to the same category as the question about authority in 11:27ff. In both instances the reply of Jesus is enigmatic and cast almost in the mold of a rabbinic question in the Mishnah.

9. Unquestionably the evangelists identify Jesus in some fashion with the Son of Man. But Jesus never in our sources said, "I forgive you," though presumably he could have done so. The unanimous consent of the evangelists is that Jesus considered the function of the Son of Man to include remission of sin, but it is important to note that nothing is indicated of a messianic character for the Son of Man. Moreover, if the form critics are in order in suggesting that the narrative was a basis for the exercise of pardoning power in the early community, then it is hard to discover any terminology other than Son of Man which could have been originally associated with power to forgive in Jesus' name. Certainly there is no foundation in presumably known sources for any function of the expected Messiah to forgive sin.

10. The crux of the argument in the narrative is made to hang upon the question of authority, as was noted in part in the note to v. 7 preceding. To pardon sin is reserved to God: the Son of Man is represented in all three synoptists as acting as God's vicegerent. But this is no more—but certainly no less—than the other manifestations of Jesus' activity in healing and exorcism, and in the inauguration of the Reign of God.

11. Our examination of the passage is further complicated by the uncertainty in textual terms of the precise location of the phrase *on earth*. In some manuscripts it is not found at all, and in some the phrase comes (as it does in Matthew and Luke) before to forgive *sins*, and even in some manuscripts between the infinitive and the substantive. It is hard to resist the conclusion that what we have here is a Markan redaction of the texts of Matthew and

Luke. But this is not the end of the matter. There is no immediate indication of the meaning of the phrase. If it is meant to be read as applying to *sins*, then there is here a statement of the obvious—plainly sin belongs to the earthly realm. Matthew, by placing the phrase immediately following *The Man*, emphasized the earthly status of the Son of Man in contrast to the authority properly belonging to the later exaltation to heaven. Since Jesus' hearers would have no knowledge of any such contrast, we are left to choose between regarding this Matthean and Markan understanding as deriving from the early community, or—because of its very improbability in contemporary circumstances—as coming from Jesus himself. But such a contrast is not necessarily what lies behind our present Matthean and Markan texts. M. D. Hooker has suggested (in *The Son of Man in Mark*, Montreal: McGill University Press, 1967, p. 91) that we ought rather to look at the authority vested in man as God's earthly representative in the creation narrative of Gen 1:26. There is indeed considerable merit in the position, so far as *authority* is concerned, but it must perforce leave unresolved the linking of that authority with the forgiveness of sin.

12. The surprise of the hearers and the spectators is clearly not a result of anything heard—it springs from the healing of the paralytic (and thus a normal ending to any miracle story), though it may also include surprise that forgiveness is linked with that healing. But it is to be noted that in the synoptic gospels no astonishment is ever adduced by the use of the term Son of Man (John 9:35ff. and 12:34 have the hearers surprised by the identification of Jesus with the Son of Man). The fact is that the synoptic gospels begin with the Son of Man assertion, and certainly not with an affirmation that Jesus *is* the Son of Man. It is possible, as is contended by many NT scholars, that we have a theological reflection of the early community intruding into the narrative.

13. The possibilities of other reasons for the text as we now have it apparently reduce in the final analysis to two: (a) The term "Son of Man" was accepted as a title for some yet-to-come personage from whom affirmations of pardon might be expected, and would only be astonishing if that personage was personally identified with Jesus. Effectively therefore the gospels—on this view—represent Jesus as asserting that he was the Son of Man, thereby producing surprise in the onlookers. (b) The term means no more than "a man," the identification with Jesus would occasion no surprise, and the whole dispute would turn on the matter of authority.

The second of the possibilities listed is not satisfactory. The attempt to reduce the term in this context to the colorless "a man" leaves far too much unanswered. The Matthean understanding of Jesus as Representative Israel can hardly have been snatched from thin air, unless we invest the early Christian community with an inventive genius of a very high order, and the term "Son of Man" has an unmistakable "representative" character about it both in Daniel and *1 Enoch.* Moreover, in both Daniel and *1 Enoch* the Son of Man does exercise dominion "on earth." We need also some explanation for the early disappearance of the term in the NT: it figures in Acts 7:56, Rev 14:14, and nowhere else, though Paul's theology of the Second Adam appears to be aware of it. Why should the synoptic tradition have been at such pains to resurrect an archaic, Semitic phrase which was effectively defunct—the more so, if we consign the gospel writings to that historical limbo of the last two decades of the first century? (Cf. C. P. Ceroke, "Is Mark 2:10 a Saying of Jesus?" *CBQ* 22.4.1960, pp. 369-90 and Taylor, pp. 200ff.)

Finally, both episodes in all three traditions have been finely honed and reduced to bare, easily memorable details.

11. The Calling of a Levite
(2:13-17) = Matt 9:9-13; Luke 5:27-32

2   [13] He went back to the seashore. All the crowd came to him and he taught them there. [14] As he walked along, he saw a Levite, son of Alphaeus, at his place in the customshouse, and said to him, "Follow me." And he got up and followed him. [15] Later on, when at table in the house, there were many tax collectors and nonobservant Jews gathered together with Jesus and his disciples, for many people followed him. [16] Some Pharisee-lawyers observed him eating in the company of tax collectors and nonobservant Jews, and protested to his disciples: "He eats with the tax collectors and nonobservant Jews!" [17] Jesus heard this, and said to them, "It is not the healthy who need a physician, but the sick. I did not come to call the self-righteous, but sinners."

Comment

This account is important for several reasons. First of all, we note the fact that lists of the inner circle of the disciples in the gospels are confused and confusing. There may well have been a larger group than is designated "the Twelve," and the designation may have been an accommodation to the tribal division of Israel (cf. Matt 19:28, Luke 22:30). The lists of names (cf. Matt 10:2ff., Mark 3:16-19, Luke 6:13-16) are as confused as the identification of the twelve tribes in the OT. But here in the parallel of Matthew with Mark we have a name, whereas in Mark we have what has been translated here as *a Levite, Son of Alphaeus*. Given the very fluctuating use of the definite article in Aramaic in the first century, it would hardly be surprising if a translator/scribe on being confronted by *Levi* in his original concluded that it was a proper name (it was common enough as such at this time) and so rendered it in the Greek of Mark and Luke. At all events, this solution does remove the confusion between *Matthew* and *Levi* in the lists. Second we notice Mark's *Pharisee-lawyers* in v. 16 (literally "scribes of the Pharisees") in contrast with Matthew's "Pharisees." Attention has already been called to the importance of scribes (cf. note on 1:22) as patient collectors and preservers of oral traditions of law. Third in all the synoptic traditions the call of the Levite is closely linked with questions about nonobservant Jews, and whatever the precise historical circumstances of each episode, the association may well have been made because of the disdain felt by Pharisees for a Jew who would engage in a trade such as tax collection. As mentioned before, both episodes in all three traditions have been reduced to easily memorable dimensions. The bare injunction *Follow me,* whatever other attendant details there may have been in the original oral tradition, represents both for the Levite and the early post-resurrection Christian the abiding imperative of Jesus. Similarly, however extended the narrative may originally have been in vv. 15-17, the emphasis lies in the assertion of Jesus' table fellowship with people normally considered to be beyond the pale.

Notes

13. *the seashore:* The note of place is indeterminate and is certainly editorial. But the constant attendance of crowds listening to Jesus would have made him a familiar figure to the tax collector.

14. *customshouse:* This would be a tax-collection service for Herod Antipas, collecting taxes on goods passing through his territory from the neighboring jurisdictions of Herod Philip and the Ten Towns.

and followed him: It has more than once been pointed out by commentators that a decision to follow Jesus would have been irrevocable for a tax official, whereas the disciples called in 1:16-20 could easily on occasion have returned to fishing.

15. *at table* (Greek *katakeisthai,* literally "reclining"): The Hellenistic custom of reclining on the left elbow at table was widespread in the time of Jesus, though opinion as to whether this was common, or reserved only for formal occasions, is disputed.

the house: It is not clear from our texts whose house this was. It can be read as meaning the Levite's house, or a house Jesus was using while in Galilee.

tax collectors: A distinction must be made between these officials (Greek *telōnai)* and the tax farmers (Greek *architelōnai,* Latin *publicani)* whose responsibility it was to forward taxes when collected. But in either case, the employment of a Jew would have been treated by scrupulously observant Jews as disgraceful: not only did the task involve the handling of coins with pagan symbols and even human representations on them, the work was also being performed for the wholly unacceptable family of the Herods and ultimately for Rome.

nonobservant Jews (Greek *hamartōloi):* The older, common translation of "sinners" simply will not suffice. The sense here is far from the use in Paul denoting those separated from God by rebellion. The synoptic use of the term often means "Gentile" (cf. Mark 14:41, Gal 2:15). The charge of "nonobservance" would obviously derive from a Pharisaic view of the Law and its oral tradition.

disciples (Greek *mathētēs):* The plural in the synoptic tradition commonly denotes the inner circle of Jesus' followers—the Twelve—and though found in classical Greek, is not found in *LXX* except in variant readings of four verses in Jeremiah. The Hebrew *talmîd* is found only in 1 Chr 25:8 but is later found in wide use in rabbinic Judaism.

Mark's introduction of the disciples is sudden, since so far there has been mention only of the call of five to the inner circle. But in order to deal with much material later, Mark must now refer to those closest to Jesus with the generic "the disciples."

It is conventional wisdom among most NT scholars, and certainly on the part of the upholders of the two-document hypothesis, that the picture painted of the disciples in this gospel represents them as totally lacking in understanding, often dull-witted, and altogether unworthy of the trust placed in them by Jesus. This unfavorable picture, it is asserted, is mitigated and softened by the (later) evangelists. The present writer finds this position unacceptable. Given the legitimacy of the arguments set forth in the Introduction (Part 2, "The Purpose of Mark's Gospel") then, we suggest that "the disciples" in Mark as a generic term serves a two-fold purpose: First the disciples themselves are represented as coming slowly—but inevitably and inexorably—to an understanding of the ministry of Jesus in which persecution, suffering, and death were inevitable, and not at all seeing God's vindication of Jesus as more than a faint possibility. Second the emphasis in Mark on failure and lack of faith (present in Mark's own tradition from Petrine reminiscences?) is deliberately intended to sustain a community already under persecution, and one which needs reassurance that a *theologia crucis* is indeed part and parcel of the faith. An early Christian community increasingly under attack could well evoke sympathy for doubting whether indeed Jesus had been the agent of God, let alone whether he was Prophet of the Last Days. Third it is certainly an unnecessary exercise—and even futile, in the absence of any supporting documentary evidence—to compass sea and land in order to discover hypothetical "enemies" or "heresies" as objects of attack by the evangelists. With an abundance of classical polemical material at hand, it is surely pertinent to ask why Mark resorted to such tedious length in order to disquiet critics—and to have done it in such obfuscatory a fashion as to leave it to the mid-twentieth century to discern his purpose. Finally we need some kind of explanation—given the "enemies" or "heresies" hypothesis—as to why this polemical literature should have been labeled a "gospel" by its author.

It must be noted that the term "disciples" is not all-embracing in Mark: it includes the Twelve, and can also be used to describe a wider circle of Jesus' immediate followers. Instances of the term will be noted, and where necessary examined, in the course of the commentary.

By far the most apt modern treatment of the subject is that of Ernest Best, "The Role of the Disciples in Mark," *NTS* 23.4.1977. It is free of the current quest for discerning conflicts and heresies of various kinds. The bibliography in that article is a useful compendium of writing on the subject. Cf. further C. H. Turner, "The Twelve and the Disciples," *JTS* 28.1927, pp. 22-30; K. Kertledge, "Die Funktion des 'Zwölf' im Markusevangelium," *TTZ* 78.1969, pp. 193-206; S. Freyne, *The Twelve: Disciples and Apostles* (London and Sydney: Sheed and Ward, 1968); J. B. Tyson, "The Blindness of the Disciples in Mark," *JBL* 80.1961, pp. 261-68. The principal proponent of the "heresy" hypothesis is T. J. Weeden *(Mark: Traditions in Conflict,* Philadelphia: Fortress Press, 1971).

16. *Pharisee-lawyers* (literally "scribes of the Pharisees," found only here in Mark —cf. Acts 23:9): Both Matthew and Luke prefer "the scribes and the Pharisees." The phrase here simply identifies scribes who belonged to the Pharisee party. Mark's normal identification of influential groups on the contemporary scene are "scribes" (twenty-one times), "the elders" (seven times), and "the chief priests" (fourteen times). The origin of the term "Pharisees" is obscure. They were certainly the inheritors of the struggle of the Hasidim ("the devoted ones") to maintain the integrity of the Law in the time of the Maccabean revolt. The commonly accepted understanding of the word as meaning "Separatists" can be understood as meaning those who separated themselves from the spread of Hellenization, and also—later—from their scrupulous regard for the Law, from the "people of the land," whose observance of the Law and its oral traditions was regarded as unsatisfactory. It has also been suggested that the word may come from the Hellenized version of the Aramaic for "Persian"—thus calling attention to the emphasis placed by the Pharisees on retribution or reward in the afterlife, on angels and spirits, and on the providence of God— all held to be intrusions into Jewish thought from the time of the Persian exile (cf. Taylor, p. 206). It is important to be scrupulously fair to the Pharisees contemporary with Jesus. Our own gospels hardly leave us with the impression that the Pharisees were a highly regarded, patriotic "party of the common people"—yet such was the case. Given the inroads of Hellenism, care for and anxiety about the distinctiveness of Judaism as exemplified in the Torah could hardly, in the Pharisaic view, be exaggerated. In spite of such care, Hellenistic and Roman loan words abound in the Mishnah, though so far none has been discovered in the Essene writing of Qumran (also a spiritual descendant of the time of the Hasidim). See Albright-Mann, AB *Matthew,* Introduction IX, pp. cvi-cxxiii.

"He eats. . . .": We have treated this as an accusation, reading *hoti* with the Revised Version as the introduction to an accusation. Some scholars have argued for *hoti* as *ti hoti* (why), thus accommodating Mark to the tradition of Matthew and Luke *(dia ti,* "why").

17. *heard this:* More precisely, "heard of this." It would be very unlikely, given the circumstances outlined above, that Jesus' critics would have been at table with him.

the healthy: The proverb about the sick and the healthy was well known in classical writings.

righteous . . . sinners: In the singular, and in a generic sense, the words are common in the Qumran literature (Hebrew *ṣaddîq* and *rāshāʿ).* The form here in Greek does not mean the "righteous" in the sense of those devoted to the Law, but those satisfied with their own rectitude. The saying, ironic in tone, appears to be directed at the scribes. Luke understands the saying as a call to repentance—which has found its way into some manuscripts of Mark. But if *kalesai* (call) is used in the sense of "invite," then there is another possible explanation for the saying: Jesus will then be the host of a feast, the messianic banquet, a common theme in Jewish literature (cf. *Pirqê Abôth* 3:20; *2 Enoch* 42:5) and in the NT (Matt 8:11, 26:29; Luke 14:15-24; Rev 3:20, 19:9). In this event the saying is not specifically directed to Jesus' critics but asserts that what is demanded of the would-be entrant into the messianic fellowship is the loyal trust of faith. Entrance into fellowship with Jesus is not a reward for moral rectitude, in strong contrast to Essene practice for which entrance into the community was subsequent to a righteousness already attained.

12. Fasting
(2:18-22) = Matt 9:14-17; Luke 5:33-39

2   18 Once, when the Pharisees and John's disciples were fasting, some people came to him asking, "Why are the disciples of both John and the Pharisees fasting, but your disciples are not?" 19 Jesus said to them, "Do you expect the bridegroom's friends to fast as long as the bridegroom is with them? While the bridegroom is with them, they cannot fast; 20 but the time will come when the bridegroom is taken from them. When that day comes, then they will fast. 21 No one sews a piece of unshrunk cloth on an old himation, for if he does the new patch will tear away from it, and so leave a bigger hole. 22 And no one puts new wine into discarded wineskins. If he does, the wine will burst the skins, and then both wine and skins will be lost—[no, fresh wineskins for new wine!]"

Comment

All possible notes of time, place, and circumstance have been lost in the initial saying on fasting. So too with the saying on the old and the new which follows it—both appear to have been attracted to their present location by the conflict of Jesus with his critics in the preceding section. It is difficult to imagine the discussion about fasting taking place at an early stage in Jesus' ministry; indeed it is more realistic to suppose that this incident may belong to a time after the death of John.

The short narrative is an almost perfect example of what happens to an often-repeated story in the process of oral transmission, and the handling of the tradition by the three synoptists is instructive. Matthew baldly introduces it as a question from John's disciples, while Luke has received simply the saying and framed it with a hypothetical question beginning "and they said." Mark can only make the incident intelligible by making it dependent on a fast which is unidentified and unidentifiable. (See notes ad loc.) Indeed, it has been widely held that 18a is the work of a redactor; in that case Mark would have inherited the Matthean tradition. There has been the further suggestion that 19b-20 are an addition to the narrative. That is indeed possible, and if so the verses as an isolated saying have been attracted to their present location at some stage in the late oral tradition or in the early written tradition.

Notes

18. *John's disciples* (cf. 6:29; Matt 11:2 = Luke 7:18; Luke 11:1; Matt 14:12; John 1:35,37; 3:25): The usual view is that the two sets of people—John's disciples and the Pharisees—were sharing a common fast. But if *the Pharisees* has been assimilated to the text by attraction from the second half of the verse, as seems highly likely, then originally the fast may have been that of mourning after the execution of John.

were fasting: The Greek phrase is periphrastic and does not mean "were accustomed to fast." The only statutory fast known to the Law was that of the Day of Atonement (Lev 16:29), but Luke incidentally testifies to Pharisaic customs of fasting on Mondays and Thursdays (Luke 18:12).

19. *bridegroom's friends* (literally, "sons of the bride-chamber"—Greek *numphōn* —a rare word): In Matt 22:10 it is the room where the marriage is celebrated. Taylor (p. 210) regards the phrase as "translation Greek," close to an Aramaic original.

bridegroom: The word is common in the OT (cf. Isa 54:4ff., 62:4ff.; Ezek 16:7ff.; Hos 2:19) in contexts where God is the groom and Israel his bride. From such passages there developed the idea of the bridegroom as being in some sense identified with the messiah. The idea is certainly present in the NT (cf. John 3:29; 2 Cor 11:2; Eph 5:32; Rev 19:7, 21:2). The problem in this passage is to determine whether or not Jesus is *represented* as identifying himself with the messianic bridegroom, and further whether Jesus did in fact imply that such he was. It is not enough to say that the primitive community so regarded Jesus—it is surely necessary to inquire as to the origin of that conviction. At the least Jesus implies that the Reign of God is proleptically present in his own person, and therefore the present time is one of joy and not of fasting and mourning. This need not demand an explicit public claim of messiahship.

Verses 19b and 20 are often dismissed as a late addition to the text by the Christian community, but even if that view is accepted, v. 19a (with its possible messianic overtones) must still be explained. Critical opinion tends to suggest—by implication— that the Proclamation of an imminent Reign of God was in some sense a commonplace in the period immediately prior to the ministry of Jesus, with that ministry being but one of many such examples. (See J. Jeremias, *Neutestamentliche Theologie,* Teil I;

English translation as *New Testament Theology*, Part 1, by John Bowden, New York: Scribner, 1971, especially pp. 32-33.) The Essenes may well have been the only group anticipating such an eschatological Proclamation, but so far as is presently known the phrase "Reign of God" is found only three times in their writings. The Proclamation of Jesus (and that of John before him) was revolutionary in its time, and he can hardly have been unaware of the near predictability of a violent end for anyone making such a Proclamation. Such an end could with safety be foretold for the proclaimer, either at the hands of a suspicious Roman authority, or of a disappointed mob.

Matthew and Luke do not have *while. . . . they will not fast*. The phrase is redundant, or is an addition to the text, or Mark added it to his sources to emphasize for his distressed community that Jesus knew a time of distress was to come.

20. *is taken from them* (cf. Matt 9:15; Luke 5:35): On the parallel between the Greek verb *apairō* (remove) and Isa 53:8, see Lohmeyer, p. 60. A violent death seems to be meant here. In this verse, commentators generally agree on the use of *numphios* (bridegroom) as allegorical, and hence—by comparison with v. 19a, where "when the bridegroom is with them" is intended to be read as "during the marriage feast"—it is often suggested that this verse is not genuine. The argument is odd: there may be allegory in both verses, or the two verses in question may be an example of the well-known Hebraic phenomenon of parallelism. Moreover the use of "bridegroom" in the third person certainly parallels the use by Jesus of "The Man" in the third person when speaking of himself. To suggest, as some do suggest, that the two verses are a device to undergird the ascetic practices of the early Church is to strain out a gnat—the emphasis is not on fasting, but on mourning. The criticism that the material may not be genuine because it injects a passion motif into the narrative far too early is hardly worth noticing, save to remark that in other circumstances the evangelists are assumed to have collected isolated sayings into groups by a loose process of association. (Nineham, 1963, p. 102, regards the verse as an intrusion.)

It remains to make note of the possible connection between v. 20 and Isa 53:8. It is accepted wisdom that the links between the Servant Songs of Isaiah and the ministry of Jesus were the work of the early community and retrojected into our present gospels. This may be so, but for the present commentator there remains the far more distinct possibility of religious genius in the person of Jesus. For further discussion on vv. 19-20, cf. G. Braumann (" 'An jenem Tag' Mc 2.20," *NovTest* 6.4.1963, pp. 264-67) and A. Feuillet ("La controverse sur le jeûne [Mc 2.18-20, Mt 9.14-15, Lc 5.33-35]," *NRTh* 90.2.1968, pp. 113-16 and 90.3.1968, pp. 252-57).

that day . . . they will fast: The sense changes from the indefinite phrasing of "as long as" to "that day," and the cryptic character of the saying renders any precise solution difficult, if not impossible (cf. Lohmeyer, p. 60). It has been commonly suggested that the saying refers to the Passion and death of Jesus. The criticism that this reference to the Passion is a prophecy after the event (cf. Bultmann, *History*, p. 19), on the grounds that such a prediction is too early in the Markan scheme, is somewhat weakened in the face of the suggestion now commonly made that the saying belongs to a later stage in the ministry. The attempt to reinforce the argument by objecting that the reference to fasting is certainly a community saying not only disregards other sayings of Jesus (cf. Matt 6:16), but if (with Lane, p. 112) we interpret the word as "sorrow," the objection fails.

21. There is no obvious connection between the preceding verses and vv. 21-22, except that Mark inherited his material from the Matthean order and that the discussion now passes from John's disciples to Jesus and his own community. In what circumstances the sayings were first used, we cannot know, though they may have been part of pronouncement stories from which they were taken in the process of oral transmission. As Taylor rightly points out (p. 212), the sayings are revolutionary, demanding that a radically new message demands a radically new means of expression. The view occasionally expressed, that the stark contrast posed between the old and the new is so reminiscent of Pauline and other NT writings that it must have come from such sources, fails to put the matter another way: Is the originality of thought so displayed first characteristic of Jesus, and then developed in the teaching of Paul?

unshrunk cloth (Greek *hrakosis agnaphon*): The phrase means a piece of cloth that has not been treated. Matthew's phrase is the same, but Luke has "the patch will tear away from the himation."

sew: The verb in Matthew and Luke is *epiraptei,* a relatively late word, which Mark changes to *epiballei* (place upon).

himation: The Greek word has been left standing, as there is no precise modern equivalent. The garment was an outer cloak, generally of goat or camel hair, and was the dress which might not be retained as a pledge overnight (cf. Exod 22:26). It was put aside when working or folded for quick movement. It could be laid on the ground as a rug or carpet for a distinguished person (cf. Matt 21:8), and when folded it could be used as a saddle.

The incompatibility of the old with the new is simply stated, but it is impossible to determine the circumstances in which the saying was first uttered. It is joined by a simple conjunction to the succeeding saying about new wine.

22. *new* (Greek *neon*): The word means freshly made, and therefore still fermenting. Pouring such wine into old leather wineskins would result in the loss of both wine and skins. Matthew and Luke agree in separating the destruction of wine and skins separately; Mark bears all the signs of a conflated text, Streeter (p. 311) notwithstanding. The words enclosed in brackets are omitted by some manuscripts, but Streeter explains that the line divisions in D (Codex Bezae) are such that the words *oinos askos* (wine, wineskin) would have been found in each of three successive lines, separated by only a few words. According to this view the manuscript omissions are due to this homoioteleuton.

For all the fact that we cannot know in what circumstances the sayings in vv. 21 and 22 were spoken, some questions must be asked. Was the contrast between the old and the new intended as a criticism of John's disciples, or of the Pharisees? Or was there an even more radical view being expressed—that Jesus could not accept the continuance of the normative Judaism of his own time alongside his own community? But if the Matthean *and both are preserved* (Matt 9:17) is indeed in context, then the two communities—Judaism and the new messianic sect—were envisaged as continuing together. Whether Jesus foresaw any spread of his movement into the broader Hellenistic world must be a matter of debate (cf. J. Jeremias *[Jesus' Promise to the Nations,* London: SCM Press, 1956 and 1958], perhaps the most persuasive argument in favor of the thesis). See also T. W. Manson (1964). A Samaritan mission certainly was undertaken by Jesus, and taken up by the early Jerusalem community, but this could easily be argued as being to "the lost sheep of the house of Israel." It was left to the theological insight of Paul to build on the premise: Since sin is a universal human phenomenon, then God's redeeming act in Jesus must also be of universal human significance.

It seems safest to assume that the saying here is meant to apply to the disciples of John, in the face of Jesus' Proclamation of the dawning Reign of God. The spread of Baptistic sects through the Mediterranean world is well known. But while the NT never betrays Jesus as displaying anything but the highest regard for John, the position of John's followers who had embraced his message and attached themselves to his memory was altogether a different thing. If such loyalty and attachment carried with it a refusal to give allegiance to Jesus, then it had to be made clear that, the messianic kingdom having been proclaimed, there could be no room for the new community *and* the Baptist's community existing in uncomfortable parallel. (Cf. K. Stendahl in *Peake's Commentary on the Bible,* rev. ed. edited by H. H. Rowley, London: Nelson, 1962, p. 782a.)

13. The Sabbath (i) The Wheatfields (2:23-28) = Matt 12:1-8; Luke 6:1-5

2   23 On one Sabbath, as he was going through some wheatfields, his disciples as they walked began to pluck the ears of wheat. 24 The Pharisees said to Jesus, "Do you see that what they are doing is forbidden on the Sabbath?" 25 "Have you never read," he replied, "what David and his men did when they were hungry and had nothing to eat? 26 He went into the house of God, when Abiathar was high priest, and ate the bread of the presence—which is not allowed, save to priests—and even gave it to his men. 27 The Sabbath," he added, "was made for the sake of man, not man for the Sabbath. 28 The Man, therefore, is lord even over the Sabbath."

Comment

The purpose of this pericope is to answer with a pronouncement outlining the controversies and doubts in the early community about one of the salient features of observant Judaism—the keeping of the Sabbath, and its validity for members of the new community. The disciples could glean and eat, and that was legitimate (cf. Deut 23:25). What was not legitimate under Mosaic

Law was plucking grain (i.e., reaping) on the Sabbath (cf. Exod 34:21), heavily underscored in the Mishnah (cf. *M Shabbath* 7:2; Strack-Billerbeck, Vol. 1, pp. 615-18, 623-29; and E. Lohse in *TWNT,* 1964, pp. 11-14).

There seems no good reason to see in the details of this pericope any note of time, as Taylor does (p. 216), for "ripe grain" ready for milling is purely incidental to the narrative. In any event, grain ripens early in parts of the Jordan valley, and it is unwise to see any reference here to a chronological note about Passover (officially the beginning of the harvest season). Cf. Lane (p. 114, n.70).

We can see both from the incident, and from the account in 3:1-6, how important a question the Sabbath posed for the early Christian community. From the earliest days the first day of the week, as the day of Jesus' resurrection, assumed paramount importance, but such importance by no means diminished the continued impact of the Sabbath on Jewish Christians. As the use of phrases such as "the Lord's day" (Rev 1:10) for the first day of the week came into use the challenge about the continued observance of the Sabbath would certainly not diminish.

The Markan text is a very good example of the conflation methods of the evangelist. All the essential elements are present, but the colorful details of Matthew and Luke are absent.

Notes

23. *as he was going through:* Reading *paraporenesthai* (to pass by) with Taylor (p. 215) and Lohmeyer (p. 62). Mark here has an independent tradition of *kai egeneto* (and it happened) with the infinitive. Matt 12:1 has *eporenthe,* and Luke 6:1 has *diaporenesthai* ("he passed through" and "to pass through," respectively).

as they walked began to pluck. The Greek *hodon poiein* (to make a way) could be read as meaning that they made a path through the field of grain as they walked through it. Here again, Mark uses an older independent tradition and not those of Matthew and Luke. It is clear from what follows that the disciples' offense was not working on the Sabbath, or of going beyond the limits imposed on journeys on the Sabbath, but of collecting and eating grain on the Sabbath. The manuscript evidence is in confusion—evidence of the difficulty experienced by copyists with Mark's style.

ears of wheat (Greek *stachuas):* The meaning is clearly that of grain ready for harvest. The word regularly appears in farm accounts in the papyri.

24. The verse literally reads "See! They are doing what is not lawful on the Sabbath!" The Greek *ide* (See!) was by NT times little more than an interjection.

forbidden: Gleaning was permitted on the Sabbath (cf. Deut 33:24), but the action of the disciples was considered reaping and eating. For the different kinds of work forbidden by the rabbis on the Sabbath, cf. *M Shabbath* 7.2 and also Strack-Billerbeck Vol. 1, pp. 615-18, 623-29. The question was addressed to Jesus as being responsible for the actions of his disciples.

25. "Have you never read . . .": The technique of question and counterquestion was a familiar exercise in rabbinic argument.

David and his men (cf. 1 Sam 21:1-6): The example is given as calling attention to the care of David for his men. There is no call to see in this example a contrast between one messianic figure and another (cf. Rawlinson, p. 34).

when they were hungry: The phrase is peculiar to Mark.

26. Mark omits Matthew's *pōs* (how) or Luke's *hōs* (as, how, when) in the beginning of the verse.

house of God: The title is that used in *LXX* for the tent in which the ark was kept.

Abiathar: The Markan account differs in detail from the narrative in 1 Sam 21:1-6. Not only so, but the accounts in Matthew and Luke omit all mention of Abiathar. The statement in Mark is incorrect, for Ahimilech his father was high priest at the time. Either this name is a primitive gloss, supplied by a copyist, or Mark himself disregarded the absence of names and supplied one well known for his association with David. The narrative further suggests that David himself entered the sanctuary (in contrast with 1 Sam 21:6, cf. also 2 Sam 8:17).

bread of the presence (cf. Exod 40:23; 1 Sam 21:6): The phrase refers to the twelve newly baked loaves placed on a table each Sabbath in the Tabernacle and later eaten by the priests.

which is not allowed (cf. Lev 24:9): The prohibition *may* be later than the time of David, though given the conservatism of most ritual prescriptions, it is not safe to make this statement unreservedly.

27. *he added:* Scholarly opinion is divided as to whether the saying on the Sabbath belongs to this section, or is an independent saying from another source attracted to this context. But belonging here or not, the saying has generated its fair share of controversy. The translation given here is an attempt to indicate that the Greek *kai elegen* (and he said) may be no more than a connective phrase, since the saying in v. 26 may be regarded as the climax of the pericope.

It is of course the saying about The Man which has so divided the commentators. It is often said that the saying is inauthentic because (a) there is no reference to suffering connected with The Man, nor yet of eschatological glory, both characteristic of "authentic" sayings in Mark; (b) the saying is certainly attributed to Jesus, though it is not addressed to the disciples but to his critics; (c) it comes (as did the saying in 2:10) before the passion predictions.

To assert that the phrase means simply that "mankind" is lord of the Sabbath is certainly ostensibly easier than employing The Man in 2:10, but it is doubtful if the apparent ease is warranted. It is improbable that Jesus could have said that *any* man could dispense the Mosaic Law, in spite of rabbinic assertions that "the Sabbath was delivered to you, and not you to the Sabbath." Furthermore the Sabbath was a peculiarly Israelite tradition, so the attempted rendering, "mankind is lord of the Sabbath," is singularly inappropriate. Alternatively it can be suggested that while v. 27 is acceptable (on the lines of Midrash *Mekilta* 109b on Exod 31:14, attributed to Rabbi Simeon b. Menssya (c. A.D. 170), v. 28 is an addition by the primitive community reflecting a desire on the part of that community to assert the lordship of Jesus over the Sabbath.

The problem is compounded by the absence of v. 27 in the Matthean and Lucan tradition, which may indicate that originally vv. 27 and 28 were two distinct sayings. But if ever this could be proved, it would fatally affect the view that The Man in v. 28 is a mistranslation of "man." Significantly both Matthew and Luke retain the saying, which is often confidently asserted to be a fabrication of the early community, while omitting a verse which is generally thought to be an authentic saying of Jesus. F. W. Beare (The Earliest Records of Jesus, New York and Nashville: Abingdon Press, 1962, pp. 130-36) places the origin of both verses in the early community. The authenticity of v. 27 need not detain us—Jub 2:23ff. could equally have said the same thing, bearing in mind the desire of that book to retroject the keeping of Sabbath to the creation, though not revealed until later times. Equally the identification of "mankind" with "Israel" would not have occasioned any comment—it is the troublesome v. 28 which causes all the problems.

We must now take up again the relationship between the sayings in vv. 27 and 28 and the preceding story about David. The Sabbath rules, designed to safeguard the sanctity of the Sabbath, were set aside for a person in a special position—one already anointed for service—and "for those who were with him." So in the case of Jesus, the rules are put aside for one in a special position, and for those who are with him. We may wish to conclude, with Lane (p. 120) that this represents a Markan interpretation of the needs of the early community. Unhappily this explanation leaves us still in the position of explaining the origin of the detached sayings of vv. 27 and 28. Furthermore the absence of v. 27 in Matthew and Luke still puzzles. For Matthew certainly there is no question of the dominion of The Man, with his especial emphasis on Jesus as "Representative Israel." Though the notion of corporate personality centered in Jesus is not so emphatic in Luke, neither he nor Matthew would have felt any urgent necessity to include v. 27. For Mark the situation (as it was outlined in Part 2 of the Introduction) was far different, and a dispirited community had to be reassured that Jesus was and always had been Lord, even of the Sabbath.

The Man in these sayings in Mark is nowhere explicitly identified with Jesus, though The Man is asserted to have authority. The identity may be implied, in that Jesus is questioned about his followers and appeals to the authority of The Man as far exceeding that possessed by any other. The context does leave open the possibility that The Man was regarded as a corporate term.

One final concern calls for brief discussion: the possibility that the Sabbath as "rest" had implications of salvation and possession (cf. Deut 3:20, 12:9; Josh 1:13-15 as identifying the Sabbath with entry into the Promised Land and Isa 14:3 or Jer 30:10 as identifying the Sabbath with restoration). In the NT, apart from the identification of the Sabbath and salvation in Heb 3:7-4:13, we must take into account the links between the Sabbath and the healing ministry of Jesus (cf. especially John 5:16-18, which has close thematic links with Mark 2:23-28 and 3:1-5). Jesus' use of the Sabbath in John 5:16 clearly states that for him, as for God, the Sabbath has been set aside in favor of the activity of the new creation. (In this connection cf. A. G. Hebert, 1941, pp. 145ff.) For further discussion cf. A. Hultgren, "The Formation of the Sabbath Pericope in Mark 2:23-28," JBL 91.1.1972, pp. 38-43.

The difficulty in all this is that in the case of David the Law is acknowledged, but special circumstances are pleaded as a reason for setting the Law aside. But in the narrative before us there are apparently no special circumstances: hunger could not be

pleaded as a reason for setting aside the rule. Perhaps there was no emergency of any
kind at all, and Jesus' disciples were simply being lax in observance. Something far
more was involved, but the compressed style of the narrative hardly allows us to do
more than guess. Perhaps the parallel to be drawn is that if David could demand
special consideration under a set of special circumstances, then the inbreaking of the
Reign of God was itself a special circumstance par excellence, and the Agent of God
in this time of inbreaking is his own authority. But this by no means implies a messianic abolition and messianic suspension of the Sabbath.

I am now indebted to Dr. Charles A. Kennedy for the suggestion that the name
Abiathar, so far from being a mistake which Matthew and Luke corrected by omission, is the result of a scribal correction of what the scribe assumed to be a simple case
of dittography. In other words, the original text of Mark would have been Ab(ba)-
Abiathar (the father of Abiathar), in much the same way that in Arabic custom at the
present time a father may be known by the name of a more famous son (e.g., Abu-
Omar = the father of Omar). Dr. Moses Aberbach confirms this with three examples
from the Babylonian Talmud: *Berakoth* 18b; *Yoma* 29a; and *Taanith* 26b. In the first
of these, one of the disciples of Judah the Patriarch is known as "the father of Samuel"
while the third speaks of "the father of R. Zera." While it is true that these are not
Palestinian examples and are second and third century in date, they may be testimony
to a long-standing custom in Aramaic. As stated, the tentative solution can be adduced to support either the familiar two-document hypothesis (a scribe had changed
what he thought to be a dittography, and Matthew and Luke then omitted what they
took to be ignorance on the part of Mark) or the Griesbach hypothesis (Mark, noticing that his two authorities did not supply the name of the high priest, supplied a
familiar Semitism).

14. The Sabbath (ii) The Man with the Withered Hand
(3:1-6) = Matt 12:9-14; Luke 6:6-11

3 ^{1} On another occasion he went to synagogue, and there was a man
there who had a withered hand. ^{2} They watched him closely to see
whether he would cure him on the Sabbath, so as to bring an accusation against him. ^{3} He said to the man with the withered hand, "Come
and stand out here." ^{4} He then asked them, "Is it allowed on the
Sabbath to do good—or to do evil? To save life—or to kill it?" They
were silent, ^{5} and looking at them with anger, but sorrowing for their
obdurate stupidity, he said to the man, "Stretch out your hand." He
stretched it out, and it was restored. ^{6} The Pharisees, however, on

leaving the synagogue, met with some members of Herod's party and began plotting to destroy him.

Comment

The story preceding is not easy to classify. At first sight it appears to be a straightforward healing story, but the question in v. 4 immediately suggests another classification—that of "pronouncement," having to do with the attitude of Jesus toward the Sabbath. The narrative is further complicated in interpretation by the more extended versions in Matthew and Luke and the use by Luke of one of Matthew's verses (12:12) in another context (Luke 14:1-6). If we accept that this pronouncement story took shape in the exigencies of the Palestinian community, then we must also take notice of some features of the Markan narrative which have all the marks of a tradition based on eyewitness reminiscence (vv. 2,3,5,6), which will be the subject of commentary in the notes. Mark's independence of Matthew and Luke is striking, but far more striking, on the customary hypotheses, would be the independence of Matthew and Luke from the supposed Markan source.

Notes

1. *went to synagogue:* Mark uses the colloquial expression, in much the same way as we would speak of "going to church," whereas Matthew and Luke both have the definite article. We have translated Mark's *palin* (again) by *on another occasion* as being better than attempting to make some artificial connection with the preceding narrative.

withered hand (Greek *xeraino*): Compare also 4:6; 5:29; 9:18; 11:20,21. The Greek implies an inability to use the hand. We cannot determine from Mark's *exerammenēn* whether the condition had existed from birth, though the Greek of Matthew and Luke does not carry any such necessary indication.

2. *watched him closely* (Greek *paratereō*): The verb implies a sense of hostility, almost a sense of "lying in wait for," and certainly bears far more the marks of an eyewitness account than the question posed in the Matthean account.

so as to bring an accusation (Greek *kategoresōsin*): The term is a technical one (compare 15:3,4).

3. Taylor (p. 220) correctly sees in the action of Jesus in bringing the man into the midst of the assembly a note of original narrative.

4. The reference is to the Mosaic Law. The Matthean version, with its direct question from Jesus' critics, loses the drama of the account in Mark, and Luke (6:8) explicitly states that Jesus understood the mental processes of his potential accusers. Mark's version is an indirect question. The Pharisees permitted the rescue of an

animal on the Sabbath, but the Essenes apparently did not. The challenge to Jesus was whether he would observe the rabbinic rule allowing relief to the sufferer when life was in danger (compare *M Shabbath* 18:3 and *Yoma* 8:6). According to Jerome, the *Evangelium ad Hebraios* described the man as deprived of his livelihood as a mason. Matthew's version specifically refers to the Pharisaic permission (12:11) as an example of *qal va-homer* (arguing from the lesser example to the greater) as giving him entitlement to heal on the Sabbath. There is further the underlying and unspoken challenge that the dawning of the Reign of God carried with it implications of a new creation— and what more appropriate day to herald the new act of God than the Sabbath.

do good (Greek *agathapoieō*): The word, common in the New Testament, is found in the Septuagint and later Greek. It is formed on the same principle as *kakopoieō* (to do evil). In many cases the verb "to do good" is associated with saving life, as of deliverance from sickness, sometimes of the salvation of the self from judgment.

life (Greek *psuchē*): There are three uses of the word in Mark—

a. The sense of mundane existence, "the self"—8:35, 10:45, 14:34.

b. The inner self of feelings and emotions—12:30 and perhaps 14:34.

c. Simple earthly existence—8:36,37.

Here it is the first: "Is it lawful to save a person, or not?"

save (Greek *sozō*):

a. To rescue from death—15:30-31.

b. To preserve life—3:4, 8:35a, and (passively) to survive death.

c. To heal, or cure—5:23,28,34.

d. To save (in the theological sense)—8:35b(?), 10:26, 13:13, 16:16.

they were silent: The silence seems to imply that the simple question of doing good as opposed to doing evil carried a further note: to what extent was it lawful to watch for the life of another, as the critics were doing at that moment? (Cf. Rawlinson, p. 36; Lohmeyer, p. 69.) The criticism has sometimes been made that this interpretation is altogether too subtle, but Taylor (p. 222) is surely right in saying that if it were merely a question of a general principle being involved, Jesus' critics could well have replied that the healing could be postponed until the next day. As it was, the critics were reduced to silence. And, as with the previous narrative, there could be no more appropriate day for the messianic work of restoration than the Sabbath.

5. *looking at them:* The Greek *(periblepō)* is a Markan usage, and in all cases except 9:8 it implies the sense of a swift and appraising glance at enemies or friends. The remainder of the phrase *(but . . . stupidity)* is not found in Matthew or Luke; nor is *anger.* The word we have translated by "sorrowing" (Greek *sunlupeō*) demands a sense of "be aggrieved with," but there is no contemporary evidence for such a meaning. W. L. Knox *(Some Hellenistic Elements in Primitive Christianity,* London: H. Milford for the British Academy, 1944, p. 6) suggests a Latinism here: he calls atten-

tion to the sense already being attributed to the Latin *contristari*. Perhaps this is as good an interpretation as we shall find, and Latin influence in Mark's gospel has long been recognized.

Matthew and Luke, but especially Matthew, are concerned with a presentation of a case (Jesus versus his critics about Sabbath observance), while Mark has chosen to make full use of an eyewitness (Petrine?) account known to him and thereby to focus more on the person of Jesus himself.

obdurate stupidity (Greek *pōrōsis*): linked with *anger*, is a faithful translation but has the advantage (as some other translations do not) of emphasizing the impatience of Jesus with those whose devotion to the law was coupled with moral obtuseness.

Stretch out your hand: The Markan narrative from this point follows Matthew and Luke far more closely. The healing would appear to have taken place immediately after the man obeyed. The vivid details of 5a apart, the main interest focuses on the Sabbath controversy, and whether the man begged for relief we cannot know.

it was restored: The details which we customarily find in miracle stories are absent from this narrative, since all the emphasis is on the "pronouncement" element in the account.

6. *The Pharisees . . . some members of Herod's party.* The Pharisees are introduced for the first time in this Markan pericope, whereas in Matthew and Luke they are the principal critics. Strictly speaking, the Greek *Hērōdianoi* does not mean "party" as such, but rather the friends and supporters of Herod Antipas (cf. Josephus, *Ant* 14.15.10). If it might be objected that an alliance of Pharisees and Herodians is improbable, then it should be remembered that a common enmity can make some strange bedfellows. Historical examples abound. On the Herodians, as consisting of those friendly to Herodian rule, and at the same time even of some influence and authority in the community—cf. W. J. Bennett, Jr., "The Herodians and Mark's Gospel," *NovTest* 17.1.1975, pp. 9-14; and Lagrange, p. 55. Mark's text has the word *euthus* (immediately) to describe the meeting of the Pharisees with the Herodians, as if to indicate that they lost no time in plotting the downfall of Jesus.

began plotting (Greek *sumboulion*): The whole phrase is awkward, for the translation assigns to *sumboulion* the meaning of "counsel," instead of "council," apart altogether from the odd use of *edidoun* as "take," for which there is no precedent in contemporary Greek. Luke never uses the construction, and Matthew prefers *sumboulion lambanein*. W. L. Knox *(Some Hellenistic Elements)* maintains that the influence of the Latin *consilium* on vernacular Greek can be discerned here, suggesting that two Latinisms, both *hapax legomena* in meaning, in one short narrative indicates a passage from Greek (or Aramaic) into Latin and back again into Greek before finding its present place in Mark.

Wherever the story belonged in the original tradition—and Mark follows Matthew's order—we have reached a climax in the ministry. From this point in the narrative the threat of death is never far away.

15. The Crowd by the Sea
(3:7-12) = Matt 4:24-25; 12:15-16; Luke 6:17-19

3   ⁷ Jesus went away with his disciples to the lakeside. Great crowds
followed him—from Galilee, ⁸ Judaea and Jerusalem, Idumaea and
Transjordan, and the region of Tyre and Sidon. This great crowd came
because they heard of the things he was doing. ⁹ So he told his disciples
to have a boat ready for him so that he would not be crushed by the
crowd. ¹⁰ He had cured many people, so that all who had diseases kept
crowding in upon him to touch him. ¹¹ The unclean spirits, too, when
they saw him would fall before him and scream, "You are God's son!"
¹² but he insisted that they should not make him known.

Comment

With this short summary statement, we are prepared for the climax of the
Galilean ministry in the succeeding narrative. The style and vocabulary are
Mark's adaptations of his sources. The material, as summary, may appear to
be longer than strictly necessary, and there are no links to the preceding
material. The summary, by including such items as the crowds, the demon-
possessed, the boat, and the desire of the people to touch Jesus, as well as the
incidental mention of teaching by the lake, look forward to succeeding material. It seems probable that Mark in condensing and conflating the material
before him deliberately formulated this summary to follow on the beginnings
of the plot against Jesus. Thereby he supplied the public theme seen against
the background of private and underground threat.

This material has occasionally been cited as an example of a compilation of
material from pre-Markan sources, together with Markan editorial notes. (Cf.
L. E. Keck, "Mark 3:7-12 and Mark's Christology," *JBL* 84.3.1965, pp.
341ff.; and T. A. Burkill, "Mark 3:7-12 and the Alleged Dualism in the
Evangelist's Miracle Material," *JBL* 87.4.1968, pp. 409ff.) Most simply Keck
argues that 3:7-12, 4:35-5:43, 6:31-52, and 53-56 make up a cycle of traditional material, all of it reflecting a Hellenistic *theios anēr* concept of a god-
man figure using thaumaturgic powers for the benefit of mankind. All of this
material is to be carefully distinguished from the rest of the Markan miracle

narratives, which (he argues) are more closely associated with the Palestinian milieu and the Proclamation of Jesus in its original setting. Keck pursues this theme by asserting that 3:7-12 is not related structurally to what follows, but instead is a thematic summary of the preceding material. This attempts to prove altogether too much, as Burkill correctly observes. Putting on one side the always perilous argument in favor of a Hellenistic god-man figure, the pericope before us takes up themes which look forward to 4:35-5:43—the crowd, the boat, the lakeside, the demoniac, the desire of people to touch Jesus. A comparison of the Greek of this section with Matt 12:15-21 and Luke 6:17-19 suggests that the evangelist used the sense, and some of the vocabulary, before him to expand from that material his own preface to the ministry ahead.

Notes

7. Mark ignores the links provided by Matt 12:15 with the preceding synoptic pericope, constructing this pericope to serve as an introduction, not as a sequel.

went away (Greek *anachōrēsen):* Regularly used of withdrawal from peril in the classical authors (a sense which seems demanded in Matthew's text), it is also found in the papyri, as indicating the desertion of a village in the face of an impending visit by tax collectors. So far as Mark's text is concerned, it seems more likely to mean a withdrawal from towns and villages into the countryside.

Our own translation *to* (the lakeside) follows the Greek reading *eis* instead of *pros* (toward). Similarly, we read—though Taylor omits—*ekolouthēnen* (followed). In some manuscripts the verb follows *from Judea,* as though to distinguish two elements in the crowd: those from near at hand, and those from more distant parts. We also read *polus ochlos* (great crowds) in this verse, since Mark generally used the word *ochlos* as a noun for a crowd. *Plethos polu* has been rendered *this great crowd* in v. 8. For a fuller explanation of the textual problems, cf. Taylor, p. 226. Taylor omits *plēthos polu,* but it seems to be demanded by the construction of the whole, with a period after *Sidon* where Taylor has a comma. All in all, Mark exhibits all the signs here of an accommodation to both Matthew and Luke (6:17-19), and textually this explains the difficulties of the pericope.

8. *Jerusalem* (Greek *Ierosoluma):* Cf. 3:22, 7:1, 10:32ff., 11:1, 15:27, 15:41. Mark does not use the Semitic *Ierousalem.*

because they heard: The phrase strongly suggests rumors and stories as they passed from one group to another.

Both vv. 7 and 8 demonstrate Mark's concern to witness to the extent of the ministry. For the first time, we hear of *Judaea and Jerusalem.* Similarly, to the south we have *Idumaea* (Edom), the home of the Herods, and from the time of John Hyrcanus the territory had been Jewish. The region of *Transjordan* is Peraea, between the Jabbok and the Arnon. To the north, the country closely linked with Galilee is mentioned. Samaria is not mentioned, and we do not hear of the Ten Towns until v. 20.

9. The phrase introduced by *hina* (literally, "in order that") *proskarterē* indicates

command, not purpose, and this use of the subjunctive is common in vernacular texts in *koinē* Greek.

boat (Greek *ploiarion*): The Greek is a diminutive, a usage characteristic of Mark, but it can hardly have been meant literally.

so that he would not be crushed: The phrase is peculiar to Mark and argues for eyewitness reminiscence behind the tradition.

10. The vivid narrative is heightened still further in this verse, and it is measurably more graphic than the stilted parallel in Matt 12:15 and Luke 6:17-18. It would be reading far too much into the Markan text to exaggerate the difference between Matthew's *pantas* (all) in 12:15 and Mark's *pollous* (many) in this verse.

he had cured many: The word translated as *many* should not be taken to indicate "most, but not all," and too much can be made of the emphatic "all" *(poulas)* in Matt 12:15 or Luke 6:19. The word *pollous* could be, and was, used to indicate "all." In fact Mark is being very literal: not all of the crowd was in need of healing. Mark tells of the touch of Jesus in 1:41, and here we have an eagerness on the part of people to touch him (cf. 5:27ff., 6:56). Luke supplies the explanation that power went out from Jesus to heal (cf. Mark 5:30).

who had diseases: The sick are described by the evangelist as being scourged, afflicted.

touch him: Cf. 1:41, 5:27, 6:56. Luke adds (in 6:19) that power went out from Jesus for healing, and Mark records a similar thought in 5:30.

11. *unclean spirits:* Cf. 1:23.

saw (Greek *theoreo*): Cf. 5:15,38; 12:41; 15:40,47; 16:4. The word generally implies something more than a mere glance, and "take account of" would equally serve the meaning here.

"You are God's son!": This is the evangelist's attempt to give meaning and interpretation to the terrified cries of the possessed. It does not imply recognition of messiahship. See also 14:51, 15:39.

12. *not make him known:* The injunction to silence in Mark has been dealt with in 1:25,34,44. Mark's version here closely follows Matthew. But for Mark, the pericope is but introduction, whereas for Matthew it both concludes a preceding section and introduces a new demon conflict. Matthew, therefore, has a quotation from Isa 42:1-4 as a text central to both narratives.

16. Choosing the Twelve
(3:13) = Matt 5:1 (3:14-15) = Matt 10:1
(3:16-19) = Matt 10:2-4; Luke 6:14-16; Acts 1:13

3 13 He then went into the hill country and called to himself the men he wanted, and they went to him. 14 He appointed twelve to be with him, to send them out to make the Proclamation, 15 and with authority

to cast out demons. [16] So he appointed the Twelve: to Simon he gave the name Peter; [17] then there were the sons of Zebedee, James and his brother John, to whom he gave the name Boanerges (Sons of Thunder), [18] then Andrew, Philip, Bartholomew, Matthew, Thomas, James the son of Alphaeus, Thaddaeus, Simon the member of the Zealot party, [19] and Judas Iscariot, the man who betrayed him.

Comment

This pericope not only presents us with familiar difficulties connected with the names of the Twelve, it also raises the question of its sources. The details of the location are vague; there are none of the vivid details which we associate with this evangelist, and all in all it has the marks of a very early fixed tradition. Nor is this all: the functions of the Twelve are very different from those ascribed to the apostles and elders in Acts 15, and this in turn raises the question (to which no answer seems possible at present) as to how far the lists of the Twelve in the synoptic gospels represent a highly formalized account of what was a loose association of some followers who were close to Jesus, but who may have been more than twelve in number.

Some things can be said with accuracy:

1. The synoptic tradition is that Jesus chose an inner circle of disciples for commissioning to a special and separate task as evangelists, and the appointment symbolizes a new era in the spiritual history of Israel, of which "the Twelve" are a symbol.

2. There was nothing unusual in the choosing of circles of pupils to safeguard and disseminate teaching—cf. Isaiah and Jeremiah in the Old Testament.

3. The silence of the epistles regarding the Twelve has been frequently used as an argument to cast doubt on the authenticity of the narrative. But against this, the very simplicity of the narrative is its own argument, and the list as it stands contains features which the older tradition did not attempt to explain —e.g., the appellation *Boanerges,* and the term *Iscariot.* There is an element of restraint about the narrative, and the description of the appointment in v. 14 precisely fits the Galilean ministry.

4. The contrast with the Matthean narrative is marked. Matthew speaks of the Twelve as an already recognizable company, and the commissioning in Luke 10:1 is a delegation of authority. Mark's version is much closer to Luke in seeing the action of Jesus as choosing the inner circle for the first time. Mark is evidently here choosing between his sources and not relying on details which only an eyewitness could have supplied.

The unanimity of the four gospels and the Acts on the central place of the

Twelve (the title is especially common in John) obscures the fact that we know little of the inner circle. It is more than likely that their function (cf. Acts 8:1) was exclusively within the framework of the Jerusalem community, and when Jewish Christianity came to an end c. 64-70 the Gentile communities may not even have known the names of the Twelve with anything approaching accuracy. The emphasis on "the Twelve" in the literature of Qumran is of some significance. (Cf. C. S. Mann, "The Organisation and Institutions of the Jerusalem Church in Acts" in J. Munck, *The Acts of the Apostles,* AB, Garden City, N.Y.: Doubleday, 1967, pp. 276-85.) Matthew's version of the delegation of authority explicitly refers to the Twelve as "apostles" (10:2)—a term used only twice in this gospel. Here again, whatever the original identification of "apostles" and "the Twelve" (at least for Jerusalem), the term "apostles" underwent considerable change with the conversion of Paul. (Cf. Johannes Munck, "Paul, the Apostles and the Twelve," *ST* 3, Lund: Gleerup, 1949; Joseph Baumgarten, "The Duodecimal Courts of Qumran, Revelation, and the Sanhedrin," *JBL* 95.1.1976, pp. 59-78.)

Notes

13. *called to himself:* The qualifications of the men Jesus chose are not mentioned, but perhaps one qualification was that of having been with Jesus from the beginning of his ministry. Mark frequently uses the verb *proskaleomai* (to call) with reference to the disciples, the crowds, or a summons of Pilate to a centurion (15:44). The implication of this verse is plainly that a larger number of people was present from whom Jesus chose the Twelve. Luke's version has it that this choice was preceded by a vigil of prayer in the hills.

14-15. The function of the Twelve, apart from close association with Jesus, is simply stated: *to make the Proclamation, and with authority to cast out demons.* The phrase "and to heal the sick and" is read by a few manuscripts after *authority,* but this is probably a later manuscript assimilation to Matt 10:1. There are difficulties in the account as we now have it. The commission to evangelize and exorcise is not acted upon until 6:7, which may indicate Mark's desire to suggest that there was indeed a time of close companionship with Jesus before the mission. But our present text has two instances of *he appointed,* here and in v. 16, though some manuscripts omit the second use. The position is complicated further by the fact that the manuscripts which omit the second *he appointed* are the very ones that also omit "whom he also called apostles." All we can usefully say is that the original text—whatever it may have been —is now corrupted beyond our recovery.

16. The Greek text is confusing. It begins abruptly with *to Simon,* when we might reasonably have expected some introduction of Simon before the giving of the name, as is done with James and John in the following verse. The construction of the Greek is odd, for while the abrupt introduction of Peter appears to demand an introduction in the accusative case (e.g., "first, he called Simon, to whom he gave the name . . ."),

the case in which all the other names occur, we have a dative instead. Taylor (pp. 16-17) finds himself compelled to expand the existing text to *"prōton simōna (kai epethēkem onoma to simōna petrou)* . . ." ("First, Simon, and he gave the name Peter to Simon . . ."). Our translation attempts a reflection of the present confused state of the Greek text. *Simon,* the Greek form of the Hebrew *Shimeon,* is common in Josephus and the New Testament.

Peter: the Greek *petros* (a rock) is the Greek equivalent of the Aramaic *kepha* (cf. Greek *kephas* of John 1:42; 1 Cor 1:12, 3:22, 9:5, 15:5; Gal 1:18, 2:9,11,14). This Aramaic form is not used in Mark. Peter is, however, consistently used in Mark (Simon is the solitary exception in 14:37).

17. The following of Peter's name by the two brothers gives appropriate emphasis to the importance attached to them in conjunction with Peter throughout the narrative. The title *Boanerges* represents a so far unsolved problem. Presumably the word should be divided as *Boane-rges* in the Greek text, but while the first part of the word can be easily understood as a rendering of the Hebrew *Bene* (sons of), there is no word similar in Hebrew or Aramaic to explain the second part as "thunder." Perhaps the best suggestion is still that of Lagrange (p. 65), that the Arabic *radjas* did mean "thunder" and that the word may have passed into common usage. Some texts assign the designation to all the Twelve, and perhaps there is to be found some connection (certainly not clearly understood by Mark) with the cult of twins. This reading would seem to indicate the possibility that the disciples were called in pairs.

Possibly some enlightenment is to be found in the fact that the title was in Hellenistic times associated with the cult of twins. This is interesting in that Matthew's version links all brothers in pairs in this list. If then, with the four Western manuscripts which give the title to all the Twelve, we could be certain that Jesus called them in pairs, we could even associate the name with pairs. But in the absence of any such knowledge, we can only conclude that Mark found a complicated word and made of it what sense he could.

18. As in Acts 1:13, *Andrew* is mentioned after *James* and *John.* (Andrew is a Greek name, but this must not be taken to indicate that he or any of the others was a Greek.) In Matthew and Luke, Andrew is named immediately after Peter, and if the "pairing" procedure was followed, this is where we would expect it. But this Markan order occurs also in 13:3 and is based on the desire to emphasize the priority given to the three principal members of the Twelve—Peter, James, and John (cf. 5:37, 9:2, 14:33).

Philip: This name is also in Greek. Apart from fairly frequent references to him in John, Philip is mentioned only in the lists of the Twelve in the synoptic gospels and Acts. He is often confused in the early Christian tradition with another Philip (Acts 6:5, 8:5-40, and "the evangelist" of 21:8).

Bartholomew: The name is Aramaic *Bar-Tolmai.* The name *Tolmai* is attested in South Arabic and Nabataean as the normal transcription for Greek *Ptolemaios.* Hence Bartholomew's father was Ptolemy. Bartholomew is sometimes identified with Nathaniel (John 1:45), but this is purely conjectural.

Matthew is an abbreviated form of Mattathias (cf. 1 Chron 15:21, 1 Macc 2:1) and derived from a Hebrew word *(mattān,* from the root *ntn)* meaning "gift." Matt 10:3 adds the word "tax-collector," so identifying him with "Levi," and in some manuscripts of Mark the word has been added by assimilation. It is not proposed to argue at length here the point that Levi was early in the tradition regarded as a proper name, whereas (given the cavalier treatment of the definite article in New Testament Greek) it should properly have been read as *ho levitēs* (the Levite), thus identifying one of the Twelve as "Matthew the Levite." (Cf. Albright-Mann, AB *Matthew*, Introduction, p. clxxix.)

Thomas (cf. Matt 10:3; Luke 6:15; John 11:16; 14:5; 20:24,26f.,28; 21:2; Acts 1:13): The name in Aramaic *(tōmā)* signifies twin. The name is not Greek. The apocryphal *Acts of Thomas* speaks of him as "Judas Thomas," while John 14:22 carefully distinguishes "Judas, not Iscariot."

James, the son of Alphaeus: This name is mentioned only here in Mark. Cf. also Matt 10:3, Luke 6:15, Acts 1:13. Sometimes identified with James the Less (cf. 15:40) or even with Levi (cf. 2:14), he may be the brother of Matthew the Levite. Some commentators identify him with Klopas (cf. John 19:25) or with Kleopas (Luke 24:18). Alphaeus is the Greek form of Aramaic *Ḥalfai* (shortened from a common rabbinic form *Ḥalafta).*

Thaddaeus (Aramaic *Taddai):* On the basis of some satisfactory Aramaic etymologies, it could be a place name. We know nothing of this disciple, and the obscurity is compounded by the fact that some manuscripts substitute *Lebbaeus.* Matthew (10:3) attempts to preserve both traditions by writing, "Thaddaeus (called Lebbaeus)." Both names are typical Aramaic shortened forms (hypocoristica). In Luke's list (6:16) Lebbaeus/Thaddaeus is replaced by Judas/Jude. There is no good reason that the list of "the Twelve" should always have been confined to the same persons (until after the defection of Judas).

Simon the member of the Zealot party: For all the discussion on the relative merits of the variant manuscript readings *(kananaios* [Canaanite] and *kannaios* or *kanaios* [Zealot]), the solution lies in the transmission of the Hebrew/Aramaic. In normal transcription the Hebrew *qof* was always *k* and the aspirated *kaph* always *chi.* The reading therefore is *qannāyā*, "Zealot," which is the appellation in Luke. The introduction of an additional *a* is simply explained: two *n*'s between two *a*'s could very easily produce an extra *a.* If this passage were being dictated, *kananaios* and *Chananaios* would soon be hopelessly confused. "Canaanite" seems to the present writer a very weak candidate for any description of a disciple of Jesus. It is far more likely that more than one Zealot would have been attracted by the teachings of Jesus, and that one of them would have been identified in this list. Luke 6:15 reads *Simōn ton kalonaienon Zēlōten,* presumably to put the matter beyond doubt (cf. Acts 1:13, *Simōn ho Zēlōtēs).* The Zealots as an organized party belonged to a somewhat later time and were particularly active in leading roles in the first Jewish War (70 A.D.). But they were preceded by many groups, especially in Galilee (including left-wing Pharisees), with strong nationalist passions. The term "zealot" would appropriately have been applied to such people before any formally organized party came into being.

19. *Judas Iscariot:* Mark leaves the word *Iskariōth* (14:10, cf. Luke 6:16) or *Iskariōtēs* (14:43, Matt 10:4, 26:14, Luke 22:3, John 6:71, 12:4, 13:2,26, 14:22) unexplained. Various attempts have been made to explain the term ("man from Keriotes," "assassin"—from the Latin *sicarius,* "knife"), but few carry anything like conviction. *Judas* alone is useless as an identification, as would be any name used without a patronymic

in a Muslim country. The best explanation is that of Harald Ingholt, from the near unanimity in later iconography depicting Judas as red-haired. His technical discussion and conclusions can be found in "The Surname of Judas Iscariot," *Studia Orientalia Johanni Pedersen,* edited by Einar Munksgaard, Hannie, 1953, pp. 152ff. On the basis of Palmyrene inscriptions he demonstrates that Iscariot cannot have been a geographical appellation and suggests that the word derives from the Hebrew-Aramaic *sqr,* which varies in meaning from "reddish-brown" to "ruddy." What we have, therefore, is a nickname.

17. Jesus and Beelzebul
(3:20-30) = Matt 12:22-32; Luke 11:14-23; 12:10

3 20 He went into the house: once more, such a crowd of people collected that they were unable to eat. 21 On hearing of this, his family set out to take charge of him, for people were saying that he was out of his mind. 22 But some scribes who had come from Jerusalem said, "He is possessed by Beelzebul," and "He casts out demons by the prince of demons." 23 So he called them to himself and spoke to them in parables: "How can Satan drive out Satan? 24 If a kingdom is divided against itself, then that kingdom cannot stand. 25 And if a house is divided against itself, then that house cannot stand. 26 If therefore Satan is in rebellion against himself, he is divided and cannot stand— that is the end of his power. 27 But no one can break into a strong man's house and take away his belongings until he first ties up the strong man; only then can he plunder his house. 28 Truly, I tell you that all things can be forgiven to men—their sins and the blasphemies they use; 29 however, anyone who blasphemes against the holy Spirit can never be forgiven but is guilty of an eternal sin." 30 He said this because they were saying, "He has an unclean spirit."

Comment

The vividness of the Markan narrative, adding what would appear to be eyewitness detail to the stylized pericopae of Matthew and Luke, provides us with an insight into the controversial ministry of Jesus as seen through the eyes of members of his family. It is possible that this account of the family's hostility has been added in this context by the evangelist, but this does not for a moment suggest that it was a free composition of the author and still less of the early community.

Notes

20. There are few devices used by this evangelist in contrast with Matthew's narrative of the ministry, and *crowd* and the *house* are two of them. There are no parallels in Matthew and Luke to 20-21.

21. We have translated the Greek *hoi par autou* by *his family*. The Greek phrase covers all manner of meanings, from "envoys" and "adherents" to "neighbors and family." The sense is correctly conveyed by the Vulgate *sui* (his own). The reference is to immediate family, and not to disciples, still less to critics. Two concerns are at stake in this confrontation with Jesus: first, a concern (and the lesson) that Jesus was not taking sufficient physical care of himself, and secondly a total lack of sympathy for the fashion of Jesus' ministry. The phrases about Jesus' family are strong and definite: they set out to *take charge (kratēsai)*—a verb used several times in chapters 6 and 14 with the meaning "to arrest." Furthermore the expression *people were saying* in its Greek form *(elegon)* could equally well include members of his family.

out of his mind (Greek *exestē):* Paul uses the same verb in 2 Cor 5:13, speaking of himself in contrast to his correspondents, and it is used of Paul by Festus (Acts 26:24).

We must not rule out the possibility of fear on the part of Jesus' family that his activities would draw unfavorable attention to them on the part of Roman authority. (Cf. Richard J. Cassidy, *Jesus, Politics, and Society,* Maryknoll, N.Y.: Orbis Books, 1978.)

A suggestion was made by H. Wansborough ("Mark 3:21—Was Jesus Out of His Mind?" *NTS* 18.2.72, pp. 233-35) that the proper subject of *exestē* was the crowd, and not Jesus, so that the verse would in his view read, "When they heard it, his followers went out to calm it down, for they said it was out of control with enthusiasm." The author points to Mark's often careless use of *autos,* which Wansborough wishes to refer to the crowd and not to Jesus. This suggestion is supported by D. Wenham in "The Meaning of Mark 3:21," *NTS,* 21.2.75, pp. 295-300. Wenham further suggests that Matt 12:23-24 and Luke 11:14-15 support the idea of the crowd's being out of its mind. The suggestion is interesting, for if true it has Mark drawing on a separate tradition (as we suggested in the comment above) and at the same time attaching it to the traditions before him. But the verb *kratēsai* has far stronger implications than "calm," as we have seen. Moreover Matt 12:23 certainly indicates astonishment on the part of the crowd, but hardly uncontrolled enthusiasm, while the Greek *hoi par autou,* in conjunction with the verb *exēlthon* (set out) hardly suggests followers who were with him—rather, those who had heard from some distance of what was happening.

We must hazard some suggestion as to what the critics—and Jesus' family—had heard and were saying. It is, to begin with, almost impossible to catch from the somewhat leisured English of many of our translations the air of driving urgency which informed the ministry and mission of Jesus. Even the phrase "the Reign of

God" has over the centuries been debased by one kind of identification or another, from domination by the ecclesiastical authority on the one hand to some of the simplicities associated with the "social gospel" on the other. It is perhaps not too much to suggest that Jesus would not feel too comfortable with the bland inoffensiveness of much that passes for Christian worship and instruction. It is at the least possible that Jesus would have more sympathy with the enthusiasm of some forms of "charismatic renewal" in our own time. At all events, in this context it is worth giving some attention to the suggestions in J. D. G. Dunn *(Jesus and the Spirit,* Philadelphia: Westminster Press, 1975). We have lost—in part thanks to the measured prose of some translations of the New Testament—the dramatic urgency of the Proclamation of the Reign of God by Jesus, the excitement of religious fervor which our New Testament sources demonstrate as having been engendered by the very presence of Jesus. From our perspective, "enthusiasm" is all too often suspect, even allowing for the undoubted excesses and condescension of so many charismatics among us. We should bear in mind additionally the testimony of John 7:5 that "his brothers did not believe in him."

22. We can infer from various parts of the narrative that there was a firmly grounded tradition in the oral period of transmission of the charge that Jesus was in league with demonic powers. In this pericope, vv. 28-30 appears to belong to a different strand of the tradition from vv. 22-23, but both have coalesced in this gospel around the opening vv. 20-21. Matthew and Luke attach the tradition to the casting out of a demon from a dumb man, an attachment commonly assigned to Q in the two-document hypothesis. Mark prefers a straightforward account of the charge and does not allow his narrative to be distracted by the sayings tradition recorded in Matt 12:27 or Luke 11:17.

scribes . . . from Jerusalem: Presumably the ministry of exorcism in Galilee had attracted the attention of authorities in Jerusalem, who sent a semiofficial investigating team from the Sanhedrin. Provision for such investigation can be found in *M Sanh* 10.4 (cf. also Acts 5:27-40). Matthew speaks of "the Pharisees," where Luke mentions "some of them" as though they were bystanders in the crowd.

Mark has omitted the story of the dumb demoniac, which in Matthew (12:22ff. = Luke 11:14) preceded the charge of an alliance with Beelzebul. The charges were distinct and were constantly being made—*said* (Greek *elegon)* is an imperfect tense. The first charge was of alliance with Beelzebul (cf. 3:30) and the second that Jesus' exorcisms were performed by the power of Satan, here called *the prince of demons.* Interestingly Matthew and Luke in combining the charges identify Satan with Beelzebul. The identification may also be present in Matt 12:27 (= Luke 11:19). It should be added that Jewish literature nowhere identifies Satan with Beelzebul, although other names (Mastema, Sammael, Asmodaeus) are applied to him.

Beelzebul: The confusion in the Greek text is reflected in modern English translations. Continued decipherment of Ugaritic texts makes it clear that Beelzebul is the original Canaanite form and is to be preferred to the "Beelzebub" of the Hebrew Bible (2 Kgs 1:2). The name means "Baal the Prince." This was the title of the god of Ekron (2 Kgs 1:2ff.), but in the Canaanite epic he was *Zubulu* (Prince, Lord of the Earth). In later Jewish demonology he became chief of the demons.

23. *So he called them:* This is an editorial device of the evangelist as preface to some succeeding material (cf. 3:13).

parables: The material in vv. 23-25 more than adequately illustrates the meaning we have given to the word (cf. Introduction, "Parables," pp. 145-53). What is presented here is a "case" demanding an answer and response, even though the saying is presented almost in hyperbolic terms.

Satan: There is no question that Jesus accepted the views of all his contemporaries that evil was personified and hypostasized in individual spirits, of whom the chief was Satan. Similarly he accepted the possibility of demoniacal possession. The development of "Satan" in biblical literature is interesting, as demonstrating the way in which evil is treated. The Hebrew figure of the *śāṭān* appears in the prologue of Job as a member of the heavenly court, as a kind of legal prosecutor. This material may be as early as the seventh century B.C. and is certainly no later than the fifth century. Ps 109:6 (pre-exilic) depicts the *śāṭān* as a prosecutor. A slight change of emphasis comes in Zech 3:1-2 and represents a development in which the prosecutor can easily be a malign figure. (It must be remembered that the parallels are innumerable, and when the state is unpopular, the prosecutor can easily be seen as actively hostile. In the time of Persian domination this would certainly appear to be the case to a Jewish writer.)

The intertestamental writings, under the influence of Iranian dualism, contrast a dominion of God and a beneficent providence with a dominion of evil, and from this emerges in *Jubilees* the *mastema* as an active opponent of good. In addition, the *śāṭān* in that literature is wholly evil, and no longer a member of the heavenly court. In what fashion the *śāṭān* became "the devil" in Greek *(diabolos)* we cannot precisely say. But in the New Testament the *diabolos* figure is head of the dominion of evil, bent on the destruction of humanity by temptation. The Greek *diabolē* is "a calumny" and *diabolos* "an accuser"; the Septuagint uses the word *diabolē* mainly in the sense of "calumny," though occasionally as the equivalent of "enmity." The Septuagint does use *diabolos* for *śāṭān,* but rather in the sense of "opponent." Josephus never uses *diabolos* or any other word for Satan. Care must be taken to distinguish *diabolos* from *daimōn* (demon), which can be either good or bad, or even neutral.

Essene theology was developed in dependence on Zoroastrianism in some form, and in the Essene system we have a complete dualism which (though ultimately under God's dominion) still placed the "good Spirit" and the "evil Spirit" in total opposition to each other.

In its present form v. 23 is peculiar to Mark but is not materially different in sense from Matt 12:26 ("If, therefore, Satan exorcises Satan, he is thereby divided against himself"). If Mark has no parallel here to the statements in Matt 12:25 and Luke 11:17 (that Jesus knew the thoughts of his opponents), he has nevertheless implied as much in 2:8. The general notion of a Satan divided is illustrated by two hypothetical cases, each cast in a conditional clause. Both Matthew and Luke agree in using *erēmoutai* ("falls into ruin," Matt 12:25 = Luke 11:17) against Mark's *ou dounatai stathēnai* (cannot stand)—an indication that Mark had his own sources in addition to Matthew and Luke.

24. Two parallel situations are used to illustrate the absurdity of thinking that Satan can be at enmity with himself: the divided kingdom and the divided house, followed in v. 26 by the circumstances presupposed in this verse being fulfilled. Mark's

against itself (vv. 24,25,26) is found in Luke 11:17, but Matt 12:25 has a different Greek idiom with the same meaning. Matt 12:25 and Luke 11:17 have *erēmoutai* (is laid waste) in place of Mark's *cannot stand,* and in Luke's version the fall of the house is part of the fall of the kingdom. Matthew and Mark preserve a Semitic parallelism which Luke discards.

26. The argument reaches final form in this verse. In spite of the Griesbach hypothesis, it does not seem possible to make any firm judgment about dependence in this climax. Where Mark is *clearly* following the order of either Matthew or Luke, the verbal affinity between Mark and Matthew, or between Mark and Luke, is clear. When, however, he is dealing with texts in both Matthew and Luke which are verbally very similar, the evangelist is far freer in his adaptations. Both Matthew (12:26) and Luke (11:18) end with "how can his kingdom stand?" and Mark heightens the effect with *that is the end of his power.* The concluding sayings contained in Matthew and Luke ("and if I cast out demons by Beelzebul . . .") are omitted by Mark.

27. Once again, Mark freely adapts the two traditions before him, being far closer to the text of Matt 12:29ff. than the corresponding and more prolix Luke 11:21ff.

In our present texts the sayings about the strong man are historically situated and in all texts attached to the charge that Jesus is in league with demonic powers. But the whole tenor of the saying is strongly eschatological, and we may safely assume that in its original setting it referred to the end-time. But its presence here witnesses to the conviction of the evangelists that in the exorcisms of Jesus a frontal assault was made on the fortress of the strong man. Isa 49:24-25 appears to lie behind the description of Satan as the strong man—but if Satan is indeed *ho ischuros* (the strong man), then Jesus in his healings and exorcisms is *ho ischuroteros* (the strongest one).

belongings (Greek *ta skenē autou):* Some commentators see in this an identification of the possessed, but while the word is indeed used in 2 Cor 4:7 and 1 Thess 4:4 of the body, it seems best to preserve the primary meaning of the Greek.

ties up (Greek *dēsē):* Apocalyptic literature abounds in the idea of binding evil powers (cf. Isa 24:22ff.) or of casting Satan to the earth (cf. Rev 22:9). See further H. Kruse, "Das Reich Satans," *Bib* 58.1.1977, pp. 29-61.

28. *Truly* (Greek *Amēn):* The phrase which opens this saying is one of considerable solemnity, almost like an oath, and is found only in the sayings of Jesus (cf. 8:12; 9:1,41; 10:15,29; 11:23; 12:43; 13:30; 14:9,18,25,30). It is found thirty times in Matthew, six in Luke, and twenty-five in John (with a repeated *Amen).*

all things can be forgiven: There is a translation difficulty here. The word *panta* (all) can be used, by shifting the punctuation to qualify *sins,* whereas there is also the perfectly legitimate use, adopted here, of *panta* as the subject of *can be forgiven,* and *their sins and the blasphemies they use* as in apposition to *all.*

sins: No distinction is made in Mark between sinfulness in general (Greek *hamartia)* and *hamartēmata,* used here, meaning specific acts of sin.

Before examining the meaning of the text before us, it is well to look for a moment at the synoptic relationships here.

An examination of the relationship between the synoptic gospels at this point will illustrate the difficulty of attaching too definite a shape to the material commonly known as Q. At the same time it will indicate the relatively fixed state of the tradition from which the evangelists worked.

$$
\begin{array}{rcl}
\text{Matt } 12{:}22\text{-}23 & = & \text{Luke } 11{:}14 \\
24\text{-}26 & = \text{Mark } 3{:}22\text{-}26 = & \text{Luke } 11{:}15,17\text{-}18 \\
27\text{-}28 & = & \text{Luke } 11{:}19\text{-}20 \\
29 & = \text{Mark } 3{:}27 = & \text{Luke } 11{:}21\text{-}22 \\
30 & = & \text{Luke } 11{:}23 \\
31\text{-}32b & = \text{Mark } 3{:}28\text{-}30 & \\
43\text{-}45 & = & \text{Luke } 11{:}24\text{-}26
\end{array}
$$

Mark's 3:22-30 is omitted where one might have expected it in Luke (6:19 or 8:4), but as the table demonstrates, most of it is found later. Luke combines a request for a sign (which occurs later in Mark) with the accusation of alliance with demons. Luke's vv. 27-28 have no equivalent in Matthew, and Matthew's vv. 31-37 have no equivalent in Luke 11. Matthew's vv. 39-42 = Luke 11:29-32.

The parallels of Matthew and Luke are in verbal agreement in the Greek as compared to Mark, especially in Matthew's v. 25 (Luke's v. 17) and Matthew's v. 26 (Luke's v. 18). But even in their parallel to Mark 3:27, Matthew's tradition is far closer to Mark than to Luke. In Matthew there are two incidents, the first a reply to an accusation and the other Jesus' reaction to a demand for a sign; in Luke both are combined, but with interposed material at 11:27-28, without any parallel in Matthew.

The parallels cannot without grave difficulty be met by the presumption that Matthew and Luke both had access to Mark *and* to an independent source.

to men: The justification for the translation is given above *(all things . . .),* but attention must be paid to the Markan *tois huiois toū anthrōpou* (literally, "to the sons of men") where Matthew's text plainly demands the emphasis on a contrast between blasphemy against The Man, and blasphemy against the holy Spirit—the former capable of being forgiven and the latter not. Mark's text is a highly condensed version—Matthew's saying about blasphemy against The Man being forgivable is in the verse before us. All three gospels, however, share the problems of the succeeding verse.

29. *against the holy Spirit* (for "holy Spirit," cf. 1:8, 12:36, 13:11): The Greek of Matt 12:31 and Luke 12:10 is similar in meaning to the Markan text, though the vocabulary and structure are different.

In classical Greek *blasphēmeō* implies irreverence toward the gods and enmity against men, but monotheism in Judaism and Christianity invested the nominative *blasphēmia* with an increased sense of arrogant defiance of God. Such defiance could also be employed against God's spirit, against his name and his will, and all could by extension be counted blasphemous. The ministry of Jesus also results in an extension of the meaning of the term (cf. Acts 26:11 and probably also 15:29). The blasphemy under discussion here is that of attributing the positive good of works of healing to an evil agency.

can never be forgiven: (literally, "has no forgiveness to the ages of ages"). The *never* is emphatic, and Mark's phrase is an attempt to render Matthew's text even more emphatic. The following clause, with its mention of an *eternal sin,* is peculiar to Mark but merely repeats the warning of the preceding part of the sentence. The phrase is omitted by some manuscripts, but even without the phrase the sense is emphatic.

Commentators are rightly hesitant about interpreting this saying. Matthew's gospel appears to draw a distinction between blasphemy against The Man, as meaning the messianic ministry in *this* age, contrasted with blasphemy against the Spirit in the *coming* age. It must be confessed that this is hardly convincing. Possibly two conclusions may be drawn: First to attribute to the powers of evil what is manifestly the work of God in healing is indeed blasphemy against God in his act of salvation; second the saying may refer to "the Spirit" as meaning Jesus' earthly ministry, and not referring to any future activity. We are perhaps faced with the language of very strong hyperbole (cf. Num 15:30f., 1 Sam 3:14), but it must be said that this by no means clears up the difficulties inherent in the saying. See further R. Scroggs, "The Exaltation of the Spirit by Some Early Christians," *JBL* 84.1.1965, pp. 360-65; and M. Eugene Boring, "How May We Identify Oracles of Christian Prophets in the Synoptic Tradition?" *JBL* 91.4.1972, for the view that the saying in present form owes much to early Christian community attitudes toward those who were not believers. The monograph of E. Lövestam *(Spiritus Blasphemia: Eine Studie zu Markus 3.28f par Matthäus 12:31f, Lukas 12:10,* Scripta Minora Regiae Societatis Humaniorum Litterarum Lundensis, 1966-67, Lund: Gleerup, 1968) should be read in conjunction with the reviews of E. Bammel *(JTS* 22.1.1971, pp. 192-94) and F. Lentzen-Deis *(Bib* 51.4.1970, pp. 587-90). Reference should also be made to Taylor, p. 244, and to Lane, pp. 144-45.

30. *because they were saying:* The use of the imperfect tense underlines the serious character of the condemnation by Jesus in the preceding verses. To persist in attributing works of mercy to the instrumentality of Satan was to persist also in an obduracy of mind which—in its blind refusal to give glory to God—was blasphemy.

18. The Family of Jesus
(3:31-35) = Matt 12:46-50; Luke 8:19-21

3 ³¹ Then his mother and brothers arrived, and standing outside sent in a message asking for him. ³² A crowd was sitting around him, and they told him, "Your mother and brothers are outside asking for you." ³³ "Who is my mother?" he answered, "and who are my brothers?" ³⁴ Then, looking around at those sitting with him, he said, "See! Here are my mother and brothers. ³⁵ For whoever does the will of God is my brother, sister, and mother."

Comment

Originally a detached story in the oral tradition, this saying of Jesus that his
family consists of those who do the will of God seems to have found place
here by attraction to vv. 21ff. and is in its present place a sequel to the earlier
story. All unnecessary elements have been stripped away to concentrate on
the single saying. Comparison with a wholly different narrative (Luke 11:27f.)
seems to underline the possibility that on several occasions Jesus expressed
ideas about true kinship as distinct from physical parentage or relationship.

Notes

31. *mother and brothers:* Mary appears here only in Mark. It has generally been
assumed that the lack of reference to Joseph implies that he was dead. We must give
some passing notice here to the questions raised by *and brothers.* Three main positions
have been traditionally espoused:

1. The brothers were blood brothers, a view generally termed Helvidian, after
   Helvidius (c. 380), who first propounded it.

2. Epiphanius (c. 382) gave his name to the Epiphanian view—that the brothers
   so mentioned were sons of Joseph by a former marriage.

3. The Hieronymian view (from Jerome, c. 383) was that the brothers were in
   fact cousins, being sons of Mary the wife of Clopas, sister to Mary the mother
   of Jesus. This he based on the assertion that *adelphos* could be used in Greek
   to indicate a far wider relationship than that of blood kinship. This was certainly true, but the Greek *anemsios* (cousin) was the regular word, and
   adelphos would hardly have been substituted for it. Moreover, not only are the
   brothers of 3:31-35 not members of the Twelve, they are in active opposition
   to Jesus (cf. Mark 3:21, John 7:5). In addition they are never associated in our
   texts with Mary the wife of Clopas. Indeed in John 19:25 four women are
   mentioned, and we have no reason to think that Mary of Clopas was sister to
   Jesus' mother.

   The first two views claim some antiquity, and the Epiphanian hypothesis goes back
to the second century. The Epiphanian hypothesis has some doctrinal implications, in
that it safeguards belief in the perpetual virginity of Mary.

   asking for him: The request to speak to Jesus is connected with the earlier report
that Jesus was beside himself, but Mark allows the unit of narrative to stand by itself,
not connecting it (as does Matthew) with the preceding narrative. Luke's explanatory
note (8:19) is superfluous to Mark's purpose. (Some manuscripts add "and his sisters,"

but this is probably an assimilation to Matt 12:47 and Luke 8:20. See Lane, p. 146, n. 103.)

32. *a crowd:* The crowd is not identified as hostile, and—judging from v. 34— probably included some disciples.

33. *he answered* (Greek *apokritheis legei):* The Greek here, with its variant *apokritheis eipen,* is common in the synoptists (Mark has fifteen examples), but John prefers *apekrithē kai eipen.* The use reflects the Septuagint and Aramaic. Occasionally the classical aorist middle voice *apekrinato* is found (Mark has one example at 14:61). It has been suggested that *apekrithē* belongs rightly to early Hellenism—it is not found in the papyri after the end of the first century B.C.—and passed from Septuagintal use into the New Testament.

"Who is my mother . . . brothers?": The narrative was remembered because of this question. It is impossible to evade the sense of regretful disappointment in the question, and a sense also of rejection (in some measure) on the part of the family. To inject into a consideration of the text questions as to how far this question and the disappointment of Jesus can be accommodated to the tradition of the virgin birth is— for the Markan text—an irrelevance. It can be asked far more cogently in the Matthean and Lucan contexts.

34. *looking around* (Greek *periblepomai):* Used in Mark of a searching look (cf. 3:5). *Those sitting with him* may be taken to mean disciples, a larger group than the Twelve, and distinct from those standing on the fringes or in the crowd outside.

35. *whoever does . . . . :* Matthew has "the will of my Father in heaven" (12:50), while Luke has "the word of God" (8:21). The saying exemplifies the radical demand of Jesus upon those who are called to discipleship in his ministry, and family and kinship are set in a new framework, in which the bonds of fellowship in a common obedience to God are placed above the bonds of kinship. There is a further dimension to the saying: the fellowship of those committed to Jesus in the Proclamation of the Reign of God would constitute a family, a social group with all the inherent qualities hitherto associated with the human family.

PART III
JESUS AND THE COMMUNITY (4:1-8:26)

19. Parables (i) The Sower
(4:1-9) = Matt 13:1-9; Luke 8:4-8

4 ^{1} On another occasion, Jesus began to teach by the lakeside. The crowd that gathered round him was so large that he went into a boat on the lake. There he sat, with the whole crowd on the shore down to the water's edge. ^{2} And he taught them many things by parables. In his teaching, he said to them, ^{3} "Listen! A sower went to sow. ^{4} It happened that as he sowed some seed fell on the path and the birds came and ate it up. ^{5} Some fell on rocky ground where there was little soil, and it sprouted quickly—for there was little depth of earth. ^{6} But when the sun came up, the young wheat was scorched, and as it had no root it withered away. ^{7} Some of the seed fell among thistles, which grew up and choked the wheat and it did not bear grain. ^{8} But some of the seed fell on good ground, where it came up and grew and produced grain—and the yield was thirtyfold, sixtyfold, and even a hundredfold." ^{9} And he said, "If you have ears that are good for listening, then listen!"

Comment

The reader is referred to the section on parables in the Introduction (pp. 145-53). The aim of this collection in Mark is to explain, elicit reactions, elucidate by means of comparison with everyday things the spiritual and moral truths associated with the Reign of God. Some examples (cf. 2:21) are simple similes, while others are parables—in the sense of "cases"—and yet others are illustrative material.

We cannot assume that we always know the first application of an individual parable, and though explanations are occasionally provided by Jesus we cannot be sure that these are not in some instances the work of either the evangelist or the community (cf. Matt 13:49).

Some distinction must be made between parable and allegory: in general, a parable has but one main point in emphasis, whereas in allegory *all* the details are important as enshrining some important message. But too hard and fast a distinction between the two types of literary form ought not to be pressed to the exclusion of *immediate* reference to Jesus in his ministry (e.g., the parable of the sower).

The parable before us—the sower—is full of characteristic Markan turns of phrase, and is not dependent on Matthew. Turner (p. 250) argues that the tradition has been recorded "with great fidelity." The interpretation of the parable is as varied as the number of commentators. Four main interpretations may be noted:

1. The eschatological hypothesis, espoused by some, emphasizes the point at the end about the fullness of the harvest. The disadvantage of this interpretation is that at no point is any correlation made with the dawning Reign of God.

2. Some commentators find in this parable a theme of encouragement to the disciples, or as emphasizing the responsibilities of hearers of the word.

3. Others find here a picture of the experiences of Jesus himself as herald of the Kingdom. Certainly this may be so, but on the face of it the parable seems a very elliptical way in which to present the picture.

It is probably safe to assume that the Reign of God is in mind here, but—with some reference to item 3 above—it would seem that the parable reflects the immediate context of the Galilean ministry. Responsive listening is desperately important, but in spite of hostility, in spite of a seeming lack of response, the fields are already showing promise of an abundant harvest.

Notes

1. The opening passage is editorial, but to pick up the narrative from 3:7-12 Mark uses his own distinctive vocabulary to adapt the Matthean piece: *palin* (on another occasion), *ērxato* (began), *didaskō* (teach). There is no statement of time. The description of an increasingly large number of people is probably based on eyewitness oral tradition. There appears to have been a rising circle of people on the shore (cf. Matt 13:2). Luke's reconstruction of the scene is grammatically very different from those of Matthew and Mark.

3. The injunction *Listen!* is peculiar to Mark's account. Cf. 7:14. This injunction,

combined with v. 9, underlines the fact that parables were not expositions of the obvious but were meant to stimulate thought and response.

4. *on the path* (Greek *para tēn hodon*): The Revised Standard Version has "along" the path, which is plainly incorrect. The seed fell on the well-trodden path used by the sower walking through the fields.

5. In parts of Galilee the soil is occasionally thin, with rock not far below the surface. *Where there was little soil* is omitted in some manuscripts. Mark's text is very close to Matthew's here.

6. *the sun came up:* This is not a reference to sunrise, but to the heat of the sun high in the heavens at midday. (Cf. Jas 1:11.)

scorched: The Greek *(ekaumatisthē)* is late and is not found in the Septuagint. Luke's text omits any reference to scorching.

7. *thistles* (Greek *akantha*): In classical Greek the word is used of any thorn, including thistles. Horticulturally the picture seems to be that of a landowner who, instead of uprooting the thorns, simply cut them back, resulting in a stronger growth later.

choked (Greek *sunpnigō*): This is a strong expression, more like "throttle." Matthew and Luke have the more common *apopnigō,* though both use the verb *sunpnigō* in the interpretation (Matt 13:22, Luke 8:14).

did not bear grain (Greek *karpon ouk edōken*): The expression is from the Septuagint (cf. Lev 26:20, Ps 1:3). The more common *poiein karpon* (to produce fruit) is found in Luke 3:8.

8. By way of comparison the *some* (Greek *alla*) of this verse is plural, as though speaking of individual seeds, whereas in vv. 5 and 7 the singular *allo* is used, but some manuscripts assimilate the plural to the earlier singular. In spite of considerable loss, there is promise of an abundant harvest.

9. In somewhat differing forms, the saying of Jesus appears often in our sources. Cf. 4:23; 7:16; Matt 11:15; 13:9,43; Luke 8:8; 14:35, and even more frequently in Rev 2:7,11,17,29; 3:6,13,22; 13:9. The fact that this saying is attached to the "harvest" theme *may* indicate that the harvest is the principal emphasis of the parable.

20. Parables (ii) The Purpose of Parables
(4:10-12) = Matt 13:10-17; Luke 8:9-10

4 ^{10}]When he was alone, the Twelve and others who were around him questioned him about the parables. ^{11}]He replied, "To you has been given the secret of the Reign of God, but to those on the outside everything comes through parables, ^{12}]so that

They may go on looking, but they do not see, and go on hearing, but they do not understand; otherwise, they would turn to God and he would forgive them."

Comment

It is hard to resist the conclusion that what is before us is a community composition. The three synoptists may have received vv. 11 and 12 as an isolated saying and prefaced it by an introduction. Furthermore, if the saying referred in general to the teaching ministry of Jesus, it has been changed both by context and introduction into a generalized statement about all parables. There is perhaps an additional indication of composition in the awkwardly added phrase *the Twelve and others.*

Notes

10. *alone* (Greek *kata monas*): A classical adverb, it is found in the New Testament only here and in Luke 9:18.

parables: Originally this may have been "the parable," later amended to the plural for reasons given in the Comment above. Cf. Matt 13:10, ". . . why you speak to them in parables . . ."; and Luke 8:9, ". . . what this parable meant."

11. *secret* (Greek *mustērion*): This word is not easily rendered into English, for all its known classical and Septuagintal background. The idea of a kingdom, a Reign of God, was not only wholly familiar to Jesus' hearers—with or without messianic overtones—but it was also eagerly awaited and prayed for by Jews. What was granted to the disciples, through their obedient listening, was access to the inmost secrets of God's providence, in much the same way that the prophets had claimed access to God's council *(sôd).* This meaning of *mustērion* has been placed beyond doubt by the work of Raymond E. Brown, based in large part on the DSS. (Cf. Brown's *The Semitic Background of the Word "Mystery" in the New Testament,* Philadelphia: Fortress Press, 1968.) Those who are close to Jesus are a privileged community, seeing the Reign of God as already dawning. Mark's *to those on the outside* is considerably more harsh than the Matthean and Lucan versions.

12. Combined with v. 11, this quotation from Isaiah can be made to appear as though there was a deliberate hiding of the truth. The reader is referred to the section on parables in the Introduction, especially p. 147, where the passage from Isaiah is more fully discussed.

The difficulties in this passage are complicated by *ta panta ginetai* in v. 11, which we have translated as *everything comes* (literally, "all things happen"), which certainly does not sound like a description of teaching. Some manuscript copyists found the Greek so difficult that *ginetai* was changed to *legetai* ("are told," or "is told"), and some others omit the definite article *ta.*

The quotation from Isaiah (based on 6:9-10) is cast in the form of a command but at the same time indicates the result of Isaiah's teaching. Situated in this context, it reads as though it is Jesus' purpose deliberately to obscure the meaning of his teaching. This interpretation, however, overlooks two important considerations:

1. The context in which the Isaian passage is set (in its own text) is concerned with the faithlessness of Israel to her Lord, and the vocation of the prophet to speak and preach to a faithless people. Jesus' teaching had already met with hostility, and the appearance of the Isaian text is to that extent understandable at this point.

2. "The use of a *command* to express a result is typically Semitic" (Taylor, p. 218).

But the second consideration in no way mitigates the difficulties. Some textual notes are in order before proceeding further.

a. Mark's Greek text of the quotation departs from the Septuagint and from the Hebrew in reading *and he would forgive them*—which reading is, however, found in the Targum.

b. The forms *go on looking . . . do not see* (Greek *blepontes . . . blepōsi)* and *go on hearing . . . do not understand (akountes . . . akouōsi)* are Semitisms which in the New Testament are represented only in quotations from the Septuagint. By this means the compilers of the Septuagint strove in Greek to reproduce a Hebrew idiom of emphasis. The negatives *mē eidon* (not see) and *mē suniōsin* (not understand) are far better understood in the Greek: *blepō* is a glance without paying attention, and *akouō* is hearing as distinct from listening.

c. The final clause *mē pote,* rendered here by *otherwise,* is the crux of the problem, and we have followed Manson (p. 78f.) in taking the clause to mean "For if they did, they would repent and be forgiven." But as the clause stands in Mark, it is conditioned by *so that (hina)* at the beginning of the verse, so that in effect we have *lest by any chance* they would turn to God. The sense of this is not only at variance with the text of Matthew and Luke, it has long been severely questioned as unacceptable as describing the ministry of Jesus. Matt 13:13 has *hoti* in place of *hina,* providing a meaning that parables are used because the listeners are dull of understanding. Matthew then introduces the quotation from Isaiah but uses the Septuagint text "and I would heal them."

The fact that commentators for many years have found this Markan reading unacceptable is hardly surprising. The various arguments can be summarized as follows:

1. On the two-document hypothesis, Matthew changed the text of Mark to eliminate an improbable harshness of judgment by Jesus;

2. *hina* is used as an imperative, "let them . . .";

3. *hina* renders incorrectly an Aramaic particle which ought to have been translated as *hoi* (who).

No suggestion adequately mitigates the force of the Markan saying. All that can be safely said is that Mark does distinguish teaching to the disciples—though they are charged with blindness later (6:52, 8:17)—from helping the crowds through the obscurity of the parables. Perhaps Mark's gospel represents a later understanding of parables than Matthew's, from a time when lines of hostility between the messianic community and Jerusalem Judaism were being more and more clearly drawn. Certainly Mark would here appear to share the Pauline conviction of the hardening of Israel's heart (Rom 9-11). But while all of this may be so, the fact that this saying is attached to a parable is disturbing. The presentation of "cases" by Jesus to stimulate thought and response is characteristic of Matthew, but it is hard to reconcile the Markan use of his sources in repeating that Jesus taught many things in parables to a pressing and enthusiastic crowd with a later assertion that Jesus did this precisely to confuse and condemn his listeners.

We offer two final suggestions. It is possible, first, that Mark may have been misled by *parable* and understood it as meaning "in riddles." Secondly, the saying may originally have had nothing to do with parables at all but may have been attracted to this context by the use of *parables* in v. 11. In this case we have to conjecture a reflection by Jesus after the failure of the mission in some northern towns (cf. Matt 11:20-24, Luke 10:13-15). The inner circle could be taught openly, but the outsiders found everything he said an enigma.

It is difficult to imagine that Mark's use of the Matthean and Lucan versions is simply invention. But on either the Griesbach or the two-document hypothesis, Mark 4:11 is a *crux interpretum*.

21. Parables (iii) The Parable of the Sower Explained (4:13-25) = Matt 13:18-23; Luke 8:11-15

4   13 Then he said to them, "You do not understand this parable? But how then will you understand any parable? 14 The sower sows the word. 15 Those on the path are those in whom the Word is sown, and as soon as they hear the message Satan comes along and takes away the word sown in them. 16 Then there are those in whom the message is sown on rocky ground. As soon as they hear the message they immediately receive it with enthusiasm. 17 But it strikes no root in them, for they have no stability. When there is trouble or persecution because of the word they give up at once. 18 And there are those who receive the word among thistles. These hear the word, 19 but the anxieties of this life, and the deceptive attraction of riches, and all other kinds of desire, choke the word and it will not yield anything. 20 But there are those who receive the seed on good ground: they hear the word and accept it, and they bear fruit—thirtyfold, sixtyfold, and a

hundredfold." [21] He went on: "Does anyone bring in the lamp and put it under a measuring bowl, or under the bed, and not on a lamp stand? [22] For nothing is hidden, except to be disclosed, and nothing is covered except to come to light. [23] If you have ears, then listen!" [24] He also said to them, "Take notice of what you hear. The measure you use in judgment will be the same measure which judges you—and with something more besides. [25] For the man who has will be given more, and the man who has nothing will lose even what he has."

Comment

It is not easily possible to regard this section as being anything other than a community interpretation of the parable, representing the kind of explanation being given of parables after the ministry of Jesus had ended and the community was already in being. We have seen some reason to think that the primary emphasis of the parable of the sower was concerned with an impending abundant harvest in spite of adversity. In this explanation the emphasis has shifted from the harvest and the word to the spiritual state of those to whom the word comes. There are other indications of the secondary character of this tradition: Matthew's text has the significant wording (13:18) "Listen to the parable of the sower." Though Mark omits this incorrect phrase (the parable has little to do with the sower), his text equally misrepresents the initial meaning. Secondly, we have few recorded examples of Jesus explaining his "cases." Thirdly, in Matthew (and implicitly also in Mark) the explanation is given to those who have been told that they are privy to the prior decisions of God. Luke 8:9-10 simply states that Jesus explained the parables, while the Markan tradition has Jesus wondering at his hearers' obduracy. It was suggested in the AB *Matthew* commentary (p. 168) that the explanation arose from uncertainty about the precise meaning of the "coming" of The Man. Finally, the text before us contains words which are found only in the epistles. However, it is an *early* explanation, for the sower is not identified, and no attempt is made—as in later traditions—to allegorize the threefold level of the harvest.

Notes

13. *understand* . . . *understand* (Greek *oidate* . . . *gnōsesthe):* The distinction between the two words is not easily rendered into single words in English. The first verb is used of knowing by intuition, while the second carries the meaning of knowing from experience. Neither Matthew nor Luke has the preliminary question. If the

discussion in the previous section does issue in Mark's passing harsh judgment, then this preliminary sentence certainly blames the hearers.

14. Every point is now examined and commented upon. Taylor (p. 259) makes the suggestion that perhaps the phrases being examined should be in quotation marks.

15. *Those on the path* is the next phrase examined. The parable itself deals with different kinds of seed, whereas the explanations offered in this section are concerned with the varying kinds of soil. This is indication enough that this section is a community composition: the hearers are interested in the various types of people to whom the message comes and their varied and sometimes inexplicable responses. The translation attempts to do justice to the Greek: what is sown is of course the word, and the different kinds of soil are the varying types of people, but in the Greek it is the various types of people who are sown. The meaning is clear enough, but in this explanation as in the parallels there may be an indication that the same parable was used on more than one occasion.

Mark's conflation with the simple *Satan comes along* is a model of brevity compared with the emphasis in Matthew and Luke on "the heart."

message (cf. 1 Thess 2:13) may be simply "the teaching" or "the Christian message."

16-17. The evangelist now takes up the case of those sown on stony ground. The Lucan version is somewhat shorter, but Mark's version follows Matthew closely, though Matthew uses the singular throughout the explanation.

It is in v. 17 that we are made aware of the immediacy of the interpretation contained in this section: *thlipsis,* "trouble," is found four times in Matthew, twice in John, and five times in Acts (cf. Mark 8:19,24); *diōgmos,* "persecution," is found in Matt 13:21 and twice in 2 Timothy (cf. Mark 10:30).

give up at once (Greek *skandalizō):* Found many times in Matthew and Mark, the word is Hellenistic, derived from a bait stick in a trap. Generally translated as "stumble," the word could also suitably be translated "they are trapped"—i.e., because their faith is so insecurely founded. Luke's version mentions apostasy.

18. The change to the "sown among thorns" introduces a number of words in the following verse which belong in general to the epistles. The interpretation offered is allegorical, like all the details enumerated.

19. *anxieties* (Greek *merimna):* Cf. Matt 13:22, Luke 8:14, 21:34, 2 Cor 11:28, 1 Pet 5:7. The combining of the word with *of this life* emphasizes the kind of anxious care arising out of particular times and circumstances. In the Pauline reference, this sense of care and anxiety in the face of a troubled era is especially marked.

deceptive attraction (Greek *apatē):* Cf. Matt 13:22, Eph 4:22, Col 2:8, 2 Thess 2:10, Heb 3:13, 2 Pet 2:13. The word *riches* (Greek *ploutos)* is found far more frequently in the epistles than in the synoptic gospels, and the same holds true of *desire* (Greek *epithumia).* All in all the vocabulary appears to belong to a time of considerable stress and anxiety, when the first enthusiasm of converts was being tested severely. This probably belongs to a later period than the ministry of Jesus, but admirably suits the period immediately prior to the outbreak of the first Jewish war (A.D. 66).

20. The end of the explanation of the parable is an anticlimax. So intent are all three versions in the synoptic gospels on the failures and shortcomings of the previous

types that the triumph of the word in the fully converted is almost omitted. Certainly the harvest is left to explain itself.

The assorted sayings which follow the parable explanations are oddly placed. Two possibilities suggest themselves: either the evangelist derived them from some collection of sayings and placed them here (an odd and somewhat artificial place) or he was dependent on some framework already in existence. The framework which best accommodates these sayings in Mark is that of Matthew. An examination of the material omitted from his Matthean source, as not being germane to the purpose, brings the evangelist to Matt 13:24. This hypothesis will be examined in slightly more detail following v. 34.

21. Matt 5:15 agrees in substance with the saying in Mark, but describes the lamp as giving light to the house, while Luke 11:33 considers the lamp as being a welcoming sign to strangers. The saying is somewhat enigmatic, for making the point that the function of a lamp is to give light does not accord too well with the earlier text (4:12), which suggested that in some fashion the revelation is deliberately hidden. Perhaps— in whatever circumstances this saying was first uttered—Mark felt that it belonged properly where he found it, since the hiding of revelation (v. 22) was not final.

lamp (Greek *luchnos):* The definite article suggests a familiar household object.

measuring bowl (Greek *modios):* The word is a derivative from the Latin *modius,* a dry measure containing nearly two imperial gallons and under which the extinguished lamp was placed at bedtime.

22. The word *for* suggests a connection with the previous saying. Mark's Greek is crude and bears all the signs of an original translator's version, whereas Luke 8:17 is smoother and far less awkward. There is further evidence that Mark may be drawing upon his own source at this point. Both Matthew and Luke have this saying in other contexts, but Mark's version seems to have been attracted to this small section of miscellaneous sayings from some collection already known to the evangelist. Furthermore the apparent meaning that the kingdom is not meant to be a mystery, hidden from sight, is not wholly consistent with the apparent sense of v. 11.

23. For this saying of Jesus, see the note on 4:9. There is no parallel in Matthew or Luke.

24. The expression *he also said* may indicate that vv. 24ff. were not joined to v. 21-22 in the independent sources to which Mark had access.

Take notice: In Greek the verb *(blepō)* has the sense of a casual glance and here has none of the careful gradations of the various "seeing" verbs so characteristic of John's gospel.

The significance of the Markan saying is very uncertain. From the context it would appear to mean "What attention you give to the teaching is also the measure of the profit you will derive from it" (cf. Swete, p. 83). The connection with *Take notice of what you hear* seems forced.

will be the same measure which judges you is peculiar to Mark. Matthew has a parallel in "Whoever has, to him will be given" (cf. 13:12, 25:29), and this Matthean expression is present in Mark 4:25; there appears to be fairly clear evidence of Markan conflation here.

25. Matt 13:12 and Luke 8:18 both have this saying, though Matthew has also the

phrase noted above, and Luke has "whoever" and "who seems to have." Matthew has a second version in 25:29 and Luke in 19:26.

Possibly the saying was a popular proverb—the rich man, from a position of power, may wield influence to increase his wealth, while the poor man is (to quote Rawlinson) "fleeced to his last farthing."

22. Parables (iv) The Growing Seed (4:26-29)

4 ²⁶ He said, "The Reign of God is like a man who scatters seed on the land. ²⁷ He goes to bed, and gets up, night and day, and the seed sprouts and grows—how, he does not know. ²⁸ The ground produces a crop by itself: first the slender stalk, then the ear, and then the grain in the ear; ²⁹ but as soon as the crop is ready, he begins working with the sickle because harvest time has arrived."

Comment

There is no true parallel to this Markan parable, though the Matthean parable of the weeds (Matt 13:24-30) has some six or seven words in common with this short section.

If, in general, the parables are taken as being concerned with the Reign of God, then it is from that viewpoint that the interpretation of vv. 26-29 must proceed. But commentators have differed widely on the precise parallel between the growing seed and the Reign of God. Four prominent interpretations can be distinguished: First, that the seed represents the divine gift to the individual believer and to the community: the gift of faith or of understanding. Second, the parable represents the slow, largely unseen, but ineluctable growth of the Reign of God among humanity. Third, the emphasis here—as in the parable of the sower—is eschatological, being concerned with the harvest of the end-time. Fourth, the "realized-eschatology" emphasis would stress the immediacy of the harvest theme and the kingdom proleptically present in the ministry of Jesus. The second interpretation is important historically, as being typical of the optimistic humanitarianism of the nineteenth century. But there are elements of truth in the other three interpretations. The frequency with which this parable is adduced as teaching the unseen and silent growth of the kingdom is alarming. The age of Jesus was innocent of any precise knowledge of plant biology, and it is far more likely that Jesus is comparing the Reign of God to the phenomenon of seed and harvest in terms of pure miracle. The fourth interpretation seems to fit the situation of the ministry particularly well: God's graciousness to his people has now come to the point where already the harvest time is near. There may also be some reference to the preaching of John in the initial reference to the sower.

Notes

26. *a man:* It is unnecessary to identify the sower with Jesus, since the term used is quite general.

27. *sprouts* (Greek *blasta*): The verb form is unusual, being (probably) a subjunctive from *blastaō*, in confusion between *ao* and *eo* verbs. The verse emphasizes, by means of the picture of a man going about his daily affairs, the mysterious process from seed to full growth.

28. The emphasis on the miraculous is continued in this verse, concentrating as it does on the power of God. There is also a note of the inexorable progress of growth toward the harvest.

29. The *de* (but) in the Greek marks the emphasis on the climax of the saying. The Greek *paradoi,* translated here by *is ready,* has the sense of "permit"—i.e., so soon as the condition of the crop permits, the reaper goes to work. The remainder of the verse is based on Joel 3:13 (cf. Rev 14:15), with strongly eschatological overtones. But the allusion to the text of Joel cannot be taken as a final determinant that the meaning of the parable as used by Jesus was similarly eschatological.

23. Parables (v) The Mustard Seed
(4:30-32) = Matt 13:31-32; Luke 13:18-19

4   [30] "How shall we describe the Reign of God?" he asked, "or by what parable shall we describe it? [31] It is like a mustard seed, which when it is sown is smallest of all the seeds on the earth, [32] yet when it is sown it grows and becomes taller than the other shrubs, with such large branches that birds can make nests in its shade."

Comment

Commentators agree that this parable belongs to the undeniably authentic stratum of Jesus' understanding of the Reign of God. We find here some similarities with the previous parable in the interpretations generally offered for it. The parable can be, and has been, variously understood as embodying ideas of growth, or silent, unseen development, or the inbreaking of the Reign of God in power, or the immediate context of the ministry of Jesus. The element of growth is certainly present, but it may be questioned whether this element is the main emphasis; we should be equally sceptical of an interpretation which places all the weight on a catastrophic irruption of the Reign of God into human affairs. Two considerations are offered in this commentary: first, the Reign of God has indeed arrived in the Proclamation and ministry of Jesus, and though it is apparently insignificant in its beginnings, there is no doubt as to its future growth; second, because the Reign is already present, people are already seeking its shelter and its promise. We cannot easily identify the Reign with the end product of growth (as we possibly could in the previous parable), for we can know nothing of a *future* growth. Jesus presents his hearers with a phenomenon already present, and they are invited to see its miraculous growth in and around everything which accompanies the ministry. An interpretation of universalism, or of the inclusion of Gentiles, must be regarded as doubtful.

Notes

30. Some attention will be paid after v. 34 to the problems of synoptic relationships posed here. Mark has the double question, as has Luke, but Matthew has a single question.

31. *seed* (Greek *kokkos*): Cf. Matt 13:31, 17:20, Luke 13:19, 17:6.

mustard (Greek *sinapi*): Though proverbially used in Palestine as an example of the smallest seed, it is not so in fact. The translation here is the best we can do with a Greek duplication—literally, "which when it is sown upon the earth is the smallest of all the seeds upon earth." Lohmeyer (p. 88) offers the suggestion that two parables, or two versions of the parable, have been telescoped. Textual variants in superior manuscripts of Mark make the confusion worse.

32. This verse provides a repetition of *when it is sown,* found in the preceding verse.

grows (Greek *anabaine*): The Greek verb is a strange one to describe growth, since literally it means to "go up" or "ascend."

shrubs (Greek *lachanōn*): Cf. Matt 13:32, Luke 11:42. The word is used mainly of vegetables or garden herbs. Luke 13:19 and Matt 13:32 speak of the seed becoming a "tree," and both have the birds nesting in its branches, where Mark has *make nests in its shade.* The plant has been known to attain a height of twelve feet.

The imagery is that of Dan 4:12 and Ezek 17:23, 31:6. In these passages the tree is the equivalent of a great empire sheltering subject peoples, and it is this consideration that is the only basis upon which to suggest that Jesus was thinking of Gentiles.

24. Parables (vi) Jesus' Use of Parables (4:33-34) = Matt 13:34-35

4 ³³ With many such parables he spoke his message to them, so far as they were able to hear it; ³⁴ and he did not speak to them except in parables. But privately, to his disciples, he explained everything.

Comment

The suggestion by Taylor (p. 271) that this section originally "was more closely associated with 1-9" calls for an examination of its position in the Matthean version.

An examination of Mark 4:26-34, on the generally accepted theory that Matthew used, and then rearranged, the Markan material, cannot reasonably explain some odd factors in the theory. Why did he put Mark aside at 13:24, then use Mark 4:33-34, and, having done so, place it after the saying on yeast, rather than leave it where it was in the Markan place after the mustard seed? Moreover, according to the usual synoptic theory, Matthew omits Mark's 4:21-25 at 13:31, while the material parallel to Mark is scattered throughout Matthew. For example, Mark 4:21 = Matt 5:15; Mark 4:22 = Matt 10:26; Mark 4:23 = Matt 11:15; Mark 4:24 = Matt 7:2; Mark 4:25 = Matt 13:12. If indeed Matthew is dependent upon Mark, this distribution of Markan material is almost bizarre. But a Markan dependence on the framework of Matthew, together with an urgent concern for condensation, makes for an entirely different—and far more explicable—interpretation of the material before us.

Mark's interest in the *deeds* of Jesus, and his minimal concern for extended blocks of teaching, has been noted before. The evangelist can therefore summarize this short section of parables and pass on to his next block of material.

Notes

33,34. These verses should be taken together to appreciate the Semitic parallelism. Mark adds to the text of Matthew *so far as they were able to hear it*—Luke omits the verses. Mark has *to them*, referring to 4:1. The evangelist indicates that he has made a deliberate selection by the use of *many such*.

Verse 4:11 seems to suggest that the parables were addressed only to the crowds; the two verses here correct the impression by asserting that it was in the use of explanations that Jesus differentiated between the crowds and the inner circle.

privately (Greek *kat'idian):* The New Testament generally preserves the proper and full meaning of *idios* as "one's own" in contrast to the weakening of the word in Hellenistic Greek to little more than a pronoun. It is worth calling attention to the fact that Mark, in common with Matthew, preserves the careful distinction between two levels of teaching, while the extended use of the word "disciples" in Luke to include all followers of Jesus precludes such a distinction.

25. Miracles (i) The Calming of the Water (4:35-41) = Matt 8:23-27; Luke 8:22-25

4 ³⁵ On that day, in the evening, Jesus said to them, "Let us cross over to the other side." ³⁶ So leaving the crowd, they took him with them in the boat, just as he was. There were other boats accompanying him. ³⁷ A very strong windstorm began to blow, and the waves broke over the boat until it was almost swamped. ³⁸ He was in the stern of the boat, asleep on a cushion; they roused him and said, "Rabbi, don't you care that we are about to perish?" ³⁹ He awoke, rebuked the wind, and commanded the sea: "Be quiet! Be still!" The wind dropped, and there was a great calm. ⁴⁰ He then said to them, "Why are you frightened? Have you no faith, even now?" ⁴¹ They were awestruck and said to one another, "Who is this? Even the wind and the sea obey him!"

Comment

In the ensuing selection of miracle stories, it is clear that Mark took three units in succession from Luke 8:22-56. While there are Matthean parallels which have had some influence on Mark's text, it is far closer to the Lucan examples—especially in the accounts of the demon-possessed, Jairus' daughter, and the woman with a hemorrhage. In other words two features of conflation between two texts were at work: the use of order in one source, coupled with textual use of another.

The stilling of the storm is a miracle narrative, pure and simple, with vivid details which almost certainly belong to the earliest level of oral tradition and suggest an eyewitness (e.g., *just as he was; there were other boats; asleep on a cushion; "Rabbi, don't you care . . ."*—together with *"Be quiet!"* and *"Why are you frightened?"*).

Attempts to find parallels to the narrative, biblical and otherwise, are not convincing, whatever view is taken of the purely miraculous elements in the story. Indeed, as Taylor suggests (p. 273), the story contains parallels with the saga of Aeneas in Virgil's *Aeneid*.

The narrative makes two assertions, one about Jesus and the other about faith. According to the first, the story declares the sovereignty of Jesus over the manifestation of Satan as epitomized in the chaos of a storm (and also at another level over the sea as signifying the place of darkness and death). Secondly, the narrative is a demand for faith—not faith in Jesus as a wonder-worker, but faith in God as the creator and sustainer of nature.

Much of our modern concern is expressed by the question "What actually happened?" To that question there are many possible answers. The command *"Be quiet! Be still!"* was certainly addressed to the raging storm, but it is also an exhibition of Jesus' total abandonment to the Father. If we accept the Pauline assertion that "God was in the Messiah, reconciling the world to himself" (2 Cor 5:19, cf. Col 1:20), then without reference to later christological definitions (such as that of the Council of Chalcedon) we shall admit that in his acts there were exhibitions of divine power outside the realm of his consciousness.

Notes

35. The precise note of time, in contrast with Matthew and Luke, certainly may be accounted for by hypothesizing Mark's access to an independent source (cf. Mark 1:32,35). There are historic presents not easily rendered in translation ("says" and "they take him"), while *Let us cross over* suggests some degree of haste, the reason for which is unclear.

the other side (Greek *eis to peran):* Cf. 5:1,21; 6:45; 8:13. This generally refers to the east side of the lake.

36. *other boats:* We hear nothing further of these other boats, and presumably they dispersed in face of the storm. This detail belongs to the "reminiscence source" of Mark, in contrast with the far more formal narratives of Matt 8:23 and Luke 8:22. Matthew and Luke also represent Jesus as preceding his disciples into the boat.

37. *windstorm* (Greek *lailaps amenou):* The Greek is that of Luke 8:23 (cf. 2 Pet 2:17). Matthew has *seismos megas.* Like all inland lakes surrounded by mountains, the Sea of Galilee is subject to sudden storms which sweep down colder air from the surrounding valleys.

waves (Greek *kuma):* Cf. Matt 8:24, 14:24. The verb translated as *broke over* is a strongly expressive verb, meaning literally "hurled upon." Mark's Greek in the remainder of the verse is independent of both Matthew and Luke.

38. This verse is peculiar to Mark and has all the signs of eyewitness reminiscence. The pronoun *he* effectively points to the contrast between Jesus and his disciples. The stern of the boat, with a small seat, was the place of honor, the helmsman being placed at the very back.

The verse also has two more vivid historic presents: "they rouse him" and "they say to him," in contrast to the participles and the past (aorist) tenses of Matthew and Luke.

Rabbi (Greek *didaskalos):* The Greek equivalent is used by Mark at 5:35; 9:17,38; 10:17,20,35; 12:14,19,32; 13:1, and 14:14; he uses the Aramaic "rabbi" only at 9:35, 11:21, and 14:45, and the caritative "rabbouni" at 10:51. Sufficient evidence is available for use of the term "rabbi" in the time of Jesus to justify translating the Greek as *rabbi* in this and other instances.

The fear, even resentment, of the disciples that they may be facing death while Jesus sleeps is vividly expressed in the Markan account. Much has been made in the commentaries of the editorial methods of Matthew and Luke to present a more favorable portrait of the disciples than is given here. However, though Mark (on the hypothesis embraced by this commentary) owes much to Matthew's order and Luke's text, he plainly also had access to a very early tradition (that of an eyewitness?) and is to that extent independent of the other two evangelists.

39. *awoke:* Mark shares the Greek verb with Luke.

rebuked: The Greek implies a strong command.

"Be still!" (Greek *phimaō):* The word was used in the command to the demoniac in 1:25. It was used in the magical papyri to cast a spell to bind someone so as to make him unable to do harm.

Mark's text shares Matthew's use of the Greek in *dropped (ekopasen)*, and the text of both Matthew and Luke for *great calm (galēnē megalē)*.

The tradition is unanimous that Jesus addressed the storm in words of command. The reaction expressed in v. 41 on the part of the disciples tells us little, for much more may have been said by Jesus.

40. *frightened* (Greek *deilos):* The same word is in Matt 8:26 and indicates cowardice or timidity. The faith for which Jesus calls is faith in the provident care of God. Matthew adds "you men of little faith" to the charge of timidity, not having the second part of this Markan verse. Luke has simply "Where is your faith?" This sharp rebuke to the disciples is the first of several in Mark (cf. 7:18; 8:17,21,32f.; 9:19).

41. The verse describes the reaction of the disciples to the event, whereas Matthew's version is far more generalized. The sense is one of reverential wonder and an awestruck awareness of being in the presence of the inexplicable. The phrase *and said* is a change to the imperfect tense (literally, "they kept on saying"). Matthew and Luke use the expression "they were amazed," and both have the plural of *obey* in response to their own "winds and sea."

For further reading, see H. van der Loos, *The Miracles of Jesus* (Leiden: E. J. Brill, 1965), pp. 646ff.

26. Miracles (ii) The Gerasene Demoniac (5:1-20) = Matt 8:28-34; Luke 8:26-39

5 [1] So they came to the other side of the lake, into the country of the Gerasenes, [2] and as he left the boat he was met by a man with an unclean spirit, coming from the tombs. [3] He lived in the tombs, and no one could control him anymore. [4] Chains were useless—he had often been fettered and chained, but he had snapped the chains and broken the fetters. No one could master him. [5] So night and day he wandered among the tombs and on the hillsides; he would scream and cut himself with stones. [6] When he saw Jesus in the distance, he ran to him and threw himself down before him, [7] shouting loudly, "What do you want with me, Jesus son of God most High? In God's name, do not torment me!" [8] (For Jesus was already saying to him, "Unclean spirit, come out of this man!") [9] He therefore asked him, "What is your name?" "My name is Legion," he said, "for there are so many of us." [10] He pleaded earnestly that he would not send them out of the region. [11] Nearby, there was a large herd of pigs feeding on the hillside, [12] and the spirits pleaded with him, "Send us among the pigs, and let us go into them." [13] He gave them permission, and the unclean spirits came

out and went into the pigs. The whole herd—about two thousand—rushed over the edge into the lake and were drowned. [14] The men in charge fled and carried the news to the town and the countryside, and people came out to see what had happened. [15] They came to Jesus and saw the man who had been possessed by the legion of demons, sitting there clothed and in his right mind, and they were afraid. [16] Those who had witnessed it told them how the demon-possessed man had been cured and what had happened to the pigs. [17] They then begged Jesus to leave the district. [18] As he was embarking, the man who had been possessed by demons begged to go with him. [19] He would not permit it but said to him, "Go home to your own people and tell them what the Lord has done for you, and how he had mercy on you." [20] The man therefore left and went through all the Ten Towns, spreading the news of what Jesus had done for him, and everyone was amazed.

Comment

There are several comments to be made about this narrative. First, though the story exhibits all the signs of the miracle story familiar to form criticism (circumstances, symptoms, exorcism, the reaction of the bystanders), the story as it stands has not arrived at the highly formalized shape which miracle stories achieve when handed down through a succession of versions. Second, vv. 6-7 read almost as though an account of a separate incident has been telescoped into the present narrative. Third, the descriptive passage in vv. 3-5 belongs to a stage in the oral and early written traditions which had not yet been condensed into stylized form. Finally, the scene continually shifts from the people to the demoniac and then to the hillsides. All of these considerations suggest that the evangelist was doing his best with an embarrassment of riches by way of source material. There are many details in the story which, far from being embellishments of an originally bald statement, bear all the marks of reminiscence from an eyewitness.

We may usefully contrast the versions in the other two synoptic gospels. In Matthew and Luke we have accounts which are terse, designed for easy memorization, whereas in Mark we have a narrative in which the evangelist has access to a far livelier and more dramatic narrative—in fact, so dramatic that he finds it imperative to insert v. 8 to relieve the confusion of detail. We can find some indications of the way in which the story developed from Matthew's version, where we have two men who are demon-possessed, in contrast with the one man of Mark and Luke. All of this seems to suggest to the present commentator that Mark had two versions of the story which Matthew had originally possessed, and telescoped into one. Mark used a combination of the terse and condensed Matthean account, together with his own "reminiscence source," and produced the present narrative.

Difficulty has always been felt with the significance of the narrative as we have it now, especially with respect to the fate of the pigs. No amount of pleading that evil belongs to the abyss (represented in this story by the sea) and that swine were unclean animals removes the feeling that the whole incident as recorded represents gratuitous waste. Perhaps the only adequate hypothesis is that the man's reactions to exorcism were so terrified that his panic communicated itself to the herd of swine. Panic behavior in many species of animals is well attested, and our sources simply combine this panic behavior with an exorcism.

Notes

1. *Gerasenes:* This place identification has provided problems from the earliest time because Gerasa and Gadara are too far from the lake (thirty and six miles respectively). Matthew's text has *Gadara*, while Mark and Luke have *Gerasa*. Moreover, the landing place is not identified, and in all our texts the meaning is vague. Origen (died c. 254) in his *Commentary on John* (6.41) pointed out the impossibility of both places as a precise identification and suggested Gergesa, a place with overhanging cliffs. In Mark the reading is undoubtedly *the country of the Gerasenes*, though some texts are assimilated to Matthew. Perhaps the best we can do is to assume that all three synoptic evangelists simply wished to indicate "territory belonging to . . .." Wherever the exact location, the herd of swine indicates Gentile territory. (For fuller information, cf. Lane, p. 181n.6.)

2. *from the tombs:* The demoniac is introduced with a wealth of detail. Tombs, as being ritually unclean, were commonly regarded as appropriate dwellings for demons and the possessed. (Cf. Lohmeyer, p. 94n.3.)

3-5. Most of this material is peculiar to Mark, for Matthew and Luke simply indicate the danger the man posed to the community. Talmudic prescriptions provide four tests of madness: spending the night in a grave, tearing one's clothes, walking around at night, and destroying anything given. All such signs are present in this case.

There are words in this small section found only here in Mark: *katoikēsis* (dwelling), *halusis* (chain), *pedē* (fetter), *diaspaō* (tear apart), *damazō* (tame). In fact, all five words are rarities in the NT text. There is one possible indication of the eyewitness character of the narrative in this brief section. Mark uses the perfect tense in v. 4, as though what is being committed to writing unchanged is the oral narrative of bystanders. This is especially marked when the evangelist returns to the imperfect tense at the end of v. 5.

6. It is possible that in this verse we find some slight evidence for the two narratives telescoped in Matthew. In this verse the story is resumed, but here the demoniac sees Jesus from a distance, while in v. 2 Jesus meets him as soon as he leaves the boat.

in the distance (Greek *apo makrothen):* Cf. 8:3, 11:13, 14:54, 15:40. Matthew has the expression twice, as does Luke.

threw himself down (Greek *proskuneō):* The verb, like its derived substantive, is wide-ranging in meaning, from humble obeisance to a superior on the one hand to worship on the other.

7,8. *shouting loudly:* The scene has all the classic elements of two previous demon possession narratives (1:23ff., 3:11): the wild shouting, the obeisance, and the question which includes a confession of Jesus' status. The demoniac fears that he is to be punished in some fashion apart from chains and fetters *(basanizō,* "to put to the test" or "torture"). Matthew has no equivalent to v. 6, and Luke has simply "seeing Jesus." Matthew's text has an eschatological reference in 8:29, "Have you come to torment us before the time?"

Mark's v. 8 must be regarded as editorial, perhaps as an explanation for the frantic behavior. If this explanation is rejected, there is the possibility that the author is using his Lucan version, replacing Luke's *parengelen* by *elegen (was already saying),* changing Luke's indirect speech to direct, and moving Luke's description of the demoniac to vv. 3-5. It must be said that proponents of Markan priority would reply that Luke (as a far more elegant prose writer) improved upon the text before him.

was already saying (Greek *elegen):* This imperfect tense may be used as a pluperfect, "he had been saying," or even in a Semitic sense of "command," but we have attempted here to suggest that Jesus was repeating the injunction—a simple command was insufficient, given the gravity of the case. In this view, the question in v. 9 is far more explicable.

9. *asked* (Greek *eperōtaō):* This is the first use in Mark of a verb he uses twenty-five times.

Legion: The Latin word was widely used in Aramaic and Hellenistic Greek, often as a term to describe a large number—a use that still survives in English. The question *What is your name?* is Jesus' acknowledgment of the ancient belief that knowledge of a name gave power over demons as well as enemies. The sufferer's reply, giving a number (a Roman legion was usually about six thousand men) rather than a name, suggests that he knew himself to be prey to a whole multitude of impulses before which he felt powerless. The availability of modern psychiatric vocabulary to describe the man's condition does not render his condition any the less parlous, and the change from singular to plural in this passage vividly underlines the condition.

10. The man makes his request on behalf of the demons by whom he is possessed.

region (Greek *choras):* The belief was common in the ancient world that demons were associated with a particular place (cf. Luke 11:24). This fact does not, however, remove the difficulty inherent in Luke's reading of *eis tēn abusson* (into the abyss). The abyss was the place of final punishment for demons, and this seems on all accounts to be the original meaning. G. Schwarz in a recent article—"Aus der Gegend (Markus V.10b)," *NTS* 22.2.76, pp. 214-15—convincingly argues that the difference between *choras* in Mark and *abusson* in Luke goes back to a confusion in Aramaic between *tĕḥûmā'* (district, place) and *tĕḥômā'* (the deep) with Luke 8:31b representing the original reading.

11. The precise location can only be surmised, though the herd of swine indicates a Gentile or pagan territory, and the subsequent verses demand a mountainous spot.

12. The use of *pleaded* (Greek *parekalesan*) represents a particular request or demand, as distinct from the repeated pleas in v. 10.

and let us: The clause in Greek is redundant—avoided in Matthew and Luke—and may represent an imperative with *hina* (in order that), which though unusual is not uncommon in the New Testament. Such use has been adopted here in the translation.

13. *two thousand:* Mark alone has this detail, and it is almost certainly a considerable exaggeration.

Some details of what took place are in the text, and others must be inferred. Presumably Jesus gestured to the demoniac and the demons left him, entering into the swine. It may well be, as has been suggested many times, that in a seizure accompanying the exorcism the demoniac hurled himself at the pigs, thinking that the demons who possessed him wished to enter the swine. In panic, the pigs ran down the steep hillside and were drowned. Admittedly, this is reading the narrative with twentieth-century knowledge of psychology in mind, together with established empirical data about the panic behavior of animals, but the commentator must work with the "headline" character of much New Testament narrative and supply the "fine print" not accommodated in headlines.

14. There is a contrast in the narratives of Matthew and Mark at this point. In Mark the dwellers in the countryside (Greek *agros*) come out to see the demoniac, whereas in Matthew Jesus is the center of attention. The word *agros* is frequent in the Septuagint but was becoming increasingly rare by New Testament times. Mark uses it in three ways, as meaning a field or plot of ground, in the plural for villages, hamlets, and for the rural areas as distinct from urban. The town is not identified.

15. A new section begins with a historic present. The verb *saw* (Greek *theōrousin*) implies "to have a good look at" the former demoniac. The description of the man—sitting, clothed, and rational—is given from the point of view of the beholder. Mark is here drawing on Luke's text, and *the man who had been possessed by the legion* is implied in Luke 8:35, though it is omitted by some manuscripts of Mark.

16,17. The awe induced by the sight of the cured demoniac gave way quickly to the conviction that Jesus was a dangerous person to have around the district. Matthew severely compresses his account at this point, and Luke associates with fear the request that Jesus leave.

18,19. The remainder of the narrative is purely Markan. The Greek of *begged to go with him* may be compared with 3:17.

and tell them (Greek *apangeilon):* Manuscript evidence also attests the use of *diangeilon,* a word used in Luke 9:60, Acts 21:26, and Rom 9:17 of missionary activity.

"Go home . . .": The Greek preserves a distinction not easily rendered in English translation between the man's family *(eis ton oikon)* and a somewhat wider circle *(pros tous sous),* but in the translation we have been more idiomatic than literal.

what the Lord has done: The Greek *kurios* (Lord) is used of God. The Greek preserves the difference in meaning between the perfect and aorist tenses: the first clause, in the perfect, represents a completed action with effects continuing into the present, while *had mercy on you* describes the initial, decisive act in the beginning.

20. The injunction to spread the story contrasts strongly with the opposite injunctions in 1:25,44; 3:12; 5:43; and 7:36. Perhaps the best explanation is that this was outside of Galilean territory.

Ten Towns (Greek *Decapolis): Cf. 7:31.* The Decapolis seems to have been a very loose federation of towns and villages; there is no evidence that it was ever an administrative unit or a legal entity. It seems to have been a convenient description of ten towns in close proximity, in some ways akin to "The Potteries" in Great Britain, familiar from the novels of Arnold Bennett. (Cf. S. Thomas Parker, "The Decapolis Reviewed," *JBL* 94.3.1975, pp. 437-41.)

27. Miracles (iii) Jairus' Daughter; the Woman with Hemorrhage (5:21-43) = Matt 9:18-26; Luke 8:40-56

5 21 When Jesus went back to the other side of the lake, a large crowd once more gathered around him. 22 While he was by the lakeside, one of the presidents of the synagogue, named Jairus, came to him. When he saw him, he threw himself down at his feet 23 and implored him, "My little daughter is close to death. I beg you to come and lay your hands on her that she may be cured and live." 24 So he went with him, and a large crowd accompanied him, pressing in upon him. 25 There was a woman who had suffered from hemorrhages for twelve years, 26 even though she had been treated by many doctors and had spent all she had. Instead of getting better, however, she had grown worse. 27 She had heard about Jesus, so she came up from behind in the crowd and touched his clothes, 28 for she said [to herself], "If I can touch even his clothes, I shall be cured." 29 Immediately the flow of blood stopped and she knew in herself that she was cured of the affliction. 30 At the same time Jesus, aware that power had gone out of him, immediately turned round in the crowd and asked, "Who touched my clothes?" 31 His disciples said, "You see the crowd pressing in on you, and yet you ask 'Who touched me?'!" 32 But he was looking around to see who had done it. 33 The woman, trembling with fear and knowing what had happened to her, came and prostrated herself and told him the whole truth. 34 "My daughter," he said to her, "your faith has cured you. Go in peace, and be free from your affliction." 35 While he was speaking, some came from the ruler's house, saying "Your daughter has died—why bother the rabbi further?" 36 But Jesus, overhearing what they were saying, said to the president

of the synagogue, "Do not be afraid—only believe." [37] And he allowed
no one to go with him, except Peter and James, and James's brother
John. [38] They arrived at the president's house, and he found a great
commotion, loud crying, and wailing. [39] He went in and said to them,
"Why all this commotion and crying? The child is not dead—only
sleeping." [40] They laughed at him. But having put them all out, he
took the child's father and mother, and his own companions, and went
in where the child was. [41] Then, taking her by the hand, he said to her,
"Talitha koum," which means "Get up, my child." [42] The child immediately got up and continued walking about. (She was twelve years
old.) When this happened, they were all completely amazed. [43] He
gave them strict injunction not to let anyone know, and told them to
give her something to eat.

Comment

While it can be pleaded that the preceding narrative in the Matthean version
is an example of a miracle story honed and refined to essentials by community
use, this cannot be said of the pericope before us.

The wealth of detail, the anguish in the plea of Jairus, the dialogue between
Jesus' disciples(?) and the messengers from Jairus' house, together with Jesus'
refusal to turn back—all of this, with the details which follow, makes for a
very distinct personal reminiscence from an eyewitness. Comparison with
Matthew and Luke demonstrates that the evangelist, while adhering to Matthew's order, drew upon his own sources.

When we come to the salient question "What took place?" our task is
immeasurably more complicated. In the terse account of Matthew, the
daughter is dead even as Jairus comes to Jesus (Matt 9:18). And Luke makes
the fact of death emphatic by "her spirit returned" (Luke 8:55). The present
account is less clear-cut, for the messengers report the girl dead, and the
mourners are already lamenting. Presumably, therefore, Mark tells a story of
resuscitation from death. But there are other factors to be recognized. To
begin with, Jesus refuses to accept the report of death, exhorts Jairus not to
be afraid but to trust. Two possible interpretations can be attached to this
factor. Either Jesus intended to restore the dead to life, or he disbelieved the
report. This is not all. "Why all this commotion and crying? The child is not
dead, only sleeping," along with the command "Get up, my child," does not
demand any suggestion of return to life, though to be sure that could be
meant. There are other considerations germane to the discussion, not the least

of which is the prevalence, before being accurately diagnosed by modern medicine, of diabetic coma.

We are reminded in the narrative before us of restoration to life in the narratives of Elijah (1 Kgs 17:17-24) and Elisha (2 Kgs 4:18-37). Both narratives either state or at least imply that a child is dead and is revived and brought back to life. To be sure, there is ambiguity in the stories, and they may mean that the child is at the point of death, but not yet already dead. But in those instances, as in the case before us, the persons so revived are brought back again to the life which they had been living before, and they will ultimately die again.

In no way would a suggestion of a diabetic coma in the present case—as well as that of the widow's son in Luke—militate against a dramatic reversal of the natural process through Jesus' intervention. That Jesus went to challenge the fear of death would be all of a piece with the evangelists' portrait of him.

It is fitting to mention briefly here the raising of Lazarus in John 11. There is no room in this account for resuscitation, for all the details conspire to emphasize that Lazarus was dead—indeed he was longer in the tomb than Jesus. Perhaps the best that can be said in this brief reference is that the narrative was intended as an encouragement to belief in the resurrection of all true believers. For a complete discussion of the Lazarus narrative—crucial to the Johannine understanding of the theme of "giving life"—see Raymond E. Brown, *The Gospel According to John I-XII,* AB, Garden City, N.Y.: Doubleday, 1966), pp. 420-37.

Notes

21. The west side of the lake is the scene of these two episodes, but there is no indication of place or locality. In the ensuing phrases, there is very wide variation in the texts: "again" being added after *went back* by some manuscripts, and "in the boat" by others. The welcome of the crowds is in marked contrast to the attitude of the Gerasenes in the preceding pericope—indeed, the Greek of *gathered around him* is literally "gathered on top of him." Matthew and Luke both have a far more generalized narrative. Matt 9:18 and Luke 8:41 both have *kai idou* (and behold), which has been assimilated by some texts of Mark. Otherwise it must be said that Mark used his own independent account.

22. *one of the presidents:* The phrase does not imply a plurality of such office holders; it indicates simply the class of people to which Jairus belonged.

Jairus: It seems best to regard this name as coming from Luke 8:41. The construction, while normal, appears to be an intrusion in this sentence. Either it is a scribal addition, or Mark found it in Luke when using his own eyewitness source. Other than those of the disciples, Mark never uses names apart from Bar-timaeus in 10:46. The name itself in Hebrew means "he who enlightens."

Mark's independence of Matthew and Luke seems to be underlined by his use of the historic present in *came* whereas the others use the aorist.

threw himself down (Greek *piptei)*: Cf. 3:11, 5:33, 7:25. *Proskuneō* at 5:6, 15:19 also indicates the obeisance rendered to a superior, and equally in other contexts the reverence due to God.

23. *implored him:* We have chosen here to follow the reading of some manuscripts by so rendering the imperfect tense (literally, "kept on imploring him").

my little daughter (Greek *thugatrion*, diminutive of *thugatēr;* cf. vv. 34 and 6:22, 7:26-29): Presumably the diminutive is used as a term of affection.

close to death: Matthew tersely says "has just died," while Luke has "is dying." Mark's Greek is deplorable *(eskatōs echei)* and certainly indicates the independence of sources other than his own. The Greek construction of *I beg you to come* . . . is odd, meaning literally "so that, in coming, you may lay hands. . . ." The best way to treat the awkward Greek construction is as an imperative with *hina* (in order that). Cf. C. F. D. Moule, p. 144. Jesus' practice of laying hands on the sick was the precursor of ancient and modern Church practice.

cured and live: The Matthean tradition has simply "live," and the two words in Greek certainly in context seem to amount to the same thing. However, the Greek word translated by *cured* is used in contexts elsewhere when it obviously refers to salvation from sin.

24. Matthew speaks of the disciples' accompanying Jesus, while Mark sets the scene for the next episode by speaking of a *large crowd.* Unique to the gospels, the technique of an episode within an episode suggests that it rests upon a very early tradition, for there are no connecting links in the synoptic gospels, which we might otherwise have expected.

Once again we have a miracle narrative which for all the details usually associated with the genre—description of symptoms, failure of previous therapies, evidence of cure—nevertheless has all the air of an unreconstructed oral tradition. This is true even of the terse narrative of Matthew and the longer version in Luke. The account of the woman's fears, the impatient reaction of the disciples, and the portrait of Jesus himself all combine to present a compelling and strong narrative, vividly recalled by an eyewitness.

Here again we have to face the question "What happened?" Jesus was apparently aware that the woman's faith, for all her anxious self-questioning, had drawn upon his healing powers. But there is no real explanation for the question *Who touched my clothes?* Explanations for the cure in terms of psychology are interesting, but for the sufferer who had been cured, the reality was the cure, not the semiprecision of a psychological hypothesis. The narrative provides us with reason enough: the woman's faith in God's healing power had been kindled by what she had heard of Jesus and now saw of him.

25-28. These verses are noteworthy in Mark, as containing some attempt at literary Greek, with an unusual (for Mark) use of participles.

Mark's description of the woman's symptoms contrasts with the terse summary in Matthew.

25. *hemorrhages:* The woman's illness would make her ritually unclean (cf. Lev 15:19), and in consequence everything she touched would be unclean. It is important

to evaluate ritual impurity of this kind correctly. In an age that could not distinguish between a blood flow which could cause infection and one which did not, it was empirically safer to bracket all such cases together.

26. It was Lagrange (p. 140) who declared that it was an Eastern custom to consult as many physicians as possible, and with the result that the multiplicity of prescriptions given made the patient worse. Mark's harsh verdict on the doctors is from his own source. Luke says simply that the woman could not be cured by any of the doctors.

27. *she had heard . . . .:* The reports were of the healing ministry. But the Greek phrase (literally, "the things about Jesus") is reminiscent of Luke 22:37, 24:19 and 27, Acts 1:3, 17:25.

his clothes: Matthew's version refers to the tassels attached to the corners of the cloak (cf. Num 15:38, Deut 22:12). Coming secretly, because of ritual impurity, the woman's action indicates her belief that mere contact will effect a cure.

28. *to herself:* The phrase is not in the Greek of Mark (it is found in Matthew), but it is necessary in English translation to avoid the notion that the words were spoken aloud.

The person of a healer was in former times regarded as sacrosanct, and objects associated with the healer's person were held to be potent as in some way partaking of the healer's power (cf. Acts 5:15, 19:12).

29. The use of Greek tenses here is notable, as it was also in vv. 18 and 19 above. *Stopped* is an aorist form, as is *knowing,* indicating completed past action, while *she was cured* indicates lasting results. The comment about the woman's knowledge is peculiar to Mark.

30. *immediately:* A word very common in Mark, it nevertheless in context indicates the immediacy of Jesus' knowledge.

aware (literally, "knowing in himself"): Cf. 2:8, John 6:61, 11:38.

power (Greek *dunamis):* The Greek is awkward (literally, "knowing that power from him had gone out"), and we have attempted a smooth translation. But Mark's phrase is meant to describe the outgoing of a personal power in Jesus to heal, appropriated by the woman.

The word *power* is variously used in the New Testament (cf. Mark 6:2,5,14; 9:1,39; 12:24; 13:25,26 and 14:62) and as a "work of power" is used in this gospel at 6:2,5,14, and 9:39, whereas in 9:1 it is the power with which the Reign of God comes to men. In 13:25 it is used of heavenly beings, in 13:26 of the appearance of The Man, while in 12:24 and 14:62 the word becomes a substitute for God. Common in the pagan world, the word is associated with the worship of a manifestation of elemental might. In the New Testament its use is wholly determined by the majesty of the living God, or by any work which manifests that majesty.

31. *"Who touched . . . .":* Cf. 3:10, 6:56. The question implies that those who came to Jesus often wished to touch him. The impatient reply of the disciples is not found in Matthew and is more deferential in Luke.

32. *he was looking around:* Cf. 3:5. The feminine participle in the Greek of *who had done it* does not impute supernatural knowledge to Jesus; the expression comes from the viewpoint of Mark.

33. *trembling with fear:* For the same sense, cf. 16:8, 1 Cor 2:3, 2 Cor 7:15, Eph 6:5,

Phil 2:12. Luke attributes the woman's fear to the fact of her being discovered, an interpretation disavowed by the subsequent clause in Mark. It is possible that the woman's fear may have been increased by her knowledge that she had rendered Jesus ritually unclean.

prostrated herself: Mark's version does not hint at a public declaration, as does Luke's, but does say that she told the whole truth. Luke's version is much fuller than Mark's at this point (cf. Luke 8:47). Some texts of Mark have "told him all her case" (Greek *aitian),* and Taylor suggests—in view of the same word in Luke 8:47—that this may be the original reading.

34. *faith:* The woman's cure is ascribed by Jesus to her faith in the healing power of God—cf. 10:52. Faith (Greek *pistis)* in the New Testament is not a name for an inner experience, but describes primarily a committal of trust to God, which in its turn is made effective by God's response to that trust.

Go in peace: The phrase corresponds to the Hebrew of 1 Sam 1:17. Cf. Luke 7:50, 8:48, Acts 16:36, Jas 2:16. The word *peace* is found only here in Mark. The Hebrew word *shalōm* carries the meaning of wholeness, soundness, rather than the sense of an absence of strife implied by the English translation. Matthew's text has "and from that very hour the woman became well."

35. The resumption of the narrative about the sick girl is notable in that it is less literary. Participles are absent, there is no indirect speech, and there is one Aramaic phrase. Cf. Lohmeyer, p. 105.

some came: The Greek can also be translated as "there came from the ruler's house some who said. . . ."

bother (Greek *skulleis):* Cf. Matt 9:36, Luke 7:6, 8:49. The early classical meaning of *skullō* was "to flay," but this verb, like many others in Hellenistic and *koinē* Greek, took on the less harsh meaning indicated here. The manner of the question implies that the messengers from the house have no expectation that Jesus would or could resuscitate the girl. Mark follows Luke in this verse, which is absent in Matthew.

36. *overhearing:* An interesting problem arises with this participle *(parakousas).* Cf. Matt 18:17 (2). The verb can mean either hearing accidentally or hearing without paying attention, or even ignoring. This last sense is found in all seven uses in the Septuagint and in Matt 18:17. We have chosen this translation—commentators are divided—because Jesus is frequently represented as acting on what he hears.

It is implied that the father is afraid, fearing the worst. Luke adds, "and she will be made whole."

37. There is no mention in Matthew of the familiar trio accompanying Jesus. Luke (6:14) has the same order (Peter, James, and John) here, but Luke 8:51, 9:28, and Acts 1:13 have John in second place. The three form an inner circle in the group of disciples (cf. 9:2, 14:33, and—with Andrew—at 13:3). There is a striking similarity here to the inner circle of three in the council of twelve among the Essenes of Qumran.

38. Matthew and Luke agree against Mark in having "coming" (Jesus) for *they arrived.* Peculiar to Mark is Jesus' "taking in" (Greek *theōrei),* which we have rendered by *found.* But Mark's text cannot easily be translated if we retain *theōrei* as "took in," for it is followed by *commotion* and *crying.* Matthew's text has "saw the musicians and the crowd making a great noise," while Luke has "and everyone was weeping and lamenting about her." Matthew's version obviously implies professional

mourners, and this may be the case in Mark, though it is not said. *B. Chethuboth* 46b required "two flutes and one to wail," even for the poorest funerals.

39. *He went in:* Mark's vague account does not indicate whether this was the courtyard in front of the house (such as we may suppose a man of some eminence to have). This may not sound immediately important save for the words of Jesus in this verse.

". . . *only sleeping":* The verb can be used of death—and is frequently in the Septuagint—but that meaning is ruled out here by *is not dead.* We are in no position to say whether Jesus was asserting of the girl that she was dead, but that death did not have final dominion over her (which is what Matthew and Luke imply), or whether he was saying that she was in a coma. Jesus had not seen the child, and to say that his words implied a coma means a possession on his part of an intuition which is beyond our examining. Matt 9:18 and Luke 8:53 and 55 clearly indicate that death had taken place, but Mark's text appears to be almost deliberately ambiguous.

40. *They laughed* (Greek *kategelōn):* The verb is the same in all three versions, and is certainly an indication of literary relationship. The verb is not found elsewhere in the New Testament.

having put them all out translates a Greek verb which implies forcible ejection.

went in where the child was: The phrase implies that Jesus entered the room for the first time. Matthew does not mention those who accompanied Jesus, and Mark alone mentions the child's room. Luke's account (Luke 8:53) deliberately emphasizes that the child was dead.

41. *taking her by the hand:* Cf. 1:31.

"Talitha koum": The Greek is a transliteration of the Aramaic *talitha' qum.* Some manuscripts have the feminine *koumi* in place of the masculine given here, but most modern Greek texts opt for *koum.* For other Aramaic phrases in Mark, cf. 3:17, 7:11 and 34, 11:9ff., 14:36, 15:22 and 34. Luke has no parallels to any of these instances, and Matthew has only "Golgotha" at 15:22.

It has been pointed out from time to time that the use of foreign phrases or words was a common device in Hellenistic magical and miracle stories, but apart from this instance and 7:34 Mark's use of such phrases, it does not occur in contexts of the miraculous. This instance, therefore, in the face of customary usage, is far more arguably attributed to an eyewitness source.

42. The use of verbs in this verse is carefully distinguished: *the child immediately got up and continued walking.* The age is added to emphasize the walking. The Greek of *got up (anestē),* despite its New Testament associations with the resurrection of Jesus, should be treated in Mark's text with caution. Luke's Greek admits of no such hesitation, and he regarded the narrative as one of resurrection from death.

they were all completely amazed: The Greek is strongly expressive. Taylor (p. 297) calls attention to the grammatical construction (the use of a finite verb with the dative of the cognate noun) as a "Septuagintalism," and in comparing this with the infinitive absolute with the finite verb in Hebrew concludes that we find Mark using a Palestinian source. (For the same usage, cf. 4:41.)

43. The command to silence presents its own questions. It can hardly have been supposed by Jesus that the incident could be hidden, but the fact that Mark records it, in the face of the previous verse, is some testimony to the accuracy of his recording of

tradition. Cf. 1:25,44; 3:12. Matthew omits this command, while Luke substantially confirms it.

All in all, the account reads very much like a reworking of the highly stylized versions in Matthew and Luke by one who had access (as the other evangelists did not) to reliable eyewitness testimony. If Matthew and Luke represent severely condensed versions, carefully honed to essentials over the years, Mark must evidently have found—in his own sources—that he could add life and detail and so fleshed out what he found.

28. Rejection at Nazareth
(6:1-6a) = Matt 13:53-58; Luke 4:16-30

6   ¹ He left that place and went back to his native place, followed by his disciples. ² When the Sabbath came, he began to teach in the synagogue; many who heard him were astonished and said, "Where did he get all this?" and "What wisdom is this that has been given him?" or "How does he work such miracles?" ³ "Is he not the craftsman, Mary's son, brother to James, Joseph, Judas, and Simon? And are not his brothers and sisters here with us?" So they took offense at him. ⁴ Jesus said to them, "A prophet is respected, except in his native place and among his relatives and family." ⁵ He was unable to work any miracles there, except that he put his hands on a few sick people and healed them. ⁶ᵃ He was greatly surprised by their want of faith.

Comment

In contrast with what has gone before, the present pericope presents unbelief and rejection whereas 1:21 spoke of the successful inauguration of the ministry. It may be that the contrast is even more extended: cf. 1:21-39 and 6:1-2; 3:20-35 and 6:3; 4:35-5:43 and 6:4-6. But from such contrasts, impressive though they may be, it is presumptuous to assert a purely artificial narrative. There is so much detail in the material which can only be described as "biographical." The brothers and the sisters are mentioned. The word *relatives* may have some reference to those of Jesus' family who later came to prominence in the Church. There is also the bald statement that Jesus could perform no miracles in the absence of faith, and Jesus' own surprise at the lack of faith. All these factors combine to mark the narrative as belonging to the early Jesus tradition. It has been suggested that two narratives have been telescoped here, for the wonder of v. 2 is followed by the resentment of v. 3. Perhaps a sermon of the kind outlined in Luke 4:23-27 is presupposed.

Mark here takes up the Matthean order, even following the Matthean wording closely (cf. Matt 13:53-58), whereas the Lucan version of the rejection comes much earlier in the Lucan narrative (Luke 4:16-24). But Mark is indebted to Luke for associating the incident with the Sabbath. As an example of the Markan conflation method, it is interesting to observe the agreement of Mark with Matthew in wording here, as compared with Mark's dependence on Lucan wording in 4:35-5:43 (cf. Luke 8:22-56). In that last instance Mark had to deal with Matthean parallels which were in an entirely different order.

Notes

1. *native place* (i.e., Nazareth): The Greek *ekeithēn* (that place) is vague, and its use here as a connecting link with the previous narrative is very rare in Mark (three times as compared with Matthew's eleven); a dependence on Matthew's Greek seems clearly indicated.

2. *many:* Some Greek texts have the definite article *hoi polloi* (the many). If this reading is accepted, then there is a possible rendering of the technical *hā' rabbîm* ("the community of Israel"). Interesting though the possibility is, as suggesting a microcosm of Israel faced with the ministry and words of Jesus, it is best simply to take *polloi* at face value as *many*.

3. *craftsman* (Greek *tektōn*): Nothing is more persistent in the pieties of certain kinds of hymns and devotions than the mistaken idea that the Greek ought to be rendered as "carpenter," implying a lowly place in contemporary society. The Greek has a wide range of meaning, from shipbuilder to sculptor, but nearly always implies a person of considerable skill and can even be used of a physician. So far from being a village carpenter (Matt 13:55) engaged in making plows and yokes (which any peasant of his time was capable of producing), Joseph may well have been a builder of some competence, traveling over large areas of the country. Against such a background the self-renunciation of Jesus is seen as something far more impressive than the word "carpenter" would imply.

The Aramaic *naggārā* ranged in meaning from a maker of furniture to a builder, with many associated skills in between. Such craftsmen were itinerants, as by the time of Jesus they had already been for centuries. In view of the implications of Luke 4:22 and John 6:42, together with the present passage that people in Nazareth did not know Jesus by sight when he first came back after the beginning of his ministry, we must conclude that he had spent little time at Nazareth. The city itself was ideally situated for an itinerant craftsman, who could not only locate his family there but could also travel easily to coastal cities and to towns overlooking the Sea of Galilee.

Mary's son: The tone of this verse is in marked contrast to the previous one; it is possible that in this pericope we have *two* narratives and that a sermon somewhat on the lines of Luke 4:23-27 is either omitted or presupposed.

Some serious problems are posed by the use of *Mary's son.* The Matthean version (13:55) is quite different, and to describe a man as the "son of" his mother, even when the father was deceased, is often a usage of insult. We would be unjustified in seeing in the Markan phrase any implication of knowledge of a tradition of virgin birth. The textual evidence is not illuminating, for while all the uncial texts, and many minuscules, have the text we have translated here, many important texts support a version not unlike that of Matthew. Even manuscripts which have "the craftsman's son" also add "and Mary's" to the Greek. We are unlikely to arrive at any firm conclusion about the original text of Mark (the full manuscript details can be found in Turner, p. 300). But to suggest that Matthew's version represents an amendment of Mark in the interests of reverence, or because Matthew did not care to have Jesus associated with "trade," is to ignore the evangelist's use of insults on other occasions (cf. Matt 11:19, 12:24).

brothers . . . with us: We know nothing of the family of Jesus, save James (cf. Matt 13:55; Acts 12:17; 15:13; 21:18; 1 Cor 15:7; Gal 1:19; 2:9,12), Joseph (Matt 13:55—the Joses of Mark 15:40,47 is another person), Judas (Matt 13:55), and Simon (Matt 13:55). Of the sisters we know nothing whatsoever. How old the tradition is we do not know, but from the fourth century in both East and West it has been commonly held that the brothers and sisters referred to were children from an earlier marriage of Joseph. However, Matt 1:25 can certainly be taken to mean that children were born to Mary and Joseph subsequent to the birth of Jesus.

4. The proverb was apparently a common one, and there are numerous examples of it in contemporary literature. Mark alone has *relatives.* In this use of the proverb Jesus implicitly accepts the title of prophet, and he was commonly so regarded (cf. 6:15; 8:28; Matt 21:11; Luke 7:16,39. See also Luke 24:19; John 4:19; 6:14; 7:40,52; 9:17; Acts 3:22; 7:37. For *"the* prophet" see John 6:14, 7:40.). As a designation for Jesus the term passed out of currency as being inadequate. It has been revived somewhat in recent years—at all events in academic usage—as, for example, in "the prophet of the eschatological age."

5,6a. This is the strongest statement in the gospels on the limitations of Jesus, though it is mitigated slightly in the second part of the verse. Matthew's version (13:58) has been used by Mark, but somewhat expanded. Mark's version of the astonishment of Jesus reads very much like a tradition handed on by someone intimately associated with him. Here Jesus appears to take faith in God as a natural attitude and is pained by its absence.

29. The Mission of the Twelve
(6:6b-13) = Matt 10:1,5-15; Luke 9:16

6   6b He went to the villages around there, teaching, 7 and he summoned the Twelve and sent them out in pairs. He gave them authority over unclean spirits 8 and ordered them to take nothing for the journey beyond a staff—no bread, no bag, no money in their belts. 9 They might wear sandals but not an additional tunic. 10 "When you are admitted to a house," he added, "remain there until you leave those parts. 11 But at any place where they will neither receive you nor listen to you, shake off the dust from your feet as you leave, as a warning to them." 12 So they went out and proclaimed that men should repent. 13 They drove out many demons, and many sick people they anointed with oil and cured them.

Comment

Mark's redactional methods are discernible here: the evangelist takes up Luke at 9:1-6 to record the mission of the Twelve. The methods can be seen also in the wording of v. 6b at the heading of this pericope: it is difficult to say whether the coincidental wording as between v. 6b and Matt 9:35 and Luke 13:22 are copied or from memory. But though Mark is influenced by Matthew in the wording of vv. 7,8,10, and 11, it is Luke's far shorter account which Mark uses. He continued to agree with Luke in following this with the tradition that Jesus was a *Johannes redivivus.*

The severe compression of the narrative is entirely in accord with the Markan desire to limit the teaching element in the ministry to a minimum. But aside from this, the reader is left with the impression that the evangelist had little realization of the importance of the event he described. No context is provided for the brief sayings; the implication that the Twelve were extending the ministry of Jesus in exorcism is mentioned, but only in tantalizing brevity, and the nature of the Proclamation in v. 12 is not detailed.

The importance of this mission is undoubted. Whether or not Jesus deliberately formed, instituted, and set in motion a community with which we are familiar as "the Church" is a matter of considerable debate. (It would not be inappropriate to say here that the examples of Isaiah and Jeremiah were some precedent for a teacher's taking steps to preserve his teaching, while the example of the strongly eschatological community of Qumran suggests that a "messianic" Proclamation very speedily issued in a community.) But the combined testimony of three evangelists is witness enough to the importance of this event, mainly on account of the delegation of Jesus' activities to the Twelve.

The severely condensed character of Mark's narrative almost demands the parallel version. There is no note of time here, and there is no necessary connection with Herod's apprehension in the next pericope. (The incident *appears* to belong to the later stages of the Galilean ministry, though this is not necessarily so.) In striking similarity to the mission of Gehazi (2 Kgs 4:29), physical preparations for the mission are to be kept to a minimum (cf. Luke 10:4), and eating and drinking are relegated to secondary place. In Luke's version the time is that of harvest (9:2). The urgency of the mission is summed up in the highly dramatic Matt 10:23, "You will not have gone round the towns of Israel before The Man's coming."

Notes

6b. We have chosen to connect the end of v. 6 with the mission, rather than attach these few words to the account of the rejection at Nazareth. The latter conjunction would have Jesus traveling on his mission because of a denial of opportunity in the synagogue. It seems to us that 6b provides a more fitting introduction to the mission. Luke omits the words, while Mark has eliminated Matthew's "and all the towns."

7. The habit of traveling in pairs was a well-attested Jewish practice in the time of Jesus. It is attested of the disciples of John and of the missionary journeys of Paul. The passage about exorcism poses a problem, since later on (9:18) the disciples are said to be unable to exorcise a spirit, and the report in Luke 10:17 has an air of surprise about the ability to cast out demons. Presumably, for all the difficulty in 9:18, Mark is here using Matt 10:8.

8-9. The charge to the Twelve is characterized by urgency, couched as it is in a series of negatives. The suggestion that the charge derives from two selections of a "sayings source," introduced by *ordered* in v. 8 and *he added* in v. 10, seems to be gratuitously complicated. The mitigation of the severe restrictions in Matthew and Luke is noteworthy. The staff is explicitly prohibited in Matthew and Luke and is permitted in Mark. Similarly *they might wear sandals* is a departure from the texts Mark had before him. Possibly the mitigations have to do with the perils of the situation for which this gospel was written. If this is so, then the Proclamation takes on an added note of urgency.

10. The choice made by the evangelist from Matthew and Luke in this second part of Jesus' instructions was certainly of crucial importance in the years immediately prior to the first Roman campaign. The injunction of Jesus would have had critical

importance when the patriotism of the messianic sect was in question. The teaching of Jesus in this respect was taken as standard by the early Church (cf. *Didachē* 9.4f).

11. Mark's *place* in this verse is "whoever" in Matthew, and "those who" in Luke. All versions have the Greek verb *dechomai,* which means "welcome" as well as "receive." The importance, even sanctity, of the mission is emphasized by the symbolic ceremonial gesture. The shaking off of dust is not to be taken as a curse, but as a witness, intended to lead to a change of heart. The Greek specifically speaks of a warning *to them,* not an adjuration *against* them. Cf. Acts 13:51, 18:6.

The details in Matthew—the disciples are sent by Jesus from town to town, where they are to greet each household and bestow peace upon those deemed worthy, etc.— would seem to suggest that the mission was widely known. Further support for this contention is provided by the Lucan account—the missionaries are told by Jesus to remain, eating and drinking, for the laborer is worth his keep, etc. Mark's almost fragmentary treatment of these events has been discussed in the comment.

12-13. The use of words familiar from other Markan texts *(went out,* 1:29; *proclaimed,* 1:4; *should repent,* 1:15; *drove out,* 1:12; *demons,* 1:34; *sick,* 6:5; *cured,* 1:34) demonstrates that these two verses are an attempt by the evangelist to provide a narrative framework for the mission. The verb *to anoint* (Greek *aleipho)* and *oil* (Greek *elaion)* are new.

anointed: While it is well known that the use of oil as an emollient was widespread in the ancient world, Mark views it as an accompaniment to miraculous healing. That such anointing is mentioned only three times in the New Testament—here, in Luke 10:34, and in Jas 5:15—suggests that contemporary practice may have involved the symbolic use of oil in connection with healing rites. The only reference to preaching is the word *proclaimed.* Taylor suggests (p. 306) that the connection of the verb *repent* with *proclaimed* may indicate that the disciples announced the approach of the end-time and the New Age (cf. Matt 10:7; Luke 9:2; 10:9,11).

30. The Death of John the Baptizer
(6:14-29) = Matt 14:1-12; Luke 9:7-9

6 ¹⁴ King Herod heard about it, for Jesus' reputation had spread everywhere. People were saying "John the Baptizer has been raised to life—that is why these miraculous powers are at work in him." ¹⁵ Others said, "It is Elijah," ¹⁶ and yet others declared, "He is a prophet, like one of the (former) prophets." But when Herod heard it, he said, "It is John, whom I beheaded—he has been raised to life." ¹⁷ It was Herod who had sent and arrested John and put him in prison on account of his brother Philip's wife, Herodias, whom he had married, ¹⁸ John had told Herod, "You have no right to marry your brother's

wife." [19] Herodias therefore had a grudge against him, and wanted to kill him, but she could not, [20] because Herod was afraid of John, knowing him to be a good and holy man. So he kept him in safe custody, and liked to listen to him, though it left him greatly perplexed. [21] Herodias, however, found her opportunity when Herod—on his birthday—gave a banquet to his principal officials and commanders, together with the leading men of Galilee. [22] Her daughter came in and danced, and so delighted Herod and his guests that the king said to the girl, "Ask what you like and I will give it to you." [23] And he vowed to her, "Whatever you ask I will give you, even to half my kingdom." [24] She went out and said to her mother, "What shall I ask for?" "The head of John the Baptizer," she replied. [25] The girl hurried back with her request: "I want you to give me, here and now, the head of John the Baptizer on a platter." [26] The king was greatly disturbed, but out of regard for his vows and for his guests he could not refuse her. [27] Immediately therefore the king sent a guard with orders to bring John's head. The soldier went off and beheaded John in prison, [28] brought back the head on a platter, and gave it to the girl, who gave it to her mother. [29] When John's disciples heard about it, they came and removed his body and laid it in a tomb.

Comment

What follows in Mark is an account of the ministry outside Galilee; it is prefaced by two sections, one on Herod and one on John. Apart from 7:1-23 there is no public teaching in the section 6:14-8:26, and Jesus is depicted as being alone with his disciples. Not only so, but most events here recorded are outside Galilee. Works of healing are performed in private and almost (it would appear) reluctantly. The order is that of Matthew, but Mark's interests lie in forwarding the movement of his gospel toward the passion, and the extended teaching represented by Matt 10:16-15:21 has no place in the Markan scheme. There are three distinct elements in this section: the concern and fears of Herod Antipas, coupled with an account of the execution of John; the first feeding stories; and the second feeding story. With the arrival in Caesarea Philippi this section comes to an end, and the mission recorded in 6:6b-13 resumes with the return of the disciples to Jesus.

It was the arrest of John that had terminated the Judean ministry which Jesus inherited from the Baptizer. But the account of the death of John is given no time frame, and Mark is no more familiar with any historical detail than is Matthew, but simply follows him. If Luke's account (13:31ff.) of

Jesus' attitude to Herod has him displaying great courage, it is probable that Herod's initial attitude toward Jesus was one of curiosity, not unmixed with alarm. We may reasonably infer from the itinerary of Jesus (Tyre at 7:24, the Decapolis at 7:31, and the dominions of Herod Philip at 8:27) in hurrying through Galilee and making for Jerusalem by a route east of the Jordan (10:1) that the attitude of Herod Antipas was more threatening than it was recorded to be in 6:14-16. To all of this must be added the evident desire of Jesus for a measure of solitude hitherto denied him.

Notes

14. *Herod:* The son of Herod the Great and Malthace, he received the tetrarchy of Galilee and Perea. An ambitious man, his desire to be king caused his banishment by Caligula in A.D. 39. Both Matthew and Luke correctly call him "tetrarch" (though Matt 14:9 has "king"), but Mark's use of *king* here may represent local popular usage. Herod is not represented as being alarmed at a roving mission by the Twelve; it is the ministry of Jesus which alarmed him. There is no note of time, and Matthew's "at that time" (14:1) is a vague formula signifying little.

reputation (literally "name" = Greek *onoma*): Cf. also 9:37ff.,39-41; 13:6,13.

People were saying (Greek *elegon*, pl.): This reading is to be preferred to the singular *elegen* (he said) of most manuscripts. Herod's opinion comes later.

has been raised to life (Greek *egeirein*): Cf. also 6:16, 12:26, 14:28, 16:6. The other verb for raising from the dead *(anastēnai)*, with no difference in meaning, is found at 8:31; 9:6ff.,31; 10:34; and 12:23,25. The perfect tense here employed *(egēgeretai)* describes the fact perpetuated in its effects. We meet again in 8:28 the common reports that Jesus was the Baptizer *redivivus*, or Elijah *redivivus;* in both cases the common reports are important to the narrative. The phrase *that is why . . . in him* is found only here and is reproduced by Mark from his source in Matthew.

powers (Greek *dunameis*): Used here of supernatural gifts, rather than—as in 6:2—of miracles as such. Cf. also 1 Cor 12:10,28-29; Gal 3:5; Eph 1:11,20. The notion that miraculous powers were associated with those restored to life is not found either in Jewish or pagan sources. Matthew's version ascribes the saying to Herod (cf. note above on *people were saying).* Luke omits *that is why* and describes Herod as "baffled" because of the popular rumors.

15-16. For the belief in the return of Elijah, cf. Mal 3:1, 4:5, and also notes on 1:6 above. We shall deal with the identification of John with Elijah below in Chapter 9. Luke's version has "John I beheaded. Who is this about whom I hear such things?" The hostility of Herod is clearer in the Lucan version.

The following account of the execution of John is in Mark the only narrative which is not about Jesus. The historicity of the account has been debated endlessly, and it has been customary to use the word "legend" to describe the account. In the strictest etymology this word is correctly used, but many critics use the word in a derogatory sense. There are details in the account which are vivid and offer yet another insight into the character of the Herods, but for all that there are acute difficulties, chiefly concerned with the account of the Baptizer in Josephus. Mark calls the first husband of Herodias Philip; Josephus asserts that Philip was the husband of Salome. Mark's location of the scene at Tiberias (by implication) is contradicted by Josephus' placing the imprisonment at Machaerus. If the possessive *autou* in v. 22 is the authentic text, then the girl is described by Mark as a daughter of Antipas and named Herodias. In this narrative the execution of John results from the hatred of Herodias, where Josephus *(Ant* 18.5.2) places the blame on Herod's fear of John's hold over the common people, which might have issued in revolt. The difficulties and contradictions are not, however, insurmountable. We have translated v. 22 with *autēs;* it is not likely that Mark thought that the girl was the daughter of Antipas and carried the same name as her mother. The difficulty over names is fairly easily resolved: certainly Mark was mistaken if he considered the first husband of Herodias to be Philip the Tetrarch. But the Herod family notoriously repeated names, and it is even possible that the husband in Rome was called Philip. Even if Mark does place the court at Tiberias—though this is not explicitly stated—this is an honest mistake if Josephus' version is correct and could hardly be regarded as of serious dimensions. Far more serious is the difference between the reasons given by the evangelists and by Josephus. The Jewish historian, writing over fifty years after the event, was wholly concerned to trace the political ramifications which led to a war, while the gospel accounts of the death of John have about them the air of rumors and palace intrigue so characteristic of the Herods. Each account is compatible with the other, and each complements the other.

17. Mark's account would seem to imply that John's imprisonment and execution were at Tiberias, in contrast with Josephus' statement that Machaerus was the place (at the northeast corner of the Dead Sea, near the desert of Judea).

Herodias: The daughter of Aristobulus, son of Herod the Great and Mariamne, she was therefore the niece of Antipater. If Mark means that she was married to Philip, the brother of Antipas, then he is wrong. The view was expressed by Lagrange (p. 158) that possibly Herod also bore the name of Philip; while not intrinsically impossible, it is at least unlikely. (Cf. Lane, p. 218, for a useful chart of Herodian family relationships.) Josephus *(Ant* 18.5.1) asserts that the wife of Antipas, on learning of his intentions, fled to Machaerus and from there escaped to the protection of Aretas her father, king of Arabia, who in A.D. 36 defeated Antipas in battle. This was regarded by some as punishment for the execution of John.

18. Mark follows Matthew closely, both making the explanation vivid by couching it in direct speech, whereas Luke (3:18-20) contents himself with a terse statement.

"You have no right . . .": The law is found in Lev 18:16 and 20:21. It is probable that there was no personal confrontation between Herod and John, but rather that direct speech has been employed to heighten the dramatic effect.

19,20. The second of these two verses explains why Herodias could not immediately destroy John. An alternative to *was afraid* would be "stood in awe of him." Mark here departs from Matthew, who depicts Herod as being "afraid of the common people" (14:5), and instead offers us a picture of a bewildered man who liked to listen to John—the classical picture of a man drawn two ways.

greatly perplexed: We have followed what seems to be the better Greek reading here *(ēporei)* rather than using *epoiei,* which would have to be rendered as "kept it in mind." The contradictions and conflicts in Herod's character are far better preserved in the translation we have chosen, for all the impressive manuscript attestation of *epoiei.*

21. *opportunity* (Greek *eukairos*): Literally, "suitable occasion," further amplified in the following clause.

banquet (Greek *deipnon*): In Hellenistic Greek, a meal in the late afternoon. Similarly, *birthday* (Greek *genesia*) was originally a memorial feast for the dead but by New Testament times was the equivalent of another Greek word meaning birthday celebration.

principal officials . . . : The notables mentioned here would have been far more appropriate to Tiberias, in spite of Josephus' placing the event at Machaerus.

22. *her daughter:* The manuscript confusion at this point is widespread. The girl Salome, about twenty years old at this time, was Herod's grandniece and not his daughter, but some important manuscripts read *autou* (his). Some texts read "his daughter" and go on to name her Herodias, which is plainly incorrect.

There is a difficulty (far removed from the evidence for *autou* as against *autēs*) having to do with the historicity of an account suggesting that a Herodian princess should have danced before Antipas' court. The undoubted implication of the text is that the dancing was sensual and lascivious, and there is an obvious question as to whether a member of Herod's family would have been allowed to perform in the presence of strangers. The commentators have been decidedly at variance with one another, and the combination of the well-known character of the Herodian family and suggestions about the morals of oriental courts have proved irresistible to speculators. It is highly probable that the text of Esther has influenced the text: cf. Esth 5:3ff., but especially Esth 2:9 = v. 23. This is not to say that the whole story before us is fabrication.

23. *half my kingdom:* The expression is found in 1 Kgs 13:8. Cf. Luke 19:8.

24-25. The account strongly suggests an arrangement already made between mother and daughter which the daughter merely wishes to have confirmed. Even Mark's customary *euthus* (immediately), which we have assimilated into *hurried back,* carries the implication of enthusiasm. The whole reply in the latter part of v. 25 has an air of impertinence about it, as though the girl is fully aware that she has pleased a besotted king who will deny her nothing, as though there is a contractual arrangement in existence.

25. *platter* (Greek *pinax*): In Hellenistic Greek any kind of bowl or dish on which food was served. Rawlinson (p. 83) finds in this a grim witticism.

Baptizer (Greek *baptistēs*): Regularly used of John in Matthew and Luke, it is found in Josephus *(Ant* 18.5.2) but not otherwise attested.

Matthew's statement (14:8) that the girl was instructed by her mother has been omitted in Mark. This evangelist also heightens the derision of the narrative from Matthew's "Give me here . . ." to *I want you to give me, here and now. . . .*

26. *greatly disturbed:* This accords with the unanimous verdict of the synoptists on Herod's attitude toward John.

his vows (Greek *dia tous orkous*): The plural implies that the king's oath had been made repeatedly.

Matthew's version, which Mark simplifies in some respects, has Herod commanding the head of John to be given.

For references to the disciples of John, cf. John 2:18. Whatever later tradition may suggest, it is to be presumed that the body was buried near Machaerus (assuming this to be the place of execution).

Matthew's version records that the disciples came and told Jesus. The same version also has it that Jesus' withdrawal took place immediately thereafter, and also as a direct result of the execution, in contrast with Mark's account. We think that Matthew is inherently more plausible, even allowing for the fact that he has no account of any mission of the Twelve (and so no account of their return to Jesus recorded in Mark 6:36ff.). The death of John, whose mission Jesus inherited, and whose Proclamation he repeated, would of necessity demand that Jesus face once more the manner in which his ministry was to be conducted. The fate of John plainly indicated that the Reign of God was not to be inaugurated by Proclamation and the call to repentance alone. The section that follows carries the ministry farther, beyond Proclamation.

31. The Feeding of the Crowd (i)
(6:30-44) = Matt 14:13-21; Luke 9:10-17; John 6:1-14

6   30 The apostles now returned to Jesus, and reported to him all that they had done and taught. 31 He said to them, "Come away (with me) by yourselves to some lonely place where you can rest for a time." There were so many coming and going that they had no leisure even to eat. 32 So they set out privately by boat for a lonely place. 33 But many saw them leave and recognized them; so they left all the towns, came round by land, and arrived there first. 34 When he came ashore he saw a large crowd, and he was moved with pity because they were like sheep without a shepherd; and he began to teach them many things. 35 When it was getting late, his disciples came to him and said, "This is a lonely place, and it is already late. 36 Send them away, and let them go to the farms and villages nearby and buy themselves something to eat." 37 "Give them something to eat yourselves," he replied. "Do you want us to spend two hundred denarii on food in order to feed them?" they asked. 38 "How many loaves do you have?" he asked them. "Go and see." When they had found out, they said to him, "Five, and two fish." 39 He told them to make all the people sit down on the green grass, 40 so they sat down in rows, rows of a hundred and rows of fifty. 41 Then, taking the five loaves and the two fishes, he looked up to heaven, gave thanks, broke the loaves, and gave them to the disciples to distribute. He also divided the fishes among them. 42 They all ate

and had enough, [43] and twelve large baskets of scraps were picked up of what remained of the bread and fish. [44] The number of those who ate the loaves was five thousand persons.

Comment

The two narratives which follow are in Mark's account closely linked. The return of the Twelve from their mission leads Jesus to suggest that they all seek solitude. Matthew's account links the solitude of Jesus with the death of John. Mark, having included a tradition of a preaching mission, must of necessity tell of its conclusion, and the suggestion inevitably invites the question whether this mission took place coincidentally with the arrest and execution of John. This suggestion is implausible, for it was the arrest of John that had sent Jesus to Galilee in the first place.

The suggestion has been made that the details which preface this first feeding are purely artificial, since the presence of the crowds is essential to the narrative. But—it is argued—the disciples must be brought back and taken across the lake to a lonely place, while the crowd on foot arrives sooner than Jesus and the disciples, taking a direct route. Certainly here and in Matthew there are conventional details, but the account in Mark has all the signs of an original eyewitness tradition, and in this respect the evangelist has improved upon Matthew. There is a vagueness here and there in the narrative, which is characteristic of Mark: the return of the missionaries is dismissed in half a verse, and the concluding clause of v. 34 is tantalizing in its imprecision.

The account of the feeding, here consequent upon the return of the disciples and the unfulfilled quest for solitude, might well be the subject of a separate note, but it is treated here so as not to interrupt the flow of the commentary.

Both Matthew and Mark duplicate the account of the feeding (6:30-44 = Matt 14:13-21 and Luke 9:10-17; 8:1-10 = Matt 15:32-39, cf. John 6:1-14), but to assume that Mark followed Matthew in assimilating two traditions of feeding is altogether too simple, and we shall have reason to suggest that a single occasion was used by both evangelists as two separate events to make somewhat different emphases.

To treat the feeding narratives as an example of the compassion of Jesus for the hungry would set the feeding narrative wholly apart from the miracle stories in the gospels. It is plain from our gospels that the miracles were treated as signs of the incoming of the Reign of God, but also as the instruments through which the Reign of God came. Therefore, either the feeding stands alone, an exception to this understanding, or there is more to the narrative than a surface understanding. For some clues in the unraveling of this dilemma, we have to turn to the fourth gospel. John 6:15 records that after the feeding, the crowd wished to take Jesus by force and make him king. As a reaction to the feeding of a weary group of people, this can only be considered as far-fetched and even bizarre. In John's gospel, and in a more muted sense also in the synoptics, the question of messiahship is always in the background of the ministry of Jesus, and it is in this sense that John 6:15 is best understood. It is then necessary to ask what in the feeding narrative emphasized the messianic issue.

We suggest that the words of Jesus himself, in the giving of thanks, indicated that what was being done was not a simple feeding (however token that may have been), but an anticipation of the messianic Feast, a looking ahead to a future consummation in the Reign of God. We can discern that this was the way in which the New Testament writers understood it, and also the way in which Jesus interpreted it, from the occurrence of the key liturgical words "took," "gave thanks," "broke," and "gave" in:

> Matt 14:19, 15:35, 26:26
> Mark 6:41, 8:6, 14:22
> Luke 9:16, 22:19
> John 6:11 (except for "broke")
> 1 Cor 11:23-24 (except for "gave")

We are here dealing with a form of words which was fixed in the tradition very early, as witness their appearance in Paul's account of the Last Supper. We suggest that if Jesus' "giving of thanks" had any reference to the inauguration of the Reign of God, or to a new creation/new Covenant (constantly referred to in the Pauline letters), then all the ingredients were at hand in the explosive atmosphere of Galilee for a situation where an enthusiastic acclamation of Jesus as Messiah would not be out of the question.

There is much more to be said. The duplication of the tradition in Matthew and Mark attests to the crucial importance attached to the incident, though the duplicates serve divergent purposes (to be discussed in the notes).

The connection between the passion and the inbreaking of the Reign of God is clearly articulated in the gospels, particularly in John, and the feeding represented a watershed in the ministry, for it will have been clear to Jesus that the time of testing was approaching a climax. Moreover, the connection between the passion, New Covenant, and Eucharist is clear in Paul, and he can hardly have invented this but must have received it from an existing tradition. Furthermore the discourse on the bread of life in John 6 prescinds from the feeding, and if the primary thrust of the discourse is not eucharistic, that meaning is certainly present by implication.

The feeding as mere multiplication, however few or however many people were involved, seems remarkably out of character with the rest of the gospel miracles, but a token meal with strongly eschatological overtones (such as apparently obtained at Qumran) is far more satisfactory as an explanation of the reactions of the crowd in John 6:15.

Finally, attention is called to the significant article by R. H. Hiers and Charles A. Kennedy ("The Bread and Fish Eucharist in the Gospels and Early Christian Art," *Perspectives in Religious Studies* 3.1.1976, pp. 20-47) for an examination of the place of fish for the messianic banquet.

In this section Mark's text is a conflation of Matthew and Luke, though the text is closer to that of Matthew. The parallel with Matthew is strikingly illustrated by the fact that the next sixteen units are all in the Matthean order, without omitting one Matthean story (in spite of shortening some of them). The order of Matthew is broken only twice, and then to introduce two narratives of healing from another source (Mark 7:32-37; 8:22-26).

Notes

30. *apostles:* The word is used only here in Mark. It indicates a time when the word had fairly specific functional meanings, carrying the sense of commissioning for work associated with Jesus himself (e.g., preaching and exorcism).

31. *rest:* The Greek word is rarely used in this sense in classical Greek but is common in later Hellenistic Greek.

32. The identification of the *lonely place* is impossible to determine, and opinions are as varied as the commentators. The amplification of the narrative from Matthew by *so many coming and going* adds vivid detail and may be from an eyewitness account. Luke's identification of the place as "a town called Bethsaida" is interesting but is ignored by Mark.

33. *towns* (Greek *poleōn*): The term is used very loosely by Mark, as the literal sense is "cities." The vivid description of people from the surrounding countryside converging on the scene is a detail he adds to Matthew.

34. Commentators differ as to when the narrative of the feeding can properly be said to begin. Verses 33 and 34 are closely connected, so if the narrative begins at 35, it would be better to treat vv. 30-34 as a unit separate from, but introductory to, the feeding.

like sheep without a shepherd: The phrase, peculiar in this context to Mark, has parallels in the Septuagint—cf. Num 27:17, 1 Kgs 22:17, Ezek 34:5, 2 Chr 18:16.

35. If the narrative of the feeding *does* begin at this verse, it must be said that it begins abruptly, and perhaps the original form of the narrative's beginning was absorbed into the preceding verse.

getting late: The reference would appear to be to late afternoon; the note of time is essential to everything that follows.

36. *send them away* (Greek *apoluō*): This is a strong word, used in the New Testament for dismissal in divorce, though used in Mark 15:6,9,11, and 15 in the sense of "release." The imperative form of Mark is taken over from Matthew and Luke.

37. Mark heightens the Matthean narrative by omitting "There is no need for them to go away" (Matt 14:16) and leaving all the emphasis on the imperative *Give them.*

Two hundred denarii: The phrase has been left without further translation, since a modern equivalent can hardly be found. One denarius was ordinarily a single day's pay for an agricultural worker in the time of Jesus.

38. Mark's narrative again heightens the dramatic effect. Matt 14:17 is omitted, as is Luke 9:13, and the surprise of the previous verse is matched by the peremptory tone of Jesus' reply.

39-40. Again the picture is vivid, "resembling garden beds in their bright colours" (Taylor, p. 323).

all the people (Greek *pantas sumposia sumposia):* The use of the noun as distributive is matched by the repetition of the cardinal numbers in v. 7 *(duo duo:* "two by two") and—like *prasiai prasiai (in rows)* in v. 40—has often been held to be a Semitism. The commentators are divided on the issue (cf. Lagrange p. 150, Taylor pp. 60-61). *Sumposion* is found to mean a "party of guests" in the Septuagint and in classical Greek.

green grass: The point is sometimes made that this is an indication of the season of Passover, but green grass may well have been found in sheltered and watered places near the lake.

41. *looked up to heaven:* The Greek word *anablepsas* signifies the act of prayer (cf. 7:34). The phrase was later enshrined in the Gregorian canon of the Eucharist *(et elevatis oculis in caelum).*

gave thanks (Greek *eulogēsen):* The act described is that of blessing God, or giving thanks to him. Cf. the blessing of bread in Jewish practice: "Blessed art thou, O Lord our God, king of the universe, who bringest bread from the earth." In 14:22 the same verb is used, but in the parallel 8:6 and in 14:23 *eucharisteō* is used. It has been suggested that although the meaning of the words is identical the present narrative is Semitic, in contrast with a Hellenized version in 8:1-9.

It was suggested in the comment above that the "giving of thanks" may have given a clear indication of Jesus' understanding of his mission and ministry and so provoked the enthusiasm described by John 6:15.

gave them: The tense is imperfect, carrying the implication that there were several distributions of bread.

The vocabulary of this section is very close to that of the Last Supper, the only significant difference being that this present messianic Banquet in prolepsis has no mention of the death of Jesus, though it should be emphasized that the Lucan account of the Last Supper explicitly links that occasion both to the Reign of God and the death of Jesus.

42. *ate and had enough:* It is extremely difficult to avoid the element of the highly miraculous in Mark's version; by contrast Matthew's version is very matter of fact. Certainly until fairly recent times the story was treated simply as a miraculous multiplication, with only the nineteenth-century rationalists insisting that the kernel of the story was an act of kindness on the part of Jesus and his disciples in sharing their own provisions with a small number of people. Some more modern scholars have embraced the miraculous element as an act of creation. Schweitzer (p. 374) was far nearer to the treatment we have advocated in the comment. The view of this commentator is that

there was indeed a group of people seeking Jesus, the members of which—after the giving of thanks—were fed with token morsels in anticipation of the messianic Banquet.

43. The *twelve large baskets* is of considerably more importance than the purported numbers of participants: what is symbolized here is the ingathering of Israel in the Reign of God. The second feeding tradition has other concerns.

scraps (Greek *klasma*): The word means uneaten broken pieces and not dropped crumbs. The word is used in *Didachē* 9:3ff. of the broken bread of the Eucharist. The whole grammatical structure of this concluding v. 43 is so awkward that some have found suggestions of translation Greek, while Mark's addition of the fish to the remains collected seems almost an afterthought.

For further reading see J-M. van Cangh, "La Multiplication des pains dans l'évangile de Marc," in *L'évangile selon Marc: Tradition et Redaction,* edited by M. Sabbe, Bibliotheca ephemeridum theologicarum lovaniensium 34, Gembloux, Duculot and Louvain: Leuven University, 1974, pp. 309-46; I. de la Potterie, "Le sens primitif de la multiplication des pains," *Jésus aux origines de la christologie,* edited by J. Dupont, Bibliotheca ephemeridum theologicarum lovaniensium 40, Gembloux, Duculot and Louvain: Leuven University, 1975, pp. 305-29; E. Stauffer, "Zum apokalyptischen Festmahl in Markus 6:34ff.," *ZNW* 46.1955, pp. 264-66; G. Ziener, "Die brotwunder Speisung und das Abendmahl in der synoptischen Tradition (Mark 6.35-44 par., 8.1-20 par.)," *NovTest* 7.3.64, pp. 167-94; A. Shaw, "The Marcan Feeding Narrative," *CQR* 162.34.1961, pp. 268-78; J-M. van Cangh, "La thème des poissons dans les récits évangeliques de la multiplication des pains," *RevBib* 78.1.1971, pp. 71-83; J. M. Derrett, "Leek-beds and Methodology," *BZ* 19.1.1975, pp. 101-2; B. van Iersel, "Die wunderbare Speisung und das Abendmahl in der synoptischen Tradition (Mark 6.35-44 par., 8.1-20 par.)," *NovTest* 7.3.1964, pp. 167-94.

32. Jesus Walks on the Water
(6:45-52) = Matt 14:22-33; John 6:15-21

6 [45] At once Jesus made his disciples embark and go on ahead of him to Bethsaida, while he sent the crowd away. [46] After taking leave of them, he went up the hillside to pray. [47] When evening came, the boat was already in the middle of the lake, while he was alone on the land. [48] Seeing them rowing with difficulty against a head wind, he came toward them, walking on the water, somewhere between three and six in the morning. He was going to pass by them, [49] but when they saw him walking on the lake, they thought it was an apparition and cried out—[50] for they all saw him and were terrified. But at once he spoke to them, "Courage! It is I; stop being afraid," he said to them. [51] Then he

went up into the boat with them, and the wind dropped. At this, they were completely astounded, [52] for they had not understood the incident of the loaves; their minds were closed.

Comment

It is easy to treat this next narrative as a piece of purely imaginative writing, a worked-over story of some incident which had a basis in fact but was subsequently transformed into a miracle story. Against this is the close connection, both in Mark and John, between the feeding narrative and the present one. The juxtaposition of the two accounts would seem to rule out the possibility that the present narrative is a misplaced resurrection appearance. The details of the story—the hasty leaving of Bethsaida at the urging of Jesus, the struggle of the men in the ship against strong winds, and the panic reaction to the sight of Jesus—all tend to confirm that there is a basis of fact in the story. But there are other details which are not so easy to handle. The walking on the water, the sudden cessation of the storm when Jesus enters the boat, and the blindness of perception all point in the direction of homiletical concerns. To those concerns belongs the heightened element of the miraculous. If the story was originally a piece of homiletic symbolism of the death and raising of Jesus, then it has to be said that this original has long been overlaid in the tradition.

While it is comparatively easy to understand the feeding once the notion of the narrative has been divested of any interpretation of it as a mere demonstration of miraculous powers, the same can hardly be said of the walking on the water. The miracle stories properly understood are part of the inbreaking of the Reign of God and the means by which that inbreaking is done; in no sense can this present narrative be so understood. The tendency of large expanses of inland water to sudden storms would have been part of the experience of these Galilean fishermen, and the present narrative does not do more than describe one such storm in the hours before the dawn. Moreover, Jesus in this story apparently does not have rescue in mind (cf. v. 48), let alone a test of faith.

The most that can be said is that the tradition of Jesus' coming to the disciples in their fishing boat very early in the morning is an ancient tradition. But by what means or in what homiletical interests the tradition was developed we cannot know. In very sharp contrast to other miracles, Jesus here is cast in the role of a wonder-worker, even to some extent making a display of divine powers.

Notes

45. *made his disciples embark:* The Greek verb *anankadzo* literally means "to compel," and perhaps this is the word which links this present narrative with the preceding one: the tension generated in the feeding was such as to compel an early departure.

Bethsaida (cf. 8:22, Matt 11:21, Luke 9:10, 10:13, John 1:44, 12:21): Most likely the town at the mouth of the Jordan (restored by King Philip and named Bethsaida Julia in honor of Augustus' daughter) is meant. Some manuscripts of Mark have *eis to peran pros Bethsaida* (to the shores near Bethsaida), a reading which we omit here, but which was favored by *The Greek New Testament* prepared by the translators of the *New English Bible.* The difficulties occasioned by this reading led some commentators to suggest a western Bethsaida. The *eis* (into) which we read before *Bethsaida* is somewhat more exact than *pros* (near to), but notes of location in Mark are rare, and perhaps here we have a Petrine reminiscence which Mark incorporated. Matthew has no mention of Bethsaida, while Luke refers to the place in the beginning of his account of the feeding. If the feeding took place at the northeast part of the lake, then Bethsaida was fairly near at hand.

46. *taking leave of* (Greek *apotassō*): It is likely that the crowds are meant here.

hillside: Mark omits Matthew's note of the solitude of Jesus ("by himself," Matt 14:23), and the hillside is a purely formal note in Mark, though of some importance in John 6:3 and 15.

47. It is clear that the disciples began their journey in daylight, for by late afternoon they were in the middle of the lake. But perhaps the expression *en mesō* means no more than that they were well away from land. No indication is given as to when Jesus became aware of the boat in the storm, but presumably it was from some vantage point on the hillside.

48. There are difficulties attached to the following v. 48 and its surroundings. Matt 14:24 has the boat "many furlongs" from land, while John 6:19 suggests a distance of nearly four miles. John's text certainly suggests a heightening of the tradition. Moreover, the account in Matthew describes the boat as being thrown and buffeted by the waves, whereas in the Markan version it is the disciples who are in difficulty.

head wind: Presumably the wind was from the north or northeast.

somewhere between three and six (Greek *peri tetartēn de phulakī*): The phrase, as in Matthew, follows the Roman practice of four night watches (the Jewish division was three—cf. Luke 12:38).

pass by them (Greek *kai ēthelen paralthein autous*): The phrase is peculiar to Mark, and it is not without difficulty in the Greek. It can reasonably be translated by "began to pass by them" or "made as though he would pass by them." Equally, the verb without a direct object can be rendered "join," "come to . . ." Why Jesus would have passed them by we cannot know. We can only record the tradition. For additional discussion see T. Snoy, "Marc 6.48 . . . 'et il voulait les dépasser': Proposition pour la solution d'une énigme," in *L'évangile selon Marc: Tradition et redaction,* edited by M. Sabbe, Bibliotheca ephemeridum theologicarum lovaniensium 34, Gembloux: Duculot and Louvain: Leuven University, 1974, pp. 347-63.

49. *walking on the lake:* Unquestionably this is what the evangelist means, as did his source in Matthew. The Old Testament instances of divine activity in walking on the sea are relevant here (cf. Job 9:8, 38:16, and Sir 24:5), and it is reasonable to enquire how far they have influenced the present narrative.

apparition: In the darkness, the form of Jesus *terrified* them. One translation manuscript of Mark seems to have read *daimōnion* (demon) at this point. In contrast with the disciples' terror, Jesus' manner is calmly reassuring.

At this point the matter of priority in sources is of some difficulty; Matthew has a tradition at this point (Matt 14:28-31) of Peter's failure of faith on being invited to walk on the water and come toward Jesus. It is difficult—both on an assumption of Petrine reminiscences as underlying Mark, and also on any assumption of Markan dependence on Matthew—to see why Mark should have omitted the story. Moreover, since it is commonly said that Matthew and Luke treat the disciples with more respect than Mark, it is worth noting that the Matthean narrative casts Peter in anything but a favorable light. It is hardly appropriate to say that the Petrine narrative in Matthew is a homiletic expansion of Markan material, as though Mark's narrative has been untouched by homiletic considerations.

51ff. *Then he went up:* The statements in this verse are present also in 4:39, and it is hard to resist the conclusion that the present narrative is a doublet of the one in Chapter 4, dramatically heightened by purely homiletic concerns. The suggestion by Taylor (p. 330) that the point of the narrative before us—unlike the previous one—is the walking on the water is negated precisely when one has admitted the intrusion of homiletic motives.

52. Mark's explanation is that the disciples were obtuse, failing to perceive reality rather than being guilty of sheer obstinacy. Similar judgments of obtuseness in other contexts and with others in mind are found in Paul (cf. 2 Cor 3:14, Rom 11:7). If the whole point of the narrative is the walking on the water, then the commentator can only marvel at the obtuseness which made the disciples fail to see the implications of walking on the water. Furthermore Mark's explanation that they had not understood the incident of the loaves implies that the feeding was simply a multiplication miracle (as to which we have already expressed grave hesitation). If this is the meaning of the feeding narrative as the evangelist saw it, then the closed minds of the disciples must be matter for astonishment. John's gospel has far less of the element of the miraculous about it, but Matthew's version (again presumably in the interests of a homiletic concern) heightens the narrative by speaking of the disciples' reverencing Jesus and confessing him as "Son of God" (Matt 14:33).

All in all, it must be said that if this narrative is not a doublet of 4:35-41, its purpose is wholly obscure. Cf. Quentin Quesnell, "The Mind of Mark: Interpretation and Method Through the Exegesis of Mark 6:52," *JBL* 90.1971, pp. 335ff.

Appended Note

No responsible commentary can omit reference to and comment upon the thesis of José O'Callaghan that Cave VII of Qumran, among the fragments of Greek papyri discovered there, contained fragments which could with confidence be identified with Mark 6:52-53 (7Q5), 4:28 (7Q6), 12:17 (7Q7), and—possibly—6:48 (7Q15). There are manifold difficulties attaching to such confidence.

1. The fragments in Cave VII, unlike any other remains so far discovered in the area, are Greek and therefore are perhaps unrelated to the Essene Community.

2. The fragments are very small, even tiny, nineteen in all and in some cases consisting only of a single letter.

3. The first identification made proposed 7Q1 as Exod 28:4-7, with a possible date of 100 B.C., and 7Q2 could be identified as the Epistle of Jeremiah 43-44.

4. The remainder of the fragments were almost incapable of identification but by paleography could be dated 50 B.C.-50 A.D. Fragment 7Q5, which O'Callaghan identified with Mark 6:52-53, had a date approximately in the middle of the first century.

The fragment that O'Callaghan attempts to identify positively and with certainty with Mark 6:52-53 has twenty letters, though the first editorial attempts at identification yielded certainty with only seventeen of them. It is worth detailing O'Callaghan's proposed transcription:

```
          ]  e  [
        ]  utō  .  ē  [
        ]  ē  kai  ti  [
        ]  nnēs  [
        ]  thēsa  [
```

After this preliminary identification, the thesis proposed a line in the original manuscript to have contained letters on the basis of the two fragments previously identified and transcribed. In 7Q1, lines 10-13 were not intact, though the preserved lines had twenty letters each, while 7Q2 averaged twenty-one letters. On this basis O'Callaghan identified 7Q5 as Mark 6:52-53. The same methods were applied in finding 4:28 in 7Q6 and 12:17 in 7Q7. But the problems are severe: in the instances just given, only four letters are clearly distinguishable in three lines, and the size of the fragments would not appear to be capable of the certainty of identification which O'Callaghan proposes. It will be necessary to illustrate what this commentator feels to be well-nigh insuperable difficulties:

7Q6.1	7Q7	7Q15
] . [	] . [	] ntōe [
] eit . . [	] k̄a . [	] . . . . [
] . lē . . [	] tha . [	

7Q7, to which O'Callaghan links Mark 12:17, may be examined in more detail. There a line over the *kappa* is certainly a scribal sign for abbreviation, and O'Callaghan therefore reads *k(aisaros) a(podote)*. The second line has *th*, which would be part of *(eze) th(umadzon)*. But even if *kaisari, theou,* and *theo* ("to Caesar," "God's," "to God") are themselves abbreviated, the length of the resulting line is longer than O'Callaghan's stipulated norm:

> *ka (podote k kai ta theou th to th kai eze)*
> *th(aumadzon ep' autou)*
> "Give back to Caesar the things which are Caesar's and to God what belongs to God and they were amazed at him."

It has to be said that this very slender hypothesis is to the present writer unconvincing. With only photographs as assistance, it is fair to say that the size of the fragments, along with the very tentative nature of the identification, makes even speculation hazardous. The fragments may not even be biblical, and all that can be said is that the two fairly certain identifications of fragments with Exodus and the Epistle of Jeremiah provide tentative evidence that the fragments belong to the biblical and postbiblical Jewish textual history. But this is far indeed from any certainty that New Testament texts are among the fragments. Even if identification were more certain and O'Callaghan's reconstructions proved acceptable, we have no means of knowing whether we are dealing with Mark or a pre-Markan source. The best verdict that can be offered at this juncture is the ancient Scottish one of "nonproven."

The literature associated with O'Callaghan's thesis is considerable, and only a few selections can be attempted:

José O'Callaghan, "New Testament Papyri in Qumran Cave 7?" *JBL* Supp 91.2.1972, pp. 1-14; Carlo M. Martini, "Notes on the Papyri of Qumran Cave 7," *JBL* Supp 91.2.1972, pp. 15-20; José O'Callaghan, *Los Pairos griecos de la Cueva 7 de Qumran,* Biblioteca de Autores cristianos 353, Madrid: La Editorial Catolica, 1974; C. H. Roberts, "On Some Presumed Papyrus Fragments of the New Testament from Qumran," *Bib* 53.1972, pp. 91-100.

33. Healing the Sick
(6:53-56) = Matt 14:34-36

6 53 They finished the crossing and came to land at Gennesaret, where they came to anchor. 54 When they came ashore, people recognized him at once 55 and they ran through the whole district, and began bringing the sick on stretchers to any place where they heard he was. 56 Wherever he went—villages, towns, or country towns—they laid out the sick in the town centers and begged him to let them touch at least the edge of his clothes; and all who touched it were cured.

Comment

It is clear that the three episodes of the feeding, the crossing, and the landing at Gennesaret were very early linked in the tradition, for there is double attestation in Mark (6:30-56; 8:1-10) and in John (6:1-25). The word picture is vivid and in small compass characterizes the Galilean ministry. The picture is one of a peripatetic ministry, with no locations mentioned and no teaching. For all the distinctive Markan phraseology, the evangelist has heightened the impact of the shorter and stylized Matt 14:34-36, especially in v. 56. The whole piece, apart from being a digest or typical summary of the Galilean ministry, suggests that the purpose of the journey to Galilee was not to preach, but to escape attention and to be away from the jurisdiction of Herod Antipas.

Notes

53. *Gennesaret:* The Greek of this word has many variants in the manuscripts, and the original Markan reading, whether the *Gennesaret* given here (and found in Matthew) or *Gernēsera* or *Gernesar* is unknown. In any event, the location is unknown.

54-55. The verses are oddly constructed. There is first a suggestion that Jesus was recognized the moment he stepped ashore, and this is immediately followed by a description of ministry from place to place. The two descriptions do not easily fit together. The narrative reads very much like a clumsy expansion of Matthew by means of material from other sources.

56. *town centers* (Greek *en tais plateiais):* This is the best translation we could conveniently use; the phrase may refer simply to open spaces in the small villages through which Jesus passed.

34. The Law (i) Tradition
(7:1-13) = Matt 15:1-20

7   ¹ Then the Pharisees, and some scribes who had come from Jerusalem, met him and ² noticed that his disciples were eating their food with "unclean" hands—that is to say, without washing their hands. ³ (For the Pharisees, and the Jews generally, never eat without washing their hands, in obedience to traditions received from the forefathers; ⁴ and on coming from the marketplace they do not eat unless they wash all over first. They also maintain many other traditions which they have received, such as washing cups and jugs and copper bowls.) ⁵ So the Pharisees and the scribes asked him, "Why is it that your disciples do not conform to the traditions of the forefathers, but eat their food with 'unclean' hands?" ⁶ "Isaiah was right," he replied, "when he prophesied about you pettifogging lawyers—as it is written:
　'This people pays me lip service,
　but their heart is far from me:
　⁷ their worship of me is vain,
　teaching as doctrine manmade commandments.'
⁸ You put aside the commandment of God to keep the tradition of men." ⁹ He further said to them, "How well you set aside the commandment of God to uphold your tradition! ¹⁰ For Moses said, 'Honor your father and mother' and 'Anyone who curses his father or mother must certainly be put to death.' ¹¹ But you maintain that if a man says to his father or mother 'Anything of mine which might have benefited you is qorbān' "—meaning, a gift set apart for God—¹² "you excuse him from helping his father or mother. ¹³ So by this tradition which you hand on, you nullify the word of God. And there are many other similar things that you do."

Comment

Section IX (pp. cvi ff.) of the introduction to the AB volume on Matthew (Albright-Mann, 1971) attempted a summary of Jesus' attitude to the Law as seen through the eyes of one evangelist who was concerned to show at far greater length what he conceived to be the nature of the criticisms leveled by Jesus at the teachers of the Law.

Mark's version can best be described as a very brief summary of the differentiation which Jesus made between the Law on the one hand and human exigencies and oral tradition on the other.

We are justified in seeing in this narrative the outlines of the debates of the early years of Palestinian Christianity. At a time when the loyalty of Christian Jews was being called into question, both by Roman authority and by fellow Jews, the matter of the attitude of Jesus to the Law would have been crucial, not to mention the attitude to be adopted toward Gentiles seeking admission to the new community. The passage bears all the marks of the debate, for there is no typical "pronouncement," and the whole piece is disjointed, going from a complaint about setting aside oral law to a general discussion of legal tradition.

The suggestion is not made so frequently now as it was in the past that Jesus saw part of his ministry and function as propounding a "new law" or abrogating the Mosaic Law, but the reference in the first paragraph to the AB commentary on Matthew must suffice to explain the general position of the present writer.

Notes

1. There is no note of time or place, no link with the preceding narrative, but the tone of the opening verse would suggest Galilee, the *Pharisees* mentioned being probably residents locally.

2. In the second verse, *were eating their food* is important as an introduction to the material in v. 5. There are editorial remarks in vv. 3 and 4, and a note to explain the background of the controversy in v. 2—all of which would be essential to bewildered Gentiles seeking explication of something at best obscure, and at worst personally distressing if they sought admission to the community and discovered the very seeking to be a matter of intense and bitter debate.

"unclean" (Greek *koinos):* The word is used in the New Testament in the Hebrew sense of "unhallowed" or "profane." Mark adds the explanation in vv. 3 and 4 for the benefit of Gentile readers unfamiliar with Jewish custom.

It is important to notice here what Mark has done with the Matthean text, which he follows fairly closely. For Matthew the whole point is that eating with unwashed hands does not defile a man, with the "case" put in Matt 15:2 and the "decision" rendered in v. 20. But Mark has other purposes: in v. 19 the evangelist tells us that Jesus made all food clean. This would have a twofold effect: it would serve to dampen the fires of controversy between Jew and Gentile in the new community, and it would serve notice that there were more important matters at stake in a time of crisis than scrupulous observance of tradition.

3. *the Jews generally:* This phrase is unique in Mark and probably belongs to an editor. Some commentators have seen in this a reference to Jerusalem-centered Jews, as being more punctilious in the observance of the law and the traditions, but this can hardly be sustained.

washing their hands: The difficult Greek word *pugmē* has not been translated here. Literally meaning "a fist," it was early felt to be a difficulty and is omitted in some manuscripts. Various translations have been suggested: "thoroughly," "up to the elbow," or "vigorously." See M. Hengel, "Markus 7:3 *pygmē:* Die Geschichte eines exegetischen Aporie und der Versuch ihrer Lösung," *ZNTW* 60.3-4.1969, pp. 182-98; S. M. Reynolds, "PYGMHI (Mark 7:3) as 'Cupped Hand,' " *JBL* 85.1.1966, pp. 87-88.

traditions: What is here under discussion is not the Law of Moses, but oral or written tradition received from antiquity and honored because of its antiquity. The very antiquity of traditions of ritual washing has been a dispute among scholars for a considerable time. Apart from the example of the Essenes, of which we now know considerably more than was suspected by early commentators, it is generally suggested that the more pious lay people adopted the rigorous rules of purification demanded by the temple clergy. The relation of oral (and written) tradition to the Law was not, and is not, unique to Judaism, for any codification of law in written form will inevitably bring with it judicial interpretation, commentary, argument from precedent, and all manner of recommendations for living under the code in question. For any system of laws with a religious basis, there will inevitably spring up customs—some designed on a "holier-than-thou" foundation—which rapidly harden into a tradition for the devout of equal force with written prescription. With this kind of tradition the synoptic gospels record Jesus as expressing angry impatience.

forefathers (Greek *presbuterōn*): The word—often translated as "elders," but literally as "old men"—is an honorific appellation for those in the past, and even in the present, whose interpretation of the Law and tradition commanded respect.

4. This verse completes the explanation of items in the tradition which have to do with ritual cleansing. How burdensome tradition might be to the would-be observant can be best understood in terms of a peasant-farmer constantly coming into contact with unclean insects and thereby being under constant constraint to wash.

5. The narrative resumes from v. 1 with the putting of a question. Though the question is put in the form of a complaint about the disciples, it is in fact a challenge to Jesus' teaching on the Law, and the challenge is accepted by Jesus without any reference to his disciples.

conform (Greek *peripatousin;* literally, "walk"): The evangelist uses the term "to walk" in the Hebraic sense of conforming one's life. (Cf. John 8:12, Rom 8:4, and often in the Pauline letters.) Mark has amplified the Matthean version.

Isaiah was right: The quotation differs from the Septuagint in several respects, and differs too from the Massoretic Text. Matthew exhibits the same characteristics. The details of the Greek text need not detain us, but we may with some confidence ascribe the Greek to a translation of the "Old Palestinian" tradition. We no longer have this source, but its existence has been illustrated by the Old Testament material from Qumran. (Cf. Frank M. Cross, *The Ancient Library of Qumran,* The Haskell Lectures 1956-57, London: Duckworth, 1958, which provides a useful introduction to the subject.)

6. *pettifogging lawyers* (Greek *hupokritōn):* It is not proposed to offer any lengthy explanation of this translation of a word far more commonly rendered as "hypocrites." The reasons for this translation were fully examined in Albright-Mann, 1971, Introduction IX, Appendix, pp. cxv ff., to which the reader is referred.

8. Mark reproduces in other words the assertion in Matthew that the force and the intent of the Law is clouded and even nullified by surrounding it with oral tradition.

9. The contrasts in Matthew and Mark are in parallel:

Mark v. 5 Why do your disciples not conform?	Matt v. 8 You put aside the commandment
v. 10 Moses said . . .	v. 11 but you maintain

The contrast in Matthew is even less gentle, with "for God said" (15:4) instead of Mark's *Moses said* (v. 10), so making the contrast between divine command and human tradition even more direct.

10. It has been suggested that the remaining verses in this section are an isolated tradition which Mark—following Matthew—has attached to the preceding discussion of ritual purity. We cannot easily determine whether vv. 9-13 represent a reply by Jesus to a question from his audience, or whether the verses represent a challenge by Jesus to the scribes on the oral law. The contrast between *the commandment of God* and *your tradition* in the previous verse represents the challenge of Jesus in its sharpest form. The verses which follow are admittedly difficult, since we have little information contemporary with Jesus as to just how binding oaths were in common use. It is true that the Mishnah *(Nedarim)* has examples of the use of words other than *qorbān* to affirm solemn oaths, words treated as equally binding. One difficulty is to know whether the practice condemned by Jesus was common, or whether he was using an extreme and relatively infrequent example. In Mark the man is made to say that the support which his parents might rightly have expected of him is given to God or is subject to an oath (pronounced in haste or anger?) and therefore inalienable. C. G. Montefiore *(The Synoptic Gospels,* London: Macmillan, 2nd ed., 1927, Vol. 1, p. 149) maintains that the rabbinic tradition was given to the annulling of vows rather than maintaining them, and that the rabbis took substantially the same position as Jesus with respect to vows made rashly or without examining possible consequences. The point of the hypothetical case presented here is that despite the fifth commandment, any support the parents might have anticipated is rendered null and void, whether the oath was uttered rashly or deliberately.

Honor your father . . . Anyone who curses . . . .: Though the quotations agree with the Septuagint text of the two appropriate quotations (Exod 20:12 = Deut 5:16; Exod 21:16), and the Hebrew of the second passage well carries the meaning of *he who curses* or "he who makes contemptible" and would therefore fit what is said about *qorbān*, there is doubt as to whether the Greek *ho katalogon* can be translated as *curses*. A more appropriate translation of our present Greek text would be "anyone who speaks evil of . . ." (a translation favored by the RSV) and therefore something carrying less solemnity and less penalty than an oath. We have chosen to translate the Greek by *Anyone who curses* on two grounds: (1) The seriousness of the offense is implied by the words of Jesus, and cursing carried grave penalties. (2) The Greek may not reflect the original text, and hence we may have here an example of an original Aramaic text which has been absorbed into the present Septuagint quotation (cf. 7:6ff.).

must certainly be put to death: It is of considerable importance to notice that though Jesus condemns the oral tradition he regards the Mosaic prescription as binding.

11. *But you maintain . . . :* The force of *you* should not on any account be overlooked, contrasting as it does with *Moses said* in the previous verse.

qorbān (from Hebrew, literally "offering" or "dedicated to God"). The word is not found in the Septuagint, but it is in Josephus *(Ant* 4.4.4; *AgAp* 1.167). The temple treasury in Matt 27:6 is *ho korbanos*. Mark's Greek explanation *(meaning, a gift set apart for God)* does not do justice to the force of something which is "banned," or "holy." The phrase *if a man says* was a common scribal device, and the introduction of the phrase here could hardly have been of any force unless there were already examples at hand. There may even have been a contemporary incident which was notorious in Galilee. See J. A. Fitzmyer, "The Aramaic Qorbān Inscription from Jebel Hallet etTûri and Mark 7:11/Matt 15:5," *JBL* 78.1.1959, pp. 60-65.

'Anything of mine . . .' : Literally, "that by which you will be profited from me." The translation given here is the best rendering of a slightly convoluted Greek sentence, conveying the meaning that any expectation on the part of the parents is void by reason of a vow.

13. Jesus reinforces the charge that the received tradition renders the commandment of God totally inoperative. Moreover the example given, Jesus insists, is not isolated.

nullify (Greek *akuroō):* Literally, "to make a contract void." In classical Greek it is frequently used of canceling wills.

35. The Law (ii) Clean and Unclean
(7:14-23) = Matt 15:1-20

7 ¹⁴ On another occasion he called the crowd to him and said to them, "Listen to me, all of you, and understand this: ¹⁵ Nothing entering into a man from outside can make him unclean—it is the things that come out of him that make him unclean." ¹⁶ (If you have ears to hear, then listen.) ¹⁷ When he had left the people and had gone into the

house, his disciples asked him about the case. [18] He said to them, "Are you as dull as the rest? Don't you understand? Nothing that goes into a man from outside can make him unclean, [19] because it does not go into his mind, but into his stomach and then passes into the drain." So (by saying this) he declared all things clean. [20] He went on, "It is what comes out of a man that makes him unclean. [21] For from inside, from a man's mind, come evil thoughts, sexual immorality, theft, murder, [22] adultery, lust of possession, malice, deceit, fornication, envy, slander, arrogance, and folly. [23] These evil things all come from inside, and they make a man unclean."

Comment

There is no narrative to provide framework for this passage, and it is attached to the previous section by association of subject, a characteristic which Mark shares with Matthew. Perhaps the only indication of occasion is the formal statement in v. 1, suggesting that this was after a session of private teaching to the disciples. Such an indication is found more emphatically in Matt 15:10 (cf. also Mark 7:17). The saying in v. 15 bears all the marks of being genuine, since such a sentiment would not have been common in contemporary Judaism (cf. the test of "dissimilarity"). If such a saying was designed to free the infant community from an obsessive legalism, it has to be said that such freedom did not long persist, and the later penitential discipline of the Church displayed a penchant for case law every whit as impressive as that of the scribes. Furthermore it is to be noted that the sayings are in parallelism in v. 15, and characteristically are not so directly stated as our own age would prefer. If Jesus had spoken emphatically, as vv. 18 and 19 would lead us to think, it is difficult to understand how the very early disputes in Antioch and Jerusalem (and later in Corinth) could have arisen in such acute form. What we have therefore in the passage before us is a saying of Jesus which has attracted to it explanatory material intended to explicate a saying which is not immediately clear. The disciples and the retirement to the house provide a setting in v. 17, somewhat less precise than the question of Peter in Matt 15:15, but the essential interpretation has been taken over by Mark virtually unchanged. In what circumstances these explanatory glosses were produced we do not know. We can say with some confidence that the instances of inner uncleanness in vv. 21ff. appear to be more appropriate as answering questions posed by Gentiles than answering those exposed to the moral code of Judaism. It is important to notice that even in the crisis situation for which Mark

was compiled, it was yet considered imperative to include this digest from
Matthew to provide guidance.

Notes

14. The introductory words are common in Mark, especially *he called.* The command *Listen to me* is reminiscent of the parable of the sower, and insofar as what is
being discussed here is "case law," the use of the word "parable" in this context is not
inappropriate.

On another occasion: We read *palin* here, as against *panta* (which would produce the
translation "all the crowd"). *Palin* (again) is frequent in Mark, and the objection that
we cannot know to what it refers is somewhat pointless, given the comparative absence of historical notes in this gospel.

15. *unclean* (Greek *koinoō):* The word is common, being found twice here, and in
vv. 18,20,23, with five occurrences in Matthew, three in Acts, and one in Hebrews. In
classical Greek it means "to make common" and thus "to communicate or share." In
the New Testament the verb is used to denote "profane" or "to reckon as ritually
unclean." The saying in this verse carried tremendous implications and could even be
regarded as shattering in its potential impact. But the saying itself is couched in very
general and even ambiguous terms. Indeed, v. 17 describes the saying as the presentation of a "case" (Greek *parabolē)* for discussion. Matthew's version (15:11) has "goes
into the mouth" and "out of the mouth," whereas the Markan text is more enigmatic.
Even in Mark it is possible that *nothing entering into a man* and *the things that come
out* are explanatory glosses, and their deletion would not only make the saying more
"pithy," but also leave a text which would demand the otherwise unnecessary ensuing
explanatory verses.

The logical consequence of the saying in this verse, if left in the enigmatic form
"Nothing from outside can render anyone unclean," is the abolition of the legal prescriptions about kosher and nonkosher food (cf. Leviticus 11; Deuteronomy 14). But
only the explanatory glosses make this evident, for if Jesus had clearly signified the
abolition of the food laws, it is not easy to imagine the controversies between Jewish
and Gentile Christians in the early community, to which Acts, Galatians, Romans,
and Colossians bear witness. In essence the saying enunciates the principle that only
persons can be unclean, not *things.*

At this point, Matthew adds a question by the disciples (cf. Matt 15:12), followed
by a saying of Jesus about the blind leading the blind. Mark omits this note—in the
circumstances of his composition, the less extraneous material the better.

It is worth considering the relationship between Matthew and Mark and the questions involved. In Matthew, the whole debate concerns eating with unwashed hands,
and the answer is given at the end of the pericope in v. 20. For Mark the climax is the
assertion that Jesus made *all things clean* (i.e., all foods). In contradistinction from
Matthew, with its Jewish background, Mark here reflects a later stage, of more burning concern to non-Jewish Christians, and we may have here a reminiscence from the
"Roman" stage of the evangelist's career. Significantly we have a somewhat similar
situation with regard to Matthew's list of evil thoughts (15:19 = Mark 7:21-22).

Mark's list (see below) adds five words familiar from Paul's letters and two which are unique to Mark. The precept from the decalogue on false witness is omitted by Mark. Again we have a situation later than the Jewish Christianity of Matthew, where the evangelist has been more open to the concerns of Gentile Christians—presumably from his Roman residence. Finally it is notable that the Matthean condemnation of the Pharisees is not reproduced in Mark. Not only was the situation very different from the days of Matthean composition, but the evangelist may well have thought that this note of controversy paled into insignificance against the peril of his own time.

17. The introductory verse has all the signs of being used by Mark as a convenient formula for the explanatory material which ensues. The question which follows tends to confirm this view, for although Mark lays stress on the inability of the disciples to understand, the question sounds far more akin to something raised in the course of instruction.

18,19. *dull* (Greek *asunetoi):* The word means "stupid' or "obtuse," in the moral sense as well as intellectually (cf. Matt 15:16; Rom 1:21,31; 10:19).

The second part of v. 18 repeats the brief, enigmatic statement of 15a, and the explanation follows in v. 19. There are difficulties here with *he declared all things* (i.e., foodstuffs) *clean.* This phrase must have been derived from some community tradition to which Mark had access, for *katharizou* (making clean) has overwhelming manuscript attestation. But the translation we have given depends upon supplying "by saying this" in v. 19. The implications of the short enigmatic saying in v. 15 are thus stated, but without implying that Jesus said anything about making all foods clean. Matthew knows nothing of the explanatory gloss supplied by Mark, but does put on the lips of Peter a request for clarification.

20-23. A further explanation of vv. 15-16 is given in the singular, followed by an exposition. The list of things belonging to the mind in vv. 21-22 is certainly alien to any collection of sayings of Jesus and is far more familiar to us from the writings of Paul.

21. *evil thoughts* (Greek *dialogismoi hoi kakoi):* The thrust of the Greek is not so much causal linking as reflections which result in the kind of actions next described. For the list which follows, cf. Gal 5:19-21, Rom 1:29-31, 1 Pet 4:3. Examples of lists of vices were commonplaces in Greek literature. The nouns which follow—twelve in all —contain six plural examples, indicating evil actions, and six singular, describing generic vices.

sexual immorality (Greek *porneiai):* The word originally meant fornication, but later became far wider in meaning, and so to be distinguished from *moicheiai* ("adultery"—or as here, in the plural, "acts of adultery").

22. *lust of possession* (Greek *pleouexiai):* The word has associations with sexual immorality in the papyri, as is reflected in this translation, which also indicates something stronger than covetousness.

The list of vices, as distinct from specific acts, comes next. We have translated *aselgeia* by *fornication.* The history of the word is not known, but Plato uses it in the sense of impertinence of a challenging character. Later it is associated with sensuality, in the sense of shocking public morality. *Envy* (Greek *ophthalmos pouēros)* has been used to translate a word which, while literally meaning "the evil eye" (an expression found worldwide), has the suggestion of regarding men and women with malice. In the sayings of Jesus the "evil eye" (cf. Matt 20:15) becomes evil intention. The Greek *huperēphania* (arrogance) is found only here in the New Testament, though it is common in classical Greek and the Septuagint. *Aphrosunē* (folly) carries the meaning of lacking moral sense or of moral perversity.

The whole list is thoroughly Pauline; it belongs to the interpretive needs of the early community and the necessity of bringing out the implications of the original sayings of Jesus (cf. Lohmeyer, p. 142).

See further: J. Carlston, "The Things that Defile: Mark 7:14 and the Law in Matthew and Mark," *NTS* 15.1968-69, pp. 75-96; Robert Banks, *Jesus and the Law in the Synoptic Tradition*, New York: Cambridge University Press, 1975; and "The Eschatological Role of Law in Pre- and Post-Christian Jewish Thought," in *Reconciliation and Hope: New Testament Essays on Atonement and Eschatology Presented to L. L. Morris on His 60th Birthday*, edited by R. Banks, Grand Rapids, Mich.: Eerdmans, 1974, pp. 173-85. Cf. also Ernest Käsemann's contention that any denial that external impurity can penetrate to the interior being "strikes at the plain verbal sense of the Law of Moses" (*Essays on New Testament Themes*, translated by W. J. Montague, London: SCM Press, 1964, p. 147).

36. The Law (iii) Relations with Gentiles: The Canaanite Woman (7:24-30) = Matt 15:21-28

7 24 Then he left that place and went to the territory near to Tyre. He went to a house and did not wish anyone to know that he was there— but he could not escape notice. 25 For at once a woman whose daughter had a disorder of the mind heard of him, came to him, and prostrated herself. 26 (The woman was a Greek, a Canaanite by race.) She begged him to drive out the disorder of her daughter's mind. 27 But he said to her, "Let the children be fed first. It is not right to take the children's food and throw it to the dogs." 28 "Sir," she replied, "even the dogs under the table eat the children's scraps." 29 "For saying that," he said to her, "go home—the disorder has gone from your daughter's mind." 30 When she returned home, she found the child lying in bed—the demon had left her.

Comment

This narrative has all the signs of a primitive tradition where the words of Jesus have not yet been sharpened—and shortened—into a pronouncement story. The incident has a definite location, and the note that Jesus' quest for privacy was in vain is an authentic touch. The narrative records the woman's quick reply to Jesus' sharp words, and there is only a brief reference in passing to a cure.

The incident is certainly included to indicate the attitude of Jesus to the Gentiles. That Gentiles were in his mind is plain from the first part of v. 27, even though the second part follows the common tradition and attitude of his own time.

Mark's text varies greatly from Matthew's, though the evangelist is still closely following Matthew's order. It is likely that Mark is here drawing on a source common to both. The urgency of Mark's concern allows him his reference to the attitude of Jesus to Gentiles. Matthew's references are far more detailed and are omitted in this gospel (cf. Matt 10:5, Albright-Mann, AB translation; 15:24).

There are some difficulties in this narrative. The cure is assumed and is done from a distance; there is no promise of a cure—both in strong contrast to the normal Markan tradition, which is that of contact or direct command. Taylor (p. 348) correctly observes that in a parallel story (the centurion and servant, Matt 8:5ff., Luke 7:2ff.) there are reasons for thinking that the healing did not belong to the original tradition—in Luke's version we are merely told that the centurion found his servant whole and well. There are elements in the healing ministry of Jesus for which there are no parallels elsewhere. But there is here no direct encounter with the sufferer, and we must assume some form of knowledge beyond our ordinary human experience if indeed a cure does belong to the tradition. (Matthew's version is far less difficult than Mark's at this point.) We are face to face with something of which in the nature of the case we can know nothing—the human self-consciousness of Jesus. That Jesus had a sense of communion with God is reflected almost artlessly in the synoptic tradition and is almost a truism. We are, most of us, not in a position to know how such intimate communion with God can result in an immediate, intuitive knowledge. We are well aware, however, that such an immediate knowledge is possible. The most natural sense of the narrative before us is of such knowledge of the sudden recovery of the sufferer. Matthew's narrative implies a cure at a distance (Matt 15:28). If both evangelists had a common source, as we have suggested, then Mark displays far more sensitivity to the difficulties posed by an apparent miracle at a distance.

Notes

24. *Then he . . . :* Mark's use of *ekeithen* (from thence) is rare, and its presence in the text of Matthew (who uses it frequently) entitles us to assume a dependence either on Matthew's text or on a common source. The use of a geographical note is noteworthy enough in Mark to indicate a new direction in the narrative. As for *that place,* it can mean either the house from 7:17 or the countryside of 6:53-56. How far Jesus went into the pagan territory bordering on Galilee, we obviously do not know. Some texts add *and Sidon* for the first part of the verse.

did not wish anyone: This is a clear indication that the purpose of the journey was to secure privacy, not missionary activity. That the purpose of Jesus was unfulfilled because of a reputation that had preceded him from Galilee is the obvious sense of what follows, but it may be that Mark wishes us to understand that Jesus was everywhere immediately recognized. Matthew omits any mention of Jesus' crossing the border, and he has no equivalent of Mark's 24b.

25. *at once:* Mark's profuse use of *euthus* makes it impossible to determine whether the sense is as translated here or whether it means simply "So then . . ." What the woman had heard about Jesus is not stated.

disorder of the mind (literally, "an unclean spirit"): The translation is not given to demonstrate a modern scientific superiority over the (assumed) superstitious ignorance of a pre-scientific culture but to give the best equivalent for what is being described.

prostrated herself: The attitude is an indication of profound respect, as well as of supplication in distress. Matthew's version is fuller, with a note that Jesus did not immediately respond to the plea of a pagan (Matt 15:22-23), and the disciples are represented as wishing to send the woman away. At this point we are obviously faced with two versions of the tradition. Mark's emphasis on Jesus' desire for solitude calls for no mention of the disciples, whereas Matthew emphasizes their presence. From the point of view of synoptic relationships, the contrast between the two versions is illuminating. In Matthew, Jesus does not address the woman when the disciples ask him to dismiss her, but asserts, "I was not sent, except to the lost sheep of the house of Israel" (15:24). Of this additional note of exclusivity in the ministry of Jesus, Mark's version is innocent, and the Matthean version is certainly more Jewish, in all probability indicating a tradition earlier than Mark's. The narrative before us has a far different purpose: the woman may be a pagan foreigner, and Jesus asserts his obligation to his own people first, but nevertheless the woman comes in faith and the daughter is healed. In the circumstances of the compilation of Mark there were far more urgent issues than the "ethnicity" of the ministry of Jesus.

26. *a Greek, a Canaanite by race:* The Greek is literally "a Syro-Phoenician by race." The differentiation clearly marks a pagan. Phoenician was still spoken in the time of Jesus, and the native name of a Phoenician *(kena'nî)* was in Greek *Chananaios.* It is worthy of mention that in the time of Augustine of Hippo (fifth century A.D.) Carthaginian peasants called themselves Canaanites. Matthew uses the biblical term *Chananaia.*

27. This is one of the strongest assertions on Jesus' lips in our sources defining his mission as being primarily, if not exclusively, to Israel *(the children)*. The qualification *first* is—like the remainder of 27a—not found in Matthew. There is reason to think that this may be a modification of the bald statement in Matthew, though Taylor (p. 350) argues that Matthew and Mark differ in their presentation of the tradition and that no judgment can be made as to priority here. But the Markan modification—if such it is—would have been wholly appropriate to the changed circumstances of Mark's time.

Taylor (p. 350) suggests that the reference to bread in the two narrative cycles (6:30-7:37 and 8:1-26) "may indicate a catechetical interest in the Eucharist."

dogs: Although Mark uses the diminutive *kunaria* (puppies) rather than *kunes* (dogs), this should not necessarily be taken as softening the near harshness of Jesus' saying. However, the fact that the dogs in question appear to be domestic animals somewhat mitigates the saying. The woman herself responds in v. 28 with some boldness, and even (as Turner suggests, p. 350) with wit. But there was evidently hesitation in Jesus' mind as to the limits of his ministry, and the reaction voiced in this verse expresses this. The woman's reply suggests that she recognized the hesitation and took advantage of it: *Even the dogs under the table eat the children's scraps.*

28. *Sir* (Greek *kurie):* This is the only occurrence in Mark, apart from 1:40 and 10:51 (in some manuscripts).

children's: Matthew has "master's tables" and must certainly be reckoned more distinctively Jewish.

29. In Mark, there is no mention (as there is in Matthew) of faith. Jesus is seen as pleased with the woman's persistence and sends her away with the assurance that her daughter is well. If Matthew emphasizes faith (15:28; cf. 8:13 with similar words), then Mark implies simply an awareness on the part of Jesus (what we have come to call "extrasensory perception"). Matthew, both here and in the narrative of the centurion's servant, says that the sufferer was healed "from that time." It is not easy to read such a miraculous element into the Markan account, and we may well conclude that both evangelists are drawing from independent traditions, even though Mark is following Matthew's order.

30. The woman goes home and finds her daughter lying in bed, presumably in a state of exhaustion after a final paroxysm.

See further: T. A. Burkill, "The Syrophoenician Woman: The Congruence of Mark 7:24-31," *ZNW* 57.1966, pp. 1-2, 23-27; J. D. M. Derrett, "Law in the New Testament: The Syro-Phoenician Woman and the Centurion of Capernaum," *NovTest* 15.1973, pp. 161-86; W. Storch, "Zur Perikope von der Syrophonizierin Mk 7:28 und Ri 17:11," *BZ* 14.1970, pp. 256-57.

37. Miracles (iv) A Deaf Man Cured
(7:31-37) = Matt 15:29-31

7   ³¹ On his return from the territory of Tyre, he went through Sidon to the Sea of Galilee, passing through the territory of the Ten Towns. ³² Some people brought to him a man who was deaf and could hardly speak and begged him to lay his hand on him. ³³ He took the man away, apart from the crowd, put his fingers into his ears, spat, and touched his tongue. ³⁴ Then, looking up to heaven, he sighed and said to him, "Ephphatha!" (which means, "Be opened"). ³⁵ And (at once) the man's ears were opened, his speech impediment was removed, and he spoke without difficulty. ³⁶ Jesus forbade them to tell anyone; but the more he forbade them, the more persistently they spread the news. ³⁷ They were completely astonished. "Everything he does, he does well," they said. "He even makes the deaf hear and the dumb speak."

Comment

While the text is clear enough at this point, the geography is impossible to reconstruct. In fact, an exaggerated hypothetical journey with similar characteristics would have a traveler going from Baltimore to Frederick (Maryland) by way of York, Pennsylvania. The difficulty is the phrase *through Sidon,* for the place is twenty miles north of Tyre. Some manuscripts read "and Sidon," but this is a palpable attempt to deal with the geographical difficulty. The attempts of various commentators past and present to make sense of this awkward journey are often more inglorious than enlightening. The best suggestion is that of Wellhausen: from the region near Tyre to Bethsaida, thus doing away with the long journey along the coast. Jesus then would cross the border through Bethsaida into the midst of the Ten Towns. It is not as though the confusion of geography in Mark was offset by clarity in the other evangelists. The very opposite is the case. Matthew has no reference to Tyre and Sidon, nor yet to the Ten Towns, contenting himself merely with the statement that Jesus "departed from there and came by the Sea of Galilee" (15:29). It may be that Mark expresses awkwardly the sense of "the region of Tyre and Sidon." Equally Mark may have been confused and vague about an area of which he knew little or nothing. We have the possibility also that there was more than one tradition of a journey by Jesus into pagan territory, and while Matthew simply reads one return of Jesus from the region, Mark attempts to do justice to all the fragments of information he has. Cf. F. G. Lang, "Über Sidon mitten ins Gebeit der Dekapolis 'Geographie und Theologie in Markus 7³¹,' " *ZDPV* 94.1978, pp. 145-60.

The form of the narrative is that of a miracle story. The geographical notes are simply the prelude, and the narrative proper begins at v. 32. In fact the geographical note may well belong to the story of the Syro-Phoenician woman, where it stands in Matthew.

Notes

32. The words that introduce the story have no necessary connection with v. 31, and the imperfect tense of *brought* is indication enough that the narrative was self-contained in its original form.

deaf (Greek *kōphos*): Cf. 7:37, 9:25. Translated literally, the word implies someone with dull or severely impaired hearing.

could hardly speak (Greek *mogilalos*): The word is found in *LXX* at Isa 35:6. It is different in sense from *alalous* in v. 37, but the qualification *elalei orthōs* in v. 35 results in a Greek form which is best understood as "speech impairment." Some manuscripts have *moggilalou*, which means that the sufferer had a harsh or hoarse manner of speaking, thus implying that the man was not wholly speechless.

33ff. Taking the sufferer *away* is also a feature of 8:22-26. The verb *apolambanomai* is found in the papyri with the same sense of private treatment. The introduction of *the crowd* may be some indication that originally the narrative was in another context altogether. In any case we cannot explain the taking of the man away from the crowd unless it was to avoid undesirable publicity—a publicity that drew attention away from the proclamation of the Reign of God and focused upon Jesus as a wonder-worker.

put his fingers . . . . : These symbolic acts, common enough among Greek and Jewish healers, suggest to the sufferer the possibility that he might be cured. Tacitus *(Hist* 4.81) records a healing by Vespasian employing spittle. This present narrative, and those of 8:23 and John 9:6, are the only occasions when Jesus is said to have used spittle. We cannot know how the spittle was used. Various manuscripts suggest that the spittle was put on the lips, or in the mouth as a symbolic gesture, while other variants include the ears as well. The element of magic can be discounted; the actions are simply symbolic, accompanied by words of healing.

34. *"Ephphatha!"* The use of foreign phrases was characteristic of stories of wonder-workers, but this is not the case here, for Aramaic would be the normal mode of speech both for Jesus and those who reported the incident. The Greek is a transliteration of *'ethpatah,* the causative of *phatah,* "to open." The narrative suggests that the man could hear the command, if imperfectly (cf. note on v. 32 above). Cf. L. Rabino-

witz, " 'Be Opened' = 'Ephphatha' (Mark 7:34): Did Jesus Speak Hebrew?" *ZNW* 53.1962, pp. 229-38.

Attention may be called here to the gestures of prayer employed by Jesus in this account: *anablepsas* ("looking up" to heaven) and *estenaxen* ("sighed"—with compassion for the sufferer). For the latter verb, in various forms, cf. Rom 8:23; 2 Cor 5:2,4; Heb 13:17; James 5:9. At 8:12 Mark uses a stronger form of the verb.

35ff. The results of the cure are described with simple directness. The charge to remain silent is odd, since the effect of the cure could hardly have gone unnoticed. The use of the imperfect tense suggests that Jesus made more than one attempt to silence persistent stories, presumably (see note on v. 33 above) to disassociate himself from any suggestion that he was simply a wonder-worker.

37. The astonishment of those who heard the news is described in a Greek adverb *huperperissōs* found only here, though *huperperissenō* ("to exceed," "to abound") is found in Rom 5:20 and 2 Cor 7:4.

It is probable that the evangelist has Isa 35:5ff. in mind, and if this is so, he has drastically shortened Matt 15:31 with its reminiscence of Isa 29:23 (cf. Gen 1:31 and Sir 39:16).

38. The Feeding of the Crowd (ii)
(8:1-10) = Matt 15:32-39

8 ¹There was an occasion about this time when a large crowd had gathered, and as they had no food Jesus called the disciples and said to them, ² "I feel sorry for these people, because they have been with me for three days and now have nothing to eat. ³ If I send them home unfed, they will faint on the way; some of them come from a distance." ⁴ His disciples answered him, "How can anyone provide food for all these people in this lonely place?" ⁵ "How many loaves do you have?" he asked. "Seven," they replied. ⁶ So he ordered the crowd to sit down on the ground. Then he took the seven loaves, and after giving thanks to God broke them, giving them to the disciples to distribute, and this the disciples did. ⁷ They also had a few small fish, and for these he also gave thanks and ordered that these should be given to them. ⁸ Everyone ate and had enough, and seven baskets were filled with the scraps left over. ⁹ (There were about four thousand people.) Then he sent the people away ¹⁰ and at once got into a boat with his disciples and went to the district of Dalmanutha.

Comment

Mark, along with Matthew, has two accounts of feedings, whereas Luke, who avoided doublets wherever possible, has only one. Not only does Mark follow Matthew by including both feedings, but he also takes over the five units in Matthew which come between the feedings. Luke omits all five units.

In the pericope before us we have what appears at first sight to be a duplicate of the previous feeding in 6:35-44, but whether such is the case is not at all clear. The Johannine account of the feeding (John 6) emphasizes the crucial importance of the event by recording that as a result the crowd wished to proclaim Jesus king (messiah). The comment that prefaced 6:35-44 will not be repeated here, save to say that the element of the miraculous, insofar as it applied to 6:35-44, is heightened in the present pericope, since from the beginning a miraculous element appears to be presupposed. Moreover the evangelist closely follows the Matthean order in linking the feeding first with the demand for a sign and then with a saying about the *leaven of the Pharisees* and the *leaven of Herod* (cf. vv. 2-4 and 15-16).

It seems certain that the same considerations of instruction and liturgy are present here as were found in Chapter 6. The feeding here underlines that of its predecessor; it is a sign of the inbreaking of the Reign of God. To the Pharisees, however, no sign had been given, and they are seen as blindly seeking one. Even the disciples, to whom so much had been given, were not without fault. This must be regarded as editorial comment on the state of mind of the community for which Mark was writing. For a community beleaguered and faint-hearted in the face of inevitable conflict, the evangelist leaves the saying of Jesus about leaven unexplained and the question posed: "Do you still not understand?"

Liturgical and homiletic considerations are prominent in the feeding narratives and indeed dominate John's gospel. But having made that statement and the further one that Mark had an overriding didactic concern as well, the question of historicity remains. Familiar as we are in this text, as in Matthew, with the beginnings of the type of narrative so well exemplified in John (single text plus extended commentary), any commentator must provide an answer to the questions concerning the apparent duplication of the narrative. The present writer is convinced that the pericope before us is indeed a duplicate of the preceding one in 6:30-44 and that Mark followed Matthew in finding a use of the duplication in attaching it to a saying about leaven. Furthermore in Mark's account there is a suggestion that this narrative is set in a Gentile context (the Ten Towns?). The very loose phrase that begins v. 1 would tend to indicate either that Mark had no information as to time and location or to attach the narrative loosely to the preceding narrative.

The present pericope is apparently concerned simply and solely with the miracle itself. Nothing is said, as in the earlier narrative, of the reactions of the disciples or the crowds.

Notes

1. The vague introduction has already been noted. The element of anticipated miracle is emphasized by Jesus taking the initiative in calling the disciples (in contrast to 6:35). (John 6:5 has Jesus speaking to Philip.) For the verb *called,* see 3:13. The crowd is simply described as large, though most manuscripts have "again" before *a large crowd.* It must be added that a fair number of manuscripts have the word *pampollou,* a word not otherwise found in Greek scripture. Generally this is regarded as a mistaken copying of *palin pollou,* though it must be admitted that a more impressive array of manuscripts would lead us to translate *pampollou* by "huge."

2. *feel sorry:* The same sentiment of sorrow as in 6:34 is expressed in direct speech. But whereas in Chapter 6 Jesus is sorrowful because the people are like sheep without a shepherd, here the sorrow is because they have been without food.

three days: Given the importance of the phrase in New Testament writings, there is in all probability some allusion here—as there is in Matthew—to some time frame or context now lost to us. This is underlined by the fact that the disciples are mentioned again—the first time since 7:17. It is not easy to resist the conclusion that in some fashion, in the very early stages of the tradition, the saying about bread in vv. 11-13 attracted to itself a tradition of a fellowship meal with strongly eschatological overtones and that Matthew (from whatever source) assumed that there was another feeding of a crowd.

Another peculiar feature of this pericope is that Jesus puts on one side at once any notion of sending the crowds away, in contrast with the narrative in 6:36 where we have a suggestion of a dismissal by the disciples.

3. *some of them:* The implication is that some of those present were from the locality. The phrase is not found in Matthew. The text of Matthew is "I am unwilling to send them away hungry. . . ."

4. *lonely place* (Greek *erēmia):* The evangelist has used this word, in contrast with his normal *hē erēmos* or *erēmos topos,* directly from Matthew (15:33).

5. *How many . . . :* The question is in verbatim agreement with 6:38, and with Matthew's text. Fish are not mentioned, though they are referred to in v. 7. Matthew does speak of fish in this context. The perplexity of the disciples, in spite of a supposedly previous occasion, is a strong reason for thinking that this account is a duplicate. Indeed, given a previous occasion, the question in v. 4 attributes to the disciples a stupidity which can only be described as awe-inspiring.

6. The account of the seating of the crowds is sparse, with none of the detail found in 6:39ff. But the following account of the taking, giving thanks, and breaking of the bread is remarkably close to 5:41. Far more important is the use of *eucharistēsas,* or

after giving thanks, as the same usage occurs in 14:23. (See the note on that verse ad loc.) There can be little doubt of the liturgical eucharistic intent both in this pericope and in Chapter 6. Similarly the action of the disciples in distributing the bread answers readily enough to the practice in the early Church, in which the deacons administered bread and cup to the people, having received them from the hands of the presiding celebrant.

7. Mark differs materially from Matthew here. This verse has the very awkward intrusion of the fish, along with a separate thanksgiving, whereas Matt 15:36 has bread and fish together, with a single giving of thanks. In this respect Matthew is closer to the narrative of the feeding of the five thousand.

8. There is substantial agreement with 6:42 at this point, but though the sense is the same, the wording is not that of Matthew. There is, however, in the Markan text the word *perisseuma* (left over), a word found also in Matt 15:37 in the sense of "abundance." The word is found only once in *LXX* (Eccles 2:15) and is late. It is found also in Matt 12:34 = Luke 6:45.

baskets (Greek *sphuris):* Cf. Matt 15:37, 16:10, Acts 9:25. The basket described is a mat basket, used for carrying provisions (in Acts, large enough to hold a man).

A comparison of this narrative with 6:35-44 leaves the impression that the present one is a shorter version of the first, though some words peculiar to this present account would tend to suggest an independent compilation. Matthew's version is somewhat fuller and includes women and children (15:38, cf. 14:21).

10. Dismissing the crowds, Jesus embarks with the disciples for a place whose identity is unknown. The verse is a summary passage, parallel to 6:45. The place name in Matthew (the hills of Magdala) has given rise in many manuscripts to attempted accommodation between the two gospels (cf. Taylor, p. 360). The best that can be said is that some place on the west side of the lake is meant.

For further reading, cf. B. M. F. van Iersel, "Die wunderbare Speisung und das Abendmahl in der Synoptischen Tradition," *NTS* 7.1964, pp. 188ff.; B. E. Thiering, " 'Breaking of Bread' and 'Harvest' in Mark's Gospel," *NTS* 12.1970, pp. 1-12.

It is difficult to know how much to invest in the frequent suggestions (e.g., B. E. Thiering's article) that the two feedings represent a concern for Jews (the five thousand) in the first event and for Gentiles in the second. The concern of the fourth gospel, as we would expect, is for Jews alone, and therefore does not enter into this present discussion. Although Mark 8:3 specifically states that some, if not all, of the crowd had come from a distance, we have no right to assume—as has sometimes been done—that this represents diaspora Judaism. Still less is it possible to read into the evangelist's account some significance attaching to the twelve baskets in the first feeding, as though we are here in the presence of some symbolism attaching to the twelve apostles, in contrast to the seven baskets of the second feeding (= the ministry of the seven in Acts 6:1-7). If indeed such symbolism was in the mind of the evangelist, we are in no position—short of harder evidence than the text before us—to guess at precisely what such symbolism may have been.

Appended Note: Jesus and Elisha

At this point in the commentary (having reached the last of the parallels to be given below), it is fitting to give some attention to the work of G. Hartmann, *Der Aufbau des Markusevangeliums, auf einem Anhang Untersuchungen zur Echtheit des Markusschlüsser* (Münster: Aschendorff, 1936), on the parallels he found in the accounts of Elisha in 2 Kings and the ministry of Jesus in Mark. The main points are set out in parallel in the chart that follows.

For a much fuller treatment, see Raymond E. Brown, "Jesus and Elisha," *Perspective* 12.1971, pp. 85-104. The whole article richly repays study.

Whatever one may think of typology, the parallels are arresting. The principal point of interest is the oft overlooked consideration that in our Old Testament sources some care is taken to render a comparison between Elijah and Elisha, to such an extent that the latter is regarded as far outstripping his master in demonstrations of the miraculous. Whatever may have been the state of the earliest traditions of the New Testament as to the contrast between John the Baptist and Jesus, the identification of John with Elijah when taken in conjunction with Hartmann's parallels above leaves open the question as to whether there was also the implication that in Jesus something far greater than Elijah was present.

39. The Demand for a Sign
(8:11-13) = Matt 16:1-4

8 ¹¹Then the Pharisees came out and began to argue with Jesus. Testing him, they asked him for a sign from heaven. ¹²He sighed deeply to himself and asked, "Why does this generation ask for a sign? In truth, I tell you: no sign shall be given to this generation." ¹³So he left them, got back into the boat, and went across to the other side of the lake.

Elisha	*Jesus in Mark*
2 Kings	
1. 2:13-15 Divides the water and passes over. Sons of prophets do reverence to Elisha.	4:35-41 Calms the sea so that boat can cross. The disciples are awe-struck.
2. 2:19-22 Purifies the water at Jericho.	5:1-20 Heals the demoniac and drives demons into pigs. (Same situation.)
2:23-24 Calls bears against children. (Double miracle: one helpful, the other punishment of enemies.)	
3. 4:1-7 Multiplies oil for widow.	5:21-43 Heals a woman.
4:18-37 Revives Shunamite's son (Again a double miracle: first for a desperate woman, second a revival of a child.)	Revives Jairus' daughter. (Similar situation.)
4. 4:38-41 Neutralizes poisoned food, multiplies loaves for 100. (Two miracles dealing with food.)	6:30-44 Multiplies loaves for 5,000. (See second feeding in 8:1-9.)
5. 5:1-27 Heals Naaman the Syrian and punishes Gehazi.	
6. 6:1-7 Makes axhead float on water.	6:45-51 Walks on water.
6:8-23 Blinds Aramean troops. (Double miracle, one helpful, the other punishing enemies—cf. 2. Second water miracle— cf. 1.)	6:53-56 Healing of the sick. (Similar situation.)
7.	7:24-30 Heals the Syro-Phoenician woman's child.
	7:31-37 Heals the deaf-mute.
8. 6:25 Relieves famine at Samaria.	8:1-9 Multiplies loaves for 4,000. Second food miracle.
7:16 Food miracle.	

Comment

It is necessary in any preface to this section to deal with the fashion in which Mark—in the view of this commentator—dealt with his material. The demand for a sign in vv. 11-13 is complicated in its relationships. We begin with the hypothesis that these verses are a condensation of Matt 16:1-5 along with Luke 11:16 and Luke 11:29. Moreover, Matt 16:1-4 is a doublet of Matt 12:38-39, parallel to which is Luke 11:29. Now Luke in general avoided doublets, and though he has a parallel to Matt 12:38-42, the doublet of Matt 16:1-4 has only a faint trace in Luke 11:16. We suggest that Mark, with the literary units of Matthew before him and trying to incorporate elements of all of them, included Matt 16:1-4. In the process, however, he compared the Lucan parallels of Luke 11:16 and 29, and proceeded to conflate the first part of Matt 16:1-4 with Luke 11:16 and the second part with Luke 11:29, ending with Matthew's transition into the saying about leaven. The result therefore is:

Mark 8:11 = Matt 16:1a, Luke 11:16
Mark 8:12 = Matt 16:1b, Luke 11:29
Mark 8:13 = Matt 16:4a,5a

In Mark 8:12 it is far too easy to assume that the parallels are Matt 12:39 and 16:4, but the Greek text is on examination far more readily explained by the parallels we have given above. Apart from 8:12 it seems clear that the affinity of vv. 11-13 lies with Matt 16:1-5.

Using the two-document hypothesis, the picture becomes enormously complicated. In order to sustain Markan priority it is necessary to assume:

1. In addition to Mark 8:11-13 there was a Q version.
2. Luke 11:29 conflated Q with Mark.
3. Matt 12:39 took over Q, together with the Markan pericope in 16:1-5.
4. The verbal agreements of Mark 8:11, Matt 16:1, and Luke 11:16 would demand a further explication. It would be necessary to assume that Luke 11:16 was copied from Mark 8:11 and that Luke, indulging in a scissors and paste operation, separated Mark into two parts, using the later part a few verses later to conflate with Q.
5. Even on a very minor point we have to imagine Luke, in copying Mark 8:11, making sure that he agreed with Matt 16:1 in some lesser points of word order.

In short, it would demand almost incontrovertible evidence from other considerations before one could confidently assert that Mark was the prior source of Matthew and Luke in this pericope. The hypothesis that Mark depends on Matthew and Luke is a far more convincing one than the generally accepted two-document hypothesis—at least in this instance, if in no others.

Notes

11. The phrase *began to argue (ērxanto suzētein)* seems almost an afterthought. Matthew (whose order Mark follows) adds "Sadducees" to Jesus' critics.

a sign from heaven: It is important not to interpret this as a demand for a miracle. The sign, of whatever kind, was demanded as a guarantee of truth. The sign therefore would in effect be closely linked to some saying, or an utterance about the immediate proximity of the Reign of God. It is even possible that this demand for a sign in its original context belonged to the time immediately following the first feeding (with the strong eschatological overtones of that event). The Markan usage of *sign* is not to apply the word to miracles; there are seven examples in Mark, two belonging here, another in Chapter 13, and two in the nonauthentic ending of Mark.

Testing him: See 1:13, 10:2, 12:15. Jesus' enemies had already ascribed his exorcisms to Beelzebul, and so they now ask for a sign to put the matter of Jesus' affiliation at rest. The demand was intended to pose two painful choices: trying to provide a sign and failing or refusing such a sign and so losing the support of the crowds.

12. Mark (cf. 3:5) mentions the emotions of Jesus, as he indignantly demands how it is possible for such people to demand a sign.

In truth: Mark takes over the very strong negative of Matthew, the sense of which is "Perish the thought that I should do such a thing!" Mark shares the tradition of Matthew here, though in fact he makes the negative somewhat stronger than Matthew's model *(ei* for the simple negative *ou).* Both Matthew and Luke (12:39, 11:29) have the important addition "except the sign of Jonah," the plain meaning being that the message of Jesus is self-authenticating. Mark's omission of this makes the refusal even more emphatic. Mark's very tense text likewise omits Matthew's description of *this generation* as "evil."

13. Where Matthew has "he left them and went away," Mark's Greek provides us with *palin* (literally, "again"), which if taken with *apheis* (left) simply means "so, accordingly" (the translation given here), but if read with *embas* (re-embarked) would indicate that Jesus again went into the boat.

40. The Leaven of the Pharisees and Herod
(8:14-21) = Matt 16:5-12

8 [14] They had forgotten to take bread with them, and they had only one loaf in the boat. [15] He warned them: "Beware, be on your guard against the leaven of the Pharisees and the leaven of Herod." [16] They said among themselves, "We have no bread." [17] Becoming aware of this, he said to them, "Why do you talk about having no bread? Do you still not know, not understand? Are your minds so closed? [18] You have eyes—cannot you see? You have ears—cannot you hear? Have you forgotten? [19] When I broke the five loaves among the five thousand, how many baskets of leftover scraps did you pick up?" "Twelve," they answered. [20] "And how many when I broke the seven loaves for the four thousand?" They replied, "Seven." [21] "Do you still not understand?" he asked.

Comment

So far as we can judge, a saying of Jesus in v. 15 has been incorporated into a whole narrative which looks back to the two feeding narratives and contains a rebuke to the disciples for their lack of faith. Whether this present section represents a free composition by Matthew of disparate materials held together only by the feeding narratives and then copied by Mark, we have no way of knowing. There are elements which echo the tradition of the feeding (v. 14), but the warning in v. 15 is ignored after v. 16 (save for an editorial comment in Matt 16:11b-12). The two feedings are treated as separate incidents, and the warning of Jesus is attached to 6:43 and 8:8 (i.e., to subsidiary material). The same process has been at work in Matthew. What therefore we have is a curious pastiche, woven around a single saying.

We must conclude that both Matthew and Mark are at one in using the interests of instruction and worship in weaving this pattern. The only sign was the feeding—a sign to those with understanding that the Reign of God was already breaking in. But the demand for a sign on the part of the Pharisees meant that they had wholly failed to understand the significance of the sign. The interests of both evangelists at this point coincide. The message is clear enough in Mark, and it even partly explains his terse ending in v. 21, without the Matthean (editorial?) addition: if the latter-day disciples are bewildered and in disarray, then they but share the bewilderment of those nearest to Jesus in time and place. The "signs" are always there, and they are self-authenticating, though hidden wholly from unbelievers. Pursuing this theme, the historical element is pushed into the background to the point where it is irrecoverable. (This will be examined further in the notes.) The obduracy of the disciples is emphasized in the interests of the community for whom this gospel was compiled, and their total failure to apprehend the warning in v. 15 is left without a word of comment.

The feeding narratives are brought in, but seen against a background of homiletical interest: "Do you still not know?" The feeding narratives are records which are evidential and not linked with the dawning of the Reign of God. This is shared with Matthew, and whereas the Johannine version plainly hints at messianic overtones in the feeding story, the Matthean and Markan references to the feedings here make the whole episode more a "proof" reference to the person of Jesus than an authentication of his ministry.

Notes

14. The demand for a sign and the refusal of the demand are used by Matthew and Mark as preface to this episode.

They had forgotten is a strange phrase, and the failure to provide food for the voyage is hardly germane to the narrative. It is possible that the phrase has some connection with the following verse, for it is left wholly without explanation. If the saying in v. 15 is in proper context, the ignoring of it in the remainder of the narrative is even more strange. Matthew connects the incident with the arrival at the other side of the lake.

15. For the *Pharisees* cf. 2:16; for *Herod* cf. 6:14. Matthew has "beware of the yeast of the Pharisees and Sadducees" and later explains this as meaning that the disciples were to beware of the "teaching of the Pharisees and Sadducees" (16:12). Mark leaves the enigmatic statement in this verse without explanation, presumably feeling that his own sources offered no interpretation and equally that Matthew's v. 12 was not very illuminating. Luke has a parallel saying in 12:1—"be on your guard against the leaven, that is the pettifogging legalisms [Greek *hupokrisis*] of the Pharisees." If this saying was current as an isolated aphorism, then it may well have been remembered simply because of growing hostility between Gentile and Jewish Christians (cf. Gal 2:4). In that case Luke's version is particularly apposite, and Matthew's explanation is relevant. The reference to Herod in Mark is odd, indeed so odd that we must conclude that it has all the marks of authenticity.

The word *leaven* poses its own problems, for neither Matthew nor Mark interprets the phrase. In the New Testament generally, the word is used in a pejorative sense

(Matt 13:33 = Luke 13:20 is an exception): cf. 1 Cor 5:6,7,8, Gal 5:9. The rabbis were accustomed to use the word as standing for the evil inclination of mankind; cf. Strack-Billerbeck Vol. 1, pp. 728ff. Presumably Mark has this in mind too, since 7:1-23 and 8:11-13 depict the scribes and Pharisees as undermining the true intent of the Law and then compounding their error by demanding a sign. On such grounds it would be natural for Jesus to utter the enigmatic warning when leaving the scene.

Herod: Some manuscripts, admittedly not impressive ones, have *the Herodians.*

16. *said among themselves:* Unfortunately the textual state of the Greek in this verse is confused and confusing. The Greek verb refers to exchanges of views on a matter in dispute. After the italicized phrase, the Greek has *hoti* (that), generally used to introduce indirect speech. Some manuscripts so use it and read "that they had no bread." Matthew's version has the Greek *legontes* (saying, discussing, reasoning) so as to read ". . . they discussed this, reasoning 'we brought no bread.' " Now since there is strong manuscript evidence for *legontes* in Mark also, we have translated v. 16 as direct speech, but without any direct connection with the saying on leaven in the preceding verse. It must be said at once that Matthew's text does make a somewhat tenuous connection between the two verses. Mark evidently knew—as perhaps Matthew did not—that the leaven saying circulated as a separate saying. The isolated saying of v. 15 is ignored in the text—as enigmatic, though certainly belonging to the sayings tradition—and the attention of the disciples is focused elsewhere. It must be freely admitted that this is one instance where the two-document hypothesis is on the face of it more convincing as an explanation of the relationship between Matthew and Mark.

17. *Becoming aware:* Jesus could hardly have failed to notice the argument—there is no question of intuitive knowledge here. The disciples are accused of failing to understand the signs of the feeding, not the saying on leaven. The rebuking questions of Jesus are sharp, and presumably the dispute among the disciples had been acrimonious. Even so, the rebukes raise the question of the extent to which they were justified. (Matthew's order is different and the charges fewer in number—he has to find reason to connect all of this with the leaven saying and emphasizes it by repeating the saying in 16:11.)

18. *You have eyes* . . . . *:* The stinging rebuke is from the language of *LXX*—cf. Isa 6:9, Jer 5:21, Ezek 12:2. The question *Have you forgotten?* proceeds to link the whole matter to the stories of feeding in vv. 19-21.

19-21. The recalling of the incidents narrated in 6:35-44 and 8:1-9 precisely distinguishes the narratives, both by numbers and even by the type of containers employed to gather up scraps. The text of Mark in its present form, given that 6:32-44 and 8:1-9 are doublets with distinct meanings, must lead to the conclusion that these verses are redactional in a way that is not true of Matthew's version. If Mark recorded the traditions as he found them, then not only are vv. 19-21 redactional, but one must conclude that whatever saying of Jesus followed v. 18 has been lost to us.

On the above passage, see further: G. Ziener, "Das Bildwort von Sauerteig Mk 8.15," *TTZ* 67.1958, pp. 247-48; A. J. Jewell, "Did St. Mark 'Remember'?" *London Quarterly Holborn Review* 35.1966, pp. 117-20; F. McCombie, "Jesus and the Leaven of Salvation," *New Blackfriars* 59.1978, pp. 450-62. On the relations between "seeing" and "faith," both in Mark and John, see J. M. Robinson, "On the *Gattung* of Mark (and John)," *Perspective* 11.1970, pp. 99-129; Norman A. Beck, "Reclaiming a Biblical Text: The Mark 8:14-21 Discussion About Bread in the Boat," *CBQ* 43.1981, pp. 49-57.

41. Miracles (v) The Blind Man at Bethsaida (8:22-26)

8 ²² They arrived at Bethsaida, where people brought to him a blind man and begged him to touch him. ²³ He led the blind man away by the hand out of the village. After spitting on his eyes, he laid his hands on his eyes and asked him if he saw anything. ²⁴ The man looked up and replied: "I see men; they look like trees walking about." ²⁵ Again he laid his hands on his eyes; he looked hard, and now he was cured and saw everything clearly. ²⁶ He sent the man home, telling him, "Do not tell anyone in the village."

Comment

The present narrative, together with 7:32-37, forms a pair of miracle stories peculiar to Mark and presents a problem in linguistic agreement that is to say the least arresting. Even when account has been taken of the differences between the two narratives, it is hard to resist the conclusion that we have a doublet. The Greek phraseology can be set out as follows:

7:32-37	8:22-26
32. and they brought to him and they begged him to lay his hand on him	22. and they brought to him and they begged him to touch him
33. He took the man away into his ears and touched his tongue	23. He led the blind man away after spitting on his eyes he laid his hands on him
34. Then looking up and said	24. The man looked up said
36. forbade them	26. Do not tell anyone

When due allowance is made for the fact that one victim is deaf and the other blind, the verbal agreements are remarkable. When again allowance is made for the fact that in the highly stylized form of a miracle story there is a limited vocabulary, these agreements speak far more of a doublet than of two incidents in coincidental vocabulary. To be sure, Mark has a notable inclination to repeat himself, and the advertisements for medical and semimedical aids on television should remind us how limited are the word patterns in stylized narrative. Nevertheless the "doublet" hypothesis—though not capable of explaining everything—appears to be convincing. There are differences, and they should be duly noticed: (1) "looking up" in Chapter 7 applies to Jesus and in the present narrative to the sufferer; (2) there is nothing corresponding to the dramatic v. 24 in the previous story; (3) the second imposition of hands in v. 25 is without parallel in the gospels. However, confusion between two stories is certainly not unknown in our sources: cf. Matt 12:22ff., 9:32ff. with Luke 11:14.

One suggestion may be offered here with considerable hesitation. It is that Mark, anxious to emphasize that there was hope for the disciples to see the truth of the ministry of Jesus (and also need for his own community to do the same), found a fragmentary account of the healing of a blind man and adapted the narrative of 7:32-37 to the present account. That there was such a fragmentary account, we may infer from the vivid reply of the sufferer in v. 24.

Cf. the extended treatment in E. S. Johnson, "Mark 8:22-26. The Blind Man from Bethsaida," *NTS* 25.1979, pp. 370-84.

Notes

22. For *Bethsaida* cf. 6:45. It is impossible to say whether the opening phrase belongs here or to the conclusion of the preceding verse.

people brought: this impersonal plural (cf. 7:32) has been noticed in the comment.

23. *village* (Greek *chōmē*, cf. 6:6): If the fishing village is meant, then the identification with Bethsaida is possible; otherwise some other unknown location in the district of the Ten Towns must be meant.

The verbal agreements between this verse and 7:33 have already been noted previously.

eyes (Greek *ommata):* Cf. Matt 20:34. The word is a common one in poetry and is found in the papyri.

if he saw: The direct question in this form is not classical (literally, "Do you see anything?") but is common in the New Testament (cf. Matt 12:10, 19:3; Acts 1:6, 7:1). Grammatically the Greek here is the New Testament form of the direct question and is frequent in Luke and Acts. This is the sole example in Mark. We have chosen to translate it as an indirect question.

24. *looked up:* The gesture described is involuntary, and we are informed by infer-

ence that the man was not born blind—he can distinguish some objects. The sentence does not describe the beginnings of a cure.

The Greek of this verse in various manuscripts is (like v. 16) confused and confusing. The text we have used in this commentary (that of the Greek New English New Testament) is literally "I see men that as trees I see them walking." The second *see* (Greek *horō*) is omitted by some manuscripts, as is also *that* (Greek *hoti*). This omission may be a simplification, for it is not easy to see why the phrase *like trees walking about* should have been changed to the present awkward text in the principal manuscripts. Cf. C. M. Lee, "Mark 8.24," *NovTest* 20.1978, p. 74, for the suggestion that the present awkward Greek is due to a translation missing the second *d* in the Aramaic so that we can best render the sentence as "I see men that *(d)* they are like trees which *(d)* I see walking."

25. It appears that we have a story of gradual healing in this narrative, for there is a second laying on of hands in this verse. The remainder of the verse is tautologous, and no amount of verbal gymnastics will relieve this awkwardness.

looked hard (Greek *diablepō*): The word is not found in *LXX* and is infrequently found in the papyri. Matt 7:5 (Luke 6:42) uses the word in the sense of "see clearly."

saw (Greek *eneblepen*): Together with the comparatively rare adverb *tēlangōs* (clearly) the sense is that the man could now see things at a distance. The two uses of the augmented verb *blepō* show a careful distinction in tense: *diablepō* above means "to begin to see things clearly," while *eneblepen* suggests that the man fixed his eyes upon objects.

26. The man is sent away, and some editions of the Greek text would demand the translation "Do not even go into the village" (so Nestle, Tischendorf, Westcott-Hort, and Soulier). We have preferred the far more widely attested Greek version which forbade the man to speak of his cure.

PART IV
PASSION

42. Peter's Declaration
(8:27-30) = Matt 16:13-20; Luke 9:18-21

8 ²⁷ Jesus and his disciples set out for the villages of Caesarea Philippi. On the way he asked his disciples, "Who do men say that I am?" ²⁸ They replied, "Some say John the Baptizer, others Elijah, and yet others one of the prophets." ²⁹ "But you," he asked, "who do you say that I am?" Then Peter answered, "You are the Messiah." ³⁰ Then he ordered them not to tell anyone about him.

Comment

We now begin the second and major division of Mark. From this point all looks forward to the consummation of the ministry in the events of the final week. The narrative begins in the region of Caesarea Philippi (in the jurisdiction of Herod Philip) and thence in easy stages through Galilee, Peraea, and Judaea. There is no evidence that Mark had any detailed information on chronology or geography, and the whole arrangement from here to 10:52 is loose. There are four main sections:

1. The suffering Messiah (8:27-9:29).
2. The journey through Galilee (9:30-50).
3. The journey through Peraea and Judaea (10:1-31).
4. The approach to Jerusalem (10:32-52).

The first section is comprised of the confession of Peter and the first Passion prediction; sayings on sacrifice, bearing the cross, and the impending Reign of God; the Transfiguration; the descent from the mountain and second Passion prediction; and the epileptic boy.

The narrative with which this collection of four sections begins is noteworthy in that it begins the sharp division between the continued Proclamation of the Reign of God and the private teaching on The Man.

There is evidence of deliberate structure in the section 8:27-9:13, where there is a gathering of material to emphasize who Jesus is, the articulation of the meaning of his Passion and death, and an invitation to discipleship. Two authors indeed found concentric structure in the collection: A (8:27-28), B (8:29-30), C (8:31-33), D (8:34-9:1), C¹ (9:2-6), B¹ (9:7-10), A¹ (9:11-13). The parallelism, they hold, is marked not only by similarity of vocabulary, but also by similarity/contrast of content. The central passage D, on which attention is focused, is itself structured a, b, c, c', b', a. (Cf. R. Lafontaine and P. Mourton Beernaert, "Essai sur la structure de Marc 8:27-9:13," *RSR* 57.1969, pp. 543-61. Cf. also E. Haenchen, "Die Komposition von Mk 8:27-10:1 un Par," *NovTest* 6.1963, pp. 81-109.)

The narrative before us bears the marks of a witness not far from the events described. It has a natural reference to Caesarea Philippi. Peter speaks naturally and enthusiastically for the rest, and the rebuke delivered by Jesus to the same disciple has all the stamp of authenticity. The command to silence compels attention, for in the euphoria of the post-Easter experience such a command might easily have been obscured or even omitted in the oral tradition.

By the time this point in the ministry has been reached, the experience of hostility and open opposition—even violent opposition—must have focused the attention of Jesus upon the end of his ministry. There is an air of inevitability about the Passion predictions, even at the level of facing violence and without any specific interpretation of a violent end.

The confession of Peter—or a similar event—is totally necessary to explain the next and final stage in the ministry. Enough of the story of the ministry is before us in Mark, in its severely condensed form, to permit the disinterested reader to infer that speculation about Jesus has been present from the very beginning of the ministry. Here, for the inner circle, the speculation is laid to rest. Those who had accompanied Jesus from the beginnings in Galilee must often have wondered about the overtones of any Proclamation of an imminent Reign of God, and whether by such Proclamation a new day of liberation was at hand. (The presence of at least two members of the Zealot party in the number of the immediate followers is sufficient indication of at least one kind of interest aroused by the ministry.) Mark's account of the confession of Peter is terse, without any of the accompanying detail from Matthew, and nothing is done to draw attention away from the person of Jesus. In accord with Mark's purpose, it is vital to press on to explain messiahship in terms of suffering.

Mark's vocabulary is closer to Matthew than to Luke, but his account is shaped by Luke's. Mark, like Luke, omits the promise to Peter (Matt 16:17-19), but by including the anti-Petrine tradition from Matt 16:22-23 he never-

theless softens the impact by omitting "you are a stumbling block to me."
Adjustments aside, Mark is still following Matthew's order.

Notes

27. Luke has no note of place at this point, simply recording that the incident took
place after Jesus had been alone at prayer. Matthew and Mark mention the disciples
without any indication of when they joined Jesus. The mention of *villages* is odd, and
Matthew's "the district of Caesarea Philippi" is much clearer.

Caesarea Philippi (cf. Matt 16:13): The place was so named to distinguish it from
Caesarea (in Acts fifteen times), the administrative center of Roman government on
the coast. The city mentioned here, near the source of the Jordan on Mt. Hermon, was
known in ancient times as Paneas (from Greek *to paneion,* a grotto dedicated to Pan).
Near the grotto Herod the Great had erected a temple in honor of Caesar Augustus.
The city was rebuilt by Herod Philip and named Caesarea by him. It was apparently a
city of considerable splendor, in a setting of great natural beauty. It is about twenty-
five miles north of Bethsaida, whence Jesus presumably journeyed.

On the way: The question is put to elicit information and is general in character, for
the disciples had been among the people during Jesus' withdrawal in Tyre (7:24).
Matthew has "the Son of Man" for the personal pronoun in Mark.

28. Mark has a redundant Greek *legontes* (saying) after *replied,* corresponding to
Hebrew usage.

The variations in grammatical construction after the Greek *hoti* (that)—not present
in our translation—are interesting. Matthew and Luke have (literally) "who do men
say the Son of Man to be?" with the infinitive, and then the reply of the disciples
assumes the infinitive; John the Baptizer and Elijah (Matthew adds Jeremiah) are in
the accusative case, with the infinitive *einai* (to be) understood.

The various opinions held about Jesus are interesting in that apparently no one
thought of Jesus as Messiah. The opinions recall 6:14b, but despite 1:24,34; 3:11; 5:7,
nothing more than a prophet *redivivus* (Luke 9:19) is thought to be encountered in
Jesus. This is in strong contrast to the representations in John 7:28-31,41; 9:22; 14:15;
and 15:43 that common opinion speculated about the possible messianic status of
Jesus.

29. *Peter* has not been used since 5:37, but from this point the name is frequent.
The emphatic *who do you say* is in strong contrast to v. 27. Precisely what the definite
answer *You are the Messiah* implied for the speaker we cannot know, and given the
plethora of messianic speculations contemporary with Jesus, the picture is even more
confusing. All we can say is that at least Peter saw in Jesus one who would probably
fulfill the age-long hopes for the restoration of the people of God. Luke's text adds "of
God" and Matthew's "the Son of the living God." The Matthean phrase "Son of
God" has been added to the Markan text in four manuscripts, while some lesser
manuscripts add also "of the living. . . ."

Messiah (Greek *Christos*): The word is a verbal adjective used in *LXX* to translate
the Hebrew "anointed" with respect to kings, prophets, priests, the patriarchs, the
people as "chosen," Cyrus king of Persia, and finally for the ideal future king. Ps 2:2,

used by Jews and Christians alike, refers to the Davidic messiah. Whatever may prove in the end to be the best dating of the documents in question, *Pss Sol* 17:32 uses this term for the future ideal king, and in *1 Enoch* 48:10 and 52:4 the term is applied to a superhuman Son of Man. The Qumran literature speaks of two messiahs to be expected, a civil (Davidic) messiah and a priestly messiah. In the New Testament, Hebrews combines a royal and priestly messiahship (e.g., Heb 1:5-14, 4:14-5:10) and may well at some level be a reply to some who came from a sectarian Essene background.

The transliteration of the Greek by "Christ" in various English versions is without excuse, and the RSV perpetrates the KJV transliteration. In context, the answer made by Peter speaks of a commitment to Jesus as *messiah*. The fact that the Greek word is often without the definite article in NT writings after Acts ought not lead to a too hasty conclusion, such as is often made in regard to the Pauline writings, that the title "messiah" soon became a name, "Christ." The absence of a definite article, in places where we have reason to suppose an Aramaic background, makes the article conditional on context.

There was certainly some uncertainty about the precise nature of Jesus' messiahship in the primitive Christian community (cf. J. A. T. Robinson, "The Most Primitive Christology of All?" in *TNTS*, pp. 139-54), and in view of the manifold variety of expectation of a messianic or semimessianic Deliverer in the time of Jesus and in the centuries before him, this can hardly be accounted surprising. It is of course impossible to know what kind of messianic figure Peter was acknowledging. It is after the confession of Peter that Matthew has an account of a promise to Peter, in view of this response to divine revelation. Is this an embellishment, a contribution from Matthew's special sources? And given the generally held theory about Petrine reminiscences in Mark, why does Mark not include this promise to Peter? The two-document hypothesis must inevitably regard the Matthean narrative of the promise to Peter as an addition to the Markan source, though the question in the previous sentence remains. For our part, we regard the Markan text as all of a piece with the tightly controlled narrative so characteristic of this gospel. Everything extraneous to the account of ministry in action is excluded, and certainly anything which would draw attention away from Jesus.

30. The command to strict silence is couched in the same absolute terms as those employed in 1:25. The disciples are forbidden to say anything *about him*, i.e., about the possible messianic status. Both Matthew and Luke have similar injunctions. It is hardly surprising that this warning should be seized upon as yet another example of the "messianic secret" (see the note on 1:25). But it is far more convincing, and far more attuned to the times, to think that the warning had more to do with the explosive political and religious atmosphere of the times. The Proclamation of the Reign of God, with its climactic underscoring in the feeding, was more than enough to have attracted unwelcome attention from the Jerusalem establishment, apart altogether from whatever hostile construction might be placed upon events by the Roman imperial authority. To compromise the ministry at this juncture by ill-timed and disastrous rumors about messiahship would not only bring upon Jesus immediate violence but would also curtail if not render impossible any further opportunity to teach the disciples privately. The end of the ministry, its final stage (the "hour" in John's gospel) was

now in sight. The time of proclamation was ended, and so too was the time of Proclamation plus healings: in neither lay the decisive inauguration of the Reign of God. Jesus "set his face" (to quote Luke) toward Jerusalem. There and there alone would be the decisive end to the ministry.

43. Passion Prediction (i)
(8:31-38; 9:1) = Matt 16:21-28, Luke 9:22-27

8 ³¹ He then began to teach them that it was necessary for The Man to undergo great suffering, be rejected by the elders, the chief priests, and teachers of the Law, then be put to death and be raised again three days later. ³² He spoke of this very plainly. So Peter took him aside and began to reprove him. ³³ But he turned around, looked at his disciples, and reproved Peter with the words "Away with you, Satan; your interests are those of men, not those of God." ³⁴ Then he called the crowd to him, as well as the disciples, and said to them, "Anyone who wants to be a follower of mine must disown self, take up his cross, and follow me. ³⁵ For the man who wishes to preserve the self will lose it, but if a man will let himself be lost for my sake and for the Proclamation, that man is safe. ³⁶ What does a man gain by winning the whole world and losing his true self? ³⁷ What can he give to buy back that self? ³⁸ So if anyone is ashamed of me and mine in this godless and sinful age, then The Man will be ashamed of him when he comes in the glory of his Father with the holy angels."

9 ¹ He also said to them, "Truly I tell you: there are some present here who will not taste death until they have seen the kingdom of God come in power."

Comment

Still following Matthew's order, Mark takes up the narrative of Jesus' recognition of the inevitability of a violent end to his life and ministry. The introduction of the notion of suffering to the disciples is explicit—*he then began to teach them.* In what terms this was done we cannot know. There are no explicit references, for example, to Old Testament texts that would later play a definitive role in the early Christian community—e.g., Isa 53. Any possible references to the Servant Songs of Isaiah, such as figure in Matthew, are matters of dispute among academic scholars, and we cannot rightly say with total conviction that the use of those songs was Jesus' own. The one exception to this is the tradition preserved as the "ransom saying" in Mark 10:45 and parallels. The technical phrase "for the many" will be examined in its proper context, and it must suffice here to say that the phrase itself not only in all probability looks back to Isa 53:11 but also provides an interpretation of the suffering and death otherwise lacking in the passion predictions.

The Passion predictions themselves as they are preserved for us are certainly in their present form the result of post-resurrection reflection. We therefore must examine them for their irreducible basic elements. There are three sets of predictions in our sources:

	A	B	C
1.	Matt 16:21	Mark 8:31	Luke 9:22
2.	Matt 17:9	Mark 9:31	Luke 9:43-45
3.	Matt 20:19	Mark 10:34	Luke 18:31-34

The third set is the most detailed. The Son of Man will be

    a. handed over to chief priests and scribes
    b. condemned to death
    c. delivered to the Gentiles
    d. mocked, spat upon, flogged
    e. killed
    f. after three days raised.

The third precisely corresponds to the Easter experience, but there are other features also, notably the use of *dei pathein* (must suffer). There is nothing corresponding to this in Semitic usage. (It is omitted in Luke 9:22 but found in 1A and B.) Perhaps in final form the phrase was shaped in a Greek milieu (in Hellenistic Judaism?). Again the use of the verbs in 3A, 3B, 3C has some interesting features: 3B has *anastēnai,* 3A has *egerthēnai,* and 3C is the same as 3B. (The problem of the synoptic relationship does not concern us at this point.) Hos 6:2 *(LXX),* upon which we might think this vital feature to depend, has *anastēnai,* while Isa 26:19 has *egerthēsontai* for the active of the verb *qûm.* But in neither case would a Jew or a Jewish-Christian regard the "raising" as being self-induced. (The nearest to this in the New Testament is John 10:18.)

"Three days" certainly occupied the minds of the early community, but to what extent was this based on events from the Resurrection experience and to what extent on reflection about Old Testament texts? "Three days" is a frequent phrase, but even if the passion sayings in their final form were prophecies *ex eventu,* the same cannot be said of such texts as Mark 14:28, 15:29;

Luke 13:32,33; cf. John 16:16,17,19. Luke's "three" refers to the ministry and not to death and the grave, while Mark's examples are of turning points in the ministry. There are no words in Semitic usage for "several," and "three" often does surrogate for "soon." It is in light of this last statement that we must admit the weight of the thesis of C. H. Dodd *(The Parables of the Kingdom,* 3rd ed., New York: Scribner, 1961, p. 263) that we must re-examine the *parousia* sayings: Jesus made no distinction between *parousia,* resurrection, the consummation of the age, and the new temple. All these things, with their associated imagery, describe in one way or another the vindication of God, which is to come "very soon." *Parousia* and resurrection are never expressed in the same saying as two separate events, and only the Easter and post-Easter experience led to the sequence of resurrection-glory-*parousia.*

For all the possible and probable editing there are three principal reasons for regarding the passion predictions as historically based:

1. Jesus is represented to us, especially in Matthew and Luke, as being constantly at odds with authority and in some instances on issues that could involve capital charges (cf. Matt 12:24, 11:19; Mark 2:7 & par., 14:65). Two Sabbath-breaking charges are placed together by Mark, and contemporary opinion was that two warnings had to be given before witnesses before sentence could be passed. A reading of Mark 12 and 14 together, omitting the intruding Chapter 13, highlights the seriousness of speaking against the temple and all it represented. Not only did Jesus see himself as herald and prophet of the eschatological age, but it was not unusual in that time of the cult veneration of the prophets to regard them all as martyrs (cf. Luke 13:33). The tradition represents Jesus as looking at salvation history as one unbroken chain of violent death (cf. Matt 23:35). With the example of John immediately to hand, Jesus could hardly have thought of himself as an exception.

2. Jesus' own view of history and the cause of his ministry speak against the view that the predictions are fiction. Even allowing for variations in a single prediction, we are yet left with discovering the earliest stratum. There are two cautions to be entered here. First it is possible to assume too easily that Matt 20:19 deliberately changed Mark's "kill" to "crucify" (10:34). Apart from any discussion of synoptic relationships, crucifixion was a common enough sight, and if Jesus was put to death in Judea, it would be under Roman capital sentence. Second the adjustment from "after three days" to "on the third day" is best accounted for by Mark's faithfulness to tradition, and hence a deliberate change from Matthew.

All in all the solid core would seem to be 2A, 2B, 2C:

The Son of Man
will be given into the hands of men
and they will kill him
And when he has been killed, after three days he will be raised.

All of this has some interesting grammatical features. The "is delivered up" of Mark 9:31, 14:21, and Matt 26:2 is changed in Matt 17:22 and Luke 9:44 to "about to be delivered." The Aramaic form in which the saying undoubtedly came used a participle which normally had a present-tense meaning (and this is so translated in the Syriac versions). The primitive core, then, will have been a "saying"—a *māšāl* or riddle—in the form of "The Man will soon be delivered to men" with the meaning left open between a generic saying or a title. We are therefore confronted with a riddle that on the face of it could read "an individual will soon be given up to the generality of men" but that also effectively hid a time of messianic birth pangs and the eschatological final hour. The apocalyptic riddle hides the Son of Man title—as unquestionably it was meant to do. There are similar enigmatic sayings in our sources—cf. Luke 22:22; Mark 14:21 & par.; Mark 9:12; Luke 17:25, 24:7. In any consideration of the passion predictions, these should be given due weight.

3. Undue concentration on the passion predictions has had the effect of consigning to comparative limbo a whole series of "suffering" sayings of considerable importance and of widely dissimilar character:

a. Threats against God's messengers, Matt 23:34-36; woes against tomb builders for the prophets, Matt 23:29-32; and the saying against the traitor, Mark 14:21.

b. *Mesalîm* in which Jesus' own fate is central: Matt 8:20; Mark 14:7,8,22-24,36; Luke 11:29, 13:33; John 16:16.

c. Accusations against Jerusalem as the city of murderers of prophets, Matt 23:37-39, together with the warning against killing the heir, Mark 12:8 & par.

d. *Mesalîm* placing the fate of Jesus in association with the end-time, Mark 2:20 & par.—cf. 4 Ezra 10:1f.; Mark 10:38ff., 12:10 & par., 14:27 & par.; Luke 12:49, 22:35-38.

e. The sayings on the sufferings of the disciples—hardly would Jesus have predicted such sufferings dissociated from his own: Matt 10:25,28 & par., 34-36 & par.; Mark 8:34,35 & par., 9:1 & par., 10:38 & par., 14:27f. & par.

Two final considerations are offered in connection with this lengthy discussion:

1. There is a number of sayings on suffering which in the core tradition are firmly linked with the context: the incomprehension of the disciples and the designation of Peter as Satan in 8:33 forms a unity with 8:31. Similarly the disciples' expectation of glory in Mark 10:35-37 is followed by Jesus' reminding them of impending suffering in 10:38ff. The prediction of flight in a quotation at 14:27 is linked with a description of flight in 14:50, and Peter's self-assertiveness is not ignored. The narrative of anointing in 14:8 is a work of mercy (anointing the dead), and Jesus defends this as more important than a work of love, the point being that Jesus anticipates a criminal's death and burial without anointing.

2. Finally it is of some moment to consider a series of predictions that were not fulfilled. There are indications, for example, that Jesus thought he would be stoned to death: Matt 23:37 & par.; Luke 13:34—cf. Luke 4:29; John 8:59, 10:31, 11:8. Jesus certainly thought that the time of the sword would immediately follow his passion (Luke 22:35ff.) and that the disciples would be caught up in it (Mark 14:27) and even that some of them would share his fate (10:35-40). The fire of judgment would pass from the green wood to the dry—that is to say, his own suffering would be but a prelude to collective suffering. But after a short time the final event (the *eschaton)* would follow, with the journey of shepherd and flock to Galilee (Mark 14:28) and the building of a new sanctuary (14:58). None of this happened, and the disciples escaped the passion. John the son of Zebedee did not share the cup of fate, and the end was delayed. Jesus died the death of a criminal but was not buried as such. Interpretation of Jesus' death is a wholly separate question and must be dealt with in a later context.

On the whole matter of the passion predictions in Mark, cf. A. Feuillet, "Les trois grandes prophéties de la Passion et de la Resurrection des évangiles synoptiques," *RevThom* 4.1967, pp. 533-60 and 1.1968, pp. 41-74. Cf. also Morna Hooker, *Jesus and the Servant,* London: SPCK, 1959, ad loc.

Notes

31. *The Man:* The seriousness of the passion prediction is underlined by the assertion that the future Man-in-glory must suffer. (Cf. J. Jeremias, English translation by John Bowden, pp. 281-86.)

to undergo great suffering: So far, no rabbinic parallel has been found for the Greek *polla pathein* in the sense of enduring persecution. However, according to D. Meyer ("POLLA PATHEIN," *ZNW* 55.1964, p. 132), the Latin text of the *Assumption of Moses,* based on a Hebrew or Aramaic original, has the expression *multa passus est* (3,11), and the phrase is also found in Josephus, *Ant* 13.268, 13.403. G. Strecker ("Die Liedens—und Auferstehungvoraussagen im Markus—evangelium Mk 8:31; 9:31; 10:32-34," *ZTK* 64.1967, pp. 16-39) believes that apart from the introduction, perhaps the Son of Man idea and the *polla pathein* phrase 8:31 represent an original pre-Markan form of the passion-resurrection prediction and that 9:31 and 10:32-34 derive from it.

elders: These were laymen, in contrast to the chief priests (i.e., high priests, past and present, or members of the priestly families in Jerusalem). *Teachers of the Law* were scribes.

be raised again: The difference between the synoptists on the wording *three days later* are not so sharp as might appear. The phrase translated here—*meta treis hēmeras* —is found again in 9:31 and 10:34. Matthew has *tē tritē hēmera* (on the third day) at 16:21, 17:22, and 20:19 and Luke at 9:22 and 18:33. In the *LXX* and in the Hellenistic writers the phrases were identical. The phrase used in Mark may therefore mean a period less than three full days (i.e., less than seventy-two hours) or something akin to "in a very short time." However, the frequent use of *tē tritē hēmera* in the early tradition of the resurrection (cf. Matt 17:23; Luke 24:7,46; Acts 10:41; 1 Cor 15:4) raises the question whether the Matthean and Lucan texts wished to heighten reference to the resurrection. Or, to put the matter another way, did Jesus explicitly foretell his resurrection? Mark's answer—that the disciples did not understand that resurrection was meant (9:32)—is insufficient, especially since the same evangelist assures us that several times Jesus alluded to his resurrection (8:31; 9:9,31; 10:34; 14:28). But it is difficult, seeing the intensity and passion with which Jesus pursued his ministry and vocation, to suppose that for all the certainty of suffering and violent death, he did not look beyond that to the vindication of God. Certainly the idea of vocation and suffering were bound up together in the thought of Jesus, and it is thinking made up of a blend of Isaiah 53 and the future Man-in-glory.

We enter here of course into what we may gather of the human consciousness of Jesus. If Jesus was truly human, then his humanity cannot have been of a different character from our own, and learning as a day-to-day experience would have been his, as it is ours. Moreover, the faith and trust of Jesus in God, however different in degree from ours, must have been of the same kind—a loving confidence in God for the outcome of present experience. Now had Jesus known *with total certitude* that he would be raised from death, to that extent faith would be wholly absent and his humanity far removed from ours. The only OT background from which this present text about "being raised" could have been derived is Hos 6:2: "on the third day he will raise us up" (Greek *anastēsometha*). What is described here is the restoration, the vindication, of the northern kingdom of Israel, and not resurrection from death. However, a recent article (Michael Barré, "New Light on the Interpretation of Hos 6:2," *VT* 28.1978, pp. 129-41) has called attention to the fact that the Hebrew verb translated in the *LXX* commonly bears the meaning of raising from sickness and nowhere is found in any context of raising from death. We do not think that Jesus in using Hos 6:2 was looking to any particular manifestation of God's vindication of his ministry and Proclamation: steadfast faith and trust looked only to vindication, not to its manner.

Textually, the versions in Matthew and Luke agree closely, and Mark changes the *egerthēnai* of Matthew and Luke to the *anastēnai* of Hos 6:2 in *LXX*. Cf. W. J. Bennett, Jr., "The Son of Man Must . . . ," *NovTest* 17.1975, pp. 113-29. Verses 8:31 and 9:12 are alternative forms of a single saying, Semitic in origin. *Aegraptai* in 9:12 should be read in light of *dei* in 8:31; they are synonomous in the sense that both are circumlocutions for "God wills it." The evangelist is not conscious of quoting scripture (the author's attempt is to link with Ps 118:22); rather, in the context of apocalyptic sayings, it is an assertion designed to strengthen the faithful. The suffering of Mark's readers is linked to those of Jesus.

32. *plainly* (Greek *parrēsia):* The word is frequent in the New Testament; it connotes frankness in speech, boldness, freedom from ambiguity. The event was evidently decisive and represents a culmination of convictions growing out of the events of the ministry.

took him aside: The words can without difficulty mean "drew him to himself" as if to protect him. Luke omits this incident entirely, and Matthew's version is fuller.

Some old Latin manuscripts, rather in the style of Matthew, have "Then Simon Kephas, as though he pitied him, said to him, 'Far be this from you!' " The fact that one Syrian manuscript has the same wording lends weight to the possibility that something like this was in the original Markan text. Certainly its presence would be an explanation for the abrupt reaction of Jesus. Peter is represented as being almost condescending.

33. The act of turning around to face the speaker seems to have been characteristic of Jesus (cf. 5:30 and Matt 9:22; Luke 7:9,44; 9:55; 10:23; 14:25; 22:61; 23:28; John 1:38). *Away with you, Satan* is something of an expansion of Matthew's wording. It implies that the attempt on the part of Peter (and the disciples?) to deflect the inevitable course of the ministry was as insidious as any temptation in the desert. Cf. B. A. E. Osborne, "Peter: Stumbling Block and Satan," *NovTest* 15.1975, pp. 187-90; E. Best, "Peter in the Gospel According to Mark," *CBQ* 40.1978, pp. 547-58.

your interests (Greek *phronéo*): The word implies a whole direction of mind and will, not simply a momentary thought. Matthew's version adds "you are a stumbling block to me!" The whole manner of the rebuke almost demands the phrase and seems to be part of the original tradition. On the supposition that Matthew softens the attitude of Mark toward the disciples, held in some quarters, one would have expected the exclamation to be in Mark and not in Matthew.

34. This and the succeeding verses are from a collection of sayings on various occasions, drawn here by the appropriate context of v. 31. The common idea is that of continuing loyalty to Jesus, and perhaps the verses stood as a block in some collection. Preservation in this form would be wholly appropriate in a community where loyalties were being put to a severe test, and the insertion of the collection here was a stroke of editorial genius. The final saying in v. 38, referring as it does to The Man-in-glory, passes easily with the saying in 9:1 on the anticipated soon-to-be-revealed Reign of God and so to the Transfiguration narrative. It is not possible to say to what period of the ministry these sayings belong.

The editorial link of *then he called the crowd* is made plain by the mention of the crowd, which has not been in evidence since 8:6. Matthew refers only to the disciples, while Luke has "all." The phrase *as well as the disciples* is peculiar to Mark and suggests that Peter was acting as a kind of spokesman.

Of the conditions of discipleship, two are acts of committal and the third is a continuing relationship between the follower and Jesus. The first is denial of self or (following classical Greek) a "failure to see the self." The second demand is to accept the full and entire consequences of discipleship, to take up the cross as an instrument of death. Is the idea metaphorical? Did Jesus envisage that his immediate followers would suffer death with him? Or was the reference to the cross developed after the Easter experience? The saying could very easily have come from Jesus' own time, for resistance to imperial authority led all too quickly to the barbarities of capital sentence. According to Josephus, two thousand were crucified under Varus in 4 B.C. for rebellion (cf. J. G. Griffiths, "The Disciple's Cross," *NTS* 16.1970, pp. 358-64, and T. Aerts, "Suivre Jésus. Evolution d'un thème biblique dans les Évangiles synoptiques," *EphTheolLov* 42.1966, pp. 476-512). The third condition is to *follow*. Mark follows Matthew's wording, while Luke adds "daily" after *take up his cross.* All three evangelists emphasize the free will of those who would be disciples—*Anyone who wants*. In short Jesus is represented as facing the implacable hostility toward the Proclamation of the Reign of God which would be displayed when finally the ministry reached its climax.

Some manuscripts read "his self" for *self*. The Greek *psuche* as the *LXX* translation of the Hebrew *nephesh* is used in the twofold sense of a person's ordinary life and also of the true inner self or personality. G. Schwarz, " '. . . aparnēsastho heauton . . .'? (Markus 8:34 & par.)," *NovTest* 17.1975, pp. 109-12, suggests that underlying 8:34 (Matt 16:24, Luke 9:23) is the Aramaic root *nkr*, which in the pa'el form can mean "to consider oneself a foreigner" (i.e., non-Jew). Jesus' own increasing alienation from official Judaism would undoubtedly affect his followers, and they had to be prepared for it.

The saying in v. 34 follows closely on the preceding exhortation to follow—with all the consequent and final risks. The sense seems to be that even if death should be the consequence, the disciple has preserved the *true* self or has even attained it. Cf. Luke 17:30.

35. *for my sake* is omitted in some manuscripts, but this must surely be accidental for the phrase lies at the heart of the early tradition (cf. Matt 10:39, Luke 9:24).

and for the Proclamation is a Markan addition.

36ff. The value of the true self is further pursued in these verses. There is no greater gain than to find the true self, and (v. 37) no conceivable price can be placed upon it. *World* in v. 36 is used not to refer to the created order, but to the opportunities of social and commercial life.

losing (Greek *zēmioō*): The word is used often in *LXX* for "to cause loss": in the NT it is used in the passive in the sense of "to lose" (cf. Matt 16:26, Luke 9:25, 1 Cor 3:15, 2 Cor 7:9, Phil 3:8).

37. *What can he give*: Literally, "what price [Greek *antallagma*] can anyone give."

38. This saying is loosely connected with the previous sayings in the Greek by *gar* (for) and has the same form: *if anyone*. But though it, like the other sayings, is concerned with loyalty, the resemblance ends there. The Man is not the suffering Messiah but the future glorious eschatological figure. There are some notable features about this saying. The Reign of God and The Man-in-glory are side by side, linked only in the process of compilation, and while there is nothing here inherently improbable as coming from the sayings of Jesus, it is more than likely that the conjunction of which we have just spoken was made under the influence of later beliefs about the *parousia*. The Reign of God was always used in teaching the "outsiders," the casual listeners, while *The Man* was a term used only in private teaching. This sharp division begins at 8:38 and remains so until Jesus is before the Council.

The distinction between The Man and Jesus in v. 38a is significant. If the saying is original, there are two possible explanations, one of which must be true. Either Jesus spoke at some stage in the ministry of a supernatural Man-in-glory other than himself, or the expression has reference to the Community, the Elect, of which he would be head. The first seems doubtful, but the second (given a link with the "individual-and-community" figure of Dan 7:13) is not implausible. But if the latter interpretation is correct, the references by Jesus to himself as one who must suffer place this saying not in the present context but in that part of the ministry prior to the events of 8:27ff. The meaning would therefore be that those who confessed allegiance to him, or rejected him and his disciples, would be judged by the Community, the Elect at the shortly to be inaugurated Reign of God. All this would certainly illuminate the saying in Matt 19:28 = Luke 22:30. Matthew understands the saying to refer to Jesus speaking about himself as he now is, as compared with what he will be (cf. 16:27). The Lucan version (9:26) is much closer to the Markan understanding.

The saying has to do with those who are "ashamed" of Jesus and his disciples, in *this godless and sinful age* (the wording is peculiar to Mark, but the phrase "evil and adulterous generation" is found at Matt 12:39, cf. Luke 11:29). The description of a community as "adulterous" has Old Testament precedent (cf. Hos 2:2, Isa 1:4, Ezek 16:32ff.) and refers to the faulted Covenant relationship between God and his people.

glory . . . holy angels: "Glory" is used in the usual biblical sense of the splendor and majesty of God as they are demonstrated in creation. *1 Enoch* refers to the Elect One being set on the "throne of glory" or of "his glory" from which he will judge kings, the righteous, and the powerful (41:8, 62:2), but there is no phrase equivalent to *his Father* in those texts. The allusion to *angels* often occurs in conjunction with The Man (cf. Matt 13:41, 25:31; John 1:51; *1 Enoch* 61:10) and appears when Paul speaks of the *parousia* (2 Thess 1:7).

Not only is it impossible in this saying to discover whether *comes* (Greek *elthē)* is used in the sense of coming *to* the Father (in the sense of Dan 7:13), but it is far from clear to what extent we may legitimately adduce *1 Enoch* as evidence for this and similar synoptic sayings. While it is true that manuscripts of *1 Enoch* have been found at Qumran—thus establishing some outside-limit dates for the work—Chapters 37-71, containing the apocalyptic sayings concerning The Man, or the Elect One, have not so far been found there. Cf. Albright-Mann, AB *Matthew,* notes on Matt 25:31-46, pp. 306-10; and Bruce Vawter, *This Man Jesus* (Garden City, N.Y.: Doubleday, 1973), pp. 110-11. It has long been recognized that *1 Enoch* was subject to Christian influence, but the presumption remains strong that the missing section 37-71 in the Qumran manuscripts ought not to be made into a too formidable *argumentum a silentio.*

The apocalyptic sense is stronger in Matthew, who adds "when he will reward everyone according to his deeds" (16:27), while Luke's sense is somewhat weaker in reading "in his glory and that of the Father and the holy angels." Mark's text certainly represents a digest here. (E. Best, "An Early Sayings Collection," *NovTest* 18.1976, pp. 1-16.)

9:1. Some manuscripts have simply "present," whereas the majority add *here (hōde),* while yet others begin the saying with "I solemnly tell you." Without *here* the text would simply mean "bystanders" (cf. Matt 26:73, John 3:29, Acts 22:25).

who will not (Greek *ou mē)* is an emphatic negative, which is not always the case in the New Testament, especially when followed by *until they have seen.* However, the construction is common, especially in the sayings of Jesus (about sixty percent of the whole). The double negative is certainly no part of refined speech, but the emphatic sense of "by no means" is clearly present.

taste (Greek *genomai):* The word is found in the metaphorical sense in *LXX* (Job 20:18, Ps 33:9, Prov 24:13), though not in any connection with death. The remainder of the saying is a potential quagmire, even for those with some knowledge of Greek, but an attempt must be made here to explicate the grammatical structure of the words. The notes which follow therefore attempt to make the grammar understandable, leaving the interpretation to a final note.

until (Greek *heōs an):* This particle is constructed with the subjunctive, as in 6:10. In Mark the verb "to see" is used with *hoti* (that) and the infinitive when the apprehension of a fact or a set of circumstances is under discussion (cf. 2:16, 7:2, 9:25, 12:34, 15:39) and (as in the present instance) with the accusative case and the participle to describe the thing seen, the participle being part of the extended accusative: *kingdom of God* is qualified by the participle *come,* or "having come" (cf. 1:10,16; 2:14; 6:33,48f.; 9:1,14,38; 11:13,20; 13:14,29; 14:67; 16:5). With the exception of John 19:33—and that exception is dubious—this is the usage in all the gospels. The same grammatical considerations hold when the verb "to know" is employed. All of this is of crucial importance in view of the translations suggested for 9:1.

One possible translation would be "until they have seen that the Kingdom of God has come with power." This can be defended on the grammatically good ground that the accusative case *(Kingdom)* and the participle *(come)* are used in the same fashion as the familiar accusative with infinitive construction in Greek. The translation attempts to underscore an assertion not that those standing around will see the Kingdom's *coming* in power but they will become aware that the Kingdom had already come in power at some point before they became cognizant of it. In essence the debate must center on the validity or otherwise of "realized eschatology." Does the text before us, in context, point plainly to a future event? Did Jesus teach a realized eschatology? Without question, Jesus taught that in his ministry, in the very Proclamation itself and in the works of healing and exorcism, the Reign of God was already at work (cf. Luke 11:20). Furthermore the gospel of John is *the* exemplar in our New Testament sources of realized eschatology—whatever the ambiguity of the sources of that teaching, and presumably the Johannine understanding of eschatology had origins somewhere in the early tradition, if not in Jesus himself. The present writer, together with the late W. F. Albright, pleaded that Matthew's gospel had far more substantial elements of realized eschatology in its composition than is commonly realized (see AB *Matthew,* Introduction VII, pp. lxxxviii ff.; see also the notes on 25:31-46). This commentator sees no reason to change that thesis, and it is equally his view that Mark is substantially dependent on Matthew.

Perhaps the best we can do with this enigmatic saying is to suggest *either* that Jesus was mistaken in supposing that his own impending death would in some visible fashion usher in the full disclosure of the Reign of God *or* that Jesus meant that some bystanders would not die before his own suffering and death and his vindication at the hands of God.

Appended Note: "Son of Man" in 8:31,38

Generally, this saying is accepted as genuine by a majority of scholars, in contrast with the saying we examined in the appended note on Chapter 2. For those who come to the texts with a presupposition that such sayings are concerned with the *future* "Son of Man," the issue is prejudged. To others for whom the very notion that Jesus could have predicted his own passion is impossible, the confirmation of The Man in a context of suffering is a prophecy after the event. We are not concerned here to examine those positions, and it is hoped that enough was said in the appended note to Chapter 2 to indicate that the present writer cannot accept either position outlined above.

On any showing, the first of the sayings in Chapter 8 is of capital importance, for there is consensus among the synoptists that the first saying came immediately after Peter's confession and immediately before Jesus' sayings on discipleship. Moreover the rebuke of Peter is of considerable importance: either it is genuine or, if not, we must construct an anti-Petrine polemic in the early Church of considerable proportions and not a little bitterness, of which we have no trace in literature.

The picture which emerges in the first saying can be summarized as follows:

1. Jesus is the moving figure in the sayings, and the confession of Peter is only elicited by questions put by Jesus. In the same way the rebuke of Peter arises in response to Jesus' teaching. Apparently Jesus elicits from the disciples a confession of messiahship, even though Mark and Luke give us no hint that he accepted the title—certainly not in the terms of Matt 16:17.

2. Two main suggestions have been made with respect to Jesus' invitation for responses about himself and his mission: first to bring them to an acknowledgment of his messiahship and then drastically to change their understanding of messiahship, to the point of reducing such understanding to the vanishing point; second to bring them to such acknowledgment and then to deny it altogether. This seems altogether too much for the evidence. It seems very unlikely that Jesus would have provided—on his own initiative—an opportunity to confess him as the messiah unless he denied it immediately. We have no evidence whatsoever of such a denial. The command to silence in v. 30 has often been interpreted as a denial of messiahship that has been misunderstood, not simply a temporary injunction in face of misunderstanding. It is not easy, however, to see how an emphatic denial could have been misunderstood in this fashion.

3. The narrative concerned with messiahship is self-contained and self-consistent. A watershed in the ministry has been reached, and the distinction between the inner circle of the Twelve on the one hand and the crowds on the other (a distinction sharply drawn in the use of the parables) is crystallized. Peter and his companions are now privy to *the* secret of the ministry, but that knowledge must be preserved both from misunderstanding and from dissemination outside the Twelve.

4. The introduction of The Man at this juncture is to all intents and purposes sudden and without warning. Mark agrees with Luke in its use—it is not found in Matthew—and significantly Peter is seen as realizing that Jesus

uses the term of himself; Mark would have us see that the term is Jesus' self-description as Messiah.

5. The difficulty comes with the use of *dei* (must). There is nothing in the term "The Man" that carries the inevitability of suffering, whereas the whole course of the ministry had determined that *Jesus* would not only suffer but die a violent death. The problem therefore is to find a link between the suffering of Jesus and the notion of The Man as suffering. The only way in which this link can be made—and it is extremely important—is the *fashion* of the suffering as it is depicted in the crucial Daniel 7, whether corporate or individual, whether Israel or an idealized figure. The Man will suffer and Israel will suffer when the authority given to him by God is denied and the beasts and the nations are in revolt against God. The "elect of God" texts in *Enoch* exhibit the same characteristics: whereas The Man in *Enoch* is an individual person (in some instances identified with the author) and we hear nothing of his sufferings, "the elect" suffer until universal recognition is his.

6. If we are reading the evidence correctly, the recognition of Jesus by the disciples, along with his nonrecognition (even rejection) by his critics and the authorities, makes the suffering of The Man, of Jesus, inevitable. That is to say, the two questions "How *can* The Man suffer?" and "Why must Jesus suffer?" are found to be one, and the transition from the confession of messiahship to the inevitability of suffering is neither sudden nor abrupt. The broad canvas of apocalyptic vision of universal opposition found in Daniel and *Enoch* is missing, to be sure, but it is plain that Mark's intention from the beginning is to portray all opposition to Jesus as radical evil, and hence also opposition to God himself. In this sense then indeed The Man must suffer, for the confrontation between Jesus and his opponents is one between the Word of God enshrined in his Proclamation and an evil enemy. The dismay of Peter —and the rest—is precisely founded on the fact that if the authority of the one who bears the word is not recognized, their suffering is an inevitable consequence.

7. The conflict with which Mark's gospel began and the conflict theme which he has sustained throughout reach in this narrative a highly significant point. The denial of Jesus' authority is seen now for what it is: denial of God himself, arising from the opposition of the forces of evil. It must follow then that only those who acknowledge the authority of Jesus and the significance of his ministry can rightly appreciate and be taught that the outcome of denial can only be suffering. We misconceive the whole tenor of this passage if we interpret it in the sense that suffering is an inevitable part of the title "The Man." On the contrary, the suffering is a direct result of the denial of The Man. The immediate reaction of Peter is, following this premise, wholly understandable. He and the rest of the disciples have not fully understood the character of the forces hostile to Jesus and so cannot understand that failure to acknowledge The Man must involve suffering. Peter, therefore, is rebuked:

he speaks from mere human calculation and not from the viewpoint of God
and God's messianic herald.

There is a final point to be made. In this passage messiahship is linked with
suffering and The Man. We may readily concede that the views of the disciples on messiahship were far from Jesus' own and concede too that The Man
was not a messianic "title" in the sense in which we commonly use the term.
Yet with all that said, we are—albeit unconsciously—working from a background of our textbooks (from many viewpoints) on New Testament theology
and also from a presupposition that the very word "messiah" was in some
sense in the time of Jesus capable of definition. But it is unceasingly clear that
for some time prior to the ministry of Jesus the idea of "messiahship" was to
say the least vague, even though the use of the word would have an immediate significance to hearers and readers. Jesus may well have used "The Man"
to define his own interpretation of messiahship—not that The Man and Messiah are synonymous, far from it. Yet the emergence of The Man (cf. in this
context Albright-Mann, AB *Matthew,* Introduction, pp. xcvii ff.) as an *individual* champion of the people against the four kings of Daniel 7 brings the
two concepts of The Man and the messiah inevitably closer.

With respect to 9:1 possibly being linked to the Transfiguration narrative
that follows, see the important article by Enrique Nardoni, "A Redactional
Interpretation of Mark 9:1," *CBQ* 43.1981, pp. 365-84, much of which the
present writer finds persuasive if not conclusive.

44. Transfiguration
(9:2-8) = Matt 17:1-13; Luke 9:28-36

9   ² Six days later Jesus took Peter, James, and John with him and led
them to a high mountain where they were alone. In their presence he
was transfigured; ³ his clothes became dazzling white, with a brightness no cleaner anywhere could equal. ⁴ Elijah appeared to them and
Moses with him, and they were there talking with Jesus. ⁵ Then Peter
said to Jesus, "Rabbi, it is good that we are here. So let us make three
shelters—one for you, one for Moses, and one for Elijah." ⁶ (He did
not know what to say—they were so frightened.) ⁷ Then a cloud appeared, covering them with its shadow, and from the cloud came a
voice: "This is my Son, the Beloved. Listen to him!" ⁸ And now, suddenly, as they looked around, they saw no one but Jesus alone with
them.

Comment

This deceptively short pericope contains several theological motifs and not a few enigmas. For example, out of a total of seven verses in the whole, no fewer than three are concerned with Moses and Elijah, who appear with Jesus. Peter's offer to build three booths is discussed by the evangelist as the response of bewilderment. In addition the voice which announces ". . . my Son, the Beloved" apparently distinguishes Jesus from Moses and Elijah as well as from the generality of humanity. In some fashion, the two figures appear to be essential to the narrative, and the question is whether their importance is symbolic, supportive in some fashion, or simply—and crudely put—decorative.

If Moses and Elijah are symbolic figures, the symbolism ought perhaps to be open to our inspection.

(a) Is the Transfiguration narrative a prefiguration of the *parousia* and the presence of Moses as the prophet and Elijah as forerunner of the messiah then essential to the narrative? But in this interpretation, the two figures are hardly *essential,* for the Proclamation of the messiah himself immediately eliminates them, and they hardly then merit the amount of space they occupy in a very spare narrative.

(b) The suggestion has been made that in some fashion Moses and Elijah are symbolic of suffering, and suffering moreover at the hands of the people of God. But even if (as this commentator holds) Mark was written under the threat of impending persecution, neither Moses nor Elijah would immediately suggest the theme of suffering to a contemporary audience. Moreover, so far as that theme was concerned, the injunction "Listen to him!" refers to the prediction immediately preceding—it does not, and cannot, refer to Elijah or Moses.

(c) Baltensweiler (see the selected bibliography following) sees a transformed Elijah, as harbinger of the messiah, very different from the violent and even revolutionary figure known to us from scripture. His appearance therefore calls attention to a rejection of a political or zealot messiahship. This is hardly acceptable. There is no indication that the tempestuous character of Elijah as depicted in the Old Testament records has been in any way mitigated, and the role of the prophet as percursor of some future divine event in Mal 4:5-6 would apparently cast the prophet in the role of one who *imposes* peace.

Before further considering the place and importance of Moses and Elijah in this narrative, it is essential to place the narrative itself in some *Sitz im Leben* which appears to be faithful to the intention of the evangelist. That the account is intended to comment theologically upon some event seems un-doubted. The suggestion that what is being described prophetically is the appearance of the glorified Lord at the *parousia* can hardly be sustained. There is no suggestion in our sources that the early belief in the *parousia* depicted Jesus as teaching it (cf. v. 7). Furthermore, although the word "glory" is used by Mark characteristically of the *parousia* (cf. 8:38, 10:37, 13:26), the New Testament also proclaims that Jesus was glorified at the resurrection (in John, even at the passion). It is somewhat more probable to see in the Transfiguration story a deliberately misplaced resurrection appear-ance—though this by no means explains the presence of Moses and Elijah. Certainly for all the care taken by Luke to emphasize the essentially human form (and behavior) of Jesus after the resurrection, the earliest tradition as-cribes to the risen Jesus an appearance of glory. Paul equates his own conver-sion vision as being precisely the same as the appearances to Peter, James, and the rest. Paul shares with John the conviction that the resurrection was the ascent to glory and that appearances of Jesus thereafter were from the enthronement glory of heaven. Furthermore the connection between transfig-uration and resurrection is underlined by the declaration of sonship con-nected with the resurrection in Rom 1:4 (cf. Acts 13:33). There are further links between the transfiguration and the resurrection, and within the limits of seven verses for the transfiguration and eight for the resurrection, they are striking:

1. The provenance of the transfiguration as being within Mark's general notion of Galilee is underscored by 16:7: *He is going on before you into Galilee; you will see him there.*

2. The note of time may be significant. *Six days later* may probably indi-cate a Sabbath, and Mark's Greek at 15:42 and 16:2 implies that the resurrec-tion took place on the Sabbath.

3. There is verbal similarity in the two accounts, far more evident in the Greek than in translation: *hōde einai* ("to be here," 9:5) and *ouk estin hōde* ("he is not here," 16:6); *oudeni ouden eipan ephēbounto gar* ("they said noth-ing to anyone, for they were afraid," 16:8), and *ou gar ēdei ti apochrithē* ("he did not know what to say—they were so frightened," 9:6).

It seems certain that the evangelist intends to emphasize that the Resurrec-tion explains the occurrence on the mountain—but in what particular sense? Closely associated with that is the allied question: was there an *event* on the mountain, closely following upon the Passion prediction, at which the three disciples physically saw a transfigured Jesus, clothed proleptically with the glory of heaven, and alongside him Moses and Elijah similarly in glory? If an affirmative answer to this second question is given, then it is at least worthy of attention that this privileged vision apparently availed them nothing in the subsequent discourses on suffering and certainly afforded no glimmer of faith in the time of the Passion. Perhaps we shall be more successful in unraveling the meaning of the Transfiguration account if we pay due attention to another New Testament book (the gospel of John) in which "glory" is always closely associated with a whole complex—passion, enthronement-crucifixion, resurrection. The present writer maintains that *the* event emphasized and interpreted in the pericope before us is the preceding passion prediction *seen through the eyes of the resurrection experience*. Put in the simplest terms, the transfiguration narrative is not a misplaced resurrection appearance, it is *not* an event separate from the preceding account of the passion prediction and the sayings on suffering, but it *is* a theologizing of that preceding account. It is an important early example of theologizing, for it fastens on the passion prediction and provides an interpretation of the death of Jesus as triumph, "glory." Essentially in the view of the present writer it is a device far more telling than baldly stating "If we could have had faith to listen, to see, we would have interpreted the passion prediction as foreshadowing glory." The resurrection has been retrojected into the experience on a lonely hillside where fear had been the overwhelming emotion.

With all this in mind, it is possible to arrive at some tentative conclusions about the importance of Moses and Elijah. There is a clear and sharp distinction between Jesus and the two supporters, and the force of that distinction rests upon several factors:

(a) The juxtaposition of the idea of sonship with the command immediately following: *Listen to him!* involves the notion of the Son-of-God as Mark interpreted the expression. Sonship for Mark was closely associated with suffering, of which the parable in 12:6-8 is the strongest statement (15:39 may be no more than a pagan acknowledgment, and the definite article before *son* is missing).

(b) Moreover, the role of prophet of the final age is emphasized in 12:6. The disciples then had failed to recognize in Jesus at the time of the Passion prediction both the prophet and Son, and had failed to see that Jesus was speaking of his future glory, of future vindication. The disciples had therefore failed also to remember that there was witness to the prophet of the final age in the words of Moses in Deut 18:15. They had failed to hear with the ears of faith the further truths of the sayings about death and suffering, and having failed in that they had failed to see the Son. Jesus then is far superior to Moses, who foretold his coming. They had failed to see the Son-in-glory through suffering, failed too to remember that the one who had foretold the prophet-like-himself had been taken to heavenly glory, as also had the one who was to be the forerunner. Traditionally both Moses and Elijah had been translated, but Jesus came to glory through death and resurrection.

There was, then, no veridical hallucination, no vision, and we have to ask what this tradition—so firmly embedded in all our sources—was meant to accomplish in the position it occupies. What call existed at the time when our gospels were written for an assurance of the preeminent status of Jesus? To some extent, all three synoptic gospels address the same concern of interpreting the delay in an anticipated early *parousia* or manifestation in glory of the risen Lord. It is a commonplace of Lucan studies that Acts is designed (partially at all events) to assess and make provision for an extended "time of the Church"—a concern already prefigured in the same author's gospel. For all the bulk of teaching in Matthew, that evangelist too exhibits much preoccupation with a continuing community and even leaves his eschatological discourses ambiguous as between "future" and "realized" eschatology (cf. Albright-Mann, AB *Matthew*, Introduction, VI-VIII, pp. lxxxi-cv). Given the situation urged by the present writer (Introduction, 5, A and B), the crisis faced by Mark was stark and immediate. The assurance demanded by Mark's community was that the Jesus to whom they had committed their allegiance and their lives was indeed risen and was enthroned in the glory of heaven. The delayed *parousia* motif may have sufficed for Matthew and Luke, but for Mark there were far more immediate concerns. For varying reasons, all three evangelists were compelled to assert the far-excelling glory of Jesus as over against Moses and Elijah, lest in the anxieties of different situations the early Christians be led to evaluate Jesus as no more than the equal of two highly significant Old Testament figures. Significantly, though Moses occupies the attention of Luke in Acts, the person of Elijah—the one with whom Jesus might be thought to be identified—has faded from view.

What remains to be discussed is the origin of the narrative before us, especially in view of the unanimity of all three evangelists. The present writer believes that the narrative belongs to a very early strand of the tradition and that substantially it can only have come from one or all of the three disciples who had accompanied Jesus to the mountain. The three are represented in our sources as being in closer association with Jesus than the rest, and it is a reasonable assumption that on this occasion the three were privileged to hear further explanations of the predictions in the previous pericope. Their failure to understand was absolute, and the present narrative enshrines, in the enigmatic form of a vision, an acknowledgment articulated in other terms in the gospel of John, that the passion was enthronement-exaltation-glory.

The divided state of scholarly opinion on the whole matter is nowhere better exemplified than in the extensive notes and supporting bibliography in Taylor, pp. 386-88. What follows here is a highly selective bibliography and is certainly not meant to be exhaustive, but it is hoped that it contains enough material to be representative of various viewpoints. See further the recent study by George W. E. Nickelsburg, "Enoch, Levi, and Peter: Recipients of Revelation in Upper Galilee," *JBL* 100.1981, pp. 575-600.

Selected Bibliography

Baltensweiler, H. "Die Verklärung Jesu." In *Abhandlungen zur Theologie des Alten und Neuen Testaments.* Vol. 3. Zürich: Zwingli-Verlag, 1959, pp. 69-82.

Boobyer, G. H. *St. Mark and the Transfiguration Story.* Edinburgh: T. & T. Clark, 1942.

Carlston, C. E. "Transfiguration and Resurrection." *JBL* 80.1961, pp. 233-40.

Fuchs, A. "Die Verklärungserzählung des Mc-Ev. in der Sicht moderner Exegese." *TheolPrakQuart* 125.1977, pp. 29-37.

Gerber, W. "Die Metamorphose Jesu, Markus 9.2f., par." *TTZ* 23.1967, pp. 385-95.

Holmes, R. "The Purpose of the Transfiguration." *JBL* 4.1903, pp. 233-40.

Lightfoot, R. H. *The Gospel Message of St. Mark.* Oxford: Oxford University Press, 1950.

Masson, C. "La Transfiguration de Jésus (Marc 9.2-13)." *RevTheolPhil* 97.1964, pp. 1-14.

Ramsey, A. M. *The Glory of God and the Transfiguration of Christ.* London: Longman, Green, 1948.

Riesenfeld, Harald. *Jésu Transfiguré.* Acta Seminarii Neotestamentici Upsaliensis 16. Copenhagen: Munksgaard, 1947.

Rivera, L. F. "Interpretatio Transfigurationis Jesu in redactione evangelii Marci." *Verbum Domini* 46.1968, pp. 99-104.

Synge, F. C. "The Transfiguration Story." *ET* 82.1970, pp. 82-83.

Thrall, Margaret E. "Elijah and Moses in Mark's Account of the Transfiguration." *NTS* 16.1969-70, pp. 305-17.

Notes

2. *Six days:* Apart from the Passion, this is the most exact of Mark's notes of time. Cf. Luke's "eight days" (9:28). Mark follows Matthew's temporal note. Attention should be paid to the "six days" of Moses' sojourn on the mountain (Exod 24:15ff.) before the voice of God called him from the cloud. Given the need on the part of the evangelists to emphasize the sheer distance in glory as between Jesus and the two OT figures, the temporal note is surely not without significance (cf. Lohmeyer, p. 173). Cf. Foster R. McCurley, Jr., "And After Six Days (Mark 9:2): A Semitic Literary Device," *JBL* 93.1.1974, pp. 68-71.

mountain: Traditionally Mt. Tabor (ten miles southwest of the Sea of Galilee). This hill is no more than 1,000 feet high, and modern commentators often refer to Mt. Hermon (9,200 feet and some ten miles from Caesarea Philippi). But the identification of any such mountain is purely conjectural. But cf. Matt 28:16—an attractive identification if this narrative is a resurrection story.

alone: Mark's Greek expresses the desire for solitude, as does the Greek of Matthew, but Luke adds "to pray." Some manuscripts of Mark add the phrase by assimilation.

transfigured (Greek *metamorphoō*—literally, "to transform"): The word has been translated as it is here ever since Wycliffe's use (c. 1390) from the Latin *transfiguratus est.* We recall the "glorification" (Greek *deodoxastai)* of Moses' face while conversing with God (Exod 24:29), but the verb here suggests 2 Cor 3:18, where Paul contrasts the transitory glory of Moses with that of the Risen Jesus. However, in all the Transfiguration narratives, the transformation is temporary. Matthew has the same verb, with the further comment "his face shone like the sun." Luke avoids the verb and says, "his face was changed."

3. The clothing of Jesus is described as *dazzling* (Greek *stribto),* in the same fashion that polished or bright surfaces were so described in classical Greek and in the *LXX.* *White* (Greek *leukos)* is used also of the young man at the tomb in 16:5. The phrase *with a brightness . . . equal* is peculiar to Mark and further underlines his emphasis on the heavenly glory of Jesus. The absence of any reference to the face of Jesus is strange, but there is just enough variant mss. evidence to suggest that originally the text may have read "his clothing became dazzling and his face white."

4. *appeared:* The verb *horaō* is used infrequently in Mark, and the passive form *ophthē* is used here only, just as elsewhere in the NT the verb is used to describe the sudden appearance of a heavenly figure. The phrase *talking with Jesus* is illuminated in the Lucan version (9:31) by "they spoke of the departure (Greek *exodos)* which he was about to accomplish in Jerusalem." In view of the stance taken in the comment at the head of this pericope, Luke underlines the glory of the Passion despite the seeming horror. Luke further emphasizes the actual presence of Moses and Elijah by saying that the disciples saw them when they were fully awake. Matthew, however, clearly speaks of a "vision" (17:9).

5. Peter's impulsive interjection is enigmatic. The descriptive *good* might refer to joy at the present experience. But it is important to read it together with the succeeding sentence—*let us make three shelters.* The word itself (Greek *skēnē)* is not only associated with the symbolism of a dwelling place for divinity (as, e.g., in the *LXX* for the tent of meeting in the wilderness), but it has here strong eschatological overtones (cf. Luke 16:9; 2 Cor 6:1; Rev 21:3). We may be reasonably confident that the proper interpretation of the sentence may lie along these lines and at the same time accommodate the positions outlined in the comment. Providing a shelter for Jesus along with Moses and Elijah effectively places Jesus as one more eschatological messenger on the same level as the two OT prophets. Moreover Moses' promise of a future prophet was simply that, despite the use of Deut 18:15 by the Samaritans as a messianic prediction. It is surely not without significance that Peter's confused misunderstanding in v. 6 is reminiscent of the disciples' inability to say anything to Jesus in Gethsemane (14:40). Once again we have a vital link with the Passion narrative.

It is difficult to translate adequately the word *ekphoboi* (rendered here by *they were so frightened).* The word can be used to refer to religious awe, but if the considerations offered here in the comment are valid, then Mark's sense would appear to be that despite sharing the solitude with Jesus, and despite further explanations of disquieting predictions of suffering and death, the disciples did not understand. They were frightened and only later came to a realization of a lost opportunity for insight.

7. Matt 17:5 ("he was still speaking," Greek *eti autou lalountos*)—and Luke 9:34 ("as he spoke," Greek *autou legontos)* agree in using the genitive absolute, and this may originally have been the case with Mark at the beginning of this verse.

cloud: Cf. 13:26; 14:62.

covering them (Greek *episkiazō):* Cf. Matt 17:5; Luke 1:35, 9:34; Acts 5:15. Attention has already been called to the similarities in vocabulary in Luke as between the transfiguration, resurrection, and ascension. The overshadowing cloud may have reference to the cloud of Exod 40:34 which hovered over the tent of meeting, but— considering the *three shelters* of v. 5—it is far more likely that we are to understand this in the sense of Matthew's *photeinē* (bright) to describe the cloud as being that of the *Shekinah* (the presence). The readers of the gospel are therefore being assured that despite the previous warnings of suffering and death, the symbol of the divine presence (Exod 16:10, 19:9, 24:15, 33:9; Lev 16:2; Num 11:25) rests upon Jesus. It is from that divine presence that the voice speaks. Luke's narrative has already clarified the connection between the triumph of the Exodus (see the note on v. 4 above) and the overshadowing divine presence in the impending suffering and death. The voice, and the cloud of eschatological glory (cf. 13:26, 14:62, Dan 7:13, 4 Ezra 13:3, Rev 10:1) were already proleptically present in the passion predictions.

"This is my Son, the Beloved": For *Beloved* (Greek *agapētos)* cf. 1:11. For those who had ears to hear, the passion predictions were a validation of messianic sonship. Mark's readers, desperately seeking reassurance about the continuing lordship of the community in a situation increasingly perilous, were to know that God's favor rested upon Jesus at the most somber moment of his ministry. Hence the community could be assured that God's favor rested upon it, too, and there would be vindication of it as there had been for Jesus.

Mark's account follows that of Matthew in essentials. Matt 17:5 has: "In him I am well pleased," thus linking the account with the beginning of the ministry (3:17) and Matthew's "Listen to him" is reproduced by Mark. The command is linked with the prediction of 8:31 and the promise of Deut 18:15. Luke has the command to listen but replaces *the Beloved* with "the chosen one" (Greek *eklelegomenos).* The relationship between the Servant Songs of Isaiah and the self-understanding of Jesus is still a matter of uncertainty and academic debate, but Luke's choice of Greek reflects Isa 41:8, 44:1, and 48:10, thus serving to emphasize the connection between the transfiguration scene and the Servant Songs. Luke's version is far more literary and far less satisfactory than the versions of Matthew and Mark. In Luke the interjection of Peter is made as Moses and Elijah are leaving, and the fear of the disciples has nothing to do with the substance of the occasion but with their entry into the cloud. Matthew links their fear with the divine voice, and Jesus has to reassure them.

8. The narrative ends abruptly, underlined by *suddenly* (Greek *exapinēs*—cf. *exphainēs* in 13:26). For *as they looked around* (Greek *periblempsamenoi),* cf. 3:5. The remainder of the text in Greek is not straightforward. *With themselves* is read here, along with most mss., although the translation *but* depends on reading *alla* with many mss. as over against *ei mē* (except) of many equally impressive mss. We have chosen *alla* (cf. Lagrange, p. xcix), since often the more difficult reading may indicate a misunderstood Semitism—in this case the Aramaic *îla.* In any event, the occurrence of non-Markan words in vv. 3-8 may well point to an early Palestinian tradition. Matt

17:8 has "when they raised their eyes, they saw . . . ," while Luke 9:36 reads "after the voice had spoken, Jesus was found alone."

It is possible that both Matthew and Mark exhibit signs of the intrusive nature of the Transfiguration narrative. The transition in both gospels from the promise of the Reign of God (Matt 16:28; Mark 9:1) to the question about the coming of Elijah (Matt 17:10; Mark 9:11) is natural. It is hard to resist the suggestion that the speculations of the disciples about Jesus being raised (Matt 17:9; Mk 9:9-10) are commentary on the Transfiguration narrative as a further prophecy *ex eventu*. The tentative suggestion offered here is that originally the tradition passed directly from the prediction of the Passion to the sayings on the cost of discipleship (8:34-9:1 = Matt 16:24-28; Luke 9:23-27) and thence to the question about Elijah. Early in the tradition the narrative of the "missed opportunity" (the Transfiguration) was added. It must be emphasized that this is no more than suggestion, and there is no manuscript evidence for such an arrangement.

45. Passion Prediction (ii)
(9:9-13) = Matt 17:9-13

9   9 As they came down from the mountain, he ordered them not to tell anyone what they had seen until The Man had been raised from the dead. 10 They fastened on this saying, discussing among themselves what this "raised from the dead" was. 11 They put a question to him: "Why do the scribes say that Elijah must come first?" 12 He replied, "Indeed Elijah comes first, to restore everything. Yet how is it that the Scriptures say that The Man is to endure much suffering and be treated with contempt? 13 But I tell you that Elijah has come already, and they have had their way with him, just as the Scriptures say of him."

Comment

This short narrative can hardly be separated from the preceding one, yet it has concerns of its own. At the same time, it defies classification under the familiar form-critical categories. Perhaps its origin lies in the doubts, hesitations, and discussions in the community about *parousia*-expectation. In its formless and abrupt shape, it reads almost like a conversation piece from the early community debating the *parousia*. R. H. Lightfoot (*Gospel Message*, p.

92) goes so far as to suggest that we may be in the presence of a tentative construction of a "kind of philosophy of history."

Notes

9. *As they came down* . . . *:* This narrative is closely linked with the one preceding it, as it is in Matthew (whose version Mark follows closely).

what they had seen: Matthew has "the vision" (17:9), and the difference may well indicate not only the concerns of two audiences but may also give us an indication of the nature of the encounter on the mountain. Mark's audience was under far more pressure than the Matthean community, and he presents the fuller teaching about the Passion given to the three disciples as though it was a physical occurrence. The preeminence of Jesus was to be emphasized in the most direct fashion possible. Matthew's hearers, knowing of the failure of the three to understand, had the incident reported as a vision.

not to tell anyone: There are various possibilities inherent in this injunction. It may be taken as applying to the remainder of the Twelve (Lagrange, p. 234). But it may also represent an admission that the three were made privy to confidences from Jesus when alone with him and failed to appreciate their significance. It is not without interest that the Transfiguration as a historical event finds no mention in the early apostolic preaching, and indeed has no reference in the rest of the NT except at 2 Pet 2:19.

The Man had been raised: The introduction of The Man is abrupt, though it may well have references back to the *Listen to him!* of v. 7. Peter's confession of Jesus in an outburst of enthusiasm is confirmed, but that confirmation awaits the Resurrection.

raised (Greek *anastēnai):* Cf. note on 6:14.

10. *They fastened on:* Commentators and translators differ at this point, but we have punctuated the sentence with a comma after *ton logon* (this saying), leaving *among themselves* to be associated with *discussing*.

"raised from the dead": We have read here *to ek nekrōn anastenai* (and so translated as above, rather than, with some Western mss. and some early versions, *hotan ek nekrōn,* which would produce "when he shall be raised." This verse is not found in Matthew, though Luke is apparently aware of some such tradition in his 9:36. It is possible to read the verse as meaning not surprise about Resurrection, but the association of The Man with such a Resurrection; however, this seems unduly forced.

11. Mark is still following Matthew closely, and the question about Elijah seems to have been attracted to its present context by the preceding narrative (9:1-9). The difference between the two at this point (vv. 11-13) lies in the arrangement of the material. In Matthew's version, the saying about The Man and his suffering comes after the Elijah saying in v. 13 before us, and there is added an identification of Elijah with John the Baptizer.

the scribes say: The scribal opinion would be based on Mal 4:4.

12. *He replied* (Greek *ephē):* Cf. 9:38; 10:20,29; 12:24; 14:29. This is the reading in some important manuscripts, but the majority read *ho de apokritheis eipen,* which is the Matthean reading. Other manuscripts read *apokatistanei* or *apokathistanei.* The

sense is the same. We have preferred *ephē* on the ground that this may well be an
independent Markan touch, in common with his other uses of *ephē*.

Jesus allows the scribal tradition, and then the narrative suddenly changes to a
question about scriptural references to the suffering of The Man. It has been suggested
that the whole verse should be read as a question, casting doubt on the prior coming of
Elijah, and then proceeding, "Yet, how then is it written . . . ?"

13. *Elijah has come already:* The need to establish the superiority of Jesus has
already been noted. But what is somewhat surprising is the omission by Mark of
Matthew's "Then the disciples understood that he was speaking to them about John
the Baptizer" (Matt 17:13), unless it might be that Mark wished to avoid any further
confusion by the introduction of yet another name.

Appended Note: Elijah and John the Baptizer

The very fact that the Matthean text (17:13) has "Then the disciples understood that he was speaking to them about John the Baptist" adds another
dimension to any evaluation of the place of Elijah in our sources. The identification of John with *Elijah redivivus* in the early Christian tradition is enigmatic and by no means as obvious as *our* reading of the texts would have us
believe. In what follows, as in so many other matters, the present writer is
heavily indebted to his friend, the late J. A. T. Robinson, whose prescient
paper, "Elijah, John, and Jesus" (first published in 1958, and now to be found
in *TNTS*, pp. 28-53) marked a turning point in the solution of the Elijah-John
puzzle. What follows is in large part a condensation in note form of the main
contentions of Robinson's essay:

1. For Mark's audience, Jesus is the messiah, and John the forerunner is
the promised Elijah; and the lengthy saying in Matt 11:7-15 would appear to
bear this out.

2. But the only person in the first part of the Markan narrative identified
with Elijah is Jesus, not John. John in fact never mentioned Elijah, although
he did speak of one greater than himself who was "to come" (Luke 1:7 &
par.; Matt 11:3 = Luke 7:15), but we are not told when this was to be.

3. In terms of function there was one "expected one" (Mal 3:8), and he
was clearly identified with Elijah in Mal 4:5. Moreover the messenger and
Elijah are identical in Matt 11:10-14.

4. If John saw anyone as the coming Elijah, it was not himself but the one
coming after him who existed before him—i.e., the Johannine reference (1:15,
1:30) was not originally to the preexisting Word, but to the one who had been
before, Elijah.

5. The Coming One was to baptize with fire and with judgment (Matt
3:11 = Luke 3:16; Matt 3:12 = Luke 3:17; cf. Mal 3:2ff. and Matt 3:10 =
Luke 3:9; cf. Mal 4:1), and John's mission is to baptize with *water*, which all

of our sources emphasize. Above all else, in our OT sources, Elijah is a man of fire: cf. Sir 48:1-3; 1 Kgs 18:30-39; and see the textual addition to Luke 9:54.

6. But there is further evidence that the identification John = Elijah was not made by people who were witnesses to his activity, and certainly was not made by John himself. Certainly John had spoken of one coming after him, but the questions he poses from prison suggest that John had seen Jesus as the coming Elijah, and the questions were asked precisely because Jesus was apparently no longer acting in the manner which John had anticipated. So far as the witness of John's gospel is concerned, John was exactly what the Baptizer said he was not—the prophet coming into the world (John 6:14, 7:40). Interestingly, when the suggestion is made that Jesus was Elijah, it is always an alternative to the belief that he was *John redivivus.* In other words, this is evidence that folk did not identify *John* with Elijah.

7. *Our* identification of John with Elijah, both being cast in the role of forerunner, is made because we know the end of the story. But the judgment of those who were with Jesus was that *he* was the prophet and *he* was Elijah. (On this, especially the role of the prophet, see Albright-Mann, AB *Matthew,* pp. 133-34, the note on 10:40,41—admittedly based upon a new direction in translation.) The response of faith was to identify Jesus with the "Coming One" of the Baptizer.

8. Hence the question of John from prison is treated by Jesus as improperly addressed: Jesus simply turns the question back to its originator. But, knowing the end of the story, knowing the gospel narratives as a whole, we take wholly for granted the explicit statements of Matt 11:10 (= Luke 7:27) and the far more emphatic Matt 11:14. To those who heard it, the statement must have been little short of astounding: John himself was the coming one! To attempt to recapture that astonishment is for us well nigh impossible, for the *ground* of astonishment has been removed from under our feet by the very odd quotation which stands at the very beginning of this gospel: "I send my messenger" is certainly not from Isaiah (cf. 1:2); it is from Malachi 3:1, and the phrase *prepare your way* grammatically cannot agree with *his paths.* The very crude change from "his" to "your" was certainly done deliberately to inform the reader ostentatiously that all will emerge more clearly later in the book—i.e., the messenger of Malachi (Elijah) is John the Baptizer. (Parenthetically we note that the Malachi citation is neither from *LXX* nor the Hebrew but is identical with the quotation in Matt 11:10 [Luke 7:27], which strongly suggests to this writer that Mark put the quotation at the very forefront of his gospel to make his position clear about John.)

9. Our own scheme, thanks to the clue at the beginning of Mark, is clear and simple: John was the "messenger" (i.e., Elijah) who was to prepare the way of the Lord, and "the Lord" was Jesus-Messiah; hence when John asks, "Are you the Coming One?" the question means, "Are you the messiah?"

and Jesus replies, "Yes." Jesus then identifies John with Elijah, since Elijah is the forerunner of the messiah. But if all this is so, then why does Jesus then say, "If you wish to accept it, he is the expected Elijah" (Matt 11:14).

10. We appear to be at a point where we must say that the idea of Elijah being the forerunner of the messiah is one which we derive from the tradition in our sources and ultimately from Jesus himself. The process is simple when we set it in order. Jesus identified John (who was his forerunner) with the messenger of Malachi (Elijah), who was to "go before the Lord." With the use of the title "Lord" as applying to Jesus (in whatever sense), the cycle of ideas was complete.

11. What this scheme fails to acknowledge is the fact that there is no pre-Christian tradition for regarding Elijah as the forerunner of the messiah, and not even Mark 9:11 can be held to support the idea. All that we know from Malachi and Ben Sira is that Elijah would be the precursor of a day of the Lord. The present—and increasing—state of our knowledge is that "messianic expectation" was widely different and often wildly divergent—from the prophet and the Elect One to the *two* messiahs of Qumran. John's question from prison was prompted by his doubts that Jesus was fulfilling the role of the "Coming One" as John saw it, not from John's hesitations about Jesus' messiahship. Jesus was no longer acting as "Elijah"; and Jesus' own reply to John makes it clear that he had broken with the "Malachi-type" expectation, which John had provided for him (Matt 11:6 = Luke 7:23), and this had caused offense to John.

There are indications enough in our sources that Jesus was closely identified with John at the beginning of his ministry, inherited his proclamation of repentance (and the practice of baptism), and until the arrest of John largely confined his ministry to Judea. Though always eager to defend John and his work (Mark 11:29-33 & par.: Matt 11:7-11 = Luke 7:24-28, Matt 21:32) Jesus set his way of ministry in sharp contrast (Matt 11:16-19 = Luke 7:31-35). But there is more than that. We briefly alluded in the introduction (6. "Jesus in Mark's Gospel: A. Chronology," pp. 100-4) to the first stage in Jesus' ministry as an identification with John. Jesus and John were working in the same area, and Jesus preached and ministered as a disciple of John. Even the cleansing of the temple, situated where it is in the fourth gospel was—according to J. Armitage Robinson in *The Historical Character of St. John's Gospel*, London: Longman, Green, 2nd ed., 1929—placed there to demonstrate that Jesus began by implementing Malachi's scheme of things (Mal 3:1-3,8ff.). The synoptic accounts underline this connection between the teaching of John and the actions of Jesus with reference to the baptism of John and the authority which undergirded it (Mark 11:27-33 & par.). Similarly, with reference to the conversation with Nicodemus, we tend to read being born from above and with water and the Spirit (John 3:5) as meaning Christian baptism.

Perhaps this was the meaning of the evangelist; but *in context* the allusion (especially with the reference to the Kingdom of God) must be to the teaching of John.

The separation of John and Jesus upon John's arrest by no means brings to an end the Elijah theme, and John is never too far removed from the scene in thought or reminiscence. The identification of Jesus with Elijah is preserved by two disciples in Luke (9:52-56). Interestingly, the incident is located in Samaria, on the only visit to that territory of which Luke is aware. (We need the testimony of the fourth gospel here to remind us of Jesus' mission there and also that in all probability John baptized there.) The reply of Jesus to his two disciples is testimony that the pattern of ministry had changed—from a proclamation of judgment to promise of deliverance, and the Galilean ministry is adequate testimony to the change. Luke *again* provides a hint of this change: "I came to bring fire on the earth." The reflection which follows should perhaps (cf. Robinson, *The Historical Character of St. John's Gospel,* p. 44) more properly be translated as "But what do I care if it is already kindled?" The days of *that* understanding of his ministry are over, and now Jesus has a baptism to undergo, and to which his disciples are called (Luke 12:35-40). Moreover the work of the messenger of Malachi (4:6) to restore unity (i.e., the function of Elijah) is not that of Jesus—on the contrary, his ministry will provoke division (Matt 10:34-39), for the times of the end are upon them. The saying in Matt 11:11-12, "From the time of John the Baptist to this moment, the Kingdom of heaven has been under violent attack and violent men despoil it," bears witness to the violence which has already overwhelmed John, and which for the time being will assail Jesus and the disciples. All of it is recognition that The Man can only fulfill the will and demand of God through suffering and death (Mark 10:41-45)—a radical change from John's expectation of Jesus in the Judean ministry.

The role of Elijah expectation in the Transfiguration account has already been discussed in the commentary. This, however, seems an appropriate point at which to remark that the suffering of The Man is set alongside the sufferings of Elijah, and in both cases scripture is made the basis of the saying. What the scriptural basis might be for a "suffering Elijah," we have no means of determining.

The reader is commended to pursue this study further by reading the work of J. A. T. Robinson referred to above, and to which this appended note is so heavily—and gratefully—indebted. It may usefully be remarked at this point that when the late W. F. Albright and the present writer collaborated in the writing of the AB *Matthew,* the thesis propounded by Robinson was regarded with considerable hesitation by both of us. The present writer freely admits to a complete change of mind in the interval, mainly arising from a conviction that however much in our sources has been edited in the interest of "John = Elijah," there is no convincing evidence for the existence *alongside the primi-*

tive Church of anything which could recognizably be described as a "community of the Baptizer." But with all this in mind, it is instructive to go back to the appended note on Chapter 8, vv. 1-10.

46. Miracles (vi) Healing of a Boy
(9:14-29) = Matt 17:14-20; Luke 9:37-43a

9   14 When they came back to the disciples, they saw a large crowd with them, and scribes arguing with them. 15 As soon as they saw Jesus, the whole crowd, overcome with surprise, ran forward to greet him. 16 He asked them, "What were you arguing about with them?" 17 Someone in the crowd answered, "Rabbi, I brought my son to you, because he is possessed by a spirit, which makes him speechless. 18 Whenever it attacks him, it hurls him to the ground; he foams at the mouth, grits his teeth, and becomes rigid. I asked your disciples to drive it out, but they could not." 19 Jesus answered, "Unbelieving generation! How long am I to be with you? How long must I endure you? Bring him to me." 20 They brought the boy to him, and as soon as the spirit saw him, it threw him into convulsions, and he fell on the ground and rolled about, foaming at the mouth. 21 "How long has he been like this?" he asked the father. "From childhood," he replied. 22 "Often it has tried to kill him by throwing him into the fire or the water. But if you can, have pity on us and help us." 23 " 'If you can'!" said Jesus. "Everything is possible to one who has faith." 24 "I have faith!" the boy's father cried out. "Help me where faith is lacking!" 25 Jesus, seeing that the crowd was closing in on them, rebuked the unclean spirit. "Deaf and dumb spirit!" he said, "I command you to come out of him and never enter him again." 26 After shrieking out, and sending him into severe convulsions, it came out. The boy was like a corpse; in fact, many said, "He is dead." 27 But Jesus took him by the hand, helped him to his feet, and he stood up. 28 When Jesus went indoors, his disciples asked him privately, "Why could not we cast it out?" 29 "There is no way," he said, "of casting out this kind but prayer."

Comment

Though closely following Matthew's order and aware of Luke's text, Mark's account is far more detailed and even manifestly indebted to an early tradition—even an eyewitness account. However there are features in the narrative, which frankly suggest an attempt by Mark to make the whole account more vivid than the very terse accounts he found before him. The odd distinction between the disciples, the crowds, and the introduction of arguing scribes reads for all the world like an embellishment. The conversation in vv. 21-24 is far less artificial, and may argue access to a firsthand account. What is far less clear is the connection of this story with the preceding Transfiguration narrative, though the amazement of the crowd in v. 15 is typically Markan. The textual problem will be addressed in the notes. It should be noticed that the disciples appear only in vv. 14-19, and thereafter all attention is focused on the father (vv. 21-27). Yet the father has a purely subordinate role in vv. 17-19. In addition, *the spirit which makes him speechless* in v. 17 becomes *the unclean spirit* who is deaf and dumb. There are also two references to *foaming at the mouth* in vv. 18 and 20. With this kind of prolixity before us, it is possible that Mark found the account of the epileptic in Matthew and Luke, had other traditions from other sources, and combined all. What we would then have would be vv. 14-19 and 28-29 (the inability of the disciples to cure the sufferer by reason of lack of prayerfulness), the miracle story itself in vv. 20-27, which has apparently lost its conclusion, but which is found in Luke 7:43.

Notes

14. *they came:* The plural is found in many important texts, but the singular is also impressively represented. We have chosen the plural, since Mark appears to link the story with the Transfiguration.

the disciples: The bald expression without the possessive "his" is unusual in Mark, though this introductory material is characteristically Markan. It is nowhere said that these disciples are the nine, though the link with the Transfiguration already noted may imply this.

scribes: There is no definite article, the matter of the argument is unidentified, and they appear nowhere else in the narrative. The presence of official teachers of the Law in this territory seems distinctly odd. The vivid style is noteworthy. Matthew simply has "when they were approaching the crowd" (17:14), though Luke says that the incident took place "on the next day" (9:37).

15. *overcome* (Greek *exethambēthēsan*): The word has the sense almost of shock—they were not expecting Jesus to return so soon.

16. *asked them:* There are textual variants here, for some manuscripts read "the scribes," while other variants occur with the second *them,* some reading "among yourselves." Probably the question was addressed to the crowd. *Someone* (the sufferer's father) answers from among them.

17. *Rabbi:* Cf. 4:38.

son: Luke asserts that he was an "only" son. Matthew says that the father knelt before Jesus, and both Matthew and Luke have a direct request. ("Have pity on my son," Matt 17:15; "I implore you to look at my son," Luke 9:38.) Mark describes the symptoms—epilepsy (certainly Matthew's understanding) or hysteria.

18. *hurls him* (Greek *rēssei*): The Greek is somewhat uncertain. The verb is either *rassō,* to strike or throw down, or an old mistake for *rassei,* which in the sense of throwing violently suits the Markan narrative. Luke's *sparassei* is probably derived from *ressō,* with the meaning of "rend, tear."

foams (Greek *aphrizei*): The verb is not found in *LXX,* although *aphros* ("foam") from which it is derived is found frequently in medical writers of the time.

becomes rigid (Greek *xerainetai*): The word indicates total exhaustion. Luke, often credited with some knowledge of medical terminology, concentrates instead on the evil behavior of the demon.

I asked . . . : Lohmeyer (p. 186) makes the suggestion that the failure of the disciples may be (in the father's eyes) a reflection on their leader. The appeal of the father later, after another paroxysm, is made with hesitation.

19. *Unbelieving generation:* Cf. Deut 32:5. The description "perverse" (Greek *diestrammenē*) found in Matt 17:17 and Luke 9:41 is found also in a few manuscripts of Mark. The description is not meant by Jesus as applying to the crowds, the disciples, or the boy's father. Rather it emphasizes the distress of Jesus at the folk among whom his ministry was exercised (cf. 8:31 and see also Lagrange, p. 239).

20. It is characteristic of exorcism narratives that first the sufferer and then the spirit is treated as initiating some action.

threw him into convulsions (Greek *sunesparaxen*): A strong form of *sparassō,* the word is not found in classical Greek or *LXX.* Luke records that the spirit "tore" the boy (9:42). The conversation between the father and Jesus shows the father full of hesitation.

22. *But if you can* (Greek *dunē,* a late form of *dunomai)* is found often in the papyri.

help (Greek *boētheō):* Cf. 9:24; Matt 15:25; Acts 16:9, 21:28; 2 Cor 6:2; Heb 2:18; Rev 12:16. The word was frequently used in the papyri in petitions and as referring to divine assistance.

23. " *'If you can!' '':* The definite article in *to ei dunē* is a combination of quotation marks and an exclamation, in effect producing, "That expression of yours: 'If you can!' " The emphasis on faith is present here; cf. 1:15, 5:36, 11:23-24.

24. The response of the father is immediate. The Greek has *euthus,* which we have not translated.

"Help me . . .": This is not the lack of faith expressed in 6:6 but a nascent faith

plagued by doubts and hesitations. Some manuscripts add *meta dakmōn* (with tears), but this must be regarded as a scribal embellishment.

25. The reference to *the crowd* is odd. The throng is represented as being at a distance, where the first reference to the crowd in vv. 14-15 apparently puts Jesus in the middle of the people. Either then Jesus and the father had withdrawn from the crowd which ran to meet him (v. 15, Greek *prostrechontes),* or this present verse describes another crowd about to press in (Greek *episuntrecheis)* upon Jesus—in which case we may have to conclude that there were two narratives originally. There is the possibility that the original crowd was pressing in upon the epileptic boy.

The vocabulary of this verse is certainly Markan: *epetimēsen* ("rebuked," cf. v. 25), *akathartō* ("unclean," cf. 1:23), *kōphos* ("deaf," cf. 7:32), *alalos* ("dumb," cf. 7:37), *epitassō* ("command," cf. 1:27). Matthew and Luke do not reproduce the exorcism but merely mention it.

26. *like a corpse:* Cf. Acts 20:10 and perhaps 5:39-42. Just as in the case of Jairus' daughter, Jesus takes the boy by the hand and raises him. The omission by Luke of any reaction on the part of the eyewitnesses is remarkable, since such reactions are recorded by Luke in 9:43.

28-29. It is difficult to say precisely where this appendix originally belonged. It is found in Matthew, whence Luke derived it, but it is possible (cf. Taylor, p. 401) that it was misplaced from after v. 19 (Matt 17:17). It may incidentally be remarked that on the two-document hypothesis it is strange that Luke did not reproduce it, given Luke's interest in prayer. But in both Matthew and Mark this little appendix appears to be integrally part of the narrative—*when Jesus went indoors,* "thereupon the disciples came to him privately" (Matt 17:18).

The reply of Jesus in v. 29 emphasizes that the exorcist is not making use of his own power but is dependent on the power of God. Some manuscripts of Mark add, "and fasting," a reading also found in later manuscripts of Matthew, while some manuscripts of Matthew have the saying about the mustard seed (Matt 17:20 = Luke 17:6, cf. Luke 11:23). The confused state of manuscript readings at this point is evidence of the somewhat patchwork character of this pericope. So uncertain is the state of manuscript readings that "and fasting" (Greek *kai nēsteia)* is found also in Matt 17:21.

See further on this pericope Paul J. Achtemeier, "Miracles and the Historical Jesus: Mark 9:14-29," *CBQ* 37.1975, pp. 471-91: ". . . any historical picture of Jesus that does not include his activity as exorcist will be a distortion" (p. 491).

47. Passion Prediction (iii)
(9:30-32) = Matt 17:22-23; Luke 9:43b-45

9 ³⁰ They left that place and went on through Galilee. He did not
wish anyone to know, ³¹ because he was teaching his disciples and
telling them, "The Man will be handed over to men, and they will kill
him. Three days after being killed he will be raised up." ³² But they did
not understand what was being said, and were afraid to ask him.

Comment

There appears to be unanimity on the part of the synoptists that there was
another Passion prediction, associated vaguely by Matthew and Luke with
Galilee, and ascribed by Luke to a time when Jesus was at the height of his
fame. Mark presents this episode, linking it with the previous narrative *(They
left that place . . .)* as though Jesus was traveling through Galilee incognito.
There is an air of finality about the narrative. Matthew has "While they were
gathering in Galilee" (17:22); and this, coupled with the Markan note on
secrecy, indicates that to all intents and purposes the ministry in Galilee had
ended. The section on chronology in the Introduction called attention to a
threefold pattern in the mission, with the Galilean (second) part terminating
when Jesus began to reinterpret his mission in terms of suffering and death. It
is possible, for some commentators, to see in this present pericope the first
genuine Passion prediction, following on the private retreat of the three with
Jesus. But there is an entirely new note in all three evangelists in this prediction—that of being "handed over," which will be dealt with in the notes
following. That Jesus fully contemplated a violent end to his ministry, perhaps at the hands of a mob, seems clearly discernible in the first prediction.
This prediction before us seems therefore to represent a refinement, though
not as yet any statement of purpose in the suffering and death.

Notes

31. *he was teaching:* There is no difference of sense in the Greek here *(edidasken)* from that of 8:31 *(ērxato didaskein).* In both cases the implication is that repeated warnings were given. But the use of "teach" may indicate something more reflective than a simple warning. But as was pointed out above, a new element has been introduced. We may admit a stylized, formal development in the community from the oral tradition, but the community formula has been careful to preserve the new element. This preservation should warn us against attributing too much to the creative genius of the early Church: time for reflection in the mind of Jesus has permitted him to see more deeply than the mere inevitability of suffering and death.

handed over (Greek *paradidotai):* The Greek is a future present and has about it something of an air of confidence. Matthew and Luke both have *mellei paradidosthai* (about to be handed over) with a more immediate meaning. Any sense of reference to the betrayal by Judas seems weak, and Lohmeyer (p. 192) is far more convincing in his interpretation of it as a reference to all that happens in the passion, viewed eschatologically—almost as though the translation ought rightly to be "committed to all that is to happen." In this sense what is being underlined is the confrontation between Jesus and the world by the will of the Father. Cf. further A. Trecker, "Die Leidens und Auferstehungsvoraussagen im Markusevangelium (8:31; 9:31; 10:32-34)," *ZTK* 64.1967, pp. 16-39; M. Bastin, "L'annonce de la passion et des critères de l'historicité," *RSR* 50.1976, pp. 280-329.

Appended Note: "Son of Man" in 9:31

The same motif is found here as in 8:31, and is found again in 12:1-9. The dignity and the authority of The Man are alike wholly absent, and our concentration on the majesty of the figure in Dan 7:9-14 often effectively prevents our seeing that the whole context in which The Man is found in Daniel 7 is one of suffering. The representative of the holy people in Daniel 7 suffers precisely because his people suffer—they suffer on account of their obedience to God, and so therefore will The Man. The oft-made comment that the presence of "Son of Man" sayings in a context of suffering must be treated with reserve is far too cautious. If we rule out entirely the possibility of the term by Jesus as applied to himself in the time of his ministry, and allow his use of the term as designating a future figure of glory (with its application to himself a matter of doubt), we are by no means out of the dilemma. We are left with an interesting alternative: the early writers, and behind them the early community, put together traditions about the ministry around a whole complex of ideas of The Man-as-sufferer, and attributed it all to Jesus.

Few, if any, responsible scholars would defend the thesis that the evangelists were writing biography or were attempting a history of the ministry. Each evangelist was interpreting the ministry and person of Jesus in the light of his own purposes and theological concerns. Nevertheless it is pertinent to ask whence was derived the dramatic insight into the essential meaning of the ministry implied in the concept of The Man as sufferer and victim, while at the same time retaining the more usual interpretation of The Man-in-glory. In the majority two-document view, Mark is credited with the figure of suffering as one of the insights of his theological genius, leaving any description of The Man as an eschatological figure to the scene before the high priest. If we assume this common view, then the stronger emphasis on The Man-in-glory can be regarded as a restoration of a more traditional eschatological interpretation. But this is to leave unanswered questions about possible sources from which Mark might have derived the "suffering" tradition. We grant at once that his work, as a digest and conflation, has all the marks of genius. But given the circumstances of his composition as we believe those circumstances to have been, we entertain profound doubts as to his ability to see the Danielic context *solely* as one of suffering, when the exaltation of The Man appears to be so central to Daniel 7.

When it is recalled that the term "Son of Man" is found only three times outside the gospels, it becomes important to ask whence Mark derived his particular insight—those three extra-gospel references are all in terms of exaltation. If then there is here an insight from some religious genius, then there are those who will find that special genius in the creative mind of the early community. Yet Paul is aware apparently of the term "Son of Man" in a context of the ministry of Jesus (cf. his use of First Adam/Second Adam and First Man/Second Man), but it is significant that nowhere in his many references to the sufferings of Jesus does he make use of the term. If we hazard the guess that The Man-as-suffering is to be attributed to Luke (cf. Acts 8:32), we are still far from an answer to the question as to whether or not the insight belonged in the first instance to Jesus himself. The present writer holds that the insight does ultimately go back to Jesus. It was precisely the insight of Jesus to restore again to the understanding of Daniel 7 the identification of The Man with a suffering people, and an identification which bound him to the sufferings of the "holy ones of the most High."

48. Precedence (i)
(9:33-37) = Matt 18:1-5; Luke 9:46-48

9 [33] So they arrived at Capernaum, and when they were indoors he asked them, "What were you arguing about on the way?" [34] But they were silent, because they had been arguing among themselves who was the greatest. [35] He sat down, called the Twelve, and said to them, "If anyone wants to be first, he must himself be last of all and servant of all." [36] Taking a child, he placed him in front of them and put his arms around him. [37] He said to them, "Anyone who receives one such child in my name receives me; and anyone who receives me, receives not only me but the one who sent me."

Comment

This section appears to be a free composition by Mark from fragments he wished to put together in this context; the relationship between the fragments and Matthew and Luke is complicated. (The succeeding section is also complicated, suggesting that Mark, following the Matthean order, severely condensed material he gathered from Matthew and Luke and made of that condensation the results before us.)

Mark apparently wishes to tie this material to the journey through Galilee, and prescinding from the departure from the scene of the Transfiguration. But the whole complex of 9:33-50 is strung together very loosely by a series of catchwords—e.g., the expression *in my name* in v. 37.

The material can be divided as follows:

Mk 9:33			
9:34		Lk 22:24	
9:35	(cf. 10:43-44)	22:26	Matt 20:26-27; 23:11
9:36	(cf. 10:16)		18:3
9:37			10:42

The conclusion must be that in spite of what might appear to be a Petrine reminiscence in v. 33, with its mention of Capernaum, Mark's collection is a pastiche and a conflation.

Notes

33. *Capernaum:* Cf. 1:29. If there is any historical basis for this introductory re-mark by the evangelist, presumably Peter's house is meant (cf. 1:29).

The ignorance of Jesus about what was being discussed—since presumably he was walking with them—is nowhere better explained than in the contribution of Moses Aberbach ("The Relations Between Master and Disciple in the Talmudic Age") to *Essays Presented to Chief Rabbi Israel Brodie on the Occasion of His Seventieth Birthday* (London: Soncino Press, 1965). Aberbach points out that there were in the time of Jesus specific rules governing the conduct of pupil and teacher, and one rule expressly forbade a pupil walking alongside his teacher. Jesus, as Mark presents it, would have been walking in front, aware that there was heated discussion behind him, but un-aware of its subject.

34. Matthew asserts that the disciples came to Jesus with the direct question as to who was greatest (18:1), while Luke simply says a discussion arose among them on the subject (9:46) and infers that Jesus had an intuitive knowledge of their inmost thoughts. In Mark they are too ashamed to reply to Jesus' question.

35. *He sat down:* All through Mark this is the characteristic of a teacher (cf. Matt 5:1; 13:1; Luke 5:3; John 8:2). As a further example of the confused state of the Markan narrative, it is to be noticed that although Jesus had already addressed the disciples, he now proceeds to call the Twelve. The saying that follows seems to be a shortened version of 10:43, in which there is a contrast between *great . . . servant* and *first . . . slave.* The early community appears to have preserved carefully the strictures of Jesus on ambition. There is another variant of this saying in Matt 23:11 and probably another in Luke 9:48.

36. Further to complicate the pericope, Mark introduces the figure of a child being taken into Jesus' arms. The verb *enakalizomai,* rare as it is, suggests a link with the blessing of the children in 10:13-16.

37. The patchwork character is underscored more heavily by this verse. The evan-gelist takes *one such child* (Greek *paidion)* to refer to children, but in view of v. 42 *(one of these insignificant believers)* it is highly unlikely that this was the point of the original saying. It is inherently more likely that the original meaning had to do with neophytes, the more inexperienced members of the community who most stood in need of welcome and assurance. As a distillation of Mark's own v. 42 (Matt 10:40, Luke 10:16; cf. John 13:20) this can hardly be described as one of Mark's more inspired moments. The confusion is confounded by the total change of subject: in this verse it is no longer a matter of the attitude of the disciples toward others, but of their reception by others. The principle that a person's representative is also the plenipoten-tiary is a fundamental of Jewish law. The principle that to welcome *(receive,* Greek *dekomai)* the least-esteemed is to welcome Jesus is also affirmed in Matt 25:40.

Mark may have had some separate traditions at this point, but it is simpler to suppose that in the interests of conflation and compression Mark should have con-fused some disparate traditions. If it is pleaded that sayings concerning children and sayings concerning neophytes in the community could easily be confused, then it must be said that this hardly fits in this context. It would be far more suitable to find the blessing of the children (10:15) in this context than the present arrangement. In addition, Matt 18:3 must be regarded as the authentic tradition, which Mark has obfuscated in the interests of conflation. In the original Matthean version, Jesus rebuked the ambitions of the disciples by pointing to children as examples of trust. Children know that they can never have earned the gifts they are given; no more can the disciples earn entrance into the dawning Reign of God.

49. Opposition or Acceptance?
(9:38-41) = Luke 9:49-50

9 ³⁸ John said to him, "Rabbi, we saw a man who does not follow us casting out demons in your name, and we tried to stop him because he does not follow us." ³⁹ But Jesus said, "Do not stop him. No one who does a work of power in my name will be able quickly to speak evil of me. ⁴⁰ He who is not against us is on our side. ⁴¹ I tell you this: any man who gives you a cup of water to drink because you belong to the messiah will not lose his reward."

Comment

Precisely how to situate this pericope is hard to determine. On the surface it is a "pronouncement" outlining the attitude of Jesus to assistance, which came from outside the circle of the disciples. The reference to nonfollowers suggests the change of attitude exhibited as between Luke 9:50 and 11:23. The composition of this narrative is additionally complicated by v. 41 (= Matt 10:42), for which the reader is commended to Albright-Mann, AB *Matthew,* pp. 133-34. The translation of the Matthean saying is important. The immediate question is *why* this collection of material has been placed here. If v. 41 is the climax to which the previous verses point, then we are concerned with attitudes toward Jesus' ministry by outsiders and by believers, placed here at a junction where everything now moves toward Jerusalem and the Passion. But how to classify the material before us is another matter. There is no introductory *Sitz im Leben,* no question addressed to Jesus which demands an answer; and when the statement ends, the narrative is over. Was the original tradition simply vv. 38-40, at the end of which Mark found it convenient to add the Matthean saying in v. 41? Or was that verse all that Mark intended to use

from the Matthean context? The present writer, considering the introduction
of John's name in v. 38, inclines to the belief that Mark had elements of a
primitive tradition in vv. 37-50, and then inserted the material here as belonging to the end of the Galilean ministry.

Notes

38. *John:* This is the only occasion in the Markan tradition where John plays a
leading role. For *follow,* cf. 1:18; for demons, cf. 1:34. There is a textual difference in
this verse. Some manuscripts read: . . . *we saw a man casting out demons in your
name who does not follow us.* We have preferred the reading given in the translation
above. Matthew Black, in a learned discussion of the textual differences, thinks that
the variants derive from the Aramaic *de,* which can either serve as a relative pronoun
or a conjunction, and from the verb, which can either be a present or an imperfect. He
therefore supposes that Mark found two renderings of the Aramaic before him and
produced a conflated text (cf. 5:23, *That she may be cured and live*—a combination
impossible in Aramaic). He goes on to say that both 4:41 and 9:38 point to an Aramaic sayings source, though both are in reported speech. Further, vv. 38-45 are in
poetic form when translated back into Aramaic (M. Black, ad loc.).

39. For connections with Chapter 5, cf. the following: *mē* with the imperative *(Do
not stop him),* 5:36; *power,* cf. 5:30. For *speak evil* (Greek *kakalogeō)* cf. 7:10. The later
record of pagan exorcists using the name of Jesus (cf. Acts 19:13) certainly does not
eliminate the possibility that there were similar instances during the ministry of Jesus.
Luke does not have the explanatory saying in v. 39b. The tolerant attitude of Jesus
exemplified in v. 40 is not reversed later in this gospel as it is in Luke 11:23.

40. *us:* Some manuscripts have "you," but the numerical weight of the evidence is
in favor of the reading adopted here.

41. Mark's penchant for appending sayings to his material is notable: cf. 2:21-
22,27-28; 3:27-29; 4:21-25; 7:14-23; 10:10-12.

This saying is important for several reasons. First of all the Greek (which we have
translated as *because you belong to the messiah)* is *en onomati Christou este* (literally,
"because you are in the name of the messiah"). Some manuscripts have *to onomati
mou* (in my name). Matthew has *eis onoma mathētou* (because he is a disciple) at
10:42. Second the Markan text is from the fuller Matthean context. The confused
Markan Greek text, in any version, suggests an unsuccessful attempt to assimilate two
separate but related ideas in Matt 10:40-42—allegiance to the messiah, and conduct
characteristic of a disciple.

The whole matter of synoptic relationships arises again. In the whole section 9:33-
40 Mark has followed Luke in omitting the temple tax account (Matt 17:24-27).
Again, in the question about greatness Luke was Mark's mentor, for along with Luke
he omitted Matthew's saying about little children (Matt 18:1-9) and immediately—
with Luke—gives an account of the exorcist, concluding with a note which is paralleled closely with Matt 10:42. What must be recognized is that from 8:27 onward
Mark has been following both Matthew and Luke in a block of material in which both

evangelists follow the same order. At first Mark kept closely to Matthew. This was natural enough, since in the whole section 6:17-9:32 there are few Lucan parallels, and those not in the same order as Matthew. Therefore, where there is agreement in *order* among all three synoptists, there is little agreement as between order and wording. A similarity of order, when exhibited by both Matthew and Luke, made Mark's work considerably easier, and any need to agree closely with what might best be called the "text of the moment" would be minimal. We submit that if the Griesbach hypothesis is rejected, then the impartial character of the section 8:27-9:41 must be set against the alternating nature of the material preceding 8:27.

50. Occasions of Sin
(9:42-50) = Matt 18:6-9; Luke 17:1-2 (cf. 14:34ff.)

9   42 "As for the man who causes offense to one of these insignificant believers, it would be better for him to be thrown into the sea with a large millstone tied to his neck. 43 So if your hand causes you to sin, cut it off; it is better for you to enter life without a hand than to keep both hands and go to hell and the unquenchable fire (44 where the devouring worm never dies and the fire is not put out). 45 And if your foot causes you to sin, cut it off; it is better for you to enter life without a foot than to keep both feet and be thrown into hell (46 where the devouring worm never dies and the fire is not put out). 47 If it is your eye that causes you to sin, tear it out; it is better to enter the kingdom of God with one eye than to keep both eyes and be thrown into hell, 48 where the devouring worm never dies and the fire is not put out. 49 Everyone will be salted with fire. 50 Salt is good, but if it loses its saltness, with what will you season it? Have salt in yourselves, and be at peace with one another."

Comment

This is an interesting point at which to take note of Markan redactional method. Up to this point, the evangelist has been fairly even-handed as between his sources in Matthew and Luke. But from 9:51 onward Luke has a lengthy section in which Jesus and his disciples are seen going through Samaria on the way to Jerusalem. Not only does this section of Luke have its own particular geographical problems, but there are parables in the section which are peculiar to Luke, some of which are paralleled in Matthew, together with many aphorisms and sayings (much of which is also to be found in Matthew). Mark's twin concerns—to conflate his sources and in the process to produce a gospel which concentrated on the works of Jesus' ministry —were faced with a special problem by this Lucan section, 9:51-19:27. It will suffice to make three points: (1) Mark took nothing from the great central section in Luke for which there was no parallel in Matthew, and (2) where such Lucan material was used, it was conflated with Matthean material. Finally, (3) Mark on the whole accords any saying derived from the Lucan central section the place which it occupied in the Matthean order.

The section before us demonstrates the manner in which teaching material was handled to make it more easily committed to memory. Matthew habitually collected materials in groups of three, five, and seven, and employed the methods of *inclusio* and *chiasmus* to very good purpose. This section is interesting as an example of Mark's use of Matthean and Lucan material. Not the least interesting feature of the section is the way in which the repetition of key words is used as an aid to memory in the evangelist's use of the material before him, going back for this purpose to v. 37.

	Mark	Matthew	Luke
v. 37	little child	18:5, 10:40	9:48
v. 38	in my name	—	9:49
v. 39	in my name	—	9:50
v. 40	in my name	12:30	9:50
v. 41	in my name	10:42, 12:30	9:50, 11:23
v. 42	insignificant believer (or little child)	18:6	17:2,b,a
v. 43	causes you to sin, better, enter into life, fire	18:8 (5:30)	(cf. 17:3)
v. 45	causes you to sin, better, enter into life	18:8	
v. 47	causes you to sin, better, enter into life	18:9 (5:29)	

| v. 48 | salted with fire | 18:9 | |
| vv. 49,50 | salt | 5:13 | 14:34,35 |

A comparison between the key words and phrases in Mark, and the same words and phrases in Matthew and Luke demonstrates not only the skill of the Markan conflation, but also in methods not too characteristic of Mark (blocks of teaching), the studied use of repetition as an aid to memory. For example, the saying in v. 42 finds its place here because of *causes offense, better,* and *thrown,* while *in my name* connects vv. 37 and 38-40. Similarly *fire* in vv. 43 and 48 probably gave us *salted with fire* in v. 49. The order of the sayings does not give us any hint of explanation other than the catch words; there is no obvious connection, but as a method of memory retention, these connections are almost self-explanatory.

Apart altogether from the parallelism in structure so characteristic of Hebrew poetry, and characteristic in our sources of Jesus himself, we are here in the presence of the teaching methods and memory aids of the primitive Church.

Notes

42. The little narrative in vv. 38-40 is not found in Matthew, though part of a tradition known to Mark (cf. Luke 9:49-50 and 11:23) from elsewhere. If this verse was paired with v. 37 in the original tradition, then Mark inserted vv. 38-40 into his collection at this point. Both verses begin with *hos an (as for the man,* or *anyone),* and *one of these insignificant believers* is virtually but not quite the same in sense as *one such child,* and both sets of people are believers.

it would be better: Cf. 7:27. Matthew has "it would be profitable" (Greek *sumpherei),* while Luke has "it would be preferable" (Greek *lusitelei).*

into the sea (Greek *thalassan):* Mark prefers Luke's use here, in contrast with Matthew's thought of the open sea rather than a lake.

millstone (Greek *mulos, onikos;* cf. Matthew 18:6): This is the heavy millstone turned by an ass, in contrast with the small hand mill used by women (cf. Matthew 24:1 = Luke 17:35). The word *mulos* found its way into Latin as *mola.* Drowning was a Roman punishment, though there is a reference in Josephus *(Ant* 14.15.10) to Galileans who drowned some of Herod's sympathizers.

There are some interesting features about the tradition here. In the Markan saying here it is certain that the reference truly is to *insignificant believers* in v. 42, while in v. 37 the same Greek word certainly means "children." The structure of vv. 38-40 and 42-48 is easily discernible. Verses 37 and 42 are closely related, while v. 50 (in the next section) looks back to the questions in v. 49. The whole complex appears to have been based upon vv. 43-48. The saying in v. 42 (cf. v. 37) is here because of key words such as *causes offense, better, thrown,* and the phrase *in my name* in v. 37 is foundation for the narrative about the exorcist in vv. 38ff. and the saying about the cup of water in v. 41. In addition the word *fire* in vv. 43 and 48 produces the saying in v. 49, which in turn leads into the three aphorisms of v. 50. As a pedagogical device, the whole scheme is expressly designed for memorization. But of equal interest is the evangelist's faithfulness to the Matthean source. Mark (9:46-48) had already used the Lucan form of Matthew 18:1-5. Now he turns to Matthew 18:6-9, which has a parallel in Luke 17:1-2, and this he conflates with the Matthean text. It is clear that the evangelist follows Matthew, for he follows the Matthean pericope to the end and by so doing in vv. 43-47 includes material not found in Luke. The manner in which Mark dealt with his source bears the marks of an editor. Matthew, for example, carefully preserves the original meaning of *paidia* as "little children" in 18:1-6, linking it with the necessity for becoming childlike in order to enter the Kingdom. Mark's meaning of this word in v. 42 certainly refers, as we have translated it, to *insignificant believers*. A progression from "little children" to "immature believers" is precisely what we would expect in community development (a fact to which Rawlinson calls attention, p. 130).

43. The sayings before us are concerned with the sacrificial attitudes demanded for entrance into the new life proclaimed by Jesus. Obviously what is under discussion is not bodily mutilation (common though that became in times of persecution) but rather to the demand to excise from life circumstances, objects, places, which are capable of deflecting the believer from single-minded devotion to God. The phrase "occasions of sin" to describe such conditions has a long tradition in Western Christian moral theology.

without a hand (Greek *kullos;* cf. Matthew 15:30; 18:8): The meaning is "maimed" or "crippled."

life (Greek *zoē,* cf. 9:45; 10:17,30): The Greek word, understood here in the sense of communion with God, is in contrast with the Greek *bios,* meaning animal and plant life, or—in the human sense—"existence."

hell (Greek *ge'enna):* Cf. 9:45,47; Matthew 5:22,29,30; 10:28; 18:9; 23:15,33; Luke 12:5; James 3:6. This word must be distinguished from Hades (Greek *hadēs).* The reference was originally to a valley on the west side of Jerusalem where infants had been offered in sacrifice (2 Kgs 23:10; Jer 7:31, 19:5, 32:35), but which was desecrated later by Josiah and used as a place for burning refuse. (Cf. in the later literature *1 Enoch* 27:2.) The fact that Jesus embraces the accepted notions of his own time never provided, and does not provide now, any idea of eternal punishment. But the severity of the judgment of Jesus must not be eroded or explained away. The contrast between "entering into life" and "going to ge'enna" is sufficient to underscore the seriousness with which Jesus regards any levity with regard to "occasions of sin."

It is worth noting here that Deut 25:11-12 allows punishment by mutilation for certain offenses, and the rabbinic literature repeats the Deuteronomic injunction (TB *Shabbath* 88b; Midrash *Niddah* 2.1).

unquenchable fire (Greek *to pur to asbeston):* is a Markan comment (cf. Isa 66:24) presumably intended for Gentile readers. To pursue a little further the observation made in the preceding note, there is no suggestion that the place of unquenchable fire is populated by those who must suffer eternally. Perhaps the finest contribution in the English language to the whole debate on the punishment of hell is to be found in C. S. Lewis, *The Great Divorce* (London: Macmillan, 1945).

44. Some manuscripts have the words which we have retained here and in v. 46, but the manuscripts are not among the best or the most reliable. The repetition of the saying in v. 46 seems to have found place there by attraction to the word *hell* at the end of v. 45. Both instances are retained here because some readers might be puzzled by a numerical omission, and by the fact of their being accustomed to English versions which retain the texts.

47. This verse, together with v. 45, repeats the warning of v. 43. In each case *elethēnai* (to be hurled or thrown) replaces the much milder *apelthein* (to go) of v. 43. This change in the Greek has been faithfully reproduced from Matthew.

to enter the kingdom: The phrase *eiselthein eis tēn basileian tou theou* is found in Mark here, and also in 10:15,23-24,25. The implication is that the Reign of God is not simply his kingly rule but also a kind of territory in which that rule is exercised. There is therefore a twofold note here: first the rule of God experienced here and now in the circumstances of human life, and second a notion almost of territorial limits—the Reign of God has its own rules and demands to which we must be subject.

48. This verse is a free rendering of Isa 66:24 and is a picture of never-ending decay and futility. It is from the Isaianic passage that some later literature seized upon the worm as a symbol of decay and dissolution.

It is avowed by Black (p. 127b) that the translation of vv. 38-48 reveals a poetic form and pattern, while Taylor (p. 412) maintains that the repetition of hard sounds and gutturals in the Greek give fitting expression to the sayings to be found here. The relationship between these verses and the version in Matthew has been much debated: Taylor (p. 412) considers that the omission of the foot, the delineation of both eye and hand as "right," and the limitation of the sayings in Matthew to warnings, with no compensating entrance into life, makes the Matthean version secondary. Lohmeyer (p. 196) does not agree, maintaining that the Matthean version is Palestinian and the Markan version Roman.

49. The best way to describe the textual evidence for this verse is to say it is confused. The translation we have given is from the best Greek manuscripts, but another reading (attested by a considerable number of lesser manuscripts) adds "and every sacrifice will be salted with salt," and yet a third group has a slightly different word order with the same meaning. The translation of the verse as it stands presents no difficulty, but the interpretation is a very different matter, and many and various have been the attempts at interpretation. The Greek *halisthēsetai* is found only here in Mark and must (apparently) mean "will be salted" or "will be seasoned." It is generally assumed that there is here *some* reference to Lev 2:13, with salt denoting preservation and fire (if we keep the secondary reading). This does not appear to be very convincing, and the merest glance at the commentaries is enough to acquaint the reader with the attempts made to elucidate the puzzle. The most convenient way to lay out the evidence is in the following short notes:

1. It has been proposed to read *hagnisthēsetai* (shall be purified) for the existing *halisthēsetai* (shall be salted). This makes admirable sense if we are allowed to conjecture a dictated Greek manuscript. But it cannot account for the textual variants.

2. Lohmeyer (p. 197n) is inclined to allow merit to the suggestion that the Latin manuscript from Carthage (k) which reads "omnis autem substantia consumitur" from a Greek "pasa de ousia analothēsetai." The phrase adds the ending of Isa 66:24 to v. 48: "their worm shall not die, nor their fire be quenched and all their substance shall be destroyed." There is some appeal in all this, but the reading is different from the Septuagint, and in addition, the Hebrew reads "and they shall be abhorred by all mankind."

3. The suggestion of Lagrange, in an attempt to combine or connect v. 49 with v. 50, that the fire preserves the sufferers in Gehenna and so becomes the last word in punishment, is wholly unacceptable.

4. Some commentators see a reference to the fires and purification of suffering, and this may be the most helpful suggestion. The view of this commentator as to the origin and purpose of Mark leads him to suppose that there is a reference to the purging and purifying effects of the eschatological situation in which the disciples stood, and out of which they would emerge as "seasoned" protagonists.

50. *Salt* (Greek *halas):* The earlier form of the Greek is *hals,* but both forms are found in this verse. In the strictest sense, salt cannot become *analos* (lose its saltness) save by combination with other materials to the extent that it loses its nature. Possibly this hyperbole is an equivalent to "losing its reason for existence." The suggestion has been offered that the coarse salt from the Dead Sea could become damp and leave crystalline forms which had the appearance of salt but without its essential nature. The connection with v. 49 is fortuitous and artificial: the purpose of salt in this verse is to season, and it is not connected with the experience of the community in suffering.

The synoptic parallels are instructive. Matt 5:13 has *halisthēsetai,* which Mark has in v. 49, whereas the present verse *kalon to halas (salt is good)* is derived from Luke 14:34. On the other hand, Mark discards the Matthean and Lucan *mōrainō* (to make foolish), preferring instead the more straightforward *analon* (being saltless). There is the complication that *mōrainō* and *mōroomai* (to become foolish) are virtually interchangeable in Greek. This prompts the reflection that the choice of the Greek word in Matthew and Luke may have been a misunderstanding of something in Aramaic by an editor or amanuensis and which Mark corrected. There may even be word play here: *taphel* = "unsavoury" and *tabbel* = "salted."

season it (Greek *artuō):* Mark derives this from Luke 14:34, where Matt 5:13 has *halisthēsetai* (to salt).

For an Aramaic parallel ("if the salt becomes insipid, how will it be salted?") cf. TB *Bekhoroth* 8b—Strack-Billerbeck, Vol. 1, p. 236.

Have salt . . . .: The meaning of this saying is hardly obvious. *Be at peace with one another* is reminiscent of Paul's injunction in 1 Thess 5:13 and the text before us appears to be an exhortation. It is possible, however, to read the two imperatives, joined by *and* (Greek *kai)* as an imperative followed by a conditional: "Have salt in yourselves, and then you will be at peace with one another."

The Latinisms of Mark have been matters for comment by more than one commentator (see, most recently, Lane, pp. 24, 184, 222, 243, 246, 422) and two articles by J.

Rendel Harris ("A Further Note on the 'Salt' Section at the End of Mark IX," *ET* 48.1936-37, pp. 185-87; and previously, "An Unrecognized Latinism in Mark," *ET* 35.9.1924, pp. 185-87) are still worthy of consideration. Harris suggested that the evangelist seized upon the Latin *salis* (salt) in the accusative *(salem)* and made the connection between that and *salem* as "peace" in Heb 7:2. In result, we have an exhortation to the disciples to hold fast to peace *in* themselves and thereby secure peace *among* themselves. If we wish to make a connection between the present verse and v. 49, it would be necessary to carry on the thought of "seasoned," tested disciples maintaining their purpose, and so only being at peace with one another.

This section is not without interest for synoptic studies. A comparison with the Matthean text is illuminating: the Matthean parallelism in 18:8 of "hand" and "foot" is carried over into v. 9. But as can be seen in vv. 43-46 above, this has been lost, and expanded into a threefold construction concerned with *hand, foot,* and *eye,* and the result can best be described as crude. Again, a parallelism in Matthew's vv. 8-9, "enter life," becomes interpreted in Mark's text in v. 47 as *enter the kingdom of God.* It is difficult not to describe this as secondary. Similarly the explanatory v. 48 seems to be equally secondary and explanatory.

51. The Law—Divorce
(10:1-12) = Matt 19:1-12

10 [1] He then left that place and came to the region of Judea and Transjordan, and when once more a crowd was gathered round him he taught them, as he always did. [2] Some Pharisees came to him and asked him, "Is it lawful for a man to divorce his wife?" This was to test him. [3] But he asked them, "What did Moses command you?" [4] "Moses," they answered, "permitted a man to get rid of his wife by divorce papers." [5] Jesus said to them, "He wrote this commandment because of your obduracy. [6] But in the beginning, at the creation, 'he made them male and female. [7] For this reason a man will leave his father and mother (and be joined to his wife), [8] and the two will become one.' So they are no longer two persons, but a single body. [9] What therefore God has joined, man must not separate." [10] When they were indoors again, his disciples asked him about the matter; [11] he said to them, "Anyone who divorces his wife and marries another woman commits adultery with her: [12] and also the woman who divorces her husband and marries another man commits adultery."

Comment

It is hard to think of any topic dealing with conduct which has generated, and
continues to generate, more enduring controversy than the sayings of Jesus in
the synoptic gospels which deal with divorce. All ecclesiastical statements,
from all denominations, and all legislation or attempted legislation dealing
with marriage and divorce look back to, or quote, the words of Jesus on
divorce. In Mark and Luke the condemnation of divorce is absolute, whereas
in Matthew, where the condemnation is recorded twice, there is an exceptive
clause. The broad position of the Christian communities can be summarized
generally as follows:

1. The Roman Catholic Church takes the words of Jesus as normative in
   the sense that it does not recognize any possibility of breaking the
   bond of a sacramental and consummated marriage. Certain exceptions are allowed: the so-called "Pauline privilege" (1 Cor 7:12) is
   extended to nonsacramental marriages. In passing, though not with
   exclusive reference to the Roman Catholic Church, there is long over-
   due an exhaustive historical study of the origin of the application of
   the "sacramental" approach to marriage, with all the scholastic implications of "indelible marks of character."

2. The Orthodox churches take the words of Jesus to mean, from the
   Matthean text, that there is a possibility of a breaking of the marriage
   bond in the case of adultery by one partner, the innocent party being
   free to remarry.

3. The provincial character of the constituent churches of the Anglican
   Communion makes a single and simple statement impossible. The
   Church of England, for example, in general terms assumes the same
   position as the Orthodox churches, but in contrast the marriage discipline of the Episcopal Church in the United States leans far more
   heavily on local, diocesan jurisdiction in the interpretation of what is
   meant by the "indissolubility of marriage."

4. In Protestant churches, in very general terms, there is small reliance
   on the "divorce texts," and divorce can be, and is, allowed for a
   variety of reasons other than adultery. Such churches understand that
   Jesus opposed divorce but take his words not as a statement of absolute norm for Christian conduct, but as suggested Christian policy. In
   other words, Jesus wanted to discourage the possibility of divorce as
   "official" policy, but in applying his words to individual cases, such

churches would allow for some evolution in social apprehension and social conditions.

It remains to be said that for all Christian denominations at the legal and pastoral level there is always the necessity for deciding in individual cases whether in fact a true marriage had ever taken place, however stringently the normal conditions and procedures appear to have been applied.

Deut 24:1 allowed a man to put aside his wife if he discovered in her "the nakedness of a thing." This very uncertain phrase may mean something shameful, and it may historically have meant physical indecency rather than a moral offense. It cannot have meant adultery, for that was punishable by death (Deut 22:22), and the need for divorce would not arise. Two "schools" of thought were in vogue at the time of Jesus: that of Shammai, which held that the Mosaic prescription allowed for divorce in the case of a wife's sexual misconduct, including adultery (by that time the death penalty could not be inflicted by the Jewish authorities); the more "liberal" teaching of Hillel, which allowed anything shameful or disgraceful as a cause for divorce—there was considerable latitude on this score.

The Pharisees are therefore here demanding which school of thought Jesus embraces: "Is it lawful to divorce one's wife for any cause?" (Matt 19:3— where the test question is far more plainly put than in Mark). As in other disputes with Jewish leaders, Jesus' answer bypasses the immediate and goes to the root of the matter. Jesus puts aside any time-consuming discussion of Deut 24:1 and in essence abrogates it.

The differences between the Matthean and the Markan traditions are instructive. In Mark the question in v. 2 poses the legality of divorce, and Jesus' questioners entertain no doubt on the matter—*This was to test him.* In the light of Mark 7:14-23 they might have expected Jesus to call the Law in question. In Mark, Jesus demands that his critics tell him the prescription of the Law, and when they have done so he goes beyond that Law to the purpose of marriage. In Matthew, however, there is first the statement of the purpose of marriage, and another question from the Pharisees, to which Jesus replies that the Mosaic instruction was an accommodation. There are two further differences: Mark 10:12 explicitly allows (apparently) for a woman to divorce her husband, a provision not made in Jewish Law (Josephus, *Ant* 15.259 gives an exceptional example); in the Matthean tradition Jesus appears, by the clause in Matt 19:9, to hold with the stricter school of Shammai. But it is by no means easy to determine whether Jesus' stricture of the Mosaic prescription is intended *simply* as an abrogation of that prescription, or an appeal to the essence of the marriage bond as against dispensations from it. The statement taken from Gen 1:27 and 2:24 in vv. 6-7 is followed by the principle laid down in v. 9, and the whole thrust of the pronouncement story effectively ends there. There is no discussion of the effect produced and would apply only in a community which understood divorce as forbidden (cf. 1 Cor 7:10-11). It follows that any view which serves to *reduce* the words of Jesus to something akin to the school of Hillel is not legitimate.

But there remains the question of interpretation. The notion that Jesus was allowing separation, but not divorce, cannot be sustained—as Judaism had no such custom, he would perforce have had to explain it. Some scholars have attempted to interpret the Matthean exceptive clause: "Whoever divorces his wife, even when it is a case of impurity, commits adultery" or as "whoever divorces his wife, leaving aside the case of Deuteronomy 24, commits adultery." At best it must be said that the translation of the Greek exceptive clause as "leaving aside" is dubious.

So far as the Matthean text can shed any light on the problem of divorce as understood in Mark, we must next consider the meaning of *porneia* in Matt 19:9 and 5:32. The word simply means "impurity in general." There has, however, been a tendency to translate the word as "adultery." But there is a technical word for adultery—*moicheia*—and it is used in the Matthean text: "I tell you, whoever divorces his wife, save for *unchastity*, and marries someone else, commits *adultery.*" There is simply no reason to use two different words in the same text, the one very broad in meaning, for the same idea, especially in a legal question where the Pharisees would demand accuracy.

It is possible—for some commentators—to hold that *porneia* means marriages not regarded as legitimate (e.g., marriage within the prohibited relationships of Lev 18:6ff.). Such marriages were a constant problem in the early Church, since Gentiles had often contracted such illegitimate marriages. Since the Gentiles were not bound by the Mosaic Law, how could they be bound by the Levitical marriage laws? The Council of Jerusalem (Acts 15) made some exceptions to the Mosaic Law for Gentiles, but explicit mention was made of abstention from *porneia*, and it has been suggested that this precisely means prohibited marriages (in 1 Cor 5:1 Paul uses the word to describe incestuous marriage). This interpretation has some difficulties. In effect Jesus said (in the Matthean tradition), "whoever divorces his wife, except where the marriage was forbidden by the Levitical Decree, commits adultery." But this was not a problem until Gentiles began to enter the community. Jews detested all such marriages, and recognized them as unlawful. Why would Matthew (the most "Jewish" of the gospels) represent Jesus as making such an exception? Two ways remain of interpreting the exceptive clause. First there were areas of doubt concerning incestuous marriages: a man might, for example, marry a woman in ignorance that she was a long-forgotten sister. Again the Levitical prescription left some areas unresolved: a man was not allowed to marry his aunt, but nothing was said of a woman marrying her uncle. This manner of interpretation therefore has Jesus condemning divorce in all cases save those of incestuous marriages contracted in ignorance. The question remains as to whether such cases were frequent enough to demand such an explicit exception.

A final possibility is open to us. It is that Jesus, in both Mark and Luke, prohibited divorce and condemned remarriage after divorce as adultery against the divorced partner. Now although this appears to be absolute, the community, beginning with Paul, felt free to interpret and reinterpret the apparent absolute. In Mark 10:10 there is prohibition against a man divorcing his wife and marrying another woman, yet 10:11 extends the prohibition to a woman divorcing her husband—and this is wholly outside the scope of Jewish law and practice. But in the Markan community (among Gentile God-fearers?) the question arose in some context, and the teaching of Jesus was clarified. So with the Matthean exception: this belongs to a Syrian-Palestine context, after the Jerusalem Council, when questions were raised about (Gentile) incestuous marriages.

So far as the synoptic texts are concerned, we are justified in saying that unless the attitude of Jesus described here was genuinely that of Jesus himself, it is hard to imagine in what interests it was invented. On the face of it, Jewish Christians would have looked to Deut 24:1, and the attitude of Jesus is not that of Pharisaic Judaism. There is no "messianic" basis for the pronouncement, though a case might be made that a consciousness of the end-time and the onset of the eschatological age might have demanded the kind of attitude espoused by Paul in 1 Cor 7:1-7.

The bibliography at the end of the notes makes no possible claim to be anything other than suggestions for additional reading. A commentary must content itself with the scriptural texts: interpretations of moral theology must remain a matter for that discipline.

The divorce texts in the synoptic gospels may be used to shed some light on the problem of synoptic relationships. Luke 16:18 represents an acceptance of Matt 19:9 ("everyone who divorces his wife and marries another commits adultery") along with 5:32 ("anyone marrying a divorced woman commits adultery"). But he cautiously refused the Matthean assumption (5:32) that a divorced woman would necessarily remarry and therefore (for support) be forced into an adulterous relationship.

Notes

1. *that place:* Cf. Matthew 4:12,25. In Isaiah the shore is that of the Mediterranean, but as Galilee must hear the good news then that is the place where the Proclamation of the good news must be made. Matt 4:25 refers back to it, in effect producing "theological geography." If Matthew is prior, then this is a simple structure, and only

in Matt 19:1 can Jesus begin the journey to Jerusalem. The Markan text, however, is not so simple. If Mark is prior, then we might conclude that this verse triggered Matthew into recalling Isaiah. But the geographical note in Mark is vague—geographically the text is vague, and the textual evidence (cf. Taylor, p. 416; Lane, p. 351) betrays all kinds of assimilations to later political realities. Matthew, on the other hand, is straightforward: "he left Galilee and came into that part of Judea beyond the Jordan" (19:1). The translation—from the Greek text used in this commentary—simply reflects the fact that the text before us represents the evangelist as not knowing (geographically) where he was. Perhaps what Mark intended to say was that Jesus was journeying through Peraea to Jerusalem. If it is objected that this is an inverted order, then a similar inversion also is found in Mark 11:1, where Jerusalem (mentioned first) is reached last of all. Some manuscripts—reflected in the King James Version—attempt to clarify the verse by reading that Jesus came into the "coasts of Judea by the farther side of Jordan."

once more: This clearly indicates that the teaching ministry was now resumed. But apart from this the ministry is drawing to a close, with Jesus deliberately choosing to go to Jerusalem.

Mark is following Matthew's order (Luke has no parallel to Mark 10:1-12, although there is a parallel saying on divorce in 16:8), but Mark considerably foreshortens Matthew's 19:1.

2. Some manuscripts omit *Pharisees;* and if this omission is accepted, it would be preferable to read in indirect speech "Some were asking whether it was lawful . . ." However, the manuscripts which omit mention of the Pharisees are neither numerous nor particularly impressive.

"Is it lawful . . .": The word used for divorce *(apoluō),* here and in vv. 4 and 11, refers to the divorcing of a wife by her husband, which was the only kind of divorce recognized in Jewish law.

This was to test him: If Mark's manuscripts originally omitted Matthew's *peirazontes* (Matt 19:1, "testing him"), then perhaps this short explanation was added by a later scribe. The test was either (a) to bring Jesus into conflict with the Law or (b) to make him suspect in the eyes of Herod, perhaps with the expectation that Jesus would be arrested like John. The whole matter of the lawfulness of divorce and remarriage had provided an occasion for John's arrest, and Jesus was apparently at this point in the jurisdiction of Herod Antipas. We may assume that the somewhat surprising alliance of Pharisees and Herodians (first mentioned in 3:6 and then again in 12:13) is also presupposed here.

The Matthean text is far more precise: "Is it lawful to divorce one's wife for any cause?" (19:3, cf. 5:31), and this version defines the issue with stark clarity, since divorce on grounds of adultery was permitted in the Deuteronomic legislation. In other words, for Matthew the matter concerned the legitimacy of divorce itself.

3. *"What did Moses command you?":* If the intention of the test question was to discover which of the two "schools" of Hillel or Shammai Jesus embraced, then it failed of its purpose, for Jesus peremptorily put aside such a confining debate and demanded an appeal to the Law. Jesus apparently was seeking a precept, an instruction, but in reply his critics provided him with an exception and a permission. It is important to note that the Mosaic prescription simply provided for the possibility of

regularizing divorce: it made no judgment as to whether divorce was right or wrong. It also provided some measure of security and protection for the divorced woman, by providing proof that she had been divorced.

Textually, it is worth observing that Matthew and Mark preserve the meaning of the Septuagint of Deut 24:1b, which reads: ". . . writes her a note of divorce, gives it into her hands, and sends her out of his house . . . ," the verb for "send" (Greek *apolousai* in Deut) being employed for *divorce* in Mark's v. 2 and in Matt 19:1.

5. The emphasis in Jesus' reply is a condemnation of human sin: the Mosaic provision *provides* for divorce but neither sanctions it nor gives it authority. Jesus gives expression to a legal process whereby some actions are tolerated out of concession to weakness (cf. David Daube, "Concessions to Sinfulness in Jewish Law," *JJS* 10.1959, pp. 1-13). The Mosaic provision was a choice between two evils and in this case a consideration for the sake of the woman. There was no intention in the Law of making divorce *acceptable* but rather to put limits on the consequences of sinfulness. The reply of Jesus is not a wholesale condemnation of the provisions of Deut 24:1-4. Rather the purpose of the reply is to call attention to the necessity of making provision for an obduracy which refused to take seriously the divine purpose in creation expressed in Gen 1:27 and 2:24. Therefore, the sharply worded retort is to call attention to the purpose of God, and an implied question as to whether, in the face of divine intention, the Mosaic legislation could any longer stand in a dawning eschatological age. (Cf. K. Berger, "Hartherzigkeit und Gottes Gesetz. Die Vorgeschichte des antijüdischen Vorwurfs in Mc 10.5," *ZNW* 61.1970, pp. 1-47.)

obduracy (Greek *sklērokardia):* The word is not classical but is found in the Septuagint at Deut 10:16, Jer 4:4, Sir 16:10. Cf. also Ezek 3:7.

6-8. The introduction of the creation narrative immediately raises the matter to a far higher level by appealing to the purpose of God in marriage. The quotations from Gen 1:27 and 2:24 are not meant to make an appeal to a legal decision but an appeal to the true character of human life as God intended it as against legislation based on fallen human nature. By implication, therefore, the Mosaic permission was a compromise with the order of creation.

in the beginning, at the creation: The expression is used again in 13:19. Some manuscripts add "God," some omit *in the beginning,* and six manuscripts omit *them* as the object of *he made.* Commentators differ as to the precise import of this opening phrase. One possibility is "at the beginning of his (i.e., Moses') book" or "at the beginning of Genesis" with "Moses wrote" understood. We take it, as translated here, to be two expressions in apposition.

For this reason: The second quotation follows immediately from Gen 2:24. Though the phrase in Genesis refers to the origin of the woman from the man's rib, Jesus here uses the words as referring to the act of creation: precisely because God made human beings male and female a man will leave his parents and become one flesh with his wife. The words are taken as though they are those of God himself. This accounts for Matthew's *kai eipen* (he said) at the beginning of 19:5—in assimilation, some manuscripts of Mark add the phrase at the beginning of v. 7. We have put *and be joined to his wife* in parentheses, since they are omitted in three major manuscripts of Mark.

and the two will become one: Cf. Gen 29:14, 37:27; Judg 9:2. It is from the preceding statement in v. 7 that the result, the consequence, is drawn. It is in the light of this factual result that the command in v. 9 follows (cf. Matt 19:6). This saying of Jesus is quoted in 1 Cor 7:10. It is important to note that *man* in v. 9 refers to the husband and not to any legal authority, for in Jewish Law it was the husband who effected a divorce. The spiritual reality of *no longer two persons, but a single body* is the very heart of the marriage for Jesus, and in no place perhaps have we been more guilty of treating one of his sayings as a legal prescription than in the oft-quoted v. 9.

10-12. The preceding section is complete in itself, and these three verses are essentially an appendix. Matt 19:9 makes the present v. 11 part of the narrative. Mark repeats the motif of 7:17—*When they were indoors.* The reply of Jesus is completely unqualified: anyone who divorces his wife and marries another woman commits adultery against the woman he has divorced. In this Jesus goes beyond the Jewish Law, where a man can commit adultery against another married man but not against his own wife. Our translation attempts to reflect this: *with her* refers to the wife of the second marriage, but the adultery is against the divorced wife.

12. This saying is peculiar to Mark and makes the same provision in the case of the wife: if she divorces her husband and marries another, she commits adultery. The saying is extremely difficult to exegete, for a variety of reasons:

1. The saying is contrary to the Law. There were circumstances in which a wife might *petition* for divorce (denial of conjugal relationships, impotence, or even unreasonable restrictions on liberty of movement), but even so the divorce had to be initiated by the husband. There appears to have been somewhat more freedom in the Elephantine Jewish community, but the basic provisions of the Law still stood.

2. It has been suggested that the verse is a gloss, representing an accommodation to Romano-Greek customary law.

3. One manuscript reverses vv. 11 and 12 and provides us with "The woman who leaves her husband and becomes wife to another commits adultery, and the man who leaves his wife and takes another commits adultery."

4. Burkill contends (pp. 99-101) that this saying is a primitive feature in this gospel, and Jesus is referring to Herodias, which was a well-known, even notorious case.

5. The matter is complicated by various textual considerations:

   a. A purely Alexandrian family of manuscripts reads: "and if she deserts her husband and marries another . . ." But this is by no means clear, for "she" may refer to the one in v. 11 who is divorced.

   b. A geographically wider group of manuscripts has: "if a wife should leave her husband and marry another . . ." This reading was accepted by Lagrange, p. 260.

   c. A third reading, in use in Antioch, Carthage, Gaul, Italy, and Caesarea as early as the middle of the second century, is perhaps the best. It reads: "a wife, if she goes away from the husband and marries another . . ." It can be argued that it is a modification of either *a* or *b*, altered to make the text conform to Jewish marriage customs. This is not entirely so, however, for the woman marries another, without divorce, while presumably the first husband still lives.

It is possible that both *a* and *b* represent modifications of an earlier text, and it is equally possible that each is an attempt to modify *c* in accordance with Gentile marriage customs. It is further to be noticed that the reading in *c* is in agreement with 1 Cor 7:10, where Paul enjoins, as a saying from the Lord, that a wife must not depart from her husband. Moreover, the Pauline judgment is different in vocabulary from the text before us and does not mention adultery. We cannot know with certainty the history of this Markan saying, unattested save by the parallel in Paul, except to say that it may have been attracted to this context, even though it does not mention divorce.

Appended Note: Synoptic Relationships in the Divorce Texts

The texts we have just examined provide an instructive example in the field of redaction criticism, particularly as that relates to synoptic studies.

1. Both Matthean passages (5:32, 19:9) stand in the tradition of Shammai, though 5:32 is secondary to 19:9. The assumption underlying 5:32 is that a divorced woman would seek the protection of another man and so form an adulterous union. In this text we are dealing with a Christian community in which matters of specifically Jewish concern were still very important.

2. The Lucan divorce text makes use of both Matthean texts. Luke repeats the provision of Matt 19:9 that anyone who divorces his wife and marries another woman commits adultery (Luke 16:18). But while embracing the provision in Matt 5:32b that anyone contracting marriage with a divorced woman commits adultery, he could not assume that a divorced woman would necessarily remarry and so omits Matt 5:32a with its tacit understanding that in contemporary Judaism a divorced woman was almost forced into another (adulterous) union. In the circumstances of the predominantly Gentile communities the pressure to contract another union were considerably less—especially in communities where expectations of an early *parousia* positively discouraged second unions of any kind.

3. Verbally the first part of Mark 10:11 is closer to Matt 19:9 than it is to Matt 5:32 or Luke 16:18.

4. It remains to consider v. 12 in the above section in relation to synoptic problems. If it was added late in the manuscript tradition, then we are left free to hold to the two-document hypothesis in customary form. But we have seen that this verse, peculiar to Mark, has *early* manuscript attestation. It is there-

fore possible to hold that Mark is at the end of a redactional process, where the possibility existed under Roman law for a woman to divorce her husband. This verse alone, around which there is much dispute among commentators as to whether it is primitive or late in the Markan tradition, should give us pause before concluding that Markan priority is a demonstrable fact.

Bibliography

(See also Strack-Billerbeck, Vol. 1, pp. 312-20.)

Bammel, E. "Markus 10.11ff. und das jüdische Eherecht." *ZNW* 61.1970, pp. 95-101.

Banks, R. *Jesus and the Law in the Synoptic Tradition.* London: Cambridge University Press, 1975.

Bonsirven, J. *Le divorce dans le Nouveau Testament.* Paris: Desclée, 1948.

Catchpole, D. R. "The Synoptic Divorce Material as a Traditio-Historical Problem." *BJRL* 57.1974, pp. 92-127.

Daube, D. "Concessions to Sinfulness in Jewish Law." *JTS* 10.1959, pp. 1-13.

―――. *The New Testament and Rabbinic Judaism.* London: The University of London, Athlone Press, 1956, pp. 366-68.

―――. "Repudium in Deuteronomy." In *Neotestamentica et Semitica.* Edinburgh: T. & T. Clark, 1969, pp. 236-39.

Delling, G. "Das Logion Mark X.11 (und seine Abwandlungen) in Neuen Testament." *NTS* 1.1956, pp. 263-74.

Descamps, A.-L. "Les textes évangeliques sur le mariage." *RevTheolLouv* 9.1978, pp. 259-86.

Dupont, J. *Mariage et divorce dans l'Évangile de Matthieu 19:12-13 et paralleles.* Bruges: Desclée de Brouwer, 1959.

Fitzmeyer, J. A. "Matthean Divorce Texts." *ThS* 37.1976, pp. 197-227.

Fleming, T. V. "Christ and Divorce." *JTS* 24.1963, pp. 541-54.

Lehmann, M. R. "Genesis 2:24 as the Basis for Divorce in Halakah and New Testament." *ZAW* 76.1960, pp. 263-67.

Margot, J. C. "L'indissolubilité du mariage selon le Nouveau Testament." *Rev TheolPhil* 17.1967, pp. 391-403.

RABBINIC MATERIAL

M *Gittin* 9.10.
TB *Gittin* 90a.
TY *Sotah* 1.1.16b.

52. Blessing the Children
(10:13-16) = Matt 19:13-15; Luke 18:15-17

10   [13] People were bringing children for him to touch them, but the disciples rebuked them. [14] When Jesus saw this, he was angry and said to them, "Let the children come to me. Do not try to stop them, because the Kingdom of God is for such as these. [15] In solemn truth I tell you, whoever does not accept the Kingdom of God like a child will by no means enter it." [16] Then he put his arms around them and blessed them by laying his hands upon them.

Comment

It is at this point in the pattern of synoptic relationships that Luke's great central section (made up of a collection of sayings worked in with sayings from Matthew) comes to an end, and at Luke 18:15 the evangelist follows again the Matthean order. (A glance at Orchard's table is helpful at this point.)

From 10:13 to 12:37 Mark's material follows Matthew. But the very departure from Matthean order which characterized Luke's great central section provided him with editorial problems all his own when he reached Matthew 23,24,25, and because of this, Mark's redactional activity after 12:37 became much more difficult. For the time being, however, since Matthew and Luke have—in general—a common order, Mark almost always follows that common order, using first one evangelist more than the other and then the reverse. Textually Mark follows one evangelist more than the other, but in his work of conflating his sources he always demonstrates his dependence on both. In the section which follows (i.e., 10:13-12:37), the material peculiar to Luke is omitted (Luke 19:1-10,11-27,39-44); so also is the material peculiar to Matthew (Matt 20:1-16, 21:28-32, 22:1-14). In fact the only material with single attestation which Mark incorporates consists of 11:12-14 (= Matt 21:18-19) and 11:20-25 (= Matt 21:20-22).

The pericope which follows bears all the signs of the end result of constant community use, and the finely honed product has all the characteristic elements of a pronouncement story. All details of time and place are long forgotten, and the story in present form has been attracted to its present position in

Matthew and Mark by association with the preceding discussion on marriage. Similarly a saying on the essential qualifications of entering the Kingdom has been likewise attracted to the present pericope. Luke's desire to emphasize teaching on humility has caused him to place the pronouncement story at the end of the parable about the Pharisee and the tax collector.

Notes

13. *People were bringing:* The verb is impersonal, though it is worthy of note that this impersonal use of the active, while a normal form in Hebrew and Aramaic, is distinctly uncommon in Greek. Matthew's more literary style uses the passive. Luke retains the uncommon active construction.

children: The Greek *paidia* can indicate any child from infancy to about twelve years of age. It is Luke who provides the meaning of "infants" with his use of *ta brephē.* There is no indication as to who brought the children.

to touch them: In all other cases, touching in Mark is used for the sick. Here it is sought to receive a blessing. Such touching with the hands in order to impart a blessing (cf. Gen 48:14) was common in Judaism, was carried over into the apostolic community, and is still widely used. Matthew's version has "that he might lay his hands upon them and pray," an explanation not found in Luke.

rebuked: There is no explanation as to why the disciples considered children unimportant to Jesus, or why they sought to interfere, unless it was to protect Jesus from constant attention.

them: There is ambiguity here. Was the rebuke to the children, or to those who brought them? Some important manuscripts substitute "those who brought them."

14. The response of Jesus is one of anger, a detail not found in Matthew or Luke. Is *he was angry* an eyewitness detail or a method employed by the evangelist to dramatize the reaction of Jesus? Whichever may be the case, this verse enshrines the whole point of the pericope. There are further forceful details in Mark. There is no connecting "and" between *Let the children come to me* and the succeeding *Do not try . . . ,* as there is in Matthew and Luke. The first positive command is absolute and stands on its own.

come to me: The Greek *erchesthai pros me* means literally "to approach me," but it is from such verbal usage that the familiar English "coming to Jesus" took root in the language (cf. 1:40,45; 2:3,13; 3:8; 5:15,22,27,33; 6:31; 10:50).

such as these: The Kingdom "belongs" to children in the sense that children appreciate a gift as an absolute, something which they are aware they cannot have worked to deserve. Children in this saying are at one and the same time in this verse symbolic and nonsymbolic. The children are rightful recipients because they *are* receptive. But they are symbolic in that the gift of salvation is something which cannot be earned. Concentration on this sense of the saying should not obscure one highly significant feature in this verse: the juncture of the concept of the Reign of God and the command to let children come to Jesus. The unspoken sense is that in some fashion Jesus is not simply the herald of the Kingdom but *is* the Kingdom.

15. *In solemn truth* (Greek *amēn):* The coming of the Reign of God is a gift, which must be received as a child receives a gift—simply, and without any sense of having earned the gift. It is possible, though somewhat awkwardly, to read the Greek as "accept the Kingdom of God as one receives a child." But the parallel sayings in Matt 11:25 (= Luke 10:21), 18:3 and John 3:3,5 wholly support the translation given here.

will by no means: On "entering the Kingdom" cf. 9:47. The condensation of the narrative into a "pronouncement story" leaves the sense of this verse somewhat in doubt. Is it the case that the *present* Reign is "received" and the *future* Reign "entered," so that one who does not now accept the Reign of God in the same way that a child receives a gift will not enter that Reign when it is fully established? If this distinction is indeed what is intended, then we are as close as Mark ever comes to the Matthean distinction between the "kingdom of the Son" and the "kingdom of the Father" (cf. Albright-Mann, AB *Matthew,* Introduction, pp. lxxxviii-c). This stricture on entrance into the kingdom is not found in Matthew. But Matthew has a parallel saying at 18:3, while Luke has the saying in the same words.

16. Luke does not have this verse; Matthew adds (of Jesus) "and went away." The action of Jesus emphasizes his words, and Mark's version strengthens the whole episode with *put his arms around them,* by using a strengthened verb *(kateulogei)* for *blessed.* For the phrase *laying his hands* cf. 8:25.

Note: For a highly skeptical assessment of the historicity of this passage, cf. J. Sauer, "Der ursprüngliche 'Sitz im Leben' von Mark 10:13-16," *ZNW* 72.1-2.1981, pp. 27-50. The author holds that this was a piece of tradition, built up by the early community to legitimize bringing children to miraculous healers in the Church. Sauer further believes that this pericope originated in the circle of such healers.

53. True Riches
(10:17-31) = Matt 19:16-30; Luke 18:18-30

10   ¹⁷ As he was starting on a journey, a man ran up, knelt before him, and asked, "Good Rabbi, what must I do to inherit eternal life?" ¹⁸ "Why do you call me 'good'?" Jesus said to him. "There is no one who is good, except God alone. ¹⁹ You know the commandments—'Do not murder; do not commit adultery; do not steal; do not perjure yourself; do not defraud' and 'honor your father and mother.' " ²⁰ "But, Rabbi," the man replied, "I have kept all these since I was a boy." ²¹ Jesus looked straight at him; his heart warmed to him, and he said, "There is one thing wanting in you. Go and sell all that you have, and give to the poor, and you will have riches in heaven. Then come and follow me." ²² When he heard this, his face fell and he went away

distressed, for he was very wealthy. [23] Jesus looked around at his disciples, and said to them, "How hard it will be for those who have riches to enter the Kingdom of God!" [24] The disciples were amazed at these words, but Jesus again said, "Children, how hard it is to enter the Kingdom of God! [25] It is easier for a camel to go through the eye of a needle than for a rich man to enter the Kingdom of God." [26] They were more amazed than ever, and said to one another, "Who then can be saved?" [27] Jesus looked at them and replied, "For men, this is impossible, but not for God—with God everything is possible." [28] Then Peter began to say to him, "Look, we have left all to become your followers." [29] Jesus said, "Truly I tell you: there is no one who has given up home, brothers, or sisters, mother, father, or children, or land, for my sake and for the Proclamation, [30] who will not receive in this present age a hundred times as much—houses, brothers and sisters, mothers and children and lands, and persecutions, too—and in the age to come, eternal life. [31] But many who are first will be last, and the last first."

Comment

Although in essence this is a pronouncement story, like the preceding pericope, there are details here of a fuller character than normally associated with such a story. In essence, this narrative comes with details from a source more informed than Matthew and Luke, and Mark's vocabulary is more independent of his mentors than is usually the case. But for all the detail which Mark has added to the story, he has no further information on the identity of the one who came to Jesus. Moreover the contextual attraction so noticeable in Matthew is present also here, though Mark's additional source knew a little of the attending circumstances—he was starting on a journey. The narrative is one whole piece, and attempts to find the material in vv. 23-27 and 28-31 as separate and self-contained narratives only attracted by context to vv. 17-22 are not very convincing. The unity of the passage under discussion is provided by the concern of the evangelist to delineate the nature of the Reign of God and the proper response to it. The description often given to this passage —"The Rich Young Ruler"—is misleading. Not only does the story before us suggest that the questioner was no longer a youth (in modern terms), but we owe the appellation "young man" to Matt 19:20 and the further description "ruler" to Luke 18:18.

Notes

17,18. Presumably Mark wishes us to link *a journey* with the situation described in v. 1. The whole expression here in Greek *(ekporeuomenon autou eis hodon)* is completely Markan. The details of the man's approach *(ran up, knelt before him)* are remarkably vivid, and whatever dependence on Matthean order Mark has at this point, the evangelist evidently had access to a tradition other than those found in Matthew and Luke. The expressions are Markan, especially *As he was starting on a journey,* characterized by a use of the genitive absolute, a usage favored by this evangelist.

The vivid details referred to above are all the more significant when it is recalled that all we know from Mark is *a man,* with no further information.

"Good rabbi . . .": Such a form of address would be very rare in the Judaism of Jesus' time, though the use of the word "good" as applied to God is common in the Old Testament (cf. Ps. 118:1, 1 Chron 16:34, 2 Chron 5:13), and in general the Jewish view was that God alone may be fitly described as "good," and by contrast no one else is "good" (cf. Rom 7:18). This distinction is not, however, absolute—creation is described as "good" in Gen 1:31; Paul so described the Law in Rom 7:12,16; and Jesus spoke of the differences between "good" and "evil" men. Moreover later Jewish writings were able to speak of the "good man" and the "good heart" (cf. Lohmeyer, p. 209, n.2).

For *rabbi* cf. 4:38 and for *good* see below.

It is commonly asserted that the differences in v. 17 and in the one which follows are most easily explained by the derivative character of Matthew, and the more primitive version in Mark: the harshness of the question of Jesus having been replaced with the softening of the question and answer by Matthew. Cf. "Teacher, what good thing must I do to have eternal life?" He answered him, "Why question me about what is good? . . ." (Matt 19:16,17). In fact the differences are superficial. In both traditions —that of Matthew on the one hand, and that of Mark and Luke on the other—Jesus is calling into question the presuppositions of his questioner. If Jesus is simply "Teacher" or "Rabbi," then he is calculated to know no more and no less than any other teacher about what actions are deemed "good for" entrance into the life of the age to come. If he is the "Good Teacher" (as in Mark and Luke), then he will not allow the questioner to use words or ascriptions lightly.

eternal life (Greek *zoē aiōnios):* (Cf. 10:30.) This is the *LXX* rendering in Dan 12:2, where the phrase is used in connection with the resurrection of the dead, though the origin of the phrase is eschatological—"the life of the coming age." (Cf. also *Pss Sol* 3:16; *1 Enoch* 37:4, 40:9, 58:3; 2 Macc 7:9; 4 Macc 15:3.) The sense is that this life is a gift of God by inheritance (as here), or is "entered into" (cf. 9:43,45). This is a life entered upon at the resurrection and is not to be understood in terms of immortality. The later Johannine perception of eternal life as a possession in the here and now (John 3:15) is not present in this story.

Jesus' questioner seems to suggest that there are predispositions over and above the Law, though there may be a hint in *what must I do* that the man was understood (by

Jesus or the evangelist?) to mean "How may I earn eternal life?" Matthew's version in 19:17 certainly implies this: "Teacher, what good thing must I do to have eternal life?"

19. The man is recalled to the demands of the Law. But though Jesus is always represented in our gospels as obedient to the Law, and demanding attention to its intent while repudiating pettifogging oral interpretations of it, he nevertheless challenges his questioner on how *he* views the Law.

You know the commandments . . . : The order of the commandments varies in the manuscripts. In Mark and Luke the negative Greek form is *mē* with the subjunctive, where Matthew has a simple *ou* with the future tense.

Do not murder . . . : In the Greek text adopted for translating the New English Bible (1961, Greek edition 1964, Oxford University/Cambridge University Press) the order is: "Do not murder; do not commit adultery, do not steal, do not perjure yourself; do not defraud; and honour your father and mother." This is the order used in the translation above. Of these verbs *murder, commit adultery, steal,* and *defraud* are found only here in Mark. For *perjure yourself* cf. 14:56; and for *defraud* cf. 1 Cor 6:7, 7:5; 1 Tim 6:5.

It is to be noted that the command in the Decalogue prohibits murder but not killing in warfare or by judicial execution.

The verb *apostereō,* here translated *defraud,* is used in *LXX* to mean the act of keeping back the wages of a hired hand, whereas in classical Greek the primary reference was to a refusal to return money or goods entrusted for safekeeping. In this sense *do not defraud* may be a negative form of the eighth commandment: "do not steal." Some commentators see in this a reference to the tenth commandment. This verb is not found in Matthew and Luke and is omitted by some Markan manuscripts. On the other hand, it is found in some important manuscripts and has been regarded by many commentators as genuine, on the grounds that those manuscripts which do not have it dropped it because it is not found in the Decalogue. On the other hand the inclusion of *honor your father and mother* may well illustrate a tendency to assimilation and expansion. Mark rejects the expansion found in Matt 19:19: "and love your neighbor as you love yourself."

In all of this the man who questioned Jesus has his attention drawn to a series of demands which all have to do with ordinary human relationships. In this context, the introduction *You know the commandments* is no mere reminder but part of the answer to the man's question about eternal life.

20. *Rabbi* (Greek *didaskale,* literally "teacher"): See v. 17 above and 4:38.

kept (Greek *phulassō,* cf. 15:25): Mark's grammatical usage here is not correct, and he does not follow the Greek of Matthew and Luke *(ephulaxa).* This is an indication, admittedly minor, that Mark has an independent source here, however he may follow Matthew's order. The details in vv. 17-22 are far more vivid than in Matthew and Luke. This impression of an independent source is strengthened by the detail of Jesus' reaction to the man in the following verse.

since I was a boy: The expression is common in the Old Testament—cf. Gen 8:21, 1 Sam 12:2, Ps 71:17.

21. Though the reply is more in the nature of a protestation of integrity, Jesus' answer is far from condemnatory. The translation *warmed to him* has been chosen as the best suited for *agapaō.* In Greek the verb *phileō* would seem to be more human and

agapaō somewhat more detached. What appears to be indicated here is an impression in Jesus' mind that his questioner was genuinely seeking a right relationship with God. (We are reminded of "the disciple whom Jesus loved" in John 13:23, etc.) This interesting detail manifestly betrays Mark's access to a firsthand tradition unknown to Matthew and Luke.

There is one thing wanting in you: Some manuscripts of Mark, admittedly not the most important, have the verb *hustereō* (to fail) with the dative personal pronoun *soi* ("to you," singular) in place of the grammatically incorrect accusative *se*. This obviously cannot be reflected in a translation, but both Nestlé and the New English Bible Greek text read *se*, on the grounds that the *soi* was changed in Mark by scribes to reflect the (correct) Matthean and Lucan versions. Perhaps an illustration from substandard English will explain to the reader with no Greek what is being said. To say "I will get me" (accusative case) "a meal" would be changed by a grammatically sensitive listener, mentally if not verbally, to "I will get for myself" (dative case) "a meal."

The reply of Jesus must not be read as though one more performance of a good deed is all that is necessary for the young man to inherit eternal life. In spite of the structure and order of the sentences, the operative injunction is *Then come and follow me.* The demand of Jesus is not for any specific act, but for an attitude of abandonment to loyalty to his ministry and person. Similarly the command *Go and sell all that you have, and give to the poor* is not an all-embracing demand for universal renunciation but is applicable to one single individual. Evidently Jesus sensed that there was in this particular case—probably obvious from the young man's dress—an almost insuperable obstacle by way of attachment to wealth. At the same time it must be remembered that Jesus himself chose a life of renunciation: he has no settled home (1:39, cf. Luke 9:58), he and his disciples go hungry (2:23, 8:14); his needs are provided for by devout followers (Luke 8:3), and the disciples can claim that they have abandoned everything and followed him (10:28). It would be a fair assessment to say that the ethical teaching of Jesus had a very strong element of detachment toward wealth and possessions, and Paul certainly shares this emphasis (cf. Phil 4:11-14). Jesus' own standpoint with regard to his ministry seems to lean far more toward the ascetic practices of the Essenes, even though here he is but reiterating the rabbinic demand of almsgiving to the poor. Cf. C. E. B. Cranfield, "Riches and the Kingdom of God," *SJT* 4.1951 pp. 302-14.

riches in heaven: cf. Matt 6:19-21.

22. It is instructive at this point to note that the *Gospel of the Hebrews,* in the Latin version of Pseudo-Origen based on Matt 19:22, elaborates the story with "How do you say 'I have kept the Law and the Prophets'? For it is written in the Law: 'You shall love your neighbors as yourself.' Yet many of your brethren, sons of Abraham, are clothed in filth, dying of hunger, but your house is full of good things, and none of it goes out to them."

very wealthy (Greek *klemata*): Literally "property," especially with reference to land. It is noteworthy that this is the only occasion in the gospels where we have a story of the call of Jesus being refused. Aside from the phrase *when he heard this, his face fell,* Mark's text in this verse is in complete agreement with Matthew. Luke 18:23 has "When he heard this, he was filled with sadness, for he was very rich."

23. It is perhaps reading too much into the narrative to find in this verse an echo of

the young man's distress in Jesus himself, for we have no means of knowing whether vv. 23-30 were attracted to their present location by the preceding story. Taylor (p. 430) regards the conversation on riches to be a "story [so] closely connected in the tradition . . . as to be almost part of it." The teaching on wealth in the conversation which follows certainly goes far beyond exhortations to almsgiving and certainly (so far as Jesus is concerned) contradicts any unqualified assertion that wealth is a sign of divine blessing. For the rich the difficulty lies in making a choice between caring for wealth and caring for the things of God. Cf. Matt 7:14. It is not that riches are a barrier *per se* to salvation—it is simply that they pose peculiar temptations to spiritual welfare.

hard (Greek *duskolos):* This adverb is also found in Matt 19:23 and Luke 18:24, and the comparative rarity of the adverb is a significant indication of the interrelatedness of the synoptic gospels.

riches (Greek *krēmata):* This word, meaning "things one possesses," is far more general than the word translated as *very wealthy* in the preceding verse.

24. The astonishment of the disciples is all the more noteworthy, if vv. 24 and 25 are reversed in order, as they are in the Western text, principally by the sixth and seventh century Codex Claromontanus and several Latin versions of a later date. Jesus speaks to them a second time, using the affectionate term *children* (Greek *tekna,* cf. John 13:33; 2:1,12,28; 3:7,18; 5:21; and also Gal 4:19). The words used on this second occasion are even stronger, and the mitigating texts found in some important manuscripts ("those who trust in riches") must be rejected. This v. 24 is not found in Matthew and Luke, though Matthew apparently knew the verse before us, for he uses the phrase "further, I tell you . . ." at 19:24.

25. *It is easier . . . .:* In spite of the attempts of preachers and commentators in the past to find a small gate alongside a main city gate through which a camel could not possibly pass, and in spite of a few minor manuscripts which read *kamilos* (a cable) for *kamelos* (camel), we must conclude that what we have before us is an example of hyperbole (cf. Matt 23:24, Luke 6:41-42). It is odd to find a return to the question of the rich man in this verse, after the very general statement of v. 24, and it is possible to find some merit in the reversal of the verses in some manuscripts (as noted above); by doing so, the tension in the account is heightened and leads very well into the amazement of the disciples in v. 26. The order would then be vv. 23,25,24,26-31.

26. *more amazed* (Greek *exeplēssonto):* Cf. 1:22. There is a variant reading of *one another* (Greek *pros eautous* in some manuscripts, which read *pros outon,* to him). Admittedly the reading "to him" is found in some significant manuscripts, but it misses the dramatic buildup of the passage—the excited babble of conversation with its climax in the ensuing question to Jesus: *Who then can be saved?*

It would seem that the disciples' question means: "Then who can enter the Kingdom?" Given that the possession of adequate means would appear to imply leisure enough to devote to prayer, study, and good works, Lohmeyer (p. 215) finds an eschatological dimension to the question "Who will *finally* be found within the Kingdom?" As it stands, however, the choice of meaning between present or future opportunity is open, and the framing of the question ought perhaps to put the emphasis on whether anyone *can* be saved.

27. Jesus' answer has one emphasis: the power of God. The references to *Jesus*

looked at them (which is peculiar to Mark) is the evangelist's way of emphasizing the importance Jesus attached to the reply. In essence it is that *God* saves—not faith, not works, not any human endeavor. *For men, this is impossible.* The vocabulary, and the sentiments, echo the *LXX* text of Gen 18:14: "Are any things impossible with God?" Mark agrees closely with Matthew's text, but Luke 18:27 condenses the saying into "What things are impossible for men are possible for God."

28. Taylor (p. 433) sees the conversation in vv. 28-31 as a separate piece of tradition, not linked grammatically with the preceding incident. Whether what we have in vv. 28-31 was originally a pronouncement story attracted by subject matter to its present context we cannot know, though in Matthew the connection is far clearer: "Peter then said to him in reply . . ." (19:27). Textually Mark's introduction here in this verse does not follow Matthew, and it is open to the suggestion that he has an independent (Petrine?) tradition which he prefers. The opening phrase *Look, we have left all . . .* is strongly reminiscent of Peter, though the narrative lacks a great deal of the immediacy of Petrine stories, such as 1:29-39, 4:35-5:43. But if this narrative is all of a piece with the preceding vv. 17-27, then it does have plausibility as a unit for which Mark had a tradition independent of Matthew.

If anything was needed to make a tentative suggestion of Petrine reminiscence, it would be Peter's protestation of *we have left all.* The exaggeration involved must be seen against the incident at Peter's home in 1:29 and the implied suggestions in 3:9 and 4:1 that Peter still maintained possession of a boat. Evidently Peter's detachment from home and from his former work was not wholly complete. There are references here back to 1:18 (the call) and to 2:14 (the call to "follow"): such references back are very rare in Mark but are an essential part of Matthew's treatment (cf. Matt 19:27 and 4:19; 19:27 and 9:9).

left all to become your followers: The Greek tenses are noteworthy. The first verb (Greek *aphēkamen*) is an aorist tense, with a definite sense of an accomplished fact, while the second (Greek *ekolouthēkamen*) is an imperfect tense, with a meaning of a continuing action. Matthew has at this point "What therefore will become of us?"—evidently pointing back to what the young man was unwilling to do (cf. Luke 22:28-30). Mark omits this detail: his concern is to drive a point home, with no peripheral details. Matthew's text has at this point the saying about the twelve thrones of judgment (19:28), linked to the new creation; Luke has chosen to put the saying in the context of the dispute among the disciples about preeminence (22:28-30).

29. *Truly* (Greek *amēn):* Cf. 3:28.

there is no one: (Cf. 9:39.) The reply of Jesus on abandonment is characterized by great detail, loosely the same in vocabulary as Matthew. It is notable that in contrast with v. 30, the various items are separated by *or* and not, as in v. 30, connected by *and.* In this, Mark follows Matthew and Luke. Luke omits *sisters* and *land* but adds "wife" and has "parents" in place of *mother* or *father.* Some manuscripts of Mark have "wife" by assimilation to the Lucan version.

for my sake and for the Proclamation: Some important manuscripts omit this phrase. In Greek there is a double *for my sake (kai eneken emou)*—cf. 8:35—and *for the sake of the Proclamation* (Greek *kai eneken tou evangeliou),* and this has led many commentators to suggest that the whole phrase is editorial. Matthew has "for my name's sake" (19:29), while Luke has "for the sake of the Reign of God" (18:30). Even if the three variants are editorial, they are of great significance in demonstrating that the primitive Christian community identified Jesus with both the Proclamation and Reign.

30. *who will not receive:* Our three gospels at this point display different Greek grammatical constructions, which—while of interest to the grammarian of *koinē* Greek—do not differ in sense. Matthew has simply "And everyone who has left . . . will receive . . ." It is tempting to think that Mark had an independent source at this point, for his construction is far less simple than that of the other two.

hundred times as much: Cf. Luke 8:8, 2 Sam 24:3, 1 Chron 21:3. The variant readings between different manuscripts are interesting. Luke 18:30 has (in one manuscript) *heptaplasiona* (sevenfold as much), in other manuscripts *pollaplasiona* (manifold times more); Matt 19:30 in some manuscripts has *pollaplasiona,* as in the preceding example. Apparently some scribes felt that a hundred times as much was altogether excessive.

There is a distinction in Mark and Luke between rewards in the present time and those reserved for the age to come. The phrase *en tō kairō toutō (in this present age)* is unusual. It is not found in Matthew, though Luke has it at 18:30. The more usual phrase—*ho aiōn houtos*—is found in Matt 12:32, 13:22, Luke 16:8, 20:34; but the Greek form here in Mark has its closest parallel in *ho nun kairos* (the present time) in Rom 3:26, 8:18, 11:5, 2 Cor 8:13.

Some commentators regard the whole passage from *houses* to *and persecutions* as an addition, forged partly in the sense of community in the early Church and the experience of persecution. (Lohmeyer, p. 217, is representative of this view.) Others would argue for the addition simply of *and persecutions, too.* There is much to be said for such views, but it may be doubted how cogent some of the arguments are. The mention of persecutions, for example, may well represent the experience of the Christian community in a later age. But the hardships of Paul and his companions were probably common knowledge in some circles, and little was needed by way of prescience on the part of Jesus to be aware that his followers could hardly escape calumny and ill treatment in the years after the ministry. A somewhat less impressive objection to the authenticity of the saying is the suggestion that the verse reflects the sense of close personal relationships in the early community. This objection, however, fails to take into account the impulse toward such relationships displayed by Jesus in 3:35 of this gospel: "that one is my brother, and sister, and mother." Far more important is the identification made in the saying of *eternal life* with *the age to come.* It is important to remember that the two expressions "Kingdom of God" and "Kingdom of heaven" in Matthew stand respectively for the final, ingathered Reign of God at the end of time, and for the temporary, messianic Reign of the Son. This appears to be the case even when allowance is made for the fact that in Hebrew and Aramaic the two expressions are synonymous in meaning. Now Mark has taken over from Matthew in v. 23 the saying about entrance into the Kingdom of God, but there is no indication in Mark that he shared Matthew's distinction between two "Reigns." The problem with the saying before us is that the "age to come" is regarded in our New Testament sources as being in the here and now as a result of the ministry and mission of Jesus (cf. Gal 1:4, Heb 6:5), and this is underscored by references to "life" in Mark 9:43,45 and to the Reign of God in 10:15. It is best to assume that the Matthean version (". . . will receive a hundredfold, and will inherit eternal life," Matt 19:30) is to be preferred, and the Markan version is adapted by someone unaware of the theological concerns of a later age.

The promise of Jesus is that the seeming deprivation, for his sake, will be rewarded a hundredfold in the wider fellowship of the community. The community life of part (at any rate) of the early Jerusalem Church (Acts 2:44, 4:32-37) seems to have been a reflection of this saying of Jesus.

Three matters remain for comment. The first has to do with rewards and punishments. There is no denying that in the teaching of Jesus there is an important element having to do with rewards for faithfulness and perseverance, and equally punishment for failure and apostasy. But there is nothing in that teaching which reflects a notion, found widely in the Old Testament literature, that riches and possessions were a sign of God's favor. Generally the Puritan view has been that obedience to law and diligent work will bring prosperity, in spite of much evidence to the contrary. The same view has often tended to be embarrassed by the theme of rewards and punishment in the teaching of Jesus, on the grounds that service and loyalty to the master should be disinterested. It is worth pointing out that nowhere in Jesus' teaching is there the faintest hint of the notion of accumulating merit (like an interest account) so characteristic of Tertullian and later Latin writers. On the contrary the rewards promised by Jesus so far surpass any element of performance by us as to render the word "reward" itself almost meaningless.

Second the strong emphasis in Jesus' ministry on renunciation of, or detachment from, earthly concerns and possessions was emphasized by Paul (with strong *parousia*-expectation overtones—e.g., 1 Cor 7:17-35) but has from time to time in the history of the Church been rationalized as inapplicable to a later age and culture. Reaction in favor of renunciation, when it has happened, has often been sharp and embarrassing (e.g., St. Francis of Assisi and later similar movements in the century before the Reformation). One thing can be said with certainty: the view of St. Laurence of Rome (d. 258) that the Church's treasure was the poor stands in marked contrast to the accumulation of wealth in goods and possessions which has so often characterized the later ages of Church history into our own times.

Third—and somewhat separate from the first two matters—is the vexed and complicated matter of eschatology in the gospels. Matthew's version of v. 30 above does not have *in this present age* (cf. Luke 18:30), but this should not be taken as an indication that for Matthew all blessings belong to an eternity divorced from the temporal order. Matthew's "new creation" of 19:28 says no more than is said by John 3:3-8, and the emphasis is not on the end of the temporal order but on the inheritance which belongs to the disciple in the present (cf. John 6:35-39). The life of the coming age is a common theme in Matthew (cf. 5:5, 21:38, 25:34), but the question is whether Mark intends to convey by his phrase *in the age to come, eternal life* a somewhat clumsy and easily misunderstood assimilation of the sense expressed in Matthew. The present writer finds the question intriguing but insoluble.

31. *But many who are first . . . .:* Matt 19:30 (where there is a slight verbal change of order in the Greek of Mark) is repeated in reverse order at Matt 20:16, where it forms a conclusion to a parable and also forms a chiasm, a device common in Matthew. Luke does not have the saying. The meaning of the saying here is unclear in

Mark, as it is also in Matthew. *First* may possibly refer either to rank or privilege, or to the time at which a person entered the community. Luke's somewhat similar saying (13:30) is in a quite different context. The saying may have been found in isolation, or in a collection of sayings which found its way here by attraction of subject matter. (Proponents of the two-document hypothesis will attribute Luke 13:30 to Q.) If the Greek *de* (translated here by *but)* is meant to introduce a note of criticism, then the saying may be a warning to the disciples. This, however, is impossible to determine.

54. Passion Prediction (iv)
(10:32-34) = Matt 20:17-19; Luke 18:31-34

10 ³² They were now on the road going up to Jerusalem, with Jesus leading the way. The disciples were filled with wonder, and those who followed behind were afraid. Once again taking the Twelve aside, he began to tell them what was to happen to him. ³³ "See," he said, "we are going up to Jerusalem, and The Man will be handed over to the chief priests and the scribes. They will condemn him to death and hand him over to the foreigners. ³⁴ They will mock him and spit on him, flog him and kill him. After three days he will be raised."

Comment

Mark continues to follow Matthew's order with this third Passion prediction, but it is noteworthy that this third prediction comes as an interruption of the narrative in Matthew (it comes at the conclusion of the parable of the workers in the vineyard), and it has an air of intrusion about it in Mark, too. But we may be able to hazard a guess as to the position of this prediction in Mark and possibly in Matthew too. The saying with which Matthew ended at 19:30 ("Nevertheless, many who are first will be last, and the last first") is repeated at 20:16 ("So the last shall be first, and the first last"). We called attention in the previous section to this chiasm, but there may be a further reason for the repeated saying, and this may provide us with Mark's reason for placing the third Passion prediction apart from simply following Matthew's order. Did Matthew intend the saying at the conclusion of the parable of the workers in the vineyard to refer simply to the warning of Jesus against reliance on election as a privileged possession on the part of those first called (i.e., the Jews)? Or did the evangelist wish to call attention to a deeper meaning—that Jesus was the *last* of the prophetic voices in his Passion, but the *first* in his Resurrection? If this was the evangelist's intention, then the intrusive Passion prediction in the Matthean order, followed as it is by the dispute over precedence, is explained. If this is admitted, then so too is Mark's use of only one version of the "last-first" saying in 10:31, where he found it in Matthew. With Matthew, he follows with the Passion prediction (though omitting the parable) and passes into the dispute over precedence. Matthew's version is terse, compared with Mark, but both are placed in the context of the final journey to Jerusalem. The phrase *taking the Twelve aside, he began to tell them* is Markan, but with *See, we are going . . .* he reproduces Matthew's Greek, with a slight grammatical change in *to death,* and then Mark changes Matthew's "to be . . . crucified" to *and kill him.* There is a change too in the final sentence, with Matthew reading "On the third day . . ." and Mark *After three days.* What is immediately apparent in this third prediction is its great detail when compared with the first and second (8:31, 10:31), and a comparison chart will be useful at this point.

Matt	Mark	Luke			
20:17-19	10:31-34	9:31	8:31	18:31-33	
20:17	10:32				Going to Jerusalem
20:18	10:31	9:31 (rejection 8:31)			handing over to chief priests
20:18	10:33				condemnation by chief priests
20:19	10:33			18:32	handing over to Gentiles
20:19	10:34			18:32	mocking, flogging
20:19	10:34	9:31	8:31	18:33	execution
20:19	10:34	9:31	8:31	18:33	resurrection

The relationship in detail between the third prediction and the passion narrative is so close that a definite historical connection is certain and written in the light of the passion. But it is important here not to read back into the first and second predictions details which properly belong only to the third. Even the foregoing table may be misleading, for the first prediction says simply that The Man "must suffer" and speaks only of rejection, not condemnation, by the chief priests. The second prediction speaks of "handing over" to men (unspecified). Agreement between the three is reached only with death and resurrection, and crucifixion is mentioned specifically only in Matt 20:19. Luke speaks of the fulfillment of "everything written about" The Man in

19:31. In contrast with Matthew and Mark, what is remarkable about the Lucan version is how little it draws on the subsequent passion story.

Notes

32. *on the road* (cf. 1:2, 8:3): The details surrounding this third prediction lend it an air of portent not found in the previous two. Luke's gospel gives to the occasion a definitive note, as though closing off the Galilean ministry: "Now we are going up to Jerusalem . . ." (18:31). The distinction between all that has gone before in the ministry, and all that is to follow, has led to a suggestion in a recent article that the attempt to find a symbolic Galilee-Jerusalem polarity in Mark is either exaggerated or mistaken; that there is far more of historical circumstance in Mark than an understanding of "Galilee = Galilean Christians awaiting an imminent *parousia* versus Jerusalem = the enemy of the Galilean community." (Cf. Elizabeth Struthers Malbon, "Galilee and Jerusalem: History and Literature in Marcan Interpretation," *CBQ* 44.2.1983, pp. 243-55.) Given the circumstances in which we believe Mark to have been compiled, we suggest that the urgency of composition was such that little time was invested in an examination of sectional polemics, even supposing that attitudes to the *parousia* had hardened to the extent suggested by W. Kelber *(The Kingdom in Mark,* Philadelphia: Fortress Press, 1974). The precise location of a possible *parousia* has excited the attention of several commentators—e.g., Lohmeyer, Lightfoot *(The Gospel Message),* Marxsen—but the lack of any substantial agreement among them does not inspire confidence in *parousia*-expectation as the key to the understanding of Mark.

Jesus leading the way: Taylor (p. 437) expresses surprise at the distinction here (found also in Matthew) between the *disciples* and *those who followed behind.* The explanation is partly to be found in the phrase *with Jesus leading the way.* A contribution by Moses Aberbach (see notes on 9:3) gives us examples of the precise behavior expected of disciples when walking with their teacher. They must never presume, for example, to walk beside their teacher but always to follow at a respectful distance. Here *disciples* must be understood as meaning the Twelve—Jesus calls them to himself to explain in private what was to happen. The Twelve are *filled with wonder* that the Galilean ministry was so soon to finish, while *those who followed behind*—even farther behind the Twelve—were *afraid* because they foresaw the consequences of an irrevocable decision to go to Jerusalem to face inevitable hostility. This seems to be the simplest explanation of two apparently disparate groups, but the textual evidence does allow for the two groups to be considered as one. Some manuscripts omit *those who followed.* Turner (p. 50-51) makes the suggestion that the verb we have translated as plural—*they were afraid*—should rightly be *ethambeito* (literally, "he was overcome with consternation"), since a stronger form of the verb is used at 14:33 *(full of dread).* By this means it would no longer be necessary to distinguish between the *wonder* of one group and the fear *(afraid)* of the other.

taking the Twelve aside: Matt 20:17 has the same note, and Mark shares with Matthew the distinction which Jesus made between instruction given in public to the crowds and the more intimate conversations with the inner circle. But there is clearly exhibited in this single verse an atmosphere of awesome expectation, and perhaps *those who followed behind* was a deliberate Markan note addressed to a community undergoing persecution. It may even be the case that this private address to the Twelve is intended to mark a new departure in the narrative. The repeated phrase *up to Jerusalem* (vv. 32 and 33) recalls Ps. 122, and Jesus is depicted as going to fulfill a destiny: the phrase conveys far more than a mere note of geography. This is underlined by *began to tell them what was to happen*. This is peculiar to Mark but is rooted in the biblical tradition (cf. Gen 42:4,29; 44:29; Job 1:21; Esth 6:13; see also Luke 24:14).

33. *The Man:* The abundant and precise detail of the third passion prediction, written after the event, ought not to blind us to the fact that some such teaching was in all probability given at this stage of the ministry. Significantly it comes after the refusal of the young man to act in a spirit of abandonment, and after the protestation of the disciples that they have left everything. It is important to note that when Jesus begins to explain the inevitability of what lies ahead, he clearly associates the disciples with himself, just as the promise to the disciples in v. 30 was inclusive of those who would follow *them.* The two previous passion predictions in Mark were each followed by a note of the disciples' failure to understand what Jesus was saying. The first prediction is followed in 8:32 by Peter's protest, the second by *they did not understand* in 9:32, and the instance before us is succeeded by Peter's two fellow witnesses of the Transfiguration seeking their own advancement. In its turn this will be followed by lessons in discipleship. Whether the term *The Man* has its background in Daniel or *Enoch,* the use of the term is so starkly different in the synoptic gospels that we have to conclude that we are face to face with creative religious genius. Now it is open to the strongest proponents of redaction criticism to suggest that this creativity belongs to one or more of the evangelists, whichever came first, or to a community for which an evangelist was writing. The identification of *The Man* with "the saints" in Daniel is such that the central figure is in some sense involved in the suffering and those awaiting vindication, and this appears to be also true of the example before us. *The Man,* on a common understanding, *ought* to be arbiter and judge, but he is destined to be rejected (Mark 8), and those who choose the path of discipleship will themselves be called upon to renounce self (8:34-38). *The Man* in Daniel 7 is represented as receiving dominion and allegiance, but the core of this third prophecy speaks of death. It is altogether fitting that the prediction should be followed by the stern warning that following *The Man* is a call to service and not domination. If the core of the idea of the suffering Man is to be found in Daniel 7, judged as a corporate term, then we can surely find in these passion predictions the extension of that idea into the mission and ministry of Jesus. Now given the paucity of references to "The Man" outside the gospels, we are led almost inevitably to conclude that the creative religious genius of which we spoke is Jesus himself. In this connection the reference to The Man as vindicator in Acts 7:56 has far more in common with *Enoch* than Daniel, though in his suffering Stephen seeks identification with Jesus. If there are grounds, as we believe there are, for seeing The Man in Daniel 7 as a corporate term, then the links between The Man and the fate of the disciples in the three passion predictions are no accident but are an authentic part of the Jesus tradition. On the other hand, the more traditional "Man-in-glory" sayings to be found in the apocalyptic sections of Matt 25:31-46, Mark 13:24-27, and Luke 21:25-28 are far more in tune with the individual figure

of *Enoch* but nevertheless exhibit an understanding of the term which also stresses the close link between The Man and his associates.

34. The references to *mock* (cf. 15:20,31), *spit on him* (cf. 14:65, 15:19), and *flog* are all retrojections from the narrative of the passion. As in 8:31 and 9:31, Mark has *after three days,* and *he will be raised* is found also in 9:31.

An article by R. Kinnis ("An Analysis of Mark 10:32-34" *NovTest* 18.2.1976, pp. 81-100) makes the suggestion that this third prediction was a hymn that began with "was delivered" and ended with "he will be raised." The author suggests that the middle three couplets (condemn/deliver, mock/spit, and scourge/kill) were an expansion of the idea of rejection, and in McKinnis' view was a very "Jewish-Christian anti-Jewish polemic."

55. Precedence (ii)
(10:35-45) = Matt 20:20-28

10 ³⁵ Then James and John, Zebedee's sons, approached him. "Rabbi," they said, "we wish you to do something for us." ³⁶ "What is it you want me to do for you?" he asked. ³⁷ They replied, "Give us the right to sit with you, one at the right, the other at your left, in your triumph." ³⁸ "You do not know what you are asking," Jesus said to them. "Can you drink the cup that I drink or be baptized with the baptism I am baptized with?" ³⁹ "We can," they answered. "The cup that I drink," Jesus said to them, "you shall drink, and the baptism I am baptized with shall be your baptism. ⁴⁰ But to sit at my right or my left is not mine to give; it is for those to whom it has been assigned." ⁴¹ On hearing of this, the ten were indignant with James and John. ⁴² So Jesus called them together to him and said, "You are aware that those who are recognized as rulers among the foreigners lord it over their subjects, and their great men impose their authority. ⁴³ That is not the way with you; among you, anyone who wants to be great must be your servant, ⁴⁴ and if anyone among you wishes to be first, he must be the slave of all. ⁴⁵ For The Man did not come to be served, but to serve, and to give himself as a ransom for the community."

Comment

Although this section appropriately links the fate of the disciples with that of the master, it is not easy for any form-critical analysis to describe its intent. Is it a composition of the community (especially with regard to vv. 38-40) after the events of the passion? Is it—as has been suggested—an apothegm of a somewhat extended character? Was the original form—assuming it was a community composition—vv. 35-37 followed by vv. 42-45? Perhaps such evaluations are a little too sceptical, for it may be that there is here a story from the early tradition which had not yet become fixed into "pronouncement" form. We may hazard the suggestion that there are two separate stories here, one which concerned James and John, and the ensuing vv. 41-45 attached to the original by subject matter.

Matthew's version of the incident has the mother of the two sons (20:20) asking for favorable treatment for them, whereas in the version before us, it is the sons themselves who ask for preference. It appears that the story circulated in more than one form, for Mark knows a version in which the questions are put by James and John without the intervention of the mother.

There seem to be good grounds for accepting the core of this narrative as belonging to the earliest tradition, if only because of the mention of names. Perhaps a later tradition might have had some interest in hurting the somewhat overambitious disciples. (It has been suggested from time to time that Matthew's account of the mother's request is a deliberate attempt to soften criticism of the two disciples.)

Notes

35. *James and John:* Cf. 1:19. The invariable order of these two names in our gospels would suggest that James was the elder of the two.

approached (Greek *prosporeuontai*): Mark uses the verb *poreuomai* (I draw near) and its compounds with much regularity.

we wish you: The initial request of James and John is not in Matthew's version, and here in Mark the request begins innocently enough.

36. The grammatical details of the Greek as between various manuscripts are more technical than illuminating, save for the fact that one manuscript (D) of the fifth or sixth century omits the Greek *ti thelete* (what is it that you wish?) leaving a text of "I will do it for you." Matt 20:21 simply has "What do you want?" addressed in the singular to the mother.

37. *right:* The principal place of honor was always considered to be at the right hand, and next in honor the place at the *left,* even though bad news, unwelcome

events, and even ill omens were thought to come from the left (cf. Latin *sinister* = "left").

in your triumph: It is the contention of Lohmeyer (p. 221) that Matthew's ". . . in your Kingdom" (20:21) is the original reading. But the Markan phrase before us may be intended to have some reference to a future glory beyond the ministry, in the sense of the *parousia* expectation of the early community. Whatever may be the correct tradition as between "Kingdom" and "glory," the two are represented as believing that the triumph of Jesus in a Kingdom, of which they had many times heard him speak, was very near. If the saying about "thrones" (cf. Matt 19:28 = Luke 22:30) is historically in context (though Mark omits it in the section on true riches) and so had already been spoken, then James and John wished to secure principal places for themselves. It is possible that they were thinking instead of chief seats at the messianic banquet. But in either event, the two had failed to understand the true meaning and the inevitable end of the journey to Jerusalem and the warnings of suffering and death in the words of Jesus. If our gospels are historically accurate and there had been three predictions (in whatever form) of suffering and death and of the cost of discipleship associated with that passion, then the warnings had fallen on deaf ears.

38,39. Jesus' demand that the disciples face the inevitable consequences of his suffering, coupled with the sharp rebuke that they are wholly ignorant of what they are asking, is met with the same brash confidence with which the original request had been made.

cup: As a synonym for suffering, the expression is found in 14:36 (cf. Matt 26:39, Luke 22:42). In the Old Testament the word is used both of joy (Pss 23:5, 116:13) and also of suffering (Ps 75:9, Isa 51:17-22, Jer 25:15, Ezek 23:31-34). It is found in Ugaritic as applying to a person's allotted portion or destiny (cf. in the New Testament Rev 14:9, 16:19, 17:4, 18:6). The use of the present tense in *I drink* (Greek *ho ego pinō,* literally "I am drinking") is dramatic: it speaks of an experience already begun. Matt 20:22 has "the cup I am about to drink."

baptism: Although the word (Greek *baptisma)* is not found in the Old Testament as meaning suffering, the idea of water as symbolizing disaster is often found (cf. Pss 42:7; 69:2,15; Isa 43:2) and in ordinary Greek speech it was a common expression to denote being flooded or overwhelmed. Luke 12:50 has "I have a baptism in which to be baptized" in this sense. The "cup" motif figures both in the narratives of the Last Supper and Gethsemane (14:24,36). Though it is possible that *baptism* and *cup* were thought of by Mark and his community as having sacramental significance (cf. Lohmeyer, p. 223), it is likely that this was an utterance of Jesus and not the creation of the primitive community. Rom 6:3 ("We have been baptized into his death") may be a reminiscence of this saying, but equally it may be an independent reflection of the meaning of the identification of the believer with the passion and resurrection of Jesus.

It is worthy of passing mention here that Matthew omits the "baptism" saying. If—as is generally assumed—Matthew knew the Markan tradition, then his omission of this important synonym for the death of Jesus is to say the least notable.

The judgment that what we have before us is a prophecy after the event, and a retrojection from the deaths of James and John, is to place too much confidence in the purported tradition of Papias (c. A.D. 140) that both brothers died martyrs' deaths. While the death of James is recorded in Acts 12:2, we have no certain information about the fate of John. The testimony of Papias is at the very best secondhand and from unreliable sources at that. The results can be summarized as follows:

1. An editor of the *Chronicle of Philip of Side* (c. A.D. 450) says, "Papias in the second book says that John the Theologian and James his brother were killed by the Jews." Philip of Side has never been regarded as a reliable historian, and both he and his editor may well have misquoted or misunderstood Papias. The statement said to be found in Papias is repeated by the ninth century. Gregory Hamartolus, in the interests of finding in it a fulfilment of Mark 10:39.

2. Two calendars (Syriac fifth century and that of Carthage in the sixth century) both use December 27 as the commemoration of the martyrdom of James and John the apostles at Jerusalem. It is to be noted that the Carthage calendar reads *S. Johannis Baptistae et Jacobi apostoli . . . .* , but *Baptistae* is probably a mistake for *Evangelistae.*

All in all, this so-called Papias tradition is not impressive. No tradition from Asia Minor mentions the martyrdom of John, Irenaeus is silent on the matter, and Eusebius (who had read Papias) makes no mention of any such event as a double martyrdom.

S. Legasse in a well-argued article ("Approche de l'Épisode préévangelique des Fils de Zébedée: Marc X:35-40 par," *NTS* 20.2.1974, pp. 161-77) contends that this episode of the two sons is independent of the following vv. 41-45 and is firmly rooted in Jewish and Jewish-Christian apocalyptic eschatology. In such a setting, "cup" and "baptism" are symbols of subordination to the divine will but do not necessarily imply death or martyrdom. The author finds the mention of James and John to be enigmatic; either they are mentioned as an embellishment for a saying, or they are meant to be taken as typical of all true discipleship. But the themes of suffering and future glory are taken as following upon the same themes associated with the ministry and person of Jesus. With this article, cf. V. Howard, "Did Jesus Speak About His Own Death?" *CBQ* 39.4.1977, pp. 512-77, where it is rightly observed that the content of vv. 38,39 is different from other synoptic texts that speak of the passion of Jesus. Aware of the possibility of a violent end to his ministry, he was remembered as having demanded of his disciples a willingness to share the same fate.

40. The promise is made by Jesus to share in the sufferings to come, but precedence is a matter which is not his to bestow. Matt 20:23 has ". . . but is for those for whom it is prepared by my Father"—and some Markan texts have assimilated this reading. Textually there are some interesting variations in this verse of Mark. Some manuscripts read: ". . . is not mine to give to you." Others, in copying the Greek uncials, read (in effect): ". . . it is for others to whom it has been assigned" instead of *but for those to whom.* Uncials, without marks of punctuation, could easily be read as *allois* instead of *all'hois.* It is now impossible to determine what the original text was meant to read.

assigned (Greek *hētoimastai):* The Greek merely refers to the Father's counsel and will and is not to be taken as implying any notion of predestination.

41. The remainder of this section is apparently an artificial construction of sayings,

both in Matthew and Luke, and joined to the previous narrative by *On hearing this,
the ten* . . . The saying on rank is paralleled by Luke 22:24-27 in the account of the
Passion, and in this parallel the element of narrative is small. It is probable that
teaching on what constitutes greatness was given by Jesus on far more than one
occasion, but the Lucan and Markan traditions appear to be a doublet. But of the two,
which is the original? Referring to Matthew at this point is of little help, except to
demonstrate that Mark is still following Matthew's order. *The ten* links this collection
of sayings with the two sons—who presumably are regarded as not being present—
and here we may possibly argue that Mark is following Matthew. In addition teaching
on "greatness = service" seems naturally to follow upon a dispute about precedence.
The Lucan scheme (after the Last Supper, a short discourse on service, followed by
the controversy over greatness) is impossible to credit as the original context. Luke
22:24-26 must be regarded as an insertion.

42. *those who are recognized:* There is a strong note of irony here—on this, many
commentators agree. But the Greek *(hoi dokountes archein)* is not easy to render into
English (possible translations include "so-called rulers" or "those who are supposed to
rule"), and we have chosen to use a literal translation to catch the sense of Jesus'
apparent ironic detachment. The note of irony is emphasized in Luke 22:25 (those
who are called rulers). Matt 20:25 simply has "rulers," and Luke 22:25 has "kings."

their great men: Cf. 6:21. This is in parallel to *rulers.*

impose their authority (Greek *katakurieuō):* The meaning is "to exercise total control over"—cf. *LXX* Gen 1:28, 9:1; Pss 9:26, 109:2. Matthew's verb *(katexousiazō,*
20:25) is used in its simple form at Luke 22:25, though Luke also has *kurieousin,* a
somewhat less emphatic form than Mark's verb here.

43. *That is not the way:* The present tense is emphatic and dramatic, and some
manuscripts of later dates have changed it to future tense, as in Matthew. Our suggestion is that the Matthean version is the original (cf. Luke 22:26) and that Mark's
present tense represents the urgency of his own community's situation: this is not the
time to be engaged in debate about precedence or authority.

44. Taylor (p. 444) calls attention to the parallelisms in vv. 42-44, with a similar
structure to be found in Luke 22:26 (where the grammar and vocabulary are different,
presumably reflecting independent translation from the Aramaic).

It is to be noted that there is a difference between *servant* (Greek *diakonos)* in v. 43
and *slave (doulos)* in v. 44. The difference, in this context, ought not to be pressed, for
the sense is the same.

45. This verse is without question a *crux interpretum* in the gospels, and we will
first deal with the grammatical features before passing on to interpretation.

a. The structure of the saying is a well-known feature of Semitic parallelism using
synonyms.

b. Another Semitic feature is to be found in the negative-positive *did not come to be
served but to serve.*

c. The best way to treat *For* (Greek *gar)* in the present instance is to read it as an
emphatic "For indeed."

d. The expression *did not come* is best interpreted as of Jesus looking back over the
ministry from the time of speaking.

e. *to serve* (Greek *diakoneō*) is most often used in classical and Hellenistic Greek referring to serving at table, but it is certainly not confined to that meaning.

f. *to give himself* was a fairly common Greek description for the death of soldiers, and it is found in 1 Macc 2:50 and 6:44 in a similar sense.

g. In the New Testament the word *ransom* (Greek *lutron*) is found only here and in Matt 20:28, though *antilutron* is found in 1 Tim 2:6 with a similar meaning. In classical and Hellenistic Greek the word is used in two principal technical senses: the price for the return of a captive, and the purchase price for the manumission of slaves. In the Septuagint (generally used in the plural), it carries the same meaning. Examples of the idea in later Judaism are in 2 Macc 7:37; and in 4 Macc 1:11, 17:22. Essentially the meaning is that of redemption or deliverance by purchase.

h. The word *for* (Greek *anti*) can mean either "on behalf of" or "instead of." As "instead of," it is used in the New Testament at Matt 2:22, 5:38; Luke 11:11; John 1:16; Rom 12:17; 1 Thess 5:15; 1 Peter 3:9; 1 Cor 11:15; Heb 12:16; and James 4:15.

i. The Greek word *pollōn (the community)* is crucial to our understanding of this verse. Readers of the New Testament will be aware of this explanatory clause in the accounts of the Last Supper in Matt 26:28 and Mark 14:24, both in covenantal contexts. Generally it is assumed that the Greek ought rightly to be rendered as "for all" —how else can one explain the Pauline insight that the sacrificial ministry and death of Jesus was of universal efficacy? (In fact the Pauline insight derives from the concept of the universality of sin, for which any remedy God provides must equally be potentially universal in scope; it does not derive from the phrase before us, nor from the accounts of the Last Supper.)

So far as our present text is concerned, the Greek phrase *lutron anti pollōn* which we have translated as a "ransom for the community," there is a close parallel in Isa 53:10-12. The Greek of *LXX* here has variant readings, and the Hebrew text is confused and difficult to reconstruct. What we have at present is:

> 11. "By his knowledge(?) shall the Righteous One vindicate:
> my Servant shall (. . . .) the many,
> he will bear their sins."

The first Isaiah scroll from Qumran has the same reading. Unfortunately we have at present no indication of what the missing word before "the many" might have been, though the late W. F. Albright maintained that if the text had originally read "my Servant shall redeem the many," the resulting Hebrew scansion would be good.

"The many" is emphasized in Dan 12:2,10 in a chapter which provides the background for much Essene literature. But here again in Daniel we have a confused Hebrew text, itself reflected in the Septuagint and in Theodotion's revision of the Septuagint. Theodotion has ". . . and from the righteous ones of the many" (v. 3). What can be gleaned with confidence from Dan 12:3 is "And those who vindicate the many [shall be] like the everlasting stars." It seems possible to conclude that in Isa 53:10-12 and Dan 12:2,10 we have the ultimate and the mediate sources of the Essene concentration on "the many" (Hebrew *ha-rabbîm*) as background for Matt 20:28, 26:28 and Mark 10:45, 14:24. It is from this point that we may now examine in an appended note the implications of "the many" for the text before us.

Appended Note: "The Many"

"The many" of the texts of Isaiah and Daniel, later given emphasis by the Essenes as signifying the elect Essene community, has a long ancestry as a term for the Covenant people. (The attitude of the Essenes toward non-Essene Israelites is still obscure, but there is no doubt as to the Essene claim to be "Israel.") It is possible that Matt 24:31, where membership in the messianic community by no means implies inclusion among the elect, represents a rejection by Jesus of the exclusive aspects of Essenism.

The "Righteous One" as a designation for a leader, a redeemer figure on messianic lines, has in Isa 53:10-12 a link with the "servant" which should not be overlooked, and the correlation of the two titles is in a redemptive context. In Isaiah, in Daniel, and in the text before us we find again "the many" as the object of redemptive activity, as we shall find it again in the narrative of the Last Supper. It is therefore imperative for any understanding of the New Testament that for all the emphasis (especially in Paul) on the adjective *new* to describe the results of the work of Jesus there is never for a moment a suggestion that there is a "new" Israel. On the contrary, it is necessary for salvation to be incorporated into that messianic community which is heir to, and continuous with, the Israel of the Mosaic Covenant. It is clear that "the many" (= "the community") in the interpretative liturgical texts of Matt 26:28 and Mark 14:24 was sufficient explanation of the redemptive death of Jesus.

We have very little firm information about the liturgical practices of the Essenes, but what does seem clear is that *the community* was a well-established phrase reaching back to second Isaiah if not earlier. So hallowed by time was it that, for all the obscurities of the Hebrew text of second Isaiah, it had to be used. Given the Essenes' insistence that they were Israel, then the equation *the community* = Israel has far wider implications than our modern English can hope to convey.

It will be observed that the Greek *pollōn* (many) has no definite article in the texts under consideration. But at the time of the compilation of the New Testament, there was wide variation in the use or nonuse of the definite article in *koinē* Greek, and the same wide variation or inconsistency is found in the Dead Sea Scrolls in the use of the definite article before *rabbîm* (many). In many cases the word is simply *rabbîm,* while in many others the form is (correctly) *ha-rabbîm.* We are therefore wholly justified in translating the *pollōn* of our Greek texts as *the community,* even where grammatically we might have expected *tōn pollōn.*

This is not all. It is clear from the rabbinic writings that *ha-rabbîm* was understood as meaning the generality of the Covenant people, and the phrase *rĕshût ha-rabbîm* ("the public domain," found in the Mishnah *Shabbath* 9.1) to name but one, is of frequent occurrence.

We must now pass to some consideration of the bearing of all this on the meaning of the phrase *to give himself a ransom for the community*. Is this a reference to the death of Jesus as in some sense sacrificial, or is it—in general terms—a statement of a life wholly given to the good of the Covenant people? It is not too much to say that for Matthew and Mark, and for Paul as our earliest theological commentator on the ministry, Jesus' own interpretation of his death as sacrificial was in the context of the Last Supper. Nevertheless in the phrase under consideration the words *give himself* carry something more by way of meaning than would be conveyed by "a useful and dedicated life." They are part of a whole context in which it is assumed that the service, ministry, and impending death of Jesus affected *in potentia* the whole Covenant community. In the light of all this, it is instructive to look at a passage in the *Pirqê Abôth* (v. 18, in the R. H. Charles translation of v. 21: *The Apocrypha and Pseudepigrapha of the Old Testament in English,* Oxford: The Clarendon Press, 1913; reprinted 1977, p. 709). Set against that is the translation of Albright-Mann in the AB *Matthew,* p. 245: "Everyone who clears the community of guilt, sin does not enter by his instrumentality; but everyone who implicates the community in sin, they cannot perform an act of repentance through him. Moses was free of guilt and cleared the community of guilt; the freedom of the community from guilt was dependent on it, as it is said: 'The right judgments of Yahweh he carried out in Israel' [Deut 33:21]. Jereboam son of Nebat sinned and implicated the community in sin: the sin of the community was dependent on him, as it is said: 'The sin of Jereboam the son of Nebat, by which he brought condemnation on Israel for sin' (1 Kgs 14:16)." No attribution of authorship is made in this extract, and the presumption is that it is therefore early. Absent from it is the Pharisee tradition with its sharp distinction between sinner and righteous, innocent and guilty. What we have instead is the unformed point of view with regard to vindication which we saw to be the case in second Isaiah and Daniel, coupled with what has come to be called "corporate personality" (in which connection, cf. Psalm 72). What does appear to be excluded is an "exemplarist" view, both with respect to Jesus and also with respect to Moses in the *Pirqê Abôth.* Indeed at one level of the human experience an example can be so overwhelmingly different from those called to imitate it as to call forth despair. What is being said about Jesus' life of service and about his giving of himself is that both of these affect the community in a way beyond mere example, far more in line with the "servant, the righteous one" of Isaiah 53:11. Of course aware of our common humanity, we realize that human conduct of any kind is not without its universal effects, but Mark 10:45 is far more than that. It encompasses the notion of a single, all-embracing figure in whom all the inchoate themes of sin, repentance, redemption, and vindication come together.

The foregoing considerations inevitably raise the question of the genuineness of the sayings. Inevitably the suggestion has been made from time to time that we are confronted with a particularly Pauline understanding of redemption here. This is hardly the case. As we observed earlier, the distinctive contribution of Paul to the theology of redemption was the notion of its universal applicability, and this we do not find here. On the contrary, Jesus is represented as seeing his self-giving mission and death in terms of the Covenant people (= "the many"), in much the same way that he interpreted his mission in 7:27. We may freely admit that the idea of "service to death" is found in Phil 2:7, but the word *ransom* in the Pauline corpus is never used in the restrictive sense of "the community" but "for all" (1 Tim 2:6) and "for us" (Titus 2:14). If Paul is responsible—as he is—for the theological shift from a "ministry within Judaism" to a "ministry of universal significance," he must have had a starting point within the tradition of Jesus' work and words: we suggest that 10:45 was one such starting point in the tradition. Furthermore, apart from 10:45 (= Matt 20:28), it is possible that this "ransom" saying is reflected in Luke 22:27 ("Here am I among you as one who serves").

The text is also notable for *The Man* in what can only be described as a "representative" or "authoritative" sense. We have had occasion in previous instances to see the ambivalence between The Man as a corporate term and its use as applying to Jesus only, between the term as it involved a suffering community and its use to describe Jesus as one who suffered and was now glorified. Jesus, as The Man, must pass through passion and death to glory, but part of that ministry and vocation is to serve and to give his life as a ransom for "the many." The few representatives of the Covenant people ("the saints") in Daniel have in Mark 10:45 been focused sharply on one individual, but in contrast with Daniel there is a distinction between the followers and The Man: they have been exhorted to serve others, to follow the part of humility, to copy the example he has set, but for him there is now a solitary and exclusive vocation—to be a ransom for the community. Perhaps Luke's text (22:27), to which we called attention above, is the original reading, and the saying was "I did not come to be served . . ." It is even possible that the Matthean (and later the Markan, by imitation) version of the saying is a later doctrinal modification.

The combination of "The Man" and "ransom" has occupied the attention of numerous commentators, and it will be necessary to re-examine the word *lutron* in the light of this combination, for in view of subsequent usage it is well not to read into the verse some of the dominant theological concerns of a later age. It is important to remember that in the Septuagint *lutron* and its associated verb *lutroō* there is no suggestion of a kind of substitute sin offering. On the contrary, Isa 53:11 must be read in the light of the emphasis given to the word as referring to God's mighty act by which the deliverance from Egypt was achieved (Exod 6:6, 15:16; Deut 7:8, 9:26; Isa 43:1; Mic 6:4) and of the act of deliverance from the exile (Isa 52:3, 62:12; Mic 4:10; Jer 16:14). Nowhere are the two Greek words used of a sin offering. Instead the sense is that of God as champion of his people, coming to intervene for the deliverance from slavery to freedom. This is precisely the understanding of the Proclamation (the gospel) which informed and enthused the disciples according to Luke 24:21. In that case, we are once more in the presence of an understanding of Daniel 7, with its vision of the final victory of the "saints of the most High" in association with a triumphant "Son of Man." The one who heralds the dawning Reign of God ushers in its power to save and deliver through exorcism and healing, proclaims how that his final service in freeing the community will be to give his life as servant-deliverer.

As a further link in the chain between Daniel 7, Isaiah 53, and the saying before us, and perhaps also in defense of the Lucan "servant" saying (22:27), we may refer to Morna D. Hooker *(The Son of Man in Mark,* Montreal: McGill University Press, 1967, pp. 145-46) for the illuminating suggestion that Luke links the "servant" theme with the wholly new order being inaugurated by the New Covenant in the blood of Jesus at the Last Supper (22:20), and with the Kingdom being "covenanted" to the disciples, just as it had been "covenanted" to Jesus by the Father. The reminder of Daniel 7, with the Kingdom being given to the saints, or to The Man, is—for Hooker—forcible and persuasive. The "Covenant" for Israel was based on God's redeeming act in the Exodus, and the "New Covenant" of Jer 31:31-34 belongs to a future realm of another redeeming act. Given the links seen by Hooker between the "covenanted Kingdom" of Luke 22:28,29 and Daniel 7, between the same Lucan texts and Matt 19:28 and Mark 10:45, it is not surprising to find the author saying, "If our understanding of *lutron* is correct, then it was a true insight which linked the term 'Son of Man' with the idea expressed in Mark 10:45. Once again, it is *precisely because he is Son of Man and as Son of Man that Jesus suffers.* We have here, not a 'fusion' between the term 'Son of Man' and some other concept, but an expression of something which is involved in being Son of Man." (Hooker, p. 146-47.)

If, however, we find reason to interpret *ransom* in terms of an Old Testament emphasis on the delivering power of God to rescue and restore Israel, we are far removed from later interpretations of this verse as a "proof text" for substitutionary atonement. The much-canvassed notion of vicarious suffering is but the reverse side of "exemplarist" atonement—in neither case is sinful humanity (which alone is responsible for sinful rebellion against God) involved at all. It is a far cry from the Pauline expression of our being "in Adam" (i.e., "solid with" Adam) in our sinful state to a later medieval idea of God "imputing" righteousness to us through the redeeming work of Jesus.

Paul's identification of humanity with Adam in the state of sin is paralleled by his identification of the restored and redeemed with the risen Lord—there is a metaphysical relationship between humanity/Adam and believer/Christ which is expressed in the *Pirqê Abôth* as Israel/Moses and Israel/Jereboam. It is important to notice that in the whole process of identification, whether of sinfulness or of vindication, there is neither for the *Pirqê Abôth* nor for Paul any sense of "substitution."

This is not the place to explore the roots of medieval—and later—ideas of "substitutionary" or "vicarious" atonement in Tertullian and Augustine, with their full flowering in Anselm's *Cur Deus Homo;* but here it can safely be said that Irenaeus of Lyons, both in his *Epideixis* and *Adversus Haereses,* came far closer to Paul and to the intent of *ransom for the community* than most subsequent writers. (Cf. Gustav Wingren, *Man and the Incarnation,* Edinburgh and London: Oliver and Boyd, 1957.)

Additional Reading

Barrett, C. K. "The Background of Mark 10.45." In *New Testament Essays,* edited by A. J. B. Higgins. Manchester University Press, 1967, pp. 1-18.

Buchel, F. *TWNT* Vol. 4 (English translation, 1967) art. *lutron,* pp. 340-49.

Lindars, Barnabas. "Salvation Proclaimed: VII—Mark 10.45: A Ransom for Many." *ET* 93.1982, pp. 292-95.

Moulder, W. J. "The Old Testament Background and the Interpretation of Mark 10.45." *NTS* 24.1979, pp. 120-27.

Taylor, Vincent. *Jesus and His Sacrifice.* London: Macmillan, 1943, pp. 99-105.

56. The Healing of the Blind Man (10:46-52) = Matt 20:29-34; Luke 18:35-43

10 46 They came to Jericho. As he was leaving Jericho with his disciples and a large crowd, a blind man, the son of Timaeus (Bar Timaeus), was sitting and begging by the road. 47 Hearing that it was Jesus of Nazareth, he began to shout, "Jesus! Son of David! Have pity of me!" 48 Many of the people rebuked him, telling him to be silent. But he shouted all the more, "Son of David, have pity on me!" 49 Jesus stood still and said, "Call him." They called the blind man, telling him, "Take courage; stand up—he is calling you." 50 He threw off his

himation, jumped up, and came to Jesus. [51] Jesus said to him, "What do you want me to do for you?" "Rabbi," the blind man said, "I want to see again." [52] "Go," Jesus said to him, "your faith has made you well." At once he recovered his sight and followed him on the road.

Comment

Mark is still following Matthew's order, but there are evident signs that he has used his own superior and probably eyewitness account of this incident. The precise character of the incident raises some questions. Was it intended as a miracle story? If it was, then it is still a long way from the highly stylized form which miracle narratives generally have. Is the main point of the story the climax in *your faith has made you well?* If so, the miracle is almost a secondary element.

The narrative stands—as it does in Matthew but not in Luke—immediately before the entry into Jerusalem and the final triumph of the passion. We suggest that Mark left the story here—his final miracle account—because the request of the blind man to see again precisely fitted what the evangelist thought to be the principal spiritual need of his community, to see again the main theme of his gospel—the glory and the triumph of Jesus through apparent disaster and defeat.

Notes

46. *Jericho:* The old city was in ruinous state by the first century, but the new city had been rebuilt by Herod the Great as the location of his winter palace, and by the time of this incident it was a place of great beauty. It was five miles west of the Jordan and a little more than fifteen miles northeast of Jerusalem. The road between the two cities was desolate and often unsafe (as we learn from Luke 11:30), but it was much used, especially in times of pilgrimage feasts such as Passover. The sight of a blind beggar just outside the city gates would be a common experience. Luke places the story before the arrival in Jericho (18:35), presumably because of his use of the story of Zacchaeus in 19:1-10.

the son of Timaeus (Bar Timaeus): The Greek of Mark (literally "Bartimaeus, son of Timaeus") is a conflation of the Greek with the Aramaic, so that what we have in effect is *son of Timaeus* twice. Our translation is meant to avoid the confusion. Mark alone gives the man's name, and since he very rarely provides us with names, this appears to provide us with a note of authenticity. Matt 20:30 speaks of "two blind men" seeking help, and the whole pericope revolves around the same two men. It is impossible to say whether there was originally a tradition of two blind men (which Mark ignored because he had access to a better, eyewitness tradition), or whether at some stage a scribe unfamiliar with the conflation of Greek and Aramaic changed the pericope into plural form. If the conventional wisdom of the two-document hypothesis is followed, then Mark is the original text, and Matthew has misconceived the conflation and made two men out of a single, duplicated name.

begging (Greek *prosaitēs*): Though found in John 9:8, the word is late, not being found either in classical Greek or the Septuagint. Some manuscripts of Mark substitute *prosaiton.*

47. Presumably the *large crowd* referred to in v. 46 consisted of people from Jericho or going on pilgrimage to Passover, and it is not necessary to assume that the crowd consisted simply of those accompanying Jesus.

Jesus of Nazareth: The Greek present tense is used in the phrase we have translated as *Hearing that it was* . . . (literally "hearing that it is . . .").

Son of David: Mark's use of this term is found only here and in v. 48, and the evangelist is following his sources in Matthew and Luke, but in so following them it is hard to determine what meaning Mark may have invested in this phrase. The phrase is broadly "messianic," with nationalist hope and centered on a Davidic king (cf. *Pss Sol* 17:21 or in the DSS 4Q *Patriarchal Blessings* 1:34) with some reference back to the Old Testament (cf. Ps 110:1-5, Jer 23:5-6, Ezek 34:23-24). Matthew and Luke make use of the phrase quite freely, however.

48. *rebuked him:* The man's cry for help was unwelcome to some in the crowd—because they wished to hear Jesus?—but the blind man persisted in his call for help. Whether Jesus heard the cry *"Son of David!"* we cannot know—if he did, he made no attempt to silence it. We may contrast this with 8:30, where a command to silence is made. Presumably at this stage in the ministry and its approaching climax, challenges to popular (or even individual) enthusiasm were irrelevant.

49,50. The narrative here has all the signs of an eyewitness account: Both Matthew and Luke simply provide a matter-of-fact account in indirect speech. There is none of the vivid detail of "Take courage . . . he is calling you," let alone the detail of v. 50.

threw off (Greek *apobalon*): Cf. Heb 10:35. The usage in Greek is classical and is also found in the Septuagint, though Lohmeyer (p. 285) prefers the reading *epibalon,* found in two manuscripts and which conveys the sense of "laying aside." In any event the man would not have been wearing his himation but would have left it spread on the ground to receive alms and gifts. It is possible—if we may judge from this verse that he came to Jesus without assistance—that the man was not totally blind.

51. *Rabbi* (Greek *Rabbouni*): The word *rabbouni* is found only here in Mark and is a stronger word than *rabbei,* conveying more the sense of "master" or "sir." Matthew and Luke have *kurie* (master, sir, lord), and some manuscripts of Mark have assimilated the Greek of the other evangelists. It is noteworthy that *Son of David* is the expression used by Bartimaeus before he has caught Jesus' attention, and then, when standing before Jesus, he speaks to him far more reverentially. The difficulty is to decide whether the evangelists are reproducing a tradition or refashioning the tradition for theological purposes, progressing from an enthusiastic association of Jesus with the glories of Jerusalem as a Davidic city to a recognition of Jesus as (in some sense) "lord" of healing and restoration. It seems to us far more probable that the purpose of Matthew and Mark (though not Luke) is to emphasize the importance of

"seeing" Jesus as the agent of God, and "seeing" the ensuing passion as the final act in the warfare between God and Satan.

again: The Greek verb *(anablepsō)* may perhaps imply that the man was once able to see. In John 9:11,15,18 the verb is used of the man born blind.

52. *your faith has made you well:* Matt 20:34 records that Jesus touched the eyes of the two blind men, and Luke 18:42 has the command "receive your sight," but the Markan narrative is striking in that there is no action or word of Jesus to precede or accompany the healing. For *faith* cf. 2:5—the faith in both instances is the confirming trust in God's power to heal through Jesus.

followed: The word does not imply that the man followed Jesus as a disciple and may only mean that he joined the crowd of those going to Jerusalem. The fact that Mark records the man's name may indicate that Bartimaeus was known to members of the Markan community. Lane (p. 389) thinks that the evangelist "may have in mind" a contrast between the Son of David who has among his followers the former blind man, and the King David who saw only obstacles to the conquest of Jerusalem in the blind and the lame (2 Sam 6:5). Cf. " 'And He Followed Him': Miracles and Discipleship in Mark 10:46-52," P. J. Achtemeier, *Semeia* 11.1978, pp. 115-45.

Appendix to Chapter 10: The "Secret Gospel"

One of the difficulties attendant upon writing a commentary is that the passage often renders some matters of controversy, hotly debated in their own time, matters of mere curiosity at a later date. To some the debate in the mid-seventies concerning the possibility of a secret—and ecclesiastically suppressed—edition of Mark may be no more than a passing whim on the part of some interested academic scholars. But it would be irresponsible on the part of any commentator on Mark, even at this remove, to ignore the furor caused by one scholar in 1975.

The facts in the case are not in dispute: it is far otherwise with the interpretation of the facts. The facts can be set out conveniently as follows:

1. In 1958 a scholar named Morton Smith discovered in the Greek Orthodox monastery of Mar Saba (a few miles southeast of Jerusalem) a Greek text, written in eighteenth-century script on the final blank three pages of a seventeenth-century edition of the letters of Ignatius of Antioch.

2. The first line of this text indicated that it was a letter to one Theodore (otherwise unknown), and the writer was said to be Clement of Alexandria. The attribution to Clement cannot with our present knowledge be checked, but it is fair to say that whatever the origin of the letter, it was not the work of the eighteenth-century copyist.

3. The letter from Clement complains of the Carpocratians, a second-century Gnostic sect, on the grounds that they appeal to an apocryphal gospel attributed to another writer, and Clement speaks of the relationship of this *apocryphon* to the Gospel of Mark. Clement commends Theodorus for silencing the Carpocratians and their "unspeakable teachings," and goes on to warn him that they have been saying things about the gospel of Mark which are totally untrue. Then he rehearses the beginnings of the Markan-Alexandrian tradition (Mark, having written in Rome an account of the Lord's doing came to Alexandria after Peter's martyrdom, bringing with him his own and Peter's notes). In Alexandria, Mark wrote a "more spiritual gospel" for the use of "those being perfected."

4. Of this writing of a "more spiritual gospel," the letter from Clement goes on to say that Mark did not divulge things which were not to be spoken, did not commit to writing "the secret teachings of the Lord," but that he added stories to those already written, and introduced some sayings of which he had the interpretation, and which "as a master" he knew would lead the hearers "into the inner sanctuary hidden by seven veils." To all of this we must return later. But after this account, the whole matter becomes confused and confusing.

5. The founder of the Gnostic sect, Carpocrates, suborned a presbyter of Alexandria, obtained from him a copy of this "secret gospel," and began to interpret it in accordance with his "blasphemous and carnal teaching," and "polluted it" by mixing it with "shameless lies." Theodore is then warned not to believe that the Carpocratian form is the "secret gospel."

6. Then come answers to questions posed by Theodore in refutation of the falsifications being put about. The "secret gospel" apparently inserted a story between 10:32 and 10:34, which in essence declared that Jesus came to Bethany, where a woman whose brother had died prostrated herself with the cry "Son of David, have mercy on me." Jesus went with the woman to the tomb, from which there came a great cry. Jesus then rolled away the stone, went in, and raised the youth, who looked at Jesus, loved him, and began to ask that he might be with him. Six days later Jesus told the youth what to do: the youth came to him wearing a linen cloth, stayed with him that night, and Jesus taught him the mysteries of the Kingdom.

7. The next paragraph indicates that following this version of the Lazarus story there followed: "And James and John came to him" (Mark 10:35). But "the other things" about which Theodore had enquired "are not found"—viz., "naked (man) with naked (man)." Clement

then adds that following the words "and he comes to Jericho" the secret gospel adds that the sister of the youth whom Jesus loved was there, together with his mother and Salome. However, he goes on, the "many other things" about which Theodore wrote are not found in this text and are false. The next paragraph breaks in the middle of the first sentence, and the recently discovered text ends there.

Some important points are to be noticed about the "secret gospel" of which Clement speaks:

1. Clement knew of a secret, more spiritual gospel composed by Mark.

2. This differs from the Carpocratian version.

3. There are significant reminiscences of the canonical gospels: Lazarus (John 11), and the young man of Mark 14:51-52.

Clement's letter shows clearly enough that there was a "hidden" side to Christianity from a very early stage, but we could infer that from Colossians, and there was a great deal of speculation in the worlds of both Hellenism and Judaism. Cf. *Gnosis: Festschrift für Hans Jonas,* edited by Ugo Bianchi, Martin Kraus, James M. Robinson, George Widengren, and Barbara Aland (Göttingen: Vandenhoeck and Ruprecht, 1978). Furthermore in this dimly lit landscape, there was a Carpocratian version of this secret and "informed" gospel. But the relation of either to the canonical gospels is baffling, for the insertion of the story we outlined at this place in question is highly artificial, and (save on the basis of John 11) add that Jesus should have been in Bethany with Martha and Mary. Yet the transformation of the raising of Lazarus (and the encounter with his sisters) with the raising of a young man at the instance of his mother is strange, unless the author/compiler had some ulterior motive.

Morton Smith concludes—in brief—that he has found the nature and essential character of Jesus' baptismal rites, that Jesus practiced magic and made of baptism a rite in which the neophyte became possessed by a spirit. Jesus himself, Smith contends, baptized at night, accompanied by an ecstatic experience which would appear to have included some kind of erotic union. This experience/ecstasy/union enabled the one initiated to perform the magical acts of Jesus himself and to ascend in hallucinatory fashion to heaven like the master. Here then—according to Smith—are to be found the true reasons for the persecution of Christians: (1) the pursuit of magic and (2) immoral behavior. The passage of time and the triumph of orthodoxy have alike taken care that all references to this kind of practice have been expunged.

How much evidence is there for Smith's hypothesis? The previous material has certainly established our agreement that there was a "secret gospel," but it does *not* establish a hidden gospel from which all references to Jesus' magical and erotic practices have been removed. Within the compass of a commentary intended for general interested readers and students, we must attempt to evaluate Smith's suggestions and assertions. There were two books written and published by Morton Smith—*The Secret Gospel: The Discovery and Interpretation of the Secret Gospel According to Mark* (New York: Harper and Row, 1973) and *Clement of Alexandria and a Secret Gospel of Mark* (Cambridge, Mass.: Harvard University Press, 1973). For convenience we may refer to the first in abbreviated form as *SG* and to the second as *CA*.

It is perhaps worthy of some note at the outset that Smith's predeliction is to prefer pagan and Jewish sources over Christian accounts of the origins of Christianity *(CA* p. 229), but the casual and untrained reader may find him/ herself impressed by Smith's claim that Jesus is repeatedly described as a magician in both Jewish and pagan sources—a claim which the evidence simply will not bear. Again Smith's knowledge of ancient magic is wide-ranging and impressive, and much is made in both books of the parallels between ancient magic and primitive Christianity. If some of the parallels appear to be more than a little bizarre, this is of small moment alongside the parallels and resemblances to Christianity which constantly come to our attention from many and diverse parts of the world. This should hardly surprise us, for human needs and human longings—not to mention myths—are the same the world over. What the Christian community claimed, both in the New Testament and later, was not that the faith was wholly original, but that it was the true reality transcending all myth, and giving divine credentials to what had only been the poetic form of human aspiration. But this is not all. The uncritical reader may draw the conclusion that some magical and erotic practices were firmly established in the ministry of Jesus, and that these are part and parcel of a "secret gospel" discovered by Smith but long ago rigidly suppressed by the embarrassed later Christian community. It is necessary to say emphatically that Smith found no such thing. He *did* find in a letter of Clement, discovered by accident, evidence of a secret gospel known to Clement, and of insertions into that gospel by the Carpocratian Gnostics. *Caveat emptor:* the picture outlined by Morton Smith is painted in lurid colors in the more popular of the two works, for we find it said that magic was practiced at Qumran *(SG* p. 83), there are attacks on John the Baptizer in the Qumran literature *(SG* p. 89), and the miracles and exorcisms of Jesus are those of a magician *(SG* p. 106).

Lest the preceding paragraph sound too negative, let us admit before we proceed that there are some signal contributions to scholarship in Smith's work. For example, we shall be indebted for a long time to the untiring energy with which he uncovered so much material about the followers of Carpocrates, and for the fascinating demonstration of sequences in the gospels of Mark and John—it is undeniable that possible links between the two gospels are much closer when the material from Clement is inserted.

Unfortunately we cannot let matters rest upon that congratulatory note. A simple series of inquiries among friends and students in the mid-seventies, when the two books became matters of popular (and not so popular) debate, revealed that it was *SG* which was being read, while *CA* was largely left to the side. This led to the unhappy result that the unwarranted speculations of *SG* (with its intriguing title) were being read and discussed, while the serious scholarship of *CA* was unknown or ignored. It is appropriate, therefore, given the importance of the rite in Christian tradition, to see what has been made by Smith of baptism and the basis of the letter from Clement. The rite, Smith informs us, was a "pietistic magical technique for entering the Kingdom of God par excellence, the heavens" *(SG* p. 109) and the intention of the rite was to unite Jesus' followers to him "by making his spirit possess them" *(SG* p. 108). There is more: the rite was administered by Jesus to chosen followers, singly, at night. For the neophyte, this baptismal garment was a linen cloth worn over the naked body, probably removed for the baptism proper. A footnote in *SG* pp. 113-14 informs us that unknown ceremonies followed—"manipulation, too, was probably involved; the stories of Jesus' miracles give a very large place to the use of his hands." This done, the disciple was possessed by Jesus' spirit and so was united with him. In union with Jesus, the disciple entered by hallucination into the heavens, and by this means was "set free" from the laws of the lower world. Freedom from the laws, Smith tells us, "may have resulted in completion of the spiritual union by physical union." *(SG* pp. 113-14). In any event there is a note of caution: "may have . . ." But the inferences drawn in this material from one account of a night visit are truly astounding. Smith will have us understand that the scholarly proof for all this is to be found in *CA*. This is unfair. It is one thing to suggest that there was a hidden side to some manifestations of early Christianity, but it is entirely another to avow that this can be traced back to magical—and erotic?—customs practiced by Jesus. But this is all of a piece with Smith's determination to find more accurate accounts of the origin of Christianity from among its critics and possible enemies than among its well-wishers.

If this was all, we could perhaps safely leave much of the popular *SG* on one side. But it is not. We find (p. 89) that John the Baptist "started Christianity . . . He did so by baptizing Jesus . . ." The origin of baptism itself, we are told, is as follows: "The Gospels tell us that the Baptist got his rite 'from God' (Mark 11:30ff.). That is to say, it was an 'inspiration'—his own idea—and he introduced it by his authority as a prophet (Matt 11:9 and parallels)" *(SG* p. 91). In the light of the evidence of lustral rites and practices of initiation at Qumran, this is unacceptable. Every idea has a history *(ex nihilo nihil fit),* and this applies as much to the history of baptism as to any other historical discipline. Unhappily there is little attempt at the dispassionate in Smith, and the plea in *CA* p. 229 that due attention be paid to pagan, Jewish, and "comparatively indifferent observers" is negated by Smith's preference for magic—of any kind and from whatever source.

We may be duly grateful for the thoughts in *CA* on synoptic relationships, and Smith offered us in this work some new insights into that thorny problem. There are some startling differences between the canonical Mark and the Clementine material: no one in Mark ever "stays with" (Greek *menein)* anyone else; only the blind address Jesus as "Son of David" (in the vocative); there is no "garden" in Mark; no one rolls away a stone (or anything else for that matter), and there is no "loud voice" as the subject of any sentence or statement. Smith finds in the preserved material parallels to Matthew (seventeen times), Mark (twenty-six times), Luke (nine times) and John (nine times). Perhaps at this point Smith is incautious, for he suggests that if there are items similar to Matthew, then Matthew must have known the longer (inserted) text.

The problem is to know what to make of the notorious gullibility of Clement—to which phenomenon Smith himself calls attention—and at the same time deal with the well-known fact that Alexandria itself was the source of all kinds of highly-colored imitation attempts at gospels. The inserted material, as it stands, reads more like a pastiche of elements from all four gospels and therefore of late origin.

There are, however, innuendoes in Smith's work, especially in *SG.* We are to infer—from the gospel records?—that bystanders at the garden tomb from which the young man was shouting so loudly understood that Jesus' concern for him was erotic, and that the evangelists undertook a massive deception operation to suppress knowledge of Jesus' covert initiation rites. Nowhere—though the fact is acknowledged—are we given any explanation as to why the Christian community continued the practice of baptism. If the original rites had erotic overtones, it is hardly likely that the persistence of the rite would not have set tongues wagging.

Above and beyond all this, in Smith's more popular work, there is the preoccupation with magic. Perhaps at the time when the two books appeared, there was a certain appropriateness about all this. The decade of 1965-75 was marked by a freakish dabbling in religion and the occult which also characterized the beginnings of the Christian era in the Romano-Hellenistic world. The material represented by the contents of Clement's letter would have been grist to the mill of any "religious" person of the time, critical or gullible. By way of example we have only to take account of the shifts in meaning, and coalescing of understanding, of various words in the third and fourth centuries B.C.—words such as *philosophus, theurgus, mathematicus,* and *astrologus.* While *goēs* (juggler, enchanter), *aqurtēs* (collector, fortune teller), *magicos* (one skilled in incantation), and *hariolus* (soothsayer) were virtually always condemnatory, by the second century B.C. *philosophos* and *magos* (astrologer) were in common use apparently interchangeable. Soon after the time of Cicero *philosophus* were being called "astrologers," and astrologers went by a variety of names. Wonder-workers and the stories associated with them multiplied—often for light dinner-party conversation. It is completely misleading for Smith—in spite of his vast erudition on the subject of magic—to tell us that Christians were subject to persecution on account of their magical practices. If that was so, then remarkably few areas of Roman society would have been immune. Not only was the persecution of Christians local and sporadic (it never became imperial policy until the reign of Diocletian, 284-305 A.D.), but the reasons given in various localities exhibit no single pattern. The secrecy surrounding Christianity—which arose for purposes of self-protection —could equally well have been charged against any number of contemporaneous groups; the charge of "atheism" referred to any unwillingness to accommodate to the imperial cult, and even Tacitus *(Annals* 13.32) says no more. The same author *(Annals* 15.44), when he adds to this charge against Christians the further one that Christians were hated for their "abominations," may reflect no more than a Roman of the old republican cast of mind with a distaste for something self-consciously aloof. Equally he may be indulging in the anti-Semitism never far from the surface in the minds of many influential Romans. Even the report of Athenagoras, the second-century apologist, openly admits that the enemies of the Church charged Christians with atheism, infanticide, and incest—deadly enough accusations—but nowhere does he mention magic. In truth the whole picture of magic, astrology, divination, along with the limits of civil tolerance and civil disobedience, were never clearly defined in Imperial Rome either by written law or common practice, and certainly with nowhere near the precision which Smith appears to find.

All in all, we can be grateful for the industry which has illuminated for us, if only momentarily, one aspect of the underworld of speculation which fastened, limpet-like, on early Christianity. We must not be expected to be equally thankful for speculation which has feasted on speculation.

For Further Reading
(in addition to the two books of Morton Smith):

Achtemeier, P. J. Review in *JBL* 93.1974, pp. 625-28.

Brown, R. E. "The Relation of 'The Secret Gospel of Mark' to the Fourth Gospel." *CBQ* 36.1974, pp. 466-85.

MacMullen, R. *Enemies of the Roman Order.* London: Oxford University Press; Cambridge, Mass.: Harvard University Press, 1967.

Quesnell, Q. "The Mar Saba Clementine: A Question of Evidence," *CBQ* 37.1975, pp. 48-67.

———. "A Reply to Morton Smith." *CBQ* 38.1976, pp. 200-03.

Smith, M. "On the Authenticity of the Mar Saba Letter of Clement." *CBQ* 38.1976, pp. 196-99.

PART V
ISRAEL UNDER JUDGMENT

57. The Entry into Jerusalem
(11:1-11) = Matt 21:1-11; Luke 19:28-40;
John 12:12-19

11 [1] They were now approaching Jerusalem, and when they reached Bethphage and Bethany at the Mount of Olives, he sent two of his disciples [2] with these instructions: "Go to the village opposite, and as soon as you enter it, you will find a young donkey tied up, which no man has yet ridden. Loose it, and bring it here. [3] If anyone asks you 'Why are you doing that?' say in reply, 'The Lord needs it and will send it back right away.'" [4] So they went, found a colt tied up at a doorway outside in the street, and loosed it. [5] Some bystanders asked them, "What are you doing, untying that colt?" [6] They replied just as Jesus had instructed them, and they allowed them to proceed. [7] They brought the colt to Jesus, threw their himatia on it, and he mounted it. [8] Many people spread their clothes on the road, while others spread brushwood which they had cut in the fields. [9] Those who were in front, and those behind, began to shout: "Hosanna! Blessed is the one who comes in the Lord's name! [10] Blessed is the coming kingdom of our father David! In the heights (cry out): Hosanna!" [11] He entered Jerusalem, and went into the temple, where he looked around at everything; but as the hour was late, he went out to Bethany with the Twelve.

Comment

It is a commonplace among commentators that the fourth and final section of the gospel is the most closely woven and carefully crafted of all the sections. There are many reasons advanced for this, not the least of which is that the whole story of passion, death, and resurrection was the first to be committed to written form in the interests of providing believers with a full explanation of the paradox of a suffering messianic deliverer. (In the case of Mark there was the added urgency of explaining to his own bewildered community why the supposed dawning of the New Age was so fraught with suffering and apparent defeat.) Again, it has long been contended that the Passion story took shape in the context of worship, and perhaps the most notable contribution in this area is John Bowman, *The Gospel of Mark: The New Christian Jewish Passover Haggadah,* Leiden, E. J. Brill 1965, especially pp. 254-308. An essay by David Daube on the same lines ("The Earliest Structure of the Gospels," *NTS* 5.2.1959, pp. 174-87) remains a seminal study, while Austin Farrer's *A Study in Mark* (London: Dacre Press, 1951) has suffered an undeserved neglect. In convenient form and concerned with Mark's narrative specifically, is Ernest Best, *The Temptation and the Passion: The Markan Soteriology* (SNTS Monograph Series No. 2, Cambridge University Press, 1965).

All the interest exhibited in the Passion narrative of the gospels as cultic texts is to the good, and good also in that it has generated in some quarters an interest in the possible impact of contemporary Jewish patterns of worship, especially in the field of lectionaries. But given the fact that the Markan account is roughly one third the length of the whole gospel, it is important to ask what were the essential elements of the account as the earliest Christians received them. Have we any means of discovering what those elements may have been? How much in the gospel accounts can be attributed to making propaganda points in favor of the Christian theological interpretation of the historical facts? Is there any attempt by the community or the evangelists to apportion blame; and if there is, to what extent is this justified by the available contemporary evidence, legal and otherwise? To some of these questions we can have but tentative answers or inspired guesses, and the present state of our knowledge leaves whole realms for conjecture. Assuming that Mark returned to Palestine from Rome, with the elements of a Petrine tradition of the passion, what did he think it important to correlate with that tradition from the Matthean and Lucan sources before him? The suggestion has been made that the original Markan tradition lacked 14:3-9 (the anointing at Bethany), 14:12-16 (the preparation for Passover), 14:53-65 (the appearance before the priests), and possibly 16:1-8 (the empty tomb). J. Jeremias, in an examination of the growth of the passion tradition, suggests that there was an original (Aramaic) Proclamation such as 1 Cor 15:3-5 followed by an account of the arrest of Jesus and a short Passion narrative, then later a longer narrative beginning with the entry into Jerusalem (and including the "Petrine" traditions of 14:26-52,53-55,66-72, and then finally the full version as we have it now. (Cf. ibid., *The Eucharistic Words of Jesus,* London, SCM Press, 1966, English translation by Norman Perrin of *Die Abenmahlsworte Jesu,* 3rd ed., Göttingen, Vandenhoeck und Ruprecht, pp. 95-96.)

In all of this there is something unsatisfying. It is hard to see the Passion story *in and of itself* acting as a piece of apologetic material: it demands far more explanation of the events which precipitated a brutal death. Similarly, unless we can know the liturgical context within which the Passion narrative was set, we are left with a grim account of justice perverted and little apparent vindication of or redress for the victim.

The narrative as Mark finally shaped it displays signs of stitches, or material incorporated from other traditions (e.g., the plotting of the temple clergy, 14:1-2; the betrayal plot of Judas, 14:10-11; and the anointing, 14:3-9—evidently very much an afterthought). Mark is not alone in this process of assimilation and editing, and each evangelist has his own traditions. Luke has a long conversation piece (22:21-38) after the Last Supper which draws on various sources, a tradition of a meeting between Jesus and Herod (23:8-12), and Matthew has a story of the death of Judas (27:3-9) which is in important respects at variance with Acts 1:15-20.

On the whole Passion story there is a bewildering array of special works, and the task of recommending such works is onerous. But whatever recommendations are made, a synopsis of the gospels is essential (such as that of Aland, Throckmorton, Orchard, or Swanson, to be found in the bibliographies at the beginning of this commentary). Other works will be referred to in the body of the text, and a special bibliography will be found at the beginning of the narrative of the trial of Jesus.

Although we have called this fourth part "Israel Under Judgment," it is plainly an artificial structure, and its contents are determined by being set in Jerusalem before the final drama of the arrest and crucifixion. There is a series of events, then teaching in the city, and finally the apocalyptic discourse. The whole is covered in a series of three days (see 11:1,12,19), but the teaching in the city and the apocalypse are all set in the context of the third day. Apart from the Passion narrative proper, a chronological arrangement of such exactitude is unknown in Mark. But the whole scheme is certainly the evangelist's own, for the third day is far too crowded, and the constituent parts in all probability existed as independent units before Mark began his editorial work. The second part of this scheme consists of conflict/controversy stories, which given the previous Markan block of such material in 2:1-3:6 we might have expected to find in that earlier context. Now these controversy encounters (11:27-33 and 12:13-40) are in quite appropriate contexts in Matthew and Luke, and the view is therefore advanced here that Mark decided to follow his sources and include the narratives where we now find them. For all the attraction of including them in his earlier context, the topics addressed in these confrontations certainly heighten the dramatic impact of the whole complex of the Passion story and at the same time address vital aspects of a ministry approaching its end and its climax.

Notes

1-11. *They were now approaching Jerusalem:* There are two stories intertwined here —the action of Jesus in sending for a colt and then the enthusiastic entry into Jerusalem. Two main views have heretofore been advanced about these episodes. One is that the whole complex has a messianic significance as though with conscious reference to Zech 9:9 Jesus deliberately chose not only to assert the authority of his message and ministry, but also to invest both with a claim to messiahship, and in so doing to give clear signals for those who could understand, while at the same time veiling the significance of the events from the rest. Apart from the enthusiasm of the immediate followers, the results are negative, and Roman authority did not see this as a challenge. (Luke has a tradition—19:39-40—that some Jewish critics protested at the acclamations which greeted Jesus.) Another view would hold that a messianic "legend" of interpretation has been laid over an originally simple account of an entry of enthusiastic pilgrims into the holy city, and somehow allied with this is the view of Lohmeyer (p. 232) that the story has been influenced by the Markan concern for the "messianic secret."

With all this, our difficulties are only just beginning. In spite of the vividness of the account which follows, the seeming eyewitness character of some of the details, the account succeeds in being at one and the same time messianic and nonmessianic. The whole story appears to be building to a climax, and then we experience a sense of total anticlimax with the odd circumstance that it all ends with a nontriumphal entry into the city. The supporters are highly enthusiastic—though in the overcrowded conditions of the pre-Passover season they would not be as visible as at other times—and the whole story breathes an air of tense apprehension. Yet the greetings and the acclamations are for a *coming kingdom* and not a welcome to a Messiah. The one who *comes in the Lord's name* is not named as Jesus, and John's added "even the King of Israel" (12:13) makes no attempt to identify this king with Jesus. John 12:16 specifically rules out that kind of identification, that kind of contemporary understanding. The suggestion of Taylor (p. 452) that "the contrast with Matthew's narrative is astonishing and bespeaks an earlier and superior tradition" is hardly borne out by the facts. Mark's version does not have Matthew's "fulfillment" text from Zech 9:9, but equally it does not have the very unmessianic assessment of Jesus found in Matt 21:10 ("And when he entered Jerusalem, the whole city was shaken, saying 'Who is this?' And the crowds said, 'This is the prophet Jesus, from Nazareth in Galilee' ").

Even if we assume, on the basis of Zech 9:9, that there were some messianic implications in all of the report before us, and equally assume that it represents a core of historical truth, there are features which have received little if any attention recently. From this neglect the recent work of A. E. Harvey (whose 1980 Bampton Lectures have been referred to elsewhere in this commentary) has certainly delivered us. His cautions about the synoptic account can be found in Chapter 6 of *Jesus and the Constraints of History* (Philadelphia: Westminster Press, 1982, pp. 120-29). The principal points can be summarized, but the reader is advised to read Harvey's account in full. To begin with, the wealth of detail surrounding the finding of a *young donkey tied up* could certainly be an explanation of some prearrangement (for the gospels do not apparently understand the matter as resulting from some miraculous foresight), but the attitude of *some bystanders* (not to mention the owners of the animal) is surprising. Evidently what we are being asked to understand is the exercise of the right of a ruler, or his representative, or even a prominent rabbi to requisition an animal, provided only that the rights of the owner were acknowledged (cf. J. Duncan M. Derrett, "Law in the New Testament: The Palm Sunday Colt," *NovTest* 13.1971, pp. 241-58). There may be some justification (as in the *New English Bible* margin) for translating *The Lord needs it* as "its master needs it." The Greek word for *needs (chreia* = necessity) underlines the right to requisition, and Jesus takes the donkey on loan in full accordance with the prescriptions of the Law, promising to send it back right away. Harvey calls attention to the fact that the donkey was unbroken—citing the words *which no man has yet ridden*—and comments that the evangelists wish us to understand the appropriateness of an animal of such unquestioned ritual purity for a royal personage. Mark and Luke both use the Septuagint description from Zech 9:9 that the donkey was *young* (Greek *pōlon neon),* though neither evangelist uses the Old Testament quotation. Then there is the odd circumstance of the colt being *tied up.* Certainly the animal would need to be tethered, but is this an allusion to the enigmatic reference in Gen 49:11 that a future descendant of Judah would be respected by all the nations and that he would tie his foal to a vine? The description of Jesus as being a scrupulous observer of the law on borrowing *(will send it back right away)* is precise enough, but Harvey (p. 124) suggests further that this phrase may also be a reminiscence of Moses' protestation (Num 16:15) that he "had not taken from them so much as a single ass . . ."

All of this is but preliminary, and already we have a multifaceted portrait of Jesus, with no explanation by Jesus of any of his actions. The fact of riding an animal at all on this pilgrimage to Jerusalem, instead of proceeding on foot, is simply detailed without explanation or justification. Next we come to the manner of his entering the city. *Many people spread their clothes on the road*—was this a matter of securing further guarantees of ritual purity for one entering the city and temple, or was it a gesture of respect to Jesus in recognition of his status as leader or even as king? Luke seems to imply the latter: there is no further mention of the crowds in his account, and it is Jesus' followers who are responsible for the shouts of acclamation. Mark's tradition is alone in recording that *others spread brushwood which they had cut in the fields* (v. 8). The Greek word translated *brushwood (stibadas)* is unique to Mark in the whole of scripture and means "mattress stuffing" (some manuscripts omit the phrase *which they had cut from the fields).* This is certainly from an eyewitness account and an example of Mark's independence on this occasion of his principal source in Matthew. This was apparently a purely utilitarian gesture, since the thin mattresses would help the donkey on the steep slope. Matthew and John, however, have different approaches to the significance of the occasion. John 12:13 speaks of "branches of palm"—entirely appropriate to a religious occasion, since such branches were carried in procession by pilgrims into the city on the Feast of Booths. Equally significant for John's account are the rededication of the temple under Simon Maccabaeus, when branches were carried (1 Macc 13:51), and the establishment of the Feast of Dedication (2 Macc 10:6) similarly characterized by the carrying of branches and garlands and branches of palm (2 Macc 10:7). Not only does John omit all mention of the spreading of clothing on the road, the enthusiastic crowds go out to meet Jesus with branches of palm. The intent in terms of theological interpretation of the event in the fourth gospel is quite evident. But the relationship between the synoptists is less clear. Matt 21:8 speaks of the crowds cutting branches from the trees, and Luke omits any such detail. Now it is conventional wisdom that Matthew heightens and adds to an original Markan narrative, and certainly branches from trees are more attuned to a religious procession than mattress-stuffing material from the fields. But it can equally be contended that Mark's avowed purpose is to defer any depiction of Jesus as king and deliverer, and that he deliberately chose to mute the overtones of the occasion. A recent work makes clear Mark's intent to reserve the title "king" for the climax of the passion (cf. Frank J. Matera, *The Kingship of Jesus: Composition and Theology in Mark 15*, Chico, Calif.: Scholars Press, 1983).

The differences in interpretation also extend to the acclamations attributed by the evangelists to the crowds. Readers with memories of Nazi rallies in pre-1939 Germany will recall the reiterated and orchestrated shouts in unison of "Sieg heil!" or "Ein Reich, ein Volk, ein Führer!" and baseball games in the major leagues in the United States have their own particular catch phrases of crowd enthusiasm. So it must have been on this occasion, and perhaps the single shout of *Hosanna!* was what character- ized the enthusiasm of Jesus' followers. This, given the theological predispositions of the evangelists, lent itself to a variety of interpretations and explanatory material. Luke omits the cry, and in fact the word is found in the Old Testament only at Ps 118:25 (though significantly associated with Passover, Booths, and perhaps Dedica- tion). But the word itself (Hebrew *hôsha' nā*) is a cry for deliverance, salvation ("save now!"), and was part of the ritual acclamation as branches were carried around the altar in procession. In fact the well-known liturgical chant was applied not only to the prayers but also to the branches. The acclamation, then, was well-known. Perhaps too the enthusiastic followers also sang the psalm verse which follows: *Blessed is the one who comes in the Lord's name!* There would be nothing extraordinary in singing a familiar psalm as part of the normal welcome of the pilgrims as they came to Jerusa- lem. The evangelists, however, cannot leave it there, and they have to provide their own explanations of the inner significance of the event.

All the evangelists agree in providing the Septuagint text for *Hosanna!* and the psalm verse. Mark adds *Blessed is the coming kingdom of our father David!* (v. 10). This immediately calls attention to itself as an interpolation, for no spontaneous shouting or singing by a crowd would produce such a lengthy sentiment. Furthermore the phrase is unknown to us from any existing contemporary Jewish source. The expression *our father David* (apart from the enigmatic Acts 4:25, where the word means "ancestor") is strange and appears to number David among the patriarchs. In addition to this, *the coming Kingdom* in the thought of the time (and on the lips of Jesus) was the "Reign of God," and Lohmeyer (p. 231) correctly observes that the role of David would be connected with a kingdom being restored. Whatever may have been the history of the phrase (in the Markan community?) as a liturgical utterance of some kind, it is hard to find in it anything less "messianic" than the texts of Matthew and Luke. In this connection, we notice *the one who comes* in v. 9. All three gospels have it, since all quote from the Septuagint version of Psalm 118. But was the word in Greek *(ho erchomenos)* understood in any messianic sense? Of this we cannot be sure, but there are references in the New Testament, which suggest that Ps 118:26 in combination with Dan 7:13 gave the phrase some brief use in Christian circles (e.g., Matt 11:3 = Luke 7:19; Matt 23:39 = Luke 13:35; John 1:15,27; 6:14; 11:27; Acts 19:4; Heb 10:37—using the Septuagint). Luke's version leaves us in no doubt of that evangelist's understanding: "Blessed is he who comes, the king, in the name of the Lord; in heaven peace, and glory in the highest!" (19:9).

Luke does not wish to encumber his literary Greek with an attempted Hellenizing of a Hebrew word, so we have no *hosanna* in the acclamations. But the Matthean and Markan versions present us with an impossible text in what has come generally to be translated as "Hosanna in the highest heavens!" This is simply impossible. *Hosanna* as a cry for salvation can hardly be described as an appropriate prayer in the courts of heaven. Matt 21:9 has (in many translations) "Hosanna to the Son of David! Blessed is he who comes in the Lord's name! Hosanna in the highest heavens!" The same use of *hosanna* is found here as in Mark, indicating that at an early stage the Hebrew cry for salvation had become (in Greek-speaking Christian communities) something by way of a liturgical acclamation. It is worth calling attention to the process by which this happened. Mitchell Dahood *(Psalms I, 1-50,* AB Vol. 16, Garden City, N.Y.: Doubleday, 1965-66, pp. xxi-xxii) called attention to the fact that the Hebrew *la, lĕ* often introduced a vocative (so, properly, "Hosanna! O Son of David!"), but *la, lĕ* also could be used to introduce "to" and hence be used as a dative ("Hosanna to the Son of David"). What we have attempted to do in the Markan text of v. 10 is to restore the original sense of *hosanna* as a prayer.

Some Further Notes

1. *Mount of Olives:* Cf. Zech 14:4, where the place is associated with messianic hope.

2. *donkey:* It is of some interest to observe that in the patriarchal city of Haran there was a practice of donkey sacrifice (known to us from the eighteenth-century BCE Mari texts), where such a sacrifice was used to ratify a treaty between the Apiru (= Hebrews?) and some local kings. Furthermore, the king described as coming on a donkey in Zech 9:9 is described in the Hebrew text as the Righteous One (Hebrew *ṣaddîq,* which is probably a "messianic" title of ancient lineage. Indeed, the whole complex of Zech 9:9-17 is important at this point, and not simply the half verse quoted in Matthew and John. The context in Zechariah looks to the restoration of the people by reason of God's overshadowing providence and his covenant with Israel.

There are in this section seven verbal agreements of Matthew and Luke against

Mark, but nine agreements of Matthew and Mark against Luke, and only five agreements of Mark and Luke against Matthew.

On the matter of the Law and the loan of the donkey, see the article by J. Duncan M. Derrett cited previously.

58. The Fig Tree (i)
(11:12-14) = Matt 21:18-19

11 12 On the following day, after they had left Bethany, Jesus was hungry, 13 and seeing in the distance a fig tree with leaves on it, he went to it to see if he could find anything on it. But when he came to it, he found nothing but leaves, for it was not the season for figs. 14 He said to the tree, "May no one ever eat figs from you again!" And his disciples were listening.

Comment

The previous section ended on a surprisingly muted note. After the scenes of enthusiasm and acclamation, Jesus simply *entered Jerusalem, and went into the temple, where he looked around at everything,* and then, because it was late, he went out to Bethany. This is in strong contrast to the narratives of Matthew and Luke, who record the cleansing of the temple immediately upon Jesus' entry. Mark records that Jesus went into the temple and *looked at everything.* The word used in v. 11 for *temple* (Greek *hieron,* cf. 11:15,27; 12:35; 13:1-3; 14:49) is inclusive of all the temple environs, including the sanctuary (Greek *naos),* and in all probability Mark intends us to understand that Jesus gave an all-embracing survey of all he could see (Greek *periblempsamenos = looked around)* and then left for Bethany. The courts would still be thronged, for all the fact that *the hour was late.* But Mark wishes to call our attention to impending judgment, and so deserts the Matthean and Lucan narratives (which have the cleansing of the temple immediately following upon Jesus' entry into the city).

We have titled the final part of Mark's gospel "Israel under Judgment." The episode now to be discussed is vital in Mark's context, and so too is the second episode about the fig tree after Chapter 13. Considering both context and topic, it is all too easy to conclude from the two episodes of the fig tree— given the significance of a fig tree as a symbol for Israel—that what we have is a prophetic denunciation by Jesus of his own people. This is altogether too simplistic. The gospels are not mere historical reminiscence, and the theological purpose of the author and editors must be constantly borne in mind. For the early Christian community there was no sharp division such as "Israel" and "Church," and the continuity between the people of the Old Covenant and those of the New was a prime concern of the apostle Paul. For Mark, as for Paul, judgment was not to be thought of as applying solely to Judaism, however bewildering the rejection of Jesus might be to Christian Jewish believers. Mark's purpose in using the story of the fig tree here is not from any consideration that this was its original place, and that it was later adapted by Matthew: Mark uses the narrative here because in his order Jesus is about to perform a challenging acted parable in the temple, and the challenge of the advent of the New Age must be explained.

First, however, it is necessary to deal with the evident embarrassment of some commentators on this pericope. To some there is an explanation needed for the petulance of Jesus when unreasonable demands are not met. For others the whole account is a misunderstood parable, while for many there may be a desire to acquit the human Jesus of anything approaching a mistake or misapprehension. All of this is very unsatisfactory by way of explanation, and it is difficult to resist the notion that some writers on the subject are anxious to preserve the Chalcedonian "perfect God/perfect man" concept of Jesus at the expense of the Jesus of history. To attempt a survey of the relevant literature would be interesting, but fortunately for our purposes an article of 1973 can provide the student with more than adequate references and footnotes. A recently published dissertation *(The Barren Temple and the Withered Tree: A Redactional-Critical Analysis of the Cursing of the Fig-Tree Pericope in Mark's Gospel and Its Relation to the Cleansing of the Temple Tradition,* University of Sheffield, *JSNT* Supp, Series 1, 1980) would wish to link this pericope with judgment (and more specifically with judgment on the temple), and that the bracketing of the temple scene by the two fig tree stories underscores this. This tries to prove altogether too much. Mark is remarkably little interested in the temple (as compared, for example, with Luke and John), and though Mark's community may initially have been bewildered by the conflicts which resulted in the destruction of the temple, contemporary Judaism was of such diverse complexion, and so heavily weighted numerically in favor of the diaspora, that we may ourselves be in danger of giving the temple a centrality which it may not have enjoyed. As we shall hope to show, Mark's concerns in the direction of impending judgment may have included the temple, but it was by no means paramount.

The historicity of the account has often been questioned, and more often than not attempts are made to link the story to the parable about the barren fig tree in Luke 13:6-9. While there is the common feature of the unproductiveness, the language of this pericope would appear to rule out the connection—cf. he *was hungry* (Greek *epeinasen,* cf. 2:25) and *if he could find anything on it* (Greek *ei ara ti heurēsei en autē).* There is a vividness about the narrative which is lacking in the Lucan parable, and we can almost hear the direct question implied in the conditional *if he could find anything.* Moreover the exhortation in the second part of the episode, *Have faith in God* (11:22), carries the authentic ring of the historical Jesus, and we may with confidence conclude that we have a narrative from the original tradition.

With all our legitimate concern to peel away the layers of later tradition and interpretation and in so doing to discover the Jesus of history, we are often so concerned to identify Hellenistic elements in the editing and compiling of the gospel records that we fail to ask what would have been meant, intended, or implied in the context of contemporary Judaism. The present pericope is a case in point. The article to which reference has been made above ("Figtrees in the New Testament," J. Duncan M. Derrett, *Heythrop Journal* 14.3.1973, pp. 249-65) recalls for us the importance of the rabbinic writings in interpreting New Testament material. This aid in interpretation is not without peril: the invaluable Strack-Billerbeck is notoriously lacking in the provision of dates and, therefore, of the value of the material as contemporary evidence. There are admirable cautions in Derrett's article about the indiscriminate use of rabbinic and Midrashic material, and the reader is strongly advised to be aware of those cautions.

Derrett sees some value in linking Jesus' journey to Jerusalem on a colt with the fig tree incident, in that both may usefully be illuminated by contemporary or near contemporary sources. The use of the colt, he suggests, may well have been a prophetic action, a deliberate imitation of the Zech 9:9 "messianic" prophecy, whether or not the bystanders understood what he was doing. Similarly, following upon a tentative suggestion of R. H. Hiers (" 'Not the Season of Figs,' " *JBL* 87.4.1968, pp. 394-401) Derrett calls our attention to the sentence upon the fig tree (cf. Gen 3:17) in terms which carry a punishment that the tree will not bear fruit until the end of the age (Greek *eis ton aiōna).* It is here that one of the keys to interpretation lies, for the Greek can mean "to the end of this age, this era": John 8:51-52, 12:34; 1 Cor 8:13; Heb 5:6, 7:17,24; 1 John 2:17; 2 John 2:2. Two references *must* mean "to the end of this age": Luke 1:55, John 4:14.

When Derrett's article was written, it was popularly thought, even in some circles with apparent scientific support, that plants could be encouraged in their growth by being spoken to and touched. There were suggestions that cows produced more abundant milk if exposed to recordings of classical music, with a reverse effect if the music was rock and roll. Perhaps some of this if not all was dismissed by many people as a figment of the imagination. Recently, however, we have been informed of credible scientific data that trees being attacked by gypsy moth caterpillars can and do "communicate" by chemical secretions an alarm to other nearby trees which then set up their own chemical defense mechanisms. This is well enough as yet another example of a scientific discovery at which to marvel. But Jesus talking to a fig tree to condemn it, sentence it? Communication between trees should give us pause before dismissing this pericope as another example of prescientific, or "protological" thinking (as the late W. F. Albright was accustomed to call it).

There is certainly enough rabbinical and Midrashic material which deals with the sadness of the creation at Adam's fall from grace (cf. L. Ginzberg, *Legends of the Jews,* Philadelphia, The Jewish Publication Society of America, Vols. I-VII, 1946-60—Vol. II, p. 75; Vol. V, p. 122). The same material also speaks of a barren tree as a sign of the fall of Adam. By contrast, the Messianic Age, the Age of Blessings, will cause the earth to produce abundantly and beyond human expectation, and we are familiar with pictures of the natural wonders which will accompany the time of restoration (cf. Isa 40:4-5, 45:2, 49:11, 51:10, 54:10; *Pss Sol* 11:4; 1 Baruch 5:7), and the New Testament is witness to the continuing tradition (Matt 17:10 = Isa 54:10; Matt 21:21 = Isa 49:11; Luke 17:6 = Isa 51:10) and Jesus himself requires that John the Baptizer must give heed to witnesses to the New Age (cf. Matt 11:5; Luke 7:22). Perhaps the miraculous growth of seed in the parables may have references to the abundance of the New Age (cf. Mark 10:30). But even after the fall of Adam a righteous person could bring about fruitfulness (cf. Gen 26:12), and for trees to produce abundantly in the New Age, "they must offer their crop not as a matter of biological cyclic action but in response to the need of the righteous" (Derrett, p. 254). If it is the season of figs, then this is a natural process and not the kind of thing envisaged by Haggadah. Fruit out of season may be looked for, or expected, only by one entering upon the New Age who is hungry and righteous. Hence, if we ask—in terms wholly familiar to the tradition which nurtured Jesus—why the fig tree did not immediately produce fruit, then plainly the New Age was not beginning to dawn. But even this is not a final answer, for if it is true that other trees did produce fruit, then the one approached by Jesus was wrong and furthermore was contradicting the herald and harbinger of the New Age.

The sequence in Mark's division of the story has Peter understanding that Jesus had cursed the tree (11:21), though the words used in v. 14 do not imply this. The tree was dying, if not dead, and it was *withered all the way down to the roots.* Generally it is at this point that commentators regale us with much speculation about the season, or a sudden frost, or that Jesus was not in fact at the original location on the road to the act of redemption. All such speculation is pointless in the face of the fact that this is the story as Mark saw it—he was as familiar with the story of Jonah and the gourd as he assumed his hearers and readers to be. We are left free to understand that Jesus accepted that the fig tree would not bear fruit until the New Age came into being. We shall return to this theme when we come to the sequel to this narrative (Section 60).

To those readers for whom commentary upon, and interpretation of, the biblical material in the New Testament period are matters for initial exploration, see Addison G. Wright, "The Literary Genre Midrash," *CBQ* 28.2, 1966, pp. 105-54; and *CBQ* 28.4.1966, pp. 417-57.

Notes

12. *He felt hungry* (Greek *epeinasen*): This word, vivid as it is, while underscoring to some extent the eyewitness character of the narrative, may also contain a hidden intention of Mark. The verb is the same in Matt 5:6: "Fortunate are those who hunger and thirst for righteousness . . ."—hunger for the vindication of God's will and purpose. Is Mark, in using Matthew's account, treating the incident as a sign that Jesus now confidently anticipated that his forthcoming conflict would usher in the Age of Blessings? There is a further—very tentative—suggestion to be made. The hunger of Jesus for the Reign of God is matched by *may no one ever eat figs from you again!*—as is the thirst in the Matthean tradition by *"I will never again drink of the fruit of the vine until that day . . ."* In the view of Mark (and we believe of Matthew, as well as John), that day dawned in the crucifixion/exaltation of Jesus.

Matthew's account is much shorter: he simply refers to a "single fig tree by the roadside" (21:19); he makes no reference to Jesus going to seek fruit from it and underlines the importance of the occasion by saying that after Jesus spoke to the tree, it "withered at once." We shall return to this later.

13. *for it was not the season for figs:* Sufficient attention was given to this in the comment at the head of this section. It was not as yet the time for the New Age to begin.

14. *"May no one . . ."* The expression is strong, and in fact in Greek it is stronger than in Matthew. C. F. D. Moule (p. 136) describes the expression as "most vehemently prohibitive."

his disciples were listening: This looks forward to vv. 20-25, but there is the additional sense that the Markan community must be attentive to the true meaning of the narrative.

59. The Cleansing of the Temple
(11:15-19) = Matt 21:12-17; Luke 19:45-48; John 2:13-22

11   ¹⁵ So they arrived in Jerusalem. He went into the temple and began to drive out those who bought and sold in the temple. He upset the tables of the money changers and the seats of the pigeon sellers, ¹⁶ and would not let anyone carry goods through the temple court. ¹⁷ Then he taught them, "Is it not said in Scripture: 'My house shall be called a house of prayer for all the nations'? But you have made it a 'robbers' cave.' " ¹⁸ The chief priests and the scribes heard of it and sought some way to kill him. They feared him, for the whole crowd was awestruck by his teaching. ¹⁹ When evening came, he went out of the city.

Comment

This is a convenient point at which to essay an examination of the puzzles posed by the chronology of the week of the passion and death of Jesus. We have deferred it because of the division by Mark of the fig tree incident and also because the entry into the temple effectively marks the beginning of the end of the ministry.

The differences in chronology can be summarized as follows:

	Matthew	*Mark*	*Luke*
1st day	Entry. Cleansing of temple. Return to Bethany.	Entry. Return to Bethany.	Entry. Cleansing of temple.
2nd day	Cursing and withering of fig tree. Teaching.	Cursing of fig tree. Cleansing of temple.	Teaching.
3rd day	Teaching.	Fig tree withered.	Teaching.

It is natural to suggest, according to the familiar two-document hypothesis, that Matthew and Luke shorten the Markan chronology and in effect tidy up what appears to be an unnecessarily complex arrangement. But we have given reason to suppose that there are good grounds to suggest that Mark was the editor of the other traditions, and in fact the supposed dependence on Mark is not very impressive here. Luke's two days are not even suggested by the evangelist to be consecutive, and Matthew and Luke agree only in recording that the days were engaged in teaching—the material cannot be regarded as parallel. Matthew, if he was dependent on the Markan account, transferred it wholesale: cf. Mark 11:17 *(Then he taught them)* and Matt 21:23 (the dispute about the authority of John), together with Mark 11:18 *(The chief priests and the scribes heard of it)* and Matt 22:33 ("listen to another parable").

Our difficulties do not reside merely in the Sunday-Tuesday realm. We can best summarize the matter as follows:

1. Only in broad outline do the four writers agree on the central events of this week. There are wide divergences in sequence and timing, and it is impossible now to determine which writer is factually and chronologically the more accurate in his narrative. This is not all disadvantage: we would be justified in entertaining the gravest reservations as to historical reliability were we to find that there was close and substantial agreement in detail in the four accounts.

2. The narratives we have illustrate very well the tenacity of the oral tradition in main outline as received by four men, each with his own method of handling, editing, and interpreting that tradition.

3. The differences in arrangement of material, the initial chronology of Sunday-Tuesday, are all succeeded by the impression of haste in the days immediately preceding the trial of Jesus. There is an overall sense of confusion of sequence—and this in itself is fully comprehensible in light of the fact that in the final moments of trial and death most of the eyewitnesses had fled. Subsequent reminiscence will have heightened rather than diminished the impression of confusion. In addition to this, the task of determining the sequence of events has been rendered far more difficult, though certainly more interesting, by the discoveries at Qumran. They disclose that at least two sectarian groups used a calendrical system for calculating the Passover season which was seriously at variance with the official Jerusalem calendar. It is not simply that the Qumran calendar had a far more ancient lineage, but some scholars insist that it was this sectarian calendar which Jesus and the disciples used. According to this calendar, Passover *always* fell on the night of Tuesday-Wednesday, and so this would have been the night of the Last Supper. This view was first propounded by Mme. Annie Jaubert in *La date de la cène* (Paris: Librairé Lecoffre, 1957), and it is still a subject of much debate. We shall have occasion to refer to this matter again in dealing with the Last Supper. In the meantime some succinct summaries may be found in George Ogg, "The Chronology of the Last Supper," in *History and Chronology in the*

New Testament (SPCK Theological Collections, London: SPCK, 1965, pp. 75-97) and also in Jack Finegan, *A Handbook of Biblical Chronology* (Princeton, N.J.: Princeton University Press, 1964, rev. ed. 1980, pp. 290-96).

For the interest of the reader, we give here the sequence of events as the theory of Mme. Jaubert explains them:

Official Jewish Calendar (Johannine)			*Sectarian (Ancient Priestly) Calendar (Synoptic Gospels)*
Nisan 8	Saturday	Anointing at Bethany.	Nisan 11
9	Sunday	Entry into Jerusalem. Return to Bethany.	12
10	Monday	Return to Jerusalem. Incident of the fig tree.	13
11	Tuesday	Preparation for Passover. Passover/Last Supper. Arrest. Examination before Annas. Jesus taken to Caiaphas's house.	14
12	Wednesday	Sanhedrin hearing begins.	15
13	Thursday	Sanhedrin hearing ends in early morning. Roman trial begins. Examination by Herod Antipas.	16
14	Friday	Roman trial ends. Crucifixion. Official Passover begins in evening.	17

The merit of this theory is that it accounts for the variant Johannine tradition (which places the death of Jesus at the time when Passover lambs were being slain in the temple) as that of the official Jerusalem calendar.

We are now in a position to evaluate the meaning of this event as it would have been understood in Jesus' own milieu and in his own time. Whatever doubts may be expressed from time to time about the historicity of the entry into Jerusalem as we presently have it, it is very difficult to imagine the scene before us as being invented. The attack of Jesus on the trading practices which had intruded into the temple precincts depends in part on the legitimacy or otherwise of such trading. There are grounds for supposing that such provision of services was indeed an intrusion (cf. J. Duncan M. Derrett, "The Zeal of Thy House," *Downside Review* 95.2.1977, pp. 79-94; and J. Jeremias, "Zur Geschichtlichkeit der Tempelreinigung," *NTS* 29.2.1977, pp. 179-80). But how seriously was this an attempt to close down an enterprise which at this season at any rate must have been of vast extent? Not only were there numerous colonnades in the precincts where trading could be carried on, but *the temple* referred to in v. 15 was a vast open space—the Court of the Gentiles—where animals, salt, oil, wine, were sold for sacrifices, and where money changers provided services for Jews from the Diaspora who did not have the half-shekel temple tax. (Cf. Joachim Jeremias, *Jerusalem in the Time of Jesus*, translation by F. H. and C. H. Cave of *Jerusalem zur Zeit Jesu*, Philadelphia: Fortress Press, 1969, pp. 21-26, 58-71.) In addition, in the circumstances of Passover, an incident such as is described for us in this pericope can hardly be meant to suggest that Jesus conducted a wholesale eviction of all the traders.

What, therefore, do we have? A prophetic gesture, witnessed by a few, and no more than a minor disturbance in the turbulence of the pilgrim crowds? Are we to revise our estimate of the character of Jesus in favor of a man given to violent acts? Did the bystanders remain mute in face of all that was happening? Was there any reaction on the part of the temple police, or—even more to the point—of the considerable Roman military presence stationed to overlook the crowds? If there was no reaction at all, then why not? In the absence of any *recorded* reaction, either from outraged bystanders or by the civil and military authorities, are we here confronted by a carefully edited and muted version in the gospels of an attempt by Jesus to take over the temple by violent means? We can reply that such an action is wholly out of character with the portrait of Jesus presented to us in the New Testament, but this is hardly satisfactory. The critic (e.g., S. F. G. Brandon, *Jesus and the Zealots*, New York: Scribner, 1968) may well reply—and rightly—that the New Testament writers were anxious and concerned to project an image, and they have therefore carefully expunged any elements in the narrative which would represent Jesus as a zealot, a rabble rouser. (After all, according to one interpretation, the book of Acts was written to demonstrate that Christians were law-abiding citizens of Rome.)

What then is left? The most probable explanation lies in the manner of the prophets, the prophetic symbolic gesture. From all the evidence we have, the prophetic type is the one which most easily describes the ministry of Jesus, especially in words but often in action. We are familiar from the Old Testament record of many instances of a divine command to make some particular, symbolic gesture as an intimation of the will and purpose of God (cf. 1 Kgs 11:29-39; Jer 27:1-15), but we do not read the texts as in any sense suggesting that either Ahijah or Jeremiah by so doing effected what their gestures implied. Rather the prophetic symbolism is a call to hearers and onlookers to recognize and act upon the prophet's insight into the sovereign will of God. This provides us with a clue—and virtually the only one—to what in the nature of the case can have been no more than a gesture. Yet "no more than a gesture" is but an indication of our failure to appreciate its meaning in the context of Judaism. True, Jesus could have denounced publicly the authorities responsible for the commercial enterprises in the temple, but this would in all probability have only been heard by those around him, who were probably sympathetic to his convictions. What Jesus chose to do was to make clear his denunciation by a brief attack on a small scale, momentarily disrupting business, and at the same time giving his reasons for his actions. The disruption would have been slight, but the point had been made, and judging by Mark 11:28 the reason Jesus gave is precisely that he was acting as a prophet. If the trading practices in the temple were of doubtful legality, the traders were unlikely to complain to the appropriate authorities.

If then Jesus was acting in the manner of the prophets in performing a symbolic act, we shall seriously misunderstand the import if we suppose that this was a deliberate, all-out attack on a whole established system. The traders themselves were there only because the true offenders—the temple clergy —allowed them to be there. And if this was a *wholesale* attack and intended as such, it is difficult to see what it could actually have accomplished. But seen as a symbolic prophetic action, protesting the judgment of God against the use being made of the temple, the whole episode falls into place in the ministry of Jesus and is all of a piece with an episode which must be discussed later (12:41-44). The interpretation offered by the evangelists is altogether different in tone and will be discussed in the notes following.

Notes

15. *So they arrived in Jerusalem:* It is extremely difficult to say whether this is an editorial phrase, intended to link the narrative that follows with the preceding events (cf. *after they had left Bethany,* 11:12), or whether it is the evangelist's own inherited tradition, for the phrase is absent in Matthew and Luke. This difficulty is but one of a series of doubts and hesitations as we face the events of this final week. (The difficulties of two possible calendrical uses as between the synoptists and John have already been mentioned.) In all three synoptists the events of this final week by their very nature demand a much longer time span, though for Mark the structure of his gospel positively requires that the temple incident be placed here. All the same, the link or stitch in the narrative in vv. 15 and 19 may well originally have belonged to the story of the fig tree. There is precedent for this kind of arrangement in Mark (cf. 3:22-26 on Beelzebul and 6:17-29 on the execution of John). Far more formidable is the fact that this prophetic gesture in the temple does not appear to accomplish what the evangelist intended us to understand. It is not decisive: the reference to the temple clergy in v. 18

is followed by unrelated controversy stories, and we wait until a further adversary note at 14:1 before the final denouement gets under way. Even the demand for a clarification of authority in Section 61 would seem from its language to be far more appropriate to a time soon after the execution of John, and only tenuously does the question of authority seem to belong to the temple incident. In this respect the reported confusion among witnesses at the initial ecclesiastical examination is far more intelligible (14:58) if the temple incident had happened much earlier. There is also the allied question of synoptic relationships to be considered. If as is generally agreed by the majority, Matthew and Luke built upon a Markan foundation, why (beginning their accounts as early as they do) do they not correct this Markan imbalance and place the cleansing of the temple earlier? Why is it that on so many grounds the Johannine positioning of the prophetic symbolic act is far more fitting than those in the synoptists? Of course it can be replied that neither Matthew nor Luke is particularly concerned with the temple until this incident, but this is far from the case with Luke. There remains the possibility, advocated by some (cf. Maurice Goguel, *The Life of Jesus*, English translation by Oliver Wyon, London: Macmillan, 1933, especially pp. 412-19, 507-11) that in the original oral tradition this temple narrative had no fixed place. We are left with the strong possibility that the Johannine tradition is of far greater historical value, and in fact John 10:40 may represent a time of withdrawal from Jerusalem after the cleansing of the temple, and in connection with which we have the saying about destroying the temple (John 2:19; see also Matt 26:61, Mark 14:58).

temple (Greek *hieron*, cf. 11:11): This word means the whole complex of temple buildings as distinct from the sanctuary (Greek *naos*) or holy place.

those who bought: These are pilgrims for whom services had to be provided for sacrifices. In all probability the place in the precincts is the Court of the Gentiles.

money changers (Greek *kollubistes*): The word is late, derived from *kollubos* meaning "small coin" or even "rate of exchange." The bankers sat at their tables changing Roman or Greek coinage into Jewish or Tyrian currency in which alone the half-shekel tax could be paid (cf. Exod 30:13-16).

seats of the pigeon sellers: Mark has this detail in common with Matthew and John. Pigeons were the offerings of the poor for women's purification (Lev 12:6, cf. Luke 2:22-24), for the cleansing of those with skin complaints (Lev 14:22) and other purposes (Lev 15:14,29).

16. *would not let anyone:* This verse is peculiar to Mark. There is evidence that people were in the habit of using the Court of the Gentiles as a shortcut from the city to the Mount of Olives.

Mark's Greek follows Matthew closely, but he omits Matthew's "all" before *those who bought and sold.* Luke's version goes directly from "those who sold" to "saying to them, it is written . . ." (Luke 19:45).

17. *Then he taught them:* It is worth considering whether this may not be a realization on Mark's part that the temple scene did not originally belong in this context, for he has this preface to the Old Testament quotation in place of Matthew's "He said to them . . ."

My house: The quotation (Isa 56:7) is precisely from the Greek of the Septuagint. Luke has "shall be" for Mark's (and Matthew's) *shall be called,* and both Matthew and Luke omit Mark's *for all the nations.* The description of the temple as a *house of prayer* is found in 1 Kings as well as Isa 56:7 and 60:7. Lohmeyer (p. 236), while finding the quotation as appropriate for Galileans whose view of the temple might simply be that of a principal synagogue, also points out the eschatological dimensions of the saying: cf. Isa 56:8, "I will yet bring home all that remain to be brought in."

The saying as it stands calls for further examination. In the Court of the Gentiles there were prominent notices in stone (Josephus, *Jewish Wars* 5.194) warning of the penalty of death for Gentiles entering the inner courts of the temple, and we might consider the quotation apposite. But the application of the quotation to the tradesmen is hardly appropriate; they were not the ones who bore responsibility either for the trading practices or for the prohibition of Gentiles from the Court of the Jews or the Court of Women. In any event, the quotation itself in the Hebrew text (which Jesus would have used) can hardly sustain a plea for the use of the temple for worship by everyone. The Hebrew has "I will give them joy in my house of prayer" (Isa 56:7), and the context in which the verse is situated strongly suggests (vv. 6-8) that the "foreigners" are those who will "give their allegiance" and "become my servants . . . and hold fast to my covenant" and will have ceased to be Gentiles. Matthew and Luke omit *for all the nations,* perhaps aware that Jesus could not have used the Septuagint text. For all of these reasons, it is doubtful that we are confronted by Jesus' own words as an explanation of his action.

But you have made it a 'robbers' cave': The Greek word translated here is *lēstai,* and once more we are in difficulty. The word does not mean those who take advantage by fiscal manipulation, but instead—quite precisely—means "bandits," that is to say, those who rob by violence. Moreover, as used in Jer 7:11, it was applied to the inhabitants of Jerusalem generally. There is no suggestion in the narrative that the tradesmen and money changers were behaving violently. Certainly at the time of the final composition of our gospels, the use made of the temple by bandits was notorious (cf. Josephus, *Jewish Wars* 5.402), but this quotation was hardly appropriate for the time of Jesus. What was true of the preceding quotation from Isaiah is true also of this one from Jeremiah. Both are attempts by the evangelist (or of the earlier written tradition) to provide some scriptural background, however tenuous, for the actions of Jesus. The interpretation of the Johannine narrative (2:13-22) need not detain us unduly, save to say that the quotation from Ps 69:9 is in no better case than the synoptists' choice of scriptural allusion. The reader is commended to C. H. Dodd, *Historical Tradition in the Fourth Gospel,* Cambridge University Press, 1963, pp. 157-62; and Raymond E. Brown, *The Gospel According to John I-XII,* AB Vol. 29, Garden City, N.Y.: Doubleday, 1966, pp. 114-26.

The puzzle for us is that there are other biblical quotations which are far more appropriate as interpretations of the prophetic gestures of Jesus than those provided by the evangelists (e.g., Isa 59:14-20, Hos 6:5-6, Mal 3:1-3, Neh 13:4-13). If there was a felt necessity to emphasize the "messianic" character of the act or to assert the onset of the New Age, then—to us—Mal 3:1-3 would appear to be far more suitable. But apparently the eminent suitability *we* see did not commend itself to the evangelists, and we have to reckon with the fact that the virtual cessation of prophecy (let alone prophetic ministries) would have dulled the evangelists' understanding of prophetic symbolism. It is also possible that those who preserved the original tradition understood what was happening far better than the later evangelists, who found it urgently necessary to supply scriptural authority for what had taken place. In the end everything turned on the character of the ministry of Jesus and its authority, and this is a matter to which we shall return in the commentary on 11:28.

18. This verse, added in explanation for the lack of immediate action by the temple clergy, only serves to underline our own bewilderment, for it is as though the evangelist is aware that historically the cleansing of the temple may have happened earlier in the ministry.

chief priests and scribes: The two bodies formed two principal elements in the Sanhedrin and are found mentioned together in 11:27 as well as in 14:1,43,53.

some way to kill him (literally, "how they might destroy him"): The Greek word *pos* (how) implies a question in debate, "How are we to get rid of him?" Mark adds *They feared him*—a typically Markan explanatory device introduced by *gar* (for). The fear was, from the viewpoint of the clergy and the official establishment, well-founded. Galilee, where Jesus had spent much of his ministry, was a hotbed of incendiary talk and rumors of rebellion. Certainly the crowd was *awestruck at his teaching,* but had there been all the time a veiled threat to the status quo? Aside from the impression made in Galilee, Jesus was now receiving the same kind of attention in Jerusalem.

19. *When* (Greek *hotan):* The Revised Version renders this word as "whenever," which would be accurate in classical Greek, but Mark always used the word as "when" (cf. 3:11, 11:25).

Some manuscripts read the plural "they" for *he* in this verse, and the manuscripts which have this reading are impressive. However, the pericope simply speaks of Jesus, and we have elected to translate in the singular (cf. Taylor, p. 465).

Matthew has no parallel to v. 19, but Mark found his own v. 18b in Matt 22:33. Luke's version is somewhat more complicated, and Mark made no use of it. Luke 19:47-48 has "he was teaching every day in the temple, and the high priests, the scribes, and the chief of the people sought to destroy him, and they did not discover how to do it, for the whole people heard and hung onto him."

One article at least has attempted to prove that Jesus consciously fulfilled part of the prediction of Zech 14:21b in an attempt to hasten the coming of the Day of the Lord: C. Roth, "The Cleansing of the Temple and Zechariah 14:21," *NovTest* 4.3.1960, pp. 174-81. See also J. M. Ford, "Money Bags in the Temple (Mark 11:16)," *Bib* 57.2.1976, pp. 249-53; and J. Duncan M. Derrett, "The Zeal of the House and the Cleansing of the Temple," *Downside Review* 95.319.1977, pp. 79-94.

The reader should beware of the easy assumption, often made by scholars, that the twin events of the riding into Jerusalem and the incident in the temple are manifestations of a dawning consciousness on the part of Jesus that he was fulfilling a messianic role, or that he now knew himself to be the messiah. We have no evidence that Zech 9:9 was understood by Jesus' contemporaries to refer to a coming messiah, and while Zech 14:21 refers in vague terms to a future reformation of religious institutions, it is not linked in any way to a messiah-to-come. We have urged in this commentary a prophetic interpretation of the actions of Jesus as the one which best fits the facts as they are presented to us. There is the further difficulty that, in so far as we are aware, the title "messiah" was not a common one, still less the ability of any single individual either to claim or to arrogate the title to himself. Expectations prior to and contemporary with Jesus of a New Age centered upon that New Age and its blessings and not necessarily upon its agent or agents. The Qumran concept of two messiahs may in some fashion have helped shape later Christian reflection, but if we are to be faithful to the core of the "Jesus tradition" in our gospels—i.e., the historical Jesus—as far as this can be open to us, then we must conclude that the identification of Jesus with the messiah is a result of the resurrection.

Perhaps the fullest documentation of the various views on the place of the temple in restoration, renewal, and the inauguration of the Reign of God is to be found in Richard H. Hiers, "Purification of the Temple: Preparation for the Kingdom of God," *JBL* 90.1.1971, pp. 82-90. The footnotes are invaluable.

60. The Fig Tree (ii)
(11:20-26) = Matt 21:20-22

11   [20] Early in the morning, as they passed by, they noticed that the fig tree was withered all the way down to the roots. [21] Peter, remembering what had happened, said to him, "Rabbi, look—the fig tree which you cursed has withered!" [22] Jesus answered them, "Have faith in God. [23] Truly I tell you: if anyone says to this mountain, 'Be it lifted from your place and be thrown into the sea' and has no inner doubt, but believes that what he says will happen, it will be done for him. [24] For this reason, I tell you that whatever you ask for in prayer, believe that you have received it, and it shall be yours. [25] And when you stand praying, forgive whatever you have against anyone, so that your Father in heaven may forgive the wrongs you have done. [26] (But if you do not forgive others, then your Father in heaven will not forgive the wrongs you have done.)"

Comment

Mark now takes up the delayed ending of the narrative from 11:12-14 and to the ending of the story of the fig tree are attached sayings on faith and prayer.

We find in Mark's account that Peter interpreted Jesus' words as a curse, but as we saw in the previous part of this narrative, this was not necessarily so. The withering of a plant is a commonplace in Old Testament writings, as is also the superabundance of plant life in the blessings of the Age to Come. Jesus, as we know from the gospels, used the figure of Jonah in his teaching, and he would certainly have known the story of the gourd in Jonah 4:4-11. In any event, Jesus does not say that the shriveling of the fig tree was due to his condemnation. The narrative leaves open the question of whether Jesus believed that the tree would not again flourish until the New Age.

In order to understand Mark's use of the story, we must turn to Matt 21:21-22. Mark's drastic redaction of his Matthean source leaves us with some questions unresolved, questions which would not have been so troublesome to his hearers/readers. In v. 22 before us, Jesus says *Have faith in God.* At first sight this looks like an exhortation to generate enough confidence so that the disciples can then curse fig trees with similar results, or even move mountains. But not only is this a misunderstanding, it also misdirects our attention in looking at the word *faith.* We are not dealing with magic, but with Jesus' understanding of the New Age. Matthew supplies us with two clues that Mark omits: "When the disciples saw it, they wondered and said, 'How did the fig tree wither immediately?' " (21:20) and ". . . if you have faith and do not waver . . ." The wonder and the hesitation of the disciples is intimately linked with faith, as it is in Mark, but Mark confuses us by omitting "do not waver." We are able to put together the Matthean and the Markan accounts, and the resultant picture may be explained as follows: It is not that an experiment has failed for lack of a sheer quantity of faith; rather it is that when the New Age begins to dawn, the realm of nature will be restored as it was at the beginning. But that New Age will not dawn apart from faith. The word *faith* itself (Greek *pistis* = "trust") looks to the future in sure hope and confidence (cf. Matt 17:20). But if we read the text before us as though "cursing" a fig tree was only one thing and assume that there are even greater possibilities open to them, then we shall be missing the point. Either Jesus thought that in him the New Age was dawning and that, therefore, the fig tree should already be showing signs of that age, or the fig tree was itself a demonstration that in fact the New Age was not yet ready to be ushered in. It seems to this writer that Mark is determined—as is Matthew—to make certain that his readers identify the beginning of the New Age with the whole complex of passion, death, and resurrection-vindication. (Cf. John 19:30, where the Greek reads, ". . . 'It is accomplished.' And bowing his head he handed over the Spirit.") The coming of the New Age will depend on the faith, the trust, of Jesus. But so far as the disciples are concerned, the full flowering of the age will depend on *their* faith: "When you are open to the sovereign will of God, then you will be open too to the New Age. Nature will be responding as God promised, trees will bear fruit, the desert will be a highway, the mountains leveled, and all will see the salvation of God."

Notes

20. *Early in the morning* would seem to mean the following day, though Mark does not say so. The fig tree was *withered away* (Greek *xerainō*, cf. 3:1). The vocabulary of this verse is wholly Markan, especially the careful use of the perfect tense of *xerainō* as describing lasting effects. Some manuscripts omit *early in the morning*, presumably in an attempt to join the two parts of the fig tree story into one day's incident.

all the way down to the roots: This phrase recalls our own "radical" (Latin *radix)* as an expression for something fundamental. The Greek *ek rizōn* (at the very roots) is employed in the Septuagint at Job 28:9, 31:12, and Ezek 17:9, to describe "radical destruction."

21. *Peter, remembering:* Cf. 14:72.

22. *Have faith:* Some manuscripts, including the important Codex Sinaiticus, have "If you have faith . . ." Either the Lucan form (17:6) is the original (cf. Matt 17:20, 21:21) and Mark followed his own tradition, or the reading "If you have faith" is an assimilation by later scribes to the Lucan version. The phrase *Have faith in God* (Greek *pistis theou)* is found nowhere else and is grammatically barely defensible. Generally we have faith "toward God" (Greek *pros ton theon)*—1 Thess 1:8—or "in God" (Greek *epi theou)*—Heb 6:1—or a Greek variant of "in God" *(eis ton theon)*—John 14:1.

23. *Truly I tell you:* Cf. 3:28.

has no inner doubt (Greek *mē diakrithē en tē kardia autou):* The Greek verb *diakrinō* is concerned with judgment, discernment, decision, and in the New Testament in the middle and passive voices it means "to hesitate" or "to doubt" (cf. Acts 10:20; Rom 4:20; Jas 2:4). This meaning is not found in the Septuagint. Matt 21:21 has, "if you have faith and never doubt." The relationship between the synoptists is not at all clear, and what—if anything—is the relationship between v. 23 and 1 Cor 13:2? Mark agrees with Matt 17:20 and 1 Cor 13:2 in the "mountains" reference but draws upon Luke 17:6 in mentioning the sea. The conventional view would be that Luke gives the Q version while Matthew conflates Mark and Q (cf. B. H. Streeter, p. 284). This is unnecessarily difficult. Mark is concerned with the signs of a dawning New Age, of which the incident of the fig tree is an illustration, and so draws upon sayings on *faith* to be found in his sources. Hence the "even if you have the faith of a mustard seed" of Matt 17:20 is reduced to *Have faith,* followed by the solemn saying about being *thrown into the sea* which he derives from Luke 17:6.

In the strongest terms Jesus' words in Mark are an invitation, a call, an exhortation for the disciples to exercise that faith, that trust in God, through whom alone the New Age will be ushered in. For Mark's community, in the throes of doubt and near despair, the exhortation is a call to remember that through the darkest days of the ministry and the passion, the age of the New Covenant had indeed been inaugurated by its Lord.

In the early centuries of the Christian era, the visions of the Age of Blessings, of the renewal of nature (e.g., Isaiah 40) would be reinterpreted by the Christian writers in a totally nonmaterial sense as the apparent early triumph of Christianity (along with the gradual eclipse of the Judaism which gave it birth) came face to face with the collapse of Roman order. We cannot know how far Jesus interpreted the visions of future blessings in a purely material sense, but it is surely not too much to imagine the bewilderment of the Markan community as springing in part at least from a disappointment that the time of the New Covenant had not ushered in the promised peace and harmony.

Matthew's version of Mark's saying on prayer in v. 23b is instructive. There is an echo of Matt 7:7-8: "Ask, and it will be given you, seek and you will find, knock, and the door will be opened for you. For he who asks will receive, he who seeks will find, and the door will be opened to him who knocks." Somewhat more remotely in Matt 18:19: ". . . if two of you agree on earth about any request you make, it will be done for you . . ." Mark appears to have drawn together two of the most absolute of the Matthean sayings on prayer and forged them into this exhortation to pray for the dawn of the New Age.

24. The prefatory *For this reason* closely links the sayings on prayer with the faith demanded of those who long for the Reign of God.

25. The corollary to this saying on prayer is the saying on forgiveness in v. 25. The clause *forgive whatever you have against anyone* is certainly an echo of the similar petition in the Lord's Prayer (Matt 6:12, Luke 11:3-4) and is wholly in line not only with Matt 5:23-24 but also with the teaching on forgiveness in Paul and the rest of the New Testament. The Greek of *your Father . . . may forgive the wrongs you have done* in this verse is verbally identical with Matt 6:14. This is significant, for only here does Mark use *your Father* (Greek *patēr humōn*), and only here too does he use *paraptōma* for *wrongs*. There would seem to be a clear case of Markan dependence on his source in Matthew.

stand praying: This stance in prayer was common among Jews (cf. 1 Kgs 8:14,22; Neh 9:4; Ps 134:1; Matt 6:5; Luke 18:11,13) and was almost universal among early Christians. We know of the practice of kneeling in prayer from 1 Kgs 8:54; Dan 6:10; and in the New Testament from Acts 7:60, 20:36, 21:5; and Eph 3:14.

forgive: Cf. 1:18, 2:5 for the Greek *aphiemi.*

whatever you have against anyone: Cf. Col 3:13.

26. This verse is in parentheses because it is found only in a few manuscripts and is plainly an addition from Matt 6:15. It is included here as an example of the fashion in which assimilation between the gospels' material took place. It is not found in the major manuscripts of the gospels.

One final note may be added on the fig tree material. The rabbinic suggestion (TB *Berakoth* 40a, *Genesis Rabba* 15.7) was that the forbidden tree and its fruit in the Garden of Eden was a fig. Was there a tradition that just as a beast used for sinful purposes was to be slain (Lev 20:15-16), so the tree which had provided its forbidden fruit was to be punished on some future occasion? TB *Sanhedrin* 102a suggests that the threat in Exod 32:34 means that every future calamity carried some of the punishment for the idolatry of the golden calf. Perhaps then the fig tree was destined for punishment and was so punished when Jesus had reason to be displeased with it. (I owe this suggestion to my friend Dr. Moses Aberbach.)

61. A Question About Authority: A Parable
(11:27-12:12) = Matt 21:23-27; Luke 20:1-8

11 27 So they came again to Jerusalem. As he was walking in the temple, the chief priests and the scribes and the elders came to him. 28 "By what authority do you do these things?" they said. "Who gave you authority to do them?" 29 Jesus said to them, "I have but one question to put to you. If you give me an answer, I will tell you by what authority I do these things. 30 The baptism of John—was it from God, or from men? Answer me." 31 They argued among themselves, "What shall we say? If we say, 'From God' he will say, 'Then why did you not believe him?' 32 Shall we say, 'From men'?"—but they were afraid of the crowd, for everyone held that John was in fact a prophet. 33 They therefore answered Jesus, "We do not know." And Jesus said to them, "Neither then will I tell you by what authority I do these things."

(12:1-12) = Matt 21:33-46; Luke 20:9-19

12 1 He went on to speak to them in parables: "A man planted a vineyard, put a wall around it, made a hole for the winepress, and built a watchtower. He then rented it out to winegrowers and went on a journey. 2 When the season came, he sent a slave to the winegrowers to collect from them his share of the produce. 3 But they took him, beat him, and sent him away with nothing. 4 Again, he sent to them another slave, and they beat him about the head and treated him shamefully. 5 He therefore sent another slave, and they killed that one; and many more as well, of whom they beat some, and killed others. 6 He had now only one to send, and that was a beloved son. In the end, he sent him to them. 'They will respect my son,' he said. 7 But those tenants said to one another, 'This is the heir. Come on, let us kill him and the property will be ours.' 8 So they seized him, killed him, and flung his body out of the vineyard. 9 What then will the owner of the vineyard do? He will come and kill those tenants and will give the

vineyard to others. [10] Surely you know this scripture: 'The stone which the builders rejected has become the main cornerstone: [11] This was the Lord's doing, and it is wonderful in our eyes.' " [12] Then they tried to arrest him, for they knew that he had directed this parable against them. But they were afraid of the crowd, so they left him alone and went away.

Comment

There is no note of time or place here, and this is usual with Mark. But Matthew clearly links this episode with the incident of the fig tree (21:23, "When he went into the temple . . . ," following on from 21:18, "Early in the morning, as he was returning to the city . . ."). Luke is much less definite: "Now one day while he was teaching the people in the temple . . ." (20:1). For Mark, the link between the two fig-tree incidents is vital: he is concerned, as is Matthew, with the references to be drawn, and the lessons learned, from a prophetic symbolic gesture. The question of authority, and Jesus' reference back to John, are vital signs of the meaning of Jesus' ministry.

As the first part of this narrative stands, it is an apothegm, or pronouncement story; whatever elements there may have been of description or detail have long been eroded away, and we are left with a question and answer, both of them provocative. Though Luke gives no information about the time and place of this incident, both Matthew and Mark are concerned about the signs of the Reign of God and about the place and authority of Jesus in its proclamation. For Mark—on the basis of the views expressed in the Introduction— the pressure toward the inauguration of the New Covenant and its ratification in cross and resurrection had an urgency which is lacking in Matthew. There is no awareness of such pressure in Luke, for he is already concerned with a Gentile mission and an extended "time of the Church."

Notes

27. *So they came:* This may be a kind of impersonal plural and may well be the original oral tradition. Some manuscripts have "he," thus focusing exclusive attention on Jesus.

chief priests . . . elders: Cf. 8:31; *scribes:* cf. 1:22. Only here, and in 8:31, 14:43,53, and 15:1 are the three groups mentioned together. This cannot mean the Sanhedrin, for Mark uses that technical expression when its mention is called for. We assume that this was a small and casually assembled group of all three orders.

28. *these things:* It seems reasonable to assume that this Greek word *(tauta)* refers to the symbolic gesture in the temple. It can hardly have reference to the fig tree.

authority (Greek *exousia):* Cf. 1:22. The story, in whatever original form or in whatever context, was preserved because it illustrated the belief of the Christian community that Jesus' authority came from God. In contrast to the Greek word *dunamis* (= power), this word means divine authority and "not legal or political right" (Taylor, p. 469). What is being demanded of Jesus is what claim he can make to legitimate his action in the temple. The double nature of the question is more characteristic of Socratic, Hellenistic dialogue than of rabbinical debate, and the questions may have been recast for the benefit of those unfamiliar with rabbinic convention. Luke's form of the dialogue would appear to lay equal stress on the teaching of Jesus as on his actions through the ministry. The connection between the Cleansing of the Temple and Jesus' authority is certainly made in John 2:18.

29. *I have but one question to put to you:* The Greek word for *question (logos)* is here used in the sense of "matter," or even "debating point."

If you give me an answer: The verb is imperative *(apokrithēte)*, used in the same conditional sense as the verb "believe" in v. 24.

30. *The baptism:* On the baptism of John and its significance, cf. comment and notes on 1:1-11. This question of Jesus is not a device for turning aside the question, still less a riposte to divert attention from the matter under discussion. The method of question and counterquestion was a well-known device in Hellenistic culture, and is found as early as the fifth century B.C. The form was designed to elicit the truth of a matter and could even induce an opponent to give an answer which the proponent could not elicit by a direct first question.

The plain implication of Jesus' question is that John's authority came from God. We are here in the presence of the very early core of the Jesus tradition as it was remembered by the early community. When Jesus was questioned by the followers of John, he answered that the one who authorized the eschatological baptism of John had also authorized Jesus to proclaim and inaugurate the Reign of God with all its attendant signs (cf. Matt 11:2-15 = Luke 7:18-28). The implicit demand of Jesus therefore is that his opponents and questioners decide for themselves how *they* regard the subsequent ministry and proclamation of Jesus.

(The relationship between the Greek of the three synoptists at this point is of some moment. Both Matthew and Luke agree in the Greek of "Jesus said to them" *[apokritheis de ho Jesus]* and "I too will ask you a question" *[erotēso humas kagō logon]*. Generally, this is regarded as an agreement by Matthew [21:24] and Luke [20:3] against Mark. But some important manuscripts of Mark also read *apokritheis* at 11:29, and yet others read *humas kagō* ["and I will . . . you"]. The textual history is incapable of resolution, and it must be remembered that if Mark's text did originally read *kagō* [abbreviation for *kai ego* = "and I"], then it would be unique in this evangelist.)

The episode can hardly be regarded as a creation of the primary community, for there is no trace in the New Testament, let alone subsequently, of any attempt to build the authority of Jesus on that of John (cf. Lohmeyer, p. 243).

31. The force of the dilemma can be seen by reference to Luke 7:29-30. The classes

of people who listened to John and underwent his baptism were those who would have
been regarded by Jesus' questioners as less than devoted to the Law.

argued among themselves (Greek *dialogizomai*): Cf. 2:6.

among themselves (Greek *pros eautous*): Cf. 8:16.

from God (Greek *ex ouranou*, literally "from heaven"): The word "heaven" was in
common use to avoid any word for God; cf. Dan 4:26; 1 Macc 3:18; Luke 15:18,21;
John 3:27; etc.

What shall we say? If we say . . . . : Reading the Greek as *Ti eipōmen; ean eipōmen*
. . . , though some manuscripts read *ean eipōmen* . . . *Ti eipōmen* ("If we shall say
. . . What shall we say then?").

32. The second conditional sentence breaks off, and the conclusion is replaced by
the statement that *they were afraid of the crowd*. To acknowledge, with those who had
followed John, that he was a prophet was also to acknowledge that his had been a
divine inspiration, and that Jesus as John's inheritor and successor posed the same
challenge of authority.

From men? There was nothing unique in the actual practice of baptism by John, for
the Essenes used baptism as an initiation rite, and also had a regular practice of ritual
lustration. What was unique was the eschatological reference of John's rite in its
looking to the Reign of God. But Jesus' question to his opponents encompassed the
whole ministry of John—the baptism was but the most visible symbol of it.

33. Inaction is often the refuge of the unscrupulous or the conscience-burdened,
and so is it here. *"We do not know"* is answered by Jesus' refusal to reply to their
initial question. But his refusal, with the word *authority* still left hanging almost as a
threat, implies his own conviction of final vindication for his ministry and message.
(Cf. G. S. Shae, "The Question of the Authority of Jesus," *NovTest* 16.1.1974, pp. 1-
29.)

Mark's Greek follows Matthew and Luke fairly closely, with some exceptions. In v.
31, Mark omits *hoi de* ("but they") before the verb *argued* (Mark follows Matthew in
using *dielogizonto*, rejecting Luke's *sunelogisanto*). But recasting the conclusions in v.
32 given by Matthew (21:26, "If we say 'From men' we are afraid of the people, for all
regard John as a prophet") and Luke (20:6, "If we say 'From men' the people will
stone us, for they are sure that John was a prophet"), Mark considerably heightens the
dramatic impact of the incident. Mark follows Matthew in using *We do not know*,
rejecting Luke's "So they replied that they did not know."

Comment (12:1-12)

Closely linked as is this parable with the preceding discussion on authority, it
poses great difficulties of its own, complicated by the discovery of another
version of it in the *Gospel of Thomas*. Our discussion here will focus on three
areas of concern: (a) the relationship between the synoptic versions; (b) the
apparent meaning of the parable as seen by the early community and in the
Gospel of Thomas, and (c) its meaning for Mark and his community.

The three versions can best be seen when put in parallel:

Matt 21:33-46	*Mark 12:1-12*	*Luke 20:9-19*
A man planted a vineyard and let it out to winegrowers	A man planted a vineyard and let it out to winegrowers	A man planted a vineyard and let it out to winegrowers
At the *fruit season* he sent *servants* to receive his *fruits* and they were *beaten, killed, and stoned*	At the *proper time* he sent *a servant* to receive *part of the fruit* of the vineyard and he was *beaten*	At the *proper time* he sent *a servant* to receive *part of the fruit* and he was *beaten*
He sent *another group* and the same happened	He sent *another servant* and he was *wounded*	He sent a *second servant* and he was *beaten*
	He sent *another* and he was *killed*	He sent a *third* and he was *wounded*
	He sent *many others* and some were killed and some beaten	
He sent his *son* and they *cast him out* and *killed* him	He sent his *beloved son* and they *killed him* and *cast him out*	He sent his *beloved son* and they *cast him out* and *killed* him
He will destroy the winegrowers and give the vineyard to others who will give him the *fruits when in their season*	He will destroy the winegrowers and give the vineyard to others	He will destroy the winegrowers and give the vineyard to others
"The stone which the builders rejected has become the cornerstone."	"The stone which the builders rejected has become the cornerstone."	"The stone which the builders rejected has become the cornerstone."
Therefore I say to you the kingdom of God will be taken from you and given to a people yielding *its fruits.*		

Some matters spring instantly to mind. The similarity between Mark and Luke is striking, and both agree in speaking of a *beloved son,* reminiscent of the baptism (1:11) and the transfiguration (9:7) and indicating a christological interest. Matthew, by way of contrast, simply speaks of "his son" and closes with a saying which (like most of that gospel) is in many ways more attuned to the Reign of God and its inauguration than with the herald and inaugurator of that Reign. We may further detect in all three synoptists the development of the community's interest in Jesus himself and his relationship to God in the quotation from Ps 118 *("The stone which the builders rejected . . .")*. We have reason, too, to question the authenticity of v. 9 in the passage before us: it is wholly unlike any other example of Jesus' parable teaching, with the sole exception of Luke 10:36: "Which of these three, do you think, proved himself a neighbor . . . ?"

The element of allegory in Matthew and Mark was recognized early. The influence of Isa 5:1-9 (and in the text of the Septuagint) is unmistakable. The scenario (to use a modern expression) was as follows: vineyard = Israel; owner = God; the tenant winegrowers = Israel's leaders and rulers; the various messengers = the prophets, former and latter; the son = Jesus; the inevitable punishment = the ruin of Israel; the other tenants = the Gentile Church.

The necessary attempt to penetrate behind obvious allegory to the words of Jesus seems at first sight a task easy to accomplish. But before we go further, we have to set the version in our gospels against the same parable in the *Gospel of Thomas.* In doing so, we find a totally different picture from that presented by the synoptists. In Thomas, the allegorizing details are wholly absent, as will be seen from the following *(Gos Thom* 93:1-16): "A good man had a vineyard. He gave it to winegrowers so that they would work it and he would receive fruit from it. He sent his servant so that the winegrowers would give him the fruit of the vineyard. They seized his servant and beat him; a little longer and they would have killed him. The servant came and told it to his master. His master said, 'Perhaps he was unknown to them.' He sent another servant, and they beat him as well. Then the owner sent his son. He said, 'Perhaps they will respect my son.' Since those winegrowers knew that he was the heir to the vineyard they seized him and killed him. Who has ears to hear, let him hear." (The subject of the *Gospel of Thomas* continues to generate debate, and a small bibliography is found later in this section. This manuscript, found at Nag Hammadi in Egypt in 1945 or 1946, is one of thirteen, generally considered to be the library of a Gnostic sect, but its origin is unknown. Similarly, the date of the manuscript is unknown, but limit dates of A.D. 300-400 have been proposed.)

The significant differences provide a very considerable contrast to the allegories of the synoptics. Thomas does not tell us that the owner was an absentee landlord, and we may suspect that the detail *went on a journey* (= Matt 21:33, Luke 20:9) is meant to emphasize that the owner is the invisible God. Again, the synoptic version tells us that the owner sent a slave *when the season came,* a detail omitted in Thomas. This may be an indication that the evangelists wish us to understand by the word *kairos* (= *season)* that the messenger was sent at the appropriate time in salvation history. In Mark's version we have first of all *one slave* (v. 2) sent to the vineyard, then *another slave* (v. 4), then a third, and *many more as well*. Matthew, on the other hand, has one group of three slaves who were respectively beaten, killed, and stoned (21:35); then a second and larger group which suffered the same fate (21:36). Luke, in 20:10, tells of the sending of one slave who was beaten, then a second who suffered similarly (20:11), and finally a third who returned wounded (20:12). The parable in Thomas, however, tells of only two slaves who were sent before the owner's son, and they were both beaten (93:6-11). Matthew's two groups of servants have frequently been held to be the former and the latter prophets, while Mark's *many others* may reflect the persecution of the prophets by their own people. If Luke is free of allegory, it nevertheless lacks the simplicity of Thomas. Furthermore, the sending of only two slaves before the son was held by one author to preserve the "much used Jewish triplet" (R. McL. Wilson, "Thomas and the Synoptic Gospel," *ExpT* 72.1.1960, p. 37). On the other hand, it may be that Thomas reflects the synoptists in the matter of procedure.

It is, however, the matter of allegory which makes the clear difference between Thomas and the evangelists. The vital element in the synoptic versions is the vindication of the son, and this is wholly independent of the christological note implied in the use of the *only one, a beloved son* (Mark 12:6 = Luke 20:13). We hear nothing in Thomas of a vengeance on the winegrowers, but there is present in the synoptists the all-important quotation from Ps 118:22-23 from the Septuagint. That there is here a judgment on Israel and her rulers seems a conclusion impossible to resist, and reflects the growing tensions between Jew and non-Jew in the early community. There are reflections of the Passion story in Matthew, where the son is first thrown out and then killed (21:39), and this is also the case in Luke 20:15, probably reflecting not only the place of the crucifixion as outside the city, but also the kind of early Christian tradition found in Heb 13:12 ("outside the camp"). Mark merely says that the son was *killed,* and they *flung his body out of the vineyard.* In the synoptists the Resurrection has supervened, and the whole interpretation of the parable has shifted.

It is possible to plead that the kind of detail we have in the synoptists has been excised in Thomas, and the parable compressed, but the presence of two quotations from the Septuagint makes it far more likely that what we have in Thomas is the original version, or as near to the parable as spoken by Jesus as we are likely to come. The beginning and the ending in the synoptic versions are clearly secondary, christological by intent, and give added weight to a process of allegorization already in being.

Before we examine the relationship between the synoptists, we must address ourselves to the meaning of the original parable as uttered by Jesus—assuming as we do here that the version in Thomas is as close to the primary source as we can reasonably be. If we concede that the parable as originally spoken had no allegorical significance, does it bear (as do all the other parables of Jesus) any resemblance to social reality? Contemplating the forbearance of the owner, the insufferable treatment meted out to his servants, can we believe that the tenants really had any expectation that they could obtain title to the vineyard by killing the heir? In all probability the answer must be yes, given the revolutionary atmosphere of Galilee and the profusion of absentee foreign landowners. On the grounds of the above discussion, we may reasonably construct (admittedly on the basis of the *Gospel of Thomas)* the original meaning of the parable on the lines of Jesus vindicating his proclamation to the poor, the despised, and the alienated. The tenants, the winegrowers in God's vineyard, have opposed, rebelled against God. But the day of their judgment is at hand, and the leaders and rulers (the winegrowers) will be dispossessed and the vineyard given to others. But who then is the *son* in the parable? Certainly Jesus had his own vocation, his own "sending," much in his mind throughout the ministry, but how far are we correct in identifying the son with Jesus, if in fact we do? The evangelists and the early Christian writers had no doubt in the matter, as we have seen from the christological details in the synoptic texts. But only in the loosest terms would a Jewish contemporary of Jesus have made the equation "messiah = Son of God"; that equation belongs to the early Christian community. If the owner of the vineyard, of Israel, is God, then who on the lips of Jesus might the son have been? There is a slight clue in Thomas: "Perhaps for the ill-treatment of his servants"—"Perhaps he was unknown to them." There is nothing here of the assurance of the Markan *They will respect my son* (v. 6). If we can remove the identification of the son with Jesus from our minds, we may then look at the context of this parable. Matt 21:23-27—the matter of the authority of Jesus and John's baptism—is followed immediately by the parable of the two sons (21:28-32), with the highly significant "For John came to you in the path of righteousness, and you did not believe him, which the tax collectors and the prostitutes did. Even when you saw that, you did not later change your minds and believe him." This in turn is followed by the parable we have been discussing. We have seen good reason to suppose that while Jesus sought to validate his own ministry by reference to that of John, the primary community very soon began to obscure that appeal of Jesus. Is it therefore possible that the "son" in the parable before us was intended by Jesus to be identified with John? The ending is significant in all three evangelists: Matt 21:45-46, Mark 12:12, Luke 20:19 all testify to the bitter opposition of those in authority *for they knew he had directed this parable against them.* We may conclude that this estimate is correct, but did Jesus direct this parable against them on the basis of their opposition to him, or was it rather that he was accusing them of being deliberately obtuse about John and his ministry? Significantly, we find the phrase "they feared the crowd" or "they feared the people" in much the same way as Mark records (11:27) *but they were afraid of the crowd* when challenged about John. In this commentary the parable has been subsumed under the heading "A Question About Authority" on the grounds that the parable's primary reference on the lips of Jesus was to John the Baptizer.

Bibliography

The following list is merely intended to present some introductory material on the *Gospel of Thomas* and is not meant to be exhaustive.

Davies, Stevan L. *The Gospel of Thomas and Christian Wisdom.* New York: Seabury Press, 1983.

Doresse, Jean. *The Secret Books of the Egyptian Gnostics.* New York: Viking Press, 1960.

Grant, Robert M., and Freedman, David N. *The Secret Sayings of Jesus.* Garden City, N.Y.: Doubleday, 1960.

Montefiore, Hugh, and Turner, H. E. W. *Thomas and the Evangelists.* London: SCM Press, 1962.

Robinson, James M., ed. *The Nag Hammadi Library.* Leiden: E. J. Brill, 1984.

The reader who wishes to pursue further parable interpretation in the light of the *Gospel of Thomas* should consult J. Jeremias, *The Parables of Jesus* (for publication details, see Bibliography, p. 152).

We must now turn our attention to this parable as it exhibits the relationships between the three gospels. The majority and customary view is that Mark provided the first version of the parable, later elaborated and given (in Matthew's case) a different emphasis. This is far from being self-evident. For one thing, the Matthean emphasis on the Reign of God (21:43) must be regarded as being closer in intent to the proclamation of Jesus than the Lucan and Markan versions are. Again, to suggest that because the Markan account is shorter it must therefore be closer to the original is to overlook one of the known rules of conflation—that of eliminating the nonessential and peripheral and concentrating on essentials. Any attempt on Mark's part to conflate two discrete endings would not only end in failure, but would also confuse the issue. Thus, Mark's reshaping of his sources produced an ending which is much closer to the original.

Matthew's form, though far shorter than Luke's, depends for its effect on a heightening of tension: slaves, then other slaves, and finally the son, leading to the rhetorical question attendant upon the owner coming in person to the vineyard—"What will we do?" The emphasis is on the nature of the messengers sent. Luke likewise depends on dramatic effect to get his point across, but here the emphasis is on the escalating violence toward a series of messengers, and then finally the murder of the son. Mark's treatment of all this is to *combine* the series of messengers. Only in this way can we adequately account for the proliferation of the messengers in Mark's version. In result, the dramatic heightening of tension in both Matthew and Luke is missing. Hence, Mark's *ending* is certainly to be preferred *(He will come and kill those tenants and will give the vineyard to others)*. This was copied from Luke. But faced with a differing emphasis in his two predecessors as between murders of messengers and the variety of treatments meted out to them, he combined them and produced a central section to the parable which offset the dramatic ending by a wordiness uncharacteristic of his usual work. (It is to be hoped that in the not too distant future someone will undertake to examine the few Markan parables for the light they shed on his treatment of sources.)

Notes

1. The quotation *"planted a vineyard, put a wall around it, made a hole for the winepress, and built a watchtower"* comes from the Septuagint of Isa 5:1-2. The reference to *parables* is not to parables as such, but to Jesus' preferred method of teaching. For *a man,* Matt 21:33 has "householder" (Greek *oikodespotēs).*

vineyard (Greek *ampetōn):* The word is common in later Greek, in Septuagint, and in the papyri of the Hellenistic period.

winepress (Greek *hupolēniou):* This was a vessel into which the juice of the grapes ran after they had been pressed in a vessel above it.

wall (Greek *phragmos):* This was designed not so much to prevent theft as to keep out wild animals. The tower (Greek *purgos)* enabled a watch to be kept over the property.

Apart from setting the scene, the details from Isaiah have no further interest. Nothing is said of a disappointing harvest: the owner plants the property, leases it, and sets out on a journey. If the allegory is pursued at this point, the owner's absence can only be taken as referring to the invisibility of God, and not to his absence from Israel's affairs.

rented it out (Greek *exedeto*—vernacular, replaced by the more classical *exedoto* in some manuscripts): Found in Herodotus and in the New Testament, the sense is "to farm out for financial advantage."

Luke omits the details from Isa 5:1-2 and introduces the parable by saying it was addressed to the people, while Matt 21:33 has "Listen to another parable." Mark follows Matthew's Greek closely.

2-5. Mark has three slaves sent in succession, combining "his slaves" of Matthew, and Luke's three separate messengers with *many others* (Matt 21:35, Luke 20:10-12).

When the season came (Greek *tō kairō):* In Old Testament terms this would mean the fifth year (cf. Lev 19:23-25), but it is probable that the evangelists wished us to understand this term as "the time of salvation."

a slave (Greek *doulos):* If we wish to see in the various messengers the former and the latter prophets, the word is used of prophets in the Old Testament, first of Moses (Josh 14:7, Ps 105:26), then of Joshua (Josh 24:29), of David (2 Sam 3:18), and then of the prophets generally (Amos 3:7, Zech 1:6, Jer 7:25). In the treatment of the slaves there is a considerable heightening of suffering, but the Greek text is somewhat confusing. The first slave, for example, was beaten (Greek *edeiran*, which Mark took from Luke 20:10). The Greek verb *derō* originally meant "to skin" or "flay," but in New Testament times its meaning had been modified.

another slave: The translation used for the treatment of this slave *(beat him about the head)* represents the best that can be done with Mark's Greek *(ekephalaiōsan)*, the difficulty being that the Greek word in the majority of the manuscripts means "to sum up, recapitulate" and there is no example known to us of the meaning "to wound in the head." Many manuscripts, feeling that the word needs explanation, add *lithobolēsantes* (= "hurling stones"). There is no question that violent treatment is meant, for Matt 21:35 has "threw stones" (Greek *elithobolēsan)* and Luke 20:12 has "wounded" (Greek *traumatisantes)*. This is reinforced by the Vulgate: *in capite vulner-averunt* (= "they wounded him in the head"). We are left to hazard the guess that Mark used *kephalaioō* in a sense which is not attested elsewhere, or that the text is corrupt. The majority of our manuscripts do read *ekephalaiōsan,* and perhaps—as all the manuscripts in question are Alexandrian—there was an original scribal blunder and what was originally written was *ekolaphisan,* "to knock in the head." So far as is known at present, however, no manuscript contained this Greek reading.

shamefully (Greek *atimazō:* literally, "to dishonor"): Cf. 2 Sam 10:5, Acts 5:41.

another slave: There is a brief reference to the murder of the third slave, and then there is a general summary of *many more as well, of whom they beat some, and killed others*—a convenient way of dealing with the variations between Matt 21:35-36 and Luke 20:11-12. There is more than enough testimony in the Old Testament to the violence visited upon God's messengers: cf. 1 Kgs 18:13, 22:27; 2 Chron 24:20-22, 36:15, Neh 9:26; Jer 37:15.

6. The translation reflects a comma after "He had yet one, a beloved son" *(or* "an only son") in the Greek.

beloved: The Greek is *agapētos,* and as we saw earlier it reflects in both Mark and Luke the Greek of the baptism of Jesus and the Transfiguration. The equivalency of "only" and "beloved" can be clearly seen in Gen 22:2, Judg 11:34 (in A = Codex Alexandrinus), and Tob 3:10 (in Codex Sinaiticus). In the New Testament Eph 1:6 we have *ho egapēmenos* (= "the Beloved"), and in later Christian writers both *ho agapētos* and the Ephesian designation became messianic titles. With the possible exception of Luke 20:13 ("I will send my son, the beloved one") it is doubtful if any messianic meaning is intended here. Indeed, however Matthew's "his own son" (21:37) was originally meant to be understood, only the later addition of the quotation from Ps 118 changed the meaning for both the evangelists and the communities for which they wrote.

In Matthew and Mark the owner expresses a conviction: *They will respect my son,* whereas Luke 20:13 has "surely they will respect my son."

7. *heir* translates the Greek *ho klēronomos; property,* the Greek *klēronomia* (literally "inheritance").

Come on (Greek *dente):* Cf. 1:17, 6:31; see also the words of Joseph's brothers—Gen 37:20.

8. The statement *flung him out of the vineyard* may imply that the body was not

buried. Luke 20:15 ("throwing him outside the vineyard they killed him") may represent a deliberate intention to order the events to agree with the tradition of the crucifixion. Some, but not all, manuscripts of Matt 21:39 do not have this order, but read "they killed him and flung him out of the vineyard."

9. *What then . . . ?* While Mark largely agrees with Luke 20:15 in the question posed (Luke has ". . . do to them?"), Matt 21:40 has "When therefore the owner of the vineyard comes, what will he do to those tenant-farmers?" In Matthew, the hearers answer Jesus' question; in Mark (following Luke) the answer is supplied by Jesus. Recalling the ending of the same parable in the *Gospel of Thomas* ("Who has ears to hear, let him hear"), it is very difficult to determine whether this question-and-answer ending is original, or added by the evangelist to underscore Jesus' judgment on the rulers and leaders of Israel. It will be recalled that in one instance, at least, Jesus left his own question unanswered: "Does he thank the servant because he did the things commanded?" (Luke 17:9). If the parable originally had to do with the sending of John the Baptist, then it may be best to assume that the question was originally left standing without answer.

others: If Matthew (cf. 21:41) was thinking of the apostles as the legitimate heirs and successors to those who had failed so miserably, and as producing fruit where the others had failed (21:43), Mark gives no hint as to the meaning of the term. Luke's version evidently supplied Mark with his own version, but Luke adds (20:16): "and when they had heard, they said 'God forbid!' " Given the frequency of that Greek expression *mē genoito* (literally, "Let it not be!") in Paul, and especially in view of the tensions between Jew and Gentile in the Church (cf. Rom 11:1,11), is there in Luke some veiled reference to that tension and controversy? If there was, then Mark rejected the Lucan addition as wholly irrelevant to the concerns of his own suffering community. Apart from that reference in Romans, the judgment in v. 9 is clearly all of a piece with gospel sources (cf. Matt 8:11, 22:13, and Luke 13:28-30).

10-11. The preface, *Surely you know this scripture,* is in Matthew (21:42) "Jesus said to them, 'Did you not read in the Scriptures?' " and in Luke (20:17) "And looking on them he said, 'What then is this that is written?' " The variations would appear to suggest that the three prefaces are independent compositions, composed simply to introduce what had become a "proof text" in the early community. So far as Mark is concerned, his introductory preface is ample indication of the importance the community attached to the quotation. The Greek *oude tēn graphēn tautēn anegnōte* is literally "Did you not know even this writing?" It is only here that Mark uses "scripture" in the singular, but cf. Luke 4:21; Acts 1:16; John 7:38,42, 19:37; 2 Tim 3:16; Jas 2:8 (Mark 15:28 is a scribal editorial addition). Further, Mark usually introduces quotations by "it is written" (Greek *gegraptai),* and sayings by "and he said to them" (Greek *kai elegen autois).* We are here in the presence of a formula Mark found independently of his sources, or composed himself.

'The stone . . .': The quotation comes verbatim from the Septuagint, which suggests that this proof text had been in circulation among Diaspora Jewish Christians and Gentile Christian communities. But well known as the whole psalm was as a Jewish festival psalm, it is at least possible that Jesus had used parts of the psalm, or especially these verses, as part of an attack on the Jewish hierarchy in Jerusalem.

10. The stone (Greek *lithos)* which became the main cornerstone (Greek *kephatē*

gonias) drew together a series of "testimonies" in the New Testament literature around the word "stone." There are two such "stone" references in 1 Pet 2:6,8, from Isa 28:16 ("See, I lay in Sion a stone . . .") and Isa 8:14 ("a stone for stumbling . . .") and also in Rom 9:33 (from Isa 28:16). Significantly, such collections are found in early Christian writings: *Epistle of Barnabas* 6:2-4; Cyprian *(Testimonia* 2.16); Aphraat *(Homilies* 1.6); and twice Justin Martyr describes Jesus as "the stone" *(Dialogue with Trypho* 24.2 and 36.1).

In rabbinic literature the stone is sometimes identified with Abraham and sometimes with Moses. If, indeed, Jesus used this quotation in an attack on the religious establishment of his own time, it would seem likely that on his lips it meant a reversal of an existing order, and a reversal which was the work of God. To the early Christian community, the rejection of Jesus by the religious establishment and his vindication through the resurrection would very soon have produced a reinterpretation whereby any use of the quotation by Jesus would have been regarded as applying to Jesus himself.

Matt 21:43 adds to the quotation: "Therefore I say to you that the Kingdom of God will be taken from you, and given to a people which will be productive." To this, in some manuscripts, is added the Lucan (20:18) "Everyone who falls upon that stone will be crushed, but upon whomsoever it falls, it will grind him to powder."

12. Mark refers again (cf. 11:18) to the opposition of the religious authorities, using quite familiar words: *tried* (literally "sought," Greek *zēteō;* cf. 1:37), *arrest* ("seize"; cf. 1:31, Greek *kratēsai), afraid* (Greek *phebeomai;* cf. 6:41), *crowd* (Greek *ochlos;* cf. 2:4), *they knew* (Greek *ginōskō;* cf. 13:28, 15:10), *parable* (Greek *parabolē;* cf. 3:28), *left* (Greek *aphiēmi;* cf. 1:18). Matthew has another version of this sentence, and adds ". . . they feared the crowds, for all regarded him as a prophet." Neither Matthew nor Luke has the concluding *they left him alone and went away.*

On the parable, and its possible links with an ancient Jewish parable, see J. D. M. Derrett, "Allegory and the Wicked Winedressers," *JTS* 25.2.1974, pp. 426-32. See also K. P. Snodgrass, "The Parable of the Wicked Husbandmen: Is the Gospel of Thomas Version Original?" *NTS* 21.2.1974, pp. 142-44; also B. Dehandschutter, "La parabole des vignerons homicides (Mc. 12.1-12) et l'évangile selon Thomas," pp. 203-19 in *L'évangile selon Marc: Tradition et redaction,* edited by M. Sabbe (Bibliotheca ephemeridum theologicarum lovaniensium 34; Gembloux: Duculot; Louvain: Leuven University Press, 1974); and J. D. Crossan, "The Parable of the Wicked Husbandmen," *JBL* 90.4.1971, pp. 451-65.

62. Questions: 1. Taxation
(12:13-17) = Matt 22:15-22; Luke 20:20-26

12   13 Some Pharisees, together with members of Herod's party, were sent to trap him in his talk. 14 They came to him and said, "Rabbi, we know you to be an honest man, and that you court no one's favor for you pay no attention to outward appearance. You teach in all honesty the way of God. Is it lawful to pay taxes to the Roman emperor, or not? Should we pay, or not?" 15 But he saw through this casuistry and said, "Why are you putting me to the test? Bring me a silver piece and let me see it." 16 They brought one, and he said to them, "Whose portrait is this, and whose inscription is it?" "The emperor's," they answered. 17 Then Jesus said to them, "Then pay back to the emperor what belongs to him, and to God what belongs to God." They were astounded at him.

Comment

Wholly without context of time or place, save that it is set in the framework of a series of controversies about authority, this pericope is perhaps the apothegm, or pronouncement story, in its purest form. Nothing stands in the way of the stark confrontation of question/answer. All the emphasis is on what Jesus said, and perhaps the detail of his perception of motive could be eliminated without prejudice to the nature of the story. We cannot doubt that this is a genuine incident, for the reply of Jesus is wholly typical of the enigmatic character of his recorded sayings throughout the ministry.

Notes

13. We are not informed who sent the messengers to entrap Jesus, but possibly we are meant to infer that members of the Sanhedrin sent this delegation. The reference to *Herod's party* may imply that this incident belongs to the Galilean ministry. However, a tradition in Luke 23:7 records that Herod Antipas was in Jerusalem at the Passover, and the incident may belong historically in the context of this final week.

The verb translated *trap* (Greek *agrenō*) primarily means to catch by hunting or fishing. It is classical, is found in the Septuagint (Job 10:16; Prov 5:22, 6:25; Hos 5:2) and later in the papyri. Matthew uses *pagidenō*, and Luke *epilambanomai*, both with the same general sense. Matthew begins by recording a consultation of the Pharisees, and then sending some pupils, with the Herodians, to Jesus (22:15-16). Luke 20:20 connects the story with the priests' plot in 20:19, asserting that they sent spies who pretended to be honest enquirers. Given the development of a pericope *from* narrative form to the pronouncement story in its final, honed form, we must either conclude that Matthew and Luke elaborated on a simple question-and-answer apothegm from Mark, or that Mark represents the final stage in the narrative-to-pronouncement process. It will be clear by now which is the view embraced by this commentator.

14. The question is preceded by all the circumstances of flattery. Jesus is *honest* (Greek *alēthēs:* literally, "truthful") and courts *no one's favour* (Greek *melei soi oudenos:* literally, "have no regard for anyone"), for he pays *no attention to outward appearance* (Greek *ou gar blepeis eis prosōpon anthropōn:* literally, "you do not look on the form of men") but teaches *in all honesty the way of God* (Greek *all ep'alētheias tēn hodon tou theou:* literally, "you teach the way of God in truth").

You pay no attention to outward appearance. The Greek word *(prosōpon)* which we have translated as *outward appearance* was used in the common speech of this period in the sense of "person." (It was later to cause acrid debate and not a little confusion at the Council of Nicaea in A.D. 325 and again at the Council of Chalcedon in A.D. 451.) It is probable, however, that Mark's version and Luke's (20:21) "you do not consider a person" alike reflect Hebrew usage. In the Septuagint both *horaō* (to look) and *lambanō* (to receive) are used in the sense of accepting, or paying attention to, someone. (Cf. 1 Sam 16:7, Ps 82:2, Lev 19:15.) The New Testament provides *prosōpolempsia* (= respect of persons, Rom 2:11, Eph 6:9, Col 3:25), *prosōpeolēmptes* (= a respecter of persons, Acts 10:34) and *prosōpolempteō* (= to have respect to persons, Jas 2:9). There is a suggestion of favoring, of Uriah Heep, of flattering Jesus, in these substantives and verbs. The opposite attitude is to teach *in all honesty (ep'alētheias,* literally, "from the truth").

On the *way of God,* cf. Gen 6:12, Ps 1:1, Jer 21:8, Acts 18:25. "The Way" was used in the early Christian community to describe the followers of Jesus—cf. Acts 9:2; 19:9,23; 24:14,22.

taxes (Greek *kēnsos):* The Greek is a transliteration of the Latin *census,* which was a poll tax paid directly into the Roman imperial *fiscus,* or treasury. It was an object of deep resentment to Jews, not only because it was a visible sign of overlordship, but because the coinage carried the name and a representation of the emperor. The question therefore—*should we pay, or not?*—was a "no-win" problem. To answer yes would incur disfavor, and to answer no put the respondent at risk.

Some manuscripts have *epikephalaion* for *kensōs,* evidently an attempt to replace the Latin loanword by one which meant more literally "head money." The word is fairly common in the papyri.

Matt 22:17 has "Tell us, then, what you think. Is it lawful . . ." and with Luke omits *Should we pay or not?* Luke abbreviates his own source, and has (20:21) ". . . do not consider a person, but teach the way of God according to truth." He omits *you court no one's favour.*

15. *saw through* (Greek *eidōs*. Matthew has *gnous*, and Luke *katanoēsas):* The attitude of mind which Jesus sensed is described by Mark as *hupokrisis,* which we have translated as *casuistry.* Few things have been more destructive of an understanding of Jesus' critics than the translation of *hupokrisis* by "hypocrisy" and the corresponding *hupokritēs* as "hypocrite," with all the underlying assumptions of deliberate playacting. Originally, the word translated here as *casuistry* meant a hypercritical attitude, niggling, pettifogging. The reader wishing to explore this further is commended to the Anchor Bible *Matthew* (Albright-Mann, 1971, Introduction, IX, "Jesus and the Law, Appendix: *Hupokrisis, Hupokritēs, Hupokrinesthai,"* p. cxv). It is also important to remember, for all the obloquy that has attached to the word, that there is an entirely legitimate place for casuistry, concerned as it is with the bearing of the law on some particular case. To all outward appearance, there was a legitimate (and, at that time, burning) concern about handling tax money with a portrayal of a human figure on it.

In place of *hupokrisis* Matthew 22:18 has *ponēria* (= "malice"), and Luke 20:23 reads *panourgia* (= "cunning").

Bring me a silver piece: This may imply that neither Jesus nor his questioners had one, but Matt 20:19 has "Show me the tax money." This is also true in Luke 20:24—where, however, the form of the verb means, rather, "Hand me the tax money."

silver piece: This was the *denarius,* a silver coin, and the basic daily wage of an unskilled worker (cf. 6:37). Matt 22:19 reads "Show me the tax money" (Greek *to nomisma tou kēnsou,* literally "tax coin").

Some manuscripts of Mark, after *Why are you putting me to the test?* read "you casuists." This kind of address (". . . casuistry, and said . . . you casuists") is certainly typical of Mark—cf. 7:13,35; 15:4.

16. When Jesus has elicited the reply that the image and the wording belong to the emperor, he states a moral principle, but one which has in varying ways plagued the conscience of Christians and of the Church generally ever since. The verb *pay back* in v. 17 is *apodote* in Greek, and is different from the verb *pay (dounai)* in v. 14. The latter has the sense of "gift," but the verb used for Jesus' reply carries the meaning of "giving back what is due." The civil rulers therefore receive taxes as a due, not a gift. Similarly, God must be given what is his due. Later Christian attempts to reduce Jesus' statement of principle to exact legislation provided most of the material for the squalid medieval struggles between church and state. Embracing a so-called "doctrine" of the separation of church and state in no way diminishes the challenge posed by Jesus' reply.

portrait (Greek *eikōn):* The meaning of this word ranges through "image," "portrait," "statue," and "representation." Outside the compass of this commentary, we call attention to the importance of this word in the New Testament as applied to Jesus, especially in Col 1:15.

inscription (Greek *epigraphē)* (cf. 15:26; Matt 22:20; Luke 20:24, 23:38): The word is classical, and can also mean "assessment."

The emperor's: The emperor was Caesar Tiberius (A.D. 14-37) and his existing coins give the inscription *Ti(berius) Caesar divi Au(gusti) F(ilius) Augustus* ("Tiberius Augustus Caesar, son of the divine Augustus").

". . . to the emperor what belongs to him" (Greek *ta kaisaros,* literally "the things of the emperor"): "those things belonging to, or due to, the emperor"—cf. Rom 14:19,

together with "things belonging to peace" (Luke 24:19) or "things about Jesus" (Phil 1:12).

They were astounded at him (Greek *exethaumazou):* The Greek verb is a late compound, and Mark has a tendency to use compounds somewhat more expressive than a simple verb. For the same verb, cf. Sir 27:23 and 43:18, 4 Macc 17:17, and also Philo, *On Dreams* 2.70.

Jesus challenges his critics to realize that the very fact of using imperial coinage is an implicit recognition of the authority of the emperor. The attitude to the civil authorities espoused by Judas of Galilee in A.D. 6 was far different: Josephus *(Antiquities* 18.1.1) informs us that Judas held that the census undertaken by Quirinius as governor (for taxation purposes) was tantamount to slavery. In the New Testament, obligation to civil authority is explicitly commended in Rom 13:7 and 1 Pet 2:13-17 as justified by the peace and security provided by the state. But the situation envisaged by Rev 18 is one of a civil authority hostile to the Christian community and therefore to be rejected.

For an introduction to further readings on this topic, see John Howard Yoder, *The Politics of Jesus* (Grand Rapids, Mich.: Eerdmans, 1972).

Synoptic Relationships

The position taken by this writer is that generally speaking, with the gospels of Matthew and Luke before him, Mark combined the two texts whenever those texts were sufficiently close to make this possible. In the case of the pericope we have just examined, Mark made no unnecessary deviations, but as between phrases in Matthew and Luke he chose to use Luke, and when there was a significant difference in content Mark chose the longer text of Matthew. This was done as follows:

1. On the usual two-document hypothesis, Matthew changed the order of Mark's 12:14. Mark's order has four separate items: (a) *We know you to be an honest man,* (b) *You court no one's favor,* (c) *You pay no attention to outward appearance,* and (d) *You teach in all honesty the way of God.* Matthew, it is said, transferred (d) to a position between (a) and (b) and reworded it, though not significantly. Luke, on the other hand, retained Mark's order, but omitted (b) while rewording (a) and (c) and only copied word for word the last one (d). For this kind of rearrangement of the Markan material there is no explanation other than mere whim. Why should Matthew change the order of the four items—or, for that matter, introduce an insignificant change in wording in one after reproducing three? This is difficult enough to explain, but the Lucan editorial method (on the two-document hypothesis) is the wording of (a) and (c), reproducing the precise wording of Mark's (d) and omitting (b), while retaining the Markan order. Certainly, so far as I am aware, no suggestion has been made that there was here a special Lucan source.

2. On the theory of synoptic relationships generally espoused in this com-

mentary, the pericope is open to far easier analysis. Luke generally—though not always—used the Matthean text quite freely: changing the order of a phrase or a verse, rewording—often radically—and omitting phrases which appeared to interrupt the flow of a narrative. In this instance, however, fidelity to Matthew has been all but abandoned. Luke's transposition of the phrase "and teach truthfully the way of God" to the end of the sentence (Luke 21:21) is characteristic of his use of "the Way" in Acts to designate the Christian community. Luke, by this transfer, provides "the Way of God" as a climax to the whole, while in Matt 22:16 it is a minor theme. Luke's omission of Matthew's "you pay no attention to outward appearance" (Matt 22:16) is compensated by "you do not consider a person" (20:21).

3. Conflation is a process of editing in the synoptic gospels accepted by all critics as a commonplace, and this is especially true in the case of textual criticism. But what is claimed in the present instance is that the theory of Markan priority, far from simplifying the quest for rational order in synoptic relationships, results in Matthew and Luke acting at whim and in an almost irrational manner.

63. Questions: 2. Resurrection
(12:18-27) = Matt 22:23-33; Luke 20:27-40

12 ^18 Then Sadducees (who say there is no resurrection) came to him, questioning him. ^19 "Rabbi," they said, "Moses laid it down for us that if a man's brother dies and leaves a wife, but no child, then his brother must marry the widow and so raise up children on the brother's behalf. ^20 Now there were seven brothers. The first took a wife and died childless. ^21 Then the second married her, and died childless. So too with the third, ^22 and all seven—and left no children. After all the rest had died, the woman died too. ^23 In the resurrection, whose wife will she be? For they all married her." ^24 Jesus said to them, "You are mistaken, and surely it is because you do not know the Scriptures, or the power of God. ^25 For when the dead rise, men do not marry, and women are not given in marriage—in this, they are like the angels in heaven. ^26 But so far as being raised from the dead is concerned, have you not read in the book of Moses, in the passage about the bush, how God said to him, 'I am the God of Abraham, and the God of Isaac,

and the God of Jacob'? [27] God is not God of the dead, but of the living. You are very much mistaken."

Comment

At first sight this question put to Jesus might well have come from any period in the ministry. However, when we come to the close of this section of four questions—three asked of Jesus and one asked by Jesus—at the conclusion of 12:37, we shall have occasion to ask whether this grouping was deliberate.

This pericope, like its predecessor, is a typical pronouncement story, with a bare minimum of narrative detail. All the ideas contained here come from the heart of the Judaism of Jesus' time and we can be sure that we are not here dealing with a question raised in the early Christian community.

Notes

18. *Sadducees:* Mark, in common with his sources, offers minimal explanation about this group. He assumes that his reader will be fully aware of the kind of people subsumed under this name, and will also be aware of their main positions.

Even the etymology of the term *Sadducee* is uncertain. Some scholars maintain that the name derives from "Zadokite" (i.e., a descendant of the priestly family of Zadok, the high priest who anointed Solomon). Others suggest that the term comes from the Hebrew *ṣaddîk* (= "righteous"). Our only recorded information about this group comes from the New Testament and from Josephus. They were the priestly aristocracy in Jerusalem, along with their family, dependents, and followers. Both Acts (23:6-8) and Josephus *(Antiquities* 18.1.4) testify that they denied the existence of angels and spirits. It is uncertain—since the Sadducees accepted as scripture only the Law of Moses (Pentateuch)—whether they had any expectation of a messiah. Given that the Sadducees were a priestly party, we might have expected them to have some links with Qumran; but given the conviction of the Essenes that the Jerusalem priesthood had been hopelessly compromised and the high priesthood rendered suspect under the Hasmonean kings, this is highly unlikely.

We are not certain of the historical background of the Sadducees, but we may with some confidence ascribe their origin to the time of the Persian domination of Palestine from the time of Cyrus the Great (559-529 B.C.) to the Hellenistic conquest. The high priesthood was accepted by the Persians as the representative of the Jews, and this naturally gave the clerical families a considerable degree of preeminence and secular influence. Later, under the Hasmonean kings (A.D. 135-63), the Sadducees were to all intents the ruling class in the land. While it would be incorrect to describe them as a political party, they nevertheless did stand for retaining a comfortable status quo under the Roman power, and avoided the extremist separatism of Pharisees and Zealots alike. Stability and accommodation to authority being their hallmark, it would have been natural for wealthy merchants and landowners to be allied with them. The destruction of the temple in A.D. 70, and with it the disappearance of the priesthood, saw also the end of the Sadducees. The Judaism which emerged after A.D. 70 was totally independent of priesthood and sacrifice and was Pharisaic and rabbinic.

(who say there is no resurrection): The question as to the extent of belief in a resurrection-life in first-century Judaism is a vexed one, and depends to a large degree on a belief in the universality (or otherwise) of a resurrection-life among groups who acknowledged such a life. The Samaritans, along with the Sadducees, denied a resurrection. The rabbinic writers went so far as to accuse the Samaritans of deleting possible references to resurrection from the Pentateuch, and the same writers appealed to the Pentateuch in support of a doctrine of resurrection.

questioning him: This of course concerns the resurrection, but it is also couched in such a way as to discredit Jesus.

resurrection (Greek *anastasis):* This word is very seldom used in classical Greek of "rising from the dead," and in the Septuagint only in the later books (2 Macc 7:14, 12:43) and in the title to Ps 65. It is, however, freely used in the New Testament. Mark follows Matthew and Luke closely, though he omits "on that same day" (Matt 22:23) and he ignores Luke's qualifying "some of the Sadducees" (20:27).

On the above pericope, see F. Dreyfus, "L'argument scripturaire de Jésus en faveur de la résurrection des morts (Marc xii 26-27)," *Rev Bib* 66.2.1959, pp. 213-25; E. E. Ellis, "Jesus, the Sadducees and Qumran," *NTS* 10.2.1964, pp. 274-79; F. G. Downing, "The Resurrection of the Dead: Jesus and Philo," *JSNT* 15.1982, pp. 42-50.

19. *Rabbi* (Greek *didaskale* = "teacher"): The address is the same as in the previous story, without the flattering comments made by the Pharisees. The question—a scribal one, compared with the political one which preceded it—is put in typical fashion by a quotation from the Law with the introduction *Moses laid it down for us.*

laid it down (Greek *egrapsen hēmin;* cf. the more usual *gegraptai* in 7:6): The quotation which follows is a very loose rendering of Deut 25:5 (in fact it is more like Gen 38:8-9) but omits the limitation "if brothers dwell together" and omits also "and have no son." The Deuteronomic law was concerned with the maintenance of property within the family, but this is not the concern of Jesus' critics.

dies (Greek *apothanē):* cf. 3:4.

leaves (Greek *katalipē):* cf. 10:7.

raise up (Greek *exanastēsē):* cf. Luke 20:18, Acts 15:5.

children (Greek *sperma,* literally "seed"): cf. Gen 38:8.

The Greek of Matthew and Luke is similar to Mark, but Mark has modified and combined Matthew's "If a man dies having no children his brother must marry . . ." (22:24) and Luke's ". . . having a wife . . ." (20:28) and ". . . he himself was childless . . ." (20:28). Mark's Greek, though less elegant, is far more direct.

20-23. The method of argument is typically rabbinic and concerns the legitimacy or otherwise of a literal interpretation of the Law. But the intention here is not to demand interpretation; rather, it is to call in question the whole notion of resurrection.

The variations in grammatical structure are interesting in their own right, even though in translation they are inevitably lost. For example, in v. 20 we have *apothnēskōn ouk aphēken* (literally, "at his dying, he did not leave issue," and in v. 21 *apethaneu mē katalipōn* (literally, "he died, not leaving issue"). There is a Semitism in

v. 23: *en tē anastasei, hotan anastōsin* (literally, "in the resurrection, when they rise
. . ."), though some manuscripts omit the second part. Matt 22:28 does not have this
second part, while Luke 20:33, though it reads "in the resurrection" with Matthew,
recasts the sentence and (like Matthew) adds "therefore."

As has been noted before, confident assertions about the extent and nature of belief
in a resurrection-life in this period are to be avoided. However, the Sadducees' skepticism about such life depended on the fact that life after death finds expression in the
Old Testament only in the later, post-exile books: cf. Dan 12:2; Isa 25:8, 26:19; Ps
73:24; and (possibly) Job 19:25-27. How much of this belief in life after death belongs
to Persian exilic influence is difficult to say, but the older belief centered on a kind of
half-life of a very vague kind in Sheol, a place of darkness and inactivity (cf. Isa 14:10;
Job 7:9-11; Ps 6:5, 115:17; Sir 17:27).

"You are mistaken" (Greek *planasthe,* the passive form of *planaō,* "to lead astray"):
common in classical Greek and the Septuagint.

24. *"surely it is because . . .":* Jesus accuses the Sadducees of ignorance of the
Pentateuch on which they rely for denying a resurrection-life.

surely it is because (Greek *dia touto):* Matt 22:29 has "You are wrong because you
do not know the Scriptures," to which there is no parallel in Luke.

you do not know . . . (Greek *mē eidoles):* The expression is a present indicative, as
expressing not simply a past ignorance, but a present state of affairs.

the Scriptures (Greek *hai graphai,* literally "the writings": cf. 12:10): Ignorance is
everywhere deplored in the New Testament (cf. 1:21, John 5:37-43, 1 Cor 15:34, Gal
4:8); it is not, however, an ignorance of factual knowledge which is condemned, but a
refusal to draw the moral consequences of what can be known.

power of God (Greek *dunamis):* Cf. 5:30. The power is that of giving life, and
especially God's power over both life and death.

25. *when the dead rise . . . :* The error of the Sadducees, for Jesus, was in making
the resurrection-life a mere extension in another realm of earthly life and earthly
relationships. But the resurrection-life is of a wholly different order, and scripture—
for all its imagery, poetic or homespun—never makes the kind of confusion of which
the Sadducees are guilty. God, Jesus suggests, who through the Law provided for the
regulation of marriage and the raising of children, cannot be unaware of the points
raised in this "test case." In any case, the *power of God* is not confined to the very
mundane matters raised by the Sadducees. In the resurrection-life, marriage and birth
are irrelevant to the discussion.

when the dead rise (Greek *ek nekrōn anastōsin,* literally "when they rise from the
dead"): Cf. 6:14.

men do not marry (Greek *gameō;* cf. 6:17) . . . *are not given in marriage* (Greek
gamizō): Cf. Matt 22:30, 24:38; Luke 17:27; 1 Cor 7:38.

they are like the angels in heaven: It would appear from this expression that Jesus
means simply the resurrection of the righteous, and if he held any view of universal
resurrection it does not find expression here. The comparison of resurrection-life with
that of angels is expressed in 1 Cor 15:35-44. This accords with both contemporary
and later Jewish ideas—cf. *1 Enoch* 104:4; *Apoc Bar* 51:10.

Mark's Greek agrees with Matt 22:30, though Matthew has "in the resurrection" at
the beginning of Jesus' reply. Luke's version, however, is much different: "The sons of

this age marry and are given in marriage, but the ones counted worthy to attain that age and the resurrection from the dead neither marry nor are given in marriage" (20:34). Luke's version goes on to say "they cannot die any more" as they are "sons of God, being sons of the resurrection" (20:36). This gives the impression of being a parallel but independent account.

26. From the manner and fashion of resurrection-life, the narrative now passes to the fact of resurrection.

being raised (Greek *egeirontai:* literally, "about the dead, that they are raised . . ."): Cf. 1 Cor 15:16.

have you not read (Greek *ouk anegnōte):* Cf. 2:25, 12:10. This is not so much a question as an accusation.

the book: The word is used of the Law, implying reverence. Cf. 2 Chr 35:12; 1 Esdr 5:49; Luke 3:4; Acts 7:42.

in the passage about the bush (Greek *epi tou batou* = at "the bush"): This was a customary way of referring to a well-known narrative—cf. Rom 11:2.

how God said to him (Greek *pōs eipen autō ho theos):* Though this is a factual reference to a context in Hebrew scripture, and to what is said in that context, Jesus would have regarded the Law as authoritative, for himself as for all his people. Mark's version is a simpler version than Matthew's "Have you not read God's word to you?" (22:31). Luke 20:37 reads: ". . . when he says that he is the Lord God . . ."

'I am the God . . .': The quotation is from Exod 3:6 *(LXX).* The argument is that of contemporary exegesis, and the argument may not appeal to us as particularly cogent, but would have been impressive in its own time. The argument is that while the Scriptures acknowledged by the Sadducees do not mention resurrection, that cannot be held to eliminate any idea of it. Moreover, when God speaks to Moses of *Abraham, Isaac,* and *Jacob,* he speaks of them as still living. For our purposes it is important not to read into this answer of Jesus some Greek notions of immortality and the nature of the soul. Christian faith in a resurrection-life, though founded upon the resurrection of Jesus, also has roots in the biblical idea of fellowship with God as a perduring relationship: cf. Pss 16:8-10, 49:15, 73:23-25, and 4 Macc 7:19, 16:25. This is expressed with particular force in *God is not God of the dead, but of the living.*

With *You are very much mistaken,* the Markan narrative ends. This is a simple and effective conclusion. But we may well ask whether these are the words of Jesus or whether they are a free composition of the evangelist faced with a suffering community—a community, moreover, among whose members were some who doubted whether the struggle for integrity had any reward at all.

Matthew has in 22:33 an account of the astonishment of those who listened, while Luke 20:38 has after *but of the living* the comment "for all live in him," followed by a commendation from "some of the scribes," who said, "Rabbi, you have spoken well." Mark 12:32 picks up this phrase of Luke in the next section.

64. Questions: 3. The Great Commandment
(12:28-34) = Matt 22:34-40; Luke 10:25-28

12   28 Then one of the scribes, who had heard all the discussion and had noted how well he answered, came forward and asked him, "Which commandment is first of them all?" 29 Jesus answered, "The first is, 'Listen, Israel: the Lord our God is the one Lord; 30 you shall love the Lord your God with all your heart, with all your being, with all your understanding, and with all your strength.' 31 The second is this: 'You shall love your fellow man as yourself.' There is no other commandment greater than these." 32 The scribe said to him, "Rabbi, you are right; you have rightly said that he is one, and there is no other beside him. 33 And to love him with all one's heart, and with all one's understanding, and with all one's strength, and to love one's fellow-man as oneself—this is far more than all whole-burnt-offerings or sacrifice." 34 When Jesus saw that he answered thoughtfully, he said to him, "You are not far from the Kingdom of God." After that, no one dared ask him any question.

Comment

At first sight this appears to be another pronouncement story, giving the reply of Jesus to a question about the commandments. Yet there are elements of the "controversy story" as well, not to mention the elements which we might expect to find in an account of a discussion between teacher and student. The Lucan version of the incident (10:25-28) certainly belongs to this last type, while Matt 22:34-40 combines elements of controversy (". . . one of them, a lawyer, tried to trap him . . .") and also of a discussion (" 'Teacher,' he said, 'Which is . . .' "). For all the similarities, the relationship between the synoptic versions is not easily disentangled. For example, Luke 10:27—the Lucan parallel here—has the lawyer quoting Lev 19:18, but this may well have been done deliberately as a prefix to the parable of the Good Samaritan (10:29-37).

Matthew has the Pharisees coming together to meet Jesus on hearing that he has silenced the Sadducees, and the scene is set for an adversary situation.

The Markan account is much fuller than the others, has far more detail, and is far more in the nature of a narrative: it is difficult to resist the conclusion that we have here an eyewitness account. There is no evidence of the familiar Markan conflation and economy of words. On the other hand, on a theory of Markan priority it is difficult to see why Matthew and Luke succeeded not only in providing a controversy story (Matthew) and a pupil-teacher discussion (Luke) but also in omitting the Markan details of Jesus' commendation of his questioner.

Why is the account here, and not in some other context? Mark 11:18 refers to the crowd being *awestruck by his teaching,* which Matthew has in 22:33, and which in Mark's case is tied to the entry into Jerusalem. But the incident before us might well have come from any period in the ministry, and we shall be concerned when we reach the end of the fourth major inquiry (on messiahship) with some explanations by a distinguished scholar as to why these narratives are grouped together in Matthew and Mark, though dispersed in Luke.

In connection with time and location, Lohmeyer (p. 261) suggests that the story may properly belong to the Galilean ministry, on the grounds that the boldness of both question and answer is better seen in Galilee than against a background of Jerusalem Pharisaism. Yet the reference to *burnt offerings or sacrifice* would certainly seem to be in keeping with some incident in the temple precincts.

Notes

28. There are distinctive Markan features in this opening verse—namely, three participles *akousas (had heard), idou* (literally, "seeing" = *noted)* and *proselthōn* (literally, "coming" = *came forward).* This may well be a Markan adaptation of a narrative which originally began, ". . . and coming to him, they asked him . . ." (cf. Lohmeyer, p. 257).

scribes: Cf. 1:22.

how well (Greek *katōs):* Cf. 7:6. The friendliness of the scribe is distinctively Markan, contrasting with the hostile lawyer in Luke 10:25-28 who seeks to entrap Jesus (cf. Matt 22:35).

"Which commandment is first . . .": Luke's version is "What shall I do to inherit eternal life?"—which is far more reminiscent of the story of the rich man in Luke 18:18-23.

Two grammatical notes illustrate the seeming carelessness of *koinē* Greek as compared with classical or Hellenistic Greek. The word translated as *which* is *poia,* which properly means "What sort of . . ."; since Jesus can hardly have been asked to separate one sort of commandment from another, it is likely that *poia* stands for the more usual *tis* (= "which"). Secondly, *first of them all* is in the Greek *protē pantōn,* where grammatical usage would be more accurately *protē pasōn;* but the latter reading is supported by few manuscripts. It is possible, as has been suggested, that this was an expression in common use—"first-of-them-all." Similarly, the omission of the definite article before *commandment* (Greek *entole)* is reflected in Eph 6:2. (Does that passage mean ". . . which is *the* first commandment with a promise" or "which is *a* foremost commandment, and has a promise . . ."? Cf. C. F. D. Moule (1953, p. 113).

The whole matter of the most important commandment and the relative "lightness" of some commandments were often subjects of discussion among the rabbis, leading to the kind of debate on mortal and venial sins which characterized medieval and later Western Christian traditions. Hillel the Elder (c. 40 B.C.-A.D. 10), when asked by a Gentile to summarize the Law, gave a famous reply—"What you yourself hate, do not do to your neighbors: this is the whole Law, and the rest is commentary. Go and learn it" (TB *Shabbath* 31a).

29. Jesus' reply consists of the first part of Deut 6:4, the closest approximation in Judaism to what in the Christian tradition are called "creeds." The *Shema*—from the first word in the Hebrew text, "Hear . . ."—plays a significant and very substantial role not only in theological discussions among the rabbis, but also in personal piety, as *TDNT* i.41 rightly points out. Jacob B. Agus, in *The Vision and the Way* (New York, Ungar Publ., 1969, observes (p. 134): "The love of God is the climax of piety, not its beginning," and the command to love God is an aspiration expressed as an injunction.

Listen, Israel: the Lord our God is the one Lord (Greek *kurios ho theos hēmōn kurios heis estin):* There may be two clauses here, with *is* implied in the first—"The Lord is our God." But the verb *estin* at the end of the second clause does not define the relationship of the second *kurios (Lord)* to *heis (one),* so we may have a meaning of "is the one Lord" or "the Lord is one." No assistance is provided by the Hebrew of Deut 6:4, for that too is variously translated. The question therefore remains whether this is an assertion about the nature of God—that he is one—or his relationship to Israel (that he alone is our God). We cannot know whether it was originally meant one way and then understood in another way. Only Mark has the opening words from Deut 6:4, and this must be regarded as a distinct improvement on Matt 22:37 and Luke 10:27, for the command to love God is a response of aspiration to the assertion that God is one: one, in contrast to the multiplicity of pagan gods, and one in that he has chosen Israel.

Textually, the quotation is closely conformed to the Septuagint, and reads *kardia (heart)* and *psuchē (being),* but Mark has *dianoia (strength)* for *dunamis.* The differences between the evangelists are instructive. Matt 22:37 has *en hote te kardia* (with all your heart) and *en hote te psuchē* (with all your being), and it may rightly be pleaded that the construction *en* with the dative is far closer to the Hebrew *b* even though Luke and Mark agree in reading *ek* with the genitive (which is much better Greek). The Hebrew reads: ". . . with all your heart, with all your being *(nephesh)*— and with all your strength." The Markan text must be regarded as a conflate, and secondary.

It is important to remember that what is being asserted in Deuteronomy, and reiterated by Jesus, is the full response of the whole human personality. There was certainly no thought in the Hebrew mind of aspects, or qualities, of personality.

Lord (Greek *kurios):* Cf. 1:3.
love (Greek *agapaō):* Cf. 10:21.

heart (Greek *kardia):* Cf. 2:6.

being (Greek *psuchē):* Cf. 3:4.

understanding (Greek *dianoia):* The word is common in the Septuagint.

strength (Greek *ischus):* This also is found in the Septuagint and in Hellenistic Greek.

It is worth observing how infrequent are references in Scripture to human love for God. Indeed, this is the only instance in the synoptics, and there are only five such examples in the Pauline Corpus (Rom 8:28; 1 Cor 2:9, 8:3, 16:22; Eph 6:24). This reserve is wholly appropriate, for the stress in Scripture, in both Testaments, is on the free love of God for his people, the undeserved outpouring of his care and compassion for sinful humanity. It cannot be earned, and cannot be manipulated. The characteristic Greek word in the New Testament for God's love—*agapē*—is best translated as "self-giving," and for us this self-giving, this self-denying quality is an aspiration. We are capable of "friendship" with God (Greek *philia),* or even of a passionate attachment to God (Greek *erōs),* but the pilgrimage to which we are called is one in which we may hope to be fashioned by the *agapē* of God and purged of self-regarding taint in our *philia* and *eros,* for him, so that we may respond to love with love. The inevitable human tendency to follow up on the question "How do I know that I love God?" by responding "Because I do his will" immediately provokes the further question "How do I know the will of God?" The well-nigh inevitable absolute equation of the will of God with the Law can, and frequently does, end in a kind of auditing process by which one's conformity to the prescriptions of Law is used as a means of determining one's love for God. Paul knew the insidious menace of establishing righteousness through legal obedience, but it must immediately be added that the Christian centuries have seen little mitigation of the menace. On this score, some of the more dismal sides of medieval penitential discipline may stand as witness. A quotation from the late H. H. Kelly must suffice: "Love is not a thing you do or come to. It comes to you, overcomes you . . . where faith meets hope, love is born."

31. The questioner had asked about the *first of them all* among the precepts. Jesus adds, *The second is this.* Matthew 22:38 reads "This is the first and greatest commandment," and then adds, "The second is like it." Luke merely connects the two by "and."

The Greek of the second precept agrees with the Septuagint of Lev 19:18—*You shall love your fellow man as yourself.* The Greek adverb *plēsion* with the definite article translates the Hebrew for "fellow" or "the other"; linked with the preceding verse in Leviticus ("You shall not take vengeance upon, nor bear a grudge against, the children of your people"), it must refer to a fellow member of the Covenant people. It is also undeniable that the New Testament use of the word *agapē* is always in the context of community relationships. But the narrow and restricted application of love of one's fellow was always transcended, as the writings of the rabbis and the early Christian writers abundantly testify.

Precisely how "love of fellow" is to be defined or interpreted has occupied commentators and writers all through the centuries, and some account must be given here. Is this love an outpouring of concern for one's fellow, an expression of God's love which one has already received? Is it—as the text might possibly suggest—simply a higher form of self-love? We must necessarily begin with the text in Lev 19:18. The command cited by Jesus is set over against a command not to nurture hatred against one's fellow, not to take vengeance or to bear ill-will. At the very least, therefore, we have enlightened self-interest in the sense of regard and concern for one's fellow in not wishing for him or her what we would not wish for ourselves. Perhaps the best translation of *agapē* (given the current debasing of the word "love" in contemporary English) is "sacrificial compassion." It is this sense which the whole teaching ministry of Jesus reflects, and nowhere perhaps better than in the parable of the Good Samaritan (Luke 10:29-37). The Pauline letters amply demonstrate the way in which this emphasis of Jesus was understood, and Gal 5:14 asserts that the command to exercise compassion in Lev 19:18 fulfills the whole Law (cf. also Rom 13:9; Jas 2:8). Cf. H. Montefiore, "Thou Shalt Love Thy Neighbour as Thyself," *NovTest* 4.3.1962, pp. 157-70.

The juxtaposition of the two commandments of Jesus has often given rise to speculation as to whether this was unique in Judaism. So far as our present knowledge goes, the union of the two precepts by Jesus stands alone in the Judaism of his own time, but it may well be that in oral rabbinic discussion the dependence of love for neighbor on love for God was stressed.

32. The reply of the scribe is peculiar to Mark. There are no grounds for questioning the authenticity of this brief dialogue, and it is therefore all the more impressive as serving to dispel the all too common belief that the Judaism of Jesus' day was one of hidebound legalism. To be sure, a cursory reading of Paul's letters (especially Galatians and Romans) is often a trap for the unwary, seeming to support this view. (In this connection, however, see W. D. Davies, *Paul and Rabbinic Judaism*, London: SPCK, 1955, esp. pp. 86-226). It is well to bear in mind that the scribe's response to Jesus is rooted in the Old Testament tradition: cf. 1 Sam 15:22, Hos 6:6. There is no judgment on his part as to what is or is not essential, and certainly no repudiation of the sacrificial system which was a present reality, but the scribe asserts the primacy of love of God and of fellow. Jesus' reply appears to suggest that the view expressed by the scribe would have been foreign to most of his contemporaries, but there is no implication in this narrative that *he answered thoughtfully* was a cold calculation.

he is one: The scribe, in accordance with the Jewish usage of his own time, omits the name of God. Cf. contemporary Jewish practice in using the reverential "The Name" *(ha shēm)* for God. Some lesser manuscripts of Mark supply the word "God," but these are secondary sources. Though the scribe repeats Jesus' reply, the wording in the Greek is not the same. For *dianoia (understanding)* we have *sunēsis* (cf. Luke 2:47, 2 Tim 2:7) which is found in both classical Greek and the Septuagint.

whole-burnt-offerings (Greek *holokautōma):* The word is from the Septuagint and translates the Hebrew *olah.* It is to be distinguished—as the sacrifice par excellence—from *sacrifice* (Greek *thusiai),* which refers to sacrifices in general.

34. The grammatical structure of the beginning of this verse reads, literally, "And Jesus seeing him that he answered thoughtfully . . ." The use of the accusative *him* as anticipating the subject of the dependent clause is found also in 7:2, 11:32, in one version of Luke 9:31, and in Luke 24:7.

Jesus' reply brings us once again to an enigmatic statement about the Kingdom of God. The idea is certainly that of a realm in which the sovereign will of God will be unquestioned and his reign unchallenged. But in this context, is *You are not far from the Kingdom of God* being understood in some future, eschatological sense, or does Jesus mean it to be understood as a present or almost present reality? It appears somewhat odd to suggest that the man is well on the way to being found acceptable and ready when the Reign of God dawns, and the present writer finds it impossible to resist the conclusion that the Reign of God is presented by Jesus as a present reality. The scribe is *not far from the Kingdom* in two senses: he recognizes the total claim of the sovereignty of God and morally has already submitted himself to its demands, and also (since the Kingdom is almost at hand) he stands ready for its manifestation. Of considerable importance on a different level is Jesus' own understanding of the imminent dawn of the Reign of God. There is, as we have said, no ground for disputing the authenticity of this dialogue. Yet to understand Jesus' reply as implying "futurist" eschatology seems to stretch the meaning unbearably. We are therefore faced with yet another saying which carries plain implications of "realized" eschatology. Lucan— and later—interpretations in terms of a delayed *parousia* have entered into the tradition of Christian theology, but they ought not without very good reason to be retrojected into the teaching of Jesus.

thoughtfully (Greek *nounekōs):* Though classical, the word is not found in the Septuagint. Its meaning in the classical authors is "discreetly" or "sensibly."

far (Greek *makran):* The accusative case of *makros,* used adverbially, is classical, and is also found in the Septuagint. In Isa 57:19, *hoi makran* = exiled Jews ("those from afar") and in Eph 2:13 is applied to Gentiles.

no one dared ask him: Cf. v. 28. This is Mark's link with the preceding controversies, and in the next encounter Jesus himself poses the questions. Matthew has the formula at the end of the question about messiahship (22:46), and Luke at the end of the resurrection controversy (20:40).

For further reading, see W. Diezinger, "Zum Liebesgebot Mark xii 28-34 und Parr.," *NovTest* 20.1978, pp. 81-83.

65. Messiahship
(12:35-37) = Matt 22:41-46; Luke 20:41-44

12 ³⁵ As Jesus was teaching in the temple, he asked, "How can the scribes say that the Messiah is 'son of David'? ³⁶ David himself, inspired by the holy Spirit, said, 'The Lord said to my Lord, "Sit at my right hand until I put your enemies under your feet." ' ³⁷ David himself calls him 'Lord.' How then can he be David's son?" There was a great crowd, and people listened eagerly.

Comment

This final incident in the controversy series differs from its predecessors in that it is Jesus who poses the question. We are accustomed to regarding this questioning by Jesus along with the quotation from Ps 110 in v. 36 as though it was used by Jesus as proof of his Davidic descent. But it is just as easily interpreted as casting doubt on the whole idea. That the expected messiah-deliverer would be of Davidic lineage was a commonplace in some sectors of Judaism and could claim Old Testament support, and among the Essenes a priestly messiah and a Davidic (kingly) messiah were expected. But in either case, publicly to court a messianic title was an invitation to Roman intervention. By asking the question, Jesus was inviting his critics to question one possible assumption—that he was a perfervid nationalist seeking to enlist popular support. By the time Mark's gospel was finally committed to writing the kind of question posed by Jesus had been overtaken not only by the events of the final week of the ministry but also by the first stirrings of the Jewish revolt against Rome. By then, Jewish Christians had either fled or were under pressure to declare themselves for or against the nationalist cause.

Whatever the original context of these question-and-answer controversy stories, we are now in some position to assess their present place in Matthew and Mark. (As we have already seen, Luke's account of the Great Commandment is not in the context given by the other two synoptists.) On this grouping of questions, considerable light was cast by David Daube in "The Earliest Structure of the Gospels" (NTS 5.3.1959, pp. 174-87). The author suggests that our series of four questions is derived from the pattern of questions associated with the celebrations on the eve of Passover. (This contention is entirely independent of whether the Last Supper was a Passover meal or not. "Even if it was not, once Jesus was believed to be the Messiah, the new deliverance must have ranked at least equally with the old. In fact, if it was not a Passover meal, the Passover features conferred on it by New Testament writers would testify the more strikingly to the influence of this ceremony"— Daube, p. 175.)

Daube goes on to deal with the four questions, which have no logical or historical connection. But—citing TB Niddah 69b—the rabbis linked four types of questions in the early part of the Passover Haggadah: (1) questions of "wisdom," about points of law, (2) flippant and mocking questions, principally about bodily resurrection, (3) questions about the "way of the land," on matters of simple piety, and (4) questions about apparent contradictions in scripture. The questions in Mark, the article goes on to say, fall precisely into these four categories. But there is more. Of the four, three questions are put to Jesus, while the fourth is asked by Jesus himself—again, a feature of the Passover-eve Haggadah, where when the son does not know how to ask, the question is posed by the father or master. "Whoever brought the Markan questions together did not merely adopt the rabbinic categories in general; he adopted the specific applications of these categories occurring on Passover eve" (Daube, p. 182). Even the position of the parable about the vineyard which precedes the questions is used by Daube on account of the benediction preceding the questions in the Haggadah, for that blessing gives thanks for God's gift of the Law to Israel.

All of the above raises two further considerations, each connected with the other. The first concerns the primitive character of the arrangement of the material, if Daube's thesis is correct. If it is, then we are in the presence of primitive Jewish Christianity reinterpreting Passover in terms of a new deliverance, the Haggadah seen through the eyes of those who saw the narrative of Passion/Resurrection as further—and final—manifestation of the Covenant-love of God.

Secondly, in terms of synoptic relationships we are bound to ask (since Matthew and Mark share the same narrative framework here) which evangelist's work is prior in time. There is no disputing the fact that of the three synoptists Matthew is more "Jewish" in tone and in content, while Mark is often depicted as having a Roman background. Yet Mark apparently shares with Matthew (according to Daube) the same concern to reproduce the order and the format of the Haggadah questions. It seems on the face of it improbable that the most distinctively Jewish of the three synoptic gospels should have copied this feature from an evangelist whose initial sources may have been Roman (Petrine?). Luke is understandably less concerned with such matters, and the arrangement organized by Matthew and Mark would have been alien to the Gentile mission with which he was concerned.

Notes

35. *in the temple:* Mark may have found a reference to the temple in one of his independent sources, for he has already referred to the temple in 11:27.

he asked: Neither Mark nor Luke identifies the listeners. Matthew, however, in a phrase reminiscent of Ps 2:2, speaks of the Pharisees being "gathered together," and Matthew will use the same phrase from the Septuagint in 26:3. This Matthean device, and the enemies being "gathered together against the Lord and against his anointed" (Ps 2:2), are rejected by Mark, for he delays this final confrontation until the trial.

"How can the scribes say . . .": Apparently there was some kind of scribal opinion that the messiah would be a son of David—i.e., a descendant of the Davidic house. But the question as posed by Jesus, together with the enigmatic question in v. 37, fails to reveal whether Jesus himself subscribed to this opinion. The Davidic descent of the

messiah certainly finds expression in the Old Testament tradition: cf. Isa 9:2-7, 11:1-9; Jer 23:5-6, 33:14-18; Ezek 34:23-24, 37:24; Ps 89:20-37; and see also John 7:42. But what is not at all clear is whether by the time of Jesus the designation "son of David" meant a physical descendant of the Davidic house or whether the term would be applied to anyone who effectively established a claim to be the messiah. The question asked by Jesus does not offer us any help at this point. At the same time, it is uncertain whether Jesus is in *any* sense claiming to be *"son of David,"* either by physical descent or by messianic claim. It can be argued that if Jesus was intending to attack a scribal dictum about messiahship this might have constituted ground for further attacks on his teaching. The claim of Davidic sonship is made for Jesus in early Christian writings (cf. Rom 1:3; 2 Tim 2:8, and in the genealogies of Matt 1:1-17 and Luke 3:23-38), but once again we cannot be absolutely certain that the term "son of David by human descent" in Rom 1:3 refers to physical genealogy and is not an honorific designation. Whatever the case may finally prove to be, for lack of further evidence we are compelled to leave the matter as incapable of resolution. (The reader is referred to J. A. Fitzmyer, "The Son of David Tradition and Mt. 22:41-46 and Parallels," in *Essays on the Semitic Background of the New Testament,* London: G. Chapman, 1971, pp. 113-27.)

36. There is no grammatical connective, and the question in v. 35 is followed immediately by what David said under the inspiration of *the holy Spirit.* The omission of any connecting particle has sometimes been quoted as an asyndeton betraying Semitic usage, but this cannot be proved. A similar plea is also made on behalf of the use of *autos* "he," as a pronoun anticipating the use of the noun (cf. Lohmeyer, p. 262n.). But it seems far more natural to assume that what we have is the familiar Greek idiom of a pronoun used for emphasis. This is reflected in our translation of *David himself.*

inspired by the holy Spirit: Cf. 1:8,10,12, 3:29. The reference to the holy Spirit conveys the meaning that David was speaking as a prophet. The quotation which follows comes from the Septuagint version of Ps 110:1, though Mark—in common with Matthew—has *hupokatō (under)* for the Septuagint *hupopodion* (foot stool), which Luke has. For *under your feet,* cf. Ps 8:7.

at my right hand: Cf. 10:37.

enemies (Greek *echthros):* Cf. 6:11.

Instead of *inspired by the holy Spirit,* Luke has "David himself says in the book of Psalms" (20:42). At the time the Davidic authorship of the psalms was unquestioned, though parts of the Psalter predate David and parts of it are exilic and post-exilic. David was regarded as the patron of temple music, and the musical guilds may well have owed their origin to the time of David. (Cf. W. F. Albright, *Archaeology and the Religion of Israel,* 5th ed., Garden City, N.Y.: Doubleday, 1968, pp. 124-25ff.) In the opinion of Mitchell Dahood *(Psalms III,* Anchor Bible, Garden City, N.Y.: Doubleday, 1970), the affinities of Ps 110 with Ps 2 seemed to indicate a tenth-century date for these psalms, which were "probably composed to celebrate a military victory" (p. 112). On the other hand Taylor (p. 491) favors a time in the Maccabean period, with special reference to Simon Maccabaeus who was "high priest and a friend of kings" (1 Macc 13:36, 14:41).

The importance of Jesus' question, and of his reply to his own question by way of quotation, does not depend on either authorship or date. Rather, the significance of the saying lies in the insight it provides into the way Jesus understood messiahship as it was propounded in his own time. But is this interpretation correct? Or is it rather that two separate issues are to be found here? First of all, we may be in the presence of Jesus' own hesitations and doubts about an incipient idea of messiahship which was gaining some attention. In that case, these three short verses tell us nothing of Jesus' understanding of himself in any messianic terms, and—to the contrary—may well indicate his belief that in any discussion of messiahship physical Davidic descent was even irrelevant. There is the indubitable fact to be reckoned with—little if at all discussed in the literature—that the Davidic house had to all intents been eliminated by the Persians during the Exile. Lohmeyer (p. 263) goes so far as to suggest that Jesus is really looking to the apocalyptic literature, finding there an equivalence between the messiah and an expected agent of God whose origin and nature are unknown. To this we must add that, so far as we know, the interpretation of Ps 110 in messianic terms was unknown in rabbinic literature until the second century, though it may well be that this silence was due to the freedom with which the New Testament writers had used Ps 110 in a messianic sense as applying to Jesus. Secondly, we must be aware that whatever the original intent of Jesus in posing the question and providing his own answer, the early community understood this in terms of Jesus' making explicit claim to both Davidic descent and messiahship. We should note, for example, the use made of Ps 110 in the New Testament literature: Acts 2:34, 7:56; Rom 8:34; 1 Cor 15:25; Eph 1:20; Col 3:1; Heb 1:3, and 13, 8:1, 10:12; 1 Pet 3:22; Rev 3:21.

The problems raised by all these considerations are incapable of resolution. There is a certain attractiveness about the suggestion of Lohmeyer noted above, as indeed there is in the idea espoused by some writers that Jesus is articulating some speculation about the future messiah as Son of Man, an archetypal ruler or a supernatural being. In this event, we are left wholly uncertain as to what precise relationship Jesus envisaged for himself as against this future messiah. We appear to be face-to-face once more with the much-canvassed "messianic secret" said to be inherent in Mark, as well as with the unfathomable mystery of the self-consciousness of Jesus. As to the second, we can know virtually nothing, while the first—in this instance—may involve nothing more than a rejection of all messianic hopes which center on the purely mundane and political.

On the basis of this admittedly inconclusive discussion, we can only say that the whole episode bespeaks the highly allusive character of much of Jesus' teaching. It is wholly lacking in self-concern; it waits upon the will of God and looks in faith to the vindicating act of God, however that might be expressed. We are here in the presence of the historical Jesus, for the primary community was anything but hesitant in its proclamation of Jesus as Son of God through God's act in raising him from death. Only if we recognize that we are confronted here by the admittedly allusive words of Jesus himself can we explain the freedom with which Ps 110:1 was used in the early Christian community (cf. Lohmeyer, p. 263).

Further studies may be pursued in David Daube, *The New Testament and Rabbinic Judaism* (Jordan Lectures, 1952, University of London Athlone Press, 1956), pp. 158-

59; R. H. Fuller, *The Foundations of New Testament Christology* (New York: Scribner, 1965), pp. 19, 111, 119, 134, 188, 189, 199; and B. Chilton, "Jesus *ben David:* Reflections on the *Davidssohnfrage" JSNT* 14.1982, pp. 88-112.

66. Judgment on the Scribes
(12:38-40) = Matt 23:1-36; Luke 20:45-47

12 ³⁸ As he taught them, he said, "Watch out for the scribes, who like to walk up and down in long robes, and who like to receive deferential greetings in the marketplace, the best seats in the synagogues, ³⁹ and places of honor at banquets. ⁴⁰ As for those men who appropriate widows' houses, while they offer long prayers for appearances' sake, they will receive a greater condemnation."

Comment

The narrative before us consists of a brief introduction, followed by an extract from the longer compilations of Matt 23 and Luke 11:37-53. The narrative itself is beset with difficulties, with which we must deal before examining the interpretation of the passage.

1. Assuming—as this commentary does—the validity of the Griesbach hypothesis on synoptic origins, what use does this narrative make of existing sources? First we must examine what use Luke makes of Matthew. By the time Luke arrived at 20:45 in his gospel, he had come to the lengthy condemnation of the Pharisees in Matt 23:1-34. But some of this material Luke had already used in an appropriate context in 11:39-52, and he contented himself therefore with extracting the last two verses of Matt 23:5-7, which we now find in Luke 20:46. Then he goes on to lay the charges that the scribes "devour widows' houses" and "for a pretense make long prayers" (20:47). The change from the Matthean text is instructive. Matt 23:5 ("They make large phylacteries, broaden the hem of their garments . . .") would have been instantly understood by a Palestinian Torah-conscious audience, whereas Luke's version ("they walk about in long robes . . .") would have been perfectly well understood by Gentiles as describing pure ostentation.

2. Once this has been accepted, then the improvements in Mark's style and grammar said to have been made by Matthew and Luke are seen for what they are—original sources which Mark cast in his own rough-and-ready style.

No one has ever maintained that Mark attempted to write careful literary Greek, and the present instance is no exception. When Mark is following Matthew and Luke closely, especially in matters of great importance, he is very careful. But in cases where he has independent sources of his own (sometimes eyewitness accounts) or is anxious to pass on to the next topic, he is far less careful. We have an example here, in v. 38. The evangelist has *tōn thelontōn en stolais peripalein,* so that the sentence literally reads: "Beware of the scribes, of those liking to walk up and down. . . ." In other words, the Greek verb *thelō,* "to like," is used here in participle form *(theloutōn),* followed by the infinitive *to walk up and down* and then by the accusative *aspasmous (deferential greetings).* This kind of construction is common enough in the papyri, where we would not expect to find literary Greek; but so far from Luke improving Mark in his 20:46, Mark exhibits all the signs of taking shortcuts by omitting Luke's "loving" before *deferential greetings.* In other words, Mark makes the participle "liking" do duty for both an infinitive and an accusative case. Matthew's Greek at 23:6 is differently constructed and is of no assistance at this point.

3. Mark's highly selective extracts from Matthew and Luke serve a vital purpose here, for the evangelist is anxious that no one should miss the connection between the denunciation in this pericope, with its reference to widows, and the pericope which follows. Lohmeyer correctly observes (p. 261) that the scribes are Jesus' principal opponents in this gospel, and they are frequently mentioned (twenty-two times in all: 1:22; 2:6,16; 3:22; 7:1,5; 8:31; 9:11,14; 10:33; 11:18,27; 12:28,32,35,38; 14:1,43,53; 15:1,31)—as contrasted with the Pharisees (twelve times), the high priests (fourteen times), the elders (five times) and the Herodians (twice). The present instance is the only recorded example of Jesus inveighing against the conduct of the scribes, as distinct from their teaching. Although the scribes and the Pharisees are linked in the condemnation of legalism in Matt 23:1-36, it is important to draw a proper distinction. Whereas the Pharisees had an established position and an honorable one as interpreters of the Law and its traditions (and were also regarded as highly patriotic), the scribes as "bookmen" (Hebrew *sopherîm)* were regarded largely as recorders or collectors of opinions and less authoritative than the Pharisees. As is often the case with those of lesser status, they are represented in the New Testament as not only argumentative, but—in the present instance—given to ostentation to magnify their public image. (Cf., on this whole subject, M. J. Cook, *Mark's Treatment of the Jewish Leaders, NovTest* Supp 51, Leiden: E. J. Brill, 1978.)

4. The vocabulary in this pericope has a strong Markan stamp, especially in two instances. First of all, the verse immediately preceding—*There was a great crowd* (Greek *polus ochlos;* cf. 5:21,24; 6:34; 8:1; 9:14)—is common in Mark, and secondly, one expression *(listened eagerly,* Greek *hedeōs ēkouen)* is found nowhere else in the New Testament. Thirdly, there is the characteristic

Markan inheritance from Matthew of the use of the verb "to teach" (Greek *didaskō,* sixteen times, as against thirteen in Matthew and fifteen in Luke) and the noun "teaching" (five times, as against three in Matthew and fifteen in Luke). The word "teaching" is an important concept for Mark, ranging from parables (4:1-2) to replies to opponents (12:35), and the same word can be used to cover the whole spectrum of Jesus' ministry (6:6). So here the attack on the scribes is held by Mark to be part of "teaching" activity.

Notes

38. *"Watch out . . ."* (Greek *blepete):* This is a particular Markan usage of the Greek word "to see" in the sense of "beware." (Cf. 4:24; 13:5,9,23,33.)

long robes: Considerable discussion has been generated by this phrase in Mark. The Greek *stolē* (plural *stolai)* originally referred to personal equipment, and later meant "clothing" or "a robe" (in the Septuagint, cf. Exod 31:10; Jonah 3:6; Esth 8:15; 1 Macc 6:15). But so uncertain is the precise meaning that Lohmeyer (p. 263, n. 2) opted for the very poorly attested Greek *stoais*—for which admittedly a scribal error could produce *stolais*—so as to read "they walk around in the porticoes" (of public gathering places). Unfortunately, the poor attestation (only in the Syriac) means that *stoais* was read precisely because *stolais* was seen to be problematical.

Does Mark here intend to summarize or provide equivalents for Matt 23:5 ("They make large phylacteries, broaden the hem of their garments . . .")? This seems the most obvious solution, though Mark generally explains Jewish customs for non-Jewish members of his audience. This omission (if such it is) of an explanation is not as impressive as it appears, for by the time Mark committed his gospel to writing such minor matters as represented here would hardly have been worthy of urgent explanation.

From time to time it has been suggested *(pace* Strack-Billerbeck, Vol. 2, pp. 31-33) that the word for *long robes* indicates the *tallît,* originally an outer piece of clothing which became in time the prayer shawl used by Jews in the Middle Ages and into our own times. There are objections to this suggestion. First of all, though the Greek *stolē* was translated variously and even transliterated, it was never used in any sense as equivalent to *tallît.* Secondly, there is no tradition that the *tallît* was in origin a peculiarly religious article of clothing, and still less that it was especially associated with the scribes. K. H. Rengstorf, in an article in the Otto Michel *Festschrift* ("Die STOLAI der Schriftgelehrten: Eine Erläuterung zu Mark 12.38," in *Abraham unser Vater: Juden und Christen im Gespräch über die Bibel,* edited by Otto Betz, Leiden: E. J. Brill, 1963), takes the view that in the first century special clothing for the Sabbath was just coming into use, and the scribes sought this way of marking the Sabbath, presumably as a means of distinguishing themselves from folk who could not afford such observances. This sounds an admirable suggestion, but unhappily we have no first-century attestation for special Sabbath clothing.

The whole tenor of Jesus' condemnation, coupled with his many confrontations with the scribes elsewhere in Mark, leads to the conclusion that here we have an example of ostentation on the part of those seeking the kind of awesome respect paid to the Pharisees. If *stolai* in this context means—as it does elsewhere (Mark 16:5; Luke 15:22; Rev 7:9,13)—clothing befitting dignity and honor, then essentially Mark is saying no more than the charge (". . . broaden the hem of their garments") in Matt 23:5. (It is well to remember that *stolē* in the Septuagint is used to refer to royal and priestly raiment.) Implied in this scribal quest for recognition, reinforced in the remainder of this verse and in v. 39, is the whole question of authority, never far below the surface in Mark. It is well here to recapitulate the challenges to Jesus on the part of the scribes so far encountered in this gospel: 1:22,27; 2:6-7,10-11; 11:27-33. At this point in Mark, then, the challenge of Jesus is clear. He has authority, in contrast to the scribes. They are claiming the service of honor, which he will not.

deferential greetings in the marketplace . . . *:* The charge against the scribes continues with their desire to have honor paid to them in public places. Though the charges are identical in Matthew and Luke, there are differences: Luke 11:43 has "Alas for you Pharisees . . ."; Matt 23:6 reverses the order of *best seats in the synagogues* and *places of honor at banquets,* and his address is to scribes and Pharisees.

There are further and more important differences, some of which led one author to posit a possible use by Mark of "Q": see Harry Fleddermann, "A Warning About the Scribes (Mark 12:37b-40)," *(CBQ* 44.1.1982, pp. 52-67). This contention is worth examining for its validity depends on the priority of Mark and a supposed dependence of Matthew and Luke on Mark. The matter can be summarized as follows:

1. Matthew and Luke agree against Mark in using the definite article before the direct objects, and in the order of the objects. The order of the objects is not a very impressive argument, for anyone who has ever undertaken a digest of two documents (such as we contend Mark to be) is well aware of how easily order can be misplaced. The matter of the definite article is a slender foundation upon which to build any New Testament argument, for *koinē* Greek often displayed a carelessness in the use of the article which mirrored (for our purposes) its near-disappearance in contemporary Aramaic. No one claims literary excellence for Mark: on the other hand, some care in this regard is expected of Matthew and Luke. (See further on this whole question C. F. D. Moule, 1953, pp. 106-18.)

2. Matthew and Luke agree against Mark in using two words for "love" or "delight in" to describe the desire of the scribes for recognition, where Mark uses *like to* (Greek *thelō)* or "wish for." Now the use of two Greek words for "loving" or "caring about" in place of Mark's *like to* deserves more attention than Fleddermann gives it. To begin with, it is hardly surprising to find *phileō* in Matthew—he uses the verb four times as against Luke's one. In the same way *agapaō* in Luke is to be expected, for he uses it almost twice as much as Matthew. Furthermore, there is a difference in meaning between the verbs *agapaō* and *phileō,* for while the first generally means "to have regard for" or "to desire," the second has a more emotional overtone, in the sense of "to have affection for." Since it is commonly said that Matthew and Luke improve upon, elucidate, or expand Mark, we are entitled to ask which of the other two evangelists escalated with his own favorite word Mark's *like to.* In fact,

Mark's verb is precisely what we would expect to find when a writer, faced with two documents which use different verbs to express a strong desire for some object, compromises by using *like to,* and this we maintain is what Mark did.

3. There is a further suggestion in the article cited that "the saying stood in Q as well as in Mark" (p. 58). Aside from the well-known difficulties of determining the precise contents of Q, we are witnessing here a small but surely significant breach in the defenses of the two-document hypothesis, and one made, moreover, by one who presumably holds to that hypothesis. It is insufficient to say that we can construct the Q form of the saying from the material which is before us. The author's contention is that Luke places this Q saying in a series of woes (11:37-54) addressed simply to the Pharisees, whereas Matthew "brought the Q discourse to the place of Mark's warning to the crowd" (ibid.). Then, as Matthew soon has a whole series of "woes" (23:13-26), the author suggests that the saying was probably a "woe" saying in Q, but offers no proof for this. While it is true that Luke's warning was against the Pharisees, it is altogether too much to suggest that Matthew, having found this warning and placed it in its present position, "combines Mark's scribes and Q's Pharisees" (ibid., p. 58). The combination of scribes and Pharisees is found in Matthew before this juncture as a composite array of Jesus' critics (5:20, 12:38, 15:1, 23:2) and Mark quite patently singles out the scribes as Jesus' principal enemies from the beginning. The combination of scribes and Pharisees is not unknown in Luke, so we are nowhere nearer the mysterious Q, and this agreement of Matthew and Luke does not provide us with information that Mark knew the sayings held to be embodied in it.

the best seats (Greek *prōtokathedria*): Cf. Matt 23:6; Luke 11:43, 20:46. The reference is to the bench before the ark which contained the scrolls, and (since the bench faced the people) a desirable location in which to be highly visible.

39. *and places of honor at banquets* (Greek *prōtoklisia*): Cf. Matt 23:6; Luke 14:7, 20:46). This Greek word (literally, "first reclining couches"), like the word for *best seats,* is first found in the New Testament. The charge of ostentation, of a desire for public adulation, is all the more cogent in Mark in that the disciples are constantly being warned against pride and self-seeking (cf. 9:35; 10:31,43-44).

40. *appropriate widows' houses:* This verse has over the years provoked considerable debate, and it will be well to deal with matters of vocabulary before dealing with the sense. Grammatically, *hoi katesthontes,* "the ones appropriating," is in agreement (in the nominative plural) with *houtoi,* "they," of the last clause, and not in agreement with *tōn grammatōn (of the scribes,* v. 38), to which unquestionably it refers. We have therefore made a translation where *hoi katesthontes* agrees in sense with *thelontōn (who like)* in v. 38, in accordance with most commentators. Mark's haphazard grammar is corrected in some manuscripts, in assimilation to Luke's *hoi katesthiousin,* "they who appropriate" (20:47). There may, however, be another explanation for the apparent grammatical carelessness. The nominative participle *katesthontes (those who appropriate)* may be a dependent case, resumed in the pronoun *they* at the end of the sentence, thus avoiding a break after *proseuchomenoi* (literally, "praying"). But in this

case we are led to the conclusion that v. 40 may well have been a saying from a quite
different source, but which Mark is determined shall be connected, and connected
plainly, with the scribes of 12:28-34,35-37,38-40, and the following vv. 41-44. This
connection is wholly lacking in Matthew, who has the judgment on the scribes (along
with the Pharisees) in a long series of indictments, and does not have the important
story of the widow's offering. Luke's saying against the scribes and lawyers is contained in his Chapter 11, but he does maintain the connection between the scribes and
the widow's offering. Mark was, however, fully determined, as he confronted his
principal sources, that no one should miss the point that in his view the scribes were
Jesus' principal enemies. It is therefore highly probable that the verse before us,
careless as its grammar may be, is intended to avoid Luke's somewhat ambiguous *hoi
katesthiousin,* "they who appropriate" (20:47), by using a participle, *hoi katesthontes,*
"those appropriating ones," to match the participle with which the judgment began
(those who like). Precisely what was the source of v. 40 we cannot know, and it has no
parallel in Luke. The section, which began with a condemnation of overweening
vanity, ends in a condemnation of wholesale greed; but in Mark it is a vital link to the
succeeding section (cf. Lohmeyer, p. 263).

What is meant by the charge that the scribes are those who *appropriate widows'
houses,* and what connection does this have with the conjoined charge that these same
people *offer long prayers for appearances' sake?* The Old Testament and the deuterocanonical literature agree in condemning extortion against widows and the helpless (cf.
Exod 22:22; Isa 1:17,23, 10:2; *Pss. Sol.* 4:11,13,15,23, and 12:2-4). At the same time,
the statement of Josephus *(Ant* 17.2.4) that the Pharisees convinced people that they
were favored by God (and could on that pretext look to women for support) must be
balanced by the support given by women to Jesus as an itinerant rabbi (cf. 14:3-9,
15:40-41; Luke 8:2-4, 10:38-42). Such expectations of support were then, and always
have been, liable to abuse. But the word *houses* (Greek *oikias)* has been the subject of
an inquiry by J. D. M. Derrett (" 'Eating up the Houses of Widows': Jesus's Comment
on Lawyers?" *NovTest* 14.1.1972, pp. 1-9) on the grounds that there was a charge by
Jesus of serious breaches of Jewish inheritance laws. Unfortunately, brilliant though
the suggestion is, we have no evidence contemporary with Jesus for any legislation
which would allow trustees for the property of orphans to exploit estates for their own
benefit. Furthermore, the scribes were not in the strict sense lawyers, as were the
Pharisees.

The whole complex of this charge must be seen as a unit. The condemnation is
wholesale, with no mitigation. The charge that the scribes *appropriate widows' houses*
is linked with the further accusation that they *offer long prayers for appearances' sake,*
and the latter accusation has its logical conclusion for Mark in the following section.
The reference to *long prayers* can hardly mean ostentatious private prayers made in
public, and it can hardly refer to synagogue practice. The synagogues, however many
there were in Jerusalem at this time, were not primarily places of worship while the
temple still stood, but rather places of learning and instruction. We therefore conclude
that the scribes, considered primarily as teachers of the common folk, are being singled out by Jesus as those concerned with emphasizing, in season and out, the need to
maintain the magnificence of the temple as *the* place of prayer, with its constant
observances and sacrifices. We shall have occasion to discuss this at greater length in

the next section, but we stress here the contrast between prayer and the temple cult which seems to underlie so much of Mark. Here, the demands of the scribes for support of the temple and its worship are regarded by Jesus as the equivalent of depriving widows of their property.

greater condemnation: The rest of the New Testament fully supports this judgment: cf. Rom 3:8; Gal 5:10; 1 Tim 5:12.

67. The Widow's Offering
(12:41-44) = Luke 21:1-4

12 ^{41} As Jesus sat by the treasury, he watched as the crowds put money into the treasury. Many rich people put in large sums. ^{42} A poor widow came, and dropped in two copper coins, together worth less than one cent. ^{43} He called his disciples to him. "I tell you truly," he said, "this poor widow gave more than all those who are contributing to the treasury. ^{44} They have given from their superfluity, but she, out of her poverty, has put in all she had, all she had to live on."

Comment

It has been suggested that Mark's gospel exhibits a consistent animosity toward the temple and its institutions (most notably in J. R. Donahue, *Are You the Christ? The Trial Narrative in the Gospel of Mark,* SBL Dissertation Series 10, 1973, and D. Juel, *Messiah and Temple: The Trial of Jesus in the Gospel of Mark,* SBL Dissertation Series 31, 1977). This is to fall into the same error as saying that the fourth gospel is "anti-Semitic." Neither assertion can be made without severe qualification, and in both cases (in Mark and in John) it is far nearer the mark to say that both evangelists represent Jesus as passionately concerned about the righteousness of God and impatient with anything, be it institution or people, which serves to obscure it.

In the present narrative, we have a continuation of Jesus' condemnation of the scribes, in that they are held responsible for the exactions which effectively destroyed widows' estates, all on behalf of a temple still in building and soon to come to an end. Now, one of the salient features of Jesus' confrontations with the scribes in Mark is the connection the evangelist makes between them and the temple. While we may protest that the costs of the upkeep of the temple and its round of sacrificial observances were the concern of the clergy, Mark's gospel firmly lays responsibility for extravagance and excess at the door of the scribes, and they are the enemies of Jesus before the clergy enter the picture. The scribes in and around Jerusalem are quite regularly associated with the clergy (8:31; 10:33; 11:18,27; 14:1,43,53; 15:1,31) and even, at one point, almost indistinguishable from them (11:18,27-33). Any challenge by Jesus to the temple system and its clergy is accepted by the scribes as a challenge to their standing.

It is in this light that we are to understand the charge that the scribes *offer long prayers.* It is not that they are responsible for the worship and the liturgies of the temple, but that they consistently urge upon people the fundamental necessity of keeping the interminable round of observances in being. Perhaps we ought to understand *for appearances' sake* not as an indication of pretense, but as a judgment on Jesus' part that the observances themselves were but an outward show without substance.

The narrative before us has been the subject of countless exhortations, sermons, and expositions by commentators. The commentaries often reflect an embarrassment not always felt by preachers and expositors. The comment by Taylor (p. 496) may well serve as a starting point: ". . . the story is in harmony with His teaching elsewhere." But what is this teaching? It is here that the embarrassment of many writers begins. Was Jesus commending total and sacrificial giving at the expense of ordinary human prudence, which he commended elsewhere (cf. Luke 14:28)? Was Jesus contrasting those who patently could afford to give as against those who could not, to the detriment of the former? Does the phrase *gave more than all* indicate simply that Jesus was providing a scale of values in giving, dismissing the contributions of the wealthy in favor of the poor widow who *put in all she had?*

Such speculations have been effectively ended by the contribution of Addison G. Wright ("The Widow's Mites: Praise or Lament?" *CBQ* 44.2.1982, pp. 256-66), to which the reader is commended for a complete treatment of the pericope. As we have insisted throughout the material from the beginning of Chapter 11 onward, context is all-important in evaluating Jesus' actions and teaching, and so it is here.

1. The narrative, which can hardly be described as a 'pronouncement story,' is a continuation of the previous attack on the scribes, and their part (as Mark sees it) in the whole official establishment of Judaism in Jerusalem.

2. The judgment of Jesus in vv. 37-40 was that the scribes were like leeches on the Jewish faithful, and not the least of their sins was their insistence on the support of the temple system (and all that it implied), even to the sacrificing of widows' property.

3. Jesus does not commend the widow at all for sacrificing *all she had:* rather, the story should be read as a lament for a system which could end in a *poor widow.*

4. We would ourselves be rightly outraged (or ought to be) at any religious system which appropriated the property of the poor and the near-destitute in order to perpetuate "the system." Unhappily, it is not comforting to reflect how little effect the lament of Jesus has had on Christian history and how many estates (and even people) have been devoured by a near-adulation of "the system." It seems appropriate to close this note with a quotation from Wright's article: "Critical exegesis is supposed to inform preaching, piety, and church thinking; but one wonders to what extent preaching, piety, and church interests have affected critical exegesis in the history of the interpretation of this text" (p. 265).

5. The episode recounted here is followed immediately by the vivid account of the admiration evoked in the disciples by the magnificence of the temple buildings. Jesus' reply is to dismiss the magnificent display as—in the context of his ministry and mission—a massive irrelevance. One is reminded forcibly of Matt 23:23, not to mention Mic 6:8.

6. I am irresistibly reminded of the remark of a former colleague, speaking of the conflict of understanding between Jesus and the scribes and Pharisees: "After all, people are only people: it's the system that counts."

Notes

41. The opening description is vague, and there is no note of time.

the treasury (Greek *gazaphoulakion;* cf. Luke 21:1, John 8:20, and also 2 Kgs 23:11): Generally, commentators refer to a number of trumpet-shaped vessels, placed around the walls in the Court of Women, into which people were accustomed to place their offerings. Cf *DCG* 2.748-49, but see also Strack-Billerbeck, Vol. 2, pp. 37-45.

The order of the Greek words in this verse differs in some manuscripts: some have "Jesus was standing," others insert "Jesus" after the participle *kathezomenos,* "was sitting," evidently in an attempt to smooth Mark's grammar.

watched: The Greek verb *(etheōrei)* has the sense of "looking at," "taking in," rather than a mere glance.

money (Greek *chalkos):* Cf. 6:8. The word is frequent in the papyri. The reference to *many rich people* is hardly necessary, in view of *large sums,* but it gives added point to the *poor widow.*

42. *A poor widow:* Mark uses the cardinal number *mia* (= "one") where one might have expected *tis* (= "a certain"), but this was a common usage in contemporary Greek. In addition, Mark wishes to call attention to one particular incident—*came,*

and dropped in. This is a somewhat unusual grammatical care in Mark, for he uses three different tenses from vv. 41-43 for *ballō* (= "to throw," or "put in"): there is the present tense in *the crowds put money*, the imperfect tense in *rich people put in* (literally, "were in the habit of putting in"), and the aorist tense for *dropped in* (indicating completed action). The use of the perfect tense in *gave* (Greek *beblēken)* indicates a past action with continuing effects in the present.

two copper coins (Greek *lepton,* pl. *lepta;* cf. Luke 12:59, 21:2): The word (which literally means "peeled off") was used in later Greek literature for the smallest coins. Mark adds the explanation *ho estin kodrantes* ("that is, a *quadrans"),* giving the Latin equivalent. This coin was one quarter of an *as,* and we have provided the best equivalent open to us. (The *as,* or *assarion,* has been estimated as one sixteenth of a *denarius,* itself the equivalent of a day's wage for an agricultural laborer.) Luke does not have this explanation. Given the mobility of various kinds of coinage in the Roman world, there is little to be said for the suggestion that Mark provided this note of equivalence for the benefit of Roman readers. Matthew has the same word, *kodrantes,* at 5:26, and Matthew can hardly be described as addressed to Romans.

43. *called* (cf. 3:13,23) *his disciples* (cf. 2:15): The usages are Markan, as is *I tell you truly*—cf. 3:28; 6:11; 8:12; 9:1,41; 10:15,29; 11:23; 13:30; 14:9,18,25,30. Luke has the word *amēn,* "truly," only half as often as Mark, whereas Matthew uses it thirty times.

gave more: Some important manuscripts use the aorist tense, but we opt for the reading of the perfect tense, even though the difference can hardly be expressed in English (see note on v. 42).

Luke's account omits *all those who are contributing.*

44. *They have given* . . . (Literally, "For all they have put in from the superfluity which is theirs . . ."): For *superfluity* (Greek *perisseuon)* see 8:8, where Mark uses *perisseuma.*

poverty (Greek *husterēsis):* Cf. Phil 4:11. The word is not found in classical Greek, and Luke uses the more usual *husterēma* (21:4), which is represented in the Septuagint (Judg 18:10, 19:19; Ps 33:10; Eccl 1:15; 2 Esdr 6:9). The history of Mark's Greek word is obscure; it occurs in only one version of the Septuagint, and the route by which *husterēma* became *husterēsis* is not known.

all that she had (Greek *panta hosa):* Cf. 6:30, 11:24.

all she had to live on (Greek *bios):* Another translation, also preserving the meaning of *bios* as "life," would be "livelihood." A fourth-century Syriac manuscript from St. Catherine's monastery omits the phrase, but it was clearly formed from Luke's *panta ton bion hon eichen,* "all the livelihood she had" (21:4).

It is pointless to ask how Jesus knew how much money the widow put into the treasury, for the whole importance of the story lies in the words of Jesus. The evangelist plainly is not concerned to satisfy our curiosity, but in contrast with the suggestion sometimes made that this pericope was originally a parable the whole tenor of the narrative suggests a historical reminiscence. After this final judgment on the scribes, this incident provides Mark with an introduction to the prophecy of the destruction of the temple.

Note on the Relationship Between Mark and Luke

W. R. Farmer (1964, pp. 266-70) offers the suggestion that we can best understand Mark's version of this incident against Luke's by reference to the Greek biographical device known as *chreia,* a small literary unit of biographical detail originating in a concrete situation, with a definite person as subject. (The reader wishing to pursue examples of *chreia,* in both classical and postclassical times, may consult the references in Farmer, p. 266n. 15, or—in short form—R. Grant, *The Earliest Lives of Jesus,* Harper & Row, 1961, pp. 17-18, 99-101.) The object of the *chreia* was to preserve the absolute essentials of an incident for easy memorization: once committed to memory such literary units could be fleshed out with additional reminiscences and even expounded.

Farmer is entirely correct in saying that the literary unit thus described was commonplace. But it is possible to rely too heavily on such evidence, as we hope to show. We consider, however, that there are good grounds for regarding Mark 12:41-44 as an expression of Luke 21:1-4.

1. Luke's interest in Jesus' ministry among women is well known, and needs no comment. But in that area of the ministry, Luke mentions widows in no less than six chapters (2, 4, 7, 18, 20, 21), while Mark betrays no interest in the matter until we come to the judgment on the scribes at 12:40 and in the pericope before us.

2. The above note, in and of itself, would prove little about the relationship of Mark to Luke, still less about any dependence of the former on the latter. Luke, with his concern for women manifested throughout his gospel, might easily have fastened on this item in Mark and incorporated it. Yet, given Luke's obvious exploration of traditions open to him for demonstrating Jesus' concern for women, it would be very strange if the incident he records had been discovered only in one small pericope in a gospel not otherwise concerned with women. If therefore we regard the Lucan account as one of a number of *chreiai* used by the evangelist, then Mark bears all the signs of an expansion of the material, even to the extent of the familiar Markan *he called his disciples to him.* Moreover, for Mark the style is prolix: there are, for example, no less than three uses of *treasury.* Finally, the Lucan version exhibits all the signs of a story stripped of extraneous detail. We maintain that Mark's uncharacteristic mention of the widow is solely intended to underline an anti-scribal bias to be found all through his gospel.

Having said all of the above, we ought to be wary of embracing too readily the *chreia* concept as an acceptable solution in various problem areas. We had occasion, in dealing with the parable of the wicked tenants (12:1-12), to call attention to that parable as it is represented in the *Gospel of Thomas.* Now, it has often been suggested that this version most closely approximates the parable originally uttered by Jesus, and that our synoptic versions represent that parable as worked over by the early tradition in favor of an incipient christology. Yet no one has claimed that the manuscripts of Chenoboskion are older than our earliest manuscripts of the synoptic gospels, and the parables in the *Gospel of Thomas* evince not the slightest interest in the Reign of God—the central theme which informed all of Jesus' parables. If therefore we posit the *Gospel of Thomas* as the earliest form of a parable, with the synoptists serving the interests of a later development, it may be useful to say that the same process was at work as between the Lucan and Markan traditions with respect to the widow's offering. But manifestly the shorter, simpler version of the parable of the wicked tenants in the *Gospel of Thomas* is far later than the core tradition of the synoptic versions. It is therefore a matter of some importance, where evidence of dating *is* available, to exercise caution in evaluating different versions of the same incident on the basis of brevity in composition.

68. The Destruction of the Temple
(13:1-2) = Matt 24:1-2; Luke 21:5-6

13 ¹ As he was leaving the temple, one of his disciples said, "Rabbi, look—what great stones, and what wonderful buildings!" ² Jesus said to him, "You see these great buildings? There will not be left here one stone upon another that will not be thrown down."

Comment

In the nature of the case, material preceding the commentary on Chapter 13 will be lengthy, for the debate about the authenticity of this apocalyptic material has produced a voluminous literature apart from the commentaries. The thrust of the chapter is seen by most commentators as apocalyptic material concerned with the End and in some fashion closely linked to the fall of Jerusalem, the end of the old order of things, and an expectation of divine intervention in favor of the elect. But substantial questions remain, even when that interpretation has been admitted.

Allowing that what we have in this chapter (and its parallels in Matthew 24 and Luke 21) represents substantially the words of Jesus, to what extent did he anticipate either that the end of his own ministry would herald the End or that an anticipated fall of Jerusalem would usher in the sufferings of the final days? We had occasion to examine this briefly in a prefatory note to the bibliography on "The Reign/Kingdom" in the Introduction (p. 153-58). A very wide spectrum of opinion is represented in that bibliography, short as it is, and after many years of debate the question posed at the beginning of this paragraph appears to be no nearer solution. In this extended comment to this chapter we propose to give an account of three things: the form of the chapter, its background in the OT, and finally some suggestions as to its origin.

The form of Mark 13 is dictated by the question posed by the disciples. Jesus' impatience with their wonder at the temple buildings is followed by a prediction that those very buildings are nearing the end of their life. All of this comes hard on the heels, in Mark and Luke, of Jesus' condemnation of the present state of Israel's institutional religious life as represented by the temple (see Comment on 12:41-44). The full force of all this must be appreciated. Contemporary Judaism was concerned with the aggrandizement of the temple, with an external glory, while Jesus had been demanding attention to the inner meaning of Israel and her vocation before God. The disciples are presented to us as grasping the eschatological meaning of Jesus' prophecy, but they are now confronted with the fact that *as Jews* they must contemplate the destruction of a shrine thought to be inviolable as the shrine and center of the divine presence. In that well-nigh unthinkable event was the *sign* to be a single omen, the "Desecration" of v. 14, or was this but an introduction to all that would follow? Moreover, the overthrow of the heart and core of Judaism must inevitably mean the end, the fulfillment, of an era—as had been the case in the fateful year of 586 B.C. The disciples are shown as wanting assurance about such things, for they would be involved in the inevitable distress.

In all of this there is an air of necessity: *such things are bound to happen.* They are to be on their guard. For in the language of eschatology and apocalyptic war is a common theme. The wars and the distress are almost accidental, and they are no sign of the End, though they may be part of a larger canvas of God working in power. War, pestilence, and famine, all associated in some fashion with the visitation of God—all were to be borne patiently. In the midst of the turmoil there would be false messianic movements, on the part of those claiming to act with the authority of the Messiah, and the members of the infant community were not to become involved in such movements. For all the trials and tribulations, the community must watch, pray, and trust.

Such, in essence, is the message of this chapter. But even a glance at the marginal references in an English Bible reveals an abundance of Old Testament allusions, quotations, and semiquotations. The chapter is at times reminiscent of the commentary style of the Essenes—e.g., the Habbakuk scroll. A further examination, as against the rest of the gospel, discloses that this apocalyptic discourse is so weighted by Old Testament references and allusions as to make all other chapters appear barren of Old Testament allusions. This is so signal a circumstance that we are compelled to seek some explanation for it. The question of its authenticity as a collection of sayings of Jesus has already been raised, and we shall return to it. What follows is a breakdown of the chapter before us, with parallels, followed by two columns. The first column lists either direct quotations from, or allusions to, Old Testament material, while the second column contains OT material which has a bearing on the text but is not so direct as the preceding column.

Mark 13	Matt 24	Luke 21	1	2	
5	4	8	Jer 29:8		Take care
6	5	8	Jer 29:9	Deut 18:17-18 Jer 14:14, 21, 23:25	my name
6	5	8	Exod 3:14 Deut 32:39 Isa 41:4 47:8,10	Isa 14:13 Dan 7:8,25 8:9,10	"I am"
6	5,11		Jer 23:13,32 Ezek 13:10	Dan 8:24 11:32	mislead many
6	7	9	Mic 3:5 Dan 7:21 8:24 9:26 11:4-27	Jer 4:19 Dan 2:39,40	when you hear of wars
7	6	9	Dan 2:28-30 8:19		bound to happen
7	6	9	Dan 11:27	Dan 9:26 11:35	end of the age
8	7	10	2 Chr 15:6	Dan 11:25-27 Jer 6:22 51:27	nation against nation
8	7	10	Isa 19:12 Dan 11:25-27	Jer 51:27	kingdom against kingdom
8	7	10	Dan 2:40	Isa 24:18 29:6 Ezek 38:19 Hag 2:22	earthquakes
8	7	10	Deut 28:48 32:24 Jer 14:12 15:2		famine
8	8			Isa 13:8 21:3 Jer 22:23 25:29	birth pains

9	9	12	Dan 7:25		deliver you up
9	18	13	Ps 119:46 Dan 6:13		testimony
9	18	12	Ps 119:46	Deut 31:26	for my sake
11	19,20	14,15	Dan 7:25 Exod 4:11	Jer 1:7	do not worry
12	21	16	Mic 7:6	Isa 9:19 19:2 Ezek 38:21 Amos 1:11 Hag 2:22 Zech 7:10 14:13	brother will betray brother
12	21	16	Mic 7:6	Ezek 22:7	children against parents
12	9	16	Dan 11:33		put to death
13	9	17	Mic 7:6	Ps 25:19 69:7 105:25 106:41 Isa 66:5	hated for his sake
13	13	[19]	Dan 11:32,35 12:1,12 Mic 7:7		he who endures will be saved
14	15		Dan 11:31 12:11	Dan 9:27 Ps 74:4	"abominable desecra- tion"
14			Dan 11:31		set up (Mark)
	15		Dan 9:27	Isa 60:13	in holy place (Matthew)

Mark 13	Matt 24	Luke 21	1	2	
14	15			Dan 9:23,25	(let the reader understand)
14	16	21	Gen 19:17	Ezek 7:16 Jer 50:8 51:6,45 Zech 2:7 1 Macc 2:28	. . . those in Judea . . .
15	17			Exod 12:4 Isa 46:2 Jer 10:17 Ezek 7:16	roof
16	18		Gen 19:17	Amos 2:16	in the field
17	19	23		2 Kgs 15:16 Lam 4:4 Hos 14:1 Amos 1:13	Alas . . .
18	20 (Sabbath)			Exod 16:29	Pray that . . .
19	21	23	Dan 12:1 Jer 30:7 Hab 3:16	Deut 31:17,21 2 Chr 15:6 Zeph 1:2-5	the distress
20	22		Dan 12:1	Dan 9:24 Isa 65:9,15	if the Lord had not cut short
21	23			Deut 13:4,9-10 Jer 23:16	do not believe it
22	24		Deut 13:2	Deut 18:20 Isa 9:15 Jer 2:13 5:31 23:15	false prophets, Messiah
22	24			Deut 31:6 Dan 8:24	mislead

24	29		Joel 2:10	Isa 13:10 Ezek 32:7 Joel 3:3	In those days . . .
24	29	25	Isa 13:10	Ezek 32:7 Joel 2:10 3:15	sun, moon
24	29	25	Isa 34:4	Isa 13:10 Ezek 32:7 Joel 2:10 3:15	stars will fall
25	29	26	Isa 34:4		powers in the heavens
	30		Isa 11:10	Isa 18:3 66:19	ensign of the Son of Man
	30		Zech 12:12, 14	Isa 13:7,8 Ezek 32:9	tribes of earth mourn
26		27	Dan 7:13	Isa 19:1	they will see The Man
26	30	27	Dan 7:14		great power and glory
27	31		Isa 27:13		send his angels
27	31		Deut 30:3,4	Ps 106:47 Isa 27:12	gather the chosen
27	31		Zech 2:10	Isa 43:5 49:5	farthest bound . . . of earth
27	31			Isa 56:8 Jer 29:14 30:10 31:8 32:37	farthest bound of heaven

Mark 13	Matt 24	Luke 21	1	2	
27	31			Ezek 28:25	farthest
				34:12-14	bound
				37:21	of heaven
				Zech 2:10	

Even a cursory examination of an English synopsis of the gospels (such as Throckmorton's) will demonstrate that Mark is far closer to Matthew, and (save for vv. 9-13) follows his order. Furthermore, there is material in Luke not found in either of the others, while the special Matthean material is more extensive. If one had to make a demonstration of conflation and digest, Mark 13 would serve as an admirable example of an economy of words in choosing between Matthew and Luke. But even allowing that Luke had material of his own—as did Matthew—does not bring us nearer to any hypothesis about the source or sources of the material. To this we must now turn.

The nearest material we can find in the literature with the same wealth of Old Testament allusion is in Daniel and 2 Esdras. In both there are visions, in both the visions are explained by an angel, and in both there is a chief character or agent (in Daniel it is Michael and in 2 Esdras the "Son of Man"). In both books, as in the chapter before us, the chosen are the passive recipients of divine action, and the only demand is that they be on their guard. There are significant differences, however. Both 2 Esdras and Mark 13 have references to trials and to possible martyrdom, far more akin to 2 Maccabees, whereas in Daniel the trials belong (ostensibly) to an earlier period and are not connected with any "end-time." Again, 2 Esdras and Mark 13 are alike in their ideas of when the events will take place—soon, but not yet. Daniel has various sets of "days" and is far more connected with the history of the Ptolemaic and Seleucid dynasties, but it is fair to say that 2 Esdras and Mark 13 are innocent of historical connection (despite Mark 13:30). If, then, Mark 13 (and the parallel material) is ahistorical, is a free composition and a pastiche of Old Testament allusions and quotations, and if the material is here and there reminiscent of the Qumran *War Scroll,* then we must next ask in what circumstances it was composed, for what audience, and what purpose it serves in its synoptic locations.

The view espoused here is that Mark 13 (and parallels) is a fairly typical apocalyptic composition, of which we have examples in Daniel 7-13, 2 Esdras, and the *War Scroll.* The New Testament Book of Revelation belongs to the same genre, and—apart from occasional references to Jesus—does not appear to be distinctively Christian in origin. It is commonly said that apocalyptic literature is designed to sustain and encourage the afflicted in times of doubt and distress, to proclaim the inevitability of the triumph of God; and it is often said that such literature is intended for some kind of elite or representative leaders of some group. Such propositions are incapable of demonstration, unless one opts for some literal sense in 2 Esdr 14:46 ("the seventy books are to be kept back and given to none but the wise"). In the case of the synoptic material before us, restriction to an elite poses peculiar difficulties, unless we are to assume that the oral tradition in its final fixed form was committed to writing purely for the edification of such an elite. Against such a notion is the witness of all four gospels that the preaching and teaching of Jesus was always a public matter, and if the disciples were the recipients of private teaching nevertheless his proclamation of the Reign of God was never done secretly.

Mark 13 is crucial to his gospel. This was examined at some length in Chapter 2 of the Introduction, and it will not be repeated here. If Mark came back to Palestine, finding on his return a distressed and suffering community full of doubts and misgivings, then his composition of this chapter as a compact digest of the material he found in Matthew and Luke betrays an acute sense of theological timing. Certainly it was addressed to a suffering community, but it was addressed to that community as a whole, not to an esoteric elite. It is equally certain that the synoptic material which he found and used was not a free composition of any one of the evangelists: the roots are far too deep in apocalyptic tradition.

The situation of Matthew 24 and Mark 13 is such that the chapters in question serve to introduce the Passion narrative as *the* eschatological/apocalyptic event by which all human actions are and will be weighed. Was the community suffering in an agony of doubt and physical torment? So did its Lord. Was the community to believe that there would in the end be vindication? Its Lord so believed. But what was that vindication, and when would it be? That was in the hands of God and it was a vindication to which Jesus looked. Were there any hints of the outcome? The passion and death of Jesus had been the final, all-availing battle in that warfare against sin and death which for Mark characterized the ministry. And beyond that? There had been the raising of Jesus by God. Then why was there no resurrection narrative? "For they were afraid" was said of the women at the tomb: Mark's community was afraid, too, but by that simple device of the ending in 16:8 that community was driven to ask what was the basis of its faith. Luke's location of the apocalyptic material in a variety of positions has somewhat limited the effects of the whole, but perfectly fits his theme of a "time of expectation." Mark has far more in common with Matthew, having made a judicious choice of the material before him.

The matter of the composition of the "synoptic apocalypse" is probably beyond solution, and we have already noted the ahistorical framework of the whole. Whatever sayings of Jesus are embedded in the material are—in the view of this commentator—minimal. Even the fairly common assertion on the part of some authors that the basis of the Markan (and Matthean?) material is an apocalypse of Jewish or Jewish-Christian origin meets with no agreement as to the precise limits of such an apocalypse. Estimates vary between the following limits in Mark: 7-9,14-20,24-27,30-37; 6-8,14,17-20,24-31; 7-9,14-20,24-27,30; 7-10,12,14-22,24-27; 5-9,14-20,24-27. It will be seen that the stable constant is 7-9,14-20,24-27. But what modifications were made to this material is beyond agreement: the various suggestions are examined in Beasley-Murray's works listed in the bibliography at the end of Part VI. The present commentator hazards the suggestion that the core of the work is pre-Jesus, that *some* sayings of Jesus are incorporated in the final product, and that perhaps the completed material was used as a separate entity to encourage the faithful before being fitted into the framework of either Matthew or Mark.

Some very considerable—and insoluble—puzzles remain, however. The following brief list will give some idea of the complexity of the problems. What is the relevance of Luke 21 to the composition of Mark? Can we identify authentic words of Jesus, and if so, how? What circumstances dictated the placing of the material in its present positions in Matthew and Mark? Why is the prophecy of the fall of Jerusalem placed *before* the discourse, and not as a climax at the end? Who are the deceivers in vv. 5-6 and vv. 21-23, and why are these two sections not joined together? Did the reference to persecution (vv. 9-13) originally belong to the discourse, or was it added later? Is it possible that the reference to Jerusalem in Luke 21:20 is earlier than the "Abominable Desecration" in 13:14? Why—in contrast to, e.g., Daniel—is there no reference to the final triumph of God over evil? What is the significance of the injunction to "watch"? In a discourse which begins with the assertion that certain signs will herald "the End" (however understood), is there also ignorance of the "day" (13:32)? One of these questions *may* admit of an answer: we had reason to think that the story of the widow's offering in 12:41-44 was connected with Jesus' impatience with Jerusalem institutionalism. It may well be, therefore, that *when will all this happen* as an introduction to the discourse did not originally refer to the destruction of the temple—a prophecy much more closely linked with 13:28-31 than with 13:5-23.

The various sections are: 1-2, The Destruction of the Temple; 3-4, The Question of the Disciples; 5-8, Warnings About Deceivers, Wars; 9-13, On Persecution; 14-23, The Great Distress and False Messiahs; 24-27, The Coming of The Man; 28-37, On Watchfulness. It is possible that Matthew and Mark use the two words *when* (Greek *hotan*—Matt 24:15,32; Mark 13:7,11,14) and *then* (Greek *tote*—Matt 24:9,23,30; Mark 13:14,21,26) intending these words as introductions to a new subject or idea, rather as though the words were pegs with loops in between.

Although Mark exhibits remarkable fidelity to his Matthean *outline*, it should be noted that the relationship between the two evangelists is far more complex, and that Mark's use of the apocalyptic material is determined by the use Luke had made of Matthew. It will be convenient at this point to set out the relationships in tabulated form.

1. The parallels between Matthew and Luke are as follows: Luke begins at 21:5 to make use of Matt 24:1-7,15-19,29-35 in the order in which he found the material. However, the evangelist does make changes by way of omission and a very important insertion. Up to 21:11b, Luke was following Matt 24:1-7, and then discovered that the following unit in Matt 24:13 had the phrase "the one who stands firm to the end will be saved," which is a doublet of Matt 10:22. Luke promptly opted for Matt 10:17-22, probably because this section referred to "you will be hated by all" as against "you will be hated by all *the Gentiles*" in Matt 24:9. Luke—on the hypothesis of Matthean priority —had already used Matt 10:19-20 in his own 12:11-12, and so in vv. 14-15 he paraphrased what had already been used (a device to which he resorted in 21:22, partly used already in 17:31). W. R. Farmer *(The Synoptic Problem,* p. 272) rightly points out that a writer using a narrative source moves forward, and—if the writer skips material in moving forward—then, discovering material already used, will either omit it or paraphrase it.

2. The next stage in the formation of the material is the use Luke made of Matt 24:15-22 in his own 21:20-24. Here there are references to Jerusalem being surrounded by armies, in place of the Matthean "Abominable Desecration." Dating is of prime importance here. If we are to maintain the Griesbach hypothesis, then the Markan "Abominable Desecration" may be a natural reference to the placing of Roman imperial eagle standards within the temple precincts on the fall of the city in A.D. 70. This, of course, places Mark's composition after that date, with knowledge of the historical fact. Given the dating suggested in the Introduction, it appears at first sight that the two-document hypothesis, along with Markan priority, will best explain the "Abominable Desecration" in Matthew as derived from Mark, and the reference to the siege of Jerusalem as reflecting the date of Luke. This is to say too much. To begin with, the "Abominable Desecration" probably has no historical reference, and was simply derived from Daniel. Secondly, the late W. F. Albright constantly maintained that no particular gift of prescience was called for to predict an investment and siege of Jerusalem before the end of the century.

3. It is hard to resist the conclusion that Luke had access to sources of his own in his treatment of Matthew 24 (e.g., Luke 21:22,24). When Luke in Chapter 21 is using Matthew 24, he either omits anything

paralleled earlier in his own gospel or (as in the case of Luke 21:21 =
Matt 24:17-18) he paraphrases Matthew. What we have, in effect, is a
block of apocalyptic material preserved as a whole in Matt 24, but
found distributed in other contexts in Luke. One example will suffice.
Having used Matt 24:23-28 in compiling 17:21-24, Luke omits it,
proceeding in his Chapter 21:25-33 as parallel to Matt 24:29-35.
However, having used Matt 24:36-42 in his own 17:26-27,30,34,35,
Luke omits the material. This is not all. Luke omits Matt 24:45-51
(the ending of the discourse) because he has already used it in his own
special section on repentance (Luke 12:35-13:9) and combined it with
a parable from his own sources.

4. All the above serves to explain the use Mark makes of the material.
The Lucan parallels to Matthew 24 which are not used in Luke 21 are
in Luke's central section, of which Mark makes no use. In effect, the
Markan use of Matthew 24 is confined to material also found in Luke
21. In the main, Mark follows Matthew 24 far more closely than did
Luke, though the verbal agreement between all three is striking (thus
confirming the existence of the apocalypse as a prior and independent
text). The agreements between Matthew and Mark against Luke are
considerable, while the agreements of Matthew and Luke against
Mark are slight and haphazard, as is also the case for agreements
between Mark and Luke against Matthew.

5. Once more, we are faced with the familiar maze of the synoptic problem. On the familiar Markan-priority hypothesis, there are minor but
important agreements of Matthew and Luke against Mark in Matt
24:1-7,30-35, and on the two-document hypothesis these must be attributed to Q. On the same premises, it seems that Matt 24:26-28,37-
41,43-51 must likewise be attributed to Q. After all, those units are
neither in Mark 13 nor in Luke 21, but are in Luke's central section.
Why, then, on the two-document hypothesis, do we find Mark omitting from Q those elements which Luke does not have in parallel with
Matthew 24, but does have in his central section? Mark—on the hypothesis we are examining—cannot possibly have known how Matthew and Luke would use material they drew from Q independently
of each other, and it is not easy to explain the use which Luke makes
of Q in the order in which he does so. The majority opinion on
synoptic origins compels us to imagine a procedure in which Matt
24:1-7 = Mark + Q, 24:8-25 copies Mark (though vv. 17-18 *may* be
from Q), 24:26-28 = Q, 24:29-35 = Mark + Q, 24:36 = Mark, and
finally 24:37-51 = Q. This is imaginable—barely—but only with a
very elaborate "scissors and paste" technique. An even odder circumstance, however, is the reference to the Sabbath in Matt 24:20, absent

in Luke and in Mark. It is far more probable that what we have in Matthew 24 is early Jewish (or Jewish-Christian) material than it is to suggest that Matthew drew upon Mark and then added a reference to the Sabbath—all of this at a time when the diffusion of the community into the Gentile world was making the Sabbath of less moment.

Enough has been said for the time being on the complications of synoptic relationships in Mark 13—an argument that will be further elucidated in the body of the notes. It is sufficient here to say that whenever Luke followed Matthew, Mark used the common text: agreements of Matthew and Luke against Mark are without importance. But whenever Luke was at variance with Matthew, Mark followed Matthew, and as a result the textual agreements of Mark and Luke against Matthew are equally without importance.

Mark's gospel as a whole is a tightly written document, however much the purist may deplore the literary style. And Mark 13 preserves in microcosm the purpose of the evangelist. He had no time, in the situation for which he was writing, for extended supporting material (such as characterizes Matthew 24), nor yet for the artifice of Luke in avoiding duplication of material. Unfortunately, we have no means of knowing whether Luke is to be taken literally when he speaks of "many others" in the very first sentence of his gospel; but it is possible that Mark's community knew of more than one or two gospels, each with a viewpoint and an emphasis (theological or otherwise) of its own. (The "Jewishness" of Matthew as against the comparative cosmopolitanism of Luke is ample illustration.) So far as the evangelist Mark is concerned, the two sources for consideration in compiling a gospel were Matthew and Luke, and it is these two which Mark uses (together with his own special source for minor details). The *purpose* of Mark's digest/conflation is best exemplified by his emphasis on the urgent necessity of watchfulness both at the beginning and at the end of the discourse—adding "watch" at 13:9 and at 13:33. In the latter case we are confronted with a now familiar matter of interpretation. Taylor (p. 523) rightly insists that the saying is immediately applied to the case of the man leaving home and entrusting his affairs to servants as introduction to the relationship between the Lord and the Church in v. 35. But is this application of the parable directly attributable to Jesus, or is it rather an intent of the evangelists? Has this parable been attracted to its present context by the theme of watchfulness? Was the parable originally intended as a warning of the immediacy of the Reign of God in the preaching and teaching of Jesus, without its present apparent concern for signs of the End?

We earlier concluded that the discourse, like Daniel 7, is divorced from historical context and has no historical reference (with the possible exception of Luke 21:20). Whatever the origins of the discourse, with some isolated sayings of Jesus interspersed, this commentator regards the saying in Mark

13:30-31 and parallels as vital. The difficulties of interpretation are, in the present state of our knowledge, well-nigh insuperable. The opinion hazarded here is that this *is* a saying of Jesus, that it referred to the consummation and vindication (in whatever form) of his mission and ministry, and that the saying is incorporated in the apocalypse as having reference to signs of the End. Familiar to the academic scholar and to the serious student of the NT, the issue of "realized" versus "futurist" eschatology will not soon or easily disappear.

Notes

It is comparatively easy to determine the relationship between the synoptic gospels in this section of the apocalypse, and the reader without Greek who uses a single translation (KJV, RSV) can follow the steps of composition in Mark. The verbal agreement in this segment of all three gospels is very close, but the closest agreement is between Matthew and Mark (and against Luke), and though Mark has drawn upon both sources, his principal dependence is on the longer version in Matthew, but with a significant Markan emphasis on watchfulness which he develops from v. 5.

1. *what great stones:* Whether this little introduction originally belonged in this context, or whether in some original source it was a free composition to act as introduction to the synoptic apocalypse, we cannot determine. But in its present position it is part of a linked series of sayings on what may conveniently be called "institutional Jerusalem Judaism" (see above on 12:41-44). Here the disciples are seen as pilgrims— Galileans awestruck by the magnificence of the temple buildings, still being adorned and still being completed in the time of Jesus. (For a convenient summary of all this, see J. Jeremias, *Jerusalem in the Time of Jesus,* * Philadelphia: Fortress Press, 1969, especially pp. 21-27). The temple was not completed until A.D. 66.

In context, Jesus seems to be appealing to an inner spirit of Judaism as against an institutionalism which had completely outlived its usefulness and must give place to something new. Jesus' mind, as expressed in all his sayings, is reminiscent of Mic 3:12, even when he insists that he had not come to destroy the Law.

2. *You see . . . . :* Matthew's Greek *(ou blepete tauta panta:* "Do you not see all these things?") is recognizably more akin to Mark's *blepeis tautas tas megalas oikodomas* (= "You see these great buildings?") than Luke's *tauta ha theoreite* (= "as for those things you are looking at").

There will not be left . . . . : The reply of Jesus with its double *will not* is far more emphatic in the Greek than our English is able to render. No remarkable insight was demanded to foretell the destruction of Jerusalem and the temple, and Jer 26:6,18 and Mic 3:12 could have provided Jesus with Old Testament precedent for the saying. Apart from any consideration such as Jesus' passing judgment on institutional Judaism, the political climate in which he lived provided material enough for grim forebod-

---

* English translation by F. H. and C. H. Cave of *Jerusalem zur Zeit Jesu,* Göttingen: Vandenhoeck & Ruprecht, 1967.

ings. The decades after c. A.D. 40 saw the rise of the fiercely nationalist Zealot movement in Palestine and parts of the eastern Mediterranean, and Jewish Christians were faced with exceedingly difficult choices in the time of the first Jewish War (A.D. 64-70). It must have been clear to any observer that once Roman imperial authorities regarded the Parthian frontier as secure they would turn their attention to a resolution of the turbulent Palestinian situation.

one stone upon another: Josephus *(Jewish Wars* 6.4.5) tells us that the temple was destroyed by fire, and further (ibid. 7.1.1) that nothing was left to persuade the later visitor that anything had even been there. Some few manuscripts add "and after three days, another will be raised without hands." (Cf. 14:58, John 2:19.) This is clearly an interpolation. See below, under 14:58, for further discussion.

PART VI
THE FUTURE

69. The Beginning of Distress
(13:3-13) = Matt 24:3-14; Luke 21:7-19

13 ³ When he was sitting on the Mount of Olives, opposite the temple, Peter, James, John, and Andrew questioned him privately. ⁴ "Tell us, when will all those things happen and what will be the sign when the fulfillment of all these things is near?" ⁵ Jesus began: "Take care that no one misleads you. ⁶ Many will come, using my name and saying, 'I am he!' and they will mislead many people. ⁷ When you hear the noises of war, both close at hand and far away, do not be alarmed. Such things are bound to happen, but the end of the age is still to come. ⁸ One nation will make war against another nation, and one kingdom against another kingdom. There will be earthquakes in various places, and there will be famines. This is but the beginning of the birth pains. ⁹ But as for you—be on your guard. They will deliver you up to councils and synagogues. You will be flogged. Because of me you will stand trial before rulers and kings, to testify before them. ¹⁰ But the Proclamation must first be made to all the nations. ¹¹ So when they arrest you and deliver you up to trial, do not worry beforehand about what you will say, but when the time comes say whatever is given you to say. It is not you who will be speaking, but the holy Spirit. ¹² Brother will betray brother to death, and the father his child; while children will turn against their parents and hand them over to be killed. ¹³ Because of me, all men will hate you; but the man who holds out to the end will be saved."

Comment

The previous short section (13:1-2) may be regarded as self-contained, attracted to its present location by the concluding vv. 38-41 of the preceding chapter. But verses 3 and 4—whatever the origins of the remainder of the chapter—are plainly meant to be introductory. Unlike Matt 24:3 (= Luke 21:7—without any note of location), Mark's *the fulfillment of all these things* appears to point solely to the destruction of the temple, "when all this will happen and what will be the sign of your coming . . ." Luke's "what will be the sign when this is about to take place?" replaces Matthew and Mark as introduction to the whole dialogue. Here Mark would appear to be using a source of his own.

Notes

3. *Peter* . . . The four disciples are those whose call was described in 1:16-20. Precisely what this formula means, as a connection with the call in 1:16-20, we cannot determine with certainty, but see Notes at the end of Chapter 13. Matt 24:3 has "the disciples" and Luke 21:7 has "they."

4. *these things:* Cf. Dan 12:7. The catastrophic character of the prediction has been fully grasped, and the disciples are presented to us as demanding an answer, in terms of *the sign.* Was this to be a single portent, in some fashion linked with the *Abominable Desecration* (v. 14), or is there to be some *sign* to serve as an introduction to the End? The temple was the center and the symbol of Judaism, and its overthrow could only mean some kind of *fulfillment*—but of what? The translation provided here—*these things* (Greek *tauta*)—indicates the prophecy of the destruction of the temple, and so looks back. But *all these things* (Greek *tauta panta*) looks forward to the material yet to be unfolded. Matthew's version is clearer and separates the two subjects distinctly. It is possible that Mark's original tradition referred only to the fate of the temple, and that the phrase *all these things* was an addition to accommodate the apocalyptic material which was inserted later. We note further that the ensuing dialogue was a result of a private question, as is also the case in Matthew. Luke's "they asked him" (21:7) has no such indication.

5. *"Take care* . . .*":* The expression *(blepein mē)* was very common in colloquial Greek in New Testament times. It is well represented in our sources: Matt 24:4; Luke 21:8; Acts 13:40; 1 Cor 8:9, 10:12; Gal 5:15; Col 2:8; Heb 3:12, 12:25; 2 John 8. The exhortation is to beware of being deceived.

6. *using my name and saying, 'I am he':* The meaning of this, following on the warning in v. 5, is far from clear. Was there originally a warning against a belief in the inviolability of the temple as the shrine of the Shekinah (literally "presence"), to

which the warnings against false messianism were added later? For *using my name*, cf. 9:37,39.

The *many* is enigmatic. Are we to understand this to mean false messiahs (cf. Matt 24:5) or those claiming the authority of Jesus, or even some claiming to be Jesus himself (in the light of the resurrection tradition)? The phrase *using my name* is most easily understood as "claiming my authority." Matt 24:5, alone of the gospels, explicitly says "I am the Messiah," while Luke here is the same as Mark. Now, although it is true that the earliest explicit messianic claimant we know was Bar Kochba (endorsed as Messiah by his contemporary the Rabbi Akiba), c. A.D. 132, nevertheless the first century of our era was ripe for messianic exploitation of various kinds. Something of the atmosphere may be glimpsed from Acts 21:38, where "the Egyptian" was (according to Josephus) a rebel. Judas of Galilee (Acts 5:37) was a Galilean revolutionary, while Theudas (Acts 5:36) is said by Josephus *(Antiquities* 20.5.1) to have made claims to be a prophet. What is not clear is the meaning of *'I am he'* or its relationship to the first part of the verse. While *using my name* is the equivalent of a claim to delegated authority, *'I am he'* would appear to be either a claim to act as a divine emissary or a claim to a kind of self-designated divinity. There is nothing here which *necessarily* points to Jesus himself: many will come using his name as authority to claim falsely a dignity which was not theirs to claim. Apart altogether from Exod 3:14, there are other texts which the false claimants might use—Deut 32:39; Isa 41:4, 47:8 and 10. Cf. also, on the claims of those who would mislead, Dan 7:8 and 25, 8:9 and 10; and on the community subject to such false claims, cf. Dan 8:24, 11:32; Jer 23:13 and 32; Ezek 13:10. This is by no means the end of the matter. What still remains to be explained is not only whether the *many* are false teachers and false claimants using Jesus' name, but also whether *'I am he'* indicates they are additionally claiming to be the Messiah. Or will they be claiming under Jesus' authority that the definitive hour has arrived and the revelation of final glory is imminent? The problem with the second of these choices is that in our sources (and in Acts) "I am" or "I am he" is always used of the speaker and not of another (cf. Mark 6:50, 14:62), and in John (whatever the dignity of style attaching to "I am" sayings) the expression is always used of the speaker. If it were not for Luke's version, and the plain understanding in Matt 24:5 that there would be many messianic claimants, Mark's verse would be best understood as following the Matthean lead. But Luke 21:8 has "I am he" followed immediately by "The time is at hand!" and the warning "Do not go after them" (cf. Matt 24:26). Luke's text apparently combines *two* expectations—the advent of the Messiah, and the approach of the *parousia.*

There is no adequate explanation which will cover all the difficulties in this verse. We have no information of such false teachers claiming Jesus' authority in our New Testament sources. Lohmeyer (p. 270) regards the *I am* as a traditional formula for an expected eschatological Deliverer, but this appears to be going beyond the contemporary evidence available to us. Of all the material contained in this chapter from v. 5 to v. 28, perhaps here we are nearest to a saying of Jesus, but one which has been obscured in the process of inclusion in the apocalypse. The cause of the obfuscation is perhaps to be found in uncertainty in the early community, not only as to whether Jesus was the Messiah, but also whether—given the circumstances of the ministry and the passion—he had yet to be revealed as Messiah.

7. *When you hear the noises of war:* Cf. Dan 2:28-30, 8:19, 9:26, 11:27 and 35, and also 2 Chr 15:6; Jer 6:22, 23:19, 51:27. Textually, all three evangelists agree closely in these two verses, save that Luke adds "uprisings" (21:9), "pestilences" (21:11), and "terrors and great signs from heaven" at the end (21:11). The theme of war, conflict, and tumult, is common in apocalyptic literature; cf. (in the Pseudepigrapha) *Sib Or* 3:635; *Apoc Bar* 27:7, 70:3 and 8; Rev 6:8, 11:13, 16:18, 18:8; and, in the Old Testament, Isa 8:21, 13:13, 14:30, 19:2. Because of its nature the composition does not demand historical reference, but the period of the ministry of Jesus and the decade immediately following it gave ample justification for those looking for "signs": there were uprisings in Palestine, there were earthquakes in Laodicaea (A.D. 61) and at Pompeii (A.D. 62) and we know from Acts 11:28 of a famine in the reign of Claudius Caesar.

If the picture presented in these verses is common to the literature of eschatology and apocalyptic, it was important for the community not to be alarmed and not to misinterpret what was happening. Such things are *bound to happen,* but any notion of a messiah coming armed in the panoply of war is excluded. The hearers/readers are not to *be alarmed.* Here again we are in the realm of all apocalyptic and eschatological literature, where the faithful are exhorted to be faithful and trusting in the face of catastrophe. (Mark follows Matthew's Greek words *mē throeisthe,* from the classical and Septuagint *throeō,* "to cry out," used in the passive in the New Testament for being alarmed or disturbed.) The *end of the age* was still to come, and war, pestilence, and famine were not to be regarded as signs of the coming of the messiah. Significantly, the same kind of warnings are found in Paul's exhortations to the Thessalonians (2 Thess 2:3-10) and we are unhappily in no position to state whether the Thessalonian passage in any way contributed to the arrangement of the synoptic apocalypse, if not to its vocabulary.

There is a break at the end of v. 8. What has been described is only the *beginning of the birth pains,* and warnings have already been given against any rash following of those who would claim either divine or messianic authority. (Matthew, in his own version of the apocalypse, underlines the possibility of such claims—24:26—by specific references to "the desert" and to "storehouses." The first may be a caution against making common cause with Essenes, and the second against joining the Zealots with their storehouses of weapons.)

This is but the beginning . . . In differing fashion the three evangelists use the apocalypse as warning against easy assumptions that turbulent political and social upheavals were in and of themselves sufficient signs of the end-time. The phrase *the beginning of the birth pains* (Greek *archē ōdinōn tauta)* has been much debated. *Ōdin* is the Hellenistic form of *ōdis,* which means a sharp pain or pang (cf. Matt 24:8; Acts 2:24; 1 Thess 5:3). It is associated often with the pains of childbirth, especially in the plural. But whether the later rabbinical expression "the birth pains of the Messiah" was current in the time of Jesus is open to some doubt, and in fact the rabbinical usage is not found in the plural. It is true that in the prophetic literature the pains of birth are a sign of divine judgment, frequently in an eschatological context (cf. Isa 13:8; Mic 4:9-11; Hos 13:13; Jer 4:31, 6:24, 13:21, 22:23, 49:22, 50:43); and if the saying here *is* meant to convey the sense of the later rabbinic expression, then it has been derived from the prophetic books. In context it is a warning that there will be more distress before the time of deliverance dawns.

9. Cf. Dan 7:25. The readers and hearers are now warned that they cannot be mere observers of the turmoil around them, watching events—they are warned: *be on your guard*. The test of faithfulness is already upon them. Commentators call attention to the structure of vv. 9-14. Lohmeyer has suggested (p. 270) that there may be a poetical arrangement in three strophes, each of four lines, with prose sentences inserted at 10,11b, and 13. Small in compass though this section is, it poses problems of its own, not the least of them being grammatical.

Our translation, *They will deliver you . . . synagogues*, reflects our treatment of the Greek in *deliver you up* (Greek *paradidōmi*). We have elected to translate as in the text, rather than using the equally possible (though in our view less likely) "They shall deliver you up, in councils and synagogues you will be flogged." All here depends on the use of *paradidōmi* as absolute, or as qualified by the Greek *eis*, "to." The full Greek text is *paradōdousin humas eis sunedria kai eis sunagōgas darēsesthē*. While it is true that *eis* is used in *koine* Greek for "in," that usage is not nearly as common as the translation we have employed—"to."

councils: (Greek *sunedria*). On the establishment of local councils, each being called a "sanhedrin," cf. E. Lohse, *TWNT*, Vol. 7, pp. 864-65. Any town with a (Jewish) population of 120 or more was entitled to such a council. Given the character of this apocalypse it is safe to assume that such a council was meant, though later Greek usage applied the word *sunedrion* to an official assembly of any kind.

before rulers (Greek *epi hēgemenōn*): Cf. various references to the word (sometimes translated "governors") in the gospels, Acts, and 1 Pet 2:14. These were Roman provincial governors, and the two procurators Felix and Festus (Acts 23:24, 24:27) carried the designation. Luke (Acts 13:7 and 12, 18:12, 19:38) uses the title *anthupatoi* for the proconsuls Sergius Paulus and Gallio, though they would customarily have been entitled to the word used here.

kings: Mark uses the term loosely, but rather than seek some historical context it would seem preferable to understand the meaning in the general sense of Ps 119:46. Given the (probable) Jewish origin of the core of the apocalypse, there is no good reason to look for applications beyond Palestine.

This is a convenient point for looking once more at Mark's methods of composition. The exhortation in this verse—*be on your guard*—is not found in Matthew and Luke, but it is characteristic of the Markan ending to the apocalypse in vv. 33-37. That ending is itself a composite, based on the Matthean (24:42) ending as well as on like material from Matt 25:13-15 and Luke 21:34-36. It was at this point—the end of v. 9 —that Mark found himself dealing with Lucan material which had sought to use Matt 10:17-22 instead of the (parallel) material in Chapter 24. Mark's editorial work can be summarized as follows:

Matt 10:17-22 = Luke 21:12-19 = Mark 13:9-13   conflated, closer to
                                                 Matthew's text

[Matt 10:19-20 = Luke 21:14-15 (a paraphrase, but also found in Luke 12:2-9 =
                                Matt 10:26-33), and omitted in Mark]

Matt 10:18   = Luke 21:13   = Mark 13:9, conflates "witness" saying in
                                      13:10

Matt 10:19-22 = Luke 21:14-17 = Mark 13:11-13, omitting Luke 21:18

From this point (Matt 24:15 = Mark 13:14) Mark very closely adheres to the text of Matthew, and the next twenty verses are almost identical, the differences being minor. However, there are four significant omissions by Mark of Matthean material (Matt 24:10-12,26-28,30,37-51), and the material so omitted is not found in Luke either. The textual near-identity of Matthew and Mark and the nearly identical format of Luke and Mark indicate editorial work of a high order, and we are not dealing with a mere copyist.

9. *to testify before them:* Undoubtedly, historical circumstances have shaped the selection of material included in the synoptic apocalypse (e.g., v. 13 in the light of the Passion), but it is important not to exaggerate this element. Setting aside the passion predictions altogether, as well as the fate of John the Baptizer and the hostility displayed by official Judaism toward his ministry, there was ample justification for Jesus to anticipate that his followers would be subject to the hostility he had himself endured.

The phrase *to testify before them* is not without its difficulties. It is possible to read the Greek as meaning "to testify against them," and some commentators have so understood it. But, more important, an impressive array of manuscripts connect the phrase with the following verse. It is necessary to bear in mind the Greek word order in the last sentence of v. 9 and the following v. 10: *eis marturion autois* (for a witness to them) *kai eis panta ta ethnē* (and to all the nations). What would then be understood would be a testimony to Jews and Gentiles. The fact that most of the manuscripts mentioned above also have *de* (but) would then limit v. 10 to "But the Proclamation must be made first." This is an attractive reading in some ways, but given the character of apocalyptic material with its all-embracing divine message to friend and foe alike, we have elected to translate as above. Luke 21:12 is plainly an independent tradition at this point.

10. *But the Proclamation . . . . :* It will be observed in the chart of background material proposed earlier (see comment, p. 520) that no material in the Old Testament remotely parallels this verse in Mark. We see no reason to dispute the view of many commentators that this verse is a Markan insertion, whatever its original source may have been.

1. The vocabulary is completely Markan: *ta ethnē (the nations), dei (must), prōton (first)*.

2. This is a prose sentence interrupting the flow of poetic structure in vv. 9 and 11-13, and also breaks the link between *deliver you up* in v. 9 and the same phrase in v. 11.

3. No obvious interest in any Gentile mission can be found in Mark's gospel, and the isolated instance of the cure of a Gentile (7:24-30) portrays Jesus as expressing reservation and hesitation (v. 27).

4. Luke does not have the saying; it is not found in Matt 10:18, though it is found in another form and with different meaning in Matt 24:14. Mark's preoccupation with the conclusion of Jesus' ministry, as portrayed in Chapters 11 and 12, appears to rule out any interest in a Gentile mission. While the verse before us *may* be a saying of Jesus from some other context, it is almost impossible to discern the purpose of the saying in its present context. We have previously argued (see note on previous verse) for the translation given above, and this is not wholly on the grounds of acceptable readings of the most important manuscripts. We have in mind also the well-known canon of interpretation which generally prefers the more difficult reading as being the more likely to be correct.

11. (Cf. Dan 7:25; Jer 1:7; Exod 4:11.) *do not worry* (Greek *promerimnaō*): This word may be a Markan invention. It is neither classical nor found in the Septuagint, and is taken up later by Church writers. Matthew uses the common *merimnaō*, and Luke (as we might expect) the classical and literary *promelataō*, "to rehearse beforehand." The injunction is not against proper thought and preparation but against a faithless anxiety.

what you will say: God had in the past taken care of the testimony to be given before rulers—cf. Exod 4:12; Num 22:35; Jer 1:9—so in the times of distress to come *say whatever is given you to say*. For *when the time comes* (Greek *en ekeinē tē hōra*), cf. Luke 22:12.

It is not you who will be speaking: Apart from word order, the phrase is the same in Matt 10:20, though some commentators have found Mark's word order in the Greek an indication of "translation Greek" from Aramaic.

the holy Spirit: The question arises now whether the reference to the holy Spirit is a secondary reading, reflecting first-century Christian views, or whether this is original. The various forms in the synoptics may be of some help at this juncture, and a comparison chart will be useful:

Matt 10:20	Luke 12:12	Mark 13:11
to pneuma tou patros (the Spirit of your Father speaking in you)	*to hagion pneuma* (the holy Spirit will teach you what to say)	*to pneuma to hagion* (it is not you who will be speaking, but the holy Spirit)

Luke 21:15 = Mark 13:11

ego gar dōsō humin stoma kai sophein (I will give you a mouth and wisdom)

There are many difficulties here. Luke's interest in the Spirit is such that we cannot easily think of him substituting the saying in 21:15 in the apocalypse unless the saying was already current in his community. Yet Taylor is surely correct (p. 509) in his view that this saying has a "distinctly Johannine ring and appears to reflect the doctrine of the Exalted Christ." The Markan version has its own problems, if we assume that the apocalypse has historical reference. One of the signs of the age of blessings, the messianic age, was to be the free gift of the Spirit (cf. Isa 11:1-3, 41:1; Joel 2:28); equally, one of the characteristics of the early Christian community was the conviction that its members were speaking and acting under the guidance of the Spirit. What then do these references to the Spirit in the synoptists indicate—that these references were a later introduction into an original saying, or that the sayings themselves are in some fashion prophetically original? Against the latter argument is the fact that the sayings of Jesus make very few references to the Spirit, and those we have are in accordance with Old Testament references to the Spirit of God. A further question arises as to when Jesus thought the messianic age would break in upon his followers. The Reign of God had indeed been inaugurated through the ministry of healings and exorcisms (cf. Matt 13:16 = Luke 10:23), but all the evidence from his ministry suggests that any thought of an age of blessings belonged in his view to the end—and vindication—of his ministry. Furthermore, v. 8 of the section before us indicates very strongly that for the compiler(s) of the apocalypse the times of suffering and anguish belonged to the birth pains of the New Age—i.e., to its first dawning. One final note must be added: the absence of any Old Testament background material in the preceding chart (p. 518) must in our view be regarded as decisive. While the Matthean version ("the Spirit of your Father") is certainly nearer to Old Testament models, and although both Luke and Mark are secondary, the passage appears to reflect theological concerns later than the ministry of Jesus, and comes much nearer to Pauline and Johannine concepts than to the remainder of the apocalypse.

12. *Brother will betray brother* (cf. Mic 7:6 and also, secondarily, Isa 9:19, 19:2; Ezek 38:21; Amos 1:11; Mic 7:2 and 5; Hag 2:23; Zech 7:10, 14:13): The word translated as *betray* is the same Greek verb *(paradidōmi)* in vv. 9-11. With this situation of strife within families, cf. Matt 10:21 and Luke 21:16, from which vv. 12 and 13 are taken, and of which the Markan version is (cf. Taylor, p. 509) a "secondary version." The divisions created within families by strained loyalties and by outright rejection of God is a common theme in apocalyptic literature (cf. 4 Ezra 5:9, 6:24; *Jub* 23:19; *Apoc Bar* 70:3, in addition to the references cited above). Evaluating the material in this verse and in v. 13 is not easy. Being put to death (cf. Dan 11:33) in familial and fratricidal strife is common enough in the contemporary literature, and to be hated for the sake of a righteous cause *(Because of me)* is well attested in the Old Testament literature (cf. Mic 7:6, and secondarily Pss 25:19, 69:5, 105:25, 106:41; Isa 66:5), but are we justified in seeing here a reminiscence of a saying of Jesus? What casts doubt on any affirmative answer to that question is the theme of *universal* hatred. This is far more attuned to the realities of a later age, or even—historically—to the Neronian persecutions in and around Rome (from A.D. 64 onward). Classical and Christian authors testify to the detestation of Christians engendered by hostile local authorities in widely separated places (cf. Tacitus, *Annals* 15.44; Justin Martyr, *Apologia* 1.4; Tertullian, *Apologia* 2; Pliny, *Epistolae* 10.96ff.). If we wish to tie these two verses to sayings of Jesus, then the best we can do is to call attention to the fact that Jesus' words elsewhere in this gospel invoke his name *(because of me)* in terms of the loyalty

demanded of discipleship (9:37,39,41) and not in terms of a *universal* hatred on account of his ministry and person. The closest thing we have in Mark to the sentiments of v. 13 is the saying in 10:30, but that is addressed to the immediate circle of the disciples and does not speak in universal terms. It best fits the evidence of the rest of this chapter to conclude that v. 13 is part of the anonymous apocalyptic material which the evangelists used, with the addition of a universalist note not found in the original.

13. *the end:* Cf. Dan 11:32,35; 12:1,12; Mic 7:7 (Greek *telos*). In spite of the eschatological dimension of *will be saved,* it is highly unlikely that *the end* is meant as anything but "final endurance" or "complete endurance" (cf., in the NT, Luke 18:5; John 13:1; 1 Thess 2:16). The differences between the three synoptists are interesting. Matthew provides Mark with his Greek text (cf. Matt 24:21 but also 24:9a), though Mark changes the text of Matt 24:9b from "all the nations" *(hupo pantōn tōn ethnōn)* to the simpler *hupo pantōn.* It is arguable that the Matthean Greek should be translated "all the Gentiles," though it can mean, equally with Mark, *all men.* Mark also preserves the original apocalyptic note of doom, and eliminates the Lucan contribution (21:15): "for I will give you a mouth and wisdom which none of your adversaries will be able to withstand or contradict." Mark also omits another Lucan saying which appears to argue a happy outcome: "But not a hair of your head will perish" (Luke 21:18).

70. The Great Distress
(13:14-23) = Matt 24:15-28; Luke 21:20-24

13   [14] "But when you see the Abominable Desecration set up where it ought not to be"—let the reader understand!—"then those in Judea must take to the hills. [15] If anyone is on the roof, he must not come down into the house to take anything out, [16] and anyone in the field must not come back for his himation. [17] Alas for pregnant women in those days, and for mothers nursing small children! [18] Pray that it may not happen in the winter. [19] For the distress of those days will be such as has not been from the beginning of the creation which God made until now—and will never be again. [20] If the Lord had not cut short those days, no human being could survive. But for the sake of the elect whom he has chosen, he has cut short those days. [21] Then, if anyone says to you, 'Look, here is the Messiah!' or 'Look! There he is!' do not believe it. [22] For the pseudo-messiahs and pseudo-prophets will arrive on the scene, and they will produce signs and wonders to mislead

God's chosen, if that was possible. [23] But as for you—be on your guard! I have warned you beforehand."

Comment

This section introduces a new note into the apocalyptic discourse, and in the Notes below we shall once more have to discuss whether there are to be found here genuine sayings of Jesus—and, if so, what historical reference they may have, and whether two contemporary developments have colored what we have so far regarded as an anonymous apocalyptic composition.

Notes

14. *when:* Cf. vv. 7,11,29.

Abominable Desecration: Cf. Dan 11:31, 12:11, and also Dan 9:27 and Ps 74:4. This single verse presents difficulties both for those who seek some historical reference in this chapter and for those who see this as simply one item among many in a pastiche of Old Testament allusions constituting an apocalyptic manifesto. This phrase, taken directly from Daniel, refers in its original context to the pagan altar erected by Antiochus Epiphanes on the site of the altar of burnt offerings in 168 B.C. (compare 1 Macc 1:54). Originally, therefore, the quotation refers to the desecration of the temple, and not to its destruction. Anyone seeking historical reference in this verse can find it in the emperor Caligula's attempt to have his statue placed in the temple in A.D. 40. But this attempted desecration was effectively delayed by the then proconsul Petronius, and in any event was rendered nugatory by the assassination of the emperor in the next year (cf. Josephus, *Ant* 18.8). A further objection to this possible historical identification is that the participle *set up* (Greek *hestēkota)* is masculine, in contrast to the neuter of *Abominable Desecration* (Greek *to bdelugma tēs erēmōseōs),* thus suggesting that the profanation of the temple is being considered in personal terms. The participle is not found in Matt 24:15 or in Luke 21:20. Consequently, according to some commentators, Luke's Greek demands that a personal desecration, perhaps on the lines of 2 Thess 2:3-10, is intended. Is this, then, a Christian understanding of the apocalyptic material in terms of Antichrist? But this must not be seen in isolation. Apart from the masculine participle, there is Mark's use of Matt 24:15 and his alteration of it: *set up where it ought not to be* instead of "standing in the holy place," but reproducing *let the reader understand.* If we put this alongside Luke's "But when you see Jerusalem surrounded by armies, then know that its desolation is near," we can see that the material may be concerned with far more than the temple.

let the reader understand: Cf. Dan 9:23,25. Generally this phrase has been interpreted as pointing to references in Daniel (cited above) to the Abominable Desecration, and this (it is thought) is underscored by Matt 24:15 ("spoken of by Daniel the prophet"). At the same time, other commentators interpret the phrase as referring rather to the apocalypse from which Matthew and Mark are quoting. It is doubtful that either explanation will suffice; there is an air of hidden meaning here, almost of menace, as though a clue had to be hidden from the prying eyes of outsiders. This would match well the circumstances of 2 Thess 2:6-12 or the hidden reference in Rev 13:18. If we are looking for historical references, we shall conclude that the temple which was openly mentioned in 2 Thess 2:4 must now be disguised by *where it ought not to be*, or even by the somewhat clearer "in the holy place" of Matthew 24:15. In pursuit of this historical frame of reference, we might then suppose that in a time of persecution, such as that initiated by the emperor Nero, more precise language had been muted in case the apocalyptic broadside fell into unsympathetic hands. By this interpretation, *where it ought not to be* in Mark, and "in the holy place" in Matthew, have been rewritten to eliminate more precise language about an impending siege of Jerusalem. We would then conclude that all the details of havoc and uncertainty described in vv. 15 and 16 belong to wartime and are to be linked with the birth pains which would herald the Messiah.

This attempted explanation must be rejected, in the opinion of this commentator, as altogether too facile. In the first place, there is Luke 21:20. Does this belong to a time (assuming we are looking for a historical *Sitz im Leben*) when open warfare had dispensed with all need for cryptic references and an editor therefore recast Matt 24:15 and Mark 13:14 into a more contemporary mold, a prophecy after the event? Against this, there is substantial critical opinion that Luke 21:20-36 represents an independent source, in spite of elements in common with Matthew and Mark. Again, Luke 21:20 need have no historical reference whatsoever. As already noted in another context, little prescience was demanded to predict that an exasperated Roman imperial power would sooner or later lay siege to Jerusalem; and to deny that prescience to Jesus, in the political and social climate of his own time, is to be somewhat hypercritical. But we meet further and more formidable obstacles in seeking a historical setting for this initial verse. First of all, the verses which follow it (vv. 15-19) would well fit any apocalyptic threat of war in the Middle East: long centuries of experience in Palestine had sharpened apprehension of war to a point where these verses might have been written by almost anyone engaged in compiling an apocalyptic manifesto. Secondly, there is the matter of dating. Critical assumptions very commonly assign Matthew and Luke to the latter part of the first century, even though Mark, under the same assumptions, is generally assigned to the sixties of that century. Given the totally catastrophic character of the fall of Jerusalem in A.D. 70, and the severe blow to many religious and theological assumptions bound up with the continued existence of the temple, it is at the least a matter of wonder that no evangelist called attention to this in terms of "But Jesus prophesied all this." We may hope that this factor in dating our New Testament books (cf. J. A. T. Robinson *Redating the New Testament*, Philadelphia: Westminster Press, 1976, especially pp. 12-29) will in the future receive far more attention than has been the case in recent years. In short, when all the material before us has been examined, there appears to be no convincing reason to find in it any necessary historical reference; the present writer does find, however, that the quotation from Daniel in v. 14 has led to a far too easy assumption that we have here an absolute identification with the events of A.D. 70.

then those in Judea: Cf. (as background) Gen 19:17; Jer 50:8, 51:6,45; Ezek 7:16;

Zech 2:7; 1 Macc 2:28. The conditions so vividly described in these few verses are all pitched in a tone of crisis engendered by warfare and/or civil strife, and all that is left to the ordinary man or woman is flight. Those on the roof (Greek *dōma*, the flat roof to which folk went for sleep or prayer, or to stand guard—cf. 1 Sam 9:25; Isa 22:1; Jer 10:17, 19:13; Ezek 7:6) must not stop to collect household items, and the field hand (cf. Gen 19:17; Amos 2:16) is not to come back for his laid-aside clothing. (N.B.: the Greek varies slightly from Matt 24:17 and Mark 13:15, and some manuscripts of Mark omit *into the house*. This would leave the somewhat odd conclusion that while everyone was being exhorted to flee, an exception was being made for those on roof-tops.)

in the field: The Greek *(agron)* seems to have been much favored by those translating from Hebrew or Aramaic. So, also, *back* (Greek *opisō*) is often found in the Septuagint to translate "behind" or "back" (cf. Luke 9:62, 17:31; John 6:66, 18:6, 20:14). For *himation,* cf. 2:21.

So far all this material reflects the agricultural countryside, and indicates that the material has been gathered from various sources. If the focus of attention had been Jerusalem, we might have expected references to urban dwellers and their immediate concerns, but the reference to Judea in Matt 24:16 (= Mark 13:14) suggests composition elsewhere. (Mark 13:3 appears to indicate the Mount of Olives.) Luke 21:20-24, apart from the reference to those in Judea, has nothing in common with the other evangelists, though Luke 17:32 ("Remember Lot's wife") emphasizes the theme of flight in the face of danger.

17. *Alas for pregnant women:* Cf. 2 Kgs 15:16; Lam 4:4; Hos 13:16; Amos 1:13. The Greek for the last two words *(en gastri echousa)* is common in medical writings, is found in the Septuagint, and is used in the New Testament in Matt 1:18,23, and 24:19; Luke 21:23; 1 Thess 5:3; Rev 12:2. The Greek used in *for mothers nursing small children (thēladzō),* means "to suckle" or "to suck," and can be used either of nursing mothers or of children.

18. *Pray that it may not . . . :* At the end of the commentary on this chapter we shall have something to say on the place of the apocalypse in Mark's thinking. Here we shall merely call attention to the grammatical structure and its similarity to the scene in Gethsemane in 14:35 and 38. The subject of the prayer is the *distress* (Greek *thlipsis),* though the word can mean "winter" or "storms." Matthew clarifies his source by saying "that your flight may not be in the winter" (24:38) and adds "nor on the Sabbath." Luke does not have this exhortation to prayer, and his parallel in 21:22 is quite generalized: "for these are days of vengeance, to fulfill all that is written." Taylor (p. 513) raises the question whether vv. 17-18 depict the conditions imposed by war, or whether these two verses are to be regarded as representing the general character of the whole apocalypse. He adduces Luke 23:29 ("For, look, the time is coming when they will say, 'Happy are the childless, the wombs that never bore children, the breasts which never suckled children!' ") as parallel material to the verses before us. Against this, it must be said that war is part, and only part, of the general distress associated with the birth pains, and we are justified in seeing these two verses not as an isolated saying taken into an apocalyptic context, but as part of the whole apocalyptic manifesto.

19. *For the distress . . .* (cf. Jer 30:7; Dan 12:1; Hab 3:16; and secondarily Deut

31:17,21; 2 Chr 15:6; Zeph 1:2-5): This verse begins as though summarizing all that
has gone before, particularly by the use of *those days*. Reading this material, it is
difficult to imagine this "summary verse" and at the same time to exclude vv. 17-18.
The key word *distress* (Greek *thlipsis;* cf. 4:17, 13:24), taken from Dan 12:1 ("there
shall be a time of distress, such as never was . . ."), is appropriate to the times before
the End or as associated with the birth pains of the Messiah (cf. Rev 1:9, 7:14). The
verbal contribution provided by Dan 12:1 suggests a period of unbridled hatred. Matthew's version is much simpler ("There will be great distress," 24:21), but Mark
appears to be anxious for us not to miss the point. There is a typically Markan—and
probably Semitic—tautology *(from the beginning of the creation which God made)*, of
which other examples are to be found at 2:19, 4:30, 11:28, 12:14. For *from the beginning of creation,* cf. 10:6.

The emphasis on the magnitude of the *distress*—that such has never been seen
before and will not be seen again—takes us outside considerations of warfare and
siege: the language is eschatological. This is confirmed by the succeeding v. 20, where
the notion of the mercy of God has cut short the distress. Otherwise *no human being*
(Greek *pasa sarx,* literally "all flesh") would survive. This mercy for the elect is also
typical of much eschatological and apocalyptic writing—cf. Dan 12:7, *Enoch* 80:2, 4
Ezra 4:26, *Apoc Bar* 20:1. For the verb "to *cut short"* (Greek *koloboō),* cf. Matt 24:2.
Our translation *could survive* somewhat obscures the Greek verb *sōzō* (to save), but it
has been allowed to stand at this point because of its ambiguity. It is possible that the
sense is eschatological, as in v. 13 (cf. 3:4). *The elect* (Greek *hoi eklektoi)* refers to the
members of the community for which the apocalypse was written; but in this context,
as edited and arranged by the synoptists, it refers to the Christian community. The
term has a long history in the Old Testament tradition as applied to the people of the
Covenant—cf. Ps 105:6; Isa 42:1, 43:20, 65:9. In the Pseudepigrapha, *1 Enoch* equates
the elect with the righteous ones who will inherit the kingdom (1:1, 38:2-4). In our
New Testament sources the term is applied to the Christian community (Luke 18:7;
Rom 8:33; Col 3:12; 2 Tim 2:10; 1 Pet 1:1, 2:9). From the point of view of the language
employed (i.e., the tautology of *the elect whom he has chosen),* cf. the note on a similar
case in v. 19. Matthew's version—"for the sake of the chosen"—is far more direct
(24:22). Dependent though he is generally on Matthew, Mark here appears to be
relying on his own sources. Luke's 21:23-24 is wholly different in character: "For great
distress shall be upon the earth, and wrath upon this people; they will fall upon the
edge of the sword and be led captive among all nations. Jerusalem will be trodden
down by the Gentiles until the times of the Gentiles are fulfilled."

20. In this verse we are dealing with characteristically Hebrew and Old Testament
concepts. The idea of the elect as the people of the Covenant we have noticed above.
Now (cf. Dan 9:24; Isa 65:9 and 15) we find the notion of the mercy of God cutting
short the time God himself allotted for misery and distress. Taylor (p. 515) calls
attention to two features characteristically Hebrew. The first is the use of *Lord* (Greek
kurios) without the definite article in Old Testament quotations (cf. 1:3, 9:9,
12:11,29,36; Luke 1:5-2:52). This is not as impressive as it might appear, since *koinē*
Greek notoriously sat lightly to the use of the definite article, notably in omitting it
before *Christos* throughout a great deal of the New Testament material. The second
feature, Taylor suggests, is the Hebrew idiom to be found in this verse in the Greek
ouk an esōthē pasa sarx (literally "not would be saved all flesh"), with *ouk* ("not" or

"no") . . . *pasa* ("all" or "every") corresponding to the Hebrew *lô* . . . *côl* ("no one") and *pasa sarx* to the Hebrew *côl bâšâr* ("all flesh"). This is impressive as indicating something of the background of the synoptic apocalypse; but the kind of material presented here has no parallel elsewhere in the teaching of Jesus and cannot be regarded as anything other than an earlier composition used by the evangelists to introduce the passion story.

21-23. It is difficult to resist the conclusion that this small section is a doublet of vv. 5-6,9a, and the presence of *the chosen* in v. 22 suggests that this material is secondary, as does also the presence of a repeated *be on your guard*. The arrangement of the material, granted that it derives from an anonymous apocalyptic, is less easily understood. The material in vv. 5-6 (= Matt 24:5; Luke 21:8) is notable in saying *many will come* with false claims, but the suggestion is inescapable that in v. 21 the claims are even now being made, and this is the understanding of Matthew. Luke's use of the material, in the doublet at 17:20-21, has been transformed into a saying concerned with the Reign of God and its presence among the hearers.

On the majority critical view, it would be maintained that v. 21 represents a genuine saying of Jesus, being found in the Q source of Luke 17:23 and Matt 24:26, while v. 22 with its apocalyptic speculations is derivative and secondary. But we have already noticed the very heavy dependence of this apocalypse on Old Testament ideas and even quotations and allusions. In this regard, the two verses before us are not significantly different from the rest of the material. (For v. 21—*do not believe it*—cf. Deut 13:4,5, and Jer 23:16; for v. 22—*pseudo-messiahs and pseudo-prophets*—cf. Deut 13:2-4 and 18:20, Isa 9:15, and Jer 2:8, 5:31, 23:15; and for *mislead*, cf. Deut 13:6; Dan 8:24.) It appears to us that the attempted distinction between vv. 21 and 22 will not bear examination.

Pseudo-messiahs and *pseudo-prophets*, while at first glance suggestive of a later age and later concerns, were always a danger to the community—certainly there is no lack of testimony in the Old Testament prophetic tradition to the menace of false prophets. Jesus speaks of such in Matt 7:15 and Luke 6:26, and they figure in Acts 13:6; 2 Pet 2:1; 1 John 4:1; Rev 16:13, 19:20, 20:10. (The possibility that the original behind Revelation *may* have been a Jewish apocalyptic document should warn us against assuming that *pseudo-prophets* betokens a later Christian concern.) *Pseudo-messiahs* as an expression has its own problems. In spite of the evidence from the intertestamental period showing a great deal of speculation about impending divine deliverance through the agency of semidivine, semihuman figures, we have as yet no reliable data as to whether the term "messiah" was ever applied to any single historical person. Speculation among the Essenes at Qumran as to two future messiahs (one civil and the other priestly) is hardly in the realm of historical identity so far as we know. (For a convenient summary, see Raymond E. Brown, "The Teacher of Righteousness and the Messiahs," in *The Scrolls and Christianity*, edited by Matthew Black, SPCK Theological Collections 11, London: SPCK, 1969, pp. 37-45.) It is perhaps in the light of Essene speculation that this warning against *pseudo-messiahs* was inserted. Matthew's 24:26 seems to be an explicit warning against joining with either Essenes or Zealots in a false pursuit of the Reign of God.

Signs and wonders is notable in that here only does Mark use *wonders* (Greek *terata*), and he derives this from Matthew's version. The whole phrase is common in the New Testament (Acts 2:19,22, and 43, 4:30, 5:12, 6:8, 7:36, 14:3, 15:12; Rom

15:19; 2 Thess 2:9; 2 Cor 12:12; Heb 2:4). The whole phrase *produce* (literally "give") *signs and wonders* is from Deut 13:2. *To mislead* (Greek *pros to apoplanan*) is a verb found only here in Mark (derived from Matt 24:25, though with a different Greek construction) and in 1 Tim 6:10. *God's chosen* was discussed above (see v. 20). The warnings of v. 22 follow naturally on v. 20, and Mark's dependence on Matthew seems to be expressed here; for v. 21 looks like an insertion, until it is recalled that in both Matthew and Mark the previous warning about those claiming divine authority refers to future claims, while in v. 21 (again, in both Matthew and Mark) the threat of such claims appears to be vividly present.

But as for you is a Markan device, calling attention to the four disciples whose presence introduced the apocalypse. The rest of this section is written in the third person, apart from vv. 14 and 21. The *you* is emphatic in both parts of the verse, and it incorporates again the warning *be on your guard*. The use of *I have warned you beforehand* (Greek *proeirēka*) is common to describe prophetic pronouncements (cf. Acts 1:16; Rom 9:29) and also to emphasize teaching already given (2 Cor 7:3, 13:2; Jude 17). The verse is editorial, as it is in Matthew, and refers to the signs of the beginning of the birth pains.

We shall have occasion, in the passion narrative, to refer again to the importance of the phrase *be on your guard,* for it serves to explain the function of the apocalypse in Mark, whatever may have been the case with the other two evangelists.

71. The Man's Coming
(13:24-27) = Matt 24:29-31; Luke 21:25-28

13   24 "In those days, after that distress, the sun will be darkened, the moon will not give its light, 25 the stars will be falling from the skies, and the powers in the heavens will be shaken. 26 Then they will see The Man coming in clouds with great power and glory. 27 He will then send the angels and gather the chosen from the farthest bounds of earth to the farthest bounds of heaven."

Comment

In the part of the Introduction devoted to the Kingdom (or Reign) of God, we called attention not only to the great diversity of interpretation of that phrase within the Christian tradition, but also to the enigmatic character of the sayings of Jesus which relate to the coming of the Reign of God. In the four verses before us the problem is accentuated by the motif of another "coming"—that of The-Man-in-glory. To what extent, if at all, did Jesus identify himself with this figure, and if so in what sense? To this question, cast in such direct and simple terms, there appears to be no easy answer. We have concluded that this chapter is an apocalypse which predates the composition of the gospels, and the wealth of Old Testament allusions in this very short section serves to underline that conclusion. Apart from the passion narrative, this depiction of The-Man-in-glory stands alone in Mark's consistent portrait of The-Man-in-suffering, or in contexts of conflict. It is reasonable to suppose that this short section has a definite purpose in the Markan scheme, and it can be conveniently summarized.

A suggestion from this writer to the Reverend Laurence F. X. Brett (editor of *Share the Word)* led to his constructing the diagram below:

MARK'S ESCHATOLOGICAL DISCOURSE

Presetting -12:41-13:2 "taking a seat opposite the treasury . . ."
Setting -13:3-4 "seated . . . facing the temple"

(Presence of four original disciples indicates a new beginning; after their call, they accompanied him as he taught; now, called "Teacher," he speaks.)

1. *"When* will all this occur?"
2. "Sign *when* all this is coming (to an end)?" (Greek *hotan)*

PART I WHEN (13:5-23)

"Be on your guard" 5   23 "Be on your guard"
false claims quoted 6   21-22 *false claims quoted*
"WHEN you hear" 7-10   14-20 "WHEN you see"

11-13
"WHEN they take you into custody"

(Three "When" paragraphs form central portion; central command of vv. 7-10 is "Be constantly on guard" *(blepete)* at v. 9; central command of vv. 14-20 is "keep praying" *(proseuchesthe)*—cf. 14:38—at v. 18. These two sections "frame" central portion. Central statement of middle section is "Brother will *hand over* brother for execution, and likewise the father his child," which *might* prepare further for agony/arrest scene.)

PART II THE SIGN (13:24-27)

"sun, moon, stars, 24-25   27 "winds, bounds of
skies, heavens"   earth and sky"
26
"YOU WILL SEE THE SON OF MAN coming in glory"—cf. 14:41d,e

PART III   THE EXACT HOUR (13:28-37)

a parable "the fig tree"	28-29	34-36	a parable "master of the house"
(statement about time "*when* you see")	29	33	"Be on your guard" repeated

30-33
timeless assurance of Christ's words

PART IV   CONCLUSION: "Be on guard"

The parable of the master of the house prepares for the agony/arrest scene, when "master" comes and "catches them asleep." Even the reference to "when the cock crows" prepares us for what will happen to *one* of the disciples who were with Jesus in the garden—the one to whom Jesus spoke, namely Peter (14:37).

It will appear that Mark 13 is like a necklace with pendants, the most important of which, and the central one, is the present pericope. We shall have occasion to examine the distinctively Markan *be on your guard* when we reach the scene in Gethsemane. Moreover, the sayings about the *master of the house* in vv. 33-36 will be under discussion at the same time. As a preliminary observation, then, we can say that Mark imposed his own crisis-laden interpretation upon the material, even to the extent of ending his gospel at 16:8.

In what sense are we to understand the "coming" of The Man? Is this to be interpreted as the end-time, the winding up of the natural order? Or is it intended as pictorial imagery for some final judgment (cf. Matt 25:1-26)? Or is Mark's use of his material an indication of quite different concerns?

1. This writer has never conceived of any adequate reply to the contentions of J. A. T. Robinson *(Jesus and His Coming,* 1957) that the early community misunderstood and misinterpreted the whole notion of the "coming." The point is further explored by the same author in TNTS, especially in "The Most Primitive Christology of All?" (pp. 139-54). Search as we will, we can find no tradition in the Judaism of Jesus' time of a messiah coming *from* God: on the contrary, the common view was that the identity of the messiah would not be known until he was taken up by God. We do not wish to attempt any facile identification of The Man with the figure of the Messiah, but we must take seriously—given the indebtedness of Chapter 13 to Daniel—the fact that The Man is represented as "coming to" the Lord of Time in that book. It is easy to understand, in the light of the Passion story, how the earliest Christians came to assume that in some fashion Jesus

was his own forerunner as Messiah (and as The Man?) and that when the Messiah was manifested he would be Jesus.

2. The specific contribution of the gospel of John in all this debate must be taken into account. For John, the Cross is the enthronement, the Passion is glory, and at the moment of Jesus' death John says of him that he "handed over the Spirit" (John 19:30). No student of the New Testament will need reminding that judgment, for John, is here and now, in the ministry of Jesus, and there is no call for great white thrones and a summoning of the elect. The summons is constant in the ministry and a central feature of it. But are we to regard these characteristics of the fourth gospel as an aberration, a sport or mutation of an otherwise constant New Testament witness that there will be a *second* manifestation of Jesus-in-glory as The-Man-in-glory, as God's glorified messiah? We tend to overlook how very slender—let alone how constant—is this New Testament witness. Paul's Thessalonian letters are full of this prospect of a second manifestation, but the apostle's interest in it noticeably wanes after those letters, and we are entitled to ask whence he derived his Thessalonian theology of expectation. Was it from some contact with a Lucan community with the Lucan interest in a delayed *parousia* and a "time of the Church"?

3. While some of the underlying concerns in "realized eschatology" may well have to do with safeguarding a presumed infallibility in the utterances of Jesus, it is nevertheless imperative that we apply the methods of form criticism and redaction criticism evenhandedly. If the writings of a single author (Paul) can exhibit a very sharp decline in emphasis on an imminent return of the Risen Lord, then we may ask at the same time whether the influence of "he shall come again in glory to judge the living and the dead" has caused us to misinterpret the synoptic gospels. We cannot expect uniformity or consistency between the various New Testament writers, nor sometimes from a single writer, but we must do our best to understand what particular theological concerns each evangelist is seeking to emphasize in the words of Jesus, and also what editorial material he may impose upon the tradition. In the case of the chapter before us, it is at least possible that we have underestimated the plain message of a highly organized writer.

4. There is not discernible in Mark the same escalation of the call to "see" as there is in Luke, and not the same hierarchy of Greek verbs for "seeing" as may be found in John. This writer believes that the combination of Chapter 13 with the enigmatic pronouncement of 9:1, together with a demonstrable connection between Chapter 13 and the

Gethsemane narrative, is an indication of Mark's overriding concern. Chapter 13 consistently demands watchfulness: it warns against rumors and suggestions which the disciples may *hear,* but it is emphatic that even in apocalyptic tribulation *they will see The Man.* The link between v. 26 and the emphatic quotation of Dan 7:13 in Mark's 14:62 has been argued for many years. Now, on the most skeptical assessment of the quotation from Daniel (as not having been made by Jesus), the fact remains that for all three synoptists the quotation from Daniel is vital as a theological motif. But it is permissible to ask precisely what the hearers and readers of this material were to "see" with the eyes of faith. For this commentator the conclusion is irresistible that attention is being called to the passion narrative and all that this implies as *the* eschatological revelation of the purpose of God. The contrast in this apocalypse, as framed by Mark, between *when you hear* and *when you see* is in our view too pointed to be missed. Mark's community might in distress hear many things and be tempted by many rumors, but there was a distinction to be made by members of that suffering community between rumor and the definitive revelation of God's purpose in the Passion. We suggest that this is in no way modified or mitigated by the words in vv. 32-37.

Notes

24. *In those days* . . . (cf. Joel 2:10, 3:14,15; also Isa 13:10, Ezek 32:7): The phrase also comes at v. 17, and there are frequent references to *days* in the apocalypse (vv. 17,19,20, and 32). The artificiality of the whole construction in its present position in both Matthew and Mark is such that to attempt to discover why we now have celestial signs after the terrestrial manifestations is to fall into the trap of providing historical context for material which in the nature of the case is metahistorical. The phenomena associated with *sun* and *moon* both here and in Isa 13:10 are connected with a "day of the Lord"—and this would certainly be all of one piece with Mark's understanding of the Passion, and would be fitting commentary on Dan 7:13. Significantly—as Taylor (p. 517) admits—there is nothing to be found in the discourse about the overthrow of evil, nor yet of any final judgment.

Various attempts have been made to explain the apparent disconnection of different parts of the apocalypse. For example, was v. 8 originally followed by vv. 24b-26, and the two sections vv. 9-13 and 14-23 inserted later? Against this, it may be argued that the Old Testament citations and allusions in the Comment which began this chapter will reveal that the quotations from Daniel in vv. 9-13 and 14-23 are in a rough progression, and the same holds for the references to Micah. It is only when v. 26 is reached that Mark retraces his steps to Daniel 7. Furthermore, the generally accepted critical view that Matthew is dependent on Mark must somehow explain why Matthew does not rearrange the Markan sections. Why—on the two-document hypothesis

—did not Matthew (an "arranger" if ever there was one) look at the Markan apocalypse and move the two sections 9-13 and 14-22 (23?)—his own 24:9-14 and 15-22—to a position preceding the "Abominable Desecration," and then place the present section before 25:31-46 as fitting prelude to the last judgment? The "insertion" theory must be judged inadequate. In our view, the apocalypse—in which Mark follows Matthew closely—was a whole body of material, inspired in part by Daniel, and compiled to encourage Palestinian Jews facing the certainty of Roman imperial vengeance. It was ready at hand for Christians to use, but with the significant and decisive interpretation that the ministry and mission of Jesus had indeed been the manifestation of The Man.

The signs and celestial portents are a common feature of apocalyptic literature and are interpreted as signs of God's activity, and to look for precise historical contexts there, or above all in the terrestrial phenomena, is to misconceive the function of the literature and its imagery. Whatever the background of Revelation, we do not use the work to discover suitable historical frames of reference for the hyperbole of the language, and we ought not to do so here. Additional difficulties stand in the way of seeking a historical basis for every utterance in the apocalypse. Why is there no further mention of the Abominable Desecration? And in this section what is the hidden meaning of the gathering of *the chosen?* Given the predictions of distress earlier in the chapter, why is there no mention of the reactions of the inhabitants of earth in vv. 24 and 25?

The Greek vocabulary here betrays the non-Markan origin of the section. The second part of v. 24 is virtually a quotation from Isa 13:10 and 34:4, and some words are not found elsewhere in Mark: *sun* (Greek *hēlios)* only here and 1:32; *will be darkened* (Greek *skotisthēsetai),* only here (cf. Matt 24:29, Luke 23:45); *moon (selēnē),* only here (cf. Matt 24:29, Luke 21:25); *light* (Greek *pheugos),* only here (cf. Matt 24:29, Luke 11:33); *stars* (Greek *asteres),* only here (cf. Matt 2:2,7,9,10, and 24:29); *will be shaken* (Greek *salegthēsontai),* only here (cf. Matt 11:7, 24:29). The words are equally unusual in Matthew and Luke.

25. Cf. Isa 11:10, 34:4. It is not possible to determine whether the original compiler(s) or (in context) the evangelists intended us to understand astronomical phenomena or the elementals thought to have some influence on earthly affairs. The *powers in the heavens* (cf. Gal 4:3; Col 2:8,20; 2 Pet 3:10,12) is used in other parts of the New Testament to denote elemental spirits.

Mark follows Matthew closely, but Luke 21:25-28 is wholly independent, save for v. 26b = Mark 13:25b. Luke also has the vitally important "coming" of The Man in his own 21:27.

26. *Then they will see . . . :* Cf. Dan 7:13, Isa 19:1. The contrast between the injunctions to watchfulness in the first part of the apocalypse *(when you hear)* and the present assertion that it will be possible to *see The Man* in *power and glory* has been remarked on already. But whereas the figure in Dan 7:13 as the subject of a vision has already been seen ("In my night's vision I saw . . ."), in this passage the future tense is used by all three synoptists. The presence of this quotation from Daniel in the crucial Mark 14:62, as well as here, suggests very firmly that at the very heart of the apocalypse we have an important saying of Jesus. With some confidence, we may assert that we are not dealing with a compilation of the primitive community here, for

so far as we can determine that community had no theology of "Son of Man." It is arguable, from Paul's use of Adam-Christ typology, that he knew the term from the oral (written?) tradition; but apart from Acts 7:56 and Rev 1:13, 14:14, our earliest sources attribute all "The Man" sayings to Jesus himself.

The language of this verse, like 14:62, does not in our view encompass any expectation on the part of Jesus of a return to the scene of his ministry in exaltation-glory. What this language does suggest is a dramatic expression of the faith in God's vindication of his mission and ministry. Moreover, elsewhere there are sayings which underscore his conviction that this vindication would shortly take place, and that in and through his trials and sufferings God would inaugurate his reign. The evidence for this is too significant to be ignored. For whatever elements of future expectation there may be in the earliest Pauline letters, the sayings of Jesus in the synoptics and John give such expectation no support. On the contrary: the note of immediacy is constant. Jesus speaks of release from constraint (Luke 12:50), of his being made "complete" (Luke 13:32), of his exaltation to the seat of power (Mark 14:62), of his entering upon his reign (Luke 23:42) and his glory (Mark 10:37, Luke 24:26); and when he does so speak, or speaks of his "coming" (Mark 14:62) with the clouds of heaven, the point of reference is invariable. It is not to some future return, or some *parousia* event, but to a soon-to-be-accomplished end—the fulfillment of his ministry in the Reign of God and the inauguration of a New Covenant in his own blood (Luke 22:16,28-30, and also Mark 14:24 and Luke 22:20). Jesus' assertion was that God would "vindicate his elect speedily"—he would not delay (Luke 18:7-8). Significantly, Jesus goes on to ask whether, at his coming, he would find faith—trust, perception. If the primitive community, in some important respects and in some areas, misread the "coming" of which Jesus spoke, this is hardly surprising, and Mark's gospel adequately deals with the disciples' lack of understanding. That there is widespread disagreement about a possible future judgment in the New Testament is not open to doubt. What we are concerned with here is Jesus' own expectation, and the importance of the Greek in Matt 26:64 *(ap'arti*—"from now on") and Luke 22:69 *(apo tou nun*—"from this moment") is vital to the discussion. If Mark 14:62 does not have that emphasis on the present moment, he does follow Matthew in asserting that those present *will see* The Man as the cloud-rider. Jesus is portrayed for us in the synoptics, both here and (above all) in the Passion narrative, as seeing vindication and inauguration through his own death. This tradition they share with John, even though not expressing it in Johannine vocabulary. The plain language of Jesus admits of no deferred "event." Matthew's tradition (24:30) underlines the immediacy of the saying about *The Man coming in clouds* by allusions to Isa 11:10, 18:3, 66:19, and follows this up with the distress of the unseeing "tribes of the earth" (cf. Zech 12:12,14; Isa 13:7-8; Ezek 32:9).

great power and glory: The figure in Dan 7:13, whether considered as a single individual or as a representative figure of the "holy ones," is brought to the Lord of Time to receive a kingdom, dominion, and glory. Similarly, The Man in the synoptic apocalypse comes to the Father for vindication and the inauguration of the Reign of God. Like the figure in Daniel, he is invested with the symbols of divine authority and comes *in the clouds* as outward signs of God's dignity and honor.

27. The passion predictions in Mark have prepared us for the association in the tradition not only of suffering with glory, but also the association of The Man with his

"elect," his *chosen* in all that befalls him. The present verse is the equivalent in the synoptic apocalypse of the gathering of the "peoples, languages and nations" of Dan 7:14. In the verse before us, those who are associated with The Man in his triumphant vindication, *the chosen,* those who *will see,* are gathered together by *the angels.* It is to be noted that the triumph depicted in the preceding verse carries with it the authority to *send* God's messengers.

The verse is a conglomerate of ideas and words from a wide variety of Old Testament sources and from the Pseudepigrapha, and some of the words and ideas are to be found also in 1 Thess 4:15-17 and 2 Thess 2:1. For *gather the chosen,* cf. Deut 30:3-4, Ps 106:47, Isa 27:12. The theme of *send the angels* is probably from Isa 27:13. The phrase *from the farthest bounds of earth to the farthest bounds of heaven* may be odd in the Greek *(ap'akrou gēs heōs akrou ouranou:* literally, "from the corner of earth to the corner of heaven"); but the basic notion comes from Zech 2:10, though there are similar expressions in Deut 30:4, Ps 116:7 and Jer 12:12, and see also *1 Enoch* 57:2. Other Old Testament allusions will be found in Isa 43:5, 49:5, 56:8, Jer 29:14, 30:10, 31:8, 32:27, and Ezek 28:25, 34:12-14, 37:21. The concept of *the chosen* being scattered to the four points of the compass, from which they will be gathered again, is familiar in Old Testament hope and anticipation: cf. Deut 30:4, Isa 11:11,16, 27:12, Ezek 39:27, Zech 2:6-11, Pss 116:7, 147:2; and it can be found also in the deuterocanonical books (Tob 13:3, Bar 5:5-9, 2 Macc 2:7, and also *1 Enoch* 57, *Pss Sol* 11:3, 17:26).

The verse itself must be dissociated from its predecessor. For while v. 26 is central to the theme of the whole apocalypse as adapted by the synoptists, and in its present place is possibly an insertion from 14:62—with parallel treatment by Matthew and Luke—the verse before us exhibits so many of the characteristics of apocalypse that it cannot be regarded as exemplifying the manner in which Jesus is known to have used scripture. But Mark's *He will send* effectively links the vindication of The Man in coming to God with the assembling of the chosen, the faithful, who had faith to see through distress, disaster, and death, to the inauguration of the Reign of God.

72. The Lesson of the Fig Tree
(13:28-31) = Matt 24:32-35; Luke 21:29-33

13 ²⁸ "Learn a lesson from the fig tree. When its branches become green and tender and come into leaf, you know that summer is near. ²⁹ So too, when you see this happening, you know that he is near, at the very gates. ³⁰ In truth, I tell you that this generation will not pass away until all these things happen. ³¹ Heaven and earth will pass away; my words will never pass away."

Comment

What appears to be a question of relationship in Chapters 11:12-14:52 may conveniently be examined at this juncture. The pattern was first suggested by the Reverend Laurence Brett (to whom I am indebted for the diagram which appears in the comment to the previous section). Further discussion and elucidation would seem to bear out Brett's contention that the projected relationship could and should be defended.

See chart on page 535.

Various items in the accompanying chart will be discussed as we proceed into the passion story, but we are immediately concerned with the illustrative use of the fig tree to illuminate the apocalypse.

The significance of this example is partly due to its predictability. The gradual emergence of the fig tree into leaf in spring is always the first *definite* sign of the season: the almond tree, by contrast, may often flower prematurely and then have the flowers cut by a late frost.

The connection in our gospels between fig trees and the dawning of the New Age has already been explored in the comment on 11:12-14 and will not be examined again here. But the chart amply justifies our asking what the saying about the fig tree in the section before us adds to our understanding. This is not a parable or a saying of Jesus somehow misplaced in the tradition —it is vital to the interpretation of the central part of the apocalypse. The point is that Mark here, following Matthew, wishes us to understand clearly the distinction between the natural order as we observe it and that same order as it responds to the New Age, the Coming of The Man.

Once more we have the dilemma propounded earlier in this commentary— the dilemma of choosing between manifestation in the here and now and manifestation in some delayed future, but each in its own fashion identified with the Age to Come. Nothing in our sources provides us with easy answers. While for us summer is known by the emergence and unfolding of foliage and warming temperatures, all that we are told here is that when the followers of Jesus see *this happening,* then they will know that *he is near, at the very gates.* This simply leaves us—in our present age, almost two millennia after the ministry—with ambiguity. Is this problem anywhere near resolution if we postulate the ambiguity as being between Jesus' own ministry as the beginning of the Age to Come on the one hand, and, on the other, a new "Coming" in the future as the true beginning of the Messianic Age? What is *near* is already *at the very gates,* already in the here and now; but is this meant in some indeterminate, imperfect sense? We can possibly translate the Greek as "it," as the subject of *estin* (= is), but a case can equally well be made for the

STRUCTURE OF 11:12-14:52

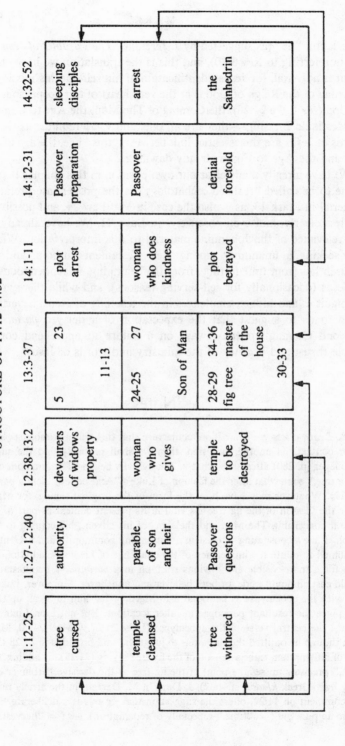

11:12-25	11:27-12:40	12:38-13:2	13:3-37			14:1-11	14:12-31	14:32-52
tree cursed	authority	devourers of widows' property	5		23	plot arrest	Passover preparation	sleeping disciples
temple cleansed	parable of son and heir	woman who gives	24-25	11-13	27	woman who does kindness	Passover	arrest
tree withered	Passover questions	temple to be destroyed	28-29 fig tree	Son of Man	34-36 master of the house	plot betrayed	denial foretold	the Sanhedrin
				30-33				

translation "he" (as suggested by J. Jeremias, *The Parables of Jesus*, pp. 119-20, in referring to Rev 3:20), and this is the translation we have chosen. The point is not vital, for Jesus' identification of himself and his mission with the dawning of the Reign of God is at the very heart of our gospel sources. Reign of God (see Luke 21:28), the Coming of The Man, the Age to Come, the Age of Messianic Blessings—they are all one, and v. 31 reminds us that the very words of Jesus are the essential link between "this" age, the age of the ministry, and the Age to Come already dawning.

We have already made clear our own position in this chapter that what has come to be called "realized eschatology" is the proper interpretation of the material in Mark 13, as is also the case in Matthew 24, and possibly (though far less clearly, and even obscurely) in Luke 21. We have already discussed the relevance of the Johannine material to this interpretation. While we are not seeking a unanimity among New Testament authors, and while the Church has from time to time, from the beginning, misunderstood the words of Jesus (occasionally for self-serving reasons), and while there are manifest ambiguities and hidden challenges in the teaching of Jesus, nevertheless it is open to us to suggest that the expectation of a delayed *parousia* or of a "Second Coming" rested always on a failure to apprehend correctly the whole thrust and urgency of the ministry and words of Jesus.

Notes

28. *Learn a lesson . . . :* If we conjecture that this was a parable spoken in some other context, on another occasion, then we shall probably find the suggestion of Lohmeyer (p. 280) attractive—that v. 28 originally began "The kingdom of heaven is like a tree," somewhat after the fashion of Luke's "And he told them a parable . . ." (21:29). Whatever may have been the form of the original saying, for Matthew and Luke the "lesson of the fig tree" is vital in its present context as part of the central section concerning The Man and the signs of his advent, his coming to God in triumph. Luke's consuming interest in a continuing community and a Gentile mission combined to dilute the immediacy of the challenge of Passion-Exaltation into a concern for a more visible and obvious triumph in a *parousia*, a manifestation, which would cast all doubt aside for both believer and unbeliever. Moreover, Luke's discomfort with the apocalypse as he found it in Matthew led him to break up the material and place the resultant pericopae in other locations. But not even Luke felt free to change the central verse of the apocalypse (Luke 21:27 = Matt 24:30, Mark 13:26), even though he omitted the summons to judgment and provided in 21:28 the expectation of redemption. Luke's version of the fig-tree saying (21:29), by adding "and all the trees," precisely misses the point of the fig tree as the decisive harbinger of summer.

fig tree (Greek *klados*, cf. 4:32): J. Duncan M. Derrett, in the article referred to in the comment on 11:22, offers the suggestion that *fig tree* is a deliberate Hebrew and Aramaic pun: *qys* (= "time," especially of redemption), *qes* (= "harvest," Aramaic *qîṣā, qîṣṣa* and *qayiṣ).* If this is so, then Luke's reference to "redemption" in 21:28 may make some deliberate link with the fig-tree saying which follows.

tender (Greek *hapalos:* cf. Matt 24:32): The word is common to both classical Greek and the Septuagint.

come into leaf (Greek *ekphuō:* cf. Matt 24:32): The verb and its precise translation are of interest to grammarians, for it can be translated as it has been here, or as "its leaves are brought into being."

29. *So too, when you see . . . . :* The whole saying is here related to the disciples—and in later circumstances to the reader/hearer, both by this phrase and by *you know.* We call attention again to the distinction between the warnings at the beginning of the apocalypse *(When you hear)* and the present emphatic verbs of observation and understanding. There is a problem with this verse, however, to which we now turn.

at the very gates: We called attention in the comment at the head of this section to the difficulty inherent in translating either "he" or "it" as the subject of the concluding part of this verse.

But there is a further difficulty, having to do with *when you see this happening* (Greek *tauta ginomena).* Mark is following Matthew's Greek closely in this section, but Matthew has *panta* (all) before *this* in his own 24:33. Luke's version is differently constructed, for while he has *you know* twice in common with Matthew, he has "when you see these things taking place" (Luke 21:31) for Matthew's "when you see all these things"; also, he omits *at the very gates* and (as we have seen) has his own contribution about the nearness of the Reign of God. But what is meant by *these things?* It seems an unusual phrase (and even more unusual in Matthew's "all these things") to describe a single sign of summer. This question is rendered more acute by Luke's "when you see for yourselves" in 21:30: this can hardly mean that in the circumstances of the day a rural community commonly relied on hearsay to indicate the first sign of summer! It is well-nigh impossible to avoid the conclusion that there was a fig-tree parable in the early tradition, oral and written, and its position here is used by Matthew and Mark to give added and pointed significance to the crucial sayings about The Man which had been inserted into an existing apocalypse, where the following v. 30 was entirely appropriate to all that had preceded v. 26.

30. The sayings subsequent to *at the very gates* assert that all that has been predicted will take place in *this generation.* The implications of this verse and the succeeding one cannot be overestimated. Was v. 27—as has been suggested—the original ending to the apocalypse, with vv. 28-36 added later by the Christian writers? The fact that the massive contributions from Old Testament sources come to an end with v. 27 certainly seems to support that view. At the same time *all these things* looks back to *when will all these things happen?* at the beginning of the chapter, although these words are from the disciples and not from the main body of the apocalypse. The question for us is: Does *all these things* refer in some prophetic fashion to the woes, distresses, persecutions, and the birth pains examined earlier, or does the phrase have much narrower focus?

It seems clear to this writer that we are dealing with a commentary, and a genuine saying of Jesus, looking back to 13:26 if not to the immediate framework in which that verse is set. Jesus is about to accomplish the fulfillment of his vocation, and his death/vindication would initiate the Reign of God, which would be consummated at the end of time. In facing that vocation he had seen with clarity all through his ministry the inexorable courses of history, and in that history the divine necessity of the renewal of humanity. The prospect of a violent death had been in his mind (according to Mark's account) almost from the beginning. This saying simply underscores his faith in the divine purpose and in his own vocation within that purpose, and so he faces what lies ahead with confidence. Having seen the advent of the Reign of God through his own imminent suffering and death and looked beyond both to his vindication, he declares that the "last times" of the old order have already begun. Judgment is already being enacted on the basis of those who would *see*, as distinct from those who would only *hear* rumors and false claims.

31. Nothing could be more emphatic than this statement. But does *my words* refer to the entire preceding discourse, the apocalypse? This can hardly be so, given the character and the background of the prophecies from v. 3 to v. 23. Does the statement then apply to Jesus' teaching in his ministry or to the saying about the coming exaltation of The Man? Given the proximity to the central section, and to the restructured fig-tree saying, the latter appears more likely. Yet the absolute character of the saying before us perhaps demands an application to the whole teaching ministry. If so, then in the three synoptists we are very close to a Johannine understanding of the nature of Jesus' mission and ministry as "the Word." Are we here confronted then with a commentary on, an interpretation of, Matt 5:17-19? The apparent parallel in 8:38 is not truly such if (with some manuscripts) we omit *my words*. For all its similarity, Matt 11:27 (= Luke 10:22) is of a somewhat different character from the absolute claim apparently being made here. For any approximation to this verse, common to all three synoptists, we have perforce to go to John's gospel (cf. 5:47, 6:63 and 68, 14:10, 15:7, 17:8) for references to the "sayings" (Greek *hrēmata)* of Jesus.

Furthermore—whether this is a genuine saying of Jesus or not—the plain sense is that he who has spoken will be the Agent of the New Age, the initiator of the redemption spoken of in the saying about The Man, and that in him there will be the fulfillment of which he spoke in Matt 5:17-18.

As an exercise in synoptic relationships, we note that the Greek construction *ou mē* with the future tense in v. 30 *(will not pass away),* while common enough in Matthew, is in Mark without parallel. Mark's Greek closely follows Matthew in this section.

73. The Day and the Hour
(13:32-37) = Matt 24:36-44

13   32 "But no one knows about that day or that hour, not even the angels in heaven, not even the Son; only the Father. 33 Watch! Be alert! You do not know when the moment is coming. 34 It will be like a man away from home on a journey, who leaves his servants in charge, each with his own work to do, and orders the doorkeeper to watch. 35 Keep

watch, then, for you do not know when the master of the house is coming—evening, midnight, cockcrow, or early morning. [36] If he comes suddenly, he must not find you asleep! [37] What I say to you, I say to everyone—watch!"

Comment

Verse 32 is lacking in Luke, and the Greek of both Matthew and Mark are virtually identical. The verse is joined to its preceding section by *de (But),* yet this should not be taken as an indication that this verse is in its original location. As it stands, there is a natural tendency to apply it to the whole complex of vv. 5-37. If ever it was applied to v. 26, we have no knowledge of it. If the saying applies to what the Old Testament describes as the "Day of the Lord," then it supplies a link and a transition from v. 31 to v. 33. The verse—whatever its place in the original tradition—is important for any attempt to reconstruct the sayings of the historical Jesus. It is highly unlikely that any second-generation Christian would have invented it, and indeed the fourth-century controversies with Arius and his followers led some to discredit the verse as denying the divinity of the Son. In its present position it reminds the readers/hearers that the faithfulness of the Son to the Father's will must be mirrored in their own lives. The presence of the Reign of God was more certain than the continuance of the physical order, but the manner and the time of the End are in the hands of God alone.

Notes

32. *that day:* Cf. 14:25; Luke 21:34; 2 Thess 1:10; 2 Tim 1:12,18, and 4:8; for "the day," cf. Matt 25:13, 1 Thess 5:4; and for "the last day," cf. John 6:39,40,44,54. The phraseology belongs essentially to the Old Testament, particularly in the sense that "the day" is known to God alone—cf. Zech 14:7. Our New Testament sources also emphasize the limited knowledge of *the angels*—cf. Eph 3:10; 1 Pet 1:12.

not even the Son: This is the only use of the title in absolute terms in Mark, and is another minor sign of his dependence on Matthew. There are similar titles in Mark, however, such as the *Son of God, my Son the Beloved, Son of the Blessed One.* The comment above called attention to the controversy surrounding an attribution of ignorance to Jesus, and some manuscripts of Matthew omit the phrase.

33. Though all three synoptists have an exhortation to watchfulness, there are divergent traditions here. While Mark has drawn on the models of Matthew and Luke to provide a suitable ending to the discourse, centered on the theme of being alert, Matthew's ending refers back to the coming of The Man and the specific need not to be found wanting.

Mark's ending is a fine piece of conflation from his existing sources, and what he has done is shown in detail here:

33 = Matt 24:42   Luke 21:34
34 = Matt 25:14,30   Luke 19:12
35 = Matt 24:42,50
36 = Matt 25:5

Mark—on the assumption that he knew Matthew and Luke—has already made his point about the Coming of The Man; and the *man away from home* is not repeated in v. 35, for the evangelist must now look forward from the *master of the house* to 14:32, where the same *master of the house* has found his disciples sleeping. (This will be dealt with later in the appropriate place.)

Watch! Cf. vv. 5,9,23.

Be alert! (Greek *agrupneō*): The verb is from Luke 21:36, and it is also found in the New Testament at Eph 6:18 and Heb 13:17. The readers/hearers are reminded that the crucial time is a matter of observation, not like the rumors of *when you hear* earlier in the discourse.

C. H. Dodd *(The Parables of the Kingdom,* New York: Scribner, rev. ed., 1961, p. 164), regards this verse as referring to Jesus' impending arrest and the inauguration of his Coming. This appears to be Mark's understanding, and the Matthean parables of the talents and the waiting maidservants point to the same interpretation. It is perhaps not too fanciful to suggest that Mark's very tightly organized ending to the chapter had (as at least one aim) the purpose of restoring Matthew's material—reimposing Matthew's understanding of it—in contradistinction to Luke's concern for a (long-lasting?) continuing community and an eventual return in glory of the risen Lord to the scene of his ministry.

34-36. If anything betrays the character of Mark's gospel as a conflated document, a digest of Matthew and Luke, then this parable does. It combines Matthean and Lucan material, and the various items in the construction can be identified. One could, for example, remove *like a man away from home . . . leaves his servants in charge, each with his own work to do.* This would leave us with a simple saying about a doorkeeper given a charge to watch, which could then be linked with Luke 12:36-37: "ready to open the door as soon as he comes and knocks. Happy those servants whom the master finds awake. . . ." This, however, simply confuses the Markan purpose. First of all, the injunction is meant to be a warning to *all,* not simply to a single servant (cf. v. 37). Secondly, the emphasis on the *master of the house* is essential to the context of the later scene in Gethsemane. On the majority view of gospel origins, what we are asked to assume is the existence of (a) a Markan original, already confused in the oral tradition; (b) a source in Luke 12:36-37; (c) a somewhat similar source in Matt 25:14; and finally (d) a situation where both Matthew and Luke, with Mark before them, decide to fragment an existing Markan ending to the discourse. It is, we suggest, far more realistic to assume a Markan conflation, on the lines suggested above in the notes on v. 33. Attractive though it is to eliminate *his servants* as an alien intrusion into a saying about a single doorkeeper, Mark's ending as it stands looks both backward, to previous warnings to watch, and forward, to an occasion when the earliest disciples had signally failed to watch. Awkward though his final construction may be, the evangelist has drawn together essential elements from both Matthew and Luke to underscore a constant theme in this apocalypse.

away from home (Greek *apodēmos*): The word in classical Greek (it is not found in the Septuagint) often implies "away at some considerable distance," even in a foreign country.

servants: The Greek *(doulos)* strictly means a slave. The thought that each servant has a specific task is not developed, and attention is concentrated on the *doorkeeper* (Greek *thurōros;* cf. John 10:3, 18:16). In Hellenistic society, doorkeepers were customarily slaves, and the classical texts often call attention to their habit of sleeping on duty.

The opening of the parable appears to have been taken from the opening of Matthew's parable of the talents (especially Matt 25:14). The change from *a man* to the *master of the house* has reference to the Last Supper and Gethsemane, though it has quite a different frame of reference in Luke 12:40.

evening . . . early morning: Cf. 6:48. It is too much to use these four watches of the Roman night as support for a specifically Roman origin of any part of the Markan tradition, though the mention of all four divisions is peculiar to Mark (see also the three Jewish watches in Luke 12:38): *evening* (Greek *opse*), cf. 11:11; *midnight* (Greek *mesonuktion),* cf. Luke 11:5; Acts 16:25, 20:7; *cockcrow* (Greek *alektorophonia)* and *early morning* (Greek *prōi),* cf. 1:35.

suddenly (Greek *exaiphnēs*): Cf. Luke 2:13, 9:39; Acts 9:3, 22:6. Some manuscripts of Luke read *exephnēs.*

asleep (Greek *katheudontas):* Cf. 4:27; Matt 25:5—"they all grew drowsy and fell asleep."

37. If 34-36 represents a summary of a whole catena of parables in Matthew and Luke, and a summary of this whole apocalypse, then v. 37 must be understood to be addressed to the Markan community as well as a saying represented as originally having been addressed to the disciples. What the origin of the saying may be we cannot know, nor can we be sure that we are confronting a genuine saying of Jesus, but the urgency of it certainly fits the general tenor of many of the parables in our sources.

We are of course confronted with the problems so familiar to us in the gospels—time, the need for immediate decision, judgment in the face of decision, the immediate future, the Reign of God, and the end-time. The view espoused here is that Mark has restored the immediacy, the urgency, of Matthew (and incidentally of the fourth gospel) in the face of the more diluted expectations of Luke. Not for Mark a time of delay and then a manifestation of the risen Jesus in glory: the exhortation to see in passion, death, and resurrection-vindication *the* coming of the master of the house was addressed with urgency to the community for which he wrote.

Bibliography

This list is not meant to be exhaustive, but simply indicates the various works (apart from commentaries) which this writer found particularly helpful. The first four are indispensable, providing the reader with the best representative views on the perplexing subject of the synoptic apocalypse.

Beasley-Murray, G. R. *A Commentary on Mark Thirteen.* London: Macmillan, 1957.

————. *Jesus and the Future: An Examination of the Criticism of the Eschatological Discourse, Mark 13, with special reference to the Little Apocalypse Theory.* London: Macmillan, 1954.

————. "The Parousia in Mark." *Expository Review* 75.1978, pp. 565-81.

————. "Second Thoughts on the Composition of Mark 13." *NTS* 29.1983, pp. 414-20.

Crawford, B. S. "Near Expectation in the Sayings of Jesus." *JBL* 101.1982, pp. 225-44.

Freyne, S. "The Disciples and the *Maskillim* in Daniel: A Comparison." *JSNT* 16.1982, pp. 7-23.

Hartman, L. *Prophecy Interpreted: The Formulations of Some Apocalyptic Texts and the Eschatological Discourse Mark 13 and Parallels.* Lund: Gleerup, 1966.

Harvey, A. E. *Jesus and the Constraints of History.* Philadelphia: Westminster Press, 1982 (esp. Chap. 4, "Jesus and Time: The Constraint of an Ending," pp. 66-97).

Hooker, M. D. "Trial and Tribulation in Mark XIII." *BJRL* 65.1982, pp. 78-99.

Lambrecht, J. "Die Logia-Quellen von Markus 13." *Biblica* 47.1966, pp. 321-60.

————. *Die Redaktion der Markus-Apocalypse: Literarische und Structuruntersuchung.* Analecta Biblica. Rome: Biblical Institute, 1967.

Lane, W. L. *Commentary on the Gospel of Mark.* The New International Commentary on the New Testament. Grand Rapids, Mich.: Eerdmans, 1974, pp. 444-84.

Mare, W. H. "A Study of the New Testament Concept of the Parousia." *Current Issues in Biblical and Patristic Interpretation: Studies in Honor of Merrill C. Tenney, Presented by his Former Students,* edited by G. F. Hawthorne. Grand Rapids, Mich.: Eerdmans, 1975.

Moore, A. L. *The Parousia in the New Testament.* Leiden: E. J. Brill, 1966.

Perrot, C. "Essai sur le Discours eschatologique (Mk XIII: 1-37, Matt XXIV:1-36, Lk XXI:5-36)." *RSR* 47.1959, pp. 481-514.

Pesch, R. *Naherwartungen, Tradition und Redaktion in Markus 13.* Düsseldorf: Patmos-Verlag, 1968.

Robbins, V. K. "*Dynameis* and *Semeia* in Mark." *Biblical Research* 18.1973, pp. 5-20.

Robinson, J. A. T. *Jesus and His Coming.* London: SCM Press, 1957.

Rousseau, F. "La structure de Marc 13." *Biblica* 56.1975, pp. 157-72.

Stone, M. E. "Coherence and Inconsistency in the Apocalypses: The Case of 'The End' in 4 Ezra." *JBL* 102.1983, pp. 229-43.

Walter, N. "Tempelzerstörung und synoptische Apokalypse." *ZNW* 57.1966, pp. 38-49.

PART VII
THE PASSION NARRATIVE

Comment

What is generally known as the "Passion narrative" has been divided in this commentary into two parts: the first deals with the plots against Jesus up to the time of his arrest, and the second with the trial and sentence. Several reasons have dictated this procedure. In the first place, the parallel columns in the chart for the first section are more detailed than in the chart for the trial, and are designed to show the close relationship between Matthew and Mark. Secondly, the trial and the judicial process call for a separate and extended comment, especially in view of the controversy which has for many years surrounded the nature of the charges on which Jesus was tried. The juridical competence of Jerusalem Judaism is also a consideration which falls more suitably into the second section of the Passion narrative. Thirdly, on any showing, and whether a Passover meal or not, the Last Supper calls for its own somewhat extended notes and comment. Finally, the presentation of the first part in detailed form will be of assistance to readers who do not possess a "synopticon," or parallel texts of the gospels.

It has long been argued that the long narrative demands an early oral tradition—an oral tradition that is best preserved in Matthew (cf. N. A. Dahl, "Die Passionsgeschichte bei Matthaus," *NTS* 2.1955, pp. 17-32). Nothing is more remarkable in Mark's gospel than the length of the passion narrative as against the rest of the material. The Griesbach hypothesis partly explains this seemingly disproportionate use of material by the necessity laid upon Mark to reproduce the Matthean outline. Indeed, Mark adds to the list of the enemies of Jesus, and at the climax of the story chooses the Matthean tradition (Matt 27:54), rather than the Lucan (23:47), as being more consonant with the challenge enunciated in the first verse of his gospel.

COMPARISON OF THE PASSION NARRATIVES
PART I

	Matthew	*Mark*	*Luke*	*John*
1. Plots for arrest & death	Chief priests, elders, at Caiaphas's house to plot arrest & death (26:3-4)	Chief priests & scribes plot to seize & kill Jesus (14:1-2),	Chief priests and scribes seeking to seize and kill Jesus (22:1-2),	[Cf. 11:45ff.]
	but not on the feast because of possible riot.	but not on the feast, because of possible riot.	they feared the people.	
2. Anointing at Bethany	In the house of Simon the leper	In the house of Simon the leper	In the house of a Pharisee	In the house of Martha and Mary
	woman anoints his head.	woman anoints his head.	city prostitute anoints his feet, weeping, wipes feet with her hair.	Mary anoints Jesus' feet, wipes them with her hair.
	Disciples irritated: Why not sell perfume and give to poor?	Some were irritated: perfume could have been sold for over 300 denarii and given to poor.		Judas asks: Why not sell perfume for 300 denarii and give to poor?
				Comment on Judas' greed
	Jesus' reply: Why trouble her? She did a good thing. You always have the poor, but you do not always have me. She did it for my burial. Wherever the gospel is preached, what she has done will be spoken of as a memorial of her. (26:6-13)	Jesus' reply: Why trouble her? She did a good thing. You will always have the poor, but you do not always have me. She has anticipated the anointing for burial. Wherever the gospel is preached, what she has done will be spoken of as a memorial of her. (14:3-9)		Jesus' reply: Leave her alone, she did this for my burial. You always have the poor, but you do not always have me. (12:1-8)

3. Plan for betrayal	Judas goes to high priests, asking money to betray Jesus. They offer 30 pieces of silver and he looks for opportunity. (26:14-16)	Judas goes to high priests to betray Jesus. They are glad and promise him money. Judas seeks an opportunity. (14:10-11)	Satan enters Judas, who confers with high priests and temple police about betraying Jesus. They are glad, promise him money, and he consents, seeking opportunity away from the crowd. (22:3-6)
4. Preparation for Passover	First day of UB, disciples ask Jesus where he wants them to prepare for Passover.	First day of UB, when they sacrificed the P, disciples ask Jesus where he wants them to prepare Passover.	On day of UB, Jesus sends Peter and John to prepare Passover. They ask, Where?
	Jesus tells them: Go to the city, to the one-you-know, and tell him: "The rabbi says, 'My time has come. I will keep Passover at your house with my disciples.' "	He sent two, told them they would meet a man carrying a pitcher of water. They are to follow him to wherever he goes, and say to owner, "Where is the dining room where I am to eat with my disciples?" He will show them a large upper room ready, and they are to prepare Passover there.	He tells them to go to the city, where a man will meet them carrying a pitcher of water. They are to follow him and ask the householder: "Where is the dining room where I am to eat Passover with my disciples?" He will show them a large upper room made ready and they would prepare Passover there.
	At evening, he reclined with the twelve disciples.	They went to the city, found everything as he said and they prepared the Passover.	They went, and found it just as he had told them and they prepared Passover.
		At evening he came with his disciples.	When the hour came he sat down, and the apostles with him.
	(26:17-20)	(14:12-17)	(22:7-14)

	Matthew	Mark	Luke	John
5. The first cup			Jesus desired to eat this Passover with them before his death. He will not eat it again until it has been fulfilled in the Kingdom. Took cup, gave thanks. "Take this and share it among you. I will not from now drink the fruit of the vine until the Reign of God has come." (22:15-18)	
6. Intimation of betrayal	While eating, Jesus says one of them will betray him.	While eating, Jesus says one of them will betray him.		Jesus, troubled in spirit, says one of them will betray him. They begin to look at one another. Peter signals the beloved disciple to ask who it is. "He is the one for whom I shall dip a morsel and to whom I give it." He took it and gave it to Judas.
	They are grieved and ask him one by one, "Not I?"	They are grieved and ask him one by one, "Not I?"	"See the hand of the one on the table!"	
	Jesus replied: "The one who dipped his hand with me in the dish."	Jesus replied: "One of the Twelve dipping with me in the dish."		
	"Son of Man goes as it has been written of him. Woe to the betrayer. It would have been good for him not to have been born."	"Son of Man goes as it has been written of him. Woe to his betrayer. It would have been good for him not to have been born."	"Son of Man goes, as decreed. But woe to the betrayer."	
	Judas the traitor asks, "It is not I, Rabbi?" Jesus says, "You have said it." (26:21-25)	(14:18-21)	They began to debate among themselves which of them would do this. (22:21-23)	(13:21-30)

7. Institution of the Eucharist	While they were eating, Jesus, taking bread, blessing it, broke it; giving it to the disciples, he said: "Take, eat, this is my body."	While they were eating, taking bread, blessing, he broke it and gave it to them and said: "Take, eat, this is my body."	Taking bread, giving thanks, he broke and gave to them, saying: "This is my body that has been given for you. Do this for my memorial."	[Cf. 1 Cor 11:23b-25]
	And taking the cup and giving thanks, he gave to them, saying:	And taking the cup, giving thanks, he gave to them and all drank from it. And he said to them:	And the cup in the same way after supping, saying:	
	"Drink from it, all of you, for this is my blood of the New Covenant that is being shed for The Many for the remission of sins.	"This is my blood of the Covenant that is being shed ʾ for The Many.	"This cup is the New Covenant in my blood that is being shed for you."	
	And I say to you, I will not drink from now of this fruit of the vine until that day when I shall drink it new with you in the Kingdom of my Father."	In solemn truth I tell you, I will never again drink of the vine until that day when I drink the new vine in the Kingdom of God."	[v. 18, "For I say to you . . . has come"]	
	Having sung the hymn they went out onto the Mount of Olives.	When they had sung a hymn, they went out to the Mount of Olives.		(13:1-20) Jesus washes the disciples' feet.
	(26:26-30)	(14:22-26)		

[Intimation of betrayal—6]	Cf. 26:21-25	Cf. 14:18-21	Cf. 22:21-23 (above)	Cf. 13:21-30 (above)

	Matthew	Mark	Luke	John
8. Dispute about greatness	Cf. 20:24-27	Cf. 10:41	Contention about greatness. Jesus replies: "Kings of nations lord it over them, and those in authority are called Benefactors. The disciples are not so: the greatest is to be junior, and the ruler like a servant. The one who reclines at table greater than the servant, yet Jesus is among them as one who serves." [For v. 29, cf. Matt 19:28] (22:24-30)	Cf. 13:31-35
9. Jesus foretells Peter's denials	Jesus says they will all stumble because of him that night because of the prophecy (cf. Zech 13:7).	Jesus says they will all stumble because of the prophecy (cf. Zech 13:7).		
	After he has been raised he will go before them into Galilee.	After he has been raised he will go before them into Galilee.		
			Jesus tells Peter that Satan had wanted to sift him like wheat, but he had prayed for him that his faith would not fail. When he has been converted he is to strengthen his brethren.	
	Peter replies that if all stumble, he will not.	Peter replies that if all stumble, he will not.	Peter says he is ready to go to prison and death with Jesus.	Peter asks why he cannot follow Jesus—he

			will lay down his life for him.
Jesus replies that this night before the cock crows Peter will three times deny him.	Jesus replies that that very night, before the cock crows twice, Peter will three times deny him.	Jesus replies that today the cock would not crow until Peter had three times denied knowing him.	Jesus replies the cock will not crow before Peter has three times denied him.
Peter says even if he dies with Jesus he will not deny him. All the disciples say the same.	Peter says emphatically that if he has to die with Jesus he will not deny him. They all speak similarly.		
(26:31-35)	(14:27-31)	(22:31-34)	(13:36-38)

10. Final dialogue	[Cf. 10:10]	[Cf. 6:8] [for Luke 22:37 cf. 15:28]	[22:35-38] [22:37, cf. Isa 53:12]	(14) (15) Farewell (16) discourse (17)

11. Gethsemane	Jesus goes with disciples to a property called Gethsemane.	They come to a property called Gethsemane.	Jesus goes as was his custom to Mount of Olives and the disciples follow. He tells them to pray not to enter the time of trial.	Jesus goes across the wadi Kidron with his disciples to a garden. (18:1-2)
	Tells disciples to sit while he goes away to pray.	Tells disciples to sit while he goes away to pray.		
	Takes Peter and the two sons of Zebedee; is sad and distressed, asks them to stay and watch.	Takes Peter, James and John; is sad and distressed, asks them to stay and watch.		
	Prays that cup may pass from him, but	Prays that cup may pass from him, but	Prays that cup may pass from him, but	

Matthew	Mark	Luke	John
submits to will of the Father.	submits to will of the Father.	submits to will of the Father.	
		An angel appears, strengthening him.	
		Jesus is in agony.	
Comes back to disciples, finds them sleeping, speaks to Peter: Watch and pray that they enter not into time of trial.	Comes back to disciples, finds them sleeping, speaks to Peter: Watch and pray that they enter not into time of trial.	Gets up, finds disciples sleeping, exhorts to prayer that they enter not into time of trial. (22:39-46)	
Prays again, with same petition.	Prays again, with same petition.		
Comes back to disciples, finds them sleeping.	Comes back to disciples, finds them sleeping, and they do not know how to answer him.		
Leaves disciples, prays a third time, then comes back, tells them to sleep and rest. The hour is at hand, and the Son of Man is betrayed into the hands of sinners.	Comes a third time and tells them to sleep and rest. It is over, the hour has come, and the Son of Man is betrayed into the hands of sinners.		
Rise, let us go. (26:36-46)	Rise, let us go. (14:32-42)		

74. The Conspiracy to Arrest Jesus
(14:1-2) = Matt 26:1-5; Luke 22:1-2; John 11:45-53

14 ¹ It was two days before Passover and Unleavened Bread. The chief priests and scribes were looking for a way to arrest Jesus secretly and put him to death. ² "But not in the presence of the festival crowd," they were saying, "or there might be a riot among the people."

Comment

With this short account of the plot to seize Jesus, we meet again the problem of the dating of events in this final week of the ministry, which was discussed in the comment on 11:15-19. The problem is not one that can be easily resolved, and undoubtedly the debate will continue until some new evidence arises which will add to our present knowledge. In the meantime, two articles are commended to those interested in pursuing the matter further, as well as in response to Mademoiselle Jaubert's hypothesis about Essene calendrical observance: F. Chenderlin, "Distributed Observance of the Passover—A Hypothesis," *Biblica* 56.3.1975, pp. 369-93, and ibid., "Distributed Observance of the Passover—A Preliminary Test of the Hypothesis," *Biblica* 57.1.1976, pp. 1-24.

The first article calls attention to the almost overwhelming practical considerations in the keeping of Passover (e.g., the arrangements for the slaughter of vast numbers of lambs) which may well have led Jerusalem authorities to assign different dates in the time of the festival for different groups. Even the calendar was not as clearly defined as we might think, for "Passover" in Josephus is vague, and could mean either 14 Nisan to midnight, or that period together with the overlapping seven-day cycle beginning at midnight on 14 Nisan. Equally, the first full day of Unleavened Bread (and so the first of Passover) was 15 Nisan. Chenderlin argues that the urgent need to deal with practical details (cf. J. Jeremias, *Jerusalem in the Time of Jesus,* 1969, pp. 56-57) may have convinced the temple authorities to make use of the provisions of Deut 6:1-8 and 2 Chr 35:1-19 to ease the situation. Admittedly this is hypothesis, but the author suggests in the second article that some foundation for this may be found in our gospel accounts. Much depends on the author's perfectly proper insistence that generally speaking we use too narrow a focus in our reading of the word "Passover"—a term which was applied equally to all eight days of the feast. His suggestion is that a wider, or "distributed," rendering of the term would obviate many difficulties of chronology. We would not, for example, reject out of hand the assertion in Mark 14:12 that the disciples prepared the feast on the first day of Unleavened Bread. Similarly, the understanding of "the day of preparation" in John 19:42 would not be an insuperable "either-or" as against the synoptic usage. Again, the "distributed" understanding of Passover would allow for the flurry of nonreligious activity associated with the arrest of Jesus in a time clearly delineated in the Law as a period of rest. Finally, Chenderlin (rejecting Mlle Jaubert's suggestion of a long interval between the Last Supper and the crucifixion) would reconcile John and the synoptists by suggesting that the crucifixion took place on the day following the supper, Passover that year beginning on Wednesday and the crucifixion taking place on Friday, 16 Nisan.

The two articles, indeed, suggest a way out of the current calendrical impasse, but it must be said that we have at present no evidence to support the hypothesis of the kind of "distributed" observance Chenderlin so attractively offers. In the absence of any further information, the present commentator believes that for the time being the calendar hypothesis of Mlle Jaubert offers our best workable solution.

Notes

1. The small section evidently designed as an introductory piece to the whole Passion narrative suffers all the disabilities of the condensation we believe it to be. Confronted with the direct speech of Matthew ("You know that in two days the Passover is coming and The Man will be handed over to be crucified"—26:2) and Luke's confusion of two feasts ("And the feast of Unleavened Bread drew near, which is called Passover"—22:1), Mark chooses indirect speech, combines his sources and gives us *two days before Passover and Unleavened Bread.* Mark 14:12 mentions both feasts, but this is no help, for Unleavened Bread was three days later, not two. The Greek text does not help us *(meta duo hēmeras),* for it might well be that by Jewish reckoning "the next day" is meant. Possibly the only assistance open to us—itself slight—is that *meta treis hēmeras* in 8:31 = "the third day."

Passover (Greek *to Pascha):* This is the Greek form of the Hebrew and Aramaic found in the New Testament, in Philo, and in the Septuagint (though *phasek* and *phasech* are also found in this last). Josephus uses *pascha* and *phaska.* The name is used of the Passover lamb (14:12,14) and of the feast (here and in v. 16), and it can be used of the entire eight days. Passover might only be celebrated in Jerusalem (we have no certain information on possible observances at Qumran). In the late afternoon of 14 Nisan the lambs were slaughtered in the temple precincts, and the meal had to be eaten between sunset and midnight of that day (15 Nisan, by the Jewish practice of beginning the day at sunset).

Unleavened Bread (Greek *ta azuma—hē heortē tōn azumōn* in Luke 22:1): Originally, this was the beginning of barley harvest, during which unleavened bread was eaten—cf. Exod 34:18. In later Judaism it was celebrated from 15 to 21 Nisan (cf. Exod 12:1-20, Josephus, *Ant* 2.15.1, 14.2.1) and occasionally, in popular usage, the name also covered Passover. The two observances are mentioned together in 2 Chr 35:17 (see also Mark 14:12). Our difficulty with chronology is certainly not eased by Josephus's dating of Unleavened Bread from 14 Nisan. Matthew 26:1 omits any mention of the feast. With the admission of our difficulties as being incapable of resolution, it is nevertheless worth mentioning that we are dealing with the memory of oral transmission, committed to writing after a time of community use and reflection and then edited by four evangelists, not one of whom (with the possible exception of "the Levite," if that was Matthew) was an eyewitness to the events. For all that the passion story may well have been the first part of the tradition to have achieved a fixed form, the lapse of time between the events of the final week and the written form will not have been insignificant. Short of having access to almanacs, calendars, and calculators, how many of us can remember what day of the week was Christmas day in 1956?

The chief priests and scribes: The Greek verb translated *were looking (ezētoun)* is an imperfect tense, and implies a scheme which had been in train for some time. We are not dealing with an official policy of the Sanhedrin, but rather with a plan set in motion by some of its principal members (cf. 3:6, 11:18, 12:12).

secretly (Greek *en dolō):* The word is absent from a few manuscripts, but Matthew's use of it, given the tone of this small episode, would certainly have commended it to Mark.

2. We are confronted with two translation problems in this verse, the first one being due partly to punctuation and partly to whether we read *de* or *gar* in the Greek: (a) our earliest gospel manuscripts not only were innocent of marks of punctuation, but were also written in what are for us uppercase letters (uncials) and without spaces between the words; (b) the Greek manuscripts of this verse can be read as either

> *elegon de mē en tē heortē*
> they were saying, "But not . . ."

> or

> *elegon gar mē en tē heortē*
> for they were saying, "Not . . ."

Here it would be proper to say (cf. Taylor, p. 528) that the presence of *for (gar)* ties the quotation much more obviously to those plotting Jesus' arrest. It has been argued that the first reading, *they were saying,* is impersonal—"people were saying." However, the manuscript evidence for *de* is impressive, it is in Matthew, and we believe that the kind of plotting just described perfectly fits the caution *But not . . .*

Our second problem concerns a translation of the word for *festival.*

in the presence of the festival crowd (Greek *en tē heortē):* At first sight, this seems to be a matter of straightforward translation, particularly in the light of *or there might be a riot.* Does the plain meaning of the Greek indicate an arrest *before* the feast (the view of many commentators)? Though none of our sources gives us a precise timing for this secret scheme, all our sources place it well within the context of the final week: in that event, the interval of time would have been very narrow, and the crowds were already gathering. Some manuscripts read *mē pote en tē heortē estai* . . . instead of *mē en tē heortē, mē pote estai* . . . , thus allowing a translation of ". . . perhaps there will be a riot . . ." without indicating whether the arrest was to be made before or after the feast. Some have suggested that the offer by Judas precipitated a decision to act on what was merely, so far, a somewhat inchoate desire of the temple clergy. The translation given here reflects John 7:11, in which *heortē* indicates a festival crowd, and it is also consonant with Luke 22:6: "in the absence of the crowds." This translation is forcibly argued in J. Jeremias, *The Eucharistic Words of Jesus* (English translation by Norman Perrin of *Die Abendmahlsworte Jesu,* Göttingen: Vandenhoeck & Ruprecht: London, SCM Press, 1966, pp. 44-49). In his view, the verse before us carries no note of time. Given all the obscurities, we can only make an inspired guess; and perhaps the priests found that they were able to expedite matters, albeit *secretly,* because of the treachery of Judas.

or there might be a riot (Greek *thorubos):* The word does not mean some kind of noisy demonstration, but a full-scale, out-of-control rampage, such as would bring upon the city a massive Roman retaliation.

the people: The word is unusual for this evangelist, who generally in such circumstances prefers the word "crowd" or "crowds." The word *people* is, however, found in Matt 26:5 and Luke 22:2, in "they were afraid of the people." In the face of only two other occurrences of *people* in Mark (7:6, 11:32), our conclusion is that this small section of the gospel is purely derivative.

75. Jesus Anointed at Bethany
(14:3-9) = Matt 26:6-13; John 12:1-8 (?)

14 ³ He was staying at Bethany, in the house of Simon the leper. While he was at table a woman came in, having with her an alabaster jar of very expensive perfume, made from nard. She broke the jar, and poured the perfume over his head. ⁴ But some people there were saying to each other indignantly, "What was the use of wasting the perfume? ⁵ It could have been sold for more than three hundred denarii and the money given to the poor." They turned upon her in anger. ⁶ But Jesus said, "Let her alone. Why are you causing her trouble? It is a noble thing she has done for me. ⁷ You have the poor with you always, and you can do good to them whenever you wish; but you will not always have me. ⁸ She did what she was able to do; she has anointed my body in anticipation, to prepare it for burial. ⁹ In solemn truth, I tell you

that wherever the Proclamation is made in all the world, what she has done will be told as her memorial."

Comment

The brevity of the previous section (14:1-2), for all its problems, contrasts strongly with the vivid detail of the narrative before us. Not only does it contain a reference to place (rare in Mark), but it also suggests that behind the story lies an eyewitness account; furthermore, it contains important derivations from Matthew as well as individual items peculiar to this evangelist.

The narrative is not easy to classify. It is hardly a pronouncement story, for in spite of vv. 6 and 7 the incident has found its way here by early association with the coming suffering, death, and burial. To compound the difficulty of classification, there are signs of development, for Matthew and Mark add an anointing of the head (a sign of royal and priestly dignity) as against Luke and John, who simply have an anointing of the feet. According to some commentators, the narrative originally may have ended at v. 7—a suggestion that has some merit, for it would accommodate a classification of this narrative as a "pronouncement story" (cf. Lohmeyer, p. 291). It can equally well be argued that this narrative is part of a complex of Bethany stories whose units have been attracted to varying contexts in the course of gospel compilation.

The position of the story raises other questions. Possibly John is correct in placing the narrative before the entry into Jerusalem ("six days before Passover," 12:1) and therefore associating it more closely with Lazarus, Martha, and Mary of Bethany. Far more acute, in the light of John, is Luke's identification of the woman in the narrative with harlotry (7:36), as well as the expansion of the story into a parable (7:39-43). Luke does not identify the anointing with Jesus' burial, and for him there is a ready-made context in his recalling the women who accompanied Jesus (8:1-3). A further difficulty is that Luke apparently sets the scene in Galilee, in the house of "Simon the Pharisee" (of whom we otherwise have no knowledge). If we add the views of later piety that the woman was Mary of Magdala, the problem is then well-nigh impossible to resolve. If, moreover, we adhere to the view that Luke is dependent on Mark, then the discrepancies between the two narratives become inexplicable. In fact, the only common features in all four gospels are the anointing of Jesus at table by a woman, the anger of some witnesses at the whole incident, and Jesus' saying about the poor.

Notes

3. The verse begins with two genitive absolutes, with the same subject repeated *(ontos autou en Bethania . . . katakeimenou autou:* literally, "and he being in Bethany . . . and he sitting at table . . ."). This is highly unusual, not only because notes of place are very rare in Mark, but also because the first genitive absolute with its place-name bears all the marks of an addition to the text. In this, the suggestion of Lohmeyer (p. 292) seems to us entirely correct: Mark's narrative probably began, *In the house of Simon the leper, while he was at table . . .* In this event we must ask whence Mark derived his opening phrase, *He was staying at Bethany.* We suggest that this derived afterthought is due to Matthew, since the latter might have rejected the Johannine tradition (if he had heard of it) as belonging to another cycle of tradition having to do with another family. Of *Simon the leper* we know nothing, but we may be justified in thinking that the name was well enough known to the community to be included.

a woman: Though she is not identified (save in the Johannine naming of her as Mary, the sister of Martha and Lazarus, 12:3), there is no ground for supposing that she was a notorious "sinner" (Luke 7:37). In view of the prediction in v. 9 (if indeed this was part of the original tradition), it is strange that her name was not remembered, and equally strange that some name was not later supplied for her.

alabaster (Greek *alabastros):* Cf. Matt 26:7; Luke 7:37. The word means a spherical jar for holding perfume, and often made of alabaster. The gender of the noun varies in the manuscripts: it may be masculine or feminine, and a few minor manuscripts designate it as neuter.

perfume (Greek *muron:* literally, "ointment") . . . *nard* (Greek *nardos):* Together, these two words can be translated as "ointment of nard." The word *nardos* is derived from the name of the Indian plant *(Nardostachys jatamansi)* from which the perfume was manufactured. It is found in the classics, and also in Cant 1:12, 4:13.

expensive (Greek *polutelous):* Cf. 1 Tim 2:9; 1 Pet 3:4. Matthew's gospel has *polutimos.*

very expensive perfume: We have left subsumed in this translation the very difficult Greek word *pistikos* (cf. John 12:3), which defies all attempts to trace its derivation. Readers of English translations are familiar with "spikenard" but this only further obfuscates the issue. The word may come from *pistos* (= "genuine") or even from the same Greek word (though derived from a different verb—*pino)* through *potos,* thus giving the meaning of "liquid." Some have suggested a derivation (though corrupted) from *spikaton* = "ointment." The Vulgate appears to favor this, with the Latin *nardi spicati.* Again, there is the possibility of *piestikēs* (from *piezō)* as meaning "distilled," though this appears to be somewhat strained. And yet again, we may have a transliteration from the Aramaic *pistaqa*—which was the name for *balanus,* the ben nut—on the grounds that the oil of the ben nut was one of the ingredients of *nardinium,* or oil of nard perfume.

4. *some people:* Mark, generally concerned to identify critics of Jesus, does not identify this group of hostile onlookers. Matt 26:8 has "the disciples"; John 12:4

mentions only Judas. But it is worth recording that some manuscripts of Mark have "his disciples," while a few others combine the opening words in our Greek text so as to read "some of the disciples." These examples bear all the marks of later scribal assimilations to the Matthean text.

indignantly (Greek *aganaktountes;* cf. 10:14): There is no main verb, and we have rendered the participle by an adverb, since a literal translation would give us "there were some being indignant with each other." Many manuscripts, faced with the obscurity of a sentence without a verb of saying or speaking, have added *legontes* (= saying) *pros eautous (to each other).* For the verb *aganakteō* (to be indignant), cf. 10:14.

"What was the use . . ." (Greek *eis ti):* Literally, "To what end?" Cf. 15:35; Matt 14:31, 26:8; Acts 19:3.

wasting (Greek *apoleia):* The word is classical and is also found in the papyri. The end of the sentence *(the perfume)* is omitted in some manuscripts, and it is not found in Matt 26:8.

5. The verse begins with a redundancy: "This perfume could have been sold . . ."

three hundred denarii: Any attempt to reproduce this in terms of modern currency is fraught with difficulty, as was demonstrated in the notes on 6:37. It will be sufficient here to note that one *denarius* was the daily wage of an agricultural laborer. Matthew has no estimate of value, and the word *epanō (more than),* which is not found in some manuscripts, has been held to be a later insertion (second century?) reflecting devaluation of the currency after the reign of Nero.

the poor: While concern for the poor was a characteristic mark of Jewish piety (and indeed commanded in the Law), the episode is not to illustrate this piety but to expose the spurious reasons given by the critics for their indignation.

They turned upon her: The speakers are not identified, and perhaps they were bystanders. Mark in general does not attempt to mitigate any failure on the part of the Twelve, and it is noteworthy that he does not follow Matthew at this point. However, since *they* refers back to *some people there* in v. 4, and since the same phrase in Greek *ēsan de tines)* is used at 2:6 to indicate the scribes, perhaps we are still in the general area of Jesus' critics.

in anger (Greek *emphriaomai):* Cf. 1:43. The Vulgate *fremebant in eam*—"they lashed out at her"—implies violent and noisy disapproval by word and gesture.

6. *Let her alone* (Greek *aphete autēn):* Cf. 10:14. The succeeding question (Greek *ti kopous parechete)* is found in the papyri but is less common in classical Greek. Cf. Matt 26:10; Luke 11:7, 18:5; Gal 6:17. The final part of this verse—*It is a noble thing she has done for me*—is notable in that it lacks the terseness of the two preceding sayings.

7. Critics of one kind or another have from time to time seized upon *You have the poor with you always* as though Jesus were giving some kind of cachet to the existence of poverty as an unalterable human condition. Certainly Mark's *You can do good to them whenever you wish* (the clause is peculiar to this gospel) might be thought to underline this assumption. Yet not only must the first part of the verse be balanced by *You will not always have me;* the possibility also exists that this was a Markan contribution in the distress of his own times and of his own community. We may usefully compare the saying in John 14:16—"A little while, and you will see me no more."

8. *"She did . . ."* The woman performed the only service within her power. (For the construction—Greek *ho eschen epoiēsen*, with the verb *poiesai*—cf. Matt 18:25; Luke 7:42, 14:14; John 8:6; Acts 4:14; Heb 6:13.) It is to be noted that the situation here is far different from that described in 12:44 (she *put in all that she had*), for here Jesus commends the woman: in Chapter 12 he condemns a pseudo-piety which in effect was no better than extortion in its results.

There are textual difficulties in this verse, however, which call for attention. The Greek is awkward, though not ungrammatical as such. Matthew's version (allowing for insignificant textual variants) is: *balousa gar autē to muron epi tou sōmatos mou pros to entiphiasai me epoiesen:* "she has poured this ointment on my body to prepare me for burial." The difficulty lies with the verb *eschen* in Mark: *ho eschen epoiesen, proelaben murisai to sōma mou eis ton entaphiasmon.* We have translated it as *was able to do,* but this makes the verb *eschen* the equivalent of *dunamai* (= to be able). What is missing is an infinitive, and we would have expected *ho eschen poiesai epoiesen =* "what she was able to do, she did." As it is, Mark's text almost reads as though the woman who anointed him had gone to the very limits of her finances, in the same way as the widow in 12:44. This is not the end of the problem, for the phrase we have rendered as *anointed my body in anticipation* is not very felicitous Greek *(proelaben murisai to sōma mou).* The verb *prolambanō,* in the sense of "take care for," "anticipate," is classical, is found in the Septuagint, and is represented at 1 Cor 11:21; Gal 6:1. But this use of the verb—with the infinitive *(murisai)*—while not wholly unusual, led Lagrange to suggest (p. 345) that we may have a case here of "translation Greek" from an Aramaic original, and others have held that the construction is not classical. No firm conclusion can be reached in the matter, if only because Mark frequently sits lightly to the usage of traditional grammar and syntax.

One further note must be added, and that concerns the relationship between this verse and its Matthean counterpart (26:10-11). It is generally held that Matthew, feeling the difficulties inherent in the Markan text, recast and smoothed the construction. We suggest that this argument is not very impressive. We called attention in v. 3 to the derivative character of Mark, with its unusual note of place, and we suggest that Mark already had a tradition of his own before he was acquainted with Matthew. This circumstance may well explain not only the phenomenon of v. 3, but also the (possible) "translation Greek" of the verse before us.

Whatever the difficulties of translation, the meaning is clear: the unnamed woman has anticipated the burial rite of anointing, even though that was not her intention.

anointed (Greek *murisai):* It is quite unnecessary to go to the length of suggesting that since the anointing was omitted at the actual burial (15:46), and subsequently ruled out by the raising of Jesus (16:1), this service perforce had to be performed. The anointing for burial is the interpretation given by Jesus both in Matthew and Mark.

In view of Luke's omission of any reference to passion and death in his account (7:36-50), the present writer entertains considerable doubt as to the genuineness of v. 9. There are far too many unresolved puzzles in the account. There is the mention of Bethany: did Matthew derive this account from some early tradition which later on became associated in the fourth gospel with Martha and Mary? If (cf. Matt 26:13 = Mark 14:9) this act is to be remembered *in all the world,* why was not the woman's name remembered? The core of the story, without the interpretation in vv. 8 and 9, reaches a climax in the pronouncement saying of v. 7—a saying as enigmatic as many other sayings of Jesus—and in that context reminiscent of the enigmatic saying about duty to Caesar and to God. If the narrative originally ended at v. 7, are the two succeeding verses homiletic expansions belonging to the early community? Or does the interpretation reflect a recasting (by Matthew?) of the Lucan story? To none of these questions can there be a definite answer.

9. *In solemn truth:* Cf. 3:8.

wherever (Greek *hopou ean*): Cf. 6:10,56.

Proclamation: Cf. 1:1.

all the world (Greek *kosmos*): Despite the use of this word in 8:36, the whole phrase is singularly un-Markan. It is, however, wholly characteristic of Matthew. The phrase *eis panta ta ethnē* in Mark 13:10 is matched not only in Matt 28:19, but also in Matthew's saying on bearing witness to the nations at 10:18. Apart from material he shares with Matthew, Mark has little obvious interest in missionary enterprise.

memorial (Greek *mnēmosunon*): No entirely adequate translation of this word is possible in English. The word here suggests—as it often does to some extent—"dead" inscriptions or statuary. A whole sentence may be the best that can be done for it: "an event in the past called into the present by its effects."

76. Judas Agrees to Betray Jesus (14:10-11) = Matt 26:14-16; Luke 22:3-6

14 10 Then Judas Iscariot, one of the Twelve, went to the chief priests to hand him over to them. 11 They were delighted at what he had to say, and promised him money, while he began to look for an opportunity to betray him.

Comment

We may be grateful to the evangelist for this very stark account of the betrayal of Jesus, baldly affixing the blame for the betrayal of Jesus on one of the Twelve. He dispenses at a stroke with the sense of failure and tragedy in Matthew and Luke. Not for Mark the puzzled attempt by Luke (22:3) to apportion some of the blame to Satanic temptation, still less the motive of avarice ascribed to Judas by Matthew (26:15). Simply, in Mark, the action of Judas is presented as unadorned treachery.

The brief account follows directly from vv. 1-2, with the temple clergy hoping to arrest Jesus secretly. They now have the opportunity presented to them by no one less than a member of the Twelve. Speculation as to the motives of Judas has existed throughout Christian history. But it is relevant to remind ourselves at this juncture that there must have been something in the character of Judas which commended him to Jesus in the first place. Possibly John 12:6 gives some hint of one factor which led to the betrayal. In what sense was Judas a thief? We are not told that the money was used for personal gain. One possible explanation presents Judas as a secret—and by now bitterly disappointed—Zealot, seeking to force Jesus into an immediate and dramatic declaration of messiahship. There is, however, no proof of this, and we can do no more than guess at Judas's motives.

Notes

10. The form *Iscarioth* was examined at 3:19. This verse provides an instructive example of the gradual loss of importance of the definite article in *koinē* Greek. The phrase *one of the Twelve* is in Greek *ho eis tōn dōdeka,* and although *ho eis* (literally, "the one") is found in contemporary usage, it is strange that Mark does not use it in 14:20,43. (Matt 26:14 does not have the article.) Certainly Paul's use of the definite article before *Christos* is inconsistent at best. Mark may be using the definite article here for emphasis: "that one, the only one, of the Twelve" who proved treacherous. It is hardly likely—though admittedly possible—that *the one* is meant to distinguish Judas from the brother of Jesus (6:3). Perhaps, too, we are in the presence of a piece of early community vocabulary, for *eis tōn dōdeka (one of the Twelve)* is frequent in the gospels (cf. 14:20,43; Matt 26:47; Luke 22:47) and is found in the most telling context of all: *It is one of the Twelve, the one who is . . .* (14:20). Was the phrase *one of the Twelve* used as a designation of Judas in order to avoid mentioning his name?

hand him over (Greek *paradidōmi):* This Greek form is used consistently, rather than *prodidōmi.*

11. *They were delighted* (Greek *echarēsan):* The Greek verb *chairo* means an unqualified joy or happiness, generally in regard to some event or some unlooked-for *opportunity* (Greek *euchairos:* cf. 2 Tim 4:2).

Mark's *promised him money* is the evangelist's rendering in indirect speech of Matthew's dialogue: "What are you willing to give me," he asked, "if I hand him over to you?" The change to indirect speech succeeds in making this very sparse narrative even more dramatic.

promised him money: Matt 26:15 records that the clergy gave Judas "thirty silver pieces," a substantial sum and the traditional purchase price of a slave. John does not record any compact, and Luke 22:5 records that they "covenanted" with Judas to give him money, and he "fully consented" to the arrangement.

In Mark, Judas *began to look for an opportunity,* and 14:43 implies that some arrangement was made by the traitor for help, and that those so recruited were armed.

77. Passover
(14:12-21) = Matt 26:17-25; Luke 22:7-14,21-23; John 13:21-30

14   12 On the first day of Unleavened Bread, when it was customary for the Passover lambs to be killed, his disciples said to him, "Where would you want us to go and prepare for you to eat the Passover meal?" 13 So he sent two of his disciples with these instructions: "Go into the city, and a man carrying a jar of water will meet you. Go along with him, 14 and wherever he goes in say to the householder, 'The rabbi says, "Where is the guest room where I am to eat the Passover with my disciples?" ' 15 He will show you a large upstairs room, already furnished. Make preparations for us there." 16 The disciples set out, and went into the city, where they found everything just as he had told them. So they prepared for Passover. 17 When it was evening, he arrived with the Twelve. 18 As they reclined at table eating, Jesus said, "In solemn truth, I tell you one of you will betray me—one of you eating with me." 19 At this, they became sorrowful, and began to say to him one by one, "It is not I, is it?" 20 But he said to them, "It is one of the Twelve, one who is dipping bread in the same dish with me. 21 For The Man is going the way appointed for him in the Scriptures, but alas for the one by whom The Man is betrayed! It would have been better for him if he had not been born."

Comment

Verses 12-16 contain a whole series of parallels to material elsewhere which must be examined. The parallels are such that commentators are sharply divided as to the historical reliability of these critical verses. Not only so, but the note of time in v. 12 implies that the Last Supper was in the context of the Passover meal of 15 Nisan.

To begin with the parallels, we may first point out a somewhat similar incident in 1 Sam 10:1-4, where the newly anointed Saul is given a sign for recognition (three men going to Bethel, one carrying a wineskin). Now the story of the anointing at Bethany manifestly interrupts the flow of the narrative from 14:2 to 14:10, and we are entitled to ask whether that story in its present position was designed to call attention to the parallel with Saul. To this question there is no answer.

The parallel with 11:1-6 is more instructive, and in tabular form it is as follows (translated literally):

11:1-6	14:13-16
1. he sends two of his disciples	13. he sends two of his disciples and says to them:
2. and says to them: Go into the village, and . . . you will find . . .	Go into the city and . . . will meet you . . .
3. say . . . the master	14. say . . . the rabbi
4. and they went and they found . . .	16. and they went . . . and they found just as he had told them and . . .
6. just as Jesus had told and . . .	

On the surface, the parallels present themselves as a doublet, leaving us with the perhaps unwelcome task of deciding which set of circumstances is historical. But before concluding too easily that one or the other is a deliberate artifice, we recall Mark's habit of repeating himself, and also take note of the features which distinguish one account from the other. Some of these matters will be discussed in the notes, but we mention a few here, for they bear upon the historicity of the material. There are questions for which the evangelist provides no answers, but so artless is the composition in each case as to suggest most strongly that the very lack of information points to a historical tradition. For example, do the instructions given to the nameless disciples imply an arrangement previously made with the householder? Or again, why the insistence on a *large upstairs room,* while instructions about other preparations are entirely absent? Similarly, we are given no clear information as to whether the meal was a Passover meal or not: apart from the contextual note in v. 14, we are left in ignorance whether the proper conclusion to the preparations lies in vv. 17-21 or in 22-25.

One point should be mentioned here, and it throws some light on the parallel material we have discussed. It will be noticed that in the center of 11:1-6 Jesus is called *the master,* and in the center of 14:13-16 he is *the rabbi.* Now, if we take Chapter 11 as the starting point of the whole Passion complex, then it is noteworthy that at vital points in the narrative there are pericopae which focus on a name or title of Jesus. It is as though the evangelist had fixed a row of pegs, with the narrative consisting of a series of loops hanging from those pegs. We have, then, the following key points:

11:3	the master—repeated also at 12:14,19,32; 13:1
12:6	the son, the beloved
12:36	Son of David
14:14	the rabbi—repeated also at 14:45
14:21	Son of Man
14:27	shepherd
14:61	the Messiah, the Son of the Blessed One (also "I am")
15:2	the king of the Jews—repeated at 15:13,26
15:32	the Messiah, the King of Israel
15:39	a Son of God
16:6	Jesus of Nazareth
[16:19	the Lord Jesus]

It can be argued that in most cases the nature of the material demands that these appellations be used, but given the parallels (in the Greek) which we examined earlier there would be no obvious reason to make the change from *the master* to *the rabbi* unless the evangelist was (consciously?) arranging this vital part of his composition to include all the titles and descriptions of Jesus. The temptation to see in this series an ascending scale must be resisted, for all of the titles and descriptions have been used before 11:3. It can be remarked, however, that 1:1 begins *Son of God,* and the centurion at the crucifixion speaks of a *Son of God.*

We note in passing that the Matthean parallels all use the same designations, though Matt 28:5 has simply "Jesus" where Mark 16:6 has *Jesus of Nazareth.* There is no such precise parallel treatment in Luke. We do not find here any clear indication of Matthean or Markan priority: all that emerges is that we have a series of episodes in which a name or designation of Jesus is central.

Notes

12. *On the first day of Unleavened Bread:* This is not a clear indication of date, since the surface meaning is 15 Nisan, but the following temporal clause *(when it was customary . . .)* demonstrates that Mark means to indicate 14 Nisan. This use of temporal clauses is in fact common in Mark, with the second clause limiting the first (cf. 1:32,35; 4:35; 14:30; 15:42; 16:2). This does not wholly clear up the matter, and though Strack-Billerbeck (Vol. 2, p. 813) seems to allow—in four examples quoted— for an apparent identification of Passover with Unleavened Bread as to dating, yet it may be that the Greek *prōtē (first)* is an early misreading for *pro* (before). This would

seem to be confirmed by Josephus *(Ant* 2.317), who employs the same kind of loose
terminology when he speaks of Unleavened Bread and remarks that the feast lasted
"for eight days." While it is possible to translate the Greek as "with reference to the
first day of Unleavened Bread" and thus assume that the disciples were asking for
guidance as to the observances the next day, it is equally possible that the term was a
generic one intended to cover both festivals. But if we are to infer from this notation of
time that it was in the afternoon—or even the morning—of the day of the Passover
sacrifice, then the interval allowed for all the arrangements seems far too short, even if
the householder was partly aware of Jesus' intentions. Any resolution of the matter
must await further discoveries (if any). In any event, the information already at hand
about sectarian calendars and places of worship may in the end require drastic revision of the usual picture of a standard, centralized, and uniform Passover celebration
in Jerusalem. Certainly the Jewish colony in Elephantine had no qualms about keeping Passover in exile, and the priestly authorities in Jerusalem (at least on one occasion) acquiesced in the situation, as we know from the famous Passover Papyrus of
419 B.C. But how far a sectarian celebration of the feast would have been tolerated in
and around Jerusalem, we have no means of knowing.

for the Passover lambs to be killed (Greek *hote to pascha ethuon):* The Greek imperfect *ethuon* denotes habitual, repeated action. Luke 22:7 has "when it was customary
to kill the Passover lambs." The verb *thuō,* which is classical, and found in both the
Septuagint and the papyri, varies in meaning between "to kill" and "to sacrifice." In
most New Testament examples, its meaning is "to kill" (cf. Matt 22:4; Luke
15:23,27,30, and 22:7; John 10:10; Acts 10:13, 11:7, 14:13,18; 1 Cor 5:7, 10:20). However, in Acts 14:13,18, and 1 Cor 10:20 the verb is used of pagan sacrifice, and in 1
Cor 5:7 it is used of Jesus. The term *thuein to pascha* is the technical expression in the
Septuagint for "to sacrifice the Passover," and translates two technical Hebrew verbs.
To what extent in the time of Jesus the particularly sacrificial element was being
muted in favor of the "later" emphasis on the shared meal as a commemoration of
deliverance, we do not know. Certainly in the Old Testament the offering of the
Passover lamb was regarded as sacrificial, and the meal which followed it was viewed
as a feast upon a sacrifice. We shall have occasion to examine the sacrificial implications of the narrative of the Last Supper later in the chapter.

13-14. *two of his disciples:* Luke 22:8 names the two as being Peter and John. They
are told *"Go into the city, . . ."* for the prescription of Deut 16:7 had centralized the
observance in Jerusalem. Given the thousands who flocked to the city for the feast, we
may wonder whether the precept to keep the feast in Jerusalem really meant in practice "within the city walls" (Hebrew *homa).* There is supporting evidence for interpreting "the city" as including the (imaginary) walls of Bethphage. If the Last Supper
was a Passover meal, care was taken to eat it within the city, even if the concluding
ritual prayers were accomplished outside it (though within the limits of what we may
usefully call "greater Jerusalem"). Cf. J. Jeremias, 1969, p. 101.

a man carrying a pitcher: The whole episode suggests some kind of prearrangement,
somewhat reinforced by Matt 26:18, which reads "Go to a certain man in the city.
. . ." It is also reminiscent of the arrangement made for the entry into the city at the
beginning of the week. It is difficult to know with certainty whether the man is an
unconscious signal, unless *meet you* (Greek *apantaō)* implies some kind of greeting.

The very fact of carrying a *jar of water* rather than a waterskin would make the man conspicuous (cf. Lagrange, p. 273), since only leather waterskins were carried by male water carriers. The suggestion of prior arrangement seems to be heavily underscored by such phrases as *wherever he goes in* and *"Where is the guest room . . ."* as well as by the simple identification of Jesus as *the rabbi.* There is no suggestion in the narrative of any kind of foreknowledge, though the two disciples may have been astonished at the turn of events.

guest room (Greek *kataluma):* Cf. Luke 2:7, 22:11. The word is found in 1 Sam 1:18, and means more than a lodging place (though that is the evident meaning of Luke 2:7).

Mark draws upon Luke closely here, while Matthew omits the story of the water carrier, and his version of the message to the householder (26:18) is: "my time is almost here: I will observe Passover at your house with my disciples." The omission by this evangelist of the meeting with the man raises again the question of a possible duplication of the Palm Sunday incident (Matt 21:1-3; Mark 11:1-3; Luke 19:28-31), but the difficulty cannot be resolved.

15. *large upstairs room* (Greek *anagaion):* The word is later, or *koinē,* Greek, and is common. Cf. *huperōon* in Acts 1:13, which has the same meaning. The impression gained is that the room had been well furnished for the occasion (Lagrange, p. 374, suggests carpets and divans). In fact the Greek word *stronnuō* (= "furnish") is used to describe the covering of seats or couches with rugs (cf. Ezek 23:41). However, the same Greek verb is also used of the act of spreading clothing and reeds in the path of Jesus at 11:8, and it is possible that the whole arrangement of the room may not have been very elaborate. All that the disciples were required to do was make the final arrangements.

16. The first part of this section ends abruptly at this verse, leaving a number of questions wholly unanswered. Having been told that the disciples *found everything just as he had told them* and then that *they prepared for Passover,* we are left without any information as to *what* they prepared. Was provision made for wine, water, the bitter herbs, reclining couches, lamps? And if the meal was a Passover meal, what disposition had been made for slaughtering the lamb and then roasting it? And what, too, of the baking of unleavened cakes? If the meal was eaten on the day before, then it would have had something of the character of a festive occasion. But if the Last Supper was not a Passover meal—and Matthew and Luke agree that it was—then the account before us simply narrates what had been intended. Everything in the narrative—the treachery of Judas, the preparations for the meal—must in consequence be pushed back in time, with the result that the synoptic chronology must be received with great caution, and the conclusion that the Supper was a Passover meal must be regarded as mistaken. Now, apart from the significant matter of Jesus' vigil in Gethsemane (which, as we shall see, offers some interesting insights), it is only in this chapter (and then only in vv. 12 and 16) that this evangelist, along with Matthew and Luke, suggests that the Supper was a Passover meal.

17. With this verse we enter another realm of difficulty. What purports to be a narrative contains a prophecy of the treachery of Judas, which appears to be a very abrupt intrusion into the narrative. We would have expected some mention of the return of the two disciples, and we would equally have expected an account of the

meal after v. 16. We are justified in seeing here two separate units, both beginning (in varying forms) with *as they were eating.* Evidently something has been displaced, and vv. 17-21 inserted. What that may have been is a matter for conjecture.

None of the above militates against the historical content of vv. 17-21. John's gospel states very clearly that Jesus had insight into the minds of those with whom he dealt (2:25), and the same gospel (6:70-71) has Jesus apparently recognizing the ambivalent character of Judas rather early in the ministry. (This seems to be an exercise in retrojection, however.) What is noteworthy in this narrative-prophecy is that Judas is nowhere even mentioned, still less condemned, and there is no suggestion that the disciples have any notion who the traitor might be. Luke's version (22:23) ends with the disciples questioning each other as to the identity of the traitor. John 13:21-30 makes only the Beloved Disciple privy to the traitor's name, and Jesus tells Judas (v. 27) to do quickly what he has to do. Matt 26:25 records Judas as asking, along with the others, "Is it I?" and being answered by Jesus with "The words are yours." Presumably, we are to understand in the Matthean story that the brief conversation took place in whispers, echoing the Johannine tradition that no one at table knew why Jesus had told Judas to go about his affairs quickly.

An admittedly very slender clue may be found for the original setting of this puzzling affair in John 2:25. That verse is set in the context of a Jerusalem Passover. So, too, is this brief narrative *if* (and only *if*) we treat the phrase *reclined at table* as necessarily indicating Passover (but see below). Was there a Passover celebration at which Jesus had referred prophetically to treachery and death, and the tradition transferred to a Passover season nearer to final betrayal and death? This suggestion is offered with considerable hesitation, but the Markan tradition is noteworthy in that not even transference to the present location has brought about the introduction of Judas's name.

When it was evening (cf. 1:32): Since evidently for the synoptists this is a Passover meal, then this is the time after sunset, and technically the beginning of 15 Nisan.

the Twelve: Either we are to assume that the two disciples of v. 13 have returned, or the expression is a conventional technicality. In the remainder of the passion story the technical phrase is used only to refer to *one of the Twelve* (14:10,20,43).

18. *As they reclined* (Greek *anakeimai,* "to recline at a meal"): The rubrics of Passover originally (Exod 12:11) had commanded that the meal be eaten in haste, and standing. But later ages modified the rule, and it became customary to eat the meal reclining as a sign of freedom from slavery. However, it is not legitimate to infer from the use of the verb that this establishes the Passover character of the meal. Reclining was the custom when entertaining guests, and also on other important (and secular) occasions (cf. Matt 22:10; Luke 5:29, 14:8,10; Mark 2:15, 6:26, 12:39, 14:3).

"In solemn truth . . .": For a note on this expression, see 3:28.

We shall have occasion to deal with table fellowship and the importance attached to it in the next section. It must suffice here to call attention to the pall of sorrow and horror cast by the idea that someone *(one of you eating with me)* could break table fellowship by treachery. The phrase may be a quotation from Ps 41:9 ("one eating bread with me") and it was so understood in John 13:18. However, the phrase is omitted in a few manuscripts of Mark, and is not found in Matthew (who is generally very alert to illuminating material from the Old Testament). It is possible that this phrase found its way into the text of Mark from John 13:18. John 13:21 reproduces the Markan saying, but omits the phrase *one of you eating with me.* Luke's version is independent: he tells us that when the hour had come Jesus "reclined at table and the apostles with him" (22:14). Then, after the first cup (vv. 15-18), the prediction of betrayal is entirely different, for it reads: "However, look—the hand of the traitor is with me on the table" (v. 21).

19. The consternation of the disciples at the breach of fellowship is dramatically presented, and the phrase *they became sorrowful* is a translation of the Greek *ērxanto* (literally, "they began to be sorrowful"), as though the awful notion were beginning to seize hold of them. The Greek of *one by one (eis kata eis)* has from time to time been cited as an example of a Semitism (Turner, pp. 540-41, accepts the idea hesitantly). But the Greek here is not very different from the *eis kath' ekastos* of Lev 25:10 (reflected in Matt 26:22: *eis ekastos),* and commonplace Greek further reduced this to *katheis.* Mark's Greek could never be described as literary, and his frequent Latinisms, along with his use of very commonplace Greek and impatience with precise grammatical construction, all combine to leave the reader from time to time bewildered as to whether the evangelist has used "translation Greek" from an independent source. Certainly Mark is noticeably more careful when drawing upon Matthew and Luke.

"It is not I . . .": This is a bewildered response, and there is no attempt on the part of any disciple to accuse another. Some manuscripts add "and another said, 'Surely it is not I?'" One manuscript adds "Rabbi" to the question, while Matthew's version has Jesus addressed as "Master." All of this makes for more uncertainty in our attempts to unravel the mysterious character of Judas. For granted an insight of Jesus into some flaw in the traitor, it is puzzling that apparently no one among the rest of the disciples had any inkling that Judas was potentially untrustworthy.

20. The reply of Jesus repeats the charge, makes no direct accusation, but with *one who is dipping bread in the same dish* underlines the heinous gravity of the treachery.

one who is dipping: The Greek verb *embaptō* occurs twice in Matt 26:23 and is repeated here in Mark. It is not classical and is not represented in the Septuagint. Matthew's version is somewhat different: "One who has dipped his hand in the dish— he will betray me." The developed form of the tradition in John 13:26 is: "It is the one to whom I give the piece of bread that I shall dip in the dish." Even here, there is no identification save privately to the Beloved Disciple.

dish (Greek trublion): Cf. Matt 26:23. The vessel is a bowl, rather than a dish. The word is classical, is found in the Septuagint, and is also in the papyri. We have used the Greek *en (in),* though it is in fact found in only four manuscripts of Mark, but is present in Matt 26:23. The use of the preposition emphasizes the terrible nature of the betrayal.

Commentaries often take the view that the bowl was the one containing the Passover dish of raisins, dates, and vinegar, but this obviously depends on an assumption that the dialogue took place in the context of a Passover meal.

Apart from noting the bewilderment manifested by the disciples that any one of their number should break the bonds of table fellowship by treachery, we are liable to pass by *one of you eating with me* and simply place it alongside *one who is dipping bread in the same dish.* However, an article on this very subject suggests a far deeper meaning than is apparent on the surface. F. C. Fensham ("Judas' Hand in the Bowl and Qumran," *Révue de Qumran* 5.1964-65, pp. 259-61) suggests that there is some important parallel material from Qumran. *The Rule of the Community* (1QS vi.1-8) prescribes, when food has been prepared, a hierarchical order in the reaching out of hands for food. In the author's view, the definitive *with me* may indicate that Judas, by not waiting his turn, deliberately denied the leadership of Jesus, and hence—to Jesus —marked himself as being in rebellion.

21. A commentary on a book of Scripture is hardly the place for a discussion more appropriate to the realm of philosophy, but we are confronted here with the acceptance by Jesus of *the way appointed for him* on the one hand and the instrumentality of Judas on the other. The relationship between the death of Jesus as a destiny ordained by God—and freely accepted by Jesus—and an evil human activity is also bound up in this verse. Judas was not a mere instrument, and the responsibility for the death was his, regardless of the ultimate good which issued from his choice. If here we are confronted with questions of causality and the relationship of human deeds to that causality—to the will of God—the present verse is more obviously concerned with the divine will and purpose and is content to state this without exploration.

Aside from such philosophical considerations, there are features in this verse which give pause to any easy acceptance of it as historical. To begin with, there is the statement that *The Man is going* (Greek *hupagei*, cf. 1:44). The verb is found on several occasions in John (8:14,21,22; 13:3,33; 14:4,28) and all in a technical sense as having to do with Jesus' origin and his return to the Father. Given the strongly Johannine character of the first part of this verse, it is not easy to conclude that it refers simply to a "going away." There is in addition the verb we have translated as *appointed for him in the Scriptures* (Greek *kathōs gegraptai peri autou*, literally, "as it is written about him"). This can be translated as "just as it has been written" in the sense of "decreed," or "appointed." In that case the meaning would be the destiny marked out for him by God. However, the frequency with which the verb is used in the remainder of the New Testament to refer to Scripture should give us pause before too hastily opting in favor of the sense of "destined" or "decreed." Above all, Acts (13:29,33; 15:15; 23:5; 24:14)—to mention no other book—uses the verb and its derivatives to describe testimony from Scripture in support of some event or circumstance dealing with Jesus and/or his followers. Even if we embrace a completely skeptical view with regard to the historicity of the early part of Acts, the evidence is there of the deliberate collection by the early community of "testimony" texts, both as reinforcement for community faith and as missionary texts for outsiders (cf. Acts 8:26-35). The "fulfillment" texts of Matthew are an obvious example of the creative use of Old Testament texts by the community.

In this context, the term *The Man* presents its own problems. While the debate surrounding the Greek *huios tou anthrōpou* (literally, "Son of Man") remains unresolved, we have urged in this commentary that it is best understood in the Danielic sense of a dual identity of individual/community, the fate of each being bound up with the other. In the present instance not only is there doubt as to the whole phrase *The Man is going the way* (to death, or to glory, or to both?); neither is there an obvious connection here between Jesus and the community, but only between Jesus and the traitor.

We are compelled to conclude that v. 21 is an early (perhaps even primitive) community "testimony" about Judas, linking the exaltation of *The Man* (see below in notes on 14:62) with the instrumentality of Judas on the one hand and the divine purpose on the other. How early this verse may be, we have no means of knowing. The Greek of Mark is almost identical with Matthew, whereas Luke 22:22 has "The Man does indeed go to his fate, but alas for the man by whom he is betrayed." Luke has *poreuetai* for the Matthean and Markan *hupagei* (see above) and makes no mention of the Scriptures.

This verse appears to have an early Semitic origin. The Greek *kalon* (= good) is undoubtedly used in the comparative sense *(better for him)*; the customary Greek *an mē* (a conditional negative) is omitted by Matthew and Mark and replaced by the simple negative *ouk* before *been born*. Finally, both Mark and Luke begin this verse (14:21 = Luke 22:22) with *hoti* (because), while Matt 26:24 omits it. It is so strange as a connective with the preceding verse that—not remarkably—many manuscripts omit the word, and others supply *kai* (and). We have retained the word, translating it as *For,* to alert the reader to our view that this verse was once part of a collection of testimonies about Judas and was later attracted to this place in the narrative.

78. The Institution of the Eucharist (14:22-26) = Matt 26:26-30; Luke 22:15-20; cf. 1 Cor 11:23-25

14 22 As they were eating, he took the bread, gave thanks, broke it, and gave it to them with the words, "Take this, this is my body." 23 Then, taking a cup, he gave thanks and gave it to them. They all drank from it. 24 He said to them, "This is my blood of the Covenant, which is poured out for the Community. 25 In solemn truth, I tell you I will never again drink of the fruit of the vine until that day when I drink the new wine in the Reign of God." 26 When they had sung a hymn, they went out to the Mount of Olives.

Comment

Within the compass of a commentary it is impossible—even if admitted as desirable—to compress into a few pages whole library shelves of comments, commentary, and controversy on the Last Supper and the Eucharist. But it is incumbent on the commentator to declare his hand at the outset of the discussion, rather than attempt to leave scattered clues in a prolixity of notes. This we now propose to do in summary form:

1. Attempts to find in the Last Supper an occasion other than Passover must accommodate some very awkward realities, not the least of which is the persistent use by Paul of Paschal imagery in 1 Corinthians, together with allusions in other letters.

2. If—and the word is used advisedly—we embrace the view sometimes put forward that the Johannine and synoptic chronologies can be reconciled by making the occasion a quasi-religious meal said to have been observed by small bands of teachers and pupils, we have still not explained the persistence of the Paschal motif.

3. Research over the past three decades into Essene calendrical observances has inclined some scholars to suggest that Jesus and the disciples held to a sectarian calendar for Passover. If this could ever be proved to be so, then at once the desire of Jesus for the secrecy of such an observance in Jerusalem is understandable.

4. The New Testament phrase "Lamb of God" in John's gospel, in 1 Peter, and Revelation must be explained if we reject the identification of the Last Supper with Passover. (C. H. Dodd's suggestion that "Lamb," when applied to Jesus, meant the "bellwether" of the flock encounters far too many difficulties to be tenable. See *The Interpretation of the Fourth Gospel*, Cambridge: Cambridge University Press, 1954, pp. 230-36.) Far more satisfactory is the more recent study of Raymond E. Brown, *The Gospel According to John I-XII* (AB Vol. 29, Garden City, N.Y., Doubleday, 1966, Section 3, pp. 58-64). Whatever the origins of Passover, by the time of Jesus sacrificial ideas had taken firm hold of the festival, partly due to the centralization of the cult in Jerusalem, and partly also due to the exclusive part played by the temple clergy in the slaughter of the lambs. Nowhere in the New Testament is the sacrificial emphasis of Passover better illustrated than in Paul's arresting phrase "The Messiah, our Passover, has been sacrificed for us . . ." (1 Cor 5:7).

5. The key phrase *blood of the Covenant* (cf. Matt 26:28 and in Luke 22:20 where it is added in most manuscripts, thereby making two cups, and 1 Cor 11:25 as the source of Luke) is not easily explained apart from the dramatic rehearsal of the pre-Christian Haggadah to give it both place and meaning. The emphasis given to the same phrase in Hebrews 9 links it firmly with Sinai, but with no other covenant.

6. We call attention briefly—as lying strictly outside the realm of this commentary—to the phrase "for my memorial" (1 Cor 11:24-25 and Luke's accommodation to the Pauline tradition at 22:19-20). Unless the Last Supper was linked to a celebration which rehearsed God's acts in vindicating his people, it is difficult to see why the phrase was already fixed in the tradition by the time Paul wrote to Corinth. (For a short and useful summary in English, cf. Max Thurian, *The Eucharistic Memorial, Part II: The New Testament,* London: Lutterworth Press, 1961; Richmond, Va.: John Knox Press, 1961.) In this connection it is worth a passing notice that Passover was far more than a mere act of recollection: "In every single generation, it is a man's duty to regard himself as if he had gone forth from Egypt . . ." *(The Haggadah,* with notes by Cecil Roth, London: The Soncino Press, 1959, p. 36).

7. R. Le Deant in "De nocte Paschali" *(Verbum Domini* 41.1963, pp. 189-95) calls attention to a Targum on Exod 12:42, which speaks of the four nights of Passover commemoration: "The night when God appeared in order to create the world, the night when he promised Isaac to Abraham and Sarah, the night when Egypt was destroyed, and the eschatological night when the world will end." Here again is a link with the earliest tradition of the Last Supper (1 Cor 11:25) and perhaps also with John 13:30, not to mention Essene views of the Covenant.

8. A further discussion of the connection between Passover and the Last Supper will occur later in the narrative on Gethsemane.

It is manifestly not the task of a commentary either to provide an overview of the history of interpretations of the Eucharist down the Christian centuries; still less is it the task of the commentator to suggest ways in which such interpretations might be evaluated in the light of contemporary knowledge. But it *is* the duty of a commentator to examine the narrative of the Last Supper in the light of the best knowledge we currently have of the milieu in which the Last Supper took place, and from which the Christian institution of the Eucharist has grown. Before we begin our examination, one caution must be made. In the whole history of interpretation, both of the Last Supper and of the Eucharist, the situation has constantly been obscured and even distorted (especially in Western Christendom) by a massive and often exclusive concentration on *This is my body* and *This is my blood.* Unless we can divorce our minds from this preoccupation, we shall be in danger of isolating the Last Supper from the whole ministry of Jesus which gave it meaning.

Not only will we seriously misconstrue the character of the Last Supper if we regard it as an isolated event in the ministry, we shall also misunderstand it unless we pay careful attention to what was implied by table fellowship in the Near East and in Judaism in particular. Table fellowship was an outward sign that peace, trust, and even amnesty prevailed. (From the Old Testament some examples come to mind—Gen 26:30, 31:54, and with respect to amnesty and forgiveness, 2 Kgs 25:27-29.) The reader will recall that it was a constant complaint against Jesus that he shared meals with the socially undesirable and with nonobservant Jews, and this bears eloquent testimony of the importance attached to the symbolism of shared meals.

The distinctive feature which marked Judaism off from the surrounding cultures in the time of Jesus was the element of prayer, of "giving thanks" for fellowship at table, and for the provision of food. The formula known to us in modern Judaism has endured through the centuries, and has an ancient prayer as the head of the table takes a piece of bread and breaks it: "Blessed art thou, O Lord our God, ruler of the universe, thou who bringest bread from the earth." The symbolic sharing of the bread conveyed the blessing of peace and fellowship. Similarly, at the end of the meal there was a further blessing: "Blessed be our God, he of whose bounty we have partaken, and through whose goodness we live." After a response the one who presided over the meal took in his hand the "cup of blessing" and recited a further thanksgiving for God's goodness to the world, for the land itself, and for Jerusalem (both the city and temple). The response "Amen" and the sharing of the cup effected a community of blessing and of fellowship. The importance of all this in the ministry of Jesus is obvious. Not only was the fellowship of Jesus and his disciples so cemented and sustained, the same symbol of table fellowship provided fuel for critics who charged Jesus with sharing that fellowship with undesirables and the nonobservant.

The ministry of Jesus brought a further dimension to table fellowship. A lack of awareness on our part of the importance of table fellowship and all its symbolism may blind us to the implications which are to be found in our sources. It is not simply that Jesus finds in the fellowship of the disciples a substitute family for the families they had had to forgo (Mark 10:29-30), but he is the head of this new family and its new table (Matt 10:25, Mark 3:34), along with all those neophytes which the ministry brought in (Matt 10:25, Mark 10:24). In this context we must see the significance of the presence at the table of the "sinners" and the outcasts. For him, the eschatological age of salvation and pardon has arrived, and provides ample explanation for Zacchaeus' thankfulness (Luke 19:1-10) as also for the ire of the Pharisees (Mark 2:16).

To understand the importance of this shared blessing at meals, we recall first the conviction of Paul that the denial of fellowship at the table was a denial of God (Rom 14:1-15:3, Gal 2:11-21), but this in its turn sprang from what had been symbolized at the Last Supper. Not only did that supper have very strong eschatological overtones (v. 25), it was the gathering up of all the

meaning with which Jesus had invested the ministry. This is heavily reinforced by the acknowledgment by Peter of Jesus' messiahship (8:29). The
Proclamation of a dawning Reign of God was arresting in its simplicity,
however indebted to and inherited from the Baptizer it may have been. But
that the enthusiastic spokesman for the Twelve should apprehend some
deeper meaning to both the person and ministry inevitably meant that table
fellowship itself acquired deeper meaning. At least it meant that the coming
Reign of God must now be associated with messianic deliverance (salvation)
and pardon. The significance of the common meal as a sign of unity and peace
now perforce has added to it the anticipation of the age of blessings.

It is against all this background that we must understand the Last Supper
as the last in a whole series of meals, itself looking toward the consummation
of an already proclaimed salvation.

The earliest account we have of the Last Supper, and the earliest interpretation of its meaning, is from Paul (1 Cor 11:23-25), and even that account
exhibits linguistic traits which are not Pauline. The apostle himself tells us
that he received a tradition which he passed on to the Corinthian congregation (1 Cor 11:23), and it fully confirms the essential structure of the formal
setting of table fellowship. We have the broken bread at the thanksgiving
before the meal and the shared cup "after supper" to mark the blessing after
food. At the same time this primitive eucharistic pattern of "took, gave
thanks, broke, and gave" left its mark on the accounts of the feedings in our
gospels (Mark 6:30-44, 8:1-10 & par.). (The various texts of the Last Supper
narrative are presented in columnar form in the comment before Chapter 14,
to which the reader is now referred.)

We are of course primarily concerned with the Markan version, but there
are features in the other synoptic versions to which we must call attention.
The Markan text is verbally very close to Matthew in the Greek, though with
a change of tense in 14:22 and the omission of Matthew's (26:28) "for the
forgiveness of sins." The Lucan version (22:19-20) is much closer to Paul (1
Cor 11:23-25). But differences in the texts of the synoptics and Paul fade into
insignificance against the manifest agreement in three significant areas: (1)
They are unanimous in recording that Jesus compared the broken bread with
his body; (2) they are unanimous in recording that Jesus compared the wine
with his blood, and that through his blood the New Covenant would be
inaugurated; and (3) they are unanimous in declaring that the body/blood
will be offered for the community.

All of this is impressive unanimity, not the least in that both the stylized
liturgical formulations of Paul and the narrative forms of the synoptists carry
us back to a tradition belonging to the earliest days of the community. The
tradition then, as it has come to us in our sources, belongs to the time of Jesus
himself. But this conclusion, important though it is, leaves us with questions
arising from the tradition itself.

This final table fellowship in the ministry differs radically from all the others in various ways, however closely the key words in its narrative are linked with the feedings in all four gospels. To begin with, this Last Supper was confined to the inner circle of the Twelve. But most importantly words of interpretation are linked with the thanksgivings before and after the meal. Obviously the words announce the coming passion (the blood will be *poured out*). What is surprising to us is that, unlike the announcement of treachery, these words of interpretation apparently evoked no surprise on the part of the disciples. This absence of any sense of the unexpected becomes far more understandable if the Last Supper was to be regarded in the context of the Passover meal, and we can summarize the evidence for this as follows:

1. The prescriptions for Passover in Exod 12:26-27 and 13:8 require that at each celebration the father of the family was to explain the reasons for the gathering, and bring to mind the redemption of the people.

2. The custom of explaining the particular manner of the meal was faithfully observed and remains to this day.

3. In Jesus' time on the afternoon before the full moon of Nisan, thousands of lambs were brought to the temple courts of Jerusalem to be slaughtered, commemorating the deliverance of the Hebrews from Egypt (cf. Exod 12:21-25).

4. The Passover meal began after sunset in families and in groups such as that of Jesus and his disciples. The meal began with bitter herbs and a fruit relish. The roasted lamb was brought in but was not yet eaten. This was the occasion for the head of the gathering to explain the particular features of the meal. This obligation was treated with great emphasis, and Rabbi Gamaliel (claimed as Paul's teacher in Acts 22:3) insisted that the Passover command was not observed unless three things were explained: the Paschal lamb, the unleavened bread, and the bitter herbs.

5. Interpretations were not invariable or fixed. The unleavened cakes might be explained as exemplifying the haste with which the Hebrews left their exile (so leaving no time for the dough to rise), or as signifying the "bread of affliction" (Ps 80:5), or even as a contrast to the abundance to be expected in the Age of Blessings to come.

6. What we appear to have, therefore, in the words of interpretation used by Jesus with the bread and cup is nothing more nor less than the customary exercise by a head of household at Passover. There may be some reminiscence of Passover interpretations in the extended dialogues of John 6 and 15, but this can at best be only conjecture.

While we may be reasonably certain of the viability of our hypothesis about what have come to be called "the words of institution," we are nevertheless compelled to ask how Jesus understood the sayings. This is especially important in that these are two isolated sayings from what was presumably a more extended exposition. We are safe in asserting that the expression "body and blood" or "flesh and blood" (John 6:53) are sacrificial terms. So too is the expression "poured out" in connection with the Covenant (cf. Exod 24:8). It is difficult to imagine this very precise use of sacrificial language apart from some assumption that Jesus referred to the lambs of Passover as pointing to himself in his whole self-giving ministry, now to be consummated in death, a death which would usher in the New Covenant.

Unless this association of the Passover lamb was made by Jesus, it is difficult to explain the promptitude with which the early Christians identified Jesus as the Christian Paschal lamb. 1 Cor 5:7-8 presents us with the unleavened bread of pure self-offering because the Passover feast, the eschatological feast, has already begun, and Jesus as the lamb has already been sacrificed. We must also not overlook the salient fact that in the entire sacrificial system of Judaism the lamb was the only animal associated with *the* divine act of redemption and deliverance. Though the Greek word used for "lamb" in Revelation *(arnion)* is not the same as that used in other contexts—John 1:29,36; Acts 8:32; and 1 Pet 1:19—it is relevant to ask whence was derived the notion of the slain lamb, if not from the Passover and from its links with Jesus' self-designation.

Finally the sacrificial death of Jesus is described in our sources as vicarious. Mark follows Matthew in saying *poured out for the community,* whereas Luke follows Paul in saying "given for you." John's gospel speaks of the flesh which would be given "for the life of the world" (6:51), though this Johannine example is only marginally sacrificial. Granted that by the time of Jesus, Passover had become a feast upon a sacrifice, and sacrificial ideas were more and more associated with it, we would search in vain in the contemporaneous literature for any notion of Passover as an expiatory sacrifice. Yet Paul uses phrases such as "died for our sins" to describe the work of Jesus (1 Cor 15:3, cf. Rom 6:10). The Johannine tradition has John the Baptizer describing Jesus as "the lamb of God that takes away the sin of the world." We must, therefore, try to determine the source of this association of ideas: Jesus' table fellowship, the idea of Passover as sacrifice, or the notion of the Passion and death of Jesus as expiatory. The second has been examined already, and the Last Supper must (as we have said) be understood in the context of the other examples of table fellowship in the ministry. But the meaning of the final meal, interpreted as linking it with a sacrificial death of expiation, can only have come from Jesus himself. Paul's account in 1 Cor 11 is already a liturgical formula; it is older than our written gospel accounts, and its vicarious sacrificial element is firmly established. Yet Paul insists that he received this in the tradition of the community. Our gospel accounts of the Last Supper are in *narrative* form, and such a form by its very nature is earlier than the *liturgical* text of Paul. It is impossible—though the attempt has been made more than once—to attribute the idea of a vicarious, expiatory death to some supposed Hellenistic "savior god" myth utilized by Paul. Savior gods had never been a serious feature of Greek religion, and an attempted importation of such a motif among the predominantly Jewish members of Paul's congregations would have been an act of consummate folly.

The explanation offered by Jesus at this final Passover meal is his and his alone. Without entering into later eucharistic controversy, which concentrated (often with dire consequences) upon the so-called "words of institution," we must again beware of investing those words of interpretation with declaratory meanings they were not designed to carry. This will be examined in the notes below.

Finally, it should be noted that the Passover meal with its blessings over bread and cup was not only the principal act of table fellowship in the year but also carried an eschatological promise of a coming age of blessings. Attention should also be paid to the words of interpretation over bread and cup, and the participation of the disciples in eating and drinking. All of these words and acts, taken together, are a demonstration proleptically of a share in the Age of Blessings, but also of participation in the redemptive death of Jesus.

Notes

22. We appear to have two separate pieces of tradition joined together, in vv. 18-21 and 22-25. *As they were eating* is found in both, but which account originally stood alone we cannot determine. The Last Supper formula in 1 Cor 11:23-26 stands as a separate account, prefaced only by "in the night in which he was betrayed." Mark's use of *kai* (and) is so frequent that its use as the first word in this verse provides no help. (Parenthetically the absence from Mark of the Greek particles *de* and *gar* may indicate a Palestinian provenance for his tradition.)

he took the bread: The Greek word for bread *(artos)* can be applied to both leavened and unleavened bread and is, therefore, of no assistance in determining whether the meal was a Passover celebration or not.

gave thanks (Greek *eulogēsas*): Cf. 6:41. The prevalence to this day of the form "blessed" in many English-language eucharistic liturgies serves to obscure the fact that in Jewish usage the act is a thanksgiving to God for his blessings. Cf. "Blessed art thou, O Lord our God, King of the universe, thou who bringest bread from the earth." Luke has the participle *eucharistēsas* (22:19), which is also the word at Mark 8:6. Paul (1 Cor 11:23) has the same participle.

broke it (Greek *klaō*): Cf. 8:6,19.

gave it to them: In contrast with the accounts of the feedings in Chapters 6 and 8, it is Jesus who distributes the broken bread. Matt 26:26 adds "to the disciples."

"Take this . . .": Matthew adds "eat," and some lesser manuscripts of Mark have added this command to the Markan text. Equally one Latin manuscript, in imitation of the next verse, adds *et manducaverunt ex illo omnes* (they all partook of it).

". . . this is my body": These words of interpretation are in their shortest form in Matthew and Mark. Paul adds "which is for you" (1 Cor 11:24). Luke, following the Pauline tradition, has "which is given for you" (17:19). All the words are heavily sacrificial; the expression *my body* has reference to a final act of surrender in death. The Lucan and Pauline "which is for you" are but explanatory expansions of the bare statement *this is my body.* Even so, the explanatory phrases serve to underline the sacrificial intent of the words of Jesus. The Greek *touto (this)* clearly means the broken loaf, and *to sōma mou (my body)* points to the life of Jesus given over to death on behalf of the people of the New Covenant.

A satisfactory translation for the Greek *estin* (is) almost defies ingenuity. The verb would not have been present in Aramaic, and the provision of it in Greek and later in Latin was for many centuries responsible for doctrinal controversies occasioned by the belief that *is* was a statement of identity. The most satisfactory understanding of the phrase would seem to be "Take this: this means my body." This has the definite advantage of emphasizing the connection Jesus makes between his life, which is about to be offered, and the bread he has taken and broken. There is here prophetic symbolism, and yet more than symbolism: ". . . often the actions. . . . are 'effective representations' for bringing about that which is depicted" (Vincent Taylor, *Jesus and His Sacrifice,* London: Macmillan, reprinted 1943, p. 118). The Old Testament tradition is replete with such examples—Isa 20:2; Jer 19:10, 27:10; and Ezek 4:3. Cf. also 1 Kgs 22:11 and, in the New Testament, Acts 21:11.

The bread is to be taken and eaten, and the command heavily underscores the sacrificial intent of the words employed. The sharing of sacrificial food offered to God (or the gods) has been a religious practice from time immemorial. In the Hebrew tradition only the sin offerings and guilt offerings were outside the practice of the "feast-upon-a-sacrifice." By means of partaking of the food offered to God on their behalf, the participants also shared in the blessings issuing from the observance. It is against this background that we are to understand the actions of Jesus: the breaking of the bread, the giving of thanks, the distribution of the broken pieces to the disciples— all combined to provide the means by which they were to share in the effects of his redemptive self-offering. Understood in this sense, we are firmly in the Hebrew biblical tradition and in the post-biblical tradition of Jesus himself, and interpreting the word of the gospels without references to the tortuous debates of succeeding centuries about the "presence" of Jesus in the eucharistic elements.

23. *gave thanks:* Cf. 8:6. The identification of the *cup* (Greek *potērion*) with the noncustomary third "cup of blessing," at the Passover meal is not certain, and a similar expression in 1 Cor 10:16 ("the cup of blessing") can hardly be taken as such an identification. Matthew and Mark mention only one cup, and this has often been taken as an indication that the Last Supper was not a Passover meal. Luke certainly refers to two cups, but this of itself does not resolve the problem. Jeremias (see the appended note "For My Memorial" at the end of this section) and Lagrange (p. 379)

hold that the evidence for Passover customs in the first century is far too slight to determine the number and possible significance of the cups employed. The attempts by some commentators to identify the *cup* in this narrative with the cup of blessing for the Sabbath is not helpful: the difficulties of the timetable of this final week are formidable, without adding to them a suggestion of a kind of "anticipated" Sabbath. Enough was said earlier in the comment to this section, to make clear the conviction of this commentator that the Last Supper can most easily be explained as a Passover observance, and it will not here be argued again.

They all drank from it: Presumably this expression indicates a single cup, though this again is of no assistance in determining the character of the meal. Matt 26:27 has an injunction: "All of you drink from this." Some discussion arises from time to time as to the meaning to be attached to the narrative statement here, and the command in Matthew, with the suggestion made from time to time that what is reflected is a polemic against some practice unknown to us. This is perhaps searching for a controversy where none can be found: it is far more likely that the words reflect the sharing of the disciples in the blessings of the (New) Covenant. Furthermore in strong contrast to the material which precedes this narrative, there is no discernible note of controversy here.

24. *my blood of the Covenant* (Greek *haima mou tēs diathēkēs):* Cf. Exod 24:8, Zech 9:11. In the first of these two references, the sprinkling of the blood of the sacrificial animal secured for the participants the blessings of the Sinai Covenant. Taylor (in *Jesus and His Sacrifice,* p. 138) remarks ". . . His life, surrendered to God and accepted by Him, is offered to, and made available to men." The wine is not only the symbol of the *blood of the Covenant,* it is the sign and sacrament through which the Covenant is received and sustained (cf. Exod 24:11). We appear to have yet another link with Passover at this point: God redeemed Israel from slavery, a deliverance symbolized by the Passover blood, and now in the end-time the people of the New Covenant will be consecrated in the blood of Jesus to a new life.

Covenant (Greek *diathēkē):* Cf. Matt 26:28; Luke 1:72, 22:20; Acts 3:25, 7:8; Rom 9:4, 11:27; 1 Cor 11:25; 2 Cor 3:6,14; Gal 3:15,17; 4:24; Eph 2:12; Heb 7:22, 8:6,8,9,10; 9:4,15,16,17,20; 12:24; 13:20; Rev 11:19. In classical Greek the term means "will" or "testament" in the sense generally understood now. It is found in this sense in the papyri. It is sometimes (though perhaps doubtfully) suggested that this is the meaning in Heb 9:15,16,17. In the New Testament and throughout the Septuagint, the meaning is "Covenant," a translation of the Hebrew *b'rîth.* There is every reason to understand the term in the New Testament as carrying with it implicitly the expression "the Reign of God." The Greek word in the New Testament directly derives from the Old Testament usage. There was a word in classical Greek for "Covenant," but that word, *sunthēkē,* had far too much of the meaning of a mutual contract to render the sense of the Hebrew. In essence, the Hebrew idea of Covenant, with its ancestry in ancient near-eastern cultures, was that of the "suzerainty treaty" by which the client people bound themselves in obedience to their Lord and protector. Israel understood herself as having been chosen by God as his peculiar possession, and herself as accordingly bound to a relationship of trusting obedience. The Covenant between God and Israel was signified by the "blood of the Covenant," first in circumcision and then in the

Covenant of Sinai. Jesus makes the link with the Israelite Covenant by the use of *my* in the phrase *blood of the Covenant.*

poured out (Greek *to ekchunnomenon):* Cf. Mark 10:45; Matt 23:35, 26:28; Luke 5:37, 11:50, 22:20; Acts 1:18, 10:45, 22:20; Rom 5:5; Jude 11. The participle is used, as it would be in Hebrew and Aramaic, in a future sense (cf. Lohmeyer, p. 308).

for the Community: It is hoped that enough was said in regard to this phrase in the notes on 10:45 to obviate further discussion here. The reader is referred to those notes.

Matt 26:28 has in addition "for the forgiveness of sins" (Greek *eis aphesin hamartiōn).* The linking of forgiveness with a New Covenant is prominent in Jer 31:31-34, but it is important to remember that there is no mention of sacrificial blood in the Jeremiac context, and rabbinic writings which conjoin "blood" and "Covenant" are concerned with circumcision more often than with anything else. Jesus is never represented in our sources as inaugurating a separatist movement, and the Pauline letters (for all their insistence on the word "new" to describe God's act in Jesus) never describe the Church as "the new Israel." Jesus, then, voluntarily pours out his life for the community of Israel, and in so doing inaugurates a New Covenant for a Covenant Community already in being.

The phraseology of Matthew and Mark is almost identical, save that Matthew has *peri* instead of Mark's *huper* (for, on behalf of). In assimilation to Matthew, some lesser manuscripts of Mark add the explanatory "for the forgiveness of sins," and some other few manuscripts of Mark have taken over Matthew's *peri.* The same understanding of *for the Community* is mirrored in 1 Cor 11:24 and in Luke's "which is given for you" (22:19).

The relationship between the synoptic gospels and the Pauline accounts is, and has been for many years, a matter of debate. 1 Cor 11:25 has: "This cup is the new Covenant in my blood." Certainly "this cup" has reference to the contents of the cup. Taylor *(Jesus and His Sacrifice,* pp. 203-6) gives preference to Mark's version as more original, but Lohmeyer (p. 306) is hesitant. The Markan and Matthean versions have often been questioned on account of the impossibility of rendering *this is my blood of the Covenant* in Aramaic. J. A. Emerton has suggested new possibilities about what is, or is not, impossible in Aramaic. Jesus, he suggests, used the rare but entirely permissible "construction of genitive after a noun with a pronominal suffix" (a very common construction in later Syriac). This, the author goes on to suggest, was to avoid any suggestion that the Covenant was of Jesus' own making; he was but the instrument and the vehicle of its inauguration through his blood—the Covenant was of God's own making. (Cf. J. A. Emerton, "The Aramaic Underlying *to haima mou tēs diathēkēs* in Matt 14:24," *JTS* 6.1955, pp. 238-40, and *"to haima mou tēs diathēkēs:* The Evidence of the Syriac Versions," *JTS* 3.1962, pp. 111-17.)

The distinctive note in the Pauline form is the adjective "new," before *Covenant,* which recalls Jer 31:31. Some Markan manuscripts add the adjective by way of assimilation to the Pauline account, and the same is true of some manuscripts of Matthew. Cf. Cullmann, *The Christology of the New Testament,* English translation, pp. 64-66.

25. *In solemn truth:* Cf. 3:28.

In Matthew and Luke there are parallels to this eschatological saying, and in Paul the account of the institution of the Eucharist has ". . . you proclaim the Lord's death until he comes" (1 Cor 11:26). The Lucan account (22:16) is prefaced by "I tell you I will not eat it again until it is fulfilled in the Reign of God."

The whole vocabulary, and the ideas associated with it, are thoroughly Jewish, even to the *amēn* with which the verse opens. The notion of a "messianic" banquet in the Reign of God, apart from references in the New Testament, is well represented in the Hebrew and Jewish traditions: cf. Isa 25:6; *1 Enoch* 62:14; *2 (Apoc) Bar* 29:5; 4 Ezra 6:51; *Pirqê Abôth* 3:20. In the New Testament, cf. Matt 8:11; Luke 14:15, 22:29; Rev 19:9. Even the use of the phrase *fruit of the vine* (Greek *genēma tou ampelou)* to refer to "wine" is wholly Semitic, as is the expression *until that day.* Equally, some variant manuscripts' readings for *when I drink the new wine in the kingdom of God* shed some light on a possible Hebrew construction behind our Greek. (The English translation can hardly mirror those variant readings.) One important manuscript has *ou mē prosthō pein,* reflecting a constant Septuagintal usage of *prostheto* with the infinitive as an equivalent of *palin* (again). This is admittedly found in but one Markan manuscript. Most lean heavily either to *ouketi ou mē piō* (I will no longer drink) or *ou mē piō* (I will not drink). The first of these does render *ou mē prostho pein* correctly, but the second is a misinterpretation of the meaning. What Jesus asserts is that he will not again drink wine until the consummation in the Reign of God.

fruit of the vine: The expression is found in the Septuagint at Gen 40:17 and elsewhere. In the New Testament, the popular word *genēma* (as distinct from *gennema* = "offspring") is found at Matt 26:29; Luke 12:18, 22:18; and 2 Cor 9:10.

The Matthean version of this verse is much fuller. It has "from now on" as a qualification of "I will not drink" and the Matthean "when I drink new wine" adds "with you." Matthew characteristically has "in my Father's Kingdom" at the end of the verse. The shorter Lucan version has "I shall not drink wine until the Kingdom of God comes."

When we have said that the saying—in whatever form—looks forward beyond the death of Jesus to the fellowship of the Reign of God, and that sharing in the drinking of the cup is a token of anticipation of that Reign, we have by no means resolved all the questions which this verse engenders. Does this saying, in its present context, reflect the actual historical situation, or was the verse attracted to its present context from another occasion? What is meant by the Lucan saying of "until the Kingdom of God comes"? The uncertainty displayed in Acts and the earlier Pauline letters as to the precise meaning of the "coming" of The Man may be at work in Luke 22:16,18. The "coming" of the Reign of God, in the exaltation of Jesus to the Father, would certainly mean the fulfillment of Passover. 1 Cor 11:26 apparently reflects a shift from this primary meaning to an expected *second* manifestation of Jesus, this time in the glory of heaven. To compound the difficulties, the present writer, together with the late W. F. Albright, contended in the AB *Matthew,* pp. lxxxi-lxxxviii, that there is a discernible distinction in Matthew between the Kingdom of The Man as a temporary, messianic phenomenon on the one hand, and the final, perduring Kingdom of the Father. If that distinction is valid, then the saying in Matthew looks beyond a Reign of the Messiah to final fulfillment in the Reign of the Father. In all of this, is there a misunderstanding of an original saying, transformed by Matthew and Luke into some remote anticipation, and which Mark (by foreshortening the verse) restored to its original intent by concentrating on death/exaltation?

Two final possibilities remain, and each is offered with considerable hesitation. First the vine as a symbol of Israel is well known throughout the Old Testament. It is at least possible that behind the sayings as we now have them there may have been a saying which spoke in terms of the fulfillment of Israel in the Kingdom, in much the same way as Paul speaks of it in Romans 11. Second does this verse belong originally to the Passover season of the year *before* this final week, which in process of time and of flawed memory attached itself to the narrative of the Last Supper? Unfortunately to all of these questions we have at present no answer.

It would be fair to say that libraries have been written on vv. 22-25, and a bibliography would be daunting to the general reader. Apart from the various commentaries on the individual gospels, this writer would say without hesitation that the one indispensable tool is the work referred to more than once above: *The Eucharistic Words of Jesus* by Joachim Jeremias. It has the supreme advantage of meticulous footnotes and a thorough examination of all the theological factors, New Testament and otherwise, which have combined to make the whole topic a matter of intense debate. Reference has also been made to Vincent Taylor's *Jesus and His Sacrifice,* and Chapter 6 of Part I will serve as a good introduction to the subject. An invaluable book by Gustav Aulén *(Eucharist and Sacrifice,* translation by Eric H. Wahlstrom of *For eder utgiven,* London and Edinburgh: Oliver and Boyd, 1958) has a useful summary of the New Testament evidence, pp. 115-55. The standard reference works such as *TWNT* are indispensable for the reader who knows Greek. In general most works on the history of liturgy deal with the Last Supper and what may be gleaned from the New Testament, but many come from denominational presuppositions.

26. *When they had sung a hymn:* Assuming that this was a Passover celebration, the *hymn* would be the *Hallel* (Psalms 113-18): it is still used in the formal Jewish rite, as it was in the time of Jesus. It is misleading to attempt to accommodate the New Testament account to the modern Jewish *seder,* or indeed to any existing Passover *Haggadah.* The reader's attention is called to the suggestions made by David Daube in *The New Testament and Rabbinic Judaism* (Jordan Lectures, 1952, London: University of London, Athlone Press, 1956, pp. 186-95). Daube, accepting the common view that the Passion narrative was the first part of the tradition to achieve fixed form, suggests that Jewish Christians, in maintaining the original order of the Passover meal (ceremonial meal, questions, interpretation of the meal), so emphasized the changed nature of the observance that the whole order was deliberately changed by orthodox Jews. "By relegating the meal to the end, the rabbis took the life, or at least any undue vitality, out of it . . . The change round was a very clever means of any fundamentally new significance being attached to the meal . . ." (pp. 194-95). It is also possible that the emphasis by the Essenes on their understanding of the "Covenant" may have served to accelerate the change.

they went out: The Passover celebration was not confined to a single location. The meal could be eaten in one place, and the recital of prayers, hymns, etc., could be held in another, provided that the company remained together.

Appended Note: "For My Memorial"

Though this phrase is Lucan (22:19, Greek *eis tēn emēn anamnēsin*) and Pauline (1 Cor 11:24,25, with the same Greek used of both bread and cup) and not part of the Markan text, it has entered into the liturgical usages of many major denominations. For that reason it seems fitting to pay some summary attention to this interpretive phrase.

1. Aside from the unsatisfactory nature of most English translations, with the very poor connotation of "remembrance" confined to a mental exercise, it is inherently unlikely that the Christian community could *forget* Jesus.

2. The Hebrew vocabulary for "remembering" or "memorializing" in a liturgical setting was a recalling before God, praying that *God* would remember his mercies to his people, and in so remembering would act for his people (cf. Lev 24:7 and the titles of Pss 38:1, 70:1). Ps 132:1 is a very good example: the sufferings of David are being memorialized before God, so that God may remember and bless David. Cf. also Sir 45:9,11,16, 50:16, *1 Enoch* 99:3. In liturgical usage, now and certainly in the time of Jesus, something (generally a sacrificial offering) was brought before God, and the "memorial" prayers brought the past into the present. As God "remembers," he acts for blessing or judgment, and when God no longer "remembers" sin, he forgives it.

3. It is important to remember that the Covenant is fellowship. It looks to the past, to the establishment of the Covenant, and "memorializes" the past before God, thereby making a present reality. The Covenant also looks to the future, to the consummation of God's purposes in making it.

4. Israel memorialized the Exodus before God and memorialized the Sinai Covenant through Passover—the annual making present of a past event, calling on God to "remember" the election of the people. By so doing, the memorial looked to the future, to a consummation either in blessing or judgment.

5. The command "do this" is found as a rubrical direction for the performance of a rite in the Old Testament, and it is also found in the Qumran texts. Cf. Exod 29:35, Num 15:11-13, Deut 25:9. This rubric, in the setting of the Last Supper, can hardly refer to the words of interpretation over bread and cup and certainly cannot refer to the whole meal, since the phrase is repeated. Moreover if we are dealing with a Passover meal, it would be a totally superfluous command to Jews. The limiting clause in Paul ("as often as you eat this bread . . . ," 1 Cor 11:26) also effectively rules out an injunction to repeat the rite. What is plainly meant is the "memorial" prayers of blessing. These would not have been the customary table prayers (for which no injunction would have been necessary) but some table blessing which bound that small community together in God's saving acts through Jesus, and which looked to a future

consummation of those acts in the End. We may confidently say that the formula of blessing (whatever it may originally have been) had an independent existence from the beginning. The "breaking of bread and blessing of cup" were wholly distinctive and separated from common meals by a "memorial" which declared the meaning of what was happening. The infant community was to continue to "memorialize" before God the dawning Reign inaugurated through Jesus. The "Proclamation" of which Paul speaks in 1 Cor 11:26 was not to remind the community, but to recall to God the as yet unfulfilled hope of consummation. God is "reminded" of that sacrificial ministry of oblation, sacramentalized in the cross, which was the community's ground of hope for the future act of God for final salvation.

The above material, together with a fresh examination of the textual evidence, is meticulously scrutinized in a recent work: Xavier Leon-Dufour, S.J., *Le partage du pain eucharistique; Selon le Nouveau Testament,* Paris: Editions du Seuil, 1982.

79. Jesus Foretells Peter's Denial (14:27-31) = Matt 26:31-35; Luke 22:31-34; John 13:36-38

14   27 Jesus said to them, "All of you will stumble, for it is written:
'I will strike the shepherd down
and the sheep will be scattered.'
28 But after I am raised up, I will go to Galilee ahead of you." 29 But Peter said, "Even though all others fall away, yet I will not." 30 "In solemn truth I tell you," Jesus answered him, "this very night, before the cock crows twice, even you will disown me three times." 31 "If I have to die with you," he said vehemently, "I will not disown you!" They all replied in the same terms.

Comment

Matthew and Mark both have this short narrative following upon v. 26, *When they had sung a hymn, they went out to the Mount of Olives.* The narrative itself, in both evangelists, is composed almost entirely of sayings: a quotation from Zech 13:7, the promise to precede the disciples into Galilee, the protestation of Peter, and the prophecy of Peter's defection. The short section ends with the statement that the rest of the disciples identified themselves with Peter's vehement protest. The narrative is closely knit, though v. 28 has all the marks of an intrusion into it. The proximity of this pericope to the story of the denial (14:54,66-72) tends to suggest that the present narrative may depend on an original Petrine reminiscence, and the psychological escalation from v. 29 to v. 31 supports this. Luke 22:31-34 and John 13:36-38 represent the prophecy of denial as taking place in the course of the Last Supper conversation, but in each case the evangelist appears to stress the enormity of the possibility of denial as over against a final meal of fellowship.

The relationship between Matthew and Mark is instructive. Matt 26:30 and Mark 14:26 are identical in the Greek; Mark's v. 27 is a curtailed version of Matthew's v. 31, omitting "all of you" and "from me tonight." The quotation from Zechariah varies slightly, and v. 28 in Mark is virtually identical with Matt 26:38. Mark's v. 29 is a sparse rendering of Matt 26:33, and the same is true of v. 30 (Matt 26:30). Mark's final verse has more of the air of an eyewitness account and presents slight variations from the Matthean version which will be examined in the notes. The Lucan version (22:31-36) has almost nothing verbally in common with Matthew and Mark, save for v. 34b. It does have a protestation by Peter but with nothing of the air of vehemence found in Matthew and Mark.

The Old Testament quotation in v. 27 raises its own questions. Though the ministry has reference to Jesus' reflections on sheep and shepherds (cf. 6:34; Matt 15:24, 25:31-46; Luke 12:32, 15:3-7; John 10:11), the use of Old Testament allusions or quotations in Mark pales into insignificance compared with the extensive use made by Matthew of "fulfillment" testimonies. Why then did Mark use this particular quotation, with the manuscript of Matthew before him? Presumably this was by way of preparation for the role of Peter in 16:7, and vv. 27 and 29 essentially belong together.

The problems of interpretation are anything but simple. It can be pleaded, and with justification, that there is a connection to be made between vv. 27 and 28, especially if the verb *proago* (translated here as *go . . . ahead)* is rendered by "lead." In that case we would have a situation where the small band of disciples, scattered by reason of the fate of the shepherd, will be gathered again by Jesus after his vindication and will lead that band to Galilee (cf. John 10:4). But this plea for the unity of vv. 27 and 28 is flawed by the fact that the verb to which we called attention above does not have a rigidly fixed meaning. In 6:45 it means simply "to go on ahead" or "to take the lead." In general two main positions have been espoused: The first is to regard the saying as having to do with the appearance of the risen Jesus to his disciples in Galilee, either as an unfulfilled prediction of leading his disciples thither, or as a prophecy after the event reflecting those appearances. The second position (cf. Lohmeyer, p. 312) regards the saying as reflecting the Matthean and Markan preoccupations with Galilee in contrast with the Lucan emphasis on Jerusalem. There is a further possibility, offered here with considerable hesitation. It is that although the saying is a creation of the primitive community, it also embodies an exhortation to that community to remain faithful to the ministry as Jesus had envisaged it.

Notes

27. *"All of you will stumble"* (Greek *skandalizō*): Cf. 4:17.

"I will strike": Both in the Septuagint and the Hebrew, the imperative "Strike!" is used. This quotation from Zech 13:7 has sometimes been described as a product of early Christian reflection on the passion, but not only is Jesus reported in our sources to have used the "shepherd" motif with some regularity, it is also fair to assume that at this stage he would reflect on the fate of his band of followers.

it is written: Cf. 1:2.

scattered (Greek *diaskorpizō*): The word is late, and is found in the Septuagint and the papyri.

28. *But after I am raised* (Greek *alla meta to egerthēnai*): The use of *meta* with the infinitive is a common construction in the New Testament and later Greek generally. Cf. 1:14. Matthew has the same construction, but with *de* in place of *alla*. For other references to the resurrection, cf. 8:31, 9:9, 10:34, 16:6. The saying is not found in Luke, who is concerned to preserve his own tradition of Jerusalem appearances. Interestingly this verse is also omitted in one papyrus fragment. Perhaps the strangest thing about this saying is that Peter does not refer to the prediction in v. 28. Even allowing that Peter's impetuous nature would seize upon a prediction of distress for the little band of disciples, it is notable that he did not equally seize upon a fragment which offered some comfort beyond the distress.

29. Both Matthew and Mark (v. 27) agree on the wording of *All of you*, and Peter's reply is designed to make an exception. He does not try to brush aside the gloomy prediction of Jesus, but he does wish to claim an exception in his own case, *though all others . . . I will not*. We have translated the Greek as best we can in *though all others*, for the order of the Greek words can convey two different senses. The Greek begins *ei kai pantes*, and this construction carries the presumption that the contingency will in fact happen. Cf. Luke 18:4; 2 Cor 4:3,16, 7:8; Phil 2:17; Col 2:5. If the Greek were read as *kai ei pantes*, the sense would be that the condition in all probability would not be fulfilled (cf. 1 Cor 8:5). The latter reading is found in some manuscripts, but the vast majority reads *ei kai*.

yet I will not (Greek *all 'ouk egō*): Mark contents himself with this starkly simply dissociation from *all others*, not following the somewhat more florid Matthean "I will certainly not" (Matt 26:33).

30. Not only does Jesus preface his reply with the solemn *amēn* (cf. 3:28), but he singles out Peter with the emphatic personal pronoun. The others may *fall away*, but it is Peter who will deny knowing Jesus.

this very night, before the cock crows: This apparent tautology is easily explained. *This very night* (Greek *sēmeron*)—the word is not found in Matthew—refers to the

Jewish day, reckoned as beginning at sunset, and *before the cock crows* refers to the night of that day. The word *twice* (Greek *dis*) makes for greater accuracy; either Peter will *disown* Jesus *three times* before the cock crows twice, or the denials will occur before the bugle call of the *gallicinium* (= "cock crow") which signaled the dawn of the "Roman" day—i.e., at the beginning of the fourth watch. Both Matthew and Luke omit *dis*, as do some manuscripts of Mark, but in all probability this is due to assimilation to the Matthean and Lucan texts. In terms of our chronology, the whole phrase means between 3 A.M. and 4 A.M.

cock (Greek *alektor*): This word, which is classical and is also found in the Septuagint, is the poetical form of *alektruōn*.

crows (Greek *phōneō*): This word is normally used of human speech (= "to give voice"), but it is found in Aristotle as referring to the sounds of birds and animals. One fragment of a papyrus amends the Greek by using *kokkuxei*, an onomatopoeia which is closely associated with the crowing of birds and is fairly common in classical Greek.

disown (Greek *aparneomai*): Cf. 8:34. Luke introduces the prophecy with the vocative *Petre*, and adds ". . . deny that you know me." There is no reason whatsoever to question the authenticity of the prediction, and it is in the highest degree unlikely that the early community—let alone later tradition—would have invented such a story. It can hardly have come from any source save Peter himself.

31. The reply of Peter is instantaneous and outraged. Mark describes this in Greek as *ekperissōs*, which we have rendered as *vehemently*, the most powerful adverb available to us. The word is apparently a Markan creation (cf. *huperperissōs* at 7:37). The word is not classical and is not found in the Septuagint or later Greek literature. Some manuscripts of Mark, evidently puzzled by this word, use instead the perfectly proper *perissōs*. It is comparable in some ways to the fairly recent coinage in American English of "humongous."

"If I have to . . .": Matthew's *kan* is reproduced in full form in Mark's *kai ean*.

". . . die with you": Cf. 2 Cor 7:3; 2 Tim 2:11. The protestation of sharing in the fate of Jesus is found in John 11:16—"let us go that we may die with him." The force of the Greek in the final clause is "I will on no account . . ."

in the same terms: The effect of Peter's vehemence is seen in the enthusiasm with which *they all* associate themselves with his protest. Matthew has "all the disciples" (26:35).

80. Gethsemane
(14:32-42) = Matt 26:36-46; Luke 22:39-46

14 ³² They went to a place called Gethsemane, and he said to his disciples, "Sit here while I pray." ³³ He took with him Peter, James, and John. He began to be distressed and full of dread. ³⁴ He said to them, "My sorrow is so great that it almost overwhelms me. You must stay here and keep on watching." ³⁵ He went a little way farther forward, prostrated himself on the ground, and prayed that, if possible, the hour might pass him by. ³⁶ "Abba, my Father," he prayed, "all things are possible for you. Remove this cup from me. Yet—not what I will, but what you will." ³⁷ On his return he found them sleeping and said to Peter, "Simon, are you sleeping? Were you unable to watch for one hour? ³⁸ You must watch and pray that you may be spared the test. The spirit is willing, but the flesh is weak." ³⁹ Again he went away and prayed in the same words. ⁴⁰ Then, on his return, he found them sleeping, for their eyes were heavy; they did not know how to answer him. ⁴¹ When he returned the third time, he said to them, "Are you still sleeping and resting? Enough! The hour has come, and The Man is handed over to sinful men. ⁴² Get up! Let us go—my betrayer has come."

Comment

In this, the most dramatically articulated part of the Passion narrative, we are face to face with two widely disparate considerations—the human consciousness of Jesus and the near despair of the disciples. As far as the first matter is concerned, there are so many questions unanswered—and impossible to answer—that there seems no good reason to doubt the essential historicity of the account. Apart from the fact that they are mentioned as being together with him at vital moments in the ministry, we are not told why Peter, James, and John were asked to accompany Jesus in his vigil. Even the vocabulary is no longer wholly open to our inspection: it may even have been obscure by the beginning of the second century. For example, what is *the hour* in v. 41? Short of a reference back to the Lord's Prayer in Matthew and Luke, what are we to understand by *the test* in v. 38? Does it refer simply to the coming trial? We are familiar enough with *the cup* in the Old Testament as a symbol of suffering or of the wrath of God, but what was Jesus' meaning in v. 36? Even one word in v. 41 will give us considerable difficulty, simply because it is impossible to determine what might have been behind the Greek.

All of the questions raised above tend to reinforce very strongly the impression that we are in the presence of a very primitive written tradition. A later tradition might well have depicted Jesus, in facing death, with the same kind of calm assurance as is described of Stephen in Acts 7.

It will be recalled that we gave some attention earlier to the pivotal role of Chapter 13 in the whole complex of the events of the final week, from 11:12 to 14:52. We remind the reader at this juncture that the exhortation to watchfulness as against the coming of the master of the house (13:35-37) appears to be linked in the Gethsemane story with the sleeping disciples (14:37-40). Certainly at the Last Supper Jesus was master of the household, and if our supposition is correct, and that meal was a Passover celebration, then the celebration was still in progress in the garden scene.

Notes

32,33. *They went:* As we noted earlier, the Passover celebration would have still been in progress.

Gethsemane: The word is a good transliteration of a Hebrew word meaning "oil press." The word translated as *place* (Greek *chōrion*) means a "field" or "piece of land" (cf. Matt 26:36; John 4:5; Acts 1:18, 4:34, 5:3,8, 28:7). John 18:1 speaks of a garden *(kēpos)* on the far side of the Kidron, going on to explain that Jesus and the disciples frequently went there. Assumed to be on the lower slopes of the Mount of Olives, it may have been a plantation of olives, probably fenced in with walls. There are two Greek readings of the name: *Gethsēmanei* and *Gesamanei.* It is not certain whether the present Garden of Gethsemane is the correct location for the gospel scene, but it has been so regarded for many centuries.

"Sit here . . .": We must assume that these words were uttered as the little group came to the gateway. We may usefully compare Gen 22:5 and Exod 24:14.

As we previously noted, we are without information as to why Peter, James, and John were singled out to accompany Jesus. Certainly they are exhorted to *watch* and *pray,* and we are reminded that all the disciples were warned of the hazards of following Jesus in 8:34 and of the warning to James and John in 10:35-40. The conjecture that these three disciples were invited to share in this vigil because they had been the first to hear Jesus predict a violent end to the ministry is no more than conjecture.

He began to be distressed: The difficulties here lie not so much in translation as in interpretation. *He began to be* must be given its full force, and the two following verbs give us a picture of ever-increasing horror and agitation. For *distressed* (Greek *ekthambeisthai)* cf. 1:27 and 9:15; the word covers a whole realm of emotions, from amazement to overwhelming distress. The verb *full of dread* (Greek *adēmonein;* cf. Matt 26:37, Phil 2:26) is classical and is also found in the papyri. It describes a state of mind in which mental anguish produces a confused and restless state of shock and even of terror. It is in the highest degree probable that the very force of the words guarantees that we are here dealing with the primitive tradition. Luke does not have this dramatic depiction of Jesus' distress. Matt 26:37 has *lupeisthai* for *ekthambeisthai.*

Lohmeyer (p. 314) rightly calls attention to the horror and mental anguish encapsulated in v. 33. One temptation—to offer psychological explanations for Jesus' state of mind—is best treated with reserve. But *He began to be* demands what explanation we can bring to bear. We called attention in the Introduction to the changes in understanding of his ministry which Jesus apparently embraced at crucial points. Confronted by the stark and harrowing narrative of Gethsemane, we can but speculate that Jesus up to this moment had still the fleeting hope that God would vindicate him and his ministry without the anguish of torture and death. The fact that all the gospels present Jesus to us as facing hostility and possible violence, and the further fact of Jesus' own predictions of suffering and death, do not necessarily detract from the admittedly speculative suggestions we have just made. Taylor (p. 552) speaks of ". . . the astonishment of the Son of Man who knows that He is also the Suffering Servant of Isa 43."

34. We can easily overlook the fact that Jesus' evident distress and anguish were beginning to take hold of him while still in the company of Peter, James, and John. Now he puts even the solace of companionship behind him to pray in private. His few words to them are an echo of Pss 42:6,12 *(LXX* 41:6,11) and 43:5 *(LXX* 42:5), in the phrases "my soul is distressed within me . . ." and "why are you so distressed, o my soul?" (Greek *perilupos estin hē psychē mou).* The addition of *heōs thanatou* in the Greek (literally "almost as to death") we have rendered as *it almost overwhelms me.* The sorrow of Jesus is such that it takes hold of life itself; death is not here a desired cessation from unbearable pain. The saying may be compared with John 12:27: "Now my soul is troubled, and what shall I say?" It is possible that the saying is echoed in Heb 4:15 and 5:7.

sorrow (Greek *perilupos):* Cf. 6:26.

stay here and keep on watching (Greek *meinate,* cf. 6:10; *grēgoreite,* cf. 13:34): The translation reflects the distinction between a command for a definite act and an exhortation to a continuing attitude of mind. Once more we are reminded of the exhortations to watchfulness, especially in relation to vv. 33-37 of Chapter 13. Matthew has "stay here and watch with me."

35. *a little way farther forward:* The word *mikron* is here used of spatial distance; in 14:70 it is used of distance of time.

prostrated himself: The attitude of prostration in prayer is well exemplified in both the Old Testament and New Testament. Cf. Luke 5:12, 17:16; Matt 26:39. Luke's version here has "knelt down" (22:41).

and prayed (Greek *proseucheto):* Cf. 1:35. In Luke 22:41 Jesus is said to be parted from the disciples "as it were a stone's throw," which would agree with the *little way farther forward* of Matthew and Mark.

prayed that: Cf. 13:8.

if possible: Cf. 13:22.

pass him by: Cf. 6:48, 13:30.

the hour: Cf. 1:15, 13:32. The word here has strong eschatological overtones. It is the "hour," the time of the fulfillment of Jesus' ministry. This whole phrase *(prayed that, if possible, the hour might pass him by)* is strongly reminiscent of Chapter 13, as can be seen from the references immediately preceding.

We referred earlier, in the comment, to the difficulty of interpreting the material before us, and *the hour* is a notable example. We have maintained in the course of this work that the gospels of Matthew and Mark are best interpreted as understanding the "hour," the "day," to be focused and centered in the passion/exaltation of Jesus. (Luke's understanding is somewhat different and—thanks to his theologizing the last resurrection appearance in Acts 1—much more convoluted.) But it must be remarked that the evangelists' theological interpretations were all crafted in the light of the Resurrection of Jesus. In the present instance the evangelists are being faithful to the primitive tradition and in the process leave us completely uncertain as to the meaning of *the hour* on the lips of Jesus. Does he mean, by asking that *the hour might pass him by,* that he shrinks from death in the sense that he has work yet to accomplish? Or is he asking to be saved from the violence which he foresees as well-nigh inevitable? Yet to both of those questions we must answer that Jesus himself in our sources was constantly aware of threats of violence and foretold his own suffering and death. All in all whatever theological constructions have been imposed on the material by the evangelists, at first sight we must conclude that the prayer of Jesus is a plea for deliverance from impending agony and death. The process of tradition/interpretation can be clearly seen in John 12:27, to which reference has already been made: "What shall I say? Father, save me from this hour? But it is for this very reason that I have come to this hour." Here we have the Johannine understanding of *the hour* as that of glory, set in a framework of a dawning realization by Jesus of a new and awesome meaning in the coming agony. We shall return to this theme in the next verse.

36. *"Abba, my Father . . .":* Cf. Rom 8:15, Gal 4:6. This is the Aramaic word for "father." Matt 26:39 has "my father" and Luke 22:42 reads "father." It is probable that this is a liturgical phrase in a bilingual community, as evidenced from the instances in Romans and Galatians. This is the only instance of its use in the gospels.

all things are possible (Greek *panta dunata soi):* Cf. Matt 19:26, Mark 10:27. Matt 26:39 has "if possible," and Luke 22:42 has "if you are willing." It is possible that Mark's phrase here was a conscious reference back to 10:27.

Remove this cup: There is in this prayer an urgency which was lacking in the questions asked in 10:38-40. The *cup* (Greek *potērion)* is not only the cup of divine wrath and judgment, but it was also an expression common in the ancient world as a symbol for destiny or fate. As a symbol of suffering, cf. Isa 51:17,22; Lam 4:21; Ps 11:6. It would be a mistake to regard this prayer as simply one for deliverance from death, and it is perhaps here that we can best interpret the verbs in v. 33 *(he began to be distressed, and full of dread).* While we must beware of reading into the words before us—let alone into the human consciousness of Jesus—the concerns and interpretations of theology (however early), we have nevertheless seen in the predictions of the Passion, in the "ransom" saying of 10:45, and in the saying over the cup of v. 24, an increasing awareness on the part of Jesus of the meaning of his death. True, it is life-poured-out, but this has been true of many a martyr. For Jesus, the final saying about his death had been an interpretation: *This is my blood of the Covenant, which is poured out for the community.* The "Son of Man" sayings, as in Daniel, exhibit in the synoptics an ambivalence of meaning between an individual and an individual-for-others. Here in these last few moments before the arrest we may be correct in seeing in the words of Jesus a realization of the awesome concept of himself as sin bearer. The earlier picture of Jesus in our gospels during the ministry does not lend itself to the idea of Jesus shrinking from suffering and death, but the extension of the idea of redemptive suffering into one of vicarious sacrifice for sin was an extension which must have been for him indeed *full of dread.*

It is important at this juncture to recall that the interpretation of Jesus' death as redemptive, as sin bearing, predates our written gospels, even though the Pauline letters took the further step of seeing that sacrificial death as being of universal efficacy. Furthermore Hebrews, the one New Testament book devoted exclusively to the sacrificial ministry and death of Jesus, also has the strongest statement on the sinlessness of Jesus (Heb 4:15). We are surely entitled to ask whence Paul gained his insights into the redemptive nature of the self-offering of Jesus. To take refuge in some imaginary "redeemer myth" of Hellenistic origin is to invite questions as to whether Hellenism even dreamed of redemptive or vicarious suffering, whereas the Old Testament does provide the faint first dawnings of such an idea in Isaiah 53. To suppose that the inventive genius of Paul in some fashion imposed itself on the gospel sources is to fly in the face of the undoubtedly primitive character of the pericope before us, with its vivid picture of an anguished Jesus, and a vocabulary fraught with difficulty precisely because it is primitive. The conclusion seems inevitable that we are here in the presence of a late-dawning consciousness in Jesus that his whole mission and ministry had tended this way, and in his own person the old hopes of a sin bearer had finally come to realization. It was upon him that the burden rested.

not what I will: Matthew's grammatical Greek *(plēn ouk hōs egō thelō all' hōs su)* gives way in Mark to a near impatience with grammar: *ou ti egō thelō alla ti su.* The sense is the same, even though Mark uses the interrogative *ti* (what) instead of the relative *ho ti* (that which). Luke 22:42 has "Nevertheless let your will be done, not mine" *(mē to thelēma mou alla to sou ginesthō),* a reading which brings the prayer of Jesus closer in form to the similar petition in the Lord's Prayer.

37. The contrast between the vigil of Jesus and the attitude of those called to share that vigil is effectively summed up in the opening clauses. Luke tells us that they were sleeping from pure grief (22:45). Since Peter had been so vehement in his protestation of loyalty, it is appropriate that he be singled out. Only here and at 3:16 is the name *Simon* used.

unable to watch (Greek *ouk ischusas):* For the verb *ischuō,* cf. 2:17. This verb can mean both "to be able" and "to have strength," and we could translate the question by "Did you not have the strength of purpose . . . ?" The earlier protestations of Peter stand in stark and grim contrast to this question.

watch (Greek *grēgoreō):* Cf. 13:34.

38. *pray that you may be spared:* The Greek of *pray that (proseuchesthe hina)* looks back to 13:18 and 14:35. It is best to understand the sense as "pray, in order that . . ."

test (Greek *peirasmos):* The word is used generally in two senses—proving and

testing by suffering (cf. Luke 22:28, Acts 20:19, Gal 4:14, Jas 1:2, 1 Pet 1:6); and also
of temptation to sin, resulting from desire or from suggestions by Satan (cf. Mark
1:13, Jas 1:13-15), but neither sense fits this context. There is a note here of a peril far
beyond that of a lapse in awareness or fear of arrest. The air of grim foreboding much
more akin to the language of Chapter 13 and its atmosphere of eschatological turmoil
is reminiscent of Rev 3:10. If this is so, then what interpretation is open to us in the
present instance? We suggest that it is at this point that all the concerns expressed in
the comment to this section come together: the hour, the dread of v. 33, the sayings in
v. 34, the cup of v. 36, even the cry of desolation in 15:34 all combine to indicate that
one of the factors at work here is the realization by Jesus that all the conflicts of the
ministry, and especially the conflicts with evil in the healings and exorcisms were now
coming to a single, inexorable point. He was face to face at this hour with the power of
evil manifested in the sharpest way, and he saw the disciples as faced with the same
menace; hence he warns that they must watch and pray. Here again we are reminded
of the pivotal role of Chapter 13 in all this complex of events, from the cleansing of the
temple to the arrest of Jesus.

Frequent repetition has dulled our ears to the strongly eschatological character of
the Lord's Prayer, but the petition "Deliver us from the time of trial" is certainly no
less urgent than the exhortation of Jesus to the sleeping disciples.

All of the above issues raise again the vexed question of our understanding of
eschatology as it is expressed or implied by the evangelists. We have repeatedly urged
that the only completely satisfactory way in which to interpret Matthew and Mark is
in terms of "realized" eschatology. This is even more emphatically true of John, but
Luke's concern for a continuing community, and the parallel concern over a delayed
parousia, have in many cases muted the urgent eschatological message of the primitive
tradition—not the least in the material presently found in Mark 13. So now with the
scene before us: the vocabulary which was already undergoing transformation in the
second century (Justin Martyr is the first Christian writer to use the expression "Second Coming") was in the original tradition vested with a note of immediate urgency.
The end of the ages had indeed come into focus, in one person and in one all-embracing event.

The spirit is willing . . . . : To contemplate the eschatological "hour" in the abstract,
as an idea, was one thing, and God's Reign is upon you (1:15) could be embraced with
all manner of fervent anticipation. But to be confronted by the very moment of the
inauguration of that Reign, in all its distress and dread, was another matter. It is in
this light that we are to understand the saying. The contrast between flesh (Greek
sarx) and spirit (Greek pneuma) is a fundamental Old Testament distinction between
humanity as finite, frail, and limited, and as dependent on the sustaining spirit of God
(cf. Num 27:16, Isa 31:3). Willing (Greek prothumos) is used in the sense of "ready,"
or "eager," or "fully engaged." The word is classical and is found in the Septuagint
and the papyri.

Luke's version of this encounter is substantially different and independent; he has
no parallel to 37b and 38b. Mark's text is virtually identical with that of Matthew.

39. Some manuscripts omit in the same words, and the same manuscripts omit palin
(again) in v. 40, which we have translated as returned for the literal "coming again."

40. Mark explains that the disciples were asleep because their eyes were heavy, and

the following *they did not know how to answer him* repeats the words used of Peter at the Transfiguration (9:6). If, as this writer believes, the Transfiguration as described for us in the gospels was a retrojection from the resurrection experience, and the vision an interpretation of what the same three disciples *might* have understood from both challenge (9:5) and passion prediction (8:31-35), then this deliberate reminiscence is wholly appropriate.

We call attention here, as we did in the notes on v. 26, to the work of Daube concerning Passover celebrations. In the same work (pp. 333-35) he provides us with further insight into the emphasis on the disciples' sleeping. Under rabbinic regulations, if the members of the company fell into a deep sleep and could not answer at all, then the celebration was regarded as ended. Distinctions were drawn between a mere doze and deep sleep, and Mark's account of the episode, when Jesus came back the second time, bears this out *(they did not know how to answer him)*. Matthew's distinction is between "sleeping" (Matt 26:40,43) and "sleeping and resting" (26:45). By his reminiscence of the wording from the Transfiguration scene Mark refashions Matthew's distinction, but with consummate skill Mark refers us back to yet another episode involving the three disciples. (Luke's account does not do justice to the rabbinic distinction.) It was not simply that Jesus wished for companionship in his vigil but also that he did not wish the Passover celebration brought so soon to a close.

41. Our translation of *"Are you still sleeping and resting? . . ."* depends on a number of factors. The first has to do with the Greek, which reads *Katheudete [to] loipon kai anapanesthe,* and the word *loipon* is the problem. We have rendered it as *still,* an adverb. The New Testament provides us with a variety of possibilities (cf. Matt 26:45; Acts 27:20; 1 Cor 13:11; Phil 3:1, 4:8; 1 Thess 4:1; 2 Thess 3:1; 2 Tim 4:8; Heb 10:13). It can be "as for the rest," "finally," "therefore," or "so." In the face of all these possibilities, it seems best to translate as we have done above, giving *loipon* the meaning of *still.*

Enough! (Greek *apechei):* The commentators provide us with a rich field of speculation with respect to this word, which the Vulgate renders as *sufficit.* But is this an ironic comment about the disciples' sleeping? This seems unlikely, for there is very little evidence for an impersonal use of the word. There is some evidence in commercial use in this period and later for the word as a technical expression for a transaction completed, and to some extent this could be upheld by the second part of the verse. The suggestion has been made that the Greek was a poor rendering of the Aramaic *kaddu,* as "enough." But it has been urged—on the ground of that same word—that in Palestinian Aramaic and in Syriac it means "already." The uncertainty is reflected in the manuscripts. One important manuscript (D, Codex Bezae) reads *apechei to telos kai hē hōra* (the end is pressing, the hour has come). The reading *to telos (the end)* is certainly attuned to the eschatological motif we have seen to dominate this narrative and may well be original; the word is found in a wide geographical distribution of early manuscripts. Perhaps then we might read the second part of this verse as "The end and the hour are closing in." But so much depends on the meaning of *apechei.* It is omitted by one eighth-century manuscript, and three lesser ones. The Vulgate has *sufficit* (it is enough), but some Latin manuscripts have *adest* (it is present), while one even reads *consummatus est finis* (the end has been accomplished). To add to the complications, a fourth-century Syriac manuscript version of the Codex Sinaiticus,

along with two other later Syriac manuscripts, apparently interprets the phrase as
ēngiken (is near). Now while the reading *to telos* may possibly be correct, it is nevertheless the case that the manuscript to which we first made reference (D) omits *ēlthen*
(has come) as though there were an editorial uncertainty of what to make of the
construction. Tempting though it is to include *to telos* and then to translate the passage as "The end is closing in, and the hour has come," we opted for caution and
arrived at our translation of v. 41 in the light of two considerations: (1) Matt 26:45
does not have either *apechei* or *telos*, but does have "the hour is almost here"; and (2)
in spite of the variations in Greek and in the Syriac versions, the Latin versions
interpret the text as saying "Enough!"

   the hour: Cf. the note on v. 35 above. The intent of all that has gone before is
summed up in this verse. It would be a mistake to regard the statement *the hour has
come* as though it was all explained by *The Man is handed over.* This is the time of
climax—the vigil has been kept, Jesus' submission to the Father has been renewed,
and the Passover celebration has ended. The announcement in the next verse that *my
betrayer has come* is but the outward sign that all has been completed.

   42. *Get up!* It is difficult, in view of the dramatic content of the narrative, and this
vigorous imperative, to defend a translation such as "You can sleep on now and take
your rest. It is all over." When this is followed by "The hour has come," the translation just quoted (from *The Jerusalem Bible,* closely akin to the KJV and RV) reduces
the saying to something of a pallid insignificance. Even if *the hour* was not heavy with
eschatological significance, Jesus would hardly have suggested sleep and rest when the
traitor was at hand.

   For an article which makes the best case for interpreting *apechei* in the sense of
Judas having received the promised money, cf. G. H. Boobyer, *"Apechei* in Mark
14:41," *NTS* 2.1955, pp. 44-48.

81. The Arrest of Jesus
(14:43-52) = Matt 26:57-68; Luke 22:54-55, 63-71;
John 18:13-14,19-24

14 ⁴³ Suddenly, while he was still speaking, there came Judas—one
of the Twelve—and with him was a crowd with swords and clubs,
from the chief priests, the scribes, and the elders. ⁴⁴ The traitor had
given them a sign: "The one I kiss is the man; seize him, and get him
away safely." ⁴⁵ As soon as he arrived, he went immediately up to him,
and said, "Rabbi!" and kissed him. ⁴⁶ Then they grabbed him and
arrested him. ⁴⁷ But a certain bystander drew his sword, struck at the
high priest's slave, and cut off his ear. ⁴⁸ Then Jesus said to them,

"Have you come out with swords and clubs to take me, as though I am a bandit? 49 Day after day I was in your company while I was teaching in the temple, and you did not arrest me. But let the scriptures be fulfilled!" 50 Then all the disciples abandoned him and fled. 51 A certain young man, dressed only in a linen cloth, followed him. They tried to seize him, 52 but he left the linen cloth behind and ran away naked.

Comment

The contrast between this narrative and its predecessor is very marked. There is nothing of the drama of the preceding pericope, there are no sayings apart from v. 48, and there is an appended Markan tradition in the last two verses which may reflect baptismal practice more than any historical incident. We are not told who might have constituted the crowd in v. 43, and all attention is concentrated on Judas and Jesus. All in the Markan account is subservient to a stark brevity, and the manuscript history demonstrates a desire to embellish the original narrative. Apart from Jesus there are no names—a fact which led some manuscripts to add the name of Judas again in v. 44.

Notes

44. *Suddenly:* Not only is there this characteristically Markan word (Greek *euthus),* but the hand of the evangelist can be discerned in the participle joining this story to the Gethsemane narrative. Some manuscripts add "Iscariot" to *Judas;* others provide the adjective "great" to *crowd* (common enough in Matthew, and found also in Mark 4:1, 9:14); and yet others read "being one of the Twelve." It is clear enough from the Markan narrative which group of people was responsible for the arrest, though one manuscript has "sent by" before *the chief priests, the scribes, and the elders.*

The sparse narrative says nothing of temple police (cf. Luke 22:52), let alone Roman soldiers (cf. John 18:3,12), and we conclude that this is a mob recruited for the occasion—quite unlike the more "official" emissaries in Luke and John. In this respect, Mark follows his principal mentor (Matthew) closely, even including Matthew's lapse into clumsy Greek with the repeated *with him, with* in v. 43.

swords (Greek *machairai):* These were short-bladed weapons, more akin to long daggers than conventional swords. The word translated as *clubs* (Greek *xula)* originally meant "wood" and came to mean by extension anything made of wood. (Cf. Acts 16:24. For other references, cf. Acts 5:30, 10:39, 13:29; Gal 3:13; 1 Pet 2:24.)

Mark's reference to *scribes* is, as we have already seen, consistent with his emphasis on this group (not mentioned in Matt 22:47) as being Jesus' principal opponents. The identification of *chief priests, scribes, and elders* is intended to associate them all in the arrest and subsequent death of Jesus. Luke 22:52, whether from erroneous information or from a desire symbolically to involve the group, says that some of the principal clergy were present at the arrest, along with temple guards.

44. *The traitor:* We may be fairly certain that we are in the presence of the earliest tradition, for all that is emphasized about Judas is his treachery. Only later reflection provided room for speculation about Judas' motives (cf. John 12:6).

a sign: The significance of both the kiss and greeting should not be missed. According to contemporary usage, no disciple was permitted to greet his teacher first, since this would have implied equality. Judas' sign, therefore, was not only a final repudiation of Jesus' authority and a signal to the mob but also a calculated insult. It is possible that John 18:4-7, which does not mention the kiss, indicates ("they drew back and fell to the ground") that even those who accompanied Judas were taken aback by this treachery.

The Greek word employed by Mark *(sussēmon),* while not unusual (it is found in the Septuagint and the papyri), would hardly satisfy a classical purist and may indicate an independent source. Matthew has the more usual *sēmeion.*

kiss: All three synoptic gospels use this verb, *phileō* (to have tender regard for). The kiss as a symbol of mutual respect was common between rabbis and pupils. For its use in the early Church, cf. Rom 16:16, 1 Cor 16:20, 2 Cor 13:12, 1 Thess 5:26, 1 Pet 5:14.

seize him: Cf. 3:21 for the same verb.

get him away: Cf. 14:53, 15:16.

safely (Greek *asphalōs):* Cf. Acts 2:36 (= certainly), 16:23. There is to be no room for error. Matthew has no parallel to *get him away safely,* and Luke has no parallel to v. 44 of Mark.

45. There is perhaps a further, but minor, indication of Mark's independent source here. There are two participles, *kai elthōn* (literally "and coming" = *As soon as he arrived)* and *euthus proselthōn* ("immediately coming to" = *he went immediately),* and one is redundant. Matt 26:49 simply has *proselthōn,* and Luke 22:47 has "he came near to Jesus and kissed him."

"Rabbi!" Cf. 9:5. This is one of the titles used of Jesus in the whole complex 11:12-15:39 to which attention was called previously.

kissed him (Greek *kataphileō):* Cf. Matt 26:49; Luke 7:38,45; 15:20; Acts 20:37. This word is stronger in meaning than the *phileo* of v. 44, and it means "to embrace fervently"; certainly in Hellenistic Greek it carries a more affectionate meaning than *phileo.* The change in the verb, with its emphatic prefixed *kata,* may indicate a more than usually affectionate greeting designed to ensure that the arrest take place as quickly as possible, with no room for error. Matt 26:50 has Jesus say, "Friend, you are here." (The Greek of Matthew is not certain, and it could be rendered—though with small justification—as "Friend, why are you here?" One very slight emendation would give us "Friend, take what you have come to get.") Luke's 22:48 has "Judas, do you betray the Son of Man with a kiss?" The Markan account has no saying of Jesus.

46. With minor variation *(him* for "Jesus") Mark follows Matt 26:50b. The verb in *they grabbed* (Greek *epebalan)* occurs only here in Mark. The narrative ends at this point, and the two disparate traditions in vv. 47-50 and 50-51 are appended.

47. Of the episode recorded in this verse, it is difficult to be certain whether we are

dealing with a factual account, or with a story which, in the confusion of the events themselves with later recollection, has suffered modification and/or embellishment. The Markan version is succinct—*bystander* is a common word in this gospel (cf. 14:69; 15:35,39; and also 4:29), and the impression gained is that the evangelist looked at the sources before him and out of hesitation curtailed them. Matt 26:51 reads, "One of those with Jesus . . . ," and Luke 22:49-50 records that "a certain one" of those who were with Jesus, wishing to protest the arrest, drew his sword. John 18:10 identified the assailant as Simon Peter, and the name of the slave is given as Malchos. The fact that all four evangelists record the incident strongly suggests a historical basis, and we would rightly be suspicious of unanimity in the confusion of the arrest. But the details defy elucidation. If Simon Peter was the attacker, it is hard for us to understand why he in his turn was not arrested. True, both Matthew and Luke agree that it was someone from Jesus' company, but given Mark's interest in Peter, it is puzzling that he did not name him—if the tradition in the fourth gospel was correct. Instead Mark falls back on caution: *one of the bystanders.* Of course it is possible that by the time the Johannine tradition was committed to writing, the name of the assailant was no longer a matter of moment. It is certainly possible to read the Greek of *a certain (eis tis)* as meaning "a certain bystander whose name is known to me, but which I will not divulge . . ." Unhappily this Greek reading (which we have followed) does not have universal manuscript support, though it is strongly attested. It is found in Luke 22:50 (Matt 26:57 reads simply *eis),* and it is possible that the manuscript's support for *eis tis* is simply by assimilation to the Lucan text. We have followed the reading, noting that v. 51 simply has *tis,* leaving *eis tis* as the only example of the usage in Mark.

As we have the account in Matthew and Mark, there is an impulsive act by a bystander, presumably out of anger at the treatment accorded to Jesus, but this is wholly obscured in Luke (where there is a rhetorical demand for common action). Presumably the action was a demonstration that the slave so attacked was despicable (cf. Lohmeyer, p. 322).

ear (Greek *ōtarion):* Luke 22:50 has the usual Greek for *ear (ous),* and Mark generally uses that word (cf. 4:9,23; 7:33; 8:18). There seems no good reason why he should here resort to the diminutive, unless by example of Matthew's similar use of a diminutive *(ōtion)* in 26:51. If the weapon mentioned earlier was indeed a sword of conventional size, the wound inflicted even by a glancing blow would have been extensive, perhaps even lethal. If the weapon was a large dagger, then it is possible that the use of the diminutive for *ear* by both Matthew and Mark is an indication that only the lobe of the ear was wounded. Luke 22:51 appears to imply this by saying that Jesus touched the wound and healed it. John (who, like Luke, identifies the ear as the right ear) emphatically states that the ear was cut completely off.

This short narrative has some words which occur nowhere else in this gospel: *spaō (draw),* v. 47; *paiō (struck),* v. 47, cf. *patassō* in Matthew and Luke; *aphaireō (cut off),* v. 47.

48-49. This somewhat puzzling saying of Jesus is found in all three synoptic gospels, and it is impossible to determine by what process it attached itself to the arrest narrative. The easiest solution is to say that we have a saying detached either from the appearance before the Sanhedrin or from the trial before Pilate. A very slight indication that this may be so comes from the beginning clause in Greek: *kai apokritheis ho*

Iesous (and Jesus answered). We have translated it as *then Jesus said to them* because *apokritheis* does not invariably in Hellenistic Greek mean "answered." Assuming for the moment that this saying did come originally from the later legal process, did early reflection on Isa 53:7-8 (cf. Acts 8:32-33) cause the evangelists to emphasize Jesus' silence (cf. Mark 15:5)? Luke's version (22:52) may offer some support to this view by his assertion that this brief address was made to "the chief priests, temple officials, and the elders." It is highly unlikely that any such official would have been present at the arrest—after all, they had hired a mob to take care of the seizure. Matt 26:55 is of no assistance and "At the same time Jesus said to the crowds . . ." has all the appearance of a writer/compiler faced with an isolated saying from the Passion narrative which is not part of the received tradition. Mark simply echoes his bewilderment.

Jesus noticeably makes no protest at the treatment he has received but only protests the fashion of the arrest—*as though I am a bandit.*

The essential wording in all three accounts is the same, with minor grammatical differences. Matt 26:55 has "Day after day I was sitting teaching . . . ," whereas Luke 22:53 reads "Day by day when I was with you . . . ," but Mark has a periphrastic imperfect *Day after day I was . . . teaching.* The interest here lies in the very plain suggestion that the Jerusalem ministry of Jesus was of far longer duration than the synoptic gospels would indicate.

"But let the Scriptures be fulfilled!" This phrase is wholly out of character in Mark, and the commentator faced with *hina plērōthōsin* is immediately reminded of Matthew's common formula: *hina plērothē* (that it might be fulfilled). Matt 26:56 has *touto de holon gegonen hina plērōthōsin hai graphai . . .* (all this has happened that the writings of the prophets might be fulfilled), and the differences are minor. It will be recalled that in v. 21 we had a similar uncharacteristic reference to the scriptures in this chapter, and there, as here, it is argued that Mark was faithful to his principal mentor (Matthew). Mark has apparently made of this short saying an imperative, and we have so translated it. It is, however, possible that there was originally the participle *gegonen* in Mark's text, and this would change the meaning to "This happened that the scriptures might be fulfilled." Luke 22:53 reads, "But this is your hour, and the power of darkness."

51-52. This very short appended narrative is peculiar to Mark and perhaps is linked to the previous v. 50 precisely because of the statement that *all the disciples abandoned him.* The connection, or lack of it, prompted scribal emendations in some manuscripts, with *neaniskos de tis* (but a certain young man) in some, and *kai eis tis neaniskos* (and one young man) in others. The emendations from the text that we have translated *(kai neaniskos tis)* may well have been undertaken in the light of v. 47.

It is difficult to know what to make of *followed him.* Is this meant to emphasize a contrast with *all . . . abandoned him?* Are we to understand that this was his one exception, or do we conclude that this was someone who had followed Jesus and the disciples from the upper room? It is possible that *followed* is meant to suggest that the young man did so after the arrest and after the disciples had fled.

dressed only in a linen cloth (Greek *peribeblēmenos sindona):* Some manuscripts add *epi gumnon* (on his naked body), but though it is well represented in important manuscripts, it may well be a scribal correction inserted to explain *gumnos* (naked), which in its turn had found its way here in a few manuscripts by a misunderstanding of *sindona gumnos* in the next verse. If *epi gumnon* is omitted—as we have done—the meaning is unchanged. In any event the general expression for "over the naked body" in Greek would be *epi chrōtos* or *en chrō* (for the latter cf. the French *au naturel)*. It seems best to understand *gumnos* in this verse as "scantily clad" or "dressed only in a *chitōn"* (a short undertunic).

seize him (Greek *krateō):* Cf. 1:31.

left the linen cloth: The impression gained from the tantalizingly short story is that of a young man who had been roused from sleep by the noise and excitement and had only time to put on an undertunic.

All of this has left in abeyance any consideration of historicity. Assuming some historical ground for the story, there have been suggestions in plenty for the identity of the young man, from John, James the Lord's brother, to (in recent times) John Mark —assuming that the Last Supper took place in the house of his mother. If this John Mark was the evangelist, we would have expected far more information, and this supposition reads too much into the very sparse narrative. There is certainly an air of eyewitness information about this section, but the most we can say of vv. 51-52 is that they afford us a glimpse of a short oral narrative in the process of transmission.

Yet elements of doubt remain. The Resurrection narrative in Mark (16:5) also has a record of a *neaniskos,* wrapped *(peribeblēmenos)* in a white robe, and this in itself should give us pause. Some features of the short story are noteworthy. To begin with, the young man is linked very closely with Jesus: Mark uses the very rare word *sunakalouthō* (Mark 5:37, 14:51; Luke 23:49) for *follow,* instead of his more usual *akalouthō* (nineteen times in this gospel); Jesus is seized, *arrested,* and the same verb is used of the attempts to seize the young man; there is the *linen cloth (sindōn)* which is mentioned twice as belonging to the young man, as it is similarly mentioned twice in the account of the burial of Jesus (15:46). We have called attention already to the fact that *neaniskos,* found here and in the Resurrection account, is nowhere else used in Mark. Some grammatical notes appear to link these two verses irrefutably with the burial and Resurrection stories: the use of the perfect participle to describe the young man as *dressed* (or "wrapped around") here and at 16:5. These occurrences are notable as being the only occasions that Mark uses the verb *periballō.* Equally the verb *pheugō* (ran away) is used here of the young man as it is later of the women at the tomb.

Many and varied have been the attempts on the part of commentators to explain this "arrest-burial-Resurrection" motif.

1. Both Jesus and the young man are *seized;* both are destined to escape their enemies; both leave the *sindōn* behind.

2. There is a "Joseph" typology at work here, and the young man of 14:51-52 is identical with the young man of 16:5. The persecuted Joseph was seized, "buried," and is raised to life again, exalted to honor and enthroned.

3. There is a baptismal motif discernible: the Christian belief was that the initiate dies with, and was raised with, the risen Christ, the whole being symbolized by putting off an old garment and putting on a new one.

A short bibliography representing these views is appended for reference:

1. J. Knox. "A Note on Mark 14:51-52." In *The Joy of Study: Papers on New Testament and Related Subjects to Honor Frederick Clifton Grant,* edited by S. Johnson. New York: Macmillan, 1951, pp. 27-30.

2. A. Vanhoye. "La fuite du jeune homme nu (Marc 14:51-52)." *Bib* 52.1971, p. 402.

3. H. Waetjen. "The Ending of Mark and the Gospel's Shift in Eschatology." *ASTI* 4.1965, pp. 117-20.

4. R. Scroggs and K. Groff. "Baptism in Mark: Dying and Rising with Christ." *JBL* 92.1973, pp. 536-40.

There are difficulties with all three interpretations. The first, like the second, depends heavily on typology (for which Mark is not noteworthy), but it also takes no adequate account of the seeming identity between the young man of 14:51 and the young man of 16:5. The second, though rightly concerned with the note of triumph through suffering in Mark, presents us with a Joseph theme which would represent an Old Testament typology otherwise wholly unknown in Mark. There is a typology in the story of the young man, as we shall see, but it is wholly contained in the relationship between Jesus and his disciples, not in any Old Testament reference. The third interpretation is at first sight much more plausible and attractive, though in detail it reads too much into the text. (Cf. in this regard F. L. Cross, *I Peter: A Paschal Liturgy,* London: A. R. Mowbray, 1954.) We are familiar with Paul's many uses of the Greek prefix *sun* (with), in phrases such as "baptized with," "dying with," "risen with," to explain the relationship of the believer with the risen Christ. This is early theology, early interpretation, but it remains to ask whence this was derived, if it was not from the early tradition eventually enshrined in the gospels. In the case of Mark, we can only fall back on the passion predictions for the motif of death/vindication, and certainly a hope beyond death is expressed there. However, in respect to baptism, the only reference provided by Scroggs and Groff is 10:38-39, which, while certainly connected with the passion, does not embody the kind of dying/rising motif which their article espouses.

We may be on much more secure ground in looking again at the vocabulary of the arrest, the young man's flight, and the warnings issued by Jesus. We have already noted the word *krateō* (to seize, arrest). This is a much used Markan word, generally in the sense of "lay hold." Of fourteen examples in Mark, the meaning of "overcome," "seize," "arrest" is present throughout the Passion narrative, including no less than four occurrences in this arrest scene (vv. 44,46,49,51). Effectively, therefore, the young man is linked with Jesus by this word. Similarly the young man is linked with the disciples, who have vigorously protested that they will not fail when Jesus predicts their defection (14:27). But the final word on their protest is 14:50: *they abandoned him and fled.* So too the young man—he *ran away.* (The Greek verb is the same— *phugeō.)*

An article by Harry Fleddermann—"The Flight of a Naked Young Man (Mark 14:51-52)," *CBQ* 41.1979, pp. 412-18—in summing up the evidence from this vocabulary, calls attention to the consistent representation of the disciples in Mark as uncomprehending, untrusting, culminating in the "falling into unbelief" (p. 416) of 14:27. Therefore, far from seeing any connection between the linen cloth *(sindōn)* wrapped around *(peribeblēmenos)* the young man in v. 51 and the robe *(stolē)* wrapped around *(peribeblēmenos)* the young man in 16:5, the author sees the connection as between the nakedness of the one who fled from the garden and the nakedness of Jesus on the cross. "The unbelieving flight of the young man is opposed to Jesus' believing acceptance of the crucifixion. Confronted with the passion the disciples all flee, even the young man. Jesus, on the other hand, fully accepts God's will. It is only after the crucifixion that care can again be bestowed on Jesus. Joseph of Arimathea buys a linen cloth and . . . wraps it in the linen cloth" (pp. 417-18). This attempts to prove too much, however readily we may agree with the emphasis on the faithlessness and flight of the disciples. Why does the author find it "difficult to see any connection" between the two young men of 14:51 and 16:5? Is it not possible, given Fleddermann's premises, that this is in truth a symbol of unfaith changed to faith? Nowhere else does Mark use the word *neaniskos,* save in these two instances, and nowhere else the verb *perilambanō* to describe a manner of dressing. And why do the women flee in 16:8— do they share in the disciples' unbelief? But nowhere in the gospel does Mark link any women with unbelief, and Jesus does not charge them with it.

For all the difficulties inherent in a baptismal motif, the conclusion of this writer is that the coincidence of two young men, described as being wrapped or clothed (though in different garments), one running away and the other announcing the Resurrection, is altogether too much to ascribe to chance.

Appended Note

It will be obvious from what has been written so far on Chapter 14 that almost every section has its own distinct problems, and what follows is a very short listing of works which would well repay the attention of the student.

1. Beernaert, P. Mourlin. "Structure littéraire et lecture théologique de Marc 14.17-52." In *L'Évangile selon Marc: Tradition et redaction.* Bibliotheca ephemeridum theologicarum lovaniensium 34, edited by M. Sabbe. Gembloux: Duculot; Louvain: Leuven University, 1974, pp. 241-67.

2. Léon-Dufour, X. "Jesus devant sa mort a la lumière des textes de l'institution eucharistique et des discours d'adieu." In *Jésus aux origines de la Christologie,* edited by J. Dupont. Bibliotheca ephemeridum theologicarum lovaniensium 40. Gembloux: Duculot; Louvain: Leuven University, 1975, pp. 141-68.

3. Sloyan, G. *Jesus on Trial: The Development of the Passion Narratives and Their Historical and Ecumenical Implications.* Philadelphia: For-

tress Press, 1973, p. 43. This important work suggests that the original Markan complex consisted of 14:1-2,25-26,43,50-54,65-72; 15:1-5,15b,21,25-26,34,37. This work should be carefully compared with Taylor—Additional Note J, in his commentary, "The Construction of the Passion and Resurrection Narrative," pp. 635-64.

4. On the Last Supper narrative, cf. also N. Turner, "The Style of St. Mark's Eucharistic Words," *JTS* 8.1.1957, pp. 108-11; N. A. Beck, "The Last Supper as an Efficacious Symbolic Act," *JBL* 89.2.1970, pp. 192-98. A lecture by David Daube in 1966 *(He That Cometh),* under the auspices of the London Diocesan Council for Christian-Jewish Understanding, has the interesting suggestion that the *aphikomen* bread, so characteristic a feature of the modern Jewish Seder, had an original meaning not immediately obvious. He maintains that *"Aphiqoman* is the Greek *aphikomenos* or *ephikomenos,* 'The Coming One' or 'He that Cometh' " and refers to the hidden Messiah. The lecture has long been out of print, but it amply repays any expenditure of effort in locating a copy.

5. On the link between 14:28 and 16:7—the "Galilee" motif—cf. J.-M. van Cangh, "Le Galilee dans l'Évangile de Marc: un lien théologique?" *RevBib* 79.1.1972, pp. 59-75.

6. On the betrayal, cf. T. F. Glasson, "Davidic Links with the Betrayal of Jesus," *ET* 85.4.1974, pp. 118-19.

7. Eminently useful for background material is Ernest Best, *The Temptation and the Passion: The Markan Soteriology,* SNTS Monograph Series 2, New York and Cambridge: Cambridge University Press, 1965. It may, however, be doubted whether the suggestion of an "Isaac" theme is really to be found in Mark. There is certainly no tradition in Judaism of an *Isaac redivivus* who would be efficacious for others.

Additional Comment

We now come to Part II of the Passion narrative, the appearance of Jesus before the Sanhedrin and the Roman governor. The accompanying chart is meant only as a guide to the differences between the four gospels, and the variations in chronology exhibited by those documents. Textual matters are dealt with in the notes, as are also such things as the nature of the appearance of Jesus before the Sanhedrin and the references in all four gospels to a custom of releasing a prisoner at Passover. Even if much of the Johannine account is a result of later theological reflection (John 18:29-38, 19:9-11), there is broad agreement between the evangelists on the events which surrounded the final sentence of execution.

The bibliography which follows this section is by no means exhaustive, but it does contain a representative selection of various authors with differing views, regarding both chronology and the legal processes involved.

COMPARISON OF THE PASSION NARRATIVES
PART II

Matthew	Mark	Luke	John
26:50,57-58	14:46,53-54	22:54	18:12-16
Jesus is led to the high priest's house, Peter follows.	Peter follows to the high priest's house, enters the courtyard with attendants.	Peter follows and goes with attendants into the courtyard.	Jesus is taken to the house of Caiaphas. Simon Peter follows. The other disciple, known to the household, goes into the courtyard with Jesus.
26:69-70	14:66-68a	22:55-57	18:17-18
Peter, challenged by a slave girl, denies knowing Jesus.	Peter, challenged by a slave girl, denies knowing Jesus.	A slave girl asserts to attendants that Peter was with Jesus, which Peter denies.	A slave girl asks Peter if he was a disciple, which Peter denies.
			18:19-23
			Jesus is questioned by Annas and sent to Caiaphas.
26:71-75	14:68b-72	22:58-62	18:25-27
Peter, challenged by another man, denies knowing Jesus. Those present again charge Peter, and after a third denial the cock crows. Peter goes out and weeps.	A cock crows, a slave girl says Peter is "one of them," which he denies, and later those standing there then challenge Peter. After another denial, the cock crows a second time. Peter begins to weep.	Another man challenges Peter, who gives a denial. After an hour, another says, "He was with him." Peter denies Jesus a third time; the cock crows; Jesus turns and looks at Peter, who goes out weeping.	Peter, challenged twice by bystanders, denies knowledge of Jesus, and the cock crows.
26:59-66	14:55-64		
High priests and Sanhedrin seek witnesses against Jesus. Two "false witnesses" repeat Jesus' saying about destroying the Holy Place. Jesus, challenged, makes no reply.	High priests and Sanhedrin seek witnesses to put Jesus to death, but many witnesses' accounts do not agree. Some bear "false testimony" and repeat the saying about destroying the Holy Place. Jesus, challenged, makes no reply.	22:66-71 Jesus is challenged, "Are you the Messiah?" and replies with the "Son of Man" saying from Dan 7:13. They press him further, and he replies, "The words are yours."	

Matthew	Mark	Luke	John
Jesus, challenged on messiahship (Son of God) replies with the "Son of Man" saying from Dan 7:13. High priest describes this as blasphemy, tears his clothes, and they all agree that Jesus is guilty of death.	Jesus, challenged on messiahship (Son of the Blessed) replies with the "Son of Man" saying from Dan 7:13. High priest describes this as blasphemy, tears his clothes, and they all agree Jesus is guilty of death.	23:1 Jesus is led to Pilate.	
26:67-68	14:65		
Jesus is mocked, spat on, and challenged to prophesy.	Jesus is mocked, spat on, and challenged to prophesy.		
27:1-2			18:28
High priests, elders consult and lead bound Jesus to Pilate.	High priests, elders and scribes, Sanhedrin consult and lead bound Jesus to Pilate.		Jesus is taken in the early morning to the Praetorium, which the clergy do not enter.
(27:3-10, Suicide of Judas: cf. Acts 1:15-20)			
27:11-14	15:2-5	23:2-5	18:29-38
Pilate asks Jesus if he is King of the Jews. Jesus replies, "The words are yours." High priests and elders accuse Jesus, who does not reply, and Pilate is amazed.	Pilate asks Jesus if he is King of the Jews. Jesus replies, "The words are yours." High priests and elders accuse Jesus, who makes no reply, and Pilate is amazed.	Jesus is accused of perverting people, forbidding payment of taxes, and making himself a king. Pilate says he finds no guilt in Jesus, but the accusers say he disturbs the people.	The accusers are pressed by Pilate, who asks Jesus, "Are you the King of the Jews?" In a dialogue about kingship, Pilate asks, "What is truth?" He goes out and says he finds no guilt in Jesus.
		23:6-12	
		Pilate sends Jesus to Herod, who questions him at length, but Jesus does not reply. Herod's soldiers dress Jesus in splendid clothing, and he is sent back to Pilate.	
		23:17-23	
		Pilate calls the high priests and leaders, and says neither he nor Herod find any fault in Jesus, so he will punish and release him.	
27:15-23	15:6-14	23:17-23	18:39-40
Pilate had a custom of releasing a prisoner at	The crowd demands the usual Passover release.	In response to the Passover release custom,	Pilate refers to his Passover custom and

Passover. When assembled, he asks the accusers whom they wish released, Barabbas or "Jesus called Messiah." They, stirred by the high priests, and, in response to a question about what to do with Jesus, say, "Let him be crucified!"

Pilate asks whether they wish "the King of the Jews." Stirred by the high priests, the crowd demands Barabbas. In response to Pilate's question of what to do with Jesus, they reply, "Let him be crucified!" Pilate asks what evil Jesus he has done. The crowds again shout for Jesus to be crucified.

the crowd demands the release of Barabbas. Pilate addresses them, seeking to release Jesus. They shout, "Crucify him!" For the third time Pilate asks what evil Jesus has done, as he has found no cause of death in Jesus. The crowd, abetted by the high priests, calls for crucifixion.

asks if they wish the release of Jesus. They reject this and demand the release of Barabbas. Pilate has Jesus flogged.

27:27-30

The soldiers take Jesus to the Praetorium, put a scarlet robe on him, plait a crown of thorns, and put a reed in his right hand. They mock him as King of the Jews, spit on him, and strike him.

15:16-18

The soldiers take Jesus to the Praetorium, put a purple robe on him, plait a crown of thorns, and mock him as King of the Jews. They strike him with a reed and spit on him.

19:1-15

The soldiers make a crown of thorns, put a purple robe on Jesus, and mock him as King of the Jews. Pilate says he finds no fault in Jesus. Jesus comes out wearing the crown of thorns and the robe. Pilate says, "Behold the man." The high priests and those around shout for the death of Jesus. Pilate replies that they should execute Jesus. They reply that Jesus ought to die because he made himself Son of God. Pilate, afraid, questions Jesus and on receiving no reply speaks of his authority. In response to Jesus' reply, Pilate again tries to release Jesus, but the crowd pleads loyalty only to Caesar. Pilate leads Jesus out: "Behold your king!" The crowd demands crucifixion, as it does again when Pilate asks, "Shall I crucify your king?" Pilate hands Jesus over for execution.

27:24-26

Pilate washes his hands in public, and hands Jesus over for flogging and crucifixion.

15:15

Pilate decides to satisfy the crowd by releasing Barabbas. He hands Jesus over for flogging and crucifixion.

23:24-25

Pilate accedes to the demands of the crowd, releases Barabbas, and hands Jesus over for flogging and crucifixion.

82. Jesus Before the Council
(14:53-65) = Matt 26:57-68; Luke 22:54-55,63-71;
John 18:13-14,19-24

14   53 Then they led Jesus away to the high priest's house, where the chief priests, elders, and scribes were all assembling. 54 Peter followed him at a distance into the high priest's courtyard. There he sat with the attendants and warmed himself at the fire. 55 The chief priests and the whole Sanhedrin were seeking some evidence in order to put Jesus to death, but they were not finding any. 56 Many gave perjured testimony against him, but their evidence did not agree. 57 Then some stood up and gave false evidence against him as follows: 58 "We heard him say, 'I will tear down this man-made temple, and in three days I will raise up another, not made by men.'" 59 But not even here did their testimony agree. 60 Then the high priest stood up in the presence of everybody and asked Jesus, "Have you no reply to the accusations they bring against you?" 61 But he was silent; he gave no answer. Again the high priest questioned him, "Are you the Messiah, son of the Blessed One?" 62 "I am," said Jesus, "and

you will see The Man

seated at the right hand of power

and coming with the clouds of heaven."

63 The high priest tore his clothes and said, "What need have we of further witnesses? 64 You have heard the blasphemy—what is your opinion?" They all judged him to deserve the death penalty. 65 Some began to spit on him; they blindfolded him and hit him, calling out, "Prophesy!" The attendants set on him with blows.

Comment

The linked narratives of ecclesiastical examination, civil trial, and crucifixion are not only the longest sections of the gospel, they also enshrine the explanation of Mark's work in editing his sources.

The one who confronted the highest ecclesiastical authority was also The

Man, about to be vindicated, and also the vicegerent of eschatological judgment (13:26, 14:62). The evangelist demands that in spite of all appearances
all should see and understand this. This claim had to be made not only in the
face of an authority which had denied it all, but also in the face of those
insistently demanding of Christians where their true loyalties were. The Jesus
who had faced the religious authorities had also confronted civil authority,
mainly in silence (14:61, 15:5), allowing that same exasperated authority to
attach to the Cross a mocking title which nevertheless proclaimed the truth.
In the crisis in which Mark's community finds itself, its members also must
face the suffering which loyalty to Jesus will inevitably involve.

Our difficulty is to disentangle the theological concerns of the evangelists
(in our case especially Mark) from the strictly factual. This is by no means
easy: the early speeches of Peter in Acts (cf. esp. 2:22-24; 3:13-15) demonstrate clearly one early Christian attempt to fasten responsibility for the trial
and crucifixion on the Jewish leaders in Jerusalem. Can this be sustained in
our sources? Was Pilate supine and vacillating, responding to mob unrest, or
was he all the way through coldly calculating his own chances of survival in
an area where one false step could ruin his family and career? What was the
role of the Sanhedrin, officially or unofficially, all through this process? The
seemingly interminable debate on where blame is to be apportioned continues
unabated in both Jewish and Christian circles, and the bibliography at the
end of this comment bears testimony to this.

The fact of the crucifixion is undisputed, and the statement that Jesus
ended his life *crucifixus est sub Pontio Pilato* stands as a "secular" historical
datum in the midst of the theological statements and assertions in the New
Testament. Attested in the classical literature and central to the New Testament proclamation of Jesus, the crucifixion was a specific Roman form of
execution for a capital sentence. Outbreaks of lawlessness and occasional mob
violence apart, such an execution of sentence under Roman law could only
have been carried out by those acting under the appropriate imperial authority. All the evidence available to us combines to make it clear that crucifixion
in the time of Jesus was no arbitrary punishment but a sentence awarded for
three classes of offenders: slaves, upon information from their owners of serious offenses against life and property; habitual criminals; and conspirators
against Roman rule. Josephus *(Jewish Wars* 2:75, 241, 253) gives the third of
those reasons for the executions outside Jerusalem.

If we accept that Jesus was executed because Pontius Pilate regarded him
as an enemy of the state, and the gospels unanimously agree that the charge
was made, we must now examine the gospel evidence to see the use made by
the writers of the basic historical fact and the probable criminal charge
brought against Jesus. We must later on consider the gospel evidence for the
placard said to have been affixed to the cross, but for the moment we must
make the observation that the early Christian community would scarcely

have invented the charge against Jesus—for the most part the early community was concerned to demonstrate its law-abiding character. Not even the sometimes ambivalent attitude of Paul toward the state, not even the pervading sense of joy in Revelation at the downfall of the state, can be considered as evidence for any legacy of Jesus to the infant community which could have been called rebellious. Indeed the occasions on which Jesus was asked to declare his attitude to the Roman state were very few, and his replies such as to leave his questioners baffled by their detachment. There is more. The time in which Jesus exercised his ministry was one marked by the rise of various nationalist movements, and even if the language of such movements was not matched by overt acts of revolt, nevertheless there was no lack of those prepared to resort to the sword. Now there is not a shred of evidence to suggest that the early Christians allied themselves with such groups, and there is no evidence that the name and example of Jesus were invoked by such rebels against the Roman order.

Although our sources freely admit that Jesus was executed as being subversive—an admission in itself potentially dangerous to his followers in the succeeding decades—the portrait of Jesus provided by those same sources is wholly at variance with the charge, sentence, and execution. It can be maintained, and frequently has been, that this portrait of Jesus had been deliberately falsified so as to exclude any element which would in any way give credence to Jesus' revolutionary activities. Since the gospels are the only documentation we have for the ministry, for the trial and sentence, this argument is wholly incapable of refutation. However, the proponents of this viewpoint single out various points regarded as significant elements which escaped the process of excision. They do not turn out on examination to be of more than minor significance and certainly not enough to be regarded as tips of hidden icebergs of controversy. The cleansing of the temple we examined in context, and it certainly represented no threat to Roman order. The discussion on the legitimacy of taxation was certainly not the exclusive prerogative of subversives; the matter occurs again and again in the most innocent of contemporary classical writers. In the circumstances of the time it is difficult to imagine Jesus *not* being asked the question. That one of Jesus' disciples should have been called "the Zealot" need occasion no surprise; given the nature of the Proclamation by Jesus, it would be natural for the term "Reign of God" to interest someone attracted otherwise to political alternatives, violent or otherwise. Luke's preservation of a tradition (22:38) of two followers carrying swords immediately before the arrest, far from signaling violence to come, would have put a great many visitors to Jerusalem under similar suspicion. (The reader who wishes to examine these questions, from the standpoint of a "conspiracy of silence" on the part of the evangelists, may consult the works by Brandon and Cohn listed in the bibliography following the comments for this section.)

For those to whom the gospels are hopelessly compromised documents, no argument is possible. If, however, we accept the *substantial* accuracy of the New Testament accounts of the trial (allowing, in passing, that historians find those accounts very difficult at times), then we are bound to seek some explanation for a sentence and an execution so wholly out of character with Jesus as the gospels depict him.

We can immediately rule out the possibility of Jesus having been caught up in some antinationalist Roman military dragnet. Given the climate of the times, Jesus as the victim of such a piece of brutality would immediately have become a nationalist symbol—and of that there is no trace. In any event, such an occurrence would be entirely contrary to all that we know of the administration of Roman law in the provinces. Though substantial discretion was allowed to a governor *extra ordinem* (i.e., outside the senatorial provinces), the procedures were nevertheless precise; a sentence of death could only be imposed after trial before the governor, as a result of information brought against a prisoner. Our gospels are unanimous that such a charge (information) was made against Jesus by his fellow Jews. The questions which arise from this datum are formidable: How can it have been possible for Jews in the first part of the century to have delated a fellow Jew to the imperial authority on grounds of sedition? If the Sadducees were anxious to preserve the civil status quo, can this have been equally true of the patriotic and separatist Pharisees on this occasion? Did Pilate act strictly within the letter of the law? This question is posed by the consideration that a contemporary of Jesus (Philo Judaeus of Alexandria) in a work outlining anti-Jewish activities in Alexandria and in Palestine accuses Pilate of many executions carried out without trial *(Embassy to Gaius,* 302). That Philo records Jewish agitation to send official complaints to the emperor but underlines Pilate's well-known cruelty while in office—it also, and incidentally, underscores the contention previously made that such executions were totally illegal. We are bound, therefore, to ask whether Jesus was put to death contrary to law? There is no hint of this in the New Testament, and the spread of Christianity through the Mediterranean world would surely have evoked some response from the Jews upon whom the evangelists fasten most responsibility for the death of Jesus.

The contemporary records clearly indicate that Pilate was far from being an ideal governor, even allowing for the fact that he was attempting to administer a notoriously turbulent province with potential threats on two of its borders. Did he, in this case, respond to the passionate pleas of Jewish accusers and sentence a man whose guilt on a charge of subversion was wholly incapable of being sustained? Was the trial held in public, or was it—as John's gospel seems to hint—a private hearing? Who first handed on the details to Jesus' followers? Does the account of the silence of Jesus before Pilate owe its origins to the interest of the early community in Isaiah 53, or did that interest arise from the fact that Jesus said virtually nothing at the trial? The matter of

Barabbas raises its own questions, not the least of which is whether or not the governor had any discretionary power to release a prisoner in response to popular demand. We know of no such instance from classical sources, and it is probably unlikely that a Roman provincial governor would dare to act often with the capriciousness of—say—a Nero or a Caligula. Nevertheless, *if* this incident is historically based, then it renders much more likely the possibility that Pilate responded to clamor on the part of the Jewish leaders.

In essence the gospels all agree that one circumstance of the trial was that pressure from the Jewish authorities was brought on one precise and exact charge—that of subversion of lawful Roman authority. This is a circumstance which is by no means self-explanatory. There had been nationalist movements before, especially in Galilee, and there would be more before the final Roman intervention in A.D. 135. There was inflammatory apocalyptic literature in plenty, and the Essenes (by whatever process of interpretation) looked to a final eschatological warfare. We are, therefore, bound to ask what possible information the Jews could have used against Jesus which they did not use against anyone else. Put in another form, what was there about the mission and ministry of Jesus which evoked such venomous hostility as to bring a fellow Jew before a pagan court on a charge which inevitably carried the death penalty? It is here that we must approach the testimony of John's gospel with the utmost caution, for the reported protestation of the Jewish authorities at the trial that they were not empowered to carry out a capital sentence (18:31) has to be balanced against reports in the same gospel that there had been attempts on Jesus' life before (cf. 5:18, 7:30, 8:59, 10:31). We must beware of the protestation in 18:31 for the precise reason that the whole movement in that gospel is to a climax of enthronement, of exaltation (physically and theologically) which could not be accommodated by Jewish execution by stoning.

Since the protestation is absent from the synoptists, in some significant ways we must deal cautiously with the Johannine account, theologically loaded as it is, aside altogether from the continuing debate as to whether or not the Sanhedrin had legal jurisdiction at that time. This latter consideration cannot be resolved with our present knowledge, and any suggestion offered in any commentary will certainly fall under criticism from any one of dozens of bodies of opinion. Scholarly opinion ranges from a total denial of Sanhedrin competence at one end of the scale (e.g., Paul Winter, see the bibliography on this subject) to an affirmation at the other (cf. E. Rivkin, "Beth Din, Boulé, Sanhedrin: A Tragedy of Errors," *HUCA* 46.1975, pp. 181-99) at the other. Strobel (see the bibliography in this section) hazards the thought that the Sanhedrin might have treated Jesus as the "seducer" of Deuteronomy 13 and 17 and so could condemn Jesus—apparently in suggesting this accepting also the legal competency of the Sanhedrin. What is often overlooked is the significant variation in New Testament sources as to the precise role of the official

Judaism of Jerusalem in the legal process against Jesus. To this we must now turn.

In summary the following conclusions emerge:

1. Matthew's gospel, followed by Mark, presents us with a meeting of the chief priests, elders, and scribes at which Jesus is judged to be deserving of death (Matt 26:59-66; Mark 14:55-64), apparently on a charge of blasphemy. This is apparently supported by other statements—Matt 20:18, 27:3; Mark 10:33—though both Matt 20:18 (= Mark 10:33) is certainly a prophecy after the event.

2. This version of events is modified by Luke 22:71, which makes no mention of blasphemy as a technical charge and has nothing to say of any verbal judgment by the high priest. If we allow historicity to the speeches in Acts, the same author (13:27-28) has Peter saying that the Jews found no cause of death in Jesus. However, this is in part negated by Acts 2:23-24 and wholly so by 3:13-14. In any event the Greek of 13:27-28 is a matter of some dispute and is outside our present purpose.

3. It is significant that John has no session of the Sanhedrin, let alone a verdict, as a preliminary to the trial before Pilate. To be precise, apart from Matthew and Mark no New Testament author ever makes the statement that Jesus was condemned to death either by the Sanhedrin or by an irregular group of Jerusalem Jews. This is true even when we take into account that Luke's gospel uses the verb "hand over" *(paradidōmi)* exclusively of the Jewish people.

The above considerations provide one solid piece of evidence: Jesus was not *condemned* to death by any element of Judaism, official or otherwise. But this simply provides us with a starting point for another discussion, which has to do with linking the Roman execution with specific Old Testament prescriptions which had to do with a capital sentence. We refer to the expression "on a tree" (or, somewhat more literally, "on wood") at Acts 5:30, 10:39, Gal 3:13 (a quotation from the Septuagint of Deut 21:23), and 1 Pet 2:24. In other words there was an early tradition which sought to link a Roman penalty with a Jewish penalty carried out on the body of one executed for idolatry or blasphemy. This simply increases our dilemma. Is this testimony to a conviction on the part of three disparate writers that *had* Jesus been convicted under Jewish auspices, he *would* have been deemed worthy of the death penalty and the subsequent hanging of the body? So far as Paul is concerned, did he believe that as things stood Jesus *could* have been found guilty of blasphemy and that crucifixion carried out by the secular authorities was a sufficient implementation of Deut 21:23? Some support for this may be found in Luke, who—though insisting on the ignorance of the Jewish leaders (cf. Acts 3:17, 13:27)—nevertheless, as we have seen, insists that the "delivering up" or "handing over" of Jesus resulted in a death which bore semblance to the penalty of Deut 21:23. It is possible to read Matt 26:66 = Mark 14:64 as a condemnation, a verdict of guilty, but the wording refrains from this: *they all judged him to deserve the death penalty.* John contents himself with outlining the manifest errors of the members of the Sanhedrin.

If there is one single factor—indeed a single word—which forges these varied accounts into a single unit, it is the word *paradidōmi* (infinitive *paradidonai),* to which attention has already been called. Its meaning in Greek and to a far lesser extent in Latin *(tradere)* ranges all the way from a neutral "handing on" of something to downright treachery or betrayal. Two uses will concern us here; both are in the last analysis theological. The first of them, used frequently in the Passion predictions, in the prophecy of betrayal, in the accounts of the arrest, and in the handing over of Jesus to Pilate, is wholly consistent with the general sense of the verb. But what is its relationship to the "handing over," "giving over" of Jesus to death in the remainder of our sources, and to his being "handed over" by God? And in all this wealth of theological reflection, which came first—Isa 53:6,12 (with three uses of *paradidōmi* in the Septuagint), or the Pauline reflection in Rom 8:32? The same phenomenon is found in Gal 2:20 and Eph 5:2, and perhaps we are in the presence of a very early confessional statement which later fastened on Isaiah 53 as the embodiment of the figure of Jesus. It is here that we may be near to an understanding of the element of "self-offering" which is so manifestly a part of the sayings of Jesus in the gospels, most notably in the "ransom" saying which we examined at 10:45 and which undoubtedly underlies John 10:11.

Nothing in the above paragraph provides us with a ready-made solution as to whether Isaiah 53 was read back into our sources, all flowing from "handed over"—which would provide a sequence of betrayal, Sanhedrin, and the trial before Pilate. After all, we have no information as to the identity of any eyewitness who would have supplied all the wealth of detail which attends those events. There is one negative witness, and that is the absence of any "fulfillment" note in Matthew, where we might naturally have expected a reference to Isa 53:12. It is found at Luke 22:37 and was assimilated from there in some manuscripts of Mark (15:28). On balance we have to conclude that the New Testament sources simply used a precise word for the process whereby Jesus was "handed over" to the governor by the Jewish authorities. But later reflection—on Isaiah 53?—provided an early tradition in which was enshrined the Christian belief that this act precisely fulfilled the redemptive purposes of God.

If, as we have seen, the Sanhedrin did not condemn Jesus to death (even though finding that he deserved such a penalty), why did the authorities seek to "hand him over" to the governor for trial, sentence, and execution? What was the reason or pretext? This is all the more pressing a question in view of the well-known Roman practice of allowing wide latitude to local legal codes and practices, of which Jews in Palestine took full advantage. John 19:6 refers to the large discretionary powers of the Jewish legal authorities, along with their reply to Pilate that those powers did not include the death penalty. The explanation provided by John 11:45-54 has given a theological interpretation to a gesture designed as a sop, a kind of legal bribe, to Roman authority. But how genuine was the threat of a Roman destruction of Jewish institutions, or even of "the nation"? Certainly the threat was genuine immediately before the War of A.D. 66, as Josephus *(Jewish Wars* 2,397, 400, 421) informs us, and given the character of Pilate, the tense situation on the Parthian border, and the always turbulent nature of the province, it would not be surprising if the situation was much different in the time of Jesus.

One feature of the matter before us which deserves attention is the possibility of a severely divided Sanhedrin. This is relevant, aside from all considerations of competency. Prominent in the proceedings against Jesus is the charge of a threat to destroy the temple. In itself this is hardly grounds for consideration of a capital sentence, and far more devastating things had been predicted for people and nation by the writing prophets. (We shall have occasion in the notes on v. 58 to consider the theory of a Jewish scholar now deceased that something far more serious was underlying the charge.) Now divided legal opinion, even in the highest courts of any nation, is nothing new in the history of jurisprudence: Paul used his knowledge of such divided opinion to good effect (Acts 23:7). But do we have enough information in our sources to determine that a divided Sanhedrin, anxious to dispose of a troublemaker, simply remitted the matter to Pilate?

Matthew and Mark, in close parallel, tell us that the Sanhedrin—or some members of it—found Jesus deserving of the death penalty, where Luke leaves the matter entirely open, with no "finding" at all. John declares in effect that the decision to hand Jesus over was in essence political. Paul's description of Jesus having been "hanged on wood" *may* indicate that he thought Jesus had been guilty of blasphemy (under a law which he found inadequate even when not totally wrong). What appears to be the most acceptable and sensible solution to the often conflicting testimony is that the appearance of Jesus before the Sanhedrin was not a trial at all and not even what might be described as a "grand jury" enquiry. We repeat the caution given earlier: in our gospel sources we are not dealing with eyewitness accounts, and—short of possible information from Joseph of Arimathea—we may be reading the selective pickings of second- and third-hand reports.

What emerges from the evangelists is the reconstruction of a series of events (precipitated by the treachery of Judas?) brought about to seek some means of handing Jesus over to the Roman civil authorities. Once we reach this point, then we no longer have to deal with procedures patently illegal under Jewish law (e.g., a meeting of the Sanhedrin at night to consider a capital offense, a verdict of capital punishment delivered before the lapse of one night). What we *do* have is a hastily convened meeting, in all the circum-

stances of the preparation for Passover, to determine what could be done with
Jesus. There was certainly some semblance of an inquiry, seeking evidence on
which the prisoner might be convicted, and what followed the solitary recorded reply of Jesus was not the kind of thing normally associated with a
judicial proceeding. Certainly all three synoptic evangelists report Jesus as
speaking of The Man as the cloud rider, evoking an outraged charge of blasphemy and a response that Jesus deserved the death penalty. But the purpose
of the gathering was not an examination of theology, but to seek some political grounds on which the prisoner might be handed over to the jurisdiction of
the civil power.

The record of the evangelists is that the Sanhedrin sought witnesses who
could bring charges involving the death penalty but could not find anything
consistent. We shall have occasion to call attention to some deeply puzzling
questions in Mark's version of the saying about destroying the temple (v. 58),
but the unanimity of all four evangelists is good evidence for its authenticity.
It can only have infuriated the official Jerusalem establishment but was
hardly ground for a sentence of death. The members of the Sanhedrin must
have found convincing reason to seek a Roman court hearing and sentence.
Now the unanimity of all four gospels that Jesus' cross was placarded with a
summary of the capital charge is all the more notable in that this is the sole
example known to us of such a practice. It is hard to think of any reason—
apart from a firm historical basis—which would have prompted the writers to
include this single and strange exception. Jesus then was found guilty and
executed on a criminal charge of sedition under Roman law, one which would
hardly have been the basis for a capital charge under Jewish law. Now the
placard specifically singles out a supposed claim to be "king of the Jews"—a
prominent feature of John's gospel. How plausible then was the reasoning
which caused the prisoner to be taken to Pilate? Luke and Luke alone supplies us with some specific details (in 23:2):

1. Jesus deceived, misled the people, inciting to revolt.
2. He forbade paying taxes to the emperor.
3. He made himself the anointed one, a king.

It was the last of these, in Luke's account, which claimed Pilate's attention,
for from it might easily prescind the first and the second. But given an ele-
mentary accuracy to all of this, what was there in the ministry and teaching
of Jesus which could plausibly support the charge?

The term "Messiah" (Greek *Christos*) occurs with baffling frequency in the
gospels, especially in John. Does its early appearance in the Pauline letters
betoken a common use on the part of Jesus' followers during his ministry? If
so, the members of the Sanhedrin would have little difficulty in finding
ground for translating the term as *rex* or *Caesar,* with all the implications of a
civil rebellion in the making. But for the Jewish leaders—especially for the

Sadducees, with their rigid adherence to the Pentateuch and a desire to preserve the political and religious status quo—the quotation from Daniel will have been decisive. We have noticed throughout this commentary the ambivalence of interpretation in the sayings about The Man. Here there is no question of any involvement of the followers with the central figure: they have all forsaken their representative and have fled. So in the crisis of this Sanhedrin appearance Jesus is alone and speaks for himself alone, in a text which has assertions about sovereignty and about the real status of Jesus in the endtime.

It seems to this writer that whatever doubts or reservations might be entertained in previous instances of "Son of Man" sayings, we are right to see here *the* decisive use of it by Jesus, in a context which provided the authorities with a convenient excuse to remit a troublesome and even dangerous critic to the governor.

In summary all the evidence from the gospels goes to prove that there was no judicial or even semijudicial proceeding before the Sanhedrin, and John's gospel omits any reference to an appearance before that body. Matthew and Mark can only—at most—say that there was an agreement that Jesus "deserved" to die. Luke avoids any such suggestion. There was no verdict of guilty in any fashion which would fulfill Jewish legal codes, and the decision to find some means of handing Jesus over to the governor was a purely political one. That there were many occasions in the ministry of Jesus which roused the ire of the Jewish authorities is beyond question—the conduct of Jesus and his disciples on the Sabbath, for example, and his apparent dismissal of the food laws—and we may safely assume that the possibility of legal proceedings was more than once raised. But far more pressing than food laws or Sabbath breaking was a ministry in Galilee, which was never a model of stability and religious observance, a ministry in—of all places—Samaria, and above all potentially threatening language about a Reign of God with Jesus as its harbinger and inaugurator.

Note:

The views expressed above are not shared by all writers and commentators, and appended here are some representative works on the Sanhedrin appearance from very different viewpoints.

Catchpole, D. R. "The Answer of Jesus to Caiaphas (Matt xxvi.64)." *NTS* 17.1971, pp. 213-26.

Lohse, Eduard. *The New Testament Environment.* Translated by John E. Steeley, rev. ed. Nashville: Abingdon Press, 1976, chapters 2 and 3.

Moule, C. F. D. *The Origin of Christology.* London and New York: Cambridge University Press, 1977, especially, pp. 11-46.

Yoder, John Howard. *The Politics of Jesus.* Grand Rapids, Mich.: Eerdmans, 1972.

On the Sanhedrin appearance, Gerard S. Sloyan's work (see the general bibliography) finds evidence of a "sandwich" structure in Mark. He finds a proceeding at night, with a finding (14:64), but 15:1 suggests another meeting at which a decision was reached. The author, therefore, suggests two traditions, with this section (14:53-64) sandwiched between references to Peter's denial in 14:27-31 and 14:66-72. However, Mark often uses material as a "filling" between two other blocks of material—e.g., 6:14-29 between 6:7-13 and 30-31; 3:22-30 between 3:20-21 and 31-35. Furthermore, according to the "sandwich" theory, 14:65 is closely linked with 14:55-64, and it too has a "denial" motif. (Cf. W. G. Kümmel, *The Theology of the New Testament*, translation by John E. Steeley of *Die Theologie des Neuen Testaments*, Nashville: Abingdon Press, 1973, pp. 70-71.)

Bibliography: The Sanhedrin and Trial

This bibliography covers both the appearance before the Jewish leaders and the trial before Pilate. It is placed here for convenience of reference.

Bammel, Ernst, ed. *The Trial of Jesus: Cambridge Studies in Honour of C. F. D. Moule.* Naperville, Ill.: Allenson, 1970.

Bartsch, Hans-Werner. "Die Bedeutung des Sterbens Jesu nach den Synoptikern." *TZ* 20.1964, pp. 87-102.

Benoit, Pierre. *Jesus and the Gospel.* Vol. 1. Translation by Benet Weatherhead. London: Darton, Longman and Todd, 1973.

———. "Jésus devant le Sanhedrin." *Angelicum* 20.1943, pp. 143-65.

Bertram, Georg. *Die Leidensgeschichte Jesu und der Christuskult* Forschungen zur Religion und Literatur des Alten and Neuen Testaments. N.F. Vol. 22. Göttingen: Vandenhoeck and Ruprecht, 1922.

Best, Ernst. *The Temptation and the Passion: the Markan Soteriology.* SNTS Monographs 2. Cambridge University Press, 1965.

Black, Matthew. "The Arrest and Trial of Jesus and the Date of the Last Supper." In *New Testament Essays: Studies in Memory of Thomas Walter Manson*, edited by A. J. B. Higgins. Manchester University Press, 1959, pp. 19-33.

———. "The 'Son of Man' Passion Sayings in the Gospel Tradition." *ZNW* 60.1969, pp. 1-8.

Blinzler, Josef. "Das Synedrium von Jerusalem und die Straffprozessordnung der Mischna." *ZNW* 52.1961, pp. 54-65.

———. *The Trial of Jesus: The Jewish and Roman Proceedings Against Jesus Christ Described and Assessed from the Oldest Accounts* Translation by I. McHugh and F. McHugh. Westminster: Newman Press, 1959.

Boman, Thorlief. *Die Jesuüberlieferung im Lichte der Neuen Volkskunde.* Göttingen: Vandenhoeck and Ruprecht, 1967, pp. 221ff.

Boobyer, G. H. "The Redaction of Mark IV, 1-34." *NTS* 8.1961-62, pp. 59-70.

———. "The Secrecy Motif in Mark's Gospel." *NTS* 6.1959-60, pp. 225-35.

Borgen, Peter. "John and the Synoptics in the Passion Narrative." *NTS* 5.1958-59, pp. 246-59.

Bornhäuser, Karl. *The Death and Resurrection of Christ.* Translation by A. Rumpus. London: Independent Press, 1958.

Brandon, S. F. G. *The Fall of Jerusalem and the Christian Church: A Study of the Effects of the Jewish Overthrow of A.D. 70 on Christianity.* 3rd ed. London: SPCK, 1957.

———. *Jesus and the Zealots.* New York: Scribner, 1967.

———. *The Trial of Jesus of Nazareth.* Historic Trials Series. New York: Stein and Day, 1968.

Braumann, G. "Markus 15, 2-5 und Markus 14, 55-64." *ZNW* 52.1961, pp. 273-78.

Bultmann, Rudolf. "The History of the Tradition of the Passion." In *The History of the Synoptic Tradition.* Translation by John Marsh. 2nd ed. New York: Harper and Row, 1968, pp. 275ff.

Burkill, T. A. "St. Mark's Philosophy of the Passion." *NovTest* 2.1958, pp. 245-71.

———. "The Trial of Jesus." *Vigiliae Christianae* 12.1958, pp. 1-18.

Buse, Ivor. "St. John and the Markan Passion Narrative." *NTS* 4.1957-58, pp. 215-19.

Catchpole, D. R. "The Answer of Jesus to Caiaphas (Matt. xxvi. 64)." *NTS* 17.1971, pp. 213-26.

———. *The Trial of Jesus: A Study in the Gospels and Jewish Historiography from 1770 to the Present Day.* Studia Post-Biblica, Vol. 18. Leiden: E. J. Brill, 1971.

Cohn, H. H. "Reflections on the Trial and Death of Jesus." *Israel Law Review* 2.1967, pp. 332-79.

———. *The Trial and Death of Jesus.* New York: Harper and Row, 1971.

Conzelmann, Hans. "History and Theology in the Passion Narratives of the Synoptic Gospels." *Int* 24.1970, pp. 178-97.

Cook, Michael J. *Mark's Treatment of the Jewish Leaders.* Leiden: E. J. Brill, 1978.

Dabrowski, E. "The Trial of Jesus in Recent Research." *StEv* 4.1968, pp. 21-27.

Davies, Alan T. "The Jews and the Death of Jesus: Theological Reflections." *Int* 23.1969, pp. 207-17.

Derrett, J. D. M. *Law in the New Testament.* London: Darton, Longman and Todd, 1970.

Dewar, Francis. "Chapter 13 and the Passion Narrative in St. Mark." *Theology* 64.1961, pp. 99-107.

Dodd, C. H. *More New Testament Studies.* Grand Rapids, Mich.: Eerdmans, 1968 (especially pp. 84ff. on "The Historical Problem of the Death of Jesus").

Donahue, John R. *Are You the Christ: The Trial Narrative in the Gospel of Mark.* SBL Dissertation Series 10. Missoula, Mont.: Scholars Press, 1973.

Dormeyer, Detlev. *Die Passion Jesu als Verhaltensmodell: Literarische und theologische Analyse der Traditions und Redaktionsgeschichte der Markus Passion.* NTAbh, Neue Folge 11. Münster: Aschendorff, 1974.

Enslin, Morton. "The Temple and the Cross." *Judaism* 20.1971, pp. 24-31.

Finegan, Jack. "Die Überlieferung der Leidens- und Auferstehungsgeschichte Jesu." *ZNW* 15.1934.

Flusser, David. "A Literary Approach to the Death of Jesus." *Judaism* 20.1971, pp. 32-36.

Gaston, Lloyd. *No Stone on Another.* Supplements to *NovTest* Supp, Vol. 23. Leiden: E. J. Brill, 1970.

Glasson, T. Francis. "The Reply to Caiaphas (Mark 14:62)." *NTS* 7.1960-61, pp. 88-93.

Gnilka, J. "Die Verhandlungen vor dem Synhedrion und vor Pilatus nach Mk. 14.53-15.5." In *Evangelisch-Katholischer Kommentar zum Neuen Testament.* Heft 2. Zürich-Einsiedeln: Benziger, 1970, pp. 5-21.

Gordis, Robert. "The Trial of Jesus in the Light of History: A Symposium." *Judaism* 20.1971, pp. 6-74.

Grant, Robert M. "The Trial of Jesus in the Light of History." *Judaism* 20.1971, pp. 37-42.

Hahn, Ferdinand. "Der Prozess Jesu nach dem Johannesevangelium. Eine redaktionsgeschichtliche Untersuchung." In *Evangelisch-Katholischer Kommentar zum Neuen Testament.* Heft 2. Zürich-Einsiedeln: Benziger, 1970.

Harvey, A. E. *Jesus and the Constraints of History.* Philadelphia: Westminster Press, 1982.

Hengel, Martin. *Die Zeloten.* Arbeiten zur Geschichte des Spätjudentums und Urchristentums. Vol. 1. Leiden: E. J. Brill, 1961.

Horbury, William. "The Passion Narratives and Historical Criticism." *Theology* 75.1972, pp. 58-71.

Horvath, T. "Why Was Jesus Brought to Pilate?" *NovTest* 11.1969, pp. 174-84.

Isaac, Jules. *Jesus and Israel,* New York: Holt, Rinehart and Winston, 1971.

Jeremias, Joachim. "Zur Geschichtlichkeit des Verhörs Jesu vor dem Hohen Rat." In *Abba: Studien zur neutestamentlichen Theologie und Zeitgeschichte.* Göttingen: Vandenhoek and Ruprecht, 1966.

Jonge, M. de. "The Use of Ὁ ΧΡΙΣΤΟΣ in the Passion Narratives." In *Jésus aux origines de la christologie,* edited by J. Dupont. Bibliotheca Ephemeridum Theologicarum Lovaniensium 40. Leuven: Leuven University Press, 1975, pp. 169-92.

Kelber, Werner H. *The Passion in Mark: Studies in Mark 14-16.* Philadelphia: Fortress Press, 1976.

Kilpatrick, G. D. *The Trial of Jesus.* New York: Oxford University Press, 1952.

Knox, John. "A Note on Mark 14, 51-52." In *The Joy of Study,* edited by Sherman E. Johnson. New York: Macmillan, 1951.

Koch, Werner, ed. *Der Prozess Jesu: Versuch eines Tatsachenberichts.* Köln: Keipenhauer & Witsch, 1966.

Kuhn, Karl Georg. "Jesus in Gethsemane." *EvTh* 12.1952-53, pp. 260-85.

Langevin, Paul-Émile. *Jésus Seigneur et L'Eschatologie: Exégèse de Textes Prepauliniens.* Studia Post-Biblica Vol. 21. Paris: Desclée De Brouwer, 1967.

Léon-Dufour, Xavier. "Passion [Récits de la]." *Dictionnaire de la Bible* Supp 6, cols. 1419-92.

Lietzmann, Hans. "Der Prozess Jesu." In *Sitzungsberichte der Preussichen Akademie der Wissenschaften* (phil.-hist. Klasse), 1931, pp. 313-22.

Linnemann, Eta. "Studien zur Passionsgeschichte." *FRLANT* 102.1970.

Linton, Olof. "The Trial of Jesus and the Interpretation of Psalm CX." *NTS* 7.1960-61, pp. 258-63.

Lohse, Eduard. *History of the Suffering and Death of Jesus Christ.* Translation by Martin Dietrich. Philadelphia: Fortress Press, 1967.

Lührmann, D. "Markus 14, 55-64: Christologie und Zerstörung des Tempels im Markusevangelium." *NTS* 27.1981, pp. 457-75.

McArthur, Harvey K. "Mark XIV, 62." *NTS* 4.1957-58, pp. 156-58.

McKelvey, R. J. *The New Temple.* Oxford University Press, 1969.

Maier, P. "Sejanus, Pilate, and the Date of the Crucifixion." *Church History* 37.1968, pp. 3-13.

Mantel, Hugo. *Studies in the History of the Sanhedrin.* Cambridge, Mass.: Harvard University Press, 1965.

Marin, L. *The Semiotics of the Passion Narrative Topics and Figures.* Pittsburgh Theological Monograph Series 25. Pittsburgh: Pickwick Press, 1980.

Nörr, Dieter. "Problems of Legal History in the Gospels." In *Jesus in His Time,* edited by Hans Jürgen Schultz. Translation by Brian Watchorn. Philadelphia: Fortress Press, 1971.

O'Neill, J. C. "The Silence of Jesus." *NTS* 15.1969-70, pp. 153-67.

Perrin, Norman. "Mark XIV, 62: The End Product of a Christian Pesher Tradition?" *NTS* 12.1965-66, pp. 150-55.

Ramsey, A. M. "The Narratives of the Passion." In *Studia Evangelica III.* Berlin: Akademie Verlag, 1964, pp. 122-34.

Sandmel, Samuel. *A Jewish Understanding of the New Testament.* New York: Ktav Press, 1957.

Schenke, L. *Studien zur Passionsgeschichte des Markus: Tradition und Redaktion in Markus 14, 1-12* (Forschung zur Bibel 4). Würzburg: Echter Verlag Katholisches Bibelwerk, 1971.

Schille, Gottfried. "Das Leiden des Herrn: Die evangelische Passionstradition und ihr Sitz im Leben." *ZTK* 52.1955, pp. 161-205.

Schinzer, R. "Die Bedeutung des Prozesses Jesu." *NZTR* 25.1983, pp. 138-54.

Schneider, G. "Traditionsgeschichte von Mk 14, 43-52." *ZNW* 63.1972, pp. 188-209.

Schreiber, Johannes. *Die Markuspassion: Wege zur Forschung der Leidensgeschichte Jesu.* Hamburg: Furche Verlag, 1969.

Senior, Donald P. *The Passion Narrative According to Matthew: A Redactional Study.* Bibliotheca Ephemeridum Theologicarum Lovaniensium 39. Leuven: Leuven University Press, 1975.

Sherwin-White, A. N. *Roman Society and Roman Law in the New Testament.* Oxford: Clarendon Press, 1963.

————. "The Trial of Christ." In *Historicity and Chronology in the New Testament,* edited by Matthew Black. London: SPCK, 1965.

Sloyan, Gerard S. *Jesus on Trial: The Development of the Passion Narratives and Their Historical and Ecumenical Implications.* Philadelphia: Fortress Press, 1973.

Smallwood, E. M. "High Priests and Politics in Roman Palestine." *JTS* 13.1962, pp. 13-34.

Strecker, G. "Die Leidens- und Auferstehungsvorraussagen im Markusevangelium (Mk 8, 31; 9, 31; 10, 22-34)." *ZTK* 64.1967, pp. 16-39.

———. "The Passion-and-Resurrection Predictions in Mark's Gospel." *Int* 22.1968, pp. 421-42.

Strobel, August. *Die Stunde der Wahrheit: Untersuchungen zum Strafverfahren gegen Jesus.* Tübingen: J. C. B. Mohr, 1980.

Taylor, Vincent. "The Narrative of the Crucifixion." *NTS* 8.1961-62, pp. 333-34.

———. "The Origin of the Markan Passion Sayings." *NTS* 1.1954-55, pp. 159-67.

VanHoye, A. "Structure et théologie des récits de la passion." *NRTh* 99.1967, pp. 135-63.

Vielhauer, Philipp. "Zur Frage der Christologischen Hoheitstitel." *TLZ* 90.1965, pp. 569-88.

Viering, Fritz, ed. *Zur Bedeutung des Todes Jesu.* Gütersloh: Mohn, 1967.

Walter, Nikolaus. "Tempelzerstörung und synoptische Apokalypse." *ZNW* 57.1966, pp. 38-49.

Wead, D. "We Have a Law," *NovTest* 11.1969, pp. 185-89.

Wilcox, Max. "The Denial Sequence in Mark XIV, 26-31, 66-72." *NTS* 17.1969-70, pp. 426-36.

Wilson, W. R. *The Execution of Jesus.* New York: Scribner, 1970.

Winter, Paul. "A Letter from Pontius Pilate." *NovTest* 7.1964, pp. 37-43.

———. "The Marcan Account of Jesus' Trial by the Sanhedrin." *JTS* n.s. 14.1963, pp. 94-102.

———. "Mc 14, 53b, 55-64, ein Gebilde des Evangelisten." *ZNW* 53.1962, pp. 260-63.

———. "Marginal Notes on the Trial of Jesus." *ZNW* 53.1962, pp. 260-63.

———. *On the Trial of Jesus.* Studia Judaica. Berlin: Walter de Gruyter, 1961.

———. "The Trial of Jesus as a Rebel Against Rome." *Jewish Quarterly* 16.1968, pp. 31-37.

Notes

53. This connecting note would follow most naturally from v. 46. We may consider the possibility that Mark had originally intended this and then on returning to the Palestinian community found a vague tradition of a young man at Gethsemane and some account of a scuffle at the time of Jesus' arrest. The episode of the young man he fashioned into a theological motif, while the short outbreak of violence in the garden faced him with parallel but varying accounts in Matthew and Luke. This latter he duly inserted but in so doing broke the continuity between vv. 46 and 53.

the high priest's house: The high priest is not identified, but it was Caiaphas. He held office from A.D. 18 to 36. According to John 18:13, Jesus was taken first to Annas, the father-in-law of Caiaphas, but no reason is given for this action.

chief priests, elders and scribes were all assembling: Cf. 14:43. Some important manuscripts of Mark have *autō* (to him) after *assembling,* though many equally important manuscripts omit it. It is not found in Matthew. We have translated it by *house* as the best way of rendering the Greek. This does not read as though a formal meeting was taking place, but rather it suggests that members of the various groups of the Sanhedrin had agreed on an ad hoc discussion.

54. *Peter followed him:* It is difficult to know what to make of this seeming interpolation. One writer (E. Linnemann, "Die Verlegnung des Petrus," *ZTK* 63.1.1966, pp. 1-32) regards it simply as a natural development from 14:27-31; once the story of Jesus' prediction of Peter's denial became known, another story would follow. Yet another writer (C. A. Evans, " 'Peter Warming Himself': The Problem of an Editorial Seam," *JBL* 101.2.1982, pp. 245-49), finding the same phenomenon in John 18:18,25 as in Mark 14:54,67, concludes that we cannot posit a common source but rather a story-telling device of digression and resumption. This latter verdict was plainly not in the mind of R. T. Fortna ("Jesus and Peter at the High Priest's House: A Test Case for the Question of the Relation between Mark's and John's Gospels," *NTS* 24.3.1978, pp. 371-83). John's source, he maintains, is closer to Mark than John's gospel (one hearing, followed by all three denials) but is not identical in structure. Though Linnemann perhaps errs in the direction of scepticism, there are nevertheless obtrusive questions. If all the disciples had forsaken Jesus and run away, why did Peter remain behind? If Peter was the principal source behind the Markan tradition, why is it John who records that Peter was responsible for cutting off the ear of the high priest's servant (John 18:10), with Mark simply recording a *certain bystander?* There are no certain answers to any of the above questions, but given the suggestions of Fortna and given the agreement of the evangelists on the intrusion of this verse into the narrative, we can only suppose that it was made at a later date.

courtyard (Greek *aulē,* cf. Latin *aula):* Strictly this was an open space around which rooms were arranged, and entrance was made through the *proaulion* (14:68). Mark's Greek at this point is hardly simple. Partially he shares Matthew's and Luke's vocabulary, but his attempted combination of the two sources results in a clumsiness which is difficult to translate.

> Matt 26:58—*ho de Petros ēkoluthei auto apo makrothen heōs tēs aulēs . . . kai eiselthon eso . . .* (Peter, however, followed him at a distance as far as the courtyard . . . and entering inside . . .)

> Luke 22:54-55—*ho de Petros ēkoluthei makrothen. Periapsantōn de pur en mesō tēs aulēs . . .* (Peter, however, followed at a distance. They had lit a fire in the middle of the courtyard . . .)

> Mark 14:54—*kai ho Petros apo makrothen ēkolouthesen autō heōs esō eis tēn aulēn*

Literally translated, this would be "and Peter followed him from a distance inside into the courtyard . . ." The problem is that *esō* is relatively rare in the New Testament (it occurs eight times in all), being found only once in Matthew and once in Mark. It is not too surprising to find it in Matthew, but its presence in Mark is astonishing and can only be explained either as having been copied from Matthew or appended by very early scribal assimilation.

attendants (Greek *hupēretai):* The word has a very wide range of meaning, from lesser attendants and religious functionaries to one use describing the president of a synagogue (Luke 4:20).

at the fire: The Greek word used here *(phōs)* could be translated by "at the blaze," for in later Greek and in the Greek of this period *phōs* (light) is often employed as the equivalent of *pur* (fire).

The phrase *warmed himself at the fire* is an odd feature both here and in John 18:18 for it appears again in Mark 14:67 = John 18:25, and presumably this is an editorial seam (cf. C. A. Evans in the comment above.)

Matthew does not have the Markan note about Peter warming himself but says that Peter came and "sat with the guards to see the end" (26:58).

55. This opening formula *(the chief priests and the whole Sanhedrin)* may be treated as the opening of the official inquiry, rather than a resumption from v. 53. The Sanhedrin consisted of seventy-one members, composed of heads of the high-priestly families, scribes, and elders, the whole being under the presidency of the high priest. The Mishnah has a section on the Sanhedrin, and given the tenacity of oral tradition in Judaism we may be reasonably confident that this third-century compilation does reflect Sanhedrin practice in the time of Jesus.

Mark's language, following Matthew, appears to suggest that what took place was a formal Sanhedrin meeting, but this seems doubtful, especially if the view is taken that this was an official judicial inquiry for which the death penalty was to be sought. We argued against such an understanding in the comment, and it is important to remember that the codification of the tractate *Sanhedrin* in the Mishnah prohibits night meetings in criminal cases. Luke's version, which is fuller, has the meeting taking place in the morning (22:66-71), and John has an account of Jesus being questioned by Annas (18:19-23). The accounts of the meeting in all the evangelists depict the attitude of the inquirers as one of fierce hostility, and given a decision to find some way in which to hand Jesus over, this is hardly surprising. The attitude is also but a continuation of the attitude depicted in vv. 1,10-11.

in order to put Jesus to death: A somewhat interesting grammatical note obtrudes here. Mark uses the construction *eis to* with the infinitive, found only six times outside the Pauline letters. Generally it is used of final or remote result. Matthew has a different and more usual construction.

evidence (Greek *marturia):* Cf. vv. 56 and 59.

56. *gave perjured testimony* (Greek *pseudomartureō):* Cf. 10:19. The requisite two witnesses of Deut 19:15 apparently were not to be had. The Greek for *evidence did not agree (issai hai marturiai)* can also be rendered as "not equivalent testimony."

57. Mark may have had access to two traditions which are reflected in the general statement of vv. 55-56 followed by the particular charge in vv. 57-59. Matthew has a single tradition: "At last two came forward and said . . ." (26:60).

58. *this man-made temple* (Greek *naos):* The reference is to the sanctuary proper and not to the temple precincts, for which the word would be *hieron* (cf. 11:11). For the description of the sanctuary as *man-made* (Greek *cheiropoiēton,* literally "hand-made"), cf. Acts 7:48, 17:24, Eph 2:11, Heb 9:11,24; and *not made by man* (Greek *acheiropoiēton,* literally "not hand-made") cf. 2 Cor 5:1, Col 2:11. The former of the words is classical, is found in the Septuagint (where it applies to pagan shrines), while the latter is apparently a reference to an entirely new order of things. But apart altogether from the dismissal of the temple and its institutions by Jesus as at best irrelevant (13:1-4) and his impatience with those who represented the established

order in Jerusalem, many questions remain, even if we accept the idea that the saying refers to an eschatological new creation. Luke does not record the saying, Matthew has it as "I am able to destroy God's temple . . . ," and John 2:21 maintains that Jesus referred to the temple of his body. (Does this mean the "body" of believers, as a spiritual temple?) There seems to be no adequate reason to doubt the genuineness of the saying, even though the original form may be beyond recovery. The saying, in some form, appears to be supported by 13:2, 15:29, John 2:19, and Acts 6:14. Did Jesus make some kind of "messianic" claim that he would build a new temple? (Cf. *1 Enoch* 90:29, 4 Ezra 9:38-10:27.) Even if he did, this does not wholly explain the conflicting testimony, still less the evidently impatient anger of Caiaphas.

Those familiar with the views of the late Abram Spiro will be aware of his long interest in the Samaritan influences to be found in the New Testament (cf. the digest made by the late W. F. Albright and the present writer in Johannes Munck, *The Acts of the Apostles*, AB, Vol. 31, Garden City, N.Y.: Doubleday, 1967, Appendix V, pp. 285-300). The connection between the "man-made temple" of Mark and the same expression in Acts 7:48 was pointed out by Spiro in a letter to W. F. Albright in March 1965. A copy of this letter was given to me by Abram Spiro in 1966. Only his untimely death in 1966 prevented the completion of his work on Stephen and on Samaritan influences in the New Testament sources. It seems best to reproduce here such sections of his long letter as are germane to the saying before us.

". . . Obviously this logion caused great difficulties to the primitive church and perhaps played a part in the trial of Jesus. Now, Matthew altered the logion by making Jesus say: 'I am able to destroy the Temple of God, and to build it in three days' (Matt 26:61). Thus Jesus did not threaten to destroy the Temple but merely asserted his ability to do so. John 2:19 has it differently: 'Destroy this Temple, and in three days I will raise it up.' In verse 21, John tells us: 'He spoke of the temple of his body.' However, when I came to the Mark alteration, I was astonished for Mark 14:58 says: 'I will destroy this Temple that is made with hands and in three days I will build another not made with hands.' . . . while Matthew and John tried to weaken the force of the offensiveness of this Logion of Jesus, Mark, far from weakening it, makes it even more damaging . . . but it is quite a different story when you add a theology to it and say that the Temple is made by hands . . . Mark reflects the words of Stephen in Acts 7:48. No Jew would say that the Temple was made by hands . . . Stephen says that the Jewish Temple was made by hands. His own tabernacle, of course, was patterned by an angel; therefore, it is not handmade (Acts 7:44). Paul, on the Areopagus, calls the Temple of the Athenians handmade (Acts 17:24-25). His own Temple of Jerusalem, of course, was not made by hands but by either God or Angel; and Paul considered it holy and worshipped in it . . .

". . . the Samaritans are mentioned unfavorably in Matthew, favorably in John, and somewhat ambiguously in Luke, and again favorably in Acts, Mark is completely silent about the Samaritans . . . Looking further I noticed that in Mark, Jesus is reported as having denied that the Messiah is a descendant of David (Mark 12:35-36). As against this, one fully understands Paul's outcry that Jesus is a son of David (Rom 1:3). It was further astonishing to me to find that the idea that the Messiah is to be of David's descent is ascribed in Mark to the Scribes (verse 35).

". . . I further noticed that the Phoenician woman who was helped by Jesus is reported in Matthew (15:22) to have cried out that he was the Son of David, but this is not found in Mark 7:25-30. Likewise, at Jesus' entry into Jerusalem, he is not addressed in Mark as the Son of David (Mark 11:9-10), but he is addressed as the Son of David in Matt 21:9.

". . . Of course, many commentators have suggested that Mark's anti-Jewishness was due to the fact that he wrote for a Gentile audience. I do not believe this to be true. Had Mark been thinking of Gentiles, he would not have attributed to Jesus the words that the Gentiles are "dogs" (Mark 7:27). Obviously, Gentiles were not foremost in his mind when he wrote his Gospel. This being the case, his anti-Jewishness is not anti-Semitism, but it is Samaritanism . . ."

No one can now interpret what Spiro might have written, but in the interests of preserving his concerns for Samaritans and Samaritan influences, the parts of the letter relevant to this saying have been reproduced. The openness of New Testament scholarship in recent years to questions about Samaritanism in early Christianity was demonstrated in Oscar Cullmann's *Der Johannerische Kreis, Sein Platz im Spätjudentum, in der Jungerschaft: Jesu im Urchristentum,* 1975 (translation by John Bowden as *The Johannine Circle,* Philadelphia: Westminster Press, 1976). Later there came *The Community of the Beloved Disciple* by Raymond E. Brown (New York, Toronto: The Paulist Press, 1979), which explored the concept in terms of Johannine studies.

Assuming some validity to the thesis propounded by Spiro with reference to the saying in v. 58, it would be even easier to explain the agitation and anger of the high priest. We are constantly in danger of forgetting that in the time of Jesus the Samaritans were numerically highly significant and maintained their identity in the Dispersion. Jesus therefore—according to Spiro's understanding of Mark—would have posed a double threat, that of a prophetic troublemaker and that of a rabble-rousing sympathizer with Samaritanism.

59. This verse may be of more significance than is commonly thought. It is peculiar to Mark and may reflect the confusion felt by Mark in the face of conflicting accounts and the total silence of Luke.

60. The high priest's question was plainly intended to provoke some kind of defense from Jesus on which the members of the council might seize as a reason to send the prisoner to Pilate.

We have chosen to translate here as one question the address of Caiaphas, though it is possible (by reading *ti* = "what") to make two questions from the Greek: "Have you no reply? What are these things that they bring in evidence against you?"

61. *But he was silent:* It is impossible to know whether this represents a genuine historical reminiscence. (John 19:9 has a tradition of Jesus being silent at one point in the trial before Pilate.) It is possible that this is a detail which owes its origin to Isa 53:7, and the reflections of the early community retrojected this into the present context. Matt 26:63 simply says "Jesus was silent," whereas Mark has a double statement so typical of his style. Luke has no tradition of the silence of Jesus, and his narrative at this point is wholly independent. It is possible that the double statement of Mark is meant to emphasize the silence in suffering of his own community.

"Are you the Messiah, Son of the Blessed One?" Mark's version is far more emphatic than Matthew's ". . . tell us if you are the Messiah, God's Son" (26:64) or Luke's "If you are the Messiah, tell us" (22:67). The Greek for *you (su)* is a note not only of

emphasis but also of derision. There is one reminiscence (albeit badly rendered?) of the Jewish liturgical and semiliturgical usage "The Holy One, blessed be he."

Apart from this, serious questions arise. To what extent in the time of Jesus was the Messiah regarded as the "Son of God" other than in the adoptive sense of the language of the "messianic" psalms? If at all, this cannot have been in the metaphysical sense of later Christian formulation, and not even in the sense employed by Mark in 1:1. The formula in Rom 1:4, though it antedates the final version of our gospels, appears to be "adoptive" in form. In any event it prescinds from the resurrection of Jesus and is certainly not in the context of the trial and the passion. The oath by which in Matthew's version (26:63) the high priest charged Jesus seems to imply some account of the ministry and mission of Jesus (the proleptic messianic banquet in the feeding of the crowd, or the saying in Matt 11:27 = Luke 10:22?). Or did the members of the Sanhedrin sense that Jesus conceived of himself as encapsulating or "personalizing" Israel (which is the fashion in which Matthew and Luke understood the temptation stories)?

the Blessed One (Greek *eulogētos):* Used in the New Testament solely of God, it is found in Luke 1:68; Rom 1:25, 10:5; 2 Cor 1:3, 11:31; Eph 1:3; 1 Pet 1:3.

62. The combination of the words of Ps 110:1 and Dan 7:13 provides an eschatological setting for the psalm and is the only place in the New Testament where this is found. From the standpoint of Judaism there are hints to be found. Ps 2:7 links the terms "Son" and "the anointed one," and the Midrash on that psalm uses both Psalm 110 and Daniel 7 in explaining it. There is, therefore, some precedent for the linking of the two texts. Probably Caiaphas' question was based on Ps 2:7. But the question was posed in a Jewish setting, against a Jewish background of conventional thought, envisaging an earthly messiah (however "Son" was understood). Jesus' reply evidently looks to another interpretation of Psalm 110: the messianic conflict, however it appears at the moment, will issue in final triumph. If this was indeed the meaning of Jesus' words, then his reply could hardly have done other than inflame the situation.

It is strange that Paul Winter ("The Marcan Account of Jesus' Trial by the Sanhedrin," *JTS* 14.1963, pp. 94-102) does not make the requisite connection between Ps 72:1 and Daniel 7, through Ps 7:1, and find the conjunction of a "seated messiah" being borne on the clouds. He does, however, see the eschatological elements involved. Sloyan pp. 62-64 (see bibliography) rightly emphasizes that the appearance before the Sanhedrin was but the culmination of what had been all along (in Mark's view) constant hostility, and finally the hostility ended in seeking the death of Jesus.

"I am . . .": Matt 26:64 has "The words are yours," while Luke 22:70 reads "You say that I am." Cf. 15:2 = Matt 27:11 = Luke 23:3 for "You say so" in reply to Pilate. A substantial number of important manuscripts of Mark read "You say that I am," and perhaps our present reading represents Mark's sense of the underlying meaning in Matthew and Luke. Certainly those two evangelists represent a reserve not found in our present text (cf. Lohmeyer, p. 328). The Matthean and Lucan versions imply that Jesus' own ideas of messiahship were radically different from those entertained by some members of the Sanhedrin.

and you will see (Greek *opsesthe):* Matt 26:64 has "from now on, you will see . . ." *(ap'arti),* and Luke 22:69 has "from this moment you will see . . ." *(apo tou nun).* Surprising as it is that there is no adverbial phrase in Mark corresponding to those found in his sources, nothing could be clearer than this challenge of Jesus to his accusers that in spite of all appearances *they* will see the circumstances of Ps 110:1 and Dan 7:13 find their fulfillment in Jesus. Earlier we called attention to the importance of the verbs *hear* and *see* in Chapter 13 and in the material leading up to the passion. Here is the most important single saying in the passion complex: *You will see.* It is addressed not to friends, well-wishers, or disciples, but to enemies consumed with raging hostility. If, therefore, they are invited to see triumph and exaltation, how much more the Markan community in its time of distress? For those who—like the present writer—are firmly convinced of the validity of "realized eschatology" as interpreting the message of Jesus, this saying is more or less decisive. *This* is the moment of eschatological triumph, of glory, and though many may be asked to see it for what it truly is, only the eyes of faith can perceive it.

However, the discussion as to the historicity of the saying has been long and often acrid. The debate continues, as it will for any discernible future, centered around the continuity or discontinuity of Jesus with Judaism, around similarity in his teaching or dissimilarity over against contemporary Judaism. There are those who would maintain that vv. 61b-62 are Christian insertions, and v. 63 is the natural successor to v. 61a. Though we must attach due weight to the threat to the temple (however understood), the reaction of the high priest as described in v. 63 is surely excessive as a response to that alone. What appears to be demanded in v. 63 is not a response to the silence, nor even a response to the saying about the temple, but a response to what members of the council had heard (or witnessed?) of the ministry and teaching of Jesus, which they took to imply a claim to messiahship. In and of itself that claim hardly constituted blasphemy, but it provided a convenient excuse to delate Jesus to the governor on the grounds of seditious speech—all the more cogent if Spiro's thesis is correct.

Our readiness to ascribe religious genius to a whole plethora of characters, ancient and modern, must surely be extended to Jesus, and scepticism with regard to his own recasting of the Judaism in which he was raised is curiously misplaced. It would be as well to deny constructive genius to the Pharisaism which survived the destruction of the temple and land in A.D. 70 and 135 and remolded the religious life of Judaism. What Jesus claims in the text before us is that the glory and the exaltation belonging properly to the Anointed One will be his and will be seen to be his. (Cf. J. A. T. Robinson, 1957, pp. 43-51, 128-30).

It is right to call attention at this point to the high priest's *what need have we of further witnesses?* This cannot have been provoked by the silence of Jesus, and we are justified in assuming that the vital question of messiahship was raised and understood in an eschatological dimension.

coming with the clouds of heaven: The phrase is not found in Luke 22:69. Our ears have been so attuned over the centuries to hear this in terms of a "Second Coming" that we need to be reminded that in Daniel the "coming" is *to* the Lord of Time. It is not coming to earth in some spectacular descent from above. It is of this "coming to" God that Jesus speaks, and it was in all likelihood this expression which finally reinforced heavily the outrage of the high priest and provided enough damaging material with which to send the prisoner to the governor. Even a Roman barely tolerant of Judaism would surely understand that the whole established order was threatened.

A mere glance at the commentaries on this verse will be enough to establish how many and varied are the views espoused in response to this verse, and we here append a few representative periodical references:

Borsch, F. H. "Mark xiv.62 and 1 Enoch lxii.5." *NTS* 14.1968, pp. 565-67.

Glasson, T. F. "The Reply to Caiaphas (Mark xiv.62)." *NTS* 1.1960, pp. 88-93.

Kempthorne, R. "The Marcan Text of Jesus' Answer to the High Priest (Mark xiv.62)." *NT* 19.1977, pp. 197-208.

Linton, O. "The Trial of Jesus and the Interpretation of Ps. CX." *NTS* 7.1961, pp. 258-62.

Lövestam, E. "Die Frage des Hohenpriesters (Mc 14.62 par. Matth. 26.63)." *SEA* 26.1961, pp. 93-107.

Perrin, N. "Mark xiv.62: The End Product of a Christian Pesher Tradition?" *NTS* 12.1966, pp. 150-55.

Robinson, J. A. T. "The Second Coming—Mark xiv.62," *ET* 67.1956, pp. 336-40.

It remains to be added that Mark's community was also in the mind of the evangelist as seen by his quotation of *You will see:* apparent defeat and disaster were to be seen for what they were—only apparent. Through defeat and suffering came vindication.

63. *tore his clothes:* The ritual gesture so described (cf. 2 Kgs 18:37, 19:1) was prescribed in the time of Jesus as a response to blasphemy. Now a claim to messiahship was not so regarded, but the uttering of the divine name was definitely blasphemous. Mark does not record any such utterance, and the other gospels are silent on this point; we must, therefore, conclude that Jesus' quotation of Ps 110:1 and Dan 7:13 was given such a personal interpretation that the high priest reacted in anger. Even so, it is possible that in the time of Jesus blasphemy was not as narrowly construed as the sentence above suggested (cf. 2:7; John 5:18, 10:33; Lohmeyer p. 329). Furthermore in the highly volatile political situation of Palestine it was all too probable that a high priest—a Sadducee—would be more than anxious to put the worst possible constructions on the words of Jesus. At a minimum Jesus had connected himself with some kind of divine vindication and dominion. This seems to be reflected in *You have heard the blasphemy,* followed by (in Matthew's words at 26:66) "How does it look to you?" Somewhat surprisingly, Mark's *what is your opinion* (Greek *phainetai)* uses a Greek verb more characteristic of classical Greek than of New Testament Greek.

64. *They all judged him to deserve the death penalty:* On any showing, this can hardly be described as a sentence of death, though it does indicate a legal opinion. There is no way in which the accounts of Matthew and Mark on the one hand and of Luke on the other can be reconciled. Luke 22:66-71 has the Sanhedrin meeting in the morning, while Matthew and Mark agree on making it an evening meeting. If this was a trial, properly so-called, then the judicial rules were violated by not waiting until the following day for conviction and sentence on a capital charge. We have maintained in the comment that this was not a trial, but the kind of informal inquiry envisaged by John 18:13. No doubt the end result is the same: Jesus died as a result of hostility on the part of the leaders of the religious establishment in Jerusalem and died on a charge preferred before Pilate of covert civil rebellion.

Matthew's version (26:65-66) has "He has blasphemed! What further need have we of witnesses? Now that you have heard the blasphemy, how does it appear to you?" They all answered, "He deserves the death penalty." Luke 22:66-71 makes no mention of the high priest tearing his clothes and in v. 71 has "What further need have we of witnesses? For we ourselves have heard from his own mouth." Although in the Lucan account there is no mention of blasphemy, the evangelist appears to leave no room for any other interpretation.

65. *Some began to spit:* The brief account of the mockery has all the marks of a separate tradition. The word *some,* following on from v. 64, almost suggests that these attacks on Jesus were made by members of the Sanhedrin, but this is highly unlikely, even though Matthew has "they spat in his face" (26:67). Luke's version (22:63) is clearer: "the men who held him mocked him." The *some (tines)* of Mark may be the same as *The attendants* in the second part of the verse, if we interpret *attendants* as including those who effected the arrest.

blindfolded (Greek *perikaluptō*): The word is classical, is found in the Septuagint, and means "to cover all around."

and hit him (Greek *kolaphizō*): The word is purely vernacular, not being found either in classical Greek or in the Septuagint, and derives from *kolaphos,* the contemporary vernacular of *konduloi* (knuckles). Many important manuscripts, assimilating the Markan text to Matt 26:68 and secondarily to Luke 22:64, read: "You Messiah! Who struck you?" But even though more important manuscripts omit this assimilation, it is difficult to see what *"Prophesy!"* might mean on its own. The reference to *they blindfolded him* is superfluous unless there is some guessing game involved. Some manuscripts of Mark add "on his face" after *spit,* and yet others have "they spit on him and blindfolded his face." This latter is presumably an assimilation to Luke 22:64 —"and covering him up, they asked him . . ." The difference in the three synoptic versions can be summarized by saying that in Matthew and Luke those who taunt the blindfolded prisoner are demanding that he use prophetic powers (insight?) to give the name of the striker, whereas in Mark there is a taunting challenge to "play the prophet."

The attendants: We may reasonably assume, from Luke 22:63, that the Greek word —variable in meaning as it is—refers to those who had seized Jesus and in that sense could be described as officials attendant on the high priest.

set on him with blows: The Greek of this phrase has its own problems. It reads *hoi huperētai hrapismasin auton elabon.* In John 18:22 we have *hrapisma,* a blow on the face with the open hand, and the verb *hrapizō* is found in Hos 11:4 and Matt 5:39, 26:67. The final two words provide the difficulty and there are various attempted translations. The words can be rendered "caught him with blows" or "treated him with blows" or even "got at him with blows." The construction can only be described as a crude colloquialism, though in modern Greek it is used to render "beat him." There are differing manuscript readings of *ebalon* or *eballon,* both tenses of the verb *ballō,* in the sense of "throw" or "lay upon" or "put." But the verb *elabon* is far more widely attested in the manuscripts, and we can only conclude that *elabon* was understood as meaning *ebalon* (they went on laying blows on him). Either we have a misreading in the early written tradition or—just possibly—a Latinism where *accipere* (to receive) can easily be used as meaning that someone was "received" with violence.

In spite of some Markan dependence on Matthew, we have virtually three independent traditions of this event, though Luke's version gives the impression of being
closer to the events.

The reader wishing to pursue the history of the Sanhedrin, especially as it impinges
on the questioning of Jesus, is recommended to: Hugo Mantel, *Studies in the History
of the Sanhedrin,* Cambridge, Mass.: Harvard University Press, 1965, especially Chapter 6.

83. Peter's Denial
(14:66-72) = Matt 26:69-75; Luke 22:56-62; John 18:15-18, 25-27

14 66 Meanwhile Peter was still in the courtyard below. One of the
high priest's maids came by, 67 and saw Peter there warming himself.
She looked at him closely and said, "You were there too, with the
Nazarene, this Jesus." 68 But he denied it. "I know nothing," he answered. "I do not understand what you mean." Then he went out into
the forecourt. 69 The same maid saw him there and began again to say
to the bystanders, "This man is one of them." 70 Again he denied it. A
little while later, the bystanders again said to Peter, "Certainly you are
one of them—you are a Galilean." 71 But he began to invoke a curse
on himself and put himself under oath, "I do not know this man you
are talking about!" 72 Immediately the cock crowed a second time.
And Peter remembered that Jesus had said to him, "Before the cock
crows twice, you will disown me three times." And he broke into
tears.

Comment

It is possible to hold either that this narrative is a composition of the early
community, which grew out of the prediction of 14:30, or that the prophecy
grew from the account before us. Even though Mark is generally credited
with painting the disciples in a less than favorable light, it is perhaps difficult
to see him writing about the principal member of the band as being guilty of
dereliction or near apostasy. The very artlessness of the story, with its escalat-

ing severity in the questions, appears to have all the marks of reminiscence. Certainly it holds warnings and lessons for Mark's community, faced with all manner of temptations to go back on allegiance to the Risen Jesus. What ought not to be overlooked is that the story is also an encouragement: if the chief of the Twelve could be assailed and afflicted by doubt to the point of denial, the doubts of an afflicted community were not new. Peter not only had been restored, he was a witness to the resurrection.

Notes

66. *still in the courtyard:* It is impossible to determine whether v. 54 was originally part of this narrative, but if it was, then the first sentence of this verse might be an editorial device of resumption after the Sanhedrin inquiry. But if this is so, it remains to be asked why all three evangelists similarly divide the story of Peter, and in this regard no study of synoptic relationships is of any assistance. For if—according to the usual two-document hypothesis—Matthew and Luke found the Markan version before us, why did they not restore the unity of the narrative? On the other hand, if Mark was in possession of an independent source (Peter?), the desire on his part to use the existing framework of Matthew and Luke, together with his own far more dramatic and vivid account, makes the present arrangement explicable. Matthew 26:29, for example, has: "Peter sat outside in the courtyard" where Mark's *Peter was still in the courtyard below* has all the marks of an eyewitness who knew that the Sanhedrin was meeting in an upstairs room. Luke 22:55, referring to the fire in the courtyard and the bystanders, says, "Peter was sitting in their midst."

One of the high priest's maids (Greek *mia tōn paidiskōn*): This may have been the portress of John 18:16. The Greek word *paidiskē*, a diminutive of *pais*, by this time had come to mean a female slave.

67. *saw Peter . . . looked at him closely.* (Greek *idousa ton Petron . . . emblepsasa):* The heightening of the dramatic effect is demonstrated in the two verbs. Matt 26:69 has the maid coming up to Peter, while Luke 22:56 records that the maid saw *(idousa)* Peter but has *atenisasa* for Mark's *emblepsasa.*

The note of scorn is emphatic: *"You were there, too, with the Nazarene, this Jesus."* Matthew ("You were also with Jesus the Galilean," 26:69) and Luke ("This one too was with him," 22:56) are colorless by comparison. The dramatic tone of Mark's narrative can only be explained adequately by access to independent eyewitness testimony.

were there: Mark shares with Matt 26:69 the only instances in the New Testament of *ēstha,* the old Attic perfect form of the verb "to be," though the old imperfect form *ēs* is found several times in the New Testament. While we might easily suppose that Matthew was capable of using an archaic form, it would be difficult to imagine this of Mark, save by imitation. In fact a few manuscripts of Mark have replaced *ēstha* by *ēs.*

68. Mark represents Peter as giving an answer, but the Greek for *he denied it* (from the verb *arneomai*) rather means a disowning of interest in something, distancing oneself from the matter (cf. 8:34), and all three synoptists use the expression, with

Matthew adding in effect ". . . what you are talking about." The reply of Peter *(oute oida oute epistamai su ti legeis)* can be read more than one way. The two verbs, for example, are almost synonymous, and precision in grammar is hardly noteworthy in this evangelist. Hence we can translate the passage as "I don't know, and don't understand, what you are saying" or "I do not know him, nor do I understand what you mean" or even "I do not understand. What do you mean?" To complicate matters further, the suggestion has been made more than once that behind the Greek *oida* is the Hebrew verb *yada'* and behind *epistamai* is *ḥakam,* with the further possibility that the response might then be: "I neither know, nor am I acquainted with, the one you speak of." While this in some ways provides a possible solution for the admittedly awkward Greek, it erodes the gradual building of pressure to the climax in v. 72. Moreover an outright denial at this point, rather than the very evasive reply provided in our translation, would appear to make v. 71 wholly superfluous.

forecourt (Greek *proaulion):* Peter apparently wished to avoid further questions but could not bring himself to leave the scene and so went into the vestibule which led into the central courtyard.

Some manuscripts add "and the cock crowed," but the manuscript evidence is not impressive, even though v. 72 would appear to demand it. It is also possible that a literalist scribe inserted the cock crowing at this point because he could not imagine anything other than a precise fulfillment of Jesus' prediction. The other three evangelists do not record any cock crow. Lagrange (p. 407), evidently accepting the authenticity of the phrase, suggests that Peter either did not hear the sound, or—if he did—he persuaded himself that he had not formally denied Jesus.

69,70. The position of Peter in the vestibule, and the fact that Mark uses the phrase *The same maid,* lends weight to the suggestion that she was a portress. But this time she shares her suspicions with *the bystanders.* It is interesting to observe that the word for *bystanders (parestōs)* occurs only here and in v. 70, Mark's more usual *parestēkos* coming at 14:47 and 15:35,39.

Matthew (26:71) with "another girl," Luke (22:58) with "another one," and John (18:26) with "one of the high priest's servants" provide us with a different cast of speakers. Luke's Greek suggests a short interval between the two encounters.

Mark's use of *again* implies that Peter's replies were both essentially denials, and the tense of the verb in *denied (ērneito)* implies repetition. Matthew has "Again he denied it with an oath, 'I do not know the man' " (26:72); Luke reads "I do not know him" (22:57); and John records that Peter replied "I am not" to the charge of being a disciple (18:17).

70,71. After an interval the *bystanders* take up the challenge. They repeat the maid's charge, with the supporting *"you are a Galilean."* (Some manuscripts add "for your speech is similar," but the manuscripts in question, though numerous, are not as important as the ones which omit it.) Matthew (26:73) adds the explanation "for your accent gives you away" (Greek *gar he lalia sou dēlon se poiei).* This reference to Peter's dialect is an impressive touch. The manuscript readings are somewhat complicated in Mark, for *Galilean* on the face of it must have some reference to accent or dialect, and it cannot in context have any reference to Galilee as the milieu of eschatological fervor or nationalist aspiration. Now some manuscripts of Mark read *kai hē lalia sou hoimiazei,* and a few even read *dēlon* instead of *hoimiazei.* Added to this is the fact that some manuscripts of Matthew read *hoimiazei* in place of the *dēlon* which is given above. Two possibilities suggest themselves as explanation: (a) the clause about speech or dialect was an early addition to the text of Mark, to explain *you are a Galilean;* or (b) the explanatory phrase (either *kai hē lalia sou hoimiazei* or *gar hē lalia sou dēlon so poiei)* was taken from existing texts of Matthew. It is now impossible to determine what the textual history might have been.

began to invoke a curse (Greek *anathematizein):* The essential meaning of such a curse is "May I be accursed if what I say is not true!" Cf. 1 Sam 20:13, 2 Sam 3:9, Acts 23:12. The third accusation is the most explicit, and so too is the denial. It seems best to separate the verb *anathematizein* from *put himself under oath (omnunai),* leaving the content of the latter as *"I do not know this man you are talking about!"* It is notable that Peter does not mention Jesus by name. Matthew 26:74 has *katathematizein* and omits the phrase *You are talking about.* Luke 22:66 has no references to Peter putting himself under a curse, or to an oath, and has simply "I do not know what you are saying."

72. *Peter remembered* (Greek *anamimneskō,* cf. 10:21): The verb has the accusative case (cf. 1 Cor 4:17, 2 Cor 7:15, Heb 10:32) where good grammatical usage would demand the genitive case. The Greek of *Jesus had said to him* is awkward: *hōs eipen autō ho Iesous.* The prophecy of 14:30, with slight variations in order, is repeated.

And he broke into tears (Greek *kai epibalōn eklaien):* This short Greek text has produced profound differences of opinion. It is not found in Luke, and Matthew 26:75 has *kai exelthōn exō eklausen pikrōs* (and he went out and wept bitterly).

The difficulty lies in *epibalon* as a participle of that all-embracing verb *balō.* It will be best to examine some suggested translations:

> KJV: "And when he thought thereon, he wept" [understanding *dianoian* as "when he put his mind to it"]
> "he threw himself" [on the ground]
> "he put [his himation] around him"
> "he began to cry"—reading *epiballō,* and incidentally supported by many early versions.

The flexibility of the verb is well known, but here it is well to admit that we cannot know with any certainty precisely what Mark had in mind, and our translation reflects the best that can be done with a wide-ranging (but oddly intransigent) verb. There is no difficulty with *eklaien:* it represents a long-continued grief, following upon shattering self-discovery.

A final note must suffice about the cock crowing. The difficulties in the notes of time were discussed under v. 30, and there appeared to be an emphatic reference to two cock crowings. It is impossible to know whether the detail in this verse is a prophecy after the event, or whether the prophecy itself in v. 30 was edited in the light of a double cock crowing. All we can say is that this is a particular feature of the Markan narrative.

84. Jesus Before Pilate
(15:1-15) = Matt 27:1-2, 11-14; Luke 23:1-5; John
18:28-38

15 ¹ As soon as it was morning, the chief priests reached a decision with the elders and scribes in full council, put Jesus in chains, led him away, and handed him over to Pilate. ² Pilate asked him, "Are you the king of the Jews?" He replied, "The words are yours." ³ The chief priests were bringing many charges against him, but he answered nothing, ⁴ so Pilate again questioned him, "Have you no answer to make? You see how many charges they bring against you!" ⁵ But to Pilate's amazement Jesus made no further reply. ⁶ At the festival season he used to release for them any one prisoner at their own request. ⁷ Among those in prison was the man known as Barabbas, with the rebels who had committed murder in the rebellion. ⁸ When the crowd came up and began to ask Pilate to do for them as he had always done, ⁹ Pilate answered them, "Do you want me to set free the king of the Jews for you?" ¹⁰ For he knew that they had delivered him over out of malice. ¹¹ But the chief priests incited the mob to have him release Barabbas instead. ¹² Pilate spoke to them again, "What then shall I do with the one you call 'king of the Jews'?" ¹³ They shouted back, "Crucify him!" ¹⁴ "Why? What harm has he done?" Pilate asked. But they shouted all the more, "Crucify him!" ¹⁵ So Pilate, wanting to please the mob, released Barabbas, had Jesus flogged, and handed him over to be crucified.

Comment

What appears at first sight to be a loosely constructed chapter is in fact a characteristic Markan compilation of divisions, with a familiar Markan set of triads. There are five divisions, each with a note of time (15:1-20,21-32,33-41,42-47; 16:1-8). If we precede the first two divisions by 14:53-72 (as the first triad), we have changes of place, and in all three Jesus is mocked. The second triad provides as with death, burial, and resurrection, the details of the three-hour Roman watches, three kinds of mockers, and three women. All the construction is arranged to provide contrasts between innocence and guilt, strength and weakness (cf. for further discussion T. A. Burkill, "The Trial of Jesus," *Vigiliae Christianae* 12.1.1958, pp. 1-18).

Some commentators have considered v. 2 and vv. 3-5 to be a doublet, but it should be noticed that there is a consistent pattern in Mark's interrogation narratives. In the examination before the Sanhedrin there were three questions, of which only the first and the third were answered; in the story of Peter's denial there are three questions or accusations, and all are answered; in the trial before Pilate there are three questions (including one addressed to the crowd), and only the first and the third are answered.

All in all, the chapter—especially this first section—is a good example of Mark's use of his sources and a good example of his narrative style.

Debate continues as to the authenticity of the Barabbas story. Of the rebellion of v. 7 we know nothing, though such an event would hardly have been surprising in the climate of the times. While amnesty was amply provided for in the Roman legal system, we have no knowledge (apart from the gospels) of any customary amnesty associated with Passover. We are bound to look with some suspicion on a story in this context about a man whose name means "son of the father." However, the story is so inextricably bound up with the trial scene that we cannot now separate it from its context. Whatever historical kernel originally formed the story, we cannot now determine.

We owe a large debt to Mark for reducing the trial and Passion narratives to manageable and easily remembered essentials. Much which endears itself to speculative and psychological excursion has been excised. Matthew's mysterious story about the dream of Pilate's wife and "the Righteous One" (27:19-20), as well as the death of Judas (27:3-10) and the hand-washing by Pilate (27:24) are all omitted. Luke's story of an encounter between Jesus and Herod Antipas (23:6-12) likewise finds no place in this tightly controlled chapter. But it is in a comparison of the Markan account with the Johannine that we have reason for gratitude to this narrative for giving us the essential details.

Undoubtedly as the passion story became more widely known all manner of reminiscences, rumors, and half-recalled stories began to circulate, some of them attaching themselves to the skeleton outline of the formal narrative. The Markan account provides us simply with the skeleton outline, but all four gospels share the same purpose—to demonstrate the innocence of Jesus and the complicity of the Jewish leaders in preferring a trumped-up but plausible charge to the governor.

Notes

1. *having reached a decision:* If we take the option that a more difficult Greek reading is to be preferred, as being more likely to be authentic, then we shall read here *sumbulion poiēsantes* with the meaning "having held a consultation [or a council] . . ." But this has the effect of producing a second meeting of the Sanhedrin, or at the very least a consultation. Nothing in this verse suggests that it refers to the resumption of an adjourned meeting recorded in 14:55-65. Furthermore that meeting *had* reached a decision. This confusion of meaning is all the more notable in that Matt 26:66 has "They answered, 'He deserves the death penalty' " (Greek *enochos thanatou estin*). Mark (14:64), however, clearly says *They all judged him to deserve the death penalty*, with the important Greek word *katekrinan (judged)*. Similarly Matthew 27:1 reads ". . . [they] made plans" (Greek *sumbulion elabon)*, whereas Mark has the reading we have given above. Matthew further underlines his understanding of events by his use of *sumbulion labein* as "to take counsel" at 12:14, 22:15, 27:7, and 28:12, and we assume that this is the kind of proceeding which Mark is describing. But this is not what the majority of the manuscripts read—*sumbulion poiēsantes*. Some manuscripts of Mark (one of them of considerable importance) read *sumbulion hetoimasantes*, which is reflected in our translation above. We have accepted the reading, found as it is in the text preferred by the United Bible Societies edited by Kurt Aland, Matthew Black, Bruce Metzger, and Allen Wikgren (1st ed., 1965). It is also the reading preferred by the translators of the New English Bible in 1961. It is possible that the majority reading of *sumbulion poiēsantes* represents an attempt by Mark to combine two traditions—one of a night meeting of the Sanhedrin, reflected in 14:64, and another of a daylight meeting reflected in the present verse.

as soon as it was morning (Greek *prōi):* This would refer to the period of about 5-6 A.M. It is possible that this single expression of time is meant to cover all the events of the trial.

in chains . . . handed him over: This is the first time that Jesus is described in the narrative as being bound, in contrast to John 18:12. The expression *led him away* may reflect not only the physical act, but also may reflect a legal transference from one jurisdiction to another. The verb *handed him over* has been discussed previously. It is used ten times in the passion narrative, and in this and all other instances we may be correct in seeing an implied reference to Isa 53:4-12.

Pilate (cf. 15:2,4,5,9,12,14,15,43,44): Mark uses only the cognomen of the governor. Pilate was procurator of Judea in A.D. 26-36 under the imperial legate for Syria. Matt 27:2 describes Pilate as "governor" (Greek *hegēmenon*). A recently discovered inscription in Caesarea describes him as *prefectus judeae,* and procurator was probably a later promotion in dignity (Tacitus *Annals* 15.44 describes him as *procurator).* The titles may often have been loosely applied, and in any case the powers of the office under Roman law did not materially differ, whatever the title. Pilate had an unenviable reputation for being merciless and cruel. This portrait of Pilate is to some extent muted in our gospels, in the interest of portraying the Jewish religious leaders as being the principal guilty party in the death of Jesus. There are three occasions in Luke

(23:13-16,20,22) and in John (18:38, 19:4,6) where Pilate is represented as saying that he finds Jesus innocent and as yielding in the end to popular clamor. Matthew and Mark have no such tradition, though Matthew records Pilate washing his hands in dissociation of the whole affair (27:24). Mark's account provides us with no description of Pilate, though Pilate's vacillation is brought out, as is also the apparent conviction of the governor that he did not believe the accusations against the prisoner.

The absence of any indication of the place of the trial is indirect proof that both Matthew and later Mark wrote for those to whom the facts were well-known. It is possible that Pilate took up residence for the feast in the palace of Herod the Great, when he came from Caesarea (as one of his predecessors had done). Equally he may have made the fortress of Antonia (on the north side of the temple) his headquarters. John 18:28 speaks of Jesus being led "into the praetorium," but this does not materially assist us.

2. *"Are you the king of the Jews?"* The emphatic personal pronoun *su* is plainly scornful. The question clearly spells out the determination of the clerical party to have Jesus charged with civil rebellion. All three evangelists record the question in the same words, though it is possible that originally the words were "Are you the king of Israel?" Was Pilate seeking some way in which Jesus could be regarded as a claimant to Herod's throne (cf. Luke 23:2)?

"The words are yours" (literally "You say it"): The question did not lend itself to a plain yes or no answer, and the reply is meant to say that the speaker would have posed the question differently (cf. 14:62 and Matt 26:64). Lohmeyer (p. 335) suggests that the reply was a kind of half-affirmative, conveying the truth to those who knew Jesus was the Messiah but deliberately veiling it for the unbeliever. Perhaps this is what the evangelists wished to convey, but in the circumstances of the trial itself, this suggestion seems unlikely.

3. The reference in Mark to the accusation of the clergy is awkwardly phrased in comparison with Matthew. Literally it translates as "They asked [demanded] of him, the chief priests many things [or much]." It seems best to translate the word *polla*—as we have done above—by *many charges,* though this reads strangely if the only and principal charge was sedition. Many manuscripts add "but he answered nothing," and in spite of the manuscript evidence against it, we have included it, since Pilate's next question implies a previous silence. It is found in Matt 27:12, but it may have been omitted by some major manuscripts because the silence is implied in v. 4.

4. Jesus' silence is wholly beyond Pilate's understanding, and the Greek *palin epērota* (again continued to question him) matches the *kategoroun* (continued to bring charges) of v. 3. In Matt 27:13 Pilate's second question is substantially the same, and the silence of Jesus (as in Mark) leaves the governor astounded. Luke 23:2-5 is an independent narrative, though it does have substantially the same question as in v. 2 above. Luke 23:5 does, however, provide us with valuable information as to how the charge of sedition was framed: "He disturbs the people, teaching all through Judea, and beginning from Galilee to here." This underlines the first charge of 23:2 ("We have found this man perverting our race, forbidding us to pay taxes to Caesar, and saying that he is Messiah, a king." It is designed to persuade Pilate that the subversion was widespread. This latter is in response to Pilate's scornful opinion that he finds Jesus innocent. The Johannine narrative is far more elaborate and more highly

charged (18:28-40). The clergy refuse to enter the praetorium on the score of ritual defilement, but Pilate's question about kingship elicits a reply about earthly and heavenly kingdoms. To all of this, Pilate declares that he can find no criminal guilt in Jesus and offers to the accusers a choice between Jesus and Barabbas.

6,7. The narrative of Barabbas has plagued New Testament historians for many years and appears to be no nearer to resolution. We know of no custom for granting amnesty at the Passover season. The vocabulary is of no assistance; *apoluo* simply means *release,* without qualification. Similarly the word *prisoner (desmios)* affords no clue. The last part of the sentence *(at their own request)* is grammatically difficult but straightforward enough in meaning. The verb *parētounto* (from *paraiteomai)* is classical and is found in the Septuagint and the papyri. Here it means "to request or beg from another." It can sometimes mean "to refuse, or avoid" (as in 1 Tim 4:7, 5:11; 2 Tim 2:23; Titus 3:10; Heb 12:25) and in the negative "to beg that something not be done" (Heb 12:19) and also "to ask to be excused" (Luke 14:18, Acts 2:11). There are various manuscript readings in Mark for what is often translated as "whomsoever they desired." We have read *hon,* but there are readings of *honper etounto* (which could well be a corruption of *hon para),* of *honper an,* and of *hon an.* The essential meaning is unchanged. Matt 27:15 reads *hon ethelon* (whom they wished), and instead of Mark's *released for them* he has "was accustomed to release for the crowd."

There is abundant evidence for discretionary amnesty being granted by local Roman governors, and the term *abolitio* for the suspension of a charge was a well-known legal expression (cf. Lohmeyer p. 337 and Lagrange p. 414). There is therefore nothing inherently improbable in Pilate's action. What is surprising is the silence of contemporary and near contemporary Jewish sources.

Our difficulty comes with v. 7. The phrase in Greek found in Matthew and Mark is:

> *eichon de tote desmion episēmon legomenon Barabban*
>   (Matt 27:16)
> *ēn de ho legomenos Barabbas . . .* (Mark)
> "They held then a notorious prisoner called Barabbas"
>   (Matthew)
> *was the man known as Barabbas* (Mark)

The problem lies with the participle *legomenos.* Generally it is preceded by a personal name and then is followed by a description or title. Now while it is true that it can occasionally precede a personal name (Matt 9:9, Luke 22:47, John 9:11), what we have here is not a personal name but an epithet—*Barabbas* is the Greek rendering of *bar abba* (son of the father). In Matt 27:16,17 there are in two groups of manuscripts two readings: *Iēsoun Barabban* and *Iēsoun ton Barabban* = "Jesus Bar-abbas" and "Jesus [the] Bar-abbas." It is found also in some manuscripts of Mark, and we may reasonably conjecture that originally some form of "Jesus Bar-abbas" was found in both gospels. (Such a title was not unknown in Judaism, and the Talmud has two rabbis so named: Samuel Bar-Abba, and Nathan Bar-Abba.) But in the present context, what would that mean? It is far more likely that a later scribe would have excised the name "Jesus" than have added it. We have not reflected the name in our translation, for it seemed best to examine the matter in the notes.

Three articles have addressed the matter in the past thirty years:

Davies, Stevan L. "Who Is Called Bar-Abbas?" *NTS* 27.2,1981, pp. 260-63.

Maccoby, H. Z. "Jesus and Barabbas." *NTS* 16.1.1970, pp. 55-60.

Rigg, H. A. "Barabbas," *JBL* 64.4.1945, pp. 417-56.

In essence the three articles do not manifest any substantial differences, though there are individual refinements. The issue is of some importance not only because of the readings in the Greek text of Matthew and Luke but also for understanding the whole complex of the Passion narratives. We will therefore examine the thesis presented in the articles and respond under the various headings. (The interested reader is commended to the third article listed because of its valuable footnotes.) Accepting, therefore, as this writer does, that the oldest manuscripts of Matthew and Mark may well have contained the phrase "Jesus Bar-Abbas," understood as "Jesus Son of the Father," we summarize the thesis as follows:

1. The account of an annual Passover amnesty is a fiction. This we cannot know, but there is nothing *inherently* improbable in it, given the discretion allowed to Roman governors.

2. The custom of nicknames, or appellations, was well known in the New Testament period (Simon, called Peter; Simon the Zealot; John the Baptizer, etc.), and perhaps it is reasonable to infer that Jesus was called "Bar-Abba" in response to some aspects of his teaching. We have seen, however, that there is no ground for suggesting that the appellation was unique to Jesus, if it was indeed applied to him. If, however, there is any truth to the hypothesis that Jesus was ever known as Jesus ben-Abba, there might be some illumination here—from a quarter other than the apocalyptic saying of Ps 110:1 and Dan 7:13—of the charge of blasphemy. That Jesus addressed God as "abba" seems confirmed by the survival of the phrase in Gal 4:5 and Rom 8:15.

3. Arguing from Matt 23:8-10, Davies asserts that Jesus was never called "rabbi," since the title did not come into use until after A.D. 70, and therefore we ought to read in the Matthean text: "Nor must you be called 'abba' for you have one 'Abba' "—i.e., the Christ (p. 262). (This presupposition has been argued before.) But it is at the very least strange that the New Testament uses the term *didaskalos* = teacher = rabbi no less than fourteen times of Jesus in Matthew, Mark and John. Plainly one's viewpoint here will be influenced by one's preferred dating of the gospels. Why should the gospels have preserved this usage in days when missionary enterprise was moving into the Gentile world? But E. L. Sukenik—"A Jewish Tomb on the Mount of Olives," *Tarbiz* 1.1930, pp. 140-41—reported the finding of an unquestionably Jewish ossuary of the time of Jesus with the description of the deceased as *didaskalos.* See also Herschel Shanks, "Is the Title 'Rabbi' Anachronistic in the Gospels?" *(JQR* 53.4.1963, pp. 337-45). This is not impressive. No evidence, liturgical or otherwise, exists for any address to Jesus as *pater,* and *abba* in Rom 8:15 and Gal 4:5 is addressed to the Father.

All of the above raises far more questions than answers. If Jesus was called "abba," why has not the slightest trace of this ever been found in anti-Christian polemical sources? Why did not Jerusalem Judaism seize upon it, for example, in the period immediately after the resurrection? Why are our gospels so evidently puzzled by the Barrabas incident? (Of course it is wholly open to the critic to suggest that the New Testament evidence has been carefully manipulated and the primary historical data rendered wholly innocuous.) Assuming for the moment that there was an agitation on the part of Jesus' followers for his release, and an agitation now carefully concealed in our gospels by using his appellation of "Son of the Father," why was not this attempted deception immediately challenged? And why did the evangelists conjure up the device of making this a separate character with a history of association with rebels? Had there been such an agitation, the polemical statement in Acts 3:13 (that Pilate was determined to let Jesus go, but bowed to popular pressure) would surely have been far more forcibly stated.

All in all, we are unlikely to solve the puzzle of the prisoner with the startling appellation; and, short of some new and dramatic discovery, we must deal with the text as we find it.

7. *with the rebels* (Greek *meta tōn stasiastōn):* The word *stasiastēs* is late, corresponding to the earlier *stasiotēs*. Similarly *stasis* means a "stand" or "standing" on some issue and hence can be translated as "sect," or "faction" (cf. Luke 23:19,25; Acts 15:2, 19:40, 23:7,10, 24:5; Heb 9:8). The rebels are described as having committed murder during a rebellion, and Mark treats the facts of the rebellion as well known, whereas Matthew describes Barabbas as "notorious" (27:16).

8-10. For the first time *the crowd* is mentioned. Mark says the *crowd came up,* and the verb *(anabainō)* would seem to suggest a physical ascent, and this in turn may indicate the steps to the Antonia fortress. It seems likely that the crowd came to demonstrate support for Barabbas and not to be spectators of Jesus' trial—Jesus by this time was probably regarded as having been handed over to Pilate for some serious offense. It is impossible to know the composition of the crowd, and a comparison between the enthusiasm of Palm Sunday and the venom of the trial scene is misplaced: those who greeted Jesus on his entry into Jerusalem were festival pilgrims from Galilee, while the crowd assembled before Pilate can best be described as a mob. However, some caution is advisable: if Barabbas was a well-known partisan patriot-agitator from Galilee, a change of attitude is wholly possible. No one who lived through the years 1933-45 is likely to underestimate the fickle behavior of crowds influenced by a demagogue.

began to ask: The Greek here—far more dramatic than Matthew—must be given full weight, with its suggestion of increasing clamor. The verb *ask* (Greek *aiteisthai,* cf. 6:24) underlines this, while *as he had always done* in the Greek clearly implies the continuance of a customary action begun in the past.

"Do you want me to set free . . .": The question is clearly contemptuous, especially in the phrase *king of the Jews.* Mark's explanation for this contempt (v. 10) is wholly in character with the evangelist's custom of adding comments. Lagrange (p. 337) regards it as an addition and an awkward one at that. However, *out of malice* (Greek *dia phthonon)* is certainly not the same as the fear of the people expressed in 14:1. It is possible that v. 10 accurately reports the attitude of Pilate, for a protestation of loyalty to Caesar would be an unlikely sentiment for the Jerusalem religious establishment.

It is at this point in the narrative that Matt 27:19 has his account of the message

from Pilate's wife. The whole episode of Barabbas is omitted by Luke, and though
Matthew's version is shorter, the choice as between Jesus and Barabbas is longer and
better expressed. John 18:39 has Pilate mention the custom of amnesty, and it is he
who offers the choice.

11. *incited* (Greek *anaseiō*): The Greek word is late, not being found in the Septuagint. If—as we ventured to suggest earlier—Barabbas was a Galilean partisan, he
would have been more in favor than Jesus (who would not espouse violence). Matt
27:20 has the same sense as Mark, and he too uses the verb "to incite," but he also has
the further detail that the priests incited the people to "destroy Jesus."

12. *"What then . . ."* There is a surprising number of variants for this question in
the manuscripts. One reading is *Ti oun poiēsō ton basileia tōn Ioudaiōn* ("What then
shall I do with the king of the Jews?"). Another reading is the same, with the insertion
of *hon legete,* so as to translate as "What then shall I do with the one you call king of
the Jews?" Some manuscripts, by the use of *thelete* (wish), can be translated as "What
then do you wish me to do . . ." This may perhaps be nearer to the original meaning,
though manuscript attestation is not impressive.

It is easy to dismiss the procurator's action as weak, but he was faced with a choice
between a mob incited to an angry demonstration and a group of people hoping to
negotiate a judicial amnesty. He therefore faces them with the question—since they
have chosen Barabbas—of what he is to do with Jesus. The question is sardonic, but
having apparently decided to grant the amnesty, he is unwilling to set Jesus free. The
early community, if we may judge from Acts 3:13-15, certainly laid the blame for the
death of Jesus on Jerusalem officialdom, but it cannot be said that Pilate is on the
other hand represented in any favorable light.

In Matt 27:21 the choice is more clearly detailed: "Which of the two do you want
released to you?" After the reply of "Barabbas," Pilate's reply is in the same terms as
in Mark, save for the ending ("What then shall I do with Jesus who is called Messiah?"). Luke 23:20 simply records Pilate's wish to release Jesus, while John 18:40
records the horrifying character of the choice.

13. *They shouted back:* There is here no gradual building up of mob enthusiasm, as
in v. 8. The response is immediate. Presumably (cf. John 19:12) the taunt of "king of
the Jews" inflamed the crowd, and if Barabbas was indeed a partisan figure, then the
anger would be even further inflamed by those disappointed in Jesus.

"Crucify him!" There is no call to doubt the historicity of this clamor. Pilate's offer
having been refused and the charge of sedition being what it was, no alternative
remained. Matt 27:22 has "Let him be crucified!" while Luke 23:21 has "Crucify!
Crucify!" and John 19:51 "Take him away! Crucify him!"

14. Pilate's reply is the same in all the synoptists—*Why? What harm has he done?*
—with Luke 23:22 adding that the governor has found nothing in Jesus to warrant the
death penalty (cf. John 18:38, 19:4).

The reply from the crowd was a more frenzied outburst, and Luke 23:23 has "they
kept on shouting at the top of their voices, and the shouts were growing louder."

15. The word *wanting (boulomai)* is more emphatic than *wish (thelo)* and expresses
a deliberate decision. There is an interesting Latinism in *to please:* the Greek is *hika-
non poiēsai* = Latin *satis facere* = "to make enough, or complete." There is another
in *had Jesus flogged:* the Greek *phragellōsas* is from the Latin *flagello.* Flogging—a

very cruel punishment in itself—very commonly preceded crucifixion. Matthew and Mark describe it in a single verb, but Luke 23:16,22 has Pilate suggest it as an alternative to crucifixion, and John 19:1 has the flogging take place before the final sentence of death. It is only Luke 23:24 which states that Pilate condemned Jesus to death.

handed him over: All the evangelists use the expression, and the consistent use of *paradidōmi* throughout the narrative suggests Acts 2:23 rather than an attempt to apportion blame.

85. The Mocking
(15:16-20) = Matt 27:27-31; John 19:2-3

15 16 Then the soldiers took him inside the courtyard—that is, the governor's headquarters—and called the whole company together. 17 They dressed him in purple and, plaiting a crown of thorn branches, put it on his head. 18 They then began to salute him: "Hail! King of the Jews!" 19 They beat him about the head with a stick, spat on him, and fell on their knees in homage to him. 20 When they had finished their mockery, they stripped him of the purple and put his own himation on him. Then they took him out to crucify him.

Comment

It is very difficult to know what is to be said about this short narrative. It is possible to hold that it is an intrusion, that v. 20 simply refers us to v. 15. Equally it can be pleaded (cf. Lohmeyer, p. 340) that v. 15 simply records a decision and v. 20 refers to the implementation of that decision. The coincidence of the Greek of v. 15 *hina staurōthē (to be crucified)* and v. 20 *hina staurōsōsin (to crucify him)* is arresting, and one explanation might be that Mark is simply following his Matthean source and is not conscious of any intrusion. Matthew also has the same parallel verbs, though not the same tenses, in 27:15,31.

Far more important for our purposes are the narratives in Luke and John. There are phrases in John 19:2-6 which echo the account before us, but in John the mocking goes before the sentence of death. The Lucan material provides an enigma. Some of the details of the examination before Herod (23:11) are paralleled in the Markan narrative of Jesus' treatment by the attendants of the high priest (Mark 14:65). Luke is alone in recording the confrontation between Jesus and Herod Antipas, and it is far from easy to make any judgment about the historicity of the incident. Taylor (Note G, pp. 646-48) has a useful comment on supposed parallels in the pagan literature where a lowly or insignificant figure is made "king for the day" and subjected to all manner of indignity. To have lived in the political chaos of the latter part of the twentieth century has meant witnessing in the midst of regime and counterregime, government and insurgency, far more examples of orchestrated indignity against hapless leaders than anyone in the first century could have imagined. Historically based or not, the narrative suggests the kind of mindless violence indulged in by soldiers in a very tense situation (such as Passover in Jerusalem), where an easy victim can be found.

Notes

16. *soldiers* (Greek *stratiōtai):* These would be locally recruited soldiers, responsible to the governor, as distinct from the professional military recruits of the legions.
courtyard (Greek *aulē):* Cf. 14:44,53.
inside (Greek *esō):* See the discussion under 14:54.
governor's headquarters (Greek *praitōrion):* The word is late Greek, and a transliteration of the Latin *praetorium.* Cf. Matt 27:27; John 18:28,33, 19:9; Acts 23:35; Phil 1:13. It designates an official residence and in this instance is either Herod's palace or the fortress of Antonia (cf. 15:1).
We have translated Mark's Greek literally, and it is problematic. A courtyard is being described as if it was the whole building, and we have no other instance of a courtyard being identified as a whole complex. There is the possibility that originally the text was "into the courtyard of the praetorium" *(heōs tēs aulēs tou praiteriou),* but in that event it is hard to know how the present reading came to be. There is one place in the Septuagint (1 Macc 11:46) where *aulē* is used in the sense of "palace," but this is the only example we have. Matt 27:27 reads "into the praetorium."
company (Greek *speira):* This military term originally was applied to a cohort, a unit which might range from 200 to 500 men. In the present instance it obviously means the available members of the headquarters guard. Cf. Matt 27:27; John 18:3,12; Acts 10:1, 21:31, 28:1.
17. *dressed him in purple* (Greek *endiduskousin . . . porphuran):* The verb *endiduskō* is late Greek for *enduō* and elsewhere in the New Testament is found at Luke 16:19. *Porphura* is found at Luke 16:19 and Rev 18:12; it denotes a purple fish, or purple dye, or a cloak. Possibly it means a soldier's red military cloak which had faded (i.e., the *chlamus).* Judging by Matt 27:28 *(chlamuda kokkinē),* the word does not mean "royal purple" (i.e., deep red) but a cheaper or a faded red.
crown of thorn branches: The coins of Tiberius Caesar depict the emperor wearing a radiant circle around his head rather than the customary laurel wreath. This imitation circlet was meant to be a mockery of royal dignity (cf. 1 Macc 10:20, 2 Macc 14:4). The parallel vocabulary of Matthew and Mark in this verse *(plekeō,* "to plait"; *akanthinos,* "thorn branch") as well as in v. 18 suggests that originally Mark had the

Matthean "placed a reed in his right hand" as a mock symbol of the scepter. This is all the more likely in view of the *stick* in v. 18.

18. Mark reproduces with slight variations of vocabulary the mock homage of Matt 27:29. But the variations are worthy of note. Matthew has *Chaire, basileus tōn Ioudaiōn* in a few manuscripts, thereby producing "Hail! You king of the Jews!" But the vast majority of manuscripts (here and in Matt 27:29,37; Luke 23:37,38; John 18:39, 19:3,19,21) read *basileu tōn Ioudaiōn,* thus producing in the vocative case an acknowledgment of royal dignity. This matches the customary Latin acclamation *Ave, Caesar, victor, imperator.* It is to be noted that the phrase *of the Jews* is contemptuous.

19-20. We have translated as *fell on their knees in homage* the Greek *tithentes ta gonata prosekunoun,* though generally in the New Testament the phrase is associated with prayer (Luke 22:41; Acts 7:60, 9:40, 10:36, 21:5). Probably, therefore, a mockery of emperor or king worship was intended. The Matthean account has almost a ritual orderliness about it: the "investiture" with mock signs of regal dignity and then the indignity and violence.

The narrative concludes with Jesus being clothed again in his own outer clothing. We have read *his own,* in concurrence with many manuscripts, in contrast with the rather more vague *his himation* of some other manuscripts. Cf. *to crucify him (hina staurōsōsin)* with *to be crucified (hina staurōthē)* in v. 15.

86. The Crucifixion
(15:21-32) = Matt 27:32-44; Luke 23:26-43; John 19:17-27

15   21 On the way they met a man called Simon of Cyrene, who was on his way from the country, the father of Alexander and Rufus, and they compelled him to carry Jesus' cross. 22 They brought him to a place called Golgotha, which means "Place of a Skull," 23 where they tried to give him drugged wine, but he would not take it. 24 Then they crucified him, and

they divided his himatia,

casting lots

to see what each should get. 25 It was nine in the morning when they crucified him, 26 and the inscription against him read: "The King of the Jews." 27 Two bandits they crucified with him, one on the right hand and the other on the left. 28 (So that text was fulfilled which says he was counted among the criminals.) 29 The passers-by flung insults at him, shaking their heads. "Aha!" they said, "you were going to tear

down the temple and build it in three days! [30] Save yourself—come
down from the cross!" [31] In similar fashion the chief priests and the
scribes joked with one another. "He saved others," they said, "but he
cannot save himself. [32] Let the messiah, Israel's king, now come down
from the cross so that we can see it and believe." And those who were
crucified with him insulted him.

Comment

The account of the crucifixion of Jesus as we have it in this narrative was
obviously formed to meet the needs of the early community, and some aspects
of it suggest an accommodation to memorization. This is particularly evident
in the pattern of periods, with "punctuation" on the third, sixth, and ninth
hours. A secondary underpinning of this motif can be discerned in a pattern
of three episodes of insult. The details of the death of Jesus in the next section
have in one particular (v. 38) the same apocalyptic note as is served by Matt
27:51-53, and the account of the burial in vv. 40-41 serves to prepare the way
for the apparition at the tomb. There are only two references to the act of
crucifixion (vv. 24,25), and the account is notable for the absence of any
reference to the sufferings of Jesus. The figure of Jesus is of course central, but
theologically the emphasis is wholly on God's act in and through Jesus. We
have no means of knowing how many eyewitness accounts went into the
making of the crucifixion narratives, but the physical details of this barbarous
method of execution were all too familiar to the inhabitants of Syria-Palestine, and references are legion both in the classical literature and elsewhere
(cf. for our purposes Joseph A. Fitzmeyer, "Crucifixion in Ancient Palestine,
Qumran Literature, and the New Testament," CBQ 40.4.1978, pp. 493-514).

The task of separating the original, factual tradition from later accretion
and legend is fraught with considerable hazard. The period of oral transmission is obviously beyond our reach, though we may occasionally be able to
suggest how some items came into that tradition. To discover the core, the
central irreducible element, may prove to be illusory, but an attempt must be
made. Our concern is to see what use Mark made of his sources and what
elements he regarded as essential. We may surmise, probably correctly, that
the episode of Simon of Cyrene was no part of Mark's original tradition but
was inserted for what appeared to the evangelist to be very good reasons. To
what extent any evangelist regarded as legendary what may appear to us so to
be is a matter for conjecture. Whence was derived the account in Luke of
Jesus' meeting with the women on the way to execution (23:27-32)? Was it a
saying of Jesus from a far different context? Much theological thought is
contained in the account of Jesus' death in the fourth gospel (e.g., 19:33-36),

but to what extent did theological concerns dictate what *should* have taken place?

If we reduce the crucifixion to its barest elements in the three synoptists, we can arrive—in Mark's account—at the following sequence of verses in this section and the succeeding one: vv. 21-24,26,29-32,34-37,39. If we use the word "secondary" with some caution, making no judgment on historicity, we may then fill in the gaps in the Markan narrative with vv. 25,27,(28),32-33,38,40-41. Whatever justification this division demands can be dealt with in the notes.

Notes

21. The customary practice was for the condemned man himself to carry the *patibulum*, or crossbeam, of his cross. Whether Jesus had been so weakened by his previous ordeals that he was unable to do this for himself, we do not know. (It was not uncommon for victims to die during a Roman flogging.) According to Irenaeus *(Adversus Haereses* 1.24.4), the Gnostics seized upon this item in the tradition to assert that it was not Jesus who died but Simon. The soldiers *compelled* him (Greek *aggareuō*, "to press into public service," cf. Matt 5:41, 28:32) to perform this service.

Simon of Cyrene: Of this man we know nothing. But the part he played is firmly embedded in the tradition, important enough for the name to be one of the few (apart from the disciples) which Mark uses. The fact that Matt 27:32 and Luke 23:26 describe him as *kurenaios* (Cyrenian) affords no clue as to whether he was a Jew or a Gentile, though Acts 2:11 clearly implies that those from "round Cyrene" were Jews. Simon could well have been a Passover pilgrim. That he was *on his way from the country* may mean that he has taken up residence on a farm near Jerusalem. Only Mark tells us that he was *the father of Alexander and Rufus,* and again we assume that they were known either to Mark or to the community for which he was writing. There is a Rufus mentioned in Rom 16:13. The phrase *to carry his cross* is an echo in the Greek of 8:34 and is identical with Matt 27:32. Luke 23:26 has "they laid the cross on him to carry it behind Jesus" (cf. further G. M. Lee, "Mark 15:21: 'The Father of Alexander and Rufus' " *NovTest* 17.4.1975, p. 303).

22,23. These two verses, both in Matthew and Mark, are among the most vividly descriptive in the whole narrative, in Mark's case heightened by the use of the historic present in some tenses of the Greek.

place called Golgotha: Cf. Matt 27:33, John 19:17. A transliteration from the Aramaic *Golgoltha,* the hill was so named either from its skull-like shape or because it was a customary place of execution. It was outside the city in the time of Jesus. Luke omits the name and his Greek says "the place named Skull" (23:33).

drugged wine: Prov 31:6 has a command to give strong drink to the desperate or to one about to die. The word *drugged* is the Greek *esmurnismenon* (literally "mixed with myrrh"), and the use of myrrh was intended as an anesthetizing or stupefying agent. The verb *tried to give* reflects the Greek *edidoun.* Matthew, his memory ever alert for Old Testament undertones, builds around Ps 69:21 with "they gave him wine to drink, mingled with gall" and adds "but when he had tasted it, he refused to drink it."

24. The physical details of crucifixion, so familiar to the ancient world, are all subsumed under *they crucified him*. From the third century B.C. onward, crucifixion was used by the Roman authorities as a capital sentence for rebellious slaves and hardened criminals. The term *crux* covered a wide variety of forms: there was the diagonal X-form, or an upright with a cross piece *(patibulum)* which was set either at the top *(crux connissa)* or slightly lower *(crux immissa)* or even a simple stake on which victims were either fastened or impaled. The condemned man's arms were fastened to the *patibulum* either by ropes or nails through wrists and ankles, and the body was supported by a small saddle. Nails are mentioned in the Johannine narrative (20:25) but not in the synoptic gospels. The victim, unable to move, exposed to the elements and to raging thirst, often survived for days unless attendant soldiers ended the affair by spear thrusts.

they divided: The clothing of those condemned to death belonged to the attendant soldiers, and the well-known addiction of Roman soldiers to games of chance with dice sufficiently explains this incident without reference to Ps 22:19 (which Mark certainly had in mind). The quotation is used also in Matt 27:35 and Luke 23:34. It is foreign to Mark to use Old Testament quotations, and we assume either that he found it in his sources in Matthew and Luke, or the allusion was already firmly embedded in the early tradition of the crucifixion. John 19:24 makes a distinction between the *himatia,* the ordinary clothing of Jesus, and a special woven tunic.

We shall later on meet another quotation from Psalm 22, and the question inevitably arises as to what extent Old Testament allusions have colored the accounts as we have them, or equally to what extent the events themselves evoked reminiscences of Old Testament texts. (So far as Mark's gospel is concerned, a good summary is to be found in J. H. Reumann, "Ps. 22 at the Cross. Lament and Thanksgiving for Jesus Christ," *Int* 28.2.1974, pp. 39-58.)

Mark's version of the quotation is from the Septuagint (Ps 21:19), even to the verb form *(diamerizontai,* cf. Luke 23:24 *diamerizomenoi* and Matt 27:36 *diamerizanto).*

Matthew has the chilling comment "and they sat down there and watched him."

25. *It was nine in the morning:* We called attention in the comment to the notes of time in Mark as "punctuation marks" in the story, convenient divisions by which to memorize the progress of events. But whether we translate as we have here or give the literal "it was the third hour," we must beware of imposing on the world of the first century our own clock-dominated sense of time. The note of time here, even assuming it to rest on the evidence of eyewitnesses, is an approximation at best and a wild guess at worst. To attempt a reconciliation of this note of time with John 19:14 ("about the sixth hour") is in many ways a fruitless exercise.

The repetition of *they crucified him* is on any showing strange, the more so when it is realized that what we have translated as *when* is the Greek *kai* (and). A few lesser manuscripts read "and they watched him," which certainly makes more sense than the repeated *they crucified him*. It is tempting to think that originally there was here a statement similar to Matthew's "and they watched him there." However, the reading is represented only by a small minority of manuscripts.

26. The custom of detailing *the charge* (Greek *aitia)* was common and is referred to

in classical literature. All the evangelists have *"the King of the Jews,"* while Matt 27:37 reads "this is" before the title, and Luke 23:38 has the title followed by "this." John 19:19 reads "Jesus the Nazarene" before the title and records that the whole charge was written in Hebrew, Greek, and Latin. The same source reports that Pilate responded to criticisms by the chief priests with a sardonic "What I have written, I have written."

27. The *two bandits* (Greek *lēstēs;* cf. 11:17, 14:48) are mentioned earlier in Luke's narrative (23:32) as "criminals" (Greek *kakourgoi).* Mark is here following Matthew's outline very closely and introduces the two as a preface to the verbal insults which follow. Interestingly Mark copies Matthew's *hena ek . . . hena ex (one on . . . the other on),* which it has been suggested may be a Semitism. Mark maintains his historic present with *staurousin* (literally "they crucify"), whereas Matthew has the passive "were crucified" (27:38).

28. This verse is in parenthesis because it appears in many manuscripts of Mark, though the omission of it by the most important manuscripts would appear to demonstrate that it was at an early stage added from Luke 22:37. The manner in which the quotation is introduced is certainly not Markan, and in any event such quotations in Mark are very rare.

29. Very serious questions are raised in the verses which follow. How much of the record before us is a result of Christian piety, of reflection on Old Testament scripture? How much of the record is a *post hoc* explanation of what "ought to have happened," and how much genuine historical recollection is to be found there? The later interest of Christian liturgy in (for example) Psalm 22, Lamentations 2, and Wisdom 2 is well enough known, but how early was that reflective interest in passages which spoke of solitary suffering and which (especially in the case of Wisdom 2) appeared to mirror the experience of Jesus?

The passers-by: This refers to people from the city, not a gathered crowd at the execution. The first part of the verse invites comparison with Lam 2:15—"All those who pass by snap their fingers at you; they hiss and wag their heads at you . . ." Ps 22:7 reads "All who see me jeer at me, making mouths at me, and wag their heads . . ." The comparison invites the suggestion that the quotations of themselves explain the origin of the narrative, but it is at least possible—if the taunt in this verse is historically based—that the evangelist Matthew (always alert to Old Testament allusion) fashioned the account in texts which appeared to him to be apposite. Mark's Greek is almost identical with Matt 27:39.

"You were going to tear down the temple . . ." This saying, whatever may have been its original form or meaning, is inextricably bound up with the passion narrative (cf. note on 14:58), and it is hardly surprising to find it thrown back at the speaker. There is no good reason to suppose that we are not in the presence of genuine historical detail. The Greek translated *"Aha!" (oua)* is a word which implies real or feigned astonishment.

To the taunt in this verse Matthew adds, "If you are God's son, come down from the cross!" Jesus, they considered, had all along not only been a deceiver but was worse, a self-deceiver; and his execution was all the proof they needed.

31. All three synoptists record mockery by the *chief priests and scribes.* Granted (in Mark's case) a consuming interest in casting the scribes in the role of principal oppo-

nents of Jesus, the presence of *the chief priests* is hardly credible. This was Passover, and even granted a superfluity of clergy in and around Jerusalem, there is something strange in this scene of vengeful mocking by a class of people whom John describes as being conscious above all else of ritual purity (18:28). The vocabulary is superficially Matthean and Markan—*chief priests, scribes,* even *in similar fashion (homoiōs,* three times in Matthew, two in Mark); *joked with one another (empaizō,* five times in Matthew, five in Luke, three in Mark); and *with one another (pros allēlous,* eight in Luke, three in Matthew, five in Mark). But there is an orchestration here which is not Markan: the passers-by pick up a theme from the trial and taunt the victim; then the chief priests take this up as on a cue and then among themselves escalate the saying about the temple. And to what does *"He saved others"* refer? To healings and exorcisms? The whole complex ends on a note of sneering contempt: *Let the Messiah . . . come down from the cross* and a surprising semi-Johannine *so that we can see it and believe* (cf. John 6:30).

The construction has all the marks of artificiality, in the sense of a story transferred from an original setting and placed elsewhere for dramatic effect. Furthermore the whole episode is strikingly reminiscent of Wis 2:7—"Let us see if his words are true . . . for if the Righteous One is God's son, God will put out his hand and save him . . ." Leaving on one side for the moment the historicity of this account, it is important now to turn to Ps 22:9. (The Greek of Matthew and Mark is identical in v. 31 = Matt 27:41 save that Matthew adds "the elders" to the chorus of clergy and scribes.) The identity continues to *and believe,* to which Matthew adds "in him." Luke 23:35 is far shorter than Matthew and Mark, and to *he saved others* the Lucan conclusion is "Let him save himself if he is God's Messiah, the chosen one." Matthew's 27:43 is plainly shaped by Ps 22:8, "Does he trust in God? Then let him deliver him now, if he wants him, for he said, 'I am God's son.' "

We venture the tentative suggestion—it is obviously no more than tentative—that the mockery of the chief priests and scribes belongs not here but to the tumult of the scene at the trial before Pilate. Perhaps what we are hearing in this narrative of mockery is the entire satisfaction of the clerical party that they now had the offender in a position from which there was no escape. Certainly they would find it an irony: ". . . *joked with one another. 'He saved others,' they said, 'but he cannot save himself.' "* What an appropriate taunting response among themselves, at the sight of Jesus' helplessness before Pilate. We suggest further that it was the temple saying in that context which attracted to itself here a series of conversations (overheard by an eyewitness?) between chief priests, elders, and scribes.

This is very far from suggesting at what stage in the written tradition this transposition was made. But if it was done by Matthew, then even Luke—who has other dramatic concerns, notably that of the penitent thief—felt obliged to follow the example. This he did in spite of the fact that he has no tradition of a mocking by the passers-by.

Messiah, Israel's king: We again call attention to this example of names and titles of Jesus as we noted earlier, beginning with the entry into Jerusalem at Mark 11:1. With the exception of the soldier's exclamation at the death of Jesus, this present title ends the series.

[1:1 Jesus-Messiah: son of God]
11:10 the Coming One
11:21 Rabbi
12:14,19 Teacher, Rabbi
12:35 Son of David
13:1 Rabbi
13:26 Son of Man
14:14 Rabbi
14:21 Son of Man
14:27 Shepherd
14:45 Rabbi
14:62 Messiah
14:62 Son of Man
14:66 Jesus the Nazarene
15:2,9,12,17,18,26 King of the Jews
15:32 the Messiah, the King of Israel
[15:32 a son of God]

crucified with him: The verb *sunstauroumai* is not found outside Christian writings. It was used by Paul to describe the identification of the believer with Jesus in the Passion and death.

87. The Death of Jesus
(15:33-41) = Matt 27:45-56; Luke 23:44-49;
John 19:28-30

15 ³³ At midday a darkness fell over all the land, which lasted until three in the afternoon. ³⁴ At three o'clock, Jesus called out with a loud cry, "Eloi, Eloi, lama sabachthani?" (which means, "My God, my God, why have you forsaken me?") ³⁵ Some of the bystanders who heard this said, "Listen—he is calling Elijah." ³⁶ One of them ran and soaked a sponge in vinegar and held it up to him on the end of a stick. "Let us see," he said, "if Elijah is coming to take him down." ³⁷ Then Jesus gave a loud cry and died. ³⁸ The curtain in the temple was torn in two, from top to bottom. ³⁹ When the centurion who was standing opposite him saw how he cried out and died, he said, "Certainly this man was a son of God." ⁴⁰ There were some women present, watching from a distance. Among them were Mary of Magdala, Mary the mother of the younger James and Joses, and Salome, ⁴¹ who had all

followed him and waited on him when he was in Galilee. There were many other women also who had come up with him to Jerusalem.

Notes

33. *a darkness:* Here again, in faithful copying of Matthew, we have another of Mark's three-hour divisions. The Greek of Mark is close to that of Matthew, though there are differences. Luke 23:44 also speaks of the sun being darkened. What is being described—a natural phenomenon of some kind? If that is so, an eclipse is ruled out, being impossible at the time of a full moon. A semidarkness is often produced (as Lagrange points out, p. 432) by a sirocco blowing from North Africa, but this hardly seems to be what the evangelists have in mind. Moreover we have *over all the land* in all three gospels. Does this mean Judea? We suggest that what we have here is biblical imagery used to describe an event which for all the human tragedy involved was yet the act of God in the redemption of Israel and humanity. We recall the darkness of another deliverance (Exod 10:22), and it is significant that Matt 27:45 is nearer to the Greek of Exod 10:22 than is Mark. In addition to the darkness of the Exodus, it was a commonly held belief in the ancient world that darkness was often associated with, or presaged, the death of great men. Cf. in addition Amos 8:9, Jer 15:9, Mark 13:24. This was indeed for the early community a Day of the Lord, and we recall that Luke (9:31) at the time of the Transfiguration spoke of the "exodus" which Jesus was to perform in Jerusalem.

34. *"Eloi, Eloi . . ."* This saying is the only one recorded by Matthew and Mark, in strong contrast to the material in Luke and John. The Greek *Eloi, eloi lama sabachthanei* is the transliteration of an Aramaic original which can only be described as "Hebraized." The quotation is from Ps 22:1. The linguistic background can be seen in two manuscripts, which read *zaphthanei,* which is nearer to the Hebrew than *sabachthanei.* Presumably Mark's community would be more accustomed to the Aramaic, and this would be reflected if Mark was using a Palestinian tradition. *Eloi* may be an old Hebrew form still in use at that time for "my God." Matthew has *Eli,* which is closer to the Hebrew form of Ps 22:1. Allowing for the moment that Jesus uttered the saying, it would appear likely that it was said in Hebrew, for the comment *he is calling Elijah* makes sense only if the cry was *ēlei, ēlei,* or *ēli, ēli* rather than Mark's *eloi.* In Matt 27:45 nearly all the manuscript authorities read either *elei* or *eli,* and few read *eloi.*

While linguistically the tradition of the saying is unquestionably ancient, the very strong undertones of Psalm 22, both in Matthew and Mark, provide a whole series of questions to which answers are not readily forthcoming. The Old Testament tradition appears to have colored strongly whatever early written sources lie behind our present gospels and may well have grown through the influence of the early community and the work of the evangelists. We appear to be driven to the conclusion *either* that Jesus uttered some words from Psalm 22, *or* that Jesus died without utterance, or without utterance that was overheard, and the early tradition credited him with some words from Psalm 22. In favor of the view that this was a genuine utterance of Jesus is the fact that our gospels do not present any single view of what we have come to call "atonement." Jesus himself is presented to us as believing that he came as the obedient servant to proclaim and fulfill the demanding will of God. Only later in the ministry, and associated with predictions of the Passion and death, did Jesus begin to interpret the ministry in salvific terms. Even there, we cannot easily construct a "theory" of atonement from the ransom saying of 10:45 or the words over bread and cup at the Last Supper. Certainly nothing approaching a theory of vicarious suffering can be derived from Psalm 22, and with caution we propose to accept the view that the saying from its first verse is genuine. For one thing it underlines and emphasizes the humanity of Jesus in its fullness: the obedient servant finds himself, for all his trust and abandonment to the will of the Father, himself abandoned. The Passion predictions spoke of vindication, and to the dying Jesus this must all have seemed far away.

For further reading, from disparate viewpoints, see:

Burchard, C. "Markus 15:34." *ZNW* 74.1983, pp. 1-11.
Brower, K. "Elijah in the Markan Passion Narrative." *JNTS* 18.1983, pp. 85-101.
Gese, H. "Psalm 22 und das Neue Testament: Der älteste Bericht vom Tode Jesu und die Entstehung des Herrenmahles." *ZTK* 65.1968, pp. 1-22.
Leon-Dufour, X., "Le dernier cri de Jésus." *Études* 348.1978, pp. 666-82.
Reumann, J. "Psalm 22 at the Cross: Lament and Thanksgiving for Jesus Christ." *Int* 28.1974, pp. 39-58.

(which means . . .) (Greek *methermeneuomai):* Cf. 5:41. Mark's Greek is in general that of the Septuagint, omitting (like Matthew) *prosches me* (look on me) and using *eis ti* in place of *hina ti* for *why*. There are variant readings which demonstrate later reflection: the apocryphal Gospel of Peter reads *he dunamis mou* (my Power) for *my God,* and *kateleipsas me* (you have left me behind) for *egkatelipes me (you have forsaken me).* Some Latin manuscripts also found difficulty with *forsaken,* and we have in result *exprobasti me* (you have tested me), *me in opprobrium dedisti* (you have given me over to hatred), and *meledixisti* (you have wished me ill).

Christian history, especially subsequent to the Reformation, has been as varied as the bewilderment sensed in some Latin versions. The saying is not found in Luke or John, though it would probably be hazardous to describe either as being bewildered by the saying. Some Reformers, with a feudal view of reward and punishment which would have been rejected by Anselm, taught that Jesus was forsaken by God because Jesus was a substitute for sinners and therefore an object of wrath. To read substitutionary atonement into the Biblical literature is at best perilous and at worst indebted to a view of human nature owing more to Tertullian than to Irenaeus or Paul. There are those for whom the saying on the lips of Jesus must be in some respects rejected because it infringes on the divine nature in Jesus. This is not the place to argue the fitness or otherwise of the decrees of the Council of Chalcedon in A.D. 451. But to erode in any way the humanity of Jesus is to be on the way to producing a docetic Jesus (against which the fourth gospel and the Johannine letters wax vehement) and making of Jesus a man of certitude and not of faith, far removed from that humanity of ours which Christian faith says he shared.

35. Exactly who is being characterized as *some of the bystanders* is not clear. In v. 29 these were Jews coming out of the city. But if the cry is accurately reported

("Listen—he is calling Elijah.") then it does not seem appropriate that the one who *soaked a sponge in vinegar and held it up* should have been a Jew. In the light of John 19:29, it is far more likely to have been a soldier.

Elijah: That there was a popular belief in a coming of Elijah to aid in time of need seems well established (cf. Strack-Billerbeck, Vol. 1, p. 1042). But one manuscript reads *hēlion* for *Ēleian,* and if some of those who heard the cry mistook *Ēli* for an appeal to the sun god, then the reaction of the one who ran for the vinegar is understandable. John 19:29 speaks of a jar of *oxos* standing near the cross, and this was most probably *posca,* a sour wine often provided for soldiers and workers. Indeed the same verse may afford another hint, for if we read *hussō* (on a javelin) for *hussōpō* (on a hyssop stick) in the Johannine account, the story reads more plausibly. The *sponge* (Greek *spongas)* is found here, in Matt 27:48, and in John 19:29. Similarly *oxos* *(vinegar)* is represented in all the gospels: Matt 27:48, Luke 23:36, and John 19:29.

"Let us see" (Greek *aphete idōmen):* The expression is not an exhortation but almost an imperative. Perhaps the best rendering in idiomatic English would be "Oh, do let's see . . ." Matthew has "Let things take their course . . ."

". . . if Elijah . . .": The Greek is *ei erchetai Ēlias kathelein auton,* and *kathaireō* (cf. 15:46) is the technical term for the taking down of a crucified body. The whole expression bespeaks a doubtful possibility. Matt 27:49 has "let us see whether Elijah will come to save him." But who is speaking here? In Mark it appears to be the one who brought the vinegar *(legōn—he said,* present participle). In Matthew, however, one ran for the vinegar, "but the rest *[hoi loipoi]* said, 'Let things take their course . . .'" However, it is possible that Mark's *legōn* may be a mistranslation. G. M. Lee ("Two Notes on St. Mark," *NovTest* 18.1.1976, p. 36) suggests that in order to read *legōn,* the translator must have read *'mrw* as *'mr* by haplography, since the succeeding first person imperative would begin with *nun,* which resembles *taw.* If this suggestion is followed, then we could read *elegon* (they said) as the reaction of the bystanders to the one who went for the vinegar.

There is no particular reason, in considering the cry about Elijah, why the *bystanders* should not be understood as the attendant soldiers, and that one at least of those soldiers could have been a Jew. Whether therefore *Eli* was misunderstood as an invocation to *Hēlios,* the sun god, or as *Ēlias,* whether by Jew or Gentile, it appears to this writer that we can best understand this episode by treating *bystanders* as the attendant soldiers.

So far this has left out of the account the suggestion by some commentators that v. 36a is a parenthesis, and—on one view—inspired by Ps 69:22 (Septuagint Ps 68:22) ("When I was thirsty, they gave me vinegar—*oxos*—to drink"). The suggestion is incapable of proof, and an attempt to prove that the connection 35-36a is primary and 36b secondary must fail for lack of manuscript evidence. It is at the least possible that the tradition of v. 36a called the attention of the early community to Ps 69:22. Presumably John 19:28, in referring to the fulfillment of scripture, had this reference in mind. But given the nature of Ps 22 and the saying in v. 34, it is also possible that Ps 42:1-2 was in the evangelist's mind. There is nothing inherently improbable about the incident of the sour wine, and it is attested in Luke 23:36. It may be added that the late Dr. Jerome Webster, of Presbyterian Hospital, New York (and a long-time student of the effects of crucifixion on the human system) told me in conversation that, given the death of the victim by exhaustion and suffocation, anything given to the victim to drink would hasten the process of suffocation.

37. All three synoptists concur that the death of Jesus was preceded by *a loud cry*. Matt 27:50 has ". . . and yielded up the Spirit." Luke 23:46 has Jesus using a phrase from Ps 31:5 and ". . . he breathed his last." We have tried, by the use of the simple finality of the verb *died*, to avoid the use of euphemisms like "gave up his ghost." All four evangelists convey in one fashion or another the violence of the death. Matt 27:50 may share something of the Johannine "handed over the Spirit" (19:30) with its theological undertones of the next stage in the drama of redemption. John 19:30 has the triumphant *Tetelestai!*—"it is consummated!" Luke has Jesus voluntarily abandoning himself to death, but no evangelist uses the ordinary Greek word for "to die" *(apothnēskō)*. Mark's verb *ekpneō* is classical. It is repeated in v. 39 and is found also in Luke 23:46, but it is not represented in the Septuagint. Matthew and Mark have no tradition of any saying of Jesus.

38. *The curtain of the temple . . .* In this short verse, as in Matthew's more extended 27:51-53, we are in the presence of the language of apocalyptic. The linguistic details are as follows:

curtain (Greek *katapetasma):* Matt 27:51; Luke 23:45; Heb 6:19, 9:3, 10:20. The word is found in the Septuagint, and *to katapetasma* is the veil between the Holy Place and the Holy of Holies (Exod 27:16). The same sense is found in the *Letter of Aristeas* 86, and in Philo *(Life of Moses* 2.148). There are interpolations in the *Testaments of the Twelve Patriarchs* which also refer to this curtain *(T Levi* 10:3; *T Benj* 9:3). Commentators disagree on whether the outer curtain is meant (between the Holy Place and the Holy of Holies) or the inner one immediately in front of the Holy of Holies.

Symbolically there is agreement that the language signifies an end and a new beginning, perhaps the end of the temple system, but certainly and more importantly (as so well articulated by Hebrews) the opening of the way to God through the ministry and self-offering of Jesus (cf. Isa 64:1). Perhaps too there is an element in this verse (as there is in Matthew) of revelation of the true nature of Jesus and his mission as redeemer (cf. P. Lamarche, "La mot du Christ et la voile du temple selon Marc" NRTh 106.6.1974, pp. 583-99; and H. L. Chronis, "The Torn Veil: Cultus and Christology in Mark 15:37-39," *JBL* 101.1.1982, pp. 97-114).

By what means this eschatological motif connected with the temple came into the tradition is not open to our inspection. It is a relatively minor note in Luke 23:45 (almost as though the evangelist was undecided what to do with it) but is certainly important in Matthew as the key to the cataclysmic nature of the events he is describing. Mark is certainly not noted for including eschatological material, apart from the masterly editing in Chapter 13. The Greek of Mark's v. 38 is identical with that of Matt 27:51, save that he changed the position of *in two,* and we conclude that it was from Matthew that it was derived, even to the quite redundant Greek prepositions *ap'anōthen heōs katō (from top to bottom).*

The literature associated with the temple has its own share of stories of portents. Josephus *(Jewish Wars* 6.5.3) speaks of a light and a mysterious self-opening of the east gate of the temple forty years before its siege in A.D. 70. Jerome *(Letters* 120.8.1) tells us that the *Gospel of the Hebrews* spoke not only of the veil being torn, but also of a massive lintel falling down in fragments.

To attempt to find in any of this some element of historical reporting is to fail to appreciate the eschatological dimensions of the death of Jesus which the evangelists are attempting to communicate.

39. Mark uses the word *kenturiōn,* a Latinism found in the papyri, whereas Matthew and Luke use the equally late *hekatontarchos,* a word whose meaning is essentially the same—the commander of what we would call a "company" of soldiers. The man's position is precisely described, as *standing opposite* (Greek *ex anantias),* a precision lacking in Matthew and Luke. Matt 27:54 mentions the centurion's fellow soldiers as being overcome with awe, while Luke 23:47 describes the centurion as giving glory to God for all that happened. Aside from the mention of the curtain of the temple, which he shares with Matthew and Luke, Mark's starkly simple account links the centurion's reaction to the death of Jesus (cf. *and died* in vv. 37 and 39).

how he cried out and died: This translation is a composite of Greek readings, for some manuscripts simply have *how he died,* others have *saw him cry out,* and some omit *how.* But the best attestation, taking all things into account, seems to be *hoti houtos kraxas exepneusen,* which is reflected in our translation.

"Certainly this man was a son of God": There seems little doubt that Mark intended this verse to be a match for the very beginning of his gospel. Matt 27:54 has the same Greek, though with a different word order. As far as the soldier was concerned, this may have been a cry of admiration for a death nobly borne; the centurion may even have been a member of the Mithras mystery religion, which so admired and inculcated patient endurance in its members.

In what sense Mark understood this phrase *Son of God* we cannot know (cf. notes on 1:1), but it was certainly not in the later fully developed Christian theology. Interestingly Luke's Greek text (23:47) describing the centurion's admiration can be read as "Certainly this man was the Righteous One." This elusive "messianic" title, certainly as old as Isa 53:11 and maybe much older (cf. Albright-Mann, AB *Matthew,* p. 352). We cannot be certain what Luke intended at this point (though he does use the title in Acts 3:14, 7:52), and it may be only that Luke wished to avoid any sympathy with the pagan notion of a semidivine being that might have been implied by the centurion. Lohmeyer (p. 347) regards the saying as of the highest importance and as embodying what the Sanhedrin regarded as blasphemy.

40,41. *There were some women:* The two verses which conclude this section are in the nature of an appendix. *Among them* is a fascinating note, and the phrases *followed him* and *had come up with him* has led to the suggestion that Jesus may have had women disciples (cf. Winsome Munro, "Women Disciples in Mark?" *CBQ* 44.2.1982, pp. 225-41).

The women named appear to be three in number, but three manuscripts have the definite article before *mētēr,* and qualifying Joses. This would then give us "Mary of Magdala, Mary the mother of the younger James, the mother of Joses, and Salome."

Mary of Magdala: Cf. v. 47, 16:1. See also Matthew 27:56,61, 28:1; Luke 8:2, 24:10; John 19:25, 20:1,18. Both Luke 8:2 and Mark 16:9 record that seven devils had been cast out of her. The appellation places her as coming from the west side of the Sea of Galilee.

Mary the mother of the younger James: Matt 27:56 reads "Mary the mother of the younger James and Joseph" instead of Mark's *Joses* and is also referred to in v. 47 as

Iōsetos (Matthew describes her as "the other Mary") and in 16:1 as the mother of James. John 19:25 speaks of her as "Mary the wife of Clopas." Some Syriac manuscripts describe her as the "daughter" of James, but this is unlikely. She is presumably the mother of James and Joses, and it was a common enough usage for a woman to be known through the name of her son. The identity of these two brothers is impossible to determine, though we may assume that (like Alexander and Rufus) they were well known to the early community. It is very unlikely that they were the brothers of Jesus, for Mark would have identified Mary much more clearly as the mother of Jesus. It may be that *James* is the *son of Alphaeus* of 3:18. But quite unknown is whether *Alphaeus* is *Clopas*.

the younger: The Greek word used to describe *James* is *mikros,* which can equally mean physically smaller, and we assume in contrast to some other James, possibly the son of Zebedee. *Salome* is identified in Matt 27:56 as "mother of the sons of Zebedee." For the word *follow* (Greek *akoloutheō*) cf. 1:18; for *waited on* (Greek *diakoneō*) cf. 1:13; for *come up with* (Greek *sunabainō*) cf. Acts 13:31.

Mark has produced some very crude Greek in these two verses and appears to be following a source of his own. Matt 27:55-56 is much more polished. ("There were also many women, looking on from a distance, who had followed Jesus from Galilee and looked after him. Among them . . .") It is possible to speculate whether originally Mark's text went from v. 39 to v. 42. Luke 23:49 refers simply to "the women who had accompanied him from Galilee," though in 8:3 he mentions among the women helpers Joanna, the wife of Chuza, Herod's steward.

88. The Burial of Jesus
(15:42-47) = Matt 27:57-61; Luke 23:50-56; John 19:38-42

15   42 By now, evening had come, and as it was Preparation Day (that is, the day before Sabbath), 43 Joseph of Arimathea, a respected member of the council, a man who looked for the coming of the Reign of God, went bravely in to Pilate and asked for the body of Jesus. 44 Pilate was surprised to hear that he was already dead, so he sent for the centurion and asked him how long he had been dead. 45 When he had heard the centurion's report, he gave the body to Joseph. 46 Joseph therefore bought a linen sheet, took him down, and wrapped him in the sheet. Then he laid him in a tomb cut out of the rock, and rolled a stone across the entrance to the tomb. 47 Mary of Magdala and Mary the mother of Joses were watching and saw where he was laid.

Comment

Apart from v. 47, which has all the appearance of a later tradition preparing for 16:1-8, we have here a thoroughly artless description of the burial of a first-century Jew. Moreover the historic present in some notable instances adds to the fluidity of the narrative. Taylor (p. 599) suggests that it was compiled "in a Gentile environment," and if this is so, then we may be in the presence of an element of Mark's original Roman (and Petrine) source. Indeed a case could be made for this brief pericope as being far more careful in Greek syntax than much of the rest of the gospel. This in its turn must raise questions about the stages of compilation in Mark for which there are no more than intelligent surmises by way of answer.

There would appear to be good grounds for thinking that we are here very close to an eyewitness tradition. In view of the tortured and lingering deaths associated with crucifixion, the surprise of Pilate is wholly credible, as is also his inquiry to the centurion. Matthew has only part of this tradition, and Luke's account of the burial says nothing of it. If Matthew and Luke had access to Mark, it is puzzling to discover so many lively details being omitted from their accounts. Certainly Matthew has wholly different interests (cf. Matt 28:11-15), but his sparse account of the visit of an otherwise unidentified Joseph of Arimathea is at the least odd if he knew Mark's text. Of course this difficulty is removed if, with some commentators, vv. 44 and 45 are regarded as legendary.

Notes

42. *evening had come* (Greek *opsias genomenēs):* Cf. 4:35. This would indicate late afternoon, around 4:30 P.M. Mark goes on to explain that it was the day before Sabbath. The term *Preparation* (Greek *paraskenē,* cf. Matt 27:62; Luke 23:54; John 19:14,31,42) is a technical one and indicates the daylight hours before Passover or Sabbath (cf. Josephus, *Ant* 14.6.2). Mark in a parenthesis explains it further, *ho estin prosabbaton.* The word is found in Jdt 8:6 and in the titles to Psalms 92 and 93 in two manuscripts. Luke has "It was preparation day, and the Sabbath was near" (23:54). This adequately explains the haste with which Joseph went to Pilate.

43. This is in fact part of the previous verse, and Mark is so anxious to share his knowledge of Joseph that he has an awkward periodic sentence.

Joseph: Some manuscripts omit the definite article before *apo Harimathaias.* The student of Greek will be aware that this has the effect of stating that Joseph "came from" Arimathea, without saying that he was a native of it. However, the article is widely enough distributed to allow us to read it here. The location of Arimathea is not known, though the Syriac reads *Ramatha,* which may be the Ramathaim-Sophim of 1 Sam 1:1. The Greek form of the name may stand for the Aramaic *Ramethayga* (the two heights) also called *Rāmethā* in the Peshitta (first or second century A.D. version of the Syriac, a text in common use and perhaps done by Jewish Christians). The name was later Hellenized as Remtis, after a town some few miles north of Jerusalem.

The description of Joseph as *euschēmōn boulentēs* means "influential" and even "wealthy" (cf. Matt 27:57, *plousios).* Though used of Joseph, the word *boulentēs* was apparently not a technical term among Jews, but it is used here to indicate membership of the Sanhedrin.

who looked for the . . . Reign of God: Cf. Luke 2:25,38. This does not state that Joseph was a disciple, though Matt 27:57 describes him as "attached to" *(emathēteuthē)* Jesus. John 19:38 says that this attachment was secret, and it is John who informs us that in his work of piety he was joined by Nicodemus (19:39). Luke 23:50-51 informs us that Joseph had not consented to Jesus' death.

bravely (Greek *polmēsas) asked for* (Greek *aiteomai):* Cf. 6:24. Normally the bodies of those crucified were left hanging there to decay. Josephus *(Jewish Wars* 4.5.2.), however, informs us that the bodies of crucified criminals were often taken down and buried before evening, citing this as an example of the care taken by Jews to obey the Law (cf. Deut 21:22-23). Care was also taken that those being executed could not be secretly rescued during the Sabbath. Joseph's request was urgent (Greek *ēstēsato),* but he was aware that he was asking a favor, perhaps relying on his status as an influential member of the Sanhedrin.

44. Wholly without regard as to whether this verse was in Mark's original draft, there is a care for Greek syntax in this and the following verse which is remarkable in this gospel. The verb *surprised* (correctly, as in classical Greek, *thaumazei ei)* in proper grammatical form is found only here and at 1 John 3:13 in the New Testament. There is similar care observed in the use of tenses: *dead* (Greek *tethnēken)* is in the perfect tense, as of a persisting state of affairs, and in the use of the aorist in *how long he had been dead* (Greek *apethanen)* as describing an observed event.

The episode of the questioning of the centurion is peculiar to Mark. Matt 27:58 simply says "Pilate ordered it [the body] to be given to him." The episode has a complete ring of authenticity; crucified men often lingered for days before death supervened.

he gave (Greek *dōreomai):* Cf. 2 Pet 1:3. The verb—as witness the Septuagint of Gen 30:20, 1 Esdr 1:7 and 8:55, Esth 8:1—probably suggests an act of graciousness. The word *body* (Greek *ptōma)* is changed to *sōma* in some manuscripts but is probably original, perhaps with *sōma* being the original reading in v. 42.

46. *bought a linen sheet:* Only Mark mentions this purchase. Some have suggested that this demonstrates that Passover had not yet begun, but in fact exceptions were allowed under pressure of necessity, always provided that money did not change hands until after the festival (cf. Mishnah *Shabbath* 23.1). However, the verb *bought* *(agorasas)* is definite enough, and we are here again faced with the vexed and wholly unresolved question of chronology. In the Johannine scheme of things, this was simply preparation day, and Joseph would have had time to make the purchase.

The *linen sheet* is precisely that: a piece of new linen, not an article of clothing. (Matt 27:59 has *sindoni kathara,* "clean linen," while John 19:40 further thinks of the body being additionally wrapped in strips of cloth.) The word *wrapped* (Greek *eneilēsen)* has occasioned some question, mainly because Matthew and Luke use *ethēken,* which it is felt is more elegant than Mark's verb. In fact *eneileō* has a very wide range of meanings, from shackling a prisoner, holding people in debt, or wrapping children in clothing, to the quite neutral sense of "to wrap."

tomb cut out of the rock (Greek *en mnēmati ho ēn lelatoumēmenon ek petras):* The verb *cut* or "hewn" *(latomeō)* is late Greek. The last decades of the second temple have provided numerous examples for archaeologists of stone tombs, some containing burial chambers and some a single room with a shelf for the body. There is one notable example, that of Helen of Adiabene (the queen mother, and a convert to Judaism), with a large circular stone rolled in a trough to cover the entrance. Matt 27:60 says that the tomb was new, and Luke 23:53 emphasizes this by saying it had never been used.

We now have two quite disparate traditions in this verse. Joseph would have needed help in his task, and we have to assume his own servants assisted him. Mark certainly implies in 16:1 (cf. 14:8; Luke 23:55) that even if it was washed, the body was not anointed, and Matthew's silence points the same way. But John 19:39-40 clearly states that Nicodemus came with myrrh and aloes, and these were put into the folds of the cloth according to Jewish custom. There is no way in which the synoptic and Johannine traditions can be reconciled.

47. This may well be in the nature of a footnote to the narrative or a preface to 16:1.

The verse is notable for textual variations in the names of the women. Jesetos is read by some manuscripts, Joses by others, while some others describe Mary as the mother of James, and a few as the mother of James and Josetos.

For further reading see the following three articles in *L'Évangile selon Marc: Tradition et redaction,* edited by M. Sabbe, Bibliotheca ephemeridum theologicarum lovaniensium 34, Gembloux: Ducolot and Louvain: Leuven University, 1974.

1. Aland, K. "Der Schluss des Markusevangeliums, pp. 435-70.

2. Bartsch, H.-W. "Der ursprüngliche Schluss der Leidengeschichte: Überlieferungsgeschichte Studien zum Markus-Schluss," pp. 411-33.

3. Pesch, R. "Der Schluss der vormarkinschen Passionsgeschichte und des Markus evangeliums: Mark 15:42-16:8," pp. 364-409.

89. The Empty Tomb
(16:1-8) = Matt 28:1-8; Luke 24:1-12; John 20:1-10

16 ¹When the Sabbath was over, Mary of Magdala, Mary the mother of James, and Salome bought aromatic oils to go and anoint him, ²and very early on the first day of the week, just after sunrise, they went to the tomb. ³They were saying to each other, "Who will roll away the stone from the entrance to the tomb?" ⁴But when they looked up, they saw that the stone—big as it was—had been rolled away. ⁵Then they went into the tomb, where they saw a young man wearing a white robe sitting at the right-hand side, and they were afraid. ⁶But he said to them, "Stop being afraid! You are looking for Jesus of Nazareth, who was crucified. He has been raised; he is not here. Look—here is the place where they laid him. ⁷Now go and say to his disciples and to Peter, 'He is going on before you into Galilee; you will see him there, just as he told you.' " ⁸Then they went out and ran from the tomb, beside themselves with trembling and awe. They said nothing to anyone, for they were afraid.

Comment

Controversy surrounding this section continues and shows no sign of abating. Aside from whether the narrative before us constitutes a Resurrection story or not, debate has centered for many years on the ending at v. 8. Readers will recall that in the introduction (2. The Purpose of Mark) the view was expressed that Mark did indeed finish his gospel at v. 8, and that he had a specific and well-defined purpose in doing so. Apart from such a view (that for whatever reason the gospel did end at 16:8), the following have been some of the views espoused:

1. Ending a sentence, let alone a whole work, with *gar* (for) is highly improbable grammatically. (Cf. P. W. van der Horst, "Can a Book End with GAR? A Note on Mark 16:8," *JTS* n.s. 23.1972, pp. 121-24; C. F. D. Moule, "St. Mark 16:8 Once More," *NTS* 2.1.1955-6, pp. 58-64.)

2. The narrative of the burial in Mark belongs to the Passion tradition and is ancient. The visit to the tomb is legendary, but the visit of the two Marys is linked with the mention of the same women at the cross and at the burial, and this tradition of a triple mention may also be ancient. There is a sequence of narratives parallel to the three articles in the Pauline confession of 1 Cor 15:3b-5, and there is consequently a strong possibility that Mark added the visit to the tomb from an old tradition (cf. E. Dhanis, "L'ensevelissement de Jésus et la visite an tombeau dans l'Évangile de Saint Marc (Marc XV 40-XVI 8)" *Gregorianum* 39.2.1958, pp. 367-410).

3. While the text of Mark, as we have it now, properly ends at 16:8, there was a longer ending, but this is now lost, and vv. 9-20 are not of Markan composition. Cf. Kurt Aland, "Bemerkungen zum Schluss des Markusevangeliums" in *Neotestamentica et Semitica: Studies in Honour of Matthew Black,* Edinburgh, T. & T. Clark, 1969.

4. Attempts have been made constantly to determine the pre-Markan tradition of the raising of Jesus, based on the majority assumption of the priority of Mark. Generally there is a consensus on the part of proponents of the two-document hypothesis that the pre-Markan tradition is irrecoverable. There is on the other hand a considerable literature on the manner in which Matthew and Luke made use of Mark 16:1-8 (cf. M. D. Goulder, "Mark XVI.1-8 and Parallels," *NTS* 24.2.1978, pp. 235-40). Representative discussion on the attempts to reconstruct the pre-Markan tradition would include: E. L. Bode, *The First Easter Morning,* AnBib 25. Rome: Pontifical Biblical Institute, 1970; D. Dormeyer, *Die Passion Jesu als Verhaltensmodell,* Münster, Aschendorff, 1974 (Dormeyer views v. 8b as a gloss on the text); J. D. Crossan, "Empty Tomb and Absent Lord" in *The Passion in Mark: Studies on Mark 14-16,* edited by H. Kelber, Philadelphia: Fortress, 1976).

One of the difficulties inherent in a theory of Markan priority precisely lies in the necessity of searching for a pre-Markan tradition (admittedly in most views impossible to establish) and then seeking clues for such a tradition in Matthew and Luke—on a theory of Markan priority surely inadmissible.

If we assume that the gospel did indeed end at 16:8 and that the evangelist intended that conclusion, then there have not been wanting suggestions as to why this was so. H. Paulsen ("Mark xvi.1-8," *NovTest* 22.2.1980, pp. 138-70) argues forcibly that the earliest form was vv. 1-6,8a, and that v. 6 was the vital element in any resurrection tradition: *He has been raised, he is not here.* In the same year N. R. Petersen ("When Is the End Not the End? Literary Reflections on the Ending of Mark's Narrative" *Int* 34.2.1980, pp. 151-66) maintained that from a literary point of view v. 8 is an ironic note, is a legitimate ending, and is meant to force the reader back to Chapter 13, demanding that all must be viewed through that crucial material. Any further comment by the evangelist is unnecessary. In 1981 T. E. Boomershine ("The Narrative Technique of Mark 16.8," *JBL* 100.2.1981, pp. 213-23) rightly called attention to the habitual use by Mark of *gar* at the explanatory conclusions of 6:45-52 and 14:1-2, and other stories (9:30-32 and 12:13-17) equally explored the reactions of those involved. The final *for they were afraid* is characteristic of a Markan conclusion.

This kind of survey, limited though it admittedly is, would be incomplete without reference to an outgrowth of redaction criticism: the "polemics" school. It would demand a whole series of studies to encompass an outline of recent works on Mark within the framework of this outlook on New Testament studies. As far as Mark is concerned, the best example is W. Kelber, *The Kingdom in Mark: A New Place and a New Time,* Philadelphia: Fortress Press, 1974. With reference to the passage before us, and as a key to the thinking embodied in the "polemical" solution to the problem, we have a very good example in J. D. Crossan, "Mark and the Relatives of Jesus," *NovTest* 15.2.1973, pp. 81-113 (and see also T. J. Weeden, *Mark: Traditions in Conflict,* Philadelphia: Fortress Press, 1971). Briefly stated—and so with some risk—the position enunciated is that Mark developed his gospel as a polemic against some early Christians whose interests can be summarized as: a *theios anēr* (divine man) christology, miracles, and an appeal to Jews rather than Gentiles. Hence what we have in this pericope *(pace* Crossan) is a symbolic representation of the Jerusalem community in the persons of the women. Their failure to communicate the message of the resurrection is a clear representation of the failure of the Jerusalem community (in the persons of the disciples, especially Peter) to accept the call extended by the Risen Lord given to it by the Markan community (cf. Crossan, p. 149). The gospel, it is maintained, ends in the confrontation of Markan faith (16:1-7) and the failure of the Jerusalem community (16:8). It is very difficult to know what to make of this. Some preliminary comments must be made: The *theios anēr* motif in New Testament studies has been almost done to death in recent decades, but in essence—and certainly in technical expression—it is post-New Testament; a fascination with miracles was also characteristic of Old Testament literature —are we to expect studies in the future of polemical motifs among pre-Exilic Jewish groups? But the juxtaposition of Jerusalem-Gentile in this literature is far older than the unwary reader may imagine and has an ancestry in the nineteenth-century Tübingen School's notion of a "Peter-Paul" conflict. (The reader will also detect the inevitable hand of Hegel—"thesis-antithesis"—on which so much history tends to be written.)

In fact the women in Mark's gospel play pivotal roles, and not one of them is polemical. They are described not only as those who were with Jesus at his death, but as "followers"—a very important word in the Markan vocabulary. Further they are the very first to be mentioned after the story of Peter's denial; they are those who go to the tomb as mourners and who are the first witnesses at the tomb after the burial. So, far from being personifications of anything other than discipleship *(who followed him)*, the demand of Mark on his community is that its members identify themsclves with the women in their identification with Jesus in ministry, death, and Resurrection. Even in their alarm in v. 5 of this narrative, the Greek verb shares the agony of Jesus in Gethsemane (14:33). The fear of the women in v. 8 was certainly shared by Mark's community: that community is being urged to look beyond that fear which they share and to share also in the discipleship of the women, and also their privileged witnessing of the tomb.

There seems no good reason why this Hegelian thesis-antithesis-synthesis (Jewish community-Gentile community-"early Catholicism") should not be witnessed in yet another polemic. Why should it not be proposed (using the Griesbach hypothesis) that Mark was written as a protest against the Galilee orientation of Matthew on the one hand and the Jerusalem orientation of Luke on the other? According to this view Mark 16:1-8 leaves behind him a flat and unresolved statement of resurrection, without deciding which of the traditions before him had priority? Such a proposal, while it might generate a whole new body of literature, would still leave the ending of Mark unresolved.

Other suggestions have been made for the ending of Mark at v. 8, and these must be briefly examined. The sympathetic treatment of the fear of the women in R. H. Lightfoot *(The Gospel Message of St. Mark,* Oxford: The Clarendon Press, corrected ed., 1952, 1962) is notable. Lightfoot emphasizes that the responses of the women in v. 8—*fear (phobos); awe* or *terror (ekstasis);* and *trembling (tromos)*—are found in Mark as perfectly proper responses to healings, to supernatural events, and even to a passion prediction (cf. 2:12, 4:41, 5:15, 5:33, 5:42, 6:19-20, and 10:32). This analysis, however, does not answer the flight of the women, for previous uses of the verb to flee *(phugeō)* in 14:50-52 have prepared us for very negative connotations in Mark, and this must be all the more notable here in the face of the message in v. 6. Flight then is inappropriate: but to whom is that condemnation addressed? To a Jerusalem community resentful of a Gentile mission? And why the silence of the women, in the face of an announcement such as that in v. 6? In response to that second question, Willi Marxsen *(Mark the Evangelist,* Nashville: Abingdon Press, 1969) sees here a further development of the theme of the "messianic secret." Whereas the injunction to silence in 1:44-45 was followed by a proclamation, so in 16:7 the commission of the young man (and by implication the revelation of the messianic secret) is hindered by the silence of the women. But neither Marxsen nor R. H. Fuller, who amplifies and builds upon Marxsen (cf. *The Formation of the Resurrection Narratives,*

London and New York: Macmillan, 1971) has provided us with an explanation for v. 8. Fuller does call attention to the importance of v. 7 as a reference to the first two appearances in (e.g.) 1 Cor 15:5 and to its anticipation of the Resurrection appearances. But this is surely a somewhat unsatisfactory conclusion. Unless we are prepared to posit a proto-Markan text from some date prior to the writing of 1 Cor 15 and the traditions embodied in it, we are left wondering why (with a clear unveiling of the messianic secret in vv. 6 and 7) there are no appearances recorded in Mark.

In summary we maintain as we did in the Introduction, that Mark's manuscript was deliberately ended at 16:8, and—in the light of the discussion in this comment—for the following reasons:

1. The community for which Mark wrote, on his return to Palestine from Rome, was terror-stricken and tempted to flee.

2. Perhaps some had already fled, but the call of the messenger at the tomb was to go back to the time of loyalties, a time of discipleship characteristic of the Galilee of the ministry.

3. The silence of the community's witness is inappropriate, even in a time of peril, for *he has been raised.*

4. The women witnesses had been followers and companions of Jesus in ministry, passion, and at the tomb. The members of Mark's community are also called to be followers and witnesses, even in time of trial and distress. *"He is going on before you . . ."*

5. Mark's gospel was, in our view, specifically designed to elicit the response: "But surely there were resurrection appearances?" The message of Mark is that there were indeed resurrection appearances, but first the community must share with the trembling women all the feelings of fear, know those fears to be in the final analysis groundless, and only then can they hear the voice the women heard—*just as he told you.*

Notes

It would seem that this short pericope has no element in it of an independent Markan eyewitness tradition and consists of early "confessional" traditions of the resurrection. There are no special elements in the language, and all the words are from Mark's usual vocabulary. There are elements in this pericope which are more redolent of John than of Mark, but on the whole the account is restrained; there is no attempt (as there is in Matthew) to describe the resurrection and no account of any appearance of the risen Jesus.

1. *When the Sabbath was over:* Some time after 6 P.M. is indicated by the phrase. The *aromatic oils* (Greek *arōmata*) are accompanied in Luke's account (23:56) by myrrh.

The women are those mentioned in 15:40, and two of them are also named in 15:47. The second *Mary* is called the *mother of James,* but in 15:40 she was the *mother of James the younger and mother of Joses.* In view of 15:40, we must conclude that she is the mother of James, in spite of the fact that in v. 47 she is called the mother *of Joses.* It was probably a desire for simplification which led three manuscripts to omit the whole phrase *when the Sabbath was over . . .* to *Salome,* thus running straight through from the women in v. 47 to *Salome* in this verse. In that way the two women mentioned in the preceding verse purchase the oils. One other manuscript omits everything from *Mary* (of Magdala) to *Salome.* But the overwhelming weight of the manuscript evidence is in favor of leaving this verse as it is, with all its complications.

All the narratives mention *Mary of Magdala,* and she is the only person named by John. Matt 28:1 speaks of "the other Mary," Luke 23:55 has "the women who had come up with him from Galilee" and at 24:10 has Joanna instead of Salome. The purpose of this visit in Mark was *to go and anoint him,* which agrees with Luke 24:1, "carrying the spices they had prepared." Matthew, however, states that "they went to see the tomb" (28:1). This is a very different interpretation from that of Mark and is certainly due in Matthew's case to his story of the guard on the sealed tomb (27:62-66). In John's account, since the spices had already been wrapped in the body cloths, Mary of Magdala presumably went to see the tomb, though no reason is given. There is no suggestion in John, as there is in Mark, that the burial preparations were only temporary. The Markan account looks back to 14:8, but is 16:1 simply a reminiscence of the women who came to anoint Jesus against his burial? There does not appear to be any way to reconcile the Markan and Johannine accounts, and on the face of it, it appears improbable that the women would be going to the tomb to do the last offices for the dead after one day and almost two nights (Mark and Luke). Often it is advisable to take the more improbable option simply because it is improbable, and because its very improbability commends its veracity.

2. *early on Sunday morning:* This English phrase is deceptively simple, and once more we have conflicting accounts. *Lian prōi (very early)* would seem to suggest something between 3 A.M. and 6 A.M., with preference being given to the earlier hours (cf. 1:35). But this is contradicted by *just after (or at) sunrise* (Greek *anateilantos tou hēliou).* Luke 24:1 has *orthrou batheōs* (at first light), John 20:1 reads *prōi skotias eti ousēs* (early, while it was still dark), and Matt 28:1 has *opse de Sabbatōn, te epi phōskouse eis mia Sabbatōn* (after the Sabbath, and toward dawn on the first day of the week). The problem with Matthew's text is that *opse* can mean "after" and equally can mean "late," though presumably when followed by *epi phōskouse* it means "after." But what is the "first day of the week"? Does Matthew follow the Jewish calendar (in which case the "first day of the week" will be after about 6 P.M. on Saturday) or the Roman calendar—which would then give us 3-6 A.M. on Sunday? But even with the word "Sabbath," we are not as free of difficulty as might be supposed. In all the traditions we have either *mia Sabbatōn* or *mia tōn Sabbatōn,* and this is not as obvious an indication of a particular "day" of the "week" as might appear. By the time we

reach the *Didachē* (c. A.D. 75), the plural *sabbata* clearly meant "week" and the enumeration of the days certainly establishes Sunday as the "first day" of the week (cf. *Didachē* 6). But the notes of time in all four evangelists—not to mention the confused chronology of Holy Week—make it hazardous to say whether one or all of them wished us to understand Saturday or Sunday.

Ostensibly Luke and John agree with Mark and, just possibly, with Matthew too. But the phrase *epi to mnēmeion anateilantos tou hēliou (just after sunrise)* contradicts Luke and John and is inconsistent with *very early on the first day of the week,* especially if that indicates a Jewish reckoning of after sunset on Saturday. The difficulty was felt early: several manuscripts omit *lian (very),* one manuscript omits *prōi (early),* and several manuscripts read *anatellontos* (in the process of rising) for *anateilontos (had risen).* But these are all attempts to deal with an original reading and are manifestly secondary. It is certainly difficult to think that Mark wrote "very early on the first day of the week, after the sun had risen." Various suggestions have been made to minimize or obviate the difficulty. We can take up suggestions made in the past as to what Mark *meant* to say, such as that the women started out very early but arrived only at sunrise. This is unsatisfactory, for given only minimal accuracy in the traditional sites the distance is too small. Or perhaps Mark's Greek (never noted for grammatical purity) really was meant to read "at the sun rising," and maybe, too, *lian prōi* has been read too literally and really means "as early as could be." Even so this can hardly be made to accommodate *just after sunrise.* One possibility is to omit *and* at the beginning of v. 2, read *to go and anoint him . . . on the first day of the week,* conclude the sentence there, and start again with *Just after sunrise*—omit *and*—*they were saying . . .* Nevertheless all of this is no more than guesswork, however inspired we may think it to be, and the problem remains insoluble.

3. *They were saying:* This verse is vivid, and the action described in the verbs is continuous. But it is doubtful if the verse is historically accurate; rather the purpose must be regarded as dramatic, especially if the women's proposed action is seen as unlikely (see the note on v. 1). It is here that Matt 28:2-4 gives us a highly dramatic legendary interlude of an earthquake, the descent of a heavenly messenger who rolls away the stone and sits on it. He is described as being "like lightning, his clothing was as white as snow, and for fear of him the guards were paralyzed with fright." Whatever Mark thought of this apocalyptic intervention, we do not know, but the question *"Who will roll away the stone . . . ?"* is very strange when set alongside *But when they looked up, they saw that the stone . . . had been rolled away* in the next verse. In Luke 24:2 "they found the stone rolled away," and John 20:1 records of Mary of Magdala that "she sees that the stone has been removed." Whence then comes the question of the women in v. 3 before us? We suggest that Mark wished to eschew the highly charged Matthean account, but (unconsciously?) let slip by the fact that he knew it by *But when they looked up, they saw* that the stone of which they had been speaking was already *rolled away.* Surely if the stone was the major problem, their gaze would have been upon it?

Only Matthew provides any kind of explanation for the stone being found rolled away. It must be remembered that for many years before our written sources reached their present final form, Christian witness concentrated on the appearances of the risen Jesus. If Paul knew of any tradition of an empty tomb, he evidently found it of quite minor importance when he wrote the summary of resurrection faith in 1 Cor 15:3-8. We have seen some possible reason to think that Mark knew of Matthew's dramatic account, but Luke and John simply record the tradition that the stone had been rolled away.

they saw (Greek *theōrousin):* It is not possible to say with what precision Mark uses this verb, but in contrast with John 20:1 (where Mary "glances at" the tomb), the women "take in the fact" that the stone *had been rolled away.*

had been rolled (Greek *anakekulistai):* The perfect tense is exact—a past event, with lasting effects. Mark is capable of this striking use of the appropriate tense—cf. 15:44.

Mark provides no explanation for the event, save that a parenthetical note *(big as it was)* emphasizes the wonder. The *Gospel of Peter* 9 asserts that the stone rolled away of its own accord, after a preliminary sound from heaven, and that two men came down with a great light. The manuscript k (Old Latin, Bobiensis, fourth or fifth century) has a vivid account at this juncture of angels ascending in a great darkness on the third day—it is not wholly clear from the Latin whether Jesus is regarded as being the center of this activity—and then there was a great light. This gloss was presumably an attempt to clothe the bare Markan account with an element of drama.

Some manuscripts have the explanatory phrase *big as it was (ēn gar megas sphodra)* at the end of v. 3, but v. 8 provides us with another example of an explanation deferred to a later moment, with Mark's characteristic *gar* (for).

5. This verse raises in the most acute fashion the whole tradition of the empty tomb, but that will be deferred until we examine the text of the verse. Alone in the New Testament writings, Mark uses *they were afraid (exethaubēthēsan,* cf. 9:15) to express the women's terror. All the vocabulary is Markan, and he is composing from his own tradition. The Matthean tradition has no parallel to *they went into the tomb,* because in his account the angel is seated on the rolled-away stone. Luke 24:3 speaks of the women going into the tomb, and Mark uses the same verb (Greek *eiselthousai).* The Johannine tradition speaks of Peter and the beloved disciple going into the tomb after Mary of Magdala had looked inside and reported it as being empty.

The problem of the empty tomb, for all the studies which have been expended upon it, refuses to be resolved. The earliest confessional statement about the resurrection (1 Cor 15:3-5)—said to be the tradition Paul had received—says nothing of an empty tomb. If it is replied that the notion of "person" implied in the Hebrew word *nephesh* was such that a dissolution of the relationship between body and "spirit" was impossible, then it must be said that Paul is not so absolute. He speaks in 1 Cor 15:44 of a "spiritual body" in terms which leave little doubt that he means a radically trans- formed body. What expectations of resurrection there were—whether universal or only of the righteous—in the Judaism of the first century we do not know with any certainty. All we know is that the Sadducees denied the notion, and even there we are in ignorance of the extent to which they subscribed to a shadowy existence beyond death in Sheol. What appears to be clear from our gospels is that it was the *appearances* of the risen Jesus which first formed the Easter faith. The empty tomb motif seems to have been seized upon by the evangelists as the only explanation which would cover the conviction that God had raised Jesus from death.

If the *young man* is regarded as a heavenly being (cf. "two men" in Luke 24:4—also in the *Gospel of Peter* 9—and the "angel of the Lord" in Matt 28:2), then the impression that we are entering an imaginary realm is heightened. Even if the *young man* is a baptismal figure from the early community (cf. comment and notes on 14:51-52), then —if anything—the mark of imagination is heightened.

We are not here concerned with the theological implications of the resurrection of Jesus for later Christian theology. What we have to deal with is the thought world of the evangelists, into which we can only with great difficulty enter. The bibliography at the end of this section will not only provide further reading on the resurrection appearances as they are described by the other evangelists but will also provide some fairly recent theological reflections on the theme.

In summary it will be convenient here if this writer notes his own reflections on the New Testament material:

a. The faith of the early community was, and the faith of the Church is, that God raised the crucified and buried Jesus.

b. For the first Christians the conviction of resurrection faith was based on the appearances of the risen Jesus: the empty tomb motif was the only explanation available to them, however dramatically it was expressed.

c. The empty tomb is no *necessary* component of faith in the resurrection of Jesus, and aside altogether from the language and imagery with which the evangelists speak of it there is no way that we can either prove or disprove it.

d. If the burial chamber of Jesus should be discovered tomorrow and the unquestionably physical remains found there too, this would not disprove the resurrection.

e. It will be recalled that the passion predictions of Jesus speak of his "being raised," or—in Old Testament terms—of being physically raised. It is important to distinguish between the resuscitation of a dead body, and resurrection. Much Christian teaching, popular and otherwise, has frequently been guilty of blurring the distinction.

f. There remains the fact of the Christian community, past and present, and the fact of the New Testament. In dealing with the resurrection of Jesus, we are dealing with what has been called "metahistory," something beyond empirical verification but producing verifiable results. The teaching and Proclamation of Jesus, important though these are, would never have produced in and of themselves the radical transformation of the world of Hellenism (initially, of the disciples themselves) without something so totally compelling as Christians believe the resurrection to have been. (In this connection, cf. C. F. D. Moule, *The Phenomenon of the New Testament*, Studies in Biblical Theology, 2nd series, London: SCM Press, 1967, especially Chapter 1).

g. It would seem from the texts of the gospels that the tradition of the empty tomb was originally separate from the narratives of the resurrection appearances, though to us the movement from passion and death to empty tomb and resurrection appears natural because of the resurrection-proclamation.

The question posed most often by the enquirer puzzled by modern (and not so modern) analyses of the tradition is: Was the tomb empty? Two points deserve emphasis. The first, shorter point is the ingenuous nature of the tradition. Had the narrative been constructed of whole cloth for apologetic purposes, the very notion of women as witnesses would have cast profound doubt on the whole account. The second point concerns the well-known biblical device of the *angelus interpres* (interpreting messenger). If we strip away the explanations offered by the interpreter to the women (and also strip away our own far-too-easy identification of the messenger with a heavenly, angelic visitor), then we are left with a short narrative. That narrative is a simple account of women who went to the tomb (either, as in Matthew, simply to visit it, or, as in Mark, to anoint the body) and found it empty. The role of the messenger is simply a device to link together both the Passion and Resurrection narratives.

This writer believes that we must conclude that the tomb was empty and that the women found it so. But if the possibility envisaged in d. above did at some stage become reality, we need to remind ourselves that the Christian proclamation is that Jesus was raised from death, and not that his corpse was resuscitated. It would be well, too, to recall how poverty-stricken was the language of the New Testament period to deal with individual survival of death, much less resurrection. At the very least the gospel records are insisting, in the language available to them, that Jesus was more than his body.

6. The words used by the young man—*Stop being afraid! You are looking for Jesus* —are almost identical in the Greek of Matthew and Mark, save that Mark adds *of Nazareth* after Jesus. This is a vital reminder of the continuity between the ministry and the new state of affairs already in being. The expression *who was crucified,* in both Matthew and Mark, is almost a technical title—"the crucified one" (Greek *ton estaurōmenon*)—and is found in Paul (1 Cor 1:23, 2:2; Gal 3:1). The vocabulary is characteristically Matthean and Markan in the Greek: *you are looking for* (cf. 1:37); *of Nazareth* (1:24); *crucified* (15:13); *raised* (1:31); *place* (1:35). For *where they laid him* cf. 15:46.

He has been raised here and in Matt 28:6 is a shift in tense to the aorist, denoting an event which has but recently happened, and may be compared with the perfect tense ("was raised") in 1 Cor 15:4,20. By *the place* the narrative refers to the shelf on which the body was placed.

The somewhat breathless character of the address in this verse carries with it a very strong suggestion that what we have here is a consciously constructed drama on the part of Matthew and Mark, not a repeated tradition. The Lucan account (24:4-6) is substantially different, and though the dramatic notes are muted, the central "He is not here but has been raised" is present, though omitted in six manuscripts. The Lucan account is clearly from a separate tradition.

7. In both Matthew and Mark, though more strongly in the latter, the announcement of the resurrection is cut short with *now go and say* . . . It is likely that the emphasis on *and to Peter* may have the story of Peter's denial in mind. Again the vocabulary is commonplace in Matthew and Mark: *go* (cf. Mark 1:44); *his disciples* (cf. Mark 2:15); *Peter* (cf. Mark 3:16). Cf. also Acts 1:14, "with the women and Mary"; 1

Cor 15:5, "Kephas, one of the Twelve." The injunction to go to Galilee simply takes up the theme of 14:28, and the Greek of *he is going on before you* is a simple declaratory present—the event is already taking place. It is important to recall that 14:28 contained no promise that the disciples would see him.

The reference back to 14:28 draws attention to another matter. If *he is going before you* is a simple declaratory present tense, then it is likely that the same thing may hold true of the verb (Greek *proaxo*) in 14:28—it too probably means "I go before you."

The whole matter of *Galilee* has its own difficulties, which may not have appeared to be such to those who first heard or read the tradition, but which to us raise all manner of questions. Why should there be resurrection appearances in Galilee? Luke and John know only of appearances in Jerusalem, while Matthew and Mark only know (or only speak of) appearances in Galilee. Lohmeyer addresses the matter uncompromisingly (p. 356), concluding that this is not a matter of resurrection appearances but has to do with the fact that Galilee is the land of eschatological fulfillment— i.e., the *parousia*. This he bases on the contention that to "see" the risen Jesus in the gospels and in Acts calls for the verb *ōphthē*, in contrast to *opsesthe* here and in Matthew. While it is true, he maintains, that Paul uses *horaō* (to gaze at) in 1 Cor 9:1 and John uses the same verb in 20:18,25,29, yet "you will see him" *(opsesthe)* is the technical Johannine expression for the *parousia* (cf. 16:16,19; 1 John 3:2; Rev 1:7, 22:4). With this he compares Mark 14:62, which uses the same verb. While we may grant that Galilee was regarded with suspicion in Jerusalem as being the home of hot-headed enthusiasts, and possibly of some speculative literature, too, there is no more reason to fasten upon Galilee as the center of an expected *parousia* than there is to find it a natural place for resurrection appearances. An article by J.-M. van Cangh, "La Galilée dans l'Évangile de Marc: un lien théologique?" *RevBib* 79.1.1972, pp. 59-75, regards the word as purely redactional: Jesus always precedes his disciples, from Galilee to Jerusalem, so now he journeys back again. The Galilean mission was a veiled manifestation, but now they will see, and the Markan community must begin its work of mission in the light of the resurrection, and looking to the *parousia*.

More than twenty years ago L. E. Elliot-Binns *(Galileean Christianity,* Naperville, Ill.: A. R. Allenson, 1956; London: SCM Press, 1957) thought that the Galilee/ Jerusalem differences in the tradition could provide a key to later conflicts within Jewish Christianity. The earlier followers of Jesus in Galilee, he thought, were more open and forward-looking than the narrower Jerusalem community centered on James. One may be forgiven for finding in this a revisionist version of the Tübingen school, with its conflict between Paul and the Twelve (especially Peter), and it is no more free than the Tübingen of arbitrary reconstruction. (Much earlier B. H. Streeter in *The Four Gospels: A Study of Origins, Treating of the Manuscript Tradition, Sources, Authorship, and Dates,* London: Macmillan, 1924, p. 512, spoke of parts of Matthew as a "later Judaistic reaction against the Petro-Pauline liberalism"!) That there were tensions in the early Christian community is clear to any reader of Paul's letters, but it seems unnecessary to construct a so far undocumented conflict around the single word "Galilee."

This commentator finds himself more easily sympathetic to van Cangh's position. He believes that Mark's community was being recalled to the times of early, unfettered, and unafraid discipleship—but now knowing that for all their fears the Jesus of Nazareth and of Galilee had been vindicated, had been raised.

Matt 28:7 has "go quickly, and tell his disciples that he has been raised from the dead," but he has no such addition as Mark's *just as he told you*, though he does have "See, I have told you." The possibility must be faced, not only (as some commentators have suggested) that v. 7 is an addition to the original Markan text, but that he misread Matthew's "See, I have told you" and gave us *just as he told you*. Certainly Matthew's fondness for *idou* (see, behold), especially before important sayings, could easily have persuaded Mark that the messenger was citing a saying of Jesus. If v. 7 is regarded as secondary, v. 8 follows more naturally from v. 6 and refers to the announcement of the resurrection. As it is, their *trembling and awe* read as though these were reactions to a command to talk to the disciples (cf. Lohmeyer, p. 359n.).

8. *trembling* (Greek *tromos*): Cf.1 Cor 2:3; 2 Cor 7:15; Eph 6:5; Phil 2:12. And for the emotion of *awe* (Greek *ekstasis*), cf. 5:42. The sense of the Greek is that an overmastering fear had taken hold of them, so much so that they said nothing to anyone (literally translated, Mark has a characteristic double negative: "They said nothing to no one").

for they were afraid: The Greek ending *(ephobounto gar)* has been discussed by a massive array of grammarians, commentators, and classical as well as modern literary critics, both for and against the possibility that Mark intended to conclude his work at this point. But whether *ephobounto* suggests overwhelming religious awe, or simply terror, the consensus of those refusing credence to *ephobounto gar* as the true ending rests mainly on a view of Markan priority, thereby producing the "revisionist" endings in Matthew and Luke, together with the anonymous author of vv. 9-20. The full range of critical opinion, along with the names of principal authorities, are to be found in Taylor, p. 609.

The view of this commentator by this time will be clear: that Mark did indeed end his gospel at 16:8, with the harsh *for they were afraid.* (It is grammatically far more harsh in the Greek.) He wrote, as we have maintained, for a community overtaken by fear, a community which needed the reassurance that even those who were the first to hear of the vindication of Jesus in the Resurrection had been terrified.

Bibliography

Allen, W. "They Were Afraid: Why?" *JTS* 47.1946, pp. 46-49.

Alsup, J. E. *The Post-Resurrection Appearance Stories of the Gospel Tradition: A History-of-Tradition Analysis with Text-Synopsis.* Calwer Theologische Monographien 5. Stuttgart: Calwer-Verlag, 1975.

Bauer, J. B. "Drei Tage." *Bib* 39.1958, pp. 354-58.

Benoit, P. "Marie-Madeleine et les disciples au tombeau vide selon Joh 20:1-8." *Judentum, Urchristentum, Kirche,* 1964.

Bode, E. L. "A Liturgical Sitz im Leben for the Gospel Tradition of the Women's Easter Visit to the Tomb of Jesus." *CBQ* 32.1970, pp. 237-42.

————. "The First Easter Morning: The Gospel Accounts of the Women's Visits to the Tomb of Jesus." *AnBib,* 1970.

Bouwmann, G. "Die Erhöhung Jesu in der lukanischen Theologie." *BZ* 14.1970, pp. 257-63.

Braun, F. M. "La sépulture de Jésus." *RevBib* 45.1936, pp. 184-200, 346-63.

Brown, R. E. *The Virginal Conception and Bodily Resurrection of Jesus.* New York: Paulist Press, 1973.

Bulst, W. "Novae in sepulturam Jesu inquisitiones." *Verbum Domini* 31.1953, pp. 257-73, 352-59.

Campenhausen, H. von. *Der Ablauf der Osterereignisse und das leere Grab.* Heidelberg: C. Winter, 1958.

Carlston, C. "Transfiguration and Resurrection." *JBL* 80.1961, pp. 233-40.

Cranfield, C. E. B. "St. Mark 16.1-8." *SJT* 5.1952, pp. 282-98, 398-414.

Creed, J. M. "The Conclusion of the Gospel According to St. Mark." *JTS* 6.1955, pp. 229-33.

Dodd, C. H. "The Appearances of the Risen Christ: An Essay in Form Criticism of the Gospels." *Studies in the Gospels,* edited by D. E. Nineham. Oxford: Blackwell, 1957.

Dupont, J. "Ressuscité 'le troisième jour.' " *Bib* 40.1959, pp. 742-61.

Evans, C. F. *Resurrection and the New Testament.* London: SCM Press, 1970.

Fuller, R. H. *The Formation of the Resurrection Narratives.* London and New York: Macmillan, 1971.

Gils, F. "Pierre et la foi au Christe ressuscité." Ephemerides Theologicae Lovanienses 38.1962, pp. 5-42.

Gutwenger, E. "Auferstehung und Auferstehungsleib Jesu." *ZTK* 91.1969, pp. 32-58.

————. "Zur Geschichtlichkeit der Auferstehung Jesu." *ZTK* 88.1966, pp. 257-82.

Hayes, J. H. "The Resurrection as Enthronement and the Earliest Church Christology." *Int* 22.1968, pp. 333-45.

Leon-Dufour, X. *Résurrection de Jésus et message pascal.* Paris: Seuil, 1971.

Lillie, W. "The Empty Tomb and the Resurrection." In *Historicity and Chronology in the New Testament,* edited by Matthew Black. London: SPCK, 1965.

Lindblom, J. *Geschichte und Offenbarungen. Vorstellungen von göttlichen Weisungen und übernaturlichen Erscheinungen im ältesten Christentum.* Lund: Gleerup, 1968.

Marxsen, W. *The Resurrection of Jesus of Nazareth.* Philadelphia: Fortress Press, 1970.

Moule, C. F. D., ed. *The Significance of the Message of the Resurrection for Faith in Jesus Christ.* London: SCM Press, 1968.

————. "St. Mark 16:8 Once More." *NTS* 2.1955, pp. 58-59.

Pelletier, A. "Les apparitions du Ressuscité en teres de la Septante." *Bib* 51.1970, pp. 76-79.

Pousset, E. "La résurrection." *NRTh* 91.1969, pp. 1009-44.

Robinson, J. A. T. *The Body.* London: SCM Press, 1952.

Schnackenburg, R. "On the Expression 'Jesus Is Risen from the Dead.' " *Theology Digest* 4.1.1970.

Waetjen, W. "The Ending of Mark and the Gospel's Shift in Eschatology." *ASTI* 4.1965, pp. 114-31.

Walker, N. "After Three Days." *NovTest* 4.1960, pp. 261-62.

Walker, W. "Postcrucifixion Appearances and Christian Origins." *JBL* 88.1969, pp. 157-65.

This bibliography is but a fraction of the available material. The student and the general reader would be well advised to begin with some of the English-language books and follow up the footnotes. In this respect Fuller and Marxsen will be found helpful.

90. The Anonymous Ending
(16:9-20)

(References to the other gospels, and to other material in the New Testament, will be found in the notes.)

16   ⁹ Being raised early on the first day of the week, he appeared first to Mary of Magdala, from whom he had cast out seven devils. ¹⁰ She then went to those who had been his companions, who were mourning and in tears, and told them. ¹¹ But they did not believe her when they heard her say that he was alive and that she had seen him. ¹² After this he showed himself under another form to two of them as they were going into the country. ¹³ They went back and told the others, who did not believe them either. ¹⁴ Finally he showed himself to the Eleven while they were at table. He rebuked them for their unbelief and obduracy, because they had refused to believe those who had seen him after he had been raised. ¹⁵ And he said to them, "Go into the whole world; make the Proclamation to the whole creation. ¹⁶ He who believes and is baptized will be saved; he who does not believe will be condemned. ¹⁷ These are the signs which will follow those who believe: in my name they will cast out demons, they will have the gift of tongues, ¹⁸ they will pick up snakes and be unharmed when they drink deadly poison. They will lay their hands on the sick, and they will recover." ¹⁹ And so the Lord, after he had spoken to them, was taken up into heaven, and there took his place at the right hand of God. ²⁰ They, going out, preached everywhere, the Lord working with them, confirming the word by the signs which accompanied it.

An Anonymous Ending to Mark

Not even among writers who reject the notion that Mark deliberately ended his gospel at 16:8 is there to be found any suggestion that vv. 9-20 are from the hand of the evangelist. The vocabulary is not Markan, the whole tenor of the pericope is far different in tone from all we have seen of Mark, and even at first glance it appears to be a collage of a series of resurrection traditions. The strongest plea known to this writer for some elements of Markan origin is to be found in E. Linnemann, "Der (wiedergefundene) Markusschluss," ZTK 66.3.1969, pp. 255-87. Linnemann finds two verses of the lost ending preserved in Matt 28:16-17 followed by Mark 16:15-20. He finds two distinct strands of tradition—vv. 9-14 and 15-20. In effect, then, the evangelist drew upon Matt 28:16-17, the present Mark 16:15-18, which may be seen also in Mark 14:28 and 16:7. Mark 16:19 is a quotation from an early confessional statement known to the evangelist. This view was criticized by G. W. Trompf ("The Markusschluss in Recent Research," *Australian Biblical Review* 21.1973, pp. 15-26), who rightly—in the view of this writer—finds in the "longer ending" elements from the other three gospels, especially Luke. Yet another approach, and a very promising one, is that of H. W. Bartsch ("Der Schluss des Markus-Evangeliums: Ein überlieferungs-geschichtliches Problem," *TZ* 27.4.1971, pp. 241-54). He proposes looking back for the origins of the material to 14:62, and the kind of apocalyptic material embodied in (e.g.) Matt 27:51b-53, 28:2-5,9-10; 1 Cor 15:3-5 as belonging more to present reality than to any future expectation, and (to use a phrase of C. H. Dodd) so to "inaugurated eschatology." The anonymous author, therefore, in adding an empty tomb narrative, historicized an event which is in fact the end of history. Certain motifs, Bartsch believes, can be identified in this ending, including 1 Cor 15:3-7 and Matt 28:2-5,9-10. This commentator believes that the theological interpretation offered in this article is helpful for future study, though he does not find convincing the argument that the evangelist Mark had in fact collected apocalyptic material with a view to ending his work. Radically different is the work of J. Hug—*La finale de l'Évangile de Marc (Marc 16:9-20)*, Études Bibliques, Paris: Gabalda, 1978—which suggests that the theological motifs are the product of a Christian community in a Hellenistic environment in the middle of the second century A.D. Apart from once again raising acute problems as to dating, it may be questioned how much of this longer ending would have been intelligible in a Hellenistic environment, unless the author intends us to understand a Hellenistic-Jewish community.

The reader may be aware that this anonymous ending is rejected as

Markan on account of manuscript evidence. In pursuing this maze of problems, the two best guides available at present are:

Elliott, J. K. "The Text and Language of the Endings to Mark's Gospel." *TZ*
    27.1971, pp. 255-62.
Farmer, W. R. *The Last Twelve Verses of Mark.* London and New York:
    Cambridge University Press, 1974.

The reader or student with Greek will be well advised to use the text of the United Bible Societies in evaluating the age of the various manuscripts discussed.

In brief summary the following major manuscripts omit this ending (see the "Principal Texts of Mark," p. 159, for comparative dates): ℵ; B; k; syˢ.

The important manuscripts of the Armenian, Georgian, and Ethiopic versions omit it. Both Eusebius and Jerome report that this ending was wanting in nearly all Greek manuscripts known to them. There are further complications: this ending is combined with the so-called "shorter ending" in L and Ψ —and also in some Salvidic, Syriac, and Ethiopian manuscripts. Then there is the Freer Logion—to be given in translation later—which is found after 16:14 in W. A tenth-century Armenian manuscript has the notation *of Aristonos the elder* (or *presbyter),* generally taken to be an ascription of vv. 9-20 to the Aristion mentioned by Papias in his account of the composition of the gospels.

In fact, in all the literature before the middle of the fourth century there are only two possible allusions to this anonymous ending. The first is in Justin Martyr *(Apology* 1.45): "Going out, his apostles proclaimed" (or "made a Proclamation") "everywhere." The second is from Irenaeus, cited in Latin: "At the end of his gospel, Mark says, 'And so the Lord Jesus, after he had spoken to them, was received into heaven, and sits at the right hand of the Father.' "

Notes

9-11. This is the first of four appearances, and from its vocabulary it appears to be derived from Luke and John. The appearance is described by the verb *phainetai,* which apart from 14:64 is not used in Mark. The description *from whom he had cast out seven devils* = Luke 8:2. The time is *early,* and this word is common in Mark, but the Greek of *the first day of the week (prote sabbatou)* is different from that of 16:2. The expression *cast out of* is a Greek expression *(ekballein para)* unique in the New Testament. The reference to Mary's actions in v. 10 recalls John 20:18. The description of the disciples—*his companions*—is not Markan. Even *she . . . went,* here represented in vv. 10,12,15, is used by Mark only once elsewhere (9:30). *They (kakeinoi,* literally "and they") is never used by Mark of the disciples. Similarly *alive* in v. 11 is used only at 10:23 and 12:27, and Mark never uses the Greek verb for *had seen* (*theaomai*), though it is very common in John. The verb *did not believe* (Greek *apisteō*) is common enough in the New Testament (Luke 24:11,41; Acts 28:24; Rom 3:3; 2 Tim 2:13; 1 Pet 2:7) but is not found in Mark. The statement of the disciples' lack of faith is reminiscent of Luke 24:11 and Matt 28:17.

12-13. This verse is a reminiscence of Luke 24:13-35. While *showed himself* is a verb found in 4:22 and 16:12,14, the remainder of the vocabulary is not Markan. *After this* (Greek *meta tauta*) is common in John but is never used by Mark; the same is true of *another form (en hetera morphē)*. Two verbs are found in Mark: *going into* and *went back.* It is impossible to know what the writer meant by *another form.* Was it in the guise of a fellow traveler, as in Luke 24, or in contrast to the garden appearance of John 20:15? Or does it refer to the manner in which Jesus transcended closed and barred doors (John 20:19,26) and vanished at will (Luke 24:31)?

14-18. This is the climax of the series of appearances, but it is hardly a narrative, consisting as it does of post-Resurrection sayings. There is no note of time or circumstance, and the phrase *the Eleven while they were at table* recalls 6:26. The rebuke (cf. 15:32) is more stringent than in 8:14-21 and uses words which elsewhere are confined in Mark to critics and enemies: *unbelief* (6:6, 9:24), *obduracy* (10:5). It may be that the anonymous writer is reflecting his own time and circumstances. It is at this point that W inserts the Freer Logion. The introduction of the commission is sudden, especially after the harsh judgments of v. 14. The universalism implicit in *Go into the whole world* is a reflection of Matt 28:18-20. Whether this is simply a reflection of Matthew, or whether the fact that similar commands exist in both texts reflects an old tradition of some kind of post-Resurrection commission, we cannot know. But both here and in Matthew we are plainly in the presence of the Gentile community; if it had been otherwise, the events which led up to the scene in Acts 15 would be hard to imagine.

While *make the Proclamation* (literally "proclaim the good news") consists of common Markan words, *world* (Greek *kosmos*) is used only at 8:36 and 14:9. We have translated *ktisis* as *creation,* which is the proper sense in 10:6 and 13:19, but it probably is here better understood as "humanity" (cf. Col 1:23). In v. 16 we are in a far later stage than apostolic Christianity. The phrase *he who believes* (Greek *ho pisteuōn*) is certainly found in John 3:17, but there it is used of union with Jesus. Here we are in a baptismal-confessional era, with the underlying assumption that baptism is part of well-regulated community practice (cf. 1 Pet 3:21, Titus 3:5). To what extent this verse implies that baptism is a necessary prerequisite for the salvation of the last days, we cannot say. The verb *condemned* (Greek *katakrinō*) is used of a final judgment in 10:33 and 14:64.

17. This verse is an odd combination of synoptic vocabulary and a Johannine theme: *signs* (cf. 8:11) will *follow* those who *believe* (cf. John 14:12). But *follow* (cf. 1:18) is a strange verb to use, and although it has been translated literally, it presumably means "be associated with." All the *signs* are those to be found in the synoptic gospels and Acts: *in my name they will cast out demons* (cf. 3:15, 9:37); *the gift of tongues* (Acts 2:4, 10:46, 19:6; 1 Cor 12:28); *pick up snakes* (cf. Luke 10:19, Acts 28:3-6); *the healing of the sick* (Mark 6:13). We are again, however, in the presence of the early community and not of the post-resurrection appearances. There is no hint in the gospels of the *gift of tongues,* and if—with some manuscripts—we read "new" before

tongues, then we are in the world of "new covenant," "new creation," "new humanity," etc. While it is true that Luke 10:19 speaks of "treading on snakes," the material before us says *pick up snakes,* and some manuscripts add "in their hands." Similarly 6:13 mentions anointing the sick, and here we have *lay their hands on the sick.* Again, nowhere in the New Testament do we read of those being *unharmed when they drink deadly poison,* but according to Eusebius—an indefatigable collector of stories— Papias mentions this in several connections, notably concerning the apostle John *(Ecclesiastical History* 3.39). There are also singularities of Greek vocabulary: the adjective *deadly* (Greek *thanasimos)* is a classical word found nowhere else in Biblical Greek; *be unharmed* (Greek *ou mē autous blapsē)* is reminiscent of Luke 4:35; *the sick* (Greek *arroustos)* is used in 6:5,13, but *they will recover* (Greek *kalōs echō)* is purely classical and is represented nowhere else in the New Testament.

19. This verse has neither note of time nor of place but appears from *after he had spoken* to refer back to v. 14. The introductory *and so (men . . . de)* is represented in Mark at 12:5, 14:21,38. Perhaps if this verse does follow v. 14, it might be better to translate *ho men* by "But he . . ."

the Lord: Habitual in Luke, it is not found in Mark with the exception of 11:3. Some manuscripts have "the Lord Jesus," which is found several times in Acts and on a few occasions in the letters of Paul. It is likely that "Jesus" is an addition to the original text, by assimilation from Acts and Paul.

was taken up (Greek *anelēmphthē):* The Greek is used of the ascension in Acts 1:2,11,22, 1 Tim 3:16, and in the Septuagint at 2 Kgs 2:11 for the assumption of Elijah. Possibly this verse is part of some primitive credal statement. The derivatives of the verb are used in the service books of the Greek Orthodox Church to describe the feast of the Ascension, though the formal conciliar and credal statements of the fourth and fifth centuries use *anabainein* (to go up) or *anerchesthai* (to ascend). The substantive *analēpsis* had overtones of "assumption into another realm"—language redolent of docetic interpretations of the Risen Lord.

took his place: Cf. Ps 110:1, cited in 12:36. The theme of heavenly session has a prominent place in the language of Acts and the epistles: Acts 7:55-57; Rom 8:34; Eph 1:20; Col 3:1; Heb 1:3, 8:1, 10:12, 12:2; 1 Pet 3:22; Rev 3:21.

20. *They, going out . . .* If it is intended that we understand "from Jerusalem," we have here a statement clearly at variance with the Galilean emphasis of vv. 1-8.

Grammatically the three verbs which conclude this verse are found only in the epistles: *working with* (Greek *sunergeō* in Rom 8:28; 1 Cor 16:16; 2 Cor 6:1; Jas 2:22); *confirming* (Greek *bebaioō* in Rom 15:8; 1 Cor 1:6,8; 2 Cor 1:21; Col 2:7; Heb 2:3, 13:9); *accompanied* (Greek *epakoloutheō* in 1 Tim 5:10,24; 1 Pet 2:21).

91. The Shorter Ending

And all that they had been commanded they told briefly to those around Peter. Afterward, Jesus himself appeared to them, and from east to west sent through them the sacred and imperishable Proclamation of everlasting salvation.

The Shorter Ending

Two endings to Mark are known to us other than the conclusion at 16:8, and each in its own way bears witness to the testimony of early writers that the only ending to Mark which bore the stamp of authenticity was the ending at 16:8. But both endings now under consideration evidently arose from dissatisfaction with the existing ending. The Anonymous Ending just examined is easily seen by vocabulary alone to be non-Markan, and the same is true of the one to which we now turn.

This shorter ending is found in association with the Anonymous Ending in several manuscripts of the seventh, eighth, and ninth centuries and in a few lectionary manuscripts. There is also a possibility that B (Codex Vaticanus) was prepared to make provision for its inclusion. The only explanations which would seem to justify the existence of this ending under discussion are:

a. The author, who made no pretense of copying synoptic style or vocabulary, had a manuscript before him which ended at 16:8, and he was unaware of any other ending.

b. Perhaps the author was living in some area where inquiries about possible unknown endings to Mark were very difficult.

The manuscript tradition suggests that this shorter ending may have stood in some manuscripts before the Anonymous Ending. Although from the manuscript evidence, we can assign this shorter ending to an approximate fourth century date, there is no patristic text known to us which quotes this shorter ending, or indeed which has precisely this kind of vocabulary. The textual evidence is fully set out in K. Aland, "Bemerkungen zum Schluss des Markusevangeliums," in *Neotestamentica et Semitica,* Edinburgh: T. & T. Clark, 1969, pp. 157-80. The following words or expressions are not found in Mark:

678 MARK § XCII

briefly (Greek *suntomōs*); *those around Peter* (Greek *tois peri tou Petrou*); *told* (Greek *exēggeilan*); *Afterward* (Greek *meta tauta*); *east* ("sunrise," Greek *anatolēs*); *to* (Greek *achri*); *west* ("sunset," Greek *duseos*); *sent* (Greek *exapesteilen*); *sacred* (Greek *hieron*); *imperishable* (Greek *aphtharton*); *proclamation* (Greek *kerugma*); *salvation* (Greek *sōtērias*).

92. The Freer Logion

They replied, saying, "This age of lawlessness and unbelief is under [or from] Satan, who by means of unclean spirits does not allow the true power of God to be taken hold of. Therefore, show your righteousness now." They were speaking to Christ, and Christ replied to them, "The extent of the years of the authority of Satan has been fulfilled, but other terrible things approach, even for the sinners for whom I was delivered up to death, that they might turn to the truth and sin no more, in order that they may inherit the spiritual and imperishable glory of righteousness which is in heaven."

The Freer Logion

The date of this addition to the Anonymous Ending is not known, though the end of the second or beginning of the third century have been proposed. It was preserved in Latin by Jerome, in the course of a polemic against the Pelagians. According to him, some manuscripts of Mark existed which inserted this text before us immediately after v. 14 in the Anonymous Ending. The full text of the Freer Logion came to light in 1906 as part of a Greek manuscript of the gospels (Codex W), and the fact that it has so far been found in only one manuscript suggests that it was a purely local phenomenon. Its interest is plainly twofold: it helps modify and mitigate the harshness of v. 14, and at the same time it presents the Eleven as offering an excuse for their behavior. It was on the first of those grounds, and also because it bridges the abrupt change from rebuke to the commissioning of the disciples, that there was some disposition on the part of some scholars to consider it, at least in part, as genuine. But apart from the partial quotation in Jerome, the fact that it is known to us in only one manuscript would appear to suggest that it is a gloss.

We appear to be unlikely to discover what community was responsible for this logion. But some possibilities suggest themselves. Aside from protestations from the disciples, the reply of Jesus seems designed to afford some comfort to those who were bewildered by the seeming lack of triumph of the gospel. It also serves to answer doubts and hesitations being expressed about a delayed *parousia*, and the final judgment. It is interesting in that the advent of terrible things to afflict the community as a harbinger of salvation is a rabbinic Jewish concept.

INDEX OF NAMES

INDEX OF SUBJECTS

INDEX OF
SCRIPTURAL AND OTHER PASSAGES

OLD TESTAMENT AND APOCRYPHA

OLD TESTAMENT PSEUDEPIGRAPHA, OTHER JEWISH LITERATURE

JOSEPHUS

PHILO JUDAEUS

QUMRAN MATERIAL

RABBINIC MATERIAL

THE NEW TESTAMENT

INDEX OF AUTHORS

Ā